Eamon
De Valera

Eamon De Valera

The Man Who Was Ireland

by Tim Pat Coogan

HarperCollins*Publishers*

This book was published in Great Britain in 1993 by Hutchinson, a division of Random House Ltd.

FIRST U.S. EDITION

Library of Congress Cataloging-in-Publication Data

Coogan, Tim Pat, 1935–
   [De Valera]
   Eamon de Valera : the man who was Ireland / by Tim Pat Coogan.
     p. cm.
   Originally published : De Valera : long fellow, long shadow. London : Hutchinson, 1993.
   Includes bibliographical references (p.   ) and index.
   ISBN 0-06-017121-9
   1. De Valera, Eamon, 1882–1975. 2. Presidents—Ireland—Biography.
  3. Ireland—Politics and government—20th century.
   I. Coogan, Tim Pat, 1935–   De Valera. II. Title.
DA965.D4C66   1995
941.7082'2'092 — dc20
[B]   94-24515

95 96 97 98 HC 10 9 8 7 6 5 4 3 2 1

CONTENTS

For Barbara and Mabel

ACKNOWLEDGEMENTS

It was Frank Delaney who came up to me during the hubbub at the launching of my book on Michael Collins in Kilmainham Jail, where de Valera was once imprisoned, and suggested that I write this biography. I rejected the idea immediately; my mind was set on a work about the Irish diaspora and Irish identity which I had long planned. Apart from anything else, I was looking forward to the opportunities that the project offered for travel, away from the confines of Ireland's antique quarrel with Britain, her civil war and past dissensions.

However, some time later, while I was working with Roger Bolton on the making of the drama documentary *The Treaty*, out of the blue he too strongly urged me to make de Valera my next project. By then preparatory research for my diaspora project had confirmed for me the centrality of de Valera to many of the questions concerning identity, and the reason why, in this century particularly, there was such a large diaspora. Central too were the linked factors of both quarrel and civil war. For me and for Hutchinson it was an idea whose hour had struck.

Gail Rebuck and Neil Belton were entirely *ad idem* with Frank Delaney on the project. Throughout both Frank, and later the editorial expertise, constant cheerful helpfulness and encouragement of Tony Whittome, have been enormously enabling. Esther Jagger was a serenely efficient High Priestess of nitty gritty editing.

Others to whom I owe gratitude include those two fine journalists my son Tom and daughter Jackie, who were supportive and professional in assisting with research. John O'Mahony, that unusual being, a scholarly banker, proved himself a true friend in his help with proof-reading. Appropriately de Valera's old Alma Mater, Blackrock College, run by the Holy Ghost Fathers, was a treasure trove of advice and friendship, to say nothing of archival material and de Valera memorabilia. Fathers Sean Farragher and Michael O'Carroll, both of whom taught me and were friendly with de Valera, were of particular assistance.

In America another Holy Ghost priest, Father Mathew Farrelly, also deserves my gratitude. I must give special thanks to Mary Jordan and Kevin O'Sullivan of the *Washington Post* for their unfailingly helpful responses to my flood of inquiries. I am also deeply in debt to both Bob and Patsy Lovelock in New York for their assistance with my Roosevelt researches; in Wyoming, to Thomas Wilsted and John Brower for their help with David Gray's papers in the American Heritage Center at Laramie.

In London I must thank both Hilary Jones and Jane Leonard for their help with PRO material. In Dublin there are a great number of people and institutions to whom I am indebted. Dr Patrick Lynch, Dr T. K. Whitaker, Maurice Moynihan, Jack Lynch and some who wish to remain anonymous were enlightening and forthcoming with their comments.

Professor Brendan Kennelly was, characteristically, both generous and enlightening in donating his moving poetic insight into de Valera in his last days. Mr Daragh Connolly and his brothers are to be thanked for allowing me to use the memoirs of their father, Joseph Connolly. A great number of people who have gone ahead should also be remembered. Over the years, for various books and sometimes just for the joy of conversation I have spoken to many men and women whose conversations helped me in the production of this book. They are too numerous to mention individually, but I would like to single out the following: Vivion de Valera, Padraig O'hAnrachain, David Neligan, Gerry Boland, Sean Lemass, Michael MacInerney, Leon O'Broin, Dr John Charles McQuaid, Desmond Williams and Brendan Malin.

I cannot say enough for the kindness and professionalism of the many archivists with whom I have dealt. The National Library is simply the best club of Ireland; everyone worth knowing passes through its doors at some stage. I have reason to be grateful to all the staff with whom I have dealt, and would like to thank in particular the Director, Dr Pat Donlon, and Mr Gerry Lynne of the Manuscript Department. At Dublin University, Dr Bernard Meehan, Keeper of Manuscripts, and Felicity O'Mahony were always most helpful. So too in University College, Dublin, were the Keeper of the Archives, Mr Seamus Helferty, and his staff. Mr David Sheey, the archivist of the Archdiocesan Records of Dublin, was a font of knowledge. Nor can I say enough for the diligence and assistance of the staff at the National Archives, whose new premises at Bishop's Street were opened as I was researching this book. My special thanks are due to Ms Deidre Crowe for making available to me some uncatalogued Department of Foreign Affairs records.

I should like to thank Mr Brendan MacGiolla Choille and the Franciscan Fathers for the service they have performed in cataloguing and progressively making available de Valera's papers at Killiney. When the work is completed it will be a monumental contribution to our understanding of a man and an era. The anonymous benefactor who sent me the copies of de Valera's letters during the writing of *Michael Collins*, whom I acknowledged gratefully in that work, has earned my renewed, and increased, gratitude through the use I was able to make of his or her generosity in this one.

CHRONOLOGY

1882 De Valera born in New York, 14 October.

1885 Begins life in Ireland.

1898 Centenary of Wolfe Tone rebellion, 1798. De Valera accepted as a pupil at Blackrock College.

1908 De Valera joins Gaelic League.

1910 De Valera marries his Irish teacher, Sinead Flanagan.

1912 Home Rule crisis. Tories and Unionists make common cause to frustrate introduction of Home Rule to Ireland. Ulster Volunteers (UVF) formed. Larne gun-running.

1913 Irish Volunteers formed in response to Tory actions. De Valera enrols.

1916 Easter Rising. De Valera only commandant to escape execution. Imprisoned in England.

1917 De Valera freed. Elected as Sinn Fein representative for East Clare, President of Sinn Fein and President of reorganized Irish Volunteers.

1918 Conscription crisis. Sinn Fein victory in general election. De Valera imprisoned.

1919 First Dail meets. Michael Collins arranges de Valera's escape from Lincoln Jail. De Valera elected Priomh Aire (First Minister) of Dail. Departs for America. Michael Collins forms 'the Squad'. Evolves new form of guerilla warfare.

1920 'Year of the Terror'. Black and Tans come to Ireland. Peace feelers begin, Archbishop Clune mission etc. In America de Valera attracts much publicity as 'President of the Irish Republic' but feuds with Irish American leaders, Judge Cohalan and John Devoy and splits Irish American organizations. Launches successful bonds drive, but leaves most of the money in America on his return to Ireland at Christmas.

1921 King George V opens Parliament for six Ulster counties. Delivers conciliatory speech. Truce follows. De Valera invited to come with delegation to see Lloyd George in London. Leaves Collins in Dublin. Hears British terms for settlement. Refuses to go back to London for ensuing negotiations. However, insists that Michael Collins goes. Rejects Anglo-Irish Treaty which ultimately emerges, recognizing the two states of Ireland that exist today.

1922 Dail ratifies the Treaty. De Valera refuses to accept majority vote. Continues anti-Treaty campaign. Civil war breaks out. Arthur Griffith dies, Michael Collins killed.

1923 Civil war ends in defeat for anti-Treatyites. De Valera imprisoned.

1924 De Valera released.

1926 De Valera splits from IRA and forms new party, Fianna Fail.

1927 Kevin O'Higgins murdered. De Valera enters Dail, takes Oath.

1927–9 De Valera conducts extensive fund-raising tours in America.

1931 Uses American bonds money to help fund and launch new daily newspaper, the *Irish Press*.

1932 Forms Government, institutes various steps, including abolition of Oath and removal of Governor General, which bring about economic war with England.

1933 Period of ebullition in Irish politics begins, involving Fianna Fail, the IRA and the Blueshirt movement. De Valera ultimately successful.

1934 De Valera makes impressive contribution to League of Nations Assembly meeting at Geneva.

1937 Introduction of de Valera's Constitution.

1938 De Valera ends economic war and secures return of a number of ports ceded to England under the Treaty, thus making possible Irish neutrality in World War II.

1939–45 Ireland neutral in war. De Valera maintains strict censorship. Acts ruthlessly towards IRA. Various frictions with Allied nations. At war's end de Valera pays visit of condolence to German Embassy on death of Hitler.

1948 De Valera defeated in general election. After sixteen years in office loses power to coalition led by John A. Costello. New Government declares Twenty-six Counties a republic. De Valera embarks on world tour.

1949 Declaration of Republic results in British Government giving Unionists a guarantee that they would remain part of UK so long as a majority in the Six-county area so desired.

1951 De Valera returned to power.

1954 De Valera again defeated in general election, another coalition government formed under Costello.

1957 De Valera returned to power again. Economic situation of Republic worsening rapidly. Emigration and unemployment growing. IRA campaign in progress against Six Counties. De Valera has no remedies for economic problems but tackles IRA successfully by means of internment, and encourages Frank Aiken to pursue principled independent policies at UN.

1958 De Valera's Government adopts a plan for economic development drawn up by Dr T. K. Whitaker, Secretary of the Department of Finance.

1959 De Valera retires as Taoiseach and becomes President. Sean Lemass succeeds him as leader of Fianna Fail and as Taoiseach.

1964 De Valera addresses both US Houses of Congress, meeting in joint session.

1966 De Valera re-elected President.

1973 Ireland joins the EEC. Eamon de Valera retires from public life on completing second term as President.

1975 Sinead de Valera dies, 7 January. Eamon de Valera dies, 29 August.

LIST OF ILLUSTRATIONS

PROLOGUE

ALTHOUGH HE DIED in 1975, Eamon de Valera, generally known as either Dev. or the Long Fellow, cast a long shadow that still falls over Irish life. Quite simply the history of Ireland for much of the twentieth century is the history of de Valera. As befitted a man who sometimes seemed to model his actions on the Roman Catholic doctrine of Three Divine Persons in One God, his tangible legacies are three also: the Irish Constitution; the largest Irish political party, Fianna Fail; and the second largest Irish newspaper empire, the Irish Press Group, founded, as was so much of his political strength, on Irish America. His intangible influences can still be traced in the divisions between the leading Irish political parties, Fianna Fail and Fine Gael, and in attitudes towards Northern Ireland, Church–State relationships, the role of women in Irish society, the Irish language and the whole concept of an Irish nation. Any one of his visible creations would have been an achievement beyond the powers of most men. The three, taken together, must be accounted a rare feat indeed.

But it is perhaps in his intangible legacies that Eamon de Valera's real influence lies. The lay pontiff, the man of politics and of God, Eamon de Valera was the epitome of a land where Christ and Caesar were hand in glove. It was on his hand that the glove fitted; his hand, which, as a result, held the reins of power longer even than contemporaries such as Roosevelt, Salazar or Stalin. Yet this was not the end of his significance. In de Valera's career lies the explanation of such contemporary Irish complexities as the relationship between constitutionalism and physical force, and the ambivalence of some politicians towards violence and Northern Ireland. Approaches to education, economic planning and family law can still be measured by, with or from his policies.

Was he a Lincoln or a Machiavelli? A saint or a charlatan? A man of peace, or one who incited young men to hatred and violence? Did he seek to heal or worsen the wounds that the Irish and the English inflicted (and inflict) on each other? Was he a revolutionary or a conservative? An unscrupulous manipulator or a nice guy? The truth is that in a sense the answer to all these questions is 'Yes.' Eamon de Valera was a law-giver who helped to bring down a civil war on the heads of his people; a revolutionary who kept his country neutral in World War II. As a result of his neutrality policy Ireland was spared the horrors of war. But his playing of the Green card of nationalism also helped to create the circumstances wherein, decades later, many young Irish emigrants found themselves denied a green card. De Valera was born in America. The money he raised from Irish emigrants helped to found and fund his *Irish Press*. Yet

1

Roosevelt, who had helped him to secure these monies, became enraged at him. By the time the war was over the American Minister in Dublin, a connection of Roosevelt's, was persona non grata with de Valera and his Cabinet.

De Valera was a world figure who attempted to confine his disciples to the narrowest of cultural and intellectual horizons. Many of the challenges he confronted are still troubling the peace of Ireland and of England, disturbing relationships from Belfast to Birmingham to Boston. Some of the vexing questions of the moment are directly traceable to him: the effect of part of the Irish Constitution on Northern Ireland's Unionists; his philosophy of talking about God and the High Destiny of the Gael while practising realpolitik gave him control of the *Irish Press* and of Fianna Fail. But ownership has involved his descendants in the newspaper in some very unfortunate court proceedings. And in politics, some of those who came after him in Fianna Fail sought to profit from their opportunities by acting in ways which have spawned scandals, given rise to government inquiries, wrecked Cabinets and interfered with Ireland's ability to handle a devaluation crisis. Paradigms of modern Ireland, both the newspaper and political sagas are still evolving at the time of writing.

'Dev.' was the greatest political mover and shaker of post-revolutionary Ireland. His towering figure continues to cast shadows that are both benign and baleful. Therefore, as a biographer, I have been conscious of two linked and major problems in the course of attempting to chart the career of this extraordinary man: first, to convey a sense of his importance to Ireland and her relationships with Great Britain, America and the members of the British Commonwealth; second, while so doing to steer between the Scylla of hagiography and the Charybdis of denigration. Practically everything of substance written about him falls into one category or the other. There is no *via media* where Eamon de Valera is concerned. The problem is compounded by the fact that not only did de Valera shape history, he attempted to write it also – or, more correctly, to have it set down as he ordained. I have tried to evaluate him neither as a demon nor as a plaster saint, but as what he was: for better or worse, the most important Irish leader of the twentieth century. Doubtless my approach will leave me open to attack from both denigrators and hagiographers. Attempting a biography of Eamon de Valera, is, for an Irishman, somewhat like an Iranian sitting down to write about the Ayatollah Khomeini. Uneasy visions of Salman Rushdie occur. Nevertheless, though the reader may fault me for want of *pietas*, critical faculty or honest omission, I hope that I cannot be assailed on the grounds of fairness.

1

THE HARSH REALITY
OF A NURSERY

PERCOLATING DOWN TO us through a process of selective amnesia, recollections by contemporary admirers (and detractors), the story of Eamon de Valera's childhood and youth comes across as a combination of Aesopian fable and Lincolnesque progression from log cabin to White House, laced along the way with a liberal dash of what is known in Ireland as the 'cute hoor' approach or, in less Rabelaisian societies, peasant cunning.

In some ways de Valera's early life resembled that of his great rival, Michael Collins, who also suffered the loss of his father in early boyhood. Both leaders were reared in rural Ireland at a time of heightened nationalist sentiment, a time when two colonialisms dominated that sentiment – those of Mother England and Mother Church. On the streets was the visible sign and instrument of England's control: the Royal Irish Constabulary patrolling in pairs, their carbines slung over their backs. In the classrooms were the schoolbooks extolling the virtues of the British Empire. Less visible, but probably more potent, were the teachings from altar and confessional of a rigorous form of ultramontane Roman Catholicism that controlled the minds and hearts of the majority of the people in their part of the country. It was an Irish bishop who had recently[1] led the charge in favour of the acceptance of the doctrine of papal infallibility. And there was more than a little truth in the jest, common in clerical circles in Rome at the time, that this was entirely appropriate. For: 'Not alone do the Irish believe the pope is infallible. They believe the same of their parish priests and will beat anyone who suggests otherwise.' The parish priest was the Irish peasant's spokesman and bulwark against an unjust authority, an ever-present eternity. The consolation and support that the better priests gave their flocks was reciprocated by a respect for the clergy generally only equalled today by that accorded to an imam in a fundamentalist Arab village.

A vicious land war was petering out in the year of de Valera's birth. It left behind tales of violence, death, cattle houghing, boycotting, evictions and the creation of a peasant proprietorship. The land issue at least was, at long last, on the way to being settled. Both Collins and de Valera knew what it was to experience feelings of awe and enlightenment as they listened to the stories of these turbulent times and imbibed the wisdom of

3

their elders amidst the sights and sounds of one of the focal points of an Irish parish in those pre-television days – the local forge. Both were marked by application to 'the books', de Valera being the more obviously studious and less rumbustious of the two. And, for those with a taste in coincidence, both were influenced in their earlier careers by close female relations affectionately known as Hannie; in Collins' case his oldest sister, in de Valera's an aunt. Finally, and more startlingly, both were nearly killed in infancy through falling out of a loft.

But here one runs out of analogies, sharply. Collins' childhood was enveloped in the love of a remarkable mother[2] and of a large and affectionate extended family. His immediate family comprised seven brothers and sisters who lived on a farm of some ninety acres surrounded by neighbouring cousins, uncles and aunts. De Valera's mother largely banished him from her life, and he grew up, an ocean away from her, in the impoverished cottage of an uncle who possessed only half an acre – and no wife – for a significant part of the time that de Valera lived with him. Hannie seems to have reciprocated the affection that the infant de Valera transferred from his absent mother to her sister; but, through being forced to emigrate to America, leaving the boy behind, she was also the unwitting cause of worsening his inevitable feelings of loneliness[3] and rejection.

Why did de Valera grow up on the opposite side of the Atlantic to his mother? The answer, in a word, was poverty. On 2 October 1879 Catherine Coll of Knockmore townland, near Bruree, Co. Limerick, landed in New York, 'tired and almost penniless',[4] fleeing from a one-roomed, mud-walled, thatched cabin in an Ireland where 'famine threatened once more'.[5] The threat was a real one, as Dr Conor Cruise O'Brien has noted:[6]

> The fear of famine, or rather of having to choose between starvation and eviction, was the great underlying political reality of the late seventies and early eighties of the Nineteenth Century in Ireland. The famine of 1845–7, as a result of which a million people died and many thousands were evicted, was present in the memory or in the imagination of every Irishman. From 1878 on partial failure of the potato crop – still the staple diet of thousands of Irish tenant-farmers – and falling prices for other crops threatened a recurrence of the patterns of the forties and fifties, mass starvation, mass evictions, mass emigration.

It was in 1879 also that Michael Davitt founded the Land League. Using tactics such as boycotting – named after a Captain Boycott against whom the weapon was first used – the league eventually succeeded, with the help of the Irish Parliamentary Party leader at Westminster, Charles Stewart Parnell, in achieving its main objective, the 'three Fs' of fair rent, fixity of tenure and free sale. The settlement of the land issue created the conditions which would one day enable Catherine Coll's son to change Irish history. Thoughts of such a prospect for any child of hers would have been remote from the mind of the twenty-three-year-old Catherine as she disembarked in New York, armed for the New World with nothing more than a letter for an aunt in Brooklyn. Her father, Patrick Coll, a farm labourer, had died five years earlier when Catherine, or Kate as she was generally known, was eighteen. After her in the family were two brothers, Patrick and Edward, and a sister, Hannah (Hannie). Catherine worked as a maidservant for a local farmer, which later helped to give rise to various versions of a rumour that the reason she sailed for New York was not poverty but pregnancy. An embroidered version of this story is contained in a memoir drafted by a contemporary of de Valera's, Dick Kennedy:[7]

> The Colls were never troubled with principle to hinder their advancement . . . they transmitted that ability to Dev. . . . Pat Coll never married but he had nine Chirpauns [children of love]. Dev's mother was the first. She went as a maid to Tom Aitkinson of Glenwilliam at 17 years.
> The Sailor Coll [Pat Junior] told me that Tom was Dev.'s father. When she was going to have the child Tom sent her to America. The Sailor said Dev was born in New York Harbour just before the boat landed. She went to a friend in Brooklyn and there was a Mexican waiter who died of galloping consumption at the age of twenty-two years in same lodging so they decided to say that she was married to this waiter and called the child de Valera.

When I first read the foregoing I was strongly inclined to doubt its veracity. Apart from the obviously hostile tone of the memoir, I then had other reasons for questioning the illegitimacy story. Before going into these, let us look at the arguments advanced in its favour. An obvious one was de Valera's height and general appearance, which made him appear older than his stated age. Another was the fact that, though his mother married again and had other children, she did not extend the benefits of her new home to her first child. The Kennedy memoir states that this was because the man she subsequently married did not want the boy. And further plausibility is given to the illegitimacy theory by local[8] gossip: it was commonly said that a daughter of Atkinson's, Mrs Sybil Worteledge, 'always greeted Dev as her half-brother and boasted that he was such'.[9] Certainly de Valera had to deal with such rumours (and more besides) from his earliest days in party politics. During his first by-election campaign, in June 1917, he wrote to his wife:[10]

> Unfortunately it is no longer the preaching of ideals here but the practical work of defeating the enemy's misrepresentation – one of which is that I am a Jacobin another a letter from the Lewes Chaplain [while in Lewes Jail in England after the Easter Rising, de Valera, as part of a prison protest, had ordered his comrades not to obey an order to go to Mass, but instead to remain in their cells saying the rosary], one I haven't unfortunately been able to get a copy so far, making it appear that I was responsible for sacrilege, a third that I am illegitimate. By the way isn't 'lawful wife' in Baptism certificate. I think it is – that would be sufficient to prove the lie. . . .

It is, of course, possible that Kate could have conceived a child before emigrating. But if she did, that child could hardly have been Eamon de

Valera. He was born, as the official biography asserts, three years after Kate is said to have landed in America, on 14 October 1882, in New York Nursery and Child's Hospital, Lexington Avenue (between 51st and 52nd Streets), New York. Curiously, in view of the importance of the part the Anglo-Irish Treaty would play in de Valera's life, 1882 was also the year of the Kilmainham Treaty which freed Parnell from Kilmainham Jail. The conflict between the landlords and the Land League resulted in a 'land war' involving evictions and agrarian outrages of all sorts. Parnell was jailed, leaving 'Captain Moonlight', as he described the state of disorder, to rule unchecked. The turbulence was ended after protracted negotiations conducted between the British Government and Parnell while he was still in Kilmainham Jail.

The baptismal certificate[11] to which de Valera referred in his letter gives the date of baptism as 3 December 1882 and the venue as the church of St Agnes, near Grand Central Station. He was christened Edward, apparently because Kate's younger brother was called Edward and her baby was born on the day after the Feast of Edward the Confessor. But, in one of those gossip-provoking circumstances that surrounds de Valera's early years he was apparently registered as George. His authorized biography states[12] that this was not altered until he lay under sentence of death in 1916, when his mother procured a copy of the certificate in an effort to prove American citizenship. De Valera was to change his given name further by using his own version, with a single 'n', of the Irish form of Edward, Eamonn.

According to his biography[13] his father was Juan Vivion de Valera, a young Spaniard whom Kate first met the year after she landed; he had called on the Girauds, a French family for whom she worked. Though her subsequent treatment of her child indicates some coldness in her psychological make-up, she was obviously sufficiently well thought of by the Girauds to have been taken with them when they moved from Myrtle Avenue to Gold Street. But Kate soon opted for a change of scene and obtained a job in Greenville, New Jersey. Vivion followed, and the couple were married on 19 September 1881 in the church of St Patrick, Greenville. In the earlier part of my research, until I had learnt to mistrust de Valera's accounts of his activities, I accepted this version of his origins. In fact, the first draft of this chapter which I sent to the publishers contained the following passage:

> At this stage, in view of the persistence of the illegitimacy theory, and at the risk of stating the obvious, one should perhaps draw attention to the following. Whatever about the possibilities of godparents giving a church registrar a false name for a father 'unavoidably absent' during a christening, or perpetrating some similar fraud on a birth certificate, someone (who would have had to give proof of his identity as Vivion de Valera) had to stand before the officiating priest on that September day.
> Vivion's mother, Amelia Acosta, had died while he was young and he was raised by his father, Juan de Valera, who seems to have been in the shipping end of the sugar trade between Cuba, Spain and the USA.[14] Vivion had intended to be

a sculptor, but a chip damaged his eye and he took up first book-keeping and then music teaching to earn a living. The couple lived in an apartment at 61 East 41st Street, Manhattan, a site now dominated by the Chrysler Building. Vivion's health deteriorated, and in 1884 his father paid to have him sent to Denver where it was vainly hoped that the air would be better for him. He died there in November 1884; Kate, either for financial or for other reasons, remained in New York with the two-year-old Edward.

All the foregoing is based on de Valera's official biography. My suspicions were slightly stirred by a diary entry written by a journalist[15] whom Kate trusted. He had tried to get her talking about her first marriage, but just as she began to reply de Valera entered the room and she dried up. De Valera himself obviously obtained sufficient information about his father from Kate to be able to write the following remarks in the family Bible:[16]

> Father. born in Spain educated abroad – knew fluently Eng, German, Spanish & French. He was trained as a sculptor but chip injured his sight. He gave music lessons after marriage. Met mother in 1880 (At Greenville – village near N.Y.Bay Cemetery). Went to Denver in fall, 1880 & married mother in Sept. 1881. Died in Nov '84 (Minneapolis?) Denver. He was 5' 7" or 5' 8" in height & could wear mother's shoes. Said he was twenty-eight at time of marriage.

With the ending of the 'marriage', the young de Valera's separation from his mother is said to have begun. According to his biography,[17] 'Mrs de Valera put the child Eamon in the care of another Bruree immigrant, Mrs Doyle, and went out to work again.' The biography says that de Valera only retained 'one vivid memory of his early childhood . . . a New York apartment, 1885. Beside the fireplace sits a man. On the floor lies a small, fair-haired boy. A slim, pale-face young woman is bending over him, dressed in black. The child's eyes are fixed wonderingly on the shiny metal fittings which ornament her handbag. . . . ' This idealized account, having set the scene for the circumstances which the future President of Ireland wished to have generally accepted as the reasons why the baby de Valera found himself in Ireland in the first place, goes on to explain: ' . . . the young woman in black was de Valera's widowed mother and his mental picture was of the occasions when she came from work to visit him. This arrangement was hardly ideal; the little boy would be much happier in the friendly Bruree atmosphere. Mrs de Valera's brother, Ned Coll [Edward], who had joined her in America, was about to return home. He would take his nephew across the Atlantic to his grandmother.'

And so, aboard the SS *City of Chicago*, 'Dev. was brought to Ireland, in 1885, by an uncle who at that time was about eighteen years of age.'[18] Kate Coll's living conditions must indeed have been 'hardly ideal' if they caused her to send her only child on such an arduous journey – back to a one-roomed thatched cottage – in the care of her teenage brother. Even the journey's last lap in Ireland, from Killmallock to Bruree, had its hardships.

On 20 April 1885, the child was 'carried over the hills by his uncle in his arms as that was the shortest walking way to Bruree at the time'.[19]

Normally one would expect maternal feelings to have dictated that Kate either brought the child home herself, or explored the possibilities of his father's family assisting in the infant's upbringing so that she might have kept him. For all we know she may have done so, but we are informed that Juan de Valera called on Kate 'about a year or less after the baby had been sent to Ireland and was very angry that he had been sent. He had no interest left when he heard his grandson was gone and Dev.'s mother never saw him again. She learned that he died a year or so later.'[20] This incident would obviously be significant in itself: it indicates that, had relationships between Kate Coll and Juan de Valera been closer, young George/Edward de Valera could well have grown up in America and the course of Irish history would have been vastly different. But it has the added importance that de Valera himself spoke about it to Frank Gallagher, the journalist and de Valera apologist who was close to him for much of his life. These accounts of childhood obviously either lodged with de Valera, or were invented by him.

I do not propose at this stage to attempt an adjudication on the issue. But, on the principle of reasonable doubt, I have to say that my researches, conducted at a stage when the bulk of this book was already written, indicate that the story about Kate Coll's getting married in Greenville does not stand up. I was able to substantiate part of Kate Coll's early history in America, but not the official account of her marriage. Firstly, consultation of immigration records[21] shows that on 2 October 1879 there did arrive in New York from Liverpool, aboard the SS *Nevada*, a Kate Coll, passenger number 130. Her age is given as twenty-two and she is described as a 'spinster'.

However, not only is there no record of any Coll–de Valera marriage at St Patrick's, but there is a confusion about the church's location. Greenville is a microcosm of the American melting-pot process. It was strongly Irish in the 1880s. From the church directories one can see the churches going up throughout New Jersey in the 1860s as the Kate Colls and the Patrick Murphys, all fleeing famine, poured out of Ireland. Greenville was a small farming and fishing settlement. There was one Catholic church, St Paul's on the corner of Bergen Road and Greenville Avenue; it is still in existence, but its records show no Coll–de Valera marriage. Greenville merged[22] with Jersey City in 1873 and the church of St Patrick's, on 492 Bramhall Road, which also stands today, was built in 1869, about ten blocks outside the old Greenville boundary, in Jersey City. Most of its parishioners came from the old Greenville area, which is possibly why it could have been referred to as being in Greenville. St Patrick's records show the changes in population from the days in the 1880s, when its marriage certificates could have been for a parish in Clare or Kerry, to today; now the pastor is Haitian, as are most of the parishioners. But those records contain no record of a Coll–de Valera wedding. The other church in the area is St John the Baptist on 3026 Kennedy Boulevard, about a mile and a half away. This is also considered to be in Jersey City, not Greenville. It contains no record of a Coll–de Valera wedding either. I consulted the records in the churches[23] and there was no Coll–de Valera wedding listed in a time-span of twelve years (from 1875 to 1887) before and after the date given in the biography for the wedding, 1881.

There remained the possibility that a civil ceremony had been performed. However, enquiry at the New Jersey State Records in Trenton also failed to unearth a Vivion de Valera–Catherine Coll wedding. The Records do contain a certificate for a Catherine Coll who married a James Thompson between 1882 and 1883, and for a Joseph de Valera who married Maria Turst in Newark between 1890 and 1891. Interestingly, Joseph de Valera's country of origin is given as 'Spain', and his father's name[24] as 'August', which is not dissimilar to the 'Acosta' described as Eamon de Valera's maternal grandmother in the official biography.

The State of New York records contain two birth certificates[25] for de Valera. The first, registered on 10 November 1882, describes the child as 'George de Valero'. It states that he was born on 14 October that year at the Nursery and Child's Hospital. His father's name is again spelt with an 'o', his first name is given as 'Vivion', born in Spain, and his occupation as an artist. The mother's name is given as 'Kate'. It does not state whether or not the couple were married. The second certificate was approved as 'corrected' on 30 June 1916. It is signed by Catherine Wheelright, Kate's married name, and gives the child's name as 'Edward' and the surname as 'de Valera'. The father is again described as being an artist, born in Spain. The certificate does not say whether the couple were married. The place of birth is given as the Nursery and Child's Hospital, 61 East 41st Street.

Enquiry at the New York Historical Society[26] confirms that the Nursery and Child's Hospital did exist. It was for destitute, abandoned children, children whose parents were away, and orphans: hardly the sort of place in which a mother would have wished to leave a child if she had a home, even that of a relative in another country, in which to place it. The original de Valera baptismal record in St Agnes's has also been altered. The name was originally given as 'De Valeros', and the father's name as 'Vivian'. Someone has changed these to 'Vivion' and 'de Valera' and altered 'Edward' to 'Eamon'. I was informed that it is believed that the changes may be in the handwriting of Vivion, Eamon de Valera's eldest son. The church is something of a shrine for de Valera worshippers; one of the few things to survive a disastrous fire which destroyed it was a baptismal font with an inscription recording the fact that de Valera was baptised on it on 3 December 1882.

In de Valera's childhood, and afterwards, illegitimacy carried a stigma in

Roman Catholic Ireland. If he knew or suspected that there was a doubt about his parents' marriage the knowledge must have been a burden to him. It must have had a marked effect on his character, if even a portion of what the psychiatrists tell us about the influences of childhood be true. The death of, or abandonment by, his father, rejection by his mother, and growing up in poverty a continent away from her were the sort of experiences which either broke or toughened a man. Did they also dehumanize him? Many would say they did. A not unsympathetic historian, Dr T. Ryle Dwyer, once inscribed a copy of his biography of de Valera:[27] 'If behind the cold, impersonal countenance of the subject of this biography, there seems to be no real humanity, possibly it's because there was none.'

While conceding that there is sufficient in de Valera's career to justify that comment, it should in fairness also be noted that one may see a warmer personality emerge in the anecdotes about his early life which de Valera confided privately to Frank Gallagher. Gallagher accompanied de Valera to America on two extended tours during the 1920s when he was gathering the money to found the *Irish Press*. He became the paper's first Editor, and later Director of the Government Information Bureau. De Valera intended Gallagher to write his biography, and in various relaxed moments over a quarter of a century provided him with information about his background and with unique insights into various aspects of his career and philosophy. In the end Gallagher's health failed before he could write the book, but he left behind a large and most valuable collection of diaries, drafts and notes.[28] The drafts clearly indicate his deification of de Valera, but his diaries and in particular his notes, often made in the tiny handwriting on scraps of folded paper that one frequently finds ex-prisoners producing, contain verbatim accounts of 'The Chief's' recollections unsanitized by any attempts to present them for publication.

Symbolically enough the Colls were moving up in the world as de Valera arrived in Bruree, with the result that he had the unpleasant experience, for a child, of waking up in an empty house the morning after he arrived. The others – his grandmother, Uncle Patrick and Aunt Hannie – had forgotten about him in the excitement of inspecting the new three-room slate-roofed cottage, with a half acre of ground attached, which had just been awarded them by the state. Despite his initial scare de Valera subsequently took a pride in being 'the last occupant of his family home',[29] even if it was a one-roomed, mud-walled cabin with an open fire around which cooking and sleeping took place.

The move to the new house almost had fatal consequences for the young de Valera. There was a loft over the kitchen, and one morning the child was preparing to descend from it by ladder when his attention was distracted by the blood on a newly plucked goose-wing feather and he fell to the floor beneath. He became aware of his grandmother standing over him, calling out: 'Is he dead?', and years later he solemnly informed Frank

10

Gallagher that that was the first occasion on which he became aware that 'unconscious people could hear things'.[30] Michael Collins also had a fall through a loft trapdoor at a similar age, caused by his sisters covering it with flowers. But his fall, which was broken by a pile of hay, does not appear to have prompted any form of realization on his part. Ironically he was killed, needlessly, in a badly planned ambush staged in a place called Beal na mBlath, the mouth of flowers. As we shall see, it was his death, more than any other single circumstance, that allowed de Valera – who, coincidentally, was not far away at the time – to develop into the figure of influence he later became.

Another influential figure shortly to be removed, albeit less drastically, from de Valera's life was that of his fifteen-year-old Aunt Hannie. For about a year after he arrived in Bruree she played a mothering role, lacing his boots and dressing him up in his American velvet suit. He became 'particularly fond' of his aunt.[31] But the same economic situation that had driven her sister Kate to America drove Hannie there in 1886. Her mother's tears mingled with those of young Edward as they waved her goodbye at Bruree railway station. At the age of four he was being left behind in a strange country, bereft of the presence that had helped to make up for the loss of his father and mother.

One of the first manifestations of that strangeness that he became aware of was to have a profound effect on his entire life and career: it was the Irish language. His grandmother's friends used to speak in Irish around their firesides. He did not learn Irish as a boy and when, later in life, he took it up he learned the Connemara dialect. As a child he had not realized that the old people were speaking the Decies dialect, and he came to regret not learning this living link with his early life. Speaking in Irish three-quarters of a century later, at the opening of Ring College in the Decies (Co. Waterford) Gaeltacht,[32] he said: 'Alas, that it is not the sounds of the Decies I have, although these were the first sounds I heard when I was a young lad. Near Bruree, at that time, almost all the old people were native Irish speakers, and it was the Ring dialect they had.'

De Valera seems to have turned to the Irish language as part of a process of creating an identity for himself to compensate for the uncertainties of his early upbringing. Not only did he want to recapture his country's past – he sought to reclaim its geography also. Self, race and place were bound up in his lifelong preoccupation with the language. Significantly, he chose Bruree to make two revealing statements about how he saw Irish. At a *feis*, an Irish musical festival, which he opened on 25 June 1950, he first gave the names and meanings of various places from his boyhood and then went on: 'I am wandering like this to show you how living a link with the past the language is. The simplest place name isn't without a meaning. All you young people who want to know your country must also know your language.' And during a by-election campaign in 1955 he said on 30 October:

11

It is the bond that kept our people together throughout the centuries, and enabled them to resist all the efforts to make them English. It would be useful to us in that way today, when we have poured in upon us, from every direction, influences which are contrary to the traditional views and hopes of our people. The biggest thing that could be done for our people is to restore the language. If you do that the other things will be added to you. . . .

It might be remarked that at the time he made the speech the economy was near collapse, and unemployment and emigration were rising; but his candidate won. However, this is to anticipate and we must return to the Coll hearthside when Eamon de Valera was a small boy. Apart from the Irish language the child heard stories that:[33]

caught the secret voice of the nation. He shared the traditions of the people, their music and their songs. By winter firesides, where crickets chirped, and where the kettle hung cronawning on the crook, he heard with pride of the gallant Sarsfield; of Emmet and Tone; of the Bruree Fenians who fought at Kilmallock in '67, and left one of their number dead on the bullet-swept street. He heard of the Great Famine, and of the Land War and its evictions and clearances. . . . He heard about the hurling matches and race meetings and match-makings: about the feats of great mowers and spadesmen, about all those things that are the warp and woof of Irish life in the countryside.

De Valera did not write that description, but I commend it to the reader as being typical of the rhetoric and the psychology which would permeate his political career. It is in its way both totally accurate and fundamentally misleading. It sketches the basis for his claim in later life that he had unique insight into the minds and hearts of the Irish people – a claim which on occasion, though not always, he did justify. But while the events described in the quotation were those that the child de Valera heard discussed at his family fireside, the account is arcadian, sanitized, selective. The references to the Land War give no indication of the degradation, violence and servility spawned by the conditions of the time. At the beginning of the 1880s General Gordon wrote perceptively to the British Prime Minister, Gladstone:[34] 'I must say, from all accounts and from my own observation, that the state of our fellow countrymen in the parts I have named is worse than that of any people in the world, let alone Europe. I believe that these people are made as we are, that they are patient beyond belief, loyal, but at the same time, broken spirited and desperate, living on the verge of starvation in places in which we would not keep our cattle.'

In the year de Valera was born, the desperation of which Gordon spoke led to some of the most horrific murders in Irish history. There were some sixty agrarian or politics-related killings in the first eight months of that year alone. Amongst these were the knifing to death on 6 May 1882, the day he arrived in Ireland, of the Chief Secretary for Ireland, Lord Frederick Cavendish, and of his Under Secretary, T. H. Burke. The killings were the work of the republican splinter group the Invincibles. Some would argue that reaction in Britain to the deaths aborted progress to Home Rule for Ireland and so paved the way for revolution, partition and today's Provisional IRA. Certainly, Parnell was so shattered by the assassinations that for a while he seriously contemplated resignation. Then, in August, there occurred the Maamtrasna murders in Co. Mayo: the Joyce family were slaughtered in a clay-floored hovel shared by humans and animals. The Lord Lieutenant said: 'The house where the murders took place would not be used for pigs in England.' Here died John Joyce, his wife Breege, his elderly mother Margaret and his daughter Peggy. His two sons, Michael and Patsy, were savagely mutilated and left for dead alongside the four corpses. The neighbours, out of superstition and ignorance, left the boys in agony without doing anything to help them. One child died, and subsequently three men – one of them innocent – were hanged for the crime; five others served twenty-year sentences.

Maamtrasna and other deeds were spoken of at every fireside in Ireland. Their omission from the description of the Colls' is typical of the *suppressio veri* romanticism that would form an essential part of the de Valera hagiography. But equally essential to the de Valera saga were the violence and servility bred in the dark underside of colonial Irish peasant life. De Valera was to subsume the violence into his own political entourage, and the servility would be turned to account to depict him as the embodiment of the asexual, moralistic, free Ireland that raised the peasantry from the slime. Servility is a characteristic that Irish historians often shy away from examining; but rage at being rendered servile, and respect for one who seemed to help alleviate that condition, were important components in de Valera's popularity. One of the *cause célèbre* landlord murders which occurred when Kate Coll was thinking of going to America was that of Lord Leitrim in 1878. After killing him in broad daylight his assassins rowed to freedom across Mulroy Bay 'to be acclaimed across the land as the nation's heroes'. How colonialism and peasant morality combined to create such a metamorphosis is, as often happens, better explained through one verse from a poet than a chapter from a historian:[35]

And who are you? said the poet speaking to
The Old Leitrim man.
He said, I can tell you what I am.
Servant girls bred my servility:
When I stoop
It is my mother's mother's mother
Each one in turn being called to spread –
'Wider with your legs' the master of the house said.
Domestic servants taken back and front
That's why I'm servile. It is not the poverty
Of soil in Leitrim that makes me raise my hat
To fools with fifty pounds in a paper bank.

The verse probably also helps to explain why so many rumours

13

circulated about Kate Coll's departure from Atkinson's. And it helps to shed light on why she should choose to face the uncertainties of America rather than the subjugation of 'Domestic servants'. Kate did re-enter de Valera's life in Bruree for a brief interlude. The year after Hannie left she showed up for a 'few glorious weeks'[36] before returning to America – to get married again, to one Charles Wheelright,[37] a groom employed by a wealthy family near Rochester. Wheelright, who was English and not a Catholic, is remembered as being easy-going, fond of his beer and content to appear before the world behind a team of horses resplendent in his employer's livery. They had two children, Annie, who died at the age of ten, apparently from heart disease, and Thomas, who became a Redemptorist priest. But no call came to Bruree to bring the two half-brothers under the one roof.

As to why this should have been we can only speculate. In later life Kate Coll was described by Frank Gallagher as a 'sweet little woman . . . very very Irish'.[38] Yet a typically Irish mother would have gone through fire and water to have her son with her. It is possible that her husband did not want someone else's child. When they were first married their living quarters were rooms over the stables where he worked. However, when Gallagher met Kate and Wheelright, by then (1 April 1927) 'a heavy aging man with plenty of sport in him, though rheumatism is making him irritable',[39] he was impressed by the way 'she bossed him and he, quizzically complaining that he had to keep his job, obeyed at once'.[40] Another observer commenting on Kate said:[41] 'There was no frivolity about her and even her sister and her sister's grown children stood in some awe of "Aunt Kate". They could not catch her up on the name of a single plant or flower or bush in the fenced-in garden behind her house.'

There is a well-attested[42] story of how Kate once won a spelling bee in Rochester from other contestants who included a businessman, a lawyer and a schoolteacher. The report says there was some laughter at her plainly dressed appearance when she arrived on the platform, but she proved herself the only one able to spell all the test words correctly. In an unconscious comment on how circumstances changed for de Valera from his schooldays, in the course of an appreciation of Kate the priest who vouched for this victory told how he[43] 'administered the last rites of the church to this saintly mother of perhaps the greatest living statesman in the world. Mr de Valera surely has reason to be proud of such a mother.'

Such a mother would appear to have possessed the determination and force necessary to get her second husband to accept her child had she really wanted him to. She did, after all, succeed in persuading the Protestant Wheelright to bear the expense of making his own son a priest. But whatever the reasons for Kate's decision, what is certain is that, on the morning of 7 May 1888, de Valera set out from a motherless house for his first day at school. He was six years of age when he set off hand in hand with an older neighbouring lad, Jamsie MacEniry, to walk the mile to and from Bruree National School.

His first teacher, Thomas MacGinn, had to rely on a boy who lived near the Colls, Tom Mortell, for the spelling of his name. Consequently he was entered on the roles as 'Eddie Develera'. He was generally known as 'Eddie Coll'. His strange-sounding Spanish name puzzled the villagers; by a process of elimination they decided that, since it was neither Irish nor English, it had to be French – France being the foreign country uppermost in folk memory because of French involvement in the 1798 rebellion. It is recorded[44] that, when he had grown a little older, he foiled an attempt by two other boys to hi-jack his uncle's jennet and car. Admiring the way in which one lad defeated two, a bystander called out: 'Ha! ha! The Frenchman will do for ye!' De Valera's authorized biography says that he got into other fights by standing up for his Uncle Patrick, who was known as the 'Dane Coll'. This may have been a corrupt pronunciation of Dean, a nickname given either because Patrick was sometimes called on to perform functions in the local church, such as giving out the rosary, or because he was distantly related to a Dean Coll in nearby Newcastle West. But the de Valera version is that he would not allow any uncle of his to be stigmatized by reference to the Danish Vikings who once pillaged Ireland.[45]

The fights were not the only difficulties which the young de Valera had to contend with during his eight years at Bruree School. In years to come he found it easier to romanticize the Irish peasantry in retrospect than he did while living amongst them. A half-century later he told Frank Gallagher a story which gives a telling indication of how the coarsened texture of his childhood environment must have impacted on him. Soon after he arrived in Ireland, when he could not have been 'more than three,'[46] his grandmother took him on a pilgrimage to a holy well. As the well was situated in rough ground she left him in a cottage nearby while she completed the pilgrimage. In the cottage a young woman was feeding a baby 'goody' – bread and sugar softened in boiled milk. Having fed the child, she cleaned the spoon in her mouth and then used it to give de Valera some of the 'goody'. Sixty years later Gallagher marvelled at how he could recall both the taste of the 'goody' and his revulsion at the girl's licking the spoon.

The Coll household did not provide a great deal in the way of childish entertainment. His official biography had to concentrate on one annual event to provide a paragraph on 'Eddie's pleasures':[47] 'The race-meeting at Athlacca with its "thimble riggers", "three-card tricksters", the man in the barrel who kept bobbing his head up and down while people tried to hit him with a thrown wattle, "pigs crubeens", more sweets and cakes and, of course, the races themselves – all this was top entertainment.' And, if this 'top entertainment' was not enough to sustain a lad for a year, when the heady delights of Athlacca began to fade Bruree also provided a 'forge and the cooper's yard, producing an endless supply of firkins and barrels. There were three bootmakers, though Connor's was only for fine boots.' It is not made clear whether or not the quality of Connor's footwear deprived it of 'entertainment'. If it did, the children of the village would seem to have made up for the loss by visiting Rourke's, near Connor's, where 'a big blackbird was being trained to whistle "Harvey Duff" '. And on top of all this 'Bruree village church was a centre of much excitement'. This last was probably true enough because the parish priest, Father Sheehy, who would have been the leading figure in the village anyhow, was doubly famous for his nationalist sermons and for having served a prison sentence on account of his Land League activities. De Valera, who served Mass for him, has described sitting with his fellow altar boys 'drinking in every historic detail. Father Sheehy, eyes closed and long nose reaching his lips, retailed the golden exploits of bygone days, as if in ecstasy.'[48] This vision of Father Sheehy prompts one to speculate as to whether the good priest would have been the more moved by knowing of the path his words helped to guide his altar boy along, or by the fact that a nephew of his own was to grow up to become the celebrated arch-revisionist Dr Conor Cruise O'Brien.

De Valera developed one unusual pastime which does not appear on the official list of 'Eddie's pleasures': digging for springs. 'In the long summer evenings he and a companion often spent hours at this work.[49] It would seem a peculiar method of enjoyment, and indeed an unprofitable one', comments his sympathetic but puzzled biographer. But de Valera was so keen on this activity that he rigged up 'something in the shape of a bell which he affixed to the top of a hawthorn tree. . . . The first to arrive would pull the string and the loud metallic sound of the time-saving apparatus resounded through the ether, a reminder to the absent youth that operations had commenced.' From his late teens another loud sound came to be associated with him: the crack of a shotgun cartridge. He became so fond of fowling that neighbours remarked he seemed to have a different gun every time he came home. Prophetically he said: 'I'm afraid I shall be a soldier. I have such a love for guns.'

Near the end of his parliamentary career de Valera gave a remarkable lecture in Bruree, 'a recalling of things I heard in this very spot some 65 years ago'.[50] He spoke for an hour and a half without notes. But while he went into great and affectionate detail about history and topography, he had comparatively little to give in the way of boyhood memories. Swimming in the Maigue, being sent by the master to watch for the arrival of the school inspector, remembering a penny farthing bicycle race at the local sports, the arrival of the pneumatic tyre – but of Bruree and its life only an outline:[51]

> I would like to speak of the changes that have occurred in the sixty-five odd years since I was here. I would like if we could bring back parts of the old life I knew here, but there were other parts that were not so good. . . . We had two tailor's shops, we had shoemakers, dressmakers, stone masons, thatchers, carpenters, smiths. . . . We had here, then, a little self-sufficing community, a very pleasant community. It was a pleasant life for those who were able to make a living. . . .

Perhaps one reason why there is so little flesh on the bones of de Valera's memory is because it was consciously, or unconsciously, selective. In later life, for political reasons, he idealized the ethos of the peasant patriarchy; he never referred to the reality of the brute sexuality and near slavery that lay behind that patriarchy, and which bore particularly heavily on women. Sean Moylan, who later became a famous IRA leader and a lifelong political colleague of de Valera's, has left a memoir[52] which paints a more accurate and more uncomfortable picture:

> . . . for the farmer's wife, and particularly for the female farm servant, there was no respite. From the dawn's early light to the sunlight's last gleaming she was still unflaggingly employed . . . and fathead economists talk about the causes of emigration! It amazed me to see a slight young girl lift a huge pot of boiling potatoes from the fire and lug it into the farmyard to feed pigs and poultry. The carrying of these awkward shaped pots, weighing over fifty pounds, necessitated a posture that surely wrenched every organ in the body out of its proper alignment, with evil effect in after years.

Moylan ended his description with a plea for 'the mothers of the race whose lot on Irish farms is cast in any but pleasant places'.

But de Valera, although he invariably showed a studied courtesy to women, never showed any disposition to improve their lot in society. He would always have loyal women workers around him, but not colleagues. Perhaps the absence of a mother in his own formative years had something to do with his attitude. Grandmother Coll seems to have been closer in character to Hannie than to Kate. Years after her death there was an obvious regard in the manner in which de Valera described for Gallagher various details of her daily life: the care with which she used to tie her apron strings; how she went about her chores saying prayers; how she was always first up, collecting eggs, milking cows, getting the breakfast. In his first days at Bruree de Valera, who slept with his grandmother, used to leave her bed when she got up and he would then climb in with his uncle.

His 'hard though good uncle'[53] Patrick was obviously a man of some political talent. He served on the Killmallock Board of Guardians for three three-year terms, and was active throughout Munster in the labour movement. He thrashed the lad when he 'mitched' from school. Physical punishment was commonly meted out for misbehaviour, or what was deemed to be misbehaviour: for example, using the good reins (normally kept for driving the donkey to Mass on Sunday) to make a swing.[54] Patrick Coll's reaction to his nephew's mitching seems to have been prompted by anger at wasting time which might have been spent on the farm, rather than at lost educational opportunity – for he ensured that the boy took the fullest possible part in the labouring work of the Coll holding. In class II de Valera is recorded as being present on thirty-six days fewer than the most regular boys.[55]

One of de Valera's most famous speeches to the Dail during a perfervid moment in his career[56] gave details of his chores:

17

> There was not an operation on the farm, with perhaps one exception, that I as a youngster had not performed. I lived in a labourer's cottage, but the tenant in his way could be regarded as a small farmer. From my earliest days I participated in every operation that takes place on a farm. One thing I did not learn, how to plough, but until I was sixteen years of age there was no farm work from the spancelling of a goat and milking of a cow, that I had not to deal with. I cleaned out the cowhouses. I followed the tumbler rake. I took my place on the cart and filled the load of hay. I took milk to the creamery. I harnessed the donkey, the jennet and the horse.

His early thought was so conditioned by farming routine that when he was once given a school essay to write on 'Making Hay While the Sun Shines' he could think of nothing to say. 'What other time would you make hay?' he asked.[57] One task he did not mention in the Dail was grazing the cows along the 'long acre', the grassy roadside ditches. This was a normal method of eking out the sparse amount of grass available either on the Coll's own half acre on on what they could rent, and it involved keeping a wary eye out for the police. When they showed up, de Valera used to pretend to be driving the cattle from one field to another.

But despite all this toil, from his earliest days he seems to have been sufficiently other-directed and self-motivated to put in the study required to get him promoted from one class to another. Gallagher recorded an anecdote which shows how, even at the age of twelve, de Valera had his eyes set on wider horizons than Bruree. He and a boy some four years older were digging potatoes one day when the other boy announced that he was going to Limerick to a job. To de Valera, going to Limerick 'seemed like a great adventure and he said bitterly to himself, "and I am to remain digging potatoes all my life." '[58] Another anecdote from the period when his time at Bruree School was drawing to a close could be taken as an early illustration of his competitiveness, his cunning, his courage, his studiousness or a combination of all four. He told Gallagher:[59]

> There was to be an inspection . . . we were all preparing for it. I was the star reader but before the great day came I was down with the measles. The boy who sat next to me in class and who if I was absent the master would produce as the star came to my grandmother on the morning of the inspection. I heard him warning her how dangerous it is if anybody thinks to be allowed out with the measles. I was very sick but when that boy left I waited until my grandmother had gone off on some chore. Then I tumbled out of bed and dressing started off to school. Half way there I met the master coming to fetch me. I did my stuff but remember well how the other pupils stood well clear of me. Half the class were over to the right and the other half were over to the left with me alone in the middle.

De Valera's grandmother died in 1895, her loss being somewhat mitigated for him by the fact that Hannie had come back to Ireland once more to nurse her. It was at this stage that the boy gave a major display of that determination and self-belief that was to be the hallmark of his adult career. With the illness and death of his grandmother, his labouring chores were increased considerably: cooking was added to his list of duties. He even prepared the wedding breakfast[60] when his Uncle Patrick went through with the marriage that he had seemingly been hesitating over while his mother was alive. Coll married Catherine Dillon and they had three children, Patrick, Elizabeth and Mary.

But de Valera was determined not to 'remain digging potatoes all my life'. In his official biography he says his uncle was prepared to go part of the way towards meeting his aspirations to do something other than manual labour by urging him to become a monitor at Bruree School. Monitors were boys who had recently left school and returned to assist the teacher, in the hope that classroom experience would help them become teachers themselves. De Valera's biography says that he rejected this plan as a 'dead end unless he had enough money to pay for his teacher's training later'.[61] According to his biography, he decided that Bruree would never satisfy him and wrote to Hannie asking her to persuade his mother to bring him back to America, as an alternative to a life either as a labourer or as a monitor. But, the biography tells us, he had a hidden agenda. He wanted to persuade his uncle to send him to Charleville Christian Brothers' School which, unlike Bruree, offered the possibility of studying for an exhibition that could carry him on up the educational ladder. 'At last uncle Pat agreed to the scheme since de Valera was willing to walk the seven miles there when necessary.'

However, de Valera confided privately to Gallagher[62] that his uncle saw no need for school and that he got to Charleville by making his mother an offer she could not refuse. He insisted that either he was sent to Charleville or she sent him his passage money for America. Kate evidently shrank from bringing her first-born to the USA. Charleville it was, and Gallagher's diary notes: 'First Victory for E. de V.'[63] De Valera may have shrunk from publicly recording a deliberate refusal by his mother to accept him, or the differing versions of how he came to attend Charleville may simply stem from memory lapse – his biography was published thirty-three years after he confided in Gallagher. But certainly his two years at Charleville were a test of character that he passed with honour.

He had got the idea of going to the school in the first place through the example of an older boy at Bruree who had gone on to win an exhibition there. But this lad's home was three miles nearer to Charleville than Knockmore, and whatever inducements Kate brought to bear on Patrick Coll these did not include the provision of a bicycle. Eamon de Valera was only fourteen years old on 2 November 1896 when he started at Charleville. He may have got to school by train, but there was none back to Bruree until three hours after school ended. His biography tells how 'often on the long walk home from Knockmore he would rest exhausted against a fence, longing to throw away the heavy pile of school books. But he persisted as so often later in life.'[64] And persist he did, to such effect that in the summer after he enrolled at Charleville he was allowed a trial run at the exhibition examination, which he passed with honours. Owing to his youth he then had a year in hand, which he put to such good use that the second time around he got honours in all his subjects and was awarded an exhibition of £20 a year for three years.

His subjects were English, French, Greek, Latin, arithmetic, geometry and algebra. In retrospect it seems curious that one who throughout much of his life was preoccupied with history did not include that subject in his studies. It would, of course, have been very difficult for him to do so, as history in those imperial days largely meant British history. In their schoolbooks children learned such things as: 'On the east of Ireland is England where the Queen lives. Many people who live in Ireland were born in England, and we speak the same language, and are called one nation.' They were taught to recite:[65]

I thank the goodness and the grace
Which on my birth has smiled
And made me in these Christian days
A happy English child.

Attempts to present Irish history in the British-controlled classrooms of those days would have been looked upon as coming somewhere between heresy and sedition. De Valera would have heard far more Irish history from Father Sheehy, and at the Coll fireside, than from his own teachers. He later commented to Gallagher about the difficulties of getting Irish historians to express 'the national case'. Their training, he said, had been rather to admire the powerful empire than the little nation. He told Gallagher that he originally knew far more about early Greek history than about Irish history, and that it was from his study of Greek history that he learned to respect the little nation and the defence of its rights. This, he implied, made it easier to 'assert the full claim of Ireland'.[66] What he did not say to Gallagher was that, as will be seen, he attempted to address the issue of history teaching by making a sustained attempt to have it written to suit his own purposes.

Although de Valera did not study history at Charleville, it is important to note at this stage that the reason he was still talking about asserting the 'full claim of Ireland' fifty-six years after he first entered the school[67] was largely because of events which took place as he was growing up in Bruree. He was four years old when the constitutional movement for legislative independence from Great Britain, which had been going on throughout the nineteenth century under various guises, suddenly came to a point of crisis. In 1886 Prime Minister Gladstone, dependent for his continuation in Government on Parnell and his Irish Parliamentary Party, introduced the Home Rule Bill. This modest attempt at undoing the Act of Union of 1800, which had snuffed out the independent Irish legislature and forced Members of Parliament elected to Irish constituencies to sit in

Westminster, was received with horror by Irish Unionists, particularly those in north-eastern Ireland, where they formed a local majority. Seeing a chance of using the issue to oust Gladstone and the Liberals, Randolph Churchill played the Orange[68] card, as he put it, to begin that alliance between right-wing British Conservatives and Ulster Protestant Unionists which continues to this day, albeit in attenuated form. In one ringing phrase he formulated the policy that contains the reason why six of Ireland's thirty two-counties are still part of the United Kingdom: 'Ulster will fight and Ulster will be right.'[69]

The Churchill formula worked. Gladstone was defeated on the Home Rule issue and Salisbury replaced him as Prime Minister at the head of a Conservative Government. But the victory helped to set in train that explosion of mistrust in English parliamentary method that eventually led to Eamon de Valera taking a road familiar to many an Irish idealist – forswearing the ballot box for the bomb and the bullet. Of the Irish MPs returned in 1886 the majority in favour of Home Rule was eighty-six, with seventeen opposed. At Westminster, however, this majority became a minority which only had significance so long as circumstances allowed Parnell to deploy his followers for or against one of the two great English parties. And with his fall in 1891 this significance was to vanish for twenty formative years of de Valera's life. During that time he came to believe that constitutional methods would not induce Britain to concede justice to Ireland.

The famous Mitchelstown shootings occurred when he was five, in 1887. Police fire killed three members of a mob inflamed by proceedings at the local courthouse brought against a Nationalist MP by the Crown Prosecutor, Edward Carson, later to be the principal leader of the movement that used Randolph Churchill's policy to ensure the partition of Ireland. De Valera's earliest political memories were of fireside discussions about these shootings. He recalled a sense of delight when the subject of the Mitchelstown proceedings, the Land League leader William O'Brien, who refused to wear prison clothes, had a suit smuggled in to him. But he remembered with disappointment the aftermath of a boycotting demonstration he witnessed around the same time. The Fedamore brass band turned up to help not only make a pariah out of an unpopular local landlord, but to deafen him into the bargain with the aid of 'the biggest drum he had ever seen'. Drums filled the boy's conversation thereafter to such an extent that he was given one for Christmas – and was mortified at how tiny it was compared to the Fedamore one. The walls of his loft bedroom were covered with political cartoons fron the weekly *Freeman's Journal*.

However, there was little passion in the Coll political conversation. De Valera remembered being glad when he heard of Parnell's vindication in the Piggot forgery case. But he recalled sorrow, rather than vituperation, around the fireside when Parnell fell over the Kitty O'Shea divorce case.

The simple truth was that in his school days de Valera saw politics as an interesting phenomenon outside the reality of his daily existence. This reality was that he would break stones or dig potatoes, whether Home Rule came or not, if he did not apply himself to getting a higher education. But in the end the fact that he got one came about not so much through his own diligence as because of a chance conversation in a railway carriage between two priests.[70]

He failed to get a place at two Co. Limerick schools, the Jesuit-run St Munchin's and Mungret Colleges. But one day the local curate, Father James Liston, rode up to the door of Knockmore on his horse and called out: 'Eddie, I have news for you.' The news was that while on a holiday train journey that year he had met Father Larry Healy, the President of Blackrock College. During the meeting he had told Father Healy about his bright young parishioner, and when de Valera was refused by the Jesuits he decided to write to the President. Father Healy turned up trumps. Although the school year had already begun he replied to Father Liston[71] accepting the lad. From what was known of him, he said his new pupil would have a 'pretty brilliant career' if he applied himself. De Valera seems to have had intimations of the brilliant career himself, for when the letter was passed on to his uncle by Father Liston he wrote across it: 'Please do not let this go astray as it may be wanting. E. de V.' It was an early indication of de Valera's legendary propensity for storing documents. A notable feature of Father Healy's offer was the fact that he volunteered to take in lieu of fees the £20 prize which de Valera had won, which was a big concession, as the normal fee was £40 per annum.

But, big as it was, Patrick Coll demanded a £5 share, which must have seemed a very large sum to a labourer of the time, especially one newly confronting the problems of supporting a wife. However, de Valera's persistence not only ensured that the full £20 found its way to Father Healy, but that, amongst other necessities, he was provided with a new suit, costing seventeen shillings, and a strong tin trunk to keep his belongings in. The trunk seemed less of an asset when he arrived in Dublin the day after its purchase. A horse-drawn cab took him to O'Connell Street, in the centre of the city, after his arrival by train at Kingsbridge Station. But he had then to get himself and the heavy trunk on foot, through crowds never seen at Athlacca, to Merrion Square, about half a mile away, whence the tram left for Blackrock College – then, unknown to him, commonly known as the 'French college'. As there was also a Vincentian College in Blackrock the conductor asked him whether he meant the 'French college'; de Valera assured him that, wherever he was going, it was not to a French college. Fortunately for him the conductor decided otherwise, and so Edward de Valera arrived safely in Blackrock to a sympathetic welcome from a member of the 'French' congregation who spoke with a reassuringly broad Tipperary accent – Brother Mary Paul McGrath.

Brother McGrath's reception of the determined but confused and very gauche sixteen-year-old set the tone for what was to become for de Valera a lifelong relationship with the College. On his first night in the dormitory the boy in the bed beside him wept with homesickness. De Valera was amazed. For his part, 'he felt joy rather than sorrow'.[72] Here he was in an environment of study, free of the drudgery of Knockmore and the long walks from Charleville. An eloquent assessment of his home life came at Christmas, when he opted to stay on at the College with the clerical students, who only returned home at the summer break. He thought initially of becoming a clerical student himself, but Father Healy advised him to give the matter more thought. The idea of the priesthood occurred to him several times subsequently, yet it is a curious fact that, though many sources attest to his piety and deep religiosity, no Director of Vocations whom de Valera consulted encouraged him to become a priest. Was there a sense that, despite his obvious potential for giving valuable service to the Church, perhaps at a very high level, de Valera might create problems for authority? These hard-to-explain refusals may have been a factor in the continuing rumours about his illegitimacy since, in those days, birth on the wrong side of the blanket automatically disbarred an applicant from the priesthood. At all events, de Valera never gave the priesthood anything like the attention he bestowed on Blackrock itself.

In many ways the College epitomizes the better side of the Irish Church. Although both before and after de Valera's day ' 'Rock' has traditionally produced a high proportion of Ireland's decision-takers in the Church, civil service, Government and professions, its elitist role has always been tempered by its Father Healys and Brother McGraths. The College was opened on 5 September 1860 by French Holy Ghost Fathers, in recognition by the Vatican's geo-politicians of the growing potential for development in post-emancipation Catholic Ireland[73] and as a valuable source of missionaries with which to capitalize on the opportunities created for the Church by the scramble for Africa. By the time de Valera arrived there the school had become one of the largest in the country, excelling in sport as well as at passing examinations. Symbolically, in view of his aversion from the prospect of a life digging tubers, de Valera's first sporting triumph in Blackrock was winning the 1899 senior potato race. After his emotionally and intellectually starved existence at Knockmore Blackrock became not just an academy for him but a home, and after he married he chose to live, and ultimately to die, as near to the College as possible.

The exhibition system of payment by result, which gave de Valera and many other boys of his class their educational break, had been recommended to the British by the founder of Blackrock, Père Jules Lemann. The result was fierce competition amongst schools for a share of what little money the Government made available for scholarships; the system was attacked by many educationalists as favouring cramming and the passing of examinations at the expense of all other interests. It was, however, defended by some on the grounds that it offered pupils like de Valera a chance of entering schools other than those controlled by the British – that is, Protestant schools; and by de Valera himself on the basis that the system kept both students and teachers on their toes.

A normal day in Blackrock was as follows:

6.00 (in summer, 5.45) Rising.
6.15 (in summer, 6) To the Study Hall. Prayer, conference or spiritual reading.
6.35 (in summer, 6.20) Study.
7.45 To the Chapel. Meditation, rosary, holy mass.
8.20 Breakfast. Recreation (practice for the band). Linen room.
9.15 Class.
11.30 Lunch.
12.00 Class.
2.00 Recreation.
2.20 Class.
3.30 Dinner. Recreation.
5.00 Study.
6.45 Recreation.
6.55 Study.
8.00 (in summer 7.45) Supper. Recreation.
8.30 Prayer (in the dormitories).

Even de Valera's relief at escaping Knockmore did not save him from some adjustment problems with Blackrock and its routine. He had a difficult relationship in his first year with a Latin teacher, Father James Keawell, who repeatedly sent him to the Dean of Studies, Father Thomas O'Hanlon, to be punished. Eventually the Dean inquired of the boy why he was appearing before him so often. Hearing de Valera's side of the story he restricted his reply to asking him if he were really doing his best and, satisfied that he was, sent him back to his class, unpunished either then or subsequently. That understanding Dean saved de Valera's career, for he later told Gallagher that, had he been beaten each time he was sent to the Dean, 'I could not have stood it.' He said he would have left the school.[74] De Valera subsequently took first place in Latin in his class, defeating his teacher's favourite pupil; for this he was awarded the distinction of reading prayers at the priests' table in the refectory. Father Keawell reacted by coming up to him on his first day at the table to ask, publicly: 'Did ye copy, de Valera?' De Valera said he was 'so angry he could have struck him. Instead, having no other recourse, he left the table.' Gallagher remarked on how 'nearly fifty years later' de Valera was 'still angry with that teacher and still full of affection for the Dean'.

By Christmas he had acclimatized well enough to secure sixth place in the middle grade honours class, out of a total of eighteen, taking first place in arithmetic and religious instruction. And by the following year, 1899, he had improved to a point where in the public examinations, in which Blackrock won first place in Ireland, he got honours in Greek, Latin,

English, French, arithmetic, algebra and Euclid. In the process he secured sufficient marks both to win an exhibition to keep him at the College for the following year and to become the school's Student of the Year. This last achievement marked an important watershed in his social acceptance within the College. 'Until then he was something of an outsider among his peers, being a newcomer and otherwise undistinguished.'[75]

The Student of the Year was appointed the main reader of prayers in church, study and dormitory, and was also called upon to give religious readings during retreats when all the other students remained silent. This role brought him some teasing from the other boys, but overall it gave him increased stature and added self-confidence as a public speaker. It also gave him an opportunity to exhibit the peculiar de Valera sense of humour and a lasting love of the prayers he read out, which he later taught to his children and had recited for him in his last days. But he was lucky that his grisly sense of humour did not hasten the approach of the said days. During one lunch hour of retreat-enforced silence, his contribution to his colleagues' enjoyment of their meal was a long dissertation on death which included a vivid description of a corpse being eaten by worms. Despite this he made friends – the gentle and scholarly John d'Alton, later Cardinal of All Ireland, and in particular Frank Hughes of Kiltimagh, Co. Mayo, who like himself was fatherless. He spent Christmas of 1899 in Hughes' home, and later he and Hughes were to become best man at each other's weddings and godfathers to their respective eldest children. An illuminated verse which de Valera copied out in coloured inks and presented to Hughes[76] on 25 April 1900 commemorates their friendship:

When the evening sun is sinking
And your mind from trouble free
When of absent friends you're thinking.
Don't forget to think of me.

The sentimental note struck in the doggerel, which would have come as a surprise to some of his contemporaries, is in keeping with one facet of de Valera's character. His son Vivion once described to me how his father wept over the death of the family canary, which had escaped its cage. But two other letters of his to Hughes illustrate more dominant aspects of his character – hard-headedness in business and a self-reliance bordering in the arrogant. The first is in response to a request from Hughes for advice on what to do about some family property:

I read all the letters very carefully. My advice to you is practically what Kitty's mother thinks – take the place. I see all the difficulties before you. *Count* on no help whatever – that is the only safe way – if it comes, well and good.

Make all arrangements strong and binding, leave nothing to promises, and place no dependence on expressions of goodwill etc – however genuine now. Heaven only knows what might lead to misunderstandings later. If you take it, hard work and unfortunately something far worse, more anxiety than ye ever knew before, is I fear in store for you and Kitty. I pray that it may be less than I anticipate. Be sure about defining Kitty's position.

. . . One word – don't devote more time to the farm as if it were your main source of income – *if* this extra time is taken from your advancement in your profession.

The second perfectly illustrates the precepts of indifference to the feelings of others which in later life he would follow over and over again at moments of political crisis. It was written in response to a letter from Hughes confiding his worries about a clash between his brother, a priest, and higher ecclesiastical authority:[77]

. . . you seem to be too sensitive about the opinion of the world. I am far too much that way myself but I am not *I think* quite as bad as you are. Sensitiveness of this sort is a great misfortune. It spoils one's peace of mind more than anything else I know. Get shut of it if you can. We two are too fond of trying to look at things as we expect other people will look at them and generally go wrong in our estimate. Let what the world and your neighbour think be damned. Did you ever see the man who tried his best to be popular ever succeed except in a paltry measure – the old man and his ass just occurs to me. Aesop knew what I mean. Here's to the sunshine when the thunder is over!

It was, however, a friendship which began the following year with Michael Smithwick, a former Blackrock student who acted as tutor to the scholarship class in return for free lodgings, that most influenced his future career. Smithwick encouraged him to play rugby, to study mathematics and, most importantly, to learn the Irish language. In this capacity Smithwick was thus ultimately instrumental in both de Valera's meeting the woman he would marry, Sinead Flanagan, and in his decision to become a revolutionary.

At Blackrock de Valera took an interest in sport, chiefly rugby, javelin throwing and cycling. Blackrock was and is the great rugby school of Ireland, and de Valera developed such a love of the sport that he once shocked the purists of Gaelic football by saying that he thought rugby was the game that suited the Irish temperament best.[78] He had some athletic success, but in general he was more enthusiastic and idiosyncratic than accomplished where sport was concerned. He took up the javelin after watching some African athletes who had visited the College, and tried without success to become proficient in the sport by painstakingly hammering straight a pin from a Knockmore hay rake and 'feathering' it in an attempt to guide its flight.

In rugby he developed a passion for place kicking and, after leaving the College, was to win lasting renown (or opprobrium) for losing a match in which, as captain of the past pupils' 'seconds' team, he insisted in taking all the place kicks himself. One result of this game was that it drew his first anonymous letter, a cartoon showing a player attempting to kick a round ball; it said, amongst other things, 'Alas, alas for our blighted hopes'.[79] In running he won a reputation for chivalry by stopping to attend to another competitor who collapsed beside him during the half-mile race which some say he might have gone on to win himself, others that it was he who tripped the fallen one. The year after this he entered for the mile, and was himself nearing the point of collapse as he followed on the heels of the leading runner when it occurred to him that the other lad must be just as stressed. He forced himself to 'go one more round', and won.[80]

One of the features of Blackrock was (and still is) 'the Castle' – the former Williamstown Castle, built by William Vavassour in 1760, which was acquired by Blackrock in 1875 to provide a third-level college for students sitting civil service examinations. It was affiliated to Newman's Catholic University in 1854, and in 1882, the year of de Valera's birth, it had become a University College which it was hoped would become a recognized College of the Royal University. However it was denied this recognition, which meant that, though it prepared students for the university examinations, it got no paid professors and examiners from the Royal University. This put Castle students at a disadvantage insofar as the recognized colleges were concerned. First, because examinations were set by professors from these colleges their students knew, from the texts they recommended, what areas were likely to form the basis of questions and could prepare accordingly. Second, the Castle, depending for its income on students who could not afford to pay high fees, was itself not able to pay for qualified staff. Nevertheless the Castle presented both a scholarly and a sympathetic milieu for de Valera – and one, moreover, in which he was well placed to keep an eye out for employment opportunities. Accordingly, having completed senior grade, he enrolled in the Castle in the autumn of 1900 to spend a year doing the matriculation examination necessary before going on to take his BA.

Pausing for a moment to assess his career at Blackrock before moving on to his third-level interlude, one feels that his time in secondary school was probably best summed up by his eminent contemporary John d'Alton, later Cardinal d'Alton, who maintained a friendly relationship with de Valera throughout his long life. As an old man d'Alton recalled the first time he heard de Valera's name and the impression he subsequently made on him.[81] The Dean of Studies, Father O'Hanlon, gave the students a pep talk early in September 1898 in which he warned them that: 'You had better pull up your socks. There is a prodigy arriving from Charleville, who will set the pace.' However, the subsequent career of the prodigy caused the Cardinal to sum him up as follows: 'Dev was a good, very serious student, good at mathematics but not outstanding otherwise.'

Not surprisingly, in view of this assessment, it was on mathematics that de Valera placed his hopes of scholarships. He moved towards his objectives successfully by a combination of country cuteness and brutal hard work. The former was well demonstrated on one occasion during the year when a science teacher passed a low-voltage current through a basin of water containing a silver coin and told his pupils that the first to remove the coin from the basin could have it. De Valera let the others try first while he figured out the trick. Eventually he realized that, when the others closed their fingers over the coin, the current made them let go again. So he made no attempt to pick up the coin but used his knuckles to push it up and out of the basin.

He made up for the teaching deficiencies in the College by following a fearsome work schedule which he once jotted down on the back of a sports programme:[82] '5.45 rising, 6.00 to 7.30 Euclid. 8.30–11.30, Algebra (2 hours)–10.30 Euclid 1 hour. 12.00–12.30 Conics, 5.00–7.00 Natural philosophy, 7.30–10.30 Trigonometry and Theoretical Equations.'

His methods paid off. The following July he was awarded a £24 exhibition, coming tenth in Ireland in the matriculation examination. But he may not have adhered to the schedule as rigidly as the timetable suggests. There are a number of well-authenticated instances of his going over the wall of the College after the gates were locked to visit Keegan's pub nearby. On one such occasion the 'cute hoor' approach saved him from being 'last man over'. By the rules of an illegal but well-etablished College competition, this meant he would have had to stand treat. But he took the precaution of reconnoitring the surface of the wall before the umpire gave the signal for the line of students to race up and over: his knowledge of the toe-holds got him over without having to pay.

Obviously his finances did not allow very many sorties, but on at least one occasion it was his sense of humour, not his lack of cash, that kept him from Keegan's. As it was known that the prefect supposed to be on duty that night was in fact attending a concert, several of the students took advantage of his absence to visit the pub – but not de Valera. He went to the prefect's room and borrowed his soutane and biretta. Then, positioning himself just far enough from the wall to be seen but not near enough to be identified, he adopted the prefect's unmistakable stance. Here he stood watching as one after another the returning students dropped over the wall and, as they thought, into a trap which they expected would cost them a fine – the usual punishment for an occasional breach of regulations of that sort. There was considerable ill feeling about what was considered to be the prefect's low tactics. Next day he was greeted with derisory versions of 'The Peeler and the Goat' – a traditional indication of student displeasure at underhand behaviour which he found neither explicable nor warranted. In view of the ugly atmosphere de Valera decided not to enlighten anyone as to what had happened until more than thirty years were passed and he had become the country's Prime Minister.[83]

In 1902 he won a mathematics scholarship worth £20 and an exhibition worth £15, but he felt that these did not properly cover what he was costing the College and, to make up, took over the tutoring of two students for the solicitors' apprentice examination. It was his first teaching project and a successful one; both pupils passed with honours and, as a token of appreciation, presented de Valera with a four-shilling ticket to the Ireland v. Wales rugby international at Lansdowne Road on 8 March 1902. Characteristically he wrote on the retained portion 'given me by my first class', inscribed the names of the students and ensured that the ticket was preserved for posterity.[84]

By now de Valera was a figure of some consequence at Blackrock. At Christmas 1900 he became Secretary of the first Conference of St Vincent de Paul to be formed in the College, and took his part in visiting poor families in the Blackrock area. The following year he was elected President of the Society and was described as being 'earnest about his work in a degree beyond his fellow workers'.[85] His earnestness was attested to by the fact that in 1902 he was awarded a Bible for taking first place in the first Catholic apologetics course set up by the Fathers for university students of the College. And he was sufficiently trusted to be allowed his own room in the tower over the Castle. He asked for this room because he thought that the fresh air on the roof might counteract his tendency to fall asleep while he studied.

The sleepiness persisted all through his life. Even after he had become Prime Minister he confided to a friend[86] that he was thinking of getting himself a standing desk, because he was still falling asleep in his office. But he also said that he attributed his survival through the many crisis in his life to his fortunate ability to get a good night's sleep no matter what his anxieties were.

De Valera was also an outstanding member of the College Literary and Debating Society. Some of his contributions are of interest in the light of his subsequent career. The Society's minutes[87] summarized his views on the motion 'That the policy of free trade is preferable to protection' as follows: 'Mr de Valera was in favour of a little of both.' And, on the motion that 'Constitutional monarchy as a form of government is preferable to Republicanism': 'Mr de Valera maintained that constant elections disturbed the nation, and are not conducive to the prosperity of the people. . . .'

Time would show him markedly altering his views in this regard. He preferred monarchy over democracy because 'There is no rule so tyrannical as them all.' One of the burning issues of the day was the question of a National University for Ireland. De Valera went to a good deal of trouble to research a closely written twenty-page foolscap paper on the subject, which he delivered on 18 February 1903.[88] Some of the thoughts he expressed in this paper have a prophetic ring to them, though at this stage he was not in any sense active in the nationalist arena. Even his interest in the Irish language lay in the future. But he asked:

Is it that the problem is too hard for English statesmen to solve? They who pretend they can legislate for us better than we could for ourselves. And yet if we had but a free Parliament in College Green for the space of one single hour, this vexing question would be put to rest for ever. It seems, indeed, that Englishmen, even the most liberal amongst them, with one or two notable exceptions, have never been able to understand the needs of Ireland properly. . . .

In a passage that foreshadowed the limited role he was later to envisage for the Protestants of Northern Ireland he suggested that, as Belfast's Presbyterians were not yet ready for a university of their own, they should be given a higher technical college and come to Dublin for their degrees. Nevertheless he argued the case for 'one national university' with some large-mindedness:

> . . . if there was but one national university, it would tend to develop a strong national spirit among all students at it, whatever might be their other opinions and differences. You would have those men going out into public life with that intense common sympathy, with a common interest for which they would be ready to sacrifice their individual prejudices and inclinations. Such a spirit it is that makes patriots and constitutes the stability of a nation . . . a thing which would do much to put an end to the present religious strife in the country, while at the same time the religious training of all parties would not be neglected nor their consciences violated. . . .

He was at this stage a year away from his final BA examination, in which he hoped to achieve an honours degree. The de Valera of the punishing work schedule would normally have devoted that year exclusively to study, but an unexpected vacancy arose in Blackrock's sister college in Tipperary, Rockwell, for a mathematics and physics teacher. Because of his record in Blackrock de Valera was given first option on the job by the Dean of the Castle, Father Downey. Weighing the security of the position against the disadvantages it posed both for concentrated study and for the availability of expert tuition, de Valera decided to accept.

A former teacher of his summed up in gentle but telling terms the impression that de Valera created on the staff during his Blackrock days: 'He had a certain dignity of manner, a gentleness of disposition, a capability of adapting himself to circumstances, or perhaps I should say of *utilising those circumstances that served his purpose.*'[89] His stay in Rockwell, from 1903 to 1905, seems to have provided him with the nearest he came in life to a hedonistic interlude. 'Dev tended to look on his period at Rockwell as the happiest time of his life.'[90] This was certainly the public impression he gave of his stay there. But his private revelations to Gallagher give insights into his attitudes to College authority which are open to a more complex interpretation. He was certainly happy for most of his stay at the Tipperary school, but for all the glowing reference with which the President of the College furnished him after his two years' stay he did leave in rather headlong, unthought out fashion. And it is something of a paradox that, despite the close, friendly relationship he always maintained with Blackrock, he was not to be taken on again at 'Rock as a teacher. His only employment with the Holy Ghost Fathers after Rockwell consisted of some afternoon classes provided by his old friend Father O'Hanlon at St Mary's, the Fathers' day school at Rathmines.

While at Rockwell, apart from rugby and allied pastimes, chiefly drinking and dancing, de Valera had a short-lived romance with a local hotelier's daughter.[91] He was by now a striking figure, tall, olive-complexioned, with flashing brown eyes, a high forehead and an imperious, commanding presence that could suddenly become less daunting because of a surprisingly winning, gentle smile. But there was enough substance behind the imperious mien to cause him, by his own account at least, several brushes with the College authorities. It was in Rockwell also that he was first christened 'Dev.' – by one of the other teachers on the staff, Tom O'Donnell.

At Rockwell 'Dev.' was described as having had 'an eye for the girls'[92] – in particular for Mary Stewart, daughter of the owner of Stewart's Hotel in Cashel who, according to local legend, appears to have been fonder of him than he of her. For, although he did devise a cypher for her to prevent the local postman reading their postcards, he did not allow Mary's charms to stand in the way of the calls of career when the time came to transfer back to teaching in Dublin. But she always spoke well of him in after life and he of her.

He made several friends both at the College and in the neighbourhood. The famous rugby brothers, Jack and Mike Ryan, invited him to share their home and pastimes – shooting, fishing, card playing and 'totty twigging', the local slang for girl watching. Mike Ryan, who sometimes indulged in wrestling bouts with 'Dev.', once fell spectacularly foul of the legendary de Valera cunning. Loading a shotgun with a blank, he bet de Valera that he would not be able to hit Mike's hat from a distance of twenty yards. De Valera accepted the bet but, without Mike's noticing, switched the cartridge and blew Mike's hat to shreds.

The Ryans' presence on the Rockwell rugby team did more for its reputation than did de Valera's. On one famous occasion he took his eye off a ball so that he missed a catch which was gathered by the opposing wing three-quarter for the easiest of tries. This gave rise to the apocryphal story (it is told of many such rugby gaffes) that a former team mate of his on that occasion, hearing that de Valera had formed a Cabinet, commented: 'Jasus, I hope they didn't put him in Defence.' However de Valera in defence, as fullback, is credited with one of the longest kicks in Munster rugby.[93] Helped by a following wind, in a match at the Market Field in Limerick he kicked from his own try line to the dead ball line at the far end of the pitch.

Another rugby anecdote which Dev. told Frank Gallagher[94] contrasts strongly with the abstemious de Valera image of his later life. On a cold, raw day in Limerick Rockwell defeated the famous Garryowen team in a match in which de Valera, playing on the wing, scored a try. Because of the cold and the victory, instead of his usual few bottles of stout de Valera had eight whiskeys in Cruise's Hotel afterwards. He was argumentative in the train on the way back to Goold's Cross, where the players transferred to a jaunting-car, but escaped incident until that point. Then the jolting made him so ill that he vomited. 'Luckily nothing but the ground got it,' he remarked philosophically to Gallagher.

He was luckier still that some of the other incidents he related to Gallagher did not sharply curtail his Rockwell career in those authoritarian days. In one[95] he boasted about how he got the better of the President of the College, with whom he had agreed as part of his contract that he was to be supplied with cocoa. However, the other teachers began drinking cocoa also and, alarmed at the expense, the President ended the supply. Enraged, de Valera demanded 'fulfilment of his contract'. When the President refused de Valera made for his bike, threatening to put up in a hotel in Cashel and bill the College for his keep, and refusing to come back until he was guaranteed his cocoa. According to himself, de Valera was mounting his bike when the President called him back and said he could have the cocoa providing he did not let the other teachers see him drink it. De Valera refused the compromise, saying he would not censor his colleagues' diet, and ultimately the President caved in and restored the cocoa.

In another incident de Valera seems to have got away with deliberately damaging College property. He and some of the other teachers used to cycle to Cashel to dances and return to the college sometimes as late as 4 a.m. The authorities objected to their late return and one night the returning teachers found the door bolted against them. De Valera got into the College by climbing up to an open window. He then removed the bolt from the door, saying: 'We did not join the Rockwell staff as monks.' But on the next early morning return de Valera found the door was locked. He again climbed in through a window, and this time removed the lock and threw it in the College lake. The door was not locked again.

Not surprisingly in view of these extra-curricular activities de Valera only got a pass in his BA examination, despite the fact that he bade farewell to Mary Stewart for fourteen weeks at the end of his first year's teaching stint at Rockwell so that he could put in an intensive burst of study in the scholarly atmosphere of Blackrock. His failure to get honours effectively ruled out his becoming a university teacher, which at the time was a bitter disappointment to him. But he seems to have been a competent teacher at Rockwell at the secondary level. Amongst those whom he taught successfully were Paddy Browne, later a monsignor and President of University College, Galway, and a number of famous doctors including Michael O'Malley, Professor of Surgery at University College, Galway; Henry Barniville, Professor of Surgery at University College, Dublin; and Michael Hillery, whose son, also a doctor, would one day succeed de Valera as President of Ireland. Of his other pupils, Fionan Lynch became a Cabinet minister in the first native Irish Government after independence – opposing de Valera in the civil war – and the Leen brothers, James and Edward, became respectively an archbishop and President of Blackrock.

However, after putting in another year's teaching following his disappointing BA result de Valera decided to return to Dublin, apparently confident that he would get a part-time job at Blackrock. He had his long-standing connection with the College to rely on and, cocoa or no cocoa, the President, Father Brennan, had given him a fine reference[96] which said that de Valera's 'success and zeal as a teacher, and his ability and mastery of the subjects which he taught, and of others which he was not called upon to teach in Rockwell, deserve the highest praise that I can give; and the same may be said of his steadiness, gentlemanliness and other qualities which go to make up a thorough man and a thorough scholar'.

Was the reference in any way influenced by a desire to remove a 'difficult' man from the College? What is certain is that, Father Brennan's encomium notwithstanding, de Valera 'the thorough man' was proved to have been anything but thorough in investigating the employment situation at Blackrock. There was no vacancy for him, and he became so desperate that he went to Liverpool looking for work; but he found he could not stand living there and returned to Dublin almost overnight. Here he was lucky to pick up a temporary post at Belvedere, the Jesuit day school.

He took an active part in the sporting and extra-curricular life of Belvedere, chiefly in organizing the rugby team, but, fortunately for himself, returned to play cricket with Blackrock in the summer. Father Joseph Baldwin, who acted as confessor to the Sisters of Mercy at Carysfort Training College and who had been Dean of Rockwell during de Valera's time, was also a keen cricketer. He came to de Valera during a cricket match to tip him off that the nuns were looking for a mathematics teacher. Recommended by Baldwin, de Valera got the post.

However, it is a moot point as to whether the nuns were more interested in getting de Valera into the College or in getting the existing mathematics teacher out. This was Matthew J. Conran, later destined to be Professor of Mathematics at University College, Cork. Conran had actually tutored de Valera for his BA, and de Valera afterwards praised him for introducing him to the French approach – that of a science rather than merely a method of reckoning (le calcul). However, in the 'payment by results' climate of Irish education the nuns were less impressed by Conran's rarified view of mathematics as a method of developing the growth of a student's powers of logic, than by the fact that not enough of his students were being passed by the National Schools Board examiners.

De Valera is said to have been unhappy at replacing his old mentor, but, as so often in his career when his interests were at stake, he wrestled with his conscience and won. This was quite a significant moment in his career, and he was still not comfortable about it more than sixty years later. He told his biographers that he was 'highly critical of the way mathematics was taught . . . he found himself sorely hampered'.[97] De Valera, a part of his mind opening to the academic life, was conscious of the significance of the Latin root of the word 'education' – educare, to draw out. But de Valera the practical teacher responded to the mundane meaning that the system in which he wished to advance placed on the word 'examination'. In real terms it meant 'to get on'. And so *educare* took a back seat to the kind of approach revealed in the problems he set for some of the aspirant teachers in his care.[98]

For first year students
One hundred persons combine to buy a cow at £15, each contributing equally. If she yields an average of three gallons of milk per day for seven months (210 days, say), the average price of milk during the time being 3d per quart, what should each contributor receive altogether supposing the cow is sold at the end of seven months for £16, and that fodder, etc., during the time has cost £6. What is the gain per cent, and what rate per cent per annum interest does each contributor receive?

For second year students
At what price should a jeweller label a bracelet which has cost him ten guineas, if he proposes giving a discount of 20 per cent for cash and still wishes to gain 20 per cent? If it is ten months on his hands before sale, what rate per cent per annum interest does he receive?

The nuns' reception of this *le calcul* approach may be gauged from an assessment of his standing during his years at Carysfort by the Vice-Principal, Sister M. Malachy: ' . . . his worth was manifest and he was thoroughly appreciated by each and all of us. His devotedness to duty and his manly piety were an example to all in the College.'[99]

The post involved two hours' teaching per day, from 9 a.m. to 11.00 a.m. This was a godsend for de Valera, as it opened up options of doing other teaching work and of continuing his third-level studies. On top of this he persuaded the Holy Ghost Fathers to allow him to live in the Castle as a lodger, which meant that he now had first-class, cheap accommodation within a few yards of Carysfort. He was noted for his punctilious attendance at early morning Mass, but being neither a teacher nor a pupil at the College there was a good deal of speculation as to what his 'giraffe-like'[100] figure was doing about the place – particularly as, to overcome his tendency to fall asleep while studying, he developed a habit of reading on a seat he had fixed up for himself in a high tree in the College grounds.

But in that paradoxical combination of the 'odd bod' and the 'good ole boy' that he so frequently exhibited, de Valera made himself popular with the Castle inmates by becoming a Postman of Romance. He had an overcoat with specially large pockets for carrying books. These pockets were often used to carry letters from the Castle to the girls at Carysfort on the basis that, if challenged, de Valera would say that both the letters and their replies had been slipped into his pockets unknown to him. His sleepiness, too, may have been contributed to by his 'good ole boy' side which gave rise to late nights. For in 1907 when his mother, Kate Coll, visited Ireland again, this time bringing with her his half-brother, Thomas

Wheelright, he gave a demonstration of agility which has the ring of practice about it. Returning with Thomas to find the College gate locked, he scaled it in three movements – with his bicycle on his shoulder.

Although his official biography makes no mention of the fact, it has been stated[101] that 'his mother visited Ireland for the purpose of taking him back to America. She thought that there were better opportunities for him in the New World.' But 'having won his way through the various schools and colleges' de Valera 'had an educational career mapped out for himself and was not anxious for a change'. And so an opportunity for mother and son to spend some time together passed by – perhaps for the reasons de Valera gave, perhaps not. What we do know is that there was to be a good deal of change in his 'educational career', which hardly went the way he had it 'mapped out for himself'.

In the ten years which elapsed from the time de Valera took up his post at Carysfort to the 1916 Rising, after which he gave up teaching, de Valera occupied a variety of other part-time teaching jobs and continued his study of mathematics. It is a matter of record that he studied under a number of professors,[102] acquiring a knowledge of astrophysics, electro-optics, spectroscopy and quaternions and endeavouring to broaden his grasp of educational theory by studying philosophy under a Jesuit, Father Corcoran SJ. During this time he taught first and second arts classes (in mathematics, mathematical physics and experimental physics) in various institutions run by nuns, including the Dominicans at Eccles Street and at Loretto in St Stephen's Green, and to boys at Clonliffe College and Catholic University College, St Stephen's Green.

He told Gallagher:[103] 'I trained nearly 1,000 teachers and every time I meet them I find the old friendship exists. They at least never believe the propaganda against me. They know it isn't true.' This comment is interesting, not merely for the indication of the extent of de Valera's teaching activities, but because it ignores the fact that the matters concerning which 'propaganda' circulated about de Valera all took place after he had ceased to be a teacher. Another interesting facet of this decade of de Valera's life is that, despite all the lectures he attended under different professors, not only did he not emerge with a doctorate, he never even got his MA degree. The payments-by-results method had carried him on to a good earning plateau, but he does not appear to have had either the motivation or the aptitude voluntarily to ascend to higher academic peaks. Yet, as his mythological reputation expanded later in his career, it was claimed for him by his son Terry that Einstein said he was one of the 'only nine people in the world who really understood his theory' (of relativity).[104] Despite his teaching experience the lack of qualifications seems to have tipped the scales against him when he applied for chairs at both Galway (mathematics) and Cork (mathematical physics) in 1912 and 1913. He withdrew from the Galway contest when he realized the calibre of his opposition, but he left his hat in the ring for Cork and is said to have been beaten by only one vote on the governing body – because a supporter of his missed his train and[105] did not turn up in time.

But in 1912 he did secure a part-time, temporary post as lecturer in mathamatics and mathematical physics at the major Irish seminary, Maynooth; it was offered to him by the President of the College, Dr Daniel Mannix, who had attended Charleville School and who afterwards became one of his greatest admirers. Mannix seems to have been prompted to write to de Valera by his old Rockwell pupil, Paddy Browne, for whom the post was being kept. Though it was only temporary, the job had the incalculable value of introducing de Valera to some of the future leaders of the Irish Church who were to support him at subsequent crucial moments in his political life.

What was it in de Valera's character that prevented him from becoming a leader of the Irish Church himself? It would appear to have been a logical career for a man who in his political life could well be thought of as a sort of lay cardinal, at one level expressing and symbolizing Ireland's interface between Church and State, at another the very epitome of the thought behind the Joycean couplet:

Ireland my first, my only love
Where Christ and Caesar are hand in glove

Was it the mighty ego that could not completely subordinate itself to the dictates of a Church whose rule as a layman he dutifully followed in most aspects of his waking life? Or was there some sensual streak in his character, temporarily glimpsed at Rockwell and perhaps later in America, that heard the call of the flesh above that of the consecration bell? Did the vocation directors guarding the entrance to the halls of clericalism sense a latent *non serviam* to an authority other than that of his own will? Or was it that doubts as to whether he was born in wedlock prevented his being accepted by the Church? These questions have to be raised in any attempt to assess properly a figure who influenced his country so profoundly. But while the answers to all four would appear to be 'Yes', such judgements must remain largely speculative. What is known for certain is that, on at least four recorded occasions (and there may have been several others) during his school and teaching career, de Valera gave clear indications that he was considering the priesthood.

The first time he did so he was turned aside, as has been seen, by Father Healy. The second occurred after the first ordination in Blackrock, that of Joseph Shanahan[106] on 22 April 1900. De Valera wrote to his half-brother, Thomas Wheelright, shortly afterwards, and subsequently to his mother also,[107] telling them both that he was seriously thinking of becoming a priest. Interestingly, however, in view of his love for Blackrock and the Holy Ghost Fathers, he now directed his attentions towards the diocesan clergy and mentioned in his letters that he would have to work hard to secure the scholarships necessary to enter Clonliffe, the Dublin diocesan seminary. Nothing came of this intention; but four years later, while he was awaiting the results of his BA examinations, he 'decided that it was time to give serious consideration to a personal problem that had been nagging him for years . . . going on for the priesthood . . . that suggestion kept cropping up in his mind and even in his letters . . . he decided to do a weekend retreat with the Jesuit Fathers in Rathfarnham Castle and to discuss the matter in depth with his confessor.'[108]

De Valera kept to his decision, made the retreat and 'revealed the state of his soul to the best of his ability to his Anamchara'.[109] The result of this revelation was that once again a Father Healy-type situation unfolded, but this time with literally Jesuitical overtones, as Father Farragher's account makes clear: 'The priest in question was in talkative mood at the end of the retreat and spoke about many topics.' Whether this talkativeness was occasioned by garrulity or diplomacy we cannot be certain but, thanks to Farragher, we do know de Valera's version of what happened next: 'At last Dev, rather impatiently, asked "But what about my vocation?" "Oh! your vocation. You have what is known as an incipient vocation." Dev laughed and said "If that is all I have after all those years it is time I forgot about it." He recalled that he whistled merrily all the way as he cycled back to Blackrock!'

As Farragher points out, it was perfectly natural for de Valera to consider the priesthood at that juncture because many of his contemporaries were going on to become priests. And de Valera told Farragher that he felt 'from time to time that he had a calling to the priesthood but not the secular priesthood; he was sure of that as he felt he needed the support and the safeguards of community life'. But why inquire about those safeguards at a Jesuit, rather than a Holy Ghost, retreat, which would have been readily available? Had he already taken soundings beyond those with Father Healy and been turned away again? We cannot say with certainty at this stage; what we do know is that the account of the way his vocation testing came to an end which de Valera gave to Father Farragher is not correct. For two years later, not only did he not forget about his vocation in the summer of 1904, but he also belied his statement about feeling he needed the support of community life.

He had succeeded in getting a little regular tuition work at Clonliffe College in September 1905. How little may be gauged from an entry in the President's Diary[110] for Saturday the 9th: 'Engaged de Valera for Mature Hon Maths. 2 hrs. work at least 4/- per lesson.' Whether his relatively precarious financial position, post-Rockwell, had anything to do with his state of mind is impossible to say, but he evidently called in to see the President of Clonliffe on a rest day, Sunday, 7 January 1906, to discuss yet again his supposedly forgotten-about vocation – and this time with a view to entering the secular priesthood. The President's diary entry for that day reads: 'De Valera consults on entering eccl. [ecclesiastical] State.' The President obviously told de Valera he would need to think over his approach, for his decision was not given for another three days, on 10 January. It is described as follows: 'Another interview with de Valera. Advised him not to come in now. To give up Trinity scholarship, to read for th. [theology] and RNI [religious knowledge instruction] and to read what may be useful to begin Th. study next year.'

Was the President again deflecting de Valera from a priestly goal by delaying tactics, or was he merely influenced by the fact that de Valera had come to him in mid-term? Suggesting that he give up Trinity could have been either a test of sincerity or an example of the religious prejudices of the times – Trinity was regarded as a Protestant university. But it is difficult to believe that – especially after the type of religious formation which de Valera had already undergone – he would have required such an intensive reading course to fit him to join a first-year theological class. At all events the suggested delay appears to have had its effect, for there are no further references to de Valera's vocation in the President's Diary. His name only crops up in connection with being hired to give 'grinds' in mathematics or, in the final entry for 10 August 1908, seeking to use the President's influence. It reads: 'de Valera called to ask me to write to Fr. Byrne re vacant professorship in Training College.'

The question of the priesthood was obviously an important but unresolved part of de Valera's life. On the face of it he would have made an ideal Irish priest of the time, and would almost certainly have risen to a position of importance within the Church hierarchy. Why he did not receive greater encouragement to join the clergy we simply do not know. All that is certain is that at least three experienced priests, skilled in the field of vocation assessment, exercised caution rather than enthusiasm when confronted with the prospect of setting Eamon de Valera on a clerical career. In the event his most significant step of this decade was neither academic nor liturgical, but linguistic. In 1908 he started to learn Irish. Everything else of importance which followed flowed from that decision: his marriage, involvement in revolution and, later, his political career. As with many turning points in life, his initial interest in what became a passion was more thrust upon him than sought. Like many people of her generation, his grandmother had been a native speaker, but as the policy of the time was to downgrade Irish and regard English as the vehicle of advancement, she, as was common at the time, did not speak Irish in front of the children. However, towards the close of the nineteenth century a number of powerful Irish men and movements had set out to reverse the thrust of anglicization.

The hugely popular Gaelic Athletic Association, founded in 1884 by a former Blackrock pupil and teacher, Michael Cusack, banned the 'Garrison games' of soccer, hockey, cricket and rugby in favour of the national sport of hurling, handball, and the more recently developed Gaelic football. De Valera always believed that the game of Gaelic football originated with Cusack's experiences in the Blackrock recreation yard. As this was tarmacadamed the students could not play rugby there, because it involved tackling to the ground. A 'tip and pass out' form was evolved from which, according to de Valera,[111] Cusack developed the hand-passing, no tackling game of Gaelic football.

In the literary field the poet Yeats, the playwright Synge, and their patron and fellow playwright Lady Gregory were developing a new Irish Literature in English. They and their Abbey Theatre would one day be spoken of as having created a Celtic Dawn.[112] But nowhere did the rising rays of that dawn burn more brightly than in the Gaelic League, founded by Douglas Hyde in 1893. By 1908 the ardent young cultural nationalists of the League had become such a power in the land that Irish was made a compulsory subject for entrance to the new National University. Carysfort too began to take more notice of Irish, and as a teacher de Valera felt he could not afford to ignore the potential effect of the language on his future career.

By 1908 he had at long last moved out of the Castle and taken lodgings in nearby Merrion View Avenue where his landlady, a Mrs Russell, was a native Irish speaker from Co. Mayo. She taught him some Irish, but as her husband was a Scot who did not speak the language, classes were said to have been conducted only in his absence. De Valera decided that some more regular system of tuition was required and consulted Michael Smithwick, who by now was helping Padraig Pearse and Thomas MacDonagh to get the first all-Irish school, Scoil Eanna, off the ground. Smithwick was also a member of the governing body of the Gaelic League and an officer in the Keating branch of the League which taught Munster Irish. However, instead of advising his friend to join his branch he suggested[113] that, as Mrs Russell's Irish had been of the western, Connacht, dialect, de Valera should enrol instead at Colaiste Laighean, Leinster College, which specialized in Connacht Irish. De Valera did so, losing his opportunity of acquiring the Decies dialect, but finding to his delight that his teacher was pretty he promptly fell in love with her.

2

MARRIAGE THROUGH
THE MEDIUM

SINEAD FLANAGAN WAS four years older than de Valera. She was a primary school teacher, a well-known language enthusiast and amateur actor. Amongst the productions she appeared in was *The Tinker and the Fairy*, which was put on in the garden of George Moore's house in Ely Place, Dublin. She asked Moore should she try for a stage career. He replied: 'Height, five feet four, hair red; name, Flanagan, no, my dear.'[1] The first response of Frank Hughes, who was destined to be best man at their wedding, was equally unflattering. A breathless de Valera asked: 'Well what do you think?' 'Not much was the reply!'[2]

In return for her Irish lessons he taught her German. They became engaged and in the summer of 1909 spent their holidays together at the Irish college in Tourmekeady, an Irish-speaking district set amidst the wild beauty of the Partry-Lough Mask area of the Galway/Mayo border, not far from Maamtrasna. The couple visited Galway city, the capital of what was left of Gaelic Ireland. Here de Valera got a practical demonstration of the attitudinal difficulty involved in making the rest of the country Gaelic. An old man whom he addressed in Irish replied indignantly, 'Do you think I have no English?'[3]

During that western stay he also received a good illustration of that Irish tendency to blame all troubles on the English (a tendency, let it be said, which he would later develop himself). An old lady from whom he bought some poteen, the illegal home brew for which Connemara was once[4] justly famous, justified her prices on the grounds that they were 'because of Lloyd George's Budget'![5]

De Valera and Sinead were married on 8 January 1910 at St Paul's church, Arran Quay, Dublin. The ceremony was conducted in Irish and it cost de Valera his brand-new bicycle, because on the eve of the wedding he spent so much time fussing over comparisons of the English and Irish rituals in Gill's, the religious bookshop in Upper O'Connell Street, that someone made off with it. Sinead was a classic Irish housewife and mother of the period. She was gentle and self-effacing outside the home, but 'Mother, you know, could be quite fiery' inside it was how her son Vivion described her to me. He remembered his father telling him once: 'Listen to the women, Viv. Your mother has wonderful common sense.' She was deeply religious, lived for her home, and, though patriotic, had little time for public life – or, perhaps more accurately, recoiled against it later in the marriage when she realized how much hardship it had brought on her and how little time for family life was left over from the public activities of her husband.

In the early days of their marriage she was something of an innocent where the ways of the world were concerned. When the couple were first married they lived 'mainly in the kitchen', as de Valera put it to Gallagher, of their flat at 38 Morehampton Terrace, Donnybrook. The rent was collected by 'an old man called Byrne'[6] who awoke Sinead's sympathy by telling her that his wife had died. 'Oh, you poor man', was the response of the tender-hearted Sinead.

'Yes, ma'am,' continued Byrne – 'and I raised a monument to her memory.' Sinead's sympathy poured out anew. But then Byrne continued: 'Yes, ma'am – by marrying again.' Sinead felt her sympathy 'the most wasted thing in life'. But de Valera 'delighted himself' telling the story. This was the private, human face of the de Valeras. What the public saw was described by a contemporary biographer[7] who said that the de Valeras 'were to be met constantly in the places where the enthusiasts of the "Irish Ireland" movement congregated, talking Irish to each other as far as a limited vocabulary would allow, buying nothing that was not of Irish manufacture, and taking an active part in all the social and educational gatherings organised by the Gaelic League.'

De Valera also furthered the teaching aims which had first impelled him to join the Gaelic League, securing first place in the Leinster College teaching diploma and being awarded the diploma in Irish from the Royal University. On the strength of these accomplishments, in 1911 he was appointed director of an Irish summer school at Tawin, one of the bridge-linked islands on the shores of Galway Bay. Here he was to meet an ill-fated Irish hero,[8] the school's patron, Roger Casement, who was so impressed with him that he sent him £5 towards 'prizes of Irish make' to be awarded at the school sports.[9]

By the second year of his three-year term the de Valeras had two babies, Vivion, born in 1911, and Mairin, born in April 1912, and because of the spartan accommodation on Tawin Sinead did not accompany him. Both his 'absence makes the heart grow fonder' state of mind and the clumsy, half-guilty intensity of their relationship at that stage, probably typical of most marriages of their class and religion of the time, may be gauged from a letter he addressed, under the streaming grey skies of a wet August in the west of Ireland, to 'My dear little Mummie':[10]

> . . . I am very lonely without my own sweetheart and her babies. I'll never be a cross husband again . . . I am always thinking of you darling – yet I don't wish you here for want of proper accommodation is a desperate nuisance. I do wish I were myself at home though. There is a big big vacancy in my heart. I feel empty, joyless without you. I do not let myself think on for I know in a short time I'll have my own darling in my arms – but those weeks are horribly long. . . .

41

Ah love like ours is grand. I love you a million, billion times more now than I did when we were in Tourmakeady. When I read in the books about love – about the Speir-Bean [term used in Irish to describe the Spirit Woman or sometimes the spirit of womanhood] and all the rest I say my mummie is a great deal nicer than all that. I know what the author would like to say – but words would not do their duty for him.

I don't know what was your opinion of Amhran Chlainne Gaedheal. Several of the songs as there [sic] are arranged are clearly mixed up but there is one little gem the second one perhaps you remember it. We had it in class today I couldn't go into the meaning with the mixed class but I wished you were with me till we discuss it – you may be able to guess my thoughts as I read this verse.

Da bhfeicta an aoileann ar maidin aoibhinn ag snamh ar an gcuan
[If you were to see the beautiful woman on a delightful morning in the harbour]
A brollach scaoilte ba solas fior-ghlan i mbarr na dtonn,
[Her unfastened breast would be a true clear light on the surface of the waves.]
An eala ghlegeal nior chuibhne leithe pairt a roinnt.
[The pure white swan, she didn't think it fitting to share her affection.]
Agus codladh oidhche do bhain tu dhiom-sa e le la fada is bliadhain.
[And my night's sleep you've taken it from me this many's the day and a year.]

[Two lines omitted]

Ta na tri seoid aici is corta is deise ar bith faoi'n saoghal.
[She has the three jewels which are the most apt and nicest in the world.]
'Si is ro-ghile piop o Neili comh-chruinn ar ucht a cleibh.
[She has the most excessively bright neck since Nelly with the perfectly rounded breast on her bosom.]

These express my picture of my darling wife as well perhaps as words can do it . . . I wonder will you understand them as I did. I have felt very often whilst here that it was a great pity I was not doing some literary subjects we could talk about at home. The maths are so cold and icy.

Pad. O'Sioctain doesnt seem to be lonely at all. He has his little son with him but tho. I love viv. he would*n't* [de Valera's emphasis] be able to supply his mother's place. Ah yes sweetheart I will be a good boy to you when I go home.

I haven't forgotten the 'memorare' every night and now I pray that the Blessed Virgin may leave us all together and happy.

I can't say anything my full heart would say for love you know even our lips only poorly – I fear you will think I am only myself trying to write, but think of me when we were all and all to each other and then when your heart is full see would you be able to let me know how you feel – you will then know what I mean when I say words wont express what I want to say.

The word '*beal beosac*' came into a poem a few days ago. We translated it as 'nectar lipped' – but I understand what the poet meant. Those wild kisses.

> Goodbye darling,
> your husband and
> sweetheart, Dev.
> XXXXXXXXXXXXXX
> Kiss *our* babies.

The year before that letter was written, de Valera had discovered something decidedly unpoetic at work in Irish language circles. His rise in the ranks of the Gaelic League was checked by an organization whose existence he was then unaware of but with which he would become all too familiar in the years ahead: the Irish Republican Brotherhood (IRB). At this stage it is essential to digress for a moment so that the reader may have a grasp both of the significance of the secret IRB and of the overall course of Anglo-Irish developments which were taking place publicly as de Valera pursued his private career. The stage is now fast approaching where secret society, private life and public events all intertwine and explode.

The IRB was the hard cutting edge of nationalist Ireland's anger, distilled from the traditions of Wolfe Tone's Republican-inspired United Irishmen and the cruelly suppressed revolt in 1798; from bygone patriots like Robert Emmet, who followed in Tone's footsteps with equal lack of success; from the Young Irelanders and their unsuccessful rebellion of 1848; from the Fenians and their abortive rising of 1865; from the dynamiters who (sponsored by the American wing of the organization, Clan na nGael) bombed London in 1883, thereby setting a precedent for today's IRA. From these and many other bloodstained moments and movements in Ireland's desperate past they drew their physical force, separatist ideology and oath-bound, cell system of organization.

Just as the 'Celtic Dawn' warmed a variety of cultural and sporting activities into life, so did the physical force tradition come again to a kind of hidden strength in the early part of the twentieth century. It was partly because a group of younger men came to the fore: figures like P. S. O'Hegarty, Bulmer Hobson, Denis McCullogh and Sean MacDiarmada breathed life into what had become almost a moribund organization. And it was partly because one older figure had come back from Clan na nGael in America to continue the tradition of a rising in every generation. This was Thomas Clarke,[11] a dynamitard who, under an assumed name, had served fifteen years of penal servitude during which he had seen most of his fellow IRB prisoners either die or go insane. After his return to Dublin his little newsagent's shop in Parnell Street became the mecca of the new generation of young men who followed him into the physical force tradition. Clarke and his young lieutenants, Sean MacDiarmada in particular, saw to it that every single Irish organization of consequence was infiltrated, influenced and, where possible, controlled by the revolutionaries.

The IRB felt itself both historically and morally entitled to act in this fashion. Its members had suffered the most appalling hardships and deaths for their cause, and its leadership was seen as a sort of home-based Government-in-exile. The IRB Constitution[12] stated that:

> The Supreme Council of the Irish Republican Brotherhood is hereby declared in fact, as well as by right, the sole Government of the Irish Republic. Its enactments shall be the laws of the Irish Republic until Ireland secures absolute National Independence, and a permanent Republican Government is established. The President of the Irish Republican Brotherhood is in fact as well as by right

President of the Irish Republic. He shall direct the working of the Irish Republican Brotherhood subject to the control of the Supreme Council. . . .

However, oblivious to the existence of this 'sole Government of the Irish Republic' or to the growing strength of Fenianism, politically aware Ireland largely kept its eyes on Westminster. True, a few did have hopes for a small separatist party, Sinn Fein (We Ourselves), founded by the political journalist Arthur Griffith. His ability and integrity had attracted some intelligent attention with the publication of his book *The Resurrection of Hungary*, in which he preached the necessity to do as the Hungarians had done in the case of Austria – withdraw from the Imperial Parliament and set up a native assembly owing allegiance to a dual monarchy. In the Irish case, the arrangement would cater for the susceptibilities of the Unionists. Griffith visualized the 'Kings, Lords and Commons' applying to both Ireland and England. He preached protectionism on the lines advocated by the economist List and argued for the development of a distinctively Irish culture and system of industry. But his influence was more akin to that of an opinion group than a political party, although some advanced nationalists, Michael Collins amongst them, regarded him as the authentic Irish nationalist philosopher. Certainly this was the view of the British administrative nerve centre, Dublin Castle. Its censors saw Griffith's various publications as their chief adversaries in the 'mosquito press' and closed them down accordingly.

The mainline Dublin press, such as the *Irish Independent* and the *Freeman's Journal*, stayed open and respected by filling its columns with comment and reportage on the doings of the Irish Parliamentary Party. Through a combination of the extraordinary courage and perseverance of the party leader John Redmond, and the changing fortunes of the Liberals and Conservatives, by 1911 Home Rule was coming back near the top of the political agenda. The Tories had been out of power since 1906, but had managed to a degree to compensate for this through frustrating Liberal legislation by means of the House of Lords veto. However, the Parliament Act of 1911 largely broke the Lords' power since Bills which were passed by the Commons in three consecutive sessions would now automatically become law, whether or not the Lords rejected them. On 11 April 1912 the British Prime Minister, H. H. Asquith, dependent on Redmond and his party, moved the third Irish Home Rule Bill.

Compared to the mountain of hostility it produced, the Bill was but a legislative mouse. Dublin was to get a two-chambered Parliament, but London retained wide control in defence and fiscal matters and some Irish representation at Westminster was to continue. However, the proposal provided the Tories with another invaluable opportunity for playing the Orange card. Two days before Asquith introduced the Bill Andrew Bonar Law, the Conservative Party leader, led a distinguished group of Tory leaders to Belfast. At Balmoral, Craig's family estate, he reviewed a parade of some eighty thousand men, to whom he gave the message: 'You hold the pass, the pass for the empire.' He then went on to use Orange nomenclature to recall the siege of Derry: ' . . . your Lundys have betrayed you; but you have closed your gates, the Government have erected by their Parliament Act a boom against you to shut you off from the help of the British people. You will burst that boom, the help will come. . . .'[13]

Ulster would again fight, and Ulster would be right. This time Tory support of the Ulster Unionist resistance went very far in the direction of treason. The Conservatives had been a long time out of power; the issue was one which many within the party regarded as a prelude to the break-up of empire; and Bonar Law was so said and led by the doyenne of Unionism, Helen, Lady Londonderry, wife of the 6th Marquess of Londonderry, Chairman of the Ulster Unionist Council, that it was difficult to tell where his influence began and hers ended. Law's father had been a Presbyterian minister in Coleraine before emigrating to New Brunswick. The family originally came from Scotland and maintained a close relationship with Ulster; when the Reverend Law's health failed he returned from Canada and lived out his last five years there. Bonar Law visited his father almost every weekend during this time. The Conservative leader's natural inclination towards support for his co-religionists and upholders of a shared tradition in Ulster was heightened by his friendship with Lady Londonderry. She both acted as his hostess and regulated his social life following the death of his wife in 1908. (She was later to do the same for Edward Carson in similar circumstances.) Her London home, Londonderry House, was described by one authority as 'the social hub of the unionist party'.[14]

Nationalist Ireland could well have been forgiven for regarding the House of Commons as Unionism's political hub after Bonar Law voiced his opposition to the Home Rule proposal there on 18 June 1912:

> They know that if Ulster is in earnest, that if Ulster does resist by force, there are stronger influences than parliamentary majorities. They know that in that case no government would dare to use their troops to drive them out. They know as a matter of fact that the government which gave the order to employ troops for that purpose would run a greater risk of being lynched in London than the loyalists of Ulster would run of being shot in Belfast.

The Liberals were aghast at this introduction of what Asquith termed a new 'style of rancour' into British politics. The British Prime Minister replied to the Conservative leader in words that have an accusingly accurate relevance at the time of writing, eighty years later, as 'Ulster' bleeds on and casualties mount daily. Bonar Law, said Asquith, was creating for the future 'a complete grammar of anarchy'. A month later Asquith had to consult that grammar to find a term to describe a further Bonar Law speech, made during the traditionally demented days of the loyalist 'marching season':[15]

> We regard the government as a revolutionary committee which has seized upon

45

despotic power by fraud. In our opposition to them we shall not be guided by the considerations or bound by the restraints which would influence us in an ordinary constitutional struggle. We shall take the means, whatever means seems to us most effective, to deprive them of the despotic power which they have usurped and compel them to appeal to the people whom they have deceived. They may, perhaps they will, carry their home rule bill through the House of Commons, but what then?

   . . . I repeat now with a full sense of the responsibility which attaches to my position that, in my opinion, if such an attempt is made, I can imagine no length of resistance to which Ulster can go in which I should not be prepared to support them, and in which in my belief, they would not be supported by the overwhelming majority of the British people.

Asquith described this broadside as 'reckless rodomontade', but the Unionists took the hint about support for any 'length of resistance' very seriously. Sir Edward Carson had by now given up his prospects in British politics to become leader of the Irish Unionist MPs at Westminster and effectively leader of Ulster Protestantism's stand against Home Rule. Describing the background against which Carson saw himself carrying out his prosecuting duties in Ireland his biographer, a fellow barrister and MP, Edward Marjoribanks, said the 1871 Juries Act had 'admitted to the jury-box a class of peasants largely illiterate and quite unfitted for the discharge of judicial duties'. These jurors were known, according to Marjoribanks, as the Flowers of Tullahogue, after a well-known cheap scent.[16] He quoted a story in support of this view, to the effect that when the new jurymen were first ordered by the Clerk of the Assize to take their usual places as gentlemen of the jury 'they all scrambled into the dock . . . '.

Despite the difficulties that the Flowers of Tullahogue posed for the upholding of the standards of British justice required to bring home to the natives that they were in fact of the 'Happy English Child class', Carson was determined to ensure that the 'lesser breeds' did not remain 'without the law' – though not in the sense Kipling intended. His philosophy was based on a childhood upbringing in which, as he said himself, he was[17] 'taught to think that I ought to look upon England as the great prototype of a justice-loving, religion-loving, and in every respect a trusted nation, in which colonisation brought all its great qualities to bear on securing the happiness of the people'. Imbued with this training, Carson believed implicitly that Ireland as a whole – especially north-eastern Ireland – was better off united to England and without Home Rule. His single-mindedness brought results. Arthur Balfour, the Chief Secretary for Ireland, wrote: 'I made Carson, and he made me. I've told you how no one had courage. Everyone right up to the top was trembling. Some of the RMs [resident magistrates] were splendid, but on the whole it was an impossible state of affairs. Carson had nerve, however. I sent him all over the place, prosecuting, getting convictions. We worked together.'[18]

With such experiences in his career it was natural that Carson, who had been an Orangeman since he was nineteen, would regard the maintenance of the union as 'beneficial not only to Ulster but to all Ireland'. But where nationalists were (and are) concerned there were two fundamental flaws in this classic Ascendancy view of their country. First, the union which Carson so ardently admired was not a union between the peoples of Ireland and England, but a union between the British Government and one party in Ireland – the Protestant Ascendancy class. For Catholics, who looked to Dublin, not London, as their natural seat of leadership, the Act of Union had destroyed everything of substance in their political and cultural life, from their Parliament to their publishing houses. Second, though Carson's beloved Orange Order had its colourful parades, its convivial and welfare side (for Protestants), it also had (and has) a darker and more disruptive role, brought about through its use as an instrument for enforcing Unionist hegemony. In the words of Maurice Irvine:[19]

> . . . the Orange Order has been and is a pernicious influence in the life of Ireland and Ulster. Its drawing together of Protestants has resulted in a deeper division between them and the Catholic community and perpetuation of mutual hostility. This divisiveness is not accidental. The parades and demonstrations of the Order are designed to commemorate the battles and sieges of the seventeenth century which brought about the defeat of the Catholic-Irish interest and the consolidation of the Protestant Ascendancy. They are permeated with an atmosphere of triumphalism which reminds Catholics of their defeat and impresses on them their continuing status of inferiority.

Carson appealed unashamedly to this divisive sectarian tradition. In one of his most significant speeches, delivered at Craigavon on 23 September 1911 to an Orange crowd estimated to be fifty thousand strong, he said: 'We must be prepared . . . the morning Home Rule passes, ourselves to become responsible for the government of the Protestant Province of Ulster.' A member of the House of Commons, he was thus nevertheless encouraging a volatile audience to defy Parliament and declare a Protestant UDI which was bound to lead to bloodshed with Catholic subjects of the same Parliament. But during the Ulster crisis Carson did not merely feel he had Balfour and his Orangemen behind him as earnestly as at any time in his Crown Prosecutor days; he must also have felt he had the support of the entire Conservative establishment. In the House of Commons, apart from Balfour there were figures like Bonar Law and Walter Long; and in the House of Lords Cecil, Willoughby de Broke, Lansdowne, Londonderry, Milner, the Duke of Bedford and many others. Outside Parliament there were public figures like Sir Edward Elgar, Rudyard Kipling and Dr Jameson (of Raid fame). And behind these great names, in serried ranks, there stood the Protestant people of Ulster – dour, sincere and implacable in their belief that Home Rule was Rome Rule. When Carson headed the signatories of the Ulster Covenant, based on the old Scottish Covenant, at an impressive signing ceremony at Belfast City Hall on 28 September 1912, 471,414 people signed after him. The Covenant read as follows:[20]

Being convinced in our conscience that home rule would be disastrous to the material well-being of Ulster as well as the whole of Ireland, subversive of our civil and religious freedom, destructive of our citizenship, and perilous to the unity of the empire, we, whose names are underwritten, men of Ulster, loyal subjects of His Gracious Majesty King George V, humbly relying on the God whom our fathers in days of stress and trial confidently trusted, do hereby pledge ourselves in solemn covenant throughout this our time of threatened calamity to stand by one another defending for ourselves and for our children our cherished position of equal citizenship in the United Kingdom, and in using all means which may be found necessary to defeat the present conspiracy to set up a home rule parliament in Ireland. And in the event of such a parliament being forced upon us we further solemnly and mutually pledge ourselves to refuse to recognise its authority. In sure confidence that God will defend the right we hereto subscribe our names. And further, we individually declare that we have not already signed this covenant. God Save the King.

The Covenanters then took two other important steps. Throughout December Protestant Ulstermen were encouraged to join a force which was formalized into the Ulster Volunteer Force (UVF) at the annual general meeting of the Ulster Unionist Council on 20 January. Some ninety thousand enrolled, and were drilled and trained by leading figures in the British Army.[21] Then, the following year, on 24 April 1914, the ninety thousand were suddenly converted into a formidable force. The *Clydevalley* landed thirty-five thousand rifles and five million rounds of ammunition from Germany at Larne Harbour. Several hundred waiting motor cars had the armaments safely distributed across the province before the authorities fully realized what was happening. 'King Carson', a former Solicitor General and a practising King's Counsel, had successfully presided over 'an act of breath-taking illegality which might well have international implications'.[22]

Nationalist Ireland was not disposed to attribute the success of the landing merely to good staff work. Events of the previous month had seen to that. In the House of Lords pro-Unionist sentiment was such that, backed by distinguished soldiers such as Sir Henry Wilson,[23] their Lordships debated holding up the annual Army Act so that legally after 30 April Britain would not have had an Army with which to enforce Home Rule. But in the War Office, Wilson's influence took an even more dramatic form. An admiring biographer adjudged that his 'handling of an awkward and threatening situation . . . put an end to all possibility of the army being used against the loyal north of Ireland'.[24]

He might have added that for a short time it also put an end to civilian control over the Army. What happened was that the Government, fearing raids on Ulster arms depots, ordered certain naval and troop movements in and around the province. These, in the perfervid atmosphere of the time, provoked such a reaction that a significant segment of the officer cadre in Ireland let it be known that they would resign their commissions rather than serve against the Unionists. General Sir Hubert Gough, commanding the 3rd Cavalry Brigade at the Curragh Camp and the leading figure amongst the *non serviam* faction, was summoned to London with some of his officers for a confrontation with the Secretary for War, Colonel Seely. Following a breakfast-time briefing from Wilson, Gough extracted from Seely a written guarantee that the Army would not be used to crush political opposition to Home Rule. He was even allowed to add a paragraph in his own handwriting that 'the troops under our command will not be called upon to enforce the present Home Rule Bill on Ulster, and that we can so assure our officers'.[25] The ensuing outcry caused Asquith to take over from Seely as Minister for War and to repudiate his statement. None the less, the Army made no move against the Orangemen. So far as Nationalist Ireland was concerned the entire affair was symbolized in one word, the password used by the UVF as they distributed their weapons under the averted gaze of the British Army – 'Gough'.

While all this was happening, the Home Rule Bill was trundling around the parliamentary circuit like a punch-drunk boxer. After three rounds it obtained a favourable decision from the House of Commons in January 1913, but was knocked out by the Lords two weeks later. It re-emerged victorious from the Commons in July of that year, only to be again defeated by the Lords. However, by May 1914 it had successfully completed its third passage through the Commons and, by the terms of the 1911 Act, the Lords could no longer limit its passage into law. But against a lowering blue and orange political landscape, with, in the foreground, Tories and Unionists entwined in fearsome, near treasonable congress, and in the background the banners of world war being unfurled, the Government hesitated. Months passed before the Bill received the Royal Assent, on 18 September. By then it was caught up in the vortex of war and, although placed on the Statute Book, the introduction of Home Rule was checked by an accompanying Suspensory Act. After all that had happened, Asquith had pledged that the Bill would not come into operation until 'parliament should have the fullest opportunity by an Amending Bill, of altering, modifying or qualifying its provisions in such a way as to secure at any rate the general consent of both Ireland and the United Kingdom'.[26]

As every schoolchild knows, when one mixes blue and orange the result is green. The Tory-Unionist experiment in defying the democratic process had the same effect on de Valera's political coloration. As already seen, by 1911 he had sufficient quickening political appetite to stand for election to the Gaelic League's governing body, the Coiste Gnotha. But he had so little knowledge of Irish politics that he did not know who had defeated him. He noticed Sean O'Muirthuile, a teller during the election, 'tricking with the votes',[27] and he went home in a state of high indignation. O'Muirthuile was known to be a Sinn Fein activist, and de Valera assumed that this organization had conspired against him. Throwing the Clar (agenda) on the kitchen table, he thundered to Sinead: 'If there's one organization I will never join, it is Sinn Fein.' In fact, he would later come not just to join the party, but to dominate it. But in 1911 he was unaware that O'Muirthuile was acting on behalf of the IRB.

Nor did he realize that he himself was acting under the aegis of the IRB when he joined the Irish Volunteers two years later. Eoin MacNeill, Vice President of the Gaelic League and Professor of Early Irish History at University College, Dublin, had written an article in the Gaelic League's paper, *An Claideamh Soluis (The Bright Sword)*, proposing the formation of an Irish Volunteer Force. If the Orangemen could have an army, why should not the Nationalists? De Valera later realized that the IRB were behind the Volunteers idea. He said: 'It is not suggested, of course, that the foundation of the Irish Volunteers on 25th November, 1913, was a spontaneous act. The creation of that organisation was discussed and planned long before that date.'[28] But in 1913, for de Valera, and for Irish nationalists generally, the foundation of the Volunteers did appear to be a 'spontaneous act', an idea whose hour had struck:[29]

> So long as the Home Rule Bill was being safely piloted to the Statute Book, we took little interest in official politics . . . we thought much more of the future . . . free scope at last to organise the country's life after centuries of misgovernment and neglect. But confidence in the official leaders was greatly shaken when the Covenanting campaign produced a quite unexpected menace to the prospects of the Home Rule Bill . . . young men in Dublin discussed the possibility of organising a rival force of Nationalist Volunteers, to use the same argument which Carson had used so effectively in Ulster.

They, like MacNeill, intended the corps to be at the ready should a Conservative/Unionist attempt be made to deny the introduction of Home Rule by force. But the IRB had another agenda. They regarded the Home Rule proposals as derisory in themselves, and were anyhow dubious about British sincerity in introducing them. They saw the formation of the Volunteers as a heaven-sent opportunity to create an army which they could use to stage an uprising. MacNeill was manipulated into agreeing to act as chairman at a hugely attended meeting in the Rotunda, Dublin on 25 November 1913, at which it was openly proposed to form an Irish Volunteer Force. A Manifesto read from the platform stated the ostensible reason:[30]

> At a time when legislative proposals, universally confessed to be of vital concern for the future of Ireland, have been put forward, and are awaiting decision, a plan has been deliberately adopted by one of the great English political parties, advocated by the leaders of that party and by its numerous organs in the Press, and brought systematically to bear on English public opinion, to make a display of military force and the menace of armed violence the determining factor in the future relations between this country and Great Britain . . . such is the occasion, not altogether unfortunate, which has brought about the inception of the Irish Volunteer movement.

Some four thousand volunteers responded to the Manifesto, including Eamon de Valera. He attended the meeting in a sombre mood. A married man with responsibilities – his third child, Eamonn, was then only six weeks old – and a growing political awareness, he saw the significance of the Rotunda gathering more clearly than most. He told Gallagher that from the moment the Volunteers were set up he felt a fight was inevitable. His old parish priest, Father Sheehy, sat in the row in front of him but de Valera made no effort at recognition.[31] The time had passed for sermons. He joined the Volunteers and attended his first drill session shortly afterwards, on 6 December.

At this stage it it necessary to pause for a moment to examine two other large issues that were gathering force in Ireland and, irrespective of whether one argues that they were addressed or ignored, were nevertheless to remain on de Valera's political agenda for most of his life: they were unemployment and partition. First let us look at yet another armed force which had come into existence in Dublin in the weeks preceding the Rotunda meeting – the Irish Citizen Army. It was formed to protect striking Dublin workers from police brutality during the great labour disputes which convulsed the city in 1913. The founders of the Irish Transport Union and of the Irish Labour Party, James Larkin and James Connolly, had sought to organize workers in the face of the worst housing conditions in Europe – twenty-one thousand families each lived in one room – low wages and spiralling unemployment. The employers responded by banding together to refuse employment to anyone joining a union. A general lock-out ensued and evictions, clashes with the police and widespread hardship were the results. In this climate a Protestant Ulsterman, Captain Jack White, who had won fame during the relief of Ladysmith in the Boer War, supported Connolly and Larkin by organizing and drilling a Citizen Army. The workers were ultimately defeated and forced back to work on the employers' terms, but the Citizen Army remained in being with James Connolly as its commander.[32] Thus Ulstermen – MacNeill was an Antrim Catholic – came to be responsible for the creation of three separate armies in Ireland.

Yet, though de Valera later came to admire Connolly, his insights into either Ulster Protestantism or Dublin social conditions never led him to take any action which would enable a biographer to show that he empathized very deeply with them. St Vincent de Paul work had, of course, brought him in touch with poverty, but in those days the Church, though charitable, emphasized the doctrine of 'The poor you have always with you'. The St Vincent de Paul Society was used during the lock-out as a strike-breaking weapon, being instructed by the Church authorities not to distribute aid to the families of strikers. A Connollyite volunteer of the time remembered the reserve that some felt towards de Valera because of this: '. . . we got to learn that Eamon de Valera was in St Vincent de Paul. This was significant to us as we all remembered the role St Vincent de Paul played in the Larkin lock-out the year before in 1913.'[33]

51

And where Ulster Protestantism was concerned, even though the Orangemen's arming and drilling was the reason that de Valera took a gun in his hand, 'From the beginning he was sure that the fight for Irish freedom would not leave an insoluble problem in the north-east.'[34] Why he was so sure, we just don't know. Perhaps the numbers and temper of Southern Protestants had something to do with it. In the South Protestants comprised less than 10 per cent of the population. And though there was a certain arm's-length relationship, encouraged by the clergy of the followers of both Rome and Canterbury, in general the Southern Irish, though not what one might term ecumenical, nevertheless got on reasonably well together. In the agricultural South, as the landlord was often Protestant and the tenantry Catholic, the resolution of the land issue had put an end to any overt sectarian quotient in political debate. True, there were occasional envious Catholic eyes cast on a 'Protestant farm'. True, freemasonry and Orangism raged in the upper echelons of Dublin Castle. There was Protestant–Catholic rivalry in the trades and the professions, and it would have been unheard of for one set of Christians to put foot in the church of the other. Nevertheless the situation was totally unlike that prevailing in the North.

First, the Protestants there comprised not a minority but a majority (of some 890,000 to 690,000) in six of the nine counties of Ulster: Antrim, Armagh, Derry, Down, Fermanagh and Tyrone. Second, a ruthlessly efficient plantation by Scots Presbyterians, who were awarded Catholics' lands, had infused a grimmer, more joyless tone into the character of Ulster Protestantism than that which prevailed in the South, which was relatively untouched by 'wee-freeism'. Moreover, the concentration of Protestant capital and work ethic in the north-east had generated some flourishing industries in both field and factory – notably flax, for the linen trade, and heavy engineering, particularly shipbuilding. Since the union Dublin had become an Augustan capital of faded Palladian architecture, Belfast a Mancunian city set down in an area of Ireland that looked more like lowland Scotland – and a particularly bloodstained area at that. Throughout the nineteenth century, to the memories of the earlier ferocious Protestant–Catholic strife over land were added the newer tensions over the scramble for industrial jobs. These grew as Belfast grew, and were exacerbated by the rising temperature caused by the Home Rule Movement. As a result riot and pogrom, or attempted pogrom, erupted sporadically in Belfast through the later nineteenth and early twentieth centuries.

At Westminster, faced with a demand from one part of Ireland for Home Rule and with resistance to it in another part – which, because of Tory opportunism, threatened to trigger off civil war in England itself – it was inevitable that at some stage the idea of partition would be put forward. And proposed it was by a Liberal Unionist, T. G. R. Agar-Robartes, during one of the parliamentary circuits of the Home Rule Bill on 12 December 1912 – more than a year before de Valera enrolled in the Volunteers. The intention was to exclude Armagh, Antrim, Down and Derry. Though the amendment was rejected, at a meeting in Londonderry House Carson persuaded his principal lieutenants to support it: '. . . in doing so he opened the way for the recognition in the autumn of the following year that only the six counties with a Protestant population could make an effective resistance'.[35]

In real terms this meant that all subsequent debate – including contemporary debate – about 'Ulster' referred not to the historical province of Ulster but only to six of its nine counties: Armagh, Antrim, Down, Fermanagh, Londonderry and Tyrone. Within these six, Fermanagh, Tyrone and the city of Derry had Catholic majorities. But where Ireland was concerned, this unpublicized definition of 'Ulster' existed only within militant Unionism's decision-taking upper echelons. The nationalists as a whole paid little attention to Agar-Robartes' initiative. Partition was so unthinkable that the idea was dismissed without serious discussion. But it now appears that the Agar-Robartes proposal may have been a *'ballon d'essai'* for a policy which the Government had already agreed on.

Two months after the exclusion proposal surfaced, in August 1912, Lloyd George was in Marienbad where he had several meetings with a fellow holidaymaker, T. P. O'Connor, one of the leaders of the Irish Parliamentary Party. On the day he left the spa Lloyd George seems to have informed O'Connor that the Government had decided on partition. O'Connor was discovered 'looking the picture of despair as he sat on one of the garden seats near the wells' by a Dr Cox, physician to the Archbishop of Dublin, Dr Walsh, who was also taking the waters.[36] He confided the reason for his angst to the doctor, but swore him to secrecy. Had the news been made public, at a time when there was already growing reaction to Carson's activities, there would have been a great erosion of support from the constitutionalist, John Redmond policy, and a corresponding swing towards a more militant approach.

De Valera, like the rest of those who had joined the Volunteers, was unaware of the Marienbad disclosure, but already no one was more militant than he:[37]

> From the time de Valera enrolled he was an enthusiastic and whole-hearted volunteer. Not only did he attend his weekly drill meetings regularly; he also went to the voluntary Saturday afternoon exercises in Larkfield, at Kimmage . . . soon his diligence began to bring him to a more important position. . . . When the Donnybrook company was formed he was elected captain. . . . De Valera wrote, on request, during 1915 a manual of drill suitable for the Volunteers. He urged, however, that as a rising was imminent, the top priority should be given to training in the use of weapons.

During this time he cut a striking, rather eccentric, figure. A contemporary description of him says:[38]

> His appearance was extremely remarkable. He was exceptionally tall, considerably over six foot in height, a very serious-looking man in his early thirties with a long nose and spectacles, and a strangely foreign expression. His clothes, of rough homespun, also made him conspicuous; and he often wore a most unusual cap, with a prominent peak and a flap folded across the top, rather like an airman's helmet.

But though he turned up to the early drill sessions in his 'unusual cap' and homespuns there was nothing eccentric about de Valera's military preparations. He equipped himself with a Mauser carbine, which he bought for £5 from The O'Rahilly (O'Rahilly had awarded himself the ancestral Irish indication of distinction, a 'The'). Volunteers had to buy their own weapons, either outright for thirty shillings or by contributing threepence a week to a purchasing fund. A separate five shillings was needed to buy their haversacks, belts and bandoliers. Apart from kitting himself out fully de Valera helped in the distribution and storage of gelignite stolen from Kynoch's of Arklow, an explosives manufacturing concern whose chairman, Arthur Chamberlain, belonged to the great English Conservative family of that name. De Valera's austere manner and unusual appearance set him apart from the ordinary run of Volunteers:[39]

> He was a man we didn't care much about. He was very severe drilling, giving the orders in Irish and none of us knew Irish. He would never make free, was always grim, and we would make fun of him. He would come from Blackrock on a bicycle and, at that time, he was very thin and very tall, and he would have his full uniform on him sitting on the bike, and it looked so funny, he looked so grim on this bicycle, frowning.

In 1914 de Valera graduated from his bicycle to a motorcycle and sidecar, which he put to good use on the day the Volunteers staged their version of the *Clydevalley* exploit which had armed the UVF. Appropriately enough the English-born Irish sympathizer Erskine Childers, aboard his yacht *Asgard*, had made a rendezvous with a tug in the North Sea on the Orangemen's feast day, 12 July, to take aboard the nationalists' weapons: nine hundred old Mauser rifles and twenty-nine thousand rounds of ammunition. Twelve days later he sailed into Howth, to be greeted by a column of Volunteers which until that moment had no idea that they were taking part in anything other than a routine Sunday exercise. There was wild excitement: '. . . men rushed to the quay-side reaching for the cases and were in danger of being pushed into the water by the press of those behind. Only the severest of the officers (among whom was Eamon de Valera) succeeded in holding their companies in their place.'[40]

On the march back to Dublin the Volunteers were halted at Clontarf by a detachment of the King's Own Scottish Borderers with fixed bayonets. While Volunteer officers parleyed with the troops their men melted away, carrying their rifles. De Valera ordered two out of every three Volunteers under his command to disperse, leaving their weapons with those remaining. He then went home, picked up the motorcycle and sidecar and drove his men home, one at a time, each with his three rifles. It was dawn before he was finished. The gun-running was a triumph for de Valera and for the Volunteers. The propaganda boost given to the movement was heightened by a tragedy which occurred at Bachelor's Walk in Dublin when a contingent of the Borderers, marching back from Clontarf, fired on a stone-throwing crowd; they killed three civilians, one of them a woman, and caused thirty-one other casualties.

The contrast with the way in which the UVF arms landing had passed off could not have been more stark. Volunteers marched in military formation in the subsequent huge funeral procession, and Howth ammunition was first used to fire a salute over the graves. But the surge of support which the landings and killings brought for the Volunteers' aims was short-lived. In June Redmond, worried by the growing strength of the movement, had succeeded in adding twenty-five nominees of his own to the Volunteers' executive. The 'forward', that is IRB-controlled, wing of the executive reluctantly accepted the imposition in the interests of national unity.

But during July, in a very real sense, Irish national unity was tacitly dropped from the British political agenda and partition came out of the closet as a live option. The House of Lords made a tactical move on the 8th to counteract the Home Rule Bill, which it could no longer openly reject, by proposing that the Amending Bill, which was to have the effect of postponing it until after the war, be altered to provide for the exclusion of the entire nine counties of Ulster. This would have meant including solidly Catholic Cavan, Donegal and Monaghan in the areas which the Unionist leaders had secretly decided were the most that the Protestants could control. It was a clearly unworkable ploy, but a highly dangerous one with war looming in Europe. King George intervened to call an all-party conference at Buckingham Palace on 21 July. Here for four days the parties, in Churchill's immortal phrase, 'toiled round the muddy byways of Fermanagh and Tyrone'.[41] Asquith, with Lloyd George sitting beside him, fulfilled the prophecy of Marienbad: he proposed the exclusion of the six north-eastern counties which are today partitioned from the rest of Ireland. Redmond objected on the grounds that no area excluded from Home Rule should include a nationalist majority. Carson, who in fact wanted Home Rule neither for Ireland nor for Ulster, but with an eye on Liberal opinion, argued for 'the clean cut' of nine counties; accurately, but audaciously, he suggested that this would create a pressure towards all-Ireland unity because of the inclusion of a majority of Catholics. On 23 July the Austrian ultimatum was delivered to Serbia. The conference ended next day.

Against that background it can be imagined how severely Redmond tested Volunteer unity by swiftly making two major gestures of support for the Government while getting nothing in return, either on partition or on Home Rule. The first to this day forms a classic illustration both of the perennial 'what if?' that seems to dog the Anglo-Irish relationship at crucial moments, and of the manner in which what is good in London is perceived as bad in Dublin and vice versa. It occurred on the same day, 3 August, on which the declaration of war was announced in the House of Commons. Redmond's response to the announcement was: 'I say to the Government they may tomorrow withdraw every one of their troops from Ireland . . . nationalist Catholics will be only too glad to join forces with armed Protestant Ulstermen in the North.' A reporter who covered the occasion, W. J. Flynn, later wrote:[42]

> . . . the cheers . . . were deafening and prolonged. The scene and its conclusion baffles description. . . . I never saw before, nor have I seen since the pandemonium of enthusiasm . . . when Redmond concluded that short speech. If the House of Commons that afternoon had the decision I believe it would, by an overwhelming majority, have conceded to Ireland the largest measure of freedom it might demand. But nothing happened . . . the same evil influences that brought about Partition later made sure of that.

The IRB-controlled executive of the Volunteers did not look on Redmond's speech in the same light as did the House of Commons. His unrequited moderation was pushing them to breaking point. The point was reached within a few weeks, on 20 September at Woodenbridge in Co. Wicklow, when Redmond urged the Volunteers to take part in the fighting 'wherever the fighting extends, in defence of right, freedom and religion, in this war'.[43] The IRB faction decided that co-operation with the Redmondite nominees on the executive was impossible and a split developed between the two factions. De Valera remained with the original founders, MacNeill, Thomas MacDonagh, Eamonn Kent and The O'Rahilly.

His oratory persuaded a majority of his company to follow his lead when he addressed them on the issue on 28 September. As he and his men left the hall, which was owned by Redmondite supporters, he called out to those remaining behind: 'You will need us before you get Home Rule.'[44]

3
TAKING THE OATH

BUT AFTER THE dramatic walk-out there came anti-climax. The enthusiasm of de Valera's followers soon subsided in the disillusionment of the split. Alternative halls were hard to come by, and before long he was drilling as few as seven men – in a field near Donnybrook. But here again he showed the determination that earned him his first scholarships. This time it would win him high rank in the Volunteers.

He succeeded in getting his company appointed as the 'eyes and ears of the South City battalions'.[1] Padraig Pearse allowed him to use part of his school for drill purposes, and de Valera found it possible to attract sufficient numbers of young men to this attractive-sounding scouting corps to build his company numbers up again. Apart from scouting, Volunteers learned rifle and bayonet drill, and general field work; de Valera himself specialized in scouting, map reading and map drawing. His enthusiasm marked him out for promotion, and in March 1915 he was appointed to the rank of Commandant with responsibility for the 3rd Battalion commanding the south-east of the city.

Before appointing him formally, Pearse sounded him on what his attitude would be in the event of a rising. De Valera's answer was to the effect that as a soldier he would accept any orders he might be given. Satisfied, Pearse handed him the following letter:[2]

The Irish Volunteers, 41, Kildare St., Dublin, 11th Mar. 1915.

A Chara,
  At last night's meeting of the Executive you were formally appointed Commandant of the 3rd Batt. with Capt. Fitzgibbon as Vice-Commandant and Capt. Begley as Adjutant. I have mislaid the name of the Quartermaster, but he was also approved of. Could you let me know his name and former rank by return? (to St. Enda's?)
  Can you attend a meeting of the four Battalion Commandants on Saturday evening next after the officers lecture? There are several important matters that the Headquarters Staff wants to discuss with the Commandants.
                                        Sincerely yours,
                                        P.H. Pearse

At the meeting referred to, held on 13 March in Dawson Street, de Valera discovered that, with or without the name of the Quartermaster, detailed plans for an uprising had been drawn up. Everything had been thought of, from minutiae such as passwords and the colour of the paper (grey) on which the instructions to the Commandants to lead out their men would be written, to the overall strategy to be followed. In Dublin this involved cutting off the various military barracks on the city's outskirts so that troops could not reach the city centre. De Valera's assigned target was Beggar's Bush Barracks, and his general task was to include both neutralizing the barracks and cutting the main road and rail links between Dublin and Dun Laoghaire at or around Mount Street Bridge, Grand Canal Street Bridge and Westland Row Railway Station. From his intensive study of military manuals, to which he had applied himself with his characteristic attention to detail, he saw at once that his chances of survival were slim. The troops from Beggar's Bush could be pinned down for a time, but heavy artillery accompanied by reinforcements from England would inevitably destroy the Volunteers. When he voiced his doubts, however, he was pooh-poohed as a pessimist, chiefly by James Connolly.[3]

Some time earlier the IRB had placed Connolly under restraint and brought him to a lengthy meeting at which he was admitted to their councils. He had been threatening to stage a rising of his own with his tiny Citizen Army; Pearse and the others therefore co-opted him, fearing that otherwise he would bring the authorities down on top of them, thus aborting their plans. Connolly believed that the nation must strike off the imperial shackles before the workers could be freed from economic bondage, and so he found no ideological difficulty in the prospect of fighting alongside a collection of bourgeois poet revolutionaries. But he rejected de Valera's pessimism on the grounds that, being capitalists, the British would never shell Dublin because it would entail the destruction of capitalist property.

De Valera's response to this was: '*What!* Surely you do not believe that. Put yourself in the position of a British officer. Wouldn't he destroy every material thing if thereby he could save the life of one of his men?'[4] But Connolly refused to be moved by de Valera's argument, even though de Valera said 'he was an exceptionally clever man'. De Valera told Gallagher that Connolly was principally responsible for the rising: '. . . it was his penetrating decision, absolutely inflexible, that conveyed itself to all and where others would have doubts there were none in him. It was essential that before the war ended (afterwards Britain would be too strong to permit an Insurrection) there be an Irish Rising.'[5]

But, his high opinion of Connolly notwithstanding, de Valera still 'expressed the belief that he would not come through it alive'.[6] In fact he was the only man present at that meeting to survive; the others – Pearse, Connolly, Thomas MacDonagh, Eamonn Ceannt and Edward Daly – were all executed. Possibly his meticulous preparations for the uprising had something to do with his survival. He went about them in a characteristic blend of close study, guile and genuine compassion; every detail of his command area was studied, with the result that on the eve of the rising:[7]

He was able to tell each Company Captain what he would find to his advantage or disadvantage when he got there. . . . He was able to discuss every detail even to the places where it would be possible to procure an alternative water supply, where we could definitely find tools for such things as loopholing walls and making communications. . . . I cannot remember a query put to him that he was not able to answer immediately.

Part of this information was secured by taking walks through the district hand-in-hand with his five-year-old son Vivion, perfect cover for such reconnoitring. It was also the beginning of a practice which he subsequently continued: in an attempt to counteract the absences from his family caused by public life, he made a conscious effort where possible to take one or more of the children with him when driving to functions around the country.[8]

De Valera's diligence gained him yet another promotion before the rising: Adjutant to the Dublin Brigade under Thomas MacDonagh. This promotion caused him to join the IRB. He had hitherto fought shy of joining a secret oath-bound society, partly because of the Church's opposition to such societies and partly, in a sense, because he shared the Church hierarchical approach. With his hierarchical approach to authority he wanted to be clear where power lay and where his orders were coming from. The O'Muirthuile incident of 1911, with the rigged ballot papers, had left its mark.

Characteristically, he gave at least two separate accounts of why he changed his mind. In the first he told Dorothy Macardle that MacDonagh approached him and asked him to join.[9] He said he agreed, stipulating that he would simply take orders and take no part in IRB meetings. He allowed this version to stand for several years and for several editions of her book *The Irish Republic*, which he described as 'an excellent history'. He wrote a foreword for it and directed that it be kept in print.[10]

In the second version, which he gave in his official biography, he stated that he approached MacDonagh[11] to make a complaint. He had discovered that some Volunteers in his battalion seemed to know more about what was going on than he did. MacDonagh told him bluntly that the men concerned were members of the IRB, and that if de Valera wished to be privy to such information he would have to join. De Valera objected, saying that he was a member of the Irish Volunteers and subject to its executive; he could not serve two masters. When MacDonagh broke it to him that he would not be serving two masters because the IRB in fact *was* the executive, he says he agreed to take the oath. He repeated his stipulation about not attending meetings and added that he 'did not want to know the names of any of the members of or share any of the secrets of the organisation except those essential for the proper exercise of his command of the Volunteers'.[12]

The joining of the IRB is not the only example we shall encounter of de Valera's tendency to give differing versions of the same happening. But the incident acquires a peculiar significance later in his career on at least two occasions: first, the historic defeat which de Valera later endured over the Anglo-Irish Treaty of 1921, largely through IRB influence; and second, in relation to the prehensile logic he would one day display in connection with another, more momentous, oath-taking ceremony. Both of these will be examined in due course, but for the moment let us return to 1915–16. In those years, apart from the Easter Rising, he was involved in two other major IRB demonstrations.

The first of these was the O'Donovan Rossa funeral on 1 August 1915. The dead man had been a founder of Fenianism, and had suffered terribly in British prisons as a result. He became an icon of the physical force movement both for these reasons and because of his lifelong involvement with Clan na nGael in America. The IRB made a national event of his interment: a huge funeral procession wound its way through Dublin and culminated in shots being fired over the grave following a fiery oration delivered by Padraig Pearse, in Volunteer uniform, which concluded with these prophetic words: 'They think they have pacified Ireland. They think that they have purchased half of us and intimidated the other half. They think they have forseen everything, think that they have provided against everything; but the fools, the fools, the fools! – they have left us our Fenian dead, and while Ireland holds these graves, Ireland unfree shall never be at peace.'[13]

De Valera, also in full Volunteer uniform, was one of those who received these sentiments with approval. But he was far from approving of an incident which arose at another show of strength by the IRB on St Patrick's Day (17 March) the following year, a little over a month before the Easter Rising itself. The Volunteers took over the centre of the city for two hours, stopping all traffic, for a parade at which MacNeill took the salute in College Green. De Valera's men had cordoned off Dame Street, just below the Castle where the street passes the entrance to George's Street. A car containing an officer from the Castle, *en route* to Dun Laoghaire, attempted to force its way through 'on King's business'. De Valera refused, suggesting the officer take an alternative route as he could not get through the city centre. A policeman to whom the officer appealed also thought it wisest to do as 'the gentleman told you'.

De Valera was fully conscious that a rising was only a matter of some days away and that a premature incident could bring down the authorities on the conspiracy. Nevertheless, as was typical of him, once he had given an order he would not allow it to be challenged. He called up a group of Volunteers and instructed them to overturn the car if it made any move forward. Eventually the car drove away, along the route indicated by de Valera. The rank and file cheered but the Vice Adjutant of the Brigade, Sean Fitzgibbon, was also a member of the Supreme Council of the IRB and therefore aware of the plans for Easter and what a crack-down could do to them. Unwisely, in front of his men he criticized what de Valera had done; for his pains he was ordered back to his position. De Valera was 'mad'[14] and took up the matter with headquarters. He based his complaint less on grounds of lèse-majesté than on the fact that members of the Supreme Council should not have high military rank as this could lead to a divided command. He now knew, of course, from MacDonagh that the IRB *were* in command; what he intended was that *his* command would not be divided or diluted. But, mindful of the imminence of the rising, the IRB upheld his complaint and transferred both Fitzgibbon and another prominent IRB man, The O'Rahilly, to other duties.

At this stage the question logically arises: what were the authorities doing while all these – and many other – illegal military displays were going on? Ironically their policy in the South, and to a large degree in the North, was dictated by a man whom both Orange and Green Volunteers were united against, John Redmond.[15] He consistently advised that to make arrests would be to make a bad situation worse. But by Easter 1916 the situation had escalated to a point where the authorities could no longer stand idly by. The Volunteers' gun-running efforts had continued since Howth. In fact, only a week after Howth a further six hundred rifles had been landed at Kilcoole in Co. Wicklow from the yacht *Chotah*, belonging to another nationalist sympathizer, Sir Thomas Myles. But by Easter week intensive negotiations between the IRB in Dublin, Clan na nGael in New York and the Germans had resulted in a far larger consignment of arms than ever previously contemplated being shipped from Lübeck to the coast of Kerry aboard the *Aud*. It comprised some twenty thousand rifles and ten machine guns with ammunition and explosives. Germany was acting from the same motive that led it to permit the arming of the Orangemen: it seemed likely to make trouble for the British and so divert them from the war effort. In fact there is evidence[16] that the threat of civil war posed by the Unionists, 'The Kaiser's Ulster friends' and their Conservative allies made such an impact that 'experienced foreign observers in Berlin and Vienna certainly believed that the Central Powers calculated upon England's being unable to take any active part if war should come'.[17]

Carson had been received by the Kaiser in Hamburg in 1913 and Von Kuhlmann, the respected Counsellor of the German Embassy in London, was reported by John Dillon, the Irish Parliamentary Party leader,[18] to have been visiting leading Unionists in Belfast as close to the outbreak of war as 12 July 1914. His report, said Dillon, made the Emperor 'determined to go on with the war'.[19]

By 1916 one man determined not to go on with war was Roger Casement. He had been visiting Germany on a twofold mission: first, to raise an Irish brigade amongst captured Irish prisoners of war; and second, to raise a German expeditionary force for Ireland, led by German officers, accompanied by submarines and armed with some two hundred thousand rifles and with machine guns. In fact the IRB would have been fairly content with what the *Aud* carried. They would have welcomed some

German officers in addition to the arms, but the independent-minded approach of the conspirators to rebellion was spelled out by the Clan na nGael leader, John Devoy, during a conversation in the *Gaelic American* office in New York in which he said of an offer of money by the German Ambassador to the USA, Von Bernstorff: 'If we take their money they will expect us to take their orders, but we must retain our independence of action. If we are not willing to finance our own fight for freedom we don't deserve freedom.'[20]

Von Bernstorff had told Devoy that the Germans had too few officers to be able to spare any for the IRB, but had promised arms and German support for Ireland at the Peace Conference which would come at the end of the war. However, Casement became obsessed with the idea that the rising would be a disaster without German aid on the scale he envisaged, and succeeded in getting himself sent to Kerry in a submarine to rendezvous with the *Aud*. The Germans thought he wanted to go home to lend badly needed expertise to the projected revolution; in fact he wanted to call it off. But after landing from a punt he was captured by the British on 21 April.

Austin Stack, the Kerry Volunteer leader who was supposed to be in charge of the arms landing, went to the barracks where Casement was held to get news of him – and merely succeeded in getting arrested himself. Meanwhile the *Aud*, which had succeeded in eluding the British Navy and finding safe anchorage off Inishtooskert Island in Tralee Bay, waited fruitlessly for signals from the shore. Between Stack's arrest and a series of other misunderstandings, none came. What did come eventually was a British patrol boat, which escorted the *Aud* to Queenstown Harbour where the skipper blew up his ship. The only surprising thing about the patrol boat's arrival is that it did not occur sooner. The British had intercepted the telegrams between the German Embassy in Washington, Berlin and Clan na nGael.[21] However, the sensational proceedings off Kerry finally decided the debate which had been raging for months in Dublin Castle as to whether or not there should be a crack-down on the Volunteers. Action would have to be taken.

The IRB had been doing some cypher interception of its own, and was well aware of the risk of a swoop. Accordingly, a forged 'Castle document' was published on 20 April; its aim was to sway public opinion by indicating that, in order to prepare for conscription and renewed coercion, an attack on the Volunteers was imminent, along with the arrest of various public figures including the Archbishop of Dublin.[22] Amongst those who accepted the document's authenticity were James Connolly and Eamon de Valera.[23] It helped to steel both of them in their resolution to rebel during the splits and confusions of the next four days.

A Fianna boy scout had handed de Valera his instructions to mobilize that weekend, on the night before the document was issued. The courier's identifying password and de Valera's reply, agreed at the fateful meeting of

Commandants in March the previous year, accurately symbolized de Valera's career to that point. The password was 'Howth', the reply 'Bruree'. This was de Valera's most selfless moment. A deeply conservative man, operating in a deeply conservative society, he was abandoning a wife he loved, infant children and a promising career, to face into the gap of danger for a principle. He made his will, leaving what little he had to Sinead and praying that the insurance company would pay her the policy he had taken out on his life. His authorized biography says that 'he felt his death was almost inevitable'. Characteristically, he hid his emotion as, 'on Good Friday, he bade goodbye to his wife and four children'.[24] But a letter he wrote from prison a year later gives an indication of his inner turmoil:[25]

It is Easter Saturday and my mind naturally reverts to . . . a year ago. How I thank God that you have not the agonies before you this year which I foresaw for you at the corresponding time last year. I could not tell you then the feelings that were rending my heart on your account. But sweetheart I know you will believe me – I know you will not think it was selfishness or callous indifference or senseless optimism that made me so calm when I was about to offer up you and the children as a sacrifice. If you could have seen my heart on that terrible day of anxiety for you, Easter Sunday, you would have known – when I called to see you and found that the strain had been too much for you, I only found what I had anticipated all the day long. Could you have seen it that night when I stooped over you to give you that parting kiss you would know that though I gave it as lightly as if we were to meet again in the morning it was simply to save you, to give you some sixteen hours of respite; for in my heart I believed it was the last kiss I would give you on earth.

Yes this time last year I foresaw for you the agonies you would suffer when the rifles began to crackle and the guns to boom almost at the door. I foresaw, and endured in sympathy the terrible suspense you would endure so long as the fighting continued or till you heard definitely of my death – I saw you finally sink stunned with the leaden weight of the last news – bereft of that last thread of hope which alone made the suspense bearable.

Yet I did not foresee what was perhaps the most terrible part of all for you. The long interval from the surrender till the announcement of my sentence – made more terrible for you by the daily list of those condemned and executed, but during the time itself I knew how you were suffering and I prayed God to lighten it. I thank Him that this year you will be able to enjoy the spirit of the festival better and I pray Him to particularly gladden the hearts of those who lost their dear ones last year. . . .

De Valera's agonies that weekend were no doubt compounded by two other facts. First, Sinead was again pregnant: another son, Ruari, the Irish form of Roger, after Roger Casement, was born in November of that year. The second worrisome fact was that on Holy Thursday MacNeill had at long last found out what the IRB were planning. He at first confronted Pearse, threatening to 'do everything I can to stop this, everything except to ring up Dublin Castle'.[26] Then, on Good Friday, persuaded by MacDonagh and MacDiarmada that German arms were on the way, he changed his mind. Perhaps after all there might be a prospect of success and not simply useless slaughter. But the news of the Kerry captures made him reconsider. He published an announcement in the *Sunday Independent* addressed to each individual Volunteer, cancelling all manoeuvres for that day. No parades, marches or any other activities were to take place. To back this up he sent couriers around the country bearing similar instructions to local commanders. Whatever slim chance of succeeding the rising might have had with German arms and a united command, it was now effectively doomed.

However, at a meeting of the IRB Military Council on Easter Monday, held in Liberty Hall, HQ both of the Irish Transport and General Workers' Union and of the Citizen Army, it was decided to go ahead anyway. Pearse, Connolly, Plunkett and the other leaders reckoned, correctly, that if they did not strike first they would be rounded up anyhow. There may or may not have been another factor present in their decision to strike, one to which hitherto little attention has been paid publicly.

The IRB had officially informed the Pope that they were intent on holding a rebellion in Ireland on Easter Sunday. As to the importance attached by the men in Liberty Hall to this notification, either in terms of a potential breach of secrecy by some Vatican official or as some form of binding commitment on them to rise, we can only speculate. But, given the importance of the Church in Ireland at that time, the informing of the Pope cannot be completely overlooked. Joseph Plunkett's father, Count Plunkett – a papal Count – called at Archbishop's House in Drumcondra to inform Archbishop Walsh of the Pope's reaction to the news – at Pope Benedict's suggestion.

Archbishop Walsh was ill and the Count was received by his secretary, Father Curran. Count Plunkett informed the startled Curran of the rising and of the Pope's reaction to his mission. Not surprisingly, the Pope had shown 'profound anxiety' and asked 'was there no peaceful way out of it?' Plunkett sought to calm the Pontiff by 'assuring His Holiness that he should not be shocked or alarmed. It was a purely national movement for independence the same as every nation has a right to.' No hint of communism in the IRB! The Count then asked the Pope's blessing on the Volunteers. The Pope reacted with 'great perturbation' and asked if he had seen the Archbishop of Dublin.

Plunkett sought to calm the Pontiff by 'making it plain that it was the wish of the leaders of the movement to act entirely with the goodwill (or approval) of the Pope and gave assurances that they would act as Catholics'. Understandably, this last did not greatly reassure Pope Benedict, who again asked whether no peaceful means of achieving the objective could be found and again urged Plunkett to see Archbishop Walsh. Plunkett gave assurances that he would do so as soon as he returned to Dublin. He told Curran that he was 'just back'. But obviously the delay in the timing of the rising had a bearing on that of his notification to Archbishop's House. His visit came not on Easter Sunday but Easter Monday. As he was talking, Curran was interrupted by a phone call telling him that the General Post Office had just been attacked.[27]

Great as was Curran's surprise, it was as nothing to the shock which a similar phone call caused to a meeting which was taking place in Dublin Castle at the same time. Here the Permanent Under Secretary, Sir Matthew Nathan, and the Military Intelligence Officer, Major Ivor Price, were drawing up plans for a widespread round-up of rebels. Assisting them in arranging the commandeering of telephone and telegraph facilities was the Secretary of the Post Office, Sir Hamilton Norway. In the event it was the rebels who got in first with the communications commandeerings and took over Sir Hamilton's principal post office. At midday on Easter Monday, 24 April 1916, a small procession of some 150 Volunteers and Citizen Army men, together with one woman, Winifred Carney, Connolly's secretary, marched from Liberty Hall and took over the General Post Office in O'Connell Street. Initially much of their weaponry fitted on a single handcart, although later in the week extra men and arms did arrive at the GPO as more Volunteers flocked to the colours. Apart from the taking over of the GPO itself, the most significant activity of the day was Pearse's reading of the declaration of the republic to an amused and bemused Dublin crowd which had gathered outside. The proclamation, the foundation document for much that was to follow for de Valera and for Ireland, read as follows:[28]

Poblacht na h-Eireann
The Provisional Government
of the
IRISH REPUBLIC
To the people of Ireland.

Irishmen and Irish women: in the name of God and of the dead generations from which she receives her old tradition of nationhood, Ireland through us summons her children to her flag and strikes for her freedom.

Having organised and trained her manhood through her secret revolutionary organisation, the Irish Republican Brotherhood, and through her open military organisation, the Irish Volunteers, and the Irish Citizen Army, having patiently perfected her discipline, having resolutely waited for the right moment to reveal itself, she now seizes the moment, and, supported by her exiled children in America and by gallant allies in Europe, but relying first on her own strength, she strikes in full confidence of victory.

We declare the right of the people of Ireland to the ownership of Ireland and to the unfettered control of Irish destinies, to be sovereign and indefeasible. The long usurpation of that right by a foreign people and government has not extinguished the right, nor can it ever be extinguished except by the destruction of the Irish people. In every generation the Irish people have asserted their right to national freedom and sovereignty: six times during the past three hundred years they have asserted it in arms in the face of the world. We hereby proclaim the Irish Republic as a Sovereign Independent State, and we pledge our lives and the lives of our comrades-in-arms to the cause of its freedom, of its welfare and of its exaltation among the nations.

The Irish Republic is entitled to, and hereby claims, the allegiance of every Irishman and Irishwoman. The Republic guarantees religious and civil liberty, equal rights and equal opportunities to all its citizens, and declares its resolve to pursue the happiness and prosperity of the whole nation and of all its parts; cherishing all the children of the nation equally, and oblivious to the differences, carefully fostered by an alien government, which have divided a minority from the majority in the past.

Until our arms have brought the opportune moment for the establishment of a permanent National Government, representative of the whole people of Ireland, and elected by the suffrages of all her men and women, the Provisional Government, hereby constituted, will administer the civil and military affairs of the Republic in trust for the people. We place the cause of the Irish Republic under the protection of the Most High God, Whose blessing we invoke upon our arms, and we pray that no one who serves that cause will dishonour it by cowardice, inhumanity or rapine. In this supreme hour the Irish nation must, by its valour and discipline, and by the readiness of its children prove itself worthy of the august destiny to which it is called.

Signed on behalf of the Provisional Government,
                    Thomas J. Clarke
                    Sean MacDiarmada
                    P. H. Pearse
                    James Connolly
                    Thomas MacDonagh
                    Eamonn Ceannt
                    Joseph Plunkett

Sonorous rhetoric, heroism, unreality, compromise between Pearse's nationalism and Connolly's socialism; the Catholic South's resolutely proclaimed belief that Orange and Green could mend their differences whilst remaining 'oblivious to the differences' between them; all these were to become the *fons et origo* of Eamon de Valera's subsequent political philosophy. It was a philosophy sanctified in the public mind by the constant reminders that the men who signed the proclamation paid for so doing with their lives. But for the moment on that Easter Monday, apart from worrying about Sinead and the children, his immediate preoccupations included such problems as what to do with the Cats' and Dogs' Home and the women – not necessarily in that order.

The original plans for the rising called on the four Dublin Volunteer battalions to cover the approaches to the city. The 1st was to cover the north-west, the Four Courts and Church Street area; the 2nd the southern approaches, the Jacob's biscuit factory district. The 4th was intended to command the south-west, the south Dublin Union area, while the 3rd, de Valera's, was to close off the south-east. But that aspiration was worked out on the pre-MacNeill instruction of a battalion strength of some five hundred men. After the countermanding order appeared, only something like 130 turned up.[29] All the Volunteer commanders had to contend with similar shortages. This meant that in a nutshell the 1916 Rising largely consisted of the seizure of a number of Dublin strongpoints which were held for the best part of a week until artillery fire and superior manpower compelled a surrender. In de Valera's case, the manpower shortage meant that he could not link up as planned with the 2nd Battalion at Leeson Street. Instead he concentrated on a series of bridges in his area: Ringsend, Grand Canal Street and the one which was to pass his name into immortality – Lower Mount Street.

There is a kind of man to whom luck happens; de Valera was of that breed. His headquarters, situated near the centre of his command area, was not on the main road to Dublin from Dun Laoghaire where the troops disembarked. Hence, although only a couple of hundred yards away, it did not suffer the same type of sustained infantry attack which occurred at Northumberland Road/Mount Street Bridge, over which ran the tram tracks to Dublin. The major hazards at de Valera's post came from sniper fire and, to a degree, the tensions that his style of command generated amongst his men. Moreover, for some reason the British ceased shelling his post after a relatively slight bombardment.

Mount Street Bridge was also spared from shelling but suffered a heavy assault from ground troops. The bridge was commanded by two men, Lieutenant Michael Malone and Volunteer James Grace. As they had only single-shot rifles de Valera gave Malone his Mauser pistol and four hundred rounds of ammunition. Years later, when I was visiting Vivion de Valera at his father's old home in Cross Avenue, Blackrock, that Mauser used to be produced at a certain point in the bottle of Jameson and I would be given the honour of holding it. (The Mauser, not the Jameson.) There was every reason for the reverence: as will be seen, in a very real sense Eamon de Valera's power grew out of the barrel of that gun.

Apart from the shortage of manpower de Valera also had to contend with a shortage of woman power. He had told Cuman na mBan, the women's Volunteer force, that he would require them not as combatants but as first aid workers and cooks – because, he said, he had no weapons for them. In view of his subsequent attitude to women in public life it is equally likely that he literally did not want to see them in the front line. At all events Cuman na mBan did not report to his command post, Boland's Bakery. This vantage point commanded not only the Grand Canal and Ringsend area of the city but also Beggar's Bush Barracks, Westland Row Railway Station, the Cats' and Dogs' Home and the stables which contained the Boland's Bakery dray horses. These places, and in particular Mount Street Bridge, were all destined to pass into the de Valera legend with a veneration normally accorded only to relics of the True Cross; for one can hardly overstress the fact that, for several decades after the rising, for devout Irish nationalists Easter 1916 occupied something of the place of High Mass in the Roman Catholic religion. De Valera's place in the sacramental rite was seen as that of Supreme Pontiff. It would have been both instructive and valuable to have had from de Valera himself a record of that week which cast him in a more human role than the consistently high-heroic public figure who emerges from his authorized biography. De Valera is described as doing everything:[30]

> ... he personally saw to the removal of some essential parts from the gas works and the electricity supply station in Ringsend. ... Even in this time of anxiety, his kindness for animals was seen. He arranged that the horses belonging to the bakery were fed as long as food was available. Later in the week, when food ran out, he had them let loose on the streets to avoid suffering. The animals in the nearby cats and dogs home he also liberated. ...

The lack of a human dimension to official accounts meant that when, inevitably, differing versions began to appear the effect tended more to stigmatize an emperor for suddenly being found without clothes than to create sympathy for a brave man who found himself in an appalling situation. Because of MacNeill's countermanding order, the total number of Volunteers who initially mobilized came to only seven or eight hundred men.[31] However, in the main they fought with great gallantry. It took a week of fierce fighting and a numerical superiority of ultimately some twenty to one, backed up by artillery, heavy machine guns and an assured food supply, to force their surrender. De Valera's post, being the most isolated, took longest to receive Pearse's surrender order. It arrived on Sunday, 30 April. As he in turn took some further time having it verified, he thus became the last Commandant to yield. This fact helped both to save his life and to burnish the legendary accounts of his performance during the fighting. Two incidents in particular served to further his reputation.

The first was the heroic defence of the approach to Mount Street Bridge by Malone and his companion from No. 25 Northumberland Road on the Wednesday of the rising, 26 April. It was a defence, let it be said, which was compounded by the Western Front-like disregard for life with which the British officers committed their forces in an effort to push through to their objective, Trinity College. Because of the numerical weakness of the Irish the British met with no resistance after disembarking at Dun Laoghaire until they came within range of the Mauser:[32]

> Malone allowed the advance guard to pass No. 25 before he himself and his comrade opened rapid fire ... the officers rallied them and proceeded to carry out a concentrated attack on this post. Volley after volley was poured into the house and machine guns trained on it, but in spite of the terrific onslaught Malone and Grace kept up a stubborn fight and inflicted severe casualties on the enemy ... they actually took up kneeling positions at the end of Northumberland Rd., directly opposite Malone's position.
>
> They apparently did not know that Clanwilliam House was occupied and the men in this post opened long range fire on them, and inflicted severe casualties on them ... in spite of the fact that the house was being literally sprinkled all over with machine gun fire, hand grenades also being profusely used ... eventually Malone fell dead at his post ... the bridge presented a terrible spectacle; as did

also the greater portion of Northumberland Rd as it was actually a wriggling mass of khaki.

Malone's post and the defence of Clanwilliam House between them accounted for 4 officers killed, 14 wounded, 215 other ranks killed and wounded – half the total casualties sustained by the British during Easter week. Even though de Valera was completely cut off from this action, and took no part in it, the fact that the 'Irish Thermopylae' occurred under his command helped to send his post-rising reputation soaring.

The second incident concerned a clever piece of military thinking on his part. A high tower in an old distillery nearby overlooked his post. De Valera ordered a party to climb the tower and send out bogus semaphore signals as if it were a command post. He also caused a green flag to be flown from the top of the tower; as a result the British bombarded it during the fighting, thus both diverting artillery fire from occupied positions and destroying a vantage point which could have been used against him. Shell fire does not seem to have been employed following the destruction of the 'command post'. De Valera afterwards told Gallagher, thinking of Connolly's faith in the inviolability of capitalist property, that when the first shell boomed out his reaction was: 'That'll larn him.'[33]

De Valera's own official version of his part in the flag incident bears out this impression of coolness under fire:[34]

> Accompanied by some of his men he climbed from the roof of the distillery up an iron ladder on to the outside of the tower. Though silhouetted and an open target for the many bullets which were flying around him, he was surprised to learn that his principal fear was height. He carefully fixed a pike on a corner of the tower and attached to it a green flag with a gold harp on its centre. The ruse was brilliantly successful. The enemy's fire was diverted. . . .

But there was also an unofficial, underground, version which sharply contrasted with this picture. This version did not get any public airing until 1964 when a book by an English journalist, Max Caulfield,[35] based on interviews with survivors of the rebellion, was published. An account of the proceedings in and around Boland's Bakery, which quoted officers and men who served under de Valera, portrayed a man on, or over, the threshold of nervous breakdown. Eye-witnesses recalled seeing a tall, gangling figure in green Volunteer uniform and red socks running around day and night, without sleep, getting trenches dug, giving contradictory orders and forgetting the password so that he nearly got himself shot. In fact, according to Caulfield, one of his men did go mad, shot a comrade and had to be struck down himself. A Volunteer was quoted as saying that, 'You had a feeling that your comrades might go mad – or, what was even worse, that you might go mad yourself.'[36]

A subordinate who tried to make him sleep said de Valera's reply was: 'I can't trust the men – they'll leave their posts or fall asleep if I don't watch them.' The subordinate, Lieutenant Fitzgerald, said he then promised to sit beside him and wake him up if anything occurred. This induced de Valera to lie down, whereupon he immediately fell asleep but began to sweat and toss about. 'His eyes wild, he sat bolt upright and in an awful voice, bawled, "Set fire to the railway! Set fire to the railway!"' He then insisted that papers dipped in whiskey be used to set fire to waiting rooms and rolling stock; but another officer, Captain John McMahon, 'eventually persuaded de Valera to listen to reason and the fires were put out. De Valera quickly recovered his composure.' Caulfield also stated that it was not de Valera, but Captain Michael Cullen and three Volunteers, who carried out the flag hoisting.

These demythologizing statements did not, however, dent de Valera's reputation as one might have expected. There were a number of reasons. One is that in Ireland he enjoyed a reputation ten times that of John Fitzgerald Kennedy – *before* the books began to appear with stories about Mafia connections and womanizing. Second, all critical assessment of 1916 was drowned in the wash of adulation and commemorative ceremonies which marked the fiftieth anniversary of the Easter Rising in 1966. Third, and most importantly, the authoritative Simon Donnelly, officer commanding C company who served under de Valera at Boland's Bakery, wrote to the papers denying that he had ever spoken to Caulfield and criticizing and disputing his version of events:[37]

> I wish to make it clear that I was not consulted in any way by him or on his behalf. I was not asked for, nor did I give him, permission to use any reminiscences of mine. In fact his account of events in the sector within which I was concerned is so distorted that it is almost impossible to know where to start in pointing out the errors.
>
> Fundamentally the fault lies in the uncritical acceptance of the narrative of Volunteers who were not in a position to know more than the events within a very limited radius of their own positions.
>
> These narratives are also coloured, sometimes highly so, by the prejudices which arose from the Civil War. This is particularly so in references to the Commandant of the Third battalion, Eamon de Valera, now President of Ireland.

I remember the impact of that letter clearly for two reasons. First, because after reading it in the *Sunday Press* I suddenly understood a seemingly inexplicable incident earlier in the week when Vivion de Valera had come into the *Evening Press* office to object strongly to the paper having carried some photographs from Caulfield's book (but no text or review), which I had not then read. The pictures would normally have been prescribed material for a de Valera paper. And second, because I found on investigation that Caulfield, a careful researcher, normally used a tape recorder to augment his note-taking during interviews.

What I did not know at the time was that de Valera wrote to Donnelly on 7 April 1964, thanking him for his letter to the papers and going on to say:[38] 'So far as I know, none of the accusations made against me by certain members of B. Company were made prior to the signing of the Treaty in 1921. The members who made the accusations were those who took the Treaty side. I am glad that somebody like yourself has been able to state that they are false.'

Readers will note for themselves the significance of that 'able to *state* that they are false'. The letter does not contain a flat statement that the 'members' accusations' were false. For in fact the 'accusations' against de Valera were made before the Treaty debate. As I wrote in my biography of Michael Collins:[39]

> One of the many remarkable examples of the loyalty extended to de Valera is the way his contemporaries consistently remained silent about his crack-up in 1916. Years later, when they were in Ballykinlar Internment Camp together, Captain Michael Cullen, one of those placed in charge of him at the time, approached a fellow prisoner, Tom O'Higgins, and, warning him first that he would shoot him if he ever mentioned the story to anyone, told him what had happened and asked him for a medical opinion on de Valera's condition. At that time (1920) de Valera was publicly quarrelling with the Clan na nGael leader, John Devoy in America, and Cullen was worried that he might again have lost his reason.

But the most extraordinary feature of the letter which Donnelly wrote, or was induced to write, to the newspapers is the fact that preserved in de Valera's papers is a memoir entitled 'Mount St Bridge' by Simon Donnelly[40] which, despite using more diplomatic terminology, largely *corroborates* the accounts in Caulfield's book, although he makes no direct reference to the work. It is also significant that, unlike other memoirs in the collection, there is no accompanying note giving a correction from de Valera on any statement he disagreed with.

Donnelly says de Valera 'dispatched Capt. Cullen . . . into the tower of the Distillery. Capt Cullen had also erected a flag . . . it remained there defiant to the end.' Donnelly also turns out to have been the man who subdued the Volunteer officer who 'went mad' and fired on his colleague; Donnelly clubbed him unconscious with his revolver butt. The reason that the Volunteer became deranged was that on the Friday night de Valera had ordered a withdrawal from his bakery headquarters to the railway, which had a higher elevation. From this the men were suddenly able to see the huge fires raging elsewhere in the city. The fires, combined with the knowledge that the outpost at Mount Street Bridge had fallen the previous day, had a profoundly depressing effect on everyone, with the man whom Donnelly restrained becoming 'completely shattered'.

Then, after his men had spent some time on the railway, de Valera cancelled the withdrawal order and ordered them 'to re-occupy the bakery'. This manoeuvre was eventually carried out safely, but the reoccupation was a nerve-racking business because there was a strong possibility that the British might have entered it during the Volunteers' absence. However, it is clear from Donnelly's memoir that de Valera was too far gone in anxiety and exhaustion to evaluate such possibilities by that stage in the fighting:[41]

> Commandant de Valera had been a real live wire from the first moment we entered our position: he was for ever on the move, ignoring danger, and as a matter of fact, to my mind, taking unnecessary risks. On the Friday he presented a very worn and tired-out appearance, and in spite of several requests from different officers for him to take some rest, he declined to do so. However he was prevailed on eventually and he retired to an office he was using in the dispensary. I placed a guard over his office with strict orders that under no consideration whatever was he to be disturbed and any message coming from him was to be sent to me. However, he was not resting very long and after a few hours he was on the move again, anxious about a hundred and one different things.

Donnelly's account even casts some doubt on de Valera's 'kindness for animals'. The memoir says that feeding the bakery horses was 'rather a ticklish job and naturally took the full time of one man, which we could very ill afford. The horses were eventually turned out into the street, as there was no food for them.' But at least the memoir does not challenge the biography's claim that de Valera 'liberated' the inmates of the Cats' and Dogs' Home. Donnelly makes no mention of this episode.

The nearest de Valera himself ever came to admitting to being close to breaking point during the fighting was in an anecdote he confided more than fifty years later to Sean J. White, after he had become President of Ireland for the second time in an election he might not have won had it not coincided with the blaze of publicity attending the 1916 anniversary.[42] De Valera told White that, during one of his scouting expeditions to Westland Row Railway Station, he became so overcome by tiredness that he went to sleep in a carriage on a siding. He woke up believing himself dead and in heaven, surrounded by angels. All around him he thought he could see nymphs and cherubs. After a few moments he realized there was a very good reason for this – he *was* surrounded by nymphs and cherubs. He had been sleeping in the Royal Coach – a coach which he was later to use himself when he became President of Ireland.

Probably the most telling comment on de Valera's behaviour during 1916 is his own silence. Amongst all the recollections contained in his own collection of papers, lovingly preserved over a long lifetime, there is no de Valera memoir of 1916. This is a pity, because the man who revealed his inner agonies and sensitivities in his letter of Easter 1917 to Sinead de Valera showed a high and rare form of courage – far more so than someone without family responsibilities who went out to fight not fully understanding the dangers. De Valera understood the dangers only too well. But his was a career which in large measure observed the dictum: 'When the truth becomes legend, print the legend.'

The Saturday after the rising began was spent in preparing for what de Valera expected to be a major assault. He knew that, apart from the British forces which had broken through Mount Street Bridge, troops from the Curragh must also have arrived in the city in force. The flames from the direction of O'Connell Street made it obvious that resistance from the rebellion's headquarters in the GPO must be either over or nearly so. Isolated and as yet largely unchallenged pockets of resistance such as his command must assuredly soon be attacked. Unbeknown to him, however, Pearse had surrendered that afternoon. The biggest fire which de Valera's men had witnessed had been the blazing GPO, Pearse's HQ. De Valera was shaving the next morning when Elizabeth O'Farrell, a Cuman na mBan messenger, arrived with Pearse's surrender order. De Valera at first feared a trap because it was not signed by MacDonagh; ever the stickler for detail, he sent the messenger off to get the required signature. However, the reality of the situation soon dawned on him and he decided that surrender was inevitable.

But stories of captured soldiers being shot out of hand after surrendering on the Western Front were common in Dublin. His fear was that this fate was only too likely, particularly after the slaughter on Mount Street Bridge. His men had captured a cadet, G. F. Mackay, during the fighting. At one stage de Valera had sent word to the British who were sniping from the roof of the nearby Sir Patrick Dun's Hospital that the cadet would be shot – although he assured the cadet himself that he had nothing to worry about – if the sniping did not cease. Now de Valera decided that he would have some hope of surviving if he surrendered in the company of the cadet, living proof that the Irish did not shoot prisoners. Accordingly he marched out from his men, accompanied only by Mackay, to whom he gave his Browning automatic with the request that some day he would pass it on to Vivion. Dr Myles Keogh described the surrender scene:[43]

> Two men came out of the Poor Law Dispensary of Patrick Dun's Hospital. One was a military cadet – a prisoner – and the other was de Valera.
> 'Hullo,' cried de Valera.
> 'Who are you?' said the officer.
> 'I am de Valera.'
> 'And I am a prisoner,' shouted the other.

After the surrender, the first thing de Valera did was to demand fair treatment for his men. Addressing the officer in a tone that sounded more of victory than of defeat, he said: 'Do what you like with me, but I demand proper treatment for my men.'

His men had not asked for 'proper treatment'. Their positions had not been over-run. Not knowing that de Valera was determined on surrender they were, in the words of his official biography, 'unbroken, they would fight on'.[44] This may have been the reason de Valera did not surrender with his men. Had they known his intentions, some of them at least might not have obeyed him. His biography states that when his men had been gathered into the bakery from their various outposts they 'heard the news with incredulity',[45] and had to be convinced that the order came from headquarters before they agreed to surrender. They emerged from the bakery some time afterwards still carrying their rifles, behind a Red Cross worker holding a white flag – none of the Volunteers would carry it. De Valera gave them the order to 'ground arms' at nearby Grattan Street. Although his men had put their weapons out of action, decades after the event he told his biographer that he could still remember 'the angry crunch with which the rifles hit the street'. The surrender incident is interesting for itself, for what it tells us about the control that de Valera exerted over his men, and for the indication that it is a more calculating de Valera whom we see emerging from the crucible of 1916. Obviously there was little bonding in the relationship between him and the handful of working-class men who passed that week in hell with him. Clearly he felt it necessary to withhold, rather than to share, his decision to surrender from what were, after all, fellow Volunteers. It was the sort of occasion which, on film, would have had a commander make a speech on the lines of congratulations for past gallantry, courage in present defeat and hope for the future. In the circumstances the men's anger was understandable. Yet, beyond the manner in which his 'ground arms' order was obeyed, there is no evidence of dissent from his instruction – a fact which speaks volumes for the respect, or fear, that de Valera inspired.

After the surrender he and the other captives were marched four abreast across the bloodstained Mount Street Bridge, past No. 25 Northumberland Road where the gallant Malone had died, to a holding centre, the showgrounds at Ballsbridge. As they marched, people were coming out of their homes to give cups of tea to the soldiers. Though the Volunteers did not know it, they had also been giving the tommies assistance during the fighting. Stephen Gwynne quoted[46] a British officer who told him that his units had not needed scouts – 'the old women' had volunteered information. In all probability their sons and husbands were away 'fighting for the rights of small nations'. In some cases they were back in Dublin. Gwynne cited instances of Dubliners, in British uniform, and Volunteers shooting at each other with lethal intent, whereas before the war both sets of combatants had been in the Volunteers together. One of the first British officers killed had taken a leading part in the Howth gun landing. But in the bitterness of defeat de Valera was in no mood to ponder on such paradoxes. His attitude, overlooking the reality of the state of public feeling at the time, was that the people should have supported the insurgents 'though armed with hay forks only'.[47]

4

'WE'LL GO AHEAD WITH CONNOLLY'

THE FACT THAT de Valera was involved in the last of the firing during the rising saved him from being involved with the first to break out after it ended – the volleys of execution squads. He was taken into captivity in the Weights and Measures Dept of Ballsbridge Town Hall, which meant that he was on the opposite side of the city to the main body of arrested Volunteers who were held in places like Kilmainham Jail and Richmond Barracks. He remained in Ballsbridge during the fateful screening and court-martial procedures which claimed the lives of some of the leaders who had surrendered earlier, including Pearse, McDonagh and Clarke. The time lapse involved before he was transferred to Richmond Barracks for court martial meant that it was 8 May before his case was dealt with. By then the pendulum of public opinion was swinging against the policy of executions and in his favour. The executions, carried out in twos and threes and amounting to fifteen in all, including the signatories of the proclamation, were spread out from 3 to 12 May, longer than the period of the rising itself. The fortunes of war dictated that some of the post-rising deaths and escapes from execution were to have a crucial impact on subsequent events. Willy Pearse was executed for no reason save that he was Padraig Pearse's brother. Joseph Plunkett, dying from glandular tuberculosis, was married in his cell ten minutes before facing the firing squad. Michael Collins, the most dangerous rebel of them all, was overlooked and sent to a detention camp where he was excellently placed to rebuild the IRB amongst the inmates who on release would spread the organization throughout the four corners of Ireland. Cathal Brugha sustained so many bullet wounds in the fighting that he was not even charged because he was thought to be dying anyway. However, he recovered to turn up on crutches, an inspirational 'modern Cuchullainn',[1] at the first meeting held to reorganize the Volunteers after the rising.

But developments which the prisoners might have regarded as being of an optimistic nature were not yet general. Some of the most emotional executions lay ahead. James Connolly and Sean MacDiarmida were shot on 12 May. Their deaths followed the appearance of the following words in an editorial in the *Irish Independent* whose owner, William Martin Murphy, had obviously not forgotten Connolly's role in opposition to him during the 1913 lock-out: 'Certain of the leaders remain to be dealt with, and the part they played was worse than that of some of those who have paid the extreme penalty. Are they, because of indiscriminate demand for clemency, to get off lightly, while others, who were no more prominent, have been executed?'[2]

MacDiarmada, a particularly attractive personality, had a polio-lamed leg, while Connolly had been so badly wounded in the fighting that he had to be carried to his execution on a stretcher and then propped up on a chair before the firing squad. And Roger Casement would not be hanged until 3 August. So the barracks atmosphere was not exactly overflowing with hope. Four of the executions occurred on the day de Valera was taken to Kilmainham; one occurred the day after. His tension was added to by the gallows humour of the prisoners who shared a large room with him, and subjected him to a mock trial. This sort of game is not unknown in prison,[3] but the identity of the 'judge' who agreed to 'try' his case was extraordinary: Count Plunkett. One of his sons, Joseph, had just been executed and two others sentenced to death, later commuted to penal servitude for life. Despite this, Plunkett solemnly presided over the arraignment of de Valera on a charge of wishing to become King of the Periwinkles and Emperor of the Muglins, through having designs on the Kingdom of Dalkey Island which lies, inhabited only by goats, rats and rabbits, eight miles south-east of Dublin. It was said afterwards that, very understandably, de Valera became somewhat unnerved by the proceedings, particularly when one of the prisoners simulated execution volleys by clapping his hands. But his official biography[4] states that it was the 'advocate for the defence', Larry O'Neill, whom 'the grim game almost unnerved'. Under cover of darkness O'Neill is said to have come to where de Valera was sleeping on the floor and pressed a crucifix into his hand, whispering, 'This is terrible.'

And certainly de Valera's situation was 'terrible' at that moment. He had come through a hellish period of danger and frustration during which feelings of anxiety, guilt and exhaustion had almost unhinged him. He had psyched himself up to face death in the fighting.[5] Instead there had come the confusion, hope, and then deflation of surrender. Now ahead of him lay court martial and an inevitable death sentence. What lay ahead for Sinead, with four small children and another expected?

The court martial itself was a brief affair. Evidence was given that he was in charge of his post, that he had been born in New York and that Cadet Mackay had been treated properly whilst a prisoner. He was then taken to cell no. 59 in Kilmainham Jail to await the verdict; his comrades had been executed in the jail yard. De Valera's state of mind may be guessed at more from what he did not write, after his trial, than from what he did write. He wrote to his old friend Frank Hughes, the former rugby star Mick Ryan and Sister Gonzaga, the nun in charge of Carysfort, 'but he did not write to either his wife or his mother because there was still no definite news'.[6] Yet he acted as though the news was definite enough to warrant him addressing all his correspondents in the same strain – part stilted heart cry, part barely concealed appeal for Sinead:[7]

> Dear Sister Gonzaga,
>   I have just been told that I am to be shot for my part in the rebellion.
>   Just a parting line to thank you and all the sisters (especially Mother Attracta) for your unvarying kindness to me in the past and to ask you to pray for my soul and for my poor wife and little children whom I leave unprovided for behind.
>   Ask the girls to remember me in their prayers.
>   Goodbye. I hope I'll be in heaven to meet you.
>   Yours faithfully,
>   (sgd) E. de Valera.

Uncharacteristically, but very understandably in the circumstances, he got the date wrong in his letter to Frank Hughes, writing 'Aug. 9th' instead of 'May 9th':[8]

> Kilmainham Jail,
> Aug. 9th
>
> My dear Frank,
>   Just a line to say a last goodbye. I am to be shot for my part in the Rebellion. If you can give any advice to Sinead and the little ones I know you'll try.
>   Remember me to your wife, Mother, Aunt Stan etc. Pray for my soul.
>   DeV.

To Mick Ryan he wrote:[9]

> Just a line to say I played my last match last week and lost, I am to be shot, an old sport who unselfishly played the game. Remember me to Pat, Jack, Nora, Margaret and the Mrs. Tell Colgan we will never have another game of nap together or beat Rice's bog or the Wood. Farewell old friend, you are in my thoughts.
>   DeV.

The day after he had written these and other notes, de Valera learned that his farewells had been premature. He was reading the *Confessions of St Augustine* when an officer came to his cell to read him a statement telling him that he had indeed been sentenced to death. Then the officer proceeded to read a second document telling him that the sentence had been commuted to penal servitude for life. De Valera pretended to continue reading as he received both pieces of information with a poker-faced inscrutability that concealed his inner turmoil. The letters to Sinead and his mother would not be so difficult to write after all.

In fact the good-hearted Hughes wrote to Sinead as soon as he heard of de Valera's arrest, inviting herself and the children to come and stay in his home in Kiltimagh, Co. Mayo, until her affairs could be straightened out. As de Valera's letter to her from Lewes Jail indicates, she was shattered initially by the discovery that her husband was going to leave her, and the children, for almost certain death. But she rallied sufficiently to contact the American Consul in Dublin with a copy of de Valera's birth certificate as proof that he could claim the protection of American citizenship. In New York his mother Catherine made similar efforts, during which she discovered that on de Valera's birth certificate 'name of child' was given as George. (A 'corrected certificate' showing the name as Edward was approved by the Commissioner of Health on 30 June 1916.) Her other son, Father Wheelright, enlisted the help of the Redemptorists in a letter-writing campaign that involved approaching the White House, the State Department, Congressmen and Senators with appeals for clemency. Interestingly, de Valera's view[10] was that none of the American activity had 'the slightest influence' on his escaping execution. He said: 'What was decisive was that Tom Ashe who was also likely to be executed, and myself were court martialled on the same day and just about the time when Asquith made the public statement that no further executions would take place except those who had signed the Proclamation.'

Probably the most accurate account[11] of why de Valera escaped the firing squad is that of the man charged with having him executed, Judge Evelyn Wylie. (Wylie was the man who later did much to build up the prestige of the Dublin Horse Show and who introduced the 'Tote' to Irish racing.) He stated:

> At that time I was Crown prosecuting officer in charge of the trials of these men. A number had been convicted and executed, when Sir John Maxwell showed me a telegram he had just received from Asquith the Prime Minister. This instructed him to stop the executions as they were having a very bad political effect in England and might turn the forthcoming elections against the Government.
> Maxwell asked: 'Who is next on the list?'
> Wylie answered: 'Connolly.'
> Maxwell replied: 'We can't let him off; who is next?'
> Wylie told him: 'De Valera', stumbling over the name as he later recalled.
> Maxwell inquired: 'Is he someone important?'
> Wylie made the immortal reply: 'No. He is a school-master who was taken at Boland's Mill.'
> To which Maxwell's answer was: 'All right, we will go ahead with Connolly and stop with this fellow.'

And so James Connolly, whose leg had been shattered by a bullet, was carried to his execution, while Eamon de Valera lived to rule over a state very different from the one Connolly died for.

Understandably, all this was lost on Sinead. With her world in ruins, not knowing what was going to happen to her husband, she decided that instead of accepting Hughes' offer she would stay near Dublin with her family. She replied to Hughes, apparently on the same day that, unknown to her, de Valera's sentence was commuted – Tuesday, 9 May 1916.[12]

My dear Frank,

Very many thanks to you and Kitty for your kind offer to do so much for me. I am ever so grateful and think you are very good to write so promptly and think so much for me – at present, dear Frank, it is hard to look ahead. I have no definite news and you can fancy my mind is in a whirl. I intend going home with the children for a time at least and then I shall have time to see what I can do.

Please believe me that I shall never forget your kindness and Kitty's too, but for the present I shall keep all the poor kiddies with me – I cannot write much. I know you will all pray for us but especially for Dev. Ask your mother and Miss Hughes to get all the prayers they can. Everyone is very kind – I can think of nothing just yet.

The cutting from the *Irish Times* of April 11th only came on Sunday last. If there is anything to be done about the insurance will you please let me know. I did not know Dev got any notice or correspondence about it. [De Valera had taken out a life assurance policy. His official biographers say[12a] that prior to the rising, when making his will, he was worried about the possibility that his being an insurgent might invalidate payment. It appears from Sinead's letter that he had got some definite word from the company, probably in common with other Volunteer policy holders, that acts of rebellion were not covered.]

This is only a little word to thank you and Kitty from my heart of hearts and to beg prayers from everyone. I hope all of you are very well and happy. I shall write again later on. I shall be here in Donnybrook for a week or two. With loving thanks to you all.

Sinead.

After the commutation of his sentence de Valera was transferred to Mountjoy Jail, the first of five prisons in which he was to be incarcerated throughout the coming year; the others, all in England, were Dartmoor, Lewes, Maidstone and Pentonville. In Mountjoy he got his first bath since before the rising and received his first visit from Sinead, who was accompanied by the two eldest children, Vivion and Mairin. Mairin's recollection of her father was that: 'He looked stern and indignant – I don't think I ever hated anything (certainly I never hated anyone) as I hated the warder on duty – but my parents did not seem to take any notice of him. . . . ' Of her mother she wrote: 'We were all too young to understand the strain and worry which my mother endured. We only knew that she was altogether committed to the cause of Irish Freedom though of course we didn't understand what it was all about. At that time and throughout the years that followed she shielded us from fear and anxiety.'[13]

After a week in Mountjoy, the prisoners were sent to Dartmoor. Approaching the prison, de Valera took his pipe from his mouth and announced that he would never smoke again.[14] The drive to get his own way in all situations, implicit in his confrontation with the Castle official and his own subordinate on the eve of the rising, was now taking tangible form in a self-set leadership course. It would be seen in his application to study, in his acquiring of control over his comrades through winning their admiration by confrontation with the prison authorities, and in his attempts to influence the direction of events outside the prison. Henceforth

79

the 'good ole boy', the nice Eamon de Valera, Postman of Romance and writer of yearning love letters to Sinead, would be more and more subsumed into the skeletal resolve of de Valera, Man of Power.

Initially both study and control of events outside the prison proved to be beyond De Valera's grasp. The prison library was poorly stocked and prisoners were only allowed one letter in four months. Inside the prison discipline and silence were strictly enforced. But it was inside the prison that de Valera chose to make the dramatic gesture which first clearly set him above the other prisoners in their general estimation.

According to the official account,[15] he overheard Eoin MacNeill being admitted to the cells one evening and decided that 'he would not be isolated' because of his countermanding order in Easter Week which many of the prisoners blamed for the failure of the rising. Next morning, as the prisoners were lined up for exercise, de Valera saw MacNeill descending a staircase. We are told that: 'Immediately de Valera stepped forward and ordered the prisoners to attention. Facing towards MacNeill he saluted, at the same time commanding the Volunteers to "Eyes left." His orders were obeyed as if on a ceremonial parade.'

However, some forty years before that version was set down for posterity de Valera gave a more human account to Gallagher during an American train journey.[16] According to this, it was the strip search and anal inspection which accompanied every prisoner's admission to Dartmoor that triggered his action.

> After the indignity of the first personal search when convicts are publicly stripped naked, he decided that a fight was necessary the more so as the shyness of the Irish lads gave the impression of their being cowed. The chance of breaking out came when MacNeill was brought to the prison. Having planned it in his cell the previous night (which was typical of him) he managed to get to the top of the line the next day and at the moment MacNeill appeared he sprang from his place and shouted 'shun' to the twenty others and then 'eyes right'.
>
> They were not expecting it and did not answer smartly but at least the gauntlet had been thrown down. The Governor ordered him to his cell and followed him in there. 'Why did you do that', he asked. 'To salute my Commander-in-Chief in the proper manner,' D. answered.
>
> 'Do you not know that any such action is mutiny, the most serious crime a prisoner can commit and that flogging is the punishment?'
>
> 'I know nothing about that', D. said, 'I only know that we are soldiers and owe respect to our Commanders'.

He got a mild punishment.

By either account de Valera's action was a brave one for a man who at that stage was facing fifteen years' penal servitude. But this idealized version of his own action was typical of a characteristic that sought to place his every deed on a pedestal untainted by ordinary, unheroic human feeling or motive; a characteristic, let it be said, which caused heightened criticism of him when, inevitably, people discovered that he sometimes erred just like other mortals.

The second major act of defiance which he perpetrated at Dartmoor combined both courage and his increasingly familiar tendency to uphold his view of right and wrong whatever the consequences. He was caught in the act of throwing a small loaf across a corridor to a fellow prisoner, Jack McArdle. McArdle was given the number one punishment, bread and water for three days, but de Valera was allowed a thin gruel with his bread. He 'strongly protested to the Governor about this as the fault was really his and Jack had done nothing but catch the bread that had been thrown at him. The Governor, however, refused to change the punishment. . . . '[17]

De Valera decided to retaliate by going on a hunger and thirst strike for so long as McArdle remained on bread and water.[18] It was a hard decision to make because, apart from religious scruples about the possibility that he was contemplating suicide, he doubted his own capacity to endure the torments of such a protest. He had vivid memories of being overcome by the pangs of hunger one night after a dance during his Rockwell interlude. With the help of Frank Hughes he 'dragged himself to the nearest town, and before he could go on he consumed four raw eggs, four whiskeys and a vast amount of bread and butter'.[19] However, he managed to maintain the fast for three or four days until 'at last the Governor gave in'[20] and he was transferred to the prison infirmary. From there he was taken in chains to Maidstone Prison in Kent, where the Governor had the reputation of 'being a great hand at breaking stubborn men'.[21] It was a reputation which de Valera would one day find himself testing, but on this occasion he spent only a few weeks there before he and all the other Irish remaining in English prisons were transferred to Lewes Jail.

Around this time, Christmas 1916, certain other prisoners were released – notably those from Frongoch Camp in Wales, where Michael Collins was held, and Arthur Griffith from Reading Jail. The releases were a PR gesture aimed at stemming the growing power of Irish American criticism of Britain's Irish policies. Some of the criticism was grounded in propaganda rather than fact. Father Wheelright, for example, wrote inappropriately enough from Ulster County, New York, on behalf of his half-brother, to the Department of State, alleging that 'General Maxwell was declared insane'.[22] Nevertheless Lloyd George, who had taken over from Asquith as Prime Minister early in December, was only too keenly aware of the necessity for American men and munitions if Germany were to be defeated. The move to Lewes, where conditions were better than at Dartmoor or Maidstone, was part of an overall attempt to placate Irish American public opinion. But from the British point of view it had the demerit of bringing all the Irishmen under one roof where they could be marshalled against their jailers. To men of the Irish Republican tradition prison has always been regarded as 'the Republican University' – a different battleground wherein the fight is carried on by other means. Nor was 'University' an empty term. Throughout Irish history many a man, and woman, has entered prison a political innocent only to emerge a confirmed revolutionary as a result of contact with books and more experienced colleagues. Lewes also had the effect of concentrating the attention of politically aware Irishmen and women everywhere on the prisoners and on the man with the funny name who had emerged as their leader: de Valera.

He put the improved supply of reading material at Lewes to use in improving the quality of the diet. An article in the *Catholic Bulletin* enabled him to calculate the number of calories in the prisoners' daily food allowance. He decided that the supply of calories was insufficient and organized petitions for an increase; these resulted in the prisoners being given kippers three days a week. Then, when one prisoner was put on bread and water for talking during work, he ordered all the other Irish prisoners to stop work. The Governor caved in and directed that the man be taken off the punishment regime. Correctly anticipating that the Home Office would inevitably retaliate by dispersing the prisoners throughout the prison system to 'herd with the wife murderer and the sodomist-gone-mad'[23] he drew up plans for resistance, based on non-cooperation and destruction of prison property.

While at Lewes he also displayed a lively interest in mathematics. He read a pamphlet by a Major General Drayson on 'the motion of the pole of the Ecliptic', which prompted him to write to A. W. Conway, Professor of Mathematical Physics at University College, Dublin, asking to be recommended to 'some good work on celestial mathematics'. He wanted this to enable him to prove that Drayson's theory would:[24] 'furnish a delightfully simple astronomical explanation of the Ice Age. The maximum obliquity of 35° 25' 47" would more than double the area of the ice cap at each of the poles, and the period of the cycle etc. would fit in so beautifully with the most modern views as to the date, nature, extent etc. of the glaciations. . . .'

And even in prison de Valera did what lay within his power to influence the course of events in Ireland, principally by intervening in the issue of whether or not by-elections should be contested. In a smuggled despatch from Lewes he claimed to be badly in need of a 'clear account of the political situation in Ireland at the present time'. He said that 'the information we are able to get is very meagre and often most contradictory. We are in a complete fog.'[25] Now this is just a little strange. Cut off from Ireland, in an English prison, communication was obviously a problem. But Irish political prisoners have traditionally surmounted such problems in a host of ingenious ways, and by now these particular prisoners had had a year to set up communication channels. Granted that Michael Collins had only been on the outside for four months and had not yet had the opportunity of organizing the incredible network he was later to create, embracing everyone from dockers to policemen to prison warders to members of the British Secret Service. Nevertheless the prisoners did get letters from home, they received visits, and the changes taking place in Ireland were so far-reaching and so visible that it is difficult to believe that the hard-core revolutionaries in Lewes were not well informed about them. In fact de Valera concluded another letter to Donnelly[26] by complaining about *too much* communication: 'I wish we could censor a lot of stuff which gets out and which might mislead you.'

It is a fact of prison life that what can be got out can be got in and vice versa. One cannot dismiss the suspicion that the real origins of the 'regular fog' which de Valera complained of may be traced in another part of his letter to Donnelly: 'Many of us have a sort of instinctive feeling that there is something wrong – We can only be cured of that by being convinced by fuller knowledge that our fears are groundless.'

Was this a concealed reference to the IRB? From the time Collins arrived in Frongoch he had been reorganizing the Brotherhood. The results of his activities could already be felt in many places, including Lewes. Thomas Ashe, who had led one of the few successful engagements in 1916, at Ashbourne, was de Valera's second-in-command as leader of the prisoners. But he was also an IRB man and one of the first people to recognize Collins' qualities. Significantly, on the by-election question his views showed a divergence from de Valera's.

The by-election issue arose in January 1917 when Count Plunkett was expelled from the Unionist-minded Royal Dublin Society because of his family's connection with 1916. He retaliated by standing as a candidate in a by-election in North Roscommon. By now the British military's habit, taken up by the press, of mistakenly referring to the Easter Rising as the 'Sinn Fein rebellion' had had the effect of creating a national, and indeed international, image for Sinn Fein. Plunkett accordingly was generally regarded as a Sinn Fein candidate, but his principal appeal was to a sympathy vote. No one in the Volunteers was quite certain what he stood for – abstention from Westminster; Arthur Griffith's old Kings, Lords and Commons of Ireland; or, his own suggestion, that Ireland should be represented at the Peace Conference. But, spurred on by Collins, they campaigned enthusiastically for him, largely on the basis that what was bad for the Irish Parliamentary Party was good for them. And so it proved. Plunkett won by a majority of more than two to one and, on learning the result, declared himself in favour of abstention. This left Sinn Fein, Labour, the Volunteers and Plunkett's personal following united, in Collins' words, in a 'loose coalition' to defeat the Irish Parliamentary Party, but divided on almost everything else. So there was a background justification for de Valera's stated objection to having the Volunteers committed to candidates who stood for unclear policies and who, through running the risk of defeat, might damage the Volunteers' standing in the public eye. For the immediate occasion of his letter to Donnelly was the selection of a Lewes prisoner, Joseph McGuinness, a member of a well-known Longford family, to contest a by-election in Co. Longford on 9 May. In fact all the leading prisoners, with the exception of Thomas Ashe, felt that McGuinness' candidature was unwise. But one may also interpret his objections as stemming from a combination of fear that they might damage the Lewes prisoners' standing and resentment at such decisions being taken without consulting him. One of the reasons he gave Donnelly for vetoing McGuinness' nomination was: 'When I can avoid it I am averse to letting other people, no matter how wise they are, commit *me* to such a risk.'

His correspondence with Donnelly makes clear his feeling that the largest part of the mantle of 1916 had fallen on the Lewes prisoners in general and on his shoulders in particular. He wrote:

> Were he to be defeated and were we identified as a body formally with his policy defeat would mean the ruin of the hopes – not to say the ideals – which prompted our comrades to give the word last Easter though they knew that word was their own death knell. His defeat would mean our defeat – the irretrievable ruin of all our comrades died for and all their death had gained.
>
> To take a step absolutely in the dark is always foolish, to do so when the consequences are of such serious magnitude as the freedom of a nation is criminal.
>
> By avoiding being formally identified with the Count's movement we are still left as a reserve which while it is intact gives a hope that though he be defeated all is not lost. Our principles have not been defeated and we here are in the eyes of those at home most closely identified with our comrades who are now free.

The negative, cautious course advocated to Donnelly contrasts strongly with the writer's actions a year earlier. De Valera had left a penniless, pregnant wife with their small children while he went to take a far more serious step in the dark than that contemplated for McGuinness. And he was also, at the time, on the eve of committing himself and the other prisoners to a collision course with the authorities over the issue of prisoner-of-war status. 'To fail,' he warned his prison followers, 'to be weak – would mean dishonour to the dead – to Ireland. Friends and foes are watching you. *It must be death rather than surrender.*'[27] But above all it contrasts with the speed with which de Valera himself accepted a nomination to stand as a by-election candidate when he himself emerged from prison shortly afterwards. De Valera, Man of Power and sonorous rhetoric, was rapidly eclipsing de Valera the Nice Guy. In the event the outside leadership, principally Michael Collins, disregarded his opposition and nominated McGuinness, who won the seat, after a recount, by a tiny margin of thirty-seven votes.

It is probable that the decisive factor in his win was the fact that the issue of partition was more and more coming to the fore and redounding to the discredit of the Irish Party and in favour of Sinn Fein. On the eve of the election a manifesto denouncing partition was published in the press. It was signed by fifteen Roman Catholic bishops, three archbishops, three Protestant bishops, the chairmen of county councils and other public figures, and said: 'An appeal to the national conscience on the question of Ireland's dismemberment should meet with one answer and one answer

alone. To Irishmen of every creed and class and party the very thought of
our country partitioned and torn as a new Poland must be one of heart-
rending sorrow.'

This weighty endorsement was added to by a separate statement from
the Archbishop of Dublin, Dr Walsh, in the *Irish Independent* on 8 May,
which suggested that he remembered what T. P. O'Connor had said at
Marienbad. Having indicated that he felt that a door was being closed on
an empty stable, he said flatly: 'The country is practically sold.' The
bishops' statements showed that Collins had been correct in his assessment
that the country was turning from the Irish Party. But apart from a general
appeal to national sympathy, the McGuinness programme was short on
specifics. The campaign was summed up by his election poster: a man in a
prison uniform with a caption reading: 'Put him in to get him out.'
Nevertheless, despite the narrowness of his majority it was, as we shall see,
a victory of enormous significance. Of equal, or perhaps greater, long-term
significance was the evolution of de Valera's thoughts and actions as
revealed in this phase of his prison career. (There were to be many other
prison interludes.)

His rhetoric makes it clear that he viewed the events of Easter 1916 as
having a religious overlay – a sort of militaristic High Mass in which he was
a high, officiating prelate and Michael Malone an illustrious martyr for the
faith whose relics had been entrusted to him. Not long before writing to
Donnelly he wrote to Malone's mother, signing it with his prisoner
number:[28]

> I do not think I ever got a gift which affected me so much as your box of
> Shamrocks on St. Patrick's Day – indeed I should have said I am sure. For what
> gift could be so affecting as that of a Box of Shamrocks from an Irish Mother, on
> behalf of her Patriot Son, to a comrade whose duty it was to bid him take that
> post, in the defence of which he so gloriously fell. No wonder that Ireland is still
> unconquered. Surely that cause must be blessed, for which young men are willing
> to sacrifice their lives just budding with the promises of the future, and mothers
> the fulfilment of the dreams first dreamt by their cradles.
>   . . . Michael . . . did deeds which will be on record for ever – accomplished in a
> few hours what other men fail to accomplish in a life full of years. This Easter
> from his place in paradise he sees us still struggling through this valley of tears.
>   . . . His fate is one for envy not sorrow.
>   E. de Valera, q.95.

Behind that almost liturgical language of Holy War de Valera shows
himself aware of the realpolitik of what Malone's heroism had
'accomplished in a few hours' – a huge casualty toll that had redounded to
his, de Valera's, credit. He now set about applying that same realpolitik
from the position of prisoners' leader which Malone's actions had helped
win for him. Although he professed to be out of communication with his
comrades outside the jail over the by-election issue he was able to arrange
for a telegram to be sent to a fellow prisoner, Harry Boland, allegedly

announcing an uncle's death but in fact about outside support for a prison strike. With an eye to Irish American opinion (the USA had just entered the war) Lloyd George had called an all-party convention which was supposedly to settle the Irish issue. Sinn Fein, who were offered only a 5 per cent representation at the convention, boycotted its proceedings, thus effectively rendering them nugatory. Reckoning, correctly, that the convention would probably be accompanied by an amnesty of prisoners, de Valera decided to queer the pitch further on the pretext of seeking prisoner-of-war status – in reality, as he circularized the prisoners:[29]

> *to deprive England of any credit she may hope to gain from that release.* You are asked to engage in no forlorn hope. Preparations have been carefully made. You are *certain* to win if you be true. Remember it is not for paltry concessions for yourselves you are fighting it is for Ireland's honour. Should you have something for supper the cause will make it sweet. Your association with . . . those who died carries its obligations but the fulfilling of them will ever be your highest glory.

The 'no work' strike began on 28 May 1917. All the prisoners were directed not to work except for the cleaning squad, for reasons which contrast markedly with de Valera's protestations about being 'in a fog' over outside political happenings. His official biography states that the cleaning squad, 'always mobile, could keep them informed on events both inside and outside the prison'. A notable event held outside the prison on 10 June to publicize the prison protest resulted in the first death of a member of the Crown forces since the Easter Rising – that of a police inspector accidentally killed by a blow from a hurling stick. The fatality occurred during a proscribed meeting held in Beresford Place, Dublin, outside the ruin of Connolly's Liberty Hall which had been destroyed by shellfire during the rebellion. As a result of the demonstration Count Plunkett and Cathal Brugha were arrested – more grist to the Sinn Fein publicity mill. The strike, as expected, met with no response on the prisoner-of-war issue and the prisoners moved on to the next phase of the protest – smashing up the jail. This, as was foreseen, had the result of breaking up the Irish contingent and consigning them to the ranks of 'the sodomist-gone-mad'. De Valera fetched up back in Maidstone.

When brought to the Governor's office he refused either to stand to attention or to button his jacket. The Governor ordered the warders to take him outside and button him up before continuing the interview, but on re-entering the room de Valera tore it open again, 'sending the buttons flying'.[30] He got three days' bread and water for this, but when the Governor visited his cell during his rounds he continued his defiance by refusing to stand up. The warders stood him up forcibly, and he told the Governor that he was a 'miserable little coxcomb'. He said: 'I have more contempt for you standing up than I had lying down.'[31]

The following day he again refused to stand for the Governor and was once more forcibly stood up; but on this occasion he used his great physical strength to shake the warders off him. The Governor, thinking that he was about to be attacked, immediately got behind his men. De Valera seized his opportunity for a telling insult. Knowing that the man was of military age and that there was talk in the prison about his not joining up, he said to him:[32] ' "Aye you are running behind your warders now as you ran behind other men when it came to joining the Army." The warders were delighted, one of them telling de Valera afterwards with mingled respect and jubilation: "You gave him a queer one that time, mister." The Governor never entered his cell again.'

By way of illustrating the hold which these and similar occurrences copper-fastened on his followers' imaginations it is worth noting Gallagher's comment to himself in his diary after recording the incident from de Valera's own lips.[33] 'For a man with the certainty of fifteen years before him this stand of the Chief's was magnificent.' In fact, of course, de Valera knew that he was facing the certainty of speedy release. However, though this stay at Maidstone was to be short it was also painful. He had crushed a disc in his spine during a wrestling match at Lewes and had to lie on the flagged floor with his feet raised, resting against the wall. Looking up, he noticed that his cell window was made of glass and therefore breakable. Pain or no pain, he got up and broke the glass. It was the last protest he was called upon to make in Maidstone for, as he had calculated, the Government announced the freeing of all 1916 prisoners shortly afterwards, on 15 June. The prison chosen for bringing the men together in preparation for their release was Pentonville, where Roger Casement had been hanged; de Valera said a prayer over his grave. Perhaps in answer to it he was handed a telegram as he stepped from the jail, informing him that he had been selected as Sinn Fein candidate in a by-election in East Clare.

A further demonstration of his growing importance took place on the way back to Dublin. 'We were all paraded by Eamon de Valera on Holyhead platform opposite the Mail Boat. We formed fours, about turned, formed two deep and eventually were marched up to the 1st Class gangway.'[34] In prison de Valera had ordered his men not to show the slightest sign of emotion when the news of their release came. The order was obeyed, to the astonishment of the warders. But in public the release was to be an occasion of triumphalism. The prisoners had only been issued with third-class tickets, but de Valera decided that these were not good enough for their new-found station in life:[35] ' . . . feeling in a first class mood, Eamon de Valera decided that we should all travel 1st. Class, and we just brushed the ticket checkers aside, marched up the 1st. Class gangway and into the saloon. . . . The Captain deciding that discretion was the better part of valour decided to leave us there.'

They marched out of that saloon into a tumultuous welcome home that symbolized the extraordinary swing in public opinion which had occurred since they were marched off in disgrace after the death and destruction they had caused during Easter 1916. As Stephen Gwynne, who was himself a member of the Irish Parliamentary Party, wrote:[36] 'The Longford election had in reality been not merely a symptom but an event of great importance. It was a notice of dismissal to the Parliamentary Party.'

Before following de Valera's footsteps from the mailboat it is important to understand the events which led to that 'dismissal notice' being served. The party had begun[37] by greeting the news of the rising with, in Redmond's words, 'horror and detestation'. And when Asquith announced the executions of Pearse, MacDonagh and Clarke to the House of Commons Redmond's response fairly accurately reflected nationalist opinion at the conclusion of the rebellion. It contained the following:[38] 'This outbreak, happily, seems to be over. It has been dealt with with firmness. That was not only right, but it was the duty of the Government. But, as the rebellion has been put down I do beg of the Government not to show undue hardship or severity to the great mass of those implicated, on whose shoulders there lies a guilt far different from that of the instigators and promoters.'

However, another Irish Parliamentary Party comment on the rebellion eight days later, made this time by John Dillon, showed how swiftly this mood had changed. Dillon was speaking on the day of Connolly and MacDiarmada's execution. He pointed out that:[39]

> ... thousands of people who ten days ago were bitterly opposed to the whole Sinn Fein movement, and to rebellion, were now becoming infuriated against the Government on account of these executions. ... It is not murderers who are being executed; it is insurgents who have fought a clean fight, a brave fight, however misguided, and it would be a damned good thing if your soldiers were able to put up as good a fight as did these men in Dublin – three thousand men against twenty thousand with machine guns and artillery.

Since, of course, far fewer rebels had taken part in the rebellion than Dillon estimated, a fact which soon became known in Ireland, tales of their bravery multiplied, as did reports of the undoubted heroism with which the executed leaders met their deaths. All this coming against the backdrop of British and Orange opposition to the course which would have prevented the rebellion in the first place, the granting of Home Rule, had a marked effect on the change of attitude – particularly as the indiscriminate round-ups of suspects after the rising had succeeded in involving so many innocent along with the guilty that alienation from Westminster was given a further powerful impetus.

All these strands were brought together and publicly aired with explosive force in a letter from an unlikely source – the elderly Dr Edward O'Dwyer, Roman Catholic Bishop of Limerick, who had hitherto shown himself to be no friend of Sinn Fein. After some correspondence with General Maxwell, who wanted him to discipline two of his priests for their nationalistic activities, the Bishop addressed this almighty 'belt of the crozier' (as episcopal censure is commonly termed in Ireland) to the General in the following letter dated 17 May:[40]

... In your letter of 6th inst., you appeal to me to help you in the furtherance of your work as military dictator of Ireland. Even if action of that kind was not outside my province, the events of the past few weeks make it impossible for me to have any part in proceedings which I regard as wantonly cruel and oppressive. You remember the Jameson raid, when a number of buccaneers invaded a friendly state and fought the forces of the lawful government.

If ever men deserved the supreme punishment it was they. But officially or unofficially the influence of the British Government was used to save them and it succeeded. You took care that no pleas for mercy should interpose on behalf of the poor young fellows who surrendered to you in Dublin. The first information which we got of their fate was the announcement that they had been shot in cold blood.

Personally I regard your action with horror, and I believe that it has outraged the conscience of the country. Then, the deporting of hundreds, and even thousands, of poor fellows without a trial of any kind seems to me an abuse of power, as fatuous as it is arbitrary, and altogether your regime has been one of the worst and blackest chapters in the history of the misgovernment of this country. I have the honour to be, sir, your obedient servant,

Edward Thomas, Bishop of Limerick.

If one were to point to a single right-angled turning point in the process of conferring respectability on the insurgents, that was it. The correspondence was printed in the press and the Bishop's picture began appearing in shop windows bedecked in tricolour ribbon. Sinn Fein reprinted the correspondence in pamphlet form. Very few people apart from O'Dwyer had established the connection between Maxwell and the Jameson Raid, but a majority grasped the salient fact that a bishop was backing Sinn Fein. So did the British Government. On 30 May Asquith gave Lloyd George the job of trying to halt the slide towards Sinn Fein and, more importantly, to ward off the danger of the Irish American vote siding with the German American bloc in the Presidential election later that year. If America did not support Britain, Germany would win the war.

Lloyd George's formula was a partitionist one based on that discussed at the Buckingham Palace Conference before the war – a limited form of Home Rule for the South, from which six north-eastern counties were to be excluded. It was sold to the nationalists by the Irish Parliamentary Party leaders as a 'temporary and provisional settlement' which offered 'the best means of carrying on the fight for a united self-governing Ireland'. The Unionist leaders argued with their followers on the basis that failure to agree to a settlement would mean the Home Rule Act coming into force with no part of Ulster excluded. The attraction of settling for six counties rather than nine was that six counties would return sixteen Unionists and nine nationalists whereas nine would return seventeen nationalists and sixteen Unionists.

The Southern Unionists were, of course, unhappy at the prospect of being abandoned and felt that no settlement should be made during the war. Nor did they wish to see the Irish representation maintained at Westminster, as Lloyd George proposed (it was becoming increasingly obvious that in practice it would mean nationalist representation). It is a debatable point, although a vitally important one, as to whether Lloyd George was sincere in seeking a Home Rule solution at that stage – or, if he was, whether Asquith was sincere in backing him. Had Home Rule been pushed through, Redmond and the Irish Parliamentary Party would probably have been upheld and Ireland would have been saved from the horrors of the Anglo-Irish war and the subsequent civil war. It is impossible to evaluate at this stage what sort of backlash the introduction of conscription, or the regrouping of the IRB post-1916, might have provoked, but obviously a leader and a party with the reins of patronage in their hands would have been in a far stronger position than was Redmond after Lloyd George let him down when Tory back-bench sentiment jibbed at the Home Rule proposals. The conventional wisdom is that 'the settlement was wrecked by some of the English unionists'.[41]

But a sympathetic biographer of Lloyd George, John Grigg, reckons[42] that Lloyd George should have resigned over his failure to implement his promise to Redmond to get Home Rule through or resign. The authoritative Grigg's view is that Westminster would have accepted Home Rule had Asquith and Lloyd George really meant business. According to Grigg, Lloyd George was 'far more open to censure for what he failed to do in 1916 than for anything he did in 1921'. (That was the year in which, as we shall see, the Anglo-Irish Treaty was signed by Lloyd George.) Certainly the distrust of British politicians which Lloyd George's behaviour sowed in Irish nationalists was a factor in creating the horrors to come. While promising Redmond that he was sincere over Home Rule, and that the partition proposals were of a temporary nature which would come to an end after the war, he wrote to Carson on 29 May:[43] 'We must make it clear that at the end of the provisional period Ulster does not, whether she wills it or not, merge in the rest of Ireland.'

The backlash created by this combination of duplicity and vacillation was directed at Redmond. It was summed up in another notable 'belt of the crozier' directed at the Irish Parliamentary Party by the Bishop of Derry, Dr McHugh:[44] '. . . the worst feature of all this wretched bargaining is that Irishmen, calling themselves representatives of the people, are prepared to sell their brother Irishmen into slavery to secure a nominal freedom for a section of the people. . . . Was coercion of a more objectionable or despicable type ever resorted to by England in its dealings with Ireland than that now sanctioned by the men whom we elected to win us freedom.'

In the face of such criticism Redmond withdrew his assent to the proposals on 24 July and the scheme was shelved. But its airing meant that the idea of partition on the basis of six Ulster counties had gained greatly in acceptability in Unionist circles and that nationalists would increasingly look elsewhere for those 'elected to win us freedom'. Plunkett and McGuinness' victories followed within a year. Ireland was literally singing another song when de Valera came home on 18 June 1917. As the prisoners came down the gangway of the SS *Munster* they sang the 'Soldiers' Song', written by a 1916 prisoner, Peadar Kearney. It later became the Irish National Anthem:

> Soldiers are we whose lives are pledged to Ireland,
> Some have come from a land beyond the wave,
> Sworn to be free, no more our ancient sireland
> Shall shelter the despot or the slave,
> To-night we man the *bearna baoghail* [literally: the Gap of Danger]
> In Erin's cause come woe or weal;
> 'Mid cannon's roar and rifle's peal
> We'll chant a soldiers' song.

De Valera himself stepped out of the boat train on to the platform at Westland Row a very different person from the distracted figure who had emerged from the Royal Coach a little over a year earlier, the wraiths of anxiety and exhaustion threatening to overwhelm him. Since then he had exhibited the fortitude to endure the long, lonely hours of Lewes and Dartmoor, the leadership qualities to be looked up to by his fellows in that levelling, testing milieu, and the ego to ensure that he capitalized on that regard by becoming their accepted leader. Throughout his life one of his principal ploys in maintaining that leadership would be to give every indication that he had only reluctantly accepted it when thrust upon him. He gave a consummate display of this on the boat from Holyhead as he stood on deck with Eoin MacNeill and Dr Pat McCartan, waiting for the first glimpse of the Irish coastline. McCartan, whom British intelligence described as a 'particularly dangerous man',[45] argued strongly that he should accept the East Clare nomination which had become vacant through the death in action of John Redmond's brother, William. But de Valera demurred: 'He knew nothing, he told McCartan and MacNeill, about politics. Politics connoted Westminster, the embitterment of the post-Parnell days, the disillusionment he had himself experienced over home rule. It foreshadowed a different role altogether from military activity and he saw that the time might come when political activity would not be compatible with military activity.'[46]

Physically he showed 'a new rigidity about his mouth and a different thrust of the chin though he still looked the teacher and scholar. He was clean shaven, his hair was prison-cut like the "croppy boys" of 1798, his skin roughened and sallow.' He was the embodiment of the legends of 1916, the man the surging crowds wanted to see, to touch, to sing about:[47]

> 'Twas in Kilmainham prison yard our fifteen martyrs died
> And cold and still in Arbour Hill they are lying side by side,
> But we will yet pay back the debt for the spirit is still alive
> In men who stood through fire and blood with Convict 95.

The released men were literally carried to a line of waiting cabs and 'escorted through the city by a huge crowd of people up to Flemming's Hotel in Gardiner Place'.[48] Here de Valera headed the list of signatories to a proclamation written on Irish linen stating Ireland's case for freedom; it was addressed to President Wilson, and was being taken to America by Dr McCartan. De Valera left the exuberant 'welcome home' party with a shorter journey in mind. 'No longer did he have any hesitation left; he would stand for Clare in the by-election.'[49] There is a temptation to see a certain symbolism in his choice of companion to accompany him on his first meeting with Sinead and the children since Easter 1916 – a priest, Father Roche.

Sinead had had a bad time since he went away. In his letter to her of Easter 1917 de Valera had written in melodramatic terms of her being spared the 'agonies before you this year which I foresaw' – in other words the news of his death. But Sinead underwent other agonies which he presumably did not foresee. Years later their daughter Mairin wrote:[50]

> We still wonder how my mother lived through the months that followed the rising. She had no income, and had to leave our home and return to live with her parents, brother and sisters. She had to send Viv and me to stay with her other sister and aunt in Balbriggan – Eamonn joined us later on.
>
> My grandparents were very old and both were semi-invalids. My eldest aunt was living with them and was suffering from a very painful form of cancer. She was bedridden and because money was very scarce a nurse or other hired help was out of the question. My mother had to undertake all the work of nursing her, as well as all the housework, cooking and care of the babies. My younger aunt was a teacher and was out at work most of the day as was my uncle. He was very lame.
>
> My elder aunt died in August 1916, my brother Ruari was born in November that year and my grandmother died in January 1917.

Although Sinead did not parade her troubles, her letters do contain glimpses of the difficulties of her life at this time and of how much she missed de Valera. For example, after her mother died she wrote to thank the faithful Frank Hughes for his and his family's kindness to her during her ordeal:[51]

> My dear Frank,
> I cannot tell you how grateful I am to you, Kitty and all for the kindness and sympathy you have shown me during the troubled times. I was very glad to get your lovely letter. Please ask Kitty to keep on praying. Poor mother had a happy death. Betty, Kitty and I were round her bed as she passed away. Father has taken it very badly. The shock has been too much for him at this time of his life. His mind has become very much affected and he has such strange fancies that he is sometimes hard to manage. . . . Dev was allowed to write a special letter to me on account of mother's death . . . he seems very well and says he has treasured the names of all who were kind to me. . . . Wait till Dev comes, dear Frank and I shall show you all how much I value your friendship. . . .

Several months later, on 6 May, she was prompted to write again to

Hughes because de Valera had sent her a note for him from Lewes that she had not had time to forward. Her letter makes it clear why:

My dear Frank,

Dev sent the enclosed about a month ago and though I was anxious to write to you I could never get time. As I write now Ruary is in my arms and he makes my hand shake every way. . . . I should love to write a long letter with all the news but you have no idea of what my life is like. Father is far from well and what with him and the babies it is a constant rush. Betty is extra busy as she is going to be married next month. I wonder when will my bridegroom return. . . .

Her bridegroom returned on the afternoon of Monday, 18 June 1917. A boy whom she had taught at school rushed into the house at 34 Munster Street, Phibsboro to announce that de Valera had been sighted coming over nearby Cross Guns Bridge with the priest. However, opportunities for further sightings in the district were to be somewhat limited. By the same time on the following Friday de Valera had left home again to contest the first of his many subsequent election campaigns.

His note to Frank Hughes which Sinead had forwarded on 6 May had been enclosed with his Easter 1917 letter to her, in which he had written of his parting from her at Easter 1916: 'I know you will not think it was selfishness or callous indifference or senseless optimism that made me so calm.' Ironically, in the course of the accompanying Hughes missive he had written: 'Sinead told me how sympathetic you all were, but I have grown to regard these things as a matter of course from you Frank. . . .' Hughes' kindness was not all that he had come to regard as a 'matter of course'. From now on, Sinead and his family too were going to have to regard his ever-increasing absences in the same way. The Clare by-election interlude ushered in an era in which de Valera, Man of Power, increasingly known nationally and internationally, would take precedence over de Valera, Husband and Father.

He went to Clare via Limerick, one of his first visits being to Bishop O'Dwyer whom he called on, in the Volunteer uniform in which he conducted most of his campaigning, to thank him for his stand against Maxwell. De Valera knew which side his episcopal bread was buttered on; inside that Volunteer uniform there increasingly beat the heart of a politician. He demonstrated his growing political acuity by insisting that Eoin MacNeill accompany him on his platforms, thus both healing the split over MacNeill's countermanding order before the Easter Rising and drawing into his camp middle-of-the-road supporters of the much-admired academic. When he visited Bruree, the crowds unshackled a horse from a cart and men took turns in pulling him through the street to the accompaniment of music from the local band that brought back childhood memories of the Fedamore drum.

Now the drums were beating for him. The contrast between himself and his Irish Parliamentary Party opponent summed up the issues of the day.

Patrick Lynch KC was a former Crown Prosecutor; he came from one of Clare's leading families. Eamon de Valera came from Lewes Jail, having been prosecuted by the Crown. His campaign was marked by the public re-emergence of the Volunteers in uniform for the first time since the rising; they acted as stewards and kept order between the rival factions. Although they carried no weapons other than sticks, they were quite obviously soldierly in their bearing and prompt response to military commands. Their discipline won both widespread favourable comment and recruitment. De Valera issued no election address, but spoke with impassioned vagueness and liturgical solemnity about the proclamation of 1916 'sealed ... by ... the life blood of all its members. ... To that government when in visible shape, I offered my allegiance and to its spirit I owe my allegiance still.' He told the voters of Clare (presumably non-voters were deemed not to have aspirations): 'Every voter amongst you knows in his heart of hearts that his aspirations are ours – it will be the glorious privilege of each to boldly proclaim the truth.'[52] What exact form 'that government's ... visible shape' took, or was expected to take, we know not. Pieras Beaslai was in a position to observe de Valera closely at this stage. It was he who first[53] suggested him as the Lewes prisoners' leader, and who in turn was designated by de Valera as one of his successors should anything happen to him.[54] He described de Valera's political thought at that stage as follows: 'It was only in Lewes that he first began to study what is called "the Irish problem" closely, and in the endless prison discussions he showed that his mind was still in a state of flux. In these discussions he was inclined to treat an independent Republic as an unattainable ideal and regard what was called "Dominion Home Rule" as a fairly satisfactory compromise. At the same time he insisted that the full demand should be made in all national pronouncements.'

Stripped of rhetoric, the bottom line of de Valera's policy was that he asked the voters of Clare to vote for a man who had fought for Ireland's independence, who wanted a seat for Ireland at the Peace Conference to proclaim that independence, and who, if elected, would not take a seat in the British Parliament. On polling day, 11 July 1917, Clare agreed to his requests. He won the seat by a majority of more than two to one, 5,010 votes to 2,035. It was a historic victory in terms of both the rise of Sinn Fein and de Valera's personal reputation. From that day to our own his grip on Clare was such that he practically acquired testamentary rights to a parliamentary seat. Never once in his long career was he rejected by the electors of that county of gentle countryside and savage coastline which to this day gives its vote to the name de Valera – his granddaughter Sile represents Clare in the Irish Parliament at the time of writing.

After the bonfires and the shouting died away his first task was to secure co-operation between Sinn Fein, the Volunteers, the Liberty Clubs – as Count Plunkett's followers were known – and the Irish Nation League. This last-named organization was founded after the rising by P. J. Little and Stephen O'Mara, both of whom we shall hear of again, as a halfway house for those who opposed the Irish Party but shrank from the Volunteers' physical-force approach. After the Count's Roscommon victory these groupings had formed a loose alliance at what was known as the Mansion House Convention but, as Dr Thomas Dillon has recorded, a split threatened to develop between the Liberty Clubs and Sinn Fein, each of which was forming branches throughout the country:[55] 'At a meeting in Cathal Brugha's house in Upper Rathmines, Dublin, Arthur Griffith, whom Brugha disliked, refused Brugha's attempts to take over Sinn Fein. He said: "Sinn Fein will not give up its name. I was elected President of Sinn Fein by a convention and I cannot give up the presidency except to a convention of Sinn Fein." Brugha threatened to allow no one to leave the house (it was now approaching last tram time) until the issue was resolved.'

Dr Dillon, however, proposed that as the meeting had only two choices – to found a new organization or to work through Sinn Fein – the sensible thing to do was work through Sinn Fein. This was accepted, and Griffith agreed to dismiss half the members of the Sinn Fein Council and replace them with Volunteers' nominees. Amongst those co-opted on the spot were Dillon, who also became joint secretary, Count Plunkett, Michael Collins and Rory O'Connor, an engineer who had returned from Canada for the Easter Rising and who, having played his part in that drama, was fated for another, more tragic role in Irish history. Subsequent to the Lewes releases, other names which have either already figured in these pages, or will do so later, were added to the list. These included de Valera, Beaslai, Countess Markievicz (born Constance Gore-Booth, who had married a Polish nobleman) and William Cosgrave. Sinn Fein thus embodied in its leadership two contesting points of view – those who supported Griffith's monarchism and the upholders of the 1916 proclamation. Accordingly, after de Valera's Clare victory, the enhanced council decided to summon a Sinn Fein convention to redraft the organization's objectives.

The proclamation element found no difficulties with some of Griffith's key policies such as abstention from the British Parliament or the encouragement of native industry. But trouble arose over Griffith's strong insistence on the restoration of the King, Lords and Commons of Ireland. He felt that a kingdom was a more stable form of government than a republic, which, he claimed, was why the British encouraged republics in Europe but maintained a monarchy at home. He therefore envisaged the king of England being king of an Ireland with a strong, independent parliament of its own. Later he modified this view to allow for the enthronement of an Irish king, and cited the Swedes as his exemplars. However, this modification of view had not occurred at the time when the drafting meeting was called a week or so before the convention. As Dillon notes, the council 'had the material for a hot dispute and in fact that is what took place'. It was de Valera who saved the day. Dillon wrote:[56] 'A split would have been inevitable only for de Valera. When people got up and walked out he brought them back again. We finally got general acceptance of that extraordinary statement which was proposed as the first object of Sinn Fein.' Ironically, in view of subsequent developments, two of the walk-outs whom de Valera succeeded in bringing back were Michael Collins and Rory O'Connor. De Valera drafted the 'extraordinary statement' to which they finally agreed: 'Sinn Fein aims at securing the International recognition of Ireland as an independent Irish Republic. Having achieved that status the Irish people may by referendum freely choose their own form of Government.'

Having secured agreement on this formula, de Valera now made his decisive move towards securing the leadership of the new forces rapidly emerging in Ireland. A few days before the planned Sinn Fein convention he saw Arthur Griffith to make him an offer he could not refuse. Characteristically, the meeting took place not over Guinness in Griffith's favourite hostelry, the nearby Bailey in Anne's Street, but in a coffee shop in Grafton Street. De Valera told Griffith that he wanted him to stand down as President of Sinn Fein and to nominate him, de Valera, instead; if Griffith insisted on having a contest, he told him he would stand against him and was certain to win. In fact this was far from certain. De Valera did have the backing of the IRB and the Volunteers, but those – almost certainly the majority – who supported the new movement on constitutional grounds would have voted for Griffith. The subsequent executive elections put moderates like Eoin MacNeill at the head of the poll. Griffith's supporters headed the poll whereas the 'forward' party did badly: Michael Collins, for instance, barely secured the last place on the executive. People were prepared to vote for change, but they wished it to come by political means, not military ones.

However, although he now stood on the threshold of seeing his ideas triumph after a lifetime spent in penury in the cause of independence, for the sake of unity Griffith readily stood down. He had worked to secure influence; de Valera wanted power. Griffith ensured it for him by nominating him for the post of President when the convention was held on 25 October 1917. Count Plunkett, the only other candidate, immediately withdrew in favour of de Valera, whom Griffith introduced as a 'soldier and a statesman'. Griffith was subsequently elected as Vice President by an 'almost unanimous vote'.[57] De Valera's substantive achievement in holding the two disparate elements under the Sinn Fein umbrella together dumbfounded the Dublin Castle authorities; they had only refrained from banning the convention because their intelligence had assured them that, if it were allowed to go ahead, it would inevitably result in a split.[58]

But stylistically his performance as president and chairman of the convention – or, as it was known in its Irish form, Ard Fheis – failed to impress at least one commentator. Beaslai writes that he[59] 'made a very bad chairman. He was intensely verbose, wasting a great deal of time on elaborate explanations of the simplest points, with many repetitions, speaking in the tone of a schoolmaster to children. He commented on and explained every motion, speech or utterance of every delegate.' However, 'bad chairman' though he may have been, that unflattering pen picture nevertheless conveys the impression of a man determined to impress his stamp on the proceedings. It was in the course of his presidential address, which was delivered before reporters, that de Valera used a phrase which was subsequently frequently used against him: ' . . . we are not doctrinaire Republicans.[60] This phrase does not occur in his official biographical account of the proceedings (nor, of course, are there any comments on his style of chairmanship). What we are intended to take as the keynote passage is this:[61]

> The only banner under which our freedom can be won at the present time is the Republican banner. It is as an Irish Republic that we have a chance of getting international recognition. . . . Some might have faults to find with that and prefer other forms of government. But we are all united on this – that we want complete and absolute independence. This is not the time for discussion on the best forms of government. This is the time we can get freedom. Then we can settle by the most democratic means what particular form of government we may have.

The ambiguity contained in these descriptions of the form of government envisaged was as nothing compared to the Janus-faced policy he adopted towards the use of force. As his biography corroborates,[62] de Valera assured his audience that 'only moral means were intended' when it came to discussion of the redrafted Sinn Fein policy of making use of 'any and every means available to render impotent the power of England to hold Ireland in subjection'. However, the day after the open, two-day Sinn Fein convention the Volunteers held another convention, at the Gaelic Athletic Association at Jones's Road, Dublin, which was not open to the public. Here again de Valera was elected to a presidency – President of the Volunteers' Executive. Thus he was now President of both the constitutional movement and of the frankly militaristic Volunteers. The platform at this meeting was not a speaker's dais, but a bench of hay on which Collins and other Volunteer leaders sat. De Valera had a chair, but many of the country lads who sat facing him had to make do with planks. The rough-hewn nature of the setting was appropriate, for at this meeting the executive was empowered to 'declare war' should it prove necessary. It was generally understood that this power would only be exercised if Britain decided to enforce conscription.

But, as with the very formation of the Volunteers, there was a hidden agenda. The Volunteers had yet again been virtually taken over by the IRB. Cathal Brugha was elected Chief of Staff, but real power lay elsewhere: Michael Collins became Director of Organization, Diarmuid Lynch Director of Communications, Sean MacGarry General Secretary and 'most of the Dublin Executive were also members of the secret organisation'.[63] Collins, who also drew up a new constitution for the Brotherhood, was given the task of drawing up a new constitution for the Volunteers. Thus IRB influence permeated every level of the organization. The IRB had supported de Valera as a 'forward policy' candidate, but neither he nor Brugha wanted anything to do with the organization after 1916. As their dislike of the IRB probably had a bearing on the subsequent disastrous Irish civil war, it is worth examining here their stated reasons for their antipathy.

Brugha blamed the Brotherhood for the bungling and contradictory orders which preceded the Easter Rising: 'All the IRB in Dublin wanted was to pull their caps over their eyes, pull up their coats and be shadowed by detectives.' He also made an observation which may have had a bearing on a very wounding controversy, to be described later, in which he would one day involve de Valera against Michael Collins: 'The only two men who could keep the organisation free from graft and corruption were Tom Clarke and Sean MacDermott, and they were dead.'[64] Brugha claimed that, since the existence of the Brotherhood had been made public in the 1916 proclamation, Pearse, Clarke and MacDiarmada had thus indicated that the secret organization had outlived its usefulness and should be buried.[65] De Valera also argued that the Volunteers 'could work openly for Irish independence.'[66] His biography states that 'because his attitude was well known he was not apparently approached to continue his membership.'[67] But this does not appear to be the case according to the account of a man who took part in just such an approach, Pieras Beaslai. [68] He did so because 'there were those of us who dreaded the possibility of a later clash between de Valera and the IRB'. Accordingly Joseph MacGuinness, who was not a member, arranged a meeting between de Valera and three prominent IRB men, Beaslai, Eamonn Duggan and Fionan Lynch. Significantly, all three later opposed de Valera in the civil war. Lynch, who had connections with de Valera through Blackrock, also shared digs with Collins at this period; he later became a minister in the first Irish Government. Duggan too was close to Collins, and became one of the signatories of the Anglo-Irish Treaty which set up that government. Beaslai became a general in the new Irish Army.

Beaslai, Duggan and Fionan Lynch urged de Valera to join the IRB but he refused, giving as his reason the fact that membership of the secret society was incompatible with his religious principles. Significantly, he let it be known that he was aware that Diarmuid Lynch was using his post to organize IRB communications and that Collins was 'organising more than the volunteers'. This, as will be discussed in context later, was quite true. But the suspicion remains that his real objection lay hidden in a statement which he permitted in his biography: 'He also disliked swearing to obey an executive of unidentified members.'[69] As his progression in the nationalists' esteem since 1916 would at least have placed him on that executive, if not in charge of it as President, thus combining three

Republican Persons in one God, de Valera – a prospect which might have been expected to appeal to his nationalist and theological soul – one is left with the impression that what he feared was the prospect of not being able to *control* the Brotherhood. The demagogic gifts with which he was increasingly finding that he could manipulate public opinion could not be deployed within the ranks of a secret society. Whatever his real reason for distrusting the IRB, de Valera can hardly in logic have objected to the organization because its members espoused physical force to gain their ends.

He began his presidency of Sinn Fein by advising the Ard Fheis that each Sinn Fein club should buy a rifle so that its members might have an opportunity of studying its uses. And, as one of his most sympathetic biographers has noted, he showed in the same speech a fine appreciation of the science of 'defensive violence'. Mary Bromage describes him addressing his audience, 'his face unlighted by any smile', in the following fashion:[70] 'England, he told them with a hollow resonance, was pretending that it was not by the naked sword that she was keeping Ireland in duress. "We will draw the naked sword to make her bare the naked sword."' Nor were his fiery speeches around the country calculated to make young men turn the other cheek. At Tullamore, for example, he urged the Volunteers: 'Get every rifle you can, and those of you who cannot get rifles, get shot-guns; if you cannot get those, get the . . . pike, a very good weapon at close fighting.' When a voice from the crowd interrupted, 'We have them', he continued: 'Then get more of them. A row of ten-foot pikes will beat a row of bayonets any day.'[71]

Appropriately enough, the presentation made to him by the Tullamore Volunteers to commemorate his visit was a sword stick. But his romantic attachment to pikes – used by the 1798 insurgents – did not blind him completely to the exigencies of modern warfare. 'Start at once and purchase shot-guns and buckshot,' was his advice. 'This is much more effective at close quarters.'[72] At least one shrewd observer was under no illusion as to what his words meant. David Lloyd George, speaking in the House of Commons on 23 October 1917, said of his speeches: 'They are not excited and, so far as language is concerned, they are not violent. They are plain, deliberate, and I might also say cold-blooded incitements to rebellion. . . . This is not a case of violent, abusive and excitable language. It is the case of a man of great ability, of considerable influence, deliberately going down to the district . . . to stir people up to rebellion against the authorities.'

This analysis is a precisely accurate description of de Valera's activities at the time. A storm was gathering over Ireland. For the moment the drums of the Orange Covenanters were silent, their sound drowned by the mad roar of the guns on the Western Front. They would beat again; but now, from the ranks of the Green followers of the proclamation came the sound of pike heads being hammered out on the anvil of circumstances.

There had been another Sinn Fein by-election victory a month after de Valera won in Clare. W. T. Cosgrave defeated his Irish Parliamentary opponent by a two-to-one margin. Like de Valera, he had been sentenced to death for his part in the rising. Like de Valera's, his reprieve ensured that the spate of Sinn Fein by-election successes would catapult him into a political role which would one day confer on him the leadership of his country, albeit in opposition to de Valera. An Irish Party MP, Laurence Ginnell, gave the Sinn Fein bandwagon a further shove by announcing that he was henceforth adopting a policy of abstention from Westminster. And then, on 25 September 1917, Sinn Fein acquired its first martyr since the rising when Thomas Ashe died of clumsily administered forcible feeding while on hunger strike in Mountjoy Jail.

Ashe and some forty other prisoners had been on strike for that familiar demand from the 'Republican University', political status. They had been arrested on a variety of charges: Ashe, Fionan Lynch and Austin Stack for making speeches likely to cause disaffection, others for illegal drilling or for military displays at Sinn Fein occasions. However, all of them had fallen foul not of the ordinary criminal code but of DORA (the Defence of the Realm Act), to which the British had increasing recourse as a second authority grew within the land. As it was quite obvious that this law and those at whom it was directed, men of the calibre of Ashe and the others, were outside the common criminal code there was a great deal of public sympathy for their demand to be so recognized, even from non-Sinn Fein supporters. But the authorities took a hard line with the hunger strikers, first taking away their beds, bedding and boots so that they had to lie on cold stone floors, and then resorting to forcible feeding. The evidence at Ashe's inquest, which went on for three weeks, had a devastating effect on public opinion which was compounded when the jury brought in a verdict protesting at 'the inhuman punishment inflicted', condemning forcible feeding and urging that the practice be discontinued.

It is estimated that some thirty thousand people filed past the body as it lay in the Mater Hospital dressed in a Volunteer uniform, the shirt of which was donated by Michael Collins. The funeral, a huge affair that was part spontaneous outburst of sympathy, part show of strength by the Volunteers, brought Dublin to a halt and was marked by rifle volleys over the grave. Collins delivered a short, ominous oration after they died away: 'Nothing additional remains to be said. That volley which we have just heard is the only speech which it is proper to make above the grave of a dead Fenian.'[73]

Curiously, de Valera did not attend the funeral, putting the claims of a speaking engagement in the country before it. The independent-minded Ashe had differed from him a number of times, but he had also canvassed enthusiastically for him in Clare. Thus there was every reason for de Valera, the President of the Volunteers, to attend the most important Volunteer funeral since that of O'Donovan Rossa – particularly since during his long career de Valera was to bring the Irish political practice of funeral-going almost to the level of an art form. Whether it was the IRB character of the occasion or merely that he genuinely believed he should attend his meeting we simply don't know, but his was a significant non-appearance on this occasion.

Ashe's self-sacrifice was foretold in a verse he wrote himself. When reprinted and circulated by Sinn Fein it had an enormous effect in arousing sympathy for his cause in the Irish Catholic ethos of the time:[74]

> Let me carry your Cross for Ireland, Lord!
> For Ireland weak with tears,
> For the aged man of the clouded brow;
> And the child of tender years.
> For the empty homes of her golden plains,
> For the hopes of her future too!
> Let me carry your Cross for Ireland, Lord!
> For the cause of Roisin Dhu.

The second effect of his death was that his fellow DORA prisoners were first transferred to Dundalk Jail and then, after another hunger strike was begun, released, with only a fraction of their sentences served, on 17 November 1917. It was a momentous year for Sinn Fein and for de Valera.

Apart from his political fortunes his personal circumstances, and those of his family, improved greatly. The National Aid Association, run by Michael Collins, had given him £250 when he emerged from prison. Then, on becoming President of Sinn Fein, he was voted an annual salary of £500 – not riches exactly, but a good income by the standards of the day. Michael Collins, for instance, received £2 10s per week as Secretary of the National Aid Association. The money enabled de Valera to rent a comfortable house in the middle-class seaside suburb of Greystones in Co. Wicklow, some fifteen miles south-east of Dublin. Sinead was plagued by the constant stream of well-wishers who called to the door, but at least she had a home of her own again and a pleasant one at that, even if her husband spent increasingly little time there.

For Sinn Fein and de Valera 1918 was destined to be a watershed year. A huge pool of young men was building up in the country for two reasons: the attraction of increased prosperity on the farms through increased wartime demand for agricultural produce, and the barrier erected to emigration by fear of conscription. Sinn Fein and the Volunteers, with their rising-bestowed air of gallantry and sacrifice, were a potent draw for this pool of man, and woman, power. The authorities' reliance on banning meetings and demonstrations of nationality, such as Irish singing and dancing displays or sporting occasions, increased the flow of recruits. Ordinary crime in the country was almost nil,[75] but prosecutions under DORA soared. At one level, where the younger generation were concerned, imperialism and nationalism were set on a collision course; but on another, amongst older people, the propertied classes and some influential sections of the Roman Catholic hierarchy, the country's basic conservatism persisted. This was demonstrated in a series of three by-election defeats for Sinn Fein in February, March and April. The first and third were largely due to Cardinal Logue's opposition to Sinn Fein: he exercised his influence through the Ancient Order of Hibernians, which in South Armagh and East Tyrone conspired with the Unionists so that the Irish Party vote went to the Orangemen. The second defeat was due to the tragedy of John Redmond's death on 6 March. If ever a man died of a broken heart, it was he. His long-term colleague, John Dillon, who had become estranged from him over his moderate policies by the time he died, accurately described what had befallen him: ' . . . he faced great unpopularity and misunderstanding in Ireland in a high-minded and sincere attempt to reconcile the Irish and British people, and to serve the Empire in a time of terrible crisis and danger, and his reward was to be snubbed and humiliated in the face of his own people.'

Quoting Dillon's verdict approvingly, Dr Joseph Lee rightly commented that it 'captures the dilemma of all Irish statesmen who would seek conciliation by trusting solely to English goodwill'.[76] But Redmond's reputation in his Waterford constituency was such that his son, Captain William Redmond, retained his seat. An indication of how high feelings ran at this contest came the day after polling day, on 23 March, when Captain Redmond paid a call on the local bishop. He was told that de Valera was also in the house and would see him if he wished to meet. Redmond declined.[77] In microcosm that incident illustrated the level of political emotion in the country as a whole. Ireland was like a huge pressure cooker coming to the boil.

Most election meetings of the period – indeed any meetings connected with Sinn Fein – tended to be perfervid affairs. The potential for trouble between supporters of the Irish Party and Sinn Fein was generally compounded by the presence of strong forces of Royal Irish Constabulary on the alert for, in the words of DORA, 'speeches likely to cause disaffection'. The discipline engendered by the military overlap of Volunteer and Sinn Fein membership played a valuable part in keeping outbreaks of violence to a minimum. In fact that overlap became a source of embarrassment to the Volunteer executive in the early part of 1918 when Sinn Fein began driving cattle off grazing land in the west and renting out the ground for cultivation to small farmers and labourers. These cattle drives in one sense were quite jolly affairs, often accompanied by bands and waving tricolours; but in another they obviously contained great potential for violence should large-scale clashes develop between police and cattle drivers.[78] The stated objective was to ensure that the country would be in a position to feed itself in the face of the war-induced export of food, which was reaching such a pitch as to rekindle uneasy memories of famine. The theory behind the drives was that Sinn Fein passed on the rents to the legal landlord. But given Irish land hunger, the driving also raised fears in the Volunteer leadership that the independence movement's strength could at worst be easily siphoned off into a land war by these socialistic activities and at best alienate potential farming support. Accordingly the executive issued a directive, warning Volunteers about becoming involved in these activities which were 'neither national nor military in character'. But cattle drivers found their way to prison alongside Volunteers who had attended prohibited meetings, banned sporting occasions or Irish dancing displays, or had even been caught listening to 'disloyal bands'.

This last category of disaffection was created by a police order of 16 March 1918 which also directed the Royal Irish Constabulary (RIC) to break up the instruments belonging to such bands because 'such action was likely to have a salutary effect'. No such action had a 'salutary effect': not the bayoneting of a Sinn Fein supporter at a dispersed meeting in Clare;[79] not the shooting dead of the first two Volunteers to die in action since 1916, two young men caught raiding a barracks for arms in Gortalea, Co. Kerry;[80] not the copious application of the 'cat and mouse act', whereby hunger strikers were released from jail until they recovered and then picked up again. Sinn Fein morale and recruitment grew to such a pitch that the carrying of unauthorized weapons was prohibited in the country as a whole, and from 23 February 1918 even their possession was forbidden in the turbulent counties of Tipperary, Galway and Clare.

Clare, de Valera's constituency, grew even more turbulent and a few days later, on 27 February, was proclaimed a military area. The *Clare Champion* was banned, letters and telegrams censored and persons entering or leaving the county were issued with passports by the military. In the midst of the maelstrom de Valera pursued his course with his own distinctive blend of caution and courage. He travelled all over the country addressing meetings and reviewing Volunteer parades, often relying on public transport because he did not own a car. When the British banned one of his meetings, he simply switched either its time or venue so as to evade the terms of the order. For example, having decided to address a St Patrick's Day meeting on 17 March 1918 in Belfast of all places, he evaded the ban by starting the meeting at 11 p.m. on the night of 16 March. He was thundering that 'the spirit that has outlived centuries of oppression will outlive the Cromwells of today' when midnight struck and the police drew their batons.

But as befitted a man who should properly be thought of as a sort of lay cardinal in his own right he was more circumspect about dealing with challenges from senior clergy. During the autumn of 1917 Cardinal Logue and Dr Gilmartin, Archbishop of Tuam, made a pincer movement against him. Gilmartin attacked first. Seeing clearly the inevitable outcome of Sinn Fein's irresistible force meeting Westminster's immovable object, the Archbishop sounded alarm bells about the ethics of rebellion.[81] De Valera made a circumlocutory reply to him at Athy on 25 November, making it clear that his requirements for self-government were to dispense with Britain and to build up a self-sufficient Ireland.

Logue[82] based his attack on the 'ill-considered and Utopian' demand for an Irish republic; it was, he said, 'a dream which no man in his sober senses can hope to see realised'. In his reply, delivered in the unlikely surroundings of a concert in Roscommon, de Valera quoted Pope Leo XIII against the Cardinal. Democracy had not necessarily been all that bad, he assured his concert-going hearers, in the eyes of the Pope. And as regards Sinn Fein's republican aspirations being utopian and therefore immoral, in what way, pray, was it immoral for Belgium to make a utopian stand against Germany? But here the 'cute hoor' side of him showed itself. What he said at the concert went down well with his audience and would, he knew, also go back to His Eminence and around the Armagh diocese. There was no need for it to go much further, so he refused to give a statement to the papers.[83] Whatever form of government it would ultimately opt for – republic, monarchy or even utopia – both the Cardinal and the Archbishop had a shared worry about the central thrust of the party's policy. De Valera could not have been more explicit in spelling it out:[84] 'Sinn Feiners have a definite policy and the people of Ireland are determined to make it a success; that is, to make English rule absolutely impossible in Ireland.'

The opposition of these two high-ranking clerics and that of figures like them constituted a major brake on the implementation of this policy, as the by-elections of early 1918 showed. But in the event it was not de Valera or his colleagues who removed the brake, it was the British Government. Although boycotted by Sinn Fein, the convention for which Lloyd George had tried to create a favourable atmosphere by releasing de Valera and the other Lewes prisoners had continued its deliberations from the summer of 1917 to the spring of 1918. The official British Government line was that from this convention would emanate the blueprint for a peaceful new Ireland, brought about through agreement between Irishmen under the benevolent gaze of His Majesty's Government. Without Sinn Fein present, of course, the convention had no hope of producing any such document. The unofficial line, containing the reality of British policy, was revealed with more candour than caution by the British Government spokesman, Lord Birkenhead (the former F. E. Smith), in an interview with the *Boston Pilot* on 14 January 1918. He said that it was only a talking shop aimed at impressing American public opinion as Wilson persuaded his countrymen to go to war. Smith was quoted as saying that Lloyd George had hired some members of the convention at a guinea a day to keep them talking. This revelation overshadows the contribution of some of the participants, particularly the Southern Unionists, who made a real effort to envision a future for the Protestants of Southern Ireland under Home Rule, and *inter alia* to come to terms with the fact that their interests and outlook diverged widely from those of their Northern counterparts. Redmond and his colleagues also tried honourably to face up to the kind of Ireland which would result from Irish Catholic nationalists being given some powers of initiative in running their own country. But illness and despair at British failure to reciprocate the co-operative attitude displayed by himself and his party, compounded by the ever-increasing sound of the Sinn Fein 'noises off' described above, sapped both Redmond's judgement and his will towards the closing stages of the conference. He finally withdrew from the proceedings on 15 January.

The convention reported on 5 April. Its recommendations included an Irish Parliament more notable for the powers it would not have than those it was envisaged as exercising. It would not control anything touching on the Crown, peace and war, the Army and Navy, nor – unless Westminster decided otherwise – customs and excise. So long as the war lasted it would have no control over either the postal services or the police, and the Lower House of the proposed Parliament was to have 40 per cent of its seats reserved for Unionists. There was also a minority report which recommended a form of Dominion Home Rule considerably less than that enjoyed by the Dominions.[85] Even on their own, these morsels thrown from the troika of British, Unionist and Irish Party representatives were unlikely to have satisfied the appetites of the pursuing wolves of Sinn Fein. Accompanied as they were by an emetic, a decision to introduce conscription to Ireland, they were expelled from the body of public opinion almost as soon as they were swallowed – with no nourishment extracted from them.

In the long, sad litany of blunder and prejudice that makes up what is euphemistically termed 'the Anglo-Irish relationship', the decision to introduce conscription to Ireland in the state of ebullition then existing stands out as one of the worst ever. Granted that America had now entered the war and the need to be concerned with Irish American opinion was thus lessened, the accession of American manpower to the Allied ranks also meant that British requirements for Irish troops were correspondingly lessened. On 1 April 1918 President Wilson committed his country to providing 120,000 men a month to the Allied cause, and he underlined the importance of the Irish conscription issue in the USA by bracketing with this commitment a warning that trouble might follow in the wake of its imposition in Ireland. Even though in France the Germans were mounting a tremendous onslaught across a fifty-mile-wide front, there was as much ideology connected with the decision to flout Wilson's warning as there was military necessity.

The Tory and Unionist influence on the Cabinet was decisive. For six months they had been itching to get at the Irish manpower pool. As far back as October 1917 the Cabinet had agreed that 'with Europe in anguish' Ireland had 'no real grievance' but that 'actual rebellions and seditious acts were being promulgated'.[86] However, Irish American considerations weighed against taking any action on this opinion. There was also the consideration that from Dublin Castle came the warning that 'it would require three Army Corps to get one out of Ireland'.[87] Apparently it was the urgings of Sir Henry Wilson, Chief of the Imperial General Staff, that tipped the scales. He did not see any reason to allow 150,000 recalcitrant Irishmen to shirk their responsibility to join the ranks of the two and a half million Allied soldiers then engaged in several theatres of war. The Military Service Bill went through the House of Commons on 6 April and on that day the Irish Parliamentary Party left Westminster, never to return. What Pitt and Castlereagh had put together in 1800, Lloyd George and Henry Wilson had put asunder in 1918. The Act of Union was never the same again.

5

BEARDING THE BISHOPS

CONSCRIPTION GAVE Sinn Fein such a charge of wrathful energy that it became the dominant political force in Ireland. The Lord Mayor of Dublin, Laurence O'Neill, convened a protest meeting of public figures at the Mansion House for 18 April. This meeting may have been inspired by Archbishop Walsh, who throughout the conscription crisis secretly kept in touch with de Valera via intermediaries. He sent one of these to alert de Valera to the fact that a meeting of bishops was being called at the major Irish seminary, Maynooth, on the same day to discuss the conscription issue, and to let him know that feeling amongst their lordships was running so high that even Cardinal Logue was wavering. On the 17th the Archbishop, through Father Curran, arranged that, as if acting spontaneously, O'Neill would telephone from the meeting to Maynooth to ask to be received by the bishops. On the morning of the 18th de Valera called on Walsh, but the cunning old Archbishop decided it would be safer not to see him.[1] De Valera turned up at the Mansion House with Arthur Griffith, 'looking all the more striking, by the side of the short, moustached founder of Sinn Fein'.[2] For this meeting, not only were Sinn Fein and the Irish Party burying their differences, however temporarily; so too were the old Parnellite and anti-Parnellite rivals within the Irish Party. No longer was 'Tim Healy snarling at Willie O'Brien, squat beard against long whiskers'.[3] They were there with the contemporary leadership, John Dillon and Joe Devlin. Labour too turned up in support. De Valera was 'unawed by the older nationalists in whose company he found himself':[4] William O'Brien was no longer the revered figure whose picture had adorned his bedroom wall at Bruree; now he was a setting sun on a political landscape over which de Valera's star was rising. However, de Valera conducted himself at this watershed meeting in such a fashion that O'Brien later wrote approvingly:[5]

His transparent sincerity; his gentleness and equability captured the hearts of us all. His gaunt frame and sad eyes deeply buried in their sockets had much of the Dantesque suggestion of 'the man who had been in hell'. His was that subtle blend of virility and emotion which the Americans mean when they speak of a 'magnetic man.' Even the obstinacy (and it was sometimes trying) with which he would defend a thesis, as though it were a point in pure mathematics, with more than a French bigotry for logic, became tolerable enough when, with a boyish smile he would say: 'You will bear with me won't you? You know I am an old schoolmaster.'

Healy was somewhat more critical.[6] He remarked on the 'Castilian' features of the 'tall, spare, spectacled school-masterly' figure, whose features, he said, were of 'Jewish cast'. He was 'as chatterful as Griffith was reserved', Healy found, and his 'dats' and 'tinks' grated on the ear. 'Still a resourceful fellow', judged the old orator, though he was disturbed by the younger man's inability to pronounce the sound 'th'. However, even though de Valera spoke at such length that he had to be reminded that the bishops would not meet indefinitely,[7] there was no disagreement over the pledge which he drew up for their consideration: 'Defying the right of the British Government to enforce compulsory service in this country, we pledge ourselves solemnly to one another to resist conscription by the most effective means at our disposal.'

The next step was to get episcopal sanction for the proposal. William O'Brien suggested[8] that a delegation composed of himself, de Valera, Dillon, Healy and Larry O'Neill go to Maynooth. O'Neill, acting as though the idea were unheralded, duly went to make the prearranged phone call. In contemporary Ireland the Catholic hierarchy are regarded with considerable respect, but in those days awe would have more correctly summed up the general attitude of the people. Even the rapier-tongued Healy, who as a young man had had the temerity to criticize Parnell to his face, was daunted at the prospect of confronting the men in purple. 'I am not accustomed,' he said, 'to meeting bishops or archbishops.' But de Valera airily dismissed his qualms: 'Oh, there's nothing in that. I have lived all my life among priests.'[9] Now the years with the Holy Ghost Fathers, and the teaching at Maynooth itself, were conferring degrees of confidence and esteem that would more than make up for his lack of senior academic qualifications.

At Maynooth the delegation received 'a great ovation' from the students and found the bishops 'most friendly'. De Valera made a forceful contribution to the discussion, arguing that passive resistance was a fantasy which would inevitably lead to armed resistance, and that the British 'had a right to know the outcome if they went ahead'.[10] Where morality was concerned, the people had a moral right to resist in the face of the immorality of enforced conscription. In the face of these and similar arguments from the rest of the delegation the bishops agreed to co-operate in a number of ways, although they drew the line at sponsoring the anti-conscription pledge to be taken in the precincts of churches 'on bended knee'. Even Cardinal Logue consented to the issuing of the following hierarchical pronouncement: 'We consider that conscription forced in this way upon Ireland is an oppressive and inhuman law which the Irish people have a right to resist by every means that are consonant with the law of God.'

But the Cardinal was far from happy about giving aid and comfort to Sinn Fein. He afterwards told Archbishop Walsh: 'I fear this is the worst day's work the bishops ever did.'[11] But these reservations did not reach the wider public, who saw tangible evidence of the bishops' backing for the anti-conscription campaign, apart from their statement, in the nationwide celebration of a special anti-conscription Mass and in a chapel-gate collection for a fighting fund. It was afterwards estimated that outside the Mass, on 21 April, over one million people signed the Mansion House pledge which de Valera had drafted before setting out for Maynooth. Labour co-operated in staging a one-day national strike on 23 April, during which the country virtually closed down. Even the pubs shut, and the hierarchy added to the effect by closing down Maynooth and sending all the students home for the occasion. It was a most dramatic interlude, the Green obverse of the Orangemen's signing of their Covenant.

A harbinger of how Sinn Fein would benefit from it all came the day after de Valera's descent on Maynooth. The succession of by-election losses was halted. In Co. Offaly, Dr McCartan was returned unopposed. De Valera personally benefited enormously from the demonstrable fact that he had been more than able to hold his own at the highest level of constitutional Ireland's political and religious leadership. Men like Dillon, Healy and O'Brien might have been grey-bearded but they were household names, men who in their day had fought against incredible odds to establish the peasant on his land and themselves as his respected and skilful representatives in the greatest imperial parliament in the world. Now de Valera had shown himself not least, but honoured, amongst them all.

The Volunteers' executive was fully aware that the Volunteers might be involved in forceful resistance to conscription. Many, like Collins, had regarded their release from captivity after 1916 merely as the prelude to a resumption of the old fight. But on 26 April de Valera, with his penchant for attempting to control everything going on around him, issued his fellow executive members with a written pledge of resistance for them either to sign or to reject. 'The naked sword' was well on the way to being drawn.

The British, too, were making preparations for what seemed inevitable conflict. Home Rule on the lines of the convention report was to be offered; it would be declined, and conscription would then be enforced. In order to ensure the success of this scenario Lloyd George reshuffled his Irish team. After the rising the axe had fallen on the chief British officials in Ireland. Birrell, Nathan and the others had joined the seemingly endless list of Englishmen whose careers have suffered through contact with the Irish problem. Now their successors too were to go. Lord Wimborne, who was replaced as Lord Lieutenant by a distinguished soldier, Field Marshal Lord French, remarked afterwards that nearly anyone who had any sympathy with Irish nationality was withdrawn from the Irish executive.[12] A man stern and choleric, Edward Shortt, replaced the liberal-minded Henry Duke. The military command was shuffled around also, Sir Bryan Mahon being replaced by General Shaw. The gloves were coming off but, with America in mind, Lloyd George was concerned as to who should strike the first blow: 'Lloyd George impressed on Johnny [Lord French] the necessity of putting the onus for first shooting on the rebels. The Prime Minister, moreover, declared that he was going to table the Order in Council for conscription in Ireland at the same time as he tabled the Home Rule Bill.'[13]

Though de Valera was unaware of the fact, Lloyd George already had to hand, in the person of one Joseph Dowling, part of his excuse for going on the offensive. Dowling was one of the few Irish prisoners of war to have enrolled in the Irish Brigade which Roger Casement had tried to form during his ill-starred visit to Germany. He had been put ashore on Crab Island in Galway Bay from a German submarine with a view to making contact with Sinn Fein for the Germans. It was a German initiative which apparently only Michael Collins and a few of his intimates were aware of. Consequently Sinn Fein attached neither concern nor significance to Dowling's almost immediate capture.

De Valera was principally concerned with the conscription campaign and its effect on Sinn Fein's electoral fortunes; the party was jockeying for position with the Irish Party while maintaining a united front on the conscription issue. Yet another by-election vacancy had arisen, in East Cavan. John Dillon had tried to have an agreed candidate, Larry O'Neill, selected so that a contest could be avoided. But de Valera and his colleagues decided to reject his overture and nominated Arthur Griffith for the constituency. De Valera and Dillon shared a platform at a huge anti-conscription meeting at Ballaghadereen in Co. Roscommon, the area which returned Dillon as MP to Westminster. De Valera was invited to speak first, but with barbed courtesy insisted that, out of respect for the local man, his colleague be given the honour of opening the proceedings. He knew that Dillon would urge unity and he wanted to have the last word on the subject. Dillon duly fell for his ploy and made an appeal for unity which de Valera dismissed when his turn came:[14] '. . . there is in this cry of unity a tyranny as great in its way as the tyranny that is often exercised under the cry of liberty. We have the right unity, the unity of co-operation. The unity of amalgamation would be no unity and that we cannot have.'

His official biography says admiringly: 'Adroitly he put Dillon in the position of trying to foist an MP on East Cavan by an inter-party deal. De Valera was showing that he was an astute politician as well as revolutionary leader.'[15] In the event when polling day arrived, on 21 June 1918, Arthur Griffith won the seat. But by then East Cavan was literally of remote interest to Griffith and de Valera: both were back in jail in England. The British had made use of the futile Dowling landing to announce the discovery of a 'German plot' which justified the arrest of the Sinn Fein leadership. Dowling in fact had achieved no more than the cadging of a lift off the island from two lobster men in a currach shortly after landing from the submarine; he had then made his way to a pub and was arrested a little later. But a sonorous proclamation issued to the press by Lord French on 18 May, five weeks after Dowling's capture, announced 'drastic measures' because 'it has come to our knowledge that certain subjects of His Majesty the King domiciled in Ireland, have conspired to enter into, and have entered into, treasonable communication with the German enemy'.

By the time Dowling was picked up he had drunk so much whiskey that it would have been difficult to enter into any sort of communication with him, 'treasonable' or otherwise. Nevertheless his appearance in Galway Bay was used as a pretext to round up over eighty prominent nationalists. Apart from de Valera and Griffith they included W. T. Cosgrave, Count Plunkett, Countess Markievicz, Tom Clarke's widow, Kathleen, and the two secretaries of Sinn Fein, Darrell Figgis and Padraig O'Caoimh. By way of reconciling the Irish public to these proceedings Lord French's proclamation appealed to 'loyal subjects of His Majesty' to 'suppress this treasonable conspiracy and to defeat the treacherous attempt of the Germans to defame the honour of Irishmen for their own ends'. It apparently escaped the attention of whoever drew up the proclamation that there might be those in Ireland who would regard Britain's imprisoning so many of the country's outstanding figures as tending to 'defame the honour of Irishmen for its own ends'. For the proclamation went on to state that, in order to defend the 'safety and welfare of the empire', arrangements were to be made to 'facilitate and encourage voluntary enlistment in Ireland in His Majesty's Forces'. Cathleen ni Houlihan had been made an offer which she could not accept. Moreover, the round-up had missed the one man capable of ensuring that her non-acceptance took potent form – Michael Collins.

Although no one realized it at the time, the 'German plot' round-up began a crucially important phase of de Valera's career. It heightened his profile amongst Irishmen everywhere, but it also ultimately led to his going to America and thus being absent from Ireland during most of one of the most crucial periods in Irish history, the Anglo-Irish war. The effects of this can only be guessed at now, but they were assuredly profound. The odyssey that would lead de Valera to an eighteen-month tour of America began at a Volunteer executive meeting on the night of 17 May 1918. Michael Collins, who had already put together an important part of the intelligence-gathering machine that later enabled him to destroy the British Secret Service operation in Ireland, warned the meeting that a big swoop appeared to be only hours away.

Such alarms were frequent at the time, and the general attendance at the meeting was not disposed to react by going on the run. Because of de Valera's standing, however, there was a 'general consensus of opinion that de Valera should avoid all possible danger of arrest by staying in Dublin instead of returning to his house in Greystones'.[16] Beaslai, who was at the meeting, says that de Valera at first seemed to accept this view but then changed his mind and went home and was arrested. His official biography[17] offers a variety of pointers as to why he made the decision: the frequency of round-up reports, the fact that to 'go on the run would make work for independence very difficult', and the fact that he 'held second-class season tickets for himself and for the bicycle he used in the city'.

There was little scope for using his bicycle at his immediate destination after Greystones, a warship in Dun Laoghaire harbour. He was the first to be picked up, but as the round-up continued he was joined by the other deportees as they were swept up under the terms of DORA as persons 'suspected of acting, having acted or being about to act in a manner prejudicial to the public safety and the defence of the realm'. The ship was not ready to move off until 6 p.m. on Saturday, 18 May. It left Dun Laoghaire, or Kingstown as it was then known, to the cheers of a large crowd who defied the police to crowd on to the piers. Probably some of the enthusiasts had been amongst those who cheered de Valera and the Lewes men ashore just under a year earlier. Once more, Sinead did not know when she might expect to see her bridegroom again. Once more, she would have another baby before she did so: another daughter, Emer, was born later that summer.

It was 6 June before de Valera was able to get word home as to his whereabouts – Lincoln Jail. Conditions at Lincoln were easier than during his previous incarcerations, because the prisoners were classified as unconvicted internees and thus allowed privileges such as freedom of association and food parcels. De Valera accepted the freedom of association concession, but the Savonarola in him forbade the food parcels. He had done the same thing in Lewes, smuggling out a note to a friend:[18] 'On no account let there be any suggestions of food parcels here – they might permit it.' At that stage, whether because of wartime food shortages, or because the 1916 prisoners were agitating for recognition of their political status, or a combination of both, the authorities had cut down the prisoners' rations. Having vetoed the food parcels, de Valera went on to describe the restricted diet the prisoners were existing on:

> They cut down our food rations last week. Were we to submit to the new regime our healths would be ruined, at least that of many of us. Prison diet, as you know, doesn't stand much cutting, I own, but they have taken away about 12 ozs. of meat, 136 ozs. bread, 28 oz. potatoes per week and replaced these by 3 ozs cheese, 3½ ozs. margarine, 14 pts. of porridge, 24 ozs. Beans and Peas (Weighed after cooking and so one third or so is water.)
>
> Now the substitutes are weight for weight of less value as food and there is a loss of over 100 ozs in weight alone. Besides a number cannot digest the substitutes at all. They saw we were going to kick up a row, so they are about to change it – how far the change will be satisfactory is a question – we'll kick up a row if it isn't.

Apart from his frugal nature and the general willingness to confront prison authorities which he demonstrated after 1916, De Valera's own physical condition probably had a bearing on his cavalier attitude to food parcels: '. . . it is for the English Government to feed us properly', he wrote loftily to Sinn Fein[19] within a few days of arriving at Lincoln Jail, to which his group had been consigned. The other deportees were divided up between Usk and Gloucester. All the prisoners were initially held at Gloucester for a few days while their various destinations were being decided on. Here the prisoners staged an athletic contest and de Valera came first in the mile, a good indication of fitness on the part of a thirty-six-year-old. He made sure that he stayed fit while in jail by playing handball and rounders. When a sports day was held at Lincoln he again won the mile, from scratch, and came first in the weight throwing also. He told Sinead proudly, 'I am not quite an old man yet.'[20] He was not merely trying to reassure her when he wrote:[21] 'You need have no anxiety on my account. As I told you when in Dartmoor – there are few who can bear up against prison life as I can and the conditions here are by no means what they were in Dartmoor.' Not all the prisoners had his stamina. Two, Pierce McCan and Richard Coleman, died at Usk and Gloucester respectively, and many died prematurely after their release. One such was Joseph McGuinness,[22] whose election had caused de Valera such heart-searching.

In Lincoln de Valera had more time and opportunity to study than in Lewes, and his letters to Sinead soon began to include references such as: 'Spanish which I elected myself professor of and chapter from the Imitation in Irish!' He also taught Irish to his fellow prisoners, learned French, studied mathematics – chiefly quaternions, apparently – and applied himself to a present he had been sent: ' . . . about 18 vols. of Lecky. I wish we could read together some of them. His "map of Life" and chapters in the Histy. of European morals would greatly interest you. . . .'[23] This letter, with its scholarly references, perfectly illustrates the peculiar blend of high thinking, frugality and an almost nit-picking passion for detail that was characteristic of him:

> . . . My homespun trousers is worn through and, as I do not want to wear out the knickers, you had better send me the grey trousers I got leaving prison – It will be equally valuable as a souvenir if well worn! Send the trousers only. There is an old rain coat of a greyish colour on the back of the door of the little room over the hall. Send it along too. Mind the grey (not the green). The grey is the shorter and smaller of the two. Did you get the blackthorn stick I lost in Ballaghadereen? . . . I prized it greatly. . . . I got the cheque books. How are you for money? I could send you some if you are short. . . .

Later that month, on 18 July, he wrote again to Sinead giving more details of the course of improving reading he was pursuing (he had added economics to his earlier list) and sighing after his family in his own inimitable way:[24]

> How I wish here I had the children to teach. I would like to get Viv. and Mairin at geometry. They would be able to understand it now if the subject were properly handled with them. How is Eamonn's hearing now? Brian follows you about as usual I suppose unless Ruaidri's rivalry has made him resign his hopes of a monopoly . . . the crops in the field facing the house are still waving green I expect

– I had been looking forward to seeing the golden corn ripening there . . . now mind you be careful of yourself.

Obviously the geometry reference drew something of a rocket from Sinead, for on 2 August we find him writing to her saying: 'I am not anxious as you seem to fear as regards the children's education – what I meant in my previous letter was that prevented from doing other things now that I have leisure I should like to have the task of teaching the children. I know it is quite impossible for you to do it, except in a general way, with the amount of other work on your hands.'

Sinead was still expecting Emer, to be born on 15 August 1918, and his letters are full of solicitude for her and warnings to take care of herself. Nevertheless they frequently contained requests for her to do things for him 'When you find it convenient', as he wrote on 23 July in the course of a list of instructions as to how she might open a jammed desk which contained 'some stationery . . . particularly a notebook containing some quaternion notes and a notebook in which nothing was written but which would be useful here'. He went on to explain: 'The mechanism of a roll top desk is such that if you pull forward the top and then slap it back sharply (as if opening it roughly) it will release the catch which holds the drawers locked when the (rolling) top is in any but the well open position.' The incongruity of how this might appear to some eyes seems to have struck him here because he continues: 'Now Mr (or Miss) Censor – this is really not a secret of a new 70 mile howitzer or an air submarine – test it on your own "roll top" and do not hold this up.' Apparently the censor believed him, for the letter obviously got through – although a large percentage of his other correspondence seems to have been stopped. The censorship precluded all mention of military or political matters. But shortly after being sent to Lincoln he managed to evade it to express his delight to Sinead when Arthur Griffith won the seat in Cavan over which he had refused to horse-trade with Dillon:[25]

I have just seen the papers and the reply [to Lloyd George over the Convention Report and the German Plot arrests]. It is worthy of Breffni [the Gaelic name for the old kingdom of Breffni, which embraced what is now Cavan]. . . . I can imagine how Ireland rejoiced last night – I would like to say much but then overly much would be to have this returned. You know what we here feel and the knowledge that all is as it should be is enough to make anywhere a paradise.

But the censorship appears to have grown more lenient with time, to judge from a far more polemical letter written on 7 August.[26] It gives an interesting insight into the way de Valera viewed both England and himself. On 5 July the British had issued an order prohibiting 'the holding of or taking part in any meetings, assemblies, or processions in public places in Ireland'. This ban also applied to sporting fixtures, aeirdheachta (open air musical entertainments), Feiseanna (Irish musical or dancing contests), fetes, concerts and regattas. It was opposed by Sinn Fein, who, for example, arranged for fifteen hundred hurling matches to be held on 15 August and a similar number of public meetings to be held a week later. Many of those who addressed the meetings fetched up in jail, thus adding to the impact of the 'Republican University'. The state of disorder in the country may be gauged from the fact that in July alone the press reported eleven baton or bayonet charges by police and military. De Valera's comments were occasioned by a speech on the situation that had been made in the House of Commons by the Chief Secretary, Sir Edward Shortt. He told Sinead:

> . . . Shortt's shrift ought to pass into proverb – not because it is a new idea but as beautifully crystallising what everyone previously knew to be a fact. 'Liberty of conscience I do uphold', said Cromwell, 'but the mass I will not tolerate within this realm.'
>
> The good old brute force Tory principles of Mr. Shortt ought to be a refreshing tonic after the experience of the pharasaical whigs. The *Morning Post*'s leaders are a refreshing treat. I wish I could show you today's re reform in India – what a delightful contrast to the cant about freedom for Small nations etc. If only a decent Irish satirist would spring up – some modern Swift what excellent materials he would have at hand! What fun amidst all the tragedy. I sadly grieve at my own lack of the necessary cynicism – else I would spend my enforced leisure here on the task.

In later life at least, very few of de Valera's opponents would have agreed that he suffered from a lack of cynicism. But even his sternest critics would have to concede that his Lincoln correspondence with Sinead shows a genuine warmth of feeling for her and the children, albeit mixed up with indications of an 'odd bod' persona lurking behind that of the Family Man. Hearing from another correspondent that there were colds in the family, he was immediately consumed with anxiety and wrote to Sinead[27] instructing her always to let him know how everyone was, otherwise he would imagine the worst. He generally included in his letters some indication of love for the children such as a request that Sinead kiss them for him. Sometimes, admittedly, these declarations of affection were introduced inappropriately:[28]

> I am enclosing the income tax returns. As the post is leaving I must stop. With love to you all. I think of you and feel that though lonely you will do your best to be happy. If all the things I say to your spirit form were known to you you would understand well – all. I need not say more. Remember me to the children. Tell them Daddy is always thinking of them.

But there is no doubt that he was sincere when he wrote to Sinead after Emer's birth, saying: 'I cannot tell you how I feel being unable to be at your side just now.' Weeks earlier he had had a typewriter sent in to him and learned to type. He used his new-found knowledge to write to Sinead as follows:[29]

... we are locked up for the night and instead of gazing out through the window with my eyes as well as my heart and soul fixed on the West, dreaming of you and the children and picturing up a thousand scenes over there in the soothing calm of the glorious Autumn sunset, of you and of them, striving to divine what each of you are doing at the instant, happy in your company and enjoying those conversations in spirit which are my greatest solace when I am forced to be absent from you – instead of this feast of the imagination I decided for this evening to use this more material way of speeding to you my thoughts and my wishes.

There is something oddly cold in using this machine as the medium, I do not know if it seems like that to you, but I am using it now just to make you smile and say to yourself that the prison hasn't changed me and that the new toy has as powerful an attraction for me as ever.

His strong religious faith was of course a central reason why he was able to 'bear up against prison life' so well. His correspondence with Sinead includes several references to prayer and to serving Mass. He looked forward to the possibility of training 'Viv.' as an altar boy, and: 'As regards the Rosary we have said it in common every night since we left Ireland.'[30] To his mother he wrote:[31] 'I know you will be glad that I have served all our masses here. I feel like a little boy again and I pray that my childish faith may ever remain with me. I tell you this because I know it will give you more pleasure than anything else I could write.'

All this correspondence provides a unique insight into the thoughts of Eamon de Valera in the private realm of his family just before he entered one of the most publicized phases of his life. Outside the jail, Irish history was taking a right-angled turning. Lloyd George had succeeded in introducing neither Home Rule nor conscription before the end of the war. In the welter of bitterness over the former, and gratitude for the latter, Sinn Fein's hour struck. At the general election which followed the Armistice, held on 14 December 1918, two months to the day after de Valera's thirty-sixth birthday, the Irish Parliamentary Party were virtually obliterated, dropping from 80 to 6 seats. Overall, against a combined Irish Party, Unionist and 'others' total, Sinn Fein won 73 out of 105 seats. Only in Antrim, Armagh, Derry and Down did the Unionists command a majority. De Valera defeated the Irish Party leader, John Dillon, in Mayo and retained his own seat in East Clare without a contest. His only reverse came in a third constituency, West Belfast, where he was beaten by the Irish Party candidate, Joseph Devlin. One can imagine the cheering and exultation in Lincoln Jail when these results, and in particular their leader's own performance, were read to the Irish prisoners from a balcony. But away from the encapsulated world of family and jail comradeship, how did de Valera appear to discerning observers of that time?

Sean O'Faolain said[32] of de Valera at thirty-six that he was 'an instrument being played upon by the passions that come from love of country'. Twenty years later O'Faolain said he had turned into 'a Roman spear, with a voice like a cracked or muffled bell, and an ordered restraint in his looks, as if all lusciousness had been pared away by bitter experience

. . . the effects of memories of street-fighting, a night waiting for execution, and months in jail'.

Certainly the months in Lincoln Jail bear out O'Faolain's description. De Valera was described as 'unbending and unbreakable'[33] by Sean Etchingham, a fellow prisoner. Etchingham had fallen ill and de Valera attended to him, making toast and Bovril. But he also negotiated with the Governor on his behalf, warning that if anything happened to Etchingham there would be serious trouble in the jail. Eventually the authorities gave in and released Etchingham. Certainly, too, there was very little evidence of 'lusciousness' left in de Valera's thought if one were to judge by his entry[34] in a prisoners' poetry competition held at Lincoln on 18 September 1918. Four months to the day after the 'German plot' swoop, de Valera's thoughts, after a summer in jail, might have been expected to show some obvious hankering after female companionship. His fellow prisoners' entries contain things like:[35]

> My little lump of perfect joy,
> My two arms filled with gladness.

But de Valera's composition may be judged from the following extracts:

> When I behold thee filled am I with hope
> Quaternia
> And realms new yield my soul extended scope
> Quaternia
> Rich fruit of thought rise to a height divine
> When thou I see and know that thou art mine
> Quaternia
> And in the ages yet to rise and roll
> Until Amphiliation's awful knell shall toll
> I shall thou and I beloved find the means
> To knock algebra into smithereens
> Quaternia.

Arid, but nevertheless his verse does not seem to proceed from the simple mind described by one of his critics. P. S. O'Hegarty found him:[36]

> . . . a slow-moving, painfully uncouth, massive speaker, with a disarming habit of pouring forth as new discoveries things which had been for twenty years the commonplaces of separatist thought. His great value to the country was his honesty, and his simplicity, and his single-mindedness. He restated in plain, simple language, in speeches which were of general applications to the nations as well as of particular application to Ireland, the unassailable moral and international principles upon which Ireland's case rested; while his personality and integrity had a big influence at home in ranging all sections of Nationalist opinion behind the movement of which he was the spokesman.

O'Faolain, who fought on de Valera's side during the civil war, thought this 'a good summing up'. But he felt that O'Hegarty, one of the IRB's principal reorganizers before 1916, might have shown a 'greater degree of approbation'. In assessing de Valera's appeal, O'Faolain said that he 'was never commonplace, and never vulgar, for he has a natural human dignity of his own'. Although he did concede that de Valera could sometimes be 'exceedingly dull', his judgement was this: 'The truth seems to be that there is in every man a latent nobility which no willed effort of his own can produce; for it does not seem to infect his workaday virtues. De Valera has tapped this latent fire more persistently than any other living Irishman.'

But in these assessments neither O'Hegarty nor O'Faolain, two of the principal Irish writers and historians of their day, touch on an essential component of de Valera's philosophy which should be addressed at this stage. For it is probable, though not certain, that it was in Lincoln that de Valera began to be seriously influenced by the works of that well-known Florentine, Niccolò Machiavelli. Reading material seems to have been in short supply during his earlier prison sojourns, and his busy life on release was hardly conducive to such study. It is true that he wrote to Simon Donnelly from Lewes Jail[37] in terms which could have been taken as embodying one of Machiavelli's keynote ideas, the necessity for citizen armies: '. . . one other word, do not forget the organising and in so far as it is possible the equipping of soldiers for the Irish Nation. . . . Whatever measure of freedom Ireland will be able to secure she will need an armed body to preserve it and improve upon it.'

But on emergence from Lincoln he specifically mentioned Machiavelli to Richard Mulcahy, who was then a newly elected Sinn Fein representative and would later distinguish himself as Chief-of-Staff of the Volunteers and go on to become one of de Valera's leading adversaries both during the civil war and in their subsequent careers. He told Mulcahy:[38] 'You are a young man going in for politics. I will give you two pieces of advice – study economics and read *The Prince*.' Mulcahy told me years later that, after taking de Valera's advice, he was very disappointed to find that *The Prince* was only: 'A handbook for teddy-boys. A way for exerting gangsterism on a part of Italy.'

However, de Valera appears to have taken his own advice seriously. He took *The Prince* with him when he was smuggled to America not long after talking to Mulcahy.[39] Certainly, a year later, he quoted Machiavelli in a significant context during a long, edgy confrontation with James O'Mara, an independent-minded Limerick businessman who had become de Valera's fellow trustee of an Irish National Loan and had left behind his extensive bacon-curing business to go to America to work, living at his own expense while organizing the loan. O'Mara's daughter, Patricia, was present during the conversation which took place at Long Beach, New York. She records:[40]

> . . . a feeling of high tension and the slight discord of arguments pervading everything. The crescendo came with the discussion of the Middle Ages; the

Florentines and Machiavelli. . . . Looking back I can see that this was one of the occasions when Dad and de Valera got on each other's nerves. In all that time, in all that length of discussion, neither swayed the other by as much as an inch, though both persistently tried to do so.

But by the time Patricia Lavelle's book appeared in 1961 forty-two years had passed since de Valera gave the advice about studying Machiavelli, and he had since learned that his avowal of fondness for the Florentine did not command universal respect. Lavelle read her manuscript over to de Valera for several days[41] before submitting it for publication. What appeared was a vintage de Valera formula which bridged the gap between two opposites – his supposedly high-minded, moral approach to politics and his exemplar's reputation for amoral realpolitik. It contained an admission of both fascination and disavowal: 'The book of Machiavelli's in which de Valera was interested was, of course, *The Prince*. De Valera said that he was fascinated by this book on statesmanship because he himself believed that some foundation of good must underlie good results, and he could never find a suggestion of this kind in this book.'

By 1970, when his own biography appeared, de Valera had found a further formula for presenting his mention of Machiavelli to Mulcahy. He recalled a newspaper interview he had given[42] in which he stated that America was Ireland's main hope, that 'the Machiavellis, Lloyd George among them, might scoff, but the people of America would help to keep their President firmly to his principles. . . . Indeed quite a few politicians were Machiavellian in his eyes. He advised the Chief of Staff of the Irish Volunteers, Richard Mulcahy, that if he entered politics he should study Machiavelli and read economics.'

The question of what exactly Machiavelli's work meant has divided scholars over the centuries, and no more than a brief indication can be attempted here of how some of his central ideas may be seen at work on de Valera's thought. First, there was more to Machiavelli than is conveyed by the popular use of his name to describe someone who practises the doctrine that the end justifies the means. Like de Valera himself, Machiavelli was more complex than that. He sets forth the truth that men inevitably find it difficult to be entirely good or entirely evil, and that trying to find a middle way often results in paralysis. Therefore though he respects prudence, he extols as heroes men who have undertaken what seemed to be imprudent undertakings, in the face of moderate counsel to the contrary, and yet come out on top through a combination of their own qualities and the circumstances of the times. Machiavelli could have wished for no clearer illustration of this doctrine than the cautious de Valera's own participation in the 1916 Rising. And other, scarcely less dramatic, examples of forswearance of the 'middle way' abound in de Valera's subsequent career.

Another central doctrine of Machiavelli's was that the ideal state was the republic; after it came a principality ruled by a strong leader. There is no need to dwell on the significance which Machiavelli's fondness for republicanism would have had for de Valera, who had taken up arms under the proclamation. But one should note that the type of leader, or prince, whom Machiavelli discussed was one who had himself bounded on to the stage of influence, unaided by a power base in previous custom, history or heredity. Of the morality of such leaders, Machiavelli wrote:[43]

> A new Prince cannot observe all those things by which men are considered good, for in order to maintain his state he is often obliged to act against his promise, against charity, against humanity. . . . He should not stray from the good, but he should know how to enter into evil when necessity commands. . . . In the actions of all men and especially of princes, where there is no final arbiter, one must consider the final result.

This comes near the idea of the end justifying the means, but it is not quite that. However, as will be seen, it is very de Valera. As was Machiavelli's observation that 'men are less hesitant about harming someone who makes himself loved than one who makes himself feared . . . fear is held together by a dread of punishment which will never abandon you'.

Machiavelli also justified the use of force in political life: 'There cannot exist good laws where there are no good armies.' But he made the fine distinction that 'one should reproach the man who is violent in order to destroy, not one who is violent in order to mend things'. Again this is a thought that must obviously have struck a chord with de Valera. So would Machiavelli's preachings on the importance of a state that is internally stable and externally independent. Since he was writing in a time and place when he was benignly influenced by a Medici Pope and a Medici Duke, his admiration for the harmony of this Church–State relationship would also have been in tune with de Valera's own view of the desirability of a close relationship between Christ and Caesar.

Machiavelli's ideas might appear commonplace today, but we must remember the sense of empathy with which they would have been received by one who was himself a 'new prince' musing over the pursuit and capture of power during a time of great revolutionary change – in a prison cell. Another linked consideration is the quality of intellectual life and the level of education outside that cell. The *'le calcul'* approach permeated all aspects of education. Here is a confidential assessment of university and technical education of the time[44] drawn up for the private perusal of the Archbishop of Dublin. Having referred to the ferment of scientific activity taking place in laboratories and technical institutes internationally, it judged that 'to these scientific forces Ireland presents a void' and went on to state:

> So far as those who hold University place are concerned no man has appeared with a tradition of European thought. We have three University Colleges (excluding Trinity) and an illiterate country. With few exceptions the holders of our University Chairs are not of University standard either in the Humanities, Medical, or Science Faculties. They have not made, and are not likely to make

any contribution of worth to the National Being. . . . The whole organisation of the University is false in principle . . . what is called Technical Instruction is neither vocational nor technical; it is only an educational morass. . . .

One can imagine what a shadow was thrown across such a landscape by the tall figure of Eamon de Valera, not only a hero of 1916 and a man of proven political ability but, as he liked to be described, a *Professor* of Mathematics into the bargain. . . . All this and Machiavelli too was an overwhelming combination where the capturing of the public's imagination was concerned. And not only the public but also his colleagues, including Michael Collins, were prepared to show him remarkable friendship and loyalty. As we are now nearing a point in de Valera's career where Collins played a major role in reintroducing him to the Irish landscape, it may be helpful if we pause for a moment to examine the differences between the two men. These differences played their part in the civil war which not only devastated the Ireland of their time but has a bearing on what still divides the two biggest parties in today's Republic of Ireland.

Collins had a particular respect for teachers, partly because of his own aptitude for learning and reading and his habit of deferring to old people, and partly because as a boy a teacher had been a particular influence on him. His father's advanced age – he was seventy-six when Collins was born – may have had something to do with his attitude towards age. And his own particularly happy childhood, during which the loss of his father when he was six was compensated for by being doted on by his mother and a bevy of elder sisters, probably conditioned his easy approach to children – including de Valera's children, to whom he was notably kind. But the security of his family upbringing, so diametrically opposed to the rejection with which de Valera had to cope, also fed a self-confidence that could sometimes be tactless and abrasive. His nickname, the Big Fellow, was originally intended to convey big-headedness. If there was a row or a wrestling match in his vicinity, it was generally because he had caused it.

He was no respecter of persons or of rank. Apart from the old and the young, he admired only one other general category – fighting men; after that, individuals had to earn their respect from him. If there was work to be done, either within or near his own force field, his abounding energy ensured that it was done promptly and well – including work that others felt, often quite rightly, belonged to their sphere of influence. He had a genius for getting things done: floating an illegal, though highly successful, National Loan from the back of a bicycle, pioneering new methods of guerilla warfare, smashing the British Secret Service, organizing an underground government department. And he did all this while 'on his keeping', the most hunted, most wanted man in Ireland. But such a man leaves a swathe of bruised egos behind him. His unorthodox, swashbuckling approach was completely at variance with that of the aloof hierarchialist de Valera, with his insistence on strict procedural behaviour and observance of spheres of influence.

Moreover, a 'new Prince' was inevitably bound to come into conflict with the head of a secret society which believed that that head was in reality the Prince. And while de Valera was in jail Collins was moving rapidly towards becoming President of the IRB. The differences between the two men could be summed up in Shakespeare's 'two stars keep not their motion in one sphere', or extended almost indefinitely to give contrasts between the solitary 'giraffe-like' de Valera who climbed trees to stay awake and the gregarious Collins who tried to teach himself to do without sleep altogether so that he would not waste time.

But one fundamental difference between them should be noted: it was over the methods by which force should be applied. De Valera, as one close observer commented with equal measure of levity and acuity,[45] did not 'object to slaughter so long as it was organised'. He had a mania for uniforms and drill, orthodox, regular army organization and tactics. Whenever possible during those troubled years he devoted a good deal of his time to reviewing Volunteer displays. But where De Valera went by the military manual, Collins rewrote it:[46] 'Forget the Company of the regular army. We are not establishing or attempting to establish a regular force on the lines of the standing armies of even the small independent countries of Europe. If we undertake any such thing we shall fail.'

His experiences during the rising had convinced him that the Irish would always be beaten in 'static warfare', based on trench tactics or the seizure of buildings such as the GPO where he had spent that literally blazing week. The Irish would always be blasted out of their positions by the superior firepower of an enemy who possessed not only field pieces but other weapons such as mortars and heavy machine guns. This military reality put him in no mood to empathize with either de Valera's belief in the efficacy of pike training or his philosophical approach to combat. Instead he founded his own 'hit squad' of assassins to eliminate informers, and presided over the formation of an 'invisible army'. This army's main weapon, apart from its courage and dedication, was the incredible network of informants he built up at every level of British administration, ranging from Dublin Castle itself through the British Secret Service to the office of the head of Scotland Yard, Sir Basil Thompson.

There is an oft-repeated story about Collins which illustrates his attitude towards wearing uniforms. He was always neatly dressed himself, but far from lauding spit and polish he roasted a proud Volunteer officer who showed up in his office one day smartly dressed in the frequently worn leggings and raincoat of an IRA officer. 'What the ——— do you mean by coming up here looking like a ——— Volunteer Officer? Do you want to get yourself and us all arrested, you ———?' In a nutshell, if de Valera was inspired by Clausewitz Michael Collins built on the tactics of de Wet and the Boers in the South African War. But such differences were still far from coming to a head on a memorable day in Lincoln Jail when de Valera got word out to Collins complimenting him on the quality of the ingredients of a cake he had just received. In a real sense it contained a recipe for de Valera's success.

6

FROM LINCOLN TOWARDS
THE WHITE HOUSE

BY THIS STAGE of de Valera's incarceration, scruples about food parcels were a thing of the past. The cake in fact was the fourth in a series to be sent in to the jail. But this time it contained the correct type of blank key from which a master key to the prison's doors could be fashioned. Cakes of a high iron content had been passing into the jail since shortly after his birthday, 14 October 1918, when the prisoners had staged a concert for him. For not only had he waived his scruples about food parcels – leaving Lincoln, he decided, was worth a Mass. Accordingly he spent most of his time on the altar during a subsequent Sunday Mass trying to take the imprint of the prison chaplain's key on wax from melted down church candles. He had melted the wax before Mass, but it had cooled by the time he managed to slip off the altar into the sacristy where the priest left the key while saying Mass. He had to return to the altar and try warming the wax with the heat of his body. Eventually he succeeded and, without arousing suspicion, again left the altar and succeeded in taking impressions of the key.

The birthday concert had put into his mind a music hall song that ran: 'I couldn't get the latch key in – upon my word I couldn't'. He now got Sean Milroy, the prisoner who had done the artwork for the concert programme, to draw a seemingly innocent comic Christmas card. It showed another prisoner, Sean McGarry, trying drunkenly to fit a huge key into a tiny keyhole. A second drawing showed McGarry sitting in his prison cell looking at a very large keyhole. The captions to the pictures were 'Xmas 1917, can't get in' and 'Xmas 1918, can't get out'. De Valera then got yet another prisoner, John O'Mahony, to write out a note that he composed: 'The best wishes I can send are those de Valera wrote in my autograph book. (Field will translate).' Then de Valera wrote out in Irish the meaning of the card. The key in the picture was the prison key, the keyhole its cross-section. The plan showed typical de Valera attention to detail. The only problem was that 'Field', Michael Collins' codename, did not get the card; McGarry's wife seemingly failed to see the point, or at any rate did not pass it on.

Back at the Lincoln drawing board de Valera composed another note. This time he got one of the prisoners, Sam Flaherty, a classics student, to translate it into Latin. Again John O'Mahony sent it out, this time to a curate in Leeds, a Father Kavanagh. To make doubly sure de Valera accompanied it with a further note in Irish, drafted by him for Mrs McGarry, asking after the card and restating the instructions about the key. Irish proved no more efficacious than Latin. But on 10 January 1919 de Valera tried yet another piece of Latin in a further letter by John O'Mahony, and this time found a mark. The first key-bearing cake found its way into Lincoln. Gerry Boland, who was to prove one of de Valera's longest-serving comrades in their subsequent careers, had performed his first service for 'the Chief', as de Valera was now generally referred to by friends and followers.

Unfortunately it was not a very efficient service. The key did not work. Nor did a second which arrived in a cake two weeks later. More communication in Irish via Sean McGarry produced a third cake with a key blank for the prisoners to cut into the right size themselves. This was delivered to prison by Gerry Boland's brother Harry, Collins' closest comrade-in-arms at the time. But the blank itself was of the wrong design. Finally, six weeks after Milroy's Christmas card was sent, a woman's touch brought better fortune; Kathleen Talty, an Irish teacher, delivered a cake containing the correct type of blank.

Now at this stage it might be remarked that on one level all this trouble was unnecessary. From the time of the general election campaign of the previous year the prisoners had been expecting release, and, though disappointed at not being allowed out to take part in the actual election, de Valera had a shrewd suspicion that, once it was over, freedom lay around the corner. But he had a number of reasons for persevering with the escape plans: 'Indeed his great fear at this moment was that the Government might decide to release him before he could escape.'[1] He wanted to do as he had done with his campaign of destruction prior to the 1916 prisoners' release and deprive the British of any PR advantage which might accrue through freeing him. More importantly, he wanted to capitalize on the enormous publicity and morale-boosting bonanza which an escape would bring. Here he had a hidden agenda, which we will come to shortly.

The escape involved considerable risks for not just a few key personnel (no pun intended) but entire networks of helpers outside the jail. Collins personally supervised the setting up of a chain of safe-houses and the transportation. On the night of 3 February 1919, he and Boland cut their way through barbed wire entanglements on the jail's perimeter with the aid of a third man, Frank Kelly – who, however, got separated from them in the dark. Boland and Collins lay in a field outside the prison hoping that the prisoners had cut the key correctly, that de Valera would see their signal (a flash from Harry Boland's torch), and that they would be able to see his signalled reply (the glow from a fistful of matches). In the event, from an upstairs corridor, de Valera saw too much of their signal. Boland switched on his torch punctually at the appointed time, 7.40 sharp, but then found he could not get it to switch off again and finally had to put it in his pocket to avoid attention. Inside the jail the same sort of comic threat to the escape attempt occurred. De Valera and his two companions, Milroy and McGarry, found that the key turned perfectly in the various doors they came to. But one of Milroy's soles came loose from its upper and flapped noisily in Chaplinesque fashion as the trio tried to steal silently through the jail.

A more serious problem confronted them when they came to the final outer gate. Collins had brought a second duplicate key. But when he tried to open the gate from the outside it broke in the lock. Boland afterwards described the feeling of 'utter despair' that followed his hoarse 'I've broken the key in the lock, Dev.'[2] and stated that de Valera uttered an 'ejaculation'. Unfortunately history does not record what it was, but it definitely lacked 'lusciousness'. He did not lack self-control, however, and used his own key to push the broken one out. The rusted gate swung open with a grating sound that should have brought warders running, but the five made their way safely over the fields to Wragby Road. Ever a stickler for routine and procedures, de Valera later commented: 'I got out of Lincoln Jail through neglect of routine.'[3] In fact it was probably the diligent execution of some frequently performed routines that saved them when they reached Wragby Road. For here another threat loomed – several courting soldiers and nurses from the nearby military hospital. Fortunately, far from being neglectful, these were all engrossed in each other. The irrepressible Boland gave his heavy fur coat to de Valera, donned a light raincoat and, linking with de Valera as though they too were a courting couple, moved through the genuine pairs uttering unusually deep-voiced 'goodnights'.

The head of Collins' network in Manchester, Paddy O'Donoghue, had a taxi waiting for them outside a pub in Lincoln. This took the escapees to Worksop, where Collins and Boland caught a train to London. At Worksop O'Donoghue paid off the driver at a hotel, and then as soon as the taxi was gone, crossed the road to enter a taxi engaged by another Collins man, Fintan Murphy. Murphy had had to use his wits to get the taxi to take him and 'a party of friends' on the next leg of the journey, to Sheffield. There was a train from Worksop to Sheffield later in the evening and the driver was forbidden, under wartime petrol restrictions, to make a journey when public transport was available. However, by studying the train timetable Murphy was able to counter by saying that he and his friends had to be in Sheffield in time to catch a Manchester train, which left before the Worksop one arrived. The escapees arrived at Sheffield in their taxi without mishap.[4] Here the last link in Collins' chain, Liam MacMahon, was waiting to take them to Manchester in his own car. He took Milroy and McGarry home with him while O'Donoghue walked with de Valera to the presbytery of Father Charles O'Mahony. It was 12.05 on the morning of 4 February, exactly five minutes after Collins had planned that de Valera would arrive at Father O'Mahony's house – a remarkable logistical feat in enemy territory at a time of petrol and travel restrictions.

After about a week in Father O'Mahony's house he had to be moved again; one of Collins' friendly detectives had warned that the priest was under suspicion. Once more, Kathleen Talty provided the means of escape. De Valera was dressed in a uniform and then, fearing to take a taxi, he walked six or seven miles to his next safe house, in Victoria Park; Kathleen dutifully stepped out the distance arm in arm with her 'boyfriend'. Two weeks after he had escaped, on the 19th of the month, Collins had him smuggled back to Ireland. This time he was dressed as a priest and Kathleen Talty was accompanied by Paddy O'Donoghue and another girl, Mary Healy, when they picked him up in a taxi. They drove him to Liverpool, where he was put aboard the *Cambria* and stowed away in the second mate's cabin. In the small hours of 20 February he landed safely in Dublin where he was taken first to the home of Dr Bob Farnan in Merrion Square and then, a few days later, to a hiding place of Collins', an old whiskey distillery near the Archbishop's House in Drumcondra. The following night Father Curran sneaked him into the gatekeeper's lodge in the Archbishop's grounds. De Valera was safely back in Dublin – for the moment.

While he was in jail, just after the birthday concert that had given him the idea of escaping, de Valera wrote to Sinead:[5] 'One of my resolutions on the 14th was that I would strive to be more with you and the children in the future than in the past – but these matters are in God's hands.' And in the interpolations he made to a letter which Sinead wrote to him around this time he would appear to repeat this resolution. Sinead, of course, was thrilled by his escape, which devastated the British authorities as much as it delighted the Irish. Once word had broken of his departure from Lincoln special stop press editions of the Irish papers were issued, and de Valera sightings were reported from Paris to Skibbereen. Warrants for his arrest were issued in Amsterdam after he was authoritatively reported to be in Holland. The publicity bonanza he had hoped for was everything he had dreamed of and more. But there was a hidden cost to it all – the subtraction from his family's happiness. Sinead's letter, and his comments on it, give an indication of the pain occasioned by separation:[6]

> *a cuaisle mo chroide ba mait liom pudin beog a beit speid agam ma tagann aon beal mait.* It is much to know you are well and so well looked after. Try and take some rest. Of late I am a bit anxious that you do not take sufficient rest. Get regular sleep no matter what happens. I love the people who take such care of you. Mind that you eat well. You mustn't want to come back to your poor *maitrin* at all. [De Valera underlined all this sentence.] Don't let all the interests put me out of your heart. It is petty and selfish of me but I hate to think of my not being necessary for your happiness. And yet how little we really talked for all the years of our married life! Sometimes I get an awful longing to see you. [De Valera underlined 'longing' and interjected: 'Nothing to mine I'm certain.'] I know, dear darling, the part that God asks of me is to wait and it is an easy part compared with others but oh: it is lonely to have a husband and yet not have one. [De Valera underlined 'it is lonely . . .' and interjected: 'what would I not give to be able to see you.']

I know it is hard for you *a stoir* for you cannot see the children. I have my beloved little Emer in my arms and all the rest around me. Eamon has a beautiful disposition. He told me the other day there was no mudder like me. Mairin is lovely with the little ones. She is very clever. Fr. Flavin thinks she is 'the pick of the basket.' Brian is a very determined self-reliant character. This morning he got up and partly dressed himself. He says he will do the same in the morning and mummy will say 'Bravo'. When we ask Brian and Ruaidhri 'where is Daddy?' they say he yan [*sic*] away from pris pris. The day we heard you were in Paris poor Viv. was rather in a state. 'But mumie', said he, if he is in Paris he'll have no house to be in.

A picture man called the other day asking me to let me [*sic*] to take my picture and the children's for the screen. He was from the picture house in Brunswick St. 'Irish events'. You should hear him arguing, what value as propagandist work etc. . . . . And really it was hardly known de Valera had a wife at all and so on. Well I needn't tell you I gave a very decided but polite refusal to be pictured [de Valera underlined from 'Well' . . . to 'pictured' and wrote in the margin 'Good girl'.] When I told Viv. he seemed a bit sorry to miss the excitement. 'I suppose', said he he'd have made a comic picture of us. As I remarked to see the pictures would be bound to be comic no matter with what serious intention it was produced. I don't know whether I should waste your time with such trifles. I know your mind must be occupied with very big things just now. [Here de Valera interjected: 'But nothing can shut you out darling.] *Eire a muirsan*. Let no thought of me or the children interfere with your work. I am thinking of a number of quotations I collected and wrote down before I saw you *a maican*. They all bear on the same subject. 'I could not love you dear so much Loved I not honour more' and heaps of others. One passage from Tone's diary dealing with this subject is particularly fine. I like reading Mitchel and the others about their wives. Anything I read now I want to show you and yet when you are here how little we talk. God grant when you come home again that we may live more in each others lives. [Here de Valera wrote: 'I was thinking of writing of just this same thing.']

The children mean a lot to me – *buideceas mor le dea go bfuilid agam*, but no one my darling Dev can take your place. At dinner time the children were asking what part of the bird I'd eat. As I said the one that would pick the choice bits for me was not here. I remember a remark a country woman made to me. 'The old man I was married to for twenty six years, he'd peel the potatoe and slip it on my plate as well. I've ne'r a child will do that for me. Pray Dev dear that we'll be left together and if it's God's will and all right for the children that there won't be long between our deaths. That was one thing made me think it was easier for the mothers than the wives of the executed men. The older women in the ordinary course of events hadn't so long to wait. Perhaps Dev my birthday gift may come in June. Don't you know Dev that I love you and that it is only I think it nicer not to try see you that I don't go. Pray for us all I hope you can go to Confession. Won't you go regularly. With all my heart's love,

Sinead.

Obviously at that stage in their relationship the de Valeras had a strong, albeit inarticulate, attachment towards each other. And obviously, too, Sinead was prepared to put her own feelings to one side for the sake of the cause; but she would surely have been thunderstruck if she could have attended the first meeting of the Volunteer GHQ to take place after her husband made his escape. The principal business of the meeting was expected to be Michael Collins' account of the escape and how it might be capitalized on when de Valera got back to Ireland. Instead, the group were informed that de Valera was not coming back. He intended to go to America.

A half-century after his escape, de Valera obviously realized that his decision to go to America was not well thought out. He acknowledged this in his biography in characteristic fashion – by making no mention of the furore that his announcement caused. Pieras Beaslai was present at the meeting when Collins reported, after making his way back to Ireland having spent thirty-six hours without either food or sleep:[7]

> The statement was received by all of us with dismay. We felt that de Valera's departure would be a fatal mistake, that the country would misunderstand his motives and regard it as selfish, or even cowardly, desertion. When this view was expressed, Collins replied, 'I told him so, but you know what is to try to argue with Dev. He says he had thought it all out in prison and that he feels that the one place where he can be useful to Ireland is in America.' The meeting took the view that the place for an Irish leader was in Ireland where the strength of the fight put up would determine the support in America, and it was decided to send Brugha to England to urge de Valera either not to go at all or, failing that, to show himself first in Ireland so that the publicity value of his escape should not be dissipated.

Brugha duly went to England and succeeded in his mission of getting de Valera to show his face in Ireland first before going to the USA. Collins arranged a 'safe house' for him – the gate lodge of the Archbishop's house in Drumcondra. The version authorized by de Valera in his biography makes it appear that the Brugha mission was concerned solely with bringing de Valera up-to-date on developments in Ireland, and in particular on getting his views on a plan to assassinate British Cabinet ministers. The de Valera version is that it was only after Brugha's two-day visit on 7–9 February that: 'He began to think that the place he could best work for Ireland was in the USA where he could bring Irish-American pressure to bear on President Wilson.'[8] But Mary Bromage, whose foreword claims an acquaintanceship with de Valera extending for twenty years before she wrote her biography, indicates that he was so keen to get to the USA that he tried to get there without waiting for Collins to make the necessary arrangements: 'The hazards to which Dev exposed himself by one abortive attempt to leave for America left Collins aghast.'[9]

The reason Cathal Brugha wanted to get de Valera's sanction for assassinating British Cabinet ministers lay in an important step taken by Sinn Fein while de Valera was still in jail. Following the party's electoral success in December it had been decided to convene an Irish Parliament or Dail, as it was known in Irish, and to invite to its first sitting all the Irish representatives at liberty to attend, including Unionists and members of the Irish Parliamentary Party. History does not record what Carson said when he received his invitation, but needless to say there was no response when his name was called, nor to those of the other Unionists or members of the Irish Party. These were all marked '*as lathair*', absent, as indeed they incontrovertibly were. Another large segment of absentees, in the ranks of Sinn Fein itself, were either marked '*ar dibirt ag gallaibh*' (deported by the foreigner) or '*fe glas ag gallaibh*' (jailed by the foreigner). Collins' and Boland's names had been answered as if they were present, but in reality they were absent in England, working on de Valera's escape. In fact there were only 28 deputies present out of the 104 names called. But they transacted some very serious business indeed, adopting a Democratic Programme, sending a Message to the Free Nations of the World and making a Declaration of Independence which contained a virtual declaration of war:[10]

> We the elected representatives of the ancient Irish people in the national Parliament assembled do, in the name of the Irish nation, ratify the establishment of the Irish Republic and pledge ourselves and our people to make this Declaration effective by every means at our command.
>
> We ordain that the elected representatives of the Irish people alone have power to make laws binding on the people of Ireland, and that the Irish Parliament is the only Parliament to which people will give allegiance.
>
> We solemnly declare foreign government in Ireland to be an invasion of our national right which we will never tolerate, and we demand the evacuation of our country by the English.

The Democratic Programme of the first Dail was probably influenced by the fact that the 'German plot' had removed so many of Sinn Fein's conservative leaders to jail. A distinct whiff of socialism emanated from the document. It stated that 'all right to private property must be subordinated to the public right and welfare'. Furthermore, 'every citizen' was deemed entitled to 'an adequate share of the produce of the Nation's labour'.[11] In practice no subsequent Irish administration has ever shown itself to be unduly inspired by these principles. Brugha's proposal to shoot up Westminster was intended as a retaliation to the expected British reaction to the Declaration of Independence rather than to the Democratic Programme. De Valera seems to have given Brugha no guidance on the matter. His biography states: '. . . de Valera did not feel called upon to argue the question too closely since it was not an immediate issue'.[12] But a very potent underlining of the significance of the Declaration of Independence occurred at Soloheadbeg in Co. Tipperary as the Dail was sitting: a party of Volunteers raiding for gelignite shot and killed two RIC men guarding the explosives. From that day on the Volunteers increasingly came to be referred to as the Irish Republican Army or IRA.

De Valera did not have to spend many days in hiding in the Archbishop's grounds before being smuggled back to Liverpool to be stowed away on a ship for America. However, while he was in Liverpool the flu epidemic which was sweeping Europe had an unexpectedly beneficial side-effect on Sinn Fein. Pierce MacCan's death caused such resentment in Ireland that the authorities agreed to act on the advice of the prison doctor at

Gloucester, who said that the place was not suitable for coping with an influenza epidemic, and released all the Irish prisoners. These included Arthur Griffith, who had contracted flu in Gloucester but recovered. Griffith was hardly back in Dublin before he found himself confronted by another sort of headache. The saga of de Valera's trip to the USA had been interrupted yet again at the instigation of Michael Collins. This time Collins involved the entire Sinn Fein executive in a heated controversy.

Acting on the release of the prisoners – which he reasoned, correctly, would mean that the authorities would now call off the hunt for the Lincoln escapees – Collins placed public notices in the press announcing a huge civic reception for de Valera at the end of March. The plan called for a presentation of the keys of the city to de Valera on Mount Street Bridge by the Lord Mayor, Laurence O'Neill. De Valera liked the idea, and returned from Liverpool prepared to deliver a suitably fiery speech at the scene of Malone's heroism. However, the British banned the meeting and this touched off a fierce debate in Sinn Fein. On the one hand were those like Collins, who argued that to call off the meeting in the face of a threat would be to suffer a historic moral defeat equivalent to that inflicted on Daniel O'Connell when he cancelled a monster meeting at Clontarf because of a similar démarche. On the other hand the constitutionalists within the party, such as Darrell Figgis, argued that to defy the authorities' ban would be to jeopardize people's lives. Moreover, there was the point that Collins had placed the advertisement in the papers without the authority of the executive.

Griffith presided over the meeting held to sort out the row and, after he had consulted with de Valera, the latter withdrew his assent to the reception proposal in the following terms:[13] 'I think you will all agree with me that the present occasion is scarcely one on which we would be justified in risking the lives of citizens. I am certain we would not. . . . We who have waited know how to wait. Many a heavy fish is caught even with a fine line if the angler is patient.'

De Valera 'was very firm on the withdrawal', as Collins wrote disappointedly to another prominent nationalist, Austin Stack.[14] He was prepared to go to war if needs be, but de Valera was more disposed to go to America. 'The necessity for an American mission was never fully out of his mind', was how his biography put it.[15] What Sinead made of this 'necessity' we are not told. No hint of the yearnings of separation evidenced by their correspondence was allowed to appear in the public record. 'His wife surmised that he would never be content to go back to teaching' was the denatured response of one writer describing Sinead's reaction after he arrived home.[16] 'I could not love thee dear so much. . . .'

Between the Lincoln escapade and his departure to America in June de Valera caught up on both his family and his political activities, the latter in ways that were to have repercussions long after he had departed. Throughout March, apart from making the acquaintanceship of his new daughter, Emer, and marvelling at how the other children had grown, he devoted some of his time to drawing up a message to the Paris Peace Conference; and for the rest occupied himself by walking, receiving visitors and giving newspaper interviews. When one reporter asked him what was the truth of his involvement in the 'German plot' his response was literally Manichean. He began by giving the hypothetical example of his kidnapping the Chief Secretary on some vague, unproven charge 'like adultery'. But then he decided the example might be offensive. Instead he suggested that the reporter should suppose that he, de Valera, 'were to accuse Mr Shortt of dealing with the Devil'. At this he bethought himself of St Augustine and the Manichean heresy and told the reporter: 'That example should perhaps appeal to the English more. Though they do know that adultery exists, they are not quite so sure about the devil.'

De Valera himself permitted a little uncertainty to creep into the title of an important position which he assumed shortly afterwards on a date which some critics were afterwards tempted to invest with a certain symbolism. On 1 April, All Fools' Day, he was elected President of Dail Eireann. This title was rendered in Irish as Priomh Aire, which in English means First Minister. But before the summer was out he was being introduced to America as the 'President of the Irish Republic', a designation which would later have considerable implications for Ireland. As Priomh Aire he selected a Cabinet. Michael Collins became Minister for Finance, Arthur Griffith got Home Affairs, Cathal Brugha, who had been Priomh Aire, was appointed to Defence, W. T. Cosgrave to Local Government, Eoin MacNeill to Industry, Robert Barton to Agriculture and, at Labour, Countess Markievicz became the first woman Cabinet minister in either Ireland or England. This 'Government' immediately began trying to enforce its authority throughout the country and elsewhere. Michael Collins was empowered to float a National Loan, and plans were put in train for Sinn Fein courts and Sinn Fein county councils to take over the administration of justice and local government from the British. Dr McCartan was appointed to the Irish 'Embassy' in Washington and Sean T. O'Ceallaigh got a similar posting to Paris.[17]

Two statements made to the Dail by de Valera at this time deserve to be noted. In a reference to the Democratic Programme he effectively downgraded the priority of achieving its socialist aims by saying: ' . . . while the enemy was within their gates, the immediate question was to get possession of their country'. The other would literally have more deadly effect. The principal instrument of control used by the British in Ireland was the armed Royal Irish Constabulary – the force which had 'placed many of the Sinn Fein leaders in prison',[18] including himself, though he did not draw attention to this. As the state of unrest grew within the country, the RIC was daily coming into more and more abrasive contact with the population. Accordingly, therefore, de Valera proposed that 'members of the police forces acting in this country as part of the forces of the British

132

occupation and as agents of the British Government be ostracised socially by the people'. Eoin MacNeill seconded the motion in inflammatory terms: 'The police in Ireland are a force of traitors, and the police in Ireland are a force of perjurers.' It was carried unanimously.[19] Before long the 'ostracism' of 'traitors' and 'perjurers' would take fatal form.

De Valera had been nominated a delegate to the Paris Peace Conference at the first Dail session. The problem about this appointment, as with many other decisions taken by the first Dail, was that the British were likely to object strongly to it. With the British objecting, neither the Americans nor the French would or could entertain the idea of an Irish presence at the Conference. Article 10 of the Covenant of the League of Nations stated: 'The High Contracting Powers undertake to respect and preserve against external aggression the territorial integrity and existing political independence of all State members of the League. In case of any such aggression the Executive Council shall advise upon the means by which this obligation shall be fulfilled.'

The difficulty of being recognized internationally had been illustrated for Sinn Fein early in the New Year. Collins, Sean T. O'Ceallaigh and George Gavan Duffy had all taken part in an unsuccessful attempt to have a meeting with Woodrow Wilson as he passed through London on his way to Paris for the opening of the Conference. Nevertheless the securing of international recognition was a cardinal principle of the party's constitutional policy and accordingly, ten days after de Valera appointed his Cabinet, on 12 April, the Dail approved the following motion, proposed by Cosgrave and seconded by Collins:

The elected parliament and Government of the Irish Republic pledge the active support of the Irish Nation in translating into deed the principles enunciated by the President of the U.S. at Washington's Tomb on 4 July, 1918, and wholeheartedly accepted [by America]. We are eager and ready to enter a World League of Nations based on equality of rights, in which the guarantees exchanged neither recognise nor imply a difference between big nations and small, between those that are powerful and those that are weak. We are willing to accept all the duties, responsibilities and burdens which inclusion in such a League implies.

The motion was clearly in conflict with Article 10. Britain recognized Ireland as part of the 'territorial integrity' of the United Kingdom, not as an independent republic. And it was known that the Article was going to form part of the Peace Treaty which would emerge from the Conference. However, on 26 May de Valera, Griffith and Count Plunkett signed a letter to the French Prime Minister, Clemenceau, President of the Peace Conference, formally asking that Ireland be recognized as an independent state. De Valera was fairly certain that the request would be turned down, and equally certain that he would not be in Ireland when Clemenceau's reply was received. He was merely writing for the record. He had made up his mind to go to America to appeal to the American public 'over the head of President Wilson'.[20] Three days after de Valera sent his letter to France Collins sent off another missive, this time to one of his contacts in England, Steve Lanigan of Liverpool. It said:[21] 'I am writing to you on a most important matter, and one that may be very very urgent. We have decided here that the time is just about ripe for Dev. to get away to America, and we are therefore putting the arrangements in your hands.'

Not everyone in Sinn Fein thought the time 'just about ripe' for de Valera to leave the country. The Secretary of Sinn Fein, Padraig O'Caoimh, told a story[22] of being taken aside by de Valera one day shortly before he left and asked: 'Paddy, did you hear they're sending me to America?' To which O'Keefe said he replied: 'Be jasus they are not. It's your own ———— idea to get over there out of the trouble.' O'Caoimh's imputation of motive we may disregard, but he was certainly correct about the trip being de Valera's idea. De Valera himself wanted posterity to be clear on that much. His official biography says:[23]

> While in hiding de Valera had had considerable difficulty in deciding where he could best serve Ireland. He saw that great work could be done, at that time, both outside and inside the country. He had returned to Ireland so as to be available to present the Irish cause to the Peace Conference. If the statesmen in Paris refused to receive him and other Irish representatives, it would be clear to the world that all their altruistic professions were no more than a wartime ruse to delude their own people. . . . President de Valera decided to revert to his original plan of going to America and appealing to the people above the head of President Wilson.

This description of reverting to 'the original plan' of course overlooks two facts: Brugha had to be sent to urge him to come home after Lincoln, and the reason for his second visit to Dublin was not to be available for the Peace Conference but in order to receive the keys of the city at Mount Street Bridge. Harry Boland had been sent to the USA to prepare for his arrival a month before he drafted the letter to Clemenceau.[24] However, unaware of all this, on the morning of Sunday, 1 June 1919 the de Valera children were planning to celebrate Sinead's birthday when Collins knocked on the door with the news that the Chief would have to leave immediately.

7

PRIOMH AIRE MEETS
GALLOWGLASS

LANIGAN'S MESSENGER FROM Liverpool, a seaman called Dick O'Neill, had arrived in Dublin that morning to inform Collins that arrangements had been made to smuggle de Valera to the USA. 'They both went immediately to Greystones to interview de Valera.'[1] He was out walking, but when he returned 'Collins had no difficulty in persuading the President to take advantage of the opportunity.'[2] We are not told what difficulties Sinead encountered on hearing this bolt from the blue. After leaving home, de Valera had time to see some members of the Cabinet before setting off for America via England. Along the way he also managed to dash off a note to Sinead on a page torn from a notebook:[3]

2-vi-19

> A cuisle – I hope you were not too anxious yesterday – it may be the beginning of that birthday gift you prayed for. I have made arrangements with Sean Nunan to put to your account whatever is left after certain payments are made with the exception of £25.
> I trust you will not allow yourself to be lonely. It will be but for a short time. I have only a minute or two. Kiss the children. DeV.
> La gradh mor aron de.

The Irish political landscape was lowering with thunder clouds of Wagnerian proportions as de Valera set off from Greystones. Offences like illegal speech-making or drilling were being countered by such vigorous applications of DORA that arrests[4] had shot up above the four-figure mark in 1918 and were being added to with every day that passed since the first Dail met. Bayonet and baton charges were frequent, and the rolls of the 'Republican University' were swelling in both England and Ireland. The suppression of newspapers was commonplace. It was obvious that the 'naked swords' must soon clash, and clash they duly did. The month after de Valera crossed the Atlantic, his motion on the treatment of the RIC was translated into action by Collins' hit team, the Squad. A well-known Dublin detective, 'The Dog' Smith, a prominent member of the RIC's political section, the G-Division, was 'ostracized'[5] – with extreme prejudice. Several of his colleagues would share his fate before de Valera returned to Ireland.

But his departure was less Wagnerian than *opera buffa*. Collins had arranged that he should cross to England on the Holyhead boat from Dun Laoghaire, to be smuggled aboard the SS *Lapland* in Liverpool. His cover story was that he was going to visit Austin Stack in Manchester Jail. But on leaving Dun Laoghaire he was recognized by the prison chaplain who had attended him in Kilmainham in 1916, Father MacCarthy.[6] The priest wanted him to come to his stateroom to meet his travelling companion, an old Blackrock man, Sir James MacMahon, the Under Secretary for Ireland. Father MacCarthy thought that Sir James would be delighted to help his fellow alumnus and ex-fellow member of the Blackrock branch of St Vincent de Paul to gain access to Manchester Jail. De Valera was quite certain Sir James would, if he discovered that he was trying to slip out of England illegally, without a passport, to cause trouble in America. So, with difficulty, he declined Father MacCarthy's kind offer.

The prison chaplain was not the only one to recognize the gangling de Valera. When he and Dick O'Neill arrived in Chester they found detectives shadowing them. They thereupon took the Great Western Line as if heading for Birkenhead, but on arriving found themselves still under surveillance. They then doubled back across the Mersey to Liverpool and took a taxi unobserved to the home of Collins' head man in Liverpool, Steve Lanigan. But Lanigan was not there! He had gone to where de Valera had been supposed to arrive, Edgehill Station. It was three o'clock in the morning before he got home to find the missing Priomh Aire waiting for him. He was not there long.

At six o'clock de Valera was aboard a workmen's tram heading for the *Lapland* where another Collins man, Barney Downes, the ship's bosun, was waiting to slip him aboard as one of his newly signed-on seamen. O'Neill made de Valera carry his bag going through the docks. 'He was dressed up like a sailor, with a dark muffler around his neck. He looked very haggard and looked the part of a rather rough looking character.'[7] No sooner was he aboard than the ship was raided by detectives – not, it turned out, looking for him, but for a soldier who had killed his sweetheart. But by the time this was discovered, de Valera had been hidden 'in the bottom of the ship, rat infested – but free from detectives'. He had to stay there from seven in the morning until midnight. By the time he was brought back up on deck the rats had eaten through his jacket to get at a cheese sandwich. For the rest of the voyage he was placed in the lamplighter's cabin where amidst the lamps, wicks, ropes and other impedimenta a special bunk had been set up for him. The lamp-trimmer was a tough character, nicknamed 'the Arab' because he had grown up on the streets of San Francisco, without parents. His early experiences had left him with a hatred of policemen. Downes played on this hatred by telling him that de Valera was his cousin, fleeing to America because he had killed two policemen. The Arab took to de Valera immediately.

However, the friendly welcome failed to preserve the stowaway Priomh

Aire from seasickness. By the third day de Valera was 'deathly sick' and it began to appear that to save his life his cover would have to be blown and the ship's doctor informed. Then, at midnight on the third day without food, de Valera himself suggested that perhaps some brandy might save him. By that time the ship's bars were closed, but the bosun bethought himself of a shipment of 'special brandy' that he had seen coming aboard destined for a New York hospital. The key to the hold where the brandy was stored was kept in the mate's cabin. The bosun managed to steal this unobserved and sent the Arab for the brandy. The Arab, who liked liquor as much as he hated policemen, was delighted to oblige. He returned, 'smiling', with a case of twenty-four bottles. 'A few drops helped to bring the Chief around and after that he practically lived on Bovril until we reached New York. The Arab took a great liking to the Chief . . . and never tired of asking for details of how he shot the two cops.'

Though de Valera recovered, his trip almost proved fatal for an old sailor who had taken to hanging out his laundry close to the hiding-place. The Irishmen began to suspect him and the Arab offered to toss the sailor overboard. His offer was on the point of being taken up when the bosun thought of another way of solving the problem: '. . . we moved his clothes out of there and he never came back. . . .'

De Valera's cabin was normally kept locked from the outside. His state of mind throughout the trip may be gauged from his reaction to the bosun discovering one day that he had brought the wrong key to his cabin. He whispered this information through the keyhole and then went to get the right key. But de Valera misheard him. When the bosun came back he found that he had picked the lock, disconnected the light and disappeared to another hiding-place, thinking that something was wrong.

In New York O'Neill and Downes hunted up Harry Boland, who 'nearly had a fit when he found whom he had on board. He knew nothing about his coming over. In fact no one in New York knew about it.' At ten o'clock on the evening of 11 June 1919 de Valera 'just walked off the boat as a sailor, with a heaving line in his hand. Dressed in my boatswain's jacket I went to the gate with him. I then hurried back to change into my street clothes while he waited for me in a drug store in 23rd St.' At the corner of 11th Avenue and East 14th Street de Valera was handed over to Harry Boland and the prominent Clan na nGael leader, Joseph McGarrity from Carrickmore, Co. Tyrone.

To give him a chance of freshening up the pair first took him to a room on East 39th Street. It was rented by Liam Mellows, who had been in the USA since leading an uprising in Galway during 1916. But despite the hardships of the voyage, de Valera's powers of recuperation were such as to make a powerful impression on McGarrity in particular. 'A man who can do that must be a great guy,'[8] he said after hearing the details of the trip, and took him home with him to his large house in Chestnut Street, Philadelphia. It was the start of a friendship that was to last for a decade and a half, until McGarrity finally came to accept that de Valera was no longer heading in the same direction that first took him to Chestnut Street. A few days after he landed, while he was still incommunicado so far as the press was concerned, de Valera met another man from whom he would also part, although sooner and in more spectacular fashion – Judge Daniel Cohalan.

Cohalan was an old-style Irish American politician of the 'bossism', Tammany Hall school. He and the aging John Devoy, a legendary figure in the history of Irish revolutionary secret societies, ran the Clan na nGael in New York, which, coupled with the fact that Devoy controlled the powerful *Gaelic American* newspaper, meant that their influence carried great weight in the organization throughout the country. Cohalan gave a party for the newly arrived Priomh Aire at which he was introduced to the leading figures of the Clan. He showed them his 'little testament of the Republic'.[9] It consisted of a pamphlet put out by Sinn Fein describing the proceedings of the first Dail into which he had pasted the 1916 proclamation, the Constitution of Sinn Fein and the party's 1918 election manifesto. 'He had also brought with him, some reported, Machiavelli's *Prince*.'[10]

McGarrity, described by Padraic Colum as 'a Donegal gallowglass ready to swing a battleaxe with his long arms', was de Valera's best ally in the USA. Both he and his friend, Patrick McCartan, were born in Carrickmore, Co. Tyrone, which even to this day is one of the most republican parts of Northern Ireland. His was a classic American success story.[11] Arriving in the USA at the age of sixteen, he made fortunes in the liquor and real estate businesses and went broke on at least two occasions, probably through devoting so much time to Irish affairs that he could not keep an eye on his partners. Each time, however, he bounced back to prosperity. In his personal and business life McGarrity might appear simply to be a successful businessman who wrote poetry, collected books and was also a devout Catholic who practised what he preached through his family life and multifarious charities. But politically he was a lifelong revolutionary whose devotion to physical force as the means of bringing about an Irish republic caused the IRA to issue their statements over the pseudonym 'Joe McGarrity' for years after his death. His devotion to the Priomh Aire was such that he christened one of his sons de Valera McGarrity.

Prior to de Valera's arrival he and McCartan had been having a certain amount of difference with the Cohalan–Devoy faction, allegedly over the latter's tendency to agitate within the American system for self-determination for Ireland rather than trumpet the republic as they did in McGarrity's *Irish Press*, which McCartan edited. How much of this was a power struggle between McGarrity and Cohalan, a man who shared something of de Valera's sense of infallibility, and how much it represented the tendency of Irish political, and particularly republican, movements to split is a moot point. As a race, the Irish are quicker to recognize an insult than love. Brendan Behan once proved the point about truth often being spoken in jest. A voluntary group had agreed unanimously to adjourn for a drink to seal a bargain to forget all past differences in the cause of refurbishing Kilmainham Jail as a national monument, free of cost, as part of the commemoration ceremonies for the fiftieth anniversary of the 1916 Rising. Behan startled them by raising an objection. 'Be Jasus yiz fucking won't!' he interjected. 'Yiz are meant to be Republicans and here yiz are agreeing to paint, to plaster, to do everythin' in fucking harmony. Now yiz are all agreeing to go for a drink. We're meant to be Republicans: we'll *have* to have a split. . . . '[12]

Devoy might well be described as a 'difficult man', but he could not be regarded as less of a republican than de Valera. He had built up the Clan in the USA following his release from prison in 1871. Amongst his exploits were the rescue of Fenian prisoners from Western Australia aboard the whaler *Catalpa*, and the promotion of the New Departure, which placed the Clan behind Parnell and Michael Davitt in the struggle that ultimately defeated landlordism. In 1900 he managed to unite the Clan behind a demand for an Irish republic after a long-running internal feud over the dynamiting campaign in England which put Tom Clarke in jail. And it was he and Cohalan who had helped to bring about the 1916 Rising. But by the time de Valera arrived in America he was getting old and relied increasingly on Cohalan's advice. Michael Collins watched uneasily from afar. He had had considerable dealings with Devoy over IRB matters, and months before the trouble burst into the open wrote to a member of de Valera's entourage warning against the way things were going:[13] 'From the very beginning and indeed prior to anybody going out I knew very well what to expect from the people in command in the USA. However, the best not the worst must be made of them, and there is little doubt that eventually things will be all right.' But de Valera was not in the mood for making the best of things; as he would later demonstrate in Ireland, he had a talent for forming alliances with those opposed to his opponents. During his stay in America he joined forces with McGarrity against the Cohalan–Devoy faction, thereby leading to a split in the Irish American movement.

It was arranged that de Valera would burst upon an amazed world via a press conference at the Waldorf Astoria Hotel on 23 June. Meanwhile, as the Clan and Harry Boland cranked up the publicity machine, he went to visit his mother in Rochester. By now Charlie was retired and the couple lived comfortably enough on his pension in their own home, 18 Brighton Street, a 'pretty wooden bungalow . . . in a long avenue of framehouses'.[14] Brighton Street itself was described as being 'a block or two off the main thoroughfare'.[15] Kate was then in her sixties, dressed in black, white-haired and somewhat stooped, but still vigorous. She made him welcome, as did Charlie – who, however, threatened to break the publicity embargo by dropping heavy-handed hints to the neighbours that he knew where to find the famous Sinn Fein escapologist whom the papers were talking about. Boland had told reporters that de Valera would be at the Waldorf Astoria on the 23rd at 'five-thirty on the dot'[16] – and rather unwisely dared them to find him in the meantime.

It would be fascinating to know what mother and son had to say to each other. The once-abandoned son had passed through the crucible of revolution and condemned cell to become a figure of international status since last they had met. Yet he obviously felt sufficiently strongly towards his mother to risk spoiling the publicity arrangements through premature disclosure of his whereabouts by visiting her at that sensitive stage in the tour. For her part Kate would obviously have taken pride in her son's achievement, but did she also feel any pang of regret that it had been made possible because she had left him in Ireland? Whatever was said, Rochester must have been a pleasant interlude. He had a cluster of cousins in the area, and his Aunt Hannie too had children living close by. One of them, Mary Connolly, added to Charlie's indiscretions by dropping in for an unexpected visit to No. 18 and then racing round the clan to announce who was staying with Auntie Kate. De Valera himself spread the information net even wider by travelling to Boston to spend a Sunday with his half-brother Father Thomas Wheelright. And then the serious business began, as planned, on 23 June 1919.

Before discussing those events it is important to understand something of the two worlds within which de Valera operated: the world of President Wilson and the world of Irish Americana. De Valera was taken out of Bruree, but was Bruree ever fully taken out of de Valera? For all the international awareness which had brought him to America, there was a great gulf fixed between Woodrow Wilson and Eamon de Valera. One immediately appreciates the extent of that gulf if one visits the de Valera home in Co. Limerick, now preserved as a museum, and compares it with any one of the four houses that Wilson lived in during his Princeton years.

For example, No. 75 Library Place is by no means a grand establishment by the standard of the University. But one could place the entire Bruree dwelling in the drawing room and still have plenty of room left to serve the coffee. And one is struck not merely by the difference in scale – the difference in ambience is even greater. When the architect Ralph Adams Cram was given the task of redesigning Princeton, his brief was to model the new university on Oxford and Cambridge. And so today Gothic spires dream over the New Jersey countryside. But it is not merely the Oxbridge architecture that is replicated; the style of this elite intellectual powerhouse, as of so much of decision-taking America, was literally British. During his teaching career and presidency of the University between 1902 and 1910, a time when the young de Valera was moving from Blackrock to Rockwell to Carysfort to anti-British nationalism, Wilson's outlook was inevitably permeated by his surroundings and origins. The British Ambassador in Washington described him as being 'by descent an

Orangeman and by education a Presbyterian'.[17] He had a natural affection for the British culture which de Valera and his associates were trying to eradicate in their own country. De Valera was said, by his son Terry, to have been one of the few mathematicians in the world capable of understanding Einstein's theory of relativity. Perhaps he did, and if he had chanced to come to Princeton during the holocaust period he could have discussed the theory with Einstein himself. The great scientist had been attracted to Princeton not only for reasons of sanctuary, but by standards of excellence which Woodrow Wilson helped to found and maintain while de Valera was still cycling about on 'totty twigging' expeditions.

Apart from any reasons of personal sympathy Wilson needed British support in several important areas, particularly for the success of the League of Nations of which he was the principal architect. Here, however, his policy clashed head on with that of the majority of Irish Americans of Catholic and nationalist origin. They were strongly isolationist and suspicious of the League, which they saw as being a creature of WASP imperialists liable to involve America in foreign wars. To them the Treaty of Versailles fell between two stools, neither creating a new world order nor restoring the old.

The broad-based popular front of Irish nationalism was the Friends of Irish Freedom, founded after a two-day Irish Race Convention in Chicago on 4–5 March 1916. Its first President was Victor Herbert, the composer, and Judge John D. Moore became its Secretary (two of his sons, Richard and John D. Junior, became American Ambassadors to Ireland). But behind this respectable leadership the Clan na nGael acted as did its Irish counterpart, the IRB, infiltrating the organization and wielding *de facto* control of it. The Clan, led by Devoy and McGarrity, believed that Irish independence would only be won by physical force and were quite willing to accept support from Germany to further that policy; this Wilson regarded as treason.

His negative feelings were added to by the fact that the normally solidly pro-Democrat Irish Americans voted against him. The Irish vote was largely concentrated in cities and generally 'delivered' on a block basis, at the behest of local politicians. Wilson, though he won a convincing overall majority, only carried two of the States with large Irish populations – California and Ohio. However, America's entry to the war on 6 April 1917 meant that the Clan had to keep its head under the parapet for the duration. But once the war ended, Irish Americans again became active. On 4 March 1919 the House of Representatives passed by 216 votes to 45 a motion in the name of Thomas Gallagher of Illinois, saying 'That it is the earnest hope of the Congress of the United States of America that the Peace Conference now sitting in Paris and passing upon the claims of various peoples will favourably consider the claims of Ireland to self-determination.'

The resolution was passed early in the morning and so did not receive

Senate endorsement. Moreover, Wilson's supporters made it abundantly clear that it was an embarrassment to a President setting off to Paris. Ireland was not a victorious Allied power, nor a defeated nation, but part of Britain, America's most cherished ally. Nevertheless the importance of the resolution was exaggerated in Irish circles to the extent that one pro-de Valera historian wrote: 'The American people had instructed their President to support Ireland's claim.'[18] How far this was from the reality was borne out on the night the resolution was passed. Wilson was finally prevailed upon to meet a delegation of Irish Americans. Another Irish Race Convention had been held a few weeks earlier, on 21–22 February, and Wilson was prepared to accept the resolutions adopted at this meeting. But he was not prepared to receive them from the hand of Judge Daniel Cohalan, and only agreed to see the delegation when the judge withdrew. Cohalan had campaigned against his nomination for the presidency at the 1912 Democratic Convention in Baltimore; Wilson 'had a long memory and he never forgave or forgot'.[19]

The President was further irritated when he discovered that he was expected not merely to accept resolutions but to press Irish claims to be heard at the Peace Conference. He repeated the arguments against this course, but was more disposed to further another of the Race Convention's proposals – that a three-man delegation be appointed to go from America to the Peace Conference to lobby that Ireland's case be heard. Arrangements were made to issue the three with passports to travel to Ireland and France. The delegates were Frank P. Walsh, a lawyer and former President of Wilson's War Labour Conference Board, Michael J. Ryan, another lawyer, from Philadelphia, and Edward F. Dunne, a former Mayor of Chicago and Governor of Illinois. They received a tumultuous welcome from Sinn Fein. Patricia Lavelle has recorded what the delegates coming to Ireland meant to her and her contemporaries:[20]

> . . . their coming was a slender thread on which we hung all our aspirations of a free Ireland. . . . Out of all proportion to what they stood for, or what they could do, their arrival stirred all hearts in Galway . . . the crowning moment came when the three delegates appeared . . . we cheered till we were hoarse. I remember less of what they said than of what they meant to us, something outside of Ireland herself and working for her freedom.

However, British reaction to the speeches and activities of the Americans was the direct opposite of that described by Lavelle. Even the King wanted Wilson to furnish a 'disavowal of the action of these American citizens'.[21] When the delegation finally got to Paris – where, despite his stated objections, Wilson had worked behind the scenes and practically cleared the way for de Valera and his colleagues to come to Paris, until the British backlash set in – the three found a very fraught President. He told them on 11 June 1919:[22] ' . . . if it is your intention to go back to America and try to put me in bad, I am going to say when I go back that we were well on the way to getting Mr de Valera and his associates over here, we were well on the way, when you made it so difficult by your speeches in Ireland that we could not do it; that it was you gentlemen who kicked over the applecart.'

The Irish Americans then asked him how he could justify his attitude to Ireland in view of his celebrated wartime statement on the rights of small nations to self-determination. Addressing Congress on 11 February 1918, Wilson had expressed this noble sentiment: 'National aspirations must be respected; peoples may now be dominated and governed only by their own consent. "Self-determination" is not a mere phrase. It is an important principle of action which statesmen will henceforth ignore at their peril.' But by now, in a post-war world, the morning after a night of optimism had well and truly dawned. Wilson was beginning to realize how impossible it was to satisfy the hopes he had aroused in liberation movements in Africa, Egypt, Korea, India and many other countries. He made a heartfelt reply to the Irish American trio: 'You have touched on the great metaphysical tragedy of today.' Moreover, the Irish issue was beginning to be used by his domestic American opponents to further their opposition to his beloved League of Nations. The British Embassy in Washington was able to reassure London that a resolution passed by the Senate on 6 June, a few days before Wilson met Dunne and Co. and asking that the Irish be admitted to the Paris Conference to 'present the case of Ireland', was in reality an attack on Wilson and the League of Nations.[23]

Accordingly, as he acknowledged the cheers of the crowd while passing up Fifth Avenue in an open car on the day he returned to New York from Paris, 8 July 1919, to begin his campaign on behalf of the League of Nations, Wilson knew he had a fight on his hands. Looking out at him from the Waldorf Astoria Hotel (where, symbolically enough, he was getting a first-hand report, also fresh from the French boat but from the lips of Walsh and Dunne whom he was entertaining to lunch[24]) Eamon de Valera realized that he was going to be mixed up in that fight – opposed to Wilson. The Waldorf Astoria had become his headquarters. It was there on 23 June that he had given his first press conference in America, after a reception at which he had met the leaders of the Friends of Irish Freedom and other important Irish American figures. Twenty-third Street was thronged when he arrived to be met by Cohalan and Devoy, one carrying the Irish Tricolour and the other the Stars and Stripes of America. His statement to the press contained a shot across Wilson's bows. Its first sentence read: 'I am in America as the official head of the Republic established by the will of the Irish people in accordance with the principle of Self-Determination.'[25] It went on:

We shall fight for a real democratic League of Nations, not the present unholy alliance which does not fulfil the purposes for which the democracies of the world went to war. I am going to ask the American people to give us a real League of Nations, one that will include Ireland.

I well recognise President Wilson's difficulties in Paris. I am sure that if he is sincere, nothing will please him more than being pushed from behind by the people for this will show him that the people of America want the United States Government to recognise the Republic of Ireland.

That is the reason I am eager to spread propaganda in official circles in America. My appeal is to the people. I know if they can be aroused government action will follow. That is why I intend visiting your large cities and talking directly to the people.

De Valera thus began his campaign to win friends and influence people in the USA by telling the President of the United States that his cherished League now had yet another powerful opponent, one who regarded it as an 'unholy alliance'. Cohalan was also spearheading a drive by the Friends of Irish Freedom 'against the League, and pursuing President Wilson on his tour, from city to city, and from State to State, with half and full page advertisements in the Press'.[26] Furthermore, de Valera went on to inform the President that this new opponent who sought to interfere so directly in American politics was not an American. He was asked point-blank by a reporter:[27] 'Are you an American citizen?' To which he replied, with forthright evasion: 'I am an Irish citizen.' (Boland had just told the reporters that he was an American citizen.) But the reporter refused to be put off: 'Did you forswear allegiance to the United States?' De Valera's reply was: 'I ceased to be an American when I became a soldier of the Irish Republic.'

A sympathetic biographer commented on this exchange,[28] which his own official biography does not refer to at all: 'To his mind allegiance to the Volunteer force had automatically terminated his status as an American.' This is an over-simplified view of how the mind of a student of Machiavelli worked. De Valera was far too conscious of the benefits of American citizenship ever to renounce that status voluntarily. By the time he had finished his American visit the British had determined that if they laid hands on him they would send him back to the country of his birth. The Cabinet minute containing this decision has a note written across it: 'It is an astonishing revelation, after all the bullying H.M. Govt. have put up with from this man, to find out that he is not even technically a British subject.'[29]

In fact not only was de Valera never a British citizen – he did not become an Irish one until three years after he made the statement quoted above. And even then his Irish status was somewhat ambiguously received, because he bitterly opposed, and later replaced, the 1922 Constitution which conferred Irish citizenship on him by virtue of Irish domicile and his mother's birth in Ireland. But the 1922 Constitution's provisions allowed him to retain his American citizenship. An official memorandum prepared on his behalf by the Irish Department of External Affairs on 25 April 1946 stated:[30]

The Taoiseach [de Valera] never deliberately 'renounced' it [American citizenship] at any time. As far as I am personally aware, the Taoiseach's

American citizenship was recognised to exist, by himself and other interested parties, long after he had attained his majority (e.g. in 1916). . . . As an American citizen by birth, his American status is much more firmly rooted than that of a naturalised American . . . we may assume that no change has taken place in the Taoiseach's natural-born status.

Few native-born Americans were destined to become so great a thorn in the sides of their Presidents as de Valera would – at the head of a foreign administration. After Wilson, Roosevelt too would one day discover this, to his cost. De Valera had actually launched himself on a collision course with Wilson during a speech to the Dail[31] some weeks earlier, at a time when he knew that he was going to the USA but most of his listeners did not. He said that as the League was evolving it 'simply meant an association to perpetuate power for those who had got it, and to keep in slavery those who had been kept in slavery by international rules, as they were called, but which were simply the rules of thieves for regulating their conduct amongst themselves'. He went on to point out, perceptively, that if France gave vent to her understandable desire for revenge, then a vengeful treaty would emerge and with it a future war. But it was less to save the world from future war than to stop Ireland being regarded as an appendage of England that he embarked on his American tour. He thought the harm could be taken out of the Versailles Treaty if the 'rules of thieves' could be amended so that the victorious powers would 'surrender their colonies and possessions as mandatories of the League'.[32] And he did not object to the principle of Article 10. His view was that, if there were going to be a League, 'you must have some article in it . . . like Article 10'.[33] However, the Article had to be 'based on just conditions from the start'.

In the abstract one can commend this approach. But whereas in style de Valera couched his attacks on the League in Wilsonian-sounding rhetoric about peace, in substance he was placing his influence in the scales with that of the President's enemies while at the same time pretending he was not doing so. He wrote to Griffith[34] saying: 'I am waiting until we have got the people properly first – then even were he to attack, it would not be so deadly.' In fact he had not waited. He had already attacked 'the unholy alliance' on a number of occasions.[35] He wanted to be thought more sophisticated in his approach than Irish American leaders like Devoy and Cohalan,[36] but in fact he did not understand the American political scene as they did. He told Griffith: 'The political situation here is obscure for the moment. Am trying to give Wilson to know that if he goes for his 14 points as they were and a true League of Nations, Irishmen and men and women of Irish blood will be behind him. So Democrats and Republicans are bidding for our support – Democrats by amending the Covenant and Republicans by destroying it.'

He was in no position to overturn the ancestral antipathies to the proposed League. The vast crowds which he was already experiencing in his tour were turning out for him in the same sense as Patricia Lavelle came to hear and see the American delegates in Galway. It was not what he, or they, said, but what they symbolized: freedom, a land of their own to which, like the Jews, they might return some day. And as with the Jews their view of this land involved enormous contradictions and differences in reactions which come into focus if one exchanges the words Jewish and Palestinian for Nationalist and Unionist.

But the vast throngs who came to hear de Valera were not of a mind to worry about contradictions. True, as Dr Dwyer has written,[37] 'as the novelty of his appearances began to wear off, the crowds declined and his failings as a public speaker became more apparent. He tended to read his speeches in a dull, halting manner.' But these deficiencies were made up for by what the *Boston Herald* described as the way his 'passionate sincerity' and 'utmost simplicity' worked to 'burn their way into the consciousness of everyone who sees and hears him'.[38] Patrick McCartan, who was with him in America for much of his stay, and who showed himself prepared to be critical of him at times, judged:[39] ' . . . his bearing commanded the respect of all who met him . . . as our President he had conducted himself in public with so much circumspection and dignity as to bring to him and us universal respect'.

Although the League issue was one which it was almost impossible for de Valera to avoid commenting on, with hindsight it is clear that he would have been better to restrict his comments to a minimum and concentrate his demands on money and support for Irish self-determination. But also with hindsight, it is clear that neither he nor anyone in Dublin was entirely clear what his goals were before he set off, nor did they know a great deal about America or American politics.

His official biography opens the description of his US visit by posing the question: 'Why was the visit ever decided on?'[40] It then devotes a full page to giving different answers. One was that 'before the general release of prisoners it was considered that the moral effect of his escape would be nullified if he were to be recaptured'. This, of course, is rubbish. That short period of February–March was the time when he came reluctantly to Dublin, moved off again to England and returned for his non-event civic reception. Two other reasons given are these: 'The need for an American loan was apparent if the new Government were to operate at all effectively. . . . American public opinion must be induced to realise the relevance of the case of Ireland' (in the context of the League of Nations and the Peace Conference). The biography makes the point that in deciding to go to America 'The President . . . had the full support of the Cabinet. Arthur Griffith made this latter point clear in a statement to Dail Eireann which removed any conceivable suggestion that the President was retreating from the front line.'[41]

More than fifty years after Padraig O'Keefe made his famous caustic comment, the suggestion – almost certainly not confined to O'Keefe – that he went to America to get away from trouble was obviously still rankling with de Valera. It is as easy to see why this would be the case as it would be to accept the allegation. Leaders of countries in revolutionary ferment are frequently driven into exile. But where is one to look for examples of Presidents voluntarily departing, and staying away, before and during most of the action? And, to make the case even more extraordinary, where could one turn for examples of such a President being welcomed back to continue in respect and authority over those whom he had left behind to do the fighting? But to accept the obvious, over-simplified explanation would be misleading. De Valera's reasons for going to the USA were certainly complex, but it would be wrong to include cowardice amongst them. He was not blindly courageous, as was seen in 1916, but he was a brave man, capable of enormous resolution, once he had worked himself up to the sticking point.

The truth is that de Valera was driven to America by a combination of ego and insecurity. There is a vein in Irish public life which does not regard recognition as having been achieved until one is accepted in America – and not only in politics. Any Irish author or playwright knows what it is to be asked: 'When is it coming out in the States?' before an opinion on the work is expressed. Because of his insecure background de Valera needed the American dimension. Collins, on the other hand, resisted efforts to be sent to the USA. 'Our propaganda can never be stronger than our actions at home,' he reasoned. But de Valera both determinedly sought the international arena and equally determinedly tried to prevent people from realizing that he sought it. Even when he was honoured by being asked to address Congress in 1964, he used the occasion to make an attempt to stitch into the record his reasons for coming to America:[42]

> I was sent here with a threefold mission. First to ask for official recognition of the independence and the Republic. . . . I was sent here also to try to float an external loan . . . and finally I was asked to plead with the American people that the United States would make it clear that 'notwithstanding Article 10 of the Covenant of the League of Nations', the United States was not pledging itself to maintain Ireland as an integral part of British territory.

However, he placed a different emphasis on his mission in a letter to Arthur Griffith written the month after he landed in the USA:[43] 'My three present objectives are (1) Pressing unofficial recognition of the Republic and preparing campaign re the Treaty [of Versailles]. (2) The interest of wealthy men of the race in the industrial development of Ireland. (3) The floating of the bonds.'

In typical de Valera fashion his biography gives both sets of objectives, although separated by several pages, so that the contradictions do not readily appear and either set of reasons for going to America could be quoted as required. Of the desiderata set out for Griffith, no. 2, not surprisingly, soon dropped off the vine as a practical matter. Industrialists do not invest in war zones. Where no. 3 was concerned he was largely successful. But in view of the importance of the Republican issue in bringing about the Irish civil war, and the part it played in Irish political life subsequently, no. 1 must be our starting point in retracing de Valera's footsteps through America.

There is an obvious contradiction between the search for 'unofficial' recognition of the republic in July 1919 and the claim to Congress over forty years later that he had been 'sent. . . . First to ask for official recognition of the independence and the Republic'. One could argue that it did not matter what de Valera told Griffith, because the American mission was so much his own concept that he could very largely write his own agenda. But as the man who had devised the formula which brought the IRB-minded republicans and the Griffith monarchists under the Sinn Fein banner he was keenly aware of how much republicanism the political diet of Griffith and his supporters would accommodate: far less than the Irish Americans were prepared to force-feed them with. His letter to Griffith came a matter of days after his first American press conference, at which, as a result of the Irish American leaders' urgings, he had described himself not as Priomh Aire but as President of the Irish Republic.

In fact when he arrived in America, unaware that McGarrity and McCartan were opposing Cohalan's stance and in favour of 'Self-Determination', he described it as a 'very good policy' to a dumbfounded McCartan. His first public policy statement would have gone out extolling the virtues of self-determination had the man to whom it was given to type not referred it to McCartan first.[44] McCartan took it to McGarrity, who persuaded de Valera to drop his objections to being referred to as President of the Republic of Ireland, despite the fact that, as de Valera pointed out, he was only Chairman of the Dail. McGarrity 'contended that it was the same thing and that we had already made him President of the Republic in the minds of the American people'.[45] De Valera gave in on this upgrading of his status much more easily than he normally accepted other people's suggestions. Nevertheless he obviously understood the implications of the title change, because on the night it was announced he remarked to McGarrity and McCartan, 'I wonder what Griffith will say when he reads that I came out in the Press as President of the Republic.'[46]

In fact neither Griffith nor anyone else at that stage gave much thought to this momentous declaration. For the moment all eyes were focused on the most successful aspect of his American tour, the amount of publicity he generated. A week after his Waldorf Astoria press conference he launched a coast-to-coast tour of speaking engagements by addressing a seventy-thousand-strong crowd at Fenway Park, Boston. The next three weeks were gruelling in the extreme. He made seventeen major public speeches and a myriad of shorter addresses, receiving enormous coverage in the leading newspapers of Boston, Chicago, New York and San Francisco. Thirty thousand people turned out to hear him in Manchester, New

Hampshire; perhaps as many as fifty thousand at Cubs' Baseball Park, Chicago; and his audience at Madison Square Garden broke all records for the period, partly because the Irish-dominated New York police force allowed the fire regulations to be disregarded.

His first cross-continental tour was followed by several other forays into cities, state legislatures, universities and other circles where influence was formed. He was received with honour by cardinals, archbishops, state governors, presidents of universities and the mayors of some of America's biggest cities. But within the world of Irish Americana his fixation with the League of Nations and his attempts to signal to Wilson that he was really a supporter of the fourteen points took some of the gilt off the publicity bonanza.

In his first week of speech-making he generated a storm of booing and hissing even from the enthusiasts at Madison Square Garden simply by mentioning the President's name. He had to trim his sails a few days later at the Cubs' Baseball Park in Chicago where, before he spoke, a resolution was adopted declaring that the meeting was 'unalterably opposed' to the Covenant. He got out of allying himself with this position by stating that it was based on 'purely American grounds' and that he felt 'as a stranger and a guest here' that he 'could not presume to interfere'. This feeling soon wore off as his stay progressed, but he avoided any booing at the Cubs' Baseball Park by saying he was opposed to the League because 'it is going to do injustice to my country'. However, he was back on the Wilsonian trail a few days later at San Francisco where he told a huge convention of the Ancient Order of Hibernians that he expected America: ' . . . to make the world safe for democracy'. He then went on to make use of language in a manner which readers will later find has a familiar ring to it: he was to use a similar approach and phraseology in the face of reality during a particularly fraught moment in the run-up to the Irish civil war:[47]

> . . . you can do it even now . . . if America is determined to champion the cause of democracy in the world, that cause will triumph. If America leads the way towards true democracy, the democracy of England even and of France and of Spain and every country in the world will follow your lead . . . you are the only people that can lead and if you lead, democracy will triumph and the world will indeed be safe for democracy.

High-sounding rhetoric. But the reality was that, as we have seen, in concentrating on attacking the League as then constituted he was antagonizing Wilson on the one hand and on the other bewildering his Irish American constituency, who were opposed to the whole concept of the League on isolationist and anti-British grounds. They did not want the League reformed; they wanted it removed. The idea that America would only have one vote in the League, whereas Britain, through her Dominions, would have six, outraged anglophobes like Cohalan and Devoy, and the League issue helped to drive a wedge between them and de Valera.[48] This had demonstrably damaging political results.

It is difficult to evaluate the overall effect of the publicity he generated because so many other factors interacted to create this attention, but it certainly helped to heighten American awareness of the Irish issue. The manner in which de Valera attempted to extend his force-field throughout the continent constituted the greatest political *tour d'horizon* ever conducted in America by any Irish leader, either before or after him. One of the first appointments he made to his staff on arriving in the States was that of Kathleen O'Connell as his private secretary. It was rumoured that they had an affair; but all that can be said about their relationship with certainty is that O'Connell, then a young immigrant from Kerry, was to remain his secretary until she died, thirty-seven years later, in 1956. Her career with him could be taken as epitomizing the gift which de Valera undoubtedly possessed, when he chose to exercise it, of being able to command both devotion and efficiency from some of those who served him. She kept a record of his American peregrinations[49] which it would not be practicable to reproduce in full. However, a few extracts give an indication of their extent, of how he was received, and some of the points he made in two tours he conducted in 1919, the first a little over three weeks in duration, the second more than twice that long. Symbolically enough, the first words of Kathleen O'Connell's record are 'The Chief':

Boston, June 29, 1919
The Chief addresses 70,000 at Fenway Park. Mayor Peters, Senator David I. Walsh, and Mayor Quinn of Cambridge Mass present. Hon. Joseph F. O'Connell, representing lawyers and judiciary of Boston proposed resolutions. June 30, Dev. addresses both branches of Massachusetts Legislature.

Chicago, July 12th, 13th, 1919
Greeted by 10,000 citizens at depot. Welcomed on behalf of city by William Hael Thompson. The Mayor, present at mass meeting of 50,000, presented bouquet. Degree from St. Paul University. [Even a hostile source, the British Consulate, reported to London that a 'very impressive display both of humanity and bunting was created' and 'through organised manipulation' an ovation of nearly thirty minutes occurred when de Valera rose to speak at Chicago.][50]

San Francisco, July 17th to 20th, 1919
Met at Ferry by Mayor, city officials. At City Hall, Mayor Rolph presented a gold plaque to Dev. . . . Dev addresses National Convention A.O.H. which passes resolution calling on U.S. Govt. to recognise Irish Independence. Receives Ph.D. Degree from St. Ignatius University. Unveils Emmet Monument in Golden Gate park. Speaks at Oakland.

Butte, Montana, July 25th, 26th
Received at depot by Lt. Governor McDowell and invited to address a joint session of the State Legislature. Received freedom of the State from McDowell and of the City from Mayor. During a second visit in November when he was again the recipient of civic honours he said:
The Irish question is not a religious issue and the presence of so many

Protestants here today is the best refutation of that narrow and altogether unworthy allegation.

Second Tour.

Philadelphia, October 1st and 2nd 1919
Received at Station by Citizens Committee, with mounted escort and 300 automobiles all decorated [with Irish colours]. Mayoral welcome at Independence Hall. Visited Franklin's grave and Commodore Barry's monument. Meeting at Opera House. Present on platform [apart from prominent Irish American speakers] Bishop Yasbeck, Syrian Bishop, Dr. Robert Ellis Thompson. Presbyterian Minister, Monsignor Gerald P. Coghlan, Rector of the Church of our Lady.

Cleveland, Ohio, Oct 6, 1919
Mayor and City Council gave him an official welcome. Presidential salute fired. Parade down Euclid Ave. 500 cars. Spoke at Central Armory which was crowded out, big overflow. . . . Representative John J. Babka travelled specially from Washington for big meeting.

Indianapolis, October 11, 1919
Welcoming Committee of Five Hundred headed by J. J. Liddy. Parade through City to State House. Governor receives him. . . . Then to City Hall, received by Mayor Jewett and City Council. Bishop Joseph Chartrand received him at his palace.

St. Paul, Oct. 19, 1919
After a civic welcome he visited the Military College and said:
   If I were a young man, the one ambition of my life would be to attend a military school such as this. That is one of the pleasures of living in a free country like the United States.

Minneapolis, Oct. 20th, 1919
Spoke to 8,000 at Armory, received resolution of civic welcome. Told his audience that 'Ireland would be maintained in independence without menacing England by agreement of nations.'

St. Louis, Oct. 24, 1919
Met by Governor, given twenty-one gun salute and parade through city. Laid wreath at Washington Monument. Addressed three meetings, one a huge outdoor gathering at which he said:
   We are a peaceful people. We want peace with England and we will make peace with her if she will but withdraw the 250,000 soldiers now garrisoning Ireland.

This particular tour ended on 23 November in Los Angeles where he was escorted to his meeting, attended by an estimated twenty-seven thousand persons, by three hundred war veterans, many of them crippled and wearing their decorations. In subsequent tours many of the places mentioned above were revisited, as were a host of other,[51] new venues. His trips were generally extremely well organized. Kathleen O'Connell's lists always carefully included the names and correct titles of various dignitaries, where possible their home addresses, and the names and addresses of any other significant participants. For example, she notes that in Philadelphia on 2 October 1919 'Miss Sarah Brown (then a little child) of 1223 South 24th St. presented Dev. with 32 roses from the A.O.H. Model of Liberty Bell also presented by United Irish Societies.'

De Valera did not attend to the organization himself, but he had no hesitation in telling Diarmuid Lynch, who did (at least until he quarrelled with de Valera later in his American sojourn), just exactly what he wanted:[52] 'Every effort should be made to secure aeroplane or airship service. The advantages of the air are beyond question. The railway can be taken as a supplementary. . . . Please let me know the steps you have taken so that I may know the state of progress reached. As you are aware the success of this tour depends mainly upon your organisation. It is a case of full steam up.' He had drawn up an organizational plan which included the following:

(1) Meeting in at least one town in every state.
(2) Great care to be taken that correspondence should not become mixed up, because there are several names the same in different States.
(3) Towns should be arranged in blocks so that they can be covered in a week or at most a fortnight.
(4) Railway experts should be called in to help drawing up schedules.
(5) Efforts to be made to get invitations from Municipal State Authorities and State Legislatures making use of the Friends of Irish Freedom.
(6) Trips between towns to be arranged in the evenings with an advance agent working in with Boland ahead of his arrival.
(7) Publicity material of all sorts to be prepared to go 'hand in hand' with (6).

Whether Lynch, who was the national secretary of the Friends of Irish Freedom, as well as being a leading figure in the IRB, with years of American experience, really needed to be warned about identical patronymics amongst the Irish in the States is a moot point. De Valera was like a comet blazing across the American firmament, with other Irish stars crossing his path or following in his wake. Daniel Mannix, his old Maynooth friend, now Archbishop of Melbourne, spoke from several of his platforms across the country. At a huge banquet organized at the Hotel Astor in New York by the Maynooth Union, on 20 July 1920, Mannix said of de Valera's message:[53] 'We have listened to him here and you could almost see the sincerity of the man's soul while he picked his steps so carefully and cautiously through the morality of the fight that the Irish people have been making.' Carefully, if not cautiously, on 20 August the British sent a warship to pick up the Archbishop from a liner and thus prevent him landing in Ireland – thereby triggering further publicity explosions amongst the Irish and Roman Catholics around the world. Speakers such as Mrs Hannah Sheehy-Skeffington, the widow of the pacifist murdered by an allegedly deranged British officer in 1916, and Mary MacSwiney, the sister of the hunger striker Terence MacSwiney, added to de Valera's impact.

In the early stages of his visit his presence coincided with that of the Prince of Wales, also on a tour of the United States. De Valera wrote to Griffith:[54] 'The Mayor of Newport and Governor of Rhode Island sent me an invitation to go to Newport. I am waiting till the Crown Prince of England gets there and he is waiting till I leave there – Meanwhile all the ball dresses of the aristocracy who are ready to receive him are getting musty – most amusing.' The British tried to counteract de Valera's appeal by sending out Sir Horace Plunkett, Chairman of the Irish Convention. Carson arranged for a group of Protestant clergymen from Belfast to make a counter-tour of the States, commencing on 8 December 1919, the Feast of the Immaculate Conception. Coincidentally, though hardly out of deference to the date, paternity was denied in their case also. It was said that they had come to America under the auspices of Lord Beaverbrook, Britain's Director of Propaganda in the USA, 'to combat the teachings of de Valera'.[55] The clergymen's efforts were met by the bringing to America of another Ulster clergyman, the Presbyterian Rev. Dr J. A. H. Irwin. He spoke from de Valera's platforms in defence of the proposition that the struggle in Ireland was a national, not a religious, issue.

Between all these efforts and the activities of Lynch, Boland and the Friends of Irish Freedom de Valera's trips in the main achieved a nice balance between serious political activities and those obviously aimed at the 'human interest' angle. For example, at the Chippewa Indian Reserve in Wisconsin he was made a 'Chief' of another sort – of the Chippewa nation, with the title 'Nay, nay, ong, ga, be', which apparently translates into English as 'Dressing Feather'.[56] In Kansas City he visited a murder trial and was invited to sit beside the judge, who got everyone present to shake hands with him including the defendant, a woman who said: 'Glad to meet you, Mr President, you are the first President I ever met. So glad you came.'

Another woman who may not have been quite so glad that he went was Sinead: Greystones is a long way from Kansas City. She found it hard sometimes to follow his advice to 'do [her] best not to be lonely'[57] which he sent to her 'aboard the overland on way to Frisco' after 'strenuous days in Boston, New York and just now in Chicago'. Interestingly, he reported 'tremendous enthusiasm for our cause everywhere', which of course was true, but made no reference to the complexities of the League issue. He promised to try to get her 'a word or two every few days' from then on, gave her the Waldorf Astoria as his permanent address in the United States and, despite the brevity of his note, wrote with obvious depth of feeling: 'I am so anxious to hear from you. May God keep and guard you. Love with all my heart.' No doubt the rush and tiredness caused him to end on an unintentionally cold note. The letter ends with no salutation and is merely signed 'Eamon de Valera'.

However, a few days later he managed a warmer tone beginning '*A cuisle mo croide*' ('darling of my heart') and assuring her:[58]

> I am thinking of you and the children always. You know I will fly back as soon as ever I can. Ireland's cause is enthusiastically sympathised with by the American people – the plain people at any rate accept and recognise the Irish Republic. It is a great privilege to be an advocate for our cause which today is no less than the cause of liberty everywhere. . . .
>
> I can never write the thoughts that pass through my mind about you. Everywhere I have gone I have met Gaels who knew you in the G. League and who knew the work you did. The language is spoken by individuals in every city of America. Even in the deserts of the Rockies. It would have broken my heart were I unable to answer in our own tongue. Love and kisses to the children, Eamon.

A swing through Salt Lake City and through Montana produced an echo and a name from the days of Rockwell:[59] 'Jack Stewart (Mai's brother) got us the most varied audience, at a banquet, that I have had in America – 33rd degree masons, ministers, mormons Jews are enthusiasts for the Cause. I have sent a line to Mai.' Totty twigging was paying political dividends. Perhaps the implications of this thought struck him too, for he concluded this letter with a lyrical paragraph in Irish:

> *A Mhaitrin, a cuisle,*
>   *Gradh agus poganna. Bim ag smaoineadh ort (orraibh go leir) i gcomhnuidhe a chuisle. Raghad tar nais chom luath agus is feidir liom. Ta mo chroidhe leat. Casadh orm a lan acht ta duine amhain nach bhfuil a leithead le faghail. Go soirbhidh Dia i.*
>   *D'fhear, Eamon.*

This translates as:

> Dear little mother, darling,
>   Love and kisses. I'm forever thinking of you (all of you) my love. I'll return as soon as possible. My heart is with you. I've met many but there's one person whose like cannot be found. God bless her. [Or 'God prosper her']
>   Your husband, Eamon.

But Sinead was about to learn, as would those in his political life, that Eamon de Valera had an ability to sound warm and moderate in print or speech while acting in a hard and unyielding manner. Eamon de Valera the Nice Guy finally handed over to De Valera Man of Power during that American tour. For despite the lyricism, an ocean would lie between Eamon and Sinead de Valera for many a long day. Whether he realized this and was trying to keep the bad news from her, or whether he genuinely did not understand the length of time required to deal with the problems which were piling up in the background of his triumphal tours, it is impossible to say. Evidently Boland in the course of a trip home that summer had put the truth to Sinead with more candour than tact, for de

Valera sent her a forecast of his visit's duration which underestimated it by the order of 500 per cent:[60]

> ... Mother gave me a photo of Mairin. I have it with me always. I hope the children are real well. Do not mind Boland's *raimis* [nonsense] about remaining here a year. I'll be back as soon as ever I can get things done. I can't say when definitely however. In about a couple of more months – three I should say. . . .
>
> I wish you could come. Am asked everywhere why you don't. 'Six at home' is the only answer I can give. Yes there is no welcome like the one dear welcome. Your letters are a joy beyond all others. I am longing for them and thought they would never come . . . with all the love of my heart. Tell the children about me.
> *D'Fear Eamon. Poganna go dib go leir* [kisses to you all].

It cannot now be judged with certainty whether he knew when writing to Sinead how long he would be staying in the USA; but, as we are about to discover, he certainly demonstrated that to his mind his feuding took precedence over a return to his family and followers.

8

THE WAR FROM THE WALDORF

DE VALERA'S DIFFERENCES with Cohalan and Devoy might be summed up under three headings: ideology, money and power. We have had an insight into the first in the clash between isolation and the League. Money was shortly to bring the differences out into the open.

The ideology issue was not merely confined to isolation. At one level it centres around a perennial problem: who speaks for Ireland in the USA – the Irish Americans, or the Irish in Ireland? De Valera never acted as if he understood that the Irish Americans are Americans first. Sentiment may impel them to help Ireland, but they resent its representatives telling them how they should act in their own country. There was also the question of a personality clash. De Valera himself ascribed the difficulty to whichever reason suited him at the moment. He said the issue was 'purely one of personalities'[1] while writing to keep his Dublin Cabinet colleagues informed of his side of the argument. But in writing to Cohalan he made it clear that he expected the judge and the policy of the *Gaelic American* to be subordinate to his wishes.[2] In the course of a telling reply Cohalan pointed out that he had always acted 'as an American, whose only allegiance is to America', and asked if de Valera really believed that 'any self-respecting American will permit himself to be used in such a manner by you?'[3]

The powder keg to the blow-up over money was ignited, before de Valera came to the USA, at the Irish Race Convention held in Philadelphia on 22–23 February 1919, and sponsored by the Friends of Irish Freedom (FOIF). An Irish Victory Fund was set up, in the words of Judge Cohalan, to provide money for 'educational propaganda in America'.[4] Cohalan had two objectives – one positive, one negative. On the positive score he wanted to promote the presidential hopes of a Republican Senator, Hiram Johnson of California, who, if elected, would have appointed the pro-Irish Senator William Borah as Secretary of State; on the negative to defeat the League. But as a result of lobbying by Harry Boland and FOIF figures like Joseph McGarrity who believed that Ireland should be the main target of effort, it was decided that $250,000 should be sent to Ireland after what Boland called a 'very, very stiff fight to get any money for home'.[5] Devoy and Cohalan saw this sum as being quite sufficient. One of the three Americans whom Wilson had described as kicking over the Peace Conference applecart in Ireland, Michael J. Ryan, had reported to the FOIF that he did not see how the Dail would need more than $50,000 for its capital requirements. He thought the new assembly a piece of make-believe, whereas its founders saw it as a genuine alternative government. Consequently when de Valera proposed to float a bond loan of several million dollars the Cohalanites saw the proposal as an unnecessary infringement on their turf which might interfere with their own Victory Fund. McCartan describes[6] a meeting with Irish American leaders held in New York prior to de Valera's setting out on his first visit to San Francisco:

> Cohalan promised large sums from the Irish Victory Fund; a second Victory Fund could be inaugurated: anything and everything was promised if de Valera would only agree to abandon the idea of floating a loan. . . . President de Valera was coaxed, bullied and finally informed that 'if he did not do as the people in that room advised, he could do nothing in the United States'.
>
> Buttressed by McGarrity, President de Valera remained firm, and concluded by saying that his instructions were from the Dail, and he had to carry them out . . . so earnest was he, and so well did he state his case, that Judge Goff withdrew his opposition; told de Valera his enthusiasm was contagious; and promised whole-hearted co-operation.

Subsequent to this meeting the Victory Fund was wound up at the end of August, thus partly clearing the way for de Valera's initiative. The expenses of launching the bond drive were met by a loan of $100,000 from the $250,000 earmarked for Ireland from the FOIF Victory Fund which had already given de Valera $26,000 to help fund his American activities. Some other obstacles remained when de Valera departed for San Francisco, taking McCartan with him and leaving Harry Boland in New York to sort out the residual difficulties. Alas:[7] 'When we got back from San Francisco no progress had been made in the preparations. There seemed to be a studied effort to prove to Boland that the project was impossible. No bank would agree to accept the money; no lawyer could surmount the legal difficulties; and offices suitable for headquarters could not be rented.'

On top of all this, Judge Cohalan advised that the proposed loan would be in contravention of American anti-fraud laws which prohibited the sale of bonds on behalf of countries not officially recognized by the USA. But again McGarrity came to the rescue. A bank was found to accept the money, a headquarters to collect it established at 411 Fifth Avenue, and Cohalan was prevailed on to serve alongside de Valera on a committee which worked out a scheme for bond certificates. The idea, which seems to have originated with W. A. Maloney – who, like McCartan, was a medical doctor and was in addition one of the most able publicists in the Irish American ranks – was that these certificates could be exchanged for real bonds when the Irish republic was recognized. A New York lawyer friend of McGarrity's, Martin Conboy, thought the idea a good one, but suggested that an independent, non-Irish, opinion be obtained. Accordingly de Valera approached another rising politician, a partner in the New York law firm of Emmet, Marvin and Martin named Franklin Delano Roosevelt, and sought his advice. Roosevelt pronounced favourably on the scheme and the way was cleared for de Valera to launch a bond certificate drive, which in hindsight probably deserves to be regarded as the first 'junk bond' flotation.

Cohalan was not alone in his reservations. Senator John Sharp Williams felt that even the bond certificate device was illegal, condoned only because pro-Irish feeling was such that convictions were impossible. And at Foggy Bottom, State Department officials were outraged. One diplomat's verdict was: 'To close our eyes and do nothing to prevent our territory being used to further rebellion against a friendly nation is not very creditable to our Government and makes us morally responsible for the situation in Ireland today.'[8] The Dail had decided that $1.25 million should be raised in the USA as part of the loan, but McGarrity advised de Valera to seek more. 'Ask for $10 million and you'll get $5 million,' he advised. De Valera did not fully accept McGarrity's guidance, but on the basis of his business experience did agree to increase his Dail mandate by 700 per cent to $10 million. All he needed now was a businessman of ability and stature to organize the drive and keep its proceeds away from Cohalan and Co. This was easier said than done, given the situation in the Irish American world, so he solved the problem by sending to Ireland for James O'Mara, whose daughter would later write a book about the whole affair. In that work she included the following description of the bond drive in the American press on 2 December 1919:[9]

> . . . a 10,000,000 dollar bond-certificate issue of the Republic of Ireland will be launched about January 15th on the general pattern of the American Liberty Loan and Red Cross drives. Frank P. Walsh, Chairman of the American Commission on Irish Independence [the FOIF group which had sent Walsh and the other two members of the triumvirate to tour Ireland] will be the National Director with Headquarters opened yesterday at 411 Fifth Avenue.

De Valera also took care to stitch into the record a 'saver', the significance of which will become apparent when we examine another momentous event in his career, more than a decade later: the foundation of the *Irish Press*:

> I want to emphasize the fact that this will be a sentimental appeal and not an appeal to investors. . . . It will be distinctly understood by each subscriber to the Loan that he is making a free gift of his money. Repayment of the amount is contingent wholly upon the recognition of the Irish Republic as an independent nation. . . . The certificates will be exchangeable at par for gold bonds of the Republic at the treasury of the Republic, one month after the Republic has received international recognition and the British forces have been withdrawn from the territory of the Republic.

In the event the 'sentimental appeal' was such that McGarrity was proved right; roughly half of what was asked for was subscribed, $5,123,640, much of it by what were described in the *Wall Street Journal* as 'Irish domestic servants, and others of like or lower standards of intelligence'.[10] The bond certificates could be purchased on a scale which ascended in cost from $10 to $10,000. While the sale of the bond certificates was clearly spearheaded by de Valera's publicity appearances, the success of the drive in organizational terms was due to O'Mara, the Limerick businessman whom de Valera asked to have smuggled from Ireland on the same Downes–O'Neill route by which he had entered the United States himself. O'Mara left his wife, seven children and a demanding business, facing the growing challenge of revolution, to be helped aboard the *Lapland* pretending to be a drunken crew member. He crossed the Atlantic hidden between layers of life-saving apparatus. Only Downes and O'Neill knew he was aboard and they took turns in guarding him and feeding him through a hole they had cut between the cork rafts. Off Halifax, Nova Scotia, heat and lack of air brought on a panic attack and he had to be transferred by night into one of the lifeboats. A dock strike at Halifax meant that he was confined to the boat for ten days spent in momentary expectation of discovery. Like de Valera, he was met on arrival in New York by Boland and McGarrity. And like de Valera, he was metamorphosed from filthy stowaway into person of national consequence immediately upon setting foot in America.

O'Mara was a superlative administrator who had organized the successful 1918 Sinn Fein election campaign. Patrick McCartan described his impact on the bond drive and how de Valera combined his own charisma with O'Mara's expertise:[11]

> In Ireland, O'Mara had been a successful merchant. The Irish-American leaders in New York understood him to be a millionaire, which gave him a status with them that none of the rest of us enjoyed. In O'Mara the rank and file had confidence: they felt that the moneys he raised by the sale of bonds would go to the Treasury of the Government of the Irish Republic . . . we spoke of him as 'Ben', for he amongst us all was most like America's great business and financial envoy, Benjamin Franklin. . . .
>
> . . . O'Mara's campaign to sell the Bonds was greatly aided by de Valera's triumphal tour of the United States. If in any city he visited, no Bond committee had been formed, the enthusiasm created by his visit increased the local sale of the Bonds. O'Mara's organisers followed de Valera all over the country. To each a territory was assigned. A branch headquarters, the Benjamin Franklin Bureau, was opened in Chicago.

A notable example of de Valera's 'triumphal' touring occurred at the very outset of the drive: he received the Freedom of the City of New York and sold Mayor John F. Hylan the first bond certificate in return. As McCartan notes:[12] 'The Clan worked very hard in New York', and as a result some $600,000 was collected in that city alone. It was important for the prestige of the drive that large donations were seen to be forthcoming.

On 28 September 1919 the Friends of Irish Freedom had voted a $100,000 'present' loan to cover 'the preliminary expenses in connection with the President's tour and the Irish Republican Bond Certificate issue'.[13] In mid-February 1920 Diarmuid Lynch wrote[14] to O'Mara on behalf of the FOIF, telling him that the National Council had voted a little earlier, on the 13th, that this 'present' loan be 'applied towards the purchase of Bond Certificates in equal amount' and advising O'Mara that he could consider the letter as a bond certificate application. Lynch's letter, or the decision that gave rise to it, might be seen as giving the public support of the powerful FOIF to de Valera's project and ending a long-running dispute both about converting the loan into bonds and about the disposition of monies which FOIF branches all over the country had been holding back from the Victory Fund because of the bond drive. This in fact was how Patricia Lavelle described the position: 'Dad [O'Mara] bore the brunt of this controversy but at the end reduced opposing parties to order if not to cordiality.'[15]

But the reality was that the parties were reduced to neither order nor cordiality. In fact a most damaging public controversy had broken out between de Valera and Devoy, which proceeded to escalate into a row between de Valera and Cohalan as well, only a few days before Lynch sent his letter. Apart from the inner personality clash between the three contenders for the minds and hearts of Irish Americans the row had an outer, Congressional, dimension. Since May a Bill had been before the House in the name of Congressman William E. Mason, seeking the appropriation of funds for the 'salaries of a minister and consuls to the Republic of Ireland'. This was a device aimed at securing recognition for Irish independence by upending the normal process of diplomatic accreditation whereby the White House was the proper source of such appointments. It became a live issue when, on 12 and 13 December, the House Foreign Affairs Committee held public hearings on the Bill which ran into a great deal of opposition. One of the most powerful arguments used against it was the risk that America's loyal ally, Britain, would be endangered if Irish independence was thus conceded; anti-British Ireland might range herself alongside Britain's enemies.[16]

By way of countering such arguments de Valera began making use of the Cuban analogy, suggesting that Great Britain could do as America had done with Cuba in 1901 and conclude a treaty with Ireland whereby the Irish would guarantee that Irish independence would be no more a threat to Great Britain than was Cuba to America. It was an ill thought out argument which overlooked the reality of the political slum that was Cuba and the country's position of vassalage to America. However, he caused no particular ripples for about a week until on 6 February he gave an interview to the correspondent of the *Westminster Gazette* in which he spelled out his thoughts in some detail:

The United States by the Monroe Doctrine made provision for its security without depriving the Latin Republics of the South of their independence and their life. The United States safeguarded itself from the possible use of the Island of Cuba as a base for an attack by a foreign Power by stipulating:

'That the Government of Cuba shall never enter into any treaty or other compact with any foreign Power or Powers which will impair or tend to impair the independence of Cuba, nor in any manner authorise or permit any foreign Power or Powers to obtain, by colonisation, or for military or naval purposes or otherwise, lodgement in or control over any portion of said island.'

Why doesn't Britain make a stipulation like this to safeguard herself against foreign attack as the United States did with Cuba? Why doesn't Britain declare a Monroe Doctrine for the two neighbouring islands? The people of Ireland so far from objecting would co-operate with their whole soul.

De Valera had not realized in giving the interview that the *Westminster Gazette* had an arrangement with the *New York Globe* whereby the papers shared news. The *Globe* came out with the story on page one before it appeared in the *Gazette*, under a long heading which included both 'Compromise suggested by Irish' and 'De Valera opens the door'. Commenting editorially, the paper said that de Valera's treatment of the question of guaranteeing Britain's security had offered a 'really convincing assurance to the seemingly unanswerable argument'. However, the *Globe* went on:[17] 'This statement introduces a new principle. It is a withdrawal by the official head of the Irish Republic of the demand that Ireland be set free to decide her own international relations.'

De Valera had consulted neither friend nor foe before giving the interview. McCartan records: 'It came as a thunderbolt to us.'[18] The Devoy–Cohalan faction were enraged and an almighty row broke out during which even McGarrity, nettled at the lack of consultation, was driven to remark: 'The row may do good. It may teach him to put his feet under the table.' Devoy's reaction on 14 February was 'spread over the pages of the *Gaelic American*.'[19] He made use of the *Globe* editorial to prove that de Valera had made an offer of surrender to Britain. De Valera issued clarifications showing that he had only quoted the first Article of the Platt Amendment, on which his Cuban analogy was based; and that not only did he not subscribe to subsequent Articles which gave America rights in Cuba, including rights to bases, but that he had specifically indicated he was not in favour of British bases in Ireland. To this Devoy retorted that one could not quote part of a document and disregard the rest:[20] 'When a part of a document is offered in court or in negotiations, the whole document becomes subject for consideration.'

Instead of trying to debate with Devoy, de Valera decided on a two-pronged line of defence. One was to send an envoy to Dublin and to write to Griffith:[21]

I labour under no misapprehension as to the relations between us. They are unfortunately only too well defined by the judge's attitude from the beginning. So clear were they from the first, that I was actually considering the question of whether it would not be better for our cause that I should return, or go elsewhere. Separate as one would imagine our personal interests necessarily were – separate, too, as the parts we would naturally have to play, even in the closest co-operation here, I realised early that nevertheless, and big as the country is, it was not big enough to hold the judge and myself.

The other was to make his reply not to the *Gaelic American* but in an attack on Cohalan, to whom he sent a highly charged letter, delivered by hand by Harry Boland. Obviously the reference to court procedure in the production of documents had a bearing on his decision to see the judge's hand in the articles. But the de Valera–Cohalan exchange also shows how de Valera had arrogated to himself the divine right of kings where decision-taking was concerned in all matters Irish, and how, *per contra*, Irish Americans saw their role. He wrote:[22]

After mature consideration, I have decided that to continue to ignore the articles in the *Gaelic American* would result in injury to the cause I have been sent here to promote. The articles themselves are, of course, the least matter. It is the evident purpose behind them, and the general attitude of mind they reveal, that is the menace.

I am answerable to the Irish people for the proper execution of the trust with which I have been charged. I am definitely responsible to them, and I alone am responsible. It is my obvious duty to select such instruments as may be available for the task set me. It is my duty to superintend every important step in the execution of that task. I may not blindly delegate those duties to anyone whomsoever.

I see added force being applied, day by day, to the power end of the great lever of the American public, with which I hope to accomplish my purpose. I must satisfy myself as to the temper of the other end of the lever.

The articles in the *Gaelic American* and certain incidents that have resulted from them, give me grounds for the fear that, in a moment of stress, the point of the lever would fail me. I am led to understand that these articles in the *Gaelic American* have your consent and approval. Is this so?

The Friends of Irish Freedom Organisation is an association of American citizens, founded to assist the Irish people in securing the freedom the Irish people desire. By its name, and by its constitution, it is pledged to aid in securing recognition for the established Republic. I am convinced it is ready to co-operate to the full with the responsible head of the Republic, who has been sent here specially to seek that recognition.

You are the officer of the Friends of Irish Freedom, who, de facto, wields unchallenged the executive power of that organisation. You are the officer through whom its several resources are in the main applied. You are the officer who has accepted its most important commission, and spoken, not merely in its name, but in the name of the whole Irish race in America. It is vital that I know exactly how you stand in this matter.

The whole question is urgent, and I expect you will find it possible to let me have a reply by Monday. To avoid all chance of miscarriage, I am having this delivered by Mr. Boland, personally.

I remain, very sincerely yours,
Eamon de Valera.

No matter how sincerely he remained, Cohalan decided that de Valera was not going to be allowed to turn an exercise in damage limitation over the Cuban gaffe into an onslaught on him, and he sent back a devastating reply which de Valera found literally unanswerable:

Dear President de Valera,

Your communication dated February 20th, was handed to me by Mr. Boland on Saturday afternoon.

I was amazed at its contents. In spite of its tone, and because of the position which you occupy, I am responding to it.

The *Gaelic American* is edited, as you know, by Mr. John Devoy, for whose opinions and convictions I entertain the highest respect. I control neither him nor them.

That he has the right to comment upon, or discuss your public utterances, or those of any man who speaks for a cause of a people, I assume you will grant. In any event, it is recognised by all Americans as one of our fundamental liberties. We have no law of lèse-majesté here, nor as far as I can judge, is there talk of having one in the democratic and free Ireland in which we believe.

Into any controversy you may have with Mr. Devoy, or others I refuse to be drawn. May I venture to suggest that you evidently labour under a serious misapprehension as to the relations which exist between you and me. I know no reason why you take the trouble to tell me that you can share your responsibility to the Irish people with no one.

I would not let you share it with me, if you sought to do so. That is a matter between them and you.

What I have done for the cause of the independence of the Irish people, recently and for many years past, I have done as an American, whose only allegiance is to America, and as one to whom the interest and security of my country are ever to be preferred to those of any and all other lands. What the extent and effect of that work may be will be decided by the members of the Race and by general public opinion.

I have no appointment from you or any other spokesman for another country, nor would I under any circumstances accept one. So long, and just so long as I can continue to work thus, I shall exercise such influence and talent as I may have in the same way and for the same ideals as in the past. The people of Ireland have placed themselves unequivocally upon record as favouring complete independence for their country, and, unless and until they by vote reverse that decision, I shall regard it as final, no matter what any man or set of men may say to the contrary.

With their demand for independence I am confident all Americans will finally agree, and it is not alone just, but in line with the ideals and best interests of our country, and is essential to the permanent peace of the world, that all nations and peoples should be free.

If Ireland were to change her position, and to seek a measure of self-Government that would align her in the future with England as an ally, in what I regard as the inevitable struggle for the freedom of the seas, that must shortly come between America and England, every loyal American will without hesitation take a position unreservedly upon the side of America.

A British Monroe Doctrine, that would make Ireland the ally of England, and thus buttress the falling British Empire, so as to further oppress India and Egypt and other subject lands would be so immoral, and so utterly at variance with the ideals and traditions of the people, as to be as indefensible to them as it would be intolerable to the liberty-loving peoples of the world.

I believe the people of Ireland were in deadly earnest in declaring for absolute independence, and no voice but that of the people themselves can convince me that they intend to take a position which will put them in hostility to America.

Should they, however, take such a step – as a free people undoubtedly have the right to do – I know the millions of Americans of Irish blood, who have created this great movement in favour of Ireland's independence, which you found here upon your arrival, will once again show with practical unanimity that we are for America as against the world.

Are you not in great danger of making a grave mistake when you talk in your communication of selecting 'instruments' in this country and of 'levers' and 'power end' and 'other end of lever' through which you hope to accomplish your purpose here?

Do you really think for a moment that American public opinion will permit any citizen of another country to interfere, as you suggest, in American affairs?

Do you think that any self-respecting American will permit himself to be used in such a manner by you? If so, I may assure you that you are woefully out of touch with the spirit of the country in which you are sojourning.

You point out that I have on occasion been called upon to speak, not merely in the name of the Friends of Irish Freedom but in the name of the whole Irish Race in America. May I call your attention to the fact that it was always as an American, and for my countrymen, that I spoke?

You might have added that at those times, as at others, I have said nothing that took from the self-respect or dignity of those whom I represented, or that left any doubt upon my hearers that I believed many millions of Americans sympathised with that demand of the people of Ireland for absolute independence, which you came here to voice.

I respectfully suggest in closing, that you would be well advised if you hesitate before you jeopardise or imperil that solidarity of opinion, and unity of action, among millions of American citizens, which you found here amongst us when you came, which have been the despair of England's friends, and have already accomplished so much for America and Ireland.

Those millions do not desire to see a return of the conditions which, under the late Mr. Redmond, made political activities in Ireland a football in English party politics.

Yours very truly,
Daniel F. Cohalan

After receiving Cohalan's reply de Valera ordered McCartan back to Dublin at the end of February to explain his position to the Cabinet. He also sent back to Griffith a copy of Cohalan's letter, complaining that it was 'wilful misrepresentation of my attitude', the work of a 'tricky police court lawyer' to whom he could not send the reply that the letter merited because it might harm relationships between them to a point where they could not work together.[23] Lest this and McCartan's advocacy were not sufficient, he kept up a flow of written communications from which the following extracts at least deserve to be quoted: 'I desired that Ireland's interests should come first.' He held that the Irish in America 'were organised not in their own interests here so much as to help Ireland. I held that the money contributed was obtained in the belief that it would be used as directly as possible for Ireland'.[24] By 'organised ... to help Ireland' he clearly intended 'organised to do what I told them'. In case there should be any doubt on this interpretation, here is what he wrote a few days later:[25] 'It is sympathy for Ireland that has enabled such an organisation as the Friends of Irish Freedom to be built up. That is why the vast mass of the rank and file have joined – that is why they have contributed, and I will not allow myself to be in any hobble skirts with respect to the doings of anything which we feel certain is for the good of the Cause.'

De Valera may have been guilty of an unconscious Freudian slip in his use of the royal 'we'. For certainly neither his enemies nor his friends felt 'certain' that the Cuban analogy was good for the cause. McCartan said of the McGarrity faction's reaction to the *Gaelic American* attack:[26] 'Apart from its malice there was little Devoy said with which we could in our hearts disagree. Had he said in private what he spread over the pages of the *Gaelic American*, we might have tried to moderate his tone, but not to refute his argument.'

McCartan's personal view of the Cuban interview was that it was 'clearly an intimation that the President of the Republic of Ireland was prepared to accept much less than complete sovereignty for Ireland. ... And the choice of the *Westminster Gazette* seemed appropriate to inform Lloyd George that Ireland's President was willing to degrade her claim to the level of a domestic issue of England.' Yet, armed with false papers, he set off aboard the SS *New York* for Ireland; here Collins summoned the Cabinet to hear de Valera's explanation, which McCartan gave as follows:[27]

> First, he had wanted to start England talking, so that some basis of settlement might be considered; secondly, in the interview, he quoted only one paragraph of the Platt Amendment relating to Cuba, to show that Ireland was willing to discuss safeguards for English security compatible with Ireland's independence; and lastly that only his enemies, and Devoy and Cohalan, had put a hostile construction on the interview, in pursuance of the campaign they had started against him when he arrived in the United States, and which overtly and covertly they had since continued.

McCartan 'did not say a word about the merits or demerits of the Cuban proposal'. But Countess Markievicz, Count Plunkett and Cathal Brugha showed 'marked hostility towards the proposal'. This was countered by Collins and Griffith, who 'shut down the discussion and led in the acceptance of de Valera's explanation'. McCartan noted that the Cabinet had been watching the progress of the de Valera–Cohalan fight before ever he arrived in Dublin. This was 'evident from their informed silence and comment on my account of it. Perhaps the reports de Valera sent them dealt largely with his personal difficulties and differences.'[28]

There was no 'perhaps' about it. For example, before sending McCartan on his mission de Valera had sent a lamentation to Griffith, in which he made use of the increasingly familiar royal 'we' style:[29]

It is time for plain speaking now. A deadly attempt to ruin our chances for the bonds and for everything we came here to accomplish is being made. If I am asked for the ulterior motives I can only guess that they are

(1) To drive me home – jealousy, envy, resentment of a rival – some devilish cause I do not know what prompts.

(2) To compel me to be a rubber stamp for somebody.

The position I have held (I was rapidly driven to assert it or surrender) is the following:

(1) No American has the right to dictate policy to the Irish people.

(2) We are here with a definite objective. Americans, banded under the trade name (the word will not be misunderstood) Friends of Irish Freedom, ought to help us to obtain the objective, if they are truly what the name implies.

It was in the course of this letter that he made the point about the issue being one of personalities: 'It is not however from fundamentals like this that the trouble arises. The trouble is purely one of personalities. I cannot feel confidence enough in a certain man to let him have implicit control of tactics here, without consultation and agreement with me.' De Valera spelled out what he meant by 'consultation and agreement': 'On the ways and means they have to be consulted.' But he stipulated that he reserved 'the right to use my judgement as to whether any means suggested is or is not in conformity with our purpose'.

The kind of detail over which he claimed the 'right to use my judgement' in order to achieve 'consultation and agreement' was illustrated on at least two occasions prior to the bond certificate issue:[30] '. . . thousands of applications for these bonds . . . were presently ready for the public to sign. But before these could be sent out, President de Valera changed a word and a comma or two in the application to ensure greater definition of its purpose. The applications were then reprinted. . . .' In the second incident the pressure was the other way. Cohalan wanted de Valera to change a bond circular he had drafted in which de Valera used the words 'peasant' and 'steer', for these terms were objectionable in American usage. But de Valera held that 'peasant' had a poetic flavour and 'steer' was expressive. He got his way, and emerged from the discussion voicing his satisfaction that he 'had not given in to Judge Cohalan'. The argument had lasted for four hours. And as for his complaint to Griffith about the 'deadly attempt' to ruin the bond drive, it should be remembered that in New York, Cohalan and Devoy's home territory, the bonds brought in $600,000. Although this total was not known during McCartan's Dublin visit, it had been evident before he left that the bonds were selling well and the other two incidents had already taken place. Nevertheless, both in Cabinet and in a number of other meetings with McCartan, Collins and Griffith took the view that they had sent their elected leader to the USA and now had no option but to stand behind him in the face of what he said was a conspiracy to drive him home, based on jealousy or pride.

It was a remarkable display of loyalty all round. McCartan did not agree with what de Valera had done, and as a highly respected IRB man could easily have swayed opinion against him had he chosen to. Collins had had reservations about his going to the United States in the first place. Griffith, whom he had muscled out of the presidency of Sinn Fein, had never envisaged him either appointing himself President of the Republic when he got to America, or unilaterally deciding, without Cabinet consultation, to make the *Westminster Gazette* proposal, which decidedly lowered the presidential colours. And on top of these considerations there was the stark contrast in Dublin to the conditions in which de Valera was operating in New York.

The year 1920 was beginning to develop the pattern of events that has led to its being remembered in Irish history as the Year of the Terror. Collins' guerilla methods were achieving such success that the British had been forced to forgo normal methods of warfare also. Reprisals were being employed on both persons and property. Towns were being shot up; an undercover murder gang to counter the activities of the Squad had been set up by British intelligence. Prominent people like the Lord Mayor of Cork, Alderman Thomas MacCurtain, had already been earmarked for death. Special forces known as the Black and Tans, ex-servicemen dressed in khaki and black uniforms and not subject to the rule of law, were starting to make their presence felt – bloodily. The Auxiliaries, generally ex-officers and tough fighters, were also beginning to operate a counter-terror campaign. The Dail had been suppressed since the previous September, following the shooting of Detective Smith; but, operating underground, it was trying to exert its authority as a sort of home-based Government-in-exile. Sinn Fein courts were beginning to usurp the function of the British courts with some success. Before long Arthur Griffith would be in jail, and Michael Collins was already leading his legendary 'life on the bicycle'. He was top of the British wanted list; running his underground Dail Department, the Dail loan, his intelligence network and his communication and supply lines that crossed the Atlantic as readily as the Irish Sea; but still managing to attend with efficiency and promptitude to every call on him – except those to eat and sleep.

In addition to his other activities Collins made it a rule to visit Greystones each week to hand over de Valera's salary to Sinead, play with the children and be in a position to send their father progress reports on their welfare as well as making sure that Sinead's letters crossed the Atlantic safely. His own letters to de Valera are peppered with references like: 'I was at Greystones on Thursday evening last. All well there too, and cheerful in spite of everything.' Or, a week later: 'It would have been edifying for you to have seen me fooling with the children.'[31] One of Vivion de Valera's fondest memories ever afterwards was of 'keeping nix' (keeping watch) from a suitable vantage point up the street while Collins was in the house.[32]

Collins might have been forgiven for striking Greystones off his list, because de Valera had also tried to exercise his authority – and vent his suspicions of conspiracy – on him from across the Atlantic. Shortly after he arrived, an American newspaper cutting carrying de Valera's promise to redeem the Fenian (IRB) bonds of 1865–7 was sent to Collins who, commenting on the item, wrote to de Valera on 12 July:[33] 'That, of course, was quite right. It was worth going to America to be converted to that idea. I am serious. It was the right thing to do.' De Valera's reply, however, indicated that he found Collins' letter far from being 'the right thing': 'What did you mean by saying it was worth going to America to be "converted" to the idea of paying up the Fenian Bonds? Surely I never opposed acknowledging that as a national debt. You must mean something else. What is it?' Collins' reply on 29 August reminded de Valera of the fact that he had opposed Collins on the issue: 'I meant about the Fenian Bonds that it was worth going to America to be converted to my idea. Honestly I do not think that I was practically forced to delete a certain paragraph from the prospectus looked much in favour of the idea. For God's sake Dev. don't start an argument about its being from the prospectus only, etc. Don't please. It's quite all right.'

As an IRB man himself, Collins was mindful of the debt that his generation of Fenians owed to the previous one. He believed in continuity, and wrote later to point out to de Valera that the Fenian bonds' repayment would make the Dail responsible for an accumulation of interest at 6 per cent from the date of issue. It may have been the Fenian issue that made De Valera direct another shot across Collins' bows in connection with the Dail loan:

Only today [6 September], when I was drawing up form of application for American issue, did I notice [realize] that you propose that interest should be calculated from the day on which certificate fully paid – It should be of course from the date of the recognition and evacuation. I hope you have not made that mistake in your proposed issue in Ireland. The debt accumulated interest might be a very serious handicap later. We must look to the future.

In another letter ten days later he warned Collins that his method of calculating interest must not appear in any foreign subscription. His official biography notes approvingly how de Valera feared that the accumulated interest might make it 'difficult to keep faith with the bond-holders'.[34] As we shall see later he might well have found other, more concrete, grounds for worries about keeping faith with the bond-holders. But the biography makes no mention of Collins' reply on 6 October, which completely demolished de Valera's objections about the payment of interest:

Your remark with reference to the Interest Liability on the Loan Certificates – 'It should be, of course, from the date of recognition and evacuation' – astonishes me. So far as I am concerned, I was fully aware at the time of the liability we were incurring, and deliberately drafted the particular paragraph accordingly, Mr. Griffith, with whom I consulted today, says that he too was alive to what we were doing . . . your letter will of course come up Friday night.

When the matter came before the Dail Cabinet the result was:[35]

The entire position with regard to the Interest Payments was reviewed, and all present – Arthur Griffith, Cathal Brugha, W. T. Cosgrave and Count Plunkett – were agreed that the statement on the Prospectus accepting liability for interest from the time full payment was made was what was meant.

Collins pointed out that the loan had been thus described in Ireland, England, France and Australia and therefore: '. . . it would be very damaging if the issue in America were made on much more unfavourable terms than the issue in Ireland. I shall be eagerly waiting to hear from you on this subject'.

However, despite Collins' letters, de Valera went ahead with his own method of interest computation and issued the loan in America on 'much more unfavourable terms' than the Irish issue. In the light of all this, therefore, the decision of Collins and Griffith to back de Valera unequivocally showed a remarkably selfless inclination to put the cause of unity ahead of personal feelings. And, although one has to remember that he was partisan, one can understand why Pieras Beaslai should sum up their reaction by remarking that they were: 'to learn, to their cost, de Valera's standard of loyalty and gratitude to them at a later date'.[36] There was, of course, a severely practical political reason why de Valera should have been backed, both in America and in Ireland. As McCartan pointed out:[37]

We had built up de Valera as the sovereign symbol of our cause in the United States. De Valera as President had issued and sold Bonds of the Republic of Ireland, and as President of that Republic had asked the American people to recognise it. Our people had transferred their allegiance from the cause to him. His repudiation would irremediably injure our cause in America, lengthen the fight in Ireland, and encourage England to more murderous measures there . . . de Valera had usurped the right to speak and act for Ireland; and the situation left us without the power to challenge him.

So there was a sense in which Collins and Griffith were lumbered with their own creation: the man they had made President of Sinn Fein, elected to lead the Dail, and whom Collins in particular had helped to catapult into his position of American eminence by springing him from jail and smuggling him across the Atlantic. But Collins showed a degree of personal loyalty to de Valera that went beyond politics – though he proved himself keenly aware of the political aspect also – only a few weeks after helping to decide the *Gaelic American* controversy in favour of de Valera.

James O'Mara had offered his resignation to de Valera as loan organizer, trustee and Dail deputy.[38] His reasons were not then exclusively personality differences with de Valera. He thought that he had done what he had come for, set up a viable organization for the bond drive.[39] He did not like the tensions emanating from the split in the ranks of Irish Americans and he had a wife, family and business in Ireland which needed his presence. McCartan has recorded how O'Mara, a considerable person in his own right, gave de Valera 'the respect and deference due to a President; and would wait patiently, with sheaves of papers in his hand, till de Valera could give him an audience'.[40]

De Valera was less concerned at losing O'Mara than he was at what Cohalan and Devoy might make of his departure. He begged him to stay on:[41] 'Your resignation would be misrepresented and misconstrued. Certain persons are, as you know, but waiting for a vantage point to attack. I hate to make it so hard for you but you know I am stating the conditions as they are.' Once again he was able to count on the support of Griffith and Collins in twisting O'Mara's arm. In Dublin there was no acknowledgement that de Valera might have played any part in O'Mara's decision. His explanation that the resignation was 'purely on private grounds' was accepted uncritically. Collins wrote to Harry Boland on 19 April:[42]

> What on earth is the matter with Mr. O'Mara? There always seems to be something depressing coming from the U.S.A. I cannot tell you how despondent this particular incident has made me. No doubt I am over touchy in this matter, but yet, after a particularly hard year, every little divergence tells heavily. Mr Griffith is writing to Mr. O'Mara appealing to him to re-consider the question, as his action, if persisted in, would have a really bad effect – very much worse than the *Gaelic American* differences.

With the assistance of the pressure from Dublin in the background, de Valera again urged O'Mara not to resign by writing him a letter which broke the organizer's resistance.[43] Again he made no bones about stressing that he was concerned about what the Devoy–Cohalan clique would make of O'Mara's return to Ireland:

> My one anxiety henceforth will be to withdraw from direct political activities – so as to devote myself entirely to the winding up of the Bond Campaign. It seems to me almost a disaster that I must abandon the political objective just now. Your resignation as you see then involves a break up in my department as well as yours. Oh, do not, by unduly pressing your resignation now, spoil the ripe fruit of your devoted efforts hitherto. I . . . beg you to defer your intended departure for another month or two. . . . My entreaty is personal as well as official. You do not need to be reminded of the peculiar difficulties of the moment, you know the campaign that has been taking place underground – and how every opportunity will be seized when it is baulked in one direction to renew it in another.

In the event de Valera so completely outmanoeuvred O'Mara that he stayed on in the USA long after de Valera had gone home, only to be peremptorily disposed of when the Chief decided the time was ripe. But the unwinding of that saga must await its moment, and we must first examine what became of de Valera's anxiety to 'withdraw from direct political activities'.

His League of Nations campaign had of necessity gone into a less strident mode, partly because of his involvement in the bond drive and its attendant Devoy–Cohalan feud, and partly because the character of the League issue had been sharply altered. Wilson had been incapacitated by strokes since the previous autumn, and the whole question of American membership of the League had become increasingly doubtful through a combination of his leadership and prestige being removed from the fray and a Senate setback for the Treaty itself on 23 November 1919. By the time it came up for voting Senators had managed to adorn – or emasculate – it with no fewer than fourteen reservations. Rather than see this hybrid pass, Wilson's supporters had joined with the Republicans to kill it.

Seeking to garner whatever kudos might accrue from this defeat, de Valera made the grand gesture of cutting short his speaking tour and returned to the Waldorf Astoria from southern California. In real terms he had failed to secure either American recognition for Ireland or backing for Irish membership of the League. 'Although his contribution and that of the Irish-Americans was greatly exaggerated at the time'[44] his campaign could be – and was – represented as having had a bearing on the Senate result. This was so despite the fact that the politician described as 'the linch-pin' of the alliance between the anti-Wilson Democrats and like-minded Republicans, Senator William E. Borah, a leading member of the Senate Foreign Relations Committee, ascribed the principal credit for the defeat to Cohalan: '. . . you have rendered in this fight a service which no other man has rendered or could have rendered'. And a respected historian, Francis R. Carroll, evaluating the strength of the FOIF, has written that this evaluation was 'certainly true'.[45]

However, the Wilsonians had another tilt at the windmill on 18 March 1920. This time the Treaty had managed to acquire two further reservations, making a total of sixteen. One of these read as follows:

> In consenting to the ratification of the Treaty with Germany the United States adheres to the principle of self-determination and to the resolution of sympathy with the aspiration of the Irish people for a government of their own choice adopted by the Senate on June 6th, 1919, and declares that when self-government is attained by Ireland, a consummation it is hoped is at hand, it should promptly be admitted as a member of the League of Nations.

It was passed by 38 votes to 36, and de Valera reacted by sending a telegram in clear to Arthur Griffith which indicated that the Promised Land had been reached:[46]

A Te Deum should be sung throughout all Ireland. We thank Almighty God, we thank the noble American nation, we thank all the friends of Ireland here who have worked so unselfishly for our cause – we thank the heroic dead whose sacrifices made victory possible. Our mission has been successful. The principle of self-determination has been formally adopted in an international instrument. Ireland has been given her place among the nations by the greatest nation of them all.

Two days later he might well have sent another telegram saying: 'Hold that Te Deum.' For once more the pro- and anti-Wilsonites joined forces to kill the Treaty, Irish reservation and all, and thus America never became a member of the League of Nations. But neither then nor subsequently had de Valera the slightest intention of conceding that his telegram was either premature or unduly euphoric. Instead he wrote to Griffith five days after the Senate had killed the reservation to say that it was 'What I had always been wishing for, and it came finally beyond expectations'.[47] One biographer has judged that this reaction showed de Valera's 'inexperience in American politics because he obviously did not recognise that the resolution had been passed only as a tactical means of making the reservations so unpalatable to ensure the defeat of the actual Treaty'.[48]

But de Valera was not that simple-minded. He understood, with or without Machiavelli's teachings, that politics are about perceptions; and it suited him then and subsequently to heighten domestic Irish perceptions, amongst an unsophisticated electorate, that he was a wonder-worker who had bent the United States Government to his will. Here is the Authorized Interpretation of the significance of the Senate reservation which he first sanctioned seventeen years after cabling Griffith and subsequently took care to ensure remained in print thereafter:[49]

Ireland's position in relation to the League of Nations was thoroughly understood, and on March 18th, 1920, the United States Senate took an action on behalf of the small and struggling nation so remarkable that the gratitude of the Irish people was scarcely greater than their surprise. . . . It passed a resolution that: On Ireland's behalf the United States Senate had issued what amounted to a public reprimand to the Government of Great Britain, America's ally in the World War. It seemed as though recognition of the Irish Republic might not be too much to hope for if only the claim could be advanced with firmness and discretion by a united organisation.

De Valera's telegram to Griffith was in fact the forerunner of a familiar Irish parliamentary tactic whereby deputies caused their parliamentary questions to be reprinted in their local papers in such a way as to create the impression that they had somehow solved the problem merely by raising it. And when he wrote to Griffith in March 1920 de Valera had a very strong incentive to get him to believe that he had at least taken a major step in solving the problem of Ireland's claims, 'if only the claim could be advanced with firmness and discretion by a united organisation'. For immediately after the sending of the 'Te Deum' telegram on 19 March

Cohalan and Devoy had launched their most determined effort to get rid of him from America.

The McGarrity–McCartan faction got wind of an impending putsch when the following letter from Devoy to John McGarry fell into their hands:[50]

All the advantages, except the scandal of a fight, are on our side now . . . we'd be worse off in the end than if we fought it out now. I am also convinced that he meant to fight us all along and was only waiting for a good opportunity. He selected the wrong time and the wrong issue, because his judgement is very poor, but he is filled with the idea that the great ovations he got here were for him personally and practically gave him a mandate to do as he pleases. His head is turned to a greater extent than any man I have met in more than half a century.

. . . they wanted to make an excuse for the 'reading out of the movement' with which you know he has been threatening the Judge for some time. . . . The response he got which was the finest thing Cohalan has ever done, evidently deterred him from 'reading out' him and me. . . . His motto is the King can do no wrong . . . we cannot permit the continuance of the present intolerable relations without assuming responsibility for very serious danger to the cause.

Devoy and Cohalan decided to 'read out' de Valera at a caucus of Irish American leaders which they convened secretly in the Park Avenue Hotel, New York on 19 March. They had arranged that de Valera was to be decoyed out of the city to Chicago, where a fictitious dinner in his honour had been arranged. The findings of the caucus, repudiating de Valera, were intended to be revealed on the eve of the dinner – so that when de Valera turned up to rows of empty seats the impression would be created that the guests had stayed away in sympathy with these findings. However, Boland learned of the scheme; de Valera stayed in New York and the indomitable McGarrity pushed his way uninvited into the caucus meeting. The fiery 'gallowglass' then brushed aside all efforts to get him to leave, even though he had no invitation and attendance at the gathering was supposed to be confined to those who were allowed to sign a register after producing their credentials. The meeting had been planned as a trial of de Valera *in absentia*.

Cohalan opened for the prosecution with a tirade in which de Valera was accused[51] of alienating lifetime supporters of Ireland's cause through his arrogance and failure to consult with anyone, despite his ignorance of American politics and history. He was arraigned for wasting money through living in luxury hotels and of splitting the solidarity of the greatest movement for Ireland that had ever existed. Worst of all, he was charged with placing Ireland alongside England by his use of the Cuban analogy in a manner which could make Ireland a potential enemy of America's. Cohalan also read out his exchange of letters with de Valera over the *Westminster Gazette* interview. Then Devoy took over the case, alleging that the bond drive was being badly handled and that de Valera's advisers were 'the enemies of the leaders of the Irish race in America'. This was a reference to Maloney, whom Cohalan termed 'one of the ablest men in the

British secret service'. After an interlude of invective during which Brendan Behan would have had no cause to complain about lack of fidelity to that central Republican tenet, the Split, the gallowglass unsheathed his axe and McGarrity went into battle.

Where was de Valera, the subject of the meeting? Why had he not been invited? Two prominent New York politicians, Judge John W. Goff and Burke Cockran, thought McGarrity had a point. Cockran said that, if de Valera had made a mistake, 'it was the business of his friends to set him right, not by what might be considered abuse, but by friendly counsel.' Bishop Turner, too, thought some 'friendly counsel' with de Valera was in order.[52] Accordingly a phone call was put through from the meeting to de Valera's suit in the Waldorf. Harry Boland took it, and was disposed at first to prevent de Valera from going. But then a deputation arrived at the Waldorf from the meeting and, further and better particulars of what might be expected at the Park Avenue Hotel having been elicited, de Valera, accompanied by Boland and James O'Mara, went to confront Cohalan and Devoy.

McGarrity described him, not surprisingly, as appearing to be under a great strain as he entered the room.[53] 'His teeth were set, and he looked over the crowd, anxious, apparently to see the makeup of same.' Other descriptions were less sympathetic: de Valera's attitude was one of infallibility. The incredible meeting lasted for ten hours and was 'acrimonious in the extreme'.[54] The tension was such that at one point Harry Boland went into hysterics[55] and had to leave the room.

McGarrity says:[56]

The judge made a very clever case, keeping part of the time at least quite cool, and doing everything to irritate the President – walking close to him and pointing his finger, etc. The President was always courteous and respectful, and at one point when the Judge told the President he should repeat his assurances that he did not intend to lower the flag etc the President pointed out that he had already done so [de Valera then gave a number of occasions on which he had explained his Cuban references including a banquet at which Cohalan was present] . . . that he was quite conscious that the Judge desired to humiliate him and irritate him by making these requests to repeat and repeat . . . in the Judge's attempts to humiliate him he was only showing his own measurement to his friends.

However, McGarrity's assessment of the conference was far from being shared by everyone present. De Valera lessened the good impression he had created by repeating his observation that he had not been in the country a month before he realized that it was not big enough for himself and Cohalan. To this Bishop Turner replied that the judge could hardly be expected 'to leave his native land just because de Valera had come in'. But the respected shipping magnate John P. Grace, in a letter to a friend[57] some months after the confrontation, not only painted a far darker picture than McGarrity but raised questions about de Valera's sanity:

. . . I confess before heaven that President de Valera was that day revealed to me

174

as either labouring under some psychopathic condition or that the evil spirit himself had taken hold of the Irish movement . . . Judge Cohalan, humbling himself under insults repeated constantly during those ten hours . . . did everything humanly possible or imaginable to bridge the chasm. De Valera had not only been the aggressor, but repeatedly the aggressor, and perhaps encouraged to go a little further as each new aggression was overlooked. . . . De Valera's attitude was one of infallibility; he was right, everybody else was wrong, and he couldn't be wrong. . . . Bishops and priests, Protestants and Catholics, aged men born in Ireland and young men born here worked for those ten hours to bring President de Valera to the point of amenability. . . . I beg to repeat that not having seen him before, as for those ten hours he unfolded himself, I thought the man was crazy.

Finally, however, after both sides had stated and restated their respective positions as to who was entitled to control what in America where matters Irish were concerned, de Valera brought off a *coup de théâtre*. He announced that letters had come into his possession showing that the Devoy faction intended to send him home a discredited man. Devoy denied this, but Boland interjected to say that the man they were written to was present: 'John A. McGarry of Chicago'. Horrified at being singled out in such circumstances McGarry (to whom the Devoy letter quoted on p.173 was indeed written) was attempting to deny the charge when de Valera gestured dramatically at McGarrity and told him to: 'Get those letters.' McGarrity pretended to be about to reach into a pocket for the letters. At this, he said:[58] 'The audience became quite excited, and I fumbled in my overcoat as though going to produce the letters, when a number of persons took the floor and made an appeal . . . the incident of the letters was then dropped, in fact there was a general desire for peace.'

Judge Goff called for order, said that Cohalan had acted hastily and suggested that he was a big enough man to apologize in the interests of peace.[59] One account (McGarrity's) says Cohalan shook hands with de Valera and retracted his accusations; another (Charles Tansill's) denies this.[60] But there seems to be little doubt that in his moment of triumph he did shake hands with McGarrity and proclaim that, if he were dying in the morning, McGarrity was the man to whom he would hand over the cause of Ireland. Clearly he felt he personified the cause and that it had triumphed. Then Bishop Turner asked everyone to kneel while he said a prayer in Latin for harmony. He then persuaded the two factions to a truce and:[61] 'The meeting broke up on the understanding that henceforth de Valera would not interfere in purely American matters, and Cohalan and Devoy would keep out of essentially Irish affairs.'

The relevance of the hostilities between the warriors of the Waldorf Astoria and the Park Avenue Hotel (and the dissipation of energy and influence thus occasioned) to the actual situation in Ireland may be gauged by a brief consideration of two events which occurred a few days after the confrontation. On 29 March, 1920 the Bill for the Better Government of Ireland was introduced for its second reading in the House of Commons. It was one of the most significant pieces of Irish legislation ever brought before the House, for the Bill was the instrument which partitioned Ireland. The state of the land to which it was intended to bring 'Better Government' may be gauged from a despatch from Dublin published on the same day in the London *Daily News*. Although written by the ill-fated Erskine Childers with propagandist intent it none the less paints an accurate picture of the period:

> . . . a typical night in Dublin. As the citizens go to bed, the barracks spring to life. Lorries, tanks, and armoured searchlight cars muster in fleets. Lists of 'objectives' are distributed, and when the midnight curfew order has emptied the streets – pitch dark streets – the weird cavalcades issue forth to the attack. Think of raiding a private house at dead of night in a tank (my own experience) in a tank whose weird rumble and roar can be heard miles away. The proceedings of the raid is in keeping, though the objectives are held for the most part by women and terrified children. A thunder of knocks; no time to dress (even for a woman alone) or the door will crash in. On opening, in charge the soldiers – literally charge – with fixed bayonets in full war kit . . . in nine cases out of ten suspicions prove to be groundless and the raid a mistake. . . . Is it any wonder that gross abuses occur.

But nothing that the British could do to the Irish in Dublin was going to inhibit de Valera's campaign against the Irish American leaders in New York. He 'had no intention of upholding his side of the agreement'[62] with them. In fact the letter[63] to Griffith written after the Park Avenue confrontation formed part of his plan to escalate the war with Cohalan. He asked Griffith to get the Dail to 'secretly authorise him to spend between a quarter and a half a million dollars in connection with forthcoming elections in the United States'. De Valera made it quite clear that he did not want this demand made public because his adversaries could use it to block the bond drive: 'It is very important that there should not be an open rupture until the Bond drive were over at any rate.' To increase his leverage with Dublin, both in getting this money and in ensuring the Cabinet's continuing support against his enemies, he also sent Harry Boland to Dublin in McCartan's wake to lobby for him.

Once more Collins and Griffith stood by him, and he was again successful. On 29 June the Dail voted de Valera both a 'sum not exceeding $500,000 as he may require in connection with the election campaign for the Presidency of the United States of America' and a further sum 'not exceeding $1,000,000 to obtain the recognition of the Irish Republic by the Government of the United States'. None of this last was to be spent unless 'the recognition was assured'. One can take the vote either as a measure of the Dail's confidence in de Valera or as an indication that Sinn Fein considered it cost more to win American votes than to kill British forces – for the Dail only voted $1,000,000 to the Ministry of Defence actually to fight the war.

The de Valera–Cohalan war resumed shortly after they finished their prayers for peace. McCartan records that: 'The first aggressive move was taken by de Valera.'[64] He made an attempt to gain control of the FOIF Victory Fund through James O'Mara. On 10 April O'Mara wrote to the Friends in his capacity as a trustee (a position, of course, that he shared with de Valera) of the Dail Loan, making a formal request for a statement of account of the Fund. He quoted from a poster issued to publicize the Victory Fund and went on:[65] 'In response to this and similar appeals the money was raised. Such money morally belongs to Ireland – and it is only reasonable for the representative of the Government of Ireland to ask for a statement of account, both receipts and expenditures.'

The Friends took only six days to decide not to accede to this request, which was refused on the 16th. As a result de Valera privately included in Boland's Dublin brief an instruction to get the Supreme Council to present an ultimatum[66] to Devoy either to co-operate with de Valera or to be expelled, thus depriving Cohalan of vital Clan na nGael support. De Valera's elastic conscience was able on occasion to overcome his distaste for secret societies when it suited him. Meanwhile de Valera co-operated with Cohalan on a matter of common concern which still had to be resolved; this was the Mason Bill which had given rise to the Cuban suggestion and all the controversy which ensued.

On 8 May de Valera made a formal public declaration repudiating the right of the British Ambassador to represent Ireland in America. But what finally emerged from the smoke-filled back rooms of the Committee on Foreign Affairs on 28 May was not a Bill which would have had the effect of extending diplomatic recognition to Ireland, but a mere watered-down motion of sympathy. Patricia Lavelle describes the resolution as 'a bitter blow'.[67] McGarrity and McCartan were disgusted, and on 5 June the *Irish Press* came out with an editorial which said: 'These sympathetic Congressional farces must be ended once and for all time.'

But what emerged after the editorial appeared caused McCartan to wonder just who was responsible for the farce. For: 'It was rumoured that de Valera himself had drafted this resolution.' McCartan sought an explanation from de Valera, who 'explicitly and emphatically denied this rumour'. However, at the next meeting of the National Council of the Friends of Irish Freedom Cohalan claimed that de Valera had drafted the resolution. McCartan, who was present, naturally denied that this was so. But he was 'confounded' when Cohalan produced[68] 'a manuscript of the resolution – the first part of which – and the only part I looked at – was beyond doubt in de Valera's handwriting'.

McCartan went immediately to de Valera who then, and only then, explained to him that he had tried to draft a suitable resolution, and, having failed, threw the paper on the table. He claimed that Cohalan must have finished the resolution: '. . . a new prince cannot observe all those things whereby men are considered good . . .'[69] Having sent to Dublin for authorization to spend $1 million on securing 'recognition', de Valera did not wish to be associated with this tangible, embarrassingly personal, proof that he had given acquiescence to the fact that the Anglo-American relationship meant he had no chance whatever of securing it. This was shortly to be demonstrated again before another forum.

9

'IF THEY PROCEED WISELY . . .'

THE REPUBLICAN NATIONAL Convention met in Chicago on 9 June 1920 to choose its presidential candidate. Previously de Valera had agreed with Cohalan that at Chicago Cohalan would advocate the adoption of a plank in the Republican platform recognizing the Irish Republic. But two days before the Convention de Valera, accompanied by a large entourage, descended on Chicago before Cohalan got there and began directing the Irish lobbying attempts personally. This had the effect of creating two distinct, rival Irish camps.

Americans do not take kindly to outside efforts to influence their choice of President, and some of de Valera's closest and most loyal supporters advised that it would be 'improper for him and dangerous to intrude upon the Convention'.[1] Bishop Gallagher of Detroit begged him to leave Chicago and allow Cohalan and the FOIF to press the Irish case. Cohalan was a supporter of Senator Hiram Johnson and believed that if Johnson became President, with Borah as Secretary of State, then Ireland's cause would be greatly advanced. He felt a demand for an Irish republic would only make the US Republicans a target of attack from the anglophile press and raise the spectre of a war with England. But de Valera rejected this argument, saying that no President could give Ireland the recognition it sought unless he had a secure base in public opinion. And here again the royal plural obtruded: 'on us lies the duty of securing that opinion'[2] – by getting planks conceding recognition inserted in the main parties' platforms.

Accordingly, far from leaving Chicago, de Valera proceeded to indulge in as much razzmatazz as if he were a presidential candidate himself. Headquarters were taken, 'with huge circus posters outside'. A daily paper was published. The Irish were constantly in and out of the Republican headquarters. Leaflets were distributed. Arms were twisted. A torchlit parade was held 'with bands and banners' which, the *New York Times* commented, was 'more like old times than anything that has been seen in conventions in recent years'. De Valera addressed the marchers, telling them that: 'The Republicans must promise to recognise the Irish Republic. . . . All of Chicago wants this . . . I know the entire country wants this. I have been all over the country and I know.' McCartan considered that 'there was no chance of offending America that we did not take'. The *Chicago Daily Tribune* published a cartoon of de Valera, with a caption telling its readers that de Valera had assured the paper he 'was not a candidate for the presidency of the United States'. Of far more significance in view of what he actually did at the Convention was an interview that de Valera gave to another Chicago journalist.[3] He stated that his ambition was recognition of the Irish Republic and was then asked: 'Assuming that the Platform Committee does not go as far as you would like, would a plank something like the resolution passed in Congress be satisfactory?' To this he replied: 'At all times we have known that the American people were sympathetic. My mission is to get action in accordance with that sympathy.' Not for the last time in his career de Valera was talking soft while preparing to act tough.

He then attempted to get the Republicans not to adopt a plank favourable to Ireland as proposed by Cohalan, but one proposed by himself which contained the following words: ' . . . we favour the according by our Government to the elected Government of the Republic of Ireland full formal and official recognition. . . .' Cohalan's committed the Republicans to a 'recognition of the principle that the people of Ireland have the right to determine freely, without dictation from outside, their own government institutions and the international relations with other states and peoples'. De Valera's plank was rejected by the Republicans' resolutions committee by twelve to one; after a hard fight Cohalan's squeaked through by a margin of one vote, seven to six. On learning the result de Valera objected to Cohalan's victory and demanded that the judge's plank be withdrawn. At this the chairman of the resolutions committee became annoyed, reversed his own vote and killed the plank. De Valera's all-or-nothing attitude had got him – nothing; this was the price of his victory at the Park Avenue Hotel. He could not allow Cohalan's resolution to get through and his to fail, thereby proving Cohalan's charge that he was ignorant of American politics. He afterwards attempted to justify his behaviour by claiming that the Cohalan plank was too vague. He said it 'was positively harmful to our interests that a resolution misrepresenting Ireland's claim by understating it should have been presented'.

The following analysis by Sir Auckland Geddes,[4] the British Ambassador to Washington, is important not merely for the light it sheds on de Valera's Chicago contribution but also for its assessment of the real attitude of most American politicians to the Irish issue, as opposed to what some of them claimed, or indeed to what de Valera represented the position to be. Having described how 'conspicuous' the Irish were at the Convention, Geddes comments on how delegates were 'rather more pressingly invited than was quite politic' by the Irish into a 'large propaganda office'. He tells how:

> Cohalan drafted the plank in the first instance and made it a mild document, expressing the sympathy of small nationalities in general and of Ireland in particular. De Valera then got hold of the resolution and modified it so as to make it advocate material American assistance towards the realisation of Irish aspirations . . . it was rejected by 12 votes to 1.

Cohalan then set to work again and largely if not mainly through the assistance of Senator Medill McCormick of Illinois, had his own milder plank resubmitted to the Committee, who accepted it by 7 votes to 6, though there was a great fight on the subject, it being pointed out that in a platform the general tendency of which was aversion from foreign entanglements, such a plank would be grotesquely incongruous and expose the party to strong criticism.

The inclusion of such a plank in the programme of the party that was about to form the next American Government was obviously a matter of considerable significance. The *Chicago Tribune* thought the Republicans had gone too far in meeting Cohalan's wishes, and in fact attacked the plank for its potentially disruptive effect on Anglo-American relations, saying that it 'was in effect a recognition of the secession of Ireland from the British Empire and its recognition as independent state.'[5] But de Valera did not see it that way. Geddes goes on to describe how: 'At this point De Valera again appeared on the scene and, disavowing Cohalan's draft, advocated the adoption of his own stronger plank. Upon this the Committee replied that as the Irish leaders were quarrelling and did not seem to know themselves what they wanted, they would leave Ireland out altogether; and at the last moment the Irish plank was removed altogether from the platform.' From an Irish point of view, Geddes' shrewd summing up of this wasted opportunity is melancholy, but telling: 'The incident illustrates in an interesting manner the immense influence Irishmen can exert on American politicians *if they proceed wisely*; and how ready American politicians are to withdraw themselves from that influence if they can find some colourable pretext for doing so.'

The successful Republican presidential candidate, Warren Harding, subsequently endorsed in public the work of the American Committee for Relief in Ireland with a statement on 26 March 1921 which Geddes unsuccessfully tried to get him to disown.[6] In fact the Harding administration exerted pressure on the British to allow the Committee, an inspiration of Dr Maloney's, furthered by the Society of Friends, ultimately to distribute over $5 million in Ireland for charitable purposes. To put this in context it should be noted that the Committee, whose work was publicly supported by politicians of the eminence of Herbert Hoover and Calvin Coolidge, stayed out of the de Valera–Cohalan feuding, and from the time of its inception in December 1920 organized the sending to Ireland of two and a half times as much money as de Valera caused to be sent. He too collected some $5 million, but ordered about $3 million to be retained in America even when he left the country. One may not be too wide-eyed about the presidency which gave rise to the Tea-Pot Dome scandal, but it is legitimate to speculate on how far across the sentiment line might have strayed a President Harding who showed sympathy towards Ireland with no Irish plank in his platform, as compared to one who was subject to such a policy directive.

However, what is certain is that in the wake of the Chicago debacle,

American politicians who, in Geddes' phrase, sought 'colourable pretext' for withdrawing from the Irish issue, received ample excuse for doing so. For the Cohalan–de Valera performance received an encore at the Democratic Convention in San Francisco the following month. McCartan writes: 'De Valera now hastened there and the spectacle of another fight with the Cohalan faction was staged for the American public.' And here, at the cost of diverting briefly from the story of the development of the split, we shall get a useful insight into how de Valera dealt with dissent on the part of independently minded supporters generally in his treatment of McCartan after San Francisco. Though he was privately appalled, in public McCartan continued to support de Valera throughout the controversy, launching fierce onslaughts on 'Cohalan-Americans' in the *Irish Press*.[7] De Valera had earlier made unsuccessful attempts to get McGarrity to remove him. He now appointed him to Washington and argued that it was inappropriate for him in his role of envoy of the Irish Republic to be involved in the affairs of an Irish American newspaper.

The incongruity of this reasoning in the face of his own attempts to interfere in the affairs of the *Gaelic American* did not trouble him. Subsequent to the Washington posting, and his removal from his *Irish Press* power base, McCartan was ordered by de Valera to go as envoy to Russia. Russian emissaries and the Irish had been talking on and off, largely through McCartan, for nearly two years, but, though a treaty was drawn up, in the face of the Red scare de Valera hesitated to conclude one with Russia in advance of other countries. However, he did agree to lend the hard-up Russian contingent in Washington $20,000, accepting some jewellery as collateral in a transaction which did not come to light until nearly thirty years later when the Russians repaid the loan and got back the jewels. After the failure to conclude a treaty McCartan felt his trip to Russia would be futile, particularly as de Valera gave him no instructions as to what he was supposed to do in Moscow[8] beyond represent an Irish Republic which he himself had spent eighteen months trying to get the Americans to recognize without success. But he duly set out for Russia on 29 December 1920 for a short and, as he had prophesied, inconclusive visit. The Bolsheviks had driven out the forces which some European governments had sent in a vain effort to assist the White Russian army, and the new regime no longer had need of Ireland's support. The time when an Irish treaty could have been secured had passed. By then, in fact, the priority lay in securing a favourable trade pact with Britain.

To revert to the de Valera–Cohalan split and its effects: from early in the campaign it was clear that the Democrats were going to lose the presidential election (Harding ultimately won by roughly 16 million votes to 9 million); but, in addition, any case for emulating or surpassing the Republicans in support for Irish planks at San Francisco had disappeared because of the row at the Chicago Convention. A de Valera-favoured resolution on Ireland sponsored by the Californian oil magnate Charles

Doheny was defeated, at which de Valera issued a statement saying: 'Rejection of the plank pledging the Democratic Party to the recognition of the Republic of Ireland merely indicates that it has not yet realised how great is the volume of public sentiment in this country behind the demand for justice in Ireland.'

The Chicago and San Francisco debacles make it understandable why an Irish American historian would later write:[9] '. . . by at least 1920 a substantial body of organised anti-Irish opinion had developed as a reaction against the nationalist clamour. Indeed, it was a commentary on the exceptional vigour of the Irish-American community that the nationalist movement succeeded under these circumstances.'

The comment is just, but the 'exceptional vigour' owed much to the inflammatory effect of British activities in Ireland which tended to subsume differences, albeit after the elections. One of the charges made at the time was that the feuding gave the British a free hand to perpetrate atrocities in Ireland. McCartan, who was himself of that opinion, quoted Bishop Gallagher:[10] 'If President de Valera had remained away from Chicago and allowed Americans to run their own affairs . . . the fear of American public opinion would have stayed the murderous hand of England from commencing such murderous atrocities as Ireland has lately endured.'

One could not argue that the feud made for circumspection on the part of the British, but the interaction and nature of the forces locked in guerilla warfare in Ireland had inevitably released horror on the land anyhow. Black and Tans, the Squad, auxiliaries, regular troops and the IRA combined with sectarian violence in Northern Ireland to cause deaths in awful circumstances. Drunken soldiers fired at pedestrians from lorries. The IRA shot spies in crowded restaurants. An ambush by Volunteers was liable to be followed by reprisals on the district concerned, which could consist either of the shooting of civilians or the burning of creameries, factories or houses by 'unknown men'. Press and public opinion had forced the British to the concept of a 'police war', because a conventional military campaign in Ireland would not be tolerated. Lloyd George summed up the police-war policy at the Guildhall Banquet in London on 9 November 1920, months after the American presidential debacles:[11]

> There is no doubt that at last their [the police] patience has given way and there has been some severe hitting back . . . let us be fair to these gallant men who are doing their duty in Ireland . . . it is no use talking about this being war and these being reprisals when these things are being done [by the IRA] with impunity in Ireland.
>
> We have murder by the throat . . . we had to reorganise the police. When the Government was ready we struck the terrorists and now the terrorists are complaining of terror.

Thus while press and world opinion were scarcely edified by the ego trips to Chicago and San Francisco, it is difficult to demonstrate that they would have sanctioned any marked escalation of the violence as a result. Anything the British managed to get away with was more than compensated for by the enormous sympathy generated for the Irish struggle by events such as the seventy-four-day hunger strike of Terence MacSwiney, the Lord Mayor of Cork, who, on being arrested during an IRA meeting, went on hunger strike and died the following 25 October. The hanging of eighteen-year-old Kevin Barry, a day after MacSwiney's funeral and shortly before Lloyd George delivered his speech, also helped to illuminate, and discredit, the policy of 'murder by the throat'. The fertile brain of Dr Maloney came up with the idea of a 'court' composed of distinguished Americans, sitting under the auspices of the *Nation* newspaper to hear witnesses and prepare a report on such happenings in Ireland.

De Valera, who was wary of Maloney, was at first against the idea. But eventually Maloney persuaded him to drop his opposition, which, amongst other reasons, de Valera based on the fact that the British could swamp such a tribunal with witnesses of their choice. The *Nation*'s owner, Oswald Garrison Villiard, agreed to allow the paper's name to be used provided that a suitably prestigious committee could be formed. De Valera promised to send telegrams to influential figures in the Irish American Committee urging them to back the idea; but the response was so poor that Villiard told Maloney he was disassociating the *Nation* from the scheme. Maloney then discovered that the de Valera telegrams had not been sent: 'de Valera excitedly denied it was his fault[12] and blamed Liam Mellows for not sending them out. This was a curious reaction from a man who oversaw detail to the point of having brochures reprinted over a comma out of place. When the telegrams did go out, they drew a response that included 'Cardinal Gibbons, Archbishop Keane, and four Catholic Bishops, seven Protestant Episcopal bishops, four Methodist Bishops, the Governors of five states, eleven U.S. Senators, thirteen Congressmen, the Mayors of fifteen large cities, and college presidents, editors, and leaders of labour and industry representative of thirty-six states.'[13]

The 'court' held its first sitting on 19 November 1920. It heard testimony from, amongst others, eye-witnesses to the burning of the towns of Balbriggan, Cork and Thurles by Crown forces, and the widows of Terence MacSwiney and of Thomas MacCurtain, the Mayor of Cork whom the RIC had murdered. Several ex-members of the RIC gave evidence of the kind of instructions the 'police war' elicited, and their outcome. When the report of the 'court' was published an editorial in the *Manchester Guardian* on 31 March 1921 said:

> . . . in the main the facts, unhappily, are only too far past dispute, like those of the German reign of terror in Belgium in 1914. . . . A few men like Sir Hamar Greenwood [Secretary of State for Ireland] have landed us in the dock, without a defence, before the conscience of mankind. To dispute the few details, to point out a few excesses in this detestable American report, would only advertise its crushing remainder in truth. Our Government has put us in the stocks. . . .

The impact on Irish Americans of this 'detestable American report' more than made up for any lasting damage caused by the de Valera–Cohalan split. However, undoubtedly one of the most unlikely, and innocent, victims of the feud was Sinead de Valera. Her husband was attending the Democratic Party Conference in San Francisco when the following telegram arrived for him from James O'Mara:[14] 'To Eamon de Valera, President of Republic of Ireland, care of Liam Mellows, 504 Grant Buildings, 1045, Market St. San Francisco. Harry tells me Flanagan and family splendid. Expects Flanagan end this month, Jim.' Flanagan was Sinead and Harry was Harry Boland, back from his mission in Dublin. Decoded, the telegram meant that Sinead was on her way to America. De Valera's official biography makes no mention of this telegram, but instead gives the following description of the circumstances of her arrival which makes it appear that he knew nothing about her coming until she actually arrived, not at the end of July, but in the middle of August:[15]

> When Boland returned to Ireland in May, 1920, he decided to ask Mrs. de Valera to visit America for a few weeks. The President did not think this was wise and Mrs. de Valera was reluctant to leave the young children. Somehow Boland persuaded her. She arrived in America in the middle of August, and she stayed there for six weeks. In Washington de Valera was very surprised and perturbed, one day in August, to get a telegram that 'Flanagan' had arrived. Despite Boland's talk, he did not believe that Mrs. de Valera would be persuaded to travel and he took it that the volatile Father Michael O'Flanagan, vice-president of Sinn Fein, had landed in New York to add to the troubles already mounting up in Irish-American circles.

The account of Sinead's arrival is notable for a number of reasons other than the lack of reference to O'Mara's telegram. It also demonstrates the near-pathological preoccupation which de Valera developed for denying Collins public recognition for his services either to him or to Ireland in matters both great and small. As readers will shortly see for themselves, there were other reasons why the foregoing official account should differ from that given by Dr Dwyer below, but the tendency to suppress Collins' role in his life is well exemplified in that extract from de Valera's own authorized biography. In his decidedly unauthorized account Dr Dwyer makes this point about Collins:[16]

> Despite being the most wanted man in the country [he] regularly risked life and limb bringing Sinead money and news from America, and while at the house he would take time to play with the children. In later life she would go out of her way to tell members of the Collins family how much the visits had meant to her. Collins also arranged for her to visit the United States during 1920, though in this instance de Valera probably resented the gesture, because he told Sinead her place was at home with the children and he sent her away.

Dr Dwyer then goes on to give other reasons why de Valera might have resented Sinead's arrival in New York: 'She had actually come at a time when there were some ugly rumours circulating about his secretary, Kathleen O'Connell. They had been travelling about the country together, and rumours that they were having an affair had found their way into the press. Organising Sinead's visit would not therefore have been one of Collins' more helpful gestures in de Valera's eyes.' No, indeed! After more than seventy years have elapsed there is little to say beyond what Dr Dwyer records, namely that there were continuing and widespread rumours of an affair. These became so magnified that years later de Valera referred to them in the Dail, on 22 November 1928. After dealing with the *canard* that Sinead had left him to go abroad because 'I was supposed to be living with two or three other women', he declared 'I myself was told by a lady in Chicago that a bishop told her that my wife had to go over to America in order to keep me straight there because I was associating with women.'

The rumours about de Valera's American love-life gave rise long afterwards to one of the immortal stories[17] of Irish politics. De Valera had become Taoiseach and was leading his followers into the division lobby when from outside the chamber came the sound of the locked doors being banged and kicked. One of his more colourful followers, Donogh O'Malley, had tarried too long at the bar and was trying, unsuccessfully, to get in to vote. Next day the Chief sent for the miscreant. After a long, Mussolini-like walk to the Desk of the Presence and an even longer silence, which would have reduced anyone else to a jelly, de Valera spoke: 'Mr O'Malley, do you know what they are saying about you?'

O'Malley blandly answered: 'No.'

With an awful frown de Valera thumped the desk and thundered: 'They are saying you drink too much.'

O'Malley replied: 'Yerrah, don't mind them, Chief, sure look what they're saying about you!'

Flabbergasted, de Valera asked what they were saying.

To which O'Malley answered imperturbably: 'Sure they're saying you had an affair with Kathleen O'Connell in America.'

De Valera was caught so completely off guard that the interview turned into a long dissertation on his American itinerary which proved conclusively, to his satisfaction, that he could not possibly have had an affair as he and Kathleen were in different cities. O'Malley survived, took the pledge, and was on his way to becoming the best Minister for Education in the history of the State when he died prematurely in 1968.

But the O'Malley incident occurred in the 1950s. In 1920 Sinead de Valera seems to have had a pretty miserable visit to America. Evidently de Valera felt it necessary to concede as much, even in the Authorized Version:[18] 'He was so taken up with the serious strife with Devoy and Cohalan during his wife's visit, and was so busy with meetings and work on the Irish cause, that they had little time together. The publicity and ceaseless activity had few attractions for Mrs. de Valera. . . . ' Living in the vast Waldorf Astoria must have been daunting for her. The O'Maras (wife, O'Mara himself and Patricia) 'spent a great deal of time with them' but, significantly, Patricia notes that 'we stayed at a more quiet hotel just a block or two away'.[19] Sinead hated publicity, but 'the newspapers wished to interview Mrs. de Valera. . . . She refused but they all begged her to change her mind . . . she finally gave way and had a short interview.'[20] On 1 October Patricia, who had returned to Ireland, received a letter from her mother: 'Our Friend's wife is soon going home.' Sinead wrote to James O'Mara from Greystones, later in the month of October, thanking him for his and his wife's kindness to her: 'We pray every night for you. I know how weary and trying the time is. . . . '[21] The transformation of de Valera the Nice Guy into de Valera Man of Power was complete.

What the references to 'serious strife' boiled down to was the fact that during Sinead's visit de Valera was moving to take over leadership of the Irish Americans and their organizations. After the second Presidential Convention debacle, moves were initiated to have a conference called in an attempt to bring an end to the feuding. McCartan wrote to McGarrity[22] suggesting such a conference, but advocating that neither de Valera nor Harry Boland be invited to attend:

My experience of him [de Valera] and Harry is that they come to a conference not knowing what they want. Have an unconscious contempt or seem to have such for opinions of others. The Chief presides and does all the talking. Has a habit of getting on to side issues and shutting off people who wish to speak and thus makes a bad impression if not sometimes enemies. Tends to force his own opinions without hearing from the other fellows and thus thinks he has co-operation when he only gets silent acquiescence.

Obviously such a conference had no attractions for de Valera. He wanted one of his own moulding and wrote to the President of the FOIF, Bishop Gallagher, suggesting that an Irish Race Convention be held at a central point 'like Chicago'. He had two objects in mind in suggesting such a conference. One, unstated, was that he wanted to hold it away from New York, where the Cohalan grip on the FOIF would be weakened. Second, his letter to Gallagher stated that his aim was that 'official policy [of America] towards Ireland should come forward definitely, explicitly and above board during the coming election campaign'. He walked into a storm of controversy in the wake of this letter when it was revealed that he had got the Dail's sanction to spend half a million dollars during the election. But with his talent for seeing things black when others said they were white and vice versa he issued a statement[23] denying that he intended spending money trying to influence events: 'In public and in private I have been scrupulously careful to avoid even appearing to take sides in the party politics of the country. . . . Apart from any possible illegality, it would obviously be bad taste on my part and most inexpedient.' Blandly ignoring his interference in Chicago and San Francisco, he was still maintaining this fiction fifty years later. In his biography he had it stated that 'he never could be accused of interference with American internal politics'.[24]

But the Cohalan-leaning FOIF had been at the receiving end of de Valera's non-interference policy for too long to accept the Race Convention proposal easily. After stalling him for some months, the FOIF agreed to the holding of a National Council meeting in New York on 17 September 1920. De Valera telegraphed Council members from all round the country in order to secure majority support for a motion by him to amend the Constitution so as to dethrone Cohalan. However, the telegrams alerted the Cohalanites to his plans and he was at first prevented from even entering the meeting, only getting in after Harry Boland shouldered the doorman out of the way. Once he was inside, however, Michael J. Ryan, the Chairman, denied him the right to speak on a procedural point. One of de Valera's supporters[25] described it as 'The most disgraceful gathering of men and women that I ever attended.' At about one o'clock in the morning de Valera staged a dramatic walk-out 'amidst tumultuous scenes' and arranged with those who followed him to hold another meeting the following day in the Waldorf Astoria, at which a rival organization to the FOIF would be formed.

He told the assemblage in the Waldorf Astoria that the new organization was to be formed on democratic lines and controlled by its members throughout the country instead of by a cabal in New York. However, de Valera's version of democracy was evidently intended to be of the guided variety – the royal plural showed up remarkably freely in his short statement of policy: 'We from Ireland simply ask . . . that we should be accepted as the interpreters of what the Irish people want – we are responsible to them, and they can repudiate us if we represent them incorrectly.'

There may, or may not have been, some significance in the fact that at this stage he was observed to be 'carrying about a pocket edition of Machiavelli'.[26] His new grouping was launched in Washington DC on 16 November 1920. Called the American Association for Recognition of the Irish Republic (AARIR), appropriately enough it became generally known as Growl. It succeeded in its principal aim of supplanting the FOIF. At one stage its membership was claimed to be seven hundred thousand,[27] and at various times de Valera considered using the organization to raise huge sums of money. A levy which would have brought in a million dollars a year was proposed by him, and he also entertained thoughts of another American loan of $20 million.[28] However, an organization whose leader crosses to another continent after founding it is necessarily at some risk. When, in addition, the cause for which he has founded it seems to disappear also, as happened over the next few years, its condition becomes terminal.

The original goal of the Dail in voting de Valera the half million dollars to influence the presidential campaign was not lost sight of – rather, it evaporated. Observers of the American scene would have found this inconceivable earlier in the year. A British Embassy report drawn up in March stated:[29]

> As the election campaign draws near . . . foreign politics have become a matter of nationwide interest. It is impossible to exaggerate the extent to which the Irish question and the Irish vote dominates this situation. Other agitators such as the Germans and the Indians attach themselves to the Irish organisation and obtain from it support and a veneer of respectability.
>
> Considered in a broad manner and disregarding comparatively minor issues such as the nature of the Home Rule bill or disputes amongst Irish politicians in America, the outstanding fact is that the Irish vote in America is enormous, well-disciplined, and easily swayed by anti-British sentiment, and that at moments of crisis American politicians even against their convictions will bid for it.

Shrewdly, however, the report speculated that in the end the Irish might not succeed in worsening Anglo-American relationships because 'people are increasingly tired of having Irish grievances obtruded upon them and injected into purely American issues'. This factor and 'the disputes amongst Irish politicians' effectively took Ireland out of the campaign. Throughout it Harding was an easy front-runner for whom many Irish Americans announced their intention of voting, as against Wilson who had led them into a war. He had no compulsion to cross the line between sentiment and official policy. And when de Valera sent a formal demand for recognition of the Dail to the Secretary of State, Bainbridge Colby did not even reply. The demand was based largely on Wilson's wartime statements on self-determination. It is likely that the official silence was an eloquent commentary on the lack of wisdom (to say nothing of charity) in sending such a point-scoring document to a paralysed and incapacitated President.

Apart from weakening any chance the Irish had of elevating Ireland to the level of a substantive issue during the presidential campaign, the dispute led to a number of other damaging occurrences in the Irish American world. These were both significant in themselves and illustrative of the continuing support extended to de Valera by Michael Collins, even though one of the rows was to lead to serious trouble for him later. The first development came after the Chicago debacle. Diarmuid Lynch resigned in disgust, both as National Secretary of the Friends of Irish Freedom and as a Dail deputy. Collins sided against his IRB colleague with de Valera to the extent that he even stopped the *Irish Bulletin*, the Sinn Fein propaganda sheet which contained accurate accounts of the war in Ireland, from going to Lynch lest it gave him and the Cohalan faction a 'power to use against the President'. There was a very strong body of opinion amongst Irish Americans that the British were taking advantage of the feud to step up the military campaign. The escalation of hostilities described in the *Bulletin* could have been used to support this view.

Following Lynch's resignation, Devoy began to use the *Gaelic American* to raise the contrast between Michael Collins, 'Ireland's fighting Chief' who was risking his life in Ireland, and the other Chief in America. 'Michael Collins speaks for Ireland,' the paper said. But Collins wrote to Devoy, saying:[30] 'Every member of the Irish Cabinet is in full accord with President de Valera's policy. When he speaks to America, he speaks for us all.' Cathal Brugha, who had become so imbued with jealousy at Collins being accorded honours which he thought rightfully his, would one day use these articles to attack Collins; while de Valera, sitting close by in silent approval, made no mention of Collins' disavowal. Collins also backed Boland in the task which de Valera had set him of getting Supreme Council support from the IRB in Dublin to use the Clan in America against Devoy and Co. Initially Boland used this support to call a meeting in New York at which 'all differences were adjusted'. But then in October, as the unveiling of Growl neared, Boland went further than envisaged in Dublin and used his support from Collins to issue a statement to the press saying:

> ... we have been reluctantly compelled to sever our connections between the Clan-na-nGael and the parent body in Ireland until such time as the will of the members of the Executive becomes operative and not the will of Justice Cohalan. .... In the view of the parent organisation it is intolerable that the *Gaelic American*, well known here and in Ireland, to be the organisation's organ, should be using its circulation amongst the members to propagate misrepresentation and falsehood. . . .

Boland then went on to set up a 're-organised Clan', so that the split in the Friends of Irish Freedom was also replicated in the underground Clan na nGael. Devoy held most of his New York support and ridiculed his replacement as secretary of the executive by Luke Dillon as an example of de Valera-style democracy – the first time in history that a minority had replaced the majority. This was certainly well in an excess of anything that Collins had envisaged, and when the full circumstances became clear he later wrote to Devoy to apologize. Nevertheless, at that stage he again took the view that de Valera was Dublin's man in the USA and wrote in support of him, even though he was immersed in the preparations for one of the most complex, and horrific, operations of the entire war, Bloody Sunday, which took place two days afterwards.

On the morning of Sunday, 21 November 1920 the sounds of Dublin's Mass bells were suddenly punctuated by staccato bursts of shooting as Collins' men crippled the entire British Secret Service operation in Ireland by shooting its leadership: some nineteen officers died. One or two of the victims probably had nothing to do with spying, but the rest of the dead had been leading a counter-attack against Collins' own campaign which had come within a fraction of succeeding. Some of his best men had been captured, tortured and shot. Others had been interrogated and let go, but were obviously under surveillance. His own escapes were becoming narrower and narrower. Accordingly, on that fatal Sunday he unleashed the Squad, backed up by members of the Dublin Brigade, in the most awful, but telling, illustration of his dictum: 'England can replace a detective, but the new man cannot step into the dead man's shoes *and* his knowledge.' Some of the dead men were shot in bed, others in the presence of their wives or mistresses; one pregnant woman miscarried shortly after seeing her husband gunned down before her eyes. The Auxiliaries and Black and Tans struck back that afternoon by shooting up a crowd attending a Gaelic football match at Dublin's Croke Park. Fourteen people were killed, including one of the players (after whom the Hogan Stand is named today), and hundreds were injured.

No single event could better illustrate the atmosphere of terror and counter-terror in which Collins and the staff of GHQ fought the war in Dublin while de Valera fought his own battles in America. However, de Valera did not plan to be in America for much longer. Word had reached him of Arthur Griffith's arrest and replacement as Acting President by Collins, and there was increasing mention in the press about peace parleys being conducted between Lloyd George and Collins through the intermediacy of Archbishop Joseph Clune of Perth. If anyone was going to conduct peace negotiations with the Prime Minister of Britain de Valera intended that it should be he, not Michael Collins.

At this stage it is incumbent on a biographer to attempt to draw up some sort of political balance sheet for de Valera's eighteen months' stay in America. Was it a success or a failure? What did he achieve? The entries include some large debits and credits. These may be summarized in the sharply contrasting views of John Devoy, Liam Mellows and the poet W. B. Yeats, who heard him speak during his tour. Devoy, as we have seen, found him: ' . . . filled with the idea that the great ovations he got here were for him personally and practically gave him a mandate to do as he pleases'. Liam Mellows judged that 'de Valera changed an ignorant and either apathetic or hostile people into genuine sympathisers in two years. He made the name of Ireland respected where it was despised and the Irish Cause an ideal where it had been regarded as political humbug. . . .'[31] Yeats thought him: 'A living argument rather than a living man. All propaganda, no human life, but not bitter or hysterical or unjust. I judged him persistent, being both patient and energetic, but that he will fail through not having enough human life to judge the human life in others. He will ask too much of everyone and will ask it without charm. He will be pushed aside by others.[32]

There is a core of truth in all three evaluations. From the point of view of the Irish Nationalists the anxiety he caused the British indicates something of his worth to the Irish cause. The cost to it of his ego and power-seeking is contained in the record of the Republican Convention and the split with Cohalan, Devoy and other figures like Diarmuid Lynch.

In February 1922, by which time he had had painful opportunity of studying de Valera's character at first hand, Michael Collins wrote to John

Devoy[33] apologizing for taking sides against him in the post-Cuban interview split. He explained the understanding that he and other members of the Cabinet had of de Valera's American mission: 'Our idea was to have some sort of a world-wide federation, each separate part working through the Government, and in accordance with the laws of the country where it had its being, but all joined by common ties of blood and race. Unfortunately some of those we sent to America did not understand the vital principle of that idea.'

But it was not a question of de Valera simply not understanding the 'vital principle'; he never countenanced it for a moment. He saw himself as the Boss. The 'common ties of blood and race' in his case were subject, after all, to the fact that he was half-Spanish. Heredity must be given some role in his make-up. But whether heredity is any guide in assessing another, most important, aspect of his American tour is harder to judge. For the strange fact is that the bulk of the money raised through the bonds, supposedly the cause of his differences with the other leaders, was not remitted to Ireland. Making allowances for the expenses incurred during his tour and the fact that some monies were remitted to Ireland, he nevertheless left behind him in America something approaching 60 per cent of what was collected. Responding to questions about American financial support for the independence struggle, de Valera's loyal supporter, Sean Moylan, said in a memoir intended for posterity:[34]

> . . . were there not huge sums subscribed for the Irish Republican Dependents Fund? What about the Dail Loan and the generous subscription from the U.S.A.? I can only say that, as far as my knowledge goes, not a cent of any of those funds was devoted to the organisation of the Irish Republican Army . . . generous friends gave me my food and shelter. I needed nothing more. I didn't smoke, I drank only when wearied muscle had to be flogged to meet unexpected demands or as a remedy for complaints caught from soaking rain and chilly winds.

Obviously some of the funds that Moylan mentioned went towards arms purchase, publicity, and intangibles such as the cost of informants – invaluable in an information war, which is largely what the Anglo-Irish struggle was. But the picture painted by Moylan, an accurate representation of the lot of the average Volunteer, indicates the relief which the millions de Valera left behind him could have brought to the ranks of the IRA. And although de Valera advocated 'frugal comfort' rather than high living, his stay in the USA, while it generated a good deal of revenue for the 'cause', must also have cost a fair sum. A British officer who accompanied the Prince of Wales during his stay at the Waldorf Astoria while de Valera was also in residence at the hotel has left this description:[35]

> The Irish 'President' Valera was in the midst of his activities in New York, and his quarters, also at the Waldorf Hotel, were besieged by every species of Irishman, honourable and otherwise. The 'president' kept open house. Cigars and

surreptitious drinks were to be had for the asking, and much hard-earned money contributed by poor servant girls to 'the Cause' must have been expended in providing refreshment for stray Hibernians and the hungry priesthood.

Whatever the truth of the officer's picture – his main interest in de Valera at the time was the threat which it was assumed his presence and that of his followers presented to the Prince, who was thought to be in danger of being blown up – a note[36] in Michael Collins' accounts, as Minister for Finance, gives an indication of the level at which de Valera lived while in the USA. He entered and left America as a stowaway, of course, but Sinęad's passage is put down as costing almost $1,900. Amongst other items, de Valera lists a gold cup which he presented at a christening ceremony at Joe McGarrity's house and $385 for a dentist – not remarkable sums by American standards, but well in excess of the monies at the disposal of his Cabinet colleagues back in Ireland.

There was also an intangible cost to de Valera's US trip – the fact that, being out of touch with Ireland, he lost touch with the reality of the situation there for a crucial period. Overall he must be reckoned to have attracted some very valuable publicity for Ireland and unique adulation for himself. To sum up, therefore, it may be said that de Valera achieved a triumphal progression through America, but as with all human achievement, progress contains hidden costs.

He spent his last two days in America saying goodbye to Joe McGarrity. First he travelled to Philadelphia on 9 December, accompanied by James O'Mara, to begin the protracted, and certainly melodramatic, leave-taking.[37] McGarrity urged him not to get caught, in case capture led to his going on hunger strike and dying like MacSwiney. De Valera's reply on the use of the hunger strike weapon was that he had an open mind, ' . . . it might be again necessary to use it, that at times great sacrifices were necessary of performance as they at certain times brought results which could not be brought about by other methods'. The three talked for a long time and then travelled back to New York together. The talk continued into the night of 9–10 December until McGarrity, who was ill at the time, departed for his hotel, the Commodore. Next day in the Waldorf they resumed.

De Valera wanted to appoint McGarrity as trustee of the Dail loan in his stead and generally to have him act as his alter ego in America. McGarrity asked him to put his thoughts in writing, which produced this: 'I hereby nominate – in accordance with the terms of the deed appointing me as one of the trustees of Dail Eireann – Joseph McGarrity of 3714 Chestnut St., Philadelphia, as my substitute, entitled to act with all my powers in case I am incapacitated by imprisonment or death or any cause. Eamon de Valera. Witnessed by James O'Mara.' A covering note stated:

Dear Mr. McGarrity,
    I anticipate to be absent from the U.S. for some time. During my absence I

wish you to act for me as Trustee of Dail Eireann with regard to such funds as are at present in the U.S.

The funds referred to were the $3 million from the bond certificate drive which for some inexplicable reason he had not sent back to Ireland. However, after all the talk a spanner was thrown in the works by a member of de Valera's entourage, Diarmuid L. Fawsitt, whom de Valera had appointed Irish Trade Consul in New York. Fawsitt announced that he had taken legal advice and de Valera could not appoint McGarrity as his sole trustee. Accordingly another document was drawn up, this time bearing five signatures:

> We the undersigned, hereby acknowledge that the funds committed to our care by President de Valera and Hon James O'Mara, T.D.E. are the funds of the Irish Republican government, and we pledge our honour to surrender on the joint requisition of those two gentlemen, or their substitutes duly appointed, in accordance with the decree of Dail Eireann, by which they become Trustees, such of these funds as may be in our keeping on the date of the aforesaid requisition.
> Witnessed by James O'Mara.
> Eamon de Valera
> Jos. McGarrity
> D. L. Fawsitt
> H. J. Boland

After this document was disposed of, McGarrity notes that de Valera was 'in good spirits and seemed to be glad to get away'. He told McGarrity that he 'felt as ready and fit as he did in 1916 and he thought it was the only thing to do, to go where he would be with his people, come what may. I felt rather unworthy of the honours he has showered on me by giving of his confidence to me and such a position of trust as he has. Lord Christ Jesus and Holy Ghost grant him and give him success.' McGarrity describes the final scene thus: 'As he was to go about twelve midnight he looked a bit sad. Taking my hand he said: "give my love to the missus and children and above all I want you to promise me you will take care of your health."' McGarrity notes that in reply he counselled de Valera to stand firm and not compromise, and said that in return he and his colleagues would be with him and would win. De Valera then said something which must have given McGarrity considerable pause for thought in the years that lay ahead: 'He said, never fear there is only one policy. We will keep to it.' After this de Valera 'stepped back, stood to attention and saluted'. McGarrity acknowledged the salute and passed through the door, accompanied by Fawsitt. 'Harry Boland stood gazing at the parting scene and was much more affected than anyone in the room.'

De Valera left Harry Boland with the following message for publication:

> So farewell – young, mighty, fortunate land; no wish that I can express can measure the depth of my esteem for you or my desire for your welfare and your

glory. And farewell the many dear friends I have made and the tens of thousands who, for the reason that I was the representative of a noble nation and a storied appealing cause, gave me honours they denied to princes – you will not need to be assured that Ireland will not forget and that Ireland will not be ungrateful.

It was a message which twenty years later would cause the American Ambassador to neutral Ireland during World War II to express himself with some bitterness.[38] But after only two months had passed de Valera was writing to O'Mara in anti-climactic terms concerning his rhetoric over the bonds: 'The Dail can still sit and therefore our emergency powers as trustees are not to be used.'[39] As he was in constant touch with Dublin he knew before leaving America that the Dail could meet, albeit in secrecy, so one is tempted to wonder whether he was simply creating a psychological chariot in which to depart from a McGarrity suitably impressed at the 'honours showered' on him. What is certain, and equally anti-climactic, is that, despite the dangers hinted at in the emotional declaration that he was returning to Ireland 'where he would be with his poeple come what may', we know now that the worst threat he faced was the risk of being sent back to McGarrity. For the British Government had issued the following instruction to Geddes: 'If he applies for a visa to a passport it is to be refused. If he returns clandestinely he will be deported to his country of origin. . . . In any communication to the United States Government you should emphasisc the fact he is not a British subject . . .'[40]

At all events, Collins' network enveloped him and he was safely smuggled aboard the SS *Celtic* – only to come close to a premature death. The ship put into port *en route*, and an ensuing routine search led to friendly crew members suggesting that he hide in a large empty water tank which was never used.[41] De Valera was on his way to the tank when, with his customary caution, he stopped to send one of the crew to find out if there were any danger of the tank ever being filled. There was a delay while the sailor went off to check. He returned with the news that orders had just been issued to fill the tank. Had de Valera been in it, he would have been drowned. Again on this voyage he was so sick that his accomplices thought at one stage he had died. When he recovered they used to show him the wireless messages saying that he had absconded from America with the bond money. 'He was very much amused.'[42] There were detectives waiting at Liverpool. To prevent them finding his hiding place one of his helpers threw ropes down to another who then shouted: 'I'm coming up.' It was de Valera who came up. His escort had grown fond of him on the voyage; he was described as being 'One of nature's gentlemen.'[43] His two seamen protectors showed both courage and ingenuity as they moved him around the ship while the search was in progress. Suspected of Sinn Fein tendencies, they were subjected to fierce interrogation and told they were under arrest, but were allowed to go free. At one stage it had looked as though his guardians were going to have to shoot their way off, but de Valera 'never lost heart, however, merely saying that we would weather it'.[44] Finally only a third officer was left guarding the gangplank. He was decoyed from his post by a promise of being given two brooms and, with de Valera dressed as a seaman, his friends were 'down the gangway like a shot out of a gun'.[45]

The liner had been at sea from 13 to 22 December. But it was the short trip to Dublin from Liverpool that gave de Valera most trouble. He was taken to the cabin of the second mate, who then left him to go ashore to 'deliver some dispatches for Mick [Collins]'. Not best pleased at this, de Valera inquired what would become of him while this man was ashore. The man airily reassured him: 'That'll be alright. I'll look after you.' However, the mate was gone a long time and de Valera began to imagine he could hear voices calling the man's name. It turned out that he was not imagining things. The door of the cabin was broken in by the captain and first mate, who asked a couple of not unreasonable questions: 'Where the hell was the mate?' and 'Who the hell are you?' To these de Valera answered with 'lolling head and grunts', pretending to be drunk. The officers left in disgust and the second mate showed up soon afterwards – very drunk.

De Valera went for him bald-headed. The mate had in his pockets two bottles of whiskey which de Valera threw out the porthole screaming. 'It'll be alright! I cross the Atlantic safely and you spoil it all by getting drunk. By heavens I'll have you shot when we get to Dublin . . . etc'. But de Valera's main concern was what was going to happen when the officers returned. 'That'll be alright,' came the familiar refrain. De Valera was cut off in mid-explosion by the sound of the captain's return, and he barely made it back into the bunk before the skipper entered the cabin thundering: 'What the hell does this mean? Who is this man?'

To this the swaying second mate replied: 'Sorry sir. Thass my brother-in-law. Terrible drunkard. Always ends up in hospital at Christmas with the DTs. My sister asked me for God's sake to look after him and get him home. He's just back from America and I thought the only way I'd get him home safe was by locking him in my cabin.' Imbued with the Christmas spirit, the captain accepted the explanation and withdrew.

De Valera crossed the Irish Sea without further incident. He was met at the docks in the early hours of 23 December by Tom Cullen and Batt O'Connor. De Valera asked how things were going. Cullen's reaction was spontaneous: 'Great! The Big Fellow is leading us and everything is going marvellous.' So was de Valera's. He struck the guard rail with his hand and exclaimed: 'Big Fellow! We'll see who's the Big Fellow. . . .'

10

THE 'LONG HOOR' V. COLLINS

DE VALERA WAS installed in the safe house where Collins had held
peace talks with Archbishop Clune, the Merrion Square home of Dr
Robert Farnan, a distinguished Dublin gynaecologist whose services were
highly thought of by the wives of British officers. The first visitor he
received was Cathal Brugha, the member of the Sinn Fein Cabinet who
most hated Collins. He did not see Collins until 5 a.m. next day, Christmas
Eve. Years later he told Frank Gallagher that Brugha had[1] 'told him the
position Michael Collins and his IRB group had taken, Collins as Acting
President and sharing power amongst his own set. He Cathal had been
offered the Acting Presidency but had not taken it. "And why did you
not?" asked Dev. "It was only at your refusal that the others came in".'

De Valera told Gallagher that he found a 'deep split' between Collins
and Brugha who were, he said, 'Wholly incompatible'. Curiously, that
Christmas Eve nearly ended in disaster for Collins because, with an
uncharacteristic lack of caution, he suddenly decided to hold a Christmas
celebration for some of his closest friends in the main dining room of the
Gresham Hotel and was nearly captured by the Auxiliaries. He only
escaped by convincing the officer in charge of the raid that an entry in his
diary said 'refills', not 'rifles'. Understandably, but also unusually, on that
Christmas Eve Collins went on to break his own code of temperance and
got rip-roaring drunk.[2]

Hindsight is always 20/20 vision and it is all too easy to over-extrapolate
from past events, but Collins' survival instincts were ordinarily so finely
tuned that, whether it was de Valera's return or another reason not known
to us, his normal behaviour pattern obviously suffered a major discordancy
that day. But whatever happened that Christmas Eve, there can be no
question of over-extrapolation in assessing de Valera's first major initiative
on returning from America. It was an attempt to get Michael Collins out of
Ireland.

There were three main strands to de Valera's policy on returning from
the USA. One was to assert his ascendancy over the colleagues to whom he
was now returning; this necessitated securing dominance over Collins in
particular. His second objective was to keep control over the Irish
Americans, and his third to take over the reins of the peace process and to
work himself into a favourable negotiating position with the British.

The Collins relationship developed as follows. De Valera was visited by
Sinead at Farnan's house on Christmas Eve, but the visit does not appear

197

to have evoked any overwhelming passion to be reunited with his wife and family. Instead he besought Collins to find him a secluded house near Dublin where he could operate in secrecy. Collins arranged to have rented for him Loughnavale, a Georgian residence in its own grounds on Strand Road, bordering Merrion Strand made famous by James Joyce's hero ogling a young woman.[3] Loughnavale had the advantage that 'Passers-by could not easily see from the road what was going on.'[4] In these salubrious surroundings de Valera settled into a household described, in the decorous prose of his official chroniclers, as consisting of 'Miss Maeve McGarry as housekeeper and Miss Kathleen O'Connell, returned from America, as private secretary'.[5] Leading a 'life on the bicycle', Collins had managed to visit de Valera's family in Greystones once a week and saw to it that Sinead was supplied with the money necessary to prevent her lapsing back into the dire conditions she experienced when de Valera was in jail. However, de Valera, at liberty and in a position to set his own agenda, evidently found the once-a-week schedule beyond him. He had little to do beyond getting to know people and calling for meetings of the Dail or Cabinet. His biography makes much of the fact that he 'succeeded in holding three meetings of the Dail in the five months after his return, as many as in the whole of the preceding year'.[6] Nevertheless after six weeks back in Dublin he had managed to see very little of Sinead, and his children not at all. On 3 February he wrote to James O'Mara: 'I haven't had an opportunity of seeing my youngsters yet though I saw Madame a few times.'[7]

However, what he did have ample opportunity for was to complain about the way things had been done in his absence. From the time he arrived back in Dublin de Valera made it clear that he disagreed with the methods of warfare practised by Collins and the IRA's Chief of Staff, Richard Mulcahy. On Christmas Eve he told Mulcahy:[8] 'You are going too fast. This odd shooting of a policeman here and there is having a very bad effect, from the propaganda point of view, on us in America. What we want is, one good battle about once a month with about 500 men on each side.'

Collins' behaviour later that day becomes more understandable in the light of that statement, which not only completely failed to evaluate the nature of the unique form of guerilla warfare which Collins had initiated but was military lunacy into the bargain. The following memoir by John McCoy describes the armament of one of the most active brigades in the country:[9]

In 1919 . . . in the Newry Brigade area, embracing all South Down and South Armagh, there was not more than half a dozen rifles to fire .303 ammunition. In revolvers and automatic pistols we had not much that could be classed as serviceable in a military sense. . . .

. . . From May, 1920, onwards, we were getting a fair number of .45 revolvers of various makes. . . . There seemed to be a famine in .45 ammunition . . . we got several hundred rounds of Winchester rifle ammunition. . . . The cases had to be shortened and the ridge on the firing end of the case to be filed down or turned in a lathe so that it would fit the revolvers. . . . . The question of safety was generally solved by tying the revolver to a stake and trying out the first of the adaptations at a safe distance. . . .

Even if the Irish had wanted to revert to the old 'static warfare' tactics, they did not have the arms or the men to mount pitched battles of the type de Valera advocated. Members of even the most successful flying columns rarely had as much as thirty rounds of ammunition for their obsolete rifles.[10] Had the IRA managed to put five hundred men into the field they could have been met not by five hundred, but by fifty thousand troops backed up by heavy artillery, tanks and aeroplanes, none of which did the Irish possess. And it was precisely because they did not engage in such tactics that Lloyd George had been driven to resort to the Auxiliaries and the Black and Tans, thus losing out badly in the propaganda war.

In arguing as he did, however, de Valera was already displaying the same tactics he had used in America where, for his own purposes, he backed McGarrity rather than Cohalan and Devoy. Now he was tilting towards Brugha and Austin Stack, whom Collins had antagonized by his brutally frank criticisms of Stack's incompetence as Minister for Home Affairs. De Valera was under no illusion as to the calibre of the allies he was cultivating. He described Brugha afterwards as being 'a bit slow',[11] but conceded that he 'could be persuaded'. However, 'Austin Stack could not':[12] 'Cathal would listen and argue and at last it was possible to convince him. But Stack had a closed mind. He would not disclose his real feelings and after all you said he went on thinking the same. He was a typical I.R.B. man.' The description of Stack is interesting because, far from being 'typical', Stack in fact split from the IRB – as de Valera well knew at the time he made the comment (to Frank Gallagher). But de Valera was preoccupied with the IRB. Gallagher describes what he told him about a visit from Sean McGarry around this time:[13]

Sean McGarry, of whom he did not think much, called to see him one day and spoke to him with authority about what should be done . . . he thought it was merely Sean McG. talking big to impress D. 'So I ignored his talk and went on exercising the authority and rights of the Presidency as if there had been no break. It was only long afterwards that I realised that Sean McGarry was Head of the IRB and was considered by that body to be President. It was good I was blind to it all. Had I been aware of their plans and the complexity of the situation it would have made my part in it much more difficult. . . .'

De Valera was, of course, talking to Gallagher with an eye to posterity. But in fact, whatever difficulties he faced in ensuring that he continued to exercise 'the authority and rights of the Presidency' on his return from America, his Machiavellian approach to the task of reinstating himself in Dublin 'as if there had been no break' makes it clear that he was far from 'blind to it all'. It was not that he had come back to find Collins spinning a web of IRB-administered deceit. Collins was running everything in sight, including the IRB, because of his extraordinary ability. From the outset de Valera himself recognized that ability whenever it suited him, be it to call the Dail together or to get him a place to stay in safety. But when it did not suit him he moved against its possessor. Commenting on de Valera's attempt to get Collins to leave the country, Frank O'Connor wrote:[14] 'This was a bad beginning to de Valera's intervention in the Brugha–Collins quarrel and it is hard to see exactly what he did to curb it that would not have been better undone. By assuming the position of unprejudiced observer and electing to hold the balance between them, he really kept them divided. Of course he increased his own prestige. The contending groups were bound to bid for his support.'

Brugha disapproved of Collins' methods of war, as he did of most of his activities. He was furious at the adulation which Devoy had heaped on Collins' head and which he felt should properly have come to him.[15] He also objected to ambushes, and tried to get them banned on Saturdays, because that was shopping day.[16] Brugha's approach to fighting, going down with guns blazing in the face of overwhelming odds, was a magnificent recipe for ensuring that the Irish continued to supply history with heroes and martyrs – and the British with victories. Yet in his biography de Valera claimed that 'Brugha and Collins were the most effective Ministers and the antagonism was never open.' In his stated analysis of the differences between Brugha and Collins, de Valera had it set down that:[17]

> Cathal Brugha, Minister of Defence, was a quieter but no less determined figure [than Collins]. A director of a firm of candle manufacturers, he was able, without salary, to devote himself to the work of his department. Collins's criticism of other departments might be dismissed as the impatience of an extremely efficient young man with any form of inefficiency. But his differences with Brugha were of a different character. It has already been suggested that a conflict of authority was partly responsible. The anomalous position of the IRB had much to do with it. Brugha could be forgiven for wanting complete control of his own department, unimpeded by a secret society.

This seemingly reasoned assessment leaves out a number of vital considerations. One, Brugha's courage was unquestioned; but his ability was limited. Frank O'Connor says bluntly that he was 'useless. As Minister for Defence he should have attended headquarters meetings regularly but didn't; and when he interviewed a group of country officers it was usually to address them on the importance of studying Irish.'[18] He would cheerfully risk his life in a crazy plan to assassinate the British Cabinet, but baulked on grounds of seniority at the offer of becoming Acting President after Arthur Griffith was jailed. And his antagonism to Collins, while not 'open' in the sense of being reported in the press – at least at that stage – was very widely known in Sinn Fein and IRA circles. Sean Dowling, a knowledgeable but less engaged witness of the period, has written:[19]

'Cathal Brugha hated Collins like poison. It was pathological . . . Brugha was Minister for Defence but he never did anything. He was not able, but he was never on the run. He continued to work as manager for Lalor's candle factory on Ormond Quay. . . . Collins was so energetic that he had usurped many of Brugha's functions; he sure was hated by him. . . .'

Apart from his relationship with Brugha and Stack, de Valera also depressed Collins with his habit of holding up meetings by giving long accounts of his American trip. Undiplomatically, Collins commented on one description of the magnificence in which de Valera had travelled that had he been there no such waste would have occurred.[20] On another he boldly interrupted a reminiscence of the Chief's with: 'Oh, I have it off by heart.'[21] The two men had been living such different lives at the opposite ends of the spectrum of the Irish drama that it would have been difficult for them to relate to each other, even if de Valera had not been once more embarking on a power struggle. The price which the British had placed on Collins' head may have been as high as £4,000–5,000 – enough to get him killed several times over in the money values of the time, but insufficient to pay de Valera's hotel bills.

It was remarked after the first Cabinet meeting held by de Valera on his return, on 9 January, that Collins seemed to be remarkably 'down'.[22] In the words of his biographers, de Valera 'felt it necessary to calm Collins down'[23] and wrote to him:[24] 'I would be sorry to think that your feeling discontented and dissatisfied and fed-up was due to anything more than the natural physical reaction after the terrible strain you have been subjected to.' Having done so, he then proceeded to increase that 'terrible strain'. On 18 January Kathleen O'Connell typed up a long letter for Collins such as he can scarcely have envisaged receiving when he organized the securing of Loughnavale for secrecy and secretarial purposes at the beginning of the month. In a nutshell de Valera proposed that Collins should leave the war and go to America. He advanced several reasons for this. One was that: 'We will not have here, so to speak, all our eggs in one basket, and whatever coup the English may attempt the line of succession is safe and the future provided for.'[25] This is the reason plucked out for use in the official biography, while the others are condensed as follows:[26]

> There were indeed several reasons for sending Collins. There were money and munitions to be obtained, a boycott of British goods to be organised, and de Valera was hopeful that Collins might help to restore unity in the Irish-American forces. The Cabinet agreed and Collins, at first reluctant, became reconciled to the idea. He was somewhat disappointed when Lord Derby's visit in April made the President feel that, with the possibility of serious negotiations, Michael Collins could not be spared from Ireland.

That paragraph is in fact a near-classic example of de Valera-speak. It combines distortion with *suppressio veri* and bare-faced lying. As to the 'money and munitions', there were already millions lying idle in American banks which could have been put to this use. There is no mention in the precis of duties that one of Collins' proposed tasks was[27] 'to examine the possibilities of the US from the point of supplying material to the Minister of Defence. To make a report to the Minister on this head and as far as possible to execute any commissions which that Minister may give in relation to his own Department.'

In other words, he was to take orders from Brugha. Far from becoming 'reconciled to the idea', Collins was outraged and hurt. 'The Long Whoor won't get rid of me as easily as that,' was his reaction. Colleagues described him as being practically in tears over the proposal.[28] His outrage was mirrored in the ranks of the Volunteers, to whom he had become the symbol of the struggle. Frank O'Connor writes that de Valera's proposal 'created consternation among the officers. Several talked of sending in their commissions. There would certainly have been a serious break-up within the army, and it is unlikely that the political movement would have escaped. But Collins put his foot down at last'.[29]

Foiled for the moment, de Valera conceded that battle; but he continued to assist Brugha in his war against Collins. Having decided that a meeting of the Dail 'must be called',[30] he had written to Collins asking him to make the necessary arrangements for it to meet on the anniversary of its first sitting, 21 January. Collins did so and the deputies assembled. However Brugha objected, deciding, for reasons best known to himself, that there was an imminent danger of mass arrests. De Valera agreed with him and stayed away. To save his Chief's face Collins did likewise and the 'Dail was properly infuriated'.[31] It was a bad start for the homecoming hero and de Valera did not take long to realize this. Another meeting was hurriedly scheduled and took place on the 25th.

De Valera would appear to have wanted to take over the military as well as the political direction of events. Despite his humanitarian protestations about wishing to ease the burden on the people, he made it clear that his concerns were PR-driven rather than humanitarian. He told the meeting that the ambushes and individual shootings were having a bad effect and sought instead to have hostilities organized on regular military lines. 'One good battle involving five hundred men from each side, every month', was apparently what he proposed.[32] His proposal came against a background of three separate Irish peace initiatives which had misfied. Firstly, Roger Sweetman, the Sinn Fein deputy for Wexford, who had been appalled by the events of Bloody Sunday, wrote to the *Irish Independent* suggesting a peace conference, stating that he was 'absolutely convinced that the methods of warfare now being employed are deplorable in their results to our country, both from a material, as well as a moral standpoint'.[33] Three days later, on 3 December, Galway Urban Council passed a resolution in favour of Sweetman's proposal. And on the same day Galway County Council held a specially convened meeting which also called for a truce and the appointment of peace negotiators, saying that 'we view with sorrow and grief the shootings, burnings, reprisals and counter-reprisals taking place all over England and Ireland by armed forces of the Irish Republic'.

It was later stated that only six out of the 32 Sinn Fein members on this Council were at liberty to attend the meeting, which only discussed, but did not pass, the resolution. However, the proceedings were headlined in the *Freeman's Journal* as 'A lead from Galway' and the Council described as 'an entirely Republican body'.[34]

The effects of these reports were compounded by the contents of a wire from Father Michael O'Flanagan, Vice-President of Sinn Fein, which appeared in the *Irish Independent* on the 6th. Father O'Flanagan had been visiting London with James O'Connor, the Irish Chief Justice, who had met Lloyd George to discuss peace. Hearing what Lloyd George had told O'Connor, Father O'Flanagan sent the British Prime Minister the following on his own initiative: 'You state that you are willing to make peace at once without waiting for Christmas. Ireland also is willing. What first step do you propose?' Lloyd George's 'step' was to interpret the moves towards peace as a showing of the white feather and to call an immediate halt to the Clune initiative.

After all that had been inflicted and endured over the previous eighteen months, those present were not inclined to follow what was perceived as the disastrous 'white feather' path – especially when it was being laid down (or relaid) by someone who had been an ocean away during those terrible months. There was general criticism of the Galway County Council type of approach, which Collins summed up by pointing out that it was not the areas which had fought hardest, like his native Cork, that had been hit hardest by reprisals, but places like Galway, which had fought least.[35] Sweetman found himself so much at odds with those present that he resigned his seat. Baulked in his policy change, de Valera nevertheless sought to impress his personality on the gathering by giving the 'history of the negotiations for peace and how they had broken down'.[36] As several of his hearers had actually spoken with Archbishop Clune during his mission while de Valera was on the other side of the Atlantic, this constituted one of the more remarkable examples of de Valera's tendency to regard something as either not having happened until he said it had, or, *per contra*, not having taken place at all if he so decided.

But overall his tactics and personality had some of the desired effect. Collins well understood that the thrust of de Valera's proposals was aimed at him and, though stung into resistance at the 'ease off' approach, allowed himself to be wrong-footed to a certain extent. One of the proposals of the moment was to prevent the British from taking a census. But Collins, who exuded depression throughout the Dail session, reacted to the idea with uncharacteristic defeatism and said the British would beat them on it. Compared to his other endeavours, defeating the census was of course a simple task – as de Valera shrewdly underlined in a letter to Stack:[37] 'We are on fairly safe ground in giving an order here inasmuch as we can be certain to make it effective. Don't you think so? Our policy in my mind ought always to be to give *orders* where we are sure that the effort as a whole will be successful, but to make *appeals* only where there is any doubt.' The subsequent defeat of the census both served to bolster de Valera's general reputation for shrewdness and to improve his standing with Stack in particular. His formal air and habit of guarding his tongue also helped him to create a more favourable impression than did Collins on one of the outstanding IRA leaders of the period, Ernie O'Malley. O'Malley had just escaped from Kilmainham Jail and de Valera interviewed him at Loughnavale in the presence of Collins and Mulcahy as part of an overall strategy of getting first-hand knowledge of what and who had developed since he had left Ireland. O'Malley subsequently gave a description of the scene which goes far to explain both how the impact de Valera made on his return from the USA enabled him to assume power with such ease after his long absence and how he differed from Collins:[38]

> De Valera shook hands with me. He was tall, his lean stringy build overemphasized his height. His face was drawn and pale as if he had little exercise or was recovering from illness. The lines running to mouth edges made furrows; ridges stood out in relief. He looked worn. He smiled with his eyes. The lines on his face broke as if ice had cracked. His voice rumbled from the depths with a hard but not a harsh dryness. Dev, the Long Fellow, or the Chief had come back from the United States two months ago. He had helped to float the foreign loan of $5,000,000, and had aided the Irish vote, influenced by Article 10, that kept the States out of the League of Nations. At home he was looked up to with awe.

O'Malley was impressed with his sternness, dignity, 'definite honesty' and his 'friendly way of making one feel at ease'. But de Valera had obviously 'lost personal contact during the year and a half he had been away. . . . His questions showed that he did not know the situation in the South.' As he answered de Valera's questions O'Malley noted that 'He had not the human qualities of Collins, the Big Fellow. Dev. was more reserved, a scholarly type. He was cold and controlled. Collins might solve a problem boisterously, by improvisation, solve it by its own development. De Valera would find the solution mathematically, clearly, with logic.' After de Valera had left the room Collins asked O'Malley what he thought of the interview. O'Malley replied that de Valera 'did not know much about the Army in the South'. But the impression that de Valera had made on him was such that he was annoyed at their reaction:

> Both laughed as if amused. Collins mentioned some of the questions the President had asked; they laughed again. I felt uncomfortable. Dev. was the President. After all, I thought, how could he be expected to know the military

situation thoroughly. Cathal Brugha, the Minister for Defence, did not know the senior officers well. He worked as a traveller . . . but his position as M.D. needed all his energies. . . . I resented their jokes at the expense of the Long Fellow.

Unknown to O'Malley, the Long Fellow was on the threshold of repaying some of those jokes at the expense of the Big Fellow. Returning in de Valera's wake from America, Liam Mellows had somehow been given one of Collins' many hats, Director of Purchases. As he had been out of the country even longer than de Valera this demanding operational role, requiring a detailed knowledge of men, arms networks and the theatre of operations, must have been difficult for him. However, as his comments on de Valera's American mission would suggest, he proved to be a receptive vehicle for the views of the de Valera-Brugha side of the power struggle with Collins.[39] When Mulcahy wrote to him protesting that there would be lynchings at GHQ if it got out that nine thousand rounds of ammunition had been offered to the IRA in Scotland but refused for a lack of funds he defended the refusal: '. . . the situation reported to you . . . is quite correct. . . . As the M/D [Brugha] has stated relative to London and Manchester . . . he will debit me with amounts unless I can show goods on hand and I was not, and am not, going to put myself in the position of adding to the Glasgow muddle by making further disbursements until I saw my way clear.'

Collins had been using both IRB accounts and Volunteer monies to buy arms in the Glasgow area. The accounts had been kept with his usual meticulous care, but an aide, Tom Cullen, lost a bag containing receipts in a raid and Collins was hard put to defend his accounts when Brugha charged him not only with manipulating Volunteer funds for IRB purposes but with diverting cash to a member of his family. In an effort to get evidence to substantiate his charges Brugha had letters smuggled in to one of the prisoners in Mountjoy Jail in mid-March 1921, a time when Volunteers were being executed daily.[40]

De Valera set up an Inquiry presided over by himself; here, in the presence of Stack, Collins had to defend himself against Brugha's accusations. As might have been predicted, from the outset de Valera found the charges 'groundless'. The Inquiry was a typically de Valera ploy. He managed to convey an impression of judicial impartiality, while at the same time embarrassing his younger adversary – to the point where Collins broke down in tears – and impressing his own authority on all concerned. This last factor took precedence over the fact that the interruption in arms purchases necessitated by the magnification of the Scottish accounts issue occurred at a time when 'men were dying for lack of the few rounds of ammunition with which to defend themselves'.[41]

Possibly this consideration has a bearing on the fact that no word of the disagreeable Scottish incident occurs in the Authorized Version. Nor is there mention of the fact that subsequently de Valera effectively demoted Collins by appointing Stack to replace him as Acting President should anything happen to himself;[42] nor of the fact that his tacit support for Brugha eventually got to the stage where the resultant anger in GHQ caused Mulcahy to confront de Valera with an ultimatum: either rein in Brugha, or he would resign as chief of staff. De Valera's reply was classically disingenuous:[43] 'You know I think Cathal is jealous of Mick. Isn't it a terrible thing to think that a man with the qualities that Cathal undoubtedly has would fall a victim to a dirty little vice like jealousy.'

The answer, of course, presupposes that de Valera himself was above such a failing; but, faced with Mulcahy's ultimatum, de Valera did speak to Brugha, who promptly burst into tears and said: 'I could do no wrong.'[44] Neither could de Valera. The only indication of any of the foregoing concerning Collins to appear in his official biography is a bland statement that from April 1921 onward 'Collins did not seem to accept my view of things as he had done before and was inclined to give public expression to his own opinions even when they differed from mine . . .'.[45] However, de Valera did concede that 'he had never ceased to feel concern over Collins's high and even dominant position in the I.R.B.'. His biography states that 'For de Valera the outlook of a civil secret society was incompatible with his kind of scrupulous fidelity to principle.'[46]

In moving to change that dominant position de Valera gave a good example of what his 'fidelity' to principle meant in practice. In his customary fashion, to conceal his hidden agenda, he made it appear in public that he was acting for disinterested reasons of high policy. He first got the Dail to agree that a declaration of a state of war with England was desirable, so that the British could not represent the IRA as 'a small army of assassins',[47] and because the existence of a state of war would confer belligerent status on captured IRA men who were at that stage liable to summary execution if caught with arms. He then made a public statement on 30 March 1921 to two news outlets, the International News and the Universal Service, which was widely disseminated. It contained the following:

> This army is . . . a regular State force, under the civil control of the elected representatives, and under officers who hold their commissions under warrant from these representatives. The Government is, therefore, responsible for the actions of this army. These actions are not the acts of irresponsible individuals or groups, therefore, nor is the I.R.A., as the enemy would have one believe, a praetorian guard. It is the national army of defence.

One de Valera apologist's verdict on this statement was:[48] 'The President's statement came as an immeasurable relief and stimulus to the Republican Volunteers.' It may have – to any of the handful of young lads who paused to think of such things. But it can hardly have brought much cheer to Michael Collins. For what none of de Valera's sympathetic biographers mention is the fact that, unknown to the public, Collins had got the IRB to amend its Constitution so as to cede to the Dail the governmental powers of the Supreme Council.[49] In effect, 'civil control by the elected representatives' meant that as President of the IRB Collins had handed over control of the IRA (as the Volunteers were by now universally known) to President de Valera.

From the time he first faced the US press de Valera had accepted Joe McGarrity's advice that he allow himself to be described as President of the Irish Republic and as President de Valera, rather than use the actual title conferred on him by Dail Eireann, Priomh Aire (literally First Minister). Before leaving this phase of the Collins–de Valera relationship to examine the other strands of de Valera's post-US policies, I feel it would be appropriate to quote an assessment by Dr Dwyer of why de Valera changed his title from Priomh Aire to President and acted as he did subsequently:[50] 'Of course it was not just a question of title alone. Without power, the title would have been meaningless. He was therefore determined to show that he had more power than anybody else in the movement; he had to be clearly seen as the chief. This led to his problems with Cohalan and Devoy. In the same way it would also lead to a power struggle with Collins, which, in turn, would have disastrous consequences for the nation.'

It would indeed, but before tracing those consequences let us turn to de Valera's policy towards America. The evidence suggests that he saw America's importance lessen once he had left its shores behind him. What was important was to get the reins of American activities into his own hands. When he had arrived in America his priority had been to generate activity. Impatient to spend and to get he had encouraged the taking of offices, the building of organizations and the launching of a bond drive. On returning to Ireland he had attempted the opposite, to slow things down to a pace where, as head of the underground Government, he could have the final say in whether or not to stage 'one good battle' in any given month. Now, he decided that despite the go-getting policies he had already initiated in America, the slow-motion approach was the one he could best direct from Ireland. This phase of de Valera's American policy provides one of the best examples on record of his ability to mask his actions from those around him while pursuing an opponent. He would do so until he caused someone who might have begun, and in this case undoubtedly did begin, the confrontation in what seemed to be an unassailably strong moral and political position to put themselves in the wrong and thus become easily disposed of. He wrote to James O'Mara on 3 February:[51]

> ... it is very necessary to husband our funds and diminish expenditure in America. Operations here are much more extensive than you could imagine, and the expenditure is correspondingly heavy. We must take care not to be forced into the necessity for curtailing, for they are vital. Relief expenditure ought to be borne now altogether by a special organisation set up for that purpose, and you should try to secure a refund for any advances that have been made. The Dail can still sit and therefore our emergency powers as trustees are not to be used. Monies must be voted in the ordinary way.

Of course there had never been any suggestion of America drawing off money from Ireland; the flow had all been the other way round – very largely because O'Mara had shown himself both efficient and zealous in the raising of money and curtailment of expense. He had even gone to the extent of paying his own expenses while in the States; they came to over £10,000, worth more than thirty times that in today's values. The only suggestion of curtailing the Volunteers' activities had come from de Valera himself, and he had had to withdraw this.

O'Mara was understandably furious and composed, but did not send, a stinging reply to this communication.[52] In it he raised a number of points which illustrate the position of the Irish American movement in the wake of de Valera's activities. Were the appropriations that he and de Valera had made before the latter's melodramatic departure from the USA now *ultra vires*? Until this question was sorted out he regarded it as unwise to diminish expenditure in America. Since de Valera's departure he had advanced almost $100,000 for propaganda purposes and the expenses of an Irish Consul in America, Frank P. Walsh. He pointed out that:

> The American Association for the Recognition of the Irish Republic is growing, and threatens to become a veritable Frankenstein unless directed and controlled. To get effective work from its superabundant but now useless strength requires the services of a central bureau and the expenditure of about 200,000 dollars. You must know that all these sums are an investment in sentiment and will return sevenfold in the issue of a second loan. Knowing this it should not be difficult to convey the facts to the Dail.

But de Valera had no intention of communicating these facts to the Dail. Without waiting for a reply to his letter of 3 February he wrote again to O'Mara on 1 March, urging him to put his weight behind the AARIR and stressing the 'great needs – munitions and money to carry on'. He sought O'Mara's views on the possibility of 'raising a *further* loan' (in a later letter[53] to Harry Boland he put a figure of $20 million on this), and inquired about an audit of O'Mara's accounts and the progress of affairs at 411 Fifth Avenue, the HQ of the bond drive. Irked at the audit query and the loan suggestion, O'Mara did not reply directly but wrote[54] to Harry Boland. O'Mara asked him to pass on to de Valera 'politely' the facts that he was not responsible for the audit, but that he had asked the auditors to speed up their report; that, as de Valera knew, he had had no connection with No. 411 since de Valera had left the United States; and pointing out that he was preparing for a second loan but that this could not be attempted until the American Committee for Relief in Ireland had wound up its work.

De Valera either did not get this reply before writing[55] again, on 24 March, or quite possibly chose to ignore it, for he addressed O'Mara in terms which appear deliberately calculated to 'wind him up':

> Since I came here [to the President's Dept, Dail Eireann] and have realised the

magnitude of the world commitments of the Government I have become most anxious about the question of funds. We must cut down our running expenses in the U.S. The propaganda should henceforth be done mainly by the American organisations. . . . Will you please have the auditors send me a comprehensive summary of the state of our finances over there to date. . . . I have, as you can well understand, a number of administrative anxieties at the moment. Please do not· press your resignation from the trusteeship. I must know definitely whom I can count on everywhere. If you are not *certain* to stay on it is better to let me know. . . .

It is fine to be once more leading a natural, healthy, vigorous existence, with every moment usefully employed on the work I like best. No time to put anything on the long finger here. I am getting the education of my life. . . .

So was O'Mara, but he can hardly have felt himself leading a 'healthy, vigorous existence'. No one knew better than he that where the Dail's 'world commitments' were concerned it was principally to America and the organization which he himself had set up that Sinn Fein turned to resolve the 'question of funds'. Moreover, he had told de Valera in the plainest terms that he wanted to resign from the loan trusteeship when his term of office came up for renewal the following June; he had confirmed this in writing to his immediate superior, the Minister for Finance, Michael Collins,[56] enclosing a note and a copy of his resignation for de Valera, adding that he also intended to resign his Dail seat at the next general election. De Valera may not have been aware that a written resignation was *en route* when he sent off his communication of 24 March, but he was fully alive to what he was doing when he directed yet another lengthy missive to O'Mara on 8 April[57] in which he offered him the position of 'representative of the Republic in the U.S.A'. To make sure that this was an offer that O'Mara could not accept – and, knowing the other man's psychology as he did, de Valera must have been certain that (apart from the fact that O'Mara had been trying for a year to be released from America) there was little doubt that a refusal would be forthcoming anyhow – he put the job specification not in the letter to O'Mara, but in one to Harry Boland, of which he sent O'Mara the copy. Boland was perfectly aware of the implications of de Valera's letter. When he sent a copy to O'Mara he attached a note, written in large red letters, saying: '*Pax Domini sit semper vobiscum*, Bo.'

There was very little hope of the peace of the Lord being with O'Mara always, or ever, while he attempted to cope with the implications of the job offer contained in the letter to Boland. For his letter from de Valera included the following passage:

In considering the American situation from my own experience I know that you must alter your viewpoint in order to fit it in its proper relation to the whole. We are able to function here far more freely and effectively than anyone at the other side for a year or two can imagine. The one serious thing lacking is any adequate system of oversea communications. This lack helps to give our representatives in other countries the feeling that we are completely cut off and hemmed in, and so give them a wrong perspective. You, yourself, will need to take this particularly into account in your judgements.

The letter ended, as did all his communications to O'Mara, with polite salutations to his wife, Agnes. But the PS must have detracted very considerably from the force of the accompanying 'very sincerely, E.de V.' It said: 'The note to Harry is really addressed to you as much as to him. As trustee will you please have furnished to me an exact account of the present state of our finances at that side.' Thus amidst hints that his accounts might need checking, that he was possibly over-valuing his role in America – a nice touch from a man who had risked destroying Irish American organizations rather than have anything less than his evaluation of his own role accepted – O'Mara was asked to consider the position envisaged for him. Overall the situation envisaged 'an outlay of no more than 100,000 dollars for the maintenance of diplomatic and political side of the U.S. service during the coming year'.[58] Boland was to leave America, and O'Mara was to have a staff consisting of a secretary and two stenographers in Washington. But for some inexplicable reason, probably connected with de Valera's theories of warfare, despite the retrenchments a 'military attaché' for New York was suggested. He proposed handing over various tasks and offices to the AARIR, and the securing of 'a definite steady income from the organisation, obtained by a levy on its members' to relieve him of his 'present financial anxieties'.

As O'Mara's wife noted in her diary, it was a 'well thought out plan to provoke Jim into resignation. Move H. and the others away so as to have absolute direction direct here from the other side. . . .'[59] The plan did succeed in provoking O'Mara, but in such a fashion that de Valera was precipitated into being seen to do his own dirty work. O'Mara's main energies throughout the barrage of letters from de Valera had been devoted to helping to organize a huge convention of the AARIR. It was held in Chicago on 18–20 April, attended by five thousand delegates and, temporarily, put the seal on the triumph of de Valera's supporters over those of Cohalan and Devoy. O'Mara had been hoping that the thrust of the organization would be devoted subsequently towards lobbying Congress to recognize the Irish Republic, as the Association's name suggested. But unknown to him de Valera had cabled McGarrity asking him to propose a levy on the delegates, thus cutting across plans for the proposed new loan. And then on 29 April the letters from de Valera to himself and Boland arrived.

By then the reading of de Valera's cable at the AARIR convention had drawn a furious reply from O'Mara, one which this time he did send:[60]

My dear de Valera,
 A cable from you was read at the great Convention of the American Association for Recognition of the Irish Republic asking for a guarantee of a million dollars yearly and was translated into action by levy of five dollars a

member on every member of the Association – which practically includes every active person of our race. Neither Mr. Boland or myself was consulted on the matter.

There are nearly three million dollars lying idle here to the credit of the American trustees and at the disposal of your government. Funds were therefore not urgently required and your request at this time unnecessary.

Besides the Relief Committee, which has the enthusiastic support of Mr. Boland, your duly appointed but not accredited envoy, and which is now at the peak of its effort to collect for the relief, will be seriously handicapped by this new appeal. It is somewhat unworthy of our country to be always holding out its hat, but to hold out two hats at once is stupid.

And lastly your appeal now makes impossible any attempt later this year to raise the twenty million dollar loan which was contemplated – to use your own words when we last discussed the matter 'crops will not grow on trampled ground'.

I would advise you to promptly send someone to this country who has your confidence, if such a person exists, and having done so don't constantly interfere with his work. With kind regard I am yours sincerely.

Boland made a powerful appeal 'by the strong personal regard I have for you, to advise the President and Cabinet that you will accept the position'.[61] But O'Mara replied that he was unwilling to hold any position under de Valera, who 'claims such arbitrary executive authority' and 'in whose judgement of American affairs I have no longer any confidence'.[62] On the same day he sent off his resignation from his South Kilkenny Dail seat and on the next, 30 April, despatched the following to de Valera:[63]

Dear Mr. President

Your dispatches of April 8th obviously indicate your final decision to force through your policy which last December received the almost unanimous condemnation of the Irish Mission here. Now, as then, rather than be responsible for that policy I tender my resignation as the most emphatic protest I can make against what must be the utter disruption and destruction of American aid. . . .

. . . the progress of recent months making good your indecision and your mistakes of last year leaves me the more convinced of your error. . . .

De Valera's reaction to this whizz-bang was to send a coded cable firing O'Mara: 'Dad [O'Mara] once expressed a wish to be fired by cable, this is it, Kahn [de Valera].' Interestingly, Patricia Lavelle describes the sending of the telegram, but suppresses the scene[64] which preceded its despatch. De Valera was sitting in a small inner room of Dr Farnan's house with Kathleen O'Connell as he read the letter. It made him 'so very angry that he kicked it into the fire and in doing so his slipper shot off and hit the ceiling and rebounded on Kathleen O'Connell's head. The mark was left on the ceiling as long as the Farnans lived in the house', which was close on forty years. O'Mara may have won his point, but de Valera easily won the subsequent PR battle. At the time nobody in Ireland (or even in Britain, where the authorities confiscated the telegram, but did not know what to make of it) understood O'Mara's side of the quarrel. His wife Agnes crossed the Atlantic in a vain effort to press his case, but got nowhere. She wrote to him on 31 May:[65]

> . . . in face of the apparent impossibility of getting them to realize any point of view other than their own, combined with an ignorance of the nature of operations on your side which repulses any enlightenment, it is quite hopeless to put your views before them. The only idea prevailing is that what the Chairman decides or says must be unquestioned. . . . Unfortunately the tone of your letter quite defeated its purpose and is so strongly resented, even by your friends, that it at once creates a prejudice. . . .

De Valera's ascendancy was such that no one even thought of debating O'Mara's point about $3 million lying uselessly in banks while further begging bowls were extended. As the Sinn Feiners battled an empire they paid the homage of their understanding to their Cause and their Chief. Even O'Mara's father, Stephen, cabled another son in Toronto: 'Tell Jim not to stab his country in the hour of her agony. I am hurt beyond words.' And to O'Mara himself the old man cabled: 'Nothing matters but loyal sacrifice to duty'[66] and began making preparations to go out to America himself to replace his son. But the man finally approved by de Valera to put the seal on his American policy and replace James O'Mara was his brother Stephen O'Mara. De Valera would make use of the family, but he would never forgive the man. As the clouds of civil war gathered over Ireland the following year James O'Mara, anxious to mend the broken friendship, approached de Valera saying:[67] ' "You'll need all your friends now". De Valera responded by waving him away. "Not you anyway", he said, and walked on.'[67] The mark was left on the ceiling. . . .

O'Mara had made some curiously apt observations a year earlier when he was composing a letter for his South Kilkenny constituents explaining his reasons for resigning. He never sent the letter (dated 2 April 1921) which, with the benefit of hindsight, now reads as if it were describing de Valera's position rather than his own:[68]

> . . . I am convinced that it is not good in a struggle such as we are engaged in for any man to continue long in a position of authority and trust. Consciously, or unconsciously, the tendency to identify himself and his party with the cause for which he works is irresistible and such a mental condition in the end makes leaders and parties, not in Ireland alone but in all such movements, often put too high a value on a mere party or personal interest. O'Connell's and Redmond's parties are outstanding examples. This cannot easily happen in such a struggle as Ireland is at present engaged in, because the present effort has had little to offer either leaders or followers except personal sacrifice and suffering, and it is the pride and glory of our race that men have been found to face these dangers and hardships; nevertheless in a long-continued struggle authority develops a sense of self-importance which does not belong, and sooner or later new men should be found to carry on the old policy.

Sancta simplicitas . . . New Princes do not readily give way to 'new men'.

De Valera succeeded in putting the brakes on the growth of the Irish American movement, and the April convention of the AARIR may be taken as the high-water mark of the efforts to organize an Irish American movement in Ireland's national interest. Thereafter the civil war added to the divisions already described. Although de Valera would retain a personal following that made Irish Americans a significant factor in his own successful career, as a whole they neither developed, nor were encouraged to develop, as a powerful, co-ordinated group with links to Governments in Dublin, devoted to advancing Irish interests along, say, the lines of the Zionist lobby for Israel. It is in the realms of Irish Americana that, even today, the Long Fellow casts one of the longest shadows.

Where domestic Irish policy was concerned de Valera took a fateful step in his choice of replacement for the arrested Desmond Fitzgerald as Director of Publicity. Collins had introduced him to Erskine Childers, the man who had sailed into Howth the guns for Easter 1916 aboard his yacht the *Asgard*. Childers, an Englishman by birth and education (Haileybury and Trinity College, Cambridge), had been reared in the home of his cousin Robert Barton, a Co. Wicklow landowner. He became progressively more Irish than the Irish themselves, resigning a post on the staff of the House of Commons to advocate Home Rule for Ireland and becoming Secretary of Lloyd George's Convention. A gifted writer and propagandist, and a man of such character that de Valera said he would like to have modelled himself on him, Childers was 'above all an inflexible idealist'. That inflexibility would cost him his life, and it is a matter for speculation as to how his interaction with de Valera's own obduracy played a substantive role in the Irish civil war. What is certain is that de Valera forced his appointment through some very reluctant colleagues. Arthur Griffith, for example, thought it dangerous to trust a 'disgruntled Englishman' who was merely using the Irish cause to exercise a grudge against his own country.[69] The suspicions which Childers' appointment generated in some quarters almost certainly played a part in causing his eventual execution. But for the moment civil war was unthinkable and de Valera had secured a powerful new ally to counter-balance Collins.

The Anglo-Irish war now began to enter its final phase. Various peace initiatives flickered on and off, the most substantial since the aborted Clune mission occurring on 21 April when Lord Derby met de Valera in James O'Mara's Dublin house, 43 Fitzwilliam Place. Lord Derby arrived as 'Mr Edwards', wearing a pair of horn-rimmed glasses. De Valera came on a bicycle, as himself. He was somewhat put out because Derby had apparently seen Cardinal Logue first,[70] and the Cardinal had sent a rather dusty reply to de Valera's suggestions as to what his Eminence should say to Derby. De Valera told Gallagher that he had informed the Cardinal (probably through the Bishop of Dromore) that if the Cardinal could not bring himself to tell Derby that the Irish were behind the demand for a Republic he should at least say[71] 'that the people had elected their representatives and that these representatives alone had the right to speak for them and to voice their demands'. But alas: 'D. got back a reply which he regarded as sour and anti-national: that he [the Cardinal] got many prescriptions from doctors but instead of using them he put them on an upper shelf and was none the worse.'

Apparently Logue gave Derby to understand that the Church did not agree with de Valera's position. For de Valera wrote a letter to Dr Fogarty, the Bishop of Killaloe and his fellow loan trustee, whose contents he intended to be passed on to Logue. The gist of the Fogarty letter was the rather convoluted sentiment that if Lloyd George was the man de Valera took him to be, he would 'prise open that rift to the heart of everybody'. All in all de Valera was not overly impressed with the Derby meeting, which went on for several hours. He summed it up in a letter to Harry Boland as being a British ploy:[72] 'They are intriguing to make this an issue between ourselves and the Church – that is the real meaning of the Derby affair. . . . I saw Derby and spoke to him exactly as a journalist.'

However, an important point emerged from the Derby initiative. After reporting back to Lloyd George Derby wrote to de Valera asking whether, in a forthcoming speech to the House of Commons, the Prime Minister might say that 'those controlling the Irish movement will not consent to meet him or any Representative of the Government unless the principle of complete independence is first conceded?' De Valera immediately countered on 26 April: 'Before I reply to the unsigned note, I would like to ask the British Premier a question. . . . Will he not consent to meet me or any Representative of the Government of Ireland unless the principle of complete independence be first surrendered by us?' The question was answered obliquely. In May a *New York Herald* reporter brought a message to de Valera telling him that, in the course of an interview on the 11th, Lloyd George had said: 'I will meet Mr. de Valera, or any of the Irish leaders without conditions on my part, and without exacting promises from them. It is the only way a conclusion can be reached. The conference will lead to an exchange of opinions out of which we may find common ground upon which we can refer to our respective people for a settlement.' De Valera's response to this was: 'If Mr. Lloyd George makes that statement in public I shall give him a public reply.' And there for a time matters rested.[73]

Meanwhile, on 5 May, de Valera had held another important meeting – with the leader of the Ulster Unionists, Sir James Craig, in the Howth Road home of Tom Greene, a Dublin solicitor. Their exchange was like a game of handball played against a haystack – it yielded no return. The meeting was the brainchild of A. W. Cope, the Assistant Under Secretary for Ireland. With Lloyd George's blessing, Cope arranged for Bishop Fogarty to write to de Valera on 15 April telling him that Craig 'would welcome' a talk with him, apparently on a basis of 'fiscal autonomy for all Ireland with Partition'. But when they met, it emerged that Craig had been told that de Valera wanted to meet him. Craig had shown considerable courage in travelling from Belfast, ostensibly to see the Lord Lieutenant, and then entrusting himself to 'three of the worst looking toughs I have ever seen'. De Valera afterwards said that he 'seemed anxious and ill at ease'. Craig's account of the meeting shows that he did not feel his risk-taking was well rewarded. He said that after half an hour's discourse de Valera, who 'very much wore the look of a hunted man', had only:

> ... reached the era of Brian Boru. After another half hour he had advanced to the period of some king a century or two later. By this time I was getting tired, for de Valera hadn't begun to reach the point at issue. Fortunately, a fine Kerry Blue [terrier] entered the room and enabled me to change conversation, and I asked Mr. de Valera what announcement he was going to make to the Press about our meeting. Finally I tore off a piece of paper and wrote something down.

Craig afterwards told one of 'the toughs' who brought him to the meeting, Emmet Dalton, that de Valera was 'impossible'.[74] About the only thing the two men agreed on was that the meeting seems to have lasted for about ninety minutes. De Valera's account of what happened was as follows:

> Craigavon[74a] had been told ... that I had asked to see him and I was told that Craigavon had asked to see me. So we met rather under false pretences. We sat on opposite sides of a table and I said after the first few moments' silence 'Well?' He looked at me and he said 'Well?' I then said 'I'm too old at this political business to have nonsense of this kind: each waiting for the other to begin' and I started putting our case to him. He spoke of the Union as if it were a sacred thing. 'But', said I, 'do you not know how the Union came about?' and I started telling him about it. After a while he tore a piece from the *Freeman's Journal* which was lying beside him. 'I think', he said, after writing for a few minutes, 'we ought to issue this statement.' He had drafted it to the effect that we had exchanged our respective views on the situation. That ended the talks but I must say I liked him.

The accurate, but incompatible, accounts[75] by the two men of their one and only meeting might well be taken as symbols of the incomprehension and division of their regimes in the years that lay ahead. Both were to be borne down by what bore them up: the ancestral prejudices of their respective peoples. Craig would come to extol the virtues of his 'Protestant Parliament for a Protestant people'. De Valera would draw up a Roman Catholic Constitution for a Roman Catholic people. Ecumenicism was not a word that came trippingly from the tongue of either.

De Valera had more luck with furthering his theories at another meeting a little later that month, an IRA GHQ session which agreed to go for a spectacular operation and would yield worldwide publicity. The result could be taken as proving both his and Collins' theories of warfare; it achieved the desired publicity, but it also drew down destruction on those who conducted the raid. The target chosen was one of Ireland's finest buildings, the Custom House in Dublin, the centre of the country's income tax collection and local government administration. Collins was displeased with this venture into 'static warfare' and stipulated that both the Squad and the ASU, the Active Service Unit of full-time Volunteers which he was also responsible for creating, should only be involved in covering operations outside the building. As the Volunteers mobilized, Collins turned up on his bicycle to wish them luck. They needed it. Men went into action with only 'four or five rounds of ammunition each'.

The building and its governmental records were destroyed, but it proved impossible for several of the Volunteers to fight their way clear after the raid was discovered. Six of them were killed, twelve wounded and over seventy of the IRA's best men captured. However, these disasters were turned to de Valera's advantage because they led to a further erosion of Collins' power base. Ostensibly to make up for the Custom House losses, the Squad, ASU and Collins' crack intelligence team were all amalgamated into the Dublin Brigade. This, of course, like the rest of the Republican Army, was since the March decision under the direct control of the Minister for Defence, Brugha, and above him the President, de Valera.[76]

Throughout this period de Valera, so far as his followers were concerned, was living the life of a wanted man, only making a 'couple of surreptitious visits to his home at Greystones'. His daughter Mairin contributed a statement to the official biography in which she recalled[77] 'the excitement when my father paid a secret visit home when he was "on the run". Viv and I were allowed to see him because we were old enough to understand but the young children could not. He had to wait until they were asleep to go and look at them. During the day we were all very careful not to disturb the "important visitor in the dining room".'

In fact the British Government did not want him, as the extract given below makes clear, but they were about to get him none the less. The following account is taken from the memoirs of a British intelligence officer:[78]

> . . . the Intelligence Service had been ordered not to employ their information to secure the arrest of certain individuals, amongst whom was Mr. de Valera. It was considered better that he should remain at large, in order that the authorities might have the head of Sinn Fein organisation with whom to treat should occasion arise. This order was loyally obeyed despite the difficulty of trying not to see him. But it proved impossible to secure such a distinguished person from accidents.

To understand how such accidents occurred, we will shortly examine the political argument that raged through the British Cabinet in the months between the Clune peace mission of Christmas 1920 and the truce of July 1921. For the moment it is important to realize that, while the political and administrative wings of the British decision-taking echelons might be thought of as being divided into a peace party and a war party, the military were pursuing purely military goals, even though in de Valera's case these were pursued at a different level of intensity from the campaign waged against Collins, for example. Collins' family home was burned, and his eight motherless nephews and nieces, all under the age of twelve, left without a roof over their heads while their father was imprisoned.[79] De Valera's family were not molested, but in April a routine raid on his landlady's home turned up some receipts for the rent of Loughnavale. Hearing that they had been taken, de Valera moved with Kathleen O'Connell to Farnan's; and then, a week before the Custom House attack, into a large house in Blackrock, Glenvar. Loughnavale was raided three days after he decamped and so, one evening a month later, was Glenvar. This time he was captured, in possession of a letter, which he had got his colleagues to sign, to the effect that there was no split in the ranks of the Irish leadership. Even as the Anglo-Irish war moved towards its climax he was preoccupied with the other war which loomed large in his thoughts – that with John Devoy, who had been carrying reports of splits in the *Gaelic American*.[80] In the Irish diaspora the rivalry between Collins and Brugha-de Valera could not be hidden from an experienced old conspirator like Devoy. In fact, as we shall see, it had not been hidden from the British Government either, but their immediate concern was not with the intricacies of de Valera's feuds but with getting him set at liberty. Some four hours after he had been picked up the imposing figure of Lloyd George's man at Dublin Castle, Alfred Cope, appeared in his cell, resplendent in evening dress, to announce that de Valera was being transferred to Portobello Barracks.

Here a startled officer was moved out of his room, protesting bitterly at being dispossessed by a 'bloody rebel'. De Valera passed quite a pleasant evening reading himself to sleep with a treatise on the type of conventional warfare that he favoured, written by Marshal Foch. However the following morning, 23 June, he found himself called upon to defend guerilla tactics. According to the version he gave Gallagher[81] he encountered a high-ranking official,[82] who, indicating the coffin of a young Auxiliary, asked de Valera what he thought of the morality of shooting men from behind ditches. De Valera stated that he replied: 'Surely you as an officer know the value of cover in an attack. You use steel-sided lorries. We have only the ditches and stone walls. If you were attacking the Germans and had no other means of surprise, you'd use them.' He was set free shortly afterwards.

His reaction was characteristic of him. He told Gallagher that he was 'very despondent at his release'. He felt that he 'could now be followed and might be suspect to our own'. He felt his usefulness was gone.[83] His vision of himself as a revolutionary leader constantly eluding his enemies was shattered; his days of skulking in grandeur were over; the best thing he could do was go home. And so two years, three weeks and two days after he abandoned Sinead's birthday celebrations he returned to Greystones. At first he spoke of taking up soldiering and mentioned joining Liam Lynch's First Southern Division. But two days after his release a letter from Lloyd George gave him a better idea: to go not to Cork, but to

London, to talk peace. For de Valera, for the world at large, the letter was a bolt from the blue. As Churchill said afterwards: 'No British Government in modern times has ever appeared to make so sudden and complete a reversal of policy.'[84]

The shoots of peace had in fact been pushing upwards through the thickets of British coalition politics (composed of Liberal and Conservatives) for several months. Outside the Cabinet room, apart from the pressures of Dominion sentiment, and most importantly Irish American opinion, the voice of liberal England had been making itself heard denouncing the policy of 'frightfulness' in Ireland. Stimulated by Art O'Briain's Irish Self-Determination League many individuals and organizations had joined in the chorus: the British Labour Party, intellectuals of the calibre of Belloc, Chesterton and Shaw, influential newspapers like the *Manchester Guardian*, *The Times* and the *Daily Herald* and concerned English Catholics through Lord Cavendish-Bentinck's 'Peace with Ireland Council'. Lloyd George had begun taking a cautious, personal interest in the peace process in October 1920.

Brigadier General Cockerill MP had sent him a memo outlining a solution to the Irish problem based on a[85]

> ... Conference of fully accredited plenipotentiaries representing Ireland and Great Britain, equal in number and untrammelled by restrictive instructions and empowered by means of negotiation to make the best peace possible. . . . Pending the negotiations there should be a truce and amnesty. Once the provisions of the new Constitution were agreed they should be submitted for final acceptance or rejection, but no amendment, to the parliaments of the contracting peoples.

Cockerill published these proposals in *The Times* on 8 October 1920; they drew a response from Arthur Griffith, which led to informal contact being established between Sinn Fein and the British Prime Minister through a businessman, Patrick Moylette, who was also prominent in the IRB. Given the state of Lloyd George's dependence on the Tory members of his coalition Cabinet, the strength of the Tory Unionist relationships, and army sensitivities, these initial contacts were doomed to be short-lived. In another part of the forest the Irish Committee, reacting to the pressures of the Tory–Unionist axis, had acted on reports of the activities of the Assistant Under Secretary, Cope, with a decision that 'no person serving in the Irish Government should in any circumstances be permitted to hold communications with Sinn Fein'[86] And Lloyd George was actually interrupted in the Moylette–Griffith initiative by an unauthorized action of the military. Griffith was picked up by the army after Bloody Sunday without political authority, to the great annoyance of the British Prime Minister.[87]

But the momentum of the Cockerill-inspired initiative led to the Clune mission. This in turn foundered, as described earlier, under the weight of the Sweetman–Galway County Council–Flanagan initiatives. After a two-day review of the Irish situation involving the entire Irish executive and the top generals in Ireland, it was decided to drop the Clune approach and to accept both the military appreciation and a suggestion by Sir John Anderson. The generals felt that a truce would merely serve to give Sinn Fein an opportunity to build up its strength, particularly where intelligence was concerned. In fact this was a curiously faulty assessment of what a truce would have meant to an undercover army – it would have flushed it out into the open – and showed the inability of the brass-hat military thinkers of the age to grasp the realities of guerilla warfare. When a truce did come their principal opponent, Michael Collins, decided that resumption of the fighting was impossible. But, not knowing this, the generals convinced Lloyd George that four more months of attrition would bring victory. Sir John Anderson's recommendation was that the crucial factor would be 'the line it was possible to get the Church to take'. However, the two-day meeting ensured that the Church's reaction would be highly unwelcome to the British.

Released from his peace-making endeavours Archbishop Clune returned to Australia, calling on the Pope before he did so. He found that a papal denunciation of the war in Ireland had been drawn up in terms which would censure Sinn Fein more heavily than the British. He objected strongly and, in forthright terms, gave the Pope a first-hand account of his Irish visit, painting a highly favourable picture of the Irish leaders, particularly Michael Collins, and detailing how, amongst other atrocities, his own nephew had been murdered by Crown forces. The denunciation was postponed, after various other high-ranking Irish and Irish American ecclesiastics had confirmed Clune's analysis of the harm that such a denunciation would do in Irish Catholic circles.

And then, shortly after Clune had left for home, Cardinal Mannix too called on Pope Benedict. Clune's intervention meant that, instead of being regarded as a turbulent priest, he was asked to suggest what action the papacy might take in the circumstances.[88] Mannix advised the Pope to send a contribution to the American relief organization the White Cross, whose activities in Ireland Warren Harding had applauded, accompanied by a letter for publication. The Pope not only agreed to this, but asked Mannix to draft the letter. With customary Vatican caution it was passed through many other hands before being published. Nevertheless when it appeared Mannix shone through:[89]

> We are most especially concerned about the conditions of Ireland. Unflinching even to the shedding of blood in her devotion to the ancient Faith and in her reverence for the Holy See she is subjected today to the indignity of devastation and slaughter . . . neutrality . . . by no means prevents us from wishing . . . that a lasting peace . . . may take the place of this terrible enmity . . . we do not perceive how this bitter strife can profit either of the parties, when property and homes are being ruthlessly and disgracefully laid waste, when villages and farmsteads are being set aflame, when neither sacred places nor sacred persons are spared, when

on both sides a war resulting in the deaths of unarmed peoples, even of women and children, is carried on. We exhort English as well as Irish to calmly consider ... some means of mutual agreement.

This statement appeared on 22 May 1921 and was received with horror by the British, because it put 'HMG and the Irish murder gang on a footing of equality'. Around this time Dublin Castle's official *Weekly Summary* was referring to de Valera as belonging 'to a race of treacherous murderers'. The *Summary* went on to say that he had 'inducted Ireland into the murderous treachery of his race'. De Valera's response to this attack was a classic illustration of the elasticity of mind he could show when it suited him. Despite his protestations of Irishness in America – while at the same time retaining American citizenship – he sent the *Summary* to the Spanish Ambassador in London, accompanied by a note drawing attention to this slur on 'the honour of the Spanish race and the Spanish nation'.[90] The *Summary* attack was subsequently used 'with great effect'[91] in Spain and Spanish-speaking Latin America.

Of even greater effect was the fact that the military men's four months had passed with no sign of the promised victory. Indeed, Sir Henry Wilson was advising Lloyd George that the troops in Ireland were so worn out that it would be necessary to remove most of them by October. The prescription for victory now was full-scale martial law, in which every facet of Irish life would have to come under the control of the military. 'A foul job for any soldier' was Wilson's description of what would then follow. How the Pope would have described it, to say nothing of the Irish Americans, Sir Henry did not speculate. But two days after the Pope's letter was published the elections called for under the Better Government of Ireland Act were held, on 24 May.

These elections produced further evidence of the strength of Sinn Fein support. Of the 128 seats allotted to the 26 counties of the Catholic South, Sinn Fein won 124 without a contest. Four Unionist representatives of Trinity College were also returned unopposed. In the Protestant-dominated six-county north-eastern area, after a ferocious campaign marked by gerrymandering of constituencies, intimidation and personation the Unionists secured 40 out of the 52 seats, 12 being divided equally between Sinn Fein and the other Nationalist candidates.

Prior to the election de Valera and the leaders of the remnants of the old Irish Parliamentary Party had concluded a pact. John Dillon in the South and Joseph Devlin in the North had agreed that both wings of Nationalism would stand on a programme of abstention and self-determination. Using the proportional representation system, each side gave first preference to their own man and second to his Nationalist opponent. Although every Unionist candidate who stood in the election was elected, the Nationalist co-operation ensured that some strong pockets of Green anti-partitionist sentiment shone through the predominating cloak of Orange. In West Belfast, Joseph Devlin won a seat; Armagh returned two Nationalist deputies, one of them Collins; de Valera got 16,000 first preference votes in Down – James Craig received 30,000; and in the Fermanagh-Tyrone area four nationalists were returned. Amongst the prominent Sinn Feiners returned by the six counties were Arthur Griffith, Eoin MacNeill and John O'Mahony.[92] These Green pockets are the causes of the bloodstained images which regularly occur in the television news from Northern Ireland at the time of writing. Nevertheless, the partition envisaged in the Better Government of Ireland Act had been reflected in a clear electoral division between North and South.

Under the provisions of the Better Government of Ireland Act (BGIA) the South had been entitled to send 33 representatives to Westminster, the North 13, but Sinn Fein regarded the elections as being for the second Dail and a continuation of the abstention policy. Lloyd George thus had the clearest possible indications of international, domestic and Irish public opinion to weigh against the military men's advice. Obviously the opening of a parliament linked to Westminster in the six counties would be acceptable to a majority of the inhabitants of that part of Ireland, but what about the twenty-six counties' declaration for a Republican Dail? How could that be squared with the claims of Empire? Or with the divisions around the Cabinet table? What approach should or could the Imperialists make to the Republicans?

The Cabinet met on 26 May[93] to discuss the problem. Churchill advocated the military option, urging Lloyd George to go for a 'tremendous onslaught'. But the Conservatives were now led by a man less ideologically supportive of the Unionists than Bonar Law, who had contracted cancer. Austen Chamberlain had taken over from him and, while he was prepared to sanction force if necessary, he felt that a new offer of peace should be made. Moreover, he thought that it should contain a larger offer of self-government than that envisaged in the Better Government of Ireland Act. This view prevailed, and it was decided that, if there was not a parliament in operation in Dublin by 12 July, by which date Sinn Fein had signified its intention of allowing the BGIA to lapse, the next step should be martial law, or, in the Churchillian phrase, 'the most unlimited exercise of rough-handed force'.

The question which logically arises at this point is: how were the Sinn Feiners to be made aware of this decision? From the British point of view the contentious issue of talking to terrorists was further bedevilled by doubts as to which terrorists should be spoken to, Collins or de Valera. Who was the more moderate? Lloyd George wrongly concluded that Collins was the more hard-line Republican of the two. Collins had given two interviews to the noted journalist Carl Ackerman, a syndicated columnist, in which he dismissed the idea of a Dominion Home Rule Settlement:[94] '. . . you think we have only to whittle our demand down to Dominion Home Rule and we shall get it. This talk about Dominion Home Rule is not prompted by England with a view to granting it to us, but merely with a view to getting rid of the Republican movement. England will give us neither as a gift. The same effort that would get us Dominion Home Rule will get us a Republic.' That was in August 1920, when the effect of the interview was heightened by Devoy's reprinting it in the *Gaelic American* to prove that Collins, not de Valera, was Ireland's 'Fighting Chief'. The following April Collins again turned down Home Rule, telling Ackerman:[95] 'When I saw you before I said the same effort which would get us Dominion Home Rule would get us a Republic. I am still of that opinion and have never had so many peace moves as we have had since last autumn. Our Army is becoming stronger every day, its morale is improving and its efficiency is increasing.'

The statement was made largely for propaganda effect, because the strength of the IRA was anything but increasing. However, it contrasted markedly in British eyes with the moderate-sounding policies which had been emanating from de Valera since he had returned from America and begun to engage in the policy he had followed at the Chicago Republican Convention, publicly talking soft while privately acting tough. As Dwyer has noted, de Valera:[96] 'tended to portray a more moderate public image while privately advocating a more hardline approach. Collins tended to do the opposite. Privately he was much more moderate than was generally believed.' Closer to the realities of London than he had been in Chicago during the Republican Convention, de Valera now reversed the republican position which he had adopted in America as opposed to Cohalan's self-determination. Privately he wrote to Harry Boland explaining his U-turn:[97]

> In public statements our policy should be not to make it easy for Lloyd George by proclaiming that nothing but so and so will satisfy us. Our position should be simply that we are insisting on only one right, and that is the right of the people of this country to determine for themselves how they should be governed. That sounds moderate but includes everything and puts Lloyd George, the Labour Party and others on the defensive, and apologetic as far as the world is concerned.

That policy would, of course, have sounded equally moderate and borne more fruit had it been implemented at Chicago. But now de Valera began to give it effect, making statements in favour of self-determination such as:[98] 'If England should concede that right there would be no further difficulties, either with her or with the Ulster minority. If Ulster should claim autonomy we would be willing to grant it.' He repeated this line in an important and widely quoted interview, with the Zurich *Neue Zeitung* on 3 May, in which he said: 'The principle for which we are fighting is the principle of Ireland's right to complete self-determination.' In the same effort he gave the appearance, though hardly the substance, of being willing to accept Dominion status by adroit use of Bonar Law's name in reply to a question about his reaction if an offer of Dominion status were made on Canadian lines:

> The fact that this question is asked so often shows how skilfully England has

covered up the real issue by raising a false one. The essence of Dominion Home Rule as it exists in Canada and New Zealand is the fact that the Dominions are part of the British Empire *by their own free will*. The most conservative British statesmen, such as Mr. Bonar Law, have acknowledged the right of the British Dominions to secede should they choose to exercise it. It is obvious that when England is ready to make to us an offer with this implication she will in fact be admitting our right to have the Republic. Without the right to secede the British Dominions would not be what they are – free partners in the British Empire. The test of their status is their right to secede. By denying us that right the British deny us that status.

A little later[99] he also dusted off his old *Westminster Gazette* proposals, which had got him into such controversy over his Cuban analogy, to show how far he was prepared to go in meeting Britain's legitimate concerns over defence by guaranteeing Ireland's permanent neutrality: 'Upon recognising Ireland's independence England could at the same time issue a warning such as the Monroe doctrine, that she would regard any attempt of any foreign power to obtain a foothold in Ireland as an act of hostility against herself. . . . In the case of a common foe Ireland's manpower would then be available for the defence of the two islands.' In short, as he said himself, he was trying to convey the impression that 'we are thoroughly sane and reasonable people, not a coterie of political doctrinaires, or even party politicians, republican or other'.[100] In fact this onrush of sweet reason was so marked as to worry some of the more extreme IRA commanders, such as Tom Barry and Ernie O'Malley. Even some of the political thinkers in Sinn Fein began to get alarmed: the Republican envoy to Paris, Sean T. O'Ceallaigh, wrote to him saying: 'I hold that the firm stand we take "on an Irish Republic or nothing" needs not change but development.'[101] He received a de Valera rocket for his pains:[102] 'Our representatives abroad . . . must carry out the instructions of the Department, whether they personally agree with the policy or not . . . it is only by resignation that the representatives can find a way out.'

For Lloyd George, trying to find his way out of the Irish imbroglio, de Valera certainly sounded a better bet than Collins. He was well aware that there were differences between Collins and de Valera, and told a Cabinet meeting on 27 April that 'de Valera and Collins have quarrelled'. He obviously had an ear to the ground, for in his official biography de Valera also pointed to April as the time from which 'Collins did not seem to accept my view of things as he had done before'.[103] But Lloyd George wrongly ascribed the rift to a policy clash. His assessment was that de Valera opposed the 'gun business', but was in the grip of militants led by Collins: 'De Valera cannot come here and say he is willing to give up Irish Independence, for if he did he might be shot.'[104] Austen Chamberlain concurred in this view: 'De Valera is at the mercy of Michael Collins.' Lloyd George could clearly see the advantages of talking to Collins: 'No doubt he is the head and font of the movement. If I could see him a settlement might be possible.' But he doubted whether the 'British people would be willing for us to negotiate with the head of a band of murderers'.[105]

Thus the contending struggles for a peaceful and a military solution continued in tandem until June 1921, when the brother of an Irish patriot who had been executed on the orders of a Cabinet in which Lloyd George had held office emerged to play a fleeting but vital role in Irish history. Tom Casement, Roger's brother, had kept in touch with his old friend, the South African Prime Minister Jan Smuts, and had made arrangements to meet him when the Prime Minister arrived in London for the Imperial Conference. Word of this intention had reached de Valera and Casement's diary describes what happened next, in Dublin on 14 June:[106]

> . . . de Valera rode up on a bicycle and introduced himself. He asked me why I was going to London to see Smuts and that I had no authority from him or any official message from him. That was understood but he told me he would like Smuts to know what was required and that he would meet him if I could arrange a meeting . . . during our talk I told him that Smuts could not stand for an Irish Republic as he was Prime Minister of a Dominion, de Valera frankly told me that a Republic was out of the question. All he wanted was a Treaty between two nations. I saw that point and told him that I would put it before Smuts.

Casement later sent a copy of this diary entry to de Valera, who wrote in the margin: ' . . . this is not accurate I might have said that I was aware that it was out of the question to demand that Smuts should accept the Republican position as condition precedent to seeing me. It is probable that I indicated that the line to be pursued in seeking a settlement was that of a treaty between the two states.'[107]

Curiously, in view of this obviously for-the-record annotation, there is no mention of Casement in de Valera's official biography, which claims that 'after much preliminary spade work initiated by de Valera, Smuts and his secretary arrived in Dublin on July 5th'.[108] In fact on the day that de Valera met Casement, Smuts was already sending an historic communication to Lloyd George – not at the instigation of de Valera but at that of the King of England, George V. Smuts' description of the sequence of events in his biography[109] can be taken as indicating either Lloyd George's deviousness or the problems he faced in manoeuvring with his coalition partners. The King had invited Smuts to Windsor, where he informed him of his deep disquiet over events in Ireland. Smuts suggested that he make a conciliatory speech when he opened the Six-County Parliament later in the month. Another speech had been prepared by Balfour, which amounted to a 'declaration of war against the South'. But the King preferred Smuts' approach and suggested he put his thoughts on paper. Smuts did so, sending a copy to Lloyd George, with whom he was developing the argument that peace in Ireland was possible now that the Ulster question was out of the way.

As a result he found himself invited to a Cabinet meeting where Lloyd

George gravely discussed the draft of the King's speech which had arrived from Windsor. It was the speech which Smuts had prepared, but Lloyd George did not refer to its origins. He explained Smuts' presence at the Cabinet table as being due to the fact that he had written 'an interesting letter on Ireland'. Smuts was duly consulted as to his views on the King's speech and argued in favour of it, shrewdly basing his case on Irish American opinion. He pointed out that the most pressing defence need facing the Empire, in the wake of the Great War, lay in the Pacific. Here it was essential to Great Britain's strategy that America and Japan be drawn together. A settlement in Ireland would predispose both America and the Imperial Conference partners to see things Britain's way.

Some tense Cabinet meetings ensued, including one in which Cope was called upon to address a gathering which included not only members of the Cabinet but the highest-ranking administrative and military decision-takers on Ireland. He made such an eloquent appeal for the peace option that an enraged Hamar Greenwood urged him to 'curb his Sinn Fein tendencies'.[110] Once again Lloyd George left his Cabinet colleagues in the dark as to the real authorship of the policy under discussion, in this case himself. He had learned from Smuts that Casement could arrange a meeting between Smuts and de Valera but that a truce was essential.[111] Out of a combination of this mishmash of conflicting personalities and policies – and the King's own good instinct for peace – there emerged the decision that His Majesty's speech at the opening of the Six-County Parliament would contain the following:

> I speak from a full heart when I pray that my coming to Ireland today may prove to be the first step towards the end of strife among her people whatever their race or creed. In that hope I appeal to all Irishmen to pause, to stretch out the hand of forbearance and conciliation, to forgive and forget, and to join in making for the land they love a new era of peace, contentment and goodwill.
>
> It is my earnest desire that in Southern Ireland too, there may, ere long, take place a parallel to what is now passing in this hall; that there a similar opportunity may present itself, and a similar ceremony be performed. For this the Parliament of the United Kingdom has in the fullest measure provided the powers. For this the Parliament of Ulster is pointing the way. . . .

Thus was a new note struck in the conflict, and one of the most profound significance, but on 22 June, the very day that the King spoke, its benign effect was almost obliterated. For, arising out of the confusion in British policy described above, on 22 June the arrest of de Valera occurred. However Cope, as described earlier, succeeded in prising him out of the clutches of the military, and two days later followed Lloyd George's invitation to London stating that: 'The British Government are deeply anxious that, so far as they can assure it, the King's appeal for reconciliation in Ireland shall not have been made in vain.' However, the letter went on to make it clear that in the wake of the recent election the conference was to take place on the basis of a *de facto* recognition of partition. For, along with guaranteeing safe conduct for any colleagues whom de Valera wished to bring with him, Lloyd George also stated:[112]

> I write, therefore, to convey the following invitation to you as the chosen leader of the great majority in Southern Ireland, and to Sir James Craig, the Premier of Northern Ireland:
>
> That you should attend a conference here in London, in company with Sir James Craig, to explore to the utmost the possibility of a settlement.

De Valera found one 'quite unacceptable facet' to this otherwise welcome missive: 'It implied that the President should accept equality with Craig, the leader of the recalcitrant minority at whose demand Ireland had been partitioned.'[113] On the one hand he saw himself as the elected head of the Irish nation and wanted to be treated as such; on the other, he had already had a meeting with Craig and knew his pretensions would get short shrift in that quarter. Accordingly he resorted to a favourite tactic of his when confronted with an unpalatable decision: instantaneous procrastination. Taking advantage of his release, and the status conferred upon him by the British Prime Minister's letter, he openly set up headquarters in the Mansion House and sent a reply to Lloyd George, dated 28 June, containing the following:

> We most earnestly desire to help in bringing about a lasting peace between the peoples of these two islands, but see no avenue by which it can be reached if you deny Ireland's essential unity and set aside the principle of national self-determination.
>
> Before replying more fully to your letter, I am seeking a conference with certain representatives of the political minority in this country.

The date of the sending of this letter coincided with that on which the Southern Parliament was supposed to have opened. However, since only the fifteen senators nominated by the Governor General and the four representatives of Dublin University turned up, this Parliament was deemed to have failed to meet its statutory attendance requirements and lapsed after fifteen minutes. Whether the bulk of its members were in prison or not, the second Dail was obviously the only representative parliament in Southern Ireland. However, equally obviously it was not representative of the majority in the Northern Six Counties. But de Valera proceeded to act as though it were. He addressed a letter to five leaders of Unionism which was certain to be offensive to one of them, Sir James Craig. The others (the Earl of Midleton, Sir Maurice Dockrell, Sir Robert Woods and Andrew Jameson), being leaders of Southern Unionism, a tiny minority within the twenty-six counties, were in a different, lesser category in terms of both domicile and political status.

His letter, sent on 28 June, the same date as his reply to Lloyd George, ran as follows:[114]

A Chara,

The reply which I, *as spokesman for the Irish nation*, shall make to Lloyd George will affect the lives and fortunes of the political minority in this island, no less than those of the majority.

Before sending that reply therefore, I would like to confer with you and to learn from you at first hand the views of a certain section of our people of whom you are representative.

I am confident that you will not refuse this service to Ireland, and I shall await you at the Mansion House, Dublin at 11 a.m. on Monday next in the hope that you will find it possible to attend.

The exact set of expressions (or expletives) with which Sir James received this letter have not survived. But we do know that Lady Craig said of the missive that for 'sheer impertinence it could hardly be beaten'.[115] Craig himself described his policy, if not his reactions, in the face of de Valera's manoeuvrings to a British civil servant by announcing that he would[116] 'sit on Ulster like a rock. Let the P.M. and Sinn Fein settle it. He was satisfied with what he had got.' He did accept Lloyd George's invitation to go to London, but, unsurprisingly, not de Valera's to go to the Dublin meeting.

This was held, with typical de Valera flair for stage management, on 4 July, American Independence Day. Meanwhile Casement, continuing with his intermediary activities, had introduced Smuts' secretary, Captain Lane, to de Valera in the Mansion House on 30 June; here a meeting with the South African Prime Minister in Dr Farnan's house was arranged for 5 July. To prepare the atmosphere for discussion Cope readily fell in with a suggestion of Casement's that a number of prominent Sinn Feiners be released. Griffith, Barton, Duggan, MacNeill and Michael Staines were accordingly set free. Not surprisingly, when Casement met them at Farnan's house he thought they looked happy. The significance of the fact that there was one notable, and unhappy, absentee when Smuts arrived escaped Casement, as it did many others at the time – Michael Collins was not present.

Neither was Erskine Childers, but Smuts' biography, in describing his meeting in Farnan's house, states: 'We argued most fiercely all the morning, all afternoon until late in the night and the men I found most difficult to convince were de Valera and Childers. I couldn't convince them. Smuts probably mistook Barton for Childers, his cousin,'[117] but he identified de Valera's position correctly in his report back to Lloyd George. De Valera began by adroitly seeming to suggest that peace was impossible. He announced that he was planning to reject Lloyd George's invitation for a tripartite meeting with Craig because he saw it as a trap[118] set to get him to recognize partition. Moreover, Craig's presence would enable the British to exploit the inevitable differences between the Irish factions, giving them an excuse to blame the Irish for the conference's inevitable failure. Furthermore, if bi-partisan talks were to be held, a truce would be an essential precondition.

When Smuts asked him what he would be seeking if a truce were conceded, de Valera replied, 'A republic.' In return Smuts asked him: 'Do you really think that the British people are ever likely to agree to such a republic?' During the subsequent sparring de Valera made the case that, because of the desirability of attaining the republic, the Irish would agree to be bound by treaty limitations guaranteeing Britain's legitimate security needs. However, no such restrictions would be acceptable under Dominion status. De Valera stressed that a free choice between the two alternatives must be forthcoming, but Smuts argued that the British would never concede such a choice: 'You are next door to them.' He outlined the problems that a republic had faced in the Transvaal and made the point that, when the people had been given a chance of voting for a republic, they had voted by a large majority for a free partnership within the Empire. Smuts said: 'As a friend I cannot advise you too strongly against a republic. Ask what you want but not a republic.' However, the lengthy exchange[119] concluded on an apparently 'moderate' note. De Valera told Smuts that 'If the status of Dominion rule is offered, I will use all our machinery to get the people to accept it.'

Smuts was not overly impressed with de Valera. He had also spoken to the British commanders on the spot and his impressions of his Irish visit were recorded by one Cabinet member, H. A. L. Fisher:[120] 'Smuts back from his visit to Dev, Tudor, Macready etc. Smuts saw Dev, Duggan, Barton and Griffith. . . . All think such men quite incapable of dealing with a big situation. . . . However, Smuts was sincere in his determination to try to bring peace to Ireland. He told Lloyd George:[121] 'The present situation is an unmeasured calamity; it is a negation of all the principles of government which we have professed as the basis of Empire and it must more and more tend to poison both our Empire relations and our foreign relations.'

Lloyd George reacted to the force of the Field Marshal's convictions and to his accounts of what had transpired in Dublin by agreeing to a truce and the exclusion of Craig from the talks, leaving it to Smuts to tell de Valera about Craig. Smuts advised de Valera that 'the less said about Ulster the better for fear of giving unnecessary umbrage in that quarter and making things more difficult for yourself hereafter'. De Valera took his advice and in his reply to Lloyd George made no mention of Craig, but agreed to meet so that they could explore on 'what basis such a conference as that proposed can reasonably hope to achieve the object desired'.[122]

The truce came into effect on 11 July. Macready, the British Commander-in-Chief, was cheered to the echo by a Dublin crowd when he turned up at the Mansion House to sign the terms. One man who did not feel like cheering was Michael Collins. Knowing almost to a round of ammunition the strength, or more accurately the weakness, of the IRA, whose real power lay in anonymity, he had warned that 'once a truce is agreed, and we come out in the open, it is extermination for us if the truce should fail. . . . We shall be like rabbits coming out of their holes.'[123] He did not have long to wait before finding out what it was like to be caught out in the open by de Valera. Collins, who had single-handedly conducted the earlier negotiations with Lloyd George through Archbishop Clune, was not included as a member of the delegation which de Valera announced he was taking with him to London.

11
SAORSTAT V. PHOBLACHT

COLLINS WAS FURIOUS and argued bitterly against the slight of not being taken to London, but to no avail. De Valera said that he did not wish to give the British the opportunity of taking photographs of him.[1] Apart from the role that Collins had played in bringing the struggle to the point where the Prime Minister of Britain was prepared to sue for peace, this reasoning is hard to reconcile with de Valera's proposal of six months earlier that Collins should go to America – where the British secret service could have photographed him to their heart's content. Amongst those whom he did take to London were Griffith, Stack, Plunkett, Barton and Childers. However, de Valera did not stay in the Grosvenor Hotel with the other members of the delegation but instead moved into a private house, No. 5 West Halkin Street, with the Farnans and Kathleen O'Connell.

On the eve of de Valera's meeting with Lloyd George, Collins sat alone in his office in Dublin while cheering crowds filled the streets outside. He penned a note to a friend which contained the following:[2] 'Agreement is a trifling word or so I have come to look on it as such. At this moment there is more ill-will within a victorious assembly than ever could be found anywhere else except in the devil's assembly. It cannot be fought against. The issue and persons are mixed to such an extent as to make discernibility an utter impossibility except for a few.'

It was a gloomily accurate setting of the scene for the civil war whose seeds were to be scattered on the conference table at 10 Downing Street the following day. But, just as in euphoric Dublin, half dazed, half crazed with relief at the coming of peace, nothing in London betokened anything other than a happy ending as the curtain went up on the drama of the confrontation between Welsh Wizard and New Prince on a blazing July day at Euston Station where, as Kathleen O'Connell's diary records, the Irish party arrived.[3] 'Excited women, who far outnumbered the men, surged and fought to get near de Valera. They stopped not to cheer. They just howled and screamed in the extremity of their enthusiasm, "oh isn't he lovely" was the general comment. Meanwhile, de Valera, hatless and dishevelled, was being protected from the violent affection of the Irish crowd, by a number of stalwart policemen.' No one paused to give thought to the symbolism of the fact that the Nationalists' leader had arrived on 12 July, the Orangemen's feast day. Meanwhile in Downing Street Lloyd George was almost equally excited. His mistress, secretary and subsequent wife, Frances Stevenson, recorded in her diary:[4] 'Indeed I have never seen

230

D. [her customary description of David Lloyd George] so excited as he was before de Valera arrived. He kept walking in and out of my room and I could see he was working out the best way of dealing with de V. As I told him afterwards, he was bringing up all his guns.'

In the event Lloyd George, in Churchill's celebrated phrase 'never a greater artist than in the first moments of a fateful interview', decided that the 'best way of dealing with de V' was to use a theatrical setting in which to act out a charade for his visitor's benefit. Although, at his own request, de Valera saw the British leader by himself, the Prime Minister chose to hold the meeting, not in his study, but in the much larger Cabinet Room which still contained all the chairs set out for the Imperial Conference. A huge map, eye-catchingly splashed with the red of the British Empire, dominated one wall.

Seventy years after this historic meeting Radio Telefis Eireann and Thames TV made a lengthy drama documentary[5] which re-created the scene as accurately as possible with Ian Bannen playing Lloyd George and Barry McGovern, who looks uncannily like him, portraying de Valera. Lloyd George, all Celtic charm and personality, with an eye on the map showing 'the greatest Empire ever known', and a tremendous cascade of rolling Welsh 'rs', points out where the various Imperial Prime Ministers were seated 'in this great sisterhood of nations. There sits India, there Africa. . . . One chair remains vacant – waiting for Ireland.' He glances expectantly at de Valera who, the antithesis of climax, responds merely by blinking slightly and opening his briefcase like a schoolmaster producing the exam papers. In fact he *was* responding partly as an ex-schoolteacher – and partly as ex-convict. While the tide of Lloyd George's eloquent psychological onslaught flowed over him he was trying to concentrate on something else, as does a prisoner attempt to while away the hours – or resist his interrogators' questioning. De Valera's biography relates how he succeeded. While Lloyd George was extolling the merits of those who, from the Prime Ministerial chair, had helped to colour the map red – Pitt, Palmerston, Gladstone – and telling him that the British did not mind who occupied the seat: 'Campbell Bannerman was a Scot. I Welsh', De Valera managed to see the map from a different perspective.[6] 'His school-master's eye noted that it was a map based on Mercator's projection, which exaggerated the red markings. In any case, it was proof to him of British rapacity and certainly not an argument for re-entering the Empire.' Diamond cut diamond. Determined to persist in the anti-climactic mould, de Valera turned up for the next meeting (starting on 14 July and ending on the 21st, there were four in all) on another blisteringly hot day wearing a black tie and a black suit. Lloyd George was not the only one who could create a psychological climate when he wished. And Geoffrey Shakespeare, one of the top British civil servants involved in the Irish stituation, has left a record of the awe in which de Valera was held by his contemporaries. Shakespeare said he was[7] 'surprised at the way in which de Valera's staff treated him as royalty and walked out backwards from his presence'.

In order to make sure the climate in Dublin suited him also, he made a show of keeping Collins *au fait* with what was happening in London by writing to him later that day, 15 July:[8]

> I am sure you are anxious to hear whether any important developments have taken place. The position is simply this – that Lloyd George is developing a proposal which he wishes me to bring back in my pocket as a proposal to the Irish nation for its consideration. The meetings have been between us two as principals . . . you will be glad to know that I am not dissatisfied with the general situation . . . we will be free to consider [the proposal] without prejudice. . . .'

Outside the Downing Street theatre other actors made their contributions, notably Smuts and Craig. Of these, Smuts was both supportive and off-stage in his role playing: he called on de Valera to advise and help him in any way he could. Craig's role where de Valera was concerned neither was, nor was intended to be, off-stage or supportive. As Lloyd George was drawing up the proposals for de Valera to take home to Dublin, Craig – also in London and in touch with Lloyd George – publicly announced that[9] 'it now merely remains for Mr. de Valera and the British people to come to terms regarding the area outside of which I am Prime Minister'.

On the only occasion on which de Valera did meet Craig face to face, during the Anglo-Irish war, when Craig courageously came to Dublin under safe conduct arranged between Collins and Cope, de Valera did not score any spectacular triumph. But, more importantly, it should be remembered that, even if he had, Craig, though he led the Orangemen, did not derive all his power from them. Unlike the Nationalist leaders whose support largely came from either Irish, or Irish Americans, or both, Craig had enormously influential backing amongst the Tory establishment. De Valera might have got the better of Craig, but he was not likely to have outmanoeuvred a Unionist guru like Balfour – to say nothing of lesser but important figures like Sir Henry Wilson. Craig was frequently able to flout the Conservative–Liberal coalition Government because of Conservative support, which in those days ranged from the theological to the visceral.

Advised by his Tory mentors, Craig, let it be remembered, was able to steer clear of the Treaty negotiations, just as did de Valera. But he did so in quite different fashion. He resided openly in the Constitutional Club in Northumberland Avenue, surrounded by his ministers and receiving a stream of supporters. He cannot have been short of information concerning the course of the negotiations, and certainly he demonstrated an ability to fulfil his pre-negotiation promise to sit on his Six Counties 'like a rock'. He never came under the sort of pressure from Lloyd George which would have driven him into a united Ireland. In fact Lloyd George had to be careful not to be seen to pressurize him, lest it appear that Lloyd George were acting on behalf of Sinn Fein.

The upshot was that Craig was placated at every hand's turn, and the record shows that he was the beneficiary of undercover disbursements of arms and money on a scale proportionately far greater than anything which occurred during the Contra–Irangate affair. One result was that he was able to fund and found a militia, the B-Specials, at the British taxpayer's expense. The Specials horrified British civil servants, who pointed out to Lloyd George that in certain circumstances the Unionists had promised to use the militia against the Crown. But Lloyd George did nothing to disarm the force.[10] He knew that where the Tories were concerned Ulster could fight and Ulster would be right. De Valera looms larger in history than Craig, but he was never in a position either to cajole or to browbeat him into coming under Dublin's sway. This was probably one of the reasons he stayed away from the Treaty negotiations. He knew that Sinn Fein had no method of forcing the Conservatives not to implement the partition of Ireland.

Now, in London, challenged full frontally by Craig in his claim to be the 'spokesman for the Irish nation', de Valera wrote to Lloyd George on 19 July, the day Craig's statement appeared in the papers, protesting at the man's 'wholly inadmissible' claim that he, de Valera, only spoke for an area outside the Six Counties. He wanted from Lloyd George a 'definite statement as to whether your Government is in agreement with Sir James Craig and intends to support his view'. If the Prime Minister did back Craig, he warned that there would be 'no purpose in pursuing our conversations'. Lloyd George gave him a dusty answer: 'I am responsible neither for Sir James Craig's statement to the press, to which you refer, nor for your statement to which Sir James' purports to be a reply.' Alarmed, de Valera immediately turned to the man on whom the heaviest burden of his threat to break off the talks would have fallen, Michael Collins: 'Things may burst up suddenly so be prepared.'[11] De Valera had laid himself open to Lloyd George's retort by issuing one of his steely 'moderate' statements earlier in the discussions: 'The press gives the impression that I have been making certain compromise demands. I have made no demand but the one I am entitled to make: the self-determination of the Irish nation to be recognised.'

The realpolitik of de Valera's continuation of the talks despite the failure to get any rebuttal of Craig's position, or any indication that one might be forthcoming in the future, was to give *de facto* recognition to partition. On the related questions of Lloyd George's ability – as opposed to his inclination – to concede the rebuttal demand, the limitations on his powers over Craig, and of the threat posed to the British Prime Minister's position by Unionist and right-wing influences generally, de Valera displayed much of the incomprehension he had shown towards the workings of American politics. His biography admits that Lloyd George's position in Cabinet was 'much weaker than the Irish leader thought'.[12] On what he based his feeling that, by going to the people on the Irish issue, Lloyd George would have 'overcome the die hards' the Authorized Version is silent. Yet on 23 June, only three weeks before the talks began, the *Manchester Guardian* had revealed the extent of a plot against Lloyd George. Discontent had been simmering since the replacement (or ousting) of Bonar Law as leader of the Conservatives by Austen Chamberlain the previous March. The plot's ringleaders, Birkenhead, who (mistakenly) thought he would lead any Government arising from Lloyd George's fall, and Churchill, who was annoyed at not succeeding Chamberlain at the Exchequer, were aided and abetted by the press baron Lord Beaverbrook. In fact Lloyd George to a large extent both defused the plot by bringing Birkenhead and Churchill into the Irish negotiations at a later stage, as we shall see, and subsequently did fall from power over Ireland.

Such pressures and misconceptions obviously made for clashes during the talks. As they were nearing the end, for example, after de Valera had said he would reject Lloyd George's proposals, the Welshman unsheathed his sword and the following dialogue ensued:[13]

> Lloyd George: 'Do you realise that this means war? Do you realise that the responsibility for it will rest on your shoulders alone?'
> De Valera: 'No Mr. Lloyd George, if you insist on attacking us it is you, not I, who will be responsible, because you will be the aggressor.'
> Lloyd George: 'I could put a soldier in Ireland for every man, woman and child in it.'
> De Valera: 'Very well. But you would have to keep them there.'

A less intense but more significant exchange had taken place three days earlier, on 18 July, when Lloyd George picked up a sheet of the notepaper headed 'Saorstat na hEireann' on which de Valera had written to him and enquired with devious innocence what the word 'Saorstat' meant. De Valera explained that it meant 'Free State', and that some Gaelic enthusiasts favoured the term *poblacht* to mean republic while others chose *saorstat*. The Welsh Wizard remarked sweetly: 'Must we not then agree Mr de Valera that the Celts never were republicans and have no native word for such an idea . . . ?' According to de Valera's biography[14] Lloyd George also commented: 'Yes, there is the South African Orange Free State and the title "Free State" could be given to Ireland.' The biography states: 'De Valera is convinced that the name Irish Free State originated in this incident.' This is somewhat disingenuous. If anything can be said with certainty about the de Valera/Lloyd George versions of what transpired that fateful July there is no question that it was made clear to de Valera on that occasion just what the British intended to call the proposed Irish statelet. Given Smuts' influence on the talks – he apparently played much the same hidden role in drawing up the final proposals which emerged as he did in drafting the King's speech which led to them – and the knowledge of Ireland possessed by Tom Jones, probably Lloyd George's closest civil service confidant on the Irish issue in London, the thinking must have been obvious to a man of de Valera's intelligence.

But, as he would demonstrate on other notable occasions in his career, de Valera could sometimes specialize in seeming not to know what was going on. Throughout the talks he conveyed the impression of being a pleasant if somewhat visionary character, not over-burdened with brains. 'He wished to let Lloyd George reveal himself.'[15] He succeeded to the extent that Lloyd George was later quoted as saying that de Valera was impossible to negotiate with. 'It is like sitting on a merry-go-round and trying to catch up the swing in front.'[16] But since de Valera admitted he did not understand the Prime Minister's political position and had notified Collins at the outset that Lloyd George had announced his intention of putting down his proposals on paper, de Valera's 'cute hoor' approach on this occasion would appear to have been somewhat superfluous, a product of a combination of his reading of Machiavelli and his keen awareness of the fact that he was dealing with one of the world's wiliest politicians. But no doubt he would have appreciated Lloyd George's report on him to the Cabinet:[17]

> . . . he found it difficult to say exactly where the Irish leader stood. Mr de Valera, who had an agreeable personality, had reached the stage of asking questions in regard to such matters as the entry of Southern Ireland into the Empire, swearing allegiance in the form of an oath, the name of the new State and so forth. What he wanted was a Republic, but the Prime Minister said this was impossible, being inconsistent with the monarchy. Mr de Valera had not admitted this inconsistency . . . as the conversation progressed it became increasingly clear that Ulster was the real difficulty.

To judge from other comments made by insider civil servants such as Jones and Geoffrey Shakespeare,[18] the Prime Minister's report to the Cabinet was sanitized in the official record. Jones, obviously with the Prime Minister's sanction, wrote to Bonar Law on 22 July giving 'the P.M.'s account of de Valera': '. . . not a big man, but a sincere man, a white man and an agreeable personality. He has a limited vocabulary, talks chiefly of ideals and constantly returns to the same few dominating notions.'

In view of what Lloyd George told his Cabinet, Jones obviously misunderstood the interpretation which de Valera placed on the exchange about *saorstat* and *poblacht*: ' . . . de Valera agreed to drop the "Republic", the P.M. telling him that there was no Irish or Welsh word for it and therefore it was alien to the spirit of the Celt. . . .'

The course of Irish history and of Anglo-Irish relationships would have taken a very different course if that had been the position. The precise nature of the status which the British did propose to offer was revealed to his Cabinet colleagues by Lloyd George in the House of Commons at 5.30 p.m. on 20 July 1921. The proposal laid the foundation for modern Ireland. In a nutshell, the Twenty-six Counties were to be offered Dominion status, and partition was to remain in force for so long as the

Northerners wished. Defence of the Irish coastal waters was to remain a British preserve, and the Royal Navy was to get facilities in a number of ports. Any Irish army was to be of limited size and 'territorial' in character. The Irish were to be responsible for a proportion of the British National Debt and for preserving free trade within the British Isles.

H. A. L. Fisher's diary[19] gives a more human insight into how these proposals were prefaced by Lloyd George, and received by his colleagues, than does the official record: 'LG describes his impressions of de Valera. A nice man, honest, astonishingly little vocabulary, wants to settle but afraid of his followers. Craig also wants to settle but afraid of his followers. The document which LG had drafted with help of Balfour and Chamberlain is read out. "FE" [Birkenhead] weighs in at once saying he accepts it; Churchill and I follow.' The Cabinet then adjourned to allow fifteen minutes' private perusal of the document. On resumption, Fisher made some contributions which reveal something of the extent of the independence the proposals conferred in spite of their limitations: 'Will Ireland have an independent place in League of Nations I ask AJB [Balfour]? Yes, that follows. I get Cabinet to delete *stipulation* about recruiting in Ireland and to say "we assume that recruiting will be permitted".'

After this exchange the Cabinet turned to discussing the question of having a 'Treaty' with Ireland which Balfour, Chamberlain and Curzon opposed. However, 'LG weighed in heavily' to say that de Valera attached great importance to having a Treaty, without which the chances were weighted against a settlement. 'Eventually the words Treaty, Pact, Instrument are all used.' The Cabinet broke up at 8.10 and Lloyd George brought the document to the King. At this stage a note of comedy enters the proceedings. De Valera had insisted that he be shown the proposals in writing before meeting Lloyd George the next day. All the prior consultation and preparation of the document necessarily resulted in its being late in the evening before it was ready for transmission to the Irish. According to Lord Longford:[20] 'Barton and Childers were half undressed when suddenly their door was thrown open and "Mr. Lloyd George and Sir James Craig" were announced. . . . However it turned out to be only Tom Jones and Sir Edward Grigg, Lloyd George's secretaries, bringing the British document.'

Thereafter the document did not yield much humour. When de Valera met Lloyd George in the morning he 'flatly rejected the proposals. He said that he would not recommend them either to the Cabinet or the Dail.' The 'this means war' exchange already quoted then ensued. By the time it had concluded de Valera was outside the door of the Cabinet Room, having declared himself so appalled by the proposals that he could not be seen 'taking these things home with me'.[21] Lloyd George inquired if he were not going to give him a considered reply. De Valera answered: 'I'll give you a considered reply if you keep your part of the bargain', meaning if the truce were extended.[22] Lloyd George agreed, but by now, and not for the only time in his career, de Valera's pride had got him into a position where he could not compromise without the unthinkable occurring – his losing face. His biography frankly states that ' . . . by this time de Valera could not pick up the document without going back into the room'.[23] He left without it, to Lloyd George's chagrin. Frances Stevenson wrote: 'D was very depressed. De V. had not even taken the terms away with him.' However, the day's diary entry had a happy ending: ' . . . but now we find this was a mistake and he has sent for them – how Irish!'

At this stage let us pause before going on to see how de Valera did eventually deal with the proposals. As we are now on the threshold of one of the saddest and most significant epochs in Ireland's and de Valera's history, it may be useful to remind ourselves of the forces with which he and the British and Irish leaders of the time had to contend. The points of the eternal Irish triangle had three different colours: Orange, Green and Tory blue. Lloyd George's Cabinet difficulties have already been alluded to. To these must be added the dead weight of Conservative back-bench opinion. The throwers of bread rolls and bayers after broken glass were also baying for Lloyd George's blood because of his Irish policies:[24] 'The Conservative back benchers, for arcane reasons not unconnected with a traditional obtuseness, were determined to punish him for solving a huge Irish problem by coming to terms with the Irish.'

The 'arcane reasons', of course, included a feeling that weakening of the Union endangered the Empire. But there was also the ever-present 'Curragh Mutiny' factor. The back-benchers, representatives of the officer and gentleman class, interacted with sections of the military led by obvious figures like Sir Henry Wilson and less obvious ones like Brigadier General Prescott Decies, who was vocal in Conservative-Unionist politics and who, when sectarian violence broke out there, busied himself with lethal activities directed against Catholics in the Six Counties. Their nature may be guessed at in an assessment of his character by General Macready, the British Commander in Southern Ireland during the Black and Tan war, when Prescott Decies was an RIC district commissioner:[25] 'Strickland will have to watch the police very carefully for certainly Prescott Decies will think that martial law means that he can kill anybody he sees walking along the road whose appearance may be distasteful to him.'

The Orange portion of the triangle included many strands in its visceral determination not to be subsumed into a Catholic/Nationalist-dominated Ireland: partly that *pietas* of race and place exemplified by the slaughter of the Ulster men on the Somme; partly a desire to hold the land and the jobs they guarded against the Catholics; partly stemming from this possession, the fears and hates generated by the processes of colonialization, massacre and counter-massacre from which those possessions evolved. Where this last consideration was concerned, the memories of old bloodshed were increasingly envenomed by the contemporary shedding of new. And, running through all, the excitation of these fears by unscrupulous leaders, to be found at every level of society – political, administrative, police and pulpit, often making use of their Orange and masonic lodges – meant that not only did 'Pope' and 'Devil' become interchangeable terms, but 'Catholic neighbour' and 'dangerous menace' did so also.

In the Green corner, after a brutalizing war, much that passed for 'republicanism' was an illustration of the fact that in a fight it is generally the underdog which is positioned to bite at the testicles. Some of the more intellectually inclined amongst the leadership did have a concept of the term 'republic' which embraced the writings of figures like Paine and Rousseau. All would have equated it with 'freedom', meaning freedom from the Crown – the emblem of loyalty to the Orangeman, the symbol of suppression to the Volunteers, who associated it with famine, landlordism and the Black and Tans. Most traced their ideological lineage through the teachings of nationalist and separatist heroes such as Wolfe Tone and Thomas Davis. But a major Sinn Fein theoretician was of course the monarchist Arthur Griffith, whom many respected and followed. Few had any concept of the fears and formation of the various strands of Ulster Protestantism, ascribing their resistance to an All-Ireland Republic as being either bluff or a British-inspired stratagem. Some had a vision which felt that anything less than an implementation of the proclamation of Easter 1916 was blasphemy and betrayal. About the only common ground the Greens shared with their Orange counterparts with the fact that neither wished to see socialism rear its ugly head.

De Valera got an excellent, if bruising, first-hand experience of these differing strands of republicanism at work when he presented the Lloyd George formula to his Cabinet on Sunday, 25 July:[26]

> It was a particularly thorny meeting, and things were not helped by his poor chairmanship. His cabinet meetings lacked discipline. Instead of considering one thing at a time, he tended to deal with everything together in the hope of reaching a general consensus. This would have been extremely difficult at the best of times, but it was almost impossible in a Cabinet of eleven headstrong ministers, who were often joined by obstinate understudies. As a result the discussions tended to ramble and were usually quite inconclusive. Ministers frequently came away with conflicting opinions about the outcome of discussions.

The Dail Cabinet of 1921 certainly did contain a collection of forceful, idealistic, often brilliant personalities who more closely resembled the sort of characters met with during the days of French Revolution Assemblies than a Cabinet formed in the contemporary Europe of consensus politics. Indeed, it is impossible to resist the temptation to further the French analogy by contrasting the clash between Danton and Robespierre with that between Collins and de Valera. But there was more to de Valera's style of chairmanship than meets the eye in the judgement given above. In the first place, de Valera chose not to 'chair' the meeting, but to ask each person present to give their views in the order in which they sat at the table, beginning with Arthur Griffith and Joseph MacDonagh beside him at the top of the table and ending with Brugha facing him at the bottom. As we shall see, de Valera had his own reasons for not being identified with a positive policy on this occasion. But the foregoing assessment of de Valera's methodology at a meeting obscures the fact that in the last analysis a poor chairman is one who either does not get his own way or has something he does not wish to occur foisted upon him. De Valera took care that this did not happen either at this meeting or at the vast majority of gatherings which he chaired throughout his long life in politics. The rambling discursiveness both disguised the fact that no action was taken which he might have disapproved of, and succeeded in getting the others to reveal their minds to him without de Valera having to show his own hand. Reaction at the 25 July meeting covered the spectrum of the 'republican' movement.

De Valera had got Griffith to draft the reply for Lloyd George, rejecting the terms, although Griffith himself was personally favourable to the terms. On the conservative wing, Eoin MacNeill welcomed the offer outright. Nearer the centre, W. T. Cosgrave found it better than expected. Collins did not give a clear judgement: 'you all know my opinion' was the summing up of one observer.[27] Count Plunkett's contribution took the form of a 'masterly review of the cause for which they were fighting'. Stack, Barton, Childers and MacDonagh were all strongly opposed to the proposals. Stack was 'evidently displeased that he had gone to London'. Barton, who, like the rest of the gathering, seemingly believed that the terms had been sent by the British to Dublin Castle and then forwarded to the Mansion House, said that the President could not be the bearer of such terms to Ireland. Countess Markievicz and J. J. O'Kelly, 'Sceilig' (after a group of rocks off the coast of Kerry, his county of origin), both 1916 proclamation republicans, wanted the documents circulated so that more time could be given to their consideration. Sceilig was opposed to the whole idea of 'entering the house of the enemy', and in favour of this view cited the treatment which Brian Boru had meted out to a tenth-century rival who had been so foolish as to enter his castle. *En route* to the discussion Countess Markievicz had met the mother of a boy killed in the fighting, and had been swayed towards an aversion to doing anything which might bring similar anguish to any other mother. However, on hearing Sceilig she decided that she might adopt his viewpoint – once she actually read the documents. Ernest Blythe seemed to agree with Griffith and MacNeill and significantly, in view of his military position, Richard Mulcahy was described as sounding a 'defeatist note'.

It should be underlined that these deliberations took place amongst the members of the Ministry only, not the Dail as a whole, and were certainly not made by the Irish public, which, faced with a choice between acceptance or resumption of war, could not have been trusted to vote

239

against the proposals. One member of Cabinet, Cathal Brugha, the epitome of 1916 republicanism, did not feel that they even merited the consideration of the Cabinet. In an oft-quoted scene his reaction, when asked for his opinion, is alleged to have been:[28]

'I haven't much to add', Brugha now said looking straight at de Valera, 'except to say how glad I am that it has been suggested that we circulate these documents and consider them fully before we meet again, if for no other reason than to give you and the great masters of English you keep at your elbow an opportunity of extricating us from the morass in which ye have landed us.'

'We have done our best', half sobbed the President, 'and I have never undertaken to do more than my best.'

'We have proclaimed a Republic in arms', Cathal reminded him. 'It has been ratified by the votes of the people, and we have sworn to defend it with our lives.'

'The oath never conveyed any more to me than to do my best in whatever circumstances might arise.'

'You have accepted a position of authority and responsibility in the Government of the Republic', Cathal replied, striking the table with his fist, 'and you will discharge the duties of that office as have been defined. I do not want ever again to hear anything else from you.'

If he was accurately quoted, De Valera's final response to this was significant: 'I think I can promise Cathal that you won't have to complain again.'

The last response would seem to indicate that de Valera's mind was moving towards convergence with Brugha some six months ahead of the time when he actually did so. But, we are told,[29] he only realized in a flash of inspiration which occurred two days later just what he really wanted from Lloyd George. The latter thought he knew enough of the Irishman's mind to inform the King[30] that de Valera was 'prepared to accept the status of a Dominion, sans phrase on condition that Northern Ireland would agree to be represented within an all-Ireland parliament, otherwise de Valera insisted that the only alternative was for the Twenty-six Counties to be a republic'. This was near enough to what he had already told Smuts earlier in the month. De Valera naturally objected to partition and felt that Dominion status, apart from falling short of a republic, would mean in effect that Ireland's position of geographical proximity to England would prevent her enjoying the reality of the Dominion status of an Australia or a Canada. But in order to keep himself in a good negotiating position, while at the same time not being seen by public opinion to be looking a gift horse in the mouth, de Valera now used Smuts, whom he knew was in close contact with the Prime Minister, to send a hard-line message without incurring the odium of doing so openly:[31] 'I was greatly disappointed with the British Government's proposals. They seem quite unable to understand the temper of our people, or appear not to have the will to realise the opportunity that is now presented to them . . . suffering would seem to be in store for our people.'

Smuts tried to meet his fears about Dominion status by pointing out[32] in his reply that such status would be a bulwark to Irish independence. The other Dominions would have to come to Ireland's aid should England intervene in her affairs, because otherwise such intervention, if unchallenged, would form a precedent for intervention in Dominion affairs. On the North he counselled that the Twenty-six Counties should: 'Start as a full Dominion, make a success of self-Government in the South and it will not be long before the North will agree to join hands with you freely and willingly'. But de Valera, who was 'genuinely impressed by Smuts', nevertheless felt that while the South African's background enabled him to empathize with Irish urges towards freedom, it also seemed to 'hamper his understanding of their reasons for demanding a Republic rather than Dominion status'.[33] He said that Smuts approached the Irish question 'purely as a thinking machine. . . . Of course the principal data, the feelings and sentiments of the Irish people, he was neglecting.'[34] In other words Smuts was inclined to call a spade a spade, and give advice which de Valera would have preferred not to hear.

Accordingly he wrote[35] to Smuts on 31 July in terms that effectively ended Smuts' active involvement in the negotiations: 'unless the North East comes in on some reasonable basis, no further progress can be made'. Ireland was keen on friendship, but it was 'only in freedom that friendship could develop'. He claimed that the Irish people were 'devotedly attached to the principle of self-determination'. They were prepared 'to make great sacrifices' for their ideals, of which 'the Republic is the expression'. And he added a line of great importance to an understanding of his thinking: 'The questions of procedure and form as distinguished from substance are very important.' Smuts rightly concluded that there was no more he could do. Having sent his secretary on a last-minute opinion-sampling tour of Belfast and Dublin he decided to return to Africa, having first sent the following reply to de Valera:[36] 'Both you and Craig are equally immovable. Force as a solution of the problem is out of the question, both on your side and his premises. The process of arriving at an agreement will therefore take time.'

It would indeed; de Valera now proceeded to pull himself down by his bootstraps. He became seized of an idea which 'came to him vividly'. Two days after the Cabinet meeting which had discussed the Lloyd George proposals, he was sitting on the side of his bed at Glenvar, the large house at Blackrock he had moved into after his former residence was raided, tying his bootlaces when the word 'external' flashed into his mind. He bethought himself of a scheme whereby Ireland could be externally associated with the Commonwealth while not becoming a member. At the time, he was in a state of somewhat external association himself, having moved into Glenvar. The need for skulking had disappeared, the addiction to grandeur had not. A President, even of a self-recognized Republic, could comport himself more fittingly in the surroundings of Glenvar than in a modest home in Greystones, surrounded by a wife and children.

So far as his political external association went, he explained to listeners with the aid of diagrams, the British Commonwealth was to be thought of as a large circle. Within this circle were a number of smaller circles, 'each representing one of the self-governing countries of that group of nations'. Outside the large circle, but touching it, was another small circle, Ireland, externally associated with the Commonwealth. The concept was both far-seeing and original. Ireland would maintain sovereignty at home, but be associated with Great Britain in external affairs; would guarantee neutrality in wartime, and would, while thus meeting legitimate British concerns, escape the stigma in republican eyes of coming under the Imperial yoke. In 1921 this was decidedly advanced thinking. It was not until 1949, after a world war had brought Great Britain to her knees, that India joined the Commonwealth as a republic.

The Cabinet accepted the idea[37] and de Valera now decided to embark on another bout of instantaneous procrastination, the most ill-advised of his career:[38] 'Having won cabinet approval for external association, the President was now in no hurry to answer Lloyd George. Militarily delay was desirable and politically he felt that all the implications of his new idea should be well understood.' There is reason to question both how well understood external association really was and what, if any, steps de Valera took to ensure 'that all the implications of his new idea should be well understood'. Stack and Brugha apparently did accept the concept, and de Valera must be given credit for bringing such extreme members of the republican spectrum towards the centre. But some three months later, as we will see, Arthur Griffith had apparently never heard of the idea. There is no evidence to suggest that de Valera undertook any sort of widespread education programme to ensure that all the implications of his new idea should be well understood. What is clear is that he embarked on a 'cute hoor' style of approach to the question of negotiating with Lloyd George which guaranteed that his idea was misunderstood from the word go. He decided that the document which he had circulated to his colleagues containing the Irish reply to the British offer, and the external association idea, was 'too revealing'. The de Valera philosophy of not showing one's hand, letting the other fellow speak first, and all the other arts of the cattle jobber were brought into play. In the reply which he did send on 10 August, without troubling to consult the Dail, 'external association was indicated, but vaguely and not under that precise name'.[39] The British Cabinet decided, appropriately enough on the 13th, that this was merely 'an attempt – even though a clumsy attempt – to keep open the discussion and that the document was intended merely as a step in a prolonged discussion'.[40] Prolonged it certainly was. Some fifteen letters and telegrams were exchanged before the Irish and the British actually sat down at a table together on 11 October of that year.

This created a highly dangerous position for the Irish, militarily speaking. On the one hand de Valera encouraged a military build-up: the army mushroomed in size, becoming a paper tiger with which the far larger, better trained and equipped British forces could have easily dealt.

On the other, Collins' intelligence network became increasingly exposed and valueless. The effect on morale was incalculable. The people had taken the truce as an indication that permanent peace lay around the corner and a national carnival of relieved rejoicing broke out. De Valera later sought to have a contrary view disseminated:[41] 'The young Volunteers sternly extinguished the bonfires, silenced the clamour for release of the prisoners, took their friends angrily to task; this was a truce, not a settlement. Unless the nation maintained its morale and the army its discipline no good conclusion would come of it. Ireland must stand armed and ready for a resumption of war.'

There may have been a few isolated incidents of bonfire dousing, but in the hundreds of interviews I have conducted with survivors of the time I cannot remember any such incidents being recalled. What I did hear were accounts which bore out the descriptions of contemporary writers like Pieras Beaslai and Frank O'Connor, who said that discipline slackened where it did not break. Drinking, freeloading and commandeering of cars became commonplace. Men who were never heard of during the fighting now flocked to the colours; parties, weddings and dances were the order of the day and night. The boys 'on their keeping'[42] had beaten the British Empire. So far as the general public was concerned, expectations soared upwards like a rocket. They would come down like its stick.

12

THE 'CUTE HOOR' TRIUMPHANT

DE VALERA'S DELAYING tactics ensured that, as time passed, everyone outside of his immediate circle came to believe that the truce would end not in war but in a settlement – but what sort of settlement? Even one of de Valera's most ardent admirers, Lord Longford, judged that '. . . in the race to secure opinion favourable to the settlements that they respectively contemplated, De Valera was still waiting for the pistol while Lloyd George was half-way home.'[1]

Why did de Valera act in this fashion for months on end in one of the most critical periods in Irish history? The career of the 'Long Fellow' is such as to qualify de Valera better for the sobriquet 'long-headed' where his own interests were concerned. How did this variation in policy occur? The answer, I believe, is that the record bears the interpretation that there was no real variation in policy. De Valera acted as he did for motives of narrow self-interest:

1. He had already demonstrated that his reaction after meeting Craig once and discovering how little 'give' he might expect in that quarter was to take steps which ensured that no further meeting took place.

2. After four meetings alone with the British Prime Minister he, more than any man alive, knew what Lloyd George was putting on the table – it did not, could not and would not contain a republic. He stated in the Dail[2] shortly after meeting Lloyd George that: 'he knew fairly well from his experience in London how far it was possible to get the British government to go'. His biography, written nearly fifty years later, states quite clearly that he 'had emerged intact and unmarked from the first round. But he had no illusions about the next one.'[3]

3. Whoever went to London to negotiate with Lloyd George would be forced to compromise, and be compromised, as the diversity of opinion revealed in the Cabinet meeting of 25 July clearly showed. He needed time to make certain that he was not that person.

4. He used the whole issue of negotiation to further his secret campaign to gain supremacy over Collins.

In fact one of the rare occasions in which, prior to December 1921, the Collins–de Valera differences flickered into public view occurred in the very early stages of the negotiation process. At this stage Collins' close friend, the Longford IRA leader, Sean MacEoin, lay under sentence of death. De Valera was attempting to secure his release by secret diplomacy despite the fact, his biography assures us, that 'some members' of the

Right: Captain of the football team

Below: At Blackrock College

This is not to be exhibited however much you may feel inclined.

(Copyright)

Alas !!
Alas !!
Alas !!
for our blighted hopes; but I told you so.

Above: The first cartoon of Dev – with many to follow. This one was anonymous

Right: Dev graduates

The Home Rule Crisis 1911–1914

Right: John Redmond

Below: Carson in Belfast displays a banner emblazoned 'Mountjoy' after the ship which broke the boom to lift the siege of Derry

The UVF prepares under canvas

The Irish Response

De Valera in Volunteer uniform

Above: Erskine Childers in the British Army *c.* 1900

Left: Roger Casement, Pentonville Prison, London, 1916

De Valera in the USA

Two contrasting views: *(left)* being awarded an honorary degree from the Catholic University, July 1919, and *(below)* addressing a meeting at Los Angeles, December 1919

Above: The Adversaries: Judge Cohalan, pictured with De Valera and John Devoy, July 1919

Left: When Dev favoured top hats... with Archbishop Hayes on St Patrick's Day, New York, 1920

The Second Trip to the USA

Right: Dev alongside his mother, Catherine Coll

Below: De Valera with his half-brother, Father Thomas Wheelwright

This photograph shows the lot of Irish emigrants arriving for that Ellis Island ordeal, as experienced earlier by Catherine Coll

The Irish Treaty delegation in London. Left to right, seated: Arthur Griffith, E. J. Duggan, Michael Collins and Robert Barton. Standing: Erskine Childers, Gavin Duffy and John Chartres

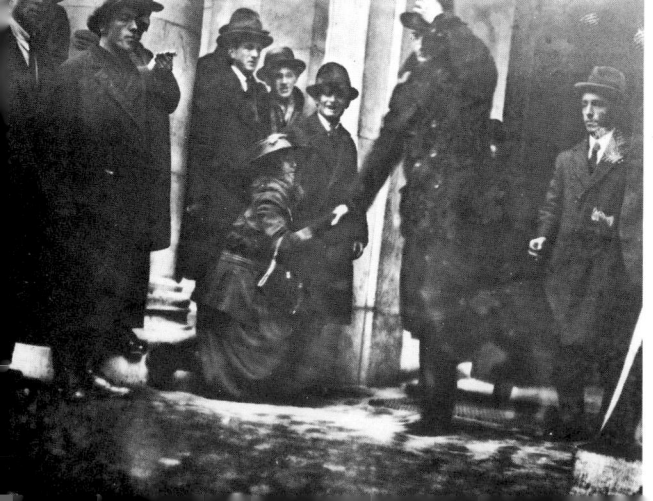

Above left: Cathal Brugha arriving at the Dail Eireann meeting at Dublin University in 1921

Above: De Valera as Chancellor of Dublin University, November 1921

Left: Genuflecting to the Chief, a woman kisses the ring of the lay Cardinal

Above: Huge crowds attend de Valera's meeting in O'Connell Street, Dublin, in February 1922

Right: The prime foe of Irish nationalism, Sir Henry Wilson (with shotgun), who was assassinated on Michael Collins' orders

Below: Armed troops of the IRA march through Grafton Street, in the heart of fashionable Dublin, in July 1922

The Civil War

Right: They're coming for me... de Valera on the platform at Ennis, Co. Clare in 1923, just before his arrest

Below: Easter Monday in Dublin, 1923. Free State troops search the trains

The fall of the Big House. Horace Plunkett's home in Kilteeragh burns in 1923

Cabinet felt that insistence on his release, 'as de Valera wanted, would jeopardise the negotiations'.[4] The biography quotes with approval de Valera's statement of 9 August to the press that 'If the detention of Commandant MacEoin is persisted in, I cannot accept responsibility for proceeding further with the negotiations.' There is no mention, however, of the fact that Collins, who of course had his own methods of gleaning British intentions in the MacEoin affair, had both embarrassed and upstaged de Valera over the issue. Without consulting anyone, the previous day he had issued a statement of his own in which he declared bluntly: 'There can and will be no meeting of Dail Eireann until Commandant Sean MacEoin is released. The refusal to release him appears to indicate a desire on the part of the English Government to terminate the Truce.'[5]

MacEoin was duly released. De Valera had been forced to issue his statement because he hesitated to challenge Collins' authority to issue such a serious warning, as he had in the pipeline a manoeuvre which we shall shortly examine, designed to superimpose his authority clearly on that of his impetuous and volatile younger colleague. But first he sent Lloyd George his rejection of the London proposals in terms which economized greatly with the truth: 'On the occasion of our last interview I gave it as my judgement that Dail Eireann could not, and that the Irish people would not, accept the proposals of your Government. I now confirm that judgement.'[6] In fact he had no intention of consulting the Irish people on the proposals and did not bring them before Dail Eireann for two weeks *after* sending the letter. And when the Dail was informed, he told the deputies that he merely wanted 'to be able to put in the first paragraph of the reply that the Dail unanimously approved of the attitude adopted by the Ministry. In other words that they could not accept those terms. It was a question of tactics that only the Ministry were involved in these replies. . . .'[7]

But this was not the only important piece of rubber stamping which de Valera wished deputies to indulge in. On 23 August he arranged for Cathal Brugha to bring before the Cabinet a motion proposing that henceforth his office be known as 'President of the Republic who shall also be Prime Minister'. Supporting the motion, de Valera pointed out that:[8] 'Though the office had been accepted it had never been constitutionally created. As a matter of fact the President was President not of the Republic but of the Ministry of Dail Eireann.'

The motion also contained a proposal for restructuring the Cabinet. Advanced on the grounds of efficiency and speeding up decision-taking, it allowed for the creation of a smaller Executive, or inner Cabinet, consisting of the President and six Secretaries of State, with a number of other ministries becoming extra-Cabinet. The Cabinet now consisted of de Valera, Griffith, Collins, Stack, Brugha, Robert Barton and W. T. Cosgrave. The Minister for Labour, Countess Markievicz, the first woman minister in Europe, was one of those moved out of the Executive, an accurate foretaste of de Valera's subsequent policy regarding women's place in public life. But Countess Markievicz was not his principal target in the manoeuvre, which would subsequently boomerang on him in a dramatic fashion that must have seemed inconceivable to him at the time. Within the restructured Cabinet, now in effect the ruling body of the Government, he appeared to have an impregnable majority. On all behaviour patterns of the time the only opponent he could possibly have foreseen having to guard against was Collins. Griffith was a man of great popular standing, but his age and health would not have indicated any likelihood of his challenging a man for whom he had already willingly stood down. Barton was not a figure of consequence; and, moreover, since he was a cousin of Childers, would naturally have been expected to follow de Valera. Cosgrave and he were particularly friendly, and Brugha and Stack were solidly ranged against Collins.

In addition to tightening his grip on the inner circle, the change of title was also designed to increase his outer sphere of influence. For de Valera, who had managed to exist in the USA without calling on the Dail to formalize his presidency, had a motive other than merely dispensing officially with the title first discarded by Joe McGarrity. He explained that the description 'President of the Republic' would mean that henceforth:[9] 'I am no longer to be looked on as a party leader. I am representing the nation and I shall represent the whole nation if I am elected to office and I shall not be bound by any section whatever of the nation.'

This rarified concept was accepted by the Dail in public session on 26 August on a motion proposed by Sean MacEoin, who had it written out for him in Irish by Michael Collins. MacEoin went on to say of de Valera:

> In no generation for more than a century has any Irish leader equalled his achievements. No one has shown himself more fitted to deal with our traditional foe. He has not been deceived by their promises nor intimidated by their threats. Eamon de Valera first met the English as a soldier and beat them as a soldier. He has been meeting them now as a statesman. The honour and the interests of our nation are alike safe in his hands.

In his own eyes, so far as the Dail and Cabinet were concerned, de Valera was now 'the symbol'[10] of the Republic. It was a piece of symbolism which Collins was to regret. For, in the week in which he had himself proposed as President, de Valera dropped a bombshell on his colleague. Eamon de Valera had indeed been 'meeting the English as a statesman', but he had no intention of continuing with the meetings. Having humiliated Collins by leaving him in Dublin while he went to London to see what Lloyd George was putting on the table, on 20 August he announced to Collins that when substantive negotiations began around that table he himself would not be there. But Michael Collins would – Machiavelli's pupil was advancing to the honours class. (Significantly, at this meeting with Collins Harry Boland was present. Collins had not realized that Boland had switched his allegiance to de Valera during his American sojourn.) Not unnaturally Collins resisted bitterly, but when the issue came up in Cabinet a few days later de Valera succeeded in using his own casting vote to counter one of Collins' principal arguments – namely that de Valera, not himself, should go. The voting was Brugha, Stack, de Valera and Barton against de Valera's going; for, Cosgrave, Collins and Griffith. De Valera himself was very well aware that it was only his Cabinet manoeuvrings which produced this result. Later in the year he admitted to Joe McGarrity that his decision to stay at home was carried 'against the will of the majority of the Cabinet'.[11] But at that stage there were too many people around who could testify to this for him to state otherwise. However, the passage of time made a different story possible some forty-two years later when dealing with a biographical questionnaire and his own reconstruction of events. In a written reply[12] to Lord Longford he lied point-blank, saying that his staying at home was 'generally accepted' and only became an issue after an agreement was concluded.

For Cosgrave did not take de Valera's refusal lying down. At the Dail meeting on 14 September[13] he argued that de Valera should go to London for a number of reasons: 'He had an extraordinary experience in negotiations. He also had the advantage of being in touch already. The head of the State of England was Mr. Lloyd George and he expected he [de Valera] would be one of the plenipotentiaries. . . . They were sending over a team and they were keeping their ablest player in reserve. . . . The reserve would have to be used sometime and it struck him now was the time they were required.' However, de Valera won the day on that occasion with two principal arguments. One, on the question of Lloyd George representing the State of England there was no analogy. They recognized themselves, but no one else did. And secondly:

> He really believed it was vital at this stage that the symbol of the Republic should be kept untouched and that it should not be compromised in any sense by any arrangements which it might be necessary for our plenipotentiaries to make. He was sure the Dail realised the task they were giving to them – to win for them what a mighty army and navy might not be able to win for them. It was not a shirking of duty, but he realised the position and how necessary it was to keep the Head of the State and the symbol untouched and that was why he asked to be left out.

This argument has been summed up by Professor Joseph Lee, one of Ireland's leading historians, as sounding 'suspiciously like an anti-Collins rationalisation. The one thing de Valera was, and that Collins was not, was President! And there would seem to have been little point remaining as symbol if there was danger that one's absence might lead to the sacrifice of the symbol in the negotiations.'[14]

Professor Lee is undoubtedly correct in his assessment of the anti-Collins rationalization, but one of the reasons that de Valera was so keen on assuming the public title of President was that Collins was already a President – of the secret IRB. And in March Collins had been a party to ceding the IRB's symbolic authority to the Dail, of which de Valera was now formally taking control. Round two of a take-over bid was in operation. Writers sympathetic to de Valera's explanations as to why he avoided going to London claim that 'unity on his side was his over-riding objective'.[15] He knew that compromise was inevitable; it is contended that he reckoned, therefore, that untarred by the brush of negotiations, when the stage of compromise was reached he would be in a position to unite the Cabinet and the nation around his 'external association' proposals. In support of this argument one may also accept the assessment[16] that since 1916 he had acted as Sinn Fein's unifying force, bringing together Count Plunkett's followers, Arthur Griffith's and those of the Volunteers and the IRB. But in the final analysis de Valera's record demonstrates that he was a unifier only when he could control the movements and personalities involved, as in the post-1916 period, or when he founded his own political party ten years after 1916. When he could not exercise control he was prepared to wreak havoc, as he did amongst the Irish American organizations and in the period of the Irish civil war which we are rapidly approaching. Despite all the rationalizations subsequently advanced to justify his failure to take part in the most important set of negotiations ever conducted between the Irish and the English, de Valera himself realized that he was acting against the wishes of most of his Cabinet.

Collins too had very powerful arguments for not going to London, but, as will be seen in the following summary by a contemporary journalist, their basis was anathema to de Valera:[17]

> For several years (rightly or wrongly made no difference) the English had held me to be the one man most necessary to capture because they held me to be the one man responsible for the smashing of their Secret Service Organisation and for their failure to terrorise the people with their Black and Tans . . . the important fact was that in England as in Ireland, the Michael Collins legend existed. It pictured me as mysterious, active menace, elusive, unknown, unaccountable, and in this respect I was the only living Irishman of whom it could be said. . . . Bring me into the spotlight of a London conference and quickly will be discovered the common clay of which I am made. The glamour of the legendary figure will be gone.

So far as de Valera was concerned, 'the only living Irishman' of that sort of Homeric proportion was himself, the 'symbol of the Republic'. When he failed to persuade Collins personally, after arguments that sometimes continued for 'up to three hours',[18] he got one of Collins' closest friends, Batt O'Connor, to carry out the task. Now as Collins' decision to go to London had even more lasting importance to Ireland than had de Valera's to stay in Dublin, it is necessary to pause to pursue his reasoning for a moment. On one level it might seem that he was simply persuaded by a bottle of whiskey and 'hours and hours'[19] of argument, which finally overcame his objections that a soldier who had fought in the field should not be expected to conduct negotiations. That, he contended, was de Valera's job. Apart from his stated objections, Collins was aware from de Valera's attitude to him ever since his return from America that there was a rivalry between them, albeit one hidden from the world at large, which did not connect de Valera with the overt Collins v. Brugha/Stack feud. Both the latter had turned down their invitations to join the team, and had not been pressed to reconsider. Moreover, with uncharacteristic lack of caution de Valera had been overheard saying of the plenipotentiaries: 'We must have scapegoats.'[20] Collins was under no illusions as to what he was being led into. 'You might say the trap is sprung', he wrote,[21] and in recorded[22] conversations between himself and Griffith it is quite clear that the two men regarded themselves as being so enmeshed in intrigue and deceit that nothing they brought back would satisfy 'the Dublinites'. His stated reasons for walking into the trap were that he acted as a soldier carrying out an unpalatable order. However, my researches into Collins' life have uncovered the fact that he had a hidden agenda.[23] Worried that the measure of independence on offer might be lost, as was Home Rule because of the change in English public opinion following the Phoenix Park killings in 1882, he decided to conclude a treaty which, once accomplished, could be used as a 'stepping stone' to a thirty-two-county Irish Republic. With the British gone, and a native Irish army to hand, he was prepared to contemplate force if necessary to end partition. In fact the record shows that he not merely contemplated, but actually used, force in an effort to accomplish this end. However, this is to anticipate. Let us continue with the selection of plenipotentiaries.

Arthur Griffith gave an account[24] of how he first heard of external association which shows how little the concept was understood. De Valera had called him to his office one day, in the company of Brugha and Stack, to persuade him to go to London. Griffith told him: ' . . . you are my Chief and if you tell me to go, I'll go. But I know, and you know, that I can't bring back a Republic.' It was then that de Valera unveiled the external association idea. 'The first I ever heard of it,' said Griffith. Following a half-hour's persuasion, Brugha gave 'reluctant consent'. Significantly Stack said nothing, but sat there 'sullen' until he and Brugha took their leave. Griffith then asked:

'Look here Dev, what is the meaning of the External Association idea? What are you getting at with it?' He replied by getting a pencil and paper and drew the line thus: [At this point Griffith too produced paper and pencil and drew a line AB at a sixty degree angle] 'That', said he, is me, in the straitjacket of the Republic. I must get out of it.' Then he drew another line, a curved line [from A] AC. 'That', said he, 'is External Association. The purpose of it is to bring Cathal along.' Then he drew another straight line. [Here Griffith drew the line AD] 'That,' said he, 'is where we will eventually get to.' Then I was satisfied, and said no more about it.

So much for the introduction to the external association concept of the leader of the delegation which was supposed to be convincing the British Empire of the merits of the idea. According to another member, Robert Barton, the delegation had 'only a hazy concept of what it would be in its final form'. They understood that 'no vestige of British authority would remain in Ireland. The compromise would be as regards our foreign relations.'[25]

The delegation consisted of Collins, Griffith, Barton, Eamonn Duggan and George Gavan Duffy, with Erskine Childers acting as the official Secretary. In a 'for your eyes only' letter to Joe McGarrity,[26] de Valera afterwards explained his team selection philosophy. He dismissed Duggan and Gavan Duffy as mere 'legal padding' – both were lawyers. Griffith and Collins he felt would accept the Crown; therefore he chose Barton and Erskine Childers to counter-balance them. Barton, he said, 'would be strong and stubborn enough as a retarding force to any precipitate giving way by the delegation. Childers, who is an intellectual Republican, as Secretary would give Barton, his relative and close friend, added strength'. He explained that he had not chosen Brugha because he would cause useless rows, and Collins and Griffith would not work with Stack. But he tacitly admitted that in reality he kept them in Dublin to check-mate anything that the delegation – by which he later made clear he meant Collins – did in London. He told McGarrity of his intention that 'the Cabinet at home should hang on to the delegation's coat-tails', leaving everything safe for a final 'tug of war' which would be resolved by means of his external association formula. His feelings of rivalry towards Collins shone through in his assessment of the danger that he most apprehended. He feared that Collins would make 'Dominion settlement appear only a step. He would have, in such a settlement, *the additional advantage that it would assure him a political future as leader of a Republican party.*' So in order to guard against the possibility of such a future de Valera deliberately built disunity and suspicion into the composition of the delegation which was faced with the most important negotiation in Irish history.

Meanwhile, as he was cobbling together the delegation he adopted a 'curiously ambiguous'[27] attitude when Brugha and Stack combined against Collins to resurrect the charges over the Glasgow accounts. During August a meeting of the old Volunteer executive, which had not met since 1920, was organized at Brugha's initiative. When it met, with de Valera presiding, Brugha unexpectedly brought up the money issue which had supposedly been found 'groundless' by de Valera the previous spring. Stack concurred, saying that 'a serious charge had been made which should be probed to the bottom'. At least one observer felt that, while appearing to hold the balance between Collins and his accusers, de Valera gave the latter a 'certain amount of tacit encouragement'.[28]

The following month he was forced to intervene in the Brugha vendetta against Collins by Mulcahy, whom Brugha had threatened to sack for opposing a proposal of his which de Valera later supported. Brugha wanted the incompetent Stack appointed as Mulcahy's deputy. When Mulcahy resisted, Brugha sent him the following:[29] 'Before you are very much older my friend, I shall show you that I have as little intention of taking dictation from you as to how I should reprove inefficiency or negligence on the part of yourself or the D/I [Collins, Director of Intelligence and as such nominally under Brugha's control] as I have of allowing you to appoint a Deputy Chief of Staff of your own choosing.' Mulcahy forced de Valera to call a meeting between himself and Brugha, at which Brugha 'burst into tears and walked out exclaiming that he could do no wrong'.[30] While thus conducting a chorus of 'noises off' to his own satisfaction, if not that of Michael Collins, de Valera continued to exchange diplomatic salvoes in public with Lloyd George which gained nothing of substance, although to the end of his life he continued to represent the exchanges as having resulted in a famous victory for him. The fundamental reality of the Irish position was that no one in the world, apart from a section within Sinn Fein and the IRA, recognized an Irish Republic. De Valera himself impressed this on the Dail after his July meetings with Lloyd George. He took the opportunity presented by a discussion on Sinn Fein policy abroad to make the point that:[31] 'The actual fact was that no nation would recognise the Irish Republic until she wanted to go to war with England.'

The British position was reiterated in a letter from Lloyd George to de Valera dated 26 August, the very day the Dail voted him President. Amidst a torrent of quotations and examples from Grattan, Parnell, Redmond, Davis, O'Connell and even Lincoln, the rock of the British position stood out. For many reasons, including the 'governing force of the geographical propinquity of these two islands', the British Prime Minister said:[32] 'I thought I had made it clear, both in my conversations with you and in my two subsequent communications, that we can discuss no settlement which involves a refusal on the part of Ireland to accept our invitation to free, equal and loyal partnership under one Sovereign.'

Nevertheless, after further communication, on 12 September de Valera sent two emissaries, Harry Boland and Joseph McGrath, to Gairloch in Scotland where Lloyd George was on holiday. They took with them a missive which included the following: 'Our nation has formally declared its independence and recognises itself as a sovereign State. It is only as the representatives of that State and its chosen guardians that we have any authority or powers to act on behalf of our people.' This did nothing for Lloyd George's holiday spirit. Even Michael Collins had warned Boland and McGrath, when he saw the letter, that they 'might as well stay where you are'. On the 15th the British Premier sent an unequivocal telegram to de Valera:

. . . the reiteration of your claim to negotiate with His Majesty's Government as the representative of an independent and sovereign State would make conference between us impossible. . . . I must accordingly cancel the arrangements for conference. . . . If we accepted conference with your delegates on a formal statement of the claim which you have re-affirmed, it would constitute an official recognition by His Majesty's Government of the severance of Ireland from the Empire and of its existence as an independent Republic.

De Valera endeavoured to climb back into the ring on the 17th with a telegram which claimed that, if self-recognition was the reason for the cancellation of the Conference, it 'seems inconsistent' for ' . . . in these conferences and in my written communication I have never ceased to recognise myself for what I was and am. If this involves recognition on your part, then you have already recognised us.' But the Scottish bagpipes were skirling 'no go the merry-go-round'.[33] On the 18th Lloyd George dismissed the self-recognition claim, pointing out that he had only invited de Valera to meet him as 'the chosen leader of the great majority in Southern Ireland' and '*you accepted the invitation*'. He went on remorselessly: 'From the very outset of our conversation I told you that we looked to Ireland to owe allegiance to the Throne and to make her future as a member of the British Commonwealth. That was the basis of our proposals, and we cannot alter it. The status which you now claim in advance for your delegates is, in effect, a repudiation of that basis.'

De Valera attempted to square the circle on 19 September with the following:

We have had no thought at any time of asking you to accept any conditions precedent to a conference. We would have thought it as unreasonable to expect you, as a preliminary, to recognise the Irish Republic, formally, or informally, as that you should expect us to surrender our national position. . . . We request you therefore, to state whether your letter of 7 September is intended to be a demand for a surrender on our part, or an invitation to conference free on both sides and without prejudice should agreement be reached. If the latter we readily confirm our acceptation of the invitation and our appointed delegates will meet your Government's representatives at any time in the immediate future that you designate.

But Lloyd George was not going to allow de Valera to slip into conference that easily. He allowed him to cool his heels for ten days before replying – normally it was Lloyd George who replied immediately, de Valera who delayed – in terms that made it clear that, whatever settlement emerged from talks, it would have to incorporate recognition of the British Empire:

His Majesty's Government . . . cannot enter a conference upon the basis of this correspondence . . . it might be argued in future that the acceptance of a conference on this basis had involved them in a recognition which no British Government can accord. On this point they must guard against any possible doubt. . . . The position taken up by His Majesty's Government is fundamental to the existence of the British Empire and they cannot alter it. My colleagues and I remain, however, keenly anxious to make in co-operation with your delegates another determined effort to explore every possibility of settlement by personal discussion. . . . We therefore send you this fresh invitation to a conference in London on 11 October, where we can meet your delegates as spokesmen of the people whom you represent with a view to ascertaining *how the association* of Ireland with the community of nations known as the British Empire may best be reconciled with Irish national aspirations.

In replying to this, de Valera was thus confined to the narrow ground of 'the people whom you represent'. The Six Counties were clearly not seen as coming within his purview. Moreover, after the clearest of stipulations as to the position of the Empire, the invitation did not seek to inquire 'if' Irish aspirations could be associated with the British Empire, but 'how'. It is therefore difficult, if not impossible, to quarrel with Michael Collins' judgement that[34] 'the communication of Sept. 29th from Lloyd George made it clear that they were going into a conference not on the recognition of the Irish Republic . . . if we all stood on the recognition of the Irish Republic as a prelude to any conference we could very easily have said so, and there would have been no Conference . . . it was the acceptance of the invitation that formed the compromise'.

That acceptance was drafted for de Valera by Arthur Griffith and despatched the very next day, 30 September: the arch-procrastinator could see that time was running out on him. Apart from anything the British might do out of exasperation, he realized that, if another section of concerned opinion – that of the Irish people, which had been ignored throughout the entire proceedings – were to be allowed to make its feelings known, he would find an overwhelming majority less concerned with republican hair-splitting than in favour of guaranteeing the continuance of peace. De Valera accepted the invitation on the following terms:

> We have received your letter of invitation to a Conference in London on October 11 'with a view to ascertaining how the association of Ireland with the community of nations known as the British Empire may best be reconciled with Irish national aspirations.'
>
> Our respective positions have been stated and are understood, and we agree that conference, not correspondence, is the most practical and hopeful way to an understanding. We accept the invitation, and our Delegates will meet you in London on the date mentioned 'to explore every possibility of settlement by discussion.'

It is understandable that de Valera should try to present his efforts at negotiation with Lloyd George in the most favourable light for posterity – that his official biographers would sum up his performance as follows:[35] 'De Valera had won his point, a conference without prior conditions. He had secured a conference without surrendering the position taken up when the Irish Republic was declared. . . . The President had surely the better of the argument; and tactically he had won a breathing space, which his soldiers thought essential. The long summer evenings had passed, the winter nights fast approached. So much was sheer gain.' But the Authorized Version did concede that this triumph did have its downside: 'By hiding his hand from Lloyd George, he had also hidden it from the public. External Association, with its distinction between the isolated and the externally associated Republic, was something not easy to grasp immediately . . . the chance to propagate it and commend it to the public was passed over in the crucial period.' And the chapter dealing with the Lloyd George–de Valera joust ends with the telling admission: 'The truce made the resumption of hostilities more difficult for the weaker side . . . British intelligence had the opportunity to become much better informed.'

It therefore need not surprise us that a knowledgeable student of the period should conclude that the correspondence had not ended in a situation favourable to Irish claims but in one in which:[36]

> Lloyd George pledges his government to discuss no settlement which involves a refusal on the part of Ireland to accept free equality and loyal partnership in the British Commonwealth of Nations. De Valera on the other hand never pledges his Government to preserve the Irish Republic, and indeed in all his messages only mentions the Republic twice . . . to Lloyd George's declaration that there can be no settlement except on Dominion lines he never makes the obvious, the only answer, that in that case there is no use in holding a conference at all, because Ireland will never renounce a Republic and accept the position of a Dominion.

What may surprise readers, however, is the fact that our 'knowledgeable student' is not a critic of de Valera's but Lord Longford, the co-author of the work which adjudged de Valera's performance to have resulted in 'sheer gain'. The change in attitude between the delivery of the judgement written as an independent author and that given as official biographer should not be assessed merely as the result of the passage of time. The conflicting opinions are but one example of how an intelligent person, looking at the facts objectively and then coming into de Valera's force field, encountering his extraordinary facility for demonstrating that black was white and vice versa, could be led to a denial of reality. It was an attribute which de Valera would later use time and time again to his own advantage to demonstrate the difference between a fact and a de Valera fact – that is, one that should be believed. But now, at this stage of his and Ireland's history, some facts which he did not wish to accept were waiting to be faced up to at Number 10, Downing Street.

13

THE SCAPEGOATS GO FORTH

DURING THE SPRING of 1921 a British statesman, Lord Cecil, wrote to the papers with the intention of setting forth his proposals for an Irish peace settlement. It was one of the many peace initiatives of the period and did not attract much lasting interest. However, unbeknownst to the peer the contents of his letter lodged with de Valera in a way that had a marked bearing on the Irish negotiators who were sent to Downing Street the following October. Writing[1] to Art O'Briain, the head of the Irish Self-Determination League in London, de Valera treated the Cecil proposals as an exercise in British duplicity. He pointed out to him how the seeming liberality of the opening paragraphs was obliterated by 'the trap', as he termed it, set by the stipulations in the concluding paragraphs. Such methods had kept the Empire over the centuries for 'these people', was his comment. It was the sort of passing judgement which any of the Sinn Fein leaders of the period might have made, but what differentiated de Valera's thought processes from those of his colleagues was that, to him, object lessons in political science were to be put to use when chance offered.

He got his chance when on 26 August 1921 the Dail appointed the plenipotentiaries, unanimously approving a resolution, which he also supported, proposed by Liam de Roiste: 'That if plenipotentiaries for negotiations be appointed by the Cabinet or the Dail, such plenipotentiaries be given a free hand in such negotiations and duly to report to the Dail.' The credentials given to the plenipotentiaries, which de Valera signed, appeared to meet the wishes of the Dail – if not the British attitude towards his self-recognition of a republic which had been expressly ruled out as a condition of allowing the negotiations to begin in the first place. The credentials described the Irish team as:[2] 'Envoys Plenipotentiary from the Elected Government of the Republic of Ireland to negotiate and conclude on behalf of Ireland with the representatives of his Britannic Majesty, George V, a Treaty or Treaties of Settlement, Association and Accommodation between Ireland and the community of nations known as the British Commonwealth.'

It might also be noted that the credentials envisaged the plenipotentiaries concluding an agreement not with the British Empire, which de Valera had agreed to in his letter to Lloyd George of 30 September, but with the British Commonwealth. This in effect meant that the Irish purported to be coming to London to discuss how they might become associated with the Commonwealth rather than be dominated by the Empire. However, it did clearly recognize the Irish negotiators as plenipotentiaries; but de Valera now, *à la* Cecil, proceeded to take back with one hand what he had given with the other. Despite the fact that he had no authority to over-ride the unanimous Dail resolution, he privately concocted a document[3] which he circulated to the plenipotentiaries limiting their freedom of manoeuvre:

(1) The plenipotentiaries have full powers as defined in their credentials.

(2) It is understood before decisions are finally reached on a main question, that a dispatch notifying the intention to make these decisions will be sent to members of the Cabinet in Dublin, and that a reply will be awaited by the plenipotentiaries before final decision is made.

(3) It is also understood that the complete text of the draft treaty about to be signed will be similarly submitted to Dublin and a reply awaited.

(4) It is understood that the Cabinet in Dublin will be kept regularly informed of the progress of the negotiations.

As Collins and Griffith had already had to cope with the effects of the disharmony which de Valera deliberately built into their delegation, it need not surprise us that this limiting document was honoured in the breach more than the observance. Point 4 was followed to a considerable degree, but when it came to the crunch points 2 and 3 were conveniently forgotten about. However, the mere fact of its existence would later enable de Valera to adopt a high moral tone at a time when allegations of breaches of faith and failure to follow instructions were being hurled at Collins and Griffith.

The other documents which he gave them were not particularly useful, either. One of them, known as Draft Treaty A, embodied the external association idea. The draft was in fact a memorandum which he had drawn up for Lloyd George on his return from the July talks, but had decided not to send. Draft Treaty B allegedly contained the terms which Ireland was prepared to accept, but in fact was intended for use as propaganda should the talks break down. Nowhere was there written down a clear, rounded statement of what the delegation was actually supposed to work towards and settle for. Neither draft was in a finished state. De Valera dismissed this lack of preparedness in the course of a letter to Griffith, in which he commented airily: 'We must depend on *your side* for the initiative after this.'[4] Thus Griffith was sent in to bat against Lloyd George with a document which de Valera had decided not to risk sending under his own name some two months earlier. Not surprisingly, Collins would write to a friend during the negotiations: 'From Dublin I don't know whether we're being instructed or confused. The latter I would say.'[5]

But what is surprising for a biographer – even after the lapse of years, even though one is perfectly aware of the fact that he did not go to London – is how little of substance de Valera contributed to this crucially important set of Anglo-Irish discussions. Years after he had died, a man who admired him, and was to follow in his footsteps as an Irish Prime Minister, Jack

Lynch,[6] remarked to me on how nit-picking de Valera was in framing answers to parliamentary questions. At an early stage in his career, as a junior minister, it was Lynch's job to liaise with de Valera in the provision of such answers. He found that 'Dev would drive you mad. He'd keep on drafting and re-drafting the answers for ever. In the end I gave up dealing with the P.Q.s [parliamentary questions] as a bad job.' Yet in London between 11 October and 6 December 1921 Ireland's entire future was drafted, and de Valera remained almost completely aloof from the process. It was totally uncharacteristic of him and completely at variance with the interventionist role he played, or attempted to play, in every other political activity he encountered during his career. The weight of evidence points inexorably towards the verdict that, during his July conversations with Lloyd George, he had seen the future and decided that it would not work for him. His formula for dealing with this unpalatable reality was: 'We must have scapegoats.'

Let us now briefly turn to examine how the scapegoats dealt with their assignments; briefly, because even though the Treaty negotiations were profoundly important for Ireland and for de Valera, his absence from the talks makes their outcome, rather than their conduct, of importance to our story. This fact in itself says a great deal about de Valera's behaviour during this period.

In London Collins and Griffith came to the conclusion that they would have to undo de Valera's work in delegation building if they were going to get anywhere. Childers, Duffy and Barton, in that order of irritation and retarding influence on their plans, would have to be excluded from the discussions. Childers they found both too fussy, and too much under suspicion of going behind their backs to de Valera, to be trusted. Duffy was not only a de Valera man but pedantic and long-winded into the bargain. Barton, stubborn but honest, laboured under the disability in their eyes of being Childers' cousin. It was probably an action of de Valera's which finally galvanized them into agreeing with the British, a little over two weeks after the talks had begun, that henceforth the discussions would take place in sub-conference, rather than plenary session.[7] Only Collins and Griffith were to be present on the Irish side. The British, too, agreed to field only two players at a time, generally Lloyd George and Austen Chamberlain, although Birkenhead and Churchill also made appearances in starring roles. It was put out at the time that the British had asked for this arrangement, but it appeared much later, after the publication of Tom Jones' *Whitehall Diaries*, that it originated with the Irish. The British were, of course, fully aware of the divisions on the Irish side. As the talks opened, each member of the British team was circulated with an intelligence memo which gave quite a perceptive outline both of the differences of opinions on the Irish side and of the reality of the Irish public's willingness to settle for far less than many in Sinn Fein professed.

The sub-conferences went into operation following a de Valera-initiated controversy which broke out on the morning of the sixth Plenary Session, 21 October 1921. The row had its origins in an exchange of telegrams between the King and Pope Benedict, expressing hopes for the success of the talks. The Pope first cabled King George as follows: 'We rejoice at the resumption of the Anglo-Irish negotiations and pray to the Lord with all our heart that He may bless them and grant to your Majesty the great joy and imperishable glory of bringing to an end the age-long dissension.' The King's reply was: 'I have received the message of your Holiness with much pleasure and with all my heart I join in your prayer that the Conference . . . may achieve a permanent settlement of the troubles in Ireland and may initiate a new era of peace and happiness for my people.' De Valera took umbrage at this, and released to the press the text of the following telegram to Pope Benedict: 'The people of Ireland . . . are confident that the ambiguities in the reply sent in the name of King George will not mislead you into believing that the troubles are in Ireland, or that the people of Ireland owe allegiance to the British King. The independence of Ireland has been formally proclaimed. . . . The trouble is between England and Ireland and its source that rulers of Britain have endeavoured to impose their will upon Ireland.'

By coincidence the de Valera telegram, which created uproar in the British press, was published just as the British discovered two major IRA gun-running attempts, one in Cardiff, the other in Hamburg. Collins knew nothing about either and went into a fury, believing that 'the Dublinites' had engineered the two escapades in order to embarrass him. In fact both were the product of the IRA's normal incessant search for weaponry. But as the sixth Session opened, the gun-runnings and the telegram produced a very uncomfortable meeting for the Irish; Lloyd George said that they had combined to 'make our task almost impossible'. The gun-running was creating a 'serious uprising of feeling' in Parliament, but the telegram was 'the gravest incident'.[8] Lloyd George said that: 'If anything comparable had been done by the Germans during the Peace negotiations those negotiations would have been at once broken off . . . if Mr. de Valera had meant to make the negotiations futile, his message was well calculated to do so. It was challenging, defiant, and, he must say, ill-conditioned, in its attitude towards the King. . . . It looked like a deliberate attempt to break up the Conference. . . .'

Somehow Collins and Griffith wriggled out of the situation by a combination of audacity and reasoned argument. Collins claimed that the Cardiff affair was really the fault of the British, who had taken advantage 'of a condition that did not exist prior to the truce'. When Lloyd George inquired into the nature of this condition, Collins told him that it was 'because our people took less precautions'! Griffith's view of the arms issue was: 'My conception of the Truce does not mean that your military forces should prepare for the end of it and we should not.' And on the telegram, he argued that de Valera was compelled to take note of the phrase in the

King's message referring to 'Troubles in Ireland'. The trouble, he reasoned, was 'not a trouble in Ireland, but is one between Ireland and Great Britain'. This was basically de Valera's own rationale. Griffith himself did not approve of the telegram, which even de Valera conceded was 'somewhat disconcerting'.[9] However, he went on to say: 'We cannot expect the Vatican to recognise us, but we have a right to expect that it will not go out of its way to proclaim its denial of recognition as it did by addressing King George alone as if he were the common father, so to speak, of both disputant nations ... the Vatican recognised the struggle between Ireland and Britain as purely a domestic one for King George.'

Possibly the key to de Valera's action lies in the theories of two well-placed Irish Vatican-watchers, Father Curran and Monsignor Hagan, Rector of the Irish College in Rome, who felt that the Pope's telegram was inspired by British diplomacy. In his memoirs[10] Father Curran claimed that word of it leaked in Rome as early as 16 October. It was said to have been inspired by Bishop Cowgill of Leeds and Cardinal Gasquet, who had got together on the occasion of Cowgill's leading a pilgrimage to Rome by the English Catholic Association. This get-together was said to have been the result of an initiative by Lord Beaverbrook. Monsignor Hagan, an admirer of de Valera's, told Curran that Beaverbrook's Rome correspondent had mistakenly spoken on the telephone to an English friend of his, a man called Welldrick who worked for Cook's, the travel agents, believing that he was talking to Cowgill. In the course of the conversation he passed on the telegram suggestion. Hagan had an audience with the Pope on 20 October, informed the Pontiff that the telegram would cause offence in Ireland, and gave him a typed copy of the Beaverbrook correspondent's message to Welldrick.

Of necessity there has to be a certain amount of conjecture about this account of the telegram's genesis. The British were certainly keenly alive to the possibility of using Vatican influence for their purposes, but until either the Welldrick transcript turns up in Pope Benedict's papers or some reference to the Hagan visit of 20 October 1921 surfaces in a papal diary, it has to be borne in mind that the Curran account is based on what Hagan told him, and is not a description of something he was involved in himself. What is certain is that with his telegram de Valera publicly aired the self-recognition issue, insulted the King and added to Collins' and Griffith's already grievous burdens at the conference table. Collins crossed to Dublin and made a vain effort to get de Valera to take part in the talks. It was in the week following this refusal that the sub-conference methodology was adopted.

Although de Valera did not go to London, he made certain that the delegation was constantly reminded of his authority in ways other than his response to the Pope's telegram. There were three instances of this in the first week of the talks alone. He refused Griffith's request to send him over an assistant of his own choosing, Darrell Figgis.[11] But, incredibly in view of

259

the man's known relationship with Collins, and his refusal to join the delegation in the first place, he attempted to send Stack[12] across as an expert adviser when a dispute blew up over the Sinn Fein courts two days after the talks began. Collins and Griffith viewed this as an attempt to install in their midst a listening post critic who would have power without responsibility, and refused. A few days later de Valera wrote to Griffith in an attempt to get one of the delegation's secretaries, Diarmuid O'Hegarty, recalled. He said he had need of him in Dublin: 'Please do not keep him an hour longer than is necessary.'[13] The President's secretarial assistance was of greater importance than ensuring that a small, divided team of negotiators, taking on the leaders of the world's largest Empire, had adequate support services.

Three days later[14] he complained, ostensibly on behalf of Brugha, that military advisers had been appointed to the delegation without consulting the Minister for Defence. He was in reality concerned because Collins had brought with him a prominent member of GHQ, Ginger O'Connell, and, as we shall shortly see, he had had it in mind to use O'Connell in his and Brugha's grand design to remodel the army to suit his purposes. Then he created a major crisis amongst the delegation by the reply he sent to the following report by Griffith on his meetings with Lloyd George and Chamberlain on 24 October:[15]

> They pressed me to say that I would accept the Crown provided we came to other agreements. It was evident they wanted something to reassure themselves against the Die-hards. I told them I had no authority. If we came to an agreement on all other points I could recommend some form of Association with the Crown. . . . I told them the only possibility of Ireland considering Association of any kind with the Crown was in exchange for essential unity – a concession to Ulster. . . . They always fell back on the impossibility of peace except on acceptance of the Crown.

The position regarding the Crown was, of course, that which Lloyd George had spelled out in detail to de Valera during their face-to-face sessions, but he responded to Griffith in terms which made his resumé appear to contain something strange, new and unthinkable:[16] 'We are all here at one that there can be no question of our asking the Irish people to enter an arrangement which would make them subject to the British King. If war is the alternative, we can only face it, and I think the sooner the other side is made to realise it the better.'

When this missive arrived in London both Collins and Griffith threatened to return home, correctly analysing the letter as an attempt to tie their hands. Collins bluntly told the delegation that Dublin was trying to put him in the wrong and get him to do 'the dirty work for them'.[17] It was again suggested that de Valera should come to London, but in a clearly unworkable way – if he could do so without publicity. Eventually a letter of protest was sent off signed by the entire delegation. It made the point that his letter was 'tying their hands in discussion and inconsistent with the powers given them on their appointment . . . it is obvious that we could not continue any longer in the conference and should return to Dublin immediately if the powers were withdrawn.' On receiving this, de Valera made a show of drawing in his horns:

> There can be no question of tying the hands of the plenipotentiaries beyond the extent to which they are tied by their original instructions. Of course a Cabinet decision cannot be withdrawn or varied except by the Cabinet as a whole . . . the delegation must understand that these memos of mine, except I explicitly state otherwise, are nothing more than an attempt to keep you in touch with the views of the Cabinet here on the various points as they arise. I think it most important that you should be kept aware of these views, for when the delegation returns there will be a question of a Cabinet decision as a policy.

Apart from the apparent climb-down, more apparent than real, de Valera's letter is of interest for the way in which it reveals how he saw the source of power in Dublin as the Cabinet – in which he believed, wrongly as we shall see, that he held a commanding majority. Consciously or unconsciously, he was excluding the body which had in fact given the plenipotentiaries their powers, the Dail, and behind the Dail the people who had returned the deputies – the Irish public. The closed circle within which his struggle with Collins was conducted was so restricted that at least one member of the Cabinet, Barton, was evidently unaware of what was going on. Years later he commented on the episode, 'I do not today quite understand what was the cause of Collins' extraordinary outburst.'[18] The fact that he did not understand the situation was probably the main reason he was included in the delegation in the first place.

Despite his emollient reply to the all-delegate protest de Valera managed to get into the record a few days later a disavowal that he was contemplating any form of compromise on the republic. His opportunity arose when he received a copy of the Irish reply to British proposals made on 27 October. The Irish document, dated the 29th, stated that it[19] 'accepted the principle that the naval and air defence of the Irish coasts would be a matter of common concern to Ireland and the British Commonwealth'. This was a variant of his own Cuban proposals, but he made no comment on the defence issue, reserving his fire for the following:

> The unimpaired unity of Ireland is a condition precedent to the conclusion of a Treaty of Association between Ireland and the Nations of the British Commonwealth. Subject to this, and . . . agreement on . . . other issues the Irish delegates are prepared to recommend that the elected Government of a free and undivided Ireland, secured in absolute and unfettered possession of all legislative authority, should, for the purposes of the association, recognise the Crown as symbol and accepted head of the combination of signatory states.

He replied to Griffith making use of the royal 'we': 'We are not quite certain what exactly the last three lines may involve, and accordingly refrain from making any comment. You know the views here from my dispatch no 7.' This was the despatch which had provoked the all-delegate letter of protest. So, without eliciting any further protest, de Valera thus managed to reiterate his earlier hard-line stance. With what forces he intended to face war, should it come, we can only hazard a guess. Collins' intelligence team were now out in the open, acting as his bodyguard in London. By coming to London, Collins believed, 'We have, mistakenly, put all our cards on the table; we have laid ourselves open to the British.'[20] And the position regarding the outcome of the negotiations was so uncertain that a plane, ostensibly hired by Canadians, was standing by to airlift Collins out of London in the event of a breakdown. Possibly de Valera reasoned that the British Government would not risk a resumption of hostilities, but he was certainly aware that the British public would not be in favour of such a resumption. However, as he did not shrink from a more destructive form of warfare, civil war, less than a year later, it is difficult not to conclude that de Valera's larger-than-life experience of life over the preceding years had left him more predisposed to be guided by the concept that he knew best than by concern with public opinion.

Yet along with this blindness a stranger, more contradictory form of blindness apparently prevented him from seeing that the drift of the negotiations was carrying them away from the 'rock of the Republic' which he seemed to cling to so determinedly. He chose not to recognize the implications of the sub-conference set-up, even though it clearly undermined the situation of checks and balances which he claimed he had tried to build into the delegation. Now Collins and Griffith were obviously acting without any influence from the other members of the team. He refused yet another entreaty to go to London when this fact, and a row over a letter from Griffith to the British, were forcibly brought to his attention.

Before dealing with a censure motion in the House of Commons from the Die-hard element – Tory back-benchers who were appalled at the spectacle of talks taking place with Sinn Fein – Lloyd George, Birkenhead and Churchill met Griffith and Collins in Churchill's house. Here, according to a report[21] which Griffith made to de Valera immediately after the meeting, Lloyd George summed up his position as follows: 'The bias of his speech had to be peace or war with Ireland. If Griffith would give "personal assurances" on the Crown, free partnership with the British Empire and coastal and naval facilities, he would "smite the Die-hards" and, more importantly, would "fight on the Ulster matter to secure essential unity".'

The Die-hards were duly smitten and Griffith attempted to give Lloyd George his 'personal assurances'. But when he informed the delegation of what he was doing, a furious row broke out. He was charged with weakening the Irish position on the Crown and Ulster, and with giving Lloyd George a document which he could use to his advantage in dealing with either Washington or Belfast. The Childers/Barton/Duffy contingent insisted that the letter be sent from the delegation as a whole; after two days of argument and redrafting it was sent to Downing Street, signed by Griffith as Chairman. Contingent on the securing of 'essential unity', Griffith was prepared 'to recommend a free partnership of Ireland with the other States associated within the British Commonwealth, the formula defining the partnership to be arrived at in a later discussion. I was, on the same condition, prepared to recommend that Ireland should consent to a recognition of the Crown as head of the proposed association of free states.'

But in the anger and confusion of the redrafting, and the subsequent side-conferences with the British over the form of the 'assurances', a bad situation had been made worse. Even though, unknown to the other delegates, the draft on which Griffith's original letter was based was drawn up by Tom Jones, it only spoke of recommending 'Free partnership *with* the British Commonwealth'. But, as sent, the letter spoke of partnership '*within* the British Commonwealth', meaning '*within* the British Empire'. The republicans' efforts at redrafting had effectively got rid of the pretence that there was any likelihood of a republic emerging from the negotiations.

Even worse was to follow ten days later: the possibility of a break over Ulster was lost and, *de facto*, partition was accepted. Just as with the republic there was very little prospect, given the strength of British military and political support for the Unionists' desire to carve out the Six Counties from the rest of Ireland, that it could ever have been prevented by the tiny, divided Irish delegation. Although, admittedly, Craig did come under heavy pressure from the Liberals during the Treaty negotiations, he had such support from the Conservative ranks – where Bonar Law had made a reappearance at the side of Balfour and the other Tudor Tories – that he was able to hold to his position that he had the Six Counties and all that remained was for the Prime Minister to conclude with Sinn Fein the arrangements for dealing with the other Twenty-six Counties. However, Lloyd George led Griffith to understand that, as a result of his greatly appreciated 'assurances' letter, he was prepared to resign should Craig prove obdurate.

Craig did prove obdurate, but Lloyd George had no more intention of resigning than he had over the promise he had first given Redmond in similar circumstances some five years earlier. Once more he utilized the approach of a Die-hard show of strength to achieve his purposes. First he sent Jones to Griffith and Collins to suggest that, because of Craig's continuing intransigence, he fully intended to resign if the Unionists did not accept that they could keep their Six-County area only if they did so under an All-Ireland Parliament. However, if he did resign, a militarist administration would surely replace him, possibly one led by Bonar Law. This would be even worse for Ireland. Accordingly he had Jones make a suggestion, giving it as his own idea, that:[22] 'Supposing the Twenty Six

Counties of the South were to be given the powers under discussion, and suppose Ulster were to be not only restricted to existing powers, but also submitted to a Boundary Commission set up to "delimit" her area? How would that strike them?'

The idea struck Griffith as having such potential that he reported to de Valera next day that the Boundary Commission would give the South 'most of Tyrone and Fermanagh, and part of Armagh, Londonderry, Down etc.' Jones, obviously sensing the enthusiasm on the Irish side for the Boundary Commission idea, returned to the fray the next day with a proposal which got Lloyd George off his resignation hook. If Ulster refused the Boundary Commission, as both British and Irish agreed they would, Lloyd George would stay in office and call a full Cabinet meeting to get the backing he would need in order to mobilize public opinion against Ulster. The Six Counties would be made to look 'utterly unreasonable' for their insistence on coercing areas that wished to be excluded. Would the Irish support such a proposal? Griffith wrote to de Valera that:[23] 'We said that it would be their proposal not ours, and we would not, therefore, be bound by it but we realised its value as a tactical manoeuvre and if Lloyd George made it we would not queer his position.'

Lloyd George built on this indication of support on 12 November, when he showed Griffith a letter from Craig in which the Unionist leader agreed 'as a lesser evil than being included in an all-Ireland Parliament' that the Northern state should have the same powers as those proposed for the South. What this meant in effect was that 'Ulster should be formed into a Dominion and pay none except voluntary contributions to England'.[24] Griffith told de Valera that this idea 'simply astounded all the principal members of the Cabinet except Lloyd George'.[25] The Boundary Commission idea was now made to appear to bear even more heavily on that part of Ulster which remained after the optings out had occurred, because in writing to Craig Lloyd George had made it clear that the area 'would have to bear the same taxation as England'.[26]

After showing Griffith the Craig letter, Lloyd George again asked him for assurances that he would not repudiate him. Having got them, he then had Jones draw up a memorandum on the British proposals which was shown to Griffith the following day, the 13th. Griffith 'briefly indicated his assent', without paying attention to the memo. De Valera's apologists have subsequently maintained that the next time this memorandum was heard of was when Lloyd George produced it in the closing hours of the Treaty drama, with such stunning effect that:[27] 'the attempt to stage the break on Ulster on which the whole Irish strategy hinged had gone by the board'.

This dramatic reminder of his promise was said to have been what led to his deciding to sign the Treaty, and the other delegates' decision followed from his. However, the assurances surfaced as a substantive matter at an important meeting in Downing Street on 23 November, and Griffith specifically referred to it in a letter to de Valera on that date:[28] 'On Ulster

Lloyd George declared that I had assured him I would not let him down, if he put up the proposals subsequently embodied in their memorandum to Craig. . . . I said that I had given him that assurance and I now repeated it, but I told him that it was his proposal – not ours. . . . He was satisfied. . . . He would put his proposal to Craig from himself only. . . .'

Whether Griffith thought Lloyd George was talking about his letter of assurance which provoked the row with the other delegates, or the subsequent memorandum of which the letter formed the base, is immaterial. Everyone concerned knew that he had pledged his word on 'assurances'. But at all events, a few days after the drawing up of the memorandum containing the Griffith assurances the Lloyd George forces duly carried the day at the Unionist Annual Conference at Liverpool on 17 November. A motion censuring the Government was defeated; the delegates were informed that a 'settlement was almost reached', on the basis that there would be no coercion of Ulster if she refused to co-operate in Dominion Home Rule. Moreover, the proposed settlement would keep Ireland within the Empire and would guarantee both the Crown and British naval interests.

While the foregoing could be read as indicating that Griffith was simply outmanoeuvred by Lloyd George, this would be an over-simplification. Unquestionably Griffith felt that his 'assurances' approach contrasted so favourably with the type of 'non possumus reply'[29] emanating from Craig that, he informed de Valera, the result was: 'The "Ulster" crowd are in the pit they digged for us, and if we keep them there, we'll have England and the Dominions out against them in the next week or so.'

De Valera also felt things were progressing 'admirably' over 'Ulster' at this stage.[30] But the reality was far darker. In fact, Collins and Griffith were aware that some of the men they were dealing with in London were actively engaged in a scheme whereby the British taxpayer would become liable for the costs of arming and paying sectarian murder gangs. The scheme was part of the Tories' overall determination to make the Six Counties so strong that they could successfully defy any move towards a united Ireland; it was actually revealed to the public in the *Irish Bulletin* on the very day that the Unionist Conference was held in Liverpool, 17 November. The paper printed the contents of a circular from a Colonel Wickham to senior members of the Ulster Special Constabulary, the B-Specials, which stated categorically that because of the 'growth of unauthorised loyalist defence forces' the Government was proposing to enrol these forces alongside the B-Specials as Class C recruits. They were to be a military force, drawn from ex-soldiers of the 'reliable section of the population'. Apart from being a clear manifestation of the old Conservative policy of 'Ulster will fight and Ulster will be right', the circular was a clear breach of the truce.

The top British civil servant in Ireland, Sir John Anderson, was horrified:[31]

Matter seems to me to be most serious. Wickham, while an officer of the Imperial Government, has not only constituted himself the instrument of another authority in a most delicate matter involving big political issues but he has done so in terms which suggest that in so acting he was carrying out instructions of the Government which employed him. I cannot understand how any British officer could get into such a position, and can only suppose that he received assurances on which he relied that the action he was taking would not be disapproved.

Not only was Wickham receiving 'assurances', he was shortly to be appointed head of a new police force which was set up in the Six Counties along sectarian lines because the Unionist–Tory alliance deemed that there were too many Catholics in the existing Royal Irish Constabulary.[32] Amongst those from whom he took instruction were the architect of the new force, Sir Henry Wilson, and Sir Laming Worthington Evans, a member of the British delegation with which Collins and Griffith were negotiating.

The Wickham incident must have given Griffith and Collins pause for thought as to the sincerity of British intentions over the Boundary Commission. Collins' intelligence network, which unearthed the circular, left him in no doubt as to the power and inclinations of those who were arming and organizing the very people who might be expected to resist the Commission, the Unionists. Meanwhile, on top of the unsatisfactory situation in Belfast, the situation in Dublin was as much a factor for Collins and Griffith as anything that happened in London. During the talks they wrote down their concerns, and had them typed and initialled. Here are some of them:[33]

Collins: How best to reconcile our ideas with the fixed ideas at present held by certain members of the Cabinet? I will not agree to anything which threatens to plunge the people of Ireland into a war – not without their authority. Still less do I agree to being dictated to by those not embroiled in these negotiations. . . . If they are not in agreement with the steps we are taking, and hope to take, why then did they themselves not consider their own presence here in London? Example: Brugha refused to be a member of the delegation.

Griffith: It is not so much a question of who is dictating to whom. It is a question of powers invested in us as representatives of our country. Sooner or later a decision will have to be made.

Collins: Exactly. What are our powers? Are we to commit our country one way or another, yet without authority to do so? . . . The advantages of Dominion status to us as a stepping stone to complete independence are immeasurable.

Griffith: Agreed, but with one question. How far can we trust the signatures of the British delegation in this matter? Once signed we are committed. But are they?

Collins: No we are not committed – not until both the Dail and Westminster ratify whatever agreement is made.

Griffith: Ratification by the Dail means what precisely? That a certain amount of power is still in the hands of those we know will be against anything which treats of Empire status.

Collins: I agree in part to the above. Supposing, however, we were to go back to Dublin tomorrow with a document which gave us a Republic. Would such a document find favour with everyone? I doubt it.

Griffith: So do I. But sooner or later a decision will have to be made and we shall have to make it – whatever our position and authority.

And so, against that background, they made their decisions. Unsupported by Dublin and deeply mistrustful of Lloyd George, whenever any chance of progressing towards Collins' 'stepping stone' presented itself they took it. Inevitably it became quite clear to the other members of the delegation what they were doing. Excluded as a result of the sub-conference methodology from making any contributions to the discussions which might have altered the direction of the negotiations, the Barton–Duffy wing decided to make a protest to Dublin. Duffy went over and saw the other members of the Cabinet, but got nowhere. De Valera acted neither on his protest, nor on one made by Sean T. O'Ceallaigh around the same time. Alarmed at reports that Griffith was prepared to recognize the Crown in return for concessions, O'Ceallaigh at first considered speaking out publicly against the 'imminent surrender'. He then left his post as Irish Republican envoy in Paris at 'two hours' notice',[34] and went to Dublin where he had an interview with de Valera, telling him that he would not stand for such a compromise. De Valera:[35] 'took him coolly, almost coldly, told him that everything was safe inasmuch as the delegates could not sign anything without first submitting it to the Cabinet and getting their approval. He wound up by telling Sean he should not have left Paris without permission and told him to return at once.'

In dismissing both Duffy and O'Ceallaigh in this fashion – to say nothing of not taking action on whatever reports he was getting from Childers – de Valera was not merely placing an over-reliance on the Cecil-type document he had given to the plenipotentiaries. His immediate priorities lay not in London but in Dublin, where he had in hand another manoeuvre which, had it come off, would have strengthened his hand in dealing with Collins and Griffith. For the New Prince was on the threshold of getting himself a New Army. In an extension of the policy which he had introduced in March when he first began exerting his influence on the Army, he now proposed a take-over of GHQ. In conjunction with Brugha he proposed a scheme whereby the Army would be recommissioned on 25 November, the anniversary of the founding of the Volunteers in 1913. Officers and men were to resign and then be offered fresh commissions – provided they took an oath of loyalty to the Dail, of which he of course was now President and Brugha the Minister for Defence.

Prior to the unveiling of this scheme there had been considerable tension in GHQ over two initiatives of Brugha's. In one he created fears that individual IRA officers would be found to have been acting outside the law when he declared that a scheme whereby local officers collected levies to support the Army was now illegal. He proposed that the National Exchequer become involved, but Collins immediately vetoed the idea as it created a potential for enormous liabilities. His second idea created not fear, but anger. He wanted Austin Stack appointed Deputy Chief of Staff. Mulcahy, who like most of the GHQ team regarded Stack as a dud, immediately wrote to de Valera on 1 November saying that he would take no responsibility for 'any position' if Stack were appointed. Collins had made way for de Valera in March by agreeing to allow the IRB to amend its Constitution to recognize the authority of the Dail, rather than that of the Supreme Council which he headed. But now, even though enmeshed in intrigue in London, he was not prepared to allow him to get away with this latest stratagem. Two days before the planned recommissioning ceremony he wrote to Mulcahy directing him to organize a meeting to discuss the de Valera ploy:[36]

> I have heard from Mr. Griffith that the Cabinet has been summoned for the 25th to meet the GHQ Staff of the Old Army (It reminds me of Napoleon). The members of the Cabinet at present in London have been asked to be present. I think we ought to have a meeting of the GHQ Staff very early Friday morning. I would strongly suggest that we should have associated at that meeting Directors of Staff who operated for a certain time in the Old Army. I mean Directors who really did operate. . . .

The fruits of that meeting were seen later in the day. Mulcahy suggested to de Valera that before the 'Old Army' was disbanded he should call in the GHQ staff, thank them for their past services and explain what was envisaged. The thanking ceremony was delayed for several hours while Griffith and Collins brought the rest of the Cabinet up-to-date on the current state of the London negotiations. It was only when they had left to return to London that de Valera called in the officers. He had thought of a way of sweetening Mulcahy's objections to Stack by agreeing that Eoin O'Duffy, whom Mulcahy wanted for the position, should be appointed, provided that Stack also be selected as 'Cathal's ghost on the Staff'. Not one member of the GHQ staff agreed, either to this suggestion or to the 'New Army proposals'. O'Duffy said bluntly that he found the proposals 'insulting'. Ginger O'Connell, more tactfully, deemed them unnecessary because GHQ were 'like a band of brothers'. De Valera, realizing that Collins and the IRB had out-manoeuvred him, lost his temper:[37] 'Rising excitedly, he pushed away the table in front of him and, half-screaming, half-shouting, said: "Ye may mutiny if you like, but Ireland will give me another army" and dismissed them all from his sight.'

However, he had to climb down. These calculated shows of temper often worked for him on a one-to-one basis, when he would bring up an array of other psychological tricks: the calculated hissing breathing through the nostrils, like a pressure cooker coming to a boil that could only be averted by doing whatever it was he wanted; the deliberate silences, the piercing, accusatory glance, the long walk to a huge desk with a chair placed in front for penitent or supplicant; the demoralizing mood switch from kindliness to anger; the unexpected hardness that always underlay his deceptively rambling circumlocutory manner in negotiation. But such approaches were of little use against the group psychology of some of the bravest men in Europe. One did not have to be a student of Machiavelli to realize that to attempt to reorganize GHQ against its wishes in the midst of a shaky truce was not good politics. A few days later he allowed it to become known that there would be no 'New Army', but that the new commissions should be accepted.

The 'New Army' rebuff was the second setback he had received on 25 November. The first was the more serious, but he had refused to accept it. In plain language, Griffith and Collins had told the Cabinet that the previous day in London they had done their best to have external association accepted but had been rejected. Failure to accept the Crown would mean war. At this stage the British offer on the table was based on Dominion status within the Empire, on the Canadian model. This involved an Oath of Allegiance to the King and guarantees on defence. True, the British had agreed to Griffith's suggestion that in any Treaty the term 'Saorstat Eireann' would be translated not as 'Republic' but as 'Free State'. But that was to be the only concession to Irish symbolism. British symbolism required that their fundamental position remained as set out in the summer-long exchange with de Valera and in a policy declaration delivered to the Irish during the negotiations:[38]

> The Crown is the symbol of all that keeps the nations of the Empire together. It is the keystone of the arch in law as well as in sentiment. . . . The British Government must know definitely whether or not the Irish Delegates are prepared that Ireland should maintain its ancient allegiance to the Throne, not as a state subordinate to Great Britain, but as one of the Nations of the Commonwealth, in close association with the realm of England, Scotland and Wales.
>
> No man can be a subject of two States. He must be either a subject of the King or an alien, and the question no more admits of an equivocal answer than whether he is alive or dead.

But 'an equivocal answer' is just what de Valera sent the plenipotentiaries back with on the day of the New Army charade. They were instructed that Ireland 'should recognise the British Crown for the purposes of Association, as symbol and accepted head of the combination of associated states'. In other words, they were to go back with what had been rejected the day before. The Canadian model was unacceptable because, as Childers in particular argued, Canada's distance from England safeguarded her from the consequences of her subordinacy to the Crown. Ireland, because of her closeness to the neighbouring island, would be subordinate not only in theory but in reality too.

On the face of it, this Charge of the Light Brigade return to Downing Street would appear to have inevitably put paid to the talks process, but Lloyd George too required a settlement, albeit one on terms that his

Conservative partners in Government would live with. Apart from the pressures he was subjected to by domestic and international public opinion he had to have regard to the situation highlighted by Smuts; the post-war balance of power in the Pacific; and how the developments, or lack of them, in Ireland might set an example in British colonial possessions elsewhere – in India, or more particularly in Egypt.

In the early twentieth century Japan began to emerge as a naval power in the Pacific, and the Japanese annexation of Manchuria in the 1930s would later provide occasion for one of de Valera's most notable speeches to the League of Nations. Professor F. M. Carroll is one of the (curiously) few writers on the Anglo-Irish conflict even to mention, however briefly,[39] the Anglo-American–Japanese relationship in the Pacific in terms of the Irish American lobby. But a knowledgeable Irish American activist of the period, J. C. Walsh, one of the stalwarts of the bond drive, accurately summed up the importance of this faraway theatre of empire to Lloyd George in the winter of 1921:[40] 'The English had to agree with the United States about warships in the Pacific and the United States would not start the conversations until something had been done about Ireland.' And where Egypt was concerned, the comments of a British Cabinet member of the time are instructive for how they illustrate both the importance of the issue and the contempt with which British imperialists regarded much of the world outside their shores. At the time he made the following diary notes[41] H. A. L. Fisher was President of the Board of Education! On 19 October he wrote: 'I ask LG [Lloyd George] how the Egyptian negotiations are getting on. "Badly, I expect," he said cheerfully. With all his merits Mr. George [sic] is not quite the man to negotiate with the inferior races.' And on 4 November: '(Re Egypt) . . . Attend Cabinet at 5 p.m. Allenby in attendance; twisted one way by Winston, another by Curzon. Most unsatisfactory. . . . Eventually a most unsatisfactory compromise agreed to. My impression is that PM is so anxious about Ireland that he dare not make concessions about Egypt.'

Nor did he dare go to Washington for the Disarmament Conference. Griffith informed de Valera[42] that, when Lloyd George sounded him about the effect his departing from London would have on the Treaty talks at this stage, he was told bluntly that they would not continue. However, Lloyd George felt that he could dare to make a concession over Ireland – a most adroit one. He first refused the reintroduction of external association point-blank; it was simply 'impossible'. The British Government which attempted 'to propose to the British people the abrogation of the Crown would be smashed to atoms'. But to get over the Childers line of objection to the Canadian or Dominion solution, which Griffith had dutifully put to him, he said that the Irish could insert in the treaty[43] 'any phrase they liked which would ensure that the Crown in Ireland would be no more in practice than it was in Canada or any other Dominion.'

It was a most important concession, which in the long term became the basis of Irish constitutional advancement. But what the Welsh Wizard was concerned with was the short-term impact, which was considerable. As Griffith wrote to de Valera, it:[44] 'knocked out my argument on the document they sent in – that the Crown in the Dominions were merely a symbol but that in Ireland it would be a reality'. However, de Valera was in no mood to face up to the reality either contained in Griffith's letter or bearing down on him as the Treaty negotiations turned into the home straight: accept or reject their outcome. For decision time was only a few days further off. Griffith warned de Valera: 'It is essential that a Cabinet meeting should be held.' Collins and Griffith may or may not have brought matters to a head deliberately by agreeing that Griffith would get his copy of the final British proposals before Craig got his. It was finally decided that Craig's copy was to be brought to him on 6 December, which meant that on that day the Irish had to face an ultimatum: sign or face war. Some pro-de Valera commentators, like Lord Longford, have argued that by agreeing to the Craig arrangement the Irish threw away their freedom of manoeuvre. But it could equally be advanced that by now Griffith and Collins were so sick of the nit-picking from Dublin that they may have reasoned that the existence of an imperative would enable them to secure half a loaf rather than no bread.

In fact, in the penultimate draft[45] which the British produced, on 1 December, they had by any reckoning secured considerably more than half. The Irish were offered a self-governing Free State with the same status as Canada. On the symbolic front there was a stipulation that the Oath only imposed allegiance to the Crown 'as head of the State and Empire', and in practical terms a highly significant alteration on defence was made. Naval defence was to be an exclusively British prerogative only until 'an arrangement has been made whereby ... the Free State undertakes her own coastal defence'. This last secured a departure from a fundamental British requirement on common citizenship: 'The essence of common citizenship is that all who enjoy it are at peace or at war together ... it is not compatible with neutrality in any form.'[46] Ironically, destiny would later enable de Valera to build on the coastal defence provision to ensure that Ireland did remain neutral during World War II. But on 2 December 1921 de Valera was preparing to reject, not build on, the Treaty proposals. Arthur Griffith had left London that morning at 8.30 to bring the document to Dublin and de Valera. According to the account of the day which de Valera gave his biographers,[47] he had driven up from Clare to meet Griffith and insisted on driving himself in order to get in some practice in case hostilities recommenced. The result was that 'the President was very tired when they arrived back at Kenilworth Sq. [the house he was now staying at in Dublin] at 10.30 p.m. The roads were very slippery.'

One is tempted to comment that the roads were not all that was 'very slippery'. For de Valera disliked the idea of engaging man-to-man with

271

Griffith over the proposals and perhaps committing himself to a supportive position where they, or Griffith, were concerned. He wanted to ensure that he had Cabinet sanction, and protection, for his manoeuvrings. Griffith was nearly twelve years older than he and had just made a racking rail and sea journey from London, having gone to bed in the small hours of the morning after an exhausting day spent, like the previous seven weeks, in tense, anxious negotiation. But it was de Valera, 'the Roman spear' which prided itself on its fitness, who pleaded tiredness. According to his account, he told Griffith that 'we could never accept these proposals'. Griffith's reply to this was that he had 'always told him that he would not break on the Crown, which was what the President now seemed to expect of him'.[48] After a two-hour discussion which failed to resolve this argument:[49] 'The President felt too tired to argue satisfactorily. He decided that the questions could be fully discussed at the Cabinet meeting fixed for the next day [i.e. later that day]. Later he was to regret the adjournment bitterly. He always reproached himself for having missed his most favourable chance of persuading Griffith of the consequences of acceptance. . . .'

However, writing to McGarrity much nearer to the discussion with Griffith, on 27 December, de Valera makes no mention of tiredness and conveys an impression of political disagreement carried on in an atmosphere of reason and objective judgement:[50]

> I told him [Griffith] definitely that I would never consent to sign any such agreement. He said he would not break on the Crown. We parted at that. Next day, Saturday, we all met at a Cabinet meeting. I criticised the British proposals in detail. . . . Dominion status nominally, with an oath of allegiance to the British King as an organic part of the Irish Constitution, and a recognition of him as head of the Irish state. The oath crystallised in itself the main things we objected to – inclusion in the Empire, the British King as King in Ireland, chief Executive of the Irish state, and the source from which all authority in Ireland must be derived.

In his biography de Valera made use of his letter to McGarrity to underscore his position for posterity: He had 'insisted that we should stand on our own proposals, and if necessary break with the British on them'. Readers will remember the vagueness of the Draft Treaties A and B that the plenipotentiaries had been given as a basis for these 'proposals', Griffith's account of how he first heard of external association, and how the British received the idea. But, just as though he were discussing a real, viable option that the Irish, rather than the British, had somehow thrown away, de Valera calmly assured McGarrity and his biographers that as a last resort he was prepared to accept 'recognition of the British King as head of the whole association, that is we could swear to recognise him as a sort of President of the whole league'.[51]

However, despite this display of magnanimity towards George V, de Valera told McGarrity that Griffith still refused to break on the Crown even though 'It was pointed out to him that the acceptance of allegiance meant a certain split – the greatest of all dangers. There was a question of my going over in person to London. The objection to this was that the British would think I had gone because I was anxious to prevent a break-down. They would accordingly not make any further advance to me but might stiffen instead.' Here his biography interjects: 'The next sentence is crucial for an understanding of de Valera's moral and tactical position.' It is indeed, though hardly in the sense in which de Valera intended. The sentence reads: 'I probably would have gone nevertheless had not Griffith, on being shown that if he accepted the Crown he would split the country, given an *express undertaking* that he would not sign a document accepting allegiance but would bring it back and refer the matter to Dail Eireann. This made us all satisfied; we were certain for our part that Dail Eireann would reject it.'

The clear impression conveyed by those words is that some reasoned argument, probably involving de Valera himself, obtained a consensus amongst those present in which Griffith concurred. The reality was very different. The biography does admit that: 'Other accounts of the seven-hour-long meeting show it to have been less orderly than the President's letter might suggest.' The meeting was in fact a monumental nit-picking session: the Mansion House resounded to the sound of seven hours of confused, acrimonious bickering. The worst scene occurred when Brugha, who of course had done nothing when Duffy paid his visit to Dublin to complain about the arrangement, inquired how it was that Griffith and Collins attended all the sub-conferences. When he was informed that the British had asked for the arrangement, he remarked that the British Government 'selected its men'. Collins contained himself, but Griffith was infuriated. Leaving his chair, he strode over to Brugha and demanded a withdrawal of his allegation. Brugha refused at first, only doing so after Griffith insisted that it be recorded in the minutes. The atmosphere was appalling. Apart from the acrimony Collins, Childers and Duffy had had no sleep the previous night, because the mail boat had had to put back to Holyhead after running down a fishing boat and causing the death of three of its crew; the plenipotentiaries only reached Dun Laoghaire three-quarters of an hour before the meeting began. Insofar as Collins was concerned the real meeting took place elsewhere in Dublin, in the Gresham Hotel, where the Supreme Council of the IRB were perusing the British offer. He would have more regard for their decisions than for the hair-splitting in the Mansion House.

Here there was a great deal of disagreement about vital decisions taken, and instructions and undertakings allegedly given and accepted; de Valera's suggestions as to what courses should be followed, as opposed to his objections to what had been produced, were amongst the most opaque put forward. A night's rest does not seem to have given him any better arguments with which to confront Griffith than he had produced the

273

previous day. He utilized his chairmanship skills on the side of confusion rather than that of clarity. The view of his contribution to this historic meeting which he wished to have posterity believe was set down later by Frank Gallagher:[52] 'In the exchange of views the Cabinet divided into two groups with Griffith, Collins and Duggan on one side and Barton, Gavan Duffy and Childers on the other. The President, who was naturally chairman, endeavoured to find a via media.' His policy as outlined to McGarrity is given above. As contained in the official record, his position was this:[53]

> He personally could not subscribe to the Oath of Allegiance nor could he sign any document which would give N.E. Ulster power to vote itself out of the Irish State. With modifications, however, it might be accepted honourably, and he would like to see the plenipotentiaries go back and secure peace if possible. He believed the Delegates had done their utmost and that it now remained to them to show that if the document was not amended they were prepared to face the consequences – war or no war. He would deal with present document exactly as with that of 20th of July – say it cannot be accepted and put up counter-proposals.

Of course, there was no going back to 20 July. The British position was as had been spelled out to him before the talks started. Now, on 3 December, he was sending others back to confront that no longer avoidable reality. Moreover, he was doing so with as little clear guidance as he could manage being committed to. Obviously somewhat deficient in a precise understanding of the concept of external association, the official record stated that:

> The President took his stand upon last Irish proposals [25 November] which meant external connection with the Crown. He suggested the following amendment to the Oath of Allegiance:
> 'I . . . do solemnly swear true faith and allegiance to the constitution of the Irish Free State, to the Treaty of Association and to recognise the King of Great Britain as Head of the Associated States.'

But neither Barton nor Childers, both of whom supported de Valera, afterwards thought that this is what he had said. Childers' notes had him saying 'King of the Associated States'.[54] Barton, however, says that:[55]

> De Valera did not exactly suggest an amendment to the oath. In the first place he was opposed to any oath being there at all, but said something like this 'well if there has to be an oath at all, it should be in conformity with our status of external association; something like this I suppose: I do solemnly swear true faith and allegiance to the Constitution of Ireland, to the Treaty of Association of Ireland with the British Commonwealth of Nations and so recognise the King of Great Britain as Head of the Association.'

The logic of de Valera's opposition to the Oath suddenly struck Childers, and he asked him whether he intended the scrapping of the Oath in the draft Treaty to result in the scrapping also of the document's first four paragraphs, which dealt with Dominion status. De Valera said: 'Yes.' However, in the general uproar nobody else heard him, and Childers and Collins had an unholy falling out in London when Childers attempted to carry out what he interpreted as de Valera's wishes. On top of all this it should be noted that de Valera subsequently gave two further, differing, versions of the oaths he proposed.[56] And he also attempted to make a virtue out of his evasiveness and lack of leadership by telling the Dail: 'I did not give, nor did the Cabinet give, any instructions to the delegation as to any final document which they were to put in.'[57]

The substantive matter at issue was, of course, the question of partition – the dismemberment of Ireland. But this did not remotely command the attention bestowed on the Oath. Griffith's 'express undertaking', for example, is not mentioned in the official record at all. Possibly the secretary to the meeting, Colm O'Murchadha, never heard the exchange in which it occurred – not between de Valera and Griffith, but between Griffith and Brugha. De Valera's 'this made us all satisfied' is simply untrue. After the meeting, the delegates were so deeply divided that they returned to London on different boats, Collins and Griffith travelling separately from Barton, Childers and Duffy.

Apart from the official record, three other participants in the discussions – Barton, Childers and Stack – recorded their impressions of what occurred. Barton points out that the official record was 'very incomplete'. Apart from omitting Griffith's 'express undertaking', it neither referred to a long discussion on the document's trade provisions nor made any mention of how two members of the Cabinet felt. 'Left out were Messrs. Cosgrave's and Stack's views upon the Treaty. Both were present at all meetings.'[58] (The meeting was broken into a morning and afternoon session.) The official record is not the only 'incomplete' account of the proceedings. De Valera's biography does not record how the issue of the Griffith undertaking arose. Barton notes:[59] 'I had made a fervent appeal to de Valera to join us in London, pointing out that it was not fair to ask Griffith to go back as leader of the Delegation to secure terms that could only be secured if we were prepared to go to war when he, Griffith, was not prepared to do so. Griffith's undertaking was given in reply to some query by Cathal Brugha. Brugha even at this juncture was still opposed to de Valera's going to London.'

The 'fervent appeal' fell on deaf ears. De Valera's official account[60] of how Brugha's 'some query' came about says that it occurred as Griffith was making a number of points in favour of the Treaty: that it was not dishonourable, that it practically gave a republic and that its first oath-bound allegiance was to Ireland. Brugha interrupted him: ' "Don't you realise that if you sign this thing, you will split Ireland from top to bottom?" The force of this seemed to strike Griffith, and he said, "I suppose that's so. I'll tell you what I'll do. I'll go back to London. I'll not

275

sign that document, but I'll bring it back and submit it to the Dail." This pledge satisfied everybody present at the meeting.'

The fact that the exchange made so little impact on the official recorder of the proceedings that he overlooked it is not mentioned. Nor is there any mention of the fact that he privately advised Childers to drive a coach and four through the entire document by scrapping its opening paragraphs. The de Valera account, like that given earlier by Longford in *Peace by Ordeal*, is largely based on that of Austin Stack.[61] It claimed that Griffith's pledge 'has usually been interpreted, and rightly, as an undertaking not to sign any document involving allegiance to the Crown or allegiance within the Empire. There was felt to be no necessity now for substitute delegates to go over and break off the negotiations. De Valera, in particular, abandoned the idea of going over himself, reassured as he was by Griffith's pledge. . . .'

But the Brugha–Griffith exchange occurred 'only minutes'[62] before the plenipotentiaries had to catch their boats. De Valera wanted history to believe that after a full Cabinet meeting, lasting seven hours in all, an exchange between two of its members, not including himself, was the determinant in his not going to London. The truth is that he had wriggled out of going to London in the months before the talks even began, and he had no intention of allowing himself to be dragged into the vortex of their dying hours. For though the Brugha–Griffith aside was missed by the secretary to the meeting, Griffith's substantive contribution obviously made sufficient impact to be faithfully recorded. It made his intentions crystal clear:[63] 'Mr. Griffith would not take the responsibility of breaking with the Crown. When as many concessions as possible conceded, and when accepted by Craig, he would go before the Dail. The Dail was the body to decide for or against war.'

Collins had somewhat masked his hand during the uproar, but he had said enough to be recorded as being in 'substantial agreement' with Griffith and with Duggan, who had said he believed the Treaty to be England's last word and that he would not take the responsibility of saying 'No.' Collins said that the non-acceptance of the Treaty would be a gamble, as England could arrange a war in Ireland within a week. This left only Barton and Duffy opposed. If de Valera, who had picked the team, had been sincere in his protestations of fidelity to the Republic, it was at that juncture that he would finally have had to throw his weight into the scrum to counteract that of Collins, Duggan and Griffith. His presence in London would hardly have moved the British side, but it would at least have shown an acceptance of the responsibilities of leadership. Instead, with an eye to the record, he settled for the following aspirational conclusions to the Cabinet meeting:[64]

> (1) Delegates to carry out their original instructions with same powers.
> (2) Delegation to return and say that Cabinet won't accept Oath of Allegiance if not amended and to face the consequences, assuming that England will declare war.

(3) Decided unanimously that present Oath of Allegiance could not be subscribed to.

(4) Mr. Griffith to inform Mr. Lloyd George that the document could not be signed, to state that it is now a matter for the Dail, and to try to put the blame on Ulster.

(5) On a majority vote it was decided that the Delegation be empowered to meet Sir James Craig if they should think necessary. (Brugha and Stack voted against this.)

(6) *It was decided that the President would not join the Delegation in London at this stage of the Negotiations* [author's italics].

Whether de Valera intended (1) above to refer to the plenipotentiary powers which the Dail conferrred on the delegation, or to his own more restrictive 'Cecil' document, is not clear. What is certain is that in political terms the Charge of the Light Brigade had a better chance of success than had his so-called *'via media'*, the reintroduction of external association to the negotiations. The Irish were not going back primarily directed to say 'No' to the substantive evil of partition, but instead to strain after what was, by comparison, the gnat of the Oath.

On the way to the boat Collins complained to the friend who drove him, Tom Cullen: 'I've been there all day and I can't get them to say Yes or No whether we should sign or not'; and he repeated, not for the first time, that he did not know whether he was being instructed or confused from Dublin.[65] By the time he reached London he was so disgusted that he did not even accompany the others on their fruitless trip to Downing Street. This ended in ignominy when Duffy blurted out that the Irish difficulty lay in coming into the Empire. Predictably the Tory leader, Chamberlain, was first to react: 'That ends it,'[66] he cried, getting to his feet; the rest of the British side followed him in gathering up their papers and walking out. Instead of putting 'the blame on Ulster' for breaking up the conference, the Irish had blundering into allowing the rupture to come over Crown and Empire, the worst possible ground from the point of view of international opinion.

However, some deft-footed intermediacy by Jones got the talks restarted. Sufficient alterations on the Oath (in line with those sought by the IRB), trade and defence followed, to make it possible to argue that points (2), (3) and (4) were addressed. Collins later told the Dail:[67] '. . . there was a document there and Mr. Griffith said he would not sign that document and a different document was signed'. Certainly the alterations met the objections which the IRB had raised with Collins, at least to the extent that the Brotherhood subsequently supported him. And finally, on 5 December, as Griffith was making a last-ditch stand on Ulster, Lloyd George played his theatrical ace.

Having had to leave the negotiating table to rummage through his trousers to find the document, he triumphantly displayed the memorandum to which Griffith had given his assent before the Liverpool Conference and challenged him to keep his word that he would not let him down. 'With staggering emphasis'[68] Griffith rose to his feet and, shaking his pencil at Lloyd George, replied: 'I have never let a man down in my whole life and I never will.' He would sign and recommend the document to his countrymen, even though no one else did. There followed one of the more melodramatic moments in the history of the Anglo-Irish dialogue. One signature was not enough for Lloyd George. Everyone must sign, on both sides of the table. He stood up, histrionically holding a letter in each hand:[69]

I have to communicate with Sir James Craig tonight. Here are the alternative letters I have prepared, one enclosing Articles of Agreement reached by His Majesty's Government and yourselves, and the other saying that the Sinn Fein representatives refuse to come within the Empire. If I send this letter it is war, and war within three days. Which letter am I to send? Whichever letter you choose travels by special train to Holyhead, and by destroyer to Belfast. The train is waiting with steam up at Euston. Mr. Shakespeare is ready. If he is to reach Sir James Craig in time we must know your answer by 10 p.m. tonight. You have until then, but no longer, to decide whether you give peace or war to your country.

Lloyd George was, of course, fully aware of the divisions in the Irish camp. Following the Mansion House nit-pick he was able to inform the Cabinet that:[70] 'Mr. Michael Collins and Mr. Arthur Griffith were greatly disappointed at the rejection of the British proposals.' It is highly unlikely that his charade of 'war within three days' was directed at either. Rather it was for their benefit, to induce the de Valera-ites on the team to drop their opposition to signing. In the taxi from Downing Street Collins announced that he was going to do so. Duggan followed Collins' lead, and so eventually, after hours of anguished debate, did Barton and Duffy. They argued for so many hours, in fact, that Lloyd George had begun to have 'doubts as to whether we would see them again'. He based his hopes that he would on Michael Collins having as much moral courage as physical courage, 'a quality that brave men often lack'.[71] But Collins was not lacking in courage of any sort. At 2.30 a.m. on Tuesday, 6 December 1921 he duly turned up and put his name to the Treaty. Birkenhead remarked after signing, 'I may have signed my political death warant tonight.' Collins replied grimly: 'I may have signed my actual death-warrant.'[72] Griffith was equally pessimistic. After appending his signature, he spent the rest of the night walking up and down the hallway of the house in Hans Place in which he was staying, his head in his hands, refusing to touch either food or drink.[73]

Curiously, in what might be termed one of the few large-minded gestures he ever made in Collins' direction, de Valera did implicitly concede the agony of mind which signing the Treaty brought in its wake to the signatories: he allowed his biographers to quote from a *de profundis* letter which Collins wrote to a friend that sleepless night:[74]

When you have sweated, toiled, had mad dreams, hopeless nightmares, you find yourself in London's streets, cold and dank in the night air.

Think – what have I got for Ireland? Something which she has wanted these past seven hundred years. Will anyone be satisfied at the bargain? Will anyone? I tell you this – early this morning I signed my death warrant. I thought at the time how odd, how ridiculous – a bullet may just as well have done the job five years ago.

I believe Birkenhead may have said an end to his political life, with him it has been my honour to work.

These signatures are the first real step for Ireland. If people will only remember that – the first real step.

But the most important figure who would not see the signatures as constituting 'the first real step for Ireland' was Eamon de Valera himself. Much of the foregoing account of how and why the Treaty was signed has, of necessity, been *Hamlet* without the Prince. De Valera's was the shadowy, off-stage presence, not that of the starring player, the role in which he should have cast himself. Now, however, it becomes increasingly important to study a performance which he should not have given in a tragic drama for which he wrote much of the script.

14
A TELEPHONE CALL NOT TAKEN

SINCE THE END of November de Valera had occupied himself in driving
about the country, giving pep talks to units of the Army; he was
accompanied by an entourage which included Brugha, Mulcahy and
Mulcahy's aide-de-camp, Michael Rynne. It is less easy to discern any
military value in these excursions than it is to link them with his aborted
'New Army' proposals and with an attempt to etch himself in the mind's
eyes of listeners, and newspaper readers, as the 'living symbol of the
Republic' – a symbol clearly distinguishable from the compromisers who
had gone to London, and set atop the 'Rock of the Republic' from which
he 'never budged'.[1] He had some of the speeches which he made at the
time quoted approvingly in his biography:[2]

> He had said at the cabinet meeting that they were prepared to face the
> consequences – war or no war. To the people of Galway he said on December
> 4th:
> 'There are things, no matter what the alternative, that those who are charged
> with the direction of affairs in this country can never give up. When we started out
> in our programme, we knew what it meant, and we counted the cost. We are not
> going to quail now, even if it be certain that the full price of our freedom has to be
> paid.'

The clear-cut nature of the 'war or no war' reference to the Cabinet
meeting has, of course, to be contrasted with the state of irritated
confusion in which Collins had driven from the Mansion House only the
day before, complaining that he was unable to elicit a straight 'yes' or 'no'
as to whether he should sign. From Galway de Valera went on to Ennis,
where he told a muster of Volunteers that:[3] 'At any moment they might be
called upon by the national Government to stand by the principles they
held.' And the next day, 5 December (the date of Lloyd George's *coup de
théâtre* ultimatum), he was in Limerick, where he and Mrs Tom Clarke, the
widow of the 1916 leader, received the Freedom of the City. De Valera
said:[4] 'No offer will be accepted by the nation if that offer deprives us of
the essentials of freedom. Now, it is not a hard thing to know what are the
essentials of freedom. Freedom is a thing that you cannot cut in two – you
are either all free or you are not free. It is, therefore, for complete freedom
that we are struggling, and we tell everybody that this nation will continue
to struggle for its freedom until it has got the whole of it.'
That paragraph is reproduced in the official biography, but it does not

include other extracts from this highly significant speech which give a very strong indication that he had already made up his mind to reject the document which he expected to emanate from London. These, taken in conjunction with his coded references to the Oath, make one wonder whether it was intended to be read in Ireland or in Hans Place and Cadogan Gardens, the London addresses where the delegation was housed:

> When certain proposals were made on 20 July, we had no hesitation whatever about rejecting them. . . . We shall have as little hesitation in rejecting the new proposals if they are not what we want or what they pretend to be. This is no idle talk on my part, because what we say we mean. . . .
> . . . We may have years of terror. We had it before, but when it was all over they were as far away from achieving their main purpose as when they started – that of obtaining from the Irish people an oath of allegiance such as Yorkshire gave to their rulers in England.
> This is not Yorkshire. It is a separate nation, and they will never – not to the end – get from this nation allegiance to their rulers.

He spent that night in the spacious O'Mara home in Limerick, accompanied by his entourage and an 'honour guard' of thirty-two Volunteers.[5] Patricia Lavelle records an exchange around the family fireside which is of the utmost significance in explaining what de Valera was building up towards:[6]

> . . . everyone's thoughts were with the delegates in London. News should come in at any time . . . de Valera asked grandfather [Stephen O'Mara, father of James]:
> 'What did you really think of Parnell?'
> 'I'll tell you what I thought of him,' grandfather replied. 'If I were crossing over Sarsfield Bridge and Parnell said to me: "Jump into the river", I would jump.' And there they had it: – the tremendous personal magnetism of a leader, dead over a quarter of a century, was brought before them.

Unfortunately they had more. They had, though they did not realize it, the spectacle of de Valera, 'The Chief', preparing to don the mantle of the original 'Chief', Parnell, in Parnell's most Homeric, but also most arrogant and destructive, phase – that which preceded his death. For, after the O'Shea divorce case had caused Gladstone to issue an ultimatum to the Irish Parliamentary Party to the effect that he could not carry Home Rule while Parnell remained its leader, Parnell:[7]

> . . . skilfully seized on the sole aspect that might be expected to gain him public sympathy in Ireland, the submission of the party to Gladstone's 'dictation'. . . . Few more arrogant demands have ever been presented to a people than Parnell's insistence that Ireland abandon all chance of apparently imminent home rule simply to maintain his leadership. . . . His behaviour revealed the personality of a spoiled child. Ireland was his toy, and he arrogated the right to smash it at his whim. . . . Granted Parnell's belief that his leadership was the only thing that mattered, compromise spelled defeat.

De Valera was about to react to Lloyd George's 'dictation' exactly as Parnell had done vis-à-vis Gladstone twenty-five years earlier. Unlike Parnell, de Valera was to live through his petulant paroxysm, but in so doing he dealt his colleagues and his country some terrible, lasting wounds. His party was still sitting at the fireside when, in the small hours of the morning, the telephone rang with the news for which the O'Mara household had been agog. It was Gearoid O'Sullivan, a member of GHQ, to inform the Chief of Staff that a Treaty had been signed. De Valera, however, continued as he had with Griffith a few days earlier in Kenilworth Square, and refused to become involved personally. Incredibly enough, although the future of Ireland had just been decided, he would not come to the telephone when invited to do so by Mulcahy.[8] He withheld this important detail when writing to McGarrity shortly afterwards:[9] 'On Monday night in Limerick I heard over the telephone that some agreement had been reached, and I felt like throwing my hat in the air. I felt certain, on account of Griffith's undertaking, that our proposals had been accepted. I was in the same high spirits on Tuesday until about 7.30 p.m. when the text of the Treaty as signed was put in my hands. . . .'

Presumably the description of the Cabinet meeting given on pp.273–6 exonerates the biographer from any further comment on the veracity of the comment about 'Griffith's undertaking', but there is no escape from pronouncing on the account which de Valera authorized in his biography. It is a blank lie. Under a photograph of the sombre group on the steps of the O'Mara home, showing a grim-faced de Valera, seemingly very far removed from any inclination to throw his hat in the air, and Brugha apparently even less so, the caption reads: 'De Valera photographed in Limerick on the morning of 6 December, 1921. Unbeknown to him, the Peace Treaty had been signed in London.' The text also furthers a false version of events:[10]

> Next morning in Limerick the first news appeared cheerful. As the President left for the railway station he was told that a telephone message had been received from Dublin saying that a treaty had been signed. His immediate reaction was one of joy and surprise. He had assumed all along that the delegates would carry out their instructions and sign no agreement that had not been submitted to Dublin in its final form. . . . Under some lucky circumstances the British must have collapsed. 'I did not think they would give in so soon,' he said.

There are differing accounts of the journey back to Dublin. In the Rynne family it is told that, on hearing that Mrs Tom Clarke was on the train, de Valera left his State Coach and went to sit with her, later sending for Brugha so that Mulcahy and Rynne were left sitting by themselves in the official coach. 'The civil war was planned on that train,' was a frequently overheard comment in the Rynne household.[11] Patricia Lavelle's account[12] does not mention de Valera leaving the State Coach, but does say that Mulcahy and Rynne sat apart from him. Obviously, whatever the truth about 'planning the civil war', the split which would shortly sunder the nation over the Treaty was to be seen in microcosm on that train journey. As the train left Limerick station a stop-press was being cried along the streets, giving the news that the Treaty had been signed.[13] It seems inconceivable that similar editions were not available in Dublin also when the train got in at 2.30 in the afternoon. But de Valera's authorized account[14] is that he drove through the city to 53 Kenilworth Square for lunch and then motored through Dublin and Bray to Greystones, where he visited his family 'for a few hours', after which he drove back to Dublin, where he was to preside at a Dante commemoration ceremony in the Mansion House, beginning at 7.30 p.m. – all without knowing what had been signed.

At the Mansion House, however, he met Brugha and Stack, who, not surprisingly, had with them a copy of the *Evening Mail* which had been available on every street corner in Dublin for several hours. He asked them 'Any news?' and in reply was shown the paper. It was then and only then, he would have us believe, that he first learned the terms of the Oath. Stack left a memoir of the occasion which de Valera had included in his biography:[15]

> He donned his [university] gown and was about to lead the way into the Round Room when who should arrive but Mr. E. J. Duggan and Mr. Desmond Fitzgerald. Duggan reached the President an envelope which the President ignored. Duggan asked him to read the contents. 'What should I read it for?' 'Oh', said Duggan, 'it is arranged that the thing be published in London and Dublin simultaneously at 8 o'clock, and it is near that hour now.' 'What', said the President, 'to be published whether I have seen it or not – whether I approve or not.' 'Oh well, that's the arrangement,' Duggan replied. The President took up the envelope, opened, glanced over the contents. ... At that moment he appeared to me to be an almost broken man.

However, another witness to the occasion has left a sharply contrasting account of what transpired. Pieras Beaslai says that when Duggan and Fitzgerald arrived they found de Valera:[16]

> ... in a towering rage. When they handed him the copy of the Treaty he laid it aside, declaring that he had no time to read it, and turned round to discuss whether he would wear his Chancellor's robe or not, muttering some remark about 'soon being back at teaching'. He presided at the Dante Commemoration without having read the Treaty. I was one of the speakers, and sat near him, and I was astonished at the state of suppressed emotion under which he seemed to labour. And all this time he had not taken the trouble to study the Treaty. Apparently the fact that a Treaty had been signed, without being first referred to him, was the source of his agitation. The nature of the Treaty, affecting the fate of the people of Ireland, was of only secondary interest to him.

A letter which de Valera himself wrote bears out Beaslai's opinion of the 'source of his agitation'. He told McGarrity that the fact that he was not consulted before the delegates finally signed might be considered as:[17] 'an act of disloyalty to their President and to their colleagues in the Cabinet such as is probably without parallel in history. They not merely signed the document, but in order to make the *fait accompli* doubly secure, they published it hours before the President or their colleagues saw it.'

However, as he was speedily to find out, whatever his estimate of his own importance as indicated by his use of the royal 'we', a majority of the Cabinet did not regard the signing as 'unparalleled disloyalty'. On the morning after the Dante commemoration he convened a meeting of the Cabinet members available in Dublin, Brugha, Stack and Cosgrave, and informed them that he intended to sack the three in London: Barton, Collins and Griffith. He knew that Brugha and Stack would support this action out of bitterness towards Collins and Griffith, and he expected that Cosgrave would do so out of meekness and affection for him.

Cosgrave had suffered a nervous reaction to the horrors of Bloody Sunday and he had taken temporary physical and spiritual refuge in the black soutane of the Christian Brothers, who ran an industrial school in Glencree in the Wicklow Mountains. It was this absence which led to Kevin O'Higgins, who would one day become the strong man of Irish politics, being first brought into the Dail Cabinet. On his return to the Dail, de Valera told Frank Gallagher,[18] Cosgrave became 'nearer to me in a personal sense than anybody in the Cabinet'. He put Cosgrave's attachment to him on a par with that of Frank Aiken, who by the time of the conversation with Gallagher had become so intensely devoted to de Valera that, in the homely idiom of a Cabinet colleague of both, he was said to believe that 'the sun shone out of Dev.'s arse'![19] Cosgrave was the one who called at de Valera's office to take him to lunch and performed other small, necessary services such as ensuring that he got his hair cut. Accordingly, feeling certain of adequate support, de Valera now confidently drafted an order dismissing the plenipotentiaries.

However, to his astonishment Cosgrave objected, saying that they should not be condemned unheard. De Valera decided 'to hold my hand'. He told Gallagher that he did so because of 'my sense of natural justice'. There was also, he conceded, the fact 'that Cosgrave was the 4th of seven'. De Valera had suddenly realized that he had misjudged both man and situation, and was now facing the unexpected possibility of being outvoted in Cabinet. As his biography states laconically:[20] 'Caution was necessary' – but only caution insofar as getting his own way within Cabinet was concerned. De Valera now proceeded to act with an enormous lack of caution concerning the likely effect of his words and actions on public order. A full Cabinet meeting was called for 8 December, but without waiting for it de Valera drafted the following statement for publication:[21] 'In view of the nature of the proposed Treaty with Great Britain, President de Valera has sent an urgent summons to the members of the Cabinet in London to report at once, so that a full Cabinet decision may be taken. The hour of meeting is fixed for 12 o'clock noon tomorrow. A meeting of the Dail will be summoned later.'

Desmond Fitzgerald, whose efforts hitherto had been devoted to telling the world that there were no differences in Sinn Fein, was surprised at the tone of the statement and suggested that: 'This might be altered, Mr. President. It reads as if you were opposed to the settlement.'

De Valera replied grimly: 'And that's the way I intend it to read. Publish it as it is.'

On the way out, Fitzgerald whispered to Stack in amazement: 'I did not think that he was against this kind of settlement before we went over to London.'

Stack replied: 'He's dead against it now anyway. That's enough.'[22]

There was, of course, no need to publish this statement. The public, if it considered the question at all, would naturally have assumed that there would have been a Cabinet meeting to discuss the issue. De Valera was deliberately beginning a campaign of opposition to the Treaty – although it was at a far greater stage of assuredness than was Home Rule – on the same lines as Parnell's ill-fated campaign. The difference was that, unlike Parnell, he was not spearheading a political civil war but was heading towards an actual war, involving death and destruction.

The Cabinet meeting was an angry rerun of the 3 December meeting: nit-pick Mark II. A source sympathetic to de Valera, Erskine Childers, has left an account of the proceedings.[23] De Valera centred his attack on the fact that the delegates had not referred to him before signing. He claimed again that he would have gone to London had it not been for Griffith's promise to consult before signature. And he also brought forward the fact that he had replied in the affirmative to Childers' query as to whether the first three clauses of the Agreement should be scrapped. He waxed eloquent on the subject of his efforts on behalf of external association, which would have satisfied those who thought like Cathal Brugha. Summing up, he charged that everything had been given away, without effort [sic], without consultation and without permission.

It was Barton who made the most spirited counter-attack. Childers noted that he 'strongly reproached the President', blaming him for giving rise to the whole situation through his 'vacillation' in refusing to go to the talks himself. But neither charge nor counter-charge produced any concession towards harmony. Kevin O'Higgins – present, but not voting, as Cosgrave's understudy – made the most constructive point of the meeting. He disliked the Treaty and felt it should not have been signed, but the fact that it had been signed created a situation in which unity was imperative. However, de Valera had no intention of working towards unity. After the meeting ended he surprised Childers by telling him privately that he intended to rely on 'extremist support' to carry his opposition to the Treaty. As we shall see, he subsequently sought to implement this policy and, having lived to realize its folly, sought to rewrite history so as to convey the opinion that his concern was to seek agreement. Frank Gallagher was a principal vehicle for the revisionism. The following is an account by him of the 8 December Cabinet meeting which took place in a room adjoining one in which Gallagher was briefing journalists:[24] 'Just as the room filled with enquiring journalists, came angry voices. . . . To every question from the pressmen I gave a voluble answer. They did not perceive the raised voices, which in my ears were again and again an orchestration to what I was saying. . . . As de Valera struggled a few feet from them, to draw back a united Cabinet to solid ground, they were as yet unaware of any division.' Kevin O'Higgins gave a different version, however:[25]

> So hasty, so precipitate, so eager was he to take action in this matter that the Minister of Local Government and myself had the very greatest difficulty in persuading him to wait until the delegates arrived before he hurled a bombshell that split the greatest political movement, the solidest the world has ever seen. He waited for twenty-four hours and the next day the fatal Cabinet meeting was held. Even some people who were not entitled to speak at that meeting spoke to the President and implored him to consider what he was doing and to consider the consequences of his act but we might as well have tried to hold the West Wind.

The hurling of the 'bombshell' occurred as follows. De Valera eventually lost his battle to have the Treaty rejected out of hand. Barton, Collins, Cosgrave and Griffith voted to have the issue decided, not by the inner Cabinet of seven, but by the Dail, which had appointed the plenipotentiaries. De Valera, Brugha and Stack were in the minority. However, in the course of a statement which gives a remarkable indication of the state of his ego at the time, de Valera subsequently lied to the Dail about what happened. He said:[26]

> There is no question of majority rule in the Cabinet, none whatever. . . . I do not ask for the resignation of the three plenipotentiaries whose actions were not, I hold, on account of the undertaking given, in accordance with the Cabinet decision. I did not do it in order not to intensify and split. No man is going to change my views, they can change my position, but not the whole of Ireland will change the opinion which I will express. Everyone has the same right. No one is going to bind me here by majority rule. . . .

In other words, he reacted to his reverse in Cabinet exactly as he had at the Republican Convention in Chicago. If he could not get his way, then he would do what he could to prevent anyone else getting theirs. Accordingly, before the Dail met (on 14 December) he indulged in one of the most destructive exercises in megaphone diplomacy in recorded Irish history by issuing the following 'Proclamation':[27]

TO THE IRISH PEOPLE
A Chairde Gaedheal [My Friends]

You have seen in the public Press the text of the proposed Treaty with Great Britain.

The terms of this agreement are in violent conflict with the wishes of the majority of this nation as expressed freely in the successive elections during the last three years.

I feel it my duty to inform you immediately that I cannot recommend the acceptance of this Treaty, either to Dail Eireann or the country. In this attitude I am supported by the Ministers of Home Affairs and Defence.

A public session of Dail Eireann is being summoned for Wednesday next at 11 o'clock. I ask the people to maintain during the interval the same discipline as heretofore. The members of the Cabinet, though divided in opinions, are prepared to carry on the public services as usual.

The Army as such is, of course, not affected by the political situation and continues under the same orders and control. The great test of our people has come. Let us face it worthily without bitterness and above all, without recriminations. There is a definite constitutional way of resolving our differences – let us not depart from it, and let the conduct of the Cabinet in this matter be an example to the whole nation.

The Cabinet's conduct did set an example to the nation, of the wrong sort. Obviously different groups had different expectations of the Treaty – expectations which de Valera, with his concentration on other activities such as his telegrammed joust with Lloyd George and his attempt to wrest the army from Collins, had done little to shape or diminish since the Truce. The die-hard republicans of the Brugha stamp were bound to be bitterly disappointed with the Oath and the enshrinement of partition. But their numbers would have been balanced by those who had supported the old Irish Parliamentary Party and now saw the Treaty confer far wider powers than envisaged under Home Rule: fiscal autonomy; an Irish Parliament free of Westminster representation; and a native Army, civil service and police force responsible to that Parliament. And for the ordinary man in the street, or field, these appeared in the welcome light of a famous victory, whereby the Black and Tans would depart and a faltering peace would be copper-fastened.

De Valera's Proclamation was the first major indication that the peace was far from copper-fastened. Beaslai wrote of it that:[28]

It is hard to speak with patience of the insane irresponsibility of a man who, entrusted with the leadership of the Irish people in a great moment of crisis in their history, could fling such a torch in the powder magazine. ... A dignified statement showing how far the Treaty fell short of national aspirations, would have steadied the country and solidified the national position. But de Valera was evidently incapable of rising to the height of a great national occasion.

When he wrote, Beaslai had no knowledge of the contents of Childers' diary. He did not realize that de Valera *was* rising to the occasion – in his own fashion. He was preparing if necessary, like Parnell, to smash Ireland like a toy in pursuit of 'extremist support' with which to repay Collins and

Griffith for presenting him with a *fait accompli*. By way of indication of the delicate balance in which peace lay as he commenced this operation it should be noted that, in the week after his issuing of the Proclamation alone, several acts of violence occurred. These included attacks on the RIC and the British Army in which two men were killed and four injured.[29] There was a raid on Michael Collins' office,[30] obviously with inside knowledge, in which money and documents were taken. And as the Dail debate on the Treaty opened, deputies were threatened by the Cork IRA that if they voted for the Treaty they would be regarded as having committed treason.[31] Beaslai's powder keg allusion was not overdrawn.

De Valera himself conceded on the first day of the Dail debate on the issue, 14 December 1921, that if a plebiscite were held the people would have accepted the Treaty.[32] But concessions to truth and reality were not high on his agenda for the course of the debate. Even though the Cabinet had voted in favour of the Treaty, he refused to have it placed before the Dail as a Cabinet measure. Instead he tried to diminish its status by insisting on Griffith, as Chairman of the delegation, proposing it for ratification. Then he opened the public session[33] by saying in Irish that he would like to have delivered his entire speech in it but that, as he did not have sufficient grasp of the language to do so, he was switching to English. However, in English he opened by saying: 'Some of the members do not know Irish, I think, and consequently what I say will be in English.' He continued his attack on the same moral plateau, by reading out the 'Cecil' document he had presented to the delegates but not their credentials from the Dail; he thus clearly suggested that the delegates had exceeded their instructions. Collins managed to check-mate this move by reading out the credentials, which showed that they did have power to sign a Treaty and refer it back to the Dail, as they were now doing. However, against the objections of Collins and Griffith de Valera succeeded in getting the discussion transferred to private session on the plea that misunderstandings could best be cleared up that way. In reality, he had twin objectives: first, to have the press excluded so that the public were prevented from making their feelings known; and second, to attempt to browbeat the Assembly into accepting a document of his own which he wished to have substituted for the Treaty and resubmitted to the British.[34]

In all, the debate occupied thirteen days of private and public session. De Valera's opening remarks maintained the pretence that he knew nothing about the signing of the Treaty until he got to the Dante commemoration, and clearly indicated that the lèse-majesté involved in not consulting him was the worst feature of the whole affair:[35] 'I have only one thing to say. One thing I feel hurt about, with respect to this delegation, and that is that a Treaty was signed in London, and when I heard of it first the signatures were appended to it. As I came in the door of the Mansion House I was given a signed copy of the document, and it had already been given to the Press in London.' He had in fact a great deal more than 'one thing' to say, attempting to dominate the proceedings both by frequent interruptions and by speaking at wearisome length. The number of pages in the Dail records taken up by his contributions is almost double that of Collins and Griffith combined: a total of thirty-nine pages for his to twenty for theirs. He made 250 interruptions, relying on his prestige to ride roughshod over the procedures of debate. In addition to this onslaught, he also mounted a campaign outside the chamber. Deputies were called in and subjected to pressure to get them to vote his way, and he made another determined effort to capture the Army GHQ. But when this was mentioned in the Dail by Mulcahy[36] he said flatly: 'I did not discuss the Treaty.' He told the Dail that he had called the meeting 'as my duty to know the strength and to find out the fighting strength of the army'.

Nobody thought to ask him why he did not think to enquire into the strength of the Army in the days before the Treaty was signed, when he was engaged in going about the country visiting Army units in the company of an entourage that included the best-informed men on the subject in Ireland. However, he did admit that he had asked the officers if they would be in favour of continuing with the fighting or not, and that it 'was only in that particular way that the question of the Treaty or anything like it came in'. It emerged in the course of the Dail exchanges that GHQ had voted with one exception in favour of ratifying the Treaty.[37] He wrote to McGarrity a few days later:[38]

> . . . MC [Collins] had got the IRB machine working. . . . It was a case of Cohalan and his machine over again. . . . Tho' the rank and file of the army is right, the Headquarters Staff clean gone wrong – a part of the machine. Curse secret societies! . . . I have been tempted several times to take drastic action, as I would be entitled to legally, but then the army is divided and the people wouldn't stand for it, and nobody but the enemy would win if I took it.

Decoded, that 'Curse secret societies' means 'Curse Michael Collins'. There appears to be little doubt that, had he succeeded in his New Army manoeuvre and not miscalculated over Cosgrave, de Valera planned to put himself in a position where he could take action if he wanted against the 'scapegoats' he had sent to London. He seems to have had it in mind to rise from the ashes of the Treaty controversy with some compromise of his own which would have both discredited the delegates and left him with the credit for making the best of a bad job. However, it was an unrealistic expectation and, frustrated on all fronts, he forgot about what the people would or would not stand for and embarked on a course that only the enemies of Ireland could have rejoiced in.

Divorced from the tension of the moment and the effect of his mesmeric personality, his logic during the talkathon does not come across impressively in print:[39]

> You will all admit that my duty would have been were it not for another point of

289

view to have been with the delegation. I was captaining a team and I felt that the team should have played with me to the last and that I should have got the last chance which I felt would have put us over and we might have crossed the bar in my opinion at the high tide. They rushed before the tide got to the top and they almost foundered the ship; and as I was captain I have a right to show that it was not through my fault as captain that it has been done. It was a *fait accompli*. . . .

Collins' comment on this was 'A captain who sent his crew to sea, and tried to direct operations from dry land.'[40] De Valera made use of woolly, sentimental-sounding language to cloak a steely purpose:

It is possible to get what will really be such as we can accept. There are differences that may be regarded as shadows, but they are more than shadows – the things that matter for us. If to the Crown and His Majesty's Ministers in this country these things are not shadows for them; but the Irish Army and Irish Ministers if they are mere shadows, why should they be grasping for the shadows, and why should not we? I wanted to clear these shadows because they mean an awful lot. We have the country supporting definite proposals. It will be the mischief to get the English out of the position they are in.

In place of the 'mischief', the Treaty, which he conceded that the country was supporting, he had his own document – another version of the external association proposals which the British had again rejected on 4 December. Collins termed this Document No. 2, and the name stuck. Document No. 2 (which can be compared with the Treaty in the Appendices to this book) omitted two things: any mention of an Oath, or of the word 'republic'. It provided that 'for the purposes of the Association, Ireland shall recognise his Britannic Majesty as head of the Association'. On partition he tried to have his cake and eat it. Paragraph 17 of Document No. 2 contained what he termed a 'declaratory phrase' denying 'the right of any part of Ireland to be excluded from the supreme authority of the National Parliament and Government'. But the rest of the paragraph, to say nothing of numbers 18 to 23, made it abundantly clear that partition was being recognized out of a 'sincere regard for internal peace, and in the desire to bring no force or coercion to bear upon any substantial part of the province of Ulster whose inhabitants may now be opposed to the acceptance of the National Authority. . .'.

He admitted that the other clauses relating to Northern Ireland were 'practically the same as the Treaty provisions,'[41] and that these contained an 'explicit recognition of the right on the part of Irishmen to secede from Ireland'. As far as he was concerned, the difficulty was 'not the Ulster question . . . this is a fight between Ireland and England. I want to eliminate the Ulster question out of it.' In other words, the substantive issue of the partition of Ireland was to be removed from the debate so that he could concentrate minds on the wrong which had been done in presenting him with a *fait accompli* and the necessity for correcting this by getting external association re-entered on the lists, via Document No. 2.

But neither the Collins faction nor the 'extremist support' which he sought to attract from the ranks of the IRA was impressed with his brainchild. Collins pointed out that, by giving Ireland the same status, the Dominions would have a vested interest in preventing Britain from setting a precedent for Imperial meddling. But there was no Dominion protection in Document No. 2. Nor was there any 'extremist support' forthcoming for a document that appeared so similar to the Treaty. De Valera was forced to concede this similarity himself:[42] 'It is right to say that there will be very little difference in practice between what I may call the proposals received and what you will have under what I propose. There is very little in practice but there is that big thing that you are consistent and that you recognise yourself as a separate independent State and you associate in an honourable manner with another group.'

He justified being prepared to go to war for such small differences as follows: 'I say that small difference makes all the difference. This fight lasts all through the centuries and I would be willing to win that little sentimental thing that would satisfy the aspirations of the country.' But he undercut even this waffling justification by admitting, almost in the same breath,[43] that there was 'only one snag' in satisfying the 'national aspirations of the country' – the Ulster question. The unease that this sort of rhetoric generated amongst some deputies may be gauged from the words of Sean Milroy:[44] 'I say that the man who asks the Irish nation to go to war and to plunge the hopes of the nation into distress and chaos on the difference between these two documents – I think that man will stand condemned at the bar of history as having committed one of [the] most gigantic blunders Ireland has known.'

And Padraic O'Maille described the de Valera document as being like:[45] 'looking for a bit of glow in the rainbow, but when you look for the rainbow you won't find the glow'. Apart from the unreality of going to war over the differences between the Treaty and Document No. 2, there was the severely practical question of the ability to wage or withstand war. Brugha assured the Dail that: 'We are in a very much better position [militarily] than we were when the Truce started . . . we are very much better off militarily than we have ever been before.'[46] However, this drew a strong corrective from Sean McEoin, a figure whose bravery was accepted as being beyond question on all sides of the house. He said:[47] 'I want everyone to realise what we are going in for, because I hold we have a duty to the civil population. . . . It [the Army] may be stronger in some points. In point of members it is a bit stronger – in training it is a bit stronger. . . . I have charge of four thousand men. . . . But of that four thousand I have a rifle for every fifty . . . and I may add that there is about as much ammunition as would last them about fifty minutes for that one rifle.'

McEoin added to the impact of this statement, which neither Brugha nor de Valera attempted to contradict, by pointing out that the Irish intelligence network was now exposed: 'They know now every officer and man from one end of Ireland to the other.' In the circumstances, even de Valera had to concede that his hobbyhorse would not trot. When the debate went public on 19 December, having achieved nothing but the generation of animosities in private, he attempted to have Document No. 2 withdrawn and tried to impose a ban on its discussion. It had seemingly dawned on him that 'the living symbol of the Republic' was in fact advocating a compromise, in which Brugha and Stack concurred. Griffith understood what he was doing and put a telling question to him:[48] 'Am I to understand, Sir, that the document we discussed at the Private Session is to be withheld from the Irish people?' However, he got no satisfaction at that stage, and the proceedings opened with Griffith proposing and Sean McEoin seconding the ratification of the Treaty.

It was now 19 December and the Treaty had been signed on the 6th. In the meantime Sinn Fein had to all intents and purposes divided into two parties. Around de Valera were grouped most of the women deputies: Mary MacSwiney, sister of the hunger striker Terence MacSwiney; Tom Clarke's widow, Kathleen; Padraig Pearse's mother, Margaret; and Countess Markievicz. Some Dublin wit dubbed his following 'the women and Childers party', but there was little else to joke about. Outside the chamber, division and disorder were spreading throughout the country and in the North a separate, sectarian horror story was rapidly building up. It was hardly an ideal backdrop for de Valera to argue, in public, for rejection of the Treaty in the following terms:[49]

> I am against this Treaty because it does not reconcile Irish national aspirations with association with the British Government. . . . I am against this Treaty, not because I am a man of war but because I am a man of peace. I am against this Treaty because it will not end the centuries of conflict between the two nations of Great Britain and Ireland.
>
> [The Treaty is] absolutely inconsistent with our position; it gives away Irish independence; it brings us into the British Empire; it acknowledges the head of the British Empire, not merely as the head of an association but as the direct monarch of Ireland, as the source of executive authority in Ireland.

And he wound up by making a revealing use of a famous comment by Parnell. Approval of the Treaty would be:[50] 'presuming to set bounds on the onward march of a nation'. Either by accident or design, he made no reference whatsoever to partition. Collins did. He said[51] he had intended basing his speech on a comparison of the Treaty with Document No. 2, but that he respected the President's wish for it not to be referred to; he went on to base his case on the merits of the Treaty only:

> In my opinion it gives us freedom, not the ultimate freedom that all nations desire and develop to, but the freedom to achieve it. . . . We have stated we would not coerce the North-East. We have stated it officially. I stated it publicly in Armagh and nobody has found fault with me. What was the use of talking big phrases

about not agreeing to the partition of our country. Surely we recognise the North-East corner does exist, and surely our intention was that we should take such steps as would lead to mutual understanding.

He did score one important debating point – by reading out the correspondence between de Valera and Lloyd George which had led to the negotiations. Pointing out that Lloyd George had made it clear that they would not be negotiating on a republic, he said: 'If we all stood on the recognition of the Irish Republic as a prelude to any conference we could very easily have said so, and there would be no Conference.'

His speech accelerated the swing of public opinion towards the Treaty. The Dail recessed for Christmas on 22 December and resumed on 3 January. In that time twenty-four county councils passed resolutions supporting the Treaty, and the press was solidly in favour. The irony of the strength of the opposition to the document within the Dail lay in the fact that its radicalism, representative of the country at large, was in no small measure due to the type of 'forward' candidate whom Collins had been instrumental in foisting on the Sinn Fein ticket while de Valera was in jail in 1918. The great swing to Sinn Fein that year had been influenced by peace, not war – the fact that the public perceived the party as having kept its menfolk from war. Now, three years later, having stood by Sinn Fein in war, the people were again looking to the party for peace. But, obvious though this was, de Valera continued on his Parnellite course.

After the recess de Valera returned to the Dail hoping to capitalize on its militant spirit with a reworked version of Document No. 2. Even close friends like Dr Farnan[52] warned him against this course, pointing out that the country could not understand the subtle differences between the Treaty and what he proposed. During the recess the Labour Party had worked out a method, which Collins supported, of dealing with these differences. The idea was that the Dail would pass legislation enabling a Provisional Government to be formed as a Committee of the Dail. This Government would then draw up a Constitution – as would be required in the event of the Treaty's being ratified. However, the Constitution would not derive its authority from the Crown, but would be an autochthonous affair deriving from the Irish people themselves. The Oath could be sworn to by the republican-minded in the knowledge that they were swearing allegiance to the Free State's Constitution, as drawn up by Irishmen. But de Valera rejected this compromise.[53] In fact, as Dr Dwyer points out, he rejected it twice. First, 'de Valera dismissed the idea because, he said, Griffith and Collins would not accept it. When they did he rejected it anyway.'[54] Instead he attempted a filibuster by trying to have his revised version of Document No. 2 accepted as an amendment to Griffith's motion that the Treaty be adopted, even though he had agreed at the commencement of the debate that there should be only one motion before the house – for, or against, the Treaty. Had he succeeded with his amendment ploy everyone in the Dail could have replied to the amendment, even though they had already spoken.

However, Griffith scuppered the manoeuvre by pointing out that Document No. 2 was now Document No. 3 because de Valera had substantially changed it from the version which the Dail had argued over fruitlessly in private session.[55] De Valera tried to impose his will on the Dail as he had done with GHQ, flying into a passion and telling the stunned deputies: 'I am responsible for the proposals and the House will *have* to decide on them. *I am going to choose my own procedure.*' An icy Griffith recalled those present to the fact that they were supposed to be democrats: 'I submit it is not in the competence of the President to choose his own procedure. This is either a constitutional body or it is not. If it is an autocracy let you say so and we will leave it.' De Valera blustered on: 'In answer to that I am going to propose an amendment in my own terms. It is for the House to decide whether they will take it or not.' Fortunately one of those sitting behind him tapped him on the shoulder and calmed him down, and the Dail went into recess. But his arrogance was to cost him dearly. Griffith decided that he had had enough of the 'Now you can see it, now you can't' Document No. 2 for which the nation was supposed to be prepared to contemplate war and, unknown to de Valera, issued it to the press.

Unaware that this was happening, de Valera sought to increase the public temperature by issuing a statement of his own to the press – another of his Proclamations to the people of Ireland:[56] 'Do not enter upon a compact which in your hearts you know can never be kept in sincerity and in truth. No matter how worthy, they are neither good friends to Ireland nor to England nor humanity who advise you to take that course. Be bold enough to say No to those who ask you to misrepresent yourselves.' And by way of practising what he preached, that night he also showed himself bold enough to say 'No' to a further initiative based on the Labour Party's peace formula. Sean T. O'Ceallaigh used the idea to invite a group of pro- and anti-Treaty deputies to his house, where they worked out a proposal that, apart from holding out a prospect of peace, demonstrated the enormous respect in which de Valera was held. Eight of the deputies – Liam Mellows abstained – 'respectfully' suggested that de Valera 'might advise abstention from voting against the Treaty'. The eight gave as their reason for making this proposal the hope that: 'the services of President de Valera be preserved for the nation'. The idea was that he would continue as President of the Dail but 'The Provisional Government would be permitted to function by the Dail, and derive its powers from the Dail.' The intention was that the Dail would exercise those powers to continue in control of the Army and other services. Both Griffith and Collins accepted the plan; not so Parnell II. Having secured the pro-Treaty acquiescence:[57] 'The whole nine Deputies then waited on de Valera, who when he received it [the Peace Plan], flew into a passion, swore, and refused to accept the terms of the agreement, again urging the acceptance of his own pet document.'

Moreover, in the same way that he had tried to prevent Document No. 2 from being discussed when it did not suit him, he and Brugha used their influence[58] to prevent the document being discussed by the Dail, even in private session. Joseph McGuinness, one of the pro-Treaty deputies, said afterwards:[59] 'The people on this side literally went on their knees to President de Valera to try and preserve the unity of the country.' A combination of his performance in the Dail the previous day, and of Griffith's revealing his 'pet document' to the paper, caused the *Freeman's Journal* to mount a journalistic onslaught aimed at bringing de Valera to *his* knees the morning after the O'Ceallaigh-led initiative.[60] The reporter who had covered the Dail said that de Valera seemed to be:

> . . . arrogating to himself the rights of an autocrat. It seems as though he wanted to wreck the Dail before a vote could be taken and then carry the devastating split as far as his influence could reach, throughout the length and breadth of the land. The worst disaster which has befallen Ireland since the Union is imminent, and can only be averted by the deputies who love their country more than they love Mr. de Valera, refusing to share his terrible responsibility.

By now the split in the Dail was clearly mirrored in the country as a whole. The big battalions – the Church, business, the bigger farmers, the press and most of the senior Army officers – were on the side of the Treaty. However, the power of the antis was not negligible. Sections of the IRA, particularly in Cork, were solidly anti-Treaty, and prominent IRA men like the commanders of the Southern Divisions, Liam Lynch and Ernie O'Malley, were opposed. In GHQ figures like Rory O'Connor, Liam Mellows, Sean Russell and Jim O'Donovan were anti-Treaty. However, it is one of the great 'ifs' of Irish history as to whether anything more than a relatively minor faction fight would have developed had de Valera not thrown his enormous prestige on to their side. His intervention brought incalculable political credibility to the militarists. And, selfless and sincere though many of the Republican dissidents were, de Valera's subsequent history of U-turns on everything he professed during the civil war era places him in history's pigeonholes marked 'pique', 'power struggle' and 'anti-Collins' rather than 'idealist'.

It was not a straightforward struggle between the White Knights (Collins and Griffith) on one side and the Black Knight (de Valera) on the other. Collins in particular had deliberately set out to bring war to Ireland out of a cold, ruthless calculation that the country ultimately stood to benefit more from war than from peace. And his actual conduct, as opposed to his fair words, on wooing the Protestants of North-east Ulster could be regarded as being equally ruthless and even more deceitful. But he and Griffith were acutely conscious of how Home Rule had slipped through the fingers of Irish leaders at other turning-point moments: the first playing of the Orange card, when Gladstone went for Home Rule in 1886; and its successful replay on the eve of World War I. Partition and the Oath were bitter pills, but now they had something tangible – more than Griffith, in particular, had once dreamed possible in his days of advocating dual monarchy for Ireland. And Collins, more than any man alive, was aware of how much of what had been achieved had come about through bluff, publicity and a now useless intelligence network, rather than by military might. In a fresh military confrontation with England, his 'stepping stone' would be too slippery with blood to stand on. The larger forces of the country realized this and the *Freeman's Journal* echoed that feeling, albeit in extravagant and intemperate language. Its political reporter's comments were accompanied by an editorial which said, amongst other things, that de Valera had made 'a criminal attempt to divide the Irish nation'. It said that Document No. 2 contained everything that was allegedly wrong with the Treaty, and that Erskine Childers was the real author of the document. The *Journal* termed it 'the curse of Ireland at this moment that its unity should be broken by such a man acting under the advice of an Englishman who has achieved fame in the British Intelligence Service'. It said: 'When the fight was on Mr. de Valera and Mr. Childers fell accidentally into the hands of the military. They were immediately released. That was the time there was £10,000 for the corpse of Michael Collins. The Irish people must stand up, and begin their freedom by giving their fate into the hands of their own countrymen.'

De Valera replied to this slur on his nationality by defending both his proposals and his background:[61]

> Now, I have definitely a policy, not some pet scheme of my own, but something that I know from four years' experience in my position – and I have been brought up amongst the Irish people. I was reared in a labourer's cottage here in Ireland. I have not lived solely amongst the intellectuals. The first fifteen years of my life that formed my character were lived amongst Irish people down in Limerick; therefore I know what I am talking about; when ever I wanted to know what the Irish people wanted, I had only to examine my own heart and it told me straight off what the Irish people wanted.

On this occasion, 6 January, he had decided that what the people wanted was for him to resign. He intended, he said, to offer himself for re-election; if successful, he would elect a new Cabinet and throw out the Treaty. It was a calculated ploy, which flew directly in the face of public opinion, to shift the debate from the issue of the Treaty against Document No. 2 to that of his own enormous popularity. In the private session held that morning he had refused to countenance either the O'Ceallaigh compromise formula or the withdrawal of his resignation, even when warned that this would mean:[62] 'a terrible disaster that would drive us back farther than we have been for one hundred years'. His reply was: 'There is no use in discussing it. The whole of Ireland will not get me to be a national apostate and I am not going to connive at setting up in Ireland another government for England.'

Behaviour like that in the situation of crisis that was then building up throughout Ireland makes it impossible to resist the conclusion of one of his biographers, Dr Dwyer, who, recalling his attitude towards the Cohalan resolution at the Republican Convention in Chicago, adjudged that:[63] 'his attitude towards the Treaty was similarly influenced by his determination to show that he, not Collins, was the real Irish leader. Hence the President's refusal to accept the Treaty even under the terms urged on him by Sean T. O'Kelly [O'Ceallaigh].'

However, the delay in moving from private to public session on that day allowed for a backlash to build up against de Valera's tactics and he withdrew the resignation threat, 'under this criticism', because, his biographers inform us:[64] 'He had no desire to do anything which could be misinterpreted as underhand, despite his feeling that those in favour of the Treaty were not themselves acting fairly.' He told the Dail, in injured tones: 'I am sick and tired of politics, so sick that, no matter what happens, I would go back to private life. I have only seen politics within the last three weeks or a month. It is the first time I have seen them, and I am sick to the heart of them. Now I am told this is a special political manoeuvre. . . . I am straight with everybody and I am not a person for political trickery. . . . ' This was a fairly breathtaking statement for a man who had worsted a Tammany Hall leader on his own political turf in America, but he capped it later on in his remarks by saying:[65] 'It is because I am straight that I meet crookedness with straight dealing. If I tried to beat crookedness with similar methods, we are undone.' But the innocent abroad pose slipped when, in the course of that speech, he gave another reason for tendering his resignation: 'There was a case in today's papers. Someone was kidnapped and the Minister for Finance [Collins] sent someone to make enquiries. *He had no right to send anybody.*'

There is a celebrated and oft-quoted assessment by Pieras Beaslai of de Valera's actions during the debate which is accurate insofar as it constitutes a description of his tactics. But it omits mention of one successful part of Machiavelli's principal Irish disciple's over-riding strategy – always to create an impression of great personal integrity. Beaslai wrote:[66] 'One of the most irritating features of Mr. de Valera's behaviour at this time was, having used every device of a practised politician to gain his point, having shown himself relentless and unscrupulous in taking every advantage of generous opponents, he would adopt a tone of injured innocence when his shots failed, and assume the pose of a simple sensitive man, too guileless and gentle for this rough world of politics.'

Beaslai was, of course, devoted to Collins and Griffith and therefore the 'generous opponents' reference has been queried, but what is undeniable is the fact that to the end of his days de Valera's followers did believe that he was 'straight' – that he did meet 'crookedness with straight dealing'. And to the end of his days de Valera continued to have it laid down that they were correct in that belief. As he said at another stage[67] of the Treaty wrangle:

297

'. . . the reputation for honesty. I want to preserve that. . .'. Dealing with his behaviour during the Treaty debates, his biography says:[68]

> To avoid hurting those who signed the Treaty, and thus antagonising them irrevocably, he tried to tone down any attacks on them for violating their instructions. The result was almost like playing with words. 'Paragraph three', he said, 'was not exceeded; but paragraph three was not carried out.' . . . His whole effort was too subtle, especially when he was denied an opportunity to propose 'Document No. 2' in a formal speech at the public sessions. It needed explanation. . . . He was made to appear a fanatic who had already compromised the position. His speeches, hampered by the subtlety of his ideas on external association and the need for a conciliatory restraint, lacked the forcefulness to maximise support.
>
> . . . The publication of cabinet and other private documents as party propaganda showed him that the divisions had ended all semblance of united cabinet responsibility. When a pro-Treaty minister interfered in the work of other ministers, he had no means of controlling him. In the circumstances, on January 6th, he tendered his resignation to the Dail.

'Paragraph three was not exceeded . . .': whatever was the truth about that classic piece of hair-splitting – which even de Valera obviously recognized for what it was – that defence is spurious. Document No. 2 was not debated in public session because de Valera would not allow it to be discussed. The 'publication of cabinet documents' reference, an allusion to Griffith's giving Document No. 2 to the press, makes no mention of the background to that decision. And the reference to the minister who 'interfered in the work of other ministers' cleverly both avoids mentioning Collins by name, lest this be taken as an evidence of bias, and at the same time gives the reader who had not read the actual debates the impression that, despite de Valera's best efforts, administrative chaos was spreading to the point where a minister was interfering in the ordinary departmental work of colleagues. But even for a de Valera there came a point where the casuistry had to stop. Make-up-minds time came on 7 January 1922, when the Treaty was voted on. De Valera attempted to obstruct matters until the very last second. Under the rules of procedure Griffith was supposed to have the last word, but de Valera interjected: 'Before you take a vote, I want to enter my last protest – that document will rise in Judgement against the men who say there is only a shadow of difference. . . .' He again began to extol the virtues of his own 'explicit document', but Collins cut him off: 'Let the Irish nation judge us now and for future years.'[69]

The voting took place in alphabetical order. Collins himself voted first – ironically for Armagh, a Northern constituency which by the terms of the Treaty was shortly to be cut off from the Dail's purview. Like the other deputies elected for more than one area, he only voted once. When the votes were counted they were found to be: for the Treaty, 64 votes; against, 57. For the first time in centuries, by a margin of seven votes, representatives of the Irish people had been in a position to take control of their own destinies. De Valera's first major contribution after the result was announced consisted of an attempt to deny them their right to do this. There were a few rather anti-climactic moments after the vote was taken during which no particular reaction occurred in the chamber. Then, as the news spread outside the building, the cheering of the crowds in the street began to be heard. Smiles and tears broke out within the assemblage. De Valera made himself heard:[70] 'It will of course be my duty to resign my office as Chief Executive. I do not know that I should do it just now.' Collins called out: 'No.' But de Valera ignored him – and, *inter alia*, the vote, which had just been taken – by continuing:[71] 'There is one thing I want to say. I want it to go to the country and to the world, and it is this: the Irish people established a Republic. This is simply approval of a certain resolution. The Republic can only be disestablished by the Irish people. Therefore, until such time as the Irish people in regular manner disestablish it, this Republic goes on.'

It was a viewpoint which was to have dire repercussions for 'the Irish people'. Collins appealed for his assistance in forming a commitee of public safety because 'when countries change from peace to war or war to peace, there are always elements that make for disorder and that make for chaos'. Some commentators believe that de Valera might have responded positively to the appeal had not Mary MacSwiney, apparently fearing this co-operation, intervened to deliver a 'Screeching tirade':[72] 'This is a betrayal, a gross betrayal; and the fact is that it is only a small majority; and that majority is not united; half of them are looking for a gun and the other half are looking for the flesh-pots of the Empire. I tell you there can be no union between the representatives of the Irish Republic and the so-called Free State.'[73]

De Valera knew that if he wanted 'extremist support' that was the sort of viewpoint he would have to accommodate. He did not answer Collins, but instead made an unsuccessful attempt at high-flown rhetoric: 'I would like my last word here to be this: we have had a glorious record for four years; it has been four years of magnificent discipline in our nation. The world is looking at us now. . . .' Here he broke down, but it would be far from his last word in an Irish Parliament. Throughout the decades which would follow he would utilize the system initiated on that day to deliver innumerable speeches. It would not be so for many others whom his actions had influenced: Collins and Boland, now on opposite sides of the chamber with Boland on de Valera's side, also had tears in their eyes. They had something else in common. Unlike de Valera, neither would live to see another 7 January.

15
'Every means in Our Power'

THE INTERPRETATION WHICH de Valera wished history to place on his behaviour before and after the signing of the Treaty was that throughout the years of struggle he was an apostle of peace and unity, who had held together the differing factions in Sinn Fein (as represented by Arthur Griffith and Cathal Brugha)[1] until they were sundered by British guile. Then the divisions created by the British set in train the conditions for a civil war which he was powerless to avert, although he did everything he could to warn everybody concerned of the dangers involved.

Nearly thirty years after the Treaty debates, when Frank Gallagher was Director of the Government Information Bureau, the following extract[2] from his book *The Four Glorious Years* appeared under his pen name, David Hogan, in de Valera's *Sunday Press*, then the largest-selling paper in Ireland:

> By a miracle de Valera had held Sinn Fein together through the vast divide. . . . A British statesman had divided the men of Ireland who had held together so magnificently, had divided them irrevocably, uncontrollably. Those who for four years had fronted every danger, never yielding, never parting, were now at one another's throats, despite every effort to turn this English victory, and the passing of the Treaty which saw Irish unity melt away and the Nation lie helpless at last before the will of her enemy was greeted only by tears. . . . The Four Glorious Years were over. . . .

The glory was certainly over – that much is incontestable; but, as should by now have emerged from these pages, there are certainly grounds for demurring at Gallagher's assessment of de Valera's contribution to harmony prior to the Treaty's being passed by the Dail. And after that the grounds multiply rather than diminish. His conduct gives rise to legitimate speculation as to precisely who, or what, was the 'enemy' that should stand arraigned before the bar of history charged with causing 'the Nation to lie helpless'. The Treaty, the British, the IRA – or de Valera? It is certainly tempting to accept uncritically the verdict of Tom Hales, Michael Collins' former close friend, who ironically was fated to command the ambush which killed Collins: 'If Dev had come back with a document that Collins didn't like there'd have been no civil war.'[3] Certainly if de Valera had reined in his ego, and supported Collins and Griffith in trying to derive benefit from the Treaty, as he did later on for his own purposes, the opposition in the country at large would have been nothing like that which he helped to generate. However, while de Valera's later political life may be taken as validating Hales' comment, in as much as many of his actions served to illustrate the truth of Collins' 'stepping stone' argument, it has to be understood that the way to civil war developed along two tracks, the political and the military. There is no gainsaying that on the political track de Valera, in pursuit of 'extremist support' from the military, did much that was harmful and little that smacked of either prudence or, occasionally, even reason. But, as we shall see, the military factor was an important one none the less.

Before examining it, let us follow de Valera along the political path which ultimately led to this cautious arch-conservative literally finding himself on a road that led to an extremist position and to his picking up the gun once more. The question which will forever hang over his reputation in Irish history is: would he have been on that road if his rivalry with Collins and his fatal streak of 'cute hoorism' had not made him shirk the responsibility of going to the London negotiations?

His first move, the day after the Treaty was passed, was to preside over the formation of a new grouping called Cumman na Poblachta, composed of the deputies who had voted against the Treaty. And then, when the Dail convened on the following day, 9 January, he resigned his Presidency. The idea was that Cumman na Poblachta would attempt to have him re-elected so that, if successful, he could sack all the pro-Treaty Cabinet members, elect his own Cabinet and then proceed to sabotage the Treaty. Collins tried to get him to agree to a Committee of Public Safety drawn from both sides of the house; but de Valera refused, giving as his reason an argument which he immediately began to demolish by his own actions:[4] 'I have tendered my resignation and I cannot, in any way, take divided responsibility. You have got here a sovereign assembly which is the government of the nation. This assembly must choose its executive according to its constitution and go ahead. . . .'

The policy he said he intended to pursue was, in the conditions of the time, akin to the captain of the *Titanic* deliberately deciding to ignore the existence of the iceberg. For, the political life of both England and Ireland having been convulsed over the issue for the previous month, de Valera now announced that he would 'carry on as before and forget that this Treaty has come'. As the Dail had already voted in favour of the Treaty, this of course was a blatant attempt to do as he had earlier been frustrated in doing: to transform the issue from being for or against the Treaty to that of his own enormous personal prestige. In the event he failed, losing by only two votes. One of those who voted for him, Tom O'Donnell, who had been the first to christen him Dev., had earlier voted for the Treaty.

Nevertheless, despite all the strain and anxiety which de Valera had caused him, both then and in the preceding months, the man who would succeed him, Arthur Griffith, greeted the vote by rising to pay a remarkable tribute to the now ex-President:[5] 'I want to say now, that there is scarcely a man I have ever met in my life that I have more love and respect for than President de Valera. I am thoroughly sorry to see him placed in such a position. We want him with us.'

De Valera responded to this generosity by stating that he had acted as he had, in effect trying to subvert the democratic principle of adherence to majority rule, because he felt that it was 'the best way to keep that discipline we had in the past'. And then he went on to utter words that he proceeded to make a mockery of in the very near future: 'I hope that nobody will talk of fratricidal strife. That is all nonsense. We have got a nation that knows how to conduct itself.' The following day he gave a foretaste of that conduct.

Griffith was proposed to succeed him, by Collins, as Chairman of the Provisional Executive. He used this title because of the curious constitutional position created by the terms of the Treaty, which did not recognize the Dail. The Treaty only officially recognized the Parliaments of Southern and Northern Ireland which had been referred to in the Government of Ireland Act of 1920. The Southern Parliament was supposed to appoint a Provisional Government to take over from the departing British administration. However, Sinn Fein had viewed the 1921 election as being to the second Dail, which drew its self-proclaimed mandate from the declaration of a Republic by the First Dail in 1919. In other words, the members of the Dail had gone before the electorate promising not to recognize the Southern Parliament. Now they had to do so in order to implement the Treaty. Accordingly de Valera objected to the proposed title on the basis that it could only be changed, like the status of the Dail itself, by the will of the people. He had not worried about the will of the people when he changed his own title of Priomh Aire to that of President while he was in America and without reference to anyone in Dublin. But now he managed to get the better of the argument. The following day Griffith told him that, if elected, he would occupy whatever position de Valera had occupied. For a moment de Valera appeared mollified. 'That is a fair answer,' he said. But he then took umbrage at Griffith's announcement that the Republic would continue in being until the Free State envisaged by the Treaty was established by way of a general election. He decided that:[6]

> As a protest against the election, as President of the Irish Republic, of the Chairman of the Delegation, who is bound by the Treaty conditions to set up a State which is to subvert the Republic and who, in the interim period instead of using the office as it should be used, to support the Republic, will, of necessity, have to be taking action which will tend to its destruction, – I, while this vote is being taken, am going to leave the House.

He then led a walk-out of his followers from what he had but recently termed a 'sovereign assembly'. The feelings that this engendered may be gauged from the following exchanges:

Collins: 'Deserters all! We will now call on the Irish people to rally to us. Deserters all!'

Ceannt: 'Up the Republic!'

Collins: 'Deserters all to the Irish nation in her hour of trial. We will stand by her.'

Countess Markievicz: 'Oath breakers and cowards!'

Collins: 'Foreigners! Americans! English!'

Markievicz: 'Lloyd Georgites!'

Outside the chamber, as Griffith proceded to appoint a Cabinet, an even more ominous exchange occurred as de Valera defended his action to a *Freeman's Journal* reporter:[7]

'We have a perfect right to resist by every means in our power.'

'Even by war?'

'By every means in our power to resist authority imposed on this country from outside.'

It should be understood that this talk of war was occurring against a backdrop of a country on the brink of civil and economic chaos. On the day that de Valera staged his walk-out the Labour Party were trying to make use of the new Parliament, whatever its constitutional ambiguities, to raise the appalling unemployment problems. There were 130,000 officially declared unemployed,[8] which masked the real total as in those days unemployment amongst women was largely ignored by the Live Register. Poverty was widespread, most notably in the slums of Dublin and in the West of Ireland. On top of this there was the effect of the destruction caused by the war, particularly the British reprisal burning of creameries, the fact that over a million acres of land had gone out of cultivation, and the imminent collapse of what industry there was in the South. Law and order had collapsed in many areas. Commandeering of vehicles and cattle 'for army purposes' was rife. Here and there throughout the country, peasant avarice resulted in land seizures and the intimidation of Protestants. The destruction of the Royal Irish Constabulary had brought normal policing to an end and the Volunteers, who were supposedly filling the vacuum, were as divided over the question of whether to destroy or uphold the new order as were the politicians.

In the North, partition meant that roughly a third of the population was now cut off from Dublin rule. This third controlled most of the country's industry and 40 per cent of its taxable capacity. But the North, where sectarian tensions were rising by the hour, also obtruded across the path of the Southern administration's ability to concentrate on building a new State. For example, as we shall see, a highly combustible incident occurred on 14 January, the very same day that Griffith attempted to get around de Valera's objections by calling a meeting of the Southern Parliament to appoint a Provisional Government. The Lord Lieutenant should have done this under the terms of the Government of Ireland Act, but to help the pro-Treatyites over the de Valera hurdle the British allowed them to dispense with this formality. This had the important consequence of obviating the need for the Oath being administered on that occasion. Griffith remained President of the Dail and his Cabinet stayed in being, but Collins became Chairman of the Provisional Government while remaining Dail Minister of Finance. Thus two Governments, both drawn from Sinn Fein and comprising the same overlapping personnel, were brought into being. The British duly began keeping their share of the bargain by handing over the reins of power to the Provisional Government.

As if to underline the dangers of the Six-County situation on the day of the Provisional Government's formation, the Northern security forces arrested a group of important IRA men in County Tyrone. One of them was the OC of the 5th Northern Division, General Dan Hogan. They were carrying arms, as they were entitled to do under the terms of the truce, and claimed that they were merely a party of footballers *en route* to take part in the Ulster Gaelic Football Championship. But the Unionists suspected, correctly, that they also intended to attempt to rescue three condemned IRA prisoners in Derry Jail.[9] The ensuing controversy was one of the factors which would ultimately lead Collins into the bizarre situation of declaring a *sub rosa* war on the Six Counties – helped by men who were opposing him in the South over the Treaty. But this comes later in our story, and for the present we must return to de Valera.

His official position in the parliamentary arena, and that of his followers, was that they would have nothing to do with the Provisional Government. They were members of Dail Eireann. However, his real policy was one of disruption without responsibility. He and his claque put down questions which afforded opportunities of criticizing the Provisional Government's activities without sharing in them. The day after the Provisional Government's formation he rejected Collins' 'stepping stone' argument in an interview with the American journalist Hayden Talbot, which he then had reprinted in his propaganda sheet *Poblacht na h-Eireann*, edited by Erskine Childers:[10] 'It is not a stepping stone, but a barrier in the way to complete independence. If this Treaty be completed and the British Act resulting from it accepted by Ireland, it will certainly be maintained that a solemn binding contract has been voluntarily entered into by the Irish people, and Britain will seek to hold us to that contract. It will be cited against the claim for independence of every future Irish leader.'

Ironically, the future would show him to be the Irish leader who did most to prove that Collins was right. But that would have seemed inconceivable to anyone studying his actions in the days following the passing of the Treaty. Outside the Parliament he operated in an atmosphere of highly charged drama that began farcically and ended in tragedy. The farce took place in connection with a visit to Paris where an Irish Race Congress was held from 21 to 28 January.

De Valera travelled to Paris on a forged passport, pretending to be Father Patrick Walsh, a friend of Rockwell days. He had made a study of

Walsh's background, noting down details of his career in his diary, and had himself photographed in London wearing a Roman collar in the somewhat unclerical purlieu of Charing Cross. In Paris he succeeded in getting himself elected President of the organization set up by the Congress, Fine Ghaedheal,[11] but in little else because the Congress foundered on the rock of the Treaty controversy. Nevertheless, undaunted: 'Behind a confessional in Notre Dame Cathedral, de Valera put on once more the Roman collar and set off for London, via Antwerp.'[12] He was back in Greystones on 3 February. Why he should have indulged in such hugger mugger his biography does not tell us. When the British captured him during the Black and Tan war they released him; despite his opposition to the Treaty they were hardly likely to deal with him more severely after seven months of truce and the conclusion of a peace treaty. Inevitably, therefore, one is inclined to interpret the dressing up in Paris as being symptomatic of the atmosphere of intrigue and unreality in which he increasingly operated during those tragic days.

But he had it laid down for posterity that:[13] 'De Valera continued to play his part manfully in the public argument.' What this means, in fact, is that on his return from Paris he began a series of huge anti-Treaty meetings throughout the country. The first, pointedly held in O'Connell Street, near the GPO where Pearse had read the declaration of the Republic in 1916, was held on 12 February. To underline the significance of the setting Pearse's mother was brought on to the platform and de Valera:[14] '. . . vehemently addressed a vast enthusiastic crowd from three platforms, and with all the vigour of his spirit assailed the London agreement'. He was introduced as 'President of the Republic', thereby showing both the same elasticity with which he had assumed the title 'President of the Republic' in America in the first place, and a scant regard for parliamentary majority rule. The title had, of course, been voted from him a month earlier. In the weeks that followed he gave similar performances throughout the country: Cork, Clare, Kerry, Limerick, Tipperary and Waterford all witnessed tumultuous gatherings.

Yet, despite the enthusiastic meetings, he was well aware that the overall situation of the country was such that the electorate as a whole were in favour of the 'London Agreement' and would demonstrate this when the elections envisaged by the Treaty were held. Accordingly he seized the opportunity presented by the holding of a Sinn Fein Ard Fheis (annual conference) on 22 February to get the elections put off. The Ard Fheis was an extraordinary one, called solely to discuss the Treaty. There were some three thousand delegates present, many of them from the Six Counties – young, fiery, committed nationalists. Collins readily conceded that there was an anti-Treaty majority present.[15] De Valera heightened the audience's emotions with an impassioned address in which he urged them 'in God's name not to give a British Monarch a democratic title in Ireland'. He proposed a motion of fidelity to the Republic, stipulating that Sinn Fein would:[16] 'put forward and shall support at the coming parliamentary elections only such candidates as shall publicly ... pledge themselves not to take an oath of fidelity to, or own allegiance to the British King'.

Griffith proposed an amendment to approve the Treaty which met with heated opposition. A split was looming when Collins rose to make a plea for unity. De Valera agreed to an adjournment until the following day, and used it to gain his price for unity. There was to be a postponement of the elections for a three-month period during which the Ard Fheis would be adjourned. Meanwhile the Dail would continue to meet regularly, and the new Constitution which was being drawn up under the terms of the Treaty would be submitted to the people as well as the Treaty. Griffith had to go to London to explain the bargain to Churchill, but he managed to convince him that the Treaty had not been breached. Accordingly on 27 February Churchill assured the House that all that was involved was a delay of six or seven weeks in the elections. The Constitution would be submitted to the people by the authority of the Provisional Government, not the Dail, and it would contain nothing which the British Government would not accept. In fact Collins was hoping that it would contain a great deal that the British might not like but that his adversaries in Sinn Fein would swallow.

Apart from buying time in order to allow for the drafting of a Constitution which might unite Sinn Fein, Collins had a more urgent motive in conceding an election postponement to de Valera. Developments with the Army had given him cogent reasons to forgo the obvious advantage of going to the polls to capitalize on the pro-Treaty feelings of the public. An open split in Sinn Fein would have led inevitably to a similar split in the IRA, causing either civil war or a cessation of the British handover of power to the Provisional Government, or a combination of both.

The Army position had been deteriorating steadily from the time Griffith replaced de Valera as President of the Dail and chose a new Cabinet, naming Richard Mulcahy[17] to succeed Cathal Brugha as Minister for Defence. De Valera immediately pressed him to state the position of the Army. Mulcahy replied that:[18] 'the Army will remain the Army of the Irish Republic.' That evening he held a meeting of senior officers in the Mansion House to which de Valera was invited. When de Valera entered the room Mulcahy ordered the men to attention, insisting that, out of office or no, de Valera was to be shown the same respect as before. De Valera urged Mulcahy to hold the Army together and not to do anything which might cause disquiet to the IRA. Mulcahy repeated what he had said in the Dail about the Army's position, and de Valera responded by asking the officers to support the new Minister.[19] But this exchange of civilities could not hide the fact that some of the most important officers present, notably Liam Lynch, were deeply troubled by the Treaty.

Their unease took tangible form the next day, 11 January, in the form of a letter to Mulcahy requesting that a Volunteer Convention be held to consider the following resolution:[20] 'That the Army reaffirms its allegiance to the Irish Republic. That it shall be maintained as the Army of the Irish Republic, under an Executive appointed by the Convention. That the Army shall be under the Supreme Control of such Executive, which shall draft a Constitution for submission to a subsequent Convention.'

The effect of the resolution, of course, would have been to place the Executive which it envisaged outside civilian control. Mulcahy bought time with a reply which pointed this out to the signatories (who included some of the most important IRA leaders in the country), but refrained from saying yes or no to the holding of the Convention. The Collins faction was hoping that the sight of the British handing over barracks and other symbols of authority to the new administration would influence the IRA.

However, there were a number of complex factors at work in the IRA. One was a simple but widespread belief that, having 'beaten the British' into conceding the Treaty offer, one more good push would bring the Republic. But in my own researches into the IRA – which extend for well over a quarter-century – during which time I talked to dozens of survivors of the period, I became very conscious of the fact that there was what might be termed an 'honour factor' at work in the minds of the Volunteers. A curious factor it might appear in our day, but it was a real one nevertheless. Certainly there were thugs who had grown used to drinking, commandeering, intimidating and swaggering. Undoubtedly there were the 'trucileers', who only emerged when the shooting stopped so as to join the enlarged Army which began to be built up after the truce was declared. And a most unhealthy growth it was, soaring between July and November from around only three thousand to more than seventy thousand.[21]

But there was also a mass of apolitical idealists. They, and their people's response to their selflessness and sincerity, had been the backbone of the movement which had led to the offer from Britain of Dominion status. But to their scrupulous, Catholic way of thinking, politics, with its inevitable compromises, was tinged with dishonour. In the first place they had come into the IRA in the spirit of the 1916 leaders, expecting to fail, perhaps to pay with their lives, but nevertheless to keep alive the tradition of a 'rising in every generation'. It seemed to be somehow ignoble to stop now, claim the Dominion spoils and leave the field. They had taken an Oath to a Republic and to a Dail, and now many felt they were being asked to go against that Oath, by acquiescing in their disestablishment. One by-product of de Valera's rivalry towards Collins, and his zeal to get control of the Volunteers, had been to expose an idealistic movement of young men and women to an overdose of oath-taking.

Liam Lynch would come to epitomize this type of thinking. Significantly, he and Collins struggled for months to bridge the gap between their respective adherents, and ultimately fell leading the opposing sides in a civil war they both detested. Mulcahy, who succeeded Collins, held de Valera principally responsible for the civil war. As Dr Maryann Valiulis has written:[22]

307

He believed that the civil war assumed the scale it did because de Valera persuaded Liam Lynch with his tremendous influence in the Southern divisions to go against the Treaty. In Mulcahy's eyes, de Valera had destroyed the wonderful harmony of the volunteer movement and led good comrades astray. For these offences Mulcahy never forgave him ... de Valera had betrayed the revolutionary movement for power, not principle. . . .

This view, the mirror image of the one de Valera would have us believe of the British responsibility for all that happened, was and is widely shared in Ireland. But as with the de Valera analysis, there are deficiencies. It leaves out the 'honour factor', the Mujaheddin quotient in the revolutionary movement. And of course it leaves out the importance of many other hardened revolutionaries like Liam Mellows, Rory O'Connor, Cathal Brugha and Ernie O'Malley who did not even bother to attend the meeting which Mulcahy called in the Mansion House. These men and others who thought like them were not impressed even by such a historic event as occurred on 16 January – Collins' taking over of Dublin Castle. The age-old seat of British dominance had fallen to the Irish, but they still persisted in their demand for an Army Convention. It was conceded, but postponed for two months. And, two days after the Castle was handed over, a watchdog Council was set up comprising two from the pro- and two from the anti-Treaty side. Its objective was to ensure that:[23] 'The Republican aim shall not be prejudiced', but its hidden agenda was to ensure that old comrades did not begin shooting at each other.

At that stage neither side wished to attack the other. But, like the political agreement concluded at the Ard Fheis, the watchdog arrangement had mixed results. It bought time, which allowed Collins to continue with the forlorn hope of drafting a Constitution which the British would agree to but which would at the same time be Republican enough to enable the two wings of the IRA to support it. And, *inter alia*, it also staved off civil war for a period, thus enabling the British evacuation to continue. However, it also had the effect that, from the time it was concluded, the British were handing over barracks to both pro- and anti-Treatyites. Two rival armies were in the process of being formed.

The Provisional Government forces established their GHQ in Dublin at Beggars Bush Barracks, which ironically enough dominated the area that de Valera had commanded in 1916. Their rivals operated all over the country raiding for arms and transport. The anti-Treatyites grew strong enough to take over the city of Limerick at the beginning of March. Only intense mediation by Liam Lynch and Stephen O'Mara, the mayor, prevented open warfare breaking out. Both sides withdrew from the city. However, in Beggars Bush and the Provisional Cabinet the compromise was looked upon as a surrender to mutineers. Further such deals were ruled out, and the postponed Convention was prohibited altogether.

Collins and Griffith feared, with good reason, that if it were held the result would be the declaration of a military dictatorship. They asked the old Irish Parliamentary Party leader Tim Healy to approach de Valera to request his support in opposing the Convention in the face of this danger. De Valera met Healy 'coolly'[24] with Boland by his side at his offices in 23 Suffolk Street. 'In another room upstairs sat Rory O'Connor and fellow officers, but Dev had tried all along to make it clear that he and O'Connor had no connection with each other apart from sharing the same address. . . .'[25] When Healy warned him that, if he lent himself to the use of force, he would be a sorry man within the year, he replied: 'I don't think so',[26] and continued to assert that he had nothing to do with the Army. He refused to accede to Healy's request. 'There's no crime in the blow that has not been struck,'[27] was his attitude. He did warn O'Connor privately against defying the Convention ban. However, it was held on 26 March, unanimously adopted the resolution which it had sent to Mulcahy on the 11th, and elected a new executive with Rory O'Connor as its leader. O'Connor then gave a press conference at which he repudiated the authority of the Dail and of GHQ. When asked if this meant the setting up of a military dictatorship, he replied in the affirmative. The executive's actions subsequently fuelled the fears raised by this statement. GHQ stopped the dissidents' pay, and they responded by organizing bank and post office raids around the country. Hostile newspapers were threatened and sometimes had their printing plants smashed, as in the cases of the *Freeman's Journal* and the *Clonmel Nationalist*. The Provisional Government's efforts to build up an unarmed police force were interfered with.

What was de Valera's role in this process? Watching the militarists pile anarchy upon chaos, Patrick McCartan wrote to Joseph McGarrity, after the O'Connor-led executive was formed, that the Volunteers were:[28] ' . . . well over the precipice but de Valera is still on the brink and no doubt will soon sling them a document or two when he makes up his mind'. In fact, as we have seen, de Valera would not have had to sling his document very far had he chosen to, as he and O'Connor shared the same building. This naturally associated him in the public mind with O'Connor – an association which he took every opportunity to further, although O'Connor showed no eagerness to endorse his political leadership. 'Some of us,' he said, 'are no more prepared to stand for de Valera than the Treaty.'[29] As de Valera had appealed to the Army to support GHQ and, *ipso facto*, the Dail, O'Connor's action was as much a repudiation of him as of the Dail. Nevertheless, throughout the period leading up to the executive's formation, and after it, de Valera failed to disassociate himself from the O'Connor faction; he also continued to fling not documents but fiery statements which had only one objective in view: the winning of 'extremist support'. These statements were the most irresponsible of his career and, taken together, certainly form solid evidence for those who would argue, like Mulcahy, that it was he who caused the civil war. Nevertheless one of his closest and most knowledgeable subordinates[30] would testify nearly sixty years later that de Valera's 'resentment of the charge of incitement to civil war was, beyond doubt, sincerely and deeply felt'. And his official biography states:[31] 'There is no evidence that his speeches, in fact, stirred up the violence they were said to encourage.' This was a cleverly worded statement because there could of course be no 'evidence' of a courtroom nature, unless the IRA took to leaving notices on bodies saying: 'Shot because of de Valera speech'.

The incitement charges began after de Valera issued a statement to the press on 15 March, formally announcing the formation of his followers in the Dail into Cumman na Poblachta. He then set off to the strongly republican South to continue his programme of public speechmaking. In Dungarvan on the 16th he said:[32] 'The Treaty ... barred the way to independence with the blood of fellow-Irishmen. It was only by Civil War after this that they could get their independence ... if you don't fight today, you will have to fight tomorrow; and I say, when you are in a good fighting position, then fight on.'

He really got into his stride during two St Patrick's Day speeches the next day. At Carrick-on-Suir, where his audience included an estimated seven hundred members of the IRA, he said:[33] 'If the Treaty was accepted the fight for freedom would still go on; and the Irish people, instead of fighting foreign soldiers, would have to fight the Irish soldiers of an Irish Government set up by Irishmen. If the Treaty was not rejected, perhaps it was over the bodies of the young men he saw around him that day that the fight for Irish freedom may be fought.' At Thurles, where again his audience was largely drawn from the IRA, many of them carrying rifles, he was reported as saying:[34]

> If they accepted the Treaty, and if the Volunteers of the future tried to complete the work the Volunteers of the last four years had been attempting, they would have to complete it, not over the bodies of foreign soldiers, but over the dead bodies of their own countrymen. They would have to wade through, perhaps, the blood of some of the members of the Government in order to get Irish freedom.

By the time he got to Killarney the next day, 18 March, he had widened his argument so that it now took in the republican 'honour factor', his objections to the 'stepping stone' thesis, the 'wading through blood' warnings and a condemnation of the principle of majority rule – 'the people had no right to do wrong'. The following is taken from the report which appeared in the *Irish Independent* on 20 March:

> Acts had been performed in the name of the Republic which would be immoral if the Republic didn't exist. . . . Men and women were shot for helping the enemy, and there would be no justification for the shooting of these if the Republic did not exist.
>   Declaring that if they accepted the Treaty, they were putting two very definite barriers in the way of achieving freedom, Mr. de Valera declared one barrier would be that they were pledging the nation's honour to a certain agreement.

Another barrier, if an Irish Government was set up, those who wanted to travel on the road to achieve freedom, *such as those men present with the rifles*, would have in the future not merely the foreign soldiers to meet, but would have to meet the force of their own brothers, their fellow country-men, who would be supporting the Government.

'Therefore, in future', he went on, 'in order to achieve freedom, if our Volunteers continue, *and I hope they will continue until the goal is reached*, – if we continue on that movement which was begun when the Volunteers were started, and we suppose this Treaty is ratified by your votes, then these men, in order to achieve freedom, will have, I said yesterday, to march over the dead bodies of their own brothers. They will have to wade through Irish blood. . . . The people had never a right to do wrong.' He was certain that the same pluck which had carried them so far would enable them to finish.

These utterances brought a storm of criticism upon him from platform, press and pulpit. He attempted to defend himself in a letter to the *Irish Independent* on 23 March in which he quoted the 'wading through blood' warnings from his Thurles speech only, saying: 'This a child might understand.' He said that his speeches were 'an answer to those who said the London Agreements gave us "freedom to achieve freedom".' He told the Editor that this editorial, 'in which you picture me as "encouraging" and "preaching civil war" and indulging in "violent threats" and "in the language of incitement", I can only characterise as villainous'.

But he made no reference to his Killarney speech with its comments on rifles and his hope that the Volunteers would 'continue'. Using his formidable personality and a display of the temper he normally only showed in private, he also attempted an outright denial in the Dail two months later.[35] Kevin O'Higgins accused de Valera of having told 'excitable young men that if they continue to go forward with their objective, as he hoped they would, it would be necessary for them to wade through Irish blood, including that of some members of the Government. . . .' De Valera interrupted him: 'I beg once more to deny that. It is an absolute misrepresentation.' After some further cross-fire the following exchange took place:

O'Higgins: 'If on looking up the press reports I find that I have misquoted the deputy, I will. . . .'

De Valera: 'I publicly denied it as a misrepresentation. I deny it now, and let that end it.'

O'Higgins: 'I am willing to accept the denial.'

De Valera: 'I denied in the *Irish Independent* that I made this statement, and the thousands of people who listened to me know it is a lie.'

The significance of that dialogue is, first, that it was provoked by the moving of a motion by Griffith proposing the holding of a general election which de Valera desperately wanted to avoid; and second, that *both* O'Higgins and de Valera could be shown to be telling the truth. The flurry in the Dail constitutes a classic example of the difference between a fact and a 'de Valera fact' – that is, one he wanted believed no matter what the truth of the matter. For in the time which had elapsed since his delivery of the Thurles speech the overall situation had become further destabilized. He had played his part in the destabilization process – which did involve the use of the phraseology O'Higgins imputed to him, although he was an accessory to some of the language rather than the user of it. Throughout those two months he had had two fundamental objectives. One was the familiar target of 'extremist support'. In this he failed. Despite his wild and swirling words, O'Connor and his men took their decisions without consulting him. The other was a basically undemocratic attempt to prevent the public from expressing their will through the ballot box. Despite his Ard Fheis Pact with Griffith and Collins on postponing the elections, a few days later he tried to get the postponement period extended. On 2 March he backed a Dail motion to extend the franchise to women on the grounds that equality of citizenship had been promised by the 1916 Proclamation. He also sought to have the electoral register revised. As he himself pointed out,[36] this would have had the effect of delaying elections for at least three months while the franchise revision was being carried out. The motion was defeated, Griffith regarding it simply as a delaying tactic. However, de Valera's sustained attempt to avoid facing the verdict of the polls finally bore fruit in the form of a written agreement with Michael Collins.

This compact – 'The Pact', as it became generally known – probably had its origins in a peace-making attempt which McGarrity made during a two-month visit to Ireland which began on 12 February 1922. McCartan gave a lunch in his honour at the Mansion House, and in a letter to Devoy afterwards gives an indication of de Valera's feelings towards Collins:[37] 'When McGarrity and Collins arrived at the Mansion together, de Valera scowled at Joe.'

Not surprisingly, no agreement emerged from the lunch, but McCartan credits McGarrity with the fact that Collins and de Valera 'parted good friends as Joe refused to let either of them out of the room when they got hot'.[38] McGarrity held discussions with Griffith also, and it was said by a knowledgeable observer that 'his presence and his influence did something to ease the strained relationships and make contacts less embarrassing'.[39] This was something, certainly, but not enough to avert war. The sequence of events and de Valera's part in them was as follows.

At Dun Laoghaire on 6 April he followed O'Connor's lead and publicly repudiated the Dail, saying:[40] 'When Dail Eireann took its rightful place as the Government of the nation, then they would have a stable government; but if they attempted to do that which they legally could not do, to set up a Provisional Government as the Government of the country, that Government would not be obeyed. That Government would not function.' In answer to a questionnaire he told the *Manchester Guardian* five days later[41] that the political aims of the anti-Treaty forces were identical with his own. However, he demurred from accepting responsibility for the O'Connorites. He said that the Republican Army was a separate body quite independent of his political party and had acted entirely on its own initiative, impelled, he was sure, by the sole desire to save the Irish people from being forced by the threats of the British Government to surrender their independence. He thought the Army was entitled to use its strength to prevent elections such as those proposed, which might well be regarded as the device of an alien aggressor for obtaining, under threat of force, an appearance of popular support for his usurped authority.

Two days after this appeared, on the night of Holy Thursday, 13 April, O'Connor's executive again 'acted entirely on its own initiative'. Anti-Treaty troops seized a number of buildings in Dublin, including the *ancien régime* Kildare Street Club, a freemason's hall, Kilmainham Jail and, most importantly, the hub of the Irish legal system, the Four Courts, which O'Connor made his headquarters. It was a rerun of the Easter-week seizure of the GPO. But instead of a reading of the Proclamation of the Republic a statement signed by Liam Mellows was issued, stating the conditions on which those inside the Four Courts would be prepared to hold discussions with those inside the Dail. These included maintaining 'the existing Republic', placing the Army (pro- and anti-Treaty) under the control of an 'elected independent Executive', disbanding the police force and handing policing over to the IRA. The final requirement was that 'No elections on the issue at present before the country to be held while the threat of war with England exists.'[42] The country had obviously moved into the ante-chamber of civil war.

And the civil war began to the sound of music. Ernie O'Malley has left a vivid account of spending an afternoon with Rory O'Connor in O'Connor's house in Monkstown, Co. Dublin, playing Brahms, Debussy and Ravel. Then, as the strains of Schumann's 'Carnival' died away, O'Connor said:[43] 'We must go down town now.' And go they did, to set up a rival Army HQ to that loyal to the Griffith/Collins faction. Conflict was thus rendered inevitable. O'Malley explained not only their action, but that of a sizeable segment of the IRA:[44] 'We had taken an oath of Allegiance to the Republic, we meant to keep it. We would fight until we wore the Free State down, or were wiped out ourselves.' De Valera's espousal of 'extremist support' carried the message from those fanatic hearts to a far wider audience than would otherwise have listened to their tune.

A Labour Party delegation met de Valera the day after the Four Courts seizure, Good Friday, to intercede with him to use his influence to avert disaster. One of the delegation, Senator J. T. O'Farrell, later told the Senate:[45]

We spent two hours pleading with him then, with a view to averting the impending calamity of the civil war, and the only statement he made that has abided with me since as to what his views were was this: 'The majority have no right to do wrong.' He repeated that at least a dozen times in the course of the interview, in response to statements that the Treaty had been accepted by a majority, and that, consequently, it was his duty to observe the decision of the majority until it was reversed. He refused to accept it on the grounds that the majority had no right to do wrong.

De Valera, after all, had been advocating electoral policies similar to those of Mellows in the *Manchester Guardian* a few days earlier. Although he still had no control over the Four Courts men, an interview given by O'Connor after the seizure must have encouraged him to believe that his campaign to win 'extremist support' was succeeding. O'Connor said that the executive was no longer associated with any political organization, but added:[46] 'I am safe in saying that if the Army were ever to follow a political leader, Mr. de Valera is the man.' De Valera now proceeded to give further evidence as to why he was 'the man'. His biography would have history believe that he thought O'Connor's repudiation of the Dail 'altogether wrong. He was in fact in a nightmarish position with little influence on events in practice.' Nevertheless he greeted the Four Courts seizure by issuing what he termed his Easter Proclamation:[47]

> Young men and young women of Ireland, hold steadily on. Those who with cries of woe and lamentation would now involve you in a disastrous rout you will soon see rally behind you and vie with you for first place in the vanguard.
>
> Beyond all telling is the destiny God has in mind for Ireland the fair, the peerless one. You are the artificers of that destiny.
>
> Yours is the faith that moves mountains, the faith that confounds misgivings. Your is the faith and love that begot the enterprise of 1916.
>
> Young men and young women of Ireland, the goal is at last in sight – steady, all together forward. Ireland is yours for the taking. Take it.

His official biography makes no mention of this Proclamation. It makes the point that he had 'no part whatever in this step. But he felt the dispute was a matter for the Minister for Defence and any interference by him would be unwelcome to either party.'[48] The Proclamation, however, is of particular significance for a number of reasons. It reveals the same sort of unreal, dramatic thinking he displayed in going to Paris in a blaze of thunderous secrecy: the same complete lack of regard for the feelings of the electorate, as opposed to that of the young men with the guns. And clearly his appeal to this last group makes nonsense of his claim that he was not guilty of incitement. 'Ireland is yours for the taking. Take it. . . . ' It was now that the chickens of his long absence in America and from the London talks were coming home to roost. His American-inflated ego made him impervious to the feelings of the majority of the Irish people, whose wishes he professed to be able to divine through his own unique process of vascular oracularity. The evasion of responsibility which had led him to attempt to make scapegoats out of Griffith and, in particular, Collins was now causing him to try evading the authority of the ballot box. If he was in 'a nightmarish position' it was not because he was pulled along by Rory O'Connor and the extremists. It was because he deliberately sought 'extremist support'. Machiavelli would not have been proud of his pupil during this period.

Nor was McGarrity much comforted, either. He composed a poem which he addressed to the leaders on both sides of the divide:[49]

Let not passion's poisoned arrow
Drive ye to embittered strife;
Stand as sisters, stand as brothers
Rally for the nation's life.

He would hardly have been cheered by the effects of his rallying call had he attended a meeting between those to whom he addressed it, called by the Roman Catholic Archbishop of Dublin, Dr Byrne,[50] in an eleventh-hour attempt to avert civil war. It took place on 29 April in the Mansion House and was attended by Collins, de Valera, Brugha, Griffith and some Labour Party delegates. Brugha's contribution to what was supposed to be a peace conference was to accuse Collins and Griffith of being British agents. Collins stood up angrily: 'I suppose we are two of the Ministers whose blood is to be waded through?' Brugha replied: 'Yes, you are two.' De Valera made no attempt either to challenge this interpretation of his words or to rebuke Brugha. As he was supposed to have stayed away from Downing Street because of the importance he attached to Brugha's statements and replies, his categorical denial in the Dail of O'Higgins' allusion to his sanguinary utterances does more to illustrate the nature of de Valera-speak than to enhance his reputation for veracity.

He and Brugha refused Collins' plea for either an election or a plebiscite on the Treaty. Collins argued that 'Every adult has a right to vote.' But Brugha dismissed this by saying that 'No nation has power to part with its nationality or barter any part of national heritage.' He said that no such issue should be put before the people while the threat of war was there. De Valera added a gloss to the plebiscite refusal, saying the sort proposed was a 'stone age plebiscite'. It had been suggested that people would signify their preference by walking through gates or barriers, mainly at churches. Later in the exchange he gave another memorable example of de Valera-speak. After he had remarked that compromise would have to be consistent with the Republican ideal, Griffith flared up: 'Was that your attitude? If so, a penny postcard would have been sufficient to inform the British government without going to the trouble of sending us over.'

When de Valera tried to explain, Griffith cut him off: 'Did you not ask me to get you out of the strait-jacket of the Republic?'

De Valera's reply was that he meant the strait-jacket of the *isolated* Republic.

Not surprisingly, the only tangible result from the Conference was a press statement from de Valera, who said: 'Republicans maintain that there are rights which a minority may justly uphold, even by arms, against a majority.' He made a justification of his refusal to co-operate in the holding of an intimidation-free election by proposing a further six-month adjournment so that: 'Time would be secured for the present passions to subside, for personalities to disappear. ... ' In six months' time many personalities *had* disappeared, permanently, including the other three principal participants in the talks – Brugha, Collins and Griffith. And the very day that he issued the statement, very large sums of money disappeared from banks all round the country as the Four Courts men collected more than a quarter of a million pounds in raids – a colossal sum in today's money values. Years after the war had ended, the poet Yeats would write:[51]

Had de Valera eaten Parnell's heart
No loose lipped demagogue had won the day
No civil rancour torn the land apart.

The quest for 'extremist support' meant that de Valera maintained his hard line internationally as well as domestically. In the course of a controversial interview he told John Steele of the *Chicago Tribune*: 'We all believe in democracy, but we must not forget its well-known weaknesses. As a safeguard against their consequences the most democratic countries have devised checks and brakes against sudden changes of opinion and hasty, ill-considered actions.' In America, he argued, a Treaty needed a two-thirds majority to pass the Senate. As Ireland had not had an 'opportunity of devising constitutional checks and brakes ... the Army sees in itself the only brake at the present time and is using its strength as such'.[52] This interview was reprinted in *Poblacht na h-Eireann*, but the day before it appeared de Valera, through the intermediacy of Harry Boland, had started to negotiate an arrangement with Collins which, had it actually gone into operation, would have provided some very dubious 'checks and brakes' on Irish democracy. On 20 May an electoral pact was announced which cut across the interests of all the other political parties in contesting the election, and was blatantly in contravention of the Treaty.

Under its terms, de Valera and his supporters were to contest the election on the same panel as those of the Provisional Government. Both sides were to be under the Sinn Fein banner, their numbers being determined by their strength in the Dail. Following the election a coalition Government was to be formed with a President and a Minister for Defence, who would represent the two wings of the Army – those operating from Beggars Bush and those from the Four Courts. The other nine ministers were to be allocated on the basis of five from the majority party and four from the minority.

Even some of Collins' most loyal supporters were appalled. It was legally impossible to have a coalition Provisional Government of pro- and anti-Treaty members. Under Article 17 of the Agreement, every member of the Provisional Government had to accept the Treaty in writing. Yet the pact would almost certainly have returned to Government such rabidly anti-Treaty figures as Brugha, Childers, de Valera and Stack. The Minister for Defence would have had to be acceptable to both the Beggars Bush GHQ and those in the Four Courts who were conducting the bank robberies and furthering a boycott of Belfast products which involved destroying goods and pouring whiskey down drains. Griffith's relationship with Collins cooled markedly[53] after the pact. The Provisional Government's Law Officer, Hugh Kennedy, drew up a lengthy official memorandum[54] pointing out the illegalities of the arrangement. And the British were outraged. Prior to the agreement being signed Churchill had got word of it and warned Collins that:[55]

> ... any such arrangement would be received with world-wide ridicule and reprobation. It would not be an election in any sense of the word, but simply a farce, whereby a handful of men who possess lethal weapons deliberately disposed of the political rights of the electors by a deal across the table. . . . Your Government would soon find itself regarded as a tyrannical junta which having got into office by violence was seeking to maintain itself by a denial of constitutional rights.

After the pact was announced, Collins and the Treaty signatories were immediately summoned to London to explain what was going on. The problem for Collins was that he was in such an appalling situation that he dared not explain what was really happening. He, and the leaders of GHQ, had entered into collusion with the Four Courts leaders to provide the Northern IRA with the weapons to launch an attack against the Six Counties. De Valera was almost certainly aware of this arrangement through his relationship with Aiken and Boland, even if he did not discuss it directly with Collins himself during the pact negotiations. Certainly the conclusion of the pact and the launching of the offensive followed on each other's heels. At the time, as Professor Lee has pointed out,[56] 'there was one armed policeman to every two Catholic families in Northern Ireland'. While the South lurched inexorably towards civil war, 'On a per capita basis Protestants were scoring four kills to every one by Catholics.' Murder gangs operated with impunity from the ranks of the Royal Ulster Constabulary, the new police force which Sir Henry Wilson had created, and from those of the B-Specials, an all-Protestant militia which the Tory component of the British coalition had succeeded in arming and paying – against the advice of senior British civil servants. Even Lloyd George conceded that this was akin to 'arming the *fascisti*'. Catholics were systematically intimidated out of their homes and jobs to pave the way for the creation of a blatantly unjust State. For the violence was but the physical manifestation of well-thought-out constitutional planning.

First, the Unionists had turned down the original British offer of Ulster in its existing nine-county form. Craig informed Lloyd George that they could be certain of controlling only six counties. Nine would have contained too many Catholics, who would have constituted a force for assimilation in a thirty-two-county Ireland. Second, the Unionists, with the aid of their Tory allies, frustrated British attempts to have a second chamber attached to the Belfast Parliament for the purposes of redressing Catholic grievances. Carson objected bitterly, threatening to take to the streets as he had done against Home Rule. The Unionists did not view their statelet as being one in which Catholic susceptibilities were catered for. What they wanted, and got, was one in which Orange hegemony was guaranteed. The third major step in ensuring this was their successful blocking of the move to introduce proportional representation to the Six Counties to parallel what was done in the Catholic Twenty-six to safeguard the Protestant minority.

Apart from his *sub rosa* activities, at official level Collins had two meetings with Sir James Craig in an effort to ease the situation. He also bombarded Churchill (the minister responsible for Irish affairs) with complaints, once reducing him to tears by showing him a photograph of the MacMahon family who had been wiped out by a police murder gang. Unofficially he introduced a whole battery of measures designed to prevent the Northern statelet functioning. The obstruction ranged from not handing over departmental files to paying the salaries of Catholic schoolteachers in primary schools from the Secret Service Fund, so that they would give their allegiance to the South. At another level still he connived at measures such as the kidnapping of prominent Orangemen as hostages against the IRA men under sentence of death in Derry. These were ultimately released, as were a party of Free State officers and men who had been sent to rescue the men under the guise of being Monaghan Gaelic football players – but not before he had sent members of the Squad over to England in an unsuccessful attempt to shoot the hangmen.

While Collins unquestionably hated partition in itself for the damage it did to Ireland, and was deeply stirred by the sufferings of the Catholics, he had two other items on his agenda of co-operation with the Four Courts men – one short-term and one long-term. In the short term the pact made it possible to secure something approaching an intimidation-free election. It also bought time to allow his drafting team to produce a Constitution which he hoped would be Republican enough to avert civil war with those who felt the Treaty had betrayed the Republic. Similar crises to that which occurred in Limerick had almost precipitated large-scale fighting in Kilkenny and Sligo in the weeks prior to the pact with de Valera. There were those in the Cabinet who believed that such fighting would have to be faced. Griffith, who had shown extraordinary courage in addressing a meeting in Sligo after the Four Courts men had banned it, told the Cabinet that if it was not 'prepared to fight and preserve the democratic rights of the ordinary people and the fruit of national victory, we should be looked upon as the greatest set of poltroons who ever had the fate of Ireland in their hands'.[57]

A majority agreed with him. In fact it would be truer to say that everyone did so with the exception of Mulcahy, who dissented through loyalty to Collins and his own awareness of how ill prepared the new

Beggars Bush Army was. But Collins went against his own Cabinet in favour of the de Valera pact – not through affection for de Valera, but for a combination of the foregoing reasons combined with a sense of loyalty to the old friends who now opposed him. A close colleague of those days has written: 'What troubled Collins was the split in the Army. There were men in the Army that he would go almost any distance to satisfy. He would rather, as he told me more than once, have one of the type of Liam Lynch, Liam Deasy, Tom Hales, Rory O'Connor, or Tom Barry on his side than a dozen like de Valera.'[58] Collins was desperate to prove to such former comrades that he really did intend the Treaty to be a 'stepping stone' to a thirty-two-county Republic. And it may be observed here that, from my researches into his life, it became quite clear that had he lived, and obtained settled conditions in the South, he fully intended to attempt to achieve that goal by military means if necessary. There is evidence that the British suspected what Collins was doing.

He was subjected to fierce pressure over the pact for giving way to unconstitutional forces. It was pointed out to him that[59] 'Boland, de Valera's secretary, represented only 2% of the Population'. He was criticized for 'making one surrender after another to the Republicans' while not obtaining 'the free opinion of the Irish people'. This last was particularly hard to take, coming from the man whose father had instituted the 'Orange card' policy which had led to partition in the face of the majority of 'the free opinion of the Irish people'. Churchill told Collins bluntly that he had been responsible for placing all the British signatories to the Treaty under 'fierce scrutiny of our actions'. And there was more than a hint of personal feeling in his warning that:[60] 'You will find that we are just as tenacious on essential points – the Crown, the British Commonwealth, no Republic – as de Valera and Rory O'Connor, and we intend to fight for our points.'

If Churchill had known at that stage that, as a result of de Valera's pressure, Collins' planned Constitution envisaged incorporating in its provisions features of the pact which would have enabled de Valera to evade Article 17 of the Treaty, the fighting might have commenced then and there. The draft proposal was for four 'Extern' ministers who would have joined the Cabinet by appointment, without taking the Oath or being subject to collective responsibility. A few days later, on 1 June, with Griffith and Collins sitting in the visitors' gallery listening to him, Churchill repeated his warnings in the House of Commons. If the Constitution was not in accordance with the terms of the Treaty, Britain would withhold ratification.

De Valera had thus succeeded in placing Collins between the anvil of his own adamantine ego and the Churchillian hammer. He sought to disclaim all knowledge of this for the benefit of posterity. His biography says that he remained hopeful of what the pact and Constitution might bring,[61] 'little realising the appalling pressures to which Collins in particular was being subjected behind the scenes'. As he was in fact a prime source of these behind-the-scenes pressures, unacknowledged guilt at his treatment of the younger man may have had a bearing on de Valera's later attitude to Collins. But it was not all gain for de Valera; Collins ultimately derived more from the pact than he did, because it enabled him to force de Valera to expose himself to the verdict of the people. The postponed Sinn Fein Ard Fheis endorsed the pact. And on 6 June de Valera joined Collins in a joint appeal for support for the pact on the grounds that: 'many of the dangers that threaten us can be met only by keeping intact the forces which constituted the national resistance in recent years'.[62] Intimidation of Provisional Government speakers at election meetings eased off, thus validating Collins' argument to Churchill that without the pact there would have been no election. De Valera was fully aware that, inevitably, the Constitution was running into trouble with the British – *Poblacht na h-Eireann* had in fact said as much – but he hesitated to speak out as he had done in his rejection of the Treaty. The election was clearly not 'in violent conflict with the wishes of the people'. The pact offered him the possibility of a place in Government, which he had no hope of otherwise. Any party standing against the Treaty was doomed to lose. The 'wading through blood' approach, which he dropped after writing the *Independent* letter, had cost him moderate support. His goal of extremist support had been somewhat advanced by the pact, to the extent that it showed that he could exert his influence to prevent intimidation. This, of course, prompts speculation as to what matters might have been like had he chosen to exert that sort of influence from the time of the Treaty's signing. However, he had little other control over the Rory O'Connor faction. So he stayed silent while Collins and Griffith made racking journeys to and from London, conducting a gallant but doomed rearguard action on the Constitution.

It may be that the challenge posed to the Treaty by de Valera and the Four Courts men would have made civil war inevitable anyway; or that Collins' designs on the Six Counties might have provoked a different and even bloodier North–South encounter later. What is certain is that the British rejection of Collins' Constitution guaranteed that civil war would break out in Southern Ireland. Lloyd George adjudged the document to have wandered so far from what he had intended as its base in the Canadian Constitution as to be a 'setting up of an independent Republic in Ireland. The Crown was only brought in under conditions very derogatory to its dignity . . . the Constitution was a complete going back on the provisions of the Treaty.'[63] After some of the toughest talking ever heard in Downing Street between the Irish and the English, Collins lost the battle. He later claimed that the[64] 'action of certain men in this country who had created disturbance from one end of the nation to the other and who had spoken threateningly against the obligation that this nation had incurred . . . had weakened the hand of our negotiators in London'. And he was supported in this claim from an unlikely quarter. Gavan Duffy, who had differed with him so strongly over the Treaty negotiations, said:[65]

320

I sympathise with the Minister who said that, because it is true that Mr. de Valera and his friends have forgotten the day when they promised us that there was a constitutional way of settling our differences, and they have forgotten the day when they promised us that if we were up against England they would be behind us as an auxiliary army. Yet there is some truth in the fact that the deplorable performances of that party have made the Government position difficult.

At all events, the Collins Constitution was drastically reworked so as to include the following. The Oath became obligatory on anyone entering Parliament. The Parliament was to consist of the King and two Houses. The King was to summon and dissolve Parliament. There was to be a representative of the King, a Governor General, whose signature was necessary before any Bill could become law. No law could be passed, and no amendment could be made to the Constitution, which was in conflict with the provisions of the Treaty.

The details of the Constitution were not published until the morning of the election, too late for de Valera to gain any benefit from them. But they had a very considerable bearing on the attitude of the militant Republicans. Collins had recognized the Constitution's likely impact by repudiating the pact two days earlier. Speaking in Cork, he said he was[66] 'not hampered by being on a platform where there were coalitionists' and urged 'the citizens of Cork to vote for the candidates you think best of'. Overall, the electorate responded by voting by a majority of nearly three to one for the candidates it thought best of – those who were pro-Treaty.

De Valera's faction lost 22 seats, being returned with only 36. The Collins–Griffith group lost 8, returning with 58. But in the scales with these there had to be reckoned the Labour Party's 17 seats, the Farmers' Party 7, 6 Independents and 4 Unionists, all pro-Treaty. In other words, as de Valera expected they would all along, the people voted for peace as soon as they got the chance. They were not, however, to enjoy it for very long.

16

BINOCULARS AND
BEAL NA MBLATH

COLLINS AND MULCAHY had been involved in negotiations with the
Four Courts men on and off since the occupation. Realistically speaking,
there was very little prospect that these would ever have been successful.
Between those seeking to run a state by more or less normal, democratic
methods, and those who seek to subvert it by any and every possible
means, there is very little common ground. The British rejection of the
Constitution ensured that what little remained was cut away. All that was
left was a shared reluctance by both sides to fire on old friends. But by
18 June the basic incompatibility of the two sides had reached a position
where it only required a spark to ignite the powder train. Negotiations had
broken down on the Four Courts men's demands, which crystallized
around a proposal that they should have the right to appoint the Chief of
Staff of the Army. On the 18th the Four Courts men held another
convention, at which Tom Barry proposed that the IRA should resume the
war against Britain. Those who supported him split from those under Liam
Lynch, who opposed it, and returned to the Four Courts. Here they chose
a new leader, Joseph McKelvey, to replace Lynch, and began making plans
for an offensive against the North and against the British Army units still
left in the South. Lynch set up his headquarters in the Clarence Hotel
across the River Liffey from the Four Courts.

The situation thus presented to Collins and his allies was that any attack
on the British would at best have halted the evacuation of British officials
from Ireland and at worst have involved the Provisional Government in
fighting O'Connor and his men alongside the British Army. Following the
election the Collins faction was now in a better position to move against the
Four Courts; and the time which had been spent in negotiation, although
infuriating to Collins' Cabinet colleagues, meant that the new national
Army being built up from Beggars Bush was now in a far stronger position
than it had been at the time of the initial seizure. But, while Collins still
hesitated, on 22 June Sir Henry Wilson was assassinated in London and the
clouds of war closed over Dublin.

It was in fact Collins who had authorized the assassination as a
retaliation for the slaughter of Catholics in the Six Counties, though this
was not generally realized at the time. A recently released letter to Collins
indicates that Wilson's death was probably sealed the previous March. The

letter, from a London informant, describes the discussion of a 'political plot' by 'certain Government officials'. The officials were quoted as saying:[1]

> Sir Henry Wilson is to act in Ulster with Sir James Craig. The Conservative element of the Coalition is to get rid of Lloyd George as Premier at any cost. They anticipate being able to get Cabinet control [they did so the following October]. When they have gained this object, civil war will break out in Ulster (preparations for same being now well in hand), and to re-establish what is considered English prestige, the reconquest of Ireland will be effected. The English public is to be doped with the idea of civil war and British troops will be invited to restore law and order in Ulster, and will later find it necessary to go over the border. The conversation ended with a laugh from one member of the group, who stated that they would exterminate the swine this time for good.

Pressed by journalists for his comments on Wilson's assassination, de Valera issued a cleverly worded statement saying:[2]

> The killing of a human being is an awful act, but as awful when the victim is the humble worker or peasant, unknown outside his own immediate neighbourhood, as when the victim is placed in the seats of the mighty and his name known in every corner of the earth. It is characteristic of our own hypocritical civilisation that it is in the latter case only we are expected to cry out and express our horror and condemnation.
>
> . . . I do not know who they were who shot Sir Henry Wilson, or why they shot him. . . . I know that life has been made a hell for the Nationalist minority in Belfast and its neighbourhood for the past couple of years. . . . I do not approve but I must not pretend to misunderstand. . . .

He managed to impute blame for the killing to the Treaty: 'In London, last December, a regard for justice would have secured a lasting peace between Ireland and England. . . . But so-called expediency and threats of war intervened and we have what we have. . . .'

But the Provisional Government's responsibility in the matter was not to be allowed to end with the issuing of a statement. The British Cabinet may have guessed the truth of the killing, but preferred to attribute it to Four Courts elements rather than to someone with whom they had signed a Treaty that was already grossly unpopular in Tory circles. Either way Lloyd George had to be seen to take action. Not only was evacuation halted; initially a resumption of hostilities was discussed with Macready, but he managed to buy time and cooler counsels prevailed. However, strong pressure was exerted on Dublin to proceed against the O'Connorites. Apart from the Wilson murder and the pressure, the election result would probably have emboldened the Provisional Government into taking action anyhow. But the Four Courts men guaranteed that that point would be reached sooner rather than later. Four days after Wilson's death they kidnapped Ginger O'Connell, the Deputy Chief of Staff of the Beggars Bush HQ, in retaliation for the arrest of one of their own officers. At 3.40 a.m. on 28 June an ultimatum was delivered to the Four Courts men, telling them to evacuate by 4 a.m. It was ignored, and twenty minutes later Collins' men started shelling the building with field pieces borrowed from the British.

The generally accepted version[3] of how de Valera learned of the shelling has him driving to Dublin from Greystones in a car loaned to him by Liam Mellows, unaware of what was happening until he was stopped at Stillorgan and warned not to go any further because people had been killing each other in Dublin since the early morning. This is reminiscent of the official version of the manner in which he first heard of the Treaty's signing, except that on this occasion we are led to believe that no one thought of making a telephone call to Greystones. At all events, he is said to have replied that if people were being killed it was all the more reason why he should carry on to town. He was saluted through a barricade manned by Government forces and drove into his Suffolk Street office, where he issued a statement saying that:[4] 'At the bidding of the English, Irishmen are today shooting down, on the streets of our capital, brother Irishmen. . . . In Rory O'Connor and his comrades lives the unbought indomitable soul of Ireland. . . . Irish citizens! Give them support! Irish soldiers! Bring them aid!'

After that there was not much he could do except bring what aid he could to the insurgents in person. He rejoined his old unit, the 3rd Battalion, again took the Volunteer Oath, and was posted to the Hammam Hotel in O'Connell Street with other notable figures on the Republican side including Robert Barton and Cathal Brugha, Austin Stack and the leader of the Republicans in Dublin, Oscar Traynor, OC of the Dublin Brigade. The concentration of leadership was symptomatic of the Republicans' lack of military expertise. Traynor had commandeered a set of buildings on the opposite side of O'Connell Street to the Four Courts, so there was no prospect of relieving the garrison. O'Connor had arranged for a tunnel to be dug from the Four Courts to allow for escape via the Liffey, but he forgot that the river was tidal which made the tunnel useless. The Four Courts surrendered on the afternoon of 30 June, an occasion marked by one of the greatest acts of vandalism ever perpetrated in Dublin. Two lorry-loads of gelignite were exploded under the Public Records Office in the Four Courts complex; for hours afterwards fragments of centuries-old documents drifted over Dublin. And for another five days Dublin reverberated to the sound of gunfire as O'Connell Street was wrecked for the second time in six years. The Archbishop of Dublin and the Labour Party attempted to mediate between the combatants, but the negotiations foundered on the Republicans' refusal to surrender their arms. De Valera escaped from the fighting, according to Mulcahy, in a Red Cross Ambulance. He later denied that he had donned a white coat to help him get away; but a hitherto unpublished eye-witness account of an encounter with him during the battle, which describes his political thinking as the crisis burst around him, comes from a St John's Ambulance man, F.

Homan,[5] who acted as a Collins–de Valera go-between. Homan had been told by Father Albert, the Capuchin monk who remained with the Republicans in the Fourt Courts during the bombardment, that a 'friendly message' from Collins would go a long way towards securing peace. He duly received an assurance from Collins which he described as follows:

> Tell these men that neither I, nor any member of the Government, nor any officer in the army (and I learned the feelings of every officer in Dublin on my rounds yesterday) not one of us wishes to hurt a single one of them, or to humiliate them in any way that can be avoided. They are at liberty to march out and go to their homes unmolested if only they will – I do not use the word *surrender* – if only they will deposit their weapons in the national armoury, there to remain until and unless in the whirl of politics these men become a majority in country in which case they will themselves have control of them.

It was not the least of Ireland's tragedies that that message was not acted upon. Father Albert, whom Homan discovered busy hearing confessions, was delighted to be interrupted with Collins' reply but left Homan to be dealt with by Robert Barton while he returned to cope with problems more pressing than a mere outbreak of civil war – the preparation of men's souls for the next world, to which the said civil war seemed increasingly likely to consign them. Barton's reaction was interpreted by Homan as: 'We want no terms save victory or death.' And there that phase of his peace mission ended. However, because of it, he was subsequently involved in the provision of a safe conduct for de Valera from the Government, and of a car to bring him to the Shelbourne Hotel where an elderly Irish American bishop, Dr O'Reilly, wanted to explore peace prospects with him.

De Valera sent back a friendly message to the old bishop, whom he had met in America, but refused to come to the Shelbourne. However, he had an interview of 'about an hour an a half' with Homan which the latter said he would not set down in full because, apart from its length, it 'would certainly not serve the cause I have been engaged in if I were to repeat vehement expressions regarding certain actions and persons'. But he did record the political *tour d'horizon* on which de Valera took him and the positions which de Valera wished to have attributed to him as shot and shell burst around himself and his listener: 'Mr. de Valera described the difficulties created for him by the Treaty, his efforts to reconcile the opposing parties in the Dail, the reasons for the two pacts and his disappointment at their results, the setting up of the Army Executive without his wishing it (indeed I gathered contrary to his wishes) although the circumstances precluded him from actively opposing it.' De Valera then went on to describe '. . . his anxiety and his efforts for peace and for the unity of the Army, the warning (which he declared his opponents were very wrong in describing as a threat) that the acceptance of the Treaty might involve the country in civil war, the unsatisfactory character of the proposed Constitution and his despair of amending it while his opponents had a majority which they were prepared to make subservient to English ministers.' Finally, Homan mentioned 'his utter inability to prevent the present outbreak, which he declared was begun by the Government in obedience to English ministers'.

Eventually Homan got round to the subject of Collins' message. De Valera pronounced it a distinct advance on what Collins had already said: '. . . let them lay down their arms and then we'll talk to them'. He left Homan to discuss the matter with 'The Brigadier' (probably Traynor), and returned to say that he would be prepared to recommend the insurgents to cease fighting on the understanding that they would be allowed to go home taking their weapons with them. De Valera said he believed that they would agree to this. He spoke feelingly of the love for his weapon engendered in each man by years of fighting, and told Homan that the right to retain his rifle (shared as it was by every other citizen) would do much to mitigate the present feeling. He did not propose that the men captured in the Four Courts should be given back their weapons, but he did stipulate that when the men in the Gresham and Hammam Hotels were allowed to return home so too should the Four Courts prisoners. In view of what subsequently befell the Four Courts leaders, this was as ironic as it was unreal.

Not surprisingly Collins rejected the proposal, pointing out the damage already done; the risk that conflict would bring the British back; and that, even if this did not happen, the credibility of the Provisional Government would be gravely undermined. 'And all for what?' he thundered. To gratify 'the alleged sentimental desire of some desperadoes to hold up the Government of the country any time they liked, and indulge in bloodshed, raids, and anarchy. He expressed amazement that any citizen should express approval of such a proposition or allow himself to become an emissary of Mr. de Valera in pressing it.'

However, Collins ultimately cooled down and parted amicably, with Homan saying that leniency in the treatment of prisoners he entirely agreed with, but that retention of weapons would be indefensible. When Homan got back to the Hammam he found that most of the occupants had departed, including de Valera who by that time was being moved from one safe house to another. Homan has left a memorable pen picture of one of the few who remained, Cathal Brugha, 'brandishing a large revolver'. Homan's description provides an accurate insight into the mind set of a classic example of the type of 'extremist support' on which de Valera had allowed himself to become dependent. Before Brugha even spoke, Homan says he realized that 'negotiations seemed hopeless. For here was a man whose resolve . . . was clearly imprinted on his face – a resolve not to leave that house alive if he could find death without committing suicide. It was not merely that he was willing to give up his life, he was determined to give it up – to get away from it. His motives (I thought I read in his face at least two, perhaps a third) – but this is not the place for them. . . .'

Brugha refused to discuss Collins' terms. 'Lay down our arms? Never. We are out to achieve our object or to die. There is no use negotiating with Mr. Collins.' Then he asked: 'What exactly did Mr. de Valera propose?' When he was told, his reaction was: 'He could not carry the fighting men with him on that, the most they would agree to would be to leave this place with their arms and go and join our men fighting elsewhere and for my part I would oppose even that. You are wasting your time. We are here to fight to the death.' He was true to his word. The next day the Hammam fell and Brugha went down firing. It would obviously have been very difficult to take him alive, but Dave Neligan told me that some of the troops opposed to Brugha had made up their minds not even to attempt to do so. He was regarded as a dangerous fanatic, and was probably shot in the back as he advanced on a barricade near the Hammam. Ever magnanimous, Collins was deeply grieved by the news of his death, but after Collins himself was killed it would be the spirit of those who shot Brugha which would permeate the Government forces rather than that of Collins.

The start of the civil war inaugurated a bad time for de Valera and an equally unpleasant one for Sinead. Their youngest child, Terry, was just a month old when de Valera made his escape from the Hammam. Once it was realized that he had done so the house was raided during the night by armed men seeking to arrest him. Sinead refused to speak to them other than in Irish. In successive raids the children learned to adopt the same technique. Vivion told me a story of those days which illustrated the turmoil and division that the family went through. Remembering how Collins had risked his life to visit them during the Black and Tan war, 'when the row started over the Treaty', Vivion said to his mother: 'Surely Uncle Mick couldn't be wrong!' He was shushed into silence and bundled out of the kitchen. Sinead could not solve all her problems so easily. She returned her husband's Dail salary to Collins and applied lessons she had learned in 1916 to making do on short commons. Eventually the raids and the isolation of Greystones caused her to move with the children to 18 Claremont Road, Sandymount.

De Valera himself moved south out of Dublin. He was now in the anomalous position of being the political leader of a movement that for the moment had no use for politics. The attack on the Fourt Courts had resolved Liam Lynch's uncertainties. He was arrested, but released by Mulcahy in the mistaken belief that he would dissuade his followers from hostilities. In fact he made his way south and became Chief of Staff of the militants. The anti-Treaty forces now became known as 'the irregulars' to their opponents, whom they termed Free Staters. And, for a time, Lynch would literally call more of the shots than de Valera, who however showed remarkable resilience in working himself back, in a matter of months only, from a very difficult situation into a position of power

The Provisional Government postponed the opening of the new Dail and set up a War Council, headed by Collins who took over as Commander-in-

Chief of the Army while Cosgrave became acting head of the Provisional Government. Initially the Republican, or irregular, forces would appear to have held the initiative in terms of both numbers and positions secured. At the start of the fighting virtually all of Munster was in their hands and Rory O'Connor claimed to represent 80 per cent of the IRA. But he and his comrades proved in practice to be so disorganized and lacking in leadership that by the time of his death, only some seven weeks after the fall of the Four Courts, Collins had broken the back of the irregulars' resistance. Seaborne landings spearheaded by a few hand-picked men from the Squad captured rebel strongholds, such as Cork and Kerry, in surprise attacks. Limerick fell to a determined assault from Provisional Government troops. From now on there was to be no 'conceding to mutineers'. The civil war would continue for several months afterwards, brutally and destructively, by means of guerilla warfare, but all hope of a win for armed resistance to the Treaty was gone within weeks of the first shots being fired.

No one was more aware of this fact than de Valera, and it forced him to adopt a contradictory twin-track approach to regaining power. On the one hand he needed to be seen by the militants to be prepared to play a soldier's role; on the other he soon realized that nothing except a peaceful policy had any long-term hope of success. Even before the civil war broke out the election result had shown the feelings of the majority, and the destruction of war intensified the wish for peace. To help bring this about he now needed not only extremist support but extremist control. De Valera met the conflicting claims of the situation in his own inimitable way. First, he did enough soldiering to show that he was not letting down in their hour of need those whom he had incited to militancy. His official biography says that:[6] '. . . while there was any chance of success, de Valera plunged whole-heartedly into the war. As he saw it, the Republican Army was throwing itself across the stampede of a nation.' An emissary sent by Joseph McGarrity to Ireland shortly after the civil war began reported back admiringly to McGarrity that she had witnessed de Valera:[7] '. . . with a rifle slung on his shoulder, towering head and shoulders above his men, similarly equipped, in a big lorry dashing out to a battle'.

Lorry-borne battles, however, were few and far between. Even the official biography concedes that[8] 'de Valera and his comrades were hustled from one position to another'. Having fled Dublin after the fall of the Hammam, he made his way to Clonmel where the Republicans had set up their GHQ. Here he was received with honour, and a contingent of Liam Lynch's men escorted him into the town. Harry Boland wrote to McGarrity:[9] 'The Chief is at G.H.Q., hale and well, the same gentle, honest, straight-forward, unpurchaseable man that you knew. All the calumny that has been heaped upon him is British inspired; they failed to bribe or intimidate him, they now try the weapon of slander.'

Around the middle of the month he was appointed adjutant to Sean Moylan, who was nominally Director of Operations. Most of the operations consisted of retreats. The advancing Free State forces had a couple of borrowed British field pieces in front of them, most of the people with them – and the genius of Michael Collins behind them. Opposing them, figures like Sean Moylan fought fairly, but reluctantly, with no real enthusiasm for what they were doing. The large question mark which de Valera placed under 'address' when asked by the butler to fill in the visitors' book on his departure from a commandeered house outside Cahir was symbolic of the uncertainty of the movement's destination as much as of his own. It was also symptomatic of the temper of the warfare of the period. The reason he signed the book that day, 29 July, was because the owner, a Colonel Charteris, was coming home from Cowes. Later in the war the Republicans adopted a scorched earth policy of burning such 'big houses'. Along with the loss of some lovely old buildings this cost the country many collections of priceless antique furnishings and works of art. The only recorded damage done by de Valera's men, however, was to the panelling in the hall which suffered in the course of target practice.[10]

The day after he left that house a loss occurred which was more indicative of the cost of civil war. Harry Boland was fatally wounded in a scuffle in a hotel in Skerries, Co. Dublin; he was buried on 5 August. Arthur Griffith, whom strain and exhaustion had consigned to a Dublin nursing home, died of a brain haemorrhage on 12 August. Michael Collins was killed in an ambush on 22 August. Each of these blows hit de Valera hard and for different reasons. Boland's death, Kathleen O'Connell recorded, cost him 'his most faithful friend'.[11] His own diary shows that Griffith's elicited a jumble of responses. Memories of their earlier association, of Griffith's selflessness, their more recent differences – and a significant indication of guilty pride. Why had Griffith signed the Treaty without referring back to him? 'Did he think when it was signed I'd accept the fait accompli?'[12] Whatever answer he gave himself, no one was in a better position than de Valera to evaluate how much his own stubborn reaction to the affront to his ego posed by that *fait accompli* had contributed both to Griffith's stress and the situation in which he, and the nation, now found themselves. Collins' death generated all the reactions caused by the earlier deaths, compounded and heightened by the linked facts that his course of conduct had both left him unable to influence events and exposed him to the very real danger of retribution from Collins' comrades. De Valera now suffered a nervous fit similar to the one he had experienced in 1916. Before describing it, however, it is necessary to back-track for a few weeks in order to understand his position at that stage vis-à-vis the fighting men he sought to bend to his will.

His biography makes the point that: 'At no time during the civil war did he rank as a military leader.'[13] But he was obviously a figure of importance in the Republican GHQ. He moved less to any directive of his nominal commander, Sean Moylan, than he did of his own volition. At this stage the irregulars still held Cork, where they had taken over the *Cork*

Examiner and placed Frank Gallagher in charge as Editor. De Valera decided to 'fight a propaganda war'.[14] To help him do this he assembled a team consisting of Childers, Robert Brennan and Kathleen O'Connell, who managed to issue editions of *Poblacht na h-Eireann* printed on a handpress. In addition to these propaganda activities de Valera took the extraordinary step of having Vivion sent down from Dublin 'to stay near him in the home of a friend'.[15] Whether this step was taken to give the boy a holiday in those unlikely surroundings, or so that his son's presence in the vicinity would be a safeguard for Sinead against gossip concerning O'Connell, it is impossible to say. Dc Valera did try to take the children with him on normal election campaigns; but in this case he brought his eldest son, a twelve-year-old, into the war's cockpit. Apart from the danger for the boy, this was a highly uncharacteristic security risk for a man whose behaviour during both the Anglo-Irish war and the civil war was notable for his almost obsessive concern for disguise and for not giving clues as to his whereabouts. Even during this period he[16] 'put on horn-rimmed glasses and grew a beard, wearing habitually a trench-coat and a cap pulled over his face'.

De Valera did take part in one major act of military destruction that recalled his advocacy of the Custom House burning – the blowing up of the Ten Arch Bridge carrying the Dublin–Cork railway over the Blackwater near Mallow. It was Childers' idea to make it difficult for the Free Staters to catch up with irregular troops retreating to Kerry. But de Valera refused to intervene to halt the demolition, which caused major disruption of economic and social activity in the county. A county surveyor who interceded with him 'met only obduracy'.[17] The demolition 'would save thousands of lives,' de Valera argued; in fact it cost the irregulars a great deal of support. Later he acknowledged this, but without changing his attitude. Looking at the ruins of the bridge from the riverside home of William O'Brien, the old Irish Party stalwart, whom he called on shortly afterwards:[18] 'Dev volunteered that his was the most hated Party in Ireland but a party that intended to go on fighting'. He certainly was one of the most hated figures in Ireland at that moment. English booksellers cancelled their orders for a biography of him by David Dwane, which before the fighting had been a bestseller, and Free State soldiers raided bookshops to destroy existing copies.

De Valera sought to convince O'Brien that he had been a[19] 'constitutionalist from beginning to end' but was now in a dilemma about what he should do next. He began to deliver a dissertation on the Treaty's genesis, saying: 'In the London negotiations I should have preferred to make our first stand upon the integrity of Ireland, and the inclusion of the Six Counties. . . .' O'Brien cut him off by asking why had he not gone to the negotiations. De Valera responded[20] 'as if a nerve had been touched' to the effect that he had remained in Ireland as a reserve in case the British behaved badly. He argued that 'all the world would have been with us' had the envoys not given in over partition; even Craig would have seen the light and come under the sway of a united Ireland. He again repeated the point he wished to have accepted ever afterwards:[21] 'Now that it was war, he was only a soldier again and the military men were in command.' The remains of the shattered bridge, clearly visible through the window, formed an appropriate backdrop for that statement. He left after two hours, adding to his reputation for asceticism, as he was wont to do on occasion, by studiously refusing all offers of food or drink. Outside the house a car and driver waited to take him to his next port of call. It was the day Arthur Griffith died.

The manner in which de Valera departed from O'Brien's house, juxtaposed with Griffith's death, symbolized his political role at that moment. Tragedies and matters of great moment were taking place around him, which he was sometimes in a position to influence – but not to control. He was a figure of consequence, but not of command; more responsible than he suggested to O'Brien, but still not in control. When he first joined the GHQ he had urged Lynch to negotiate, to seek a truce while he was still in a position of strength. But a number of factors told against him. First, as a sympathetic biographer has noted,[22] the 'intricacies of the proposals he expounded as he paced the floor were incomprehensible to the fighters coming and going at the field headquarters'. Also, in the early stages of the fighting the strength of the Republicans was such that Lynch saw no need to negotiate; later, as defeats mounted up, he grew more stubborn and determined to fight on. But the most important difficulty facing de Valera at this stage was the fact that he was himself undecided as to which was the best policy – to fight on, or to desist. According to a note he made in his diary[23] on the day he spoke with O'Brien, his analysis was: 'Any chance of winning? If there was any chance, duty to hold on to secure it. If none, duty to try to get the men to quit – *for the present* [author's italics]. The people must be won to the cause before any successful fighting can be done. The men dead and gloomy – just holding on.'

This is what it is averred he wrote privately. But publicly he gave at least one witness to understand that his main preoccupation was with the reaction of the British and Michael Collins. Peter Golden, an American who was guided to his farmhouse hiding-place near Gougane Barra, described finding him:[24] '. . . heartsick and distraught at the terrible things which had come to the nation and its people . . . he is overweighed with grief. He speaks with great kindness of Arthur Griffith. He is fearful that the next step will be a military dictatorship set up by Mick Collins taking his orders from England.'

This dictatorial portrayal of Collins, of course, leaves out one inconvenient fact: Collins had had to manoeuvre de Valera into allowing an election to be held at a time when he was supporting Rory O'Connor, who had openly declared in favour of a military dictatorship. All the contradictions of his position came home to roost in the circumstances surrounding the death of Collins ten days later. Two days earlier the irregulars had held a crucial meeting in Ballyvourney, a remote beauty spot in West Cork. They had agreed Lynch's plans for abandoning the type of static warfare in which they had fared so disastrously to date, and reverting to the old guerilla tactics that, ironically, Collins had been foremost in developing. One of those who argued against this decision was Tom Hales, a man who, rather than betray Collins, had once resisted British torture that drove his fellow prisoner mad.[25] It would be his karma to lead the ambush which killed 'The Big Fellow'.

The Ballyvourney meeting had brought many prominent leaders of irregulars to the area, including Childers and de Valera. Two days after the Ballyvourney decision a meeting of the officers of Cork Nos 1 and 2 Brigades was in progress, in Long's pub at the entrance to a little valley called Beal na mBlath, the mouth of flowers, when word reached de Valera that Collins was in the area. He was apparently revisiting the scenes of his boyhood while on a visit to Cork in an attempt to establish contact with the irregulars. On hearing that Collins was about, de Valera drove to the scene of the IRA meeting and discovered that Collins had indeed driven past the pub a little earlier. As a result, plans had been made for the first major application of the new guerilla warfare policy – an ambush had been laid in case he returned to Cork via Beal na mBlath.

De Valera was angered and upset.[26] He wanted to take the opportunity of Collins' presence in the area to try to negotiate peace terms with him. He pointed out to the IRA men that the option of surrender had to be considered. According to an account by his ADC which I have seen, he 'virtually pleaded with them' that they were far more likely to get benign terms from Collins in his own county than from his colleagues in Dublin. However, he was bluntly told that his rank in the area was merely that of a staff officer subject to Liam Lynch, whose directive on guerilla warfare they intended to implement. De Valera then 'stormed out of the meeting in a rage'.[27] Later that night, when he heard the news of Collins' death, he was described as[28] 'furious and visibly upset'. By then Michael Collins' brains were seeping through a gaping head wound on to the shoulders of men who had to carry his body across fields and ditches in the darkness because of the irregulars' bridge-blowing activities in which de Valera had participated.

The next day de Valera awoke fully alive to the peril of his position. Collins had friends to whom the taking of life presented little problem. Taking his would have been a great pleasure to some of them at that moment. He was reviled in press, pub and pulpit. One Cork priest, Canon Cohalan of Bandon, preached a sermon in which he said:[29] 'The day Michael Collins was shot, where was de Valera? Ask the people of Beal na mBlath and they will tell you. There was a scowling face at a window looking out over that lonely valley and de Valera could tell you who it was.'

He had spent the night in Fethard in Co. Tipperary. An eight-man escort of armed men had been provided to get him to Callan in Co. Kilkenny, and the leader of the escort has recorded his behaviour that day. He asked to be allowed to travel without being spoken to. Accordingly the bulk of the party went ahead to form a scouting party, while only the leader remained within earshot of, but not talking to, de Valera. The party took a cross-country route of some fifteen miles on foot. During the journey:[30] '. . . de Valera seemed very distressed and he appeared to be talking or muttering to himself. Several times when he spoke out loud, not addressing me or anybody in the escort, I distinctly heard him say, "I told them not to do it, even pleaded with them, but they wouldn't listen to me and now what will become of us all". Dev was so distressed when he spoke out that I felt he was crying.'

However, he was not long about drying his tears. Discovering that he had left his binoculars in the house near Beal na mBlath to which Canon Cohalan alluded, he wrote to his hostess asking that they be sent on to him in Dublin. He failed to get them, but another request he made around the same time was more successful. His reason for returning to Dublin was to see what use he could make of his political party in view of the fact that the opening of the Dail that should have taken place following the elections was now definitely fixed, after many postponements, for 9 September. Lynch had not replied to a written request that he had made to be allowed to talk to each member of the IRA executive individually. He wanted to weigh up the support, or lack of it, that he might expect from the fighting men for any political initiatives he might take. If he could not be sure of the 'extremist support' he had courted to the point of picking up a gun once more, he knew that at that stage he was out on a political limb.

Accordingly, in the absence of any communication from Lynch he sought a meeting with Richard Mulcahy, who had succeeded Collins as Commander-in-Chief of the Free State forces. According to his official biography:[31] 'Still bent on reconciliation, de Valera agreed to meet General Mulcahy . . . in Dr. Farnan's house in Merrion Square'. Mulcahy's papers give a different picture. According to him, he only agreed to see de Valera after repeated entreaties from a Monsignor Ryan of San Francisco, who assured him that de Valera was a[32] 'changed man'. Mulcahy initially refused, telling the Monsignor that: 'Mr. de Valera could stop the civil war by writing a letter to the *Evening Mail*.' But he relented after further entreaties. In so doing Mulcahy, who was also Minister for Defence, was at some distance from his Cabinet colleagues – on 5 September, only the day before the meeting took place, the Cabinet had decided to put an end to a spate of well-meaning but futile peace attempts by decreeing that there should be no more without explicit Cabinet approval.

The meeting proved to have a far more fateful outcome than appears in de Valera's official biography. The pair met under safe conduct and spoke together alone after the Monsignor had opened the proceedings by administering a blessing to them. It proved to be somewhat lacking in efficacy. With his talent for psychological scene-setting, the Long Fellow appears to have made use of his advantage in height over the short Mulcahy. For though de Valera's accounts of the meeting do not give much detail of its content, Mulcahy's says:[33]

> We met one another standing and remained standing. I took the initiative in saying that the position in Ireland was that [there] are two things to my mind that were important: 1 That somebody should be allowed to work the Treaty, and 2 That if there was to be an army in Ireland it should be subject to Parliament. Given these two things I didn't care who ruled the country as long as they were representative elected Irish men and women, and I came to a full stop. The 'changed man' still standing in front of me said:
> 'Some men are led by faith and some men are led by reason, but as long as there are men of faith like Rory O'Connor taking the stand that he is taking, I am a humble soldier following after them'.

At this, Mulcahy concluded that his mission was over. 'There was no room for discussion,' he said. A biographer who discussed the meeting with de Valera afterwards reports that:[34] 'His unaltered suggestion was to seek new terms from the British based on external association' – hardly an innovative proposal at that stage. Not surprisingly, in his diary de Valera noted: 'Couldn't find a basis. Mulcahy was looking for a basis in acceptance of the Treaty – we in revision of the Treaty.' And in a letter to McGarrity[35] de Valera later wrote airily that the meeting was 'rather amusing', but did go on to explain that acceptance of the Treaty would 'Of course mean "quit" for the Republicans and if it has to be done, it is much better [to] do it boldly without any camouflage'.

Unfortunately the outcome of the talk was far from 'amusing'. For after listening to de Valera Mulcahy also came to the conclusion that it was best to 'act boldly and without camouflage'. He deduced that, decoded, de Valera's utterances meant in practice that he was lending his authority to a policy of destruction which could only end in the ruin of the new state. To counter this he decided that reprisal executions were necessary, but that, unlike the British use of the reprisal weapon during the Black and Tan phase, the executions should be officially sanctioned. Nine days after meeting de Valera he formally placed this proposal before the Cabinet.[36] The Government accepted it and introduced a draconian Emergency Powers Bill which gave the Army permission to set up military courts which could impose the death penalty for a wide range of offences. Apart from attacks on military personnel these included arson, destruction or commandeering of property, looting, and possession of either weapons or explosives. Thus, far from leading to 'reconciliation', the talks in Farnan's house led to the introduction of one of the most fearsome pieces of legislation ever seen in Ireland. In a nutshell, it made any act of war by the irregulars/Republicans punishable by death. Cosgrave said flatly:[37] 'We are not going to treat rebels as prisoners of war.' The Irish revolutionary wheel had come full circle. The Irish were about to do unto their brothers as the British had done unto them.

But the Emergency Powers Bill was not de Valera's immediate concern. His priority was to secure a position of political authority. His brief taste of the bomb and the gun had shown him that that was not the way forward. One of his motives in meeting Mulcahy had been to tease out some guidelines on how he should react to the opening of the new Dail. Some of his followers favoured the summoning of an assembly based on those who had been deputies prior to the June elections. In their view, the Provisional Government had illegally destroyed the Dail and the Republic for which it stood. In public de Valera shared their position that the Provisional Government was an illegal junta; but he was long-headed enough to foresee the possibility of a day dawning when he might have an opportunity of entering the 'illegal' assembly, and he did not wish to tie his hands in advance with a policy directive which might prevent him taking that course. Accordingly he refused to hold a 'Dail' consisting of his followers only, pointing out that they had already, earlier in the year, attended a Parliament summoned by the said junta. But before meeting Mulcahy he promised a party worker, Colm O'Murchadha, that he would let him know the line to be followed after 'tonight's interview'.[38]

After the meeting he made his way to a typewriter and typed a message to O'Murchadha, stating that 'for reasons of principle and expediency' non-attendance would be justified when the Dail opened. His reasons of 'principle' were that it would not be a real Dail because it would derive its authority from British acts rather than from the second Dail. The second Dail had not been summoned to abolish itself formally, as should have occurred after the general election; therefore the second Dail was still technically in existence. Entry would, of course, also involve taking an oath. In plain language it would be what it set out to be, and what an overwhelming majority of public opinion expected it to be – a Parliament functioning in accordance with the Treaty. Where 'expediency' was concerned, he was worried that the IRA might regard him as having entered 'an illegal assembly in as much as it was summoned by the illegal junta called the Provisional Government'. This would reveal divisions on the Republican side. Moreover, as his faction was outnumbered they would be easily outvoted. 'Our presence at the meeting would help to solidify all other groups against us. We would be the butt of every attack. We could not explain – we would be accused of obstructing the business and "talking" when we should get on with the work.' But with an eye to the future he also wrote:[39] 'If we issue a statement it will tie our hands and if at a future time a course other than non-attendance should seem wise we might find ourselves precluded from taking it.'

With that canny 'saver' he laid the whole basis of his future political life, the formation of a new political party and his ultimate entry to the Dail. One is tempted to wonder whether there was some unconscious symbolism in the fact that he put the carbon into the machine the wrong way round. 'Naturally he swore!'[40] But then 'Punctilious about keeping a record of his recommendations yet careful not to tie himself up in knots by stating policies that might embarrass him later he wrote, "could you have a carbon made of this letter and send it to me. . . ."'[41]

His next move was to write an important letter to Joe McGarrity on 10 September, which sought his support *inter alia* for a campaign in Washington to 'revise the Treaty'.[30] In the course of an analysis of the situation he admitted frankly that a majority of the people were for the Treaty. If the Republicans acquiesced in this preference, then they had to accept the 'abandonment of the national sovereignty' and partition. The Republicans' choice, therefore, lay between 'a heart-breaking surrender of what they have repeatedly proved was dearer to them than life and the repudiation of what they recognise to be the basis of all order in government and the keystone of democracy – majority rule.'

The use of the term 'they' in this well-put description of the Republican dilemma is revealing. Even in the eye of the storm of civil war de Valera was already preparing for a future which did not include the IRA. In fact, the letter as a whole could be taken as summing up both de Valera's own view of his political contemporaries and his delineation of policies which were crucial to his success in later life. It also clearly illustrates the strength of his ego, his contempt for his political opponents and his resentment against Collins:

> The Provisional Government feel that they are strong enough now to throw away all camouflage and reveal themselves as creatures of a British institution. . . . This is all to the good for the deception of Republicans by Michael Collins, especially the men in the army, was what most secured the acceptance of the Treaty at all. There cannot be deception any longer.
>
> The personnel of the Provisional Government is very weak. Cosgrave is a ninny. He will however be egged on by the church. Were it not for Mick's lead, there is no doubt in my mind that Mulcahy's policy would have been 'unity against the enemy', as the primary consideration. . . .

He wrongly accused Collins of having tried to have him assassinated: '. . . two of Mick's special men were sent down South to "get" me. One was ambushed and from what I have heard he will not be able to "get" anybody for some time. The other is down south still.'

The ambushed man was Frank Thornton,[42] one of Collins' principal intelligence agents, who had been sent south on a mission which had nothing whatever to do with de Valera. He was to have arranged safe conducts for irregulars with whom Collins wished to hold peace talks. It may be taken that the second man, whoever he was, was on a similar mission. De Valera went on to indicate to McGarrity his dissatisfaction with having to trail in the wake of the Lynch forces' policy, and he did so in a way which indicates how little of substance but how much of pride there was between his approach to the Treaty and that of Collins:

336

... the present position places upon me the responsibility for carrying out a programme which was not mine. The programme, 'Revise the Treaty' would be mine. . . . We will have a number of people shouting as before, what is the difference between Document 2 and the Treaty? You know of course that it is the difference between Peace and War. . . .

If the Free State should become operative, and . . . the present physical resistance fails, I see no programme by which we can secure independence but by a revival of the Sinn Fein idea in a new form. Ignoring England. Acting in Ireland as if there were no such person as the English King, no Governor-General, no Treaty, no oath of Allegiance. In fact acting as if Document No. 2 were the Treaty. Later we could act more independently still. Whilst the Free State were in supposed existence would be the best time to secure the unity of the country. . . . If we can get a single state for the whole of the country, then the future is safe.

Leaving aside the bland overlooking of the vast obstacles raised against the getting of a 'single state for the whole country', the foregoing raises one central question. In real terms, what was the substantive difference between Collins' acceptance of the Treaty as a 'stepping stone' towards full independence and a programme of 'Revise the Treaty' aimed at securing the same objective? The answer lay in the mind and personality of Eamon de Valera, and was certainly a causative factor in bringing about the civil war. The letter ended with an interesting indication of how de Valera could speak of someone who backed him, Harry Boland, as opposed to someone like Collins who opposed him:

Had the Coalition come into existence, I'd have nominated Harry as one of the Ministers from our side – and then he would have had his chance. Very few here understood Harry's worth. If I live I will write an account of what he did in the United States for Ireland. Loyal, generous, big-souled, bold, forceful Harry – Harry of the keen mind and broad sympathies. Incapable of the petty or the mean. Typical of the best in the Irishman, Harry was fit to be anything.

Interestingly, de Valera never did get round to writing that account, which raises the suspicion that some of the warmth in the tribute may have been generated by a consciousness of Boland's high standing in McGarrity's eyes. What is certain is that possibly the most significant evidence of de Valera's long-headedness occurs in a postscript to the letter. It deals with an injunction which the Provisional Government had taken out restraining him from drawing on the monies he had left behind in America: 'We have asked John F. Finnerty to watch the case for us. We may have to ask him to come over to get the material for the case. We are anxious to get their title contested, if only to expose their illegalities. It is we who are the constitutional party, properly so called, not they. They tore up and ignored the constitution. In fact their action has been a coup d'etat, nothing less.' What that copious use of the royal 'we' obscures is the fact that de Valera was setting in train an action which, as we shall see in Chapter 20, would lead to his founding what in effect became a family business.

But this is to anticipate. To return to September 1922: having sounded Mulcahy as to Free State policies, directed his own followers accordingly, and attempted to do the same for McGarrity and his American friends, de Valera now turned his attention to Lynch, who around this time had sent him a brief and unsatisfactory reply to his request of the previous month for a meeting with the Army executive. It stated that, because of the conditions prevailing, the executive had not met and was not likely to meet. Furthermore, Lynch concluded on a note which exasperated de Valera:[43] 'I would, however, be only too pleased to have your views at any time on the general situation, and matters arising out of it, and they will have my earnest consideration.'

De Valera did not take kindly to this brush-off. He was seeking authority, not mere 'consideration' for his views. He let it be known to the Suffolk Street faithful, via O'Murchadha,[44] that: 'This is too good a thing and won't do. If I don't get the position clear I shall resign publicly.' He issued some IRA men who visited him around this time with a not very heavily veiled threat of resignation:[45] 'If it is the policy of the party to leave it all to the army, well, then, the obvious thing for members of the party to do is to resign their position as public representatives.' And he told his political followers that the fact that the IRA had withdrawn its recognition from all political authority was the party's biggest stumbling block. Despite what he had said to Mulcahy about O'Connor, he painted a different picture for Cumann na Poblachta: 'Rory O'Connor's unfortunate repudiation of the Dail, which I was so foolish as to defend even to a straining of my own view in order to avoid the appearance of a split, is now the greatest barrier that we have.'

Of course he had not merely defended Rory O'Connor at the time of the Four Courts seizure. He had urged young men and women to join him in taking over Ireland. But what he was now doing, though more subtly than during the Treaty debates, was moving the goalposts towards the issue of his own great personal prestige and away from the question of the IRA's autonomy from political control. On 13 September he issued a letter to the members of Cumann na Poblachta and to the IRA executive which made Lynch an offer he could not refuse: in effect to share power with him or face the loss of his support and that of his followers. The letter proposed three courses of action:[46] 'Either (a) The Republican Party must take take control, acting as the legitimate Dail. (b) The Army Executive take control and assume responsibility. (c) A joint Committee be formed to decide policy for both.' In order to forestall any charges of a take-over bid he professed himself as being in favour of (b). He reasoned that the IRA would not support a political party, and that even if it did it had insufficient strength to make the Dail work. He said that (b) was 'most in accord with fact'. But then he went on to outline a scenario in which the IRA took full responsibility for both the fighting and his resignation:

> . . . the Army Executive must publicly accept responsibility. There must be no

doubt in the minds of anybody on the matter. This pretence from the pro-Treaty Party that we are inciting the army must be ended by a declaration from the army that this is not so. The natural corollary to this is that we, as a political party should cease to operate in any public way – resign in fact. This is the course I have long been tempted to take myself, and were it not that my action might prejudice the cause of the Republic, I'd have taken it long since. Our position as public representatives is impossible.

It took some time for this missive to be digested by the largely apolitical IRA executive. Their youth and conditioning predisposed them more towards focusing on the problems of a guerilla war that was going badly for them than on the formulae of a student of Machiavelli. However on 17 October de Valera got his way. An executive meeting held in a remote farmhouse in Ballybacon, near the Glen of Aherlow in Co. Tipperary, agreed to the issuing of the following proclamation which he drew up:[47] 'We, on behalf of the soldiers of the Republic in concert with such faithful members of Dail Eireann as are at liberty, acting in the spirit of our oath as the final custodians of the Republic, have called upon the former President, Eamon de Valera, to resume the Presidency and to form a government which shall preserve inviolate the sacred trust of National Sovereignty and Independence.'

Thus empowered, at a meeting in Dublin on the 25th de Valera duly formed a 'Government' which regarded itself as the second Dail.[48] For good measure he also formed a twelve-member Council of State. His Cabinet consisted of Austin Stack, Minister for Finance; Robert Barton, Minister for Economic Affairs; Liam Mellows, Minister for Defence; Sean T. O'Ceallaigh, Minister for Local Government; and P. J. Ruttledge, Minister for Home Affairs. As Mellows was in jail de Valera and Lynch arranged to co-sign all documents relating to the Department of Defence. De Valera's official biography sums up this performance by stating:[49] 'The Emergency Government came into being.' What in fact had happened was that de Valera had climbed back into the saddle. True, his horse had to gallop to the pace set by Liam Lynch, but he was astride none the less – even if his seat of power was an unreal sort of home-based Government-in-exile.

But there was nothing unreal about the grim life-and-death steps being taken by the Provisional Government while all these manoeuvrings were taking place. Following a short period of amnesty, the drastic Emergency Powers Bill came into force on 15 October. During its passage through the Dail, Provisional Government speakers had made it quite clear that one of its principal targets would be Erskine Childers. Kevin O'Higgins referred to him as keeping 'steadily, callously and ghoulishly at his career of striking at the heart of this nation, striking deadly, or what he hopes are deadly, blows at the economic life of this nation'.[50] His influence on de Valera during the Treaty negotiations; the subsequent Dail debates in which he was thought to be the real author of Document No. 2; his propaganda efforts; and his encouragement to the IRA to concentrate on economic targets like the Cork bridges – all these had made him a particular figure of hate.

De Valera unintentionally exposed him to this hate. Having set up his underground Government, he sent for Childers to become its secretary. Childers made his way successfully from Cork until he got to Robert Barton's house at Annamoe, Co. Wicklow, where he had been brought up. Here he was arrested in the early hours of 11 November. He was in possession of a small pistol given to him by Michael Collins, which he had not used because there were women in the house. Hitherto no executions had taken place under the Emergency Powers regulations, but on the day of Childers' appearance before the secret military court, 17 November, four rank-and-file IRA men who had been arrested in possession of weapons some time earlier were executed by firing squad. That evening in the Dail Kevin O'Higgins spelled out the reasons for their deaths with brutal honesty: 'If they took as their first case, some man who was outstandingly wicked in his activities, the unfortunate dupes throughout the country might say that he was killed because he was a leader, because he was an Englishman, or because he combined with others to commit raids.' On the eve of his execution Childers instructed his twelve-year-old son, also Erskine, who would one day succeed de Valera as President of Ireland, never to do or say anything that would cause bitterness – an injunction which the future President obeyed throughout his life in politics.

Childers was shot on the morning of 24 November. The execution was delayed for an hour until the light improved. Before it Childers said:[51] 'I die full of love for Ireland', shook hands with each member of the firing squad and beckoned them nearer before they took aim. In this last, Childers, an ex-British officer, was literally dead right. Nerves and inexperience apparently led to hideous occurrences at some other executions of the period.

Another man for whom political activity with de Valera was also said to have almost had fatal consequences that month was Ernie O'Malley. He had escaped after the fall of the Four Courts and become Assistant Chief of Staff of the IRA, using a house in exclusive Ailesbury Road as his headquarters; it was owned by Sheila Humphries' mother, a sister of The O'Rahilly. O'Malley had been staying in the house for six weeks and 'returned late that night',[52] although he was to have spent the night in another house so as to have a fitting for a badly needed new suit. The house was raided at 7.30 the next morning, 4 November, and O'Malley received some twenty-three wounds. Sixteen bullets were taken from his body. Incredibly, he survived not only this trauma but a subsequent forty-day hunger strike while in prison, recovering to write some of the best literature of the troubled times.[53]

The Ailesbury Road incident added to de Valera's mythic reputation. Even though he was nowhere near when the shoot-out occurred, the following account of the raid was written by an American academic, Mary Bromage, after several interviews with him some forty years later:[54] 'Everyone at the meeting was a wanted man but the Chief, the others knew, was the most wanted of them all. He managed to reach a rear exit while O'Malley in the hall drew the fire. . . . A few days afterwards, from an unknown spot, the newly acclaimed Republican President issued a statement of defiance to offset persistent rumours of peace: "Victory for the Republic or utter defeat are now the alternatives."' The writer prefaced her biography by saying: ' . . . the actual happening, the word written close to the moment and incontrovertible outcome have been the criteria in my view of this man and the country he made his'. She might have added: ' . . . and the history he made his'.

The truth is that following his rejection of the Treaty, if not in the months before then, but certainly for most of the civil war period, de Valera's normal shrewd judgement appears to have deserted him.[54a] In a letter to McGarrity dated 12 October 1922, commenting on Lloyd George's fall, he says:[55] 'L.G. has resigned. How strong we would have been now had they maintained the Pact.' In fact, of course, the opposite was the case. The Tories were the traditional allies of the Unionists. The supplanting of the Liberals by the Conservatives, while not leading to the scenario envisaged by Wilson, meant that, far from gaining strength, any influence that Irish nationalists had with the British Government was sharply lessened.

But, notwithstanding Bromage's remarks, there was nothing mythic about the era ushered in by the judicial murder of Erskine Childers. From then on the civil war entered a vile and violent phase that poisoned Irish public life for fifty years and set Irish political parties in a mould that to a large extent still exists as this is written. The following brief extract from the unholy litany of horrors will indicate why this should be so, and illustrate also the background against which de Valera tried to carry out the contradictory policies of urging both peace and war.

Following the Childers execution and those that preceded it, on 30 November the IRA had issued a warning threatening a wide variety of categories of persons with destruction of property and/or death. De Valera, as the Republican President with responsibility for the IRA, and who, of course, had specific co-responsibility with Lynch for the Ministry of Defence, was by definition a party to this warning. Its targets included judges, journalists and every member of the Provisional Parliament who had voted for the Emergency Powers measure which had set up the military courts. The Free State Constitution came into operation on 6 December, with Cosgrave being returned unopposed as President of the Executive Council. Next day the IRA translated the warning into action by shooting two members of the new Free State legislature – fatally in the case of Sean Hales, a close friend of Collins and a brother of the leader of the ambush which shot him. The other, Padraig O'Maille, Deputy Chairman of the Dail, was badly wounded. The Free State met terror with terror in a swift, ruthless and totally illegal action. That night four irregular leaders who had been in prison since the fall of the Four Courts and had no connection whatever with the shootings were wakened from their sleep and told they were to be executed in reprisal next morning.

The sentences were duly carried out on Rory O'Connor, Liam Mellows, Richard Barrett and Joseph McKelvey. The circumstances attending the death of Rory O'Connor[56] in particular would seem to have fully justified Childers' stoical efficiency in beckoning the firing squad nearer. Most of the squad aimed at him, setting his clothes on fire; nevertheless it is said that he had to request a number of pistol shots from the officer in charge of the squad before death finally came. In addition, the concentration of fire on him meant that at least one of the other three, Richard Barrett, also required additional bullets to administer the *coup de grâce*. O'Connor's death could be taken as symbolizing the entire tragic parting of the ways represented by the civil war. He had been Kevin O'Higgins' best man at his wedding a year earlier.

O'Higgins' father was shot dead in his home a few days later. In the course of a spate of attacks on the homes of Free State deputies and senators the seven-year-old son of one prominent IRB man, Sean McGarry, received fatal burns. Out of many incidents of kidnappings and burnings, one, that involving Senator John Bagwell of Marlfield, Co. Tipperary, may be given, *Unum discet omnes*. Bagwell owned one of the finest libraries in the country, built up by his father, the historian Richard Bagwell. The library, together with an outstanding collection of china and paintings, was burned by an IRA party who said they were ordered to do so because Bagwell was 'a member of the Free State Senate'. This happened on 9 January. On the 29th he was kidnapped in Dublin by irregulars, but managed to escape the following day. The poet and author Oliver St John Gogarty had a similar experience, escaping from his kidnappers by swimming the freezing Liffey in a hail of bullets.

Against a nationwide backdrop of such incidents, punctuated by a constant stream of reprisal executions, during the month of March Kerry recorded the worst set of atrocities. They began when a Free State intelligence officer and four comrades were blown up by a mine at Knocknagoshel on the 5th. By way of reprisal, nine irregular prisoners were tied together and set to remove a deliberately mined barricade at Ballyseedy. Eight were blown to pieces but one was miraculously blown clear, living to tell the tale. At Countess Bridge, near Killarney, a similar incident blew four prisoners to bits; but again there was an incredible piece of luck for one man, blown safely clear. To ensure that this would not happen again five other prisoners who were treated in the same way on 12 March at Cahirciveen were first shot in the legs, before being blown up. In all there were seventy-seven executions, a total death roll of some four hundred and a damage bill approaching £50 million – a huge sum in the money values of the time. Apart from burnings, the Republicans' scorched earth policies included such tactics as driving trains into railway stations at full speed and wrecking essential services like power plants and waterworks. But to grasp the appallingly unstable, dangerous state of the country overall one must also bear in mind the conditions in the Six Counties of Northern Ireland. Here, in the two years from the end of June 1920 to the same moment in 1922, 428 people had been killed. It was calculated that some four times that number had received wounds of varying severity, and that 23,000 Catholics had been driven out of their homes in an Irish variant of 'ethnic cleansing'. As the Six Counties is such a small area, its approximately 600,000-strong Catholic population felt itself to be experiencing a pogrom of considerable intensity.

The independent-minded Joseph Connolly, who had returned to Ireland from America where he had been acting as Irish Consul, was horrified at the situation he found. In his unpublished memoirs[57] he describes writing to de Valera advising him to end the civil war. He admitted that because of his absence in the United States he could not 'speak with authority on all the causes and events that led to Civil War'. However, he condemned both the war and de Valera's failure to find the 'constitutional way of settling their differences' of which he had spoken. Connolly argued that, as the Free State Government was a *fait accompli*, the only 'sane course' was for de Valera and his followers to end the war and adopt the policy of political opposition.

De Valera's hitherto unpublished reply to Connolly gives a revealing insight both into de Valera's mind set at the time and the type of arguments he used to justify his rejection of the 'sane course'. It is headed 'Government of the Republic of Ireland, Office of the President':[58]

I received your letter of the 17th and accompanying memo, every line of which I read with sympathetic understanding – but the difficulties remain.

Republicans will not regard the Free State Government as an Established Government, either de jure or de facto.

The legitimate sovereign authority of the nation at this moment is the Second Dail, which the Executive had no authority to suppress. If that Dail is allowed to meet, it has power to make provision for the Government of the country pending the next election; if it is not allowed to meet, I do not know what alternative there is.

Republicans cannot permit the Free State Government and Parliament to go on establishing itself and functioning as a de facto Government whilst the Republican Government is suppressed. The people have already had enough 'accomplished facts' presented to them.

When the Articles of Agreement were brought over here, I felt as if a plague were being introduced into the country, and every effort I have since made to save the people from its effects have been met on the other side by bad faith and the miserable short-sighted tactics of party politics. Frankly I have no hope that our opponents would even now keep any contract they might enter into with us.

Heaven knows there ought to be sufficient incentive! With a little commonsense we could now apply the Sinn Fein policy of ruling ourselves without any reference to the foreigner in a way that could not have been applied before, but blindness and partisanship deprives us of the power to seize the opportunity. It is heartbreaking.

Thus, standing on Olympian principle, de Valera dismissed the plague-bearers who would have involved the soul of the nation in compromise and 'party politics'. But a few years later when he founded his own party no arguments could be found to prevent his seizing the same opportunities that existed in December 1922.

De Valera's position throughout this hurricane of violence and disorder was not an enviable one. His failure to go to London and subsequent opposition to what was brought home by those who did – the Treaty – condemned him to seek 'extremist support' and to indulge in a sustained bout of petty Parnellism that in secret must have troubled him deeply. Morally and politically, his position was untenable. As a devout Catholic, who had shown himself keenly aware of the importance of the support of the bishops during the conscription crisis, he understood better than most the political and religious implications of a pastoral issued to the press by the bishops on 10 October. It condemned the irregulars for having 'chosen to attack their own country' and containing a coded side-swipe at de Valera: 'Vanity, perhaps self-conceit, may have blinded some who think that they, and not the nation, must dictate the national policy. . . .' More importantly, it also placed the irregulars under a form of excommunication. Condemning the Republicans' campaign as a 'system of murder and assassination of the national forces without any legitimate authority', the pastoral said: ' . . . the guerilla warfare now being carried on by the Irregulars is without moral sanction, and therefore the killing of National soldiers in the course of it is murder before God, the seizing of public and private property is robbery, the breaking of roads, bridges and railways is criminal. . .'. Then the full power of the 'belt of the crozier', as episcopal condemnation is termed in Ireland, was unleashed: 'All who in contravention of this teaching participate in such crimes are guilty of grievous sins and may not be absolved in Confession nor admitted to Holy Communion if they persist in such evil courses. . . .'

De Valera was nothing if not persistent. The formation of the 'emergency Government' a week later gave his activities a coloration of legitimacy. But this 'Government', which he described in a press release as 'The Government of which I am the head',[59] also firmly identified him with the 'system of murder and assassination'. As Professor Bromage put it: '. . . he became an avowed protector of the fighting men in return for their support'. He did not disagree with the use of violence in principle, but with the choice of targets against whom it was to be used. After the attack on the McGarry home he wrote:[60] 'I am not against the burnings of offices etc., of Free State officials, particularly if these burnings are done effectively. That is direct legitimate war on the functioning of the enemy Government, but I am against such burnings as that of McGarry's which was very badly executed and which has all the appearance of a reprisal on his family, and looks mean and petty.' His official position on violence, as recorded in his authorized biography, was:[61] 'His desire was to stop the killing of all who were only indirectly responsible for the situation. Those who voted for repressive statutes and who were particularly active or aggressive had chosen their side and must accept the consequences.'

But in practice running with the gunmen while purporting to hunt with the peacemakers proved a difficult thing to do. Having clearly given his associates to understand that he was in favour of some of the more extreme measures proposed, he then tried to distance himself from them. Far from restricting the list of targets to those who had 'voted for repressive statutes', in February 1923 Lynch issued an order broadening[62] the category of 'legitimate targets'. De Valera reacted with a disclaimer written five weeks later and clearly drafted with an eye to the record:[63] 'The C/S [Chief of Staff] was wrong in thinking that I had "agreed" to the order as a definite decision. I merely indicated that I regarded it as possible that we would be forced to adopt as defensive measures some of the drastic proposals which the Staff meeting had agreed to on the understanding that the execution of the orders would be kept strictly under the control of G.H.Q. – liberty of action not being allowed to subordinate commanders.'

Privately he showed himself fully aware of the futility of the course he was embarked on. He wrote to his colleagues in both the political and military wings, setting out the impossibility of military victory:[64] 'Unless a large section of the Free State Army can be won over, or the people turn overwhelmingly to support us rather than the Free State, there is little prospect of victory which would enable us to dictate terms. . . . What guerilla warfare leads to is a desire on our opponent's part to come to terms with us provided these terms do not mean complete surrender by him to us, which unfortunately is what we require. . . .' In a letter to McGarrity, along with a characteristic concern for the financial aspect of the situation he summed up public opinion accurately, although he blamed it on manipulation of the press:[65]

> Organisation work here is extremely difficult, and we are sorely in need of funds. The 'will of the people' cry, abused though it is, for with their lying press they could make people will anything they choose, is nevertheless a terrible cry to make headway against. The country is so tired of war and fighting, and there is such a natural hatred to turning one's arms against one's own countrymen, that some of the very best are standing aside, feeling that we are right but not wishing to be involved themselves.

By writing seemingly detached, objective letters of that sort not only to McGarrity but also to other influential figures, such as Daniel Mannix in Australia, de Valera managed to do something to circumvent the Free State censorship. The *Poblacht na h-Eireann* publication, which after Childers' death was produced by a series of editors, among them Sean

O'Faolain, was only a one-page, tabloid-sized production run off on a Gestetner. But foreign newspapers also provided him with a publicity outlet. The London *Daily Mail* carried an interview with him in which he said:[66] '. . . we are in arms against and resisting now exactly what the whole nation resisted in the period 1919–21. The only difference is that in the earlier period England was maintaining her claims directly; now she is maintaining them indirectly through Irishmen. This is a continuation of the former war.' In New York, around the same time, Patrick Lord's *Irish World* printed a long statement from him in which he blamed the civil war on those who[67] 'failed to realise that the young men who were fighting and daily risking their lives to uphold the Republic and seeing their comrades die for it, would resist to the death any attempt to disestablish it at England's bidding . . . this should have been clearly before the eyes of those who had taken upon themselves the leadership of the nation, and at all hazards they should have been careful to prevent it. . . .'

A disinterested observer might well have concluded that an even more potent factor in creating the bloodshed was the manner in which de Valera fomented dissension over a document which had been signed without his being consulted. But behind the smokescreen of blaming his political opponents for the state of affairs he continued to manoeuvre in the unrealizable hope of finding a formula which would yield him both a face-saving recipe for peace and some method of reintroducing to the debate Document No. 2 and External Association. This landed him in conflict with right and left. The Cosgrave administration had issued a pamphlet illustrating the nature of his position the previous year. He replied with a public statement defending Document No. 2 and saying:[68] 'The fact that these proposals and my statements have been twisted by knaves to make a trap for fools doesn't take away from the truth that is in them.' This last was a reference to his 'wading through blood' speeches, the substance of which, though not the rhetoric, he had repeated in the *Daily Mail* interview. But Document No. 2 was the sore point with the IRA. In their eyes it was a considerable retreat from the Republic and hardly distinguishable from the Treaty. Lynch sent him a rocket, stating:[69] 'Your publicity as to sponsoring Document No. 2 has had a very bad effect on Army and should have been avoided. Generally they do not understand such documents. We can arrange peace without referring to past documents.'

This could be taken as the authentic confused, angry voice of the average militant Republican, unskilled in the decyphering of Machiavellian formulae. But that of conservative, well-educated circles more versed in dealing with sophistry was equally angry and even more scathing. The hierarchy returned to the charge against the irregulars in their Lenten Pastorals. That of Cardinal Logue summed up the general tone:[70]

Never before in the world's history did such a wild and destructive hurricane spring from such a thin, intangible, unsubstantial vapour. The difference between some equivocal words in an oath; the difference between internal and external connection with the British Commonwealth; this is the only foundation I have ever seen alleged. Men versed in the subtleties of the schools may understand them; men of good, sound, practical common sense shall hardly succeed.

But the Cardinal went further than most in including a lightly veiled attack on de Valera's motives in sponsoring the 'unsubstantial vapour': 'There may be other foundations – pride, jealousy, ambition, self-interest, even mere sentimentality; but if they exist they are kept in the background.'

Certainly de Valera's reply to Lynch indicated 'other foundations' – quite simply that he knew best:[71]

Fundamentally, this whole question is a political one and the army will have to do one of two things.

1) Either be definitely subject to the Government and leave all political matters to the Government within the wide range and the understanding with the Executive on which the government was formed; or

2) If they want to deal with the political question, and will not confine themselves to the military one, they will have to think intelligently along political lines and discuss the political problems as they would discuss military ones. . . .

. . . I know what is and what is not possible, as far as Britain is concerned. At any rate I have fixed it definitely in my own mind as a conviction that is likely to be unshaken by anything I can foresee within my life . . . and I will take no responsibility for publicly handling the situation if I have, at every turn, to account for what I say, to people who have not given a moment's thought to the whole question.

. . . Many good men have come to the conclusion that we have long ago passed the point at which we should have regarded ourselves as beaten so far as actually securing our objective is concerned. And if you were to hold that the objective was the 'isolated' Republic, I would say they were right.

He used some particularly interesting language in defending Document No. 2 to P. J. Ruttledge, who had judged that his publicizing of the proposal was unwise because some Republicans would feel let down by his compromise:[72] 'If you want honest consideration for proposals you must throw them in at a crisis which will give them the necessary prominence. The one thing that I am a convinced believer in is the indestructible character of truth and its certainty of ultimate triumph – bad politics it will be said, but to my mind the policy of fooling the gullible is despicable.'

However, any perusal of two other letters he wrote around this time, against the background of facts not known to his correspondents, will inevitably make even the most gullible wonder just who was fooling whom in the pursuit of peace. He told a Jesuit priest, Father L. McKenna sj, that:[73] 'This situation has not been brought about by my will, nor could my will end it. It has been brought about by a blind and ruthless disregard of the essentials of peace and it will continue as long as these conditions are wilfully ignored.' A few weeks later he wrote the following *cri de coeur* to a correspondent in London, Edith Ellis:[74]

Alas! Our country has been placed in a cruel dilemma out of which she could be rescued only by gentleness, skill and patience, and on all sides a desire for justice and fair-dealing. Instead we find ourselves in the atmosphere of a tempest – every word of reason is suppressed or distorted until it is made to appear the voice of passion. I have been condemned to view the tragedy here for the last year as through a wall of glass, powerless to intervene effectively. I have, however, still the hope that an opportunity may come my way.

In fact, far from his being 'powerless', an opportunity to break through the 'wall of glass' had just come his way – and he had turned it down in a particularly Machiavellian fashion. The Ellis letter was subsequently captured by the authorities and published, as his biography notes in injured tones:[75] 'apparently to give the impression that de Valera was shirking responsibility and trying to throw it on other Republicans'. That is exactly what he *was* doing. What happened was that Lynch's second-in-command, Liam Deasy, had become increasingly disenchanted with the war and felt it should be stopped. But before he had had an opportunity of communicating this view to his followers he was captured and sentenced to death. He asked for a stay of execution so that he could make an appeal to his followers to lay down their arms. The Free State authorities allowed him to write a letter for publication, on condition that he also signed and issued a prepared appeal addressed to a list of the leading Republicans headed by de Valera. The appeal was to 'accept and aid in an immediate and unconditional surrender' of both arms and men as he had done. This letter was published in the press on 8 February 1923, along with a governmental offer of an amnesty to all who complied by the 18th.

However, in a classic display of 'cute hoorism' de Valera chose not to reply to Deasy. Instead, he drafted a notice turning down the initiative, which he got Lynch to sign and issue over *his* name. Along with the statement for publication he sent Lynch a covering letter in which he advised:[76] 'Were we to lose all the lives that have been lost and get nothing of national value it would be awful.' The letter is printed in his official biography, but out of context, three pages away from the description of the Deasy incident and giving no indication that it was written with the intention of rejecting a peace move. Whatever responsibility for civil war, death and destruction de Valera might have disclaimed up to that point, he certainly shared the guilt for those lives that were lost afterwards.

Not only was he still hoping for peace on his terms; he was also backing Lynch in plans for a totally unrealistic scheme to launch a campaign in England, where the IRA had become almost non-existent after the truce. The once-powerful London IRA had become so weakened that a one-legged man had been used in the shooting of Sir Henry Wilson, with the result that both assassins were apprehended and hanged. And since the Wilson shooting Scotland Yard, aided by the Treaty split which created bitterness and informers in equal measure, had virtually wiped out the organization through jailings and deportations. Nevertheless in the same month that he wrote his 'wall of glass' disclaimer to Ellis, he also wrote to Lynch telling him that in the proposed British offensive:[77] 'the first blow should be concerted and big, followed quickly by a number in succession of other blows'. And a little later he wrote to him that: 'were we to abandon the Republic now it would be a greater blow to our ideals and to the prestige of the nation than even the abandonment on December 6th, 1921. In taking upon ourselves to be champions of this cause we have incurred obligations which we must fulfil even to death.'

He swung back towards a more prudent course a few days later, on 2 February, when he again wrote to Lynch: 'We can best serve the nation at this moment by trying to get the constitutional way adopted. In this matter it is all a question of what the Army is prepared to do.' Decoded, this meant that he was placing the blame for the continuation of the fighting on Lynch and the other executive members. In the wake of this, he immediately sent another memo to Lynch urging peace. It showed de Valera to be well aware of the state of public opinion, but still anxious to save face: ' . . . it is very much better to lead in this peace matter in which the whole country is so interested. If we make a decent peace offer which will command the support of reasonable people the others can't proceed and we shall have a victory.'

But any sort of 'victory' for the irregulars was now out of the question. The Deasy affair had marked a watershed. The upholding of a Republic in arms against the wishes of the people that the Republic was said to represent was increasingly being seen as a contradiction in terms. But how to act on the logic of that fact without losing face and 'extremist support'? De Valera had indicated his ideas on the subject in a letter to Lynch:[78] 'With the general policy embodied in "should we be beaten let us quit", I am in complete agreement. Were we to "compromise" on any essential we would have proved that we were fighting for party – not defending sacred principles.'

This was more than a little ironic in a letter which was largely taken up with defending the compromise of Document No. 2; but it provided the basis for a strategic discussion on ending the war, which took place between de Valera and the IRA leaders on 23 March. Liam Lynch had been resisting an executive meeting since January[79] but, in the wake of the Deasy incident, even some of the most determined IRA commanders were looking for a way out. On 6 February two of them, Tom Barry and Tom Crofts, had made the journey to Dublin to put the situation to him forcefully. P. J. Ruttledge, who was present, wrote to de Valera next day:[80] 'I consider that we have reached a point where it is absolutely necessary that Army Executive meet and review the situation and decide, when conversant with all circumstances, as to prosecution of war or otherwise.'

Tom Barry, who had been the most successful flying column commander during the war, also acted as the conduit for circulating to his comrades an appeal for peace signed by some of the most important Catholic clergymen in the South, including the Archbishop of Cashel, Dr Harty. The basic circumstance with which Ruttledge and the growing peace party on the Republican side wished to make Lynch 'conversant' was the impossibility of continuing the struggle. The authoritative Florence O'Donoghue reckoned that:[81]

> ... the relative strengths in the 1st Southern Division area at the time were: I.R.A., 1,270; Free State, 9,000. In the Southern Command area, which included the counties of Cork, Kerry, Limerick, Clare, Tipperary, Kilkenny, Carlow, Wexford and about half of Galway, 6,800 I.R.A. men were opposed by 15,000 troops. In the whole country I.R.A. strength did not exceed 8,000 at that time, and against them the Free State authorities had built up a force of at least 38,000 combat troops. The possession of barracks, armoured cars and artillery emphasised the overwhelming Free State strength.

Outside the military sphere, the strength of public support for the Free State was also overwhelming. Even to get to the meeting both Lynch and de Valera, who of course travelled separately, had to take extraordinary precautions – more befitting men traversing a hostile country than leaders in their own land. The meeting was held in remote Bliantas, in the Monavullagh Mountains in Waterford. De Valera was not as fit as he normally was:[82] 'After many months confined in Dublin with little exercise, he found the journey, some of it on foot over mountains, a great strain. He rode a horse over the last stages. An intelligence report stated that he had been seen crossing the Comeragh mountains on horseback, with a beard down to his toes!'

The meeting went on for four days, with Free State activity continually forcing interruptions in the proceedings. At first de Valera was not admitted and had to wait in the kitchen while the discussions continued in another room. No sooner was he let in than Free State troops were reported near by and:[83]

> ... they all marched back to Lyre, where ... the meeting continued until 2 a.m. They then went on into the Nire valley and with Free State troops reported close by, they had to climb up into the mountains where the meeting continued in the open. De Valera had with him a half loaf of dry bread. Even when the meeting adjourned and the members dispersed to billets, they could not get to sleep before they were roused and forced to move again.

In the midst of the confusion and passionate debate the discussion came down to two points of view:[84] first, that de Valera be empowered to enter directly into peace negotiations with the Free State authorities and report back to another executive meeting, and second, a motion sponsored by Barry and Crofts that 'further armed resistance and operations against F.S. Government will not further the cause of independence of the country'. The second was the more realistic. The conditions on which de Valera was supposed to negotiate were contingent on the abolition of the Oath. Before attending the meeting he had already given a written reply to a question from the IRA Adjutant General, Tom Derrig, as to what his minimum terms from the Free State would be:[85] 'The obvious answer is our minimum will be the maximum that the conditions of the moment enable us to obtain. Under conditions which it is possible to conceive, this maximum might be as low as zero.'

Years later, de Valera gave an interesting account of the much-interrupted meeting to Frank Gallagher[86] (which for some reason he did not include in his official biography); it offers a revealing insight into the difference between his and Lynch's thinking. After describing how he sat in the farmhouse kitchen while the militarists discussed the ceasefire issue, he said:

> Thank goodness I am a patient man, but as it went on I was feeling damned angry – these men had urged me to resume the Presidency and the responsibility for the struggle. Now they were coming to their decision without me. At last I was called in and after further discussion I realised that Liam Lynch and others were expecting a delivery of arms with which the struggle could be continued.
>
> I realised the arms would never come. It was arranged that if the arms did not come in a week I would issue the cease fire proposals. I got them to agree to the general terms then and to give me permission to issue the proposals if the armament had not arrived in a week.

Gallagher goes on to record de Valera's description of a scene that took place as de Valera and Lynch walked down the mountain together after this decision was reached. Lynch wondered out loud: 'What would Tom Clarke have made of this decision?' At which, Gallagher notes: ' "I stopped" (said Dev) and speaking to me (Gallagher) with great energy, "I said, Tom Clarke is dead. He has not our responsibilities. Nobody will ever know what he would do, for this situation did not arise for him."' According to Gallagher, de Valera went on: 'But it arises for us and we must face it with our intelligence and conscious of our responsibility. It would be impossible to conduct a struggle if we had always to be thinking what would Clarke do, what would Pearse do in situations they had never to meet. We know what they stood for and we should be guided by that, but each crisis has its own problems which must be decided by those living them.'

Two points may be noted about the foregoing. First, in his description of being left waiting in the kitchen de Valera omits to mention that it was he who had drafted the resolution in which the IRA had called on him to assume the presidency. Second, the official biography, which of course was written many years later, is at variance[87] with the Gallagher account in that it has the meeting ending inconclusively, with de Valera being empowered merely to investigate the chances of peace and to report back to another executive meeting fixed for 10 April.

The journey back to Dublin was both difficult and hazardous. De Valera later described how he and Aiken had to get down on their hands and knees to make headway against the ferocity of the March winds howling across the mountains.[88] His diary for the 27th reads:[89] '. . . Wildest night I ever experienced. Falling at every step. Misled by the guide. Ignored stepping stones and walked through the streams. Stuck my left leg in a boghole up to the groin. Arrived in the morning, clothes and leather jacket all ruined.' His beard saved him when at one stage the party were suddenly surrounded by Free State soldiers. No one recognized the tall man whose cover story was that he was *en route* to visit his dying wife.

As Lynch was fatally injured on 10 April while crossing the Knockmealdown Mountains, by soldiers who thought at first that they had shot de Valera, the beard may literally have been a life-saver. Lynch had been on his way to the executive meeting agreed the previous month. De Valera reacted publicly to the news of his death with a dramatic, defiant proclamation:[90]

> Soldiers of the Republic, bulwark of our nation's honour and independence, as you mourn in spirit today at the bier of your comrade and your chief – the lion heart who, with exalted soul and tenacious will, backed by his loyal allies the hills, more than any other baffled the forces of an empire and brought them to terms – you will renew your pledges of devotion to the cause for which he gave his young life and beg that the God of Liberty and Truth may strengthen you, to be faithful every one, similarly unto death.
>
> Faced in arms by former comrades who have deserted from your side, your task is a hard one and a sad. It is a task which only heroes would venture – you have to fling yourselves across the path of the stampede of a nation.
>
> But it is better to die nobly, as your chief has died, than live a slave.

Lynch was succeeded as Chief of Staff by Frank Aiken. Aiken, who had commanded the 4th Northern Division of the IRA during the Anglo-Irish war, had also played an active role in the covert operation against the Six Counties which Collins had sponsored. He had initially remained neutral in the civil war; but some of the GHQ generals decided that he was tending to become neutral against them, so they arrested him and lodged him in Dundalk Barracks. Troops loyal to him carried out a rescue operation and he returned to recapture the barracks; later he became one of the irregulars' more successful commanders. He was also one of their most realistic. Lynch had been prolonging the civil war in the hope that some mountain artillery, which the IRA were negotiating for, would have arrived from the Continent. This was of course nothing but a fantasy. Even had such heavy weapons slipped through British naval surveillance they could not have hoped to escape that of the Free State authorities. And of course such heavy weapons were completely unfamiliar to the IRA. Aiken had no such illusions. Moreover he was also very heavily influenced by de Valera who, since the 23 March meeting, had been running into a blank wall with his peace attempts.

Amongst the most interested observers of the Irish conflict were the geo-politicians of the Vatican. Ireland was the emerald in the papal crown and developments which might have had an adverse effect on the flow of Irish resources – physical, intellectual and financial – into the Roman empire were keenly studied. The Pope sent an envoy, Monsignor Luzio, to Ireland to report at first hand. Luzio attempted to mediate between Cosgrave and de Valera, but the discussions were 'abortive'.[91] However, his visit did afford de Valera the opportunity of making a number of observations for the Pope's benefit on the subject of the Irish hierarchy and the bishops' pastoral on the Republicans. He asked Luzio to:[92] 'Please give to the Holy Father my dutiful homage. Though nominally cut away from the body of Holy Church we are still spiritually and mystically of it, and we refuse to regard ourselves except as his children.' A month later he wrote again to Luzio, saying of the bishops:[93] 'Their failure to condemn ill-treatment, the torturing and the murder of prisoners, and the inflammatory addresses of some of their members . . . are scarcely worthy of Him who is Charity. . . .'

He claimed that the bishops' attitude had created the impression that the Vatican wished to keep Ireland subject to England. The role of the Vatican, he claimed, should be to persuade Cosgrave to 'adopt the open-minded generous policy that is the truest wisdom in a case like this'. And he asked that the bishops' ban of excommunication on Republicans be lifted. But whatever markers he may have laid down for the Pope, he made no impression at all on the Cosgrave administration.

The sequence of events was as follows: at an executive meeting held in Poulacappal on 20 April Aiken was elected Chief of Staff. The meeting passed a resolution empowering 'the Government and Army Council to make peace with the Free State authorities'. This was followed by a two-day meeting of 'the Government and Army Council' on the 26th and 27th in Dublin, at which de Valera presided. Here it was decided to cease hostilities. De Valera issued two documents to the press on the 27th, one signed by him as President, the other anonymously by Aiken, as Chief of Staff, announcing the suspension of 'all offensive operations' as and from noon on the 30th. However, even though the stable door was thus bolted de Valera still wanted to have a bet on the horses. On 30 April he contacted two prominent members of the Free State Senate, Senators Jameson and Douglas, with a view to arranging negotiations between himself and Cosgrave. He later attempted to deny that he had initiated the contact,[94] but as there was so much evidence to the contrary he allowed the fact that he had asked to meet the senators to be printed.[95] Jameson – who, incidentally, had been number one on a list issued by the irregulars of senators who were to be shot at sight – and Douglas agreed to act as intermediaries, not as negotiators. Cosgrave accepted their intermediary status, but refused to meet de Valera or his 'collaborators in destruction, male or female'.

Instead the senators were given terms[96] to pass on to de Valera. These included the acceptance by de Valera of the principle that political issues should be settled by majority vote, and agreement to an arms surrender which would be arranged 'with as much consideration as possible for the feelings of those concerned'. Cosgrave promised to allow a 'clear field for Mr. de Valera and his followers provided they undertook to adhere strictly to constitutional action'. After three further meetings with the senators, during which the Free Staters kept up relentless military pressure, which, apart from arrests and shootings, included two more executions, de Valera produced his own terms on 7 May. In the circumstances these were as audacious as they were unrealistic. They included at least three points which it was a cast iron certainty the Free State Cabinet would reject. One was the abrogation of the Oath – in real terms, the rejection of the Treaty which the Cosgravites had just fought a victorious civil war to uphold. A second called for the 'Assigning to the Republican forces at least one suitable building in each province, to be used by them as barracks and arsenals, where Republican arms shall be stored, sealed up, and defended by a specially pledged Republican guard – these arms to be disposed of after the election by re-issue to their present holders, or in such other manner as may secure the consent of the Government then elected.' The third indicated de Valera's concern not just for guns but for butter too: 'That the funds of the Republic, subscribed in the U.S. and elsewhere, and at present sealed up by Injunction, shall be made available immediately for peaceful efforts in support of the Republican cause, and that all property of the Republican Party seized by F.S. forces shall be restored.'

Cosgrave, whom de Valera had dismissed to McGarrity as a 'ninny', rejected these terms by letter on 8 May. He told Jameson and Douglas: 'No truck, no negotiations, unless there is a surrender of arms.'[97] If they did this, de Valera and his followers would be given every facility for taking part in an election – though not if that meant tampering with the Oath. He told the Dail on 10 May: 'You will find that as far as the party that has promoted disorder is concerned they are prepared to accept peace only if they are guaranteed a lease of political life. We are not going to guarantee them a lease of political life.'

Kevin O'Higgins summed up the attitude of the Government in an oft-quoted phrase: 'This is not going to be a draw, with a replay in the autumn.'[98] De Valera realized that it was time for an invocation of the policy of 'should we be beaten let us quit'. He arranged that Frank Aiken would issue the following ceasefire order:[99] 'Comrades! The arms with which we have fought the enemies of our country are to be dumped. The foreign and domestic enemies of the Republic have for the moment prevailed.' And on the same day, 24 May, he himself issued the following proclamation:[100]

Soldiers of the Republic, Legion of the Rearguard:
The Republic can no longer successfully be defended by your arms. Further sacrifice of life would now be vain and a continuance of the struggle in arms unwise in the national interest and prejudicial to the future of our cause. Military victory must be allowed to rest for the moment with those who have destroyed the Republic. Other means must now be sought to safeguard the nation's right.

. . . You have saved the nation's honour, preserved the sacred national tradition, and kept open the road of independence. You have demonstrated in a way there is no mistaking that we are not a nation of willing bondslaves.

. . . The sufferings you must now face unarmed you will bear in a manner worthy of men who were ready to give their lives for their cause. The thought that you still have to suffer for your devotion will lighten your present sorrow, and what you endure will keep you in communion with your dead comrades, who gave their lives and all those lives promised, for Ireland.

May God guard every one of you and give to our country in all times of need sons who will love her as dearly and devotedly as you.

The war of brother against brother was over.

17

'PUBLICITY BEFORE ALL'

ALTHOUGH HE HAD used his influence to discontinue its use, after issuing his 'Legion of the Rearguard' message, de Valera saw to it that the Republican rod was kept in pickle. He ordered that emigration by his followers should be prevented, just as during the Anglo–Irish war IRA Volunteers had been forbidden to leave Ireland without a permit. He also over-ruled the objections of those who suggested that the IRA should destroy its arms in return for an amnesty. His argument was that, so long as the arms remained in IRA keeping, the Free State authorities would not risk proceeding too harshly against the Republicans in case it sparked a new civil war.[1] But of course the retention of arms meant that the Cosgravites remained, as O'Higgins had put it, wary of a 'replay in the autumn'; as a result they continued to raid and arrest IRA supporters, so that by 1 July 1923 more than 11,000 prisoners, including 250 women,[2] were in custody, many without trial.

In order to legalize their continued detention, the Government forced through a Public Safety Bill on 2 July; it was followed on 3 August by an Indemnity Bill protecting its forces from actions resulting from the harassment of Republicans. The political joke of the hour was that the Government was not only attempting to out-Herod Herod, it was attempting to out-Higgins O'Higgins. But apart from the desire to round up people for their past civil war activities and against possible future reruns, the authorities also felt it necessary to create the right conditions for holding an election later that month. The de Valera-ites had been using a double-barrelled propaganda weapon against the Government. Barrel one stigmatized it as an usurping junta. The argument was that the previous year's elections, having been held under the pact arrangement, should have resulted in a coalition Government in which de Valera and his followers were entitled to a share of power. Barrel two was the Oath. The Government were determined that, whatever happened about barrel two, barrel one at least could be spiked by securing a fresh, stronger mandate at a general election, scheduled for 27 August.

De Valera met the situation by issuing a policy statement which appeared in the press on 24 July:

> It is not the intention of the republican Government or Army Executive to renew the war in the Autumn or after the elections. The war, so far as we are concerned, is finished. Our present purpose is to work through the Sinn Fein organisation. We intend to devote ourselves to social reform and to education, and to developing the economic and material strength of the nation.

Politically, we shall continue to deny the right, and to combat the exercise of, of any foreign authority in Ireland. In particular we shall refuse to admit that our country may be carved up and partitioned by such an authority.

If there were a free election, so that the Republicans could adequately present their programme to the electorate and, if we were elected on a majority, our policy would be to govern the country on Sinn Fein lines as in 1919, refusing to co-operate with England in any way until England was able to make with us such an arrangement as would make a stable peace possible. . . .

He decided to go forward in Clare again. After being unanimously endorsed as a candidate, he made the nomination the occasion of a ringing declaration:[3] 'Our opponents make a mistake if they imagine that we are going to remain on the run. If the people of Clare select me as their candidate again I will be with them and nothing but a bullet will stop me.' His decision was a matter of international interest, and he made sure that this attention would not be diluted in any way by other candidates coming forward. Most of the other eighty-seven Sinn Fein nominees were also on the run – but he forbade them to appear, saying that 'a reserve must be kept'.[4] His 'nothing but a bullet' statement had been made partly in response to a comment by Desmond Fitzgerald, Minister for External Affairs in the Free State Government:[5] 'As long as we are in power de Valera and every other enemy of the country will have to be on the run.' The question of his ability to exist on the run had begun to puzzle observers in other countries. A letter, which was brought to Cosgrave's attention, from a Government sympathizer in America summed up these feelings:[6]

The worst publicity from our point of view is the recrudescence of de Valera as a man immune against arrest. That he may place the State in an awkward position by appearing publicly as a candidate seems to be his present plan. . . . The outside world – always on the side of the spectacular – would sympathise with de Valera were he to appear in his old constituency and claim freedom in appealing to the electors. . . .

Failure to arrest him would damn the Government in the eyes of many of its friends. If arresting is to be done, it should not be remotely associated with the elections in point of time. . . . The longer his immunity from arrest continues, the more likelihood there is of his resurrection as a political force, and a growing certainty that his responsibility for the bloodshed will be forgotten. The government will lose in the estimation of the outside world by continued neglect to make De V. face the consequences of his criminal exploits. No one outside Ireland knows the reasons for this failure. . . .

Commending these views to the Government, the Free State Director of Publicity, Sean Lester, recommended that if it were decided to arrest de Valera[7] it would be well to 'prepare the public mind' by 'a little campaign on his personal responsibility – the death of his dupes etc.' The Government had no difficulty in falling in with this recommendation and decided that he should be arrested wherever and whenever he might be found. De Valera himself supplied the authorities with the information they required on both scores. He announced publicly that he would address a meeting in the square in Ennis on Our Lady's Day, 15 August. He did not intend to help his opponents by allowing them to arrest him away from the hustings.

Apart from his desire to corner the limelight for himself, de Valera's decision did have a safety-first component. Some of the old Collins Squad members, who were now in the political wing of the Civic Guards, operating from the Criminal Investigation Department at Oriel House, Dublin, would certainly have liked to meet de Valera on a dark night. Their boss for a period, Joseph McGrath (who later founded the Irish Hospitals Sweepstake, the organization which for several decades ran a series of lucrative sweepstakes on big horse races in Ireland and England), told me that he had to be careful to prevent his men from 'taking care of the Long Fellow', as he put it. 'A life,' he said, with considerable understatement, 'meant very little to some of those men.' The prominent IRA man Noel Lemass was captured by some of this group on 3 July. He was known to have been suspected by Collins of opening his mail, and was also the chief suspect in the Sean Hales murder. Suspicion was proof to his captors. Lemass's body was eventually discovered in the Dublin mountains the following October. No one was ever charged with the murder.

Accordingly, before going to Ennis de Valera took a number of precautions. He got advice from the IRA about the safest location for a meeting. 'In some open place away from houses', he was told. Then he made his will, appointed a substitute, P. J. Ruttledge, and drafted a statement to be issued by Ruttledge after his capture:[8] 'The manner of his arrest and renewed harassing of Republicans finally dispose of the claim that the election is free. Such recreant methods will not intimidate faithful citizens of the Republic or bend the unyielding spirit of Irish Independence.'

He set off for Ennis on the morning of the 12th, in a blaze of secrecy. The entire country was agog with interest as to whether or not he would get to Ennis without being arrested. To ensure that he did, de Valera had some disinformation put about to the effect that he was travelling to Clare by sea. Then, wearing a beard and moustache, he set off by land, guided by an IRA officer, Sean Hyde, who took him on a circuitous route that involved crossing mountain ranges and the River Shannon. It was to be his last opportunity for some time to enjoy the beauties of the Irish scenery.

De Valera had been made fully aware by Joseph Connolly[9] and others that his presence at Ennis could result in widespread tragedy and that his own assassination was a distinct possibility. However, de Valera proved adamant and Connolly agreed to make the opening speech. Curiously, in view of the dangers involved, de Valera directed that Kathleen O'Connell should also be present in Ennis. She and Connolly were duly driven there, on his instructions, by a man called Joe Delaney.

The night before the meeting he literally had a close shave: with an eye to the cameras, de Valera now removed both beard and moustache. He had got as far as Knockanira, about five miles from Ennis, and it was deemed wiser for him to spend the night there. It was a lucky change of plan, for the house in Ennis in which he had intended to stay was raided by Free State troops. The town was thronged with thousands of excited spectators who had come from all over the country to see what would happen when and if de Valera turned up. A party of soldiers were standing by to arrest him but, in the rueful words of Captain T. Power, who was supposed to arrest him:[10] 'unfortunately he got to the stage before being recognised'. Whether or not this was an attempt at a cover-up on the part of the Army one cannot say at this remove, but *The Times* report gives a completely different picture:[11] 'At a few minutes past two he appeared, driving up in an open car, preceded by a band. . . . After the usual demonstrations and rather tedious preliminary speeches, de Valera rose and addressed the crowd. He looked pale and drawn but his voice carried well. He had uttered only a few sentences . . . when an armoured car pushed its way into the crowd and troops began to move towards the hustings.'

Power noted that, as the candidate neared the stage, 'a shot was fired from it'.[12] De Valera was pulled backwards on to the floor of the stage, and a sudden sharp pain shooting through his leg made him think that a bullet had broken the limb.[13] Firing became general all over the square. Captain Power reported that:[14] 'One of the bullets fired by de Valera's supporters cut a service rifle in two in one of the private's hands who stood beside me.' But miraculously no one was hit. Much of the shooting was done by the troops firing blanks in the air to disperse the crowds. *The Times* described the scene as it was told and retold all over Ireland:

> . . . the crowd broke in panic as the troops passed towards the platform. De Valera was apparently fainting, and some of his friends rushed to him, trying to drag him away. The scene as de Valera, pale and speechless, stepped from the platform, and was instantly seized by the troops, almost baffles description. Shrieks of terror rent the air; several of de Valera's supporters leapt or fell from the platform, and Mrs. O'Callaghan, who is standing for Limerick, was thrown backwards into a quarry, but fortunately escaped without serious injury. . . .

De Valera subsequently recounted the story in more dignified terms. He said that when the pain subsided in his leg he struggled to his feet and exclaimed: 'They are coming for me. I am glad it was in Clare I was taken.'[15] He made his way down the steps and, escorted by Power and a party of soldiers, walked to the barracks through cheering crowds. That much is agreed, as is the fact that forty years later a fragment of a bullet, probably from a ricochet, was discovered in his leg.[16]

He was transferred from Ennis Barracks to spend the night in Limerick Jail. He was then taken to the Detention Barracks at Arbour Hill Detention Centre; here he spent two months strictly confined before being transferred to Kilmainham, where he had been sent after his court martial in 1916. But, having caught their hare, the Free State authorities now found themselves in the embarrassing position of not being able to discover a legal recipe for keeping him in the jug. The dilemma was well summed up in a memo from David Neligan to the Minister for Defence, Mulcahy. Neligan, Collins' old 'Spy in the Castle', was now Director of Intelligence.[17] He had been instructed to consult with Hugh Kennedy, the Attorney General, with a view to constructing a case against de Valera. He reported to Mulcahy that Kennedy, having perused the documents in the case, said[18] ' . . . there did not seem to be much in them. He was not clear as to what charge could be put against him, or as to what kind of tribunal he would be arraigned before . . . he stated that we would again discuss it, as there was no immediate necessity for a trial.'

The shrewd Kennedy had obviously divined, correctly, that de Valera was hoping for a trial which would be not 'of himself alone but of the whole system which brought the Free State into existence'.[19] He had calculated that the Free State authorities were not likely to execute him; but this was a calculation, not a certainty. A story that Neligan told me illustrates the tensions and anxieties playing about de Valera as he sat in detention. He was guarded by soldiers under four commandants who each served an eight-hour shift. One of these, a man given to drink, apparently decided to help him to escape and one night slipped the keys of the barracks to him. However, the student of Machiavelli could not accept the offer on its face value and decided that it was a plot to solve the legal problem by having him shot 'while trying to escape'. Accordingly he locked himself in his cell and threw the keys into the corridor.

Outside the jail there were tensions for Sinead also. It took over a week of anxious, frustrating inquiries before she was officially informed where her husband was being held – significantly on 23 August, the day when Kennedy informed Neligan that the case against him was slim. Next day she wrote to Kathleen O'Connell:[20] 'I was at Arbour Hill today and gave a letter and a cardigan jacket and shirt to Dev. I was told the letter would be given to him after it was sent to G.H.Q. to be censored. But I was told he cannot write to me. I want to make a parcel of his things and bring them up.' Sinead then added a paragraph remarkable not only for her concern lest someone should endanger themselves in attempting a jailbreak, but for her concern for the other woman: 'For goodness sake don't let anyone take dangerous risks for D's sake. Write again if you cannot call. I know your poor heart is broken. I, too, am anxious but keep on at the prayers.'

On the Sunday before polling day a huge meeting in College Green, Dublin which de Valera had been scheduled to attend went ahead, with Vivion standing in for his father on a platform that included Erskine Childers' teenage son, Erskine Junior. The thirteen-year-old Vivion fought off an attack of his chronic asthma, aggravated by the excitement, to read a script which said:[21] 'My father promised that he would speak to you here today and he is a man who would keep his word if he could. But he cannot speak to you for *giollai na nGall* [the ghillies of the foreigner] seized him in Co. Clare the other day. . . . I know not what they will do with him . . . but they cannot kill the spirit of freedom in Ireland.'

Sinead must have felt her prayers had been answered when the election results were made known. De Valera received 17,762 votes against the 8,196 secured by his Cumann na nGaedheal rival, Eoin MacNeill. Overall the de Valera-ites did remarkably well. A revision of the constituencies had increased the number of seats from 128 to 153, and the Government had expected to win a substantial proportion of these. In the event they only gained five and Sinn Fein took eight. The results were as follows:

Cumann na nGaedheal	62
Sinn Fein	44
Farmers' Party	15
Labour	14
Independents	17

The figures indicated that a combination of a resurrection of sectional interest politics and a backlash against the executions and the numbers in prison were having their effect. Yet balancing the sectional Me Fein [Myself Alone] factor there was also a paradoxical, and very Irish, 'ballot-box of romance' influence at work. Sinn Fein had fought the campaign with little discernible policy other than 'if there's a government we're agin it'. The election had been a torrid affair characterized by fights, intimidation, and the fact that so many of the Sinn Fein candidates were either in jail or on the run. But this disruption of the election machinery was more than compensated for by the ancestral Irish sympathy, inculcated by centuries of strife, for 'the felons of our land'. People who were not prepared to support the irregulars in violence were nevertheless willing to show that sympathy by voting for them.

Prominent Republicans like Aiken, Ruttledge, Kathleen Brugha (Cathal Brugha's widow), Austin Stack, Countess Markievicz and Mary MacSwiney were amongst those returned with handsome majorities. The first three headed the poll in their constituencies. But the main beneficiary was one Eamon de Valera. It did not matter that the Oath denied his party a platform in the Dail, and that he himself was a closely guarded prisoner. The Irish people had borne out the judgement of Gavan Duffy more than a year earlier: de Valera was demonstrably 'the greatest personality we have in public life'.

For some months after his arrest his life was far from public. He was placed in a wing separated from other prisoners and prevented from exercising in the company of anyone except the officer on duty. Sinead and Vivion were only allowed as far as the gates of Arbour Hill, bringing parcels in response either to his own requests or to Sinead's assessment of his needs. He was allowed to send and receive two letters a week. In one to

Kathleen O'Connell he asked for a number of mathematical texts, by Bromwich, Darboux, Einstein, Goursat and Niewenglowski. He told her that he was:[22] 'very lonely of course at times and anxious about Sinead and the family but I have no end of work to do'.

Some of the work included a project to produce in collaboration with O'Connell a book on the adaptation of Gregg shorthand to Irish. But this was abandoned when it was found that someone else had produced a similar book. In another letter to O'Connell he wrote:[23] 'If you want to make me happy, send me all of them [books]. It will be living life over again going through them and picking out what is of use. It will be like making the acquaintance of old friends again and what I have forgotten will come back through them more quickly than in any other way.' Like many a busy man he obviously gave his wife the impression that he talked more about books than he read them, because he continued: 'I am afraid Sinead has grown cynical about my relation to books, and will think this only another of my whims. . . . The privilege of being in jail is that one can ask to be indulged in whims of this sort. I'll be shut off as completely as if I were on another planet and these books, old or new, the only friends at hand.'

But a memory from the past intruded on his planet one day when an officer guarding him used his bayonet to cut the name 'MICK COLLINS' over his cell door. His official biography describes his reaction to this gesture:[24] '. . . his schoolmaster's heart was saddened. There were three errors in it. The capital "i"s dotted and the diagonal of the "N" was drawn in the wrong direction and "S" reversed. He decided to teach the lieutenant how to form his letters!' One is inclined to speculate as to what else he might have attempted to teach the lieutenant had opportunity offered.

Another planetarian visitor, this time in the flesh, was the American lawyer Finnerty who was allowed to see him on 3 and 4 January 1924 in connection with the action over the bond monies, left behind in New York, that he had mentioned to McGarrity in his letter of 10 September 1922. The Free State authorities bugged their conversation and hence we have on record[25] from a prison cell, following a shattering civil war defeat, two of the central components of the de Valera Man of Power philosophy that ultimately led him to triumph. In the course of explaining to Finnerty that he wanted the money 'wholly for propaganda', he said: 'The vital weakness of the Free State Government was that it knew nothing of the psychology of the people. They are incapable of feeling the nation's pulse. They have no publicity department worth talking of. *Any government that desires to hold power in Ireland should put publicity before all* [author's italics].'

His assessment of his political rivals reflects his belief that only he could possibly articulate the wishes of the Irish people. This is the 'looking into his own heart' philosophy which we have already encountered. But the second point, on the importance of propaganda, was to lead to a – perhaps *the* – classic display of de Valera's tenacity. His relentless, almost obsessive, pursuit of the means of publicity led, as we shall see when we come to examine the course of the bonds case in Chapter 20, to the foundation of a de Valera newspaper empire.

In April 1924 he was transferred back to the main part of Arbour Hill and a new and more liberal regime. The bonds case may have had a bearing on this, for now American accents were being added to the voices raised in Ireland in the traditional and ever-potent cry of 'Release the prisoners.' In the Dail the Government was under constant assault, chiefly from the Labour Party, on the issue. Outside it, Maude Gonne MacBride[26] was but one of the formidable array of Republican activists turning the Government's own prison weapon upon itself. But the American scene carried a particular patina of danger, as a report from the Free State's representative in Washington, Professor T. A. Smiddy, made clear: [27]

> Efforts are being made by the various branches of the American Association for the Recognition of the Irish Republic to bring pressure to bear upon Congress and the Executive to appeal to Great Britain for release of de Valera and others.
>
> Representative La Guardia of New York moved some time ago in the House of representatives [sic] to this effect. . . . The enclosed cutting shows the activities in Boston.
>
> What is more·serious is that Mr. Charles Murphy, Boss of Tammany,[28] is moving in the same direction: he asked Representative John J. Boylan of New York, to petition Congress for de Valera's release . . . the American Association for Recognition of the Irish Republic has strong influence in Tammany at present.
>
> It is hoped Tammany's influence will not make itself felt in the forthcoming trials of Dail Funds.

The irony of a de Valera-founded organization (the AARIR) being used to get the British to bring pressure on a sovereign Irish Government to release de Valera did not prevent Kate Wheelright visiting Washington to lobby Congressmen on behalf of her son. The AARIR made her guest of honour at a large and well-publicized function held in the city.[29]

However, even prior to the growth of the American agitation and the move to Arbour Hill De Valera had had an easier time of it than many other political prisoners. The Free State authorities did not recognize them as such and attempted to treat them as ordinary criminals, a familiar source of conflict in Irish history. Eventually, during October, the situation resulted in mass hunger strikes throughout the prison system in which de Valera did not join. Using 'the line', the generic name for the multiplicity of routes whereby Irish political prisoners have traditionally smuggled messages in and out of prisons, no matter how tightly guarded, de Valera communicated his dislike of this method of protest. Some of the prisoners on strike had been speculating as to whether he was supporting them or not. Ruttledge, in his capacity as 'Acting President of the Republic', issued a statement saying that acting on 'strict orders'[30] from the Republican Cabinet de Valera was not on hunger strike 'in the best interests of the cause'.[31] Survival was the name of the game. A number of prisoners died before intervention by Cardinal Logue led to an end to the strike and a gradual commencement of releases in November. Some had been on hunger strike for forty days and suffered permanent ill-effects. One such was Austin Stack who, according to the diary of his association with de Valera while they were in Arbour Hill together, seems to have enjoyed better health in jail than on his release. He died in 1929 at the age of forty-nine. His diary entry for 25 April 1924 records his surprise at receiving an unexpected visitor:[32] 'Who should walk into my cell but de Valera. He has just departed from me after a good chat. Evidently we are to be allowed to "associate" at long last.' Freedom of association was one of the demands for which Stack had gone on hunger strike.

De Valera must have been in good physical condition. Stack might have suffered a hunger strike of forty-one days, but he was still a former Kerry All Ireland Gaelic football player. Nevertheless the next day's diary entry (26th) notes that 'Dev beat me decisively a couple of times' at handball. De Valera also played tennis during the daily exercise periods of two hours each morning and afternoon, after which they normally went to each other's cells for a chat or to play chess. Sharing their detention area was a man called Keegan, concerning whom Stack notes that he was a 'former Free State Officer' with a 'record against the Black and Tans', who came from Leitrim and was 'a very good Catholic'.

The increasingly lenient nature of the regime is indicated by the fact that one of the lieutenants guarding the prisoners made up a foursome for strenuous handball matches with de Valera, Keegan and Stack. After one rubber consisting of eight games of doubles, two drawn, three each won, Stack was 'too tired to eat my supper'. Three days later, 25 May, Stack notes: 'Heavy rubber beaten by Keegan and de V. Lt. and self.' The diary does not give us an insight into de Valera's political or intellectual preoccupations, but records milestone sporting or jail occasions such as the handball matches, the first day the prisoners were allowed newspapers, the first news of possible early releases, and Sinead's first visit. She had written to Kathleen O'Connell on 7 May:[33] 'I wonder when will we get any good news. . . . I hope something will bring about some good luck. I'll believe he's coming out when I see him.'

The following month, on 23 June, the prisoners got their first newspapers, and four days later brought Sinead her 'good luck'. She was granted her first visit to her husband. As Stack noted in his diary, it was: 'Their first meeting since long before his arrest in August last.' Since that time Sinead, in her own words, had been living by the 'doctrine of quiet, determined, individual effort'.[34] As she had said in an election message after his capture:[35] 'No one need be a slave in heart, no matter what forces are arrayed against him.'

Another family visit interrupted the 'Arbour Hill Championships' one Sunday. De Valera and Keegan were playing Stack and Lieutenant Maguire in a rubber which had reached two games all before a 'yard full of spectators' (two policemen, as Stack noted drily) when, at 11.30 a.m., de Valera's three eldest children arrived to see their father. The championships resumed after lunch. Stack and Maguire won the rubber, four games to three. But even though Keegan was evidently tired out by this stage de Valera decided to play another five-game rubber, taking a Lieutenant Butler as his partner. Stack and Maguire won again, but Stack noted chivalrously: 'They are really better players than we are, man for man.'

From the end of June references to the possibility of release begin to crop up in the diary and de Valera was allowed to see more of his family, although Stack does not appear to have been allowed any visits. Then, on 11 July, Keegan was moved. Stack noted: 'We'll see him again D.V. [*Deo volente* – God willing].' Five days later de Valera and Stack were told they were to be released; it took them an hour to pack. Their first stop after leaving the jail, Stack notes, was a political one. They called at 23 Suffolk Street 'and saw Sean T. [O'Ceallaigh] MacEntee etc.'. Then they went to de Valera's home, after which 'de Valera went visiting'.

De Valera's subsequent life with his family followed the pattern set on that first day of freedom. It was sandwiched between political activity and heavily influenced by his opinions on the correct order of priorities. Any prisoner's return to his family generates a certain amount of tension in a household used to running smoothly without him. Terry de Valera, for example, described how Sinead ran the home while his father was away:[36] '. . . gentle but firm control, not only of the day-to-day running of the house, but very much in command of the school-work. Father, on the other hand, meant little more than the tall, dark-haired, bespectacled, severe figure who occasionally appeared on the home scene.' But when the 'severe figure' appeared on the scene on this occasion it was with strong views on school-work:[37] 'So far as the schools were concerned, the father suspected a tendency towards indiscipline and laxness. In English for example, grammar and spelling were being, he thought, slighted. In arithmetic, the children were being given a nodding acquaintance with the whole field of mathematics, whereas in the old days such essentials as the multiplication tables had been prescribed. . . .'

Sinead was given credit for the fact that Irish was spoken in the home, and the foregoing account goes on to note that 'Eamonn Junior, ten years old, displayed with pride his vocabulary.' However thirty-five years later, Eamonn, now a successful gynaecologist, recorded a different impression:[38] 'As a child, I feared my father, and resented his intrusion into our lives. He had been in prison and in America, and on his return I found it hard to accept the stricter discipline he enforced . . . although my father loves children, he has not been able to communicate well with them. Looking back, I realise that he has never really appreciated the difficulties and shortcomings of minds less gifted than his own.' As a result Eamonn felt that his mother became over-protective and, in some ways, too easy on the children. But he did marvel at her ability to manage 'with so little money'.[39] Terry put it more forcefully. He described resisting his mother's efforts to get him to take his medicine, but[40] 'that tall dark figure was at home and he decided otherwise. . . . I was all too soon aware of a slimy, foul-smelling substance sliding down my throat.' Later, climbing the stairs, Terry called back: ' . . . dirty fellow . . . filthy fellow. I wish he'd go back to jail again.'

But for the moment Eamon de Valera Senior had no intention of going back to jail again. Instead he went with Sinead to a 'gala occasion' in the Mansion House for the released prisoners. A new and growingly popular song, written in an internment camp by one of the prisoners,[41] was sung that night. Hearing its words, de Valera remarked prophetically that Republicans were no longer in the Rearguard.[42] The song's rousing chorus went as follows:

> Legion of the Rearguard answering Ireland's call
> Hark, their martial tramp is heard from Cork to Donegal,
> Tone and Emmet guide you tho' your task be hard
> De Valera leads you Soldiers of the Rearguard.

That song would become the anthem of de Valera's political party, a party that within a decade would form the longest-lived democratically elected Government in the history of nationalist Ireland.

But before following the step-by-step development of events which led to this happening let us turn for a moment to examine the situation of his opponents in government which, overall, made possible his climb to power. The economic situation of the country has already been described: it was in part responsible for a convulsion in the Army which had weakened the Government the previous March. The Army mutiny, as it was called, may be summarized[43] as centring around three related issues. The first was the Government's need to cut down its numbers. Then there was the resentment of some of Collins' old associates, notably Liam Tobin, Charlie Dalton and Tom Cullen, that pro-British elements were being advanced, the 'stepping-stone' idea was being abandoned and the Free State was becoming an end in itself. Finally there was Kevin O'Higgins' hostility towards Mulcahy, stemming from the Army's performance in the civil war and Mulcahy's revival of the IRB. Mulcahy did this partly to counter the Tobin–Dalton group's organization of another grouping within the Army, 'the old I.R.A.', but also out of a conscious desire to keep the Collins type of Republican ideal to the fore within the officer corps. The crisis came to a head on 18 March with a Mulcahy-sponsored army raid on one of Collins' principal haunts, Devlin's pub in Parnell Street. Inside were the principals in the Tobin–Dalton group, allegedly planning mutiny. Quite unjustly, O'Higgins chose to see Mulcahy's action as being part of an attempt to set up a military dictatorship. Mulcahy was outmanoeuvred in the resultant Cabinet battle and resigned, as did another leading minister,

Joseph McGrath. The holding of an inquiry defused the crisis. But, apart from the weakening after-effects of the resignations, the report of the inquiry, which was published in June, inevitably provoked further controversy and anti-Government propaganda. Apart from the chain reaction to this crisis, the Government was also buffeted by currents flowing from the Treaty settlement and the commercial consequences of independence vis-à-vis England.

The principal Treaty item of contention for the Government in the months before and after de Valera's election platform arrest stemmed from Article 12 of the Agreement, which dealt with the Boundary Commission. The Government had distanced itself markedly from Collins' 'forward' policy on the Six Counties. Within days of his death a report circulated by some of his colleagues three days before he was shot became Government policy. It recommended that[44]

> . . . all military operations on the part of our supporters in or against the North-East should be brought to an end. . . . The line to be taken now and the one logical and defensible line is a full acceptance of the Treaty. This undoubtedly means recognition of the Northern Government and implies that we shall influence all those within the Six Counties who look to us for guidance to acknowledge its authority and refrain from any attempt to prevent it working.

The Report made the point that: 'Heretofore our Northern policy has been really, though not ostensibly, directed by the Irregulars. In scrapping their North-Eastern policy we shall be taking the wise course of attacking them all along the line. . . . '

However, the 'peace policy' brought no tangible benefit or peace dividend from Belfast and the irregulars continued to attack the Government 'all along the line' over partition. To counter de Valera's propaganda the Government had taken the first step required under Article 12 to bring the Boundary Commission into being. Eoin MacNeill had been nominated as the Free State representative on the Commission in order to improve his chances against de Valera in Clare. MacNeill made several speeches on the theme of a united Ireland, and the issue grew steadily in importance – though not in the way Cosgrave had hoped. The British were supposed to nominate a suitable chairman, and the Unionists a representative of their own. But neither the British nor the Unionists showed any eagerness to make these appointments. It took sustained pressure from Dublin before the British finally nominated a South African, Judge Feetham, as chairman. But the Unionists refused to follow suit. The fear that one of the keystones of the Treaty would prove unreliable began to grow in nationalist circles. It had been an article of faith with supporters of the Treaty that the Boundary Commission would result in large-scale transfers of nationalist areas in the Six Counties from Belfast's control to that of Dublin. Now, as de Valera began picking up the pieces on his emergence from jail, Cosgrave was coming to the unpalatable realization that the Boundary Commission might prove a disappointment. He wrote an important letter to Judge Cohalan, who was at the time holidaying in Ireland.[45] It both sets forth his fears on the Boundary Commission, and gives a serving Prime Minister's account of the problems confronting the new Irish Government. It also contains an indirect acknowledgment of de Valera's immense influence not only in Ireland but also amongst the Irish diaspora:

> I am not satisfied with the developments in the matter of Article XII. There now appears to be a sort of line-up on the part of British parties with a view to getting a particular interpretation of the terms of reference to the Boundary Commission. . . . Sir James Craig and his friends are the only people in Ireland who have close associations and friendships in England . . . political events follow to a considerable extent such associations. . . .

Cosgrave then went on to describe the reality of Anglo-Irish relationships:

> Politically, no party in England has anything to gain from any dispensation of justice much less favours to us . . . our fiscal changes . . . are inseparable from our fiscal independence. . . . Our population in the last fifty years has decreased and our trade is much of a kind which spells prosperity for a few, and poverty and insecurity for the many.
>
> In dealing with this situation we have been concerned with our own advancement and progress and of necessity this must interfere with and lessen profits hitherto enjoyed by business people in Great Britain. Every step we take to improve our own position must, in the beginning at least, limit the profits hitherto earned in Ireland on sales and purchases by Britishers. In consequence we lose politically, and when such losses are sustained here by our own citizens there is also a lessening of the stability of the state.

Cosgrave pointed out that for the foregoing reasons, and the cost of the civil war, 'our administration is now more costly and less efficient than it was in the British occupation period'. But he also realistically accepted that the Government could expect no concessions from public opinion on these scores and went on:

> We now enter into this Boundary Commission proceedings with all these weighty considerations against us. We have no friends. People in U.S.A., England, Scotland, France and elsewhere are friends of Ireland, but for the people immediately responsible for the government of Ireland they have little or no use . . . many in Ireland have the same views. . . . We can tolerate criticism from without, but it is largely built on misgivings within. . . .

He appealed to Cohalan to influence US opinion towards the Free State:

> Lloyd George said opinion in the U.S.A. was now definitely with the British because of the Treaty. Well, let us have the benefit of that Treaty. If this one particular clause be tampered with, if the decision of the Boundary Commission is to be made in advance by politicians or statesmen, then the Treaty is not the

instrument signed by Collins and Griffith. . . . We want propaganda in the U.S.A. of the type of British good faith under test. . . .

He then made a request which clearly indicated the Government's appreciation and concern over de Valera's influence:

If this [propaganda] could be managed without associating your own name or that of Mr. Devoy it would be all the better. . . . I am sure that De V. or some of his following would commence operations [propaganda] if you were definitely to enter the lists and lead the way. And it would probably give rise to renewed vigour and activity by British parties, which we want to avoid.

He concluded his letter to Cohalan by developing an argument against partition which unconsciously highlights a political weakness in the Free State administration's approach to the problem. Privately he showed himself to be just as concerned for the Six County nationalists as any on the irregular side, de Valera included. But the 'peace policy' approach led Cosgrave and his party into adopting attitudes which, even within the ranks of their own supporters, caused dismay and resentment, as we shall see shortly. But where de Valera was concerned, the Cosgrave policy was an inexhaustible mine of propaganda accusations of being pro-British and selling out the nationalists. Cosgrave said:

. . . I would direct your attention to the arbitrary selection of six parliamentary counties for the constitution of the Northern Government. The British Government made that selection. The Irish people were not consulted and did not accept it. . . . Article XII was specially designed to secure that people were not placed under a Parliament against their will.

If it be contended that Nationalists in Tyrone, Fermanagh, Derry, Armagh are only to be used as filling-in stuff to enable those against Irish unity to maintain a parliament, it is not a valid excuse. They have their legitimate national rights which neither Birkenhead, Lloyd George, Sir James Craig nor anyone else has a right to take from them. . . .

The Cosgrave support came from a wide spectrum within the community: the Church, business, large farmers, old Irish Parliamentary Party members, forces of the right. It was a coalition which carried within itself the seeds of disruption, for it also included many – perhaps a majority – who were just as republican as anyone on de Valera's side, but who had accepted the 'stepping-stone' argument. They supported the Treaty, but as a means to a Thirty-two County state. An episode from the period, whose outcome can be seen everywhere in the Republic today, and in which my father figured, illustrates how sometimes insensitive applications of the 'peace policy' caused disquiet and a feeling that national ideals were being abandoned to even the most loyal upholders of the Government.

The incident may be taken as having begun on 26 April 1924 when my father, who was acting as Garda Commissioner in the absence of Eoin O'Duffy in America, received a communication[46] from the Secretary of the

Department of Home Affairs, E. O'Frighil, informing him that it had been decided to change the design of the Garda badge, or insignia, which appeared on uniforms, stationery and station walls. The existing badge incorporated the letters G.S. interwoven in the centre. These stand for Garda Siochana na hEireann (literally the Civic Guards of Ireland). But under the terms of a draft Bill embodying the Garda, then being processed, it was proposed to change this monogram to S.E. (for Saorstat Eireann, the Free State – in other words the Twenty-six Counties). My father replied on 3 May[47] to the effect that the existing wording had been adopted since the formation of the state, and that to change it would be to do away with the force's individuality. But more significantly he said: 'We who are looking ahead, look upon the guard as the Civic Guard of Ireland and not of any portion thereof. To treat the Guard as a portion of Ireland rather than a Guard for the entire country would be, to my mind, a great mistake. . . . Surely it is not seriously suggested that we must change our badges in order to make it clear that we are a police force for only 26 Counties of Ireland.'

The flurry of inter-departmental memo writing[48] which followed the arrival of this communication shows that the design had been influenced by examination of the British and, allegedly, the French police badges. But it was claimed that this did not mean that the state's 'vision is limited to the 26 Counties'. However, the bureaucrats felt that the matter was 'not very important and it can be settled without heat or misunderstanding'. My father received a letter telling him that the decision would be put on hold until O'Duffy returned, but that it would be necessary to make the change.[49] However, O'Duffy and the other senior Garda officers obviously shared my father's view that, despite what the civil servants said, the badge issue *was* important symbolically. It was left to my father to deal with. A six-month delaying action resulted before a meeting of the headquarters officers, representing the 'wishes of the Officers and men of the Garda',[50] was held at Garda headquarters on 25 January 1924. Writing at considerable length to the Secretary of the Department for Home Affairs, my father gave the 'unanimous conclusions of the Officers'.[51] He first dealt with the sentimental aspect of the badge question: 'Members of the Garda wearing this Badge have weathered the storm of the past two years, and some of them have died on duty. . . . The officers and men of the Garda put a high value, perhaps sentimental, but none the less to be appreciated, upon their badge and their uniform. To destroy its distinctiveness would be to ignore this fine feeling . . . a matter for great regret.' But he returned forcefully to the political aspect: ' . . . the Officers assembled . . . noted that the Police Forces of the Government of the Six Counties of Ulster are known as "The Royal Ulster Constabulary" and they feel that if there is any objection to the Garda appropriating the title "Garda Siochana na hEireann" there is still more objection to the Six-County Police appropriating to themselves the title "Royal Ulster Constabulary". They feel the more appropriate title would be the "Royal Six-Counties of Ulster Constabulary".' After considering 'the views set forth in the Deputy Commissioner's minute of the 31st ultimo' the Department conceded defeat:[52] 'The Minister is still of the opinion that the State Monogram "S.E." should be substituted for the interlaced letters "G.S.", but in view of the representations made by you he will not further withhold his sanction. . . .'

The 'G.S.' monogram is still in use today: its retention illustrates the strong nationalist sentiment of a body of men which was also fiercely loyal to the Government. They had set up an unarmed police force in the midst of a civil war. Members of the force had suffered abuse, injury and death, and had no love for de Valera or his followers. But when Cosgrave wrote to Cohalan he was becoming increasingly aware that similar feelings, widespread, and even more intensified, at every level of society, were in imminent danger of working against him, and in favour of de Valera, because of the Boundary Commission. And so it proved.

The Boundary Commission saga developed as follows. Hamstrung by the civil war, the Cosgrave Government had only seriously begun the process of getting the Boundary Clause of the Treaty implemented in February 1924, the month of the climb-down over the Garda monogram. Cosgrave met Craig in London that month and again in April, but without success. Craig refused to nominate a representative to the Commission. Eventually the British Prime Minister, Ramsay MacDonald, nominated Feetham; the Unionist protagonist Lord Balfour reacted by issuing to the press on 8 September the letter which moved Cosgrave to write to Cohalan. It had been sent to him by Birkenhead in March 1922 by way of explaining Article 12. Birkenhead interpreted it as meaning that the Six Counties would remain under Unionist control. Of the Commission he wrote:[53] 'I have no doubt that the Tribunal, not being presided over by a lunatic, will take a rational view of the limits of its own jurisdiction and will reach a rational conclusion.'

Lloyd George stoked the fires of controversy the following day. He too issued a letter to the press, saying that in his opinion Birkenhead's letter contained 'the only responsible interpretation of that important Clause'. He dismissed the matter as being simply 'a sectarian quarrel in a corner of Ireland'. This was one side of the familiar British policy medal on Northern Ireland. On the one hand the political leaders dismissed the issue as being a problem for the intractable Irish themselves; on the other the old Tory doctrine of 'Ulster will fight and Ulster will be right' was trotted out. On 26 September another signatory of the Treaty, Sir Laming Worthington Evans, made a speech at Colchester in which he said:[54] 'It was not intended that there should be large transfers of territory. . . . If by any chance the Commissioners felt themselves at liberty to order the transfer of one of these counties nothing would induce the Ulster people to accept such a decision and no British Government would be guilty of the supreme folly of trying to enforce such a decision.'

Hopes of Irish unity coming about through the Boundary Commission against a background of such orchestration were clearly unrealistic; Cosgrave acknowledged as much privately in his letter to Cohalan. Whatever Irish nationalist expectations might have been, once the British had taken the step of appointing a chairman they had, technically, discharged their obligations under the clause and, as Cosgrave wrote:[55] '. . . have performed their duty and are no more responsible for the decision than I am'. The British further safeguarded themselves from accusations of bad faith by meeting Craig's refusal to appoint a member to the Commission by doing so themselves. On 9 October an Enabling Act was passed, and two weeks later a prominent Belfast Unionist apologist, J. R. Fisher, a former editor of the *Northern Whig*, was appointed. The Commission held its first meeting on 6 November in London. A year later almost to the day, on 7 November 1925, a bombshell burst over nationalist Ireland. The *Morning Post* published a forecast of its likely findings.

The Six Counties were to hold what they had, apart from some slivers of Armagh and Fermanagh. Far from gaining any counties, the Twenty-six Counties were to lose a portion of Co. Donegal. The fears that Cosgrave expressed to Cohalan had been realized. For two weeks the Free State Government breasted a tide of public outrage at this blow to one of the main arguments in favour of the Treaty. Then, on 21 November, MacNeill resigned from the Commission, giving up his portfolio as Minister for Education two days later. The dominoes were falling de Valera's way as first Cosgrave and then O'Higgins crossed to London for a series of meetings, beginning on the 25th, at which they attempted to salvage some governmental credibility for the debacle. As we shall see, the agreement they emerged with, although the best they could hope for in the circumstances, helped rather than hindered de Valera's accelerating return to fortune.

But before examining how, it is necessary to return to charting the steps, taken either by himself or by his followers, which helped to interact with the Boundary Commission's report in furthering this objective. Less than a month after his release a meeting of those elected under the Sinn Fein banner, both at the previous general election and to the second Dail, was held on 7 and 8 August. De Valera was becoming increasingly aware that the sacred cow of abstention from the Free State Parliament could never be milked for power. He had decided that: 'By August 1924 . . . there was an air of fantasy in keeping it [the second Dail] in existence.' But there were many on his side, like Austin Stack and Mary MacSwiney, who regarded abstention as a matter of dogma and the second Dail as the *de jure* Government of the country. Accordingly, at the meeting de Valera set out to counter Stack and MacSwiney's 'more rigid view'[56] with his own increasingly less rigorous application of Republican Theology.

He persuaded the meeting to agree to the setting up of a Council of State which he saw as a more important body than the second Dail. It was called

Comhairle na d'Teachtai, Council of Deputies. The two groupings' respective roles were defined as follows:[57] 'For formal acts on account of continuity . . . it would be wiser to regard the Second Dail as the *de jure* government and legislature. But the whole body of elected members, including those just returned, should act as the Council of State and be the actual government of the country.' The practical effect of the creation of Comhairle na d'Teachtai was that, instead of having both feet firmly off the ground in the wraiths of the second Dail, the Council now only had one. It was at least something which existed, even though it had nothing of political substance, and it looked to de Valera, not to the second Dail, as the fountainhead of authority. But that was not how he explained his new creation to the meeting. What he said was:[58] 'The material point is whether the Second Dail should meet now and hand over its powers and authorities to the body that was subsequently elected, and whether they should meet afterwards and hand over to the body recently elected the powers they subsequently had.' Most of his listeners paid the Chief the homage of their understanding; very few attempted to translate the gobbledygook. Had they done so, the translation would have read: 'Machiavelli's pupil was beginning to draw away from "extremist support".' The fine Italian hand was evident also in a resolution passed at an IRA executive meeting held two days after the Comhairle na d'Teachtai meeting ended. It stipulated that:[59] ' . . . members of the army who went on public platforms were not to say that there would be further war or that there would be no further war. They were not to mention war at all. . . .'

One of his biographers subsequently commented:[60] 'Once more he set himself to the task of moulding public opinion, with all that apparent reasonableness and logic which had created such an invincible impression of his sincerity and integrity in the past.' And where better to begin moulding public opinion than in Ennis, on Our Lady's Day, 15 August 1924, the anniversary of his arrest a year earlier? Sinead refused to travel and did as she had done a year earlier – went to a church to pray for his safety.[61] To guarantee that safety, or more accurately to make the point that there could be a threat to it, the platform was surrounded by an IRA guard as he rose to speak in an atmosphere of great excitement. He began: 'I would disappoint a number here if I were not to start by saying, "Well as I was saying to you when we were interrupted . . .".' After the laughter had died away he did as he had done at the Comhairle na d'Teachtai meeting a week earlier, and began to give intimations of a departure in policy from the old *non possumus* second Dail doctrine. After ringing statements about the impossibility of giving 'allegiance to any foreign power or to any foreign people' he went on:[62] 'Things may be forced on us, we may temporarily have to submit to certain things, but our assent they can never have. . . . Don't forget for a moment that there is a vast difference between patiently submitting, when you have to, for a time, and putting your signature to a consent or assent to these conditions.' Decoded, this meant:

'We may have to enter a British-established Parliament, but we'll never sign our affirmation to the Oath.'

Statements similar to those already quoted from Lloyd George and other British political leaders about the Boundary Commission question provided de Valera with priceless ammunition on the partition issue. He was well aware that he was wielding a double-edged sword which could be used against him either there and then by his opponents, or some time in the future, if (and when) he came to power. He had warned the Comhairle na d'Teachtai on 7 August that:[63] 'The object of the Free State was to make it appear that we by our opposition had smashed the possibility of the North coming in. We will have to be very careful as to that. The Ulster problem will remain for us and it will be a very difficult problem.'

Nevertheless the sword was wielded with both force and frequency. He told the Ennis meeting that his reason for entering politics was to prevent partition and, at a meeting in the border town of Dundalk the following Sunday, that his reason for *not* entering Leinster House was because it was a partition Parliament.[64] As one of his biographers has noted, this was 'deliberately twisting the truth'. For, as Dr Dwyer has pointed out:[65] 'He had indicated a willingness to accept Partition before the Treaty negotiations, and he had already explained that taking a seat at Leinster House "would be a matter purely of tactics and expediency" if the oath were dropped.' In short, he was merely using the Partition issue to cloak political expediency in the hypocritical garb of principle.

But his most spectacular manipulation of the partition issue was achieved, at some cost to himself, when he managed to get sent to jail over the question of the Six Counties. A general election was scheduled in Great Britain and Northern Ireland for 29 October. In the Six Counties the old Irish Parliamentary Party was still strong, under the leadership of Joe Devlin. But the party decided to opt for abstention in the election. This was partly to highlight the position of Catholics in the area for the benefit of the Boundary Commission, and partly because the party feared the effects of Sinn Fein contesting the election. A split nationalist vote would give Unionist victories which would be both damaging in themselves and harmful in the eyes of the Commission. Accordingly, the party put up no candidates and issued a statement advising their followers not to vote.

De Valera took the opposite tack. Overlooking his comments on the 'well-known weakness of democracy' and the people 'having no right to do wrong', he issued a statement to the effect that 'elections were the only means available of making the wishes of the people clearly known'.[66] More importantly, he announced that he intended to speak in support of an anti-Treaty Republican[67] candidate in Newry. This had three results. First, he was denounced by the pro-Treaty nationalists for splitting the vote. Second, he was denounced by the Unionists for his effrontery in meddling in their election. Unionist papers warned him to stay out of the Six Counties, and the Northern Government issued an order banning him from various parts of the statelet, including Newry. It was made quite clear that he would be arrested if he tried to defy the order. He countered by announcing that he would do so, did so, and thereby produced the third result, a publicity bonanza.

He was arrested in Newry on 24 October, served with the exclusion order, and put across the border the next day. He immediately travelled to Sligo where, at a public meeting, he announced his intention of crossing the border again to 'reassert the right of Free speech in Derry'.[68] In Derry the B-Specials were more alert than the Free State troops had been in Ennis the previous year, and he was arrested before he reached the platform. Arriving in Belfast by rail under armed guard, he had to be protected by police from an angry Orange mob. Protests were made to the British Prime Minister, Ramsay MacDonald, about arresting an election candidate (de Valera was standing in South Down). These had no effect except to get more publicity for de Valera. On 1 November he was sentenced to a month's imprisonment after the following exchanges with the magistrate:

Magistrate: 'Have you anything to say in your defence?'

De Valera: 'I refuse to recognize this court because it is the creature of a foreign power and therefore has not the sanction of the Irish people. . . .'

Magistrate: 'You may make any statement you like in your defence but we can have no political speeches, and on no account can we listen to any statement showing contempt of court.'

De Valera: 'In that case I have only to say that I do not recognize the court.'

For his pains he received a month in solitary confinement. But the jail term and the defiant exchange with the magistrate in the best Robert Emmet tradition was worth nearly a thousand votes a day to him. On 18 November five by-elections were held in the South. Sinn Fein gained over 29,000 more votes than the party had polled in the same constituencies[69] in 1923 and won two of the seats. The most significant was that of South Dublin where Sean Lemass, a brother of the murdered Noel, emerged into the national limelight, doubling the Sinn Fein votes from 9,749 to 17,297 in the process. Clearly a change was taking place in the South. The Southern victories also helped to mask the damaging fact that in the North de Valera's decision to contest the election meant that the Unionists had a sweeping victory, recording easy wins even in nationalist areas such as Fermanagh and Tyrone. These were valuable gains, especially while the Boundary Commission was sitting. The realpolitik of the situation meant that partition was now copper-fastened, Boundary Commission or no Boundary Commission. Sinn Fein's vote in the North went down from 104,716 in 1921 to only 46,257. In England the election had resulted in a win for the Unionists' allies, the Tories, under Stanley Baldwin. In Northern Ireland the Unionists held not only an overwhelming political advantage, but also police and paramilitary supremacy through the strength of the Royal Ulster Constabulary and the B-Specials.

These considerations may have added to de Valera's feelings of depression in Belfast Jail. Despite the fact that he had been returned for South Down,[70] he apparently found his solitary confinement in Belfast the worst experience of his prison career.[71] One of the few books he was allowed was a volume of Francis Thompson's poetry. Perhaps someone in the prison library service thought certain lines from the poet's major work, 'The Hound of Heaven', were appropriate in his case:

> I fled Him, down the labyrinthine ways
> Of my own mind; and in the mist of tears. . . .

> I tempted all His servitors, but to find
> My own betrayal in their constancy
> In faith to Him their fickleness to me
> Their traitorous trueness, and their loyal deceit. . . .

He came out of jail paler and more furrowed-looking than ever, with a new target for attack: the Government's headgear. This example of a pernicious, pro-British predilection he stigmatized:[72] '. . . when he reappeared after his return in the same crumpled frieze coat [black] and the same rain-drenched felt hat. Referring to the formal attire of the Free State Ministers, he mocked "this wonderful tall hat, this most capacious and highly respectable tall hat." It would be no tall hat for him.' And he returned to an old target with another of those ancient Irish proverbs of which he had laid in such a plentiful supply for dealing with contemporary problems – in this case for assailing the stepping-stone argument in the context of the Boundary Commission and the Treaty:[73]

> Where is their stepping-stone argument now? They will soon have forgotten that they ever had such an idea. The stepping stones have been too slippery and they have slipped off. When I think of it, I think of what used to be in some of the old Irish tales about stepping stones. '*Fuair siad san na clocha. Fuair sinne an t-ath. Do badh iad san. Do thainig sinne slan.*'
> I am certain it will be so with the Republicans. *They* looked for the stepping stones and were drowned. *We* found the ford and we came safe.

That extract contains some of the hallmarks of de Valera's political rhetoric, such as the use of the generalized 'they' rather than a personalized attack. He rarely indulged in this form of public debate. Though he could show malice in private, as in the case of Michael Collins' reputation, he generally eschewed such behaviour in public. This apparent loftiness of character both enhanced his reputation and obscured the fact that there were several in his party who did use such tactics – unchecked by His Loftiness. Also characteristic was his bland overlooking of the fact that he might have had anything to do with adding to the adverse conditions of the moment – in this case, of course, the slipperiness of the stepping stones was in no small part due to the blood spilled in the civil war which he had played such a major role in bringing about. The use of Irish and evocation of an ancient tradition also gave him a special position in public life as being the leader who epitomized the consciousness of being Irish.

But the course he had followed in opposing the Treaty and afterwards had placed him in a position where he was unable to capitalize on his standing. In an open letter[74] to him which contained more than a hint of coalition should he mend his ways, Thomas Johnson, the Labour leader, summed up the disabilities of the abstentionist, second Dail policy: ' . . . a big proportion of the Army, Civil Service, Judiciary, would refuse to accept the direction of any authority except one constituted according to the Constitution of Saorstat Eireann . . . your economic policy would require not violence and strife but a period of peace, general good-will and united effort on the part of all who place the common good above individual self-interest. . . .' He warned, perceptively, that any revolutionary policy which seemed to challenge Britain would probably provoke not military but 'economic and financial' pressure. De Valera's activities when in power produced a reaction which certainly proved Johnson to be correct in this regard. He told de Valera bluntly that his continued defiance of the Constitution would 'destroy all hope' of accomplishing social change 'in this generation'. But he concluded by stating that the Labour Party would be 'eager to co-operate with any body of deputies *in the Dail* [author's italics]' who would work constitutionally for such change. The idea of losing the opportunity of a generation lodged with de Valera, though he did not take immediate steps to give it effect. He did not have to.

The tide of affairs continued to flow his way throughout 1925. The Army mutiny crisis had resulted in McGrath's forming from amongst the ranks of Government deputies an Adam's rib party known as the 'National Group', and contributed to a further nine by-elections being held during March. These confirmed the trend of the previous November: the Sinn Fein vote went up in each constituency, and two more Sinn Fein deputies won seats. The party now had a total of 48 empty seats in Leinster House. An indication of what might have happened had they been filled came when the Government forced through an unpopular public safety measure on 3 April. This was introduced because the IRA was reorganizing with ever-increasing vigour and inevitably coming into conflict with the forces of the state. Amongst other penalties the 'floggers' bill', as the Treasonable Offences Act was unpopularly known, provided for deportation and the death penalty. The Labour Party and other groupings, including many of the Government's own supporters, opposed it. Only thirty deputies actually voted to pass the measure into law. Had Sinn Fein been present, the Government would have been defeated. The debate with the party's ranks over whether or not to enter Leinster House intensified.

At the same time the economic situation worsened. What jobs there were in the public service went to Government supporters. The policy of

377

preventing emigration amongst those on the losing side in the civil war proved impossible to maintain. That year saw a mass exodus of Republicans, mostly to America. It was becoming increasingly clear that abstention was no answer to the problems of the hour. But the rumours that a new departure might see the policy go produced the following resolution at the Sinn Fein Ard Fheis, which began on 17 November:[75] 'Owing to the insidious rumours that Republicans will enter the Free State Parliament if the Oath be removed, we call on Sinn Fein to get a definite statement from the Government [i.e. the Comhairle na' dTeachtai/second Dail body] that they will adhere to the policy of Cathal Brugha, Erskine Childers, and their fellow martyrs and enter only an Irish Republican Parliament for all Ireland.' De Valera opposed the motion and two of his supporters, Sean Lemass and Countess Markievicz, moved a compromise amendment which was carried. The amendment stipulated that no change in policy take place, but 'no subject of discussion is barred'[76] except the 'questions of the accepting of allegiance to a foreign king and the partition of Ireland'.[77] It recommended that discussion on the issue continue, with a special emergency Ard Fheis being called if any shift were envisaged.

All this took place against the lowering cloud of the Boundary Commission, which had hung over all political debate since the thunderclap of the *Morning Post* report earlier in the month. Kevin O'Higgins, the strong man of the Government, had fainted on the day of publication – not without reason. The feelings of the Gardai at the prospect of losing their badges was magnified to the nth degree in the Army at the prospect of losing Donegal. It is said[78] that General Joseph Sweeney, who was so trusted by the Government that he had been temporarily placed in charge of the Army during the mutiny crisis, drew up plans to defend his native county against any handover. Many of the most senior officers supported him in the full knowledge that this might mean resuming the Anglo-Irish war.

Though this lurid scenario might appear to have worried the British, it was the Irish Government which was in the more vulnerable position. They were caught between the impregnability of the Tory–Unionist fortification of the border and the crossfire of criticism from both their own and de Valera's supporters. Trouble in the Government's own ranks resulted in one of its deputies, Professor Magennis, setting up a breakaway group, Clan na h'Eireann, the Children of Eireann. The Clan initially took a couple of deputies and a senator from the ruling party, but became a political orphan of the storm after the next general election when all its representatives, including Magennis, were defeated.

However, this lay in the future. For the moment, in London, Cosgrave and O'Higgins were condemned to negotiating, not on the terms of the Boundary Commission's report, but on trying to have it suppressed. The Commissioners were anxious to 'serve the report like a writ'.[79] O'Higgins put it to the Prime Minister, Stanley Baldwin, who was contacted with some difficulty at Chequers, that de Valera would come to power as a result of the crisis unless the Dublin Government emerged from the debacle with some semblance of concessions. Baldwin eventually agreed to suspend publication while the Dublin leaders explored the situation with Craig. They had little need of such exploration. He had already declared that he was just as ready as he had been in 1914 to:[80] ' . . . fight in the open against our enemies who would take away the loved soil of Ulster from any of the loyalists who want to remain there'.

He conceded nothing by way of territory, or amelioration of any of the laws discriminating against Catholics which were in the process of creating an apartheid state in the North. But he did agree to release some thirty IRA prisoners who had been in prison since the time of Collins' covert operations against the Six Counties. He was also supportive of O'Higgins and Cosgrave in negotiations on the financial provisions of Article 5 of the Treaty, which became embroiled in the controversy over the territorial provisions of Article 12. Article 5 had been hanging fire since the Treaty's signing. It said: 'The Irish Free State shall assume liability for the service of the Public Debt of the United Kingdom as existing at the date hereof and towards payment of war pensions as existing at that date in such proportion as may be fair and equitable, having regard to any just claims on the part of Ireland by way of set-off or counter-claim, the amount of such sums being determined in default of agreement by the arbitration of one or more independent persons being citizens of the British Empire.'

The Irish had baulked at the prospect of an imperial arbitrator. It is difficult to state precisely just what each side claimed from the other, but the figures have been put at £175 million by the British and £300 million by the Irish.[81] The Irish demand was on the basis of British over-taxation in Ireland. The British demand was to be reimbursed for the compensation they had been forced to pay for the depredations of their troops during the Anglo-Irish war. In addition they sought an increase in the Irish contribution to the cost of recompensing Unionists for damage to their property. The Irish did agree to a 10 per cent increase in the compensation payments and to a contribution to the war debt. This in effect meant that the Irish ended up paying for the excesses of the Auxiliaries, the Black and Tans and Lloyd George's 'reprisals' policy. The cost of the increase for the Unionists was probably about £5.5 million. Under the war debt heading, the Southern Irish agreed to pay £150,000 down and £250,000 a year for sixty years. Where the North was concerned, however, Craig's supportive attitude became explicable when it emerged that he had used the negotiations to get the Six Counties' war debt liability cancelled. Where Article 12 was concerned, the British agreed to the suppression of the Boundary Commission report and the Irish to recognize the existing border. This was in effect nothing more than a confirmation of the policy adopted in the days after Collins' death. But it was a grievous blow to the nationalists of Northern Ireland and to the prestige of the Cosgrave administration.

However, Cosgrave put a brave face on the settlement, saying in the Dail that the British had agreed to 'close all outstanding questions of controversy'. He had secured what he wanted from Britain: 'A huge 0'. He later described the settlement as a 'damned good bargain'. It was, of course, anything but a 'damned good bargain' from the nationalist point of view. Nor was it a 'huge 0', because the question of the land annuities was still outstanding between England and Ireland. The land annuities were the monies which the Dublin Government remitted each year to the British Exchequer to repay the loans raised to buy out landlords under the various Acts which resolved the land issue. The monies derived in the first instance from the farmers who worked the land and paid the annuities to the state in the same way as a mortgage repayment. The annuities question would one day prove to be one of the sharpest arrows in de Valera's quiver.

But the signing of the London Agreement found him weaponless and indecisive. Initially he met the situation by one of his favourite devices – adapting history to suit his own purposes. In a public statement[82] he said that Lincoln had been right to fight a civil war against the Southern states, which had a better case for secession than the Northern Unionists. Although the nationalists were too weak to prevent the 'outrage', they were not so weak that they would give the Boundary settlement the 'sanction of our consent'. He then went on to claim that when he met Lloyd George in 1921 he 'broke with him on this policy of partition; and had Mr. Griffith acted as I had believed he meant to act, he too would have broken on partition'. This was another classic illustration of a 'de Valera fact'. The policy which de Valera himself had set forth four years earlier in Document No. 2 had eschewed the use of force to bring the Unionists under Dublin's sway and confirmed them in their position by offering them:[83] ' . . . privileges and safeguards not less substantial than those provided for in the Articles of Agreement for a Treaty signed in London on December 6th, 1921'.

It was a time of confusion and emotion. Even Austin Stack, one of the staunchest abstentionists, toyed (temporarily) with the idea of entering Leinster House. He wrote to de Valera wondering whether enough support could be mustered if Comhairle na d'Teachtai did enter the Dail, 'Oath and all', to defeat the London Agreement and thus bring the Free State to an end.[84] Thomas Johnson, the Labour Party leader, invited all elected deputies to met at the Shelbourne Hotel on 7 December to try to find some way of blocking the settlement. Comhairle na d'Teachtai and Labour, however, found it easier to meet in the Shelbourne than in Leinster House. De Valera could not make up his mind when the Sinn Feiners met privately after the meeting; he gave no leadership to his followers one way or the other. One of them, Gerry Boland, said afterwards:[85] 'Much as I loved Dev. there were times when he could not just make up his mind.' Abstentionism ultimately condemned de Valera to ineffectual protest on 10 December, the day the agreement was sanctioned by the Dail by 71 votes to 20. His only contribution to the drama was to hold a meeting of Comhairle na d'Teachtai at the Rotunda and read out a declaration which he and the deputies signed:[86] 'In the name of the Irish nation and the Irish race, in the name of all who have stood and will yet stand unflinchingly for the sovereign independence of Ireland we, the duly elected representatives of the Irish people, by our names appended hereto, proclaim and record our unalterable opposition to the partitioning of our country.'

But as Christmas neared he began coming to a decision. On 18 December he told a meeting of Comhairle na d'Teachtai that he believed Sinn Fein should launch a campaign against the Oath so that the party could enter Leinster House without abandoning their principles. By then he had a clearer idea of the chances of this course being accepted than he had had after the Shelbourne Hotel meeting with Labour. This meeting had taken place close on the heels of an important decision by the IRA, which we will shortly examine. He had not then sufficient time to analyse its likely impact, but as the days passed and the reaction of the public to the Boundary Commission became clear, he obviously made up his mind that he could disregard the IRA's decision. The days of depending on 'extremist support' were numbered.

The abstention issue had come to a head at an IRA convention, the first since the civil war, held in Dalkey on 14 November. The atmosphere in the organization and its relationship with de Valera prior to this have been well summarized by one of the leading IRA men of those and subsequent years, Tomás O'Maoileon:[87] 'Aiken's intentions throughout 1925 were increasingly under the microscope of men like Jim Killeen, George Plunkett, Dave Fitzgerald, Andy Cooney and the rest. They felt very uneasy about the relationship of the Army to the shadow government under de Valera, Lemass and Ruttledge. Aiken was very friendly with de Valera: he fawned upon him. It was feared that he would be over influenced by him.'

Accordingly, during September Andy Cooney and George Plunkett, Count Plunkett's son, had confronted Aiken with reports that he was planning to lead the IRA into Leinster House. He refused to answer yea or nay, but promised to make an unequivocal statement at the November convention. Ironically for a man who was smoothing the path towards recognition of the State Parliament, Aiken introduced a new Constitution, which was accepted, whereby Volunteers would – as de Valera had done the previous year in Belfast – refuse to recognize the courts, North or South. It was a stipulation that greatly added to prison populations. Following discussions of the Constitution and consequent resolutions on various organizational matters, Peadar O'Donnell, the author and socialist, moved the following booby-trap resolution:[88]

> That in view of the fact that the Government has developed into a mere political
> party and has apparently lost sight of the fact that all our energies should be

devoted to the all-important work of making the Army efficient so that the renegades who, through a coup d'etat, assumed governmental powers in this country be dealt with at the earliest possible opportunity, the Army of the Republic sever its connection with the Dail, and act under an independent Executive, such Executive be given the power to declare war, when, in its opinion, a suitable opportunity arises to rid the Republic of its enemies and maintain it in accordance with the proclamation of 1916.

The discussion provoked by this resolution allowed Plunkett to demand that Aiken give his promised statement. When the Chief of Staff admitted that elements in the leadership had been discussing the possibility of entering Leinster House, if the Oath were removed, the lava poured forth. Violent language was used, and the O'Donnell resolution was passed by an overwhelming majority. A new executive was elected, and Aiken and those who supported him were all dismissed. Cooney was elected Chief of Staff and the IRA reverted to being a law unto itself, independent of political control from de Valera or anyone else. This was not what O'Donnell had intended. He told me himself[89] that his intention had been to cut the IRA away from Sinn Fein's traditional preoccupations such as the Oath, the second Dail and partition, so as to concentrate instead on socialist objectives.

However, old friendships continued and many IRA members continued to have close links with the de Valera-ites. For example, the IRA demonstrated their new-found independence with a spectacular jailbreak from Mountjoy on 25 November; George Gilmore, who planned and led the raid on the prison in which nineteen prisoners escaped, was at the time Sean Lemass's secretary. Frank Gallagher was a front page contributor to the first issue of the influential IRA newspaper *An Phoblacht*, launched earlier in the year.[90] In November de Valera himself had seen to it that a close supporter, Gerry Boland, travelled with an IRA delegation to Moscow on an arms mission. It was unsuccessful, partly because Stalin decided that the fact that the IRA had shot no bishops indicated a dearth of the necessary revolutionary fibre.[91] However, these close links and dependences had contributed to de Valera's vacillations in the eye of the Boundary Commission storm; once it blew over, he made sail straight for Leinster House. He announced in January that he would enter Parliament if he could so without taking the Oath. Arrangements were put in train for the holding on 9 March of the emergency Ard Fheis proposed the previous November to deal with the policy shift. In a memorable phrase of his own, uttered in the sail-trimming process: ' . . . the grey wisdom of the world' was calling him and those who thought like him to 'repress the warm instincts of our hearts'.[92]

But it was not calling to people like Mary MacSwiney, Austin Stack and Father O'Flanagan. The 'warm instincts' of their hearts, and of those who thought like them, was to cling on to the vision of the second Dail as the legitimate Parliament of the Republic, and the Free State and its institutions as the illegitimate offspring of Mother England. When the Ard Fheis met, they opposed the following resolution which de Valera proposed:[93] 'Once the admission oaths of the twenty-six and six-county assemblies are removed it becomes a question not of principle but of policy whether or not Republican representatives should attend these assemblies.' He argued that the issue was one not of principle, but of tactics. He called his audience's attention to the difficulty of putting principles into practice:[94] 'We are not all Thomas Aquinases. We are not all able to judge of the application of principles. . . .'

However, Mary MacSwiney replied in similar theological vein to the effect that, once Leinster House was entered, the descent into hell would be easy.[95] She and Austin Stack supported an amending resolution from Father O'Flanagan:[96] 'That it is incompatible with the fundamental principle of Sinn Fein to send representatives into any usurping legislature set up by English law in Ireland.' This was passed, narrowly, by 223 votes to 218. It was then put to the meeting as a substantive motion, but the enormous prestige of de Valera was tacitly acknowledged when it came to the vote. It was defeated by two votes, 179 to 177, with 85 abstaining. After three days of debate Sinn Fein had demonstrated clearly that it wanted the man but not his policy. Father O'Flanagan sponsored a motion, seconded by Mary MacSwiney, which was passed by acclamation, expressing '. . . the deep love and gratitude which each member feels for the man who was described by one delegate as the greatest Irishman of the century'.

However, the man wanted his policy. He told the Ard Fheis:[97] 'This is the opportune time, and I realise that the coming general election is the time. . . . I am from this moment a free man. . . . My duty as President of this organisation is ended. . . .' He had set up his own organization to oppose Cohalan and Devoy when he could not get his way in America. He had done it in Ireland when defeated on the Treaty vote by Collins and Griffith. Now he was about to do it again when beaten by MacSwiney, O'Flanagan, Stack and the others. All of the foregoing had one thing in common. They had shown him friendship, campaigned alongside him and supported him however and whenever they could. But such considerations did not weigh with de Valera Man of Power when it came to getting his own way.

18

THE WARRIORS OF DESTINY

DE VALERA KNEW that money – a great deal of money – would be needed if his new departure were to succeed. America was important here, and in particular his relationship with McGarrity. Well before the Extraordinary Ard Fheis of Sinn Fein was held in March 1926 he had foreseen that a split over abstention was inevitable, and he saw to it that he got his retaliation in first. In January Frank Aiken went to the USA to make a protracted stay, fund-raising and spreading new departure propaganda. The AARIR, de Valera's own creation, was supportive, though the organization was by now far weaker than it had been in the days before the Treaty split. But Clan na nGael was wary: it sent an observer to the Sinn Fein Extraordinary Ard Fheis, a Major Enright,[1] who watched the split unfold. Accordingly, after the Ard Fheis ended de Valera wasted no time in writing to McGarrity, putting his position on record:[2]

> Whoever else misunderstands my present line of action, I feel certain you will not. The new situation is full of hope if only it can be maintained without a bitter split.
>
> For over a year – since the nine by-elections, I have been convinced that the programme on which we were working would not win the people in the present conditions. It was too high, and too sweeping. The oath on the other hand is a definite objective within reasonable striking distance. If I can mass the people to smash it I shall have put them on *the march* again, and once moving, having tasted victory, further advances will be possible.
>
> . . . The people are very badly off. Many of our best workers have been compelled to emigrate, and the others are hard set to keep the wolf from the door . . . up to now the people could only see us as offering them fire as a retreat from the frying pan.
>
> You perhaps will wonder why I did not wait longer. It is vital that the Free State be shaken at the next election for if an opportunity be given to consolidate itself further . . . the national interest as a whole will be submerged in the clashing of the rival economic groups. It seems to me a case of now or never – at least in our time.
>
> . . . If the section opposing my view holds firm without violently obstructing I will be free to go out after the mass of the people and I believe I can win them back. . . .
>
> You may remember I wrote to you at the time of the Cease Fire Order about the military manoeuvre of 'changing to a flank in the front of an enemy'. It was successfully performed at that time, and has saved years of vain sacrifice. Perhaps it is too much to hope that such a manoeuvre can be repeated again. But if it can, and I do succeed, it will mean that we will have arrived in 1927 at what we would otherwise be attempting only a decade hence. Ten years are worth saving to the nation.

Obviously Johnson's warning about wasting a generation had weighed with de Valera. But a time would come in his later career when that last sentence would have a particularly ironic and accusatory ring to it. However, in the context of 1926 the letter already contained irony enough. De Valera was now hoping to influence his former 'extremist support' to do as he had failed to do when asked by Collins and Griffith after losing the Treaty vote: campaign without 'violently obstructing' or, better still, do as he had suggested to the Ard Fheis, treat his new grouping with 'benevolent neutrality'[3] – in other words leave the field to him.

But neither his letter nor Aiken's efforts succeeded in changing the Clan's traditional allegiance. Aiken asked McGarrity to use his influence so that the:[4] 'Clan-na-nGael organisation should confine its activities to supporting the Army [the IRA] whilst leaving the members free to support their favourite political Republican organisation'. But the Clan's official position was made clear in a statement issued on 15 June. It said:[5] 'To prevent division in our ranks it is deemed necessary that all our members stand faithful to their obligation, that revolution alone be in future our object.' And writing[6] in reply to Aiken regarding his suggestion that he should influence the Clan towards the de Valera line, he told him that the new departure was not for him. He said he could only give his personal view, but he knew that the reason for the Clan's existence was to help an armed force in Ireland. McGarrity and de Valera were approaching a parting of the ways.

Meanwhile, as these developments were taking place in America, back in Ireland de Valera pressed on vigorously with his change of direction. A month after the Extraordinary Sinn Fein Ard Fheis, on 17 April he announced to a representative of the news agency United Press the new party's policy, rationale and title. This guaranteed publicity for the new departure not only in Ireland but throughout the English-speaking world, particularly in America. He told UPI that:[7] 'The conviction on which the new organisation is based is that in the heart of every Irishman there is a native undying desire to see his country politically free, and not only free but truly Irish as well, and that the people recently divided are but awaiting an opportunity to come together again and give effective expression to that desire. They are conscious that, if real unity can be secured, Ireland is theirs for the taking.'

He explained that the name Fianna Fail had been chosen to symbolize 'a banding together of the people for national service, with a standard of personal honour for all who join as high as that which characterised the ancient Fianna Eireann, and a spirit of devotion equal to that of the Irish Volunteers from 1916–21'. Fianna Fail, literally Warriors of Destiny, was the name given by some Irish speakers to the Volunteers instead of the more commonly used Oglaig na h'Eireann or Irish Army. The Fianna were the Irish samurai. De Valera said that the purpose of the new 'Republican organisation' was the:

... re-uniting of the Irish people and the banding of them together for the tenacious pursuit of the following ultimate aims, using at every moment such means as are rightfully available:

1) Securing the political independence of a united Ireland as a republic.

2) The restoration of the Irish language and the development of a native Irish culture.

3) The development of a social system in which, as far as possible, equal opportunity will be afforded to every Irish citizen to live a noble and useful Christian life.

4) The distribution of the land of Ireland so as to get the greatest number possible of Irish families rooted in the soil of Ireland.

5) The making of Ireland an economic unit, as self-contained and self-sufficient as possible – with a proper balance between agriculture and the other essential industries.

One method of achieving all the foregoing which de Valera made clear would *not* be 'rightfully available' to his samurai was taking the Oath. 'That oath no Republican will take, for it implies acceptance of England's right to overlordship in our country.'

The new party was formally launched in the La Scala Theatre[8] on 16 May 1926. Most of those present in the packed, excited audience were aware of the symbolism of the theatre's proximity to the GPO. Very few, with the possible exception of de Valera himself, pondered on the significance of the fact that the La Scala was located in Prince's Street. He certainly managed to interject a suitably Machiavellian note into the proceedings. At the Sinn Fein Ard Fheis a month earlier he had made it clear that his aim was to retain a modicum of traditionalist 'extremist support'. He had hoped, he said:[9] ' . . . that some would reserve themselves and . . . would do everything in their power as long as we tread the path – that they would defend us and make it clear to our people abroad that we held the honour of Ireland as sacred as they did'.

In his opening remarks he sought to convince his listeners that, even though his head was answering the call of the 'grey wisdom of the world', his heart still responded to the 'warm instincts' of those whom he wished to use as a 'reserve'. Shortly before the La Scala meeting, there had been yet another daring IRA jailbreak, in which a prominent Republican, Jack Keogh, had been rescued. Early on in his speech de Valera said:[10] 'When a military commander is given a task, he feels it his first duty to "appreciate" or judge the situation correctly. . . . I am willing to wager that when the boys who rescued Jack Keogh the other day undertook their task they . . . started I am sure by finding out all they could about the conditions of his detention. They were then able to prepare their plans wisely. . . . We must act similarly in our political task.'

This was greeted with tremendous applause. In the course of a very lengthy speech he went on to urge Republicans to position themselves 'along the most likely line of the nation's advance'. He invited his audience to place themselves in the position of a young man 'with strong national feelings, honest and courageous' who examined the existing political situation. He would see:

> . . . the country partitioned . . . nearly one half of the electorate . . . shut out from having an effective voice in determining its rulers. . . . He would have no difficulty in tracing the anomaly to its source, the oath of allegiance to a foreign power acquiesced in by the majority under the duress of an external threat of war. The pretence at democracy and the misrepresentation of the real wishes of the people which that pretence covered he would recognise as the immediate obstacle to a unified national effort at home . . . the screen by which England's controlling hand was effectively concealed from a great many of the Irish people themselves and from the outside world. . . .

'To sit on the safety valve is a notoriously dangerous expedient', he told his audience. History, alas, does not record for us the numbers of lives preserved for the nation as a result of this piece of information, but it was clear by the following November when the new party held its first Ard Fheis that La Scala had launched a movement of substance. The intervening months had seen Fianna Fail Cumainn (branches) spring up all over the Twenty-six Counties. Sean Lemass's and Gerry Boland's practical administrative abilities, combined with de Valera's mesmeric presence, made inroads into Sinn Fein support. While they organized, he made off with Sinn Fein's Republican and emotional baggage. On 29 June, a month after the formation of Fianna Fail, he had stated at Clare: 'I stand for an Irish Republic, for the full freedom of Ireland, as thoroughly today as I stood nine years ago when I first came before you.'

The Ard Fheis was deliberately held on the anniversary of Erskine Childers' execution. De Valera opened the proceedings by asking everyone to rise and do honour to one who had been 'put to death for loving their rights and their liberty more than he loved himself'. He continued with his safety valve motif:[11]

> It is vain to think that the natural aspirations of Irishmen for the liberty of their country are going to be stifled now. If the road of peaceful progress and natural evolution be barred, then the road of revolution will beckon and will be taken. Positive law and natural right will be involved in the old conflict. The question of minority right will be again bloodily fought out.
>
> I have never said, and I am not going to say now, that force is not a legitimate weapon for a nation to use in striving to win its freedom. . . . But a nation within itself ought to be able to settle its polity so that all occasions of civil conflict between its members may be obviated. . . . This eternal menace of civil war was concealed in the womb of England's Greek gift of the 'Treaty'; and, of all the duties which this nation owes itself, the duty which at this moment is paramount is the duty of seeing that this menace is not passed on to the coming generation. . . .

De Valera was bringing to a fine art the process of acting constitutionally while cloaking his actions in revolutionary rhetoric. One of his first public appearances after the Ard Fheis was with Sean MacBride – whose home in

Dublin, Roebuck House, was an IRA headquarters – at a rally to protest at the conditions under which George Gilmore, a top IRA man, was held in prison.[12] But he had not a great deal of time to devote to such activities. He needed two things above all to fuel his and his party's drive for power – money and propaganda. And the best source of both was America. In the same way that he turned other national misfortunes to his advantage, he now turned to make emigration work in his favour. With the help of the Irish in America he could fund at home both his political campaigns and the founding of the newspaper he had set his heart on. And that is why, on the morning of 25 February 1927 in the Rob Roy Hotel at Cobh, an interested observer could have witnessed what some of his critics would undoubtedly have termed an exercise in role reversal – someone trying to force dope down the throat of Eamon de Valera. The someone was Frank Gallagher, who has left a description of the scene.[13] He said: 'I am trying to get Dev to take his Pollycarp dope. But I am going to have some job. When I asked him not to take too much tea at breakfast he said: "As bad to be fasting as to be dead" and he limited himself to four large cups.'

Gallagher made his diary entry as the two were waiting for the tender to ferry them to the liner which would take them to New York. The hitherto unpublished diaries of de Valera's trips to the USA are an invaluable part of the mosaic of de Valera's career and life. They afford glimpses into his appeal, his philosophy and the hard-headed commercialism that he cloaked under a guise of guileless sincerity and other-worldliness. They record the effort he put into criss-crossing America to further his aims. New York, Boston, Butte, Chicago, Cleveland, Denver, Dodge City, Kansas City, Los Angeles, St Paul/Minneapolis, Portland, San Francisco and Washington were all visited, and sometimes revisited, during the four years he spent launching paper and party.

Gallagher did not go on all the journeys with him, but his anecdotes show de Valera in activities typical of all of them. Going to Mass, browsing in book stores, checking that a show was clean (that the girls were clothed), before venturing into a Broadway theatre. (This was for a Charlie Chaplin performance.) Sometimes de Valera's stories, told in a relaxed atmosphere far from the strife of Ireland, shed light on history. For example, a group of Redemptorist priests who asked after dinner about his political memories were rewarded with the inside story of how his arch-rival Cosgrave first came to be selected as a Sinn Fein candidate – de Valera picked him to prevent Countess Markievicz splitting Sinn Fein by standing against Eoin MacNeill, the party's original choice, whom the Countess never forgave for countermanding the 1916 order.

It would obviously be impossible to give any sort of extended excerpt from the Gallagher chronicle, which in part takes the form of letters to his wife Celia, but a few extracts will help to illustrate the esteem in which de Valera was held in America and how he managed to use that standing to launch a newspaper empire and win power in Ireland. It was, as Gallagher called his diary, a 'Great Adventure'. Not the least part of the adventure was the struggle with seasickness which de Valera had to endure on the way over. Gallager makes several mentions of how ill he was, and how by sheer willpower he forced himself out of his bunk for occasional walks on deck. The seasickness may have contributed to one of the few recorded gestures of open-handedness where money was concerned in de Valera's career. A collection was taken up for a new baby born on board. When the collector, a young woman, first approached him de Valera told her that he had no money on him. She apparently disbelieved him and was inclined to treat the coin he subsequently produced as being a case of too little, too late. But it turned out to be a ten dollar gold piece, the highest contribution received.

De Valera was an object of great curiosity to his fellow first-class passengers, who obviously did not know whether they had an anarchist or a statesman in their midst. Gallagher described how de Valera won over a young woman of the school of 'Come-now Mr. de Valera what-*is*-all-this-Irish-business' with: 'The best summary of all the intricacies of the position I have ever read or heard'. Gallagher noted that he: ' . . . didn't think it was in D. to be so lucid and compressed'. For her part, the young woman was so impressed that her 'bright eyes starred him and half closed now and again in a telling intimation that she understood and sympathised. . . . Lola will make a real intelligent friend of Ireland and will be of use. . . . D. saw her value sooner than I did. . . . '

By invitation de Valera left the first-class world of private cabins and menus, which offered a choice not of meals but of banquets, to pay a visit to a concert of heartbreak given by Irish emigrants in the stuffy, crowded, third-class section filled with not just Irish, but Germans, Poles, Scots – all representatives of the poor of Europe. Behind the gaiety, the music and the dancing of the improvised *ceili* there lay, in Gallagher's phase, a shared 'sorrow at leaving, and [they were] fearful of what lay ahead'. They had every reason to be fearful. In one of his early diary entries after landing Gallagher noted, on 11 March, that two prominent Republicans, Mick Crowley and Connie Neenan, called on de Valera 'desperately anxious that the truth of the position be known back at home'. Crowley, who had been eight months out of work, was sharing digs with eight other Irishmen 'with degrees who couldn't get work anywhere'. But though de Valera also may have been apprehensive about what lay ahead, he knew that in the continuing Irish diaspora lay a source of power for him in Ireland.

His arrival in New York on 5 March was a major event in Irish circles. *The World*'s headline was: 'Welcome to de Valera' and he was besieged with requests to speak to Irish organizations. He again stayed at the Waldorf Astoria, where his relations turned up in force to greet him: 'Fr. Wheelright v. nice, much younger than Dev and eight cousins, two are very pretty and gay young ladies.' But they waited in vain for two and a half hours without seeing their famous relative. It was 2 a.m. before he managed to return to the Waldorf from a press of appointments and meetings elsewhere in the city. All through his three months' stay it was the same. Gallagher records de Valera having to cut short a visit to Macy's department store because so many people accosted him that it was impossible to shop; 'people came up to him even during Mass', Gallagher commented. There was: 'an endless stream of visitors to the hotel. Deputation after deputation. . . .'

In revealing Gallagher's own attitudes, the diary also indicates something of the completely unquestioning nature of the respect that de Valera received. On the journey over, Gallagher had read Pieras Beaslai's monumental biography of Collins. A curious choice of reading for a voyage with 'the Chief', one might have thought, for the book is as complimentary to Collins as it is critical of de Valera. However, even more curious is the fact that Gallagher departs from his normal custom when mentioning an author and passes no judgement on the work. Beaslai's manifest ability made it difficult for a contemporary like Gallagher, who knew both author and characters, to criticize him. But to praise him, even privately, given his attitude to 'D.', would have been as unthinkable as to criticize the theological basis of his Church: the delivery of a priest's sermon, perhaps, or a personal foible, but not his doctrine. Robespierre's disciples preferred to live in a world where Danton was not even mentioned. Shortly after they landed, Gallagher was walking along a New York street with de Valera when a man stopped them to ask de Valera: 'Why didn't you go to London for the negotiations?' All Gallagher records is: 'D. answered him briefly and we walked on commenting on the fact that the Irish everywhere were asking themselves the same questions as those at home.' There is no analysis and, of course, no mention of the explanation. What Gallagher does say, in a letter to his wife dated 8 March, is: 'It is clear that he is loved by everyone here.' And later: 'D. is absolutely delightful and enters into all my jokes.'

One of de Valera's most important encounters took place two days after he landed, on 7 March. It was with John Hearn, Treasurer of AARIR. Gallagher described Hearn as a 'very fine looking man, with a keen, spiritual face. He is of course opposed but I like him. He and D. had a long, long chat.' In the course of that chat – during which, Gallagher noted, several VIPs were left waiting – de Valera evidently modified Hearn's opposition. Hearn remained loyal to the second Dail, traditionalist viewpoint all his life – in fact he was the last second Dail representative in the USA – but he also agreed to continue playing a crucial starring role in de Valera's plans. De Valera had mentioned the Irish newspaper situation to him as far back as 1922:[14] 'The propaganda against us is overwhelming. We haven't a single daily newspaper on our side, and but one or two small weeklies.' He now needed Hearn's help in rectifying that situation by intervening in a drama that had been going on since 1922.

A little recapitulation is required before we see the curtain go up on one of the most important scenes in that drama, which took place on 14 March, 1927. As we saw, for reasons best known to himself, when he returned to Ireland at Christmas 1920 de Valera left in New York banks some $3 million of the monies he had solicited for the Irish cause. He specifically agreed with Collins after the Treaty split 'that this money should not be used for party purposes'.[15] I will leave it to readers to judge for themselves how his activities in New York during March 1927, and subsequently, could be made to square with that undertaking. But first let us remind ourselves that along with the external Dail loan, of which these monies formed part, there was the internal loan which Collins had administered in Ireland, 'on the bicycle'.

The Provisional Government claimed the balance of this loan in 1922. De Valera objected, in his capacity as trustee, arguing that the money had been subscribed for the maintenance of the Republic and should not be transferred. He was supported in his objection by one of the other trustees, Stephen O'Mara, and opposed by the third, Bishop Fogarty. Fogarty joined in an action brought by the Government to recover the money. On 31 July 1924 Judge Murnaghan, a Dublin High Court judge, found in the Government's favour. De Valera's side appealed, but the High Court decision was upheld by the Irish Supreme Court on 17 December 1925. In consequence some £81,000 found its way into the coffers of the Irish Free State's Department of Finance. De Valera was determined that the money he had left on deposit in New York should not follow.

For, concurrently with the Dublin proceedings, the Cosgrave administration also took action in New York. In August 1922 the Provisional Government secured an injunction preventing the banks from handing over the balance of the external loan (and its accrued interest) to de Valera, O'Mara or anyone acting for them. The Cosgravites followed up this victory with an application to the New York Supreme Court seeking a declaration that the Provisional Government was the legitimate successor of the Republican Dail and was thus entitled to the money subscribed for the establishment of an Irish Republic. De Valera contested this claim.

The position in New York was somewhat different from that of Dublin – the banks felt that the money should go neither to de Valera nor to the Free State, but should be returned to the original shareholders. De Valera himself 'had long felt'[16] that this would be the decision of the court. Therefore, following the decision in favour of the Free State in the Dublin High Court in July 1924, he moved to capitalize on the possibilities offered by a decision in favour of the bondholders. On 5 August 1925, Sean T. O'Ceallaigh, the Poblacht na hEireann envoy in New York, wrote to Hearn, who had been appointed as chairman of a 'Bondholders' Committee', advising him that it was time to enter the fray:[17] ' . . . it has now been agreed by all the lawyers, that the Bondholders Committee should get to work without further delay with a view to intervene in the present case for the preservation of the Funds for the Republic'.

Accordingly when the case finally came for hearing, on 14 March 1927 before Mr Justice Peters of the New York Supreme Court, along with de Valera and the Free State there was a third force present in the action – the Bondholders' Committee, or the Hearn Committee as it was more generally known. Gallagher notes in his diary that the Free State counsel, in his efforts to avoid the use of the word 'republic', got so tied up in references to the first and second Dails that Justice Peters interrupted him to ask in exasperation: 'If you don't know how many governments there are, how am I supposed to know?' De Valera, however, made it quite clear that he knew what he was talking about. His biography states that:[18]

> For three days he was examined and cross-examined on the details of Irish history from 1913 to 1922. With all his habitual care and precision he answered the questions put to him. The New York newspaper [not named by the biographers] said 'On the witness stand de Valera gave the impression of being meticulously honest. He would decline to identify a paper or vouch for the accuracy of a statement unless he knew of it from his own personal knowledge.' Indeed the deliberation and care which he gave to each question and to his answers appears to have tested the patience of his own lawyers on occasion.

It would take us ahead of our story to discuss the outcome of this display of meticulous honesty at this stage; we will return to the saga in Chapter 20, at its proper place in our story. For the moment it is sufficient to say that Peters' verdict, delivered the following May, bore out de Valera's predictions about the money being given back to the bondholders.

To return to Gallagher's record of his American visit, 14 March also saw de Valera speak at Carnegie Hall. Gallagher says it took 'hefty police' to get him through the crowds outside. When he did get in: 'The audience went wild . . . rose and cheered five minutes, ten minutes, a quarter of an hour. . . . He spoke very well, going over the events of the last six years step by step. He held his audience for nearly three hours. We all went home thoroughly happy. . . .'

St Patrick's Day, 17 March, began with Mass at St Patrick's Cathedral. That afternoon de Valera showed himself to the crowds gathered on Fifth Avenue for the Parade, but left before it started because 'it is a Cohalan affair,' Gallagher noted. That evening de Valera delivered a radio talk on the topic of emigration: 'It was fine. He quoted "They are going, they are going" from Eithne Carberry with extraordinary feeling.' Then began the 'pilgrimage of Irish societies'. This was preceded by de Valera administering the cut direct to a stage Irishman who had accompanied them on a tour of Sing Sing Prison a few days earlier, on the 13th. It is hard to tell from the tone of Gallagher's diary which more affected the pair, the fact that it was quite normal for as many as five people a day to be executed as Sing Sing or the 'terribly fat red-headed, bull of a man'. He drove a 'violent green' coloured car bedecked with an American and a Republican flag. Gallagher notes that, as de Valera emerged from the Waldorf

Astoria, 'Himself appeared out of the car in dress suit with an opera hat above the flames'. This is what happened next:

> On the vast face was a patronising and expectant smile, fat as any smile smiled on earth. He seemed even to open his arms. But following Father T. [Talbot, a priest friend of de Valera's] we passed him out as if he was not. Consternation in the street. There was cries of 'hallo'. D. was adamant. I want nothing to do with that man he told J.M. [John Martin, an AARIR stalwart] who was terribly distressed . . . the green car was speedily lost in the traffic . . . H.S. [Himself, de Valera] was delighted with the incident. 'I have got back my self-respect', he said.
> We visited the H.Q. of the AARIR. This was a smallish little entertainment in a smallish room which was packed to the doors.

But there was nothing 'smallish' about the next port of call, the Leitrim Men's Association.

> There were nearly five thousand people in the great hall. . . . Some of those in charge of the affair were not entirely sober [despite Prohibition, a constant source of amazement to the abstemious Gallagher]. . . . The Kerry Men were next. . . . A crowd outside the door was mainly tight and in the battle to get inside I, despite a gallant fight, was repulsed. I waited for D. to re-emerge. . . .
> The Cavan men met us at the Kerry-men's place with an escort of motor-police who shot through the city sounding their shrill police call . . . the 71st Armoury . . . an immense room . . . there must have been 8,000 people on its floor and in the galleries . . . D. was nearly killed by those trying to grasp his hand or hug him. The crowd was so great there was no chance of a quiet hearing but as three broadcasting stations were in operation D. was able to reach a bigger audience even than those in the hall. . . .

The final stop of the day was the *ceili* given by the United Councils of the AARIR: 'It was the pleasantest turnout of the lot. . . . Dev made a good speech and afterward had to shake hands with everybody. The pair managed to escape without drinking any of "the real good stuff."'

The next day they moved on from New York to Philadelphia.

> . . . were met at the station by the usual multitude who tried to trample me to death . . . arrived at the Bellevue Hotel to a charming suit [*sic*] of rooms . . . the police came with us as a guard [to the meeting] and held all other vehicles back until our procession was through . . . the hall was not completely crowded . . . this was the first disappointment, there were others. . . . Speaker after speaker got up before D. The last was the worst. He spoke for 65 minutes introducing D. . . . so heavily dosed with spoken saccharine that I writhed. . . .
> The audience had been suffering for over two hours and were mentally clubbed to death. They gave D. a royal welcome but both D. and they were worn out. Result a very poor speech by D. – the worst yet, and a thoroughly disappointed audience. . . .

Gallagher was horrified at the lack of respect shown by a pressman 'to an international celebrity'. The pressman boarded the train at Providence and then walked along shouting 'de Valera' until he found his quarry, whom he interviewed until the train pulled into Boston. Here 'we found a whole host of Pressmen and photographers awaiting us and . . . the cameras clicked for ten minutes. . . . There was an enormous crowd in the station and D., though flanked with policemen, had difficulty at times in keeping his feet. I saw people sobbing with a kind of joy when they saw him. . . . We had to scramble for our cars, then through interested streets we drive to the Copley Plaza – the finest hotel here. . . .'

Having rendered unto Caesar, by way of calls on dignitaries such as the Governor and the Mayor, de Valera then moved to ensure that Christ got his share by visiting the Cardinal. The celebrated William O'Connell, 'Gangplank Bill', so called (behind his back) because of his frequent trips abroad, 'dominated the Catholic scene in Boston'.[19] He received de Valera in his home, standing in a 'lavishly furnished' room with a 'massive dark wood top table in the centre of it and a general colour scheme of browns and yellows and reds on carpets and walls'. The Cardinal was 'very fat and jovial . . . ugly too unless he smiles'. As Gallagher notes, it was 'an interesting scene':

> The Cardinal with his taut waistband and his red skull cap, and his massive pensive face which was only occasionally lit up with a smile and an upward flash of the bright eyes. D stood a few feet from him looking marvellously slim in contrast. We . . . were lined up at a respectful distance. . . .
>
> His Eminence welcomed D., but ponderously and carefully stated that he had to remember that he was the Cardinal of all sections in Boston. He longed for Irish unity and friendship with Britain and didn't see why the half-loaf of the Treaty might not be used for a while . . . in matters of human Government principles were not so important . . . the whole speech was spoken with much music in the voice and an obvious weighing of words. . . .
>
> D. replied very quietly and gave the 'coup de Grace' to his Eminence's points. On the half-loaf he said that . . . when it was a question of pledging oneself to have nothing all one's life but half-loaves it was an entirely different matter.
>
> During D.'s statement the Cardinal stood looking up at him and his expressive eyes flashed when D. punctured something he had said. It was clear enough that the eminent heart was with us but the eminent head had to be diplomatic and as a result very colourless and flat.

Gallagher described with great glee an incident which occurred on the front steps of the house as they were leaving after half an hour of 'this by-play'. The Cardinal's housekeeper came running up to de Valera and 'taking his hand reverently kissed it, which was one for his Eminence. Indeed D. made a much nicer Cardinal at that moment.' Gallagher did well to record that moment; during much of his career de Valera behaved like a lay cardinal – though particularly on that visit to Boston.

The next day was Sunday, and after Mass in South Boston in the morning the Chief indulged in a little moralizing at lunchtime: he joined with Gallagher in attacking Sean O'Casey's right to 'defame our values'. And then it was time to attend to the central reason for the trip to the USA in general and Boston in particular – the collection after the sermon during the political High Mass of a de Valera public meeting. The door to the large hall in which this particular meeting was held had been locked for over an hour before de Valera and his party arrived. 'There was a huge mob outside the hall and despite police reserves and police horses it took us ten minutes to fight our way to the doors and a fierce struggle to get through them.' Inside, the proceedings got under way with the singing of 'The Star Spangled Banner' by a daughter of the famous Fenian, O'Donovan Rossa. De Valera was introduced and welcomed as 'the man who fought in the streets of Dublin for the independence of Ireland. We welcome you as the man who accepted the sentence of death proudly and who when that sentence was commuted fought and defeated the English in their prisons. We welcome you as the man who coming from jail unbroken rallied the Irish nation to the success of 1918. . . .'

Gallagher comments: 'It was a fine sincere speech, the best I have heard in America since I came.' And then came the punchline. 'Towards its end H. [Hughes, a cultivated Bostonian described as having a greater knowledge of Irish history than anyone living at the time] announced that a collection would be taken up.' There then unfolded, in Gallagher's words, 'a scene very novel to me':

> From all parts of the house people came carrying bundles of dollars and five dollar bills. The dais was soon littered with them. Each subscription as it was handed up was announced and the fat ones and those with a ringing covering message roused the audience to new applause. For an hour it went on. . . . When the black bag with $5,000 dollars was taken away D. stood up to speak. . . . It was magnificent and carried the house off its feet.

Gallagher would get used to that scene. It was to be repeated, with variations, in many parts of the USA both during the trips on which Gallagher accompanied de Valera and on other occasions. The network of de Valera helpers, dating back to the great 1919–20 tour, was such that he could draw on huge lists of names and addresses to ensure that those summoned to meetings were likely to subscribe.

Having tasted the fruits of Boston, de Valera convened a committee meeting at the Waldorf Astoria to plan his appeal in New York. Gallagher's diary entry for the following day, 27 March, describes the result: 'Last night D. decided to summon a meeting of old workers by postal card. This required 5,000 cards. . . . I brought back the cards to Major Kelly's Alcazar Hotel. . . . The Major's room was full of workers from all sections. A nice looking girl seated by the Major turned out to be one of the buyers of the big dress stores here who is on her way to Europe to collect summer frocks for her house.' The postcards, addressed from the Waldorf Astoria and dated 28 March, contained the following message from de Valera:

A Chara [Friend],[20]
   May I ask you as an old worker in Ireland's cause to attend a *special meeting* to
be held on Thursday next, 31st inst at 8 p.m. in the Hall at 338 East 29th St,
   Do Chara, Eamon de Valera
Please bring this card with you. It will be required at the hall.

Kelly's workers were so efficient that the postcards were ready for posting
the next day.

While this particular effort was being mounted, de Valera was of course
continuing to attend to the bonds case hearing and in addition had other,
separate, means of funding in operation. For example, on 1 April a note
arrived at the Waldorf from a priest in a parish on West 121st Street:[21]
'Dear Chief – I am enclosing $10 given me by Cecilia MacMurrough, 305,
West 55th St. for the De Valera Fund (Election).'

As a result of this kind of donation and larger amounts, on 29 March,
even before de Valera's postcard had had time to take effect, the following
entry appears in Gallagher's diary: 'Telephone calls late in the evening
announced that twenty-five thousand dollars were ready for sending to
Ireland from New York alone.' By way of counterpoint it may be noted
that the previous day Connie Neenan had called again to the Waldorf to
ask the party to do what it could to discourage emigration from Ireland.
'Hundreds of newcomers were starving.'

The organizational work involved took its toll of de Valera's nerves. On
25 March Gallagher notes that 'D. has his difficult sides'. These would not
have bothered Gallagher had he not work of his own to do, but as he had 'a
mountain' of it he felt the strain acutely. However, intensely loyal and
careful even in his private jottings, Gallagher would not set down his
feelings in writing. When it came to describing how de Valera's personality
and the pressure of work were causing him greater anxiety than he had
ever known in his life before, Gallagher switched to shorthand. Evidently
it was the bonds case which contributed to de Valera's tensions and difficult
manner, for on the 28th Gallagher says: 'D. went to court after a bout of
anxiousness over things in general. It gets rather on my nerves but I
understand him better in these things and it is easier than it was.'

But 'anxiousness' or not, organizational detail was always keenly
attended to and well in advance. Even before setting out on the main leg of
his coast-to-coast American tour, de Valera was making sure that his
arrival back home on the Irish coast would be suitably marked. On 31
March Gallagher was empowered to write to his wife Celia:[22] 'Go to Liam
Pedlar and say that it would be wise to begin at once organising a public
reception for D. at Cobh, at Cork, and at Dublin. He is scheduled to arrive
on the *Republic* on May 7th at Cobh and will probably go to Dublin straight
away with perhaps a short break at Cobh. The election will be on then and
public excitement should be ready to make D's entry a triumphal one.'

On 1 April, 'the first morning of the great trek' across the American
continent, de Valera visited his mother in Rochester before setting out for

Chicago. Kate had kept some letters for him since his 1920 visit. One was from Sinead, another from Michael Collins. The latter provoked a highly significant reaction. Gallagher says that the letter 'moved D. greatly, not in any sentimental way but in appreciation of the finer things that were in Mick'. One is tempted to wonder whether there was any remorse in that 'appreciation'. In the afternoon de Valera visited 'the aunt who was his mother' (Hannie), and in the evening addressed a 'particularly intelligent and well-set-up' audience. He told them 'that Ireland was not free, was not even enjoying the status of Canada, must have full freedom or none, and had never had a real chance of ratifying the Treaty'.

The normally efficient travel arrangements broke down at Rochester, affording yet another example of the esteem de Valera was held in by Americans. First the railway authorities, believing him to be *en route* to the station (as did Gallagher) held the train; even though if it was late arriving in Chicago, every passenger got a refund of six dollars. Then, when he did not come, 'The clerks who would have cursed and impeded anyone else went out of their way to make new arrangements for D.' Finally, after a farewell supper at the Wheelrights, there was 'one more tribute to D: Usually nobody in America is allowed past the ticket turnstiles', but the whole party were allowed on the platform. Gallagher noted: 'As I saw D. kiss his little mother I wondered would they ever see one another again. I'd have liked to have kissed her myself.'

And so to Chicago, where the object apparently was to confer with Frank Aiken, who was looking 'fat and well'. The party 'went quietly to Frank Aiken's hotel where the Chief discussed ways and means similar to those that had been successful at New York'. They left Chicago that evening and the following day found them in St Paul, where a priest, Father Jeremiah O'Connor, belied his Christian name to preach not a jeremiad but a eulogy on de Valera who, he said, was 'chosen by God to be his nation's liberator'. Gallagher commented: 'What a difference between this and churches in Ireland.' The organizer of that night's meeting, a Sligo Protestant called Richard Brown, proposed that Gallagher should make the appeal for funds. However this was changed – 'at D.'s insistence'. De Valera, after all, was the one who had been chosen by God.

The same thought had obviously occurred to the clergy of San Francisco, because Gallagher notes that when they arrived there, on Sunday, 10 April, the priest, in addition to the usual notice, 'announced D.'s meeting'. It was held in a 'huge hall . . . festooned with the city fathers'. The crowd 'went mad' when de Valera arrived, and showed their appreciation of his 'fine speech' in the way they responded to the collection. This was taken up by a namesake of Gallagher's, Andy Gallagher, with breezy, American irreverence which Gallagher did not think struck 'the right note': ' . . . Dr Brennan – twenty-five dollars – thought you were worth more than that doctor. Dr. Timothy Walsh – fifty dollars. Best coroner in town. Hope business brightens up Dr. Mr. M.J.

Spelly, one hundred dollars. Good for you Michael, you must have got that contract. Miss T. O'Byrne – twenty-five dollars – do you hear that Tommy?'

Whatever about the style of the collection, it certainly collected many of the 'right notes'. Gallagher says the performance went on for an hour. After the meeting de Valera stood on the edge of the platform: 'Shaking hands with thousands. As the half-hours passed he used both hands but never showed fatigue.' There's nothing like a good collection to give energy to a man or a campaign. The rest of de Valera's US tour was equally successful. The difference was in degree rather than kind. Organizers went ahead some weeks before his arrival at each venue to make sure that people knew he was coming. And when he came they responded. Obviously a small hall in Butte, Montana would yield less than a large one in New York, Boston or San Francisco. But it yielded nevertheless, and all the halls and all the collections added up to making his tour a triumphant success.

He left for Ireland from Commonwealth Pier in Boston (aboard the SS *Republic*) on 1 May, as Gallagher had alerted Celia, to the cheers of a crowd of some five thousand. Before him lay the election campaign which he had had his eye on as he addressed the Sinn Fein Extraordinary Ard Fheis in March the previous year. He was rested and confident after the success of his American trip. Apart from his own collecting efforts, the bonds were still putting money into his political coffers. By contrast Sinn Fein, through lack of funds, organization and candidates, could put forward only 15 candidates against Fianna Fail's 87. The luxury cruise on the *Republic* had been not just an apt piece of symbolic scene-setting but an ideal psychological and physical preparation for the fray. There was a buzz about his whole campaign which the Government lacked. War-weary and borne down by the cares of office, his opponents had to face him without their superstars, Griffith and especially Collins. There was no one to match him in the field, either in opposition or on his own team – here Brugha, Childers, Lynch, Mellows and Rory O'Connor were all dead. His programme:[23] ' . . . seemed to be offering both a panacea for Ireland's economic underdevelopment and a programme for recovering national self-respect. Its economic policies, a left variant of Arthur Griffith's programme, consciously sought to tie the struggle for full political independence to the attainment of a new and more equitable social order.'

It would not be true to say that the election campaign was a bare knuckle affair, because many activists of the period used knuckle-dusters in the furtherance of democracy and free speech.[24] It is not remarkable that this should be so. There was a real possibility of power changing hands between two sides which had faced each other in civil war five years earlier. And even during the campaign, in particularly Republican parts of the country such as Clare, Kerry and Tipperary (but by no means confined to these areas) Fianna Fail Cumainn by day drilled as IRA columns by night.

By way of contrast to the political uproar all round him de Valera added a little theological disputation to the proceedings. He clashed with a Monsignor Ryan of Cashel on the advice given by the monsignor to a Republican who had asked how he could take the oath to enter the Free State Parliament having already taken one to the Republic. The monsignor's reply was that a man was committed to his wife by the vow of marriage, but if she were dead he was free to take a vow to someone else. De Valera retorted by asking the monsignor whether that meant freedom to take a vow to a second wife with a view to proving unfaithful to her or to encompassing her death. He said that the people who now suggested lightly that the Oath be taken were the very people who would tell them 'when they had them in the trap' that they had taken an oath and must keep it.[25] Nevertheless, as one historian pointed out, the use of election material by Fianna Fail clearly indicated that, despite posturing over the Oath, the party set out to convince people that:[26] ' "Fianna Fail is going in"; and there is no doubt that many thousands of electors voted for Fianna Fail in the belief that they would take their seats, Oath or no Oath.' In the event the result was damaging to the Government, which lost 11 seats, but still not fully conclusive. The results were:

Cumann na nGaedheal	47
Fianna Fail	44
Labour	22
Independents	16
Farmers' Party	11
National League	8
Sinn Fein	5

The question of doing a deal with Labour or Republican-minded independents could not arise until de Valera was in a position to deal with them – inside Leinster House. Although he knew very well that he would not be admitted[27] and had plans prepared for the next stage of his campaign against the Oath, he decided to derive what publicity he could from a mock attempt to enter. A huge crowd had gathered in the precincts of Leinster House on 23 June when he and his followers arrived to make their gesture. It was a dramatic scene: a large contingent of Gardai kept back the excited crowd and the excitement in the air was almost a tangible thing. The Gardai cleared a passage for de Valera. He was armed, not with a weapon, but with a legal opinion prepared by three eminent lawyers[28] which proved to their satisfaction that he could not be excluded because of not taking the Oath. But it was not to the satisfaction of the officiating clerk, Colm O'Murchadha. He had a 'little formality'[29] for de Valera and the other Fianna Fail deputies to comply with – Article 17 of the Treaty, which contained the wording of the Oath that de Valera would have to take before entering the chamber. The contents of the opinion failed to impress O'Murchadha, although de Valera pressed the case with his usual forcefulness. The clerk had the doors to the chamber locked and, after some ritual expostulation, de Valera withdrew – secure in the knowledge that he had captured the next day's headlines and that he had two more cards to play.

The first was an action in the names of Lemass and Sean T. O'Ceallaigh, asking the courts to declare their exclusion illegal. The second and more promising ploy was a recourse to the provisions governing the use of the initiative in the Constitution. Under Article 48, if a petition seeking a constitutional amendment and signed by not fewer than 75,000 voters were presented to the legislature, the Government would have to hold a referendum on the question. It was a shrewd move. De Valera would not have had much trouble in securing the 75,000 signatures, and there was very little likelihood of the Irish public voting to retain an oath of allegiance to the British crown. The election had almost wiped out Sinn Fein, establishing him as the Republican standard-bearer. Opposing him in Sinn Fein, Mary MacSwiney and Count Plunkett had lost their seats. Joining him now amongst the ranks of Fianna Fail were some of the best brains from Sinn Fein. Apart from figures like Lemass, Boland and Ruttledge, already mentioned, there was Sean MacEntee; shortly there would be Sean Moylan and Oscar Traynor. And he had culled most of the outstanding women from the old organization: Mrs Tom Clarke, Countess Markievicz,[30] Hannah Sheehy Skeffington and the historian Dorothy Macardle who, before she became disillusioned with him, did more for de Valera's reputation with her pen than practically anyone else in the country with the possible exception of Frank Gallagher. Nevertheless, in a letter to McGarrity[31] he affected to be gloomy about the prospects of success and appeared more concerned about getting money for his newspaper than he was hopeful about either court case or Oath:

> Our exclusion was, even according to Free State law, illegal, and the matter will probably be put to the test in their courts.
>
> As for the Oath, we intend proceeding for its removal by way of the 'initiative' and the referendum. The newspapers here make it almost impossible to make any progress. We must get an Irish national newspaper before we can hope to win. The fight is going to be a tough and a hard one, but I am convinced that if the fight is not going to be won in our day it will not be won by any other in our generation.
>
> I wish we had the support of you all over there, as we had in 1919–21. . . .

And then, suddenly, all arguments failed before a foul deed. On Sunday, 10 July 1927, as he was walking to twelve o'clock Mass, three gunmen shot Kevin O'Higgins, wounding him so badly that he died some hours later. He died as he had lived, showing his religious training and enormous courage. Amongst his last utterances were 'I forgive my murderers' and a joking remark to his wife about going to play a harp sitting on a 'damp cloud with Mick' (Collins).[32] De Valera was politicking in Clare when he heard the news. He realized that there was nothing in the slaying for him or his followers to joke about, but very possibly the reverse. He immediately issued a statement of condemnation:

> The assassination of Mr. O'Higgins is murder, and is inexcusable_ from any standpoint. I am confident that no Republican organisation was responsible for it or would give it any countenance. It is the duty of every citizen to set his face against anything of this kind. It is a crime that cuts at the root of representative government, and no one who realises what the crime means can do otherwise than deplore and condemn it. Every right-minded individual will deeply sympathise with the bereaved widow in her agony.

Even under the pressure of the moment the statement was carefully drafted: 'no Republican *organisation*'. It was many years later that it emerged, as de Valera probably feared at that moment, that one of the gunmen, Timothy Coughlan, was a member of Fianna Fail. (Coughlan was later killed by a police informer whom he tried to assassinate in 1928.) After shooting O'Higgins he and his two companions escaped capture by driving to Kilkenny and playing in a prearranged football match. It was well for de Valera that this was not known at the time.

The Cosgrave administration was initially devastated by the news. Thomas Johnson, who met with members of the Cabinet immediately afterwards, recorded his impressions of them:[33] 'Fitzgerald, O'Sullivan ill, Cosgrave, McGilligan, Hogan worn out'. He quotes Cosgrave as agreeing that the ministry was physically incapable of conducting a strenuous election campaign. Apart from the shock of the murder, the effects of the civil war, the economic situation, the Boundary Commission and de Valera's attrition had all taken their toll. Only one member, Ernest Blythe, a Northern Protestant, presented a fiery mien, pressing for a strong response. The Army and Gardai information was that further attacks were likely, and a police backlash was rumoured. Johnson proposed an all-party coalition, but Cosgrave resisted, making a point which appeared to Johnson at the time to be merely a joke – namely that such a Government, which would have had to include Blythe and a prominent Protestant ex-Unionist like the Independent Major Bryan Cooper, would lead people to say that the country was being run by freemasons. There was some jocosity in the remark, but it was not made completely in this spirit. When a little later Cooper did join the Government party during the subsequent election campaign, de Valera's followers utilized Cooper's former Unionism by issuing posters saying: 'Cooper's Dip for Free State sheep.' But the Government's response to O'Higgins' death was no joke. The administration pulled itself together and introduced three important Bills.

The first was a drastic public safety measure giving the Government sweeping powers, including the use of military courts, against any organization which was involved in treasonable or seditious activities. The second was an Electoral Amendment Bill which would require every candidate in an election to sign an affidavit that he would take both his seat and the Oath if elected, or else be disqualified. The third abolished the initiative and referendum clause in the Constitution.

Fianna Fail members realized that they now either passed under the yoke of the Oath or they left politics. One deputy, Patrick Belton, took the Oath as soon as he read the legislation. De Valera expelled him immediately. But he knew the writing was on the wall. Cosgrave was not acting solely out of a desire to humiliate him, and perhaps to split his party, although neither he nor his administration would have been human if at that moment they had not echoed Kevin O'Higgins' own description of de Valera's attempts to have the barrier of the Oath removed from his path to power:[34] 'The man who did his damndest to cut his country's throat now invited it to commit political hari-kiri in order to save his face.' In fact, as one historian has noted:[35] 'for all his public denunciations of de Valera's assault on the oath, Cosgrave himself secretly but unavailingly sought to persuade the British Government to abolish it'. Cosgrave was principally concerned at the effect on public order of having such a large section of public opinion as that represented by Fianna Fail outside the democratic ambit. IRA violence and illegal drilling had been growing steadily since the organization hived itself off from Sinn Fein; policemen had been murdered and jurors intimidated. Far from trying to exclude de Valera from power, Cosgrave fully realized that he might be bringing him closer to achieving it.

De Valera tried to postpone the inevitable by having inconclusive conversations about co-operation with Captain Redmond's National League and with Tom Johnson of the Labour Party. As Redmond, heir to his father's old Irish Parliamentary Party, thought it would be a good idea if both Cosgrave and de Valera retired, leaving the field to him,[36] untainted by association with the civil war, it might appear on the surface that there was little meeting of minds here. But this contact, and that which followed with the Labour Party, were part of a long-headed strategy by de Valera whose significance only became apparent later in the month. Johnson had said during the election that the Fianna Fail programme was so similar to that of Labour that if Fianna Fail would enter the Dail Labour would help in getting the programme implemented. But he warned that this involved embracing constitutionalism and the Oath:[37] 'No country can be strong and healthy on a diet of revolution. A revolution is an emetic, not a food. . . .' Johnson was an idealistic Englishman whose view was that:[38]

> . . . the Labour movement in Ireland is in danger of being dominated unwittingly by the material view of life, of confining its thoughts to the attainment of material gains for the working class – meaning by the term the 'proletarian' the wage-earner. Salvation does not lie that way. We must preach the gospel of faithful service for the rebuilding of the nation materially and spiritually . . . the power to maintain our rights is increased tenfold when we also do our duty faithfully and fulfil our obligations.

A negotiation between an idealist like Johnson and the ruthless pragmatists of Fianna Fail would appear at the outset to be something of a mismatch. And so it proved. On 1 August he told Boland[39] that he would do everything possible to get the British Government to give way on the Oath, and if he failed would resign. De Valera sent Boland back to him on the 3rd to say that he 'was not strong enough on the oath'. But in the course of their discussion Boland revealed what was probably the real source of de Valera's hesitancy: the small margin which Fianna Fail and Labour could expect over the Government made the position 'doubtful'. However, on the 6th Boland informed Johnson that Fianna Fail were going to enter the Dail. He invited Johnson and other Labour leaders to meet de Valera and some of the prominent Fianna Fail personnel. Johnson did so, and discovered that de Valera had changed his mind (or said he had). No Oath, no entry. His decision was 'irrevocable'.

Nevertheless negotiations continued. On the 8th, in Sean T. O'Ceallaigh's house, de Valera gave Johnson an eight-point agenda for an 'informal' conference. Some of the points were predictable: the withdrawal of the constitutional amendment, the public safety Bill, taking immediate steps against the Oath and the holding of a referendum to bring the Constitution more into line with de Valera's thinking. But the effrontery of one proposal appears to have eluded Johnson, at least to the extent that he makes no comment on it: '*Immediately* [author's italics] make provision for the discharging of the full national obligation towards the subscribers to the External Loan of the Republic, adding for the purpose the necessary sum to the balance now being returned by the receiver appointed by the Supreme Court of New York State, and thereby *establishing National Credit* [author's italics]!' Establishing a national newspaper would have been more like it. However, Johnson made no comment on specifics in his statement of reply, in which he said: 'The entry of Fianna Fail Deputies into the Dail as suggested would make a complete change in the political and economic prospect and give new hope and inspiration to those of various parties who are less concerned with political party prestige than with the nation's future.'

On the Oath, Johnson was confident that with Fianna Fail in the Dail the British would be amenable to a 'modification' which would have the effect of rendering it 'innocuous and not mandatory'. But no agreement was reached. How much de Valera really intended by way of a pact with Labour, and how much he viewed the Johnson negotiation merely as a means of teasing out the other man's intentions, has to be a matter for speculation. Johnson was also a good conduit for finding out about the Government's intentions. He had engaged in detailed conversations[40] with Cosgrave immediately after O'Higgins' murder and knew the Government's thinking. But it appears most likely that the Johnson discussions were intended as a probing operation before launching an offensive on his real objective, the Cumann na nGaedheal Government. The outcome of events indicates de Valera's reckoning that without entering into any formal alliance he could achieve power, relying on other parties' support to oust Cumann na nGaedheal when, not if, he entered the Dail.

Ever a man to share responsibility, if not authority, he ensured that as many as possible of his party were involved in the decision. The day after the Johnson meeting he called the executive of Fianna Fail together and in effect made it an offer it could not refuse:[41] 'He explained that he saw no alternative between giving up political action and entry into the Free State Dail.' Entry it would be. The executive looked into its own heart, saw the wishes of Eamon de Valera, and:[42] 'A resolution was passed by forty-four votes to seven that the elected deputies of the party as a body be given a free hand in the matter of entering the legislature or not.' Next evening the Fianna Fail deputies met for a 'long, heart-searching meeting' which lasted until midnight. Once again it was vascular oracularity time. The meeting was a perfect example of de Valera's methodology in Cabinet later. He did not thump the table and insist on his way. He simply sat there, furrow-faced and forbidding, until he wore down all opposition and got what he wanted – the signatures of the forty-two Fianna Fail deputies present to the following statement for the press.

> It has . . . been repeatedly stated, and it is not uncommonly believed, that the required declaration is not an oath; that the signing of it implies no contractual obligation, and that it has no binding significance in conscience or in law, that in short it is merely an empty political formula which Deputies could conscientiously sign without becoming involved, or without involving their nation, in obligations of loyalty to the English Crown.
>
> The Fianna Fail deputies would certainly not wish to have the feeling they are allowing themselves to be debarred by nothing more than an empty formula from exercising their functions as public representatives, particularly at a moment like this. They intend therefore to present themselves at the Clerk's office of the Free State Dail 'for the purpose of complying with the provisions of Article 17 of the Constitution', by inscribing their names in the book kept for the purpose, amongst other signatures appended to the required formula. But, so that there may be no doubt as to their attitude, and no misunderstanding of their action, the Fianna Fail Deputies hereby give public notice that they propose to regard the declaration as an empty formality and repeat that their only allegiance is to the Irish nation, and that it will be given to no other power or authority.

De Valera's official account of the consequences of this statement is that it led to a 'nightmarish crisis of conscience . . . one of the few nights in his career during which the worry of a decision kept him from sleeping'.[43] However, as so often in his career, de Valera wrestled with his conscience, and de Valera won. Next day he went again to the Dail and presented himself before Colm O'Murchadha once more. With him as witnesses were Aiken and Dr James Ryan. He read out a speech in Irish:[44] 'I want you to understand that I am not taking any oath nor giving any promise of faithfulness to the King of England or to any power outside the people of Ireland. I am putting my name here merely as a formality to get the permission necessary to enter among the other Teachtai that were elected by the people of Ireland, and I want you to know that no other meaning is to be attached to it.' O'Murchadha replied that he was not concerned with these remarks. All he wanted was de Valera's name in a book which he indicated. De Valera noticed there was a Bible lying on the book and retorted: 'Then, what is this for?' He then carried the Bible to the far end of the room, returned to the book containing the Oath and delivered himself of a further disclaimer: 'You must remember that I am taking no oath.' He then signed his name, covering the wording of the Oath with some papers he had brought with him. He said later that 'I signed it in the same way as I would sign an autograph in a newspaper. If you ask me whether I had an idea what was there, I say "yes", but it was neither read to me nor was I asked to read it.'[45] And thus, in casuistry and humbled pride, did a new era in Irish politics begin.

But this did not appear likely at that moment. De Valera stalked out of the signing ceremony in a huff, saying that one day he would burn the book with his signature in it.[46] He turned up in the Dail the next day with his followers to combine with Labour in presenting a demand that the Electoral Amendment Bill which had brought him there be suspended pending a referendum. However, he seemingly thought better of gathering the necessary signatures (one-twentieth of the registered voters) for a petition which should have followed this demand and the Bill eventually passed into law, unique in that it had accomplished its purpose before ever entering the statute book. Four days later de Valera's purpose in entering the Dail was revealed, as was the benefit of his conversations with the National League and with Labour.

Labour and the National League agreed to form a coalition government which would be kept in power by de Valera.[47] The alliance of the ex-British officer Redmond, dependent on his appeal to ex-servicemen, and de Valera illustrates yet again the truth of the saying that in politics there are two sides – an inside and an outside. De Valera wanted to be on the inside. Judging from the disillusioned tone of a letter to him from Austin Stack,[48] he even appears to have toyed with the idea of trying to get Sinn Fein to help him achieve his ambition. Stack upbraided him for the fact that: 'In the morning you expressed anxiety to get the Treaty revised to the satisfaction of Sinn Fein and your intention to open negotiations with the British Government', but that later a different purpose appeared to emerge. He complained that 'when you did meet my colleagues you had a different idea altogether in your mind . . . it seemed as if you were only there to sound us and you had no proposals to make to us at all . . . you have gone further away from my road than I ever dreamt you could go. Can I hope for anything at all now? God grant that some unforeseen happening may save the situation from becoming what my fears tell me it is likely to turn out.'

There was an 'unforeseen happening', but not of the sort that Stack can have had in mind. Johnson moved a vote of no confidence in the Government on 16 August, the day after Stack wrote, which indicates that de Valera *had* merely been trying to sound out Sinn Fein's likely reaction to the manoeuvre. But one of Redmond's supporters objected to the bargain. Vincent Rice KC pointed out that the reality of the Government's situation would be that it would not 'last one hour except, and so long as, it obeys the behest of Deputy de Valera and his party'. He voted against the motion. His transfer of allegiance was made fatal when Major Bryan Cooper, who was from Sligo, waylaid another Sligoman, Alderman John Jinks, also of Redmond's party, with a liquid cosh. Over drinks he and Bertie Smylie, the editor of the *Irish Times* and yet another Sligoman, convinced Jinks that Sligo's ex-servicemen had not sent him to Leinster House to unhorse Cosgrave and install de Valera in the saddle. The befuddled Jinks took both their advice and the next train back to Sligo. The vote of no confidence thus resulted in a tie, and the chairman gave his casting vote in favour of the Government.

The close call obviously made de Valera think about the potential of the five Sinn Fein seats which remained untaken. The contact with Stack dashed any lingering hopes he may have had of these coming his way. But at the same time he was exposed to criticisms[49] that he had merely entered the Dail to further a Sinn Fein policy – in other words, to smash the Parliament. Speaking at Blackrock Town Hall a few days later, on 22 August, he replied to this charge:[50] ' . . . our purpose is not to destroy but to broaden and widen the Free State assembly – to free it from all foreign control or interference and make it so truly representative of the whole people as to secure for it the necessary authority and influence to have its decisions readily accepted and willingly obeyed'. And so, a civil war and almost six wasted years after the Treaty's signing, de Valera gave unspoken recognition to the validity of the 'stepping-stone' argument. For in place of 'to broaden and widen the Free State assembly' he could have said equally 'Our purpose is the stepping-stone policy', because that in effect is what he would now embark upon, with one significant addition. He also told his Blackrock hearers that he would honour 'our national obligation to the people of the United States with regard to the External Loan of the Republic . . . I say the obligation should be admitted and the debt repaid in full. The sooner the better for our national credit. If this be honourably discharged, other loans will be forthcoming when required.'

The Government then went on to win two pending by-elections. Cosgrave decided the omens were propitious and called for a snap dissolution. The calling of the election so quickly after the June poll, which had of course depleted the funds of all parties, was termed 'sharp practice' by de Valera. 'However,' he said, 'Fianna Fail is not quite as unprepared as they think.'[51] Nor was it. The party still had the organizational skills and the American support which it had been able to call on earlier in the summer. And it had de Valera. Out of the customary rough and tumble election campaign of the period the party emerged comfortably with 57 seats. Sinn Fein was too weak even to contest the election, which was held on 15 September. The National League was decimated, as was the Labour Party, Johnson's high-mindedness consigning him to the ranks of those who lost seats. The state of the parties was as follows:

Cumann na nGaedheal	62
Fianna Fail	57
Labour	13
Independents	12
Farmers' Party	6
National League	2
Independent Labour	1

Cosgrave again formed an administration, with the aid of the Farmers' Party. Fianna Fail and Labour were the opposition, with de Valera in effect the Leader of the Opposition. Thanks to Captain Jinks it would be five years before de Valera and Cosgrave changed places.

19

DE VALERA'S DECADE

WE NOW ENTER upon de Valera's decade. The ten years between 1928 and 1938 may be broken down into what he did during the first five years, when he was mostly out of power, and the subsequent five in which, in Government, he succeeded to a considerable degree in moulding Ireland – or at least his part of it – into his own image. The early five years saw the development and entrenchment of Fianna Fail as the best-organized and most effective political party in Ireland. Apart from occasional, short-lived interludes of division or inertia it has remained so to the time of writing, six decades later. These years also witnessed the launching of de Valera's newspaper, the *Irish Press*, which, interacting with the efforts of Fianna Fail and the overall economic and political situation, was the catalytic factor in bringing him to power which he held for sixteen years uninterruptedly and for a half a dozen years, intermittently, thereafter.

The second five years were also filled with activities of a significant, if not altogether commendable, nature. De Valera used them to abolish the Oath, the Governor General, the Senate and the Free State Constitution, and to introduce a new Constitution, Upper House, a political programme and – economic war with England. In those years Irish politics were bitter, passionate and frequently conducted in the streets and in the jails. Through it all de Valera consolidated his dominant position by introducing a system of control and patronage which indicates that his political mentors were not confined to Machiavelli. His career suggests that his extensive visits to America afforded him opportunities for studying the practices of Mayor Curley in Boston and of Tammany Hall in New York which he did not neglect. Once, when rumours circulated that he might not be on good terms with Curley, he had a photo of himself and Curley shaking hands published[1] over the caption: 'This photograph from the *Boston Herald* is an answer to those who invented the fiction of Mayor Curley's opposition to Mr. de Valera. It shows the Mayor and the Irish leader renewing their old friendship.'

However it was the political profit derived, not from America, but from conditions in the Twenty-six Counties which most benefited de Valera. Let us look briefly at the backdrop to the first five-year period. Economically it was the era of the great depression. As we have seen, Ireland's principal industrial base in the Six Counties was lost to the Southern administration through partition. The largely agricultural South was not in a good position to withstand the fall-out from the crash of 1929. The civil war had taken

408

grievous human and physical toll, and the mild protectionism and rigorous financial orthodoxy of the Cosgrave Government did more to uphold conservative notions of fiscal rectitude than to lower unemployment and emigration figures. The field in which the Government made sustained, significant progress – Commonwealth relationships – was not one calculated to impress the public. There were terrible pockets of poverty in the cities and in the western regions. The conditions were such that the more adventurous and better-pursed amongst the unemployed preferred to risk the conditions that Connie Neenan warned de Valera against in New York rather than stay at home. Under US immigration laws, emigrants had to have someone in America to guarantee them so that they would not become a charge on the state. Those who lacked this support, or were poorer or less adventurous, headed for England and even worse poverty and overcrowding than existed in New York. Sizeable contingents of emigrants also made their way to other parts of the British Empire, chiefly Australia, Canada and New Zealand.

Coupled with these problems, the Government also faced a serious challenge on the law and order front from the IRA. A selection of IRA activities roughly coinciding with the first five years of de Valera's decade – a list chosen for illustration purposes only and by no means exhaustive – occupies six and a half pages[2] of my book on the IRA. The wave of shootings, illegal drilling, attacks on Gardai and intimidation of jurors reached such proportions that by 1931 the ordinary courts of law were no longer capable of dealing with the situation. Jurymen and police witnesses were intimidated or shot. As one writer has noted:[3] 'IRA subversion was multiplying. Many police stations were like beleaguered fortresses.' In Dublin a police informer was shot and the *coup de grâce* administered not with a pistol but with a hand grenade, which blew away part of his head. In Tipperary a police superintendent was shot dead and, in the same county, a man who had given evidence in an illegal drilling case was also murdered. *An Phoblacht* issued an editorial on 20 June 1931 which had echoes of de Valera's own boycotting resolution of the RIC. It said: '*An Phoblacht* states that members of the C.I.D. should be treated as "social pariahs" . . . that treatment must be extended to uniformed police – to every individual who is a willing part of the machine by which Irish patriots are being tortured.'

In August an interview[4] with an IRA leader, Frank Ryan, made it clear that these sentiments were official policy. He not only justified the three killings[5] mentioned above but went on to claim that the IRA was capable of much sterner action. Gerald Boland, who became Minister of Justice under de Valera, told me that it was this interview which led the Department of Justice to advise Cosgrave to reintroduce the military tribunal. Cosgrave accepted the advice and on 20 October that year the IRA, along with a number of other Republican and left-inclined organizations, was declared an unlawful association. On the same day the

Special Powers Tribunal, consisting of five military officers, was set up. Introducing the Constitutional Amendment Bill No. 17 which made this possible, Cosgrave said:[6] 'The powers and machinery provided by this Bill are necessary not merely for this Government, but for any Government that may be in power if the will of the majority is to prevail.'

Although those were words that would one day have an uncomfortable ring for Eamon de Valera, the setting up of the military tribunal initially played straight into his hands. Frank Gallagher was arraigned before it shortly before the general election of 1932, and the publicity thus generated provided invaluable ammunition for the Fianna Fail campaigners. However, the telling of that tale must await its proper place in our story as it is bound up with the foundation of the *Irish Press* and will require another visit to America to place it in context. Suffice is to say that the IRA were of substantive benefit to de Valera in three ways: by actively campaigning for Fianna Fail, by providing the occasion for an emotive 'Release the Prisoners' agitation, and by furnishing an invaluable election plank in the shape of the land annuities issue.

The Irish Land Commission was charged with continuing the work of collecting the annuities from farmers and passing them to the British National Debt Commissioners to meet the loans raised in England to buy out landlords under the various Land Acts passed between 1891 and 1909. The Land Commission was acting in conformity with a financial agreement concluded between Britain and Ireland in an atmosphere of secrecy which can only be understood against the background of the Irish civil war. It was signed on 12 February 1923 between Cosgrave and Major John W. Willis, Financial Secretary to the British Treasury. A second agreement building on this was signed on 19 March 1926 between Ireland's Ernest Blythe and England's Winston Churchill in the wake of the Boundary Commission debacle. This was known as the Ultimate Financial Settlement, and together the payments amounted to some £5 million annually, including those made to former members of the Crown forces. As de Valera's authorized biography notes, the secrecy surrounding the 1923 agreement, which he claimed he only discovered on taking office, made for a 'story replete with political ammunition for use against former ministers'.[7] However, he had the annuities question and the secrecy issue in his sights long before 1932. Speaking at Blackrock on 22 August 1927, he said:[8] 'With regard to the financial settlement with England, that will have to be re-opened. That secret agreement was never properly ratified, and was unjust. It imposes on the country an annual exportation of income and revenue of over five million pounds a year. The community cannot bear that and prosper.'

Irish farmers had been only too well aware of the existence of annuities since the days of the Land Acts; many of them had taken the opportunity presented by the disorders of 1916, and the years which followed, to demonstrate their patriotism by refusing to pay any. As a result, by the time of the Ultimate Financial Settlement very sizeable arrears had accrued. The IRA leader Peadar O'Donnell, on the run from the police in his native Donegal during 1925–6, discovered that his neighbours were being served with summonses as a result and decided to take up the cudgels on their behalf[9] with the help of his IRA colleagues. He advised them not to pay their arrears and to hide their cattle so that bailiffs could not seize them. Colonel Maurice Moore, a brother of the novelist George Moore, who had likened the 1926 Financial Agreement to bribing a burglar after being burgled,[10] provided him with legal arguments to buttress his defiance.

The campaign spread to a number of other western counties including Clare, de Valera's own bailiwick, where it was led by a Fianna Fail councillor, Sean Hayes.[11] The campaign was a live issue while de Valera was speaking in Blackrock. He saw the potential of the issue and made the retention of the land annuities part of Fianna Fail electoral policy. It was a popular move whose appeal Machiavelli's pupil was careful not to dilute by overstressing the fact that the annuities would still be collected: what he intended was to reap them for the Irish Exchequer, not to let them lie fallow in the pockets of the farmers.

The 'Release the Prisoners' issue centred around the activities of a number of Republican-minded women: the widow of the executed 1916 leader Major John MacBride, Maude Gonne, the woman Yeats loved; Helena Moloney, the trade unionist; Madame Despard, the socialist sister of Lord French, the former Lord Lieutenant; and Hannah Sheehy Skeffington, the widow of the pacifist who was murdered by a deranged British officer in 1916. They organized a Republican 'Prisoners' Dependants Fund' and helped to generate publicity on behalf of the ever-increasing number of IRA prisoners. In jail the inevitable abrasive contact between warders and those to whom prison is just another field for carrying on the outside war yielded fertile ground for such effort.

Finally there was the active support given by rank and file IRA men to campaigning for Fianna Fail. These energetic, hard-working young men, drawn from the same background as Fianna Fail, saw de Valera's party as having the same goals as themselves. They, and the bulk of Fianna Fail supporters, were the sort of persons who in another country would have been found in a Labour Party: small farmers, labourers, tradesmen, teachers. Their support was particularly valuable in building up the party machine and at election time. They gave this support because, in the words of Peadar O'Donnell, they judged that there was:[12] 'more radical content in Fianna Fail than there was in any other organisation'. From the time of the inauguration of Fianna Fail in May 1926 de Valera was careful to ensure that the Labour current continued to flow his way. In his inaugural address he quoted James Connolly with approval:[13] 'Ireland, as distinct from her people, is nothing to me.' And he made sure that generally cordial relationships were maintained with the Labour Party itself.

But if Labour could be thought of as providing a strong current of support, militant republicanism was a high-tension cable. De Valera was particularly anxious that its power should continue to be harnessed to his electoral machine. Whatever his private feelings about the litany of disorder for which the IRA was responsible in 1925–31, he took care that his public utterances, and those of his subordinates, indicated an understanding of the IRA's shunning of the horrors of constitutionalism. Speaking in the Dail on 12 March 1928, Lemass said:

> Fianna Fail is a *slightly* [author's italics] constitutional party. We are open to the definition of a constitutional party, but before anything we are a Republican party. We adopted the method of political agitation to achieve our end because we believe, in the present circumstances, that method is best in the interests of the nation and for the Republican movement and for no other reason. Five years ago the methods we adopted were not the methods we have adopted now. Five years ago we were on the defensive, and perhaps in time we may recoup our strength sufficiently to go on the offensive. Our objective is to establish a Republican Government in Ireland. If that can be done by the present methods we have, we will be very pleased, but, if not, we would not confine ourselves to them.

Lemass had been Minister for Defence in the underground Emergency Government. Speaking on 27 February 1929 Sean T. O'Ceallaigh, also in the Dail, referred to the Cumann na nGaedheal Minister for Defence, Desmond Fitzgerald, as 'the so-called Minister for Defence'. It was Fitzgerald who goaded de Valera into making his most explicit statement on Fianna Fail's attitude towards the Free State, its Parliament and institutions. On 14 March 1929, during a Dail debate on the Central Fund Bill, he said that Fianna Fail had: 'failed so far to make clear what is their attitude towards the authority of the Government in the Dail and towards the people outside who claim the power of life and death'. In the course of a lengthy reply de Valera made the following points:

> I still hold that our right to be regarded as the legitimate Government of this country is faulty, that this House itself is faulty. You have secured a de facto position. Very well. There must be some body in charge to keep order in the community, and by virtue of your de facto position you are the only people who are in a position to do it. But as to whether you have come by that position legitimately or not, I say that you have not come by that position legitimately. You brought off a coup d'etat in the summer of 1922 . . . .
>
> If you are not getting the support from all sections of the community that is necessary for any Executive if it is going to dispense with a large police force, it is because there is a moral handicap in your case. We are all morally handicapped because of the circumstances in which the whole thing came about. The setting up put a moral handicap on every one of us here. We came in here because we thought that a practical rule could be evolved in which order could be maintained; and we said that it was necessary to have some assembly in which the representatives of the people by a majority vote should be able to decide national policy. As we were not able to get a majority to meet outside this House, we had to come here if there was to be a majority at all of the people's representatives . . .

As a practical rule, and not because there is anything sacred in it, I am prepared to accept majority rule as settling matters of national policy, and therefore as deciding who it is that shall be in charge of order . . . .

I for one, when the flag of the Republic was run up against an Executive that was bringing off a coup d'etat, stood by the flag of the Republic, and I will do it again. As long as there was a hope of maintaining that Republic, either by force against those who were bringing off that coup d'etat or afterwards, as long as there was opportunity of getting the people of this country to vote again for the Republic, I stood for it.

My proposition that the representatives of the people should come here and unify control so that we would have one Government and one Army was defeated, and for that reason I resigned. Those who continued on in that organisation which we have left can claim exactly the same continuity that we claimed up to 1925. They can do it . . . .

You have achieved a certain de facto position, and the proper thing for you to do with those who do not agree that this State was established legitimately, and who believe that as a matter of fact there was a definite betrayal of everything that was aimed at from 1916 to 1922, is to give those people the opportunity of working, and without in any way forswearing their views, to get the Irish people as a whole again behind them. They have the right to do it. You have no right to debar them from going to the Irish people and asking them to support the re-establishment, or if they so wish to put it, to support the continuance of the Republic . . . .

The Executive have been trying to use force, and have been using it all the time. If they are going to meet force by force, then they cannot expect the co-operation of citizens who wish that there should not be force.

I interviewed IRA survivors of the period[14] who told me that the 'continuity' speech invested the IRA with a particular mark of responsibility in their eyes. As the IRA's violence worsened, de Valera and his henchmen continued to pursue a policy of 'The enemy of my enemy is my friend'. In private, Sean Lemass put the position bluntly to Peadar O'Donnell, who had been pressing him to involve Fianna Fail more actively in his retention of the annuities campaign. 'Don't you see,' he said, 'that we stand to gain from your organisation so long as we cannot be accused of starting the turmoil.'[15] In public, Fianna Fail sided with the IRA when, in 1931, the Government banned the annual June pilgrimage to the grave of Wolfe Tone, the father of Irish republicanism, at Bodenstown in Co. Kildare. Thousands of IRA marchers successfully defied the ban; they were accompanied by a contingent from Fianna Fail, led by de Valera who placed a wreath on the grave. De Valera sometimes had to grope for words to indicate support without being seen to condone the indefensible. His reaction to one IRA shooting was:[16] 'They have done terrible things recently I admit, if they are responsible for them, and I suppose they are. Let us appeal to them and ask them in God's name not to do them.' But when the avalanche finally came down in the shape of the military tribunal de Valera commented:[17] 'These men are misguided, if you will, but they were brave men, anyhow, let us have for them the decent respect that we have for the brave.'

Broadly speaking, the 'enemy of my enemy is my friend' strategy worked. A few of the more perceptive IRA men argued against supporting de Valera. Michael Conway said:[18] 'I'm telling ye that fella will be as bad as Cosgrave, he'll hang ye when he gets in, mark my words, he'll hang ye.' Conway was uncannily prescient; as we shall see, de Valera nearly did have him hanged. But the bulk of the movement followed the line laid down in *An Phoblacht*[19]: 'One Movement, Two Groups.' In operating this Janus-faced policy de Valera was not merely concerned with two groups, but had to keep an eye on two constituencies – one of them in America.

Commentators have consistently overlooked the importance of the American dimension to de Valera's career. It was from America that he derived the principal source of the funding for his newspaper and very significant assistance for his party. It was the Irish American constituency that he assembled during his repeated American visits which enabled him to stand up to Roosevelt in maintaining neutrality during World War II. And it was over America that the Long Fellow threw one of his longest shadows. Because of the personalized nature of his American appeal the Irish in America became divided along pro- and anti-de Valera lines and ultimately fragmented, rather than becoming united as are the Jews for Israel. Only Clan na nGael and its successor IRA support groups remained organized in pursuit of a single goal over the years, and then in very weakened form. De Valera saw to it that his supporters were loyal to him, not to the Irish state. In fact, for the first ten years of its existence he and his followers did everything in their power to convince Irish American opinion that the state was an ignoble instrument of British policy. All of which, of course, he blandly overlooked during World War II when the main thrust of his policy was aimed at convincing Irish Americans that, under him, Ireland had become a paragon amongst the nations which must be preserved in her state of virginal neutrality.

In the years 1927–31 he probably spent as much time in the USA collecting for his newspaper (much more if one takes into account the time he spent working to set it up in Ireland) as he did in the Dail. As we saw, he spent the spring and early summer of 1927 fund-raising in America. Having disposed of interruptions to this activity, such as the need to fight election campaigns and the taking of an oath that was not an oath, he returned in December of that year to begin a further three months' collecting. And in November 1929 he again started a fund-raising drive,[20] 'staying this time for six months and setting up a whole network of committees'. He took Gallagher with him again on the second 1927 trip – after a bout of worrying out loud as to whether the necessary money could be raised for his companion's expenses.[21] Seasickness plagued him once more, Gallagher noted:[22] 'The Chief goes under regularly before each meal and has to stride the deck like a whirlwind to keep well until just before the next one.'

Nevertheless de Valera forced himself to the dinner table one evening in the middle of a storm – because he wanted to get a balloon for Terry, his

414

youngest son.[23] The gesture, coming at the commencement of a period of three months' travelling away from home on a million-dollar financial enterprise, might be taken as exemplifying either de Valera's frugality or his meanness, depending on how one wishes to interpret the incident. An even better example of the acuity of his antennae in warning him of the imminence of an approach for money occurred on 26 December in New York after he and Gallagher returned from spending Christmas with his mother at Rochester. Gallagher had been marvelling at the amount of money girls could make in New York compared to their counterparts back in Ireland, and was on the point of using the comparison to bring up the subject of Kathleen O'Connell's low wages when de Valera suddenly 'completely disarmed' him, saying, 'Yes, look at Kathleen now, it's very unfair to her.' Gallagher noted that he 'spoke in tones of deep concern . . . as if he had no way of changing her salary'.

Whatever the reasons for not intervening in the finances of the long-suffering Kathleen O'Connell, de Valera made certain that his visit to New York marked a most decisive intervention in the financing of his newspaper project. On 28 December a circular letter emanated from the Waldorf Astoria.[24] It began by wishing its recipients 'all the seasons greetings' and then went on to state that his visit was concerned with 'the establishment of an Irish daily newspaper' for which the total capital needed would be £250,000 or $1,250,000. Of this amount he proposed to raise £150,000 in the United States. 'I want therefore 1,000 people in the United States who will each invest at least $500 in the enterprise,' he announced. His plans were temporarily disrupted by the death of Charlie Wheelright on the day the circular was issued, which necessitated his return to Rochester for the funeral. But his committees were so efficient that by 12 January it was possible to hold what Gallagher termed 'an invited meeting' of about 150 people in the roof garden of the Waldorf Astoria. De Valera addressed those present on the political developments which had occurred in Ireland since his last visit and outlined his plans for a newspaper. Gallagher notes:[25] 'Twenty-four people subscribed $500 dollars each and others undertook to get other subscribers. Twelve thousand for one evening was good.'

In the depressed circumstances of the time, 'good' seems a somewhat understated description. De Valera's principal helpers in the fund-raising effort were the lawyers Frank P. Walsh, Martin Conboy and John Finnerty, together with Garth Healy and Major Eugene Kincaid – all of whom had been prominent in his 1919–20 activities. They and their associates co-ordinated a campaign based on the roof garden approach across the country. For example, a sympathizer[26] in Detroit received on 25 January, some days after the New York meeting, a letter signed by a committee headed by Father Peter McGuinness, President of the Friends of Irish Freedom. It told him that a 'conference of the friends of Ireland will be held in the Adams Room on the 11th Floor of the Hotel Tuller, on

Sunday afternoon, January 29th, at 3:00 P.M. for the purpose of planning means whereby we may aid in the establishment of a national daily paper in Ireland'. The sympathizer was extended 'a hearty invitation to be present' as a friend of de Valera's and a friend of Ireland. But at that stage de Valera was wary of publicity and the letter concluded by saying that 'Mr. de Valera's visit is private and the conference will not be open to the public.'

Apart from the obvious reason of not wishing his enemies to learn what he was doing, he had reason to doubt whether a section of his allies were best pleased with his newspaper plans. De Valera had barely landed in New York when McGarrity let him know on 23 December that:[27] 'The Clan', with which McGarrity agreed, 'is not in harmony with the policy of the Republican members entering the Free State Parliament and taking the Oath.' This would hardly have come as a surprise to de Valera, but he was less concerned with the Clan's reaction to his Oath-swallowing than with the organization's likely reaction to the second strand to his fund-raising policy. For this strand involved getting control of the funds which he had left McGarrity in charge of when he made his melodramatic exit from New York during another December eight years earlier – the bonds money which had been the subject of Justice Peters' decision earlier in 1927. The judge ruled that receivers should be appointed to ensure that the subscribers to the loans got back whatever was left in the American banks after expenses had been met – in effect 58 per cent of the face value of the bonds. De Valera had greeted this decision with a carefully worded statement:[28]

> As a trustee I am not dissatisfied with the decision of the Court to return the money to the subscribers. I believe my co-Trustee, Mr. Stephen O'Mara, will feel similarly about it. Taking into account the conditions under which the moneys were subscribed and all the circumstances of the present moment the decision of Justice Peters was more natural than any other for a neutral Court to take.
>
> The Free State's claim to these monies was audacious merely, and altogether untenable in the light of the explicit representations made to the subscribers when the money was being solicited. My action, and that of Mr. O'Mara, as Trustees was confined to resisting that claim. Our resistance has been successful.
>
> Between the Bondholders Committee and the Trustees there was no conflict. The latter intervened as a precaution lest by any chance there should be a misdirection as giving to the Free State money which had been subscribed for the purpose of a Republican Government only.
>
> I am certain that the subscribers who, by Justice Peters' decision, will receive only a part of the moneys originally subscribed by them, will not ultimately suffer. I cannot conceive of any national Irish Government worthy of the name refusing or neglecting to make good to the subscribers the moneys that were advanced by them and used in the national effort from 1919 to 1921.

The Free State Government was not the only party to the case to whom the term 'audacious' might be applied. Contrary to what he said in his statement, the intervention of the Hearn Committee which he had masterminded meant that part of the bond money had been allocated away from his adversaries, the Cosgrave Government, and towards a group which he could manipulate. The money which, by his own admission, had been subscribed 'for the purpose of a Republican Government only' he now intended to divert to quite a different purpose. Furthermore, decoded, 'any national Irish Government of the name' meant 'when I get into power I'll see to it that the other 42 per cent is paid over'. He in fact saw to it that much more than 42 per cent was paid. But why should he do this, and how could such payments benefit him?

The answer is given succinctly in a circular letter drafted by him and issued over the name of Frank P. Walsh, Chairman of the American Branch of Irish Press Ltd:[29]

> Dear Friend:-
> The money which you gave in the years 1919 to 1921 to help the cause of Ireland is about to be given back to you. You are probably one of those who gave your money at that time as a free gift expecting no other return for it than the satisfaction of participating in a just cause and aiding the people of Ireland in a time of need. I feel accordingly that when you read this leaflet you will be disposed to make this money available a second time – again in a good cause and for the benefit of Ireland.

The 'good cause' was the establishment of the *Irish Press* to break 'the stranglehold' imposed on the Irish people by an 'alien press'. Accompanying the Walsh circular there were a number of other documents, one a facsimile of a letter in de Valera's own writing. It said:

> In the past you proved that you understood and sympathised with the desire of our people, not only to restore Ireland to its place among the nations, but to make it as the homeland of a great race in every way worthy of that race as well as of the sacrifices that had been made and the sufferings endured so that its distinctive spiritual individuality might be pursued. I cannot doubt that you understand and sympathise still and that you will give promptly the aid that is required.

The 'aid that is required' was spelled out in Walsh's circular:

> ... many ... like yourself ... have informed Mr de Valera that on receipt of their checks [as a result of the Peters judgement] they will immediately endorse them and turn them in to his account, so as to be available for the establishment of the needed Irish newspaper.

But, Walsh went on, it was not necessary 'to wait for the actual distribution to take place. . . . This work can be proceeded with now, provided that the Directors of Irish Press, Limited, have the assurance, *by the legal assignment of a sufficient number of Bond Certificates to Mr. de Valera* [author's italics], that the balance of the sum they require will become available when the Republican Loans are repaid.' In order to provide the directors with the required 'assurance', recipients of the circular were invited to sign a power of attorney form[30] which gave not only de Valera but 'his executors, administrators and assigns, all my right, title and interest in the Bond Certificate (or Bond Certificates) of the Republic of Ireland Loans . . . and *all* sums of money, both principal and interest now due, *or hereafter to become due on* . . . said Bond Certificates [all italics author's]'.

The form empowered de Valera to 'take all legal measures which may be proper and necessary for the *complete recovery* [author's italics] on, and enjoyment of, the assigned Bond Certificate (or Certificates)'. The form probably merits consideration for entry into the *Guinness Book of Records* as 'The Blankest Blank Cheque of All Time'. For, as was pointed out to the Free State Government, which was at the time weighing up the question of redeeming the bonds:[31] 'The nett result is that holders who transfer their Bonds on these terms hand the proceeds to Mr. de Valera to be used at his sole discretion – in other words although the transfer is obtained on the basis of supporting Irish Press Ltd, Mr. de Valera can, once the transfer is made, use the proceeds for any other purpose without legal responsibility.'

Those with a taste for symbolism might be forgiven for dwelling on the fact that by this time the de Valeras had moved again – to a house in Serpentine Avenue.[32] Certainly Joe McGarrity and the Clan were more inclined to view the *Irish Press* project as an adder that counselled wary walking[33] than to see its title as a compliment to McGarrity's old paper which had inspired the name. Despite this effort to curry favour with him, McGarrity told de Valera bluntly:[34] 'The Clan as an organisation and I may safely say as a whole, are cold to the proposition which they consider a part of the political effort in which they have no faith whatever and I must say I am in hearty agreement with their opinion.' De Valera responded – enclosing a prospectus – in effect chiding McGarrity, but at the same time not acknowledging any differences between them:[35] 'I am sure you will understand how necessary a newspaper is for our present line of fight and that you will try to get our old friends to support this enterprise. To make any progress we must try to get co-operation between all the forces working for a free Ireland. The imperialist forces here are all co-operating. It is heart breaking to think we are not.'

So long as de Valera was out of office and attempting to get the *Irish Press* launched he was zealous about 'co-operating', or at least being seen to co-operate, with the Clan wing of his American constituency. In a letter[36] to Gallagher, Sean Moynihan, who accompanied de Valera on his 1929 visit in place of Gallagher, indicates the circles in which they moved: 'The Chief has gone to Philadelphia to see Luke Dillon. I have also met several of the Kerry I.R.A. lads. It has been worth coming to see them all.' After McGarrity, the eighty-one-year-old Dillon was probably the Clan's outstanding figure. He had placed a bomb in the Palace of Westminster during the 1883–4 dynamite campaign in Britain and had served fourteen years for trying to blow up the locks of the Welland Canal in Ontario in an attempt to prevent supplies reaching the British during the Boer War. Dillon was in his final illness at the time Moynihan wrote to Gallagher; enclosed with the letter was an obituary for inclusion in the Fianna Fail weekly newspaper, the *Nation*.

The subscriptions of Clan supporters were also obtained by using prominent IRA figures like Ernie O'Malley as fund-raisers to augment de Valera's efforts. Those efforts were remarkable. He criss-crossed the United States, collecting money and calling at newspaper offices to see how they were run. His basic arguments appealed to anti-British sentiment:[37]

> The existing daily press is consistently pro-British and imperialistic in its outlook. In foreign affairs it invariably supports British policy and strives to arouse hostility against all possible rivals of Great Britain, not excepting the United States. During the European War it was the main vehicle of lying British propaganda and was the sole agency in luring young Irishmen into a war in which 50,000 of them lost their lives.

He quoted a prominent Jesuit writer, Father Devane sj, as saying that: 'A glance at the counter of any newspaper shop . . . will convince even the most sceptical that we are in a condition of mental bondage . . .' Apart from stemming the flood of 'objectionable' English publications into Ireland, the *Irish Press* was also advanced as an antidote to 'perhaps the most serious aspect of the problem . . . that presented by juvenile literature'. This tended to 'turn the minds of Irish boys and girls definitely away from Irish ideals, to make them despise Irish culture and the Irish national tradition. Many of the boys' papers are, in effect, recruiting agencies for the British boy scouts,[38] which, in turn, are a recruiting agency for the British Army and Navy.'

One of the questions most often asked by de Valera as he toured American newspaper offices in his Savonarolaesque zeal to protect Ireland from the baleful influence of the boy scouts was: 'How do you control it?'[39] He satisfied himself on this point where the *Irish Press* was concerned in a manner that might be taken as demonstrating either his preoccupation with matters theological or his 'cute hoorism'. He solved the problem of control by appointing himself the journalistic equivalent of the Three Divine Persons in One of the Catholic teaching of the time: God the Father, God the Son and God the Holy Ghost.

This is how he did it. Irish Press Ltd was formally incorporated in Dublin as a limited liability company on 4 September 1928. Margaret Pearse, mother of Padraig and Willy, pressed the button to start the rotary presses rolling to produce the first edition of the paper on 5 September 1931, under the editorship of Frank Gallagher.[40] The board of directors consisted of seven prominent Irish businessmen[41] and a controlling director, Eamon de Valera. Immediately after the incorporation of the company, advertisements were placed in papers[42] throughout Ireland soliciting share capital. Two hundred thousand ordinary shares were offered at £1 each. This much was in bold type. But the bulk of the advertisements consisted of a mass of very small type which amongst other things set out the purpose of the new venture, and explained how the money was to be paid. More than halfway down in this block of type it was stated that: 'The business of the company will be managed by a Controlling Director and the Directors. The powers of the Controlling Director are set out in Articles 76 to 78 inclusive, of the Articles of Association.'

Had a reader of, say, the *Tuam Herald*, the *East Galway Democrat*, the *Connacht Tribune*, the *Mayo News* or the *Derry Journal* made his or her way to the Companies Office in Dublin Castle and obtained a copy of the Articles of Association they would have found that the powers of the controlling director covered everything – staff, policy, premises, the lot. He could hire and fire every member of the staff from the copy boy to the managing director. He had authority over every function of the paper from its content to the workings of the circulation department. The controlling director could also assume the profane equivalent of the Three Divine Persons in one God. In addition to being controlling director he could also be editor in chief and managing director. The Articles of Association stipulated that:[43]

> The Controlling Director shall have sole and absolute control of the public and political policy of the company and of the editorial management thereof and of all newspapers, pamphlets or other writings which may be from time to time owned, published, circulated or printed by the said company . . .
>
> The Controlling Director can: appoint, and at his discretion remove or suspend all editors, sub-editors, reporters, writers, contributors or news and information and all such other persons as may be employed in or connected with the editorial department and may determine their duties and fix their salaries and or emoluments. Subject to the powers of the Controlling Director the directors may appoint and at their discretion remove or suspend managers, editors. . . .

Needless to say, de Valera's followers in Tuam and throughout the country did not go to the Companies Office. Instead they either bought shares themselves or, under the auspices of the Fianna Fail Cummain, went out collecting vigorously for the new paper.

However, to make doubly sure de Valera also conducted an arcane operation in Delaware in May 1931, where he set up the Irish Press Corporation. This creation in effect acquired a controlling interest in the Irish company (roughly 47 per cent at the time of writing). The Delaware Corporation had two types of shares. First there were non-voting A shares, bought by Irish Americans and newly arrived emigrants in the manner already described. Then there were some two hundred B shares, which carried the voting rights. These de Valera himself acquired, and established a holding trust with Sean Nunan to administer them. All that is required to be said about this trust since its foundation is that it did what it was set up to do. It held the *Irish Press* for de Valera, and later his son and grandson, against all comers.

By now enough should have been said about the impact that de Valera made on people's imaginations to make explicable the extraordinary respect for him which made the *Irish Press* manoeuvre possible. But before leaving the American end of this saga to return to Ireland for the final stages of the sequence of events which placed him in power, there is one aspect of his appeal which should be touched on. An anecdote of Gallagher's helps to illustrate it, even though de Valera himself is not directly concerned in the story. De Valera's half-brother, Father Tom Wheelright, showed them over the Redemptorist school in Pennsylvania at which he taught. Gallagher noted:[44] 'When I came to the great study where young lads sat at desks to which were attached bookcases I hungered for a chance of a decent education and felt lonely and lost without it.' That was the reaction of one of the greatest journalists produced by Ireland in this century. Despite the traditional Irish love and respect for learning, formal education was in very short supply in those days, the prerogative of the few. De Valera was not merely a teacher, but Chancellor of the National University. This was how he had himself described in the advertisements soliciting funds for the *Irish Press*. Who could think of questioning the integrity of a *Professor*? Certainly not the ordinary Sean or Mary Citizen.

Although he paid close attention to his wider, American, constituency in the run-up to the 1932 election de Valera saw to it that his name and that of Fianna Fail were also kept well to the fore in domestic Irish politics. One of the least pleasant but most effective methods of so doing for any Irish politician is to get himself arrested on a 'national' issue. This happened to de Valera on 5 February 1929. The exclusion order served on him five years earlier was still in force. Nevertheless he accepted an invitation to speak at a function hosted by the Gaelic Athletic Association and the Gaelic League in Belfast in the knowledge that he would 'be arrested the moment he reaches the Border'.[45] As a result of his defiance he received a month in jail and some invaluable publicity. In Dublin Tom Johnson chaired a protest meeting at Leinster House and a large public gathering was organized by Fianna Fail. At this, Sean MacEntee told his hearers that Fianna Fail was working for the day when the Republican flag would fly over the Six County Parliament and called down maledictions on the Northern statelet:[46] 'Let the grass grow on the streets of Belfast. Let the mills be silent. . . . The people who built up Belfast were not Irish but English and Scottish and they would not be Irish until the people of the South showed them they were stronger than they.'

Vitriolic as these sentiments were, they differed little from those entertained towards the Dublin Parliament by Fianna Fail. This attitude was defined by the *Nation* as follows:[47] 'We entered a faked parliament which we believed in our hearts to be illegitimate and we still believe it; and we faced a junta there which we did not regard as the rightful

Government of this country. We did not respect, nor do we now, such a Government or such a Parliament ... Our presence in the "Dail" of usurpers is sheer expedience, nothing else.'

Fianna Fail's behaviour in the Dail certainly indicated that a majority of the deputies agreed wholeheartedly with the foregoing. The party was so imbued with bitterness and intent on bringing down the Cosgrave administration that its whole concept of parliamentarianism was distorted. Both Sean Lemass[48] and Gerald Boland told me that they considered it a good thing that the party was in opposition for those five years as it gave the Warriors of Destiny a chance to settle into parliamentary ways and learn the business of democracy. While this slow, sometimes painful, but ultimately beneficial process was at work, the Government was continuing with another successful long-term political strategy that was even slower and more difficult but, ironically enough as we shall now see, was ultimately of considerable benefit to de Valera. While he was busy portraying his opponents as lackeys of British imperialism in both Ireland and America the Cosgrave administration had been quietly striking off the imperial shackles in international relationships.

They had begun with the Treaty itself as far back as 1923. They joined the League of Nations in that year (a significant gesture of independence in itself) and in 1924, in the teeth of British objections, succeeded in having the Treaty registered with the League. The British argued unsuccessfully with Cosgrave that:[49] 'the action of the Free State Government raised questions of very great Constitutional importance between the component parts of the Empire ... the Treaty was not, in their opinion, an instrument proper to be registered ...'. The British view was that the League had no role in 'the relations inter se of the various parts of the Commonwealth'.[50] This gesture of independence was accompanied that year by another notable 'first'. Professor T. A. Smiddy was accepted by the Americans as the Irish 'Minister Plenipotentiary' to Washington. As Professor D. W. Harkness has noted, this acceptance meant that:[51] 'The Irish Free State had penetrated the diplomatic unity of the Empire, successfully establishing in the American capital the first Dominion ambassador.'

The Irish were regarded as being amongst the most active and impressive delegates to the various Imperial Conferences held during the twenties. Desmond Fitzgerald wrote two revealing letters to his wife from the Imperial Conference held in London in 1930:[52] 'MacDonald and Thomas [the British delegates] were badly briefed so the discussion wandered into byways, with self and P. MacG. [Patrick MacGilligan] acting as general advisors to the whole lot. Fortunately it gave me a sense of confidence I have never had before, though I haven't read a document.' And the following day he wrote:[53] 'It is irritating to be dealing with men who are so badly briefed. They were discussing matters and had (or pretended to have) the wrong end of the stick. I told them I had dealt with the matter in '26 and what the circumstances were. MacD. said I was wrong and proceeded to prove it by reading from the report and landed on a sentence that just proved what I said. That sort of thing happens constantly – and makes them irritable.'

Those references to the work of the Imperial Conferences indicate the position the Free State had achieved when de Valera arrived in power to use that position for his own ends. They also indicate the unimpressive calibre of British representatives against whom he found himself pitted. This was an important consideration, because he had the additional advantage of working with the same team of Irish diplomats who had studied and helped to outmanoeuvre the British over the previous decade. The chief architects of the Irish achievement were three civil servants, two of them diplomats, and three politicians. One of the civil servants was Diarmuid O'Hegarty, in effect the Government's secretary. The diplomats were Joseph P. Walshe of the Department of External Affairs, and E. V. Phelan, an Irish civil servant with the International Labour Office at Geneva who used both his position and his expertise in the service of his countrymen at various crucial junctures. Walshe deserves to be regarded as the father of modern Irish diplomacy. His memoranda in the early days of the state formed the basis for much of Ireland's subsequent policy. The politicians were Desmond Fitzgerald, Patrick McGilligan and, until he was murdered, Kevin O'Higgins.

These men created an impact on Commonwealth development which was out of all proportion to the size of the Irish Free State. But, while their work was of fundamental importance in the development of the independence of the Dominions, it had very little impact on the ordinary domestic politics of the Free State. For example, as part of its settled policy of eradicating British governmental influence from the state's affairs the Irish devoted considerable time and effort to wearing down determined British opposition to getting direct access to the King and, as a corollary, to authenticating documents not with a British Seal but with the Great Seal of the Irish Free State. On 19 March 1931 the Irish got their way. McGilligan was received at Buckingham Palace by the King personally, without having to go through a British minister, and he secured the royal signature to a treaty concluded between the Free State and Portugal, stamping it with the Irish Great Seal. This apparently largely symbolic action was later described by Professor Berriedale Keith as being of 'fundamental importance' (readers will remember from Chapter 17 the importance attached by my father and his colleagues to their seals and badges) because it removed[54] 'a power which the British Government formerly possessed in law of securing consideration of any proposed action which might injure the rights of other Dominions or of the United Kingdom'.

The royal access issue also serves to illustrate the philosophical difference in approach to the Crown between de Valera and the Cosgravites. The latter made a distinction between the symbolism of the

Crown in Irish affairs, traditionally synonymous with oppression, and the equally strong tradition of affection shown by the Irish to the royal family. (Although the murder of Lord Mountbatten might indicate otherwise, it is true to say on the basis of past experience – which admittedly predates the revelations concerning 'Fergie' and the state of Prince Charles's marriage – that scarcely a man in Ireland, North or South, could look forward with confidence to a hot meal on the day of a royal wedding. The women of Ireland were glued to TV and radio sets.) The Free State representatives were also mindful of the importance of the Crown for the Northern Unionists. De Valera, however, took the high, stony Republican ground of making no concession to Unionist sentiment and of being seen to wish to extirpate the King's influence from Irish affairs.

But two other successes in the external field which the Irish achieved in the first post-Treaty decade were of particular benefit to de Valera – the first for the international platform which it gave him, the second for its assistance in his domestic programme. The two developments were the election of Ireland to the Council of the League of Nations on 17 September 1930 and the passing into law of the Statute of Westminster on 11 December 1931, which gave effect to the resolutions of the Imperial Conference of 1930. The Statute was the culmination of efforts initiated by Kevin O'Higgins at the Imperial Conference of 1926 and continued by his successors at succeeding Commonwealth forums. It was the Irish who bore 'the major responsibility of drawing up the Statute of Westminster from 1926 onwards'.[55] Where Ireland was concerned, its important provisions were the following:[56]

> 1) No law made by the Parliament of a Dominion shall be void and inoperative on the grounds that it is repugnant to the law of England, or to the provisions of any existing or future Act of Parliament of the Parliament of the United Kingdom, and the powers of the Parliament of a Dominion shall include the power to repeal or amend any such Act, order rule or regulation in so far as the same is part of the law of the Dominion.
>
> 2) The Parliament of a Dominion has full power to make laws having extra-territorial operation.
>
> 3) No future Act of Parliament of the United Kingdom shall extend to a Dominion unless it is expressly declared in that Act that the Dominion has requested and consented to its enactment.

Churchill realized the potential of these provisions for Ireland and opposed the Bill on its second reading, on 20 November 1931. He argued correctly that, if it became law, the Dail could repudiate everything in the Treaty including the Oath. The Free State Constitution could be repealed and the state become an inexpressible anomaly. He supported an amendment proposed by Colonel Gretton to guard against these evils.[57] Cosgrave became alarmed and took the unusual step of intervening in the debate. A letter from him to the British Prime Minister was read out in the House of Commons. It said:[58]

I have read the report of last Friday's debate in the House of Commons on the Statute of Westminster Bill, and am greatly concerned at Mr. Thomas's concluding statement that the Government will be asked to consider the whole situation in the light of the debate. I sincerely hope that this does not indicate any possibility that your government would take the course of accepting an Amendment relating to the Irish Free State.

... the happy relations, which now exist between our two countries is absolutely dependent upon the continued acceptance by each of us of the good faith of the other ... the Treaty is an agreement that can only be altered by consent.

... there seems to be a mistaken view in some quarters that the solemnity of this instrument in our eyes could derive any additional strength from a Parliamentary law. So far from this being the case, any attempt to erect a statute of the British Parliament into a safeguard of the Treaty would have quite the opposite effect here, and would rather tend to give rise in the minds of our people to a doubt as to the sanctity of this instrument.

The sub-text of that letter might be read as 'For God's sake do not put another arrow in de Valera's quiver'. The amendment was overwhelmed by 360 votes to 50. Despite the initial British grumblings at the Irish registration of the Treaty with the League of Nations, it was now clearly a bilateral international agreement. The British had voluntarily removed their own right to intervene in Ireland under British law. As was said afterwards,[59] the Statute 'may be said to have put the goblet of freedom into Ireland's hands to be drained at her discretion'. The dissolution of the Dail less than two months after the enactment of the Statute meant that that discretion would lie in the hands of Eamon de Valera.

Cosgrave and McGilligan had tried unavailingly to pour away two parts of the goblet's contents. These were the abolition of the Appeal to the Judicial Committee of the Privy Council, and the Oath. Publicly, McGilligan had announced the Government's intention of removing the influence of the Privy Council from Irish affairs.[60] But various delays ensured that this tasty morsel remained for de Valera to gobble up in 1933. Privately, Cosgrave had pressed the British to remove the Oath, but without success. He sent a senior civil servant[61] to London with a blunt message: 'Either remove the Oath or de Valera wins the next election. It has become a burning issue in Ireland and a major weapon in the Fianna Fail armoury.' Cosgrave, however, was in the honourable, but weak, position of attempting to amend the Treaty by negotiation, for which he needed British co-operation – always an unreliable prospect for Irish moderates. He had to mute his quite substantive triumphs in Anglo-Irish relations, lest he give aid and comfort to both British Conservative and Irish Republican critics. His defence of the constitutional position, which appealed to Unionist elements, provided de Valera with the opportunity for attacking him as being pro-Unionist. De Valera was in the far stronger position of threatening unilateral action against the ancient enemy. Despite the spirit evinced in the House of Commons by the vote on the

Statute of Westminster, that in the corridors of power remained as unsympathetic to the sensitivity of the Dublin Government's position as it was at the time of Cosgrave's letter to Cohalan. Cosgrave's plea was turned down, and the Oath card remained for de Valera to play.

The reality of the position was that, despite the pro-British label which de Valera and his colleagues attempted to fasten on the Government, Cosgrave and his colleagues had:[62] 'worked unremittingly to remove from Irish affairs any form of interference by the British Government. This work was seen to be effective. De Valera carried it on to a conclusion. To the civil servants of the Department of External Affairs there was no dramatic break in 1932. Work proceeded in a straight line until December 1936 when External Association became a reality.'

De Valera himself once, privately, passed a notable judgement on the general performance of the Cosgrave administration which is worth quoting in the light of the foregoing. I referred earlier to his habit of taking his children on country drives when he could. After coming to power he was accompanied on one such occasion by Vivion, then in his twenties. Vivion told me that he had been waxing eloquent on the iniquities of the 'Free Staters' in the approved Fianna Fail fashion of the time when, to his great surprise, his father stopped him frowningly. 'Yes, yes, yes,' de Valera said testily, waving his forefinger, 'we said all that, I know. I know. But when we got in and saw the files . . . they did a magnificent job, Viv. They did a magnificent job.' De Valera was too intelligent a man to allow his intellect to be clouded by his own rhetoric. The years of the civil war when he had done so for a time, with disastrous results, were now long behind him. It would be too much to expect that he would have spoken publicly as he did to Vivion. During the election he had made damaging use of the propaganda to be gained from the fact that Cosgrave's campaign had received financial support from a committee that included ex-Unionists. In the week before polling the *Irish Press* had used a four-column cartoon on page one showing a huge wave about to crash down on Cosgrave in a tiny vessel flying a flag inscribed 'Help'. He was shown reaching for a lifebelt inscribed 'Aid from ex-Unionists' and exclaiming: 'Look, look, that lifebelt may save us.' That theme was pursued up and down the country. But de Valera did make one significant public admission concerning the Treaty. Speaking in the Senate,[63] while he was still familiarizing himself with the files, he said: 'There have been advances made that I did not believe possible at the time [during the Treaty debates].'

But, as has been noted earlier, these 'advances' were not made in standards of living. Indeed it would have taken a remarkable leap of the imagination on the part of any Government to have achieved such progress. It was the era of the Great Slump – the year of the enactment of the Statute of Westminster was also the year in which Britain came off the Gold Standard. The Cosgrave administration had many admirable qualities, but a flair for economic innovation was not one of them. In fact de Valera was confronted by adversaries who had made some colossal blunders in the socio-economic sphere. Overall, against a background of general European unrest, Cosgrave and his team had established a democratic, legal and political stability out of chaos. They had replaced the RIC with an unarmed police force in the midst of a civil war, and established the Local Appointments Commission which went far to achieving what was, in the existing Irish circumstances, a contradiction in terms – ethical and professional standards in state appointments. Merit was also shown to take precedence over a Unionist background where appointments in the judiciary and the civil service were concerned.

Individual members of the Government had performed outstandingly well: Cosgrave himself in holding the centre together with courage and common sense, and O'Higgins in the realms of domestic security as well as international diplomacy. Fitzgerald and McGilligan had made notable contributions in the latter category. McGilligan, despite certain ill-judged remarks of his, mentioned below, also deserves credit for the jobs he generated through his pioneering work on the Shannon hydro-electric scheme which ultimately led to general Irish electrification. Patrick Hogan, as Minister for Agriculture, had also been a success in that portfolio, although contemporary assessments have queried his vision of an agriculture-led economy based on mixed farming. As Minister for Finance Ernest Blythe had certainly balanced the books, but at a human and political cost of which de Valera was the principal beneficiary.

The Government's problem was mainly attitudinal, reflecting the values of British-trained civil servant mandarins and the middle-class, professional and business backgrounds of some of its key figures, notably Hogan, McGilligan and O'Higgins. Soon after his appointment in 1924 as Minister for Industry and Commerce, McGilligan made statements which were garnered as Fianna Fail ammunition that was still being hurled with wounding effect in the 1932 general election campaign. Speaking against an appalling backdrop of unemployment, slum housing and, predictably, infant mortality, he told the Dail that, while he himself of course did not wish to see such things happen, nevertheless:[64] 'People may have to die in this country and may have to die from starvation. . . . If it is said that the Government has failed to adopt effective means to find useful work for willing workers, I can only answer that it is no function of government to provide work for anybody.'

The civil servant C. J. Grigg, who was loaned to his friend Cosgrave by the British Board of Inland Revenue to set up the new Irish civil service,[65] 'ensured that the service would bear the stamp "made in England"'. However, it is worth pausing for a moment to examine the 'made in England' label. To affix it too readily on the naturally cautious civil service, as there is a tendency to do amongst some Irish historians, lets the politicians off the hook. For it was not the English mould of the civil service which determined policies and influenced the quality of Irish life so much as the Catholic cast of mind of the politicians and their policies. The Catholic legislation which emanated from the Cosgrave regime – on censorship, divorce and so on – was initiated by the hierarchy, not by the civil servants. Nationalistic policies, such as the restoration of the Irish language, were not civil servant-inspired. The civil servants only came into their own when the politicians ran out of ideas and fell back upon them, as happened very noticeably during de Valera's later years in power.

It is true that, as Professor Basil Chubb has pointed out, like many of the states which sprang from the British Empire:[66] 'From the beginning the architects of the Irish state adopted the political institutions and procedures of Great Britain . . . the Irish system can best be classified as belonging to the British Commonwealth pattern.' But Irish leaders, and de Valera in particular, did not hesitate to disregard the civil servants' advice when it conflicted with their own ideas. No responsible Department of Finance official would have counselled de Valera to adopt the economic policy we will shortly encounter him pursuing towards Britain, for example. What circumscribed the Cosgrave administration far more than the Treasury training of its civil servants during its early days was the attitude of the banks:[67] 'The banks' reluctance to accommodate the government in 1923 left something of a sour taste in Cosgrave's mouth . . . Cosgrave felt there was a good deal of profiteering on the part of the Irish banks . . . and thought their rates considerably in excess of the rates charged by English banks.'

Such considerations, the difficulty of obtaining credit in England, the British political attitudes he outlined in his letter to Cohalan (Chapter 17) and the fear that there might be a run on the Irish banks had their input into the financial orthodoxy of the early Cosgrave governments. This was where the loss of Collins to the infant Irish state comes across sorely. He had shown a passion for trying to import what could be learned from the best of European and world example rather than slavishly copying everything English. He had proved himself to be an excellent Minister for Finance who would have controlled, rather than been led by, the two able men whom Grigg left to run the Irish Department of Finance on his return to London in 1924. Both were cast in the British Treasury mould. But one, under the influence of his charismatic personality, had already surreptitiously provided Collins with position papers during the Treaty negotiations, although he was working in Dublin Castle at the time. This was Joseph Brennan, who became the Secretary of the Department of Finance. The other was J. J. McElligott, the Assistant Secretary who later succeeded him. However, Blythe, the Free State Minister for Finance, uncritically adopted the orthodoxy option. In three years Government expenditure was reduced from £42 million in 1923–4 to £24 million in 1926–7. Income tax was lowered to sixpence in the pound less than the English rate (from five to three shillings). Alas, in the economic climate thus produced capital tended either to lie idle in the banks on deposit or to be exported. The Irish exported £195 million in 1926–7 and only attracted in some £73 million. Professor Lee has summed up the position succinctly:[68] 'Low income tax tended to attract rentier rather than risk capital, and it was risk capital and entrepreneurship that Ireland lacked. Rentiers didn't know what to do with their money in the country, except to export it.'

Thus with Collins gone, and the Government firmly set in the mould of orthodoxy, de Valera operated in an economic climate ever more favourable to an Opposition leader. Blythe's policies also resulted in a series of electoral lunacies including cuts in pensions for the elderly and the blind. The effects of these were added to by announcements in the run-up to the election that the Government intended to effect economies by cutting the pay of both police and teachers. In addition, married women were to be rendered ineligible to be teachers. With enemies like these, de Valera hardly needed friends. His advocacy of an interventionist policy as opposed to the Government's laissez-faire, as he put it,[69] made a dramatic impact. He argued:[70] 'You must actively interfere. We hold, unlike the Ministers opposite, that active interference is necessary by the Ministry if we are going to get the country out of the rut in which it is at present.'

By the time of the general election in 1932 the country was in an even bigger 'rut' than it had been when he enunciated that principle in 1928. But, as if to ensure his victory, the Government launched a final own goal of monumental proportions, which will be discussed shortly. The kick was originally aimed at the *Irish Press* which, from the day it was first published, had had a spectacular impact on Irish society. De Valera had presided over the final stages of the paper's birth like a somewhat distracted mother heron. His official biography states that:[71] '. . . while he was overseeing preparations for the first edition of the *Irish Press*, he delegated most of the Fianna Fail party work to others; but within the paper office he saw to everything, including the difficulties of early dispatch by train to the country'. A brief note in his papers[72] in his own handwriting referring to the late nights in the *Irish Press* does indicate the stress of the period. He records, obviously for his eyes only, how hard he found it to keep his temper. But out of all the creative tension a splendid newspaper emerged.

Frank Gallagher and his team raised the standards of Irish journalism, particularly in investigative journalism, literary criticism and sports coverage wherein the *Irish Press* pioneered the reporting of Gaelic games, thereby generating a new audience for both Gaelic football and hurling and the paper itself.[73] This particular field was momentarily jeopardized by a celebrated howler which appeared in the first edition of the paper. The publication date had been timed so as to benefit from the next day's All-Ireland hurling final. The new sports editor, Joe Sherwood, an Englishman and a brilliant sports journalist, had a panel inserted on page one giving the game's starting time. It said: 'Kick-off 3 p.m.'. Hurling, Ireland's national game, is of course a stick game which begins with the 'throw-in' of a tennis ball-sized leather 'sliotar'. This function was usually performed by a member of the hierarchy. For some time afterwards de Valera had to deal with irate queries as to the authenticity of his paper's commitment to spreading a knowledge and love of Gaelic games!

He had more serious commercial stumbling blocks to overcome in the rivalry of the existing Dublin papers. The *Irish Independent*, for example, used its financial muscle to ensure that the *Irish Press* was not allowed on to the early morning newspaper train from Dublin that brought the country editions to the provinces. This setback was overcome by the improvisation of two legendary circulation executives, Liam Pedlar, the circulation manager, an old de Valera worker in America and an ex-Clan na nGael gun-runner, and his assistant Padraig O'Criogain. Pedlar drew on his gun-running experiences to ensure that the *Irish Press* arrived in Ballyfaremote in the arms of either a Fianna Fail bus driver or commercial traveller. Here it might be sold in one of the fiercely partisan shops that sold the *Press* or its rivals, but not both together. Or it might be taken on to a more remote townland by the Fianna Fail postman, or by a small farmer returning from the morning journey to the creamery. In one celebrated case in North Kerry it was brought on up the side of a mountain by a man with a 'good Fianna Fail ass and cart'. Padraig O'Criogain, who vouched for that story, also told me that he remembers periods in the early days when he worked seven days a week, averaging from three to four hours' sleep a night. The result in terms of opening up new circulation areas was summed up in a story told by my father who was on holiday in the west at the time. He went into a shop seeking an *Independent*. The old lady who owned the shop was astounded to learn that there was another newspaper published in Dublin. She thought that there was only 'Mr de Valera's *Irish Press*'. The standards set by men like the literary editor, M. J. MacManus, were such that an Assistant Professor of Education at Maynooth, Eamon Behan, who came from the Kerry Gaelic-speaking district of Ballyferriter, told me that he and his classmates in primary school learned their English from the *Irish Press* leading articles. They were too young to realize that their teacher, like many at the time, was a 'great Dev. man'. Nor did they note the frequency with which the names Cosgrave, or Cumann na nGaedheal, occurred in proximity to certain words. But they learned the spelling and usage of terms like 'traitorous', 'imperialistic', 'obnoxious' and so on!

One can understand the impact that such a publication made in unsophisticated, rural Ireland at the time; and the even greater impact of the news that the Government was prosecuting the Editor of that publication before the military tribunal for seditious libel. What happened was that through their IRA links Aiken and Dr Jim Ryan had kept Gallagher well primed with juicy copy concerning the treatment of IRA suspects by warders and detectives. Along with printing these, Gallagher had nettled the authorities by a series of attacking leading articles on prison conditions. For historical reasons, allegations of police brutality strike a particular chord in Ireland at the best of times. These were not the best of times. Policemen and jurors had been murdered and in certain cases interrogation of suspects was regarded by the police as a legitimate method of ensuring that they got in their retaliation first. These misdeeds were covered up by the simple expedient of lying. For example, de Valera took up the case of a well-known IRA man in Clare, T. J. Ryan, who had not merely been beaten, but practically pulped, before being left unconscious after a detective had been murdered. The police said his injuries were caused by being 'kicked by a cow'. The Minister for Justice, Fitzgerald-Kenney, replying to de Valera on 31 July 1929, said that he accepted their explanation; as a result the detectives were known from that time onwards as 'Fitzgerald-Kenney's cows'. Incidentally, the sequel to this case probably says all that needs to be known about police–IRA relationships of the time. The detectives involved hired a boat with the intention of kidnapping Ryan and drowning him. They were baulked when word of the plot was conveyed to David Neligan,[74] Collins' old informant in the Castle who was now in charge of the CID.

In this sort of atmosphere, with polling day fixed for 16 February 1932, Gallagher was summoned before the tribunal on 5 February. He argued that his articles were fair criticism of the Government for being harsh with their prisoners. The evidence of more than fifty witnesses who testified over the next eleven days caused a large body of public opinion to agree with him. Counsel for the defence concluded his address on the eve of the election with the ringing declaration that he doubted not but[75] 'that the members of the Tribunal would secure to their countrymen the right and liberty of exposing injurious, tyrannical power by speaking the truth'. The officers virtually took his advice. A slap-on-the-wrist fine of £100 each on Gallagher and the newspaper was imposed, the day *after* polling day, and the prosecution's costs were refused. *Irish Press* readers responded by sending in unsolicited contributions to pay the fines. For de Valera it was as though his opponents had provided a sort of Irish Watergate, eleven days before an election, which yielded fresh lead stories for his (already popular) newspaper every day until it was all over. The circulation rocketed from the mid-70,000s to 115,000. As one de Valera-ite, Donnchadha O'Briain, said in the Dail a year later in the course of a bitter controversy (see p. 441): 'The *Irish Press* settled Cumann na nGaedhael.' It is a reasonable assumption that that staunch *Irish Press* distributor in North Kerry with the 'good Fianna Fail ass and cart' would have been moved to use this valuable asset to bring incapacitated neighbours to the polls on 16 February. Certainly the rest of the *Irish Press* network, that of Fianna Fail itself and large sections of the IRA did all that lay within their power to get the vote out.

In Dublin, for instance, where Sean Lemass liaised with the IRA officer David Fitzpatrick, voting lists were given to IRA activists who scurried about the city voting for the sick, the dead and the emigrated. Some of those more dedicated to the pursuit of democracy were reputed to have voted as many as fifty times each.[76] In the event only one person actually died in the contest: a Cumann na nGaedhael candidate was shot dead in the Sligo-Leitrim area. But, in the words of the official biography:[77] 'The culprit turned out to be a non-political lunatic.' So that was all right. De Valera's theatrical flair resulted in some spectacular personal appearances. 'The Chief', the star turn of the Fianna Fail circus, entered some country towns[78] 'escorted by a volunteer cavalry, the manes of the horses braided with Republican colours', preceded by fife and drum bands. The sight of de Valera in flowing black cloak, mounted on a white horse, sometimes accompanied by a torchlight procession, made a lasting impact on the Irish political landscape. Some of this impact translated into lasting electoral support; and some, courtesy (or discourtesy) of Irish humour, into even more long-lasting folklore. For example the story of how Pat, watching a typical cloak and swagger entry to a country town, turned to Mike and said disgustedly: 'Jasus! Will you look at the long bollocks on the horse.'

To which Mike replied sweetly: 'That's not a horse. That's a mare!'

However, despite the jokes the election campaign was bitter, hard-fought, bare-knuckled. On any day one could read a description such as that which appeared in the *Irish Press* on 10 February 1932: 'The meeting was characterised by repeated interruptions, and by fist fights between rival partisans.' However, some more prosaic content described the instrument which in the last analysis probably did most to bring about de Valera's victory – his election shopping basket, dated 9 February 1932, wherein he sought a mandate to:[79]

1) Remove the Oath.

2) Retain the land annuities in the State treasury. On 2) he claimed there was no contractual obligation to pay the annuities and that the three millions involved could be used to relieve farmers 'completely of the rates on their holdings'. Another million would be freed for 'the relief of taxation'.

3) Get legal opinion on the need to continue such payments as the R.I.C. component of the Ultimate Financial Settlement. He claimed that 2) and 3) together amounted to more than 'the burden imposed on the German people by war reparations'. To continue shouldering the burden would make 'economic recovery almost impossible'.

4), 5) and 6) taken together reflected the influence of Arthur Griffith's protectionist, self-help philosophy. Native industry and agriculture were to be built up under protection and a preference sought on the British market for Irish agricultural produce in return for Irish purchases of the British machinery necessary to facilitate 4) and 5).

7) In effect promised to abandon the Government's cuts in the lower reaches of State employ but to make the upper echelons take a cut.

8) Aimed at saving the Irish language and the Gaeltacht dwellers 'from the emigrant ship'.

De Valera also promised to do all he could to end partition, but promised not to exceed his mandate in the field of international relations without consulting the people first. Because of the fears aroused in some quarters by the prospect of a Fianna Fail victory he reassured the electorate that he would not 'pursue a vindictive course against any minority, but ... govern fairly in the interests of all sections of the community. All citizens will be treated as equal before the law, and the individual will be protected in his person and in his property with all the resources at the Government's command.'

He also stated that the party was not in favour of communism, or a land tax for farmers, but did believe 'in the diffusion of property and ownership'. The communist disavowal was necessary because, in addition to the other excitements and rancours of the time, there was something of a red scare about. From the enpurpled ranks of the Irish hierarchy there had recently crashed forth a salvo directed against the reds.[80] The draconian Public Safety Bill had also been aimed at whatever existed of communism in Ireland. De Valera's pledges included the decentralization of government and the ruralization of industry as opposed to its concentration in large cities. On paper it all added up to a far more coherent and attractive programme than that of an administration intent on cutting the pay of the police and the teachers. In the words of one authority, Cumann na nGaedheal:[81] 'based its platform squarely on law, order, religion and the "red scare"'. In practice, as we shall see, de Valera's shopping basket contained at least one large time-bomb. His proposals created not a preferential position in Britain for Irish agricultural products, but their virtual exclusion for a time. However, few looked into the future. De Valera's campaign had generated so much buzz and electricity that an estimated thirty thousand people turned out for his eve-of-poll rally in Dublin. The next day, 16 February 1932 the country voted for change. Fianna Fail gained 16 seats. Cumann na nGaedheal lost 9. The outcome of the election was as follows (pre-election strengths in brackets):

Fianna Fail	72 (56)
Cumann na nGaedheal	57 (66)
Independents	11 (13)
Labour	7 (10)
Farmers' Party	4 (6)
Independent Labour	2 (2)

The figures meant that, with the aid of Labour, de Valera would be able to form a Government. He could expect to control a total of 79 seats to his opponents' 74. But for a moment it appeared as though his opponents' prayers had been answered and that, whatever the aberrations of the Irish electorate, God at least had kept his head. For the emotional and physical strain of the campaign took its toll and de Valera fell ill. It was an extraordinary anti-climax. At the peak moment of the greatest triumph of his life, at the centre of a vortex of unprecedented change and upheaval, de

Valera became so ill that he 'was unable to meet anyone for a week'.[82] However, with the aid of a prepared questionnaire and recording apparatus he did manage to conduct both an interview with John Steele of the *Chicago Tribune*[83] and a broadcast to America.[84] He was too weak even to take part in the by-election campaign in Sligo-Leitrim, which had been postponed for a fortnight because of the tragedy (the seat was won by the murdered man's widow). But, just as he had done in 1916 in the face of the even greater strain and danger, he forced himself to resume command, even though he was now sixteen years older. By the morning of Tuesday, 8 March he was strong enough to exclude the Labour Party from his Government.

The election had cost the party the seat of its old leader, Tom Johnson. However Johnson accompanied its new leaders, William Norton, who succeeded him, and William Davin to the meeting, with de Valera, Gerald Boland and Sean T. O'Ceallaigh. De Valera went through his election manifesto again and said that he expected Labour would not wish to be represented in Cabinet![85] As his was the only social-sounding agenda on offer from the bigger parties, a Labour Party which had just suffered reverses which included the loss of its leader was in no position to declare to the contrary. Norton said afterwards[86] that for ten years the Labour Party had 'pleaded in vain' with Cumann na nGaedheal, 'Fianna Fail at least promises it will tackle social and economic problems.' In fact Norton had laid down the condition that Fianna Fail should not exceed its stated programme. He also seems to have secured assurances from de Valera that he would not victimize his opponents. He held a meeting[87] with the Garda Commissioner and the Head of the Special Branch (General O'Duffy and David Neligan) to assure them they would have nothing to fear if they served the new administration in a proper professional manner; it was not until de Valera freed himself of the need for Labour support the following year that he took action against the two officers. The official biography, however, solemnly informs us:[88] 'They [Labour] agreed. The resulting independence, de Valera considered, was best for both parties. No conditions were laid down for Labour support, but it was clear that the party would support him.'

What was not entirely clear to some in Fianna Fail was whether certain elements in Cumann na nGaedheal would support a peaceful transfer of power.[89] It was known that General O'Duffy had been lobbying certain of his colleagues in the Gardai and in the Army with a view to preventing a de Valera take-over. Rumour fed on word of these overtures and there was, to use de Valera's own term, talk of a coup d'état. But it was only talk. In the Gardai, close colleagues like Neligan and my father would have nothing to do with the proposal. Their view was that they had upheld democracy against de Valera in 1922 and they were not going to threaten it in 1932 because of him. The same view prevailed in the Army. The Chief of Staff, General Michael Brennan, took steps to transfer disaffected officers who might have acted otherwise. Cosgrave himself would not have countenanced any anti-democratic actions. He was always wary of O'Duffy, unlike Collins who thought so highly of him that he regarded him as his most likely successor. In fact, Cosgrave had only persuaded my father to act as Deputy Commissioner in the first instance because he convinced him that a counter-balance was needed to someone whom he regarded as a 'wild man'. Hearing the coup rumours, Cosgrave inquired of those whom he could trust as to their validity. He was assured, correctly, that there was no need to worry, but seemingly decided that if he was returned to power O'Duffy would be shifted. When it became apparent that he was going to lose the election Cosgrave bowed out not just gracefully but nobly. His acquiescence in the verdict of the ballot box, and Eamon de Valera's forbearing interpretation of that verdict, ensured that democracy survived in at least twenty-six of Ireland's thirty-two counties.

De Valera showed himself to be aware of the problem. In a speech to the first Fianna Fail Ard Fheis held after he took office, on 8 November 1932, he said:

> We came into office . . . to take over an army that had been opposed to us in a civil war, a Civil Service that was built up during ten years of our opponents' regime. We came into office determined to be fair to everybody. The army of our opponents loyally came in as the army of the State and are prepared to serve the State loyally. We took over the police force under similar conditions, and, while here and there there are complaints, still, to the credit of the men in the army, to the credit of the Civic Guards and the Civil Service, the civil services and the forces of the State are prepared to serve elected representatives of the people. That is a great achievement.

The achievement was that of the services, of course, not his. He was the one who had resisted the setting up of the state and made strenuous efforts to subvert it. However, having correctly diagnosed the problem, he was then faced with the difficulty of implementing his post-acquisition-of-responsibility diagnosis, as compared to his earlier incarnation when he sought 'extremist support'. One result of this behaviour was:[90] '. . . when the election results became known in Listowel, Co. Kerry, the local IRA Battalion marched to the town police station and ordered its occupants to vacate the premises, telling them a new republican police force was due in a matter of days'.

His performance in snubbing the Garda Siochana in Skibbereen, while taking the salute from an IRA guard of honour, symbolized his moral dichotomy. But there was nothing dichotomous about his pursuit of power. The cacophonous unsophisticates who formed the rank and file of Fianna Fail wanted 'that crowd' turfed out, *simpliciter*. De Valera marched to a less obvious, more effective drum. The Patronage of Replacement was his metre. Unless, as with O'Duffy or Neligan, a direct challenge could be adduced, removals were kept to a minimum. Replacements and promotions, however, proliferated.

In the Gardai, the Army, the civil service, the higher and lower slopes of the law and medicine, a cult of de Valera was enshrined. The new rate collector, local government appointee, postmistress – all were Fianna Fail nominees. Knowledge is power, and all information was filtered upwards. *Per contra*, of course, nothing leaked from the meetings of the local Fianna Fail Cumainn. The cult of *omertà* was as scrupulously observed in Paulstown as in Palermo. But every local fact of value was passed on to the next level of authority. The original impetus of Sinn Fein was freedom, a selfless impulse which garnered unto itself all sorts of elements – courage, intelligence, organization, self-sacrifice, brutality. Sean T. O'Ceallaigh described how it was done:[91] ' . . . there was scarcely a constituency in Ireland in which we could not give any authorised enquirer the number of votes that a Sinn Fein Candidate was likely to receive. In a great many constituencies, where the parish had been canvassed over and over again, the figures we had in our records closely approximated to the figures published officially after the General Election of Dec. 14th, 1918.'

De Valera invested the Fianna Fail bandwagon with all the trappings of patriotism enjoyed by the Sinn Fein machine and refined it down to one omnipotent formula: Innocence + Organization + Patronage = Power. The formula worked, applied at whatever level of veniality – the parish pump, editorial chair or law library. In the words of an admirer of de Valera, albeit a Corkonian, it meant that the brushstroke was interspersed with that of the scalpel:[92]

> The man who urged the Supreme Council of Sinn Fein in 1917 to 'smother every petty or selfish interest' and to 'taboo the chicanery, the intrigues and the cliques which are the characteristics of modern party machine politics', came in due course to preside over the most professional machine Irish politics had yet seen, its multiple 'mafias' flourishing under the benignly blind gaze of the Incorruptible. Correctly resisting pressure to dismiss pro-Treaty civil servants and army officers when he came to power in 1932, he encouraged the gradual growth of an insidious, if initially discreet, spoils system in the army, the police, the judiciary, and the state sponsored bodies . . . and responded to pleas for reform by delicately holding his nostrils. Like his countrymen in general he combined a rigid concept of private morality with a more selective one of public morality. . . .

However, the photographs of de Valera's tense features as he entered Leinster House at 2.30 on Tuesday, 9 March 1932 might be taken as indicating that he was not completely certain how matters would work out. His son Vivion accompanied him, armed with a revolver, and some of his senior colleagues were also 'carrying'. Before the entry Aiken had dished out a supply of revolvers to his colleagues. De Valera told his biographers that he was concerned about the possibility of assassination (though it was later suggested in *Irish Press* circles that his worried expression was really caused by his knowledge of the standard of Vivion's marksmanship). But once inside, all cause for worry evaporated. Cosgrave did not stand for the presidency of the Executive Council, and when de Valera was nominated his winning margin, 81 to 68, was even higher than expected. Three of the independents voted for him. One of these was James Dillon (a son of the old Irish Parliamentary Party leader, John Dillon) who was destined to become one of de Valera's principal parliamentary adversaries. And so, at the end of a ten-year period, Eamon de Valera, at the age of fifty, had achieved the most remarkable double transition – from triumph to disaster, and from disaster back to triumph – in the history of Irish politics. He had done it by a combination of faith in himself, an obsessive, almost disturbed, concentration on the pursuit of power, opportunism, relentless hard work in two continents, and shrewd, long-headed planning.

To make matters even easier for him in his hour of glory, the Governor General, James McNeill, a brother of Eoin McNeill, spared him the indignity of a journey to the Viceregal Lodge in Phoenix Park to have his appointment confirmed. His Majesty's Representative in Ireland came to the Dail himself. It was a formal act of courtesy which de Valera must have appreciated personally but, as we shall see shortly, most emphatically did not reciprocate in a political sense. When forming his Cabinet de Valera retained the portfolio of Minister for External Affairs for himself. Henceforth he would not shirk going to London for negotiations. He knew, by looking into his manifesto, if not his heart, that London would soon figure large in the agenda of External Affairs. The rest of his appointments were as follows: Vice-President and Minister for Local Government and Public Health, Sean T. O'Ceallaigh; Minister for Finance, Sean MacEntee; Minister for Industry and Commerce, Sean Lemass; Minister for Agriculture, Dr James Ryan; Minister for Lands and Fisheries, Patrick J. Ruttledge; Minister for Justice, James Geoghegan; Minister for Defence, Frank Aiken; Minister for Education, Thomas Derrig.

De Valera and this team largely remained intact for several years. It will assist us in our interpretation of what they achieved, or failed to achieve, if, before proceeding to examine the record, we pause for a moment to consider some important reflections by de Valera on the subject of negotiation. He was talking to Gallagher[93] about the Treaty and the pre-1921 settlement relationship with Britain, but his words illuminate his strategy in the years afterwards, particularly the 1930s. Gallagher notes:

> He said the greatest danger of all in negotiation is reasonableness. The others have an objective and mean to obtain it, those who are anxious to be accommodating are lost. He said it was useless for the Irish to think they could get in between the English and the North, the affinity was too great.
>
> Another great danger was the desire to finish the job. This was what happened to Redmond. He wished to complete something and something became everything. A leader should try to move even a little nearer the ultimate aim rather than hasten to completion of something temporary.
>
> He thought the Southern Irish were much nearer the English in character than the Northerners were. He personally felt very much at home with the English. Outside of religion they seemed to have the same general outlook.

When Lloyd George had tried to get into his good graces by dismissing
Redmond and his party, he said – but was not their failure due to your having
betrayed them?

All the elements contained in those four, slightly disjointed, paragraphs
were present in his approach to Britain for the next sixteen years:
inflexibility; a willingness to abort negotiations and endure – or, possibly
more accurately, cause others to endure – short-term hardship for long-
term gain; an ability to convince some British statesmen that, although he
seemed to be attacking them, he was really their friend; and, where
partition was concerned, a paralyzingly pessimistic belief that, as the
British would always support the Northerners, any concessions from
Dublin were bound to be rejected and therefore there was no use making
any.

De Valera's first notable gesture on taking office was to cut his own pay
and that of his ministers; in his case the drop was from £2,500 to £1,700.
This was a leading-by-example step in the direction of his stated goal of
fulfilling James Connolly's ambition of getting 'the workers of Ireland the
living they were entitled to in their own country'.[94] The kind of living he
had in mind was, he said, 'decent frugal living'.[95] Defending his policy of
protectionism, he argued that 'over eighty thousand people could be
employed in manufacturing and producing goods that we import
unnecessarily'.[96] He accepted that 'certain costs will go up'[97] but denied his
opponents' charges that he intended to introduce a 'hair-shirt' policy.
Speaking in the Dail[98] he told the opposition that 'theirs was the silk-shirt
policy for some and the hair-shirt policy for others. If there are to be hair
shirts at all, it will be hair shirts all round. Ultimately I hope the day will
come when the hair shirt will give way to the silk shirt all round.'

It was, of course, somewhat easier for de Valera to contemplate a vista
of hair-shirted 'frugal living' than it was for many of his countrymen. He
gazed upon the prospect through the windows of Bellevue, the new home
he had moved to 'surrounded by some four to five acres'[99] in the choice
residential district of Blackrock, Co. Dublin. And, although it has not been
established that he ever used the money to pay for the services of either
milkman or mistress, the very existence of the fruits of his American and
other fund-raising activities must have conferred the balm of at least
psychological comfort on any hair-shirt induced sorenesses. In fact he took
advantage of the uproar, generated by his abolition of the Oath and the
retention of the land annuities, to increase the store of balm before the end
of his first year in power. Let us now observe how he did it.

20

PULLING A STROKE

DE VALERA'S ANNUITIES policy meant that in effect an economic war was brewing between Ireland and England; it would particularly affect the Irish farming community. Jockeying for position before the formal declaration of hostilities, both sides sought to influence American public opinion. On 15 December, Britain seized the opportunity presented by the fact that a number of European countries had defaulted on their war debt obligations to the USA[1] to bring off a propaganda coup at de Valera's expense. The Chancellor of the Exchequer, Neville Chamberlain, announced in the House of Commons that Britain would pay her dues on time, despite the fact that Parliament would have to be asked to sanction a supplementary estimate. The supplementary estimate was said to be required not only for increased unemployment benefits but also because of the loss of revenues from the Irish annuities. This announcement was extremely well received in an America shocked by the Great Depression and angered at the European defaulters. The *New York Times* ran a laudatory report under the headline: 'Irish land issue and relief put Britain out £21,420,955.'[2] To Americans, unversed in the intricacies of the Anglo-Irish relationship, Ireland seemed to be defaulting towards Britain in the same way that the Europeans were treating the United States. De Valera met the situation in his own inimitable way. One biographer has described his reaction as follows:[3]

> For de Valera, who was always particularly conscious of American opinion, the whole thing was particularly disturbing, especially at this time, but it did not take him long to pull a propaganda stroke of his own. Within a week he announced that the Irish Free State was repaying the Republican loan which he had launched in the United States during the war of Independence. Although the money would not become due until Ireland was recognised as an independent republic, he announced that it was being repaid immediately with a twenty five per cent premium added.
>
> The timing of his gesture was impeccable. While the furore was still raging over the other nations defaulting on their war debt payments, the Irish were moving to pay their debt in full, even before it was due. As a result, the story made front page news throughout the country.

That assessment is accurate, so far as it goes. For, in common with every other biographer of de Valera hitherto, it omits all mention of the effect of de Valera's 'stroke' on the holdings of the controlling director of the *Irish Press*. That this was substantial is made clear in a press statement[4] issued by the Free State's representative in America years later, when, after the publicity bonanza had been thoroughly exploited, de Valera actually authorized the payment of the bonds money. In addition to paying $1.25 to any bondholder who had not applied for a refund as a result of the decision by Judge Peters in the New York bonds case, the statement promised that 'the balance of .67 cents will be paid to those who have already received .58 cents to the dollar'.[4a]

The effect of this press release on pre-TV American public opinion may be gauged from the following excerpt from a transcript of a popular radio programme of the period:[5]

> For the next few days, the Irish Free State, through its Washington Minister, Michael MacWhite, will be paying off the first part of a five million, two hundred thousand dollar debt to America. Not to the American government, but to Johnnie Q. Public, U.S. taxpayer and foreign bond investor. It is, says Mr. MacWhite, 'redemption of a pledge guaranteed by no legal security but considered by the Irish people to be a debt of honour'. . . . No legal bond was offered. Only the most sacred bond of all – an Irishman's word that he would repay what he had borrowed. Today with the Irish Free State an established fact – the word of honour is being kept.

The enthusiastic commentator went on to describe Ireland as being little in size but 'mighty big in character'.[5a] We can but speculate as to what the broadcaster would have said of the character of Eamon de Valera, 'mighty big' in size, if he had had sight of the power of attorney described in Chapter 19 whereby bondholders had agreed to appoint: 'EAMON DE VALERA my true and lawful attorney, in my name, place and stead, to receive from the Receivers for the Benefit of Bond Certificate Holders of Republic of Ireland loans which is (are) or *shall* [author's italics] be due and payable to me on said Bond Certificate (or Certificates) of said Republic of Ireland Loans'.

Some of his Irish critics who had seen the documentation objected strenuously to his diversion of taxpayers' monies to the *Irish Press*. But they were despatched as dust beneath the de Valera chariot wheels in the course of a two-day debate on the issue in the Dail.[6] It was an acrimonious and lengthy affair, occupying over 250 columns of the official Report, and immediately followed the holding a few days previously of an even more acrimonious *Irish Press* annual general meeting. No balance sheet had been provided, but accounts had been circulated, which Desmond Fitzgerald read out to the Dail. These showed the paper to have debts of around £100,000. By a curious coincidence there was a general acceptance throughout the debate that the amount which would come de Valera's way as a result of paying off the bonds was £100,000. Sean McEntee, as Minister for Finance, disclosed that the total bill for discharging the bonds, including those outside de Valera's control, would be some £1.5 million.

The debate unleashed all the frustration that his opponents felt at their loss of power and at the methods and style by which he had triumphed. In the course of the debate de Valera sustained the most personalized criticism ever levelled at him in Dail Eireann; in turn he replied to it with some of the bitterest language of his career. The occasion had a nastier tone to it than anything which had occurred during the Treaty debates. His behaviour was likened to Lloyd George's involvement in the Marconi scandal.[7] He was charged by Patrick McGilligan with 'looting of the public purse for a party organ'. Frank MacDermott thought it 'an indelicate thing' for the President to 'go around canvassing bondholders to assign their rights to him'. Desmond Fitzgerald accused him of putting a huge charge on the taxpayer so that he might get a percentage. Cosgrave pointed out that the state had no obligation to pay the money at all because of the Peters decision (as the Free State was not awarded title to the bonds it did not acquire either their benefit or their obligations).[8] Batt O'Connor summed up the resentment that he and his colleagues felt at being constantly labelled pro-British, lacking both the patriotism and the high moral standing of de Valera. It was O'Connor, a close friend of Collins, who, under pressure from de Valera, had finally persuaded Collins to go to London for the Treaty negotiations. Collins had so trusted O'Connor that, to hide some of the loan monies from the British, he had them converted into gold so that O'Connor, a builder, could concrete the ingots into his kitchen floor, hidden in a baby's crib.[9] Neither Collins nor he had ever visualized any of the money going to fund a newspaper for de Valera. Now, all O'Connor's anger at de Valera welled up. He protested at the way he and his friends were being labelled 'John Bulls' with 'no love for Ireland' by a 'Great White Chief' who sat surrounded by 'yes-men' who swallowed de Valera's 'dope'. After pointing out that he had subscribed more than anyone on the Government benches to National Loans, with no thought of gain, he said: 'The indecent haste about it is that you want to get control of the money to help you out of your difficulties with your daily paper. . . . Think of the conditions of the farms . . . the cutting of the salaries of the teachers and the civil servants . . . and now you pass a Bill to pay £1.5 million . . . put country before party politics and a party newspaper.'

De Valera's defence was a classic exercise in casuistry, claims of high-mindedness and vituperation. He said there was no comparison between the *Irish Press* and the Marconi scandal because in the latter: 'members of the Government were taking shares in a concern in which the Government was directly interested'. This has to be regarded as a de Valera fact because he and his Government were engaged in an attempt to put money into a concern in which he and some of his colleagues *already* had shares. He claimed that he regarded his control of the bonds and of the *Irish Press* as part of a sacred 'trust' to safeguard the values of the Irish people. He could not understand how someone of Desmond Fitzgerald's low calibre ever came to be chosen as a publicist for Sinn Fein. Replying to Fitzgerald, he said: 'The vilest and most contemptible thing I have ever listened to was the suggestion that the Irish people should pay in order that a small enterprise get a small percentage of it . . . money was lawfully and legally due to the *Irish Press*.' He took the charge of corruption to his critics in extraordinary terms. On the Opposition benches he said there were 'men who could be guilty of corruption were they in a position to do so. . . . I know it is gall and wormwood to them that they are not here to do it, and that is the whole trouble. They are not here to do it and it is the great and supreme pleasure of my life to know they will have to digest the gall and wormwood.'

Neither he, his son Vivion, nor the other directors received 'one penny' in directors' fees, he said. In the event numbers told and the Bill went through the Dail. The great respect in which people held him, combined with the use of the word 'trust', not only in the debate but on many subsequent occasions, coupled with his disclaimers about directors' fees, misled many people into thinking that the *Irish Press* was run on non-profit-making lines like, for instance, the Nuffield or Observer Trusts, which had been set up to further particular philosophies. A note from an unknown admirer[10] sums up the mixture of innocence and admiration which enabled him to float the *Press* and keep it floating: 'I know you will do it. You do all the work. You support the *Press*. You pay for everything that comes your way. . . . Take great care of yourself: for you are now "The Cause" and on your health may easily lay in great part the fate of the Irish issue in America.'

In fact de Valera never displayed any great eagerness to 'pay for everything'. The *Irish Press* managed to accumulate the reserves to found lucrative Sunday and evening stable companions, but never paid a dividend to shareholders during his tenure as controlling director.[11] Wages and conditions were appalling. Frank Gallagher's duties occupied him from 11.30 a.m. to 3. a.m. the following day.[12] For this he received £850 a year. When de Valera appointed him he asked for a four-year contract at a salary of £1,000 a year rising by £50 per annum to £1,200. However, de Valera sidestepped him by getting him to write to the board of directors officially seeking the appointment without reference to their discussions. As a result Gallagher got a one-year contract and £850 a year.[13] In the month in which de Valera forced the bonds payments through the Dail, July 1933, Gallagher was driven to offering his resignation to him – not because of his own strains but because of the treatment meted out to the staff.[14] Amongst the many cases of parsimony cited by Gallagher was that of the behaviour of Harrington, an American whom de Valera had appointed to the business side of the paper to reassure American subscribers. He attempted to fire the person acting as women's editor because she had used agency 'copy' for a fortnight, contributing nothing of her own. It emerged that she was on holiday and had prepared the material in advance to save the expense of providing a replacement.[15] Ten pounds a week was all that was allowed to pay for contributors to a page which appeared six days a week.[16] Gallagher finally resigned in 1935. Recalling that early period, in the thirties, the acting women's editor, Maire Comeford, said: 'I was working so hard then, I do not like, even now, to think about it.'[17] One thing which can be said about the *Irish Press* is that there was no discrimination between the sexes. Men were treated on a plane of equal injustice to women!

Brendan Malin, who was political correspondent of the *Irish Press* before helping to found the Irish News Agency and subsequently going on to a distinguished career with the *Boston Globe*, recalled the conditions, and de Valera's attitude to them, as follows:[18]

> Although a back-breaking schedule of 'markings' with the Long Fellow through the years brought the two of us reasonably close – as close as one might expect to get to the New Jesus in a Black Coat – he never discussed *Irish Press* staff or wage-condition matters with me. This is understandable, I suppose, since the 'wage scales' throughout much of the period were a disgrace, while the absence of anything approaching established hours of work was tantamount to sustained oppression, or, in the words of the American Bill of Rights, 'cruel and unusual punishment'.

Joseph Walshe, my predecessor as Editor of the *Irish Press*, also accompanied him on political campaigns and his abiding recollection was that de Valera 'never spoke to anyone on the staff'. De Valera got away with this attitude and treatment of journalists for two reasons. One, the paper had a policy of employing young staff who, when they failed to get pay increases, generally moved on to be replaced by another youngster. For this reason the *Irish Press* became one of the greatest nurseries of journalistic talent in the English-speaking world. The second reason was that inevitably a percentage of senior men stayed on because they were imbued with what Gallagher termed:[19] 'the democratic and republican outlook which is the essential mark of this paper'. Their treatment, when they came to pensionable age, was often quite disgraceful. By the time I became Editor in 1968 de Valera had had no formal contact with the paper for almost a decade and the National Union of Journalists had forced improvements in conditions. But there were still a number of older men on the staff, formerly brilliant journalists, now beyond pensionable age but unable to retire because the pension arrangements were so inadequate. Until their presence became highlighted by productivity agreements, I used to hide them in cubby-hole offices where they did not draw attention to themselves and spent their nights sub-editing Letters to the Editor or attempting to write leading articles which often had to be rewritten.

I have abiding memories of two particular cases. One was that before I took over the Irish editor was only paid half what other executives of the same standing, such as the literary editor and foreign editor, received. The post was deemed to be one occupied for love of the language only. The other was that of an old Republican called Paddy Clare, the 'night town man' for over thirty years. He remained on duty throughout the night until near dawn checking hospitals and fire stations and recording what befell during darkness. A great reporter and 'character', he was justly famous for the scoops he brought off and the times he saved the paper from being beaten by rivals, often with large staffs on duty. But he was never placed on the permanent staff, and around 1974 fetched up with an ex gratia pension of £1,500 a year. A few years later he rang me up to tell me he had a lung complaint which was making the Irish winters intolerable for him. Could his pension be augmented by an extra £5 per week which would enable him, living cheaply, to winter in Spain? My representations on his behalf were turned down. 'Frugal comfort' could mean different things to the de Valeras and to those who served them.

A biographer fastened on a statement of de Valera's during the Dail debate on the *Irish Press* and paying the bondholders: 'The Irish people know full well that I personally never got one penny out of anything I did as far as Ireland was concerned.'[20] She wrote:[21]

Nor did his son Vivion, who became a director, receive any money from the newspaper. There never had been any expectation, Cosgrave's supporters went on, that the money should be repaid to the bondholders. Not to be deflected, Dev held out that the original pledges must be repaid, that no one was going to prevent the *Irish Press* from getting what was legally due in the process, and in his complicated financial scheme he won. He now had a newspaper in daily circulation to serve as Fianna Fail's mouth piece.

Joseph Connolly, who became a director of the *Irish Press*, said of the new paper's importance to de Valera and to Fianna Fail:[22]

The early morning of 5th September, 1931, when the first copies of the *Irish Press* began to come off the machines, was a memorable one for de Valera, probably the most notable date in his diary next to Easter Monday, 1916. The new paper gave an added impetus to the already considerable growth of Fianna Fail all over the country. While it adhered firmly to its motto of 'The Truth in the News', it was nevertheless frankly a party paper and as such was zealous in spreading the gospel of Fianna Fail. . . . It was the necessary coping stone to all the speeches, lectures and propaganda of the movement.

De Valera's extraordinary ability to mask what he was doing from even his closest associates was demonstrated by his handling of his and Connolly's association with the paper. One of his methods of impressing the public with the new administration's honesty had been to announce before forming a Government that no member of the Ministry would continue to hold directorships in any commercial concern. In pursuance of this edict Connolly, after discussion with de Valera, resigned his *Irish Press* directorship. His memoirs note with approval that de Valera also resigned as chairman. Connolly evidently had not realized that de Valera still held the much more significant position of controlling director.

De Valera did indeed win the battle of the bond certificates for the *Irish Press*. In fact what he created was not a Fianna Fail, but a de Valera 'mouthpiece'. When Bromage's biography, quoted above, was published, in 1956, far from not receiving any money from the paper, his son Vivion had progressed from his unpaid directorship of 1933 to being the well-paid managing director of the company. Three years later he succeeded his father as controlling director and he would one day pass on the lucrative newspaper group to his own son, Eamonn. But to follow the fortunes of the *Irish Press* further at this stage would take us too far ahead in our story. Let us return now to the turbulence of the Oath and land annuities controversies of the 1930s.

These, and some related issues which we will encounter later, like the Governor-General controversy, the Blueshirts upheaval and the enactment of the Constitution of 1937, were in fact outcroppings of de Valera's row with Griffith and Collins over the Treaty – attempts to implement his external association theories to prove himself right and his opponents wrong. In fact, everything he did was within the framework of the state and the opportunities created by the Treaty. In office he created a mini-rerun of the Anglo-Irish war, a war of words, bullocks and butter rather than one of bombs and bullets. It was a war which highlights the bloody futility and harmful consequences of the civil war he helped to create by his rejection of the 'stepping stone' argument.

Naturally de Valera's election was viewed with both interest and apprehension in London. His election campaign and subsequent radio broadcasts to America had left the British in little doubt that he intended to take action over the Oath and annuities issues. Nevertheless his first contact with a senior British official was encouraging. On 14 March 1932 he received William Peters, the British trade representative in Dublin. Peters reported that de Valera 'was not a firebrand'. He wanted an 'independent Ireland on the best of terms with her neighbour'. Peters told de Valera that, now that he had access 'to all the relevant facts', he would be able to 'appreciate that the "hidden hand"' of Britain so often referred to did not exist. In reply de Valera barefacedly disclaimed any anti-British sentiment and, without using so many words, made the remarkable admission that he appreciated what his predecessors had achieved but that he dare not say so publicly: 'He said he had never been one of those who attributed everything to any "hidden hand". He sitting in the centre of things in the Government could appreciate the degree of independence enjoyed but no statesman could go out to the people and tell them this because he simply would not be believed.'

What de Valera did not say was that he was perfectly free to 'go out to the people'. But he could not do so and enjoy 'extremist support'. However, Peters reported to the Dominions Office[23] that he was 'pleasantly surprised' by de Valera, at his 'absence of heaviness and the glint of humour in his eye'. Another Dublin correspondent who offered his assistance was Dr R. J. Oldham, principal medical officer of the Ministry of Pensions in Ireland. He proposed his appointment as a delegate to deal with de Valera because: 'I have the medical knowledge which I deem essential for dealing with the psychological problem presented by Mr de Valera's mind.'[24]

But the man in charge of the Dominions Office was not impressed by either trade or medical approaches. J. H. Thomas, the British Secretary of State for Dominion Affairs, made the British position on the Oath clear in an internal policy document:[25] 'In our own interests and also in loyalty to others, namely those who, like Mr. Kevin O'Higgins, have given their lives for the Treaty, and those who, like Mr. Cosgrave, have risked, and are still risking, their lives and political fortunes for it, we should stand absolutely by the sanctity of the Treaty. On this there should be no compromise; our attitude should be clear and definite.' With his mind running on these lines Thomas called in J. W. Dulanty, the Irish High Commissioner in London, to find out what de Valera intended doing. Dulanty was recalled to Dublin for a briefing and on 22 March 1932, reading from a prepared script,[26] formally stated to Thomas that the Oath was not mandatory under the Treaty. Amendments to the Constitution were 'purely a domestic matter'. Relaying the words of the Master, Dulanty said that relations between the two countries 'should naturally be close and friendly'. However: 'The abolition of the Oath was the principal and the dominating issue before the electors. It has been the cause of all the strife and dissension in the Irish Free State since the signing of the Treaty. The people, and not merely those who supported the policy of the present Government, regard it as an intolerable burden, a relic of mediaevalism, a test imposed from outside under threat of immediate and terrible war.'

Thomas replied to de Valera on 23 March that the British Government's view was: ' . . . that the Oath is an integral part of the Treaty made ten years ago between the two countries'. Furthermore, although de Valera had avoided mentioning the annuities issue in the presentation which he authorized Dulanty to make, Thomas stated that: ' . . . the Irish Free State Government are bound by the most formal and explicit undertaking to pay the land annuities to the National Debt Commissioners, and the failure to do so would be a manifest violation of an agreement which is binding in law and in honour on the Irish Free State, whatever administration may be in power, in exactly the same way as the Treaty itself is binding on both countries'.

Further cannonading across the Irish Sea in a manner reminiscent of the Lloyd George–de Valera exchange which preceded the Treaty negotiations failed to produce a meeting of minds. On 20 April de Valera introduced a Bill in the Dail to remove the Oath. Speaking on the 27th, he brazenly made use of the Cumann na nGaedheal achievements in the field of foreign affairs to justify his proposal. In furthering his case he made use of his predecessor's move to remove the appeals to the Privy Council and the achievement of the Statute of Westminster, and even went to the extent of quoting Michael Collins:

They proposed the removal of the article of the Constitution which provided for appeals to the English Privy Council. . . . The basis of their argument was that the status of the Free State was not fixed at a special period and kept there, and the fact that we had advanced was given recognition to, not very long ago, when the Statute of Westminster was passed. . . .

When the Treaty was being put before the old Dail, one of the arguments put forward in favour of it was that it gave freedom to achieve freedom. Are those who acted on that policy now going to say that there is to be a barrier – and a perpetual barrier – to achievement? Let the British say that if they choose. Why should any Irishman say it, particularly when it is not true?

It was an extraordinary, bare-faced demonstration of the use of de Valera fact, whereby truth could only be acknowledged when it suited him to do so. Now de Valera, who had used 'wading through blood' terminology in an effort to show that the Treaty was a barrier to freedom, had decided that the time had come to recognize it instead as a stepping stone to independence. He was even prepared to adapt the famous Collins argument to his purpose 'In my opinion, it [the Treaty] gives us freedom, not the ultimate freedom that all nations desire and develop to, but the freedom to achieve it.'[27] Unsurprisingly, if somewhat ignobly, the Opposition were not prepared to assist him on the road to Damascus,[28] and there was a parliamentary battle royal before he forced the measure through the Dail on 19 May 1932 with the aid of Labour. The Opposition centred their arguments on his failure to negotiate with the British on the issue; the fear of what form British reaction might take; and the sanctity of existing agreements. Fundamentally, however, the Opposition was in a weak position, because though they were naturally enraged at de Valera's stealing of their electoral clothes, the logic of their position was that they were opposing him for adopting their policies. This remained a crippling weakness for Cumann na nGaedheal throughout the thirties, driving them to adopt ever more pro-British positions and thus abandoning the high ground of nationalism to de Valera.

When the Bill went to the Senate for ratification on 25 May 1932 reservations were also voiced about the wisdom of not negotiating with the British. Nor was much credence placed on de Valera's argument that once the Oath went the Republicans who still did not recognize the Parliament would drop their objections to the legitimacy of the state.[29] The irrepressible Senator Oliver St John Gogarty managed to transform the issue of the Oath into a dissertation on the qualities needed in a Republican leader, who, he said, would have to dress:[30] 'like the manager of the Cats' Home; he had to look grave; he had to be filled with the milk of human kindness, but touched withal by a gentle melancholy on account of the dope he must administer in the end'. Irrepressible, but not irreplaceable. De Valera's anger was roused by the Senate's decision to use its powers of delay to hold up the Bill, which took a year and another election before passing into law on 3 May 1933. He gave a broad hint[31] that if the Oath were not abolished the Senate would be; and, as we shall see, this threat was ultimately put into practice.

However, the Oath disappeared into the dustbin of history a good deal faster than did the annuities issue, which lasted from 1932 to 1938. Apart from involving Ireland and England in economic warfare, with very unpleasant consequences for both sides, the dispute helped to revive civil war passions with pro- and anti-Treaty forces, represented by the IRA and followers of Eoin O'Duffy, clashing both with each other and with the Government. We have seen how Thomas bracketed the annuities and the Oath issues in the exchanges described earlier. In his reply of 5 April 1932,[32] de Valera asked what was the basis of the British assertion that the Irish had given an 'explicit' undertaking to pay the land annuities. He claimed that: 'The Government of the Irish Free State is not aware of any such undertaking, but the British Government can rest assured that any just and lawful claims of Great Britain, or of any creditor of the Irish Free State, will be scrupulously honoured by its Government.' In his reply, dated 9 April, Thomas professed himself to be 'at a loss' as to how de Valera could be unaware of the justice of the British position. Thomas drew attention to the heads of the Ultimate Financial Settlement of 1926, which we have already encountered, arising out of the Boundary Commission Settlement. He pointed out that the Ultimate Settlement confirmed the Financial Agreement of 12 February 1923 between the British and Irish Governments, in which the Irish had agreed to pay 'the full amount of the annuities'. The first item in the Ultimate Financial Settlement read: 'The Government of the Irish Free State undertake to pay to the British Government at agreed intervals the full amount of the annuities accruing from time to time under the Irish Land Acts, 1891–1909, without any deduction whatsoever on account of income tax or otherwise.'

De Valera had already taken legal advice on the 1926 document and had been confirmed in his view that the annuities payments were not legally binding.[33] Similar annuities were being retained by the Six County Government; and, moreover, the Agreement had not been ratified by the Dail. But the Thomas reference to the 1923 Agreement started a fresh hare. De Valera ordered a search to be made for this document, and it was eventually discovered in a 'Secret' file in a very dilapidated condition. De Valera later told the Dail:[34] 'It is literally in tatters, half-pages, parts of pages not typed, interlineations and so on. Honestly I never saw a contract of any kind presented in such a form. There is not even an Irish signature to it.' Cosgrave had apparently signed the British copy. But the 1923 Agreement's strange features did not end there. De Valera subsequently told a public meeting in Dun Laoghaire[35] that the Cosgrave Government had refused a British request that the document be published in connection with a court case heard in 1925. Agreement to having the document presented in court was only granted on condition that the portion dealing with the land annuities be pasted over. Later still, in 1931, the Cosgrave administration had concealed the existence of the document from its own lawyers.

Where his British opponents were concerned, de Valera developed some different ammunition. He argued that the Ultimate Settlement only referred to the land annuities insofar as it freed them from Irish income tax. Furthermore, even if it was ratified – which it was not – it only made Ireland liable under the 1923 Agreement. But these liabilities had been cancelled by the 1925 Boundary Commission settlement, which had ended Irish obligations[36] to the British public debt. Legalistically speaking, de Valera's position was thus not unjustifiable. Politically and emotionally, whatever his opponents might argue about the sanctity of agreements, the Irish public were mindful of the fact that the annuities question arose over land which had been confiscated by force from the natives in the first place. Chamberlain was uneasily conscious of the risk that 'an arbitrator might hold that Mr. de Valera is right from a purely legal and technical point of view'.[37] But the British were determined to stand on the high Imperial ground. What was done in Dublin was noted in the Dominions, Egypt and India. The nomenclature used in the Thomas–de Valera exchanges accurately reflects the differing philosophies of the Irish and the British. De Valera wrote on behalf of 'The Government of the Irish Free State'; Thomas, on behalf of 'His Majesty's Government in the United Kingdom', addressed himself to 'His Majesty's Government in the Irish Free State'.

On 11 May 1932 Thomas fired a shot across de Valera's bows in the House of Commons. He read a tough statement, drafted by Chamberlain, saying in effect that if the Treaty were abrogated by the removal of the Oath the British would make no further agreements with Dublin – in other words with de Valera. There have been suggestions[38] that this statement was prompted by urgings from Cosgrave that the British should take a firm line with de Valera. But it was very much in line with overall British policy of the time, albeit heightened by a feeling in Whitehall that one of Britain's arch-enemies was now installed in power across the Irish Sea. De Valera refused to be intimidated. Only after he had shunted the Oath Bill through the Dail, to what everyone realized was but a temporary siding in the Senate, did he deign to take heed of the Noises Off emanating from London. He did so with a characteristic hauteur that won grudging admiration even from opponents of the calibre of his critical biographer, Denis Gwynn:[39]

He announced that he was quite willing to discuss the matter, but that the British Government which claimed the annuities must send delegates to Dublin to state its case. . . . Not since Parnell had any Irish leader adopted so high-handed an attitude. . . . Cosgrave and his friends appeared as timid and futile Ministers who had never dared even to put forward the claims which de Valera was triumphantly vindicating. For years they had tried to frighten the country into believing that such questions could not even be discussed without provoking disaster.

De Valera's stock soared even higher when two real live British Cabinet ministers showed up in Dublin on 6 June. 'They were to confine themselves only to stating their case for payment of the land annuities. That, at least, was the general interpretation put upon the carefully worded formula of their mission.'[40] The two ministers were Thomas and Lord Hailsham. The latter, apart from a record of hostility towards the claims of Irish nationalism, was also the Minister for War; the implicit threat contained in his portfolio helped to push up the public temperature, but it also served to underline de Valera's daring. However, the actual meeting was something of a damp squib. De Valera and Sean T. O'Ceallaigh conferred inconclusively with the two Englishmen on 7 June for about an hour and a half. No progress was made beyond arranging for a continuation of the talks in London three days later. The British account[41] of the encounter contains a monumental misjudgement of de Valera's character. He was described as: 'A complete dreamer with no grasp of realities'. Nothing could have been further from the truth. Joseph Connolly described de Valera's work rate and application in his early years of Government in these words:[42] 'De Valera, working from early morning until the early hours of each succeeding day, never let up. Save for the few hours of sleep he snatched, it was a continuous round of work. From a meeting of the Cabinet over to the Dail and from there back to his office desk. We all felt the strain but by far the greatest burden rested on him and only an iron constitution could have carried it.'

The London meeting did not result in a reconsideration of this verdict. The British fielded a larger team, which augmented the presence of Hailsham and Thomas with that of the Prime Minister, Ramsay MacDonald, the Conservative leader, Stanley Baldwin, and the Home Secretary, Herbert Samuel. De Valera and O'Ceallaigh were accompanied by the Secretaries of the two Departments which de Valera represented – Sean Moynihan of the President's office and Joseph Walshe of External Affairs – and by John Dulanty, the Irish High Commissioner in London. Once again de Valera raised the issue of external association, this time by suggesting that both parts of Ireland would probably agree to be freely associated with Great Britain once a Thirty-two County Ireland had been declared. This was not what the British Cabinet representatives wished to hear from the leader of His Majesty's Government in the Irish Free State. Nor did they wish to be told that 'come what might'[43] the Oath was doomed. Thomas warned de Valera:[44] 'Don't think, Mr. President, that the day you declare a republic you will be met by British guns and battleships; you will be faced with the possibility of your people in England being aliens – with the return to your country of thousands of civil servants and thousands of unemployed people now receiving public assistance. That will be Great Britain's answer, and it is for you to realise it.'

Republicanism apart, the British felt that they had the same right to the annuities in particular as they had to their Empire in general. Giving up the one established a precedent for the other. De Valera was informed that if by 16 July the annuities were not handed over they would be recouped by the imposition of a 20 per cent tariff on Irish imports. The British were willing to have the issue decided upon by arbitration, but they wished the arbitrators to be drawn from the Commonwealth countries. De Valera, mindful of the role of the South African, Feetham, during the Boundary Commission debacle, proposed instead the International Court at The Hague. Despatches exchanged between the two sides[45] failed to resolve the issue. De Valera adopted a hard man, soft man approach. On 2 July he informed Thomas that the dispute was 'not only in regard to the Land Purchase Annuities but in regard to all other annual or periodic payments, except those made in pursuance of agreements formally ratified by the Parliament of both states'. The other 'annual or periodic payments' included RIC pensions, judicial and civil pensions and a variety of other payments arising under several different Acts. However, on the 4th he informed Thomas that the disputed monies were not being withheld, but merely placed in suspense accounts pending arbitration.

On 14 July he sanctioned the acceptance of an invitation to London from the rising Labour front-bencher, Sir Stafford Cripps, to the Labour leader William Norton. He told Norton:[46] 'We are prepared to accept a Commission of four (two nominated by each party) to receive evidence and prepare a report on all the facts and circumstances which either party may wish to lay before them relating to the financial disputes and differences between the Irish Free State and Great Britain, this report to be the basis of negotiation for a settlement and you can so inform Sir Stafford Cripps.' The British did not accept this proposal, but the Cripps invitation resulted in de Valera's going to London the next day. The newspapers reported that as he alighted from his train at Euston at 5.30 p.m. a demonstrator called out: 'Who killed Mike Collins?' The catcall had the same sort of wounding irrelevancy to the course of the dispute as did de Valera's subsequent heated meeting with Ramsay MacDonald.

De Valera at first refused to go to Downing Street unless he could see the Prime Minister alone. MacDonald demanded that the Lord Chancellor and Attorney General be present. De Valera countered by stating that he would not go unless he could see the Prime Minister alone, 'at any rate in the first instance'.[47] MacDonald agreed to this. In all, the Downing Street meetings lasted for over three hours. They concluded with the issuing of a communiqué which said that 'neither party was able to depart from the position taken up on the published dispatches'. MacDonald did see de Valera alone for an initial fifteen minutes, but had to leave for about an hour to attend a dinner, leaving de Valera with the Chancellor and the Attorney General. In the course of the acrimonious discussions MacDonald denied that he had asked de Valera to come to London, and de Valera accused the British of trying to force him into an election defeat. He warned the British that this was a 'profound mistake'. The Irish people were in a 'resolute mood'. Neither side would accept the other's terms for settlement. In the words of an official record, de Valera:[48] '. . . made it

451

plain that he wished to go behind the two agreements of 1923 and 1926, stating that he was of opinion that a fair settlement would not merely leave the Irish Free State under no liability to make any payment but would require the British Government to pay a considerable sum to the Irish Free State'.

Less stilted accounts[49] quote him as threatening the British with trouble from the Irish miners in the Lancashire coalfields. This proved the breaking point in the talks. As de Valera stalked out, MacDonald called after him that he hoped they would meet again. No doubt mindful of his own dictum that the greatest danger in negotiations is reasonableness, De Valera replied: 'I don't think so.' MacDonald's verdict was that: 'So long as de Valera is there, there is no way out.' Seeing de Valera as a man who relished the notion of violent confrontation to achieve his aims, he wrote:

> Behind it all is the romance of force and of arms – shooting, murdering and being murdered. It is the gay adventure of the fool put into a china shop in hobnail boots with liberty to smash.
>
> He begins somewhere about the birth of Christ and wants a commission of four picked solely to give individual opinions and all he demands is a document, a manifesto, a judgement as from God himself as to how the world, and more particularly Ireland, should have been ruled when they were cutting each other's throats and writing beautiful missives at the same time. It makes one sick.

And so began the economic war. The annuities were not paid on the following day. The British implemented the threatened 20 per cent levy, and the Irish responded with similar levies on British goods coming into Ireland. On the face of it, the dispute should have destroyed both de Valera and Fianna Fáil, for at the time Britain accounted for some 96 per cent of Irish exports. At one stage in the hostilities de Valera declared openly that this market was 'gone for ever'.[50] Yet, incredibly, the economic war worked in his favour. More accurately, he made it work by a portfolio of measures in which he made use of patronage, the Pope, propaganda, protection and a variety of doles, grants and subsidies; Mayor Curley of Boston could not have bettered de Valera's use of the state's revenues to purchase popularity.

In his first year in office he increased public spending by roughly 20 per cent, from approximately £24 million to £29 million. The money went to unemployment relief in a number of areas, including housing, road works, health care and the provision of free milk for schoolchildren. Agricultural rates were cut and subsidies used to cushion the effects of the British duties on agricultural exports, chiefly cattle, butter, eggs and pig meat. The bigger farmers, those hardest hit by the tariff blizzard, were largely Cumann na nGaedheal supporters anyhow. But amongst the smaller men the reduction of the annuities, and the funding of arrears for three years or longer, won many hearts and minds. The grumbles at the slaughter of the unsaleable calves of the bigger farmers were counterbalanced by the plaudits of the poor who benefited from the distribution of free meat. Efforts to encourage arable farming, so as to make the state self-sufficient in food production, notably flour, were not in the long run successful, but they helped to divert attention from the effects of the crisis.

An unlikely alliance with Fianna Fail was forged, between the poor and the would-be businessmen, through a vigorous industrialization policy spearheaded by Sean Lemass. In de Valera's first year in office protective duties were imposed on no fewer than forty-three different categories of imports. But the protection/subsidy policy had its drawbacks. The consumer was often exploited by the newly created Irish entrepreneur who could get away with shoddy goods and services in the absence of competition. The doles and subsidies encouraged a dependency culture amongst small farmers, particularly in the Fianna Fail stronghold of the Irish-speaking west. Here a tradition of appalling poverty was somewhat alleviated, from the 1932 election onwards, by the giving of small hand-outs for all sorts of things including speaking the Irish language. The language was not revived, but, cynics averred, children's first English phrase became: 'How do I get the grant?' However, overall, although much of the subsidization was introduced on an ad hoc basis to counter the effects of the British tariffs, there was a benign and lasting core to early Fianna Fail policy. It put a human face on Government that was lacking in its predecessors.

De Valera also saw to it that his Government wore a pious face in the run-up to the annuities confrontation. The thirty-first International Eucharistic Congress was held in Dublin in June 1932, and de Valera and his ministers derived untold benefit from the principle of piety by association. Newspapers were filled with pictures and descriptions of the once excommunicated Warriors of Destiny hobnobbing with cardinals and bishops. De Valera personally welcomed the Papal Legate, Cardinal Lauri, on his arrival at Dun Laoghaire on 20 June. At a gala reception in Dublin Castle the next day he extended felicitations to the Legate in a manner which adroitly suggested both that the Pope was on the side of Fianna Fail and that the Warriors were his loyal children. After recalling how for centuries the Irish had repeatedly suffered through war, and, significantly, confiscation, he declared:[51] 'But repeatedly also did the successors of St. Peter most willingly come to our aid, in the persons of Gregory XIII, Clement VIII, Paul V, Urban VIII, Innocent X and many others of the line of Roman Pontiffs down to the present day. Today with no less favour and good will, His Holiness, Pope Pius XI has turned his august regard to our country. . . .'

He went on to remind his hearers that the occasion also commemorated the apostolic mission to Ireland of the national saint, St Patrick. 'Who,' he asked, 'can fail on this day to recall to mind the utterance of our apostle, recorded of old in the Book of Armagh: Even as you are children of Christ, be you also *children of Rome* [author's italics]'. His subsequent course of action indicates that he was aware of the significance of the fact that Cardinal Lauri's rise to Eminence followed a sojourn at Rome's College of Propaganda. Where propaganda was concerned, de Valera had little to learn from the Vatican. He organized well-attended meetings throughout the country, preaching a gospel, faithfully disseminated by the *Irish Press*, compounded in equal parts of appeals to patriotism, mythology, anti-British sentiment, support for a Buy Irish campaign and – his own particular brand of mathematics. This last was particularly effective. He proved to his own satisfaction that the £5 million involved in the annuities issue was the equivalent of £330 million in British terms. As a contemporary wrote:[52] 'The figure was certainly impressive; and the agitation in Ireland has since been kept up in the belief that de Valera is fighting to abolish a foreign tribute which is equivalent to almost half what the English tax-payers have to pay in their whole Budget.'

'What is there in this fight?' he thundered at a Fianna Fail Ard Fheis.[53] 'There is this in it, that, if the British Government should succeed in beating us in this fight, then you could have no freedom, because at every step they could threaten you again and force you again to obey the British. What is involved is whether the Irish nation is going to be free or not.' He made that speech the day after Sean Lemass sent him a memo[54] warning him that the country was facing 'a crisis as grave as that of 1847 [the year of the Great Famine] and I feel strongly that our present efforts are totally inadequate to cope with it'. But de Valera was not directing his appeal to the present. As Dr Ryle Dwyer has written, de Valera:[55]

> ... exploited historical tradition to instil in the people a pride in their Irishness and a sense of their own greatness, which had a distinct appeal to many of those raised as part of the British Empire. . . . The strength of his appeal was not found in magnetic oratory or in the logic of his message, but in the passionate sincerity he projected. . . .
>
> Those who did not believe in what he was saying were nevertheless convinced he believed it himself. As a former teacher he knew the value of simplicity and repetition, and he used his own political calendar of anniversaries to trot out again and again various myths about Ireland's past glories, cultural greatness, spiritual resilience and the indomitable determination of her people to secure their freedom against overwhelming odds.

Add in a few black cloaks, white horses and torchlight processions, and the Eamon de Valera Show was a very tough act indeed for his adversaries to follow. He made it even tougher through his use of a laser-beamed instinct for the political jugular that he sometimes used to cut through the aura of sanctity, sincerity and Celtic mythology with sudden, devastating effect. Such an occasion was looming up in the New Year of 1933. De Valera faced trouble on both the constitutional and unconstitutional fronts. Overall, rhetoric and placebo remedies were proving to have their limitations in cushioning the effects of the economic war and of the Great Depression. In the Dail a new and threatening coalition of forces was forming as a result of the annuities crisis. On 6 October 1932, two leading independents had come together to form a new political party. These were James Dillon, a son of John Dillon who had succeeded John Redmond as leader of the Irish Parliamentary Party, and Frank MacDermott, an ex-British Army officer and New York banker. Their new National Centre Party, largely representative of the larger farmers, had the settlement of the annuities dispute as one of its foremost aims. MacDermott, who was selected as leader, found wide support for his view that partition could only be addressed when Dublin–London relationships were normalized. He argued that, whatever the merits, or demerits, of leaving the Commonwealth, there was nothing to be said in favour of remaining in while having the drawbacks of being outside.[56] Concurrent with this development, a feeling began to grow that the time had come for a more powerful new party to be formed by amalgamating all the existing constitutional opposition parties on a basis of friendship with Great Britain and independence within the Commonwealth. This idea was articulated in a letter to the papers on 28 December 1932 from Senator Vincent, the leader of the independents in the Senate. The following day the Lord Mayor of Dublin convened a meeting in the Mansion House at which representative professional men passed a resolution endorsing this idea. Meanwhile the highly unconstitutional opposition party, the IRA, were becoming more and more of a problem. De Valera knew that as the economic war bit deeper both forms of opposition were bound to grow stronger. His reliance on the Labour Party was becoming irksome. According to Gallagher it was J. H. Thomas who prompted him to take action. The Dominions Secretary made a speech on the annuities issue in which he questioned de Valera's right to act for the whole Dail when he had only 72 members out of 153.[57]

De Valera decided to nip in the bud all threats to his position. Without telling anyone of his intentions – least of all his colleagues – he called a snap general election four days after the Mansion House meeting, on 2 January. 'He sent for each Minister individually and informed him of his decision. It came to them as a great surprise, as they had not suffered a defeat in the House and a dissolution might in fact jeopardise the position of the party.'[58] His opponents were caught off balance when he made his decision public at a dramatic midnight press conference. Their disequilibrium was added to by his election pledge to cut farmers' annuity payments by half. And lest anyone should think that his months in Government had been sullied by any whiff of communism, the *Irish Press* assured its readers that:[59] 'there is not a social or economic change Fianna Fail has proposed or brought about which has not its fullest justification in the encyclicals of either Leo XIII or the present Pontiff'.

However, as the campaign progressed, further disbursements on the social front were promised by Fianna Fail. The *Irish Press* was able to claim that the party was the only one which cared for the poor.[60] As a result, one

Conservative opponent of de Valera's noted in horror that:[61] 'It was the first general election held in Ireland in which class issues were raised.' But the appeal to poor, pocket and Pope had their effect. On polling day, 24 January, de Valera gained five seats and, as the economic war worsened, could thus confront his enemies with increased rather than diminished strength – not a bad result for a 'complete dreamer with no grasp of realities'. But before proceeding to examine how he exercised his new mandate, it is necessary to return briefly to our examination of how he exercised his old one. Linked to the annuities and Oath issues was the question of the Governor General.

De Valera's intention to demean, and eventually dispose, of this office first came to public attention through an incident at the French Legation on 23 April 1932. Earlier, he had privately informed the IRA leadership,[62] as part of his effort to win that organization's support for his programme, that he intended to make a Sean naScuab[63] out of the Governor General. But at the Legation the Governor General's arrival was taken as the occasion for a calculated snub by the two Fianna Fail ministers present, Sean T. O'Ceallaigh and Frank Aiken, who left as soon as he arrived. Naturally the incident made the papers, the report in the *Irish Press* being the most significant. Its version of events read: 'Later the Governor-General arrived. This was a surprise, and Mr. O'Kelly and Mr. Aiken then left.'

The official British position, of course, was that Aiken and O'Ceallaigh were part of 'His Majesty's Government in the Irish Free State', a Government which had received its seal of approval from the Governor General. After the *Irish Press* report appeared, McNeill wrote to de Valera on 26 April complaining about:[64] '... a considered policy that the Governor-General be treated with deliberate discourtesy by members of your Council and by the newspaper which you control'. De Valera's reply was uncompromising: 'As regards the Ministers; the incident was no less embarrassing for them than for the Governor-General, and the publicity which ensued might have seriously affected the public interest. . . .' He went on to make McNeill an offer which he could not accept: 'If the Governor-General's social engagements are communicated to me in advance, such an incident will certainly not occur in the future.' Decoded, this read: 'Please co-operate with the Government in organizing a boycott of your functions.' McNeill declined to co-operate and in his reply, on 2 May, continued to press for an apology: ' . . . not merely on my personal or official account, but with regard to the honour and self-respect of Irish public life'. No apology was forthcoming; de Valera's reply merely stated that: 'he regarded the whole affair as unfortunate and regrettable, and one that should not have been permitted to occur. Further than this I am unable to go.' Later in the month more friction arose – or more accurately, was generated by de Valera – over the Governor General's position.

McNeill had made long-standing arrangements to invite some dignitaries to stay with him in the Viceregal Lodge during the Eucharistic Congress.

Although he had sought clarification on how the incoming administration would regard his issuing such invitations, de Valera delayed giving a decision until McNeill had committed himself to inviting his guests. Then External Affairs informed him that the invitations were an embarrassment to the Government. McNeill wrote to de Valera on 24 May protesting at the delay in telling him where he stood. But the only tangible result was two further snubs. Neither McNeill, nor his party, was invited to the state reception in Dublin Castle at which de Valera invoked the Pope's influence on his policies. He was invited to a civic reception given by the Lord Mayor at the Mansion House, but when Aiken was informed of this he refused to allow the army band to play there.

McNeill waited until the Congress was over before writing to inform de Valera, on 7 May, that unless he got his apology the correspondence would be published. De Valera formally directed him not to do so, but on 10 July McNeill had the letters delivered to newspaper offices. De Valera sent police around in their wake warning against publication. He succeeded in intimidating the Irish papers, but Fleet Street was unbowed and the correspondence appeared in Britain. De Valera made an unsuccessful attempt to prevent the British papers being distributed in Ireland. When this failed, he issued an authorization for publication in Irish newspapers also, and the full correspondence duly appeared in the columns of the Irish dailies on 12 July. The dispute then followed a subterranean course for some time.

Using the path of direct access to the monarch opened by his predecessors in Government, de Valera had a submission[65] made to the King on 9 September 1932 asking that McNeill's appointment be terminated and that the Irish Chief Justice, Hugh Kennedy, should carry out his functions until a successor was appointed. By now the British Prime Minister, Ramsay MacDonald, was more inclined to take a Thomas view where de Valera was concerned than a Peters one. His irritation surfaced in a letter to the Archbishop of York[66] on 13 September; it contained an assessment of de Valera (which incidentally, as we shall see, appears not to have been studied by MacDonald's son, Malcolm, prior to his subsequent dealings with de Valera). MacDonald said that, like Gandhi, de Valera possessed:

> . . . a mentality which simply baffles one in its lack of reason. Whatever he may have said to one or two people who have gone to him strenuously desiring peace, the position is that where we have tried to get him to face the real facts of the situation he refuses to do so, and his generalities about goodwill have no existence in reality. His undisclosed actions (although some of them came out in rather an unpleasant prominence during the Eucharistic Congress [i.e. the McNeill affair]) really are the key to his mind. He will do nothing except what is a step to an Irish Republic and is undoubtedly a complete prisoner to the Irish Republican Army . . . we are doing everything we can to get something done, but up to now, Dev does not budge.

The British did try to get 'something done'. The King's reply to de

Valera suggested a compromise: McNeill should be allowed to resign and given longer notice to vacate his office – he had held the post since 1928, and in any event his term expired on 3 February 1933. De Valera agreed and instructed the Irish High Commissioner in London, Dulanty, to inform the King that if McNeill resigned by 1 October 1932, he could stay on for two more weeks, until the 15th. This was acceptable to the King, but not to McNeill. When Dulanty, who had been instructed by de Valera to bell the cat, called on McNeill to advise him to resign, the Governor General dug in his heels and announced that he was going to the King himself. However, the King too advised him to resign. McNeill then did so, on 2 October, managing to prise another two weeks out of de Valera before his resignation took effect on 1 November. Now de Valera's plans hit a snag: Kennedy demurred at taking the oaths involved. He told de Valera:[67] 'If the Chief Justice, or if a group of Judges, were to be constituted the King's agent in the Saorstat [state], I believe that the prestige of the Courts would be greatly damaged and they would be exposed to a species of attack which would seriously shake, if not destroy, their authority.'

When the Dominions Office was informally apprized of Kennedy's objections it 'chose to convey an almost official "objection" to any procedure which would allow the Chief Justice to act without first taking the prescribed oaths'.[68] The Irish riposted, again informally, by telling the Dominions Office that the question of informing the King about the Governor Generalship 'was not one in which British Government had any standing or interest'.[69] Two further Irish stratagems failed: first, that the Chief Justice be appointed to act as Governor General on a form of royal warrant which would permit him to act by virtue of his existing office. As this would not have met Kennedy's objections to the effect of the Governor Generalship on the prestige of the courts, it becomes increasingly obvious that de Valera had entered the lists without giving much thought to how he was going to get out of them. The British also vetoed his next proposal, namely that a Commission be set up consisting of the Chairmen of the Dail and Senate – and himself. When this idea landed in Whitehall:[70] 'objections to a Commission which would include the President of the Executive Council were raised . . . the British Government gave obstructive advice to the King in the matter'. It is difficult to envisage a British Cabinet giving any other sort of advice to a King concerning a proposal that Eamon de Valera take on the duties of Governor General.

However, having tried once more, unsuccessfully, to put pressure[71] on Kennedy to act in an interim capacity, de Valera finally resolved the situation by adopting a proposal made by an Englishman to Kennedy. Alarmed at newspaper reports that either he or a panel of judges might be called on to adopt the duties of Governor General, Kennedy had sent a memorandum to de Valera on 6 October. It contained the following:[72]

I happened, some years ago, to discuss the Office of Governor-General with an Englishman who formerly held a position of great importance and influence

[Kennedy said he could not divulge his name. It may have been Birkenhead, who had died not long before the memo was written]. . . . I mentioned to him that one of the great objections in Ireland to the Vice-Regal and Governor-General position was the inevitable re-creating of the old sham Court, gathering round it all the hovering sycophants and certain social types alien to the National life of the country and the rotting effect of this on social life generally by creating false social values and distracting from National realities. . . .

He said to me, 'Why should not the Office be conducted as a purely formal office by a man residing in an ordinary residence in the city, say in Fitzwilliam Square, in such circumstances that nothing of that kind could arise. Then there should be no expectations created either of entertainment or social privilege, round the position. He should be an officer with a bureau for transacting the specific business with which he was entrusted, and his Office would begin and end there.

De Valera thanked Kennedy for the suggestion, saying:[73] 'I appreciate the importance of the matter in question, and if your idea can be worked out it would be of very great value.' Having failed to persuade Kennedy to take up the post, de Valera decided on 25 November that the 'officer with a bureau idea' could be 'worked out'. The King was advised that the Government had decided to appoint as Governor General a colourless Fianna Fail supporter, Donal O'Buachalla, who had been defeated in far more electoral contests than he had ever won. In line with his policy of using to the maximum the advances made by his predecessors, de Valera directed that:[74] 'the Signet Seal to be used on the Commission will be that approved by His Majesty for use in the Irish Free State'. Next day the requisite oaths were administered to O'Buachalla by Kennedy, in Irish and in the presence of only two officials. Instead of moving into the Viceregal Lodge O'Buachalla, a retired Maynooth shopkeeper, was installed in a modest Dublin house, as suggested by Kennedy's anonymous English friend, and functioned purely as outlined in the Kennedy memo. In place of McNeill's £24,000, O'Buachalla received only £2,000 a year for the remaining four years that the Governor Generalship continued in being. And so the symbol of British rule in Ireland was removed at the suggestion of an Englishman, redounding greatly to the credit of Eamon de Valera on the grounds of both national prestige and economy.

Of course the question which logically arises in the Governor General issue, as with so many other constitutional advances made under de Valera, is: could the office not have been disposed of without all the rancour and controversy? The answer is that of course it could, but one may as well ask whether all the constitutional progress he made could have come about without the civil war. De Valera had made a nice calculation that the confrontational method, wherein he could be portrayed in heroic guise, taking on the might of Empire, carried greater electoral advantage for him than the 'sanctity of agreements' approach of his predecessors. The support he would lose amongst the staid he would more than make up for amongst the poor and the radically inclined. Like the battle of Waterloo, it was a close-run thing, as the development of the National Centre Party, and the subsequent Mansion House protest, showed. But de Valera's boldness and sense of timing in calling the January election proved to be the decisive factors.

21
DE VALERA STANDS TALL

DURING HIS EVENTFUL first term in office de Valera also played a controversial but non-partisan role in the wider arena of external relations, that of the League of Nations, which brought credit to his own and his country's reputation. As we saw, the Free State had been elected to the Council of the League in 1930. The result in terms of de Valera's prestige was akin to the timing of the Eucharistic Congress. As matters fell out, the Irish were accorded by rote both the presidency of the Council and the acting presidency of the Assembly for the thirteenth session of the League at Geneva in September 1932.

Since he was the man chosen to accompany de Valera to Geneva, and to hold the fort there for him while de Valera returned to Dublin to look after Dail business, Connolly's views on his British adversaries were important in helping de Valera to decide his economic war strategy. They were not flattering. After an evening spent in the 'childish activity' of playing bagatelle with Ramsay MacDonald and Sir John Simon, Connolly declared himself: '. . . worse than bored. I had the staggering realisation that this man who had just been entertaining me was the Prime Minister of Britain and that his attendant henchman was Foreign Secretary. The former was either tired and exhausted or a completely spent force, and his Foreign Secretary was a "yes man" politician keeping in step without marching.'

De Valera's anti-League posture in America during his first tour was well known in Geneva, and when he rose to speak in the Assembly:[1] '. . . there was no handclap to welcome him. The formal politeness customarily shown to any chairman was absent.' He had been provided with a script prepared by the League Secretariat, but disregarded this in favour of a 'naught for your comfort' document of his own. It was received 'in stony silence'.[2] But this may simply have been due to the fact that his audience did not realize at first that he had finished. One correspondent adjudged him no orator:[3] 'He keeps his chin down, mumbles and stumbles over his lines, has no sense of the dramatic.' But in the lobbies afterwards his speech, and his courage in delivering it, were unreservedly praised.

He spoke against the background of the ongoing, and ultimately futile, Disarmament Conference; the impending, and equally futile, Economic and Monetary Conference in London the following year; and the continuing Japanese onslaught on Manchuria. His speech, made on 26 September 1932, combined the themes of the challenges facing the League, the expectations the world placed in it, the disappointing reality with which these expectations were met, and the fact that Ireland in particular wanted peace – 'In spite of the opinions you may have formed from misleading reports.' He said:[4]

> Out beyond the walls of this Assembly there is the public opinion of the world, and if the League is to prosper, or even survive, it must retain the support and confidence of that public opinion as a whole . . . People are becoming impatient and starting even to inquire whether the apparently meagre, face-saving results of successive League conferences and meetings justify the burden which contributions to the League Budget, and the expense of sending delegation after delegation to Geneva, impose upon the already overburdened national taxpayer . . . there is a suspicion abroad that little more than lip-service is paid to the fundamental principles on which the League is founded . . .
>
> Ladies and gentlemen, the one effective way of silencing criticism of the League, or bringing to its support millions who at present stand aside in apathy or look at its activities with undisguised cynicism, is to show unmistakably that the Covenant of the League is a solemn pact, the obligations of which no state, great or small, will find it possible to ignore.

Press coverage was divided as to the merits of his speech. The *Daily Express, Manchester Guardian* and *New York Herald Tribune* said that it was badly received. The last-named declared:[5] 'It was all true enough, but the words come with a strange sound from Mr. de Valera – himself the flaming embodiment of that excessive nationalism which more than any other single force has been responsible for the League's present state.' However, the *Daily Herald* thought that de Valera had made the 'best speech'[6] ever heard from a League President. The *New York Times*[7] reckoned that the speech, taken together with the way de Valera had presided over the Assembly's difficult deliberations on Manchuria, 'unquestionably made him the outstanding personality of this session'. Thus did de Valera seize the opportunity to make the point that it was not only the O'Higginses and the Fitzgeralds who could wear Ireland's colours with distinction on the international stage. And to ensure that no lingering accusations of hostility stemming from his anti-League utterances in the USA during his 1919–20 tours could be made against him, he gave a further address on 2 October[8] in which he made the point that he had spoken: 'Not as an enemy of the League but as one who wishes the League to be strengthened and developed as the best visible means of securing peace among the nations and of solving the major political and economic problems which face the world today'.

All this was fine and large and helped to win adherents to the swelling prologue of the Republican theme which de Valera sought to develop during his early days in office. A politician of his calibre understood full well the art of crafting speeches so that what was said abroad resounded satisfactorily at home. However, there was one section of the Republican fraternity which was not too impressed by either attendances at international conferences or valour shown at domestic receptions in the

462

teeth of oncoming Governors General – the IRA. As we have seen, the activities of this organization had resulted in a sizeable amount of bloodshed, turmoil and jailings in the run-up to the 1932 election in which de Valera first won power. Immediately on being confirmed in office by the Governor General, de Valera began paying his campaign dues for 'extremist support'. Within hours of being appointed Frank Aiken and James Geoghegan, the Ministers for Defence and Justice respectively, were despatched from Leinster House to the military prison at Arbour Hill. Every IRA man was visited in his cell. It was noted that Aiken spent a particularly long time talking to George Gilmore. The visit rang up the curtain on a stage which many in Cumann na nGaedheal, and in the police force, gazed upon with foreboding.

The day after the Aiken-Geoghegan visit, 10 March 1932, all the IRA prisoners were released to a tumultuous welcome on the streets of Dublin. Two days later the formerly banned IRA newspaper, *An Phoblacht*, was republished. More importantly, less than one week afterwards, on the 18th, the military tribunal was suspended and the orders which had rendered unlawful the IRA and a political organization formed from its ranks, Saor Eire, were both revoked. These developments took place while statements made at an IRA show of strength a few days earlier were still ringing in the ears of former members of the Government. On Sunday the 13th a huge demonstration had been held in the heart of Dublin, in College Green, to welcome home the prisoners. During the rally the IRA's Dublin Brigade were deployed in military formation, and Cumann na mBan appeared in uniform and Sam Browne belts. Sean MacBride told the meeting that, while the days of coercion were over, the IRA would not disband and intended to continue towards its objectives. But what really put Cumann na nGaedheal temperatures up was a statement by one speaker, Sean McGuinness, who declared that:[9] 'The members of the defunct Executive Council were ... a menace to society and the independence of Ireland, and it behoved all Republicans to unite and wipe out that menace at all costs.'

The IRA policy statements were not all that cheering for de Valera either. *An Phoblacht*'s first reissue, on 12 March, carried articles from what might be regarded as the right- and left-wing leaders of the movement. Maurice Twomey, the Chief of Staff, an old-style Fenian, wrote that: 'Fianna Fail declares its intention to chop off some of the imperial tentacles; every such achievement is of value and will be welcomed. Notwithstanding such concessions, the Irish Republican Army must continue its work, and cannot escape its role as the vanguard of the freedom movement.' And from the left Peadar O'Donnell had even more unpromising (and perceptive) things to say:

> ... tell the working farmers to keep their annuities in their pockets ... [Fianna Fail] is not the leadership of a real government for freedom: it can lead to greater freedom from humiliating Imperial restrictions but the furtherest the road can

> lead is an externally associated double-headed 26-County Republic . . . they are
> not going to blast these interests [big business, land-owners etc.] out of the way
> but make a new bargain on their behalf, in the name of us all, with British
> Imperialism.

De Valera had let a genie out of the bottle. How was he going to get it back in again? Had the IRA pondered the significance of James Geoghegan's becoming Minister for Justice, it might have guessed the answer. Geoghegan was a former member of Cumann na nGaedheal whose appointment to de Valera's Cabinet had come as a surprise. It might have been taken as a source of potential reassurance to Cumann na nGaedheal and Unionist elements; but it could also have been analysed (correctly) as indicating that de Valera saw the possibility of unpopular security measures down the line and wished to distance himself from them. His grasp of the realities of power meant that he was keenly aware of the fact that 'two stars keep not their motion in one sphere'.

He held private meetings with representatives of the IRA leadership on a number of occasions. His objective[10] was to get them to agree to his programme of a piecemeal dismantling of the Treaty: the abolition of the Oath, the removal of the Governor Generalship, and the restriction of the King's role in the appointment of Irish foreign representatives. With all this done, the declaration of a republic would be only a formality; there would 'only' be partition left to deal with. He wanted the IRA to disband and accept the principle of majority rule.

However, the IRA countered with an offer of a united front against 'British aggression'. In America, McGarrity was pondering the wisdom of having the Army oath changed to pledge allegiance to the nation as a whole. This would allow the IRA to join the Army without loss of principle and with a view to taking it over.[11] On majority rule, the IRA reminded de Valera of his own record on the issue. The majority had opposed 1916, supported the Treaty and, within the ranks of Republicans, opposed his breach with Sinn Fein. Majority rule was all right in a free country, but Ireland was not free. 'The people have no right to do wrong . . .' De Valera must have felt his own arguments coming back to haunt him.

However, these agonizings were unknown to the public. To many, de Valera's early days in power seemed to indicate that, far from supporting the police against the IRA, his policy was aimed the other way round. This was in marked contrast to his studied wooing of the permanent civil service and, in one case, the impermanent. Johnny Collins, Michael's brother, had been worried because his temporary civil service status had not been confirmed at the time of the Fianna Fail take-over. In a shrewd PR move, de Valera sent word to him through Sean T. O'Ceallaigh, who had interceded on his behalf, that he would be made permanent. However, he went out of his way to spread alarm and despondency amongst the Garda Siochana. He had two objectives in this: one to show O'Duffy, and any supporters he might have, who was boss, and the other to woo 'extremist support'. His two aims combined to contribute to a very nasty confrontation in Irish society, centring on a by-road in Irish political development, the Blueshirt movement, which we will encounter shortly through following the Machiavellian path of de Valera's IRA policy.

Along with substantive steps such as the suspension of the military tribunal, de Valera introduced less obvious baits to attract IRA support. Word went down the line in the Gardai to go easy on the organization; the old coercive policy was frowned on, and it became harder to obtain sanction to bring charges. Meanwhile, as this policy was percolating downwards, much of the rank-and-file IRA membership could see no obstacle on the road to a Thirty-two County workers' republic beyond that presented by the local sergeant of the Gardai. They assumed that 'their' side had won when the 1932 election results became known. IRA men starting giving orders to Garda sergeants in places like Galway and Kerry. Some of the more thuggish began spitting on Gardai, or jostling them in the streets. As one historian of the period has written:[12] 'De Valera was adept at playing to this gallery. Shortly after the election he visited Skibbereen, in County Cork, on a victory tour. On arrival he found the local police had assembled to greet him on one side of the road while the IRA had paraded its own guard of honour on the other. Without hesitation he paused in front of the IRA, took their salute and passed on into town completely ignoring the small group of Gardai.'

De Valera's policy of leniency towards the IRA, coupled with the public's fear of the organization, made the courts increasingly ineffective in dealing with the situation. There was national controversy over a case heard in the Dublin Circuit Criminal Court on 14 July 1932. A jury declared Gerald Dempsey, an IRA officer, 'not guilty' of the illegal possession of guns and ammunition. He refused to recognize the court and said that the weapons had been stolen from him. On hearing the jury's finding, the judge said to him:[13] 'How you regard that verdict I don't know. Possibly you have the same contempt for it I have.' He then sentenced Dempsey to three months for refusing to recognize the court. *An Phoblacht*[14] sternly demanded his release and three days later James Goeghegan, the Minister for Justice, made an order setting Dempsey free.

Inevitably some of the Gardai took matters into their own hands. A month after the Dempsey case, on 14 August, T. J. Ryan, of kicking cow fame, and George Gilmore were badly assaulted by detectives in Clare. The detectives involved were suspended, following an Inquiry which also led to David Neligan's downfall. He took up a collection for his suspended subordinates and was removed from office in consequence, eventually winding up in a dead end job in the Land Commission. While these events were taking place, *An Phoblacht* continued to preach the doctrine that: 'Free speech and the freedom of the press must be denied to traitors and treason mongers.'

De Valera eventually became alarmed and appealed to his supporters to 'set their face against action which would prevent our opponents from being heard'. This had as little effect as his statement that the removal of the Oath would remove any excuse for IRA men to refuse to obey the rule of law. Frank Ryan answered him directly on 10 November: 'No matter what anyone says to the contrary, while we have fists, hands and boots to use, and guns if necessary, we will not allow free speech to Irish traitors.' And, speaking at the same meeting, Peadar O'Donnell said: 'The policeman who puts his head between Mr Cosgrave's head, and the hands of angry Irishmen, might as well keep his head at home.'[15] By this stage many of Cosgrave's supporters had not only come to the same conclusion, but had decided to do something about it.

In March 1932, three days after the big IRA rally in College Green at which McGuinness made his reference to the defeated Government's being a 'menace to society', a body known as the Army Comrades Association had held a convention which set up a National Executive to reorganize itself. Hitherto the ACA had claimed to be nothing more than a benevolent society, securing work for ex-Free State soldiers in county councils and so on. Now, under the leadership of Dr T. F. O'Higgins and Richard Mulcahy, the organization began soliciting members on a plank of free speech, a free press and democratic methods of election. But its fundamental *raison d'être* was the belief that de Valera was allowing the IRA to run riot. By the end of the year it was claiming a membership of some thirty thousand. Recruitment was accelerated by the disruption of a Cosgrave meeting in Cork in May and by other similar incidents directed at anti-Fianna Fail speakers. There is no doubt that initially the ACA did secure a hearing at public meetings for both Cosgravite speakers and, later, National Centre Party spokesmen which they would not otherwise have had. I interviewed several Garda members, both officers and men, of that period who corroborated this. Through either shortage of resources or deliberate policy there were not enough police at meetings to prevent IRA/Fianna Fail supporters disrupting them.

De Valera denied this in the Dail,[16] saying that the resources of the state were both adequate and being utilized. But out of their own experience a number of Opposition speakers rebutted him. E. J. Duggan, one of the Treaty signatories, told of a meeting in Trim at which he would have been 'run out of town' had it not been for the ACA. And another speaker commented: 'A Civic Guard would be murdered if he went to interfere.' Certainly many members of the force believed this to be true at the time.

The ACA and IRA began coming into increasingly abrasive contact towards the end of 1932 when the IRA declared war on Bass ale. There were raids on pubs, window-smashings and commandeerings of lorries. This was partly because of the movement's traditional hostility to British products and partly because an executive of the company had made disparaging comments about Ireland. After a lorry-load was destroyed on 14 December the ACA provided the brewers with protection for their shipments. The election campaign of the following month was one of the roughest in the history of Irish politics. Again there were violent clashes between the IRA and the ACA. Frequently only the ACA's presence won a hearing for opponents of de Valera. James Dillon, who was not then associated with the ACA, testified[17] that were it not for the fact that the organization 'wiped the square of Macroom' with a crowd of about fifty men he would have been prevented from speaking. The fifty had been chanting 'up de Valera' and refused to desist until induced to do so by the ACA's interpretation of the term a 'ballot box'.

The atmosphere of fear and suspicion which all this engendered worsened sharply in February 1933. On the 19th de Valera sanctioned the arrest of Inspector E. M. O'Connell, the deputy head of the Special Branch, and an Army colonel, Michael Hogan, a brother of the former Minister for Agriculture. Three days later O'Duffy was sacked as Commissioner of Police. Eamonn Broy, who had been appointed to succeed Neligan, took over both as head of the Special Branch and as O'Duffy's successor. O'Connell and Hogan were held in jail until the end of March, when they were charged under the Official Secrets Act. The country was swept with rumours that either O'Duffy and company were planning a coup, or de Valera was plotting a dictatorship.

But when Hogan and O'Connell appeared in court the mountain of rumour merely produced a ridiculous mouse. The gravamen of the charge was that some data on subversive organizations taken from Special Branch files had been passed on to another Hogan brother, James, a Cork University history professor. James Hogan, a theoretician of the right, used the information to produce anti-de Valera articles, and, eventually, after a trial, a booklet, 'Could Ireland Go Communist?'[18] In this he pointed to the fact that, in Russia, every blow that Kerensky struck against the Tsar resulted ultimately in the Bolsheviks coming to power. He argued that in Ireland de Valera's depredations against Cumann na nGaedheal could bring about a 'communist-IRA' take-over.[19]

The jury acquitted both Hogan and O'Connell. What O'Duffy had to do with the affair was not made clear. It was known that James Hogan had been his intelligence officer in the civil war, but no charge was brought against him and de Valera offered him a post at the same salary elsewhere in government service. O'Duffy, however, refused on the grounds that if he could not be trusted in the police force he could not be trusted anywhere. De Valera never gave any reason for O'Duffy's dismissal. When Cosgrave tabled a censure motion in the Dail, de Valera's reply was:[20] 'We say this, whether it be the Governor-General or the Chief of Police, that as long as we are responsible for public policy we will have men in whom we have confidence . . . Let us note that without any of the bunkum, full confidence.'

De Valera obviously chose that moment of increased strength to move against the Gardai as part of his general process of tightening his grip on the levers of power. The public were unaware of the fact that he had got information from the IRA (and, I understand, possibly from Broy) about O'Duffy well in advance of his dismissal. However, de Valera's response had been that he felt O'Duffy was loyal to the Government. When he was reminded about this after the sacking he stated that he believed O'Duffy would have been loyal had not a new set of circumstances been created in the meantime.[21] He obviously wished to suggest that it was the IRA's fault that the situation had deteriorated, but it is a moot point whether de Valera himself, or the IRA, had done most to stir up public passions. Certainly in the ranks of those opposed to him there was a widespread feeling that O'Duffy had been hard done by. People who were unaware of how relationships between de Valera and the IRA had deteriorated were all too conscious that O'Duffy had been a hate figure to *An Phoblacht* which 'for months'[22] had demanded his removal. The feeling that O'Duffy had been martyred as a result of an IRA–de Valera pact was a major contributory factor in his being offered the leadership of the ACA the following July – a move which, as we shall shortly see, was to result in the Free State's political blood pressure shooting up very considerably.

But first let us return to charting the course of the IRA–de Valera relationship. The IRA had helped to put de Valera in – in order to get Cosgrave out. That was all. The more realpolitik-minded amongst the leadership realized that a Second Authority arising in the country would inevitably conflict with the Government of the day. This feeling was reflected in editorials in *An Phoblacht*, from which extracts have already been quoted. By 18 February 1933 a collision was being foreshadowed in a secret Army Council document[23] circulated to 'The Commander of Each Independent Unit'. It contained the following:

> In dealing with England, the Fianna Fail 'Government' agreed to submit the question of the payment of tribute to arbitration. The payment of any tribute to England is an encroachment on the sovereignty of Ireland, which sovereignty is, and must remain, non-judicable. . . .
>
> In its economic policy the Fianna Fail 'Government' has upheld and bolstered the capitalist system so that the economic war with England is being used for the advancement of both British and Irish capitalism within our shores.
>
> . . . these facts bring us to the realisation that the policy of the Fianna Fail Government is not directed towards the achievement of our aims. . . . In brief, it makes the same claims as regards the control of arms, and as regards its legitimacy, as the Cosgrave 'Government'.

Relations between de Valera and the IRA deteriorated progressively after this. There was an increasing deployment of the state's forces of law and order against the movement, on top of which de Valera used two other tactics – bribery and subversion. He introduced pensions for those who had fought against the state in the civil war in the same way as the Free State had pensioned its soldiers. And he set up a new Army Volunteer Reserve, with a uniform said to be the same as that intended by Casement for his ill-fated Brigade. This undoubtedly siphoned off a sizeable amount of potential manpower from the IRA; but not from O'Duffy's new force.

During the spring of 1933 some members of the ACA had begun wearing a distinctive blue shirt. One stalwart of the period told me that this was merely because unfortunate errors of a knuckle-duster nature sometimes occurred during clashes in the absence of a form of identification. But, disturbingly, for those looking to the Europe of the dictators, the ACA also developed the habit of the one-armed 'Hitler salute'. Both salute and shirt were adopted officially by the movement after 20 July 1933, when Dr O'Higgins handed over the leadership to O'Duffy. The ACA changed its name to the National Guard. It promised to keep within the law, saying that: 'illegalities will not be tolerated, physical drill will be practised only as a means of promoting good health, character, and discipline.' The goal of a corporate state might have been discerned lurking behind its promise to organize employers and employed so that:[24] 'judicial tribunals will prevent strikes and lock-outs and harmoniously compose industrial differences'.

The harmonious composition of differences was not the hallmark of the Blueshirt era. De Valera reacted almost immediately to the formation of the National Guard by revoking all firearm certificates. Following the murder of Kevin O'Higgins many public figures, including O'Duffy and the ex-Cumann na nGaedheal ministers, carried legally held firearms. De Valera ordered all these called in, and the homes of former ministers were visited by revolver-collecting police over the weekend of 30 July. Challenged in the Dail on 1 August, de Valera said that O'Duffy was aiming at a dictatorship, but that the Government would not tolerate private armies. This gave James Dillon the opportunity of asking him to declare his attitudes towards the IRA. De Valera replied to the effect that there was now no need for the organization because the Oath had been removed and soon people would come to realize this; it was simply a question of time. But the National Guard was 'not a body which has any roots in the past, not a body which can be said to have a national objective such as the IRA can be said to have'.

This certainly sounded like one law for the left and another for the right. O'Duffy's adherents complained that their legally held weapons were taken from them while the IRA was left unmolested in possession of unlawfully held weapons. Events moved rapidly thereafter. O'Duffy announced his intention of holding a march past Leinster Lawn outside Government Buildings in Merrion Street on Sunday, 13 August. The stated objective was to revive a custom practised by Cumann na nGaedheal, but not by Fianna Fail, of laying wreaths at a cenotaph on the lawn in memory of Collins, Griffith and O'Higgins.

De Valera elected to believe that O'Duffy's march would be along Mussolini lines. It might not go past, but into Government Buildings. He decided that the time to find out was before, not after, O'Duffy got to Merrion Street. He banned the parade, and used it both as a pretext to ban the National Guard and, more importantly, as a cause to revive the military tribunal which he had so decried under the Cosgrave regime. Moreover, he created the world's most speedily recruited police force. This grouping, formally known as the S-Branch and popularly described as the Broy Harriers, consisted of Fianna Fail supporters who had fought against O'Duffy's side in the civil war. Some of these men had been active in breaking up Cumann na nGaedheal meetings. They were recruited in some cases by a knock on the door at midnight, followed by an invitation to come immediately to the Castle to join a new police force. Their principal qualifications were that they were good shots and could be relied upon to fire on, rather than side with, O'Duffy.

The country went into a state of red alert while it waited to see whether or not O'Duffy would defy the ban. It would have been even redder had the public been aware that the IRA Army Council had drawn up plans for a major ambush of the marchers when they got to the high buildings on either side of Dublin's Westmoreland Street. At the last moment O'Duffy decided to do as as de Valera himself had done in the case of the Mount Street Bridge reception many years earlier, and chose discretion before valour; he cancelled the march.

De Valera had won an important battle of nerves, but the war went on. On 8 September the movement which he had temporarily aborted through his calling of the snap election was successfully concluded. Cumann na nGaedheal and the National Centre Party decided to join forces – this time with the National Guard, or, as it was renamed to get around the banning, the Young Ireland Association. All three groupings were to accept the leadership of O'Duffy and fuse into the United Ireland Party, more generally known by its Irish name, Fine Gael. Although he continued as the parliamentary leader, accepting the overall leadership of someone he termed 'a wild man' cannot have pleased Cosgrave. But there are two sides in politics, an inside and an outside. After two election defeats O'Duffy, who had a wide popular following, appeared to offer a better prospect of a route back to the inside than did the view from the Opposition benches. On the face of it this created a classical right v. left situation in Irish politics. On the right were the UIP, big farmers, many business and professional people, and ex-Unionists, all under the banner of O'Duffy, although he held no seat in Parliament. On the left there was Fianna Fail, the Labour Party and the IRA.

The ripple effect from the Eucharistic Congress meant that religious fervour shot up sharply throughout Ireland. Bishops became concerned that communism meant the 'nationalisation of women and children'. They encouraged the setting up of Vigilance Committees to ensure that places like Knocknagoshel and Bruree did not turn red. Cardinal Logue feared that:[25] 'Like a plague Bolshevism seems to be spreading. It is time that all of us should feel called upon to prepare ourselves for this trouble that seems to be coming.'

In order to prepare for the trouble, many on the right began causing it. During the spring and early summer known IRA activists and left-wing groups were attacked by vigilantes on the streets of Dublin. On 27 March fiery sermons from a number of Dublin pulpits resulted in even more fiery scenes on the streets outside as mobs attacked and burned known IRA and socialist meeting places. Professor Hogan commended those responsible as Catholic citizens who had taken the law[26] 'into their own hands in default of Government action'. In this climate O'Duffy went on a[27] 'raging, tearing campaign throughout the country, enlisting recruits, using fascist symbols and the fascist salute, announcing to the people that the object of his movement was to save the country from Communism. The Blueshirt flag, he declared, would soon be flying beside the tricolour on Government Buildings.' The fascist patina given to the emergence of an organized, shirted, right-wing movement was added to by utterances in the Blueshirt press. Another Hoganesque figure in the movement, Professor Michael Tierney, later President of University College, Dublin, wrote:[28] 'The corporate state must come in the end to Ireland as elsewhere.' And a correspondent, 'Oghanach' ('Youth'), suggested that at rallies Blueshirts should greet their leaders as the Nazis did by giving:[29] 'three sudden staccato bursts of mass cheering, each burst consisting of one sharply ejected syllable . . . the word may be Heil (Hail) pronounced sharply or it may be Hoch (Up)'.

This sort of thing provided priceless propaganda for Fianna Fail, as did photographs of O'Duffy in the *Irish Press* reviewing displays of blue-shirted men all giving the 'Hitler salute'. But the Irish generally and Fine Gael in particular were not fascists. The Blueshirt movement was an outcropping of the civil war and of the more ancient Irish custom of faction fighting. De Valera, who also had big farmers and businessmen in his retinue, had just as much fondness for the theatricality of power, and making the trains run on time, as had O'Duffy. During a visit to Genoa, he was quoted in the *Irish Times* on 5 June 1933 by a Reuter correspondent as having given a statement to the press in which he 'spoke of his great admiration for fascism'. And when he approached Dun Laoghaire at the end of his holiday, the care which we have already seen him display, while in the USA with Gallagher, to ensure that his return to Cobh in 1927 was properly marked, displayed itself in spectacular fashion. He was greeted with a nineteen-gun artillery salute.

But he was a far better political strategist than O'Duffy. He ground down the Blueshirts by a combination of attrition and manipulation of the movement's internal weaknesses. For several months after the formation of Fine Gael rural Ireland was a scene of violence and commotion. As a protest against the economic war some of the bigger farmers withheld their annuities and sometimes their rates. In retaliation the Government distrained their cattle, selling them at auction to defray the arrears. The Blueshirts helped to obstruct both seizures and sales. Roads were trenched, telegraph wires cut and trees felled across roads. Blueshirt meetings were turned into riots by attacks from Fianna Fail and IRA supporters. De Valera's attitude to these attacks was:[30] 'It is up to the Government to see that opportunities for free speech are given. But the Government cannot possibly make people or causes popular.'

It is just possible that de Valera himself did not realize the hardship he caused. Father Farragher told me a revealing anecdote. One day while he was being interviewed[31] de Valera talked of his youth. He described being so tired one day that on the way home from school he slept standing up. 'Ye don't realise how hard it was,' he remarked to the priest. Father Farragher came of a farming family that had had Blueshirt leanings – not out of any remote attraction to fascism, but because of the havoc wreaked upon their standard of living by the economic war. Despite himself he felt all the bitterness which had swirled around him in boyhood stirring to life again. 'I remembered the way that everything a farmer had was lost and, though I kept my temper and was polite about it, I told Dev. about those days and about how we knew all too much about hardship.' De Valera was momentarily taken aback, but replied in oracular terms: 'The generation that does not suffer for its country leaves no mark on history.' This blindness may have made it easier for him to persevere with his policies.

De Valera allowed the anarchy to continue until he calculated that the public had had enough of it. Then on 30 November 1933, he struck. Police raided the homes of hundreds of UIP supporters and the party headquarters. No arms seizures were reported, but the raids turned up some damaging political ammunition which was probably the real target of the raids. A letter from an O'Duffy supporter to a British Conservative MP was read out in the Dail on the day of the raids. It contained some very disparaging judgements both on Cosgrave's party and on MacDermott. Fault lines were clearly developing in the Blueshirt alliance.

Then on 8 December – a significant date, being the anniversary of the execution of Rory O'Connor and his three colleagues – de Valera struck again. An order was issued declaring the Young Ireland Association to be unlawful. No mention was made of those who followed in O'Connor's footsteps, the IRA. However, tentative steps had been taken towards curbing the organization earlier in the month. On 1 December twelve IRA men were sentenced to jail for periods of four to six months each in connection with a riot at Tralee the previous October. The fighting was caused by an attempt to prevent a Fine Gael convention being held. O'Duffy's car was burnt out and he and his deputy, Commandant Cronin, were attacked in the street. Amongst other assaults, O'Duffy was struck on the head with a hammer and during the convention a Mills bomb was thrown at a skylight but it bounced harmlessly off some wire netting.

One might have thought the sentences would have been perceived as justified in the circumstances. But civil war memories were so bitter in Kerry that de Valera had to travel to Tralee to ward off a storm of protest from the Fianna Fail organization, which threatened to culminate in a one-day strike for the release of the prisoners. At the Fianna Fail Ard Fheis on 8 November he had had to respond to unprecedented criticism when he was attacked for not being Republican enough and for being too lenient with Fianna Fail's opponents. In the course of a spirited reply, which silenced his critics, he said that had he not attended the debates earlier in the day he could have prepared a speech showing the many advances Fianna Fail had made. In fact he had prepared a lengthy typescript,[32] the contents of which help to illustrate a part of his appeal. He made his point in 'cute hoor' fashion, in effect telling his followers that since they had been bold enough to criticize him they would have to pay for their sins by allowing their enemies to make criticism also. Nevertheless a basic decency and a concern for democracy and fair play peep out. He told the Ard Fheis:[33]

> ... we cannot have it both ways, and I am afraid there are in our organization a number of people who would like to have it both ways. They want to be free to criticise us themselves, but they want to deny that right to other sections of the people. Now, you cannot have that. If you claim within your organization, as you have a right to claim, the liberty of free criticism of us as the Government of the people or the free criticism of us as your Executive – because there is a difference – but if you want to claim that privilege for yourselves, you dare not deny it to others.

However de Valera, Nice Guy, could not hold the stage long from de Valera, Man of Power. The United Ireland Party responded to the banning of the Young Ireland Association by changing its name to the League of Youth. The UIP then brought and won a High Court action, on the grounds of free speech, declaring the new organization lawful. Temporarily foiled, de Valera had O'Duffy himself arrested with two colleagues at Westport on 17 December. His arrest and detention were declared illegal by the High Court on the 21st, but the attrition continued relentlessly. O'Duffy was immediately served with a summons to appear before the military tribunal on a charge of belonging to two unlawful associations (the National Guard and the Young Ireland Association) and with incitement to murder de Valera.

These charges too fell by the wayside. Worse, the High Court decided that the military tribunal was a court of limited jurisdiction which was not exempt from prohibition. One of de Valera's most important tools was, it seemed, in danger of turning in his hand. In the Dail, on 2 February 1934, one of Fine Gael's leading lawyers, John A. Costello, declared that the Blueshirts would be:[34] 'victorious in Ireland ... [as] ... the Blackshirts were victorious in Italy ... the Hitlershirts ... victorious in Germany'. Costello would one day become Prime Minister after a career in law and politics which demonstrated a fidelity to democracy rather than demagoguery. But it was an era in which people saw reds under the bed and blues above it.

473

On 11 February the Blueshirt–IRA conflict took a particularly vicious turn. The home of a Blueshirt supporter in Dundalk was bombed after he had given evidence before the military tribunal identifying men who had robbed him of United Ireland Party funds. Two children were badly injured in the blast, and his mother fatally so. On the same day there was a ferocious riot in Drogheda as police used tear gas and fired over the heads of a Fianna Fail–IRA mob which tried to attack a Blueshirt gathering.

Something had to be done, but once again de Valera elected to do it to the Blueshirts, not to the IRA. On the 23rd he introduced the Wearing of Uniform (Restriction) Bill. It prevented the use of badges, uniforms or military titles in support of a political party; the carrying of weapons, including sticks, was also declared illegal. The Bill contained an extraordinary provision that offenders under the proposed law would be tried by district courts only. This was an attempt to get around the problems posed by the High Court itself and by its limitations on the military tribunal. There was to be no appeal to the High Court.

De Valera said the measure was necessary to end 'this tomfoolery of Blueshirting'. He forced it through the Dail under the guillotine on 14 March 'after a stormy and destructive debate'.[35] Many of the Fine Gael deputies attended the Chamber in their blue shirts. The mood of the exchanges may be gauged by a clash between Dr O'Higgins of Fine Gael and Fianna Fail's Sean MacEntee. When O'Higgins referred to the fact that some Fianna Fail TDs were said to have been seen laughing over the murder of a Cork Blueshirt, MacEntee's reply was: 'Any Deputy with the name O'Higgins has no right to talk about murder.'

De Valera's contribution to that debate can be examined under two headings: one, the tough, resolute manner in which he challenged the Opposition, the Blueshirt movement and O'Duffy himself head on; the other, the almost hysterical way in which he found it necessary to launch off at a tangent to defend his own origins, showing as he did so how vulnerable he must have felt concerning them. His fundamental mind set – that he ruled so correctly that it was incorrect of anyone to challenge him – was also revealed at various junctures during the debate.[36] His basic argument was that the Bill was necessary to avert civil war. It was pointed out to him (by Frank MacDermott) that the Blueshirts did not have arms. He replied that arms were available if they wanted them. At which Dillon broke in: 'Arrest every man who has arms and we will support you.' At this he lost control of himself momentarily to retort that the Cosgrave party 'were using the machinery of the law to defeat and prevent . . .'. The idea that he found it distasteful that the Opposition should use the democratic process (that is, the High Court actions) to oppose him provoked derision from his critics. But once the laughter had subsided he returned to the charge with his customary tenacity: the Opposition were guilty of 'using the courts to hamper the Executive'.

In a memorable display of de Valera fact he moved the goalposts of the

Blueshirts' origins completely away from the uncomfortable reality of his supporters' thuggery at public meetings to focus exclusively on the O'Duffyites' anti-communist stance. This last he demolished by the dubious method of using confidential reports to the Government from the former Chief of Police, General Eoin O'Duffy himself, to prove that communism was virtually non-existent in Ireland. He went on:

> This country is not a natural breeding ground for communism and everybody knows it. It is opposed to our religion; it is opposed to our individualistic tendencies; it is opposed to our whole scheme of life. If there is one country in the world which is unsuitable soil for Communism, it is this . . . I have never stood for Communism in any form. I loathe and detest it as leading to the same sort of thing that I loathe and detest in the type of State that General O'Duffy would set up, because they are both destructive of human liberty.

In fact the same arguments could have been used against fascism taking root in Ireland. Although the authoritarian basis underlying fascism could be found in some forms of Irish Catholicism, the temper of the people, their individualism, and the divisions caused by the civil war militated against the growth of forces such as, say, a united, right-wing agrarian movement. And there simply were not sufficient big businessmen in Ireland to provide the leadership or backing for a capitalist movement.

However, de Valera's animadversions on communism in Ireland at least contained reasoned arguments. Now, suddenly, as his speech continued, emotion took over and he switched from the dangers of civil war to allegations of slurs on his ancestry. He showed both an extreme sensitivity to these and a continuing preoccupation with the gossip surrounding his relationship with Kathleen O'Connell at the time of Sinead's visit to America:

> In this House on one occasion I have had to speak on a personal matter. I did it, not because I cared a snap of my fingers regarding what anybody says about me personally, but because I am jealous, as long as I occupy this particular position, that my antecedents and character shall not be attacked. Before, they went and soiled the steps of God's Altar; the same campaign is going on now in another guise, and I know that in order to get some basis for their Communistic attack on us they are suggesting that I am of Jewish origin.

He told the House that an allegation concerning his supposed Jewish ancestry had been made at a meeting which had been reported in the *Cork Examiner*. There was, in fact, a rumour that he was the illegitimate son of a Spanish Jew. However, as a rumour printed in a Cork paper would hardly have attracted national attention the suspicion arises that he was using the same tactic that he had attempted during the Treaty debate: trying to transfer the focus from the stated issue to that of his personal standing. At all events, he went on excitedly:

> There is not, so far as I know, a single drop of Jewish blood in my veins. I am not

one of those who attack the Jews or want to make any use of the popular dislike of them. But as there has been, even from that bench over there, this dirty innuendo and suggestion carried, as I have said formally to God's Altar, I say on both sides I come from Catholic stock. My father and mother were married in a Catholic church on September 19th, 1881. I was born in October, 1882. I was baptised in a Catholic church. I was brought up here in a Catholic home. I have lived among the Irish people and loved them, and loved every blade of grass that grew in this land. I do not care who says or who tries to pretend that I am not Irish. I say that I have been known to be Irish and that I have given everything in me to the Irish nation.

At all events, whatever his motivation in making it, the appeal to emotion failed. Having had to use the guillotine to get the Bill through the Dail, de Valera then suffered the mortification of seeing it rejected by the Senate. As the vote approached, he made his contribution in the face of the inevitable. Donal O'Sullivan, who was the clerk of the Senate at the time, says:[37] 'His voice was vibrant with anger, and he thumped the table to emphasize his points.' One of these points was that: 'To-morrow if we wanted to do it we would get ten shirts to your one in the country. There is not the slightest doubt about that. There will be, if necessary, a special force established to protect the country and preserve public order, under the control of the popularly elected Government of the Irish people.' He had been challenged to go to the country on the Bill but he claimed that if '*we* did, *we* would not be able to maintain order at the present time'. He concluded: '*We* put on you definitely the responsibility for depriving us, the elected representatives of the people, of the powers which *we* deem necessary to preserve public order on the one hand and the public safety on the other [author's italics throughout]'.

O'Sullivan would not remain clerk of the Senate for long. The following day, 22 March 1934, de Valera introduced a Bill in the Dail to abolish the Senate. He would see that through, but he was not to need the Uniforms Bill which precipitated it. The Blueshirt movement began to self-destruct after a disastrous showing in the local government elections held on 30 June. The Senate had proved a delaying factor for legislation introduced on 26 April 1933 (the Local Government (Dublin) Bill), and 10 May of the same year (the Local Government (Extension of Franchise) Bill). These Bills had aimed to improve Fianna Fail's chances by removing the commercial register for the Dublin County Council and taking away the existing ratepayer stipulation by extending the franchise to everyone over twenty whether or not they paid rates. In the absence of these two pieces of legislation O'Duffy assumed that Fine Gael would do well, and incautiously made the local government elections a test of Fianna Fail popularity. He predicted[38] that Fianna Fail would lose twenty out of the twenty-three councils. In fact the result was exactly the other way round: Fine Gael won only three. Behind the uproar of Blueshirt–IRA clashes de Valera's social policy was proving to be the real attraction for the Irish electorate. The Irish vote for bread and butter policies, not bomb and bullet ones – these are matters for the ballad, not the ballot box. Like his IRA counterpart, a Blueshirt could expect a friendly voter to give him a bed for the night, or a blind eye to illegal activity, a gift of money perhaps, or the loan of a car – a sympathy born of history; but not a contemporary mandate from the polls. O'Duffy's prediction showed his fundamental inability to grasp these facts of Irish political life, and revealed how lacking he was in political skills when compared with de Valera.

The Marsh's Sale Yard incident in Cork city, later in the summer on 13 August, helped to accelerate the growth of public disenchantment with the violence attendant on Blueshirt activity. The violence was in fact inflicted by de Valera's hastily formed Broy Harriers and occurred on the occasion of a sale of cattle seized from farmers who had withheld their annuity payments. The general run of farmers or local butchers would not buy these cattle; the purchasers were generally jobbers who gave fictitious names and bought the cattle for a song, and they were protected by the Broy Harriers from the wrath of the farmers and Blueshirts. At Marsh's a large crowd was kept back from the yard where the actual sale took place by a cordon of uniformed police. Suddenly a lorry containing fifteen men armed with sticks broke the cordon and smashed through the main gate into the yard. Three or four members of the crowd, including a fifteen-year-old boy, managed to follow the lorry into the yard before the Gardai reformed the cordon. There were forty ordinary Gardai inside the yard, including ten armed detectives. The lorry and its occupants were thus trapped by superior numbers inside a police cordon, and prevented from using the lorry by cattle pens. However the Broy Harriers opened fire, killing the fifteen-year-old boy and wounding seven other people.

The superintendent who was nominally in charge of the Gardai that day was subsequently sued by the boy's father, as were three of the S-Branch. In a written judgement[39] Mr Justice Hanna dismissed the charges against the superintendent, awarded damages to the plaintiff, and said that the evidence disclosed a prime facie case of manslaughter. He found there was no 'justification for sending fusillade after fusillade of revolver and rifle shots into the men huddled in the lorry and at the three or four men running to escape', and concluded that the Broy Harriers' principal qualification was that they knew how to handle guns. He said: 'These S-Men are not real Civic Guards. They are an excrescence upon that reputable body.' Many of the regular force at the time would have agreed with the judge. Fianna Fail's reaction, however, was to have two of the S-Branch men involved at Marsh's Yard promoted to the rank of sergeant, to sanction an unsuccessful appeal to the Supreme Court against Hanna's findings and to ensure that no manslaughter charge was ever brought by the Attorney General.[40]

However, the Blueshirts' activities were reaching a crescendo of tree felling and obstruction of sales and seizures which was disturbing to many of the more conservative members of Fine Gael. The tragedy at Marsh's

Yard heightened these anxieties. Then at the League of Youth Congress held five days after the shooting, on 18–19 August, with O'Duffy presiding, a resolution was passed calling on farmers to withhold both annuities and rates. That was the breaking point for the conservatives. Developments following on a heated meeting of the national executive of the United Ireland Party (Fine Gael) on the 31st showed that whether or not it was fascist-inclined, the party was certainly not united. James Hogan resigned from the executive and issued a statement that he did so as:[41] 'the strongest protest I can personally make against the general destructive and hysterical leadership of its President, General O'Duffy . . . in politics I have found him to be utterly impossible. It is about time the United Ireland Party gave up its hopeless attempt of saving General O'Duffy from his own errors.'

The party agreed. On 21 September O'Duffy was manoeuvred into announcing his resignation as chairman of the party. The party also deemed him resigned from the post of Director-General of the League of Youth and appointed Commandant Cronin in his stead. Cronin was the man who had first used the Army Comrades movement to protect Cosgrave at a meeting in Cork; he was also the originator of the Blueshirts. However, O'Duffy refused to accept his appointment and there was a further split in the Blueshirt movement, with each man drawing adherents to himself. O'Duffy's wing held on to their blue shirts but eventually, on 8 June, became known as the National Corporate Party.[42] The cumulative effect of the rows and splits was to cause irretrievable damage to both the strength and the prestige of the Opposition. Cosgrave scrambled back into the saddle of Fine Gael leadership rather shamefacedly. The alliance with O'Duffy and Blueshirtism had been a disaster. There might be jokes about the 'long bollocks on the horse', but de Valera, not O'Duffy, was unquestionably the man on the white horse in Irish politics. O'Duffy disappeared from the headlines after leading an Irish contingent to fight in the Spanish Civil War under Franco. On the right, therefore, de Valera was left free to deploy the military tribunal and the Broy Harriers as he wished, to curb the annuities retention campaign. On the left, dissensions within the IRA, coupled with his own increasing pressure on the movement, would shortly leave him with a clear field also. His period of maximum power and freedom of manoeuvre was rapidly approaching.

The IRA break-up may be described relatively quickly under three headings: the movement's own inner tensions which led to a split; the movement's impact on the public that ultimately provoked the backlash against it which enabled de Valera to suppress it; and, finally, what might be termed de Valera's own relationship with the IRA and McGarrity. The IRA's involvement with the anti-Blueshirt campaign obviously deflected it from its stated goal of setting up a Thirty-two County Irish Republic. This caused a good deal of heart-searching and debate[43] within the movement, exacerbating the perennial problem for the IRA of force v. constitutional action. The left were unhappy at the wasteful deployment of the movement's energies, the right at the inevitable alliance with communist opponents of the Blueshirts.

A convention was held in Dublin on 17 and 18 March 1934 to resolve the issue. On the casting vote of Maurice Twomey it voted against setting up a new party. The left-wingers walked out, led by George Gilmore, Peadar O'Donnell, Frank Ryan and Michael Price. On 8 April, at Athlone, they formed the Republican Congress Party which called on 'Workers and working farmers [to] unite on to the Workers' Republic'. Far from uniting with anybody, the two wings of the IRA came into open conflict at Wolfe Tone's grave at Bodenstown during the annual pilgrimage on 17 June 1934, when the Congress wing lost their banners to the right-wingers. However, the new movement initially took a good deal of strength from the Twomey–Sean MacBride wing.

But the Republican Congress soon suffered a split itself. On 29 and 30 September, at a convention in Rathmines Town Hall, Michael Price differed from his colleagues on methodology. Should the movement openly involve itself in politics and join in strikes, as he advocated, or form cells and infiltrate parties and trade unions as the others recommended? Neither aim of the Congress commended itself to the Irish people, and much of what was left of the energy of the movement was eventually siphoned off into an IRA contingent that went to Spain to fight against Franco. By the end of 1934 the IRA was thus considerably weakened, but de Valera continued to proceed against the movement with a cautious implacability which is illustrated by the records of the military tribunal.[44] These show that 349 Blueshirts were sentenced that year as opposed to only 102 IRA men. But in 1935 the Blueshirt threat had abated, so that only 74 were sentenced as compared to 112 IRA men. The Blueshirts disappeared from the purview of the tribunal altogether in 1936 but 129 IRA men were sentenced in that year, which was also the year when de Valera finally declared the IRA an unlawful organization. By the end of 1937, when neither Blueshirts nor IRA any longer presented a threat de Valera's balancing act, use of the tribunal came out perfectly. The tribunal had sentenced exactly 434 Blueshirts and – 434 IRA men.

De Valera was finally moved to proscribe the IRA by a combination of the movement's increasing loss of influence – accelerated by the loss in numbers caused by the acceptance of pensions and by the attractions of the National Reserve – and by a series of IRA outrages, in particular by three murders. The first, on 9 February 1935, was that of twenty-one-year-old Roderic More-O'Ferrall, who was shot during an IRA raid on his father's house near Edgeworthstown, Co. Longford during an agrarian dispute in which the IRA had become involved. A week after the death, Frank MacDermott challenged de Valera in the Dail to declare the IRA an unlawful association. He replied that this was not necessary. When pressed by MacDermott that the real source of IRA strength was their belief that Fianna Fail secretly supported the movement, de Valera replied that such a belief, if it existed, was without foundation.[45] De Valera's own circumstances at the time certainly did not support such a belief: he was accompanied constantly by an armed bodyguard ten to fifteen strong. This led to a telling shaft about the Government's position from James Dillon:[46] 'They have seen turned against themselves the very self-same methods of insolence, aggression and intimidation that they rejoiced to see turned against us in the past . . . the blackguard and the intimidator were clearly shown that they had the sympathy of the Government so long as they confined their activities to attacking ordinary citizens who were members of our organisation.'

Point was given to Dillon's comment about insolence, at least, the following St Patrick's Day, 17 March 1936. After taking the salute at a military march-past de Valera made a radio broadcast: it had become his custom to use St Patrick's Day for his own version of a state of the nation broadcast. The state on this occasion was well illustrated by an IRA jamming operation. Much of his speech was rendered inaudible, and a voice interjected at one stage to say: 'Hello comrades! For the last half-hour we have just witnessed a very fine display of English militarism.'[47]

The following week the IRA threw down another gauntlet before de Valera, this time a bloodied one. In Castletownsend, Co. Cork, seventy-two-year-old, retired Vice-Admiral Somerville, a brother of Edith Somerville, the co-author of *Memoirs of an Irish RM*, was shot dead because he had been in the habit of giving local lads references to enable them to join the British Army or Navy. Ironically, though it was not known at the time, he was shot on the order of a famous Cork IRA leader who had himself been trained in the British Army – Tom Barry.[48] Even if he had known who was responsible, de Valera would not have had much time for pondering the ironies of the Irish physical force tradition. A month later the tradition claimed another victim. On 26 April John Egan of Dungarvan, Co. Waterford was shot dead by the IRA on the mistaken suspicion that he was an informer. On 21 July the military tribunal sentenced Michael 'Micksie' Conway[49] to be executed for the murder on 12 August. However, on 24 July de Valera sanctioned a reprieve and commutation of the sentence to life imprisonment. But there was to be no reprieve for the organization to which Conway belonged.

With his position growing stronger by the day, de Valera no longer needed 'extremist support'. On 18 June an order had been made declaring the IRA an illegal organization. The following day the forthcoming Wolfe Tone Commemoration at Bodenstown was banned and Maurice Twomey, the IRA Chief of Staff, was sentenced to three years' penal servitude for membership of an illegal organization. It was left to Gerald Boland, the Minister for Justice, to spell out the new policy in the Dail in uncompromising terms:[50] '". . . the fact that these murders have occurred makes it clear that stern action must be taken . . . I now give definite notice to all concerned that the so-called Irish Republican Army, or any organisation which promotes or advocates the use of arms for the attainment of its objects, will not be tolerated . . .". The next day he boasted that " . . . we smashed them [the Blueshirts] and now we are going to smash the others [the IRA]".'

De Valera had decided that the time had come when the IRA could no longer 'claim exactly the same continuity that we had claimed up to 1925'. Naturally his political opponents reminded him of such utterances as he made the break with his former associates. Replying to Opposition point-scoring in the Dail on 23 June 1936, he came as near as he ever did to admitting he had been wrong:[51] 'Do I regret that policy? If that policy has led in any way to the murder of individuals in this State I regret it. I cannot say whether it is that policy that has done it but, if it has, I must regret it.'

All of the foregoing forms part of de Valera's public association with the IRA and could be followed through the newspapers and Dail debates. We now turn to examine his private relationship with the IRA. What was the answer to the question he himself posed in the Dail as to whether his policy contributed to killings? The short answer has to be: 'Yes, but'. Inasmuch as he contributed to the strength of the IRA for his own ends, the answer is simply: 'Yes'. De Valera and Fianna Fail literally stood shoulder to shoulder with the IRA at Bodenstown in 1931 when Cumann na nGaedheal banned the Wolfe Tone Commemoration which now, in 1936, he was banning once more. A major difference between the 1936 ban and the one that Cumann na nGaedheal imposed in 1931 was that there was no question of the leader of the Opposition laying a defiant wreath on Wolfe Tone's tomb. Cumann na nGaedheal would certainly taunt de Valera over his past policies, but unlike Fianna Fail in Opposition, would resolutely refuse to make use of the IRA to regain power.

The 'but' stems from the fact that, from the moment he won power, de Valera's support of the IRA became more apparent than real. He calculated that if he could get a public IRA declaration of support for Fianna Fail he would be able to avoid entering into coalition with Labour, since his ability to keep the peace would be made manifest. Accordingly, two days after the election he informed the IRA of his plan to set up a National Reserve, which members of the organization could join without taking an oath but by making a declaration of support for the Government. His other proposals contained the following:[52]

> All the usual reactionary forces will be whipped up to force Labour and ourselves to agree to this coalition, and the levers of the Eucharistic Congress, trouble with England, world depression, etc., will be used for all they are worth. We will be on the defensive and may fail to secure the reins of Government unless you come to the National rescue by showing that you will accept our authority when the oath is removed . . .
>
> If the way is not cleared for a fusion of forces we are doomed to a period of indecision and weakness in dealing with the urgent international, financial, and economic social problems which will lead to a defeat of the Fianna Fail Government, if it should get control, and the anti-national reactionary forces will again get control.

> I appeal to you for God's sake and for the sake of the people of Ireland to clear
> the way by making the announcement *at once* [author's italics] that you are
> prepared to accept and act up to the principles which the men who fought the civil
> war agreed upon.

Inevitably this appeal fell on deaf ears. He wanted IRA support to help
him control the Twenty-six Counties; but the IRA was wedded to the
concept of a Thirty-two County republic. In that context gestures such as
removing the Oath, or even releasing the prisoners, as he did immediately
on taking office, were merely cosmetic to the IRA, albeit disturbing to a
large segment of public opinion. The Army Council's reply to his overture
said, in part:[53]

> We have always been prepared to obey and support a *Government for all-Ireland*
> [author's italics] elected by the Irish people and functioning 'without faith or
> fealty, rent or render to any power under heaven.' Indeed the Organisation is
> such that once the Republic as we know it is again proclaimed and functioning,
> the organisation as we know it dissolves. We state this fact to dispose of the
> calumny so energetically circulated by our enemies that the Irish Republican
> Army does not visualise any conditions under which it would give allegiance to an
> established government.

In the event, as we saw, de Valera did not have to enter into a formal
coalition with Labour. Whether he had really expected the IRA to co-
operate with him is doubtful. He knew enough of the character of men like
Twomey, Gilmore and the others to calculate the chances of success of a
bribe like the National Reserve on men who were prepared to kill or be
killed in order to attain their objectives. However, while the Army Council
reply ended any hope of formal support for Fianna Fail, it did not end
Fianna Fail's exploitation of the IRA to further its campaign against what it
termed 'reactionary forces'. These, it spelled out in the negotiations, were
'Cumann na nGaedheal, the Senate and the banks'.[54]

Twomey wrote to McGarrity complaining about de Valera's tactics.[55]
Fianna Fail, and especially de Valera, were making public statements
about 'majority rule' which, decoded, meant that the IRA should disband.
Worse, the IRA was becoming involved in the attacks on Blueshirt
meetings. Twomey said:

> The fact is that the opposition is spontaneous, and that these attacks are largely
> made by members of the Fianna Fail organisation and active supporters of Fianna
> Fail. As a matter of fact we have ordered Volunteers not to take part as units in
> these attacks, while saying that if there is opposition they should, of course, join
> in with others who resent the preaching of treason and surrender. But the point is
> that Fianna Fail leaders are using the commotion their own followers are largely
> responsible for creating to attack us.

De Valera too appealed to McGarrity.[56] After condemning the IRA's anti-
Bass campaign as a 'damn foolacting business' and giving a resumé of the

state of mounting disorder in the country which demanded 'united action and almost fierce organisation on the part of everyone who wants to win this fight', he played the familiar anti-British, Green card: 'You know the British are in all this; that they are in touch with the opposition leaders; that a definite plan of campaign is being followed and that disaster awaits the country if the stupidity that is manifesting itself is allowed to continue. On the other hand if we win this fight England will never attempt to squeeze us this way again.'

McGarrity's letter began 'My dear Chief' and explained that he had taken a few days to reply because of business problems. These were in fact horrendous. He had been defrauded by a partner and, though he was himself blameless, had lost both his fortune and his place on the New York Curb Exchange. As a consequence he was being snubbed in Philadelphia and at the time of writing was waiting hopefully for the results of intercession by Sean T. O'Ceallaigh with Martin Conboy, the pro-de Valera lawyer, whom he hoped would take his case. But it was the rest of the letter which concerned de Valera:[57]

> We have all been vexed and alarmed here on reading that the government had acted against the people [at] home who are trying to stop the use of English goods in Ireland. We realise the importance of winning the fight on the annuities, and feel that any compromise on that point would be a betrayal. We feel the sooner you exclude everything English the quicker you will win the fight. Lord Guinness is one of their own and will not be taxed by the English nor have his product excluded.
>
> . . . as long as the papers report jailings of Republicans by the Free State Government, it creates a chill in all concerned. Your own organisation [the AARIR] is ashamed of it and our members denounce it [Clan na nGael]. Their answer, when we counsel patience, is 'he started the economic war, our men do their share in it by the boycott and are bludgeoned and jailed for their efforts. If Cosgrave would jail men for this offense, he would be one of the loudest in protest, and now he does same kind of work himself and thinks it quite in order.' To be frank, it is apparent that an agreement between your forces and the forces of the IRA is a national necessity. They can do things you will not care to do or cannot do in the face of public criticism, while the IRA pay no heed to public clamour so long as they feel they are doing a national duty.

He concluded: 'God bless your family, yourself, and all who are true to Ireland.'

De Valera was so furious that he did not reply to the letter for three months.[58] And then he made no mention of his former mentor's business anxieties.[59] McGarrity was 'deeply hurt'[60] by the delay. When the letter did arrive it was marked 'strictly personal and confidential' and began 'My Dear Joe':

> I refrained from replying to your letter of October 2nd. The fact is that to reply to it would require a book, that is, if I wished the reply to be convincing. You suggested that you would possibly be coming here. I hoped you would, so that I

might give you the 'talking to', which as I re-read your letter I would give the world for an opportunity of doing.

I do not think I ever got a letter which required such patience to read through. There was a pain in every line of it. . . . You talk about coming to an understanding with the IRA. You talk of the influence it would have both here and abroad. You talk as if we were fools and didn't realise all this. My God! Do you not know that ever since 1921 the main purpose in everything I have done has been to try to secure a basis for national unity.

It has taken us ten long years of patient effort to get the Irish nation on the march again after a devastating Civil War. Are we to abandon all this in order to satisfy a group who have not given the slightest evidence of any ability to lead our people anywhere except back into the morass.

We desire unity, but desire will get us nowhere unless we can get some accepted basis for determining what that national policy shall be *and where leadership shall lie* [author's italics] . . . Those who are barring our path now are doing exactly what Cohalan & Co. did in 1919 to 1921.

Unknown to McGarrity, de Valera did make one further unsuccessful effort to come to an agreement with the IRA.[61] He saw Sean Russell secretly in April 1935. According to the account which Russell later gave to McGarrity: 'Russell asked, or rather promised co-operation with the Fianna Fail Party in every way for a period of five years from that date if Dev would promise to declare a Republic for all Ireland at the end of the five-year period. Dev refused to agree to that saying: "you want it both ways."' Twomey put de Valera's rejection rather more bluntly:[62] 'With this, de Valera angrily dismissed him.' McGarrity himself saw de Valera during Christmas 1935. But as he recorded:[63] 'He had little heart to enter into discussion for, as he phrased it, his written answer to my appeal . . . gave *no* [author's italics] encouragement for unity except on Dev.'s terms.'

McGarrity said later that he would have 'talked frankly',[64] had he known that de Valera had seen Russell. But de Valera did not enlighten him. The end came for Joseph McGarrity on 13 September 1936. On that day a young Limerick IRA man, Sean Glynn, somehow managed to commit suicide by hanging himself with a towel from a low shelf in Arbour Hill prison. He had been arrested aboard a commandeered lorry attempting to get to the Wolfe Tone Commemoration which de Valera had banned the previous June. In his diary McGarrity describes IRA prisoners being:[65] 'so unmercifully treated that young Glynn was found hanging in his cell in Arbour Hill Prison Dublin. . . . This was the last straw for me.' The conditions in Arbour Hill were undoubtedly harsh. The prisoners were kept in solitary confinement, forbidden to speak and, to ensure that silence was maintained in the jail, the warders wore rubber-soled shoes. McGarrity was so moved that he actually criticized de Valera publicly for:[66] '. . . selling out his former friends and repressing all freedom of thought in Ireland with the ruthlessness of a dictator'.

And so Joseph McGarrity and Eamon de Valera came to a parting of the ways. They had travelled a long way since de Valera stepped off the SS

Lapland in 1919. But it was only some six months before he died, writing to his friend Mick McDonnell,[67] that McGarrity acknowledged that throughout the period of their friendship he and de Valera had in fact been pursuing different goals: 'Dev! His very name makes me sick. What has he not done in reverse of everything he taught? We made him a little god here, and I now believe, and have for some time, that after Easter week [1916] he was through with any physical contest against England.'

Making allowances for McGarrity's choice of language, no doubt influenced by his state of mind at that moment – he was writing to tell McDonnell that he had just been diagnosed as having throat cancer – it was a perceptive judgement. After his crack-up in Boland's Bakery de Valera had had enough of physical force. His espousal of McGarrity and the IRA after the signing of the Treaty came about through the injury to his pride inflicted by Collins and Griffith. Had it not been for that fateful rush of blood to the head on hearing of the Treaty's signing he would have parted from him and his associates far earlier. His goal had been 'extremist support', not the extremists' objectives.

Before leaving the hidden world of de Valera's relationship with the IRA to return to his continuing public disagreement with England, one tragic bond which he did share with McGarrity should be commented on. In the period of de Valera's first four years in power (1932–6), while he and the IRA were moving towards their inevitable estrangement, both he and McGarrity suffered the loss of a son. In August 1932 McGarrity's son Joseph died unexpectedly and in February 1936 de Valera's boy, Brian, was killed in a riding accident in Phoenix Park. Brian had been a promising student at Blackrock, particularly of mathematics; he was described as being 'brilliant in that direction'.[68] His death at twenty-one was a terrible blow to both Sinead and Eamon. The furrows on de Valera's face seemed to increase, but Catholicism, stoicism and the tumultuous events of 1936 left the public man little time for private grief. For, apart from the crackdown on the IRA, that year also saw de Valera take his most decisive steps towards moulding the country into his own image.

22

THE UNIQUE DICTATOR

THE YEAR 1936 saw de Valera abolish the Senate and utilize the abdication of King Edward VIII as a stepping stone towards the introduction of a new Constitution, thus creating a republic that was not a republic and embodying many of the concepts of Document No. 2 and of external association. He had heralded this as far back as 23 April 1933 when, speaking at Arbour Hill, at the annual Easter Commemoration over the graves of the executed 1916 leaders, he had announced his intention of removing British forms step by step so that:[1] 'this State that we control may be a Republic in fact; and that, when the time comes, the proclaiming of the Republic may involve no more than a ceremony, the formal confirmation of a status already attained'.

As we have seen, his predecessors' work on the Statute of Westminster facilitated the abolition of the Oath in May 1933. In November of that year their preparatory work also assisted him in disposing of the right of appeal from Irish courts to the British Privy Council. He himself disposed of the Governor General in that month. Following McNeill's resignation he transferred some of the Governor General's powers to the Executive Council – in real terms, to himself. These were the Governor General's prerogatives in regard to recommending money Bills and his power to withhold his assent, if he chose, from a Bill of any sort. There was thus no fear that de Valera's choice for Governor General, Donal O'Buachalla, would withhold his signature when one of de Valera's favourite pieces of legislation came before him on Friday, 29 May 1936. This was the Constitution (Amendment No. 24) Bill, 1934 which de Valera had at last succeeded in battling through the Dail and Senate. It was this legislation which abolished the Senate. Thus, between his tinkerings and those of his predecessors, the Constitution was assuming a very different character from that which the British had forced Michael Collins to accept in 1922.

So were the politics of the Twenty-six Counties. By 1936 de Valera's position was accurately summed up in the title of a favourable biographical work published that year, *Unique Dictator*, by Desmond Ryan.[2] He controlled the level of power, the Government, a powerful newspaper and the largest political party. His opponents in Parliament, already increasingly ineffectual, were further weakened by the death of Patrick Hogan in a motor accident. The new Fine Gael Party was becoming an increasingly attenuated version of the old Cumann na nGael. Outside Parliament the Blueshirts and the IRA were disintegrating. The Senate, the last bastion of Unionist and Cumann na nGaedheal opposition to his policies, was abolished. The annuities dispute with Britain had settled into a bloodless version of that most blessed distraction for rulers throughout the ages, a foreign war. He decided that the time was ripe for the introduction of a new Constitution.

However, he refused to be drawn by opponents who scented that he had some such scheme in mind throughout the long drawn-out Senate battle. But he did give an indication of his intentions in Clare on 29 June 1935 when, speaking in Ennis, he said:[3] ' . . . before the present Government left office they would have an Irish Constitution from top to bottom'. What he did not say was that the previous April he had directed the legal adviser to the Department of External Affairs, John Hearne, to begin drafting a Constitution incorporating the idea of external association. Drafting was sufficiently far advanced by June 1936 for him to send Dulanty, the Irish High Commissioner, to the King with a memorandum indicating his intentions:[4] ' . . . establishing conditions for permanent peace and harmony amongst the Irish people and providing a more secure basis for friendship and co-operation with the people of Great Britain . . . .' To this end he intended: ' . . . to introduce a Bill for the purpose of setting up a new Constitution . . . leaving unaffected the constitutional usages relating to external affairs. Among the provisions of the new Constitution will be the creation of the office of the President, elected by the people, and the abolition of the office of Governor General.' The next day, 8 June, he set up a Commission to examine the question of bicameralism and report on the type of Upper House which might replace the vanished Senate. But all constitutional plans were soon to be temporarily disrupted by the abdication crisis, a disruption which de Valera was to use to his advantage.

Under the terms of the Statute of Westminster:[5] ' . . . any alteration in the law touching the Succession to the Throne or the Royal Styles and Titles shall hereafter require the assent as well of the Parliaments of all the Dominions as of the Parliament of the United Kingdom'. Accordingly the British Prime Minister, Stanley Baldwin, sent Sir Henry Batterbee to Dublin on 29 November to seek de Valera's opinion on the three alternatives faced by the British Cabinet:

(1) That Mrs Simpson be recognized as Queen.

(2) That she should not become Queen but that the King need not abdicate.

(3) That the King abdicate in favour of the Duke of York.

De Valera recommended the second option on the grounds that divorce was recognized in England. Unlike the other Dominion Prime Ministers, who made their views known directly to the King, de Valera merely asked that he be kept informed of the King's intentions. He did not inform the British of what he intended to do himself in the event of an abdication. When Batterbee pressed Joseph Walshe, the Secretary of the Department for External Affairs, for information he was told, on 10 December:[6]

' . . . we are going to amend the existing constitution, so that the law would exactly express the realities of the constitutional position in regard to the functions exercised directly by the King. The precise manner in which this is to be done, has not yet been determined.'

When the British discovered that de Valera did not intend to summon the Dail for a week Malcolm MacDonald, the new Secretary for the Dominions who had replaced Thomas, rang to ask him to convene Parliament immediately. The British were concerned that if this did not happen there would be a week in which Edward VIII would still be King in Ireland, making of the Free State an independent monarchy, albeit of only a week's duration. De Valera in fact had this legislation prepared and on 10 December summoned his deputies by telegram to appear at the Dail the next day, sending them copies of the proposed Bills by post; several country deputies must have left for Dublin before the post containing them arrived. This was the moment when his abolition of the Upper House was of greatest benefit to him. The two Bills were put forward under a guillotine motion whereby the first, entitled the Constitution (Amendment No. 27) Bill, 1936, had to be passed through all stages between 3 p.m. and 11 p.m. The second, the Executive (External Relations) Authority Bill, had also to be passed on a single day, 12 December.

Bill number one got rid of the King and of the Governor General. But in order to avoid problems over diplomatic representation, particularly with the USA and the Vatican, the Crown was retained for external purposes in Article 51 of the Constitution: 'Provided that it shall be lawful for the Executive Council, to the extent and subject to any conditions which may be determined by law to avail, for the purposes of the appointment of diplomatic and consular agents and conclusion of international agreements of any organ used as a constitutional organ for the like purpose by any of the nations referred to in Article 1 of this Constitution.'

One would have thought that, whatever diplomatic problems there were, this section would have caused nearly insuperable translation difficulties, but de Valera knew what it meant (the King was the 'organ') and that was enough. Throughout the debate the Opposition lawyers won most of the debating point battles, but de Valera won the war. This was perfectly underlined just as the first day's debate was concluding. One change proposed by the new legislation was that the Chairman of the Dail was henceforth to summon the Dail. Just as the guillotine was about to fall, a Fine Gael lawyer, deputy Cecil Lavery, pointed out that once the Dail was dissolved there would be no Dail Chairman and thus no person to call it into being again. This caused a flurry of consternation in the ranks of Fianna Fail. The Attorney General tried to move an amendment to cope with the situation, but the Opposition objected, pointing out that under the terms of the guillotine the motion had to be passed within the next few minutes. The Chair upheld the objection – but the Bill passed by 79 votes to 54.

Bill number two also went through the next day. This stated that:

> So long as Saorstat Eireann is associated with the following nations, that is to say, Australia, Canada and Great Britain, New Zealand and South Africa, and so long as the King recognized by those nations as the symbol of their co-operation continues to act on behalf of each of those nations (on the advice of the several Governments thereof), for the purpose of the appointment of diplomatic and consular representatives, and the conclusion of international agreements, the King so recognised may, and is hereby authorised to, act on behalf of Saorstat Eireann for the like purposes, as and when advised by the Executive Council so to do.

The reasoning behind this was 'de Valera's view that the keeping of this shadowy link with Britain might help towards the ultimate reunification of Ireland.'[7] This passed by 81 votes to 5. In the course of the two-day debate Frank MacDermott asked a very good question to which no one provided an answer:[8] 'How would it be if the new King said – as I would if I were in his shoes – "Go and be damned; I'm not interested in acting as your deputy for certain purposes while I am not recognized as King of the country."' The short answer is that de Valera's legislation would have collapsed. But, as we shall shortly see, the British were moving towards a more conciliatory position over the annuities dispute and other matters, and no such eventuality arose.

The way was now clear for de Valera to set about introducing his new Constitution. Little else in his career throws such a shadow over contemporary Ireland. Apart from the efforts of Hearne and other civil servants he solicited drafts from religious figures. This involved him (not surprisingly) in turning to Blackrock and to a Holy Ghost Father, John Charles McQuaid, who (not surprisingly) was found to be a most acceptable candidate in the eyes of the state when a vacancy occurred in the Archdiocese of Dublin some years later. De Valera also consulted a well-known Jesuit writer of the time, Father Edward Cahill SJ. Before the Constitution was published he had consulted personally with all the leaders of the major Irish Churches and sounded the Pope as to his reaction. The latter expressed no opinion on the religious provisions of the Constitution, which he was given sight of before the Irish electorate. But his neutral stance enabled de Valera to ward off a 'triumphal recognition',[9] sought by Cardinal MacRory who had also appealed to the Pontiff. His official biography states that he expected[10] 'no trouble' with the religious article. 'This however proved to be a delusion.' He had considerably difficulty in persuading some of his Cabinet colleagues on the one hand, notably Gerry Boland, that the provisions were not sectarian and offensive to Northern sentiment, and the Catholic Church on the other that he was doing enough to acknowledge its special position in Ireland. In the end the 'special position' was exactly what he recognized in a Constitution that gave less evidence of republicanism than it did of the influence of that other Irish colonial power, the Holy Roman Catholic and Apostolic Church. It visualized a state that, while democratic in practice, would be theocratic in precept; and neither at the time of its enactment, nor in today's Ireland, is it a source of enthusiasm for Irish Protestants.

In its final form Article 44 read:

> The State recognises the special position of the Holy Catholic and Roman Church as the guardian of the faith professed by the great majority of the citizens. The State also recognises the Church of Ireland, the Presbyterian Church in Ireland, the Methodist Church in Ireland, the Religious Society of Friends in Ireland, as well as the Jewish Congregations and the other religious denominations existing in Ireland at the date of the coming into operation of this constitution.

As we shall see, Article 44 was later abolished; and, at the time of writing, some of the Constitution's other provisions are a source of national and, indeed, international, controversy. These will therefore be examined in some detail later. In general, however, de Valera's Constitution has withstood both the test of time and its baptism of fire during its passage through the Dail. As he said himself, despite much criticism:[11] 'The amendments made to the draft, during the course of discussion in the Dail . . . have affected details only.'

The Constitution embodies the various changes made by both himself and the Cosgrave regime in the relationship with Britain, and it removed the quotient of ambiguity from Fianna Fail's recognition of the state. A party which enacts a democratic Constitution and actively solicits support for that Constitution could no longer be regarded as a 'slightly constitutional party'. From 1937 onwards Fianna Fail, by word as well as deed, had left 'extremist support' behind. Articles 4 and 5 declared that (4): 'The name of the State is Eire, or in the English language Ireland.' Ireland (5) was described as a: 'sovereign, independent, democratic state'. Indeed, the Constitution proved to be so democratic in spirit as to be an embarrassment to the abandonment of 'extremist support'. In 1939 High Court Judge Gavan Duffy ruled that the Offences Against the State Act, which de Valera had introduced that year to curb the IRA, was repugnant to the Constitution. A number of IRA men were freed as a result. Much later, in 1973, in a move which would almost certainly have been even more unwelcome to him, the High Court ruled in the McGee case that it was contrary to the spirit of the Constitution to prohibit the importation of contraceptives, a milestone in the protracted battle to legalize contraception in Ireland.

De Valera himself regarded the Constitution as a keystone achievement, a 'great work'. He said:[12] 'As long as I live anyhow, it will always be a matter of pride for me that I was the head of the Government that was able to get a majority of the Irish people to support and pass that Constitution.' He said of one of its articles (1) that: 'I would be very glad indeed at the hour of my death to stand over it.'

He was speaking at the Fianna Fail Ard Fheis of October 1937, as usual claiming to be 'unprepared' because of pressure of work, and then going on to deliver a closely reasoned address that occupied over thirteen long pages.[13] The reason for the lengthy address was deeply rooted in his own psychology, in his attitude towards women, and in his ever-present awareness of the need to preserve the image of being the keeper of the Holy Grail of Republicanism. Mrs Tom Clarke, widow of the 1916 leader, had accused him of 'slipping' from Republican principles in the drafting of the article. As other provisions in his Constitution will shortly demonstrate, de Valera had no feeling for feminism. Nor was he eager to see women advance in politics. Nevertheless he had a profound respect for women's insights into human nature. 'Listen to the women, Viv,' was one of his frequent exhortations to Vivion. His view of women – as teachers, guardians of the social order, mothers and nuns – could be described as conservative, sexless or even, in a way, dehumanized. But it interacted powerfully with his view of certain women who had been touched by the revolution. These, as his letter from jail to Mrs Malone, the mother of the 1916 hero, indicates, he viewed with an especial reverence as coming somewhere on the political spectrum between the Mother of Sorrows and the Keepers of the Sacred Flame. It was no accident that he chose Margaret Pearse to start up the *Irish Press*. Mrs Tom Clarke was the keeper of one of the most sacred Republican flames of all. A criticism of his Constitution from her was akin to a papal disapproval of a new Mass.

That is why his reply was so careful. He pointed out that the first aim of Fianna Fail itself was to secure the unity of Ireland as a republic. He went on to say of the Constitution:[14] 'as far as we are concerned, certainly as far as I am concerned, on the basis of that Constitution the next move forward must be to get within that Constitution the whole of the thirty-two counties of Ireland'. Whether this was really his ambition, or whether his ego demanded that he have his own document rather than one drafted under Michael Collins, must remain a matter for speculation. What is certain is that his Constitution contains statements grossly offensive to the Irish Protestant tradition, particularly the North of Ireland Protestants whose assent or opposition to unity is so fundamental to the question of partition.

De Valera showed himself to be keenly aware of the essential nature of partition, as opposed to the customary windy anti-British Fianna Fail platform rhetoric of the period. Some two years after the enactment of his Constitution he had a conversation with Frank Gallagher[15] which is summarized as follows: ' . . . that the position of the majority was one of a group now in power fearing to become a minority inside a temperamentally different State'. Readers may judge for themselves whether the Preamble to the Constitution and its first three articles reflected an approach to a 'temperamentally different' minority, or a consciousness of the need to trail behind him clouds of 'extremist support' as he came before the bar of his own party to answer critics like Mrs Clarke. The Preamble states:

> In the name of the Most Holy Trinity, from Whom is all authority and to Whom, in our final end, all actions both of men and States, must be referred,

We the people of Eire,

Humbly acknowledging all our obligations to our Divine Lord, Jesus Christ, Who sustained our fathers through centuries of trial.

Gratefully remembering their heroic and unremitting struggle to regain the rightful independence of our Nation.

And seeking to promote the common good, with due observance of Prudence Justice and Charity, so that dignity and freedom of the individual may be assured, true social order obtained, the unity of our country restored, and concord established with other nations.

Do hereby adopt, enact and give to ourselves this Constitution.

On 12 July an Orangeman will be found 'gratefully remembering' the 'unremitting struggle' for a different nation from that envisaged by de Valera, when he recalls, in the words of a popular Orange song, how his forefathers 'fought for the freedom of religion, on the green, grassy slopes of the Boyne'. In considering the effect of Article 1 of the Constitution on the said Orangeman, it should of course be borne in mind that he already had his 'own form of Government' and that he had every intention of doing all within his power to ensure that it continued to operate 'in accordance with its own genius and traditions'. Article 1 states: 'The Irish nation hereby affirms its inalienable, indefeasible, and sovereign right to choose its own form of Government, to determine its relations with other nations, and to develop its life, political, economic and cultural, in accordance with its own genius and traditions.'

While we may speculate as to the effect of the foregoing on our Orange friend, we are on surer grounds with the next two articles: we know for certain that he and his like strongly object to them. Article 2 states that: 'The national territory consists of the whole island of Ireland, its islands and the territorial sea.' While Article 3 says: 'Pending the re-integration of the national territory, and without prejudice to the *right* [author's italics] of the Parliament and Government established by this Constitution to exercise jurisdiction over the whole of that territory, the laws enacted by that parliament shall have the like area and extent of application as the laws of Saorstat Eireann and the like extra-territorial effect.'

De Valera defended Articles 2 and 3 stoutly. He said that the Dail, on behalf of the nation, had a duty to assert a moral claim and right to such jurisdiction since there was no doubt that:[16] 'the vast majority of the people of this island would claim that the nation and the State ought to be coterminous'. One need not be too solicitous about the susceptibilities of the Northern Unionists; their mutually exploitative relationship with the Tories has produced malign results for both Ireland and England, and there is no need for expatiation on the carnage that continues as this is written. Moreover, until it was dissolved in 1972, the apartheid of the Irish-un-Free State which was created in Belfast was every bit as unlovely as what was done to black Africans by the South African Orange Free State. But, instead of an entirely legitimate and justifiable aspiration to unity, to put in such unsustainable *claims* in a Constitution which could only apply to twenty-six of the thirty-two counties was an act of coat-trailing provocation. Worse, as things have since evolved, to take these claims out, which could only be done by referendum, would be to create a highly combustible sense of abandonment and outrage amongst Six County nationalists, and, at best, a highly divisive referendum campaign in the Twenty-six Counties. After all the carnage in Northern Ireland, such a campaign would not by any means be certain of success.

The dangers of putting in these articles was foreseen by at least one knowledgeable person of the time, the redoubtable J. J. McElligott of the Department of Finance. McElligott was a nationalist of impeccable credentials, he had fought in the GPO and his personality was such that he was described as possessing the wisdom of the serpent and the mildness of the dove.[17] He drew the attention of the small group of civil servants who were engaged on drafting the Constitution to the dangers inherent in the claim.[18] Articles 2 and 3, he said, seemed 'rather to vitiate the Constitution, by stating at the outset what will be described, and with some justice, as a fiction' – a fiction, moreover, which would 'not contribute anything to effecting the unity of Ireland, but rather the reverse'. His submission on a second draft of the Constitution was even more pungent. Claiming territory which 'does not belong to Saorstat Eireann' enshrined in the Constitution a:[19] 'claim to "Hibernia Irredentia". The parallel with Italy's historical attitude to the Adriatic seaboard beyond its recognised territory is striking and in that case it is likely to have lasting ill-effects on our political relations with our nearest neighbours.'

But – and here readers may recall my disagreement with Professor Lee's assessment of civil servants' influence – it proved 'Impossible to change Dev's mind'.[20] He proved as unwilling to accept McElligott's personal warning that 'no good fruit'[21] would emanate from Articles 2 and 3 as he did the Finance man's *private*[22] assessment that the economic war was damaging and unnecessary. It is very difficult to separate de Valera's real mind on the Six Counties from his public posturing. Apart from his remarks to Gallagher another close confidant, Maurice Moynihan, had a recollection of his speculating on the unworkable[23] nature of a repartition. He made speeches a-plenty, but these do not help us to uncover evidence of original thought on the issue. There are no examples of error on the side of generosity to the Protestant community in Ireland, which would have meant ruffling either nationalistic or clerical feathers. The reverse is true, in fact. Articles 2 and 3 carry us back to his original decision to go for 'extremist support'; they may be regarded as the IRA component of his Constitution. He paraphrased Parnell to fend off a group of Republican-minded members of Fianna Fail who lobbied him to declare a full frontal republic in the Constitution, saying: ' . . . there would be no words in the new constitution that could possibly place bounds to the march of a nation'.[24] Then Eamonn Donnelly, the principal sponsor of the Republican demand, forced a vote on the issue at a Fianna Fail National Executive of

3 November 1937. The vote was defeated by 21 votes to 4. But the issue was so embarrassing for de Valera that he made the rare gesture of taking the chair at the meeting himself. Donnelly's resolution called flatly for Fianna Fail backing for a Six County plebiscite of the kind de Valera had been seeking in 1923; this had as its objective the returning of Northern nationalist representatives to a Dublin Parliament.[25] It was this pressure from Fianna Fail republicans, coupled with a desire to seduce IRA support, that made it necessary for de Valera 'to include as a minimum, his irredentist claims in the Constitution'.[26]

In the course of his introduction of the Constitution in the Dail, he was asked by Frank MacDermott what it contained by way of concession (MacDermott had earlier drawn attention to the anomaly of professing unity while acting in a way that made it more difficult to attain) that would not be there if the Northern problem did not exist. To this de Valera replied threateningly:[27] 'The Deputy had better not ask me to go into the origin of a number of other things that would possibly be in this Constitution if the Northern problem were not there. If it was not there, in all probability there would be a flat, downright proclamation of the republic in this. That is one.' And he went on to say that: 'You cannot go farther than we have gone in this Constitution to meet the views of those in the North without sacrificing, to an extent that we are not prepared to sacrifice, the legitimate views and opinions of the vast majority of our people.'

In other words he was not prepared to take on the Church. Nor did anyone on MacDermott's side of the House show any inclination to do so either. A Catholic state for a Catholic people was in an advanced state of growth. During his Ard Fheis speech that year de Valera said that he would:[28] ' . . . urge both Fianna Fail and the Irish people to move forward on the basis of the Constitution to secure the unity of their country. That was intended to indicate the utmost limit of concession which they in this part of the country were prepared to make in order to meet the sentiment of the people in the North.' But the only vestige of 'concession' one finds in the Constitution appears to lie in Article 29.4. This states: ' . . . the Government may . . . avail of, or adopt, any organ, instrument, or method of procedure used or adopted for the like purpose by the members of any group or league of nations with which the State is or becomes associated for the purpose of international co-operation in matters of common concern.' In plain language, there might be occasions when the Crown could be made use of – hardly a blindingly large-minded concession to the Protestant and Unionist tradition.

The other great area of controversy in the Constitution lies in its attitude to women. It is admittedly an area which throws a longer shadow over contemporary Ireland, wherein the absence of divorce is a live issue at the time of writing, than it did over the 1937 era in which de Valera introduced the Constitution. But to some it read like a feminist's nightmare, even

494

then. Under Personal Rights, Article 40.1 declared: 'All citizens shall, as human persons, be held equal before the law. This shall not be held to mean that the State shall not in its enactments have due regard to differences of capacity, physical and moral, and of social function.' When this is taken in conjunction with the succeeding Article it immediately becomes apparent that de Valera was worsening the lot of women in the Ireland of 1937. Article 41 deals with the family:

1 1 The State recognises the Family as the natural primary and fundamental unit group of Society, and as a moral institution possessing inalienable and imprescriptible rights, antecedent and superior to all positive law.

2 The State, therefore, guarantees to protect the Family in its constitution and authority, as the necessary basis of social order and as indispensable to the welfare of the Nation and the State.

2 1 In particular, the State recognises that by her life within the home, woman gives to the State a support without which the common good cannot be achieved.

2 The State shall, therefore, endeavour to ensure that mothers shall not be obliged by economic necessity to engage in labour to the neglect of their duties in the home.

3 1 The State pledges itself to guard with special care the institution of Marriage, on which the Family is founded, and to protect it against attack.

2 No law shall be enacted providing for the grant of a dissolution of marriage.

3 No person whose marriage has been dissolved under the civil law of any other State but is a subsisting valid marriage under the law for the time being in force within the jurisdiction of the BV government and Parliament established by this Constitution shall be capable of contracting a valid marriage within that jurisdiction during the life time of the other party to the marriage so dissolved.

When the draft Constitution was published it suddenly dawned on some women how these clauses affected the principle of sex equality when taken in conjunction with other steps de Valera had taken or was taking. First, under the Conditions of Employment Bill he had introduced the right to restrict (or completely debar) women working in industry. The object of this piece of legislation was to:[29] 'protect the interests of the male workers who, without such restrictions, might have been swamped by lower paid women in the new industries'. Second, his provisions on women did away with an existing guarantee in the Collins Constitution, Article 3 of which said: 'Every person without distinction of sex, domiciled in the area of the jurisdiction of the Irish Free State shall within the jurisdiction of the Irish Free State enjoy the privileges and be subject to the obligations of such citizenship.'

De Valera's clauses were also in stark contrast to the promises contained in the 1916 proclamation: 'The Republic guarantees religious and civil liberty, equal rights and equal opportunities to all its citizens.' In a widely quoted article he was accused of having 'an innate prejudice against women anywhere outside the kitchen'.[30] Professor Mary Hayden said: 'What is proposed by the new Constitution is not a return to the Middle Ages. It is something much worse.' De Valera argued[31] that he had deliberately deleted the phrase 'without distinction of sex' from the existing Constitution because he considered it 'a badge of their [women's] previous inferiority'.

He found it necessary to train the guns of the *Irish Press* on Mary S. Kettle, the chairman [*sic*] of the Joint Committee of Women's Societies, when she pointed out that the cumulative effect of the various articles he was introducing was to ensure that 'no woman who works . . . will have any security whatsoever'. In a rather unworthy editorial[32] the paper claimed that Ms Kettle was following the lead of the Fine Gael lawyer, John A. Costello, and knew little about drafting a Constitution; it quoted the opening words of Article 40 to show that they contained the same guarantees as contained in the 1916 proclamation: 'All citizens shall, as human persons be, held equal before the law.' However, the paper left out the qualifying words which followed ('This shall not' etc. – see above). Many women's organizations protested, but without effect. They included the Women Graduates' Association, the National Council of Women of Ireland, the International Alliance of Women for Suffrage and Equal Citizenship, the Mothers' Union and the Geneva-based Six Point Group which said de Valera's clauses were based on:[33] 'a fascist and slave conception of woman as being a non-adult person who is very weak and whose place is in the home'.

One of the most noticeable broadsides directed against the Constitution came from the pen of Louie Bennett, the much-respected secretary of the Irish Women Workers' Union. In a letter to de Valera[34] she reiterated all the objections detailed above and focused in particular on yet another area, Section 4 (2) of Article 45, which reads as follows: 'The State shall endeavour to ensure that the strength and health of workers, men and women, and the tender age of children shall not be abused and that citizens shall not be forced by economic necessity to enter vocations unsuited to their sex, age or strength.' Louie Bennett described this Article as being: 'the most indefensible in the Constitution. It takes from women the right to choose their own avocation in life. The State is given power to decide what avocations are suited to their sex and strength. It would hardly be possible to make a more deadly encroachment upon the liberty of the individual than to deprive him or her of this right.'

But the most significant protest from any woman was an unpublished one. Dorothy Macardle did send a short letter of support for Louie Bennett to the *Irish Press*,[35] but her major fire was reserved for a private communication to de Valera. Macardle has been rather slightingly described as the 'hagiographer royal to the Republic'.[36] The term could perhaps be defended by reference to her mammoth work *The Irish Republic*, which took her seven years to compile, much of that time spent writing in an isolated house in a lonely Wicklow glen. But the work, which contains a mass of invaluable detail, is not so much a paean to the republic as a hymn to de Valera. Significantly, it was reprinted by the Irish Press in 1951. Macardle, who came of an old Protestant brewing family, had shown considerable courage and journalistic talent in documenting in a famous pamphlet, 'Tragedies of Kerry', atrocities committed against the irregulars by Free State forces in Kerry. For her to take issue with de Valera was akin to one of the four Gospel authors falling out with Christ. But she told him:[37] 'I find myself in absolute agreement with Miss Louie Bennett's published letter to you. The real crux is the question of employment. The language of certain clauses suggests that the state may interfere to a great extent in determining what opportunities shall be open or closed to women, there is no clause whatever to counterbalance that suggestion or to safeguard women's rights in that respect.' Having suggested an alternative wording of her own (which de Valera did not accept), Macardle went on to sound a McGarrity-like note of disillusionment and accusation: 'As the Constitution stands, I do not see how anyone holding advanced views on the rights of women can support it, and that it is a tragic dilemma for those who have been loyal and ardent workers in the national cause.'

But as the Constitution stood then it stands now, for de Valera refused to accept the Bennett–Macardle analysis. His interpretation of women's place in Irish society remained that of his constitutional adviser on the subject, John Charles McQuaid, CSSp, President of Blackrock College. Writing from the College on objections such as Macardle's, McQuaid advised de Valera[38] that the feminists were 'very confused. Both Casti Connubi and Quadragesimo Anno [papal Encyclicals] answer them'. McQuaid told de Valera that it was 'incorrect' to state that 'men and women have equal right to work of the same kind. Men and women have equal right to *appropriate* work.' His assessment was that: ' . . . the law of Nature lays diverse functions on men and women. The completeness of life requires this diversity of function and of work. This is diversity not an inequality of work. In the desire to cut out unfair discrimination against women, diversity of work is being constantly confused with inequality of work.' The 'diversity' argument was one which was to hold sway, not only in the Constitution, but in Irish life generally for many years after de Valera had retired from politics.

De Valera also refused to accept the advice of Catholic writers[39] who pointed out to him that his clauses on marriage (Article 41, section 3, subsection 30) denied Catholics rights which the Church permitted – that is, remarriage in Ireland, following a lawfully granted civil dissolution abroad, after a civil marriage to a non-Catholic. Why he should have been so adamantine on all these issues must necessarily be a matter of conjecture. Various reasons have been advanced: his desire to show himself as an irreproachable Catholic; the experiences which befell him in childhood after his mother went out to work; his dislike of the unholy habit, shared by many of the spirited women he met in politics at the time, of standing up to him and questioning his decisions. Probably there was an element of all these factors in his reasoning. What is certain, however, is that the state which evolved under him did very little of substance to make a reality of the situation allegedly envisaged for either women or the family in his Constitution. The Kate Colls of Ireland who found themselves forced to look for work before his Constitution was enacted saw no improvement in their condition, or that of others like them, after it came into force.

The Dail approved the draft Constitution on 14 June 1937; on the same day de Valera dissolved Parliament and announced that the vote on the Constitution, and a general election, would both be held on 1 July. It is not clear whether he was fearful that worsening economic conditions would tell against him if he allowed his term in office to run for the further six months or so to which he was entitled, or hopeful that the Constitution would bring him increased popularity. More likely he was relying on the activities of a Cabinet committee on constituency revision set up after the 1933 election to strengthen his position.

As he sat on the committee himself this would not have been an unreasonable expectation. The other members were Lemass, Jim Ryan and Sean T. O'Ceallaigh. The committee abolished six university seats, four of which Fine Gael held, and reduced the overall number of seats to 138 from 153. These changes had the result of greatly increasing the number of independents who went forward, because there were not enough places for all the former Dail members to be officially adopted as candidates. Frank MacDermott did not go forward; he had been having personality differences with his colleagues, with whom he took issue over the Commonwealth. But despite this further weakening of the opposition de Valera did not do as well as he had expected. The results were:

Fianna Fail	69 (previously 80)
Fine Gael	48 (previously 53)
Labour	3 (previously 80
Independents	8 (36 stood, 12 were previously elected)

The election result meant that de Valera was back to relying on Labour support. Insofar as the Constitution was concerned, it passed by 685,105 votes to 526,945. The percentages were 39 per cent for and 30 per cent against; 31 per cent did not vote. Spoiled votes were unusually high – roughly 10 per cent or nearly 170,000 voters; this, taken with the fall in Fianna Fail support, indicates that a lot of people regarded the Constitution with little affection. It is thought that many Protestants abstained or spoiled their votes, ensuring, ironically, the Constitution's passage. As the Constitution lays claim to the whole island it is interesting to look at how the percentages recorded would have come out if applied to all-Ireland. The total number of registered voters in the Twenty-six Counties that year was 1,775,055; that across the border, 822,860.[40] This would give a total electorate of 2,597,915. In percentage terms (on the basis of those given above) this makes 26 per cent for, 20 per cent against, 22 not voting and, to take account of the border, 32 per cent ineligible to vote. In the circumstances the numbers 26 and 32 have a certain ironic symbolism.

It would be wrong to think of de Valera as being anti-Protestant. He was simply pro-power. In deciding to tear up the Constitution which Michael Collins had initiated he had given hostages to fortune. With the Roman Catholic Church's strength growing by the hour within his jurisdiction it was inevitable that the new Constitution would be more rather than less Catholic than its predecessor. In fact, once the Constitution had passed into law he showed a certain laudable consistency in putting into practice a doctrine which he had enunciated in the *Nation* during a nasty little local exercise in parish pump politics, interlarded with sectarianism, which had escalated into a national *cause célèbre* some years earlier:[41] 'The Irish people are made up of men and women of different religious beliefs and for the majority to insist upon appointments for men and women of their faith only is unjust and anti-national.' However the article, which dealt with the controversy surrounding the appointment of a Protestant lady,[42] Letticia Dunbar-Harrison, to a librarian's post in Co. Mayo, then went on to cop out: 'In Miss Dunbar's case there was the obvious and fatal flaw that for a Gaeltacht appointment she had no knowledge of Irish . . . .' Ms Dunbar-Harrison was subsequently transferred, in December 1931, to the Library of the Department of Defence, and in the general election of the following year de Valera's fence-sitting republicanism was rewarded by Fianna Fail's winning an extra seat in Co. Mayo.

Looking at the results of the constitutional referendum, which were generally conceded to have reflected the fact that those Protestants who did vote 'voted heavily against the constitution',[43] de Valera decided that a spot of tokenism was called for. He asked Douglas Hyde to become the first President of Eire, or, in the English language, Ireland (or, in reality, twenty-six counties thereof, formerly known as the Irish Free State). The seventy-seven-year-old Hyde was a Protestant, founder and former President of the Gaelic League, known in Irish language circles as An Craoibhin Aoibhinn, 'the little mellow branch'. His nomination was received with an all-party mellowness and on 4 May 1938 he was duly declared elected in the board room of the Department of Agriculture. The Viceregal Lodge, which had lain unoccupied since 1932, was to be his official residence. After accompanying him to inspect it, de Valera then took him to meet his next door neighbour, the Papal Nuncio, Monsignor Pascal Robinson, over afternoon tea.[44]

Alas for this portent of ecumenicism, the underlying reality of Protestant–Catholic relationships in the state which Hyde now presided over, courtesy of de Valera's Constitution, may be gauged from some of the responses to a questionnaire addressed by the Government to the Archbishop of Dublin, Dr Byrne:[45]

Q. Whether it would be proper, from the point of view of the Catholic Church, that a Catholic Aide-de-Camp should be present in attendance on the President in a non-Catholic Church.

R. It would not be proper; particularly in this country where the danger of a grave scandal would be always present.

Q. What ecclesiastical honours or courtesies would be paid to a Catholic Head of the State present at Mass or other religious ceremony; b) Which, if any, of these would be omitted in the case of a non-Catholic Head of the State.

R. A Catholic Head of the State receives the 'pax' (kiss of Peace) and incensation. These are not given to non-Catholics.

Dorothy Macardle did not give de Valera the kiss of peace either. An intellectual Republican, to whom Jefferson, Paine and the Rights of Man had something to do with the concept of Republicanism, she was deeply wounded by the manner in which de Valera's Constitution had rendered unto reaction the things that were Republican. Maurice Moynihan told me[46] a story which reveals how she took her discreet and lady-like revenge. An eponymous film based on her novel *The Uninvited* was shown at the Savoy. Suddenly, without warning, de Valera – who quite obviously had some foreknowledge of the subject matter – exclaimed one afternoon: 'Why don't we go?' 'And up they got!' remarked Maurice Moynihan wonderingly. 'I made a phone call to the Savoy and off we went, myself, Dev. and Kathleen in the official car.'

The film turned out to be allegorical. There was a good fairy, lightsome and beautiful, giving off a pleasant odour. There was also a bad fairy, ugly and smelly. But, as it turned out, appearances were deceptive. The good was bad, and the bad was good. 'Typical Dorothy', was de Valera's reflective comment. A remark of Macardle's was more revealing. She told Moynihan that 'writing *The Irish Republic* represented seven wasted years'. Dorothy Macardle's evident faith in the ultimate redemption of the feminist soul of Ireland, orphaned by de Valera's Constitution, was not paralleled by a belief on de Valera's part in her own redemption. She died, in December 1958, in Our Lady of Lourdes Hospital in Drogheda, after a long illness during which de Valera visited her and prayed constantly, but without success, for her conversion from Protestantism to Catholicism. 'He was very disappointed,' Maurice Moynihan told me.[47]

Macardle was neither the first nor the last author to discover that a writer suffers through involvement with politicians. The role of a writer within de Valera's firmament was that of a propagandist. He was a straight-up 'Art should serve the State' empiricist. His interests were power, politics, man management, religion, the Irish language and, by way of relaxation, walking and mathematics. A list of seventy-seven books[48] and pamphlets which he left behind him in America in 1920 contains only one novel, *The Oregon Trail* by Francis Parkman; the rest include volumes of Franklin, Webster, law journals, Irish dictionaries, works on Irish history, patriotic Irish ballads and Arthur Griffith's *The Resurrection of Hungary*.

De Valera certainly liked books. Gallagher noted[49] that during their tour of America it 'was not safe to let him into a bookshop'. But his instinct for power and politics was so strong that it dominated his literary tastes. Gallagher kept a note of a significant statement made by de Valera in this regard.[50] He said: 'If there is any man whom I would like to be in Irish history it is Thomas Davis.' He went on to point out that 'they' said Davis's style was rhetorical and his poetry inferior. However, de Valera noted, Davis 'appealed to the people not through their heads, but through their hearts. His poetry accomplished the stirring of the people and thus it was good poetry.' De Valera is not passing literary judgements here, he is telling us that he admired Thomas Davis because he was an effective propagandist. Art was serving the state.

Interestingly, therefore, one of the few people successfully to stand up to de Valera during his decade of sustained triumph was the poet W. B. Yeats. This came about less through acknowledgement by de Valera that matters creative were outside his ken than because of the fact that Yeats, who was also possessed of remarkable political skills, was as tenacious in defence of artistic freedom as was de Valera over external association. The formidable pair came into conflict over the Abbey Theatre's 1932 tour of America. Although an artistic and financial success, this tour had elicited a number of protests from Catholic Celtic ideologues along the lines of a Fianna Fail group in New York who objected:[51]

> That plays such as *The Playboy of the Western World*; *Juno and the Paycock*; the *Shadow in the Glen* and others are anything but elevating to the Irish character . . . that the money of the Irish taxpayers be not spent to subsidize the Abbey Theatre in Dublin, which is responsible for presenting these plays, with their filthy language, their drunkenness, murder and prostitution, and holding up the Irish character generally to be scoffed at and ridiculed by people of other races . . . .

De Valera passed the parcel to Sean MacEntee, who as Minister for Finance was responsible for paying the Abbey's grant of £1,000 a year. MacEntee, a cultured figure whose literary tastes and predilection for writing poetry – not exactly the distinguishing mark of a Fianna Fail Cabinet member of that or any other era – did not normally inhibit his legendary prowess as a political in-fighter, failed to enter the ring personally on this occasion. The conduct of hostilities was entrusted to J. J. McElligott who, on 27 February 1933, in best civil service-ese, made known the Government's concern at the fact that 'representations had been made to the Minister for External Affairs' (de Valera) concerning 'certain plays'. McElligott warned that if the repertoire were not cleansed of objectionable material the grant might not be paid. He also sought assurances that when the Abbey went on tour the following year a 'competent company' would be maintained in Dublin and that the grant, which in any case was being reduced to £750, would not be used for tour expenses. Furthermore he sought the deletion from the tour programmes of the phrase: 'By special arrangement with the Irish Free State Government'. And on top of all this he concluded by stating that his Minister had 'consented to the appointment of Professor W. Magennis' as a replacement for the government representative on the board of directors, Dr Walter Starkie, who had resigned some time earlier. This last was probably the unkindest cut of all, as Magennis had proven himself to be relentlessly on the side of reaction on issues involving censorship.

Yeats rose to the challenge magnificently. He replied to McElligott on 1 March, pointing out that one play, *The Playboy of the Western World*, was the 'theme of lectures in American universities and schools, certainly the most popular play in our American repertory, a world famous Irish classic'. The other, *Juno and the Paycock*, 'has packed the Abbey again and again'. He recalled that circles similar to those cited by McElligott had rioted and caused attacks on the Abbey from press and pulpit during their 1911 tour of America. These had elicited the 'powerful support of Theodore Roosevelt' for Yeats and Lady Gregory.[52] On the more recent tour, however, although Yeats had spoken at several universities, including 'the great Catholic University of Notre Dame', he had heard 'not one word of protest'.

Significantly, the first intimation of protest had come, the day after he arrived back in Ireland, 'from a reporter of the *Irish Press*'. Remarked Yeats: ' .. . cows beyond the water have long horns'. However, even if there had been such protest it would have been resisted: 'There never has been an imaginative and intellectual movement that has not faced and fought such opposition.' Of the Government's demand that the Abbey should drop from its tour repertory 'The chief work of Synge and O'Casey', Yeats thundered: 'We refuse such a demand; your Minister may have it in his power to bring our theatre to an end, but as long as it exists it will retain its freedom.' He went on to deal with the Magennis proposal:

> Your letter adds that 'the Minister has consented to the appointment of Professor W. Magennis . . . as a government representative on the board of directors.' Who asked for his 'consent?' We never heard of Professor Magennis' candidature until we received your letter. I find that word 'consent' interesting. We refuse to admit Professor Magennis to our Board as we consider him entirely unfitted to be a director of the Abbey Theatre. It is not necessary to state our reasons for this opinion as my Directors empower me to say in their name and in my own that we refuse further financial assistance from your Government.

The only concession that Yeats made in his letter was to drop the 'special arrangement' reference from the programmes of the projected tour. De Valera hesitated to be seen to withdraw the Abbey subsidy altogether: there was more opprobrium than political gain to be derived from being portrayed as the man who attempted to close this uniquely well-loved and respected Irish theatre. The Senate could be axed, but not the Abbey. Matters dragged on until the following spring when the Abbey directorate, in effect Yeats, sought an interview with him to clear the air concerning the projected US tour. At first de Valera fought shy of the meeting,[53] but he changed his mind after receiving a letter from MacEntee stating that he saw no objection to the Abbey's American tour, 'on the understanding that a reasonably good Company remains in Dublin'. He proposed to tell the Abbey this, subject to a proviso. The last line of his letter to de Valera said coyly: 'I would be glad to hear whether you agree to this course.' De Valera did not agree to this course: he changed his stance about seeing the Abbey directors and held a meeting with them. It brought him little joy.

Despite de Valera's control of the *Irish Press* and the Government Information Service, Yeats won the propaganda war. An unflattering report of de Valera's position during the meeting, from a Special Correspondent, appeared in the *Irish Independent* on 7 April 1934. It quoted 'some people associated with Mr. Yeats'. Yeats was reported as being willing to give up the state subsidy rather than have 'the liberty of the Theatre curtailed by the Government'. Moreover, 'authoritative persons' were cited as saying that de Valera had declared that 'he had never set foot in the Abbey Theatre' and had no knowledge whatever of the plays produced there. The said 'authoritative persons' furthermore declared that having 'obtained the views of competent representatives of the Irish opinion in America' de Valera had made his intentions 'very plain': 'neither Synge's *The Playboy of the Western World*, nor Sean O'Casey's *The Plough and the Stars* was to be included in the repertory'. Yeats was quoted as having stated that 'he had fought the political societies before and was prepared to do so again, if the necessity arose . . . the Abbey Theatre was not to be regarded as a minor branch of the civil service'.

The following day in the London *Sunday Times*[54] the foregoing points were repeated in an unsigned piece which described de Valera as 'The Playboy of the Free State'. 'If only', it reflected, 'Mr de Valera could see himself as others see him in the light of this silly little interference.' De Valera was not amused. He had demanded a list of the plays which the Abbey intended to put on in America. Pausing in the midst of dealing with Blueshirts, IRA, Cumann na nGaedheal, the British Government and other lesser opponents, he used the list in a vain attempt to grapple with Yeats. Yeats had not deigned to send him the list directly. Another director, Lennox Robinson, had transmitted it. A Roland for an Oliver, a Robinson for a McElligott. De Valera was reduced to replying to Robinson in the third person:[55]

> The President observes that three plays by Mr. Sean O'Casey are included in the list. All three touch upon the struggle for national independence in a manner which tends to create a false and unfavourable opinion of the motives and character of men who during that struggle risked their lives in the service of their country. Whatever may be said to justify the production of these plays in Ireland, where the audiences are sufficiently familiar with the history of the independence movement to be capable of making allowance for the element of caricature and

503

exaggeration in Mr O'Casey's representation of it, it appears to the President that their production abroad is likely to injure the reputation of the country and would certainly arouse feelings of shame and resentment among Irish exiles.

The letter went on to refer to the 'inaccurate account' of the meeting with the Abbey directors which had appeared 'in certain Irish and English newspapers'. The President regretted that Dr Yeats 'appears to have issued no denial or correction of the inaccuracies . . . '. Robinson's reply[56] on behalf of the Abbey continued the impersonal tone. It said that if the company went to the States: 'we undertake to have printed on every programme a statement to the effect that, though our Theatre receives a subsidy from the Free State Government, that Government is in no way responsible for the plays presented'. This was, of course, merely what Yeats had offered years earlier. The only consolation proffered concerning de Valera's complaint about a rebuttal of inaccuracies was a reminder that 'Dr. Yeats has personally explained the matter to you'.

And there, with some little skirmishing fire, the matter rested. The *Irish Press*[57] did give suspiciously large coverage under a massive headline to a Dominican priest who declared that the state had lowered 'national prestige' by financing 'its nationals even indirectly to lower its prestige before externs'. But in October, still in possession of the subsidy, the Abbey sailed for America with *The Playboy, Juno*, and, for good measure, *The Plough and the Stars* in its repertory. The battle won, Yeats magnanimously demonstrated Yeatsian fact to be the equal of de Valera fact. The *Irish Press* account of the Abbey's departure was accompanied by a letter from Yeats referring to the *Sunday Times*:[58]

Mr. de Valera has not 'demanded' the withdrawal of any play by Synge or by O'Casey, nor have I 'insisted' upon their presence there. We are on friendly terms with the Irish Government . . . . Mr. Yeates [*sic*] is reported to have retorted that rather than submit to the dictation of politicians or to the idea that the Abbey Theatre is a minor branch of the Civil Service he would reject the State subsidy. No such statement was necessary, no such statement was made.

The battle lost, de Valera showed himself equally magnanimous and, albeit in private, made a virtue out of necessity. To an objector to the tour he replied[59] defending the Abbey subsidy on grounds that were part cultural, part spinal Fianna Fail anti-British doctrine:

It is being continued for the purpose of enabling the Abbey Theatre to carry on the valuable cultural work which it commenced on its foundation thirty years ago . . . . The Abbey Theatre has . . . produced a distinctive school of acting, which is probably one of the finest in the world, and, although some – relatively very few – of the plays in its repertory have aroused strong objection, the repertory on the whole has been acceptable to the Irish people. The proximity of Ireland to Great Britain and the fact that our people are mostly English speaking have resulted in a strong tendency to import British plays and actors. The Abbey Theatre has been the chief agency in countering this tendency . . . .

Nor did Yeats concede to de Valera on the director issue. Magennis, whom another Abbey director, Frank O'Connor, described as a 'windbag with a streak of malice',[60] was eventually given a more appropriate post. He was appointed to the Censorship Board.

It is a pity that de Valera's official biography does not mention the duel with Yeats. One would be interested in assessing whether the poet's brief, but much commented on, dalliance with the Blueshirts, and his promise of a marching song for O'Duffy, was in fact prompted more by anti-de Valera feelings than by the temporary inclination towards fascism attributed to Yeats by some critics. However, while the silence on the Abbey incident could, perhaps, be justified on grounds of political unimportance, the failure to refer to another interesting event which began to unfold in March and April 1934 when de Valera was grappling with both O'Duffy and Yeats is eloquently significant. For in these months he was planning the setting up of a Banking Commission. Whatever view one takes of the Commission's activities, it was an important body; and the omission of any reference to its existence in de Valera's recollections is an interesting comment on his rating of matters economic in his career. At the time of the Commission's gestation de Valera gave at least one powerful observer the impression that he was not in favour of changes in the Irish financial world and was only going along with the Commission's appointment to placate his own extremists.

The observer was Lingard Goulding, Governor of the Bank of Ireland. Demonstrating his flair for the dramatic, de Valera suddenly summoned him to Government Buildings by telephone on a Saturday. Then he informed the startled Goulding of the impending Commission and handed him a list of suggested members. In those days the Bank of Ireland had a dominant position in the Irish banking world, occupying in effect the role of a Central Bank – a dominance and a role which Goulding and his colleagues wished to see continued. De Valera was able to reassure Goulding on this point to such an extent that, according to the historian Ronan Fanning,[61] Goulding reported to his colleagues a few days later, on 13 April, that: 'the list of personnel had been modified by the removal of several names [Fanning suggests that one of them may have been Maynard Keynes] to which he had taken exception. In the Governor's view the President considered a commission should sit and report, but he did not think any alteration in the system was necessary, he was being subjected to pressure from a large section of his party which he would probably be unable to resist.'

In convincing Goulding, de Valera succeeded in ensuring the co-operation of the other banks, and despite some grumbling in the banking community the commission was formally appointed by Sean MacEntee on 20 November 1934. The Commission's terms of reference were:[62] 'to examine and report on the system in Saorstat Eireann of currency, banking, credit, public borrowing and lending, and the pledging of state

505

credit on behalf of agriculture, industry and the social services, and to consider and report what changes, if any, are necessary or desirable to promote the social and economic welfare of the community and the interests of agriculture and industry.'

Its majority report appeared in March 1938 and its minority reports were complete by August of that year; the conservatively weighted Commission found in favour of the status quo. De Valera accepted this finding and ignored some discreetly worded suggestions on state credit which in effect would have meant doing away with his self-sufficiency policy and his housing programme. In a word, the British Treasury-style approach favoured from the foundation of the state was endorsed. A similar Commission set up under Cumann na nGaedheal in 1926 had summed up its view of the Free State in an interim report[63] which said: 'The Saorstat is now, and will undoubtedly continue to be, an integral part of the economic system at the head of which stands Great Britain.'

However, far from behaving 'like an integral part', throughout the entire period of the second Banking Commission's sittings de Valera had been conducting an economic war against that economic system. After the successful passing of the Constitution and his return to office with a diminished power base, it had become clear to de Valera that the most pressing item on his agenda was the economic war. His frequent visits to Geneva left him under no illusion as to the direction in which events in Europe were heading – war. At home the annuities dispute was contributing to the economic conditions which had thrown him back on Labour's doorstep. As far back as 1934 Professor Berriedale Keith had prepared a secret memorandum[64] for him on the annuities question in particular and the Irish Free State's relationship with England in general. It concluded by saying: '. . . if there were even a moderate amount of statesmanship available on either side, an effective accord should be possible'. One of those rare moments in the Anglo-Irish relationship was approaching in which there was to be a display of statesmanship on both sides. Not only would it pave the way for the ending of the annuities dispute – it would result in the handing back to Ireland of the ports retained by Britain under the Treaty, and thus facilitate de Valera's supreme display of Irish sovereignty: neutrality in World War II.

23

MAKING FOR PORTS,
VIA THE KITCHENS

AS FAR BACK as 1935 de Valera had dropped a fly at the British over the linked issues[1] of the ports retained by Britain under the provisions of the Treaty, and the economic war. Joseph Walshe was authorized to tell Sir Anthony Eden, the British Foreign Secretary, that Dublin would welcome any peace initiative from the British on the economic front. In the course of the Eden encounter, which took place in October during a League of Nations meeting at Geneva, on the eve of a British general election, Walshe also brought up the issue of the ports. He showed himself mindful of the need for 'close co-ordination'[2] of the British and Irish efforts on defence. Walshe also suggested that, if it proved possible to revise the Treaty, Dublin would 'set aside the necessary money to carry out the defence of the ports'[3] with the help of British experts. De Valera followed up the Eden approach with a round of press briefings in Dublin during which he had it bruited abroad that he and Eden had 'discussed matters'[4] at Geneva.

One of these briefings yielded the following from the correspondent of the London *Times*:[5]

> The Government is most anxious to get the warships out on purely sentimental grounds, and I believe that it would be ready to give Britain a very firm undertaking as to its attitude in time of war in return for a voluntary withdrawal. . . . Britain's security would hardly be affected by a withdrawal from Lough Swilly and Bantry Bay, particularly if the Free State Government should promise to allow free access to the British Fleet in time of war. In fact, the Free State Government probably would be willing to negotiate a treaty of mutual defence. . . .

That report is better read as an example of de Valera's habit of talking softly while acting tough than as a true indication of 'Free State Government' policy. For in fact de Valera's real policy was far from being directed towards the giving of a 'firm undertaking' to Great Britain on a 'treaty of mutual defence'. In reality he was manoeuvring towards a position of being able to stay aloof and neutral from Britain's entanglements 'in time of war'. Although the British do not appear to have realized it, he made this clear in a number of statements throughout the period of the economic war.

507

In the course of the debate[6] on the setting up of the Volunteer Reserve in 1934 he had said that the new force, together with the regular Army, was being formed with an eye to outside threats. Should an invasion occur: '. . . the invading force will have a very hot time while amongst us . . . the power that tries to establish its rule here in a permanent way will find it impossible to do so'. In the same debate Aiken referred to the Irish defence forces as being 'sufficient to make even strong *neighbours* [author's italics] respect a country'. In the month in which he authorized Walshe to initiate an approach to Eden de Valera also spoke publicly[7] about the need for national defence. Privately he set up departmental and political committees[8] to deal with the sort of problems which might arise in wartime – censorship, supplies and so forth. The world took a step nearer to confronting such issues in the summer of 1936 when the League of Nations washed its hands of the Italian invasion of Abyssinia. Viewing the abandonment of the sanctions policy, de Valera declared:[9] 'All the small states can do, if the statesmen of the greater states fail in their duty, is resolutely to determine that they will not become the tools of *any* [author's italics] Great Power, and that they will resist with whatever strength they may possess every attempt to force them into a war against their will.' He followed this up with an important statement to the Dail in which he made what were, for him, unusually unambiguous references to neutrality:[10]

> If we held the whole of our territory . . . our attitude would be . . . that we have no aggressive designs against any other people. . . . We would strengthen ourselves so as to *maintain* [author's italics] our neutrality. . . . We have no aggressive designs. . . . We have no imperial ambition of any sort. But we are in this position, that some of our ports are occupied, and, although we cannot be actively committed in any way, the occupation of those ports will give, to any foreign country that may desire a pretext, an opportunity of ignoring our neutrality.
>   . . . The first thing that any government here must try to secure is that no part of our territory will be occupied by any forces except the forces that are immediately responsible to the government here. . . . We are prepared to meet the necessary expense and to make the necessary provision to see that the full strength of this nation will be used to resist any attempt by any foreign power to abuse our neutrality by using any portion of our territory as a base. . . . We want to be neutral.

Yet despite these clear indications of policy the British proceded to assist him in securing what was to prove, for them, a most vexatious neutrality. There were three factors in this decision. The first was that the British general election, which occurred just after de Valera made his first overture to Eden, resulted in Malcolm MacDonald replacing J. H. Thomas as Dominions Parliamentary Secretary. Ramsay MacDonald's son was then only thirty-four years old. He had previously been Parliamentary Under Secretary at the Dominions Office where he had been repelled by Thomas's hostility to de Valera. According to Thomas, de Valera was 'the

Spanish onion in the Irish Stew'.[11] In contrast to Thomas, MacDonald felt a strong urge to do something to encourage a friendlier relationship with Dublin. The second factor was the appeasement policy which gained strength as Neville Chamberlain rose to power; the third, a seeming desire on the part of British military decision-takers to slant their military appreciation of the ports' worth to coincide with Thomas's political evaluation of their place in Anglo-Irish relationships.

MacDonald later told Robert Fisk[12] that he was 'much too "wishful thinking" about the kind of agreement' he could get with de Valera. 'This has always been one of my faults,' he said. In fact he admitted to the Irish Situation Committee that his assessment of de Valera was based 'more on instinct than on any direct evidence'.[13] The ISC included a number of ministers, including the Premier, Ramsay MacDonald. He and most of his ministers were heavily influenced by a number of factors against de Valera in particular and Irish nationalism in general. MacDonald's friendship with the influential Unionists Lord and Lady Londonderry gave him an added edge to the widely shared antipathy within the Cabinet towards de Valera. The Irish leader was bracketed with Gandhi as a troublemaker. As Deirdre McMahon points out,[14] 'the words "lunatic", "visionary", "dreamer", "crank" ("nemesis" too, which was more apposite), were sprinkled in letters, diaries and minutes'. But he did have some hard-headed reasons for his approach. Hitler had begun his rearmament programme the year before MacDonald succeeded Thomas. Italy's butcheries in Abyssinia began shortly afterwards, throwing into stark relief the impotence of the League of Nations. With war looming MacDonald had an impression, albeit a 'vague'[15] one, that 'Ireland might become an enemy'.[16] The whole thrust of de Valera's policy at the time seemed designed towards leaving the Commonwealth; if so, Canada might have supported the Free State and South Africa might have gone even further and followed in Dublin's secessionist footsteps.

Accordingly, mindful of de Valera's approach to Eden, MacDonald put it to Stanley Baldwin, the British Prime Minister, that a meeting should be arranged with de Valera. Baldwin was agreeable to the proposal, but as both men knew that at least one member of the Cabinet would not be – Hailsham, the Lord Chancellor and a staunch Unionist – it was decided not to inform the Cabinet of MacDonald's intentions. The Committee of Imperial Defence was directed to prepare a report on how Ireland affected British defence requirements, while John Dulanty, the Irish High Commissioner and a friend of MacDonald's, was asked to sound de Valera on the idea of meeting MacDonald. 'Rather guardedly',[17] de Valera agreed. His eyesight had begun to trouble him and he suggested that he could see MacDonald in London *en route* to Switzerland to visit an eye specialist.

The meeting took place privately at the end of March 1936 in de Valera's rooms in the Grosvenor Hotel. MacDonald was conveyed by Dulanty through the tradesmen's entrance, into the kitchen and up the servants' back stairs. He later judged[18] de Valera 'by far the most rigid, obstinate man I have ever negotiated with as well as being the most charming and genial'. Nevertheless the strangely matched pair got on well. They began by doing as they were to do many times subsequently – agreeing to differ on the first point raised between them, partition. De Valera countered MacDonald's assertion that the British Government would not change its view on the issue by replying that neither could he. The conversation then moved on to matters constitutional, economic, and the question of the ports. Further meetings were scheduled and a process set up whereby over the next two years, despite the tensions created by the introduction of de Valera's Constitution in the middle of the talks, an agreement was eventually reached between the two countries.

Its starting point was the report from the Imperial Defence Committee which MacDonald had asked for, and received from the Deputy Chiefs of Staff in February.[19] The military men elected to disregard what de Valera had said in his keynote speech to the Dail on neutrality and concentrated instead on other remarks which he had made in the course of that speech, indicating that Ireland would not be allowed to become a base for an attack on Britain. He had said:[20] 'We are prepared, and any government with which I have been associated has always been prepared, to give guarantees, *so far as guarantees can be given* [author's italics], that that will not happen.' Ironically, in saying this de Valera was using an argument first put forward by Michael Collins during the Treaty negotiations:[21] 'namely that England would be more safeguarded by a friendly and neutral Ireland than by an Ireland resentful and in spirit hostile as she had been in the last War'. Unmindful of irony, the Deputy Chiefs of Staff reported that de Valera's 'guarantee' was satisfactory although it did not go far enough. The object of securing the Treaty ports had not been to prevent Ireland being used as a base for hostilities against England, but to ensure that:[22] 'our Fleet and Air Force would have all the facilities which they would need in time of war for use against the forces of an enemy, more especially in the protection of the vital trade routes concentrated off the Irish coasts, in the security of which the Irish Free State is almost as much concerned as the United Kingdom'.

But after stating this the report went on to contradict itself by saying that 'the present time seems a propitious one for the transfer since the immediate importance of the reserved ports has somewhat decreased in view of the recent re-orientation of the defence policy of this country'. What made the moment 'propitious', apparently, was the belief that in future the important theatre of warfare would be the air, not the sea. In addition, Britain had just concluded an agreement with Germany allowing Hitler to build a navy no bigger than one third the size of its own. The pace of Hitler's subsequent rearmament, of course, made nonsense of this and all other defence pacts affecting Nazi expansion, but in February 1936

Great Britain's military strategists concluded that: 'Provided improved relations are assured, despite the risks involved, it would be desirable to hand over the complete responsibility for the defence of the reserved ports to the Irish Free State.'

Armed with this and fortified by his meeting with de Valera – its style rather than its substance, one imagines – MacDonald moved on to confront his Cabinet colleagues in the Irish Situation Committee on 12 May with a memorandum proposing that negotiations be opened with de Valera. The memorandum declared that:[23]

> The most serious aspect of Inter-Imperial relations at present is the absence of agreement on various important matters. This state of affairs between the United Kingdom and a dominion is unsatisfactory in itself, and inevitably tends to weaken the moral authority of the British Commonwealth of Nations in world affairs. Moreover, if matters are allowed to drift they may well end before long in a more serious breach between the two countries. On the other hand, I think the time has come when, despite the well-known difficulties, a careful effort to reconcile differences between the countries has some prospect of meeting with success.

MacDonald thought his case was holed beneath the waterline when, at a 'very tense'[24] meeting in Baldwin's room in the House of Commons, not only did Hailsham make 'a brilliant attack on everything in the paper'[25] but the division bells sounded before he could reply. However, much to his surprise Chamberlain, soon to succeed Baldwin as Prime Minister, invited him later in the day to state what he would have replied to Hailsham had the division bells not interrupted. After listening to MacDonald's case, Chamberlain told him that he too was in favour of negotiations. '"You can count on my help," he said.'[26]

From then until December 1937 the two countries inched both towards and away from agreement. The 'towards' was largely by means of meetings between de Valera and MacDonald, and between British civil servants and John Dulanty; the 'from', British hesitancies and ultimately ineffectual protests over de Valera's proposed Constitution, and a far from ineffectual British resolve that there could be no 'give' on partition. The British position was summarized in a letter, drafted jointly by the Dominions Office and the Treasury and signed by Sir N. Warren Fisher, Permanent Under Secretary to the Treasury, to Dulanty on 14 September 1936: 'the Constitution of a State would not be consistent with membership of the Commonwealth if it did not recognise the King as Head of the Commonwealth, of which the State forms a part, and the special relationship of its citizens to the King. If this point were adequately provided for, we feel that there would be room for discussion about the part which the Crown takes in legislation as Head of the Executive.'

Trade and financial advances were hinted at in the letter. Defence – in other words, the ports – also showed possibilities of movement, though on the basis that the ports should automatically be made available to Great

Britain in time of war. Dulanty had to disobey de Valera's express instructions to talk over this communication with him; to preserve secrecy de Valera had forbidden him to come to Dublin, or to use the telephone to discuss the talks – communication had to be by means of the diplomatic bag only. However, Dulanty crossed to Dublin to see de Valera, who subsequently approved his record of the conversation; this may be accepted as summarizing the Irish position.[27] De Valera saw the Fisher document as indicating: 'failure on the part of the British to appreciate the real character of the problem . . . they must face the issue of a United Ireland. No agreement on the basis of Partition would be acceptable to the Irish people. . . .' On the ports de Valera: 'made it clear that no country could be given an automatic right to them. Neither could he accept an arrangement with Britain by which Ireland would be involved in hostilities whenever and wherever Britain was at war . . . If no common interest were at stake, our attitude [would be] that of benevolent neutrality.'

Dulanty's note of de Valera's assessment of the impact of his Constitution on the Orangemen's minds indicates a confidence in its powers of attraction that was not grounded in reality:

> In the absence of any proposal for an all-Ireland settlement, President proposes to proceed with the Constitution on which he has already made unequivocal statements in public. The President's aim in this Constitution is to establish such a relationship with the members of the British Commonwealth of Nations that, in the event of the Six Counties voluntarily accepting union with the rest of Ireland, the Constitution would not require amendment.

Typically, de Valera sought to limit his responsibility for the Irish position: 'De Valera noted on Dulanty's first draft of this record: "The above notes only the President's *personal* views *verbally* [both italics author's] expressed on the Fisher letter and indicate [*sic*] the lines on which solution should be sought. The Executive Council in the first instance and then the pol. party would have to be satisfied before any agreement could be brought to the Dail."'

In fact de Valera's need to defer to the wishes of his colleagues appears to have been based on tactical considerations, designed to impress the British with his great difficulties in concluding any sort of an agreement, rather than on reality. His dominance of the Irish political scene was such that an authoritative observer in Dublin,[28] concerned about reports of de Valera's failing eyesight, wrote: 'There is a complete absence of leadership when Mr. de Valera is away. The truth is there is no one among his advisers to take his place . . . to whom will they turn if de Valera is to lose his eyesight and gradually be "liquidated"?' And when MacDonald asked Sean Lemass what happened when the Cabinet and de Valera differed, Lemass replied with accuracy: 'The Cabinet then takes its decision by a minority of one.'[29] Not surprisingly, therefore, the position that Dulanty noted remained official Irish policy throughout the rest of 1936, the abdication crisis and de Valera's introduction of his new Constitution. Largely through the urgings of MacDonald, the British were persuaded to swallow their objections both to Articles 2 and 3 of the Constitution, and to the implications of external association. MacDonald argued that it was better to turn a blind eye to these than to risk derailing the peace process.[30] However, further meetings with de Valera and between civil servants from both sides of the Irish Sea failed to produce any resolution of the matters at issue until, in November 1937, de Valera took the initiative as he had originally done in Geneva, more than two years earlier, and moved to break the deadlock.

Chamberlain had taken over the premiership from Baldwin on 28 May that year, and de Valera had had friendly meetings with both Eden and MacDonald in Geneva during League of Nations meetings in September. In a note which he took of his conversations[31] de Valera wrote that he saw little point in civil servants' meetings, but felt that meetings of ministerial delegations would be 'worse than useless unless there was a reasonable prospect that a settlement could be made'. Now, on 24 November 1937, he reversed this opinion and wrote to MacDonald suggesting inter-governmental meetings to 'consider important matters that would arise in case of war'.[32] The threat of war was increasing daily and the cost of the economic war approaching that of the civil war – £47 million by the time it ended in 1938. Unemployment had risen from 28,934 in 1931 to 138,000 by 1935. Some of this was caused by the fact that the handout system which de Valera had introduced allowed small farmers to qualify for the dole from 1933 onwards. Nevertheless doles have to be paid for. With a shooting war approaching, a continuation of economic warfare was obvious lunacy.

Chamberlain was receptive to de Valera's approach. He needed a friendly Ireland behind him as he contemplated an increasingly unfriendly Germany before him. He also believed that the value of an Irish settlement would 'not be found in black and white. . . . The great gain would be that the attitude and atmosphere in Eire would be altered.'[33] Accordingly on 17 January 1938, in a manner reminiscent of the Treaty negotiations, the political leaders of imperial England and of nationalist Ireland sat down at No. 10 Downing Street to attempt to settle the enmities between the two peoples. Unlike Lloyd George during the 1921 negotiations Chamberlain had the advantage of leading, and indeed at that stage dominating, the Conservative Party. His team included, apart from MacDonald, the Chancellor of the Exchequer, Sir John Simon; the Home Secretary, Sir Samuel Hoare; the Minister for the Co-ordination of Defence, Thomas Inskip; the Minister for Agriculture, Stanley Morrison; and the President of the Board of Trade, Oliver Stanley.

For his part de Valera did not shirk his responsibilities as he had done in 1921 but led, and also dominated, the Irish delegation. This consisted of Sean Lemass, Industry and Commerce; Sean MacEntee, Finance; and James Ryan, Agriculture. De Valera's official biography states that:[34]

'These ministers represented in particular the departments involved in the financial and trade difficulties.' What it does not allude to is the fact that the minister concerned with the central issue, defence (the ports) – Frank Aiken – his most devoted colleague, was not included. This controversial omission is only referred to in the Irish translation of the biography.[35] Whether or not this was due to the fact that Aiken represented the wing of Fianna Fail which believed in adopting a forward policy on partition is a moot point. On this wing, Eamonn Donnelly, like Aiken an Armagh man, sponsored a move to get Fianna Fail to contest elections in the Six Counties. Donnelly's agitation came to nothing, but he caused de Valera some embarrassment following the talks by doing as de Valera himself had done at an earlier period – getting himself arrested in Newry under an exclusion order served several years earlier.

De Valera himself had by now settled for a policy of verbal, as opposed to militant, Republicanism. He had refused to grant seats in the Dail to two leading northern Nationalists, Joe Devlin and Cahir Healy, who had privately asked him to do so. He wanted to damp down, not stoke, the fires of militant Republicanism and he had successfully opposed a resolution at the 1936 Fianna Fail Ard Fheis which sought to allow the 'elected representatives of North East Ulster to sit, act and vote in Dail Eireann'.[36] His ascendancy over his colleagues was such that he could easily have suppressed any dissent within his team. As MacDonald commented afterwards,[37] the British soon learned that de Valera was 'the only man we had to deal with'. Perhaps by 1938 de Valera had learned from his own misdeeds in 1921 when he deliberately built dissension into the composition of the delegation which he sent to London. Or it may well have suited him to have used Aiken and the Republican element within Fianna Fail as he had failed to do with Michael Collins – Collins had unsuccessfully urged that he be allowed to stay in Dublin as the alleged bogeyman who had to be placated by the extraction of concessions at the negotiating table. De Valera's attitude towards what MacDonald termed 'immense concessions' was that he would do his best to persuade his colleagues to give him more room for manoeuvre – although he would have been in a stronger position to do this had the offer been better![38] Throughout the talks he justified his intransigence by constant reference to what had befallen an earlier Irish leader who had trusted the British, John Redmond. He knew that the two areas in which he stood to gain were the ports and the ending of the economic war.

Nevertheless he proceeded as if his principal ambition was the ending of partition – on which he had already conceded *de facto*, if not *de jure*, that no progress could be made. At his very first meeting with a senior British official after taking office (William Peters, on 14 March 1932) he is reported as saying:[39] 'There was . . . no question of an immediate settlement of the problem of unity. And although this stood at the back of everything it had to be left out of account so far as immediate relations with Great Britain were concerned.' More than five years later, at one of the last meetings he held with MacDonald before writing to suggest the inter-governmental conference – his letter contained no mention of partition – MacDonald's note[40] of the conversation records him as concurring that there was no possibility of ending partition 'in the near or even the more distant future'. MacDonald notes that he was 'very sorry . . . but he must accept the fact'. De Valera's own note[41] of the conversation acknowledges MacDonald's 'steadfast view' that the 'partition solution would have to wait'. De Valera's reply merely consisted of saying that consequently he would have to 'consider a campaign to inform British and world opinion as to the iniquity of the whole position'. He drew up a political balance sheet containing the points which he put to MacDonald in which partition, though as usual at the top of the list, was dealt with in very general terms compared to the specifics on the issues he obviously did expect movement on (the annuities and the ports). It read as follows:

1. That the ending of Partition was absolutely necessary for the good relations we both desired.
2. That we could not consent to paying a penny of the land annuity money.
3. That we could not consent to any commitment to invite the British to our ports for the defence of their supplies in time of war.
4. That the line to pursue for a solution was to find how our increased commitments in regard to defence (so as to make good the policy of preventing a foreign power from using our island as a basis of attack against Britain) would be held to equate the payments on which a compromise could be made.
5. I indicated that I was willing to meet representatives of their Government, for the purpose of hammering out the financial agreement, once the main lines were fixed and it was certain that an agreement could be arrived at.

Nevertheless, both privately and publicly, de Valera set about the negotiations as though partition was his primary aim. At the conference table he impressed a sense of 'spiritual mission' on his hearers, speaking of 'my people' and 'the people of Ireland' in a 'mystical way'.[42] Privately, also, he so impressed John Cudahy, the American Ambassador to Dublin, with his arguments that the British could and should put pressure on the Unionists to end partition that Cudahy wrote to Roosevelt[43] urging him to put pressure on the British to do so. De Valera directed the Irish Minister to the USA to keep in touch with Cordell Hull, the American Secretary of State, over the progress of the talks. He also sent Frank Gallagher to Roosevelt with a letter asking him 'to consider whether you could not use your influence to get the British Government to realize what would be gained by reconciliation' and to 'give him the facts of Partition'.[44]

Roosevelt's reaction was delayed and minimalist. He replied to Cudahy[45] saying that, while a solution of the Irish problem would represent an 'incalculable gain', nevertheless: 'I am not convinced that any intervention – no matter how indirect – on our part would be wise or for that matter accomplish the effect we had in mind.' After taking a month to make up his mind, he wrote to de Valera recalling the days 'long before either one of us thought of the possibility of becoming a President'.[46] But he then went on to state that he could do nothing officially, not 'even discuss the matter'. However, mindful also of Irish American influences, he informed de Valera that he had asked the newly appointed American Ambassador to the Court of St James, Joseph Kennedy, to tell Chamberlain how happy he would be 'if reconciliation could be brought about'. After the talks de Valera elected to believe that Roosevelt's intervention was decisive. He did not reply to the US President for two months, by which time the negotiations were over. But when he did so he averred that:[47] 'The knowledge of the fact that you were interested came most opportunely at a critical time in the progress of the negotiations. Were it not for Mr. Chamberlain personally the negotiations would have broken down at that time, and I am sure that the knowledge of your interest in the success of the negotiations had its due weight in determining his attitude.' It is more probable that Chamberlain acted as he did from convictions arising out of his appeasement policy than through any pressure from Joseph Kennedy. But, at this stage, de Valera was eager to gain whatever kudos might be forthcoming from a little judicious flattery of the President of the United States. Ironically, as we shall see, his success in the talks led to a sharp coolness in Dublin–White House relationships.

Prior to the talks, de Valera gave a press conference in Dublin on 13 January at which he announced that partition would be on the agenda. And as the talks progressed he gave interviews to the *Manchester Guardian*, the *New York Times* and the International News Agency of America, all drumming up support for the idea of an end to the problem. But his use of the partition ploy helped to stimulate, rather than weaken, Unionist resolution to uphold the border. Craigavon, reading his morning newspapers in bed, reacted to de Valera's 13 January press conference by declaring a general election. Contemplating a result which would inevitably show a majority in favour of partition, de Valera was forced to adopt a policy of abstentionism which angered Six County Nationalists. He did not contest his own Six County seat and saw to it that Donnelly's plans were scrapped. As his publicity had heightened Northern Nationalist expectations he had to face suggestions of betrayal[48] after a group of Six County Nationalist MPs visited him in London during the talks. Their questioning, which lasted almost all of 24 February, had elicited a truer picture of de Valera's intentions towards the minority for whom he avowedly had such deep feelings than had his public utterances. Evidently worried about what might emerge from the MPs' descent, he indulged in a little pre-emptive damage limitation where Irish newspapers were concerned. Patrick Quinn, political editor of the *Irish Independent*, sent a cable to his Editor on the 23rd which read as follows:[49]7 'De Valera asks as a personal favour that movements Nationalist MPs be published without linking up Irish delegation with them for he has not asked them to come

De Valera with Frank Aiken prior to entering the Dail

Below: The debate over the Oath continues in the newspapers and at big public meetings (*Irish Independent*, 27 May 1927)

FRIDAY. **Irish Inde**

PITHY PRO

FAIL

DE VALERA AND THE OATH

QUESTION FOR
THE PEOPLE

PLY TO MR. HOGAN

G MEETINGS IN ENNIS
AND MULLINGAR

Imperialism. He stressed the costly administration of the Government.

Mr. M. J. Kennedy, Mr. J. J. Killane, and Mr. Jas. Victory, three of the candidates, also spoke.

CANDIDATE AND A
COALITION.

WICKLOW MEETING

Mr. J. Layery,
has been appoint
bane.

Bangor magistra
Murdy, C.P.S.,
his marriage.

Armagh City C
Mullan in place
signed.

De Valera inspects an Irish cavalry unit, 1932

Above: De Valera's 1933 Cabinet. Left to right, seated: Joseph Connolly, Sean T. O'Ceallaigh, Eamon de Valera, P. J. Ruttledge, Sean Lemass. Standing: Conor Maguire, Gerald Boland, Thomas Derrig, Frank Aiken, Sean MacEntee, Dr James Ryan and M. Moynihan

Right: The President and Sinead de Valera receive guests at a Dublin state function

Below: Frank Gallagher

Sinead de Valera

Relations with the British and the Americans

Left: At Euston Station with Malcolm MacDonald, Dominions Secretary, after talks in London, 1938

Below: With Sir Stafford Cripps to discuss the Anglo-Irish trade agreement, 1947

Sir Winston Churchill

Right: With Clement Attlee

Below: Speaking at the Cambridge Union in 1948, where the motion 'That this House would welcome a reunification of Ireland' was lost

President F. D. Roosevelt

The carefully cultivated de Valera public image is well exemplified by this election poster

At the Roscommon crossroads the old IRA men who fought with de Valera in the civil war formed a torch-lit guard of honour

Two Sides of the Long Fellow: *(left)* charming delegates at the Council of Europe at Strasbourg, and *(below)* every inch the solemn statesman at his desk

Kathleen O'Connell, de Valera's secretary and confidante

Above: The 1951 Cabinet. Front, left to right, Maurice Moynihan, Frank Aiken, Eamon de Valera (Premier President Sean T. O'Ceallaigh, Sean Lemass, Sean MacEntee, Dr James Ryan, Thomas Derrig. Second row, left to right, Patrick Smith, Thomas Walsh, Sean Moylan, Gerald Boland, Oscar Traynor, Erskine Childers. Back row, Colonel O'Sullivan, Cathal O'Daly Eamonn Dunphy

Left: Eamon de Valera opens the new manuscript room at Trinity College, Dublin, 1957

Standing for the National Anthem at Crooke Park with Jack Lynch, another successor as Taoiseach. On the right is Patrick Fanning, President of the Gaelic Athletic Association.

Left: Although blind, de Valera strikes a characteristic pose for the camera as he 'inspects' a statue of Robert Emmet in 1966

Below: He exercises similar skills at hurling before King Baudouin, watched by Frank Aiken, at Aras an Uachtarain. He surprised spectators by the length he drove the ball

Above: Contrary to popular belief, de Valera enjoyed an occasional drink, particularly in later life

Right: De Valera kisses the ring of Cardinal Roncalli, later Pope John XXIII

Right: Eamon and Sinead de Valera celebrate their golden wedding anniversary

Below: Vivion, de Valera's eldest son

Above: Eamon de Valera on his 88th birthday with his grandson Eamonn

Right: De Valera in close-up as an old man

and knows nothing of their plans.' Quinn, however, knew something of de Valera's plans. He was close to the Irish delegation all through the talks. As early as their second day, 18 January, after briefings from Dulanty, Walshe and some of the Irish ministers he had cabled his Editor that Walshe did not expect the talks to fail on partition:[50] ' . . . looks like shelving Partition in favour of settlement of other issues . . . De Valera [Quinn said] clearly shows he is accepting settlement – with Partition shelved . . . Irish ministers are in hopeful mood tonight. Dev all smiles and looking very composed. Lemass and MacEntee like schoolboys.'

Two days later, however, an article in the *Irish Independent* from Mary MacSwiney, warning against any sell-outs of the national position in London, disrupted both the pleasant mood and the flow of leaks about shelving partition. Commenting on the article, de Valera told Cudahy:[51] 'No leader would dare go counter to such sentiment . . . '. What he meant was no Fianna Fail leader with his background could be seen to go against such sentiment. It was the Mrs Tom Clarke syndrome all over again. The spectre of Mary MacSwiney's and his own earlier repudiation of Collins must have haunted him for the rest of the talks.

Overall, however, de Valera's continued use of the partition issue succeeded on two fronts. One, it presented an air of ideological constancy which prevented anyone emerging from the ranks of Fianna Fail to split the party, as he had done with Sinn Fein over the outcome of the London talks of 1921. Two, in the course of the negotiations themselves it enabled him to place the burden of concession squarely on Chamberlain's shoulders. Chamberlain was taken by surprise at de Valera's use of the partition issue. On the first day of the talks he noted that he had 'never contemplated . . . any lengthy discussion'[52] on partition. Throughout the talks de Valera continually made use of the leverage offered by partition. As the British made it more and more obvious that they were prepared to concede on the ports and the annuities, but required some concession from him on allowing access to Southern markets for Six County goods, he refused even this. 'The Six County government had shown no inclination to treat the minority justly. Until it did so he saw no reason why it should be presented with free entry into the main Irish market.'[53] As his biographers have noted:[54] 'Throughout he refused to be cornered into bargaining one right against another. He stressed that Ireland had nothing tangible to give way on; that her people regarded the defended ports and other items which the United Kingdom were proposing to concede as theirs by right; and that they were only recovering what had been wrongfully taken away from them.'

Watching the talks unfold, Quinn briefed his Editor by telegram on 14 March:[55] 'Nothing doing on partition – there never was and de Valera knew there never could be.' But to the end de Valera comported himself as though he believed there was. His position was that[56] 'The annuities and tariffs . . . were insignificant.' It was partition which was of 'vital importance in any conception of an Irish nation'.[57] He made the offer of a return of the ports appear such a trivial matter compared to the ending of partition that Chamberlain was driven to exclaim: 'Is Mr. de Valera trying to make it appear that we were thrusting a burden upon Eire in making her take over the defended ports? I am lost in admiration of Mr. de Valera's skill in dialectics.'

De Valera's animadversions on the cost of maintaining the ports were such that Chamberlain suggested it might be better 'to spare Mr. de Valera the embarrassment of having the Treaty ports offered to him'. Not surprisingly, both quotes appear in de Valera's official biography.[58] But less favourable remarks, such as Chamberlain's feeling that de Valera and Hitler resembled each other to the extent that as 'it was no use employing with them the arguments which appealed to reasonable men', did not.[59] In fact Chamberlain's passing irritations were as nothing compared to his belief in the overall efficacy of his appeasement policy which he saw applying to Ireland as to other trouble spots. For him: 'appeasement did not mean surrender, nor was it a policy only to be used towards the dictators. To Chamberlain it meant the methodical removal of the principal causes of friction in the world.'[60] So it was logical for him to tell the Irish Situation Committee a month before he talked to de Valera that: 'Even an agreement which fell short of being completely satisfactory would be better than the insecurity of the present situation.'[61]

The advice which finally decided him to conclude such an agreement had come from the Joint Chiefs of Staff on 13 January 1938. It was of the same twin-pronged nature already given to Thomas. On the one hand the military leaders advised that 'the life of the nation would be greatly imperilled' if the ports were not available to Great Britain. On the other, they reckoned that it would require a British division at each port, accompanied by anti-aircraft batteries, to defend them against attack from the Irish Army. Weighing up these two considerations, the Chiefs of Staff decided that:[62] '. . . it would be preferable to waive insistence on a formal undertaking which might be politically impracticable for Mr. de Valera to give, and which would not necessarily have any value in the event, if by so doing we could secure a satisfactory agreement with Ireland'.

Chamberlain accepted this portion of the Chiefs of Staff's verdict. After many alarums and excursions – apart from hiccups over partition, the talks were stalled during February by a British governmental crisis over Sir Anthony Eden's resignation – an agreement was signed on 25 April. Under its terms Ireland got back the ports, without concluding a defence agreement. Britain waived any rights she might have claimed from the Twenty-six Counties during a war. The dispute over the annuities ended with the Irish making a single payment of £10 million. De Valera made no concession to Six County trade, or on the Twenty-six Counties' normal protectionist duties. Only the special penal duties, imposed by both countries at the outset of the economic war, were removed under the agreement. The Unionists also gained. To placate their anger at the concessions to the South a separate agreement was concluded with Craigavon, which included benefits on agricultural subsidies and an increased share in armament manufacture.

In Ireland the result was generally seen, outside the ranks of Unionists, Nationalists and militant Republicans, as a triumph for de Valera. But he was canny about blowing his own trumpet and did not overtly trade on his achievement in public. As Cudahy wrote to Roosevelt, de Valera was:[63] 'too experienced a negotiator to make much of the agreement with England, but it is a wonderful triumph'. Nevertheless, while soft-pedalling his achievement he wasted no time in cashing in his electoral chips. A defeated Dail motion on the setting up of an arbitration board on civil servants' conditions gave him the opportunity of going to the country less than two months after the signing, on 17 June 1938. He was returned with 77 seats, a majority of 16 over all over parties, which enabled him to dispense with the services of Labour.

With one very notable exception the agreement was generally popular in the British press and political circles also. The exception was Winston Churchill, who gave his reaction during the House of Commons debate on the issue on 5 May. His anger was directed both at the prospective wartime loss of British naval operating range represented by the denial of the ports (400 miles in the case of the Cork ports, 200 for Lough Swilly) and at de Valera. Churchill was, after all, a principal architect of the Anglo-Irish Treaty which de Valera was so successfully eroding. In the course of a celebrated Commons address – in which, significantly, he referred to Collins as 'a man of his word' – he declared:[64]

> These ports are, in fact, the sentinel towers of the Western approaches, by which the 45,000,000 in this Island so enormously depend on foreign food for their daily bread, and by which they can carry on their trade, which is equally important to their existence.
> . . . we are to give them up, unconditionally, to an Irish Government led by men – I do not want to use hard words – whose rise to power has been proportionate to the animosity with which they have acted against this country, no doubt in pursuance of their own patriotic impulses, and whose position in power is based upon the violation of solemn Treaty engagements.

Then he asked the key question: what guarantee did Britain have that 'Southern Ireland' would not declare neutrality if Britain was engaged in war with a powerful nation? The answer, which of course Churchill did not receive from Chamberlain, was that not only did Britain have no such guarantee, it had a *de facto* certainty that 'Southern Ireland' would declare its neutrality. For, as Robert Fisk correctly observed,[65] de Valera had come to a 'realisation that Irish possession of the ports was not just a symbol but an essential physical requirement of an independent foreign policy in a European war'. The scale of the extraordinary coup which he pulled off in securing this requirement became evident during World

War II. Describing how the German Ambassador to Ireland worked to 'support the consolidation of Irish neutrality' during the war, Joseph Carroll remarked with both truth and understatement:[66] 'It was, after all, quite an achievement for German diplomacy for one of the countries of the British Commonwealth headed by the king to remain neutral, and German diplomacy right through the war worked for the continuation of this state of affairs.'

De Valera's approach to Chamberlain during the negotiations revealed the Nice Guy and Man of Power facets of his character. He claimed that he came to have a genuine regard for the Englishman and for Malcolm MacDonald, in whose home he stayed during part of the negotiations. As his biography states:[67] 'He never ceased to pay tribute to Chamberlain and Malcolm MacDonald.' But during the negotiations he shocked Cudahy with his cold-blooded approach to Chamberlain. He admitted that men meant nothing to him. He said that Chamberlain, like himself, was merely the proponent of a cause. Therefore: 'the individual who projected the cause was merely an instrument'. Cudahy noted that he had never heard:[68] 'a more cold-blooded analysis of the human equation in negotiation'. Deirdre McMahon records that during the negotiations he maintained the attitude of coldness even while visiting MacDonald at his Essex country home:[69] '. . . a photograph of the occasion shows de Valera fixing the camera with a look of alarming grimness. According to MacDonald's butler, de Valera was in "an aggressive mood . . . never smiled . . . and looked as if he meant to murder somebody."'

MacDonald suffered for his hospitable approach to de Valera: 'Churchill regarded MacDonald as "rat-poison on account of his connection with [the Eire] ports"'.[70] After giving him an opportunity to attempt the forlorn hope of persuading de Valera to return the ports after war had broken out, Churchill removed MacDonald from the Cabinet and despatched him to Canada as High Commissioner. But for de Valera the thirties had to be seen as an era of almost pure gain, with only two exceptions: the cost of the economic war and of the copper-fastening effect that his policies had on partition. The irony is that everything he achieved – from winning power, to abolishing the Governor General, to introducing his Constitution, to getting back the ports – was made possible by using Michael Collins' 'stepping stone', the Treaty he worked so assiduously to dismantle. The thirties were an offset, and a very considerable one, against the debit of the civil war on de Valera's historical account. But they serve to highlight, rather than obliterate, that entry.

24

BLIND COURAGE

THE DETERIORATION in the world situation in the months following his London triumph helped to strengthen further de Valera's determination to remain neutral in the looming war. Maintaining neutrality would both spare the Twenty-six Counties the horrors of war and demonstrate the state's sovereignty. Curiously, my own abiding memory is that the people who had the most principled and, at the same time, the most insightful support for neutrality were the Anglo-Irish. Brian Inglis, author of *West Briton*,[1] biographer of Roger Casement and the best Editor in the *Spectator*'s history, to my knowledge, joined the RAF at the outbreak of war and was sent to Rhodesia. Here, hearing of Churchill's rumblings, he made a pact with a fellow Anglo-Irishman that, if the British violated Ireland's neutrality, they would both immediately resign their commissions, refuse to fight, and face jail or firing squad if necessary.

Most people had little enough grasp of the sovereignty issue, nor of the principled position which Inglis, and those like him, deliberately undertook. Nor had they much grasp of the hideousness of war. Nevertheless de Valera's policy won almost universal acceptance as the war progressed. One of the principal insiders of the time, F. H. Boland of the Department of External Affairs, described the evolution of opinion which occurred:[2] 'Up to May, 1940, a lot of people – even official people – were sceptical about the neutrality policy and thought we would be eventually in the war. After the fall of France and Italy's entry, people came round much more to the view that our neutrality was the right policy and should be defended at all costs. Many people who were anti-German were not anti-Italian.'

Boland's analysis is expressed in less formal language by one of the best stories of the period. An old farmer is said to have declared at the war's outset that his ambition was to see Britain 'not bate, but nearly bate'. Initially that would have been a fairly commonplace view. Most Irish adults, in or out of the legislature, could remember the Black and Tans. Nevertheless as the war progressed, the London blitz and visions of the Gestapo overlay those memories. The determination to stay out of the war increased rather than decreased. De Valera's own personal position is probably best summarized as being at first one of apprehension about the war's outcome, tilting eventually towards a guarded preference for an Allied victory.

Gallagher records two anecdotes which support this judgement. 'Late in

'41 de Valera commented: "I wish there was some way of knowing who will win this war. It would make decisions much easier."[3] Some time afterwards, on hearing of 'a high State official making a pro-German statement at a reception where it was sure to get back to British or American ears', de Valera's reaction surprised Gallagher. He replied: 'That will be useful. I am more the other way and it will create a balance.'[4]

It is impossible to estimate the saving in Irish lives which neutrality represented. The results of the two raids which the Germans made on fortified Belfast (see p.584), which supposedly had RAF protection also, give some indication of the carnage which might have been wrought on the handful of unprotected Southern Irish cities. The down-side of de Valera's neutrality policy did not appear for many years afterwards: the lasting ill effects on partition, the end of his dream of self-sufficiency, and a very diminished Irish share in the benefits of post-war European reconstruction that left Ireland lagging behind western Europe in both cultural and economic isolation. Irish problems during the 'emergency' were in general those of irritation rather than desperation. But the irritations were not slight by any standards. Whether one agrees or disagrees with the stand he took, de Valera's maintenance of his position throughout World War II has to be accounted a diplomatic feat of a high order and a remarkable display of sustained, obdurate courage. Ireland, after all, lies so close to Britain that on a clear day a person with a pair of binoculars standing on Wicklow's Sugar Loaf Mountain can see ships entering and leaving Holyhead Harbour in Wales.

De Valera himself could not have done this, because for most of the war he suffered from blindness. His demeanour in dealing with this particular affliction certainly merits Hemingway's definition of courage being grace under stress. The war brought various shifting pressures to bear upon de Valera. Apart from his failing eyesight, his problems in maintaining neutrality included supplies, pressures from the belligerents – in practice, Germany, Britain and America – and the activities of the IRA. Although all these factors interacted, as will be demonstrated, they developed separately, and it will assist readers in following their twists and turns if they are dealt with separately also, beginning with the IRA.

The IRA began its return to the centre of de Valera's attention after his break with Joseph McGarrity. Having finally abandoned his hopes that de Valera would initiate a physical force policy against the Six Counties, McGarrity turned to supporting the IRA leader Sean Russell. From 1936 onwards Russell had been arguing within the movement in favour of a new target for militarism: not the Six Counties, but Britain itself. Ironically his plan received the assent of the IRA's executive at a secret meeting in Dublin, attended by McGarrity,[5] in March 1938, while de Valera and the British were entering the final weeks of the negotiation over the ports which was supposed to improve relationships between the two countries. Later in the year Russell's schemes achieved a further accolade, that of the second Dail. The surviving members of 'The Government of the Republic of Ireland' handed over[6] their 'authority' to the IRA's Army Council, headed by Sean Russell. Although largely ignored by the general public, this move was of great significance to Republican purists. The hand-over meant that Russell was now entitled, as de Valera himself had once done, to claim that the authority of the national Parliament (the Dail) now lay outside that assembly. A statement, written by McGarrity but signed by Russell and the Army Council, was issued on 16 January 1939. 'In the name of the unconquered dead and the faithful living' it called on Britain 'to withdraw . . . from all of Ireland.'[7]

The derisory laughter which this document elicited was drowned by the sound of home-made IRA bombs going off throughout Britain. By midsummer 1939 de Valera judged that the situation warranted a new crack-down on the IRA. He introduced legislation before the British did: the Offences Against the State Act became law on 14 June.[8] This allowed for the setting up of a military tribunal, imprisonment and detention without trial. The annual IRA march to Bodenstown was banned and the Army was called out to enforce the ban. Speaking in the Seanad on 24 July, a day on which suitcase bombs were going off at left luggage depots in London, de Valera said: 'No one can have any doubt as to the result of the campaign in England, and no one can think that this Government has any sympathy with it.' The military tribunal came into operation the following month, on 22 August.

The worst single episode of the fifteen-month campaign occurred three days later. At 2.30 in the afternoon of Friday, 23 August 1939, a bomb placed on the carrier of a bicycle exploded in crowded Broadgate, a thoroughfare in Coventry. It killed five people, badly injured twelve more, and inflicted lesser injuries on forty others. The bomb was not intended for Broadgate but was abandoned there by a bomber who panicked *en route* to his real target.[9] The ill-conceived and badly organized campaign had no hope of success, but it did have a considerable psychological effect. Bombs went off in public lavatories, letterboxes, telephone boxes, railway cloakrooms, post offices and cinemas, which were sometimes emptied also by the use of tear gas.

To have such activities carried on, in Ireland's name, by an organization which claimed to speak with a greater moral authority than he, would have been a serious challenge to de Valera at any time, whatever his own earlier ambivalent record towards the IRA. But occurring when they did, they presented him with a double source of aggravation. First, they effectively destroyed an anti-partition campaign which he had been driven to sponsor towards the end of 1938 under pressure from both the Donnelly wing of Fianna Fail and Northern Nationalists disenchanted with their poor share of his ports bargain. The vehicle for his campaign was the Anti-Partition League. In a series of newspaper interviews he defined the League's objective as ending the 'cruel wrong of Partition'.[10] To do this he proposed setting up an All-Ireland Parliament which would have allowed the Six Counties – for an interregnum period only – to have continued to exercise most of the powers then enjoyed by the statelet. Speakers from various walks of Irish life were bringing the anti-partition message to the ears of a not unsympathetic British public when the IRA bombs started to go off.

The second, more major issue was that the IRA campaign was making a mockery of his promise that Ireland would never be used as a base from which to attack England – and this on the eve of a world war in which he hoped to stand neutral. On 1 September 1939 Germany invaded Poland and the world was at war. The following day de Valera summoned the Dail in order to introduce two Bills, both of which speedily passed into law. These were the First Amendment of the Constitution Bill and the Emergency Powers Bill. The first, on which the enactment of the second depended, extended the meaning of the term 'time of war' to allow emergency legislation under Article 28.3.3. of the Constitution to include:[11] 'a time when there is taking place an armed conflict in which the State is not a participant but in respect of which each of the Houses of the Oireachtas shall have resolved that, arising out of such armed conflict, a national emergency exists affecting the vital interests of the State'. Thus was born the immortal description of World War II as 'the emergency', as it was always henceforth referred to in the Twenty-six Counties. More importantly, there also came into being the following day the Emergency Powers Act. This quite simply gave de Valera's administration power over everything in the state: censorship, military matters, supplies, agriculture and transport. Explaining the need for such powers, de Valera said of his neutrality policy:

> . . . it brings up for the Government of a nation that proposes to be neutral . . . problems much more delicate and much more difficult of solution even than the problems that arise for a belligerent . . . . It is not . . . sufficient for us to indicate our attitude or to express the desire of our people. It is necessary at every step to protect our interests in that regard, to avoid giving to any of the belligerents any due cause, and proper cause of complaint . . . a small state is always open to considerable pressure . . . .

To ensure that belligerents did not derive 'due cause' from any seeming inability on his part to control the IRA, on 8 September de Valera followed up the enactment of this legislation by appointing the hard-line Gerald Boland as his Minister for Justice in place of Patrick Ruttledge. Both the Special Branch and Military Intelligence were reorganized.[12]

Within a few days of the war's outbreak, therefore, de Valera had placed himself in a position from which he was able to confront the IRA with both legislation, and the means to implement it, that had not existed since the days of the civil war. In fact the position of the IRA was weaker than during the civil war, for he had the benefit of a much stricter censorship than had existed then, and public opinion was now more fully united against the movement than in 1922. In addition arms were in shorter supply; and, last but not least, there was no leader even remotely approaching his stature to encourage young men into the organization by advising them that Ireland was theirs for the taking.

Nevertheless partition meant, and means, that the physical force tradition in Ireland is not easily crushed, and the IRA continued to embarrass de Valera during the early months of the war. On 9 November 1939, speaking in the Dail, he opposed a Labour Party resolution urging him to release IRA prisoners on hunger strike because one in particular, Patrick McGrath, was near death. He said: 'The alternatives we are forced to face are the alternatives of two evils; one to see men die that we do not want to see die if we can save them; the other to permit them to bring the State and the community as a whole to disaster.' However, he modified this stand on the 15th, in the face of widespread pressure, when it appeared that McGrath, a hero of the Anglo-Irish war, was indeed about to die. McGrath was transferred to Jervis Street Hospital, where he recovered, and a nolle prosequi was entered in his case on 7 December.

This action followed a serious legal reverse for de Valera in that week. On 1 December, Justice Gavan Duffy put a coach and four through the Offences Against the State Act by granting a habeas corpus application for an IRA prisoner on the grounds that his detention under the Act was unconstitutional. The following day de Valera was forced to release fifty-three prisoners held under the same legislation. Then on 23 December the IRA raided the Magazine Fort in Dublin's Phoenix Park and made off in thirteen lorries with most of the Irish Army's stock of ammunition – just over a million rounds. A policeman was shot dead in Cork on 3 January 1940, and on the 5th de Valera moved to close the Gavan Duffy loophole: the Emergency Powers (Amendment) Act 1940 was brought into law. Under this measure persons were held to be detained under emergency, that is, wartime, legislation and therefore could legally be held without trial until the war's end. Unlike the Offences Against the State Act, which was passed before the war commenced, the emergency legislation was not subject to judicial review. The aged President Douglas Hyde referred the Act to the Supreme Court and refused to sign it into law until the court pronounced it constitutional on 9 February. From this point onwards de Valera showed little leniency towards the IRA. The detention camps filled up, prisoners were executed by firing squad, and in one case the English hangman, Pierrepoint, was brought to Ireland to execute an IRA man. The mantle, or nemesis, of the civil war executioners had finally descended on to the shoulders of Eamon de Valera.

Discussing the wartime period with Vivion de Valera, I found that whenever the subject of the IRA executions came up he used his father's description for them: 'Gerry Boland's executions'. In fact the executions seemed to have been unanimously agreed upon by the Cabinet. Maurice Moynihan, who was present at all the discussions concerning the executions, recalls that they were discussed as a disagreeable necessity. Everyone had their say. No one appears to have dissented. And everyone at the Cabinet table appears to have had a shared concern (understandable in view of the party's background) that failure to execute members of an organization who had killed policemen would have had repercussions in the Gardai.

We must turn now to another essential component of de Valera's wartime experience, Germany. His strong-arm treatment of the IRA convinced at least one influential observer that he was serious about neutrality, and as a result Hitler was advised to support his position. The observer was Eduard Hempel, the German Minister to Ireland. In giving his advice Hempel was pushing something of an open door, because Hitler believed[13] that nothing could be done in Ireland without de Valera's agreement. But his reports to Berlin helped to convince Ribbentrop, the German Foreign Minister, that respecting de Valera's neutrality policy, rather than supporting the Abwehr's clumsy attempts to send spies to Ireland to liaise with the IRA, was the right approach. A handful of spies were sent, but they were easily captured, and no serious fifth column threat from an IRA–Nazi link-up ever materialized.

Hempel was not a Nazi, but a career diplomat who is remembered as having behaved correctly and fairly throughout his assignment. He had been an officer in the German Army during World War I, later studying law and, after taking his doctorate, entering the foreign service in 1927. Most commentators pinpoint his meeting with de Valera on 31 August 1939 as being of central significance to the course of Berlin–Dublin relationships during World War II. Hempel reported that 'the Government's aim was to remain neutral', but that in the circumstances the Irish would have to 'show a certain consideration for Britain which in similar circumstances they would also show to Germany'. This in effect was the policy which Germany accepted and acted upon for the duration of the war. However, for reasons which will soon become clearer when we come to assess the attitude adopted by the American wartime Minister to Ireland, David Gray, it will be of value to go back a few days earlier in August, to the 26th, to consider in some detail another report of Hempel's. This makes it clear that de Valera had already laid down the Irish-German ground rules for neutrality and that he, not the Germans, had initiated the Hempel contact of 31 August. Hempel is describing an approach made by Joseph Walshe:

> He stated definitely that Ireland would remain neutral except in the case of a definite attack, for example dropping bombs on Irish towns. He could not think that such a thing could happen through us, as it would not appear to be in the German interest, while on the other hand Irish sympathy, especially in view of the strong, perhaps decisive influence of the American Irish against an American British alliance, could not be a matter of indifference to us . . . .
>
> He also expects that Britain in view of the American Irish will do everything to avoid violating Irish neutrality . . . .

He repeats the suggestion that in case of German acts of war against Britain involving Ireland, any suffering incurred should be kept to a minimum, and at the same time a formal declaration should be made that Germany has no aggressive aims in Ireland, but on the contrary has sympathy for Ireland and Irish National aims, mentioning if necessary Northern Ireland, and that she regrets Irish suffering and will attempt to keep this to the unavoidable minimum. Avoid internment of Irish Nationals in case of war.

Gray's interpretation of Walshe's message was both stark and debatable: 'In the language of diplomatic implication, de Valera wanted Northern Ireland and was ready to sell the vital interest of the United States as well as British survival to get it.' Of course Gray did not have access to the German cables until after his Irish mission had ended, probably not until 1952[14] when he was in his eighties. But it is instructive of the spirit in which that mission was conducted to reflect that his judgement of Walshe's proposal occurs in an unpublished book which Roosevelt suggested he should write. In the early months of the war Roosevelt judged that:[15] 'All things considered, the Irish Free State since it was set up has done an amazingly good job.' But at that stage Roosevelt was not aware that de Valera did not want to see him re-elected. Hempel, the German Minister, was made aware of this because he cabled Ribbentrop on 31 July 1940 stating categorically that 'the possible re-election of Roosevelt . . . is not in favour with the Government here'. Hempel said the Irish viewpoint was that the British could proceed more easily to an invasion of Ireland if Roosevelt were in the White House. However as the war progressed Roosevelt's attitude changed, and he suggested to Gray that he produce a book on: ' . . . Irish-American relations during the war years. It was to portray de Valera as a "Free Rider", that is a neutral who rode free instead of working his passage. It was to be in the nature of a "White Paper", published by the State Department.'

Roosevelt died before the project (which also involved other neutral countries) could be completed. Even if he had lived, one wonders if it would ever have appeared with State Department blessing. Its splenetic tone was such that the reaction from de Valera followers would have eclipsed the reaction to Salman Rushdie's *Satanic Verses*. However, this said, it must be acknowledged that Gray's position, his relationship with the American President and the diaries he kept make 'Behind the Green Curtain' a valuable historical document. Gray wrote it as 'fulfillment of a personal obligation'; he felt that German documents which the Allies captured after the war 'disclosed a situation not of Free Riding but secret hostility'.[16]

Gray notes that on 29 August Ribbentrop replied to Hempel's cable containing Walshe's outline of de Valera's policy instructing him that:

. . . you should now make the declaration to the Irish Government which you suggested . . . call on Mr de Valera without delay and make the following statement:

527

> In accordance with the friendly relations between ourselves and Ireland we are determined to refrain from any hostile action against Irish territory and to respect her integrity, provided that Ireland for her part maintains unimpeachable neutrality towards us in any conflict. Only if this condition should no longer obtain, as a result of a decision of the Irish Government themselves, or by pressure exerted on Ireland by other quarters, should we be compelled to safeguard our interests . . . in the sphere of warfare.
>
> You are requested to deliver this statement in clear yet definitely friendly terms and in doing so you can refer (without expressly mentioning Northern Ireland) to the wide sympathy felt in Germany for Ireland and the national aspirations of the Irish people.

Here Gray notes that Ribbentrop's reservations about Northern Ireland were conditioned by the fact that at that stage Hitler was still hoping to conclude a pact with Britain against Russia. Such an alliance would have meant that 'hard commitments to Northern Ireland might later cause embarrassment'. Moreover, Ribbentrop's 'advices from Irish Republican Army agents in Berlin could not have increased his confidence in de Valera'. However slight Ribbentrop's confidence in de Valera concerning Northern Ireland, Ribbentrop's instructions to Hempel indicate that he believed in de Valera sufficiently where Southern Ireland was concerned to accept his terms on neutrality. The issue of how far that acceptance would have carried had the Nazis changed their minds about Ireland need not detain us; the German record of trampling on the rights of small states is well known. However, in describing the meeting on 31 August at which, in reply to Germany's requirement for 'unimpeachable neutrality', de Valera made his stipulation to Hempel about showing a 'certain consideration for Britain', Gray goes on to say that that this meant in effect that de Valera was securing the 'right to deceive the British Government by publicly condemning Germany in order to ensure supply and freedom from military intervention'.

Whatever he may have wished Hempel to infer from his conversation, de Valera made himself unmistakably clear to the Minister on a number of 'danger points': ' . . . any violation of Irish territorial waters, exploitation of the anti-British radical nationalist movement [the IRA] . . . any hostile action against the population on the other side of the Northern Ireland frontier who wanted to return to the Irish state [the Six Counties nationalists] . . .' He also asked for a public announcement from the Germans that 'in view of friendly German–Irish relations that 'the Reich Government had promised respect for Irish neutrality'. In transmitting these requests to Berlin, Hempel said that his overall impression of de Valera was of 'a sincere effort to keep Ireland out of the conflict, but of great fear, which de Valera discussed in his usual doctrinaire fashion which betrays his rear weakness'. The 'doctrinaire' we can accept, but there is very little sign of weakness in de Valera's final demand: 'The Government also wanted a short announcement in the press that, in view of friendly German–Irish relations, I [Hempel] on behalf of the Reich Government had promised respect for Irish neutrality . . . . The Government consider it important that our announcements be identical and simultaneous.'

De Valera got his way. The following day, 1 September, a telegram arrived for Hempel from Berlin: 'We are in agreement with a press announcement as proposed by de Valera', but stipulating that the words 'conditional on a corresponding attitude by Ireland' must be added. The next day de Valera secured approval from the Dail for his neutrality policy and for his Emergency Powers legislation. Gray's interpretation of the deputies' reaction was: 'They did not suspect they were approving a promise to deliver to Hitler Irish influence in the United States described as "perhaps decisive", to the end of blocking American aid for Britain, or that the price was to be Northern Ireland. In his statement to the Dail on September 2, 1939, his studied omissions create the impression that the German negotiation had been limited to the practice of neutrality.'

Although the British exerted severe pressure during the war, particularly by restricting supplies, and Churchill was throughout a rumbling volcano always liable to erupt over the loss of the ports, de Valera was to enjoy happier relationships with the British Minister during 'the emergency'. To chart these we must go back a little in time. De Valera was a man of Munich. He supported Chamberlain's appeasement policy, both because he had done well out of it and because he hoped to do better – drawing a parallel between the German claim to the Czech Sudetenland and his own irredentist demands on north-eastern Ireland. Moreover, as in most of Eamon de Valera's policy initiatives, he had a hidden agenda. He was determined to maintain his neutrality policy and he wanted British military aid to help him do so.

Characteristically he cloaked all these objectives in a high moral tone designed to appeal to British, and in particular Chamberlain's, susceptibilities. It is said that he spent sleepless nights wondering if he should try to mediate with Hitler over the Sudeten issue. But when Chamberlain announced that he was going to visit Hitler in Berchtesgaden de Valera immediately cabled his congratulations on 'the greatest thing that has ever been done'. In his capacity as President of the Assembly of the League of Nations he broadcast from Geneva over Radio Nations on 25 September, praising Chamberlain for putting peace before pride:[17] 'Not always will we have someone to do what Mr. Chamberlain has done [that is, go to see Hitler at Berchtesgaden on 15 September and a week later, on the 22nd, at Godesberg] and shall find that we shall have had one crisis too many.' He appealed for 'something like a general European peace Conference, or at least a conference between the great powers'. This suggestion was aimed at Roosevelt and American public opinion. He said pointedly that now, twenty years on, was the time to attempt to fulfil Woodrow Wilson's 'ideals and his programmes'.[18]

Chamberlain was grateful for the broadcast and de Valera followed it up with a telegram to him on the eve of the Munich debacle: 'Let nothing daunt you or deflect you in your effort to secure peace. The tens of millions of innocent people on both sides who have no cause against each other but who are in danger of being hurled against each other with no alternative but mutual slaughter are praying that your efforts may find a way of saving them from this terrible doom.' The Munich surrender was signed in the small hours of 30 September 1938, the day the Assembly ended. In his closing address de Valera hailed Chamberlain as a:[19] 'knight of peace', who had 'attained the highest peak of human greatness, and a glory greater than that of all the conquerors'.

He attempted to realize this investment in adulation on his return from Geneva via London, where a portfolio of Irish desiderata was produced. De Valera had ideas about partition, Anglo-Irish defence co-operation, neutrality and the importance of not introducing conscription to Northern Ireland should this prove necessary on the UK mainland. In an attempt to impress the British he produced a map and statistics showing the extent of the injustices being perpetrated on Nationalists by means of discrimination and the practice of gerrymandering.[20] He wanted London to withdraw the subsidies which enabled Belfast to maintain this 'ghastly mess'. And by way of underscoring his complaints he told Malcolm MacDonald's Under Secretary, the Duke of Devonshire, that he had entertained thoughts of moving his troops across the border 'just as Hitler was doing'.[21] However, despite this minatory note, Chamberlain's record[22] of his conversation with de Valera shortly afterwards says that de Valera 'did not ask for autonomy or for cession of territory'. However, he did urge that the nationalist minority be given 'such safeguards as were being claimed for other minorities'.

In fact de Valera never asked the British to cede to the South the nationalist areas contiguous to the border which he claimed, correctly, would opt for rule from Dublin rather than Belfast if they had the choice. One historian has judged that he:[23] 'wanted all of the six counties or nothing, and he was only harping on the northern Nationalist grievances for propaganda purposes'. Some would go so far as to say that he did not even want the Six Counties, because he would then be faced with the uncomfortable presence of a large number of Protestants in the Dail. David Gray subscribed to this view in his unpublished book, and he quoted a number of de Valera's Irish opponents in support of his contention.

Propaganda was certainly one of de Valera's motives in belabouring the British with the partition issue. But another was to try to ensure that, should war come, England's difficulty should not prove to be the Northern Nationalists' opportunity for staging a rerun of the 1916 Rising that could spill over to the South and involve him in another round with the British. This was why he asked for – and, as we shall see, subsequently got – the Six Counties excluded from conscription. De Valera had been one of the principal architects of John Redmond's downfall, and he had no intention of seeing the weapon of conscription turned against himself by some youthful contemporary Republican rival. It is a legitimate speculation that by now police reports of increased, and very open, IRA drilling and preparation must have alerted him to the fact that a new IRA campaign was in the offing (to say nothing of individual Fianna Fail–IRA friendships, still widespread despite the official crack-down). The speculation is one which the murky and disturbing Stephen Hayes affair, which we shall encounter in Chapter 29, does nothing to diminish.

While de Valera's post-Munich descent on London did not then result in concrete Anglo-Irish defence arrangements, it did yield two interesting developments in this area. One was a report which the British prepared in response to an Irish request for information about the requirements needed to put the ports into a state of wartime readiness. The British calculated that the replacement of the existing heavy artillery and the overall modernization of defences could take as long as nine years to implement.[24] It is a calculation which, to say the least, is difficult to equate with the value which the British subsequently put on the ports. The second item of interest was a proposal by de Valera that a French officer be appointed as military adviser to the Irish Army. His reason was that:[25] ' . . . since political expediency made the appointment of a British officer impossible . . . a high military officer of our ally . . . would be a clear indication to Germany and the world that Eire was on the side of the Western democracies'. Any French officer whom the British suggested would do. The British did not suggest one, fearing that knowledge of 'certain devices and equipment' [probably radar] might come to 'the knowledge of a potential enemy' because 'the French are not very good at keeping secrets'. This British assessment of their principal ally is only slightly less surprising than that made by de Valera of one of his principal supporters. The Irish High Commissioner, Dulanty, who conveyed his request for a French officer to the British, said that de Valera was anxious for immediate action on the ports and on the officer suggestion because he was acting as Minister for Defence due to Frank Aiken's illness. It was important 'to get action taken while Mr. Aiken was away', Dulanty told the British, because he would be unwilling to undertake such work. Aiken was also represented as the bogeyman when Dulanty turned down a British proposal to appoint an Australian Catholic officer. De Valera, he said, would veto this because: 'Mr. Aiken represents the IRA Organisation and Mr. de Valera relies upon him to keep the IRA lot quiet and behind the government . . . . ' As a result Dulanty: ' . . . did not think any Dominion soldier or sailor would be agreeable to Mr. Aiken.[26]

Curiously, out of his entire Cabinet it was this same 'bogeyman', Aiken, whom de Valera would entrust with a most delicate mission to America when the war did break out. Aiken undoubtedly had all the attitudes one would expect of an Armagh-born former Chief of Staff of the IRA. But in dealing with the British de Valera brought to a near art form the practice of magnifying his domestic difficulties in order to secure external objectives.

Another nominee whom de Valera turned down for the post of adviser was General Sir Hubert Gough, the leader of the Curragh Mutiny during the Home Rule crisis of 1914. The proposer was Gough himself, who said on a number of occasions that 'his services were at the disposal of Mr. de Valera'.[27] We may accept without further analysis that Aiken would have entered a demur in this case!

De Valera continued to uphold the virtues of appeasement even after the emptiness of the Munich promises had been exposed by the sight of Hitler's troops on the streets of Prague on 15 March 1938. Chamberlain's own note of his last conversation with de Valera, at Chequers, less than two weeks afterwards, reads as follows:[28] ' . . . notwithstanding Hitler's recent actions, he had not changed his views that Munich was right and that in fact we had no other alternative but war. He said he had maintained this thesis against all critics, but added that he hoped very much that what had happened would not deflect me from the policy of appeasement . . . . In particular he hoped that I would not be tempted to embark upon a preventive war.' Chamberlain assured him on the last point and counter-attacked when de Valera again brought up the subject of partition and his own fear that war might mean he would suffer John Redmond's fate because of loyalty to the Empire. He wanted some concession on partition or else, he threatened, he would have to up the rhetorical ante during a projected tour of America. Chamberlain was not intimidated by the prospect of a de Valera propaganda campaign. He pointed out that earlier in the year de Valera had himself refused to make a gesture towards the North over trade and went on: '. . . he had himself done and said many things which had embittered feelings in Northern Ireland and made things worse than ever; in fact he had so conducted his affairs that he had not got a single friend in Northern Ireland'.

As so often happens when Irish and English leaders discuss Northern Ireland, the two men were talking through glass: they could see each other but were not communicating. To Chamberlain Northern Ireland meant the Unionists amongst whom de Valera did not have a friend. To de Valera the statelet meant the Nationalists to whose pressure he was responsive. Dulanty informed London that:[29] 'no man sitting in his chair could stand out of the partition campaign. If he did not enter into it and keep some sort of control over it it would get into unconstitutional hands'. Where Northern Ireland is concerned that is a familiar justification for taking an extreme course, another way of saying: 'I am the leader. There go my people – I must follow them.' Where de Valera was concerned it was yet another reminder of the price of 'extremist support'.

The spectre of being involved in the payment of that price worried both the British and the Americans. De Valera had been invited by Roosevelt to visit the United States, so that he could open the Irish pavilion at the World's Fair in New York in 1939. Malcolm MacDonald was appalled at the prospect of his visiting Irish cities in the USA; he supposed 'Mr. de

Valera would make some frightful speeches'. Dulanty tried unsuccessfully to soothe him by telling him that de Valera's advice for the tour was that 'he could not raise the fiery cross this time'. A civil servant's note on MacDonald's minute of the conversation gives an interesting illustration of the Dominions Office's combined irritation and lack of knowledge of both de Valera and Irish affairs:[30] 'I seem to remember that Mr. de Valera is still liable in certain states of the USA to penalties with regard to his $10,000,000 independence loan of 1920. But he can be left to steer clear of these and other entanglements himself.' By then, of course, de Valera had successfully steered his loan 'entanglements' into the coffers of the *Irish Press*, facilitated by the initial friendly advice of one Franklin Delano Roosevelt. But Roosevelt was not destined to remain friendly for long.

John Cudahy, the American Minister to Dublin, thought highly of de Valera personally. He told Roosevelt that when he met de Valera:[31]

> You will be impressed by Dev (as we call him). He has strength and a moral stature that one feels on first contact. Martin Conboy, who is staying here with his family, has great admiration for him. Together we agreed last night that our own President and Dev were the only statesmen of the democracies in this generation. I have often said that if de Valera were Prime Minister of Great Britain it would be a different world today. He has your quality of showing the way instead of being shown.

To Cudahy de Valera was:[32] 'that rare individual whose word can be taken at face value. I believe him to be entirely honest.' But for all his Kilkenny ancestry Cudahy was an American first. He was mindful, as he said,[33] of the danger that in 'foreign countries American representatives sometimes fall in with the sentiment of the country to which they are accredited, instead of being zealously, exclusively mindful of American interests'. And in the gathering storm that was soon to break over the world America's interest lay in upholding Britain. And so, in discussing the forthcoming tour of America by de Valera, 'that rare individual', Cudahy wrote to Roosevelt saying:[34]

> I had a talk with de Valera and did my best to impress upon him the fact that he must not talked too much about Partition and unity with Northern Ireland during his American tour . . . I told him very emphatically that if he were to dwell in his speeches upon any movement which would be considered an attack upon England this would be resented by the people in our country and would react to the detriment of the Irish cause.
>   . . . I wish you would hammer home to him the necessity of treading very lightly on any controversial issue directed against England. I need not tell you this is written in greatest confidence and would be fatal to me here if you were to disclose to Mr. de Valera what I have written you about this matter.

Thus, by the ineluctable dialectic of realpolitik, America's course was set even before war came and David Gray replaced Cudahy, who had asked for a transfer. Ineluctably, also, de Valera's politics would once again place him in an adversarial relationship to an American President. At the time of Cudahy's communication Roosevelt was anglophile, anti the dictators, and breasting a tide of isolationism as he swam for the distant shore of intervention. After Pearl Harbor America's interests and those of Great Britain were inextricably bound up in a world war. Neutrality, a different culture, would once again place de Valera and the White House as far apart as in Woodrow Wilson's time. Once more he would be dependent on an Irish American minority, vulnerable to the charge of assisting America's enemies. Bruree had as little in common with the horizons of Roosevelt, his grandee friends and neighbours in Dutchess County and their opulent estates along the Hudson in upstate New York as it had with Princeton. In the event, however, de Valera did not go to America.

On 26 April 1939 Chamberlain announced the introduction of compulsory national service. Craigavon immediately sought to have this conscription extended to the Six Counties, and the pot boiled over – there was a tremendous Nationalist outcry. De Valera cancelled his American trip. This step may have had more repercussions than was thought at the time. Roosevelt obviously had plans to talk to de Valera alone. He had intervened to 'make a change in the usual procedure' in the arrangements for the state dinner planned for de Valera, to provide that:[35] 'at 9.45 the President and President de Valera will retire alone to the President's study. The rest of the dinner party will then retire at their convenience.' The meeting in Roosevelt's study might have made for a meeting of minds that would have changed the course of Irish–US relationships during World War II. Who knows? At all events it never happened, and de Valera stayed at home to protest 'in the strongest terms' to the British Government. Since the Constitution laid claim to the entire island, the conscription of Irishmen would be 'an act of aggression'.[36] He was supported in his outrage by, amongst others, Cardinal MacRory, Six County trade union leaders, a host of Irish American societies and – Adolf Hitler. Roosevelt had sent an open letter to the Führer asking for assurances that he would not invade a list of thirty-one countries including Ireland. Hitler replied to this on 28 April:[37] 'He . . . asks for a statement that Germany will not attack Ireland. Now, I have just read a speech by de Valera, the Irish Taoiseach, in which, strangely enough, and contrary to Mr. Roosevelt's opinion, he does not charge Germany with oppressing Ireland, but he reproaches England with subjecting Ireland to continuous aggression.'

Chamberlain was himself subjected to 'continuous aggression' in the press whose tone may be determined from two publications at opposite ends of the spectrum, the *Manchester Guardian* and the *Daily Mirror*. The former noted that 'Herr Hitler, as he sarcastically reminded us yesterday, keeps a close eye on this rather vulnerable spot in our heel.'[38] The latter inquired: 'Is it credible that the British Government can even dream of repeating in 1939 the hideous blunder of 1918, and of forcing conscription in any part of Ireland?'[39] Chamberlain decided that it was not credible and summoned a distraught Craigavon to London to explain to him how it was that realpolitik sometimes meant that 'loyalty' was an embarrassment. He asked Craigavon:[40] 'Is Ulster out to help Britain in her war effort?' After the hapless Craigavon had spluttered out all his indignant proofs that 'Ulster' was indeed amongst the most helpful nations of the earth in the Empire's hour of need, Chamberlain sadly delivered the knock-out blow: 'If you really want to help us, don't press for conscription.' As Lady Craigavon resentfully recorded:[41] 'What else could J. do than say, "Very well, I won't!"' The British Government were, she noted: ' . . . frightened of the issue being complicated by de Valera kicking up the dust, though Ulster affairs have nothing to do with him. American opinion, as ever, had to be considered, too.' The Irish Americans might not be able to thwart the administration's anglophile drift overall, but they could be of powerful nuisance value on the isolationist side of the scales.

Something else, with a contemporary ring to it, also had to be considered: 'The military authorities in Belfast also advised against it, on account of the trouble that might arise in the Falls Road when forcibly going to enlist people . . . . ' By way of illustrating what that 'trouble' might have entailed, during the blackouts which followed the declaration of hostilities later in the year the Falls Road lights, including street lights, were frequently switched on at night. However, other sources of energy were not so immediately available to de Valera, or to anyone else in Southern Ireland, as the lights began going out all over Europe. In the month when the conscription crisis erupted the Twenty-six Counties' supply position was officially summed up as follows:[42] ' . . . if war should break out we are very largely at the mercy of other countries, and particularly of the United Kingdom . . . the economic activities of this country could in such circumstances be completely paralysed.'

The statistics on which this judgement was based include the following: all the Twenty-six Counties' coal came from Britain, 94 per cent of their iron piping, 84 per cent of their pig iron, 78 per cent of the state's most used cattle feed. Other harsh realities included the fact that Britain alone carried 64 per cent of the shipping tonnage on which Ireland depended. Wheat, maize, petroleum and timber were all carried into Irish ports by non-Irish vessels. Irish ownership of shipping tonnage was only some 5 per cent of the whole. The bottom line was that Britain was the source of 50 per cent of Ireland's imports and the destination of 90 per cent of her exports. Had the Twenty-six Counties wished to make a major shift in the purchase of imports (assuming that, in wartime, another country existed to import from), a further fact to be taken into account was that almost all their £200 million foreign reserves were in British securities.

Insofar as military security was concerned, the Twenty-six Counties were in an even more parlous position. De Valera had reached agreement with Aiken in the autumn of 1938 regarding various increases in Irish defence spending. However Sean MacEntee, the Minister for Finance, warned that these 'heavy commitments' meant either cutting back in essential services elsewhere, or 'an increase in taxation'. New proposals for defence cuts speedily emanated from the Taoiseach's Department. The Cabinet minutes for 1 December 1939 show that the Government actually decided to cut the Army strength, which it had just built up to 19,783 men, by some four thousand. Seeking electoral support for a policy of neutrality, which in part derived its appeal from the fact that people were not quite certain 'who they were neutral against', was one thing; putting up income tax for extraneous matters such as world wars was another. De Valera's reductions in defence spending were to have two effects. One was that the Twenty-six Counties came out of the 'emergency' relatively better off than other neutral, and stronger, economies. Another was that he turned his military weakness into a strength by insisting that it left him no option other than to cling fast to neutrality.

Neither advantage won him any popularity in the British Government. Here the advent of war meant that, as the stars of the men of Munich set, those of the anti-appeasers rose: Eden and, more significantly, Churchill returned to the Cabinet – Eden to the Dominions Office, where he replaced MacDonald, and Churchill to the Admiralty. Within two days of the outbreak of war Churchill called for a report on 'the so-called neutrality of the so-called Eire . . . . If they throw bombs in London, why should they not supply fuel to U-boats?'[43] After two weeks of hostilities he informed the Cabinet that U-boats had sunk twenty-eight British ships. To add to the attractions of being able to use the Southern Irish ports to extend the Royal Navy's range against submarines preying on the south-western approaches, there would also shortly come a powerful inducement to operate from the Northern port of Lough Swilly in Co. Donegal. On 14 October a U-boat sank the battleship *Royal Oak* at Scapa Flow naval base in Scotland. Access to the alternative, the huge sheltered fjord in Donegal which had been available in the 1914–18 war, instantly became desirable to the Admiralty.

As these disasters mounted, Churchill grew more and more angry at de Valera. A report drawn up by Sir William Malkin, the Foreign Office's Law Officer, on the legal problems presented by Irish neutrality provoked this Churchillian broadside:[44]

> So far as 'legality' counts the question surely turns on whether 'Eire is to be regarded as a neutral state.' If this is conceded then the regular laws of neutrality apply. But is the neutrality which Mr. Devalera [*sic*] has proclaimed a valid condition, and on all fours with, the neutrality of, say, Holland or Switzerland?
>
> It is to this point that attention should first be directed. What is the international juridical status of Southern Ireland? It is not a Dominion. They themselves repudiate this idea. It is certainly under the Crown. Nothing has been defined. Legally I believe they are 'At war but Skulking.' Perhaps Sir William should examine this thesis.

Malkin had simply pointed out the obvious – that if 'Eire' was to be regarded as neutral and 'if Mr. de Valera is determined to be really neutral there is from the legal point of view no more to be said'.[45] Eden agreed with Malkin rather than Churchill. His note on the Law Officer's report reads:[46] 'I fear that it becomes every day clearer that it is scarcely possible for "Dev" to square neutrality with the grant of the facilities for which the Admiralty ask. And at least 80% of the Irish people favour neutrality. Altogether a pretty problem.'

The man chosen by the British to attempt to solve the problem with de Valera was Sir John Loader Maffey. At six foot four he was even taller than de Valera, and his professional standing was such that he was brought out of retirement five years after relinquishing the Governor Generalship of the Sudan. Previous to that he had had wide experience in the Indian colonial service. As Chief Commissioner of Peshawar he had won particular renown for negotiating the freedom of an English lady, a Miss Mollie Ellis, from captivity by the Afridis tribe. This had proved an easier task than the freeing of the ports from the hands of de Valera. Yet, despite the incompatibility of the policies pursued by the two men, Maffey's diplomatic skills were such that he survived his Dublin posting without impairment of his personal relationship with de Valera.

The first hurdle to be crossed was that of Maffey's job description. The Irish wanted an Ambassador, but the British objected to the idea of appointing an 'ambassador' to a country that was supposedly part of the British Commonwealth. Eventually the British suggested that as a compromise there should be a 'United Kingdom Representative in Eire'. When the wording was placed before de Valera he hesitated for a moment, then crossed out 'in' and substituted 'to'.[47] It would be difficult to find a more symbolic piece of nit-picking nonsense to characterize much of de Valera's relationship with Britain than this incident. For if one takes the trouble to turn to the Irish Cabinet minutes wherein the Maffey appointment is formally approved,[48] one will find Sir John described, over de Valera's signature, as the British Diplomatic Representative 'in Ireland'. And so the Representative 'to' found himself 'in' Dublin confronting de Valera for the first time on 14 September 1939. This meeting, and two others stemming from it, may be taken as setting the tone for the entire British–Irish relationship of the war. De Valera opened the proceedings by getting his retaliation in first. Before Maffey could bring up the small matter of Irish neutrality, de Valera pounded him with a series of grievances.

The receiving of a United Kingdom Representative in Dublin 'would be a battle cry for the IRA and Extremists'.[49] Every action of his was severely scrutinized, he told Maffey, by men bitterly opposed to any rapprochement with Britain and quick to pounce on the slightest deviation from neutrality. Pointing to a map of Ireland coloured 'Eire jet-black, Northern Ireland a leprous white',[50] he declared: 'All this happens because you maintain the principle of Partition in this island.' As Maffey, correctly, described the scene later,[51] the Irish leader and the British envoy 'always performed a circle, the President saying that Eire could not consider any policy today except in the light of the crime of partition, while I said that the prospects of readjusting partition must be affected by the policy of Eire today'.

Eventually Maffey managed to break the circle to raise the matter he most wanted to discuss, an aide-memoire which de Valera had ordered Dulanty, the Irish High Commissioner in London, to deliver to the Dominions Office two days earlier. This contained the list of 'dos' and 'don'ts' which de Valera wished the British to observe for the maintenance of Irish neutrality. The list, which invoked the Hague Convention, was, effectively speaking, a catalogue of 'don'ts'. Not only was the Royal Navy's use of the ports banned, so too was any use of Ireland's coastal waters. And the RAF was excluded from Irish air space. The list applied equally to all belligerents, including Germany. De Valera blandly told Maffey that he was trying to be 'helpful' to Britain. He wanted to do what he could against submarines, but if he made an order against submarines his enemies would say that he was being anti-German and ask what he was doing about planes and ships.

Maffey asked him not to publish the document because it would arouse deep feeling in England and add to Chamberlain's problems. At the mention of Chamberlain's name de Valera's manner changed; he became admiring of and sympathetic to the British Prime Minister who, he said, had done 'everything that a man could do to prevent this tragedy'. But he refused to give any guarantee of non-publication. He pointed out to Maffey that an RAF plane had recently come down at Skerries, in north Co. Dublin, but had been allowed to take off again. Censorship had prevented the incident being reported, but it had been widely commented on. How could he hope to get away with taking action against German submarines while allowing British planes into Irish air space?

At this precise moment in the conversation de Valera's phone rang. A British plane had come down at Ventry in Co. Kerry. What was he to do? Whatever the ownership of the plane, the crew would have to be interned. Maffey's report continues: 'The President was greatly disturbed in mind and we were both much relieved when the telephone rang again an hour later to report that the plane had managed to get away – or rather had been allowed to get away. Clearly problems of this kind lie ahead of us.'

The fundamental problem which lay ahead for the two countries was thoroughly aired in the de Valera–Maffey discussion. Maffey's position was that: 'in this struggle at last there was an ideal for which England and Eire could stand together and that from that association a new chapter in our history would start'. However de Valera, who conceded that two-thirds of his people were anti-German, and said that 'personally' he had 'great sympathy for England', removed the conversation from the struggle against Nazism to the fate of John Redmond and the partition issue. Why did not the British prevent the Unionist injustices, he asked, going on to point out the advantages that a united Ireland would bring. Maffey summarized these as follows:

> ... the effect in America where the Irish element had ruined and would ruin any possibility of Anglo-American understanding! ... it was not a matter of religion. The petty tyrannies and oppressions now going on in Northern Ireland must lead to disaster. 'If I lived there', he exclaimed with heat, I should say 'I'll be damned if I'll be ruled by these people'. He went on to voice the fear that if the war went on for long the danger of a physical clash between the rival forces in Ireland could not be averted .... 'My friends in America say to me "Why don't you take a leaf out of Hitler's book and work the Sudeten Deutsch trick in Northern Ireland?"'

His summing up of this meeting was that de Valera: 'at present does not wish any consideration to obscure his vision of neutrality. The only line possible at present is to retain his goodwill and to render his neutrality as benevolent as possible.'

Maffey's description of his first meeting with de Valera could be taken as a thumbnail sketch of the subsequent wartime relationship between Ireland and Britain. But it also illustrates the subtle difference between de Valera's playing of the American Irish card with the Germans and with the British. With the former, Walshe hinted that American influence was something which de Valera could control and was prepared to consider delivering to the Germans in return for support for national aspirations; whereas with the British de Valera was both sympathetic and concerned about an 'Irish element' which by inference existed outside his sway. In a sense this was of course true, but equally it could be advanced that no man alive had demonstrated an ability to rival de Valera's own when it came to manipulating Irish American support.

After digesting both Maffey's report and de Valera's list of prohibitions Eden came to the conclusion that little could be done in practice to challenge de Valera's proposals. However he was concerned about the principle involved in a member of the Commonwealth becoming a neutral. Nor could the question of Irish bases or coastal waters being used to shelter attackers on British shipping be taken lightly.[52] Accordingly, Maffey was instructed to hand de Valera a letter from Chamberlain on 20 September 1939 outlining these fears. His eyesight had worsened so much by this stage that Maffey had to read the letter to him. In the discussion that followed de Valera mooted a procedure which was to become standard practice during the war: the repatriation of British pilots and aircrews who, in the words of Maffey, occasionally landed 'like exhausted birds on Irish shores'. De Valera also announced that when U-boats were spotted the Irish coastguard service would wireless this information 'to the world', uncoded. This of course was a clear advantage to the British, but de Valera stipulated that it would be done simply as a matter of routine and that he would so inform the German Minister.

De Valera also proposed another 'little device' which, Eden noted, 'worked smoothly through the war years'.[53] This was the provision of dumps of civilian clothing for Irish citizens serving in the British forces, so that they could change at Holyhead *en route* for Ireland. Thousands of Irishmen and women joined up during the war, and the civilian clothes dumps spared de Valera the embarrassment of having to countenance widespread displays of khaki on Ireland's green landscape. In fact this meeting with Maffey paved the way for a whole range of British–Irish co-operative measures on security which will be discussed in context later. But, having made these initial conciliatory proposals, de Valera overcame his failing sight for a final characteristic flourish. Maffey said he:[54] ' . . . led me to his black map of Ireland with its white blemish on the North-East corner and said: "There's the real source of all our trouble." He could not let me go without that.'

Neither could the British allow the ports issue to go at that. Apart from Churchill's increasingly sulphuric response to what he termed 'the odious treatment we are receiving',[55] the deteriorating war situation prompted a further approach to de Valera on 21 October 1939. Shipping losses were mounting, reports of U-boat sightings around the Irish coast were multiplying, and the Germans had begun to attack neutral Scandinavian shipping. This time Maffey was briefed by Chamberlain and Eden to tell de Valera that, while the 1938 ports hand-over had of course been unconditional, nevertheless:[56] 'There was nothing in the agreement to prevent the Government of Eire from according facilities to the Royal Navy to make use of Eire ports.' The United Kingdom Government had: ' . . . always felt . . . that in their view a state of emergency might arise which rendered it imperative in the interests of both countries, that such facilities should be accorded. These circumstances have now arisen.'

Not so far as Eamon de Valera was concerned. Maffey glumly reported that his:[57] 'uncompromising answer to every line of approach was a categorical "non possumus" . . . . I was talking to a man whose mind was made up.' When Maffey put it to him that, in the ports agreement, 'the path of generosity had been followed as an act of faith and in the belief that in the hour of need the hand of friendship would be extended', de Valera replied that the British had 'no right to expect to derive advantage from what was not ours. Such a view would justify the encroachment by Germany on Holland or Belgium.' Along with these cheerless statements, Maffey had also to contend with the disconcerting effect of de Valera's phone. Once more it rang in the middle of an interview. This time a reporter from the French news agency Havas wanted to know whether it was true that the British were demanding the ports. De Valera denied that anything of the sort had occurred, and then pointedly turned back to listen to His Majesty's Representative to Dublin explain why the ports should be returned.

Partition was Maffey's final card: 'Who could see any hope for a united Ireland on the lines of our present conversation? What British

Government would ever surrender the ports of the North after this experience?' The Great Adamantine remained unmoved. He again professed his admiration for Chamberlain, but turned down the offer of a meeting with the British Prime Minister because 'it could not in any way alter matters'. Nevertheless he was in 'full agreement' with everything Chamberlain had done. 'England,' he said, 'has a moral position today.' He conceded that Hitler might have his 'early successes, but the moral position would tell'. Of course, he added, if Britain were to move against the Irish ports its moral position too would suffer. When Maffey shrewdly countered: 'Not if help were voluntarily conceded,' de Valera's reply was: 'No, but that would stir up trouble which would quickly compromise your moral position.' And on that note of moral concern the neutrality issue subsided into a resentful quietude on Britain's part until June of the following year, when Malcolm MacDonald was sent to do battle with de Valera – unsuccessfully. Maffey did some sampling of Irish public opinion on the neutrality issue, and wrote to Eden on 23 October 1939:[58] 'The policy of neutrality commands widespread approval among all classes and interests in Eire. It is remarkable how even the "pro-British" group, men who have fought for the Crown and are anxious to be called up again, men whose sons are at the front today, loyalists in the old sense of the word, agree generally in supporting the policy of neutrality in Eire.'

Meanwhile, a figure who would loom larger in de Valera's thoughts than either Maffey or MacDonald had arrived in Dublin – David Gray, the American Minister. His importance, or nuisance value, to de Valera may be gauged from the fact that there are more references to him in de Valera's official biography, covering his seven years in Ireland, than there are to Sean Lemass, who shared a lifetime with de Valera and ultimately succeeded him as Taoiseach.

25

GRAY AMIDST THE GREENERY

DAVID GRAY WAS seventy years of age when he arrived in Dublin on 8 April 1940, into a situation which set the tone for much of his stay. In good faith he had told reporters that he would not be staying in the Embassy occupied by his predecessor, formerly the home of the British Secretary of State in Phoenix Park; at the same time the State Department were not planning to release these draughty premises (when they did move in, Gray's wife found the heating in the bathroom superior to that elsewhere in the house and moved her bed into that room). When the British learned that 'The Park' might be available they expressed an interest in acquiring it for Sir John Maffey. De Valera got an apocalyptic vision of headlines proclaiming 'De Valera lets British back into Viceregal Lodge'. Accordingly when Gray stepped ashore in Dublin an American diplomat shook him warmly by the hand and, maintaining a smiling countenance, hissed in his ear:[1] 'Say it was a misunderstanding. You're *not* giving up the house. Explain later.'

There were many misunderstandings subsequently and Gray did not give up the house – much to de Valera's ultimate chagrin. A Harvard graduate, who had subsequently been conferred with a doctorate of letters, he had also acquired a legal training and achieved some success as a playwright and journalist. He was married to the former Mrs Maude Livingston Hall Waterbury, an aunt of Eleanor Roosevelt. As he stated frankly in his unpublished book 'Behind the Green Curtain', his appointment could be considered 'nepotic'. His friendly relationship with Roosevelt was such that his personal correspondence with the President sometimes included material not usually associated with diplomatic pouches. The letters, which Roosevelt obviously appreciated, include a detailed account[2] of seances conducted by a writing medium, Miss Geraldine Cummins,[3] at which, amongst others, Roosevelt's mother, the former President Theodore Roosevelt and the former British Prime Minister Arthur Balfour sent messages to Gray. Balfour is quoted as telling Gray that 'the fact that de Valera asked some time ago for your removal from Eire was the highest compliment any American diplomat has ever been paid'. Roosevelt's reaction to the medium's messages was: 'Those are real contributions and I hope you will continue.'[4] On another occasion Gray wrote to the President that: 'If the American Ambassador to the Court of St. James has not sent you the following he is not on the job. Replace him with a good man.' This was 'the following':[5]

Mussolini gave the order to advance against the foe
So forth to Abyssinia all the organ grinders go.
But now they are incapable of any sort of grind
For they're back from Abyssinia with their organs left behind.
The hordes of Abyssinia have returned to hearth and home,
With knick-knacks for the mantel-shelf imported straight from Rome.
While the Pope is inundated with requests to join the Choir
From men whose normal voices are at least an octave higher.
Mussolini mounts the rostrum as the regiments return
With the Unknown Eunuch's ashes in a truly Roman urn –
Says he – This State occasion for recognition truly calls
What shall we give the heroes – and the heroes answer – Balls.

But de Valera saw little that was humorous in Gray's mission. After Roosevelt was safely dead in 1945, he made several efforts to have Gray removed. Joseph Walshe was instructed to write to Robert Brennan, the Irish Minister in Washington, asking that he use his contacts to 'put an end to Gray's career'[6] because of the 'continued unfitness of David Gray for promoting good relations between this country and the United States. It would be quite inconceivable for any other country in the world to send and maintain a Minister who has been doing so much harm to his country as this gentleman.' Walshe averred that examination of Gray's despatches would disclose[7] 'an attitude of constant bias against this country as well as a marked personal hostility to the Head of Government. Mr. Gray has for a long time been persona non grata to the Irish government.'

De Valera did not dare make such representations while Roosevelt was alive. In fact Gray's official communications are professional in tone, and correspondence between Secretary of State Cordell Hull and Roosevelt arising out of his despatches indicates that he was reflecting official American attitudes to de Valera. Gray himself wrote privately:[8] 'The Department and the President have backed me up in the most wonderful manner in this job and we are reaching a point where Mr. de Valera has to fish or cut bait.' (Roosevelt himself also used this phrase about the Irish in a letter to Gray.)[9] The point then at issue was the passing of the Lend-Lease Bill, after which Gray judged that, as America's and Britain's interests were so closely allied, 'being anti-British here is going to be tantamount to being anti-American for the purposes of the war'.

In a way de Valera's criticisms of Gray – that he was inexperienced in diplomacy and mixed with the wrong people, the Ascendancy elements – mirrored Gray's strictures on de Valera's sources of information:[10] 'His foreign office is very weak and they have evidently relied on what they have heard from the Irish-American pressure groups which were out to beat the President in the recent elections.' In fact de Valera knew the United States very well, as his early travels there indicate, but the Irish wherein lay his power base were not those who inhabited Roosevelt's social circle. What Gray was criticizing, though he did not realize it, was the fact that to all intents and purposes de Valera, who was his own

Minister for Foreign Affairs, largely was the Irish 'foreign office'. His wartime policy was mainly formulated by a triumvirate consisting of himself, Joseph Walshe and another outstandingly able diplomat, Frederick H. Boland.[11]

Gray began his assignment quite well disposed towards de Valera and his domestic policy. His diaries show that he entertained a very wide circle of Irish contacts, including government ones. But de Valera *was* to a large extent the Government, and in addition the minister with whom a diplomat would normally most frequently deal. Consequently when he withdrew his favour from Gray, the latter's social and political circles rapidly became restricted to members of the Opposition and his own fishing, golfing and racing friends. Gray initially told Eleanor Roosevelt:[12] 'The great thing the de Valera government has done and is doing, is to govern in the interest of the underprivileged as far as possible. They have a real new deal here which is altogether admirable. . . . ' However:

> In regard to relations with the outside world, especially England, even the Prime Minister lives in a dream-wish world . . . Mr. de Valera defends this illusion with the genius of a Jesuit attorney always shifting his ground in argument to a position in which he is unassailable on moral grounds . . . he has the unfailing escape of charging it [the problem of the moment] to England's imperialistic arrogance.
> . . . The politician in Ireland who has the custody of the Lion's tail is the one who retains power. If Mr. de V. ever let that object out of his hands he would be lost. But with the tail, his very high personal honesty as to money, his genuine sympathy for the underdog he will be very difficult to defeat. I like him very much though I despair of coping with him. He has it all over me like a tent.

But by the end of the war relations between the two men had deteriorated so much that, in his unpublished book, Gray depicts de Valera as having been possessed by the 'NeoGaelic Afflatus' after 1916:[13]

> Since that time there is no record of his having done what was generous or noble or wise, only what he believed served 'the Cause' . . . he regarded himself as 'The Cause'. . . . What was good for de Valera became good for Ireland. There was no honest view other than his . . . he dedicated himself to justifying his mistakes and making them stand in history as not having been mistakes . . . .
> In retrospect I know that I was never at ease with him. There was never honest meeting of the eyes except when his were blazing with anger. I now know that during the seven years of our relation he was always tricking my country, but I believe that there was an honest basis for the charm that he exerted and the affection he inspired. It was as if some 'Better Self', habitually kept under restraint, escaped to the window and beckoned. One recognised good will and went forward but found the window barred and what had been behind it vanished.

But though Gray's view of de Valera was unquestionably unflattering it is not true, as de Valera used the Department of External Affairs to urge, that Gray's attitudes were responsible for negative American reactions to

Irish policy. Prior to Pearl Harbor many Irish Americans tended to be isolationist. The blend of ancestral nationalism directed against England, and the growing comity of British and American interest, produced a serious policy dichotomy between Southern Ireland, the Irish societies in America and the US administration. A senior American official who took note of these complexities made a suggestion concerning the Lend-Lease controversy[14] which, had it been followed, would have eliminated some of these tensions:

> Failure to bring Ireland in under the Lease Lend programme is probably a mistake which should be corrected as soon as possible .... The attitude of Ireland to the war is a crucial point in American public opinion with respect to the administration's foreign policy . . . up to now the public has gotten the impression that . . . lease lend aid [is being used] only as a sort of club to force Ireland into line with British policy . . . out of question to expect Irish to respond favourably . . . suggest offer of limited lend-lease with no strings attached [accompanied by a publicity campaign].

This approach found favour neither with Roosevelt nor with his arcane inner circle. FDR was fully in agreement with Gray. On one occasion, 4 February 1941, the Minister wrote to FDR saying that the Dail reminded him of the 'Supervisors meetings that I used to report in Monroe County when I worked on the *Rochester Union and Advertiser*'. But in the same letter he asked the President to let him know if he was being too vigorous in his advocacy of American interests. Should he 'be careful'? Roosevelt wrote back:[15]

> I think you are unfair to the Board of Supervisors of Dutchess County or of Monroe County. Almost all of them were highly practical people.
> Over here we also have people who live in a world of unreality, but they take it out in talk and represent very definitely a minority.
> You need not 'be careful.'

Had Roosevelt lived, Ireland's and de Valera's post-war history might have taken very different courses from the manner in which they did develop. Both Gray and Roosevelt hoped that the war would provide the means of destroying the influence of 'the professional hyphenate Irish-American politician'. They wished to see an end to such Mayor Curley-like figures for reasons of domestic politics and as a method of removing 'serious difficulty in the way of putting Anglo-American relations on a firm foundation'.[16] At a lunch given by Churchill in Downing Street, attended by de Gaulle, Gray said openly that he believed 'the British and American Governments should accept the Irish claim to separatist independence, but should then say in effect, "Supply and protect yourself," . . . this was the only antidote that I could see to the decade of de Valera's preaching to Irish youth that Eire was essentially self-sufficient and reliant.'
Roosevelt's reaction to Gray's report of the lunch was revealing. He

liked the idea that 'Ireland must have self-government imposed upon it – with all the responsibilities that that implies'.[17] But Roosevelt also wanted it brought home to the Irish that 'they will never be permitted to allow any other nation to use them in a military way or otherwise against the United States or Britain'. The denial of Ireland to an enemy of Britain's was of course what de Valera had promised all along, but Roosevelt clearly saw the loss of the ports as occurring 'in a military way'. He made clear his lack of sympathy with de Valera and offered a glimpse of what the future might have held for de Valera and for Ireland had he lived: 'It seems to me that during all these years it has been a pity that Ireland has lived in a dream under the rule of a dreamer. They do not know the facts of life and it will take a rude awakening to teach them.' Roosevelt was perfectly prepared to provide that rude awakening: 'If and when we clean up Germany, I think that Mr. Churchill and I can do much for Ireland and its future – *and I think that he and I can agree on the method with due consideration of firmness and justice* [author's italics].'

Dutchess County was going to sort out South Boston, the Bronx and the Ancient Order of Hibernians once and for all. In the event, however, it was de Valera, 'the dreamer', who was destined to remain in power long after Churchill and Roosevelt. However, during the war this formidable duo presented him with two serious threats – the fear of invasion and the cutting off of supplies vital to his state's existence. The former eventually passed off harmlessly, but the second was given substantive form. Let us first examine the question of invasion, which in 1940 appeared to be looming from the direction of Germany also.

Germany's onslaught through Belgium, Holland and Luxembourg in the early hours of 10 May 1940 spurred Maffey into action without waiting for direction from London. He saw de Valera later that day[18] and put it to him that there was a 'maniacal force' loose in the world and that the time had come for Ireland to cease being 'neutral in the cause of freedom'. The discussion, however, progressed little beyond the by now familiar leitmotiv of Anglo-Irish discussion, partition. Maffey reported to London that:[19]

> . . . we always travelled back to the old prejudice, to Partition, to the bitterness in the hearts of the active and extremist elements. I suggested that with clear leadership the adventurous spirits would respond to a better call. But Mr. de Valera held to his narrow view. He seems incapable of courageous or original thought and now on this world issue and in every matter he lives too much under the threat of the extremist . . . not a strong man and his many critics here know that well . . . .

And de Valera reminded Maffey that the British were stalling on Irish requests for arms which would have enabled the Irish to ensure that no threat of attack on England from Ireland would materialize. He also refused to antagonize the Germans by agreeing to Maffey's request to close the German Legation. But he did antagonize the Germans by a concession that he indicated to Maffey before their unsatisfactory interview concluded. He told him that he would say something about Hitler's recent aggressions the next day at Galway, where he was attending a Fianna Fail convention to select a by-election candidate. At Galway he said:[20] 'I was at Geneva on many occasions. . . . The representatives of Belgium and the representatives of The Netherlands were people that I met frequently, because we co-operated not a little with the northern group of nations. Today these two small nations are fighting for their lives, and I think I would be unworthy of this small nation, if on an occasion like this, I did not utter our protest against the cruel wrong which has been done them.'

It was de Valera's first public condemnation of Germany and David Gray was amongst those who took the brave-sounding words at their face value:[21] ' . . . a statement of first importance. It was brave and explicit. It nailed the Irish flag to the masthead of Western Democracy.' He sent de Valera a letter of congratulation which was not acknowledged. In his unpublished memoirs Gray writes bitterly:[22] 'Later when we found out what had happened, we could understand why.' When the German diplomatic telegrams of the period were uncovered, it was found that privately de Valera had retreated from his public utterances. Without waiting for instructions from Berlin, Hempel called at the Department of External Affairs on 14 May to lodge a formal protest about the speech (thereby anticipating instructions to do so, which arrived on the 16th). Amongst other things he was told 'in an apologetic manner' by F. H. Boland, the deputy head, that the Department had not had the opportunity of vetting de Valera's speech! The impression that the Galway speech was an unguarded slip which did not represent policy was heightened by the account of the affair given to a German Foreign Ministry official by the Irish Chargé d'Affaires in Berlin, William Warnock:[23]

I mentioned to the Irish Chargé d'Affaires today the protest which our Minister in Dublin had made . . . respecting the speech of de Valera. Mr. Warnock had already been informed by his Government, and expressed in a similarly apologetic manner as the deputy of the Irish Foreign Minister [de Valera was, of course in addition to being Taoiseach, 'the Irish Foreign Minister'] had done to our Minister. The Chargé d'Affaires added the remark that Ireland wished to maintain neutrality towards all Powers and said personally that Ireland, in the last war against England, had struck too early. This mistake would not be repeated. In view of the German successes the question, however, was whether Ireland would not come too late.

Woermann.

It might be noted that de Valera's official biography gives the impression that there may be doubt concerning what the Germans recorded about German–Irish diplomatic exchanges. It could be inferred from the account of the Warnock conversation described above that de Valera, that most meticulous controller of detail, did not know exactly what was conveyed to the Germans. The biography says of Hempel's protest over the Galway speech: 'F. H. Boland received him on de Valera's behalf. He poured oil on troubled waters and *apparently* [author's italics] instructed Warnock to do the same.'[24] One encounters phrases such as 'according to the German records – but not to the Irish'[25] and 'There is, however, no confirmation of this on the Irish side'. It does not state that one reason for the lack of confirmation is the fact that de Valera ordered records of discussions with foreign diplomats to be destroyed.[26] The reason he gave, when the Battle of Britain was raging, was that Germany might use them after an invasion to justify her actions, as she had done with Holland. But why the destruction should have continued throughout the war, long after the threat from Germany had receded, must remain a matter of speculation. 'Of course,' as Boland himself afterwards noted,[27] 'a great many things happened in the period which never found their way into documents at all.'

What we do know is that, the day after Warnock delivered the view from Dublin in Berlin, Dublin received a jolting indication of how things could develop in Ireland as viewed from Berlin. A German spy, Dr Hermann Goertz, got away one jump ahead of the law when police raided a house in the prosperous suburb of Tempelogue in Co. Dublin. The house was owned by an Irish businessman of German ancestry, Stephen Carroll Held. In it police found a radio transmitter, a code book and some £20,000. Most disturbing of all was a cache of papers concerning the preparations for an airborne attack. There were details of Irish military installations, airfields, bridges, roads and harbours. The Germans, it seemed, were coming.

The Goertz operation ultimately turned out to have been merely an Abwehr bungle, precisely the sort of thing which Hempel had warned against. Its long-term effect was to ensure that the Hempel-sponsored, Foreign Ministry attitude of 'hands off' towards Irish neutrality triumphed over secret service adventurism. But in the immediate aftermath of the discovery de Valera decided to abandon the lion's tail for the moment and instead opted for some protection under its paw. The day after the Held discovery, on 23 May, he informed the British Government what Irish policy would be in the event of a German invasion:[28]

> The twenty-six counties would fight if invaded by Germany and would call for assistance from Great Britain as soon as this appeared necessary.
> The British would not be invited until after fighting had begun. If they arrived before it he could not be responsible for the political consequences.
> He was not under threat from internal dangers such as fifth columnists. All potential subversives were under surveillance.

On the same day that this message was delivered he despatched Joseph Walshe and Colonel Liam Archer, the head of Irish Military Intelligence, to London, where they met with representatives of the Dominions Office and of the service departments. It is clear from the minutes[29] of the meetings that the Irish had been given instructions to deal openly and co-operatively with the British. When the War Office representative, Major

G. D. G. Heyman, voiced an anxiety that the Germans might drop paratroops to link up with the IRA, Walshe made no attempt to magnify the extent of the extremist problem as de Valera normally did in his jousts with British representatives. He stated that the IRA were not a 'serious threat' which required assistance from the UK and gave evidence of de Valera's ruthless determination to deal with the organization.[30] This, as we shall see later, was indeed ruthless. Walshe said 'that the Government of Eire anticipated no difficulty in dealing with the IRA. In fact the outbreak of specific disturbances were the kind of opportunity which they were seeking in order to crush finally the organisation.'

As a result of these meetings detailed co-operation (described in the Appendix) with Great Britain in its war efforts was agreed; this, by any reckoning, must be regarded as going far beyond 'a certain consideration' for the United Kingdom. The co-operation included a pooling of information of all sorts: the routing of German and Italian official communications through Britain: the use of Shannon Airport for British purposes, and the turning of a blind eye to British overflights of Irish air space or to 'hot pursuit' in Irish territorial waters; and the use of extra 'secret' transmitters in the British Legation. In other negotiations the Irish agreed to co-operation in joint purchasing of commodities, and to shared arrangements in shipping and in petrol rationing which the British took advantage of to use as pressure points in the continuing dispute over neutrality (see Appendix B). All these arrangements, together with the sale of surplus Irish food and the contribution made by Irish man, and woman, power to the British war effort caused Maurice Moynihan to write at the foot of a 'most secret list' (Appendix A) detailing them: 'We could not do more if we were in the war.'

While the British and Irish representatives were meeting at the operational level in May and June of 1940, the British decided to make a major approach on neutrality to de Valera at Cabinet level. Two factors in particular decided this initiative: one was the spate of German successes in Europe; the other was the effect on the Cabinet, and on Churchill in particular, of lurid reports about IRA–Nazi activities in Ireland from Sir Charles Tegart, an Anglo-Irish graduate of Trinity College and former security adviser to the Palestine Police, who had been information-gathering in Ireland. Had he been briefed to provide disinformation he could not have done better. His visit resulted in both Chamberlain and Churchill, who had become Prime Minister of the wartime coalition on 11 May 1940, being informed that:[31] ' . . . the German Gauleiters of Eire are already there . . . up to 2,000 leaders have been landed in Eire from German U-Boats and by other methods since the outbreak of war'.

Accordingly, yet another effort to put pressure on de Valera was agreed upon. Ironically, by now it was Chamberlain rather than Churchill who was most hawkish towards de Valera. Chamberlain was suffering from cancer and had not long to live. His health and the ruin of his appeasement hopes were not conducive to his accepting with equanimity an Irish neutrality which his gift of the ports had helped to create. Churchill had not become any more well disposed towards either de Valera or neutrality. But he had tried and failed to get Roosevelt to send an American squadron on an extended visit to Irish ports to act as a deterrent to a German invasion. Thus he was mindful of the need not to stir up Irish American reactions which might rebound against Roosevelt in an election year. Accordingly the attempt to get de Valera to abandon neutrality was made by means of the carrot of an offer on Irish unity rather than the stick of an invasion threat.

Malcolm MacDonald was chosen to see de Valera on the basis of his earlier acquaintance with him; the two men had three meetings between 17 and 27 June. MacDonald's report of the first meeting, which occurred three days after the fall of Paris, gives an indication of the pressures on de Valera at the time:[32]

> He was in one way the old de Valera . . . His mind is still set in the same hard, confined mould as of yore. But in another way he appeared to have changed. He made no long speeches; the whole procedure was more in the nature of a sustained conversation between two people than sometimes used to be the case. He seemed depressed and tired, and I felt he had neither the mental nor the physical vigour that he possessed two years ago.

In that first meeting MacDonald's objective was to get Ireland to abandon neutrality. He argued that to wait until the Germans landed would give fifth columnists the opportunity of sabotaging road and rail communications so that, despite the operational plans drawn up by their two countries, the British would not be able to come to his aid in time. His fall-back position was a suggestion that de Valera invite British troops and warships to guard strategic areas. But de Valera turned down these proposals, arguing that they would breach neutrality and with it the 'national unity which had been achieved between the various parties in the country'.

This 'national unity' requires some explanation. The day before seeing MacDonald, de Valera had addressed a huge meeting in Dublin to drum up support for a recruiting drive for the Irish security forces which was then in progress. With him on the platform were the leaders of the opposition parties, William Norton of Labour and, more importantly, W. T. Cosgrave of Fine Gael. This was a significant indication to the public that the situation was so grave as to warrant the putting aside of civil war animosities. Privately, also, de Valera made a gesture – it was scarcely more than that – towards involving the opposition parties in a National Defence Conference. Fine Gael's nominees to the conference were James Dillon, T. G. O'Higgins and Richard Mulcahy. Labour nominated Norton and William Davin. Aiken, Boland and Oscar Traynor represented Fianna Fail – or, more accurately, de Valera. Blind, 'depressed and tired' or no, he was not having anything approaching a wartime coalition Government. Mulcahy once described the Opposition's minimalist, and purely advisory, role on the conference as being 'like hens scratching'[33] for facts.

However, the public political face of all-party unanimity, 'national unity', on neutrality gave de Valera a convincing-sounding reason for turning down MacDonald's opening gambit. He accompanied his refusal by some 'hen scratching' of his own in the form of an appeal to MacDonald for arms so as to be able to resist a German invasion 'with all their might'. MacDonald reported back to the War Cabinet in London on 20 June. It was an emotional meeting at which Chamberlain speculated about the possibilities of taking back the ports by force, while Churchill urged restraint.[34] The upshot was that MacDonald found himself back in Dublin the following day, without the arms that de Valera had asked for, but with a new proposal on unity:[35]

> That there should be a declaration of a United Ireland in principle, the constitutional and other practical details of the union to be worked out in due course; Ulster to remain a belligerent, Eire to remain neutral at any rate for the time being, if both parties desired it, a joint Defence Council to be set up at once; at the same time in order to secure Eire's neutrality against violation by Germany, British naval ships to be allowed into Eire ports, British troops and aeroplanes to be stationed at certain agreed points in the territory, the British Government to provide additional equipment for Eire's forces, and the Eire Government to take effective action against the Fifth Column.

This de Valera rejected on the grounds that the arrival of British troops in advance of German forces would lead to 'unfortunate skirmishes'. He proposed instead that:

> Eire and Ulster should be merged in a United Ireland, which should at once become neutral; its neutrality to be guaranteed by Great Britain and the United States of America; since Britain was a belligerent, its military and naval forces should not take any active part in guaranteeing that neutrality, but American ships should come into the Irish ports, and perhaps American troops into Ireland, to effect this guarantee.

MacDonald turned this down, pointing out the difficulties of drawing up a Constitution – difficulties, moreover, multiplied by wartime conditions – which would be acceptable to all parties. However, while neither side was conceding anything, a position had been arrived at wherein the most substantive proposals of the century concerning the possibility of a British withdrawal from Ireland were about to emanate from London. When MacDonald returned to Dublin on 26 June for his third and final meeting with de Valera he brought with him the following memorandum drawn up by Chamberlain:[36]

> 1) A declaration to be issued by the United Kingdom Government forthwith accepting the principle of a United Ireland.

2) A joint body including representatives of the Government of Eire and the Government of Northern Ireland to be set up at once to work out the constitutional and other practical details of the Union of Ireland. The United Kingdom Government to give such assistance towards the work of this body as might be required.

3) A joint Defence Council representative of Eire and Northern Ireland to be set up immediately.

4) Eire to enter the war on the side of the United Kingdom and her allies forthwith, and, for the purposes of the defence of Eire, the Government of Eire to invite British naval vessels to have the use of ports in Eire and British troops and aeroplanes to co-operate with the Eire forces and to be stationed in such positions in Eire as may be agreed between the two Governments.

5) The Government of Eire to intern all German and Italian aliens in the country and to take any further steps necessary to suppress Fifth Column activities.

6) The United Kingdom Government to provide military equipment at once to the Government of Eire . . . .

Like Maffey earlier, MacDonald had to read this to the nearly blind de Valera. But de Valera's political vision was sufficiently keen for him to spot the snag immediately. MacDonald reported that his reaction was that 'Eire was to enter the war immediately, but a United Ireland was to be a deferred payment'. As MacDonald struggled to convince him that Britain would not renege on her undertakings, de Valera's other fears emerged. The Germans would savagely bomb Ireland to make an example of her to other neutrals. Moreover, MacDonald reported:[37] 'One of the decisive influences on Mr. de Valera's mind now is his view that we are likely to lose the war.'

The next day de Valera described the proposals to his Cabinet, which found them 'unacceptable'. He was empowered to tell MacDonald so in the company of Lemass and Aiken; it proved to be a hard man, soft man type of encounter. MacDonald said afterwards that whenever Lemass 'began to develop at any length an argument that might have led to some compromise, one or other of his colleagues intervened with a fresh uncompromising statement'. Fear of Germany and the shadow of Irish history lay across the discussion, precluding any leaps of the imagination. The Irishmen were influenced by experiences in their own lifetimes such as the Curragh Mutiny and the fate of John Redmond, who had encouraged thousands of young Irishmen to their deaths for a Home Rule that never materialized. De Valera wanted to know: 'What guarantee . . . did the British have that the Northern Ireland Government would agree, even if they had accepted the plan in principle, to join a United Ireland in practice?' MacDonald assured him that the 'United Kingdom Government would take full responsibility to the Eire Government for seeing that our obligations under the plan were carried out to the full'.

Meanwhile, in another part of the forest, a telegram was shortly to be delivered which both illuminated that exchange and helped to illustrate the foredoomed nature of the entire British unity initiative. Although he was its author, Chamberlain had entertained no very sanguine hopes of its success. As he had stated from the outset, the whole thing depended on 'the assent of the Government of Northern Ireland'. To this end he had sent a copy of his proposals to Craigavon on the day that MacDonald began his third assault on de Valera. In his covering letter Chamberlain told Craigavon, who like himself, was nearing his end:[38] '. . . if they accept you are still free to make your own comments or objections as you may think fit'. Craigavon thought fit to telegram the following reply: 'Am profoundly shocked and disgusted by your letter making suggestions so far-reaching behind my back and without any pre-consultation with me. To such treachery to loyal Ulster I will never be a party.' So far as Belfast and Dublin were concerned it was game, set and – mismatch. Another telegram from Craigavon to Chamberlain a few days later, on 29 June, contained these words: 'De Valera under German dictation and far past reasoning with. Stop. He may purposely protract negotiations till enemy has landed. Stop. Strongly advocate immediate naval occupation of harbours and military advance south.'

Insofar as London was concerned, de Valera summarized his arguments against the British initiative in an official letter of rejection which Dulanty delivered to Chamberlain on 5 July. It contained de Valera's version of Craigavon's 'not an inch':[39]

> We are unable to accept the plan outlined, which we note is purely tentative and has not been submitted to Lord Craigavon and his colleagues.
>
> The plan would involve our entry into the war. This is a course for which we could not accept responsibility. Our people would be quite unprepared for it, and Dail Eireann would certainly reject it.
>
> We are, of course, aware that the policy of neutrality has its dangers, but, on the other hand, departure from it would involve us in dangers greater still.
>
> The plan would commit us definitely to an immediate abandonment of our neutrality. On the other hand it gives no guarantee that in the end we would have a united Ireland, unless indeed concessions were made to Lord Craigavon opposed to the sentiments and aspirations of the great majority of the Irish people.
>
> Our present Constitution represents the limit to which we believe our people are prepared to go to meet the sentiments of the Northern Unionists, but, on the plan proposed, Lord Craigavon and his colleagues could at any stage render the whole project nugatory and prevent the desired unification by demanding concessions to which the majority of the people could not agree. By such methods unity was prevented in the past, and it is obvious that under the plan outlined they could be used again.
>
> The only way in which the unity which is so needed can in our view be secured is . . . by the immediate establishment of a single sovereign all-Ireland Parliament, free to decide all matters of national policy, internal and external – the Government which it would elect being responsible for taking the most effective measures for national defence.
>
> I regret that my proposal that the unity of Ireland should be established on the basis of the whole country becoming neutral is unacceptable to your Government. On the basis of unity and neutrality we could mobilise the whole of the manpower of this country for the national defence . . . .

Apart from de Valera's points about neutrality, the reference to the Constitution is highly significant. Despite his constant use of partition in negotiation – and his perceptive analysis of the real nature of the problem to Frank Gallagher – de Valera was not prepared to risk going further than his Constitution position to abolish the border. Articles 2 and 3, and the Special Position of the Roman Catholic Church, were the parameters of his fiefdom to extreme Republicanism and the Church. He subsequently gave further, differing, reasons for turning down an offer which would almost certainly have led to bombs falling on Dublin in the 1940s, but might have prevented them going off in Belfast and Dublin in the 1990s. He told Maffey that:[40] 'It had gone hard with him to . . . turn down the dream of his life. But that in present circumstances it was impossible. It would have meant civil war.' He later told his official biographers that it was because of the doctrine of 'equal holds'. In Bruree it had been the custom amongst his boyhood companions to keep 'equal holds' when engaged in a swap. 'Each was to have a firm grip on what he was to receive before he loosened his grip on that with which he was parting.'[41] He did not feel that Chamberlain's offer gave him 'equal holds'. Chamberlain died the following November. De Valera sent his widow a telegram:[42] 'Mr. Chamberlain will always be remembered by the Irish people for his noble efforts in the cause of peace and friendship between the two nations.' Perhaps she was comforted by it.

26

IN THE EYE OF THE STORM

CONCURRENT WITH THE strains generated by the Chamberlain–MacDonald initiative in the wake of the Held affair, de Valera also had to contend with pressures exerted by the Germans – pressures which he adroitly turned to his advantage. The Nazis had instituted a blockade of British shipping, and Hempel was instructed to make it clear to Dublin that the war was now 'entering upon its decisive stage'.[1] The Irish were expected to show 'the greatest possible understanding' of any difficulties which this caused them. Hempel was also instructed to deliver a 'warning' that the Held case should be treated in a 'careful manner' – in other words, news of it should be censored.

Hempel carried out his orders in a two-part fashion. He saw Walshe on 17 June, the date de Valera began his talks with MacDonald. As Walshe would have reported to de Valera before he saw MacDonald later that day, the German visitation may have contributed towards the mood of depression which the Englishman detected. Walshe sought a declaration that the Germans were not contemplating an Irish invasion. Hempel replied that it was impossible to give this in the face of the military situation. But he informed Walshe that Berlin expected 'complete and realistically wise understanding on the part of Ireland in case of any collision between Irish interests and our measures'. For Walshe this was at least better than being told that invasion was imminent and 'the conversation went off in a very friendly way', with Walshe expressing 'great admiration for the German achievements'. Hempel reported that Walshe commented on a recent interview of Hitler's (with Karl von Wiegand, published in English in the *New York Journal-American* on 14 June 1940) in which the Führer disclaimed any intention of destroying the British Empire. Walshe was concerned that this might mean the abandonment of Ireland. Hempel reassured him about the importance of a German victory 'for the final realisation of Irish national demands'. He commented, astutely, that he expected to be summoned by de Valera after Walshe had made his report.[2]

The summons came a few days later. In the course of what Hempel described as a 'lengthy conversation which was held in the presence of Walshe in a forthright and pleasant manner', de Valera made the following points.[3] Anxiety had recently increased in Ireland that the Germans might be planning to invade with the co-operation of the 'weak minority' opposed to the Government, the IRA. However, he had only obtained the ports from Britain on the understanding that Ireland would not become a 'point of departure for an attack against England. To this he would adhere.' He had told the British that any 'English intervention on Irish territory would meet with the same determined resistance'. Except for 'the strong economic dependence of Ireland on England', Ireland stood in exactly the same position towards Germany as towards England. Hempel reported: 'If the English invaded we [Germany] would fight with Irishmen against the English, in a German invasion the English would fight along with the Irish.' Hempel concluded that de Valera was 'carrying out a completely realistic policy and regarded determination to resist any attacker to the utmost as the only possibility to reduce the danger'.

De Valera followed up this conversation by directing F. H. Boland to inform Hempel the next day 'in strict confidence' that:[4] 'English pressure for the abandonment of Irish neutrality – apparently accompanied by the bait of future concessions in respect of Northern Ireland – had recently increased again, but that de Valera had rejected all advances "most vehemently".' Hempel correctly interpreted all this as meaning:[5] 'It is therefore very possible that de Valera is, in his usual clever way, exploiting incidents such as the case of Held which brought out the German danger, so as to be better armed also against English intentions and to strengthen his position against the largely anti-German Cosgrave opposition.'

Hempel informed Berlin that, judging from the attitude of Walshe and Boland, there was a widespread realization in Ireland of 'the obvious weakness of the democracies' and a 'grave anxiety about German intentions'. He felt that the Held case had 'turned feelings against us'. His lengthy, closely reasoned despatch produced the result de Valera must have hoped for. On the eve of de Valera's final meeting with MacDonald, Hempel was instructed:[6] 'The measures against England . . . which might also affect Irish interests, are not intended to include the landing of German troops in Ireland. In order to avoid misunderstanding you may give an intimation to this effect without stressing the point.' Thus when de Valera was assessing the British offer he had at least secured a promise from Hempel that he did not have to worry about a German invasion when he decided to opt for a continuation of neutrality as against the possibility of unity.

Whatever divergence of view there may be on the morality of Irish neutrality, there can be no argument on one point: de Valera's handling of both the British and the Germans in the months of May and June 1940 gives the lie to Maffey's judgement that he was 'not a strong man'. De Valera afforded Maffey another opportunity of assessing his calibre shortly after the ending of the MacDonald mission. In its wake, fears had begun to grow that the British would tire of abortive negotiation and simply seize the ports. Accordingly, on 17 July he asked the British Representative to meet him to discuss the possibilities of improving relationships between the two countries. He cited a number of specific problems: the fear that the ever-increasing pressure on Britain would result in a thrust for the ports; the fact that a well-orchestrated press campaign was raging against Ireland in both Britain and America; the continuing refusal to supply his repeated requests for arms; and a recent case of British espionage.

Maffey's experiences with the Afridis tribe had clearly taught him the value of being prepared: he now produced two telegrams which greatly mollified de Valera. The first concerned the captured British spy, a Major Byass. It stated that the War Office had not sanctioned an instruction to the officer from a superior to collect what information he could while on leave in the Twenty-six Counties. This kind of thing would not occur again and an apology was rendered for an action taken 'in a genuine attempt to prepare ourselves for giving assistance to the Eire Government if they invited us to do so in the case of an emergency'. The second telegram was from the British Ambassador in Washington, who claimed he was doing all he could to get arms for the Irish via the British Purchasing Commission. De Valera had appealed to the Americans for weapons a month earlier and, it appeared, his request was not before the Purchasing Commission.

Maffey's report stated that the effect of the two telegrams was to make de Valera far less mistrustful. He spoke openly about the defenceless state of Dublin and appealed:[7]

> Why will you not trust us? If you think we might attack the North I say with all emphasis we will never do that. No solution there can come by force. There we must now wait and let the solution come with time and patience. If you think the IRA will get the arms I can assure you that we have no fifth column today. There is no danger in that quarter.
>
> Give us help with arms and we will fight the Germans as only Irishmen in their own country can fight. There is no doubt on which side my sympathies lie. Nowadays some people joke about my becoming pro-British. The cause I am urging on you is in the best interest of my own country and that is what matters most to me.

In fact both de Valera and the British were being disingenuous on the arms question. De Valera knew very well that the British reluctance to give him guns was not because he might attack the North; apart from their own shortages, and irritation at his neutrality policy, the British were chary of giving him weapons with which he could attack British troops should an attempt be made to seize the ports. And the Americans were highly responsive to British attitudes. An exchange which occurred in Henry Morgenthau Jnr's office the previous month[8] tells us all we require to know about how decision-taking Washington viewed de Valera's requests for arms.

Morgenthau initiated the discussion by inquiring: 'Mr. Purvis [a civil servant] said last night – he said did we turn down the requests of Ireland as to what they needed?' To which one of his aides replied:

> . . . the War Department . . . came back and said there was nothing they could

spare and unless the President said it was a 'Must' thing, that they couldn't sell it
to Ireland or to anyone else. You see, Ireland came in after the Purchasing Board
got first crack at it. What they wanted were twenty-five airplanes, a thousand
Garand rifles, twenty-five tanks, armoured trucks, a fleet of seventy-fives and
ammunition, thirty-ball ammunition, just the things that have been drained dry.

Morgenthau concluded the discussion on the Irish request by asking for
'three pieces of paper' setting forth the requirements of Canada, Britain
and Ireland. No prizes are offered for guessing what the papers revealed in
terms of priorities, but readers may draw their own conclusions from a
reference made by Morgenthau to Arthur Purvis, the man who had
initiated the evaluation exercise a year later, after Purvis had been killed in
an accident. Morgenthau told his widow:[9] 'He was worth a hundred
generals to the British.'

However, despite the 'non possumus' effect of British influence in
Washington, de Valera's interview with Maffey did produce a little 'give' in
London. The War Cabinet sanctioned the sending of a few armaments,
chiefly anti-aircraft weaponry and searchlights, to Ireland at Eden's
behest.[10] The shipment included some British steel helmets because the
continued use by the Irish Army of German-style coal scuttle helmets was
arousing both Whitehall hackles and unfavourable press comment. But on
the question of invasion fears, although the British had in fact no plans to
invade, the Cabinet refused any public declaration to this effect. On the
recommendation[11] of Lord Caldecote, the Dominions Secretary, who had
been impressed by Maffey's account of the conversation with de Valera,
the Whitehall publicity machine was temporarily switched off. However it
was switched back on again, at full blast, in November by a speech of
Churchill's.

Between July and October, German submarine warfare had wrought
havoc on British lives and shipping: 245 vessels were sunk in the Atlantic.
In November, destined to be the worst month of the year, 73 vessels were
destroyed. Speaking in the House of Commons on 6 November he said:
'The fact that we cannot use the south and west coasts of Ireland to refuel
our flotillas and aircraft, and thus protect the trade by which Ireland as well
as Great Britain lives, is a most heavy and grievous burden, and one which
should never have been placed on our shoulders, broad though they be.' In
saying this Churchill was not merely fomenting anti-Irish sentiment but was
articulating feelings that were already widespread in Britain and America.
The *Daily Mail* followed up his speech with a cartoon showing a grim-faced
de Valera riding a donkey, inscribed 'Neutrality at Any Price', past a
concentration camp. He is holding a placard saying: 'NO bases for Britain'.
The camp inmates, inscribed Norway, Holland, Belgium, Denmark and
Austria, are calling to him: 'Brother, turn back! You're heading for the
entrance.' The staid *Economist* editorialized: 'If the ports become a matter
of life and death – for Ireland as well as England – there can be only one
way out: we must take them. That would of course revive all the old

bitterness. But if bitterness there must be, let us have the bitterness *and* the bases not the bitterness alone – which is all mere "retaliation" would provoke.'

De Valera was forced to reply. He did so in the Dail, on 7 November, in what has been termed the 'finest speech of his life'.[12] It contained the following:[13]

> There has been no want of faith, good faith, as far as we are concerned . . . . It is a lie to say that German submarines or any other submarines are being supplied with fuel or provisions on our coasts . . . . I say it is a lie, and I say further that it is known to be a falsehood by the British Government itself . . . we shall defend our rights in regard to these ports against whoever shall attack them . . . .
>
> I want to say to our people that we may be – I hope not – facing a grave crisis. If we are to face it then we shall do it, anyhow, knowing that our cause is right and just and that, if we have to die for it, we shall be dying in that good cause.

The image presented of de Valera, the lion's tail grasped firmly in his strong right hand as he defied all comers, had the effect both of generating support for him and of swinging the pendulum of Irish public opinion away from fear of a German invasion towards hostility to Britain. His official biography's estimation was:[14] 'The language was less arresting than Churchill's "We shall fight them on the beaches . . . ." The spirit was precisely the same.' A somewhat different assessment of the Churchill–de Valera exchange came from the novelist Elizabeth Bowen, one of the British Ministry of Information's sources of Irish intelligence:[15] 'The flare-up of resentment and suspicion on this side . . . is all the more to be regretted because, since August, pro-British feeling and sympathy for the British cause had been steadily on the increase here . . . .'

Irish domestic response was not shared internationally. Even such a staunch supporter of the underdog as Low, the cartoonist, supported the view of the big battalions concerning Ireland and submarine warfare. A celebrated cartoon of his was reproduced for the benefit of Irish Americans in the New York magazine *The Nation*.[16] It showed a German submarine passing a coastline displaying a sign: 'Neutral Eire', and proclaimed: 'No refuelling British flotillas and aircraft to protect the trade by which Britain and Eire live.' The submarine's officers were depicted drinking a toast: 'God bless Eire's neutrality – until the Führer gets there'. This viewpoint was shared at the time by no less a personage than George Bernard Shaw, who issued a characteristic statement saying:[17]

If I were in Churchill's place I should put it more philosophically. Instead of saying I will reoccupy your ports and leave you to do your damndest, I should say – 'My dear Mr. de Valera, your policy is magnificent but it is not modern statesmanship. You say the ports belong to Ireland; that is what you start from. I cannot admit. Local patriotism with all its heroic legends is as dead as a doornail today. The ports do not belong to Ireland: they belong to Europe, to the world, to civilisation, to the Most Holy Trinity, as you might say [a reference to the theocratic nomenclature of de Valera's Constitution] and are only held in trust by your Government in Dublin. In their names we must borrow the ports from you for the duration. You need not consent to the loan, just as you did not consent to the Treaty; and you will share all the advantages of our victory. All you have to do is to sit tight and say: 'I protest!' England will do the rest. So here goes.

De Valera 'was furious and denounced Shaw in an interview with Associated Press',[18] but he was very speedily given more to think about than the animadversions of GBS. Hitler became interested[19] in the fuss and inquired of his Foreign Minister, Ribbentrop, what use could be made of the Irish situation. De Valera took advantage of his eye complaint, which was giving him serious trouble at the end of 1940, to avoid handling the poisoned chalice of a German offer of arms in direct conversation with Hempel. He used Walshe to tell the German Minister 'that the dangers of the British discovering such a shipment rendered it advisable for the question to be deferred 'until a British attack, which was unlikely for the time being, had become a fact'. Ribbentrop was not satisfied with this, and Hempel was pressurized into meeting de Valera. De Valera was at his most disarming:[20] 'With a touch of humour, which Hempel seemed to appreciate, de Valera said that the German General Staff, even without Irish participation, would presumably with German thoroughness take the measures that seemed to it appropriate in the event of a British attack. And there the matter ended.'

It was not in fact de Valera's humour which had ended the discussion on German military aid to Ireland, but German military and naval appreciation of the difficulties involved. Shortly after Churchill's 5 November speech General Warlimont had reported to the Foreign Ministry that the only two possibilities of German intervention in the event of a British swoop on the ports were a concentration of U-boats around the occupied ports, accompanied by Luftwaffe attacks. The use of airborne troops was 'out of the question'.[21] However a little later, on 3 December, Hitler speculated that: 'The occupation of Ireland might lead to the end of the war.' But Admiral Raeder thought that it might lead to a German Dunkirk. He warned of the superior strength of the British Home Fleet and the fact of Ireland's unfavourable geographical location: 'The coast of Wales and Cornwall extends like a wedge to our line of approach.' The increasing numbers of British fighter planes and the unfortified nature of the harbours meant that: 'To a defending force, cut off and left to its own devices, the topography of the country does not afford us much protection . . . without supplies and reinforcements they would soon feel the increasing pressure of a British expeditionary force brought over under the protection of British naval power; sooner or later our own troops would face a situation similar to Namsos or Dunkirk.' The Raeder–Warlimont analysis prevailed. Hitler's interest in Ireland was ephemeral. As Rudolf Hess revealed during interrogation before the Nuremberg trials: ' . . . in all his talks with Hitler the subject of Ireland had never been mentioned except incidentally'. Irish worries about the much talked about German landing were unfounded.

But this is not to say that fears of German aggression were unfounded, as a nasty incident which occurred during this period showed all too clearly. It began with a telegram from Ribbentrop to Hempel on 18 December 1940: 'In view of Dublin's increasing importance as an observation post of British military measures and results of German attacks on England, the Legation will be enlarged by the assignment of two officers and a radio operator . . . . Officers are charged internally with the duties incumbent upon military attacks.' As Gray pointed out to Walshe,[22] there tended to be a correlation between German bombing of Ireland and political developments – after various speeches of Roosevelt's warning against the dangers of neutrality in the face of German aggression, bombs fell, causing loss of life. The message was clear – the alternative to neutrality would be more of the same. The Ribbentrop proposal to install intelligence officers in the German Legation speedily provoked some politically motivated bombings. De Valera, who was in hospital receiving treatment for his eyes, responded negatively to the overture. On 20 December, two days after the request was telegraphed, bombs fell in Co. Monaghan and in Sandycove, not far from Hempel's residence in Monkstown further up the coast. An hour before they fell, German radio broadcast a denial that they were German bombs. That night Hempel met Boland at a social function and sought to further Ribbentrop's request. Boland stalled, pointing out the dangers from British and American reactions to a sudden increase in the number of German diplomats in Dublin. Hempel quoted him as making a point concerning Irish American activities which indicated the degree to which Dublin was involved in such matters. Unfavourable publicity in the USA, he said, could:[23] '. . . critically disturb the American-Irish elements' organisation and activity, developing with great vigour, directed against British attack on Ireland and U.S.A.'s entry into the war which could be fatal to Ireland.'

The logic of this statement would appear to be that de Valera reckoned America's entry into the war would forestall a British defeat, and hence the ending of partition. Boland was presumably accentuating the positive value to Germany of not disturbing the Irish American scene for the sake of a few spies. However, Ribbentrop was unimpressed. He replied on Christmas Day 1940: 'We must firmly expect the Irish Government to consent immediately to this matter of the facilitation customary in transfer of members of mission.' De Valera was still in hospital when this arrived. In fact the 'request' was more in the nature of an advice of a decision already taken. The plane with the extra staff aboard was scheduled to arrive at what was then Rineanna, today Shannon, Airport on Christmas Eve. In de Valera's absence both External Affairs and Sean T. O'Ceallaigh, the Tanaiste (Deputy Prime Minister), had tried to play for time. But Hempel, under pressure from Ribbentrop, had been unusually insistent. He took the line that this was the first request that Germany had made and it was being refused. The matter was eventually referred to de Valera, who reacted with the vigour of a man in full health. The grip on the lion's tail was temporarily transferred to the swastika. A general alert of the defence forces was ordered, and he directed that if the plane did succeed in landing the Germans were to be arrested immediately.

It was the biggest scare of the war to date, and one of the greatest of the entire period. The country buzzed with rumours of invasion, thought to be coming from the British. Ironically, as part of the co-operation with the British the runway at Rineanna had been blocked. Nevertheless on the morning of Christmas Eve a German plane flew in low over the airport and then flew away again. General McKenna, the Chief of Staff of the Irish Army, described the incident as the most alarming of the entire war.[24]

There were two sequels. The first was a confrontation between de Valera and Hempel on 27 December, a time when de Valera's physical condition obviously cannot have been good. In reply to de Valera's reiteration of Ireland's commitment to neutrality, Hempel stressed 'the gravity of the situation'. He also made the ominous point that he 'did not speak about possible concrete consequences of a negative Irish attitude'.[25]

He did not have to. The first two days of 1941 saw German bombs fall in different parts of Ireland – in Dublin itself and in Carlow, Drogheda, Kildare, Wexford and Wicklow. Three people were killed in Carlow and twenty-four injured in the Dublin raid. Previously the only fatalities had occurred when a creamery was destroyed in Campile, Co. Wexford during the summer in what was generally accepted as an accidental bombing. De Valera could not confort himself by ascribing the bombs of New Year 1941 to a lapse in German standards of thoroughness; nor could he draw any solace from reactions across the Irish Sea. Churchill's speech unleashed the hounds of Fleet Street. Public opinion grew increasingly anti-Irish, and several parliamentary questions were tabled demanding that the Government 'bring the ungrateful Irish to heel'.[26] Lord Cranborne, who was getting reports similar to Bowen's from Maffey, succeeded in having the questions withdrawn. But he failed to impress Churchill with Maffey's arguments. Churchill told Cranborne:[27]

> I think it would be better to let de Valera stew in his own juice for a while . . . . The claim now put forward on behalf of de Valera is that we are not only to be strangled by them, but to suffer our fate without making any complaint. Sir John Maffey should be made aware of the rising anger in England and Scotland and especially among the merchant seamen, and he should not be encouraged to think that his only task is to mollify de Valera and make everything, including our ruin, pass off pleasantly.

Churchill, who, as we shall see, was shortly to increase that heat on de Valera beyond merely allowing him to 'stew in his own juice', was correct in his statement that there was widespread anger against Ireland amongst merchant seamen. In *The Cruel Sea* the novelist Nicholas Monsarrat, pondering on the 'condoned sabotage' of a 'smug coastline', wrote bitterly:

> . . . it is difficult to withhold one's contempt from a country such as Ireland whose battle this was and whose chances of freedom and independence in the event of a German victory were nil. The fact that Ireland was standing aloof from the conflict . . . affected, sometimes mortally, all sailors engaged in the Atlantic, and earned their special loathing . . . . To compute how many men and how many ships this denial was costing, month after month, was hardly possible . . . escorts had to go 'the long way round' to go to the battlefield . . . the cost, in men and ships, added months to the struggle, and ran up a score which Irish eyes a-smiling on the day of the Allied victory were not going to cancel . . . . In the list of people you were prepared to like when the war was over, the man who stood by and watched you while you were getting your throat cut could not figure very high.

But no section of opinion took Irish neutrality so badly as did the North of Ireland Unionists. It is hardly surprising, therefore, that the most pithy condemnation of de Valera's policy came from the Belfast-born son of a Church of Ireland bishop, the poet Louis MacNeice. His poem 'Neutrality' includes these lines:

> The Neutral Island facing the Atlantic
> The neutral island in the heart of man,
> . . .
> But then look eastward from your heart, there bulks
> A continent, close, dark, as archetypal sin,
> While to the west off your own shores the mackerel
> Are fat – on the flesh of your kin.

Such writing encapsulates what may be termed the case for the prosecution against de Valera's neutrality policy. As we shall see, like many opening statements it does not fully stand up to subsequent examination of the evidence. But first let us look at how the charge was pressed home retributively – again through the inspiration of a Northern Irish Protestant pen. Colonel Wilfred Spender was one of the great stalwarts of Unionism. A founder of the Ulster Volunteer Force, he declared himself in favour of reprisals – that is, shooting Catholics – during the Michael Collins-sponsored offensive against the Six Counties in 1922.[28] Now, in 1940, the head of the Six County civil service, he followed up Churchill's speech with a suggestion of reprisals of another kind – economic sanctions.

He wrote two letters[29] to Lord Hankey, Chancellor of the Duchy of Lancaster, the first on 9 November, outlining what he had in mind. He advocated that the 'closure of the British ports' should result in 'hardships' to 'the Eire people'. He pointed out that on his trips to Southern Ireland it was possible to obtain 'unlimited supplies of petrol and practically all other imports from Overseas whilst we in the United Kingdom are severely rationed'. Along with wishing to see this situation rectified Spender wanted a tax on coal exported to Eire, an embargo on arms supplies and a reduction in shipping facilities for the South. This was to be on an eye-for-an-eye basis: 'For every British ship which is lost due to the closure of the Eire ports a ship intended to bring imports into Eire should be diverted to a British port.' His letter found its mark.

Hankey, who had circulated it amongst his Cabinet colleagues, replied[30] to Spender on 27 November informing him of his suggestions' favourable reception, especially 'in the most important quarter to which I sent it'. Presumably this meant Churchill. An encouraged Spender responded on 2 December with further pen pictures depicting the South as a land flowing with milk and honey. He also sent Hankey a copy of the *Irish Times* 'so that you may compare its 16 odd pages with the 6 small pages of the *Daily Telegraph*'. Churchill called for suggestions as to what economic restrictions could be placed upon Eire. As Robert Fisk says of Spender's initiative in his comprehensive study of Irish neutrality, *In Time of War*:[31] '. . . it does seem as if his letter helped to inspire the Cabinet's new measures'. Churchill got his punitive proposals on 16 December from Sir Kingsley Wood, the Chancellor of the Exchequer.[32]

It was proposed to end the arrangement, which had persisted since the war's outbreak, whereby the Irish chartered their ships through the British. To ensure that the Irish could not get ships elsewhere, other shipping nations were to be warned only to charter ships to 'Allies or co-operators'. Woods estimated that as a result of this scheme Eire would be 'very lucky' to get 25 per cent of its shipping needs. In addition to this, Britain could further cripple the Irish economy by not only forbidding the export of a wide range of necessities, but also freezing Eire's sterling balances so that the Irish could not buy elsewhere. This was Plan A, aimed at making the Irish feel uncomfortable. Plan B was intended to cause drastic shortages. No ships going to Ireland were to be insured. This would have meant in effect that no ships went to Ireland. Plan A was adopted and put into operation in the New Year. It was not acknowledged as a retaliation for neutrality.

In his memorandum to Churchill, Woods was careful to stipulate that when Britain was challenged on her policy towards Eire she would reply: '. . . that so long as we are subject to difficulties in the supply of certain things we cannot in present circumstances go on giving Eire the generous share that we have so far allowed her'.[33] In America Roosevelt was still battling against isolationist forces to have the American Neutrality Act amended so that he could bring in the Lend-Lease system on which British hopes of surviving Hitler's onslaught were pinned. The British were aware that the Irish Americans were still, as Maffey described them, the 'pillars of de Valera's temple'. A poll taken at this time showed that 52 per cent of first- and second-generation Irish Americans opposed an abandonment of Irish neutrality. Nevertheless the British sanctions served to send some uncomfortable chills through de Valera's temple. Petrol ran out almost immediately. All over the Twenty-six Counties people found themselves stranded after the Christmas holidays. The tea ration fell to an ounce per week, and white bread joined private motoring as a thing of the past. Most Dubliners cooked by gas, using some 3,500 tons of gas-producing coal in 1941. By the end of 1942 this was down to 1,600 tons. Domestic use of coal was first cut to a half ton a month per family and then abolished altogether. The 74,000 tons of fertilizer shipped into Ireland in 1940 fell to only 7,000 in 1941 and then stopped altogether. The 5 million tons of feeding stuffs imported in 1940 fell to a fifth of that in 1941 and then also vanished altogether. None the less, de Valera's self-sufficiency policy would prove adequate to the task of maintaining a subsistence economy. Turf production was increased so as to go some (smoky) way towards replacing coal. Irish farmers were forced to increase their acreage under tillage. Wheat growing was stepped up by the order of 1,000 per cent and the small protected industries which Lemass had laboured to encourage were able to produce some replacements for the lost imports, clothing and footwear, albeit of no very high calibre.

One point particularly troubled de Valera at the time: he had been on the point of getting American arms through the British Purchasing Committee, but the currency freeze aborted the deal. He sent for Maffey on 20 January 1941 to sound him on the sudden economic constriction generally and on the arms issue in particular. Maffey dutifully reported his concern about arms and the possibility that the economic thrust might be the precursor to a military one, but drew an unflattering picture of de Valera at this stage:[34]

> . . . Mr. de Valera is more uneasy today than he has ever been at any stage on his non-stop political career. Ireland being Ireland, in the mass ignorant and responsive to old hatreds, he is still the chosen tribal leader for their feuds. But hitherto he has used this Irish fanaticism on a bigger stage than his platform of today . . . He could stir world wide interest in the soul of Ireland. It is the soul of England which stirs the world today and Eire is a bog with a petty leader raking over old muck heaps.

Cranborne passed this on to Churchill on 30 January with the suggestion that[35] 'his [de Valera's] request for arms seems to afford us an opportunity of showing that our economic measures are not a sign of hostility against Southern Ireland, but are genuinely the result of difficulties created for us by shipping losses'. Up with this Churchill would not put. He wanted de Valera to understand that the economic measures *were* an indication of hostility. He told Cranborne on the 31st:

> . . . If we were assured that it was Southern Ireland's intention to enter the war, we would of course if possible beforehand share our anti-aircraft weapons with them, and make secretly with them all possible necessary measures for their defence. Until we are so satisfied, we do not wish them to have further arms, and certainly will not give them ourselves.
> . . . No attempt should be made to conceal from Mr. de Valera the depth and

intensity of feeling against the policy of Irish neutrality. We have tolerated and acquiesced in it, but juridically we have never recognised that Southern Ireland is an independent Sovereign State, and she herself has repudiated Dominion status. Her international status is undefined and anomalous. Should the present situation last until the end of the war, which is unlikely, a gulf will have opened between Northern and Southern Ireland, which it will be impossible to bridge in this generation.

The 'gulf' has, of course, proved impossible to bridge two generations further on. But for the purposes of our narrative the important point in the Churchill memo is that the 'present situation' did last to the end of the war. England's extraordinary triumph of the human spirit in the Battle of Britain, Hitler's mounting of Operation Barbarossa against the Soviet Union, Pearl Harbor – these epic events had the effect of bringing America into the war and transferring the weight of the balance spring of history to Russia and the Pacific. The importance of Irish neutrality dwindled correspondingly in the calculations of Allied planners.

Relationships between de Valera's Ireland and Churchill's Britain remained more or less as outlined above, give or take a few alarums and excursions. Anglo-Irish blood pressures were destined to go up during the war over arms procurement, a new conscription threat to the Six Counties, the arrival of American troops in the North, fresh rumours of a British invasion around the time of the D-Day landings, and even the possibility of an American invasion over the 'American note' controversy (see Chapter 28). But, overall, as the Irish issue's significance went down so did tempers on both sides of the Irish Sea. The worst never came to the worst, and both sides managed to muddle through the 'emergency' without actually coming to blows.

There are, however, two inter-related questions which should be teased out in a little more detail. Was de Valera's neutrality policy as harmful to the British as was alleged? And, having shown the foresight to negotiate possession of the ports in 1938 so as to be able to declare his country neutral, how, only two years later, did de Valera come to be so vulnerable in the matter of ships and supplies essential for the maintenance of that neutrality? The short answer to the first question is no, Irish neutrality was not the main reason that the mackerel grew fat off the west coast of Ireland. The real culprit was the product of a marriage of German ingenuity and lax British security. Unknown to the British, the Germans had cracked their naval codes as far back as 1936, during a visit by the Royal Navy to the Red Sea as part of the abortive League of Nations sanctions programme. It is believed that this breach was healed in the summer of 1943. But in the words of one expert:[36] '. . . for nearly four critical years Admiral Doenitz reaped a rich harvest of sunken supply ships – 11.5 million tons in the North Atlantic alone'. Nor were the Southern ports as strategically important to the British war effort as was claimed. They were still of some value – Churchill's estimate of the curtailment in operating range which their loss entailed was real enough. However, following the fall of France the British supply lanes along the south-west of Ireland became so vulnerable to attack by French-based air and sea raiders that Atlantic convoys were routed north about, towards the safety of the coast of Scotland. The sea off the north Donegal coast thus became increasingly deadly; although here, while Lough Swilly would obviously have been an asset, the British did have the fall-back of Derry.

In one facet of their war effort, their aerial campaign against shipping, the Germans did undoubtedly profit from the ports issue. It is a matter of record that in the early months of 1941 the Germans capitalized on the availability of French and Norwegian bases to make use of their Focke-Wulf Condors. These huge bombers used to take off near Brest and hug the west coast of Ireland as they flew to attack convoys. Then, low on fuel, they would head for Stavanger in Norway. They were a common sight to the inhabitants of Berehaven as they overflew the deserted port undisturbed by either ack-ack fire or fighter planes. Obviously a fighter base, whether at Berehaven or anywhere else along the Irish west coast, would speedily have put an end to the operations of the cumbersome Condors – always presuming, of course, that such a base could have been maintained against German air attacks, which is not at all certain in view of the increased German striking power provided by the seizure of French bases. But apart from this area of the struggle it is fair to say that many of the beliefs (which lingered for years after the war) about the loss of seamen's lives occasioned by the denial of the Irish ports were grounded more in the propaganda campaign against Ireland in the American and British media than in fact.[37]

To turn now to the question of Irish vulnerability to British sanctions. After the war a man who was better placed than most to assess the situation, F. H. Boland of the Irish Department of External Affairs, judged that[38] 'one of the mistakes which we were lucky to be able to correct in time was the assumption which I think we were inclined to make at the beginning of the war that we could operate a policy of neutrality and at the same time rely on arrangements with British government departments for essential supplies'. The Irish did make that elementary mistake, particularly where shipping was concerned, but there were other factors affecting de Valera's initial approach to neutrality. One was straightforward meanness. All the agonizing over arms could have been avoided in May 1939 when General Michael Joseph Costello was sent to Washington to buy arms. He could have had them were it not for 'the reluctance of the Irish Government which regarded the price of the weapons as exorbitant'.[39] As we saw at the end of that year, with the war actually in progress the Cabinet was contemplating cutting its Army strength by 25 per cent. But de Valera was to learn the hard way that there is no such thing as 'frugal comfort' in the arms trade. His planning for neutrality seems to have been almost exclusively political. As we saw, he laid down a trail of policy statements and negotiated back the ports with consummate skill. But he took no action on the sort of departmental reports discussed in Chapter 22 (see p. 535) which warned of the country's dependence on outside shipping. A memorandum, 'War, Essential Materials', produced by his own Department in 1935, spelled out with Cassandra-like accuracy what would happen if 'essential materials' were curtailed – but was simply pigeon-holed. Possibly because he was the leader of a largely rural-based, farmer-oriented party de Valera never gave any thought to an issue which was to plague him throughout the war, that of shipping. One would have thought his experiences in travelling to America, both in luxury and in hardship, might have alerted him to the need to do something about ensuring that Ireland would have ships in her hour of need, but this basic requirement was overlooked.

'Cute hoorism' also played its part. As has been indicated, the Irish did come to co-operate far more comprehensively with the British than would have seemed possible behind the cacophony of the orchestrated press campaign of 1940–1. Furthermore, as the war continued the Irish showed marked consideration and hospitality in areas such as the treatment of downed Allied fliers, who were cared for and speedily transferred across the border. A fiction was created whereby they were regarded as being on 'non-operational' missions and therefore should not be interned. German fliers, however, wound up in the Curragh internment camp and stayed there, whereas by around the middle of 1944 the Irish were not even making a pretence of holding Allied personnel. Co-operation between British and Irish forces eventually progressed to the stage where de Valera appointed his son, Vivion, as liaison officer with General Franklyn, the Commander of British Troops Northern Ireland. Franklyn and the Irish Chief of Staff, General Dan MacKenna, co-ordinated their strategies at secret meetings in Annamoe in Co. Wicklow – ironically enough in the house where Erskine Childers was captured and taken to his execution. At one point a stock of tricolours was provided for British troops to wave at Irish soldiers if they had to come south in a hurry on the heels of a German invasion.

But these co-operative measures developed over the years. During the war's early phase, when it looked as if Germany might win, Irish co-operation with Britain was curtailed. RAF planes were prohibited from overflying Irish headlands; to reinforce this ban, which was later abolished, anti-aircraft guns fired on an RAF plane that trespassed on Irish air space in Co. Donegal during December 1940. The hand of the 'cute hoor' was to be seen in operation during talks which took place between April and November 1940 on an Anglo-Irish trade agreement. This should have yielded an accord on shipping and exports which would have included a wide range of Irish agricultural products. The British were anxious to preserve the preferential position for their exports to Ireland which had been laid down in the 1938 Agreement; they also sought to curb Irish tendencies towards increasing economic independence. First the Irish, represented by Sean Lemass and James Ryan, argued that Britain was offering too little for agricultural produce. For Britain, Sir Anthony Eden countered by offering a subsidy on cattle imports. But then, with all outstanding issues apparently resolved, as the war went increasingly badly for Britain the Irish moved the goalposts. They chose to object to a hitherto uncontentious aspect of the talks, a parallel agreement on port, repair and transshipment facilities for British shipping. The Irish said that the presence of British ships in Ireland's ports would constitute a breach of neutrality which would leave those ports open to attack. On this the talks collapsed, leaving the Irish very shortly afterwards with reason to rue the absence of agreement on the vital issues of shipping and trade.

However, even if agreement had been reached there seems little reason to suppose that the British would have honoured it. They effectively double-crossed the Irish on another shipping agreement which had been made at the outbreak of the war. The far-seeing Sean Lemass had initiated a project to build an oil refinery at Dublin port which was aborted by pressure from the international oil cartels. However, part of the project resulted in Ireland being in the unlikely position of having 'probably the most modern oil-tanker fleet in the world when the war broke out'.[40] Although British-owned, the tankers were registered in Ireland. Without making conditions of any kind, de Valera's Government transferred the tankers to the British register.[41] The transfer was certainly one which would have merited the application of de Valera's 'equal holds' philosophy. For when the British unilaterally cut the Irish petroleum supply Ireland's protests to Britain had the same ineffectual ring about them as had Britain's to de Valera over the ports. The British replied that the tankers were handed over unconditionally and that anyway they were British-owned in the first place. The Irish made a similar blunder over tea supplies, agreeing in 1940 to a British request that Ireland should buy its tea through the United Kingdom to help keep prices down. At the end of the year Britain cut the Irish tea ration to less than half that of Britain's. De Valera was left with a new definition of the term 'swallowing the insult'.

Churchill told Roosevelt that:[42] 'Our merchant seamen as well as public opinion generally take it much amiss that we should have to carry Irish supplies through air and U-Boat attacks . . . when de Valera is quite content to sit happy and see us strangled.' In fact de Valera did not 'sit happy' on the shipping issue. An honest effort was made to rectify the mistake of not providing Irish ships to carry Irish supplies. Throughout the months of February and March 1941, in the teeth of world war, a state shipping company, Irish Shipping, was founded. Eight vessels were bought and five chartered, despite a good deal of obstruction from the British.[43] The fleet, all of which was renamed after trees, consisted largely of small coasters together with a sailing schooner. To hamstring the supply effort further, the British used the navicert system, which was supposed to be a means of denying neutral shipping to the Germans. In order to obtain a warrant, or navicert, the Irish ships had to call at British ports for examination on every voyage, even if they were going to America or to Spain. This meant they had to run the gauntlet of the German blockade, often with fatal results for Irish crews. Sometimes in issuing the navicerts the British stipulated routes which added 1,300 miles to the journey. When they travelled in convoy on the Atlantic routes the Irish ships were generally given the most dangerous, outside positions. Apart from the ships themselves, the navicert system was also used to put the squeeze on cargoes. The records[44] of the British War Cabinet's Committee on Economic Policy towards Eire show that it was decided that navicerts should be subject to 'delay' when required for Irish ships. Thus, between the diplomatic, economic and media pressures of the Allies, and the murderous underlining by the New Year bombings of the dangers of arousing German displeasure, the spring of 1941 found de Valera in a position of very great strain. It was soon to be added to.

27

MANY SHADES OF GRAY

DAVID GRAY NOW re-enters our story in a substantive way. He wanted Ireland in the war. His formal assessment to his superiors in the State Department of the man who was standing in the way of this ambition was:[1]

> His whole power is based on his genius for engendering and utilizing anti-British sentiment. His administration otherwise is generally unsuccessful. He is probably the most adroit politician in Europe and he honestly believes that all he does is for the good of his country. He has the qualities of martyr, fanatic and Machiavelli. No one can outwit him, frighten or blandish him. Remember that he is not pro-German, nor personally anti-British, but only pro-de Valera. My view is that he will do business on his own terms or must be overcome by force.

De Valera was not unaware of Gray's feelings. An old newspaperman, Gray spoke his mind freely to, amongst others, Frank Gallagher, whom de Valera had appointed Head of the Government Information Bureau. Nothing said in the presence of the devoted Gallagher lost anything in reaching the ears of the Chief, by way of either speed or translation. Gallagher was not totally a supplicant on the altar of de Valera's policy of the moment. De Valera's resentment at Gray's attitude surfaced in a curious incident involving Sumner Welles, the American Under Secretary for State. De Valera had instructed Robert Brennan, the Irish Minister in Washington, to see Welles to glean what could be learned of America's attitude to Ireland in the wake of Churchill's November 1940 speech about the 'burden' imposed by Irish neutrality which had led to the economic squeeze. Brennan was instructed to give Welles a copy of de Valera's reply to Churchill. The official account given in de Valera's biography of this meeting and its sequel is as follows:[2] 'Brennan found Welles friendly and reported: "He said it was very clear from both that Ireland could have no other policy and that Ireland's peace was an asset to Britain. Any clash between the two countries would be disastrous for both."'

After Brennan and Welles had met in Washington, Gray was authorized to see de Valera in Dublin. Noting that Gray 'had already aroused considerable criticism in Ireland' and that his attitude in the interview with de Valera 'was not calculated to win him a new friend', the biography goes on:

> De Valera recorded the conversation thus: 'The American Minister prefaced his statements by saying that Americans could be cruel if their interests were affected and Ireland should expect little or no sympathy if the British took the ports. He

added that, in any case, America was coming into the war in a short time and then Ireland would have to give the ports to America.'

Then, according to the biography,

Gray gave quite a different version of Brennan's interview with Sumner Welles from that which de Valera had received from Brennan. According to Gray, Welles had said to Brennan that the Irish Government, by its attitude, was jeopardising Ireland's security; that the use of the ports was essential to British naval success and that, apparently, the ports should be given to Britain. A minatory tone was clearly being adopted by Gray. He was deliberately showing his claws.

Nobody was going to show their claws to Eamon de Valera and get away with it. He instructed Robert Brennan as follows:

Gray is very imprudent. He repeats these views publicly in the diplomatic corps and amongst his ascendancy friends and has told them that he had been instructed to give the message in question to the Taoiseach. Since this attitude may give the impression here that America wants the British to seize our ports it might be as well to visit the Under Secretary once more.

The biography then goes on to say that Brennan was informed by Welles that he had not said all the things to Gray which Gray had reported to de Valera. However: 'Roosevelt had decided to let de Valera know of American public opinion. Gray had accordingly been instructed that "We are anxious to do everything possible to prevent a British defeat; one factor is that the British should have the use of the ports."' The biography concludes in the light of this that 'It would not be fair to Gray to hold him responsible for the confusion over what Welles had told Brennan', but that 'It was . . . clear to de Valera that he would be an unsympathetic reporter on Irish affairs to the State Department.'

Gray's account of this incident, in his unpublished memoir 'Behind the Green Curtain', suggests that there may have been more than one 'unsympathetic reporter' involved in the Welles incident. It differs sharply from de Valera's. Welles telegraphed him after the second Brennan visit to tell him of Dublin's claim that Gray's version to de Valera of what Welles had said to Brennan was: 'That the United States would shortly enter the war, that in such an event the naval bases in Ireland which the British desire, would have to be made available to the United States and that in consequence there was no good reason why the Irish Government should not *now* [author's italics] make these bases available to Britain.' The telegram stated that Brennan could not recall 'that Mr. Welles had made any such statement'.

Gray writes: 'The implication, therefore, was that the American Minister in Dublin had made it on his own responsibility.' However, Gray notes with satisfaction: 'The charge was easily disposed of.' For Gray had made a 'detailed memorandum' of his conversation with de Valera and taken the precaution of sending a copy to de Valera. 'It contained no suggestion of any such statements, nor did he except to it.' The memo also noted that Gray had read out a paraphrase of Welles' telegram to him in which Welles had set out his position. Gray had given the telegram to de Valera 'for his files'. When he called on de Valera to set the record straight, he pointed this out to de Valera. Kathleen O'Connell duly produced 'the pink telegram form'. Gray inquired 'who telegraphed the Irish Minister in Washington that the American Minister in Dublin had made the statements in question?' Not surprisingly, in view of the instructions given to Brennan quoted above, Gray reports that de Valera 'appeared at a loss. He said there must have been a "misunderstanding" and the episode ended there . . . for the American Minister in Dublin it was an occupational hazard.'

The episode ended there only insofar as Gray and de Valera were concerned. For the American then took the unusual step of consulting with 'X', an Opposition figure who had apparently warned him to put everything in writing when dealing with de Valera. Gray cabled Welles quoting 'X', whom he does not identify but who was most likely Mulcahy, as saying:[3]

'X' warned me several months ago that something like this would happen, that de Valera would try indirectly to weaken my position with the Department, but that he always worked through a third person and that he would get me in the end. He says that no dispatch to Brennan could have gone out without its being read to him. He says he [de Valera] counted on your not telling me of the occurrence but putting it down as an evidence of my unreliability. It appears, according to 'X,' that he framed Cosgrave on a so-called 'Secret Document' in regard to the land annuities, that never in fact existed, and that this is why Cosgrave will never again speak to him.

While de Valera was using Brennan to manoeuvre against Gray in Washington, two other issues, relating to the supplies position, were converging to create further tensions between Ambassador and Taoiseach. The first had its origins in a meeting between Gray and de Valera on 6 January 1941 at which de Valera asked about the possibilities of getting arms and shipping from America. Gray countered by suggesting that the best way to make contact with the American Government was to send out a Cabinet Minister, someone like Sean T. O'Ceallaigh. Despite the worsening supply situation, de Valera took his time about deciding on the suggestion. It was 22 February before he told Gray that he was sending not Sean T. O'Ceallaigh but Frank Aiken. One of Gray's motives in arranging a Cabinet-level visit was to expose the Irish Government to the strength of decision-taking American feeling on Irish neutrality. This objective was shared by Maffey, who cabled London hoping that 'every assistance will be given'. Maffey quoted Gray as saying:[4] '. . . main purpose [of visit] would be educational. He does not think any of Mission's visit will be achieved. From our point of view he considers Aiken a most satisfactory choice . . . .'

Just two months earlier Gray had passed on to Roosevelt[5] the opinion of an Opposition leader who had a different view of Aiken. The Fine Gael man described Aiken as having: ' . . . a mind halfway between that of a child and an ape . . . a physically huge man with the mentality of a boy gang leader playing at war with real soldiers'. Gray also suspected Aiken of pro-German tendencies. The reason he now found him 'satisfactory' lay in the operation of the wartime Irish censorship. R. M. Smyllie, the Editor of the *Irish Times*, has left this description[6] of how Aiken and the censorship operated:

> Mr. Frank Aiken . . . was well known for his anti-British feelings . . . . In theory the censorship was entirely neutral; in practice it worked almost exclusively against the Allies . . . . No paper dared to print a word in favour of the Allied cause. Even when America came in, and Mr. De Valera no longer had the excuse that it was mainly a British war, this rigid veto was maintained. Whether the Irish Government was trying to humbug the people of Eire, or was merely humbugging itself, nobody will ever know; but one thing is quite certain it was not humbugging the Germans . . . . They knew that, with the insignificant exception of a small minority of irreconcilables, the people of Southern Ireland were wholeheartedly on the side of the Allies . . . .

De Valera was fully aware of majority feeling in the Twenty-six Counties. The object of his censorship policy was to prevent the Allies from tapping that feeling. Smyllie, despite his all-too-vivid first-hand recollection of how the censorship operated, was unaware of de Valera's motivation in acting in such a partisan fashion. This, as one of his principal lieutenants in the wartime diplomatic battle, F. H. Boland, later pointed out, was occasioned by:[7]

> . . . the extremely virulent press campaign waged against us in Britain and in the United States from early in 1940 onwards. Much of this was an attempt to appeal to Irish public opinion over the head of the Government, and this enhanced enormously the importance of our press censorship as one of the main defences of our neutrality. It also greatly increased our suspicions of British intentions . . . . The censorship was one of the principal bones of contention with the Allies all through the war.

Understandably therefore, Gray, fretting over what he termed 'a newspaper press debarred from all discussion of the issues vital to the country',[8] could see great merit in Aiken's being exposed to the chill winds of American public opinion. He gave him letters of introduction to influential American friends of his, including Eleanor Roosevelt (it would have been against protocol for an appointed official to give a letter of introduction to the President), and sent him a pointed personal letter of advice. This last was in part an attempt by Gray to turn the tables on charges of being pro-Ascendancy which Fianna Fail frequently levelled at him:[9]

> I hope you will not be offended if I give you the same sound advice which I received from Irish friends in America before coming to Ireland. They said, 'Don't sit in the Kildare St. Club and imagine that you are exploring the forces that dominate Irish politics by talking with Ascendancy Unionists or even with members of the Irish Opposition. To estimate these forces you must associate yourself with the party in power, and must discover the sources of Mr. de Valera's influence and authority'. If you associate yourself with Irish Nationalist circles, which you would naturally find sympathetic, you will return knowing no more of the sources of majority opinion upon which the President's Government rests than you know now.

He concluded by saying that Mrs Roosevelt would arrange any introduction Aiken might desire. Aiken left Gray's letters behind and took with him the following communication from de Valera addressed to Roosevelt:[10]

> This will introduce Mr. Frank Aiken, Minister for Co-ordination of Defence measures in our Government. He will give you first hand information on our position and explain to you our need for defensive equipment and for certain other supplies which we wish to purchase in the United States. The things we want are unfortunately those in general demand at the present moment, but in amount they are such a small fraction of your total production that I am hopeful they can be obtained. May I once more ask for your kindly intervention on our behalf.

Somehow Gray discovered that his letters had not been taken to the United States and forwarded duplicates, but Aiken never presented any of them. What Gray did not realize was that de Valera intended the Aiken trip to be used to reach a constituency other than the one Gray had in mind. We have seen Boland's statement to Hempel concerning the orchestration of Irish American sentiment. As far back as 31 July 1940 de Valera had authorized Walshe to inform Hempel that, while taking care to 'avoid the appearance of co-operation' with the Germans, he had instructed Brennan in Washington to begin doing just that. Hempel reported Brennan's instructions:[11]

> . . . to make contact with Senators of Irish origin who are friendly to Germany, in order to take steps against the agitation against Irish neutrality . . . . Walshe indicated to me further that closer cooperation between the Irish element in the United States and the German element there, and also with the Italians, might be in the general interest, and he had also stated something like that to the Italian Minister. The Irish Government apparently believes that if the Irish element in the United States is properly used, it could constitute a powerful influence in our favour, likewise the Irish-American press.

Hempel also indicated that he had reason to believe that, apart from the

Irish American press, the Hearst chain would be receptive to such an approach. And some six months later Ribbentrop instructed German diplomats in America to 'cultivate as much as possible relations with the leading Irish there'. The reply from the German Embassy in Washington[12] stated that contact had been achieved with pro-Irish political circles and 'considerable sums' spent on increasing the sale of the Irish American *New York Enquirer* and, through the *Enquirer*, making contact with the *Gaelic American* and other Irish American journals. In a nutshell, the Irish American situation was not unlike that which prevailed prior to America's entry to World War I. Irish Americans were making similar contacts to those that Cohalan, Devoy and the *Gaelic American* had established with German diplomats. Anti-British sentiment had not yet been submerged in a tide of patriotic anti-German feeling. Aiken was going to America, exactly as de Valera had done on his first visit, to enlist the aid of isolationist Irish American societies against an American President's foreign policy.

But, unlike de Valera's long-range sparrings with Woodrow Wilson, Aiken was destined to have a blazing face-to-face row with Roosevelt in the White House. Between the initiation of the Aiken visit and his actual arrival in America a great deal of diplomatic static had built up. The British agreed to Maffey's suggestion that he and Sean Nunan should be facilitated in their passage through Lisbon, where the two Irishmen picked up the Pan-American Clipper service. But a mysterious delay occurred in Lisbon which kept them waiting for nine days before they flew on to America, via West Africa and the Amazon. They landed in the teeth of a hostile press conference, on 18 March. Lend-Lease had passed into American law on the 11th. An airsick Aiken had to face questioning about being pro-German. His answer that Ireland was neither pro-British nor pro-German was, in his own words, 'not well received'.[13] Nor was he well received in the White House.

During at least some of the time he was *en route*, cables were passing between Dublin, London, New York and Washington imputing pro-German sympathies to him. These could have originated from opposition sources in Dublin. But the well-orchestrated press conference suggests that they could equally have had their roots in the de Valera-supported German/Irish American links to which Hempel referred. At all events, a matter of hours before Aiken and Brennan were received by Roosevelt, Lord Halifax, the British Ambassador, saw the President. He had been informed 'from most secret sources' that Aiken was[14] 'not alone anti-British but also hopes for and believes in German victory'. It was a very British *coup de grâce* to a visit which had little hope of success anyhow.

Neither Aiken nor de Valera was a potential entrant to Roosevelt's charmed circle. They would not have been at home sailing off Newport with FDR in the company of Henry Morgenthau Jnr. There could be very little room for camaraderie between a representative of the uneasy arrogance of de Valera and that snobbish, anglophile Brahmin, with the instinctive sympathy for the underdog, who produced the New Deal – that Democrat whose devotion to liberal values gave him such a hatred for dictatorships that he apparently connived at the set-up of Pearl Harbor in order to bring his unwilling nation into war against them. Roosevelt's entire political vision of society was tilted against the world of Bossism, Irish Americans and their societies to which de Valera wished Aiken to appeal. It was only the resented power of that section of American political life that gained Aiken an audience in the first place. On 9 March the Americans had sent the celebrated Colonel Bill Donovan, then personal representative of Frank Knox, Secretary of the Navy, to Dublin to impress on de Valera the manner in which Irish neutrality was perceived in Washington.[15] On the 10th, a group of 129 prominent Irish Americans published an open letter to de Valera in the *New York Times*, appealing to him to preserve the 'life line between Britain and America . . . the life line of civilisation' by allowing Britain to use the ports. The signatories argued that 'only if England survives can Ireland be free'. The letter was prohibited from appearing in Ireland by the censorship.

Not surprisingly, against that background, Aiken found the President was[16] 'very antagonistic' from the beginning. Roosevelt's opening gambit was to charge Aiken with saying that Ireland had nothing to fear from a German victory. Aiken's denial of this was drowned in a tide of Roosevelt oratory about the need for Irish assistance to Britain's war effort.

It was only as an aide, Colonel Watson, entered the room to signal the end of the interview that Aiken managed to get in a request for arms. Despite the aide's coughs and watch-glancings Aiken pressed on. He managed to get Roosevelt to the point where the President offered to supply the Irish with submarine-spotting aircraft. These would, of course, have been of benefit to the British as the Irish would have transmitted word of any sightings. Aiken met the offer by saying that Ireland had no need to fear submarines. Her fear was of invasion, and he assumed that Ireland would have the President's sympathy if such aggression occurred.

'Yes,' replied the man from Dutchess County, 'German aggression.'

'Or,' said the man from South Armagh, 'British aggression.'

'Preposterous!' roared Roosevelt, but Aiken cut him off to inquire why, if it was such an outlandish thought, did the British not give the guarantee of non-aggression for which they had been asked. While this exchange was in progress Watson had despaired of bringing the proceedings to a close by normal methods, so he instructed a servant to place a cloth and cutlery on Roosevelt's desk for lunch. As the man did so Roosevelt shouted at Aiken: 'What you have to fear is German aggression.' But they make them dogged in South Armagh, and Aiken repeated: 'Or British aggression.' At this Roosevelt lost his temper altogether and, shouting 'Preposterous!' at the top of his voice, caught hold of the tablecloth and sent crockery and cutlery flying all over the White House floor.

Aiken's companion Robert Brennan probably spared Aiken from invasion by intervening to suggest that Roosevelt might point out to Churchill that the giving of such a guarantee would ease the situation considerably. Roosevelt promised the Irishmen that they would have the guarantee the following day, and there the interview ended. The gulf that exists between bland official communiqués and reality was rarely better exemplified than in Roosevelt's note to de Valera, acknowledging the latter's introduction of Aiken, subsequent to the White House meeting:[17] '. . . I was glad to receive Mr. Aiken and have the opportunity of an interesting discussion with him. I am sure that Mr. Aiken has informed you of this discussion. I heartily reciprocate the expression of good wishes contained in your letter and send you my warm regards.'

The guarantee that Roosevelt promised never arrived, but several weeks after the row with Aiken the American Ambassador to London, John G. Winant, did say to Eden that, in the event of the British deciding to take over the Irish ports, he hoped they would let the American Government know first. It was one of the more fruitful results of Aiken's tour. Back in Dublin, Gray began to get alarmed at the use which de Valera was making of the American visit and cabled a warning and two suggestions to Cordell Hull: 'The Irish Government is exploiting Aiken's mission as American approval of its policy, at the same time making political capital out of inciting anti-British sentiment . . . I believe the time has come for a firmer attitude and the demand that de Valera clarify definitely his position.'

As his cable arrived in Washington the day after Roosevelt had sent the cutlery flying, his suggestions were received as ideas whose hour had struck. Gray's second proposal was that he protest against a passage in de Valera's recent St Patrick's Day broadcast[18] to the effect that, in blockading each other, the belligerents were blockading Ireland. These St Patrick's Day broadcasts were traditionally aimed at de Valera's Irish American supporters as much as at those in Dublin. Maurice Moynihan, who would normally have had a hand in preparing such speeches, has stated that this particular broadcast was delivered with the Aiken mission in mind.[19] Accordingly on 25 April 1941, Gray received instructions which contained good news and bad news for de Valera. Gray was ordered to tell him that he was going to get two ships from the Americans, but that the offer was being made directly to him and not Aiken because:

> . . . as a result of the conversations which various officials of your Government have had with General Aiken, that the point of view of the latter . . . would appear to be utterly lacking in any appreciation of the fact, which seems to your Government completely clear, that the future safety and security of Eire depends inevitably upon the triumph of the British cause.

Hull's cable went on to state that: 'as Mr de Valera fully realises, the Government of the United States believes that the future security of democracy and liberty in the world depends upon the ultimate victory of the British Government . . . .'

Having told de Valera that the US Government was therefore pledged to support Britain, Gray was then to move on and ask for clarification of the blockading reference in the St Patrick's Day speech. He carried out his instructions on 28 April, making the point to de Valera that Britain could hardly be blockading the Irish when imports were still as high as three-quarters of those in the same period of the previous year. Moreover, Britain was the carrier of these imports, though de Valera had 'made no contribution to the safety of British sea-borne commerce'. Gray went on to make the telling point that a number of Irish vessels had been sunk by Germany whereas Britain had never attacked Irish shipping.

Gray notes that: 'At this point he flushed angrily and shouted that it was impertinent to question the statements of the head of a state.' Thereafter the interview did not quite proceed to the crockery stage, but one could hardly describe it as a meeting of minds, let alone of policies. Gray was correct in stating that the British were bringing supplies to Ireland whereas the Germans were sinking ships, hence to accuse both countries of 'blockading' was misleading. However, as Boland later observed, correctly, the British did apply the squeeze 'as far as they thought it safe to do so without disrupting our economy'.

Gray was also eager to make the point that the groups to whom de Valera was appealing in the USA had 'attempted to defeat the present administration, the Lend Lease Law and [were] now engaged in sabotaging our Aid for Britain Policy'. De Valera denied any anti-British sentiment and rejected the suggestion that he had 'any intention of trying to influence the American public against the American Executive'. He informed Gray that 'certain of his friends' thought him 'more British than the British' and that he would do better to mind American interests. Gray replied to the effect that the war meant that British interests were American interests. De Valera said that he understood this but 'others' did not.

After the interview, Gray reported to Washington that he felt:[20]

> The effect of a stiff attitude will be sobering. It is the only way to impress him that there are realities closing in on him. No one has ever taken this line with him. He always out manoeuvered Chamberlain. I no longer hope to get anything from him by generosity and conciliation. He must be made to realise that it is possible that a situation is approaching, in which if it is essential to survival, his ports will be seized with the approbation of the liberal sentiment of the world, that he will have only the choice of fighting on the side of Great Britain or Germany.

Gray later judged that the exchange with de Valera:

> . . . marked a turning point in Irish-American relations. Washington at long last had begun to resent having its English policy made in Dublin. The recent 'exchange of views' was a first step towards emancipation. For the next two years Mr. de Valera made no more broadcasts to 'our people in the United States.'

This assessment was certainly correct insofar as Roosevelt's administrations were concerned. FDR began what he termed an 'absent treatment' regime during which it was decided to show disfavour to de Valera even to the extent of not answering his Christmas card.[21] And after the war the 'special relationship' between the USA and Great Britain certainly carried infinitely more clout than did Dublin and the Irish American lobby where partition was concerned. But, in the immediate aftermath of the conversation with Gray, de Valera decided to do unto Gray what the Americans had done unto Aiken. After some two weeks' thought he communicated his reaction not to the Minister but to his Government. It took the form of a lengthy telegram despatched on 15 May 1941, which got to the point after reference to such matters as Ireland's 'Christian civilisation nearly 2,000 years old' and her 'consistent record of fighting for freedom longer perhaps than that of any other nation'. The point was that de Valera was turning down the ships although:

> Ireland's need for the ships is great and possession of them might well mean the difference between extreme hardship and a hardship which would be intolerable. The manner, however, in which the offer is made and the suggestion of implied conditions render it impossible for the Irish Government to accept. They cannot accept that the estimate of Mr. Aiken's attitude and the criticism directed against him is just.

The depth of his feelings may be gauged from the fact that on the day the cable was despatched he took the unusual step of criticizing Gray openly. He told a group of visitors, which included an Irish senator, The McGillicuddy of the Reeks, that Gray was a disaster as a representative and was doing great harm in Dublin. The party of visitors promptly did as de Valera had expected and made their next port of call the office of Sir John Maffey, where The McGillicuddy passed on de Valera's comments. Maffey immediately reported to London that de Valera 'appears to be starting a campaign against Mr. Gray'.[22] He recommended that the Foreign Office call Washington's attention to Gray's good work for 'our cause'.

But Roosevelt intended neither to be moved by de Valera's tactics not to be trapped into a position of appearing to connive at the return of famine to Ireland. The day after de Valera's cable arrived in Washington, Cordell Hull gave Brennan a memorandum which stated that:

> The offer of the American Government made through the American Minister in Dublin on April 28th to enter into negotiations with the Irish Government for the acquisition by the latter of two freight vessels was made unconditionally, and based only on the close and traditional friendship between the American and the Irish peoples. It was made despite an acute shipping shortage . . .

The President followed this up by, in effect, making de Valera an offer he could not refuse. In the course of a press conference on 20 May he announced the allocation of two cargo ships to Ireland, together with a half million dollar donation to the Red Cross to buy food. De Valera had not announced his refusal of the ships. He now found himself in a position in which he could neither admit to having done so because of the Aiken visit, nor use the censor's office to hide what he was up to. His method of dealing with the dilemma may be studied in the columns of the *Irish Press*. The report mentions that there was no official comment on the Roosevelt announcement, but notes that Aiken was in the United States negotiating for defence supplies and food – the obvious implication being that Aiken's visit had something to do with the ships.

However, Roosevelt was not prepared to let de Valera off the hook that easily. A series of bureaucratic delays held up the handover of the ships throughout the summer of 1941. These came to a head on 17 September when Roosevelt refused to sign a directive to the Lend-Lease authorities sanctioning the deal. Brennan was directed to approach the Secretary of State concerning the matter which had been:[23] 'Handled in such an extraordinary manner that it has now, after four months negotiations, reached an impasse to the bitter disappointment of the Irish Government'. My information from Washington contacts is that the 'impasse' was finally resolved through the intercession of John McCormack, the Democratic House Leader. The ships were transferred to Irish Shipping,[24] rechristened the *Irish Oak* (formerly the *West Hematite*) and the *Irish Pine* (formerly the *West Neris*), and – both sunk by German submarines with considerable loss of life. The *Irish Pine* was torpedoed after leaving Ireland on 28 October 1942, and the *Irish Oak* on the morning of 15 May 1943. It was a tragic, eerie underlining of the Gray view of the 'blockading' issue. De Valera did not protest to Germany over the sinkings, nor did he receive any more American ships. A State Department cable[25] turned down his request, made through Irish Shipping, for the purchase of the 8,000-ton SS *Wolverine*, saying:

> . . . the Axis powers are in fact making war upon Ireland while at the same time using Ireland's friendship to the detriment of the United Nations war effort. The loss of the *West Hematite (Irish Pine)* and the *West Neris (Irish Oak)* has harmed not only Ireland but the United States, to whom these vessels belonged, and the whole United Nations war effort . . . . Any further ships transferred to the Irish flag would be subject to these same hazards.

Apart from his overall antipathy to de Valera's policy of neutrality, Roosevelt's resistance to the ships' transfer was fuelled by the lengthy Aiken visit, which lasted for over three months. De Valera's official biography[26] gives a very misleading picture of its impact on the administration. There is, for instance, no mention of the row in Roosevelt's study, no reference to the priming of German/Irish American links in the USA, and specific disclaimers of either involvement with forces hostile to Roosevelt or efforts to 'influence public opinion against the American Executive'. In fact the biography states that Aiken 'carefully avoided contacts with senators and congressmen opposed to Roosevelt'.

But it makes no reference to the instruction to Brennan to cultivate pro-German politicians. Nor does it mention that Aiken threw off the cloak of 'Minister for Co-ordination Measures' and hit the old IRA-leaning, Irish American circuit which he and de Valera had made use of to such good effect in funding the *Irish Press*. Just as de Valera had ceased to be known as 'Priomh Aire' and came to be described as 'President of the Irish Republic', Aiken was referred to as 'Lieutenant General Aiken', a title which had civil war, Republican connotations. He undertook a coast-to-coast speaking tour under the auspices of the Friends of Irish Neutrality, an umbrella organization of Irish societies whose principal figure was that unrepentant Irish nationalist Paul O'Dwyer.

O'Dwyer, a lifelong Democrat, later became one of America's greatest civil rights lawyers, President of the New York City Council and New York's Ambassador to the UN. At the time of writing he is quite rightly regarded as a father figure by Irish Americans. He has been a controversial figure for most of his political life, but one thing I have never heard him being accused of is the crime of doing anything to support British policy in Ireland! (That is, if one excepts his donation of the family home in Bohola, Co. Mayo to the Cheshire Homes.) Like Devoy and Cohalan before him, he had to drop his pro-Irish, anti-British agitation as soon as America entered the war. The 'Friends' were disbanded immediately after Pearl Harbor. In 1941 O'Dwyer's espousal of Irish neutrality was anathema to Roosevelt, who regarded him in much the same light as Wilson saw Cohalan.

To have O'Dwyer sponsor Aiken after the White House row would have inflamed Roosevelt anyhow. But his anger was compounded when he began getting complaints[27] about Aiken from figures like Darryl F. Zanuck, the movie mogul who ran 20th Century-Fox. Zanuck, an important film propagandist for Roosevelt, said that Aiken was 'pleading' that the USA should stay neutral and that America was putting pressure on Ireland to enter the war on Britain's side. Zanuck noted that the Hearst papers were playing up this 'propaganda'. (Hempel had obviously been well informed.) He wondered why the American Government 'would entertain or sponsor a foreign figure on such an obvious propaganda trip'. Roosevelt thought it equally strange, and an instruction was issued on 5 June that Lieutenant General Frank Aiken was not to be allocated 'amenities and honours due his rank without specific prior approval in each case by the War Dept'.[28]

Aiken's version of his tour was that he lodged a copy of his official speech with the State Department. He told Joseph Carroll[29] that he stuck to this wherever he went. According to a script he handed out in Boston,[29a] this would have confined him to delivering a rehash of de Valera's League of Nations addresses. Aiken's official thesis was that small nations and their leaders had not been able to prevent the coming of war and that in the circumstances the best thing Ireland could do was defend de Valera's

Constitution. Aiken stated that Ireland was committed[30] 'in relation to our own soil and people in the territory over which we have control [to] the principles and aims which are set out so clearly in our Constitution'.

Eventually the vibes from America, and a number of events at home, combined to make de Valera uneasy about the Great American Aiken Trail and he decided to recall him. The following carefully worded telegram was sent, in code, to the Irish Legation in Washington:[31] 'As war moves toward crisis Taoiseach would be glad to have Frank's help at home as soon as possible unless of course he feels he must stay in United States for vitally important purpose. Please cable immediately. Frank's family in splendid form.'

The telegram failed to prevent a grand finale of Rooseveltian wrath arousal. Aiken's farewell dinner in New York was held under the auspices of the American Friends of Irish Neutrality and addressed by Judge Cohalan, who said:[32]

> ... When I first read that General Aiken was coming over here to ask for arms and food, I was a bit discouraged by what might be the outcome of his mission. I had seen America completely taken over by the propaganda of England, all our standards of traditions, ideals and interests were absolutely swept aside by the two groups representing two powerful minorities in favour of our taking over this war .... But, when it was made known that General Aiken was coming here for the purpose of buying and paying for anything he got from America, I had a different view.
>
> I want to thank him for the wonderful tactful job he has done, for making Americans understand that Ireland has not asked, is not asking, and does not intend to ask, anything from America for which she will not pay 100 cents to the dollar, and that as a neutral country she sees only an opportunity to buy what she so badly needs.
>
> If General Aiken is representative of the men who are governing Ireland today, as we believe him to be, then I must say that the country is fortunate indeed in having such leaders in the present crisis.

Roosevelt did not concur in Cohalan's assessment of Ireland's fortunate status. Any wry satisfaction de Valera may have derived from being praised by his old rival must have been dissipated by a statement[33] from Roosevelt on 27 June, the day after Cohalan's speech was cabled in clear to the Irish Department of External Affairs. It was to the effect that he had received no definite assurance that the Irish would defend themselves against an attack by Germany. This had the result of triggering off a Dail debate in which de Valera was attacked for not giving Roosevelt the necessary assurances. As a result Brennan was sent in to bat once again; on 15 July, armed with a list of de Valera's and other Fianna Fail leaders' statements showing how determined Ireland was to resist all-comers, Germany included, he fruitlessly demanded satisfaction from Roosevelt.

De Valera also sent for Gray three days after the Brennan note was delivered, asking him for an elucidation of the President's statement. But

Gray's correspondence[34] shows that he received little satisfaction from either the Minister or the State Department. Gray told him he had no special knowledge of the statement, but that if it was made as reported it probably meant exactly what it said. The official State Department reply underlined Gray's response. In effect it constituted a rejection of the request made in the letter which de Valera had given Aiken for Roosevelt on 4 March, and was the final postscript to the Aiken visit saga. It said:

> The President . . . while not doubting that Ireland would use the means at its disposal to resist German invasion, has not felt with certainty that Ireland unassisted could successfully repel a determined German attack. In such an event, arms provided to Ireland would not only reduce the available supplies so urgently needed by the United States and Great Britain, but would in all possibility fall into the hands of Germany . . . . It is perhaps unnecessary to refer to the long list of countries in Europe which, in the hope of remaining neutral, have neglected their defense plans only to fall victims of wanton German aggression . . . .

By the time de Valera sought Roosevelt's explanation he had received a horrific first-hand example of what German aggression could mean on the part of his own island. On the night of 15–16 April the Luftwaffe bombed Belfast, killing some 750 people – a far worse atrocity than the German bombing of Coventry, which claimed 554 lives. As the bombs rained down John MacDermott, the Six County Security Minister, managed to get off a telephone call to Dublin appealing for help. De Valera was awakened at 2 a.m. and, having spoken with Cardinal MacRory, answered the call almost immediately by sending thirteen units of the Dublin fire brigade to Belfast. It was, according to his official biography, 'possibly the fastest decision of his career'.[35] The crews fought the fires until just before dusk on 16 April, when de Valera recalled them. The sending of the fire engines was a technical breach of neutrality and he was concerned about German reactions; but the sending of the Dublin firemen – though it was speedily overlooked officially – was a greatly appreciated, and still spoken of, gesture amongst the working class of the Six Counties.

It certainly contrasts well with the behaviour of the RAF in the early hours of 16 April. Robert Fisk made devastating use of official RAF records to reveal[36] that its Hurricane squadrons were ordered to keep outside a five-mile radius of the city, leaving the Nazi bombers to do their work undisturbed. The British decided that it was too dangerous to venture into the confusion caused to radar signals by bomb damage to cable links between Belfast and Preston in Lancashire. The paucity of air defences over Belfast tempted the Germans back on 4 May to cause further loss of life; this time about 150 people were killed, and massive damage done to shipping and to factories in the docks area. In all, some ten thousand houses were destroyed, most of them in the poor, working-class areas of the city.

The Belfast bombings certainly underline the rationale behind de

Valera's neutrality policy. Writing to Roosevelt the following spring Gray said:[37] 'Ireland is at present defenceless, not because you do not realise that it is defenceless, but because you haven't the stuff at present to put in there.' Had the Twenty-six Counties not been neutral at the time of the Belfast bombings, the results could have been catastrophic. Speaking at Castlebar on 20 April, de Valera referred to the first Belfast raid as a 'disaster' and went on:[38]

> I know you will wish me to express on your behalf, and on behalf of the Government, our sympathy with the people who are suffering. . . . In the past, and probably in the present too, a number of them did not see eye to eye with us politically, but they are all our people – we are one and the same people – and their sorrows in the present instance are also our sorrows; and I want to say that any help we can give them in the present time we will give to them wholeheartedly, believing that were the circumstances reversed they would also give us their help wholeheartedly.

In that same month of May, Dublin too was bombed. On the night of the 30th German bombs killed 34 people, injured 90 others and destroyed 300 houses in the North Strand area of Dublin. Hempel was stunned by the raid. His immediate reaction was to call on both Walshe and de Valera to discover what was known about the bombing. He felt that it: ' . . . had been done by the British with captured German planes . . . to upset Irish neutrality and to get Ireland into the war'.[39] De Valera protested both to Hempel directly and to Berlin via Warnock. The Germans apologized for the bombings, attributing them to 'high winds' which had sent the planes away from their intended British targets. Long after the war was ended, in 1958, Germany paid limited compensation for the raid – £327,000. But 'high winds' may not have been the cause. Winston Churchill, of all people, later suggested that the raids might have been the result of a British invention which distorted Luftwaffe radio guidance beams so as to throw their planes off course.[40]

Curiously this distortion, if it occurred, did so only a couple of days after Churchill was worsted in yet another joust with de Valera. Conscription was once again the issue. The initiators of the controversy, as they had been in the question of putting an economic squeeze on the South, were the Unionists. Prior to the Belfast bombings the possibility of introducing conscription to augment home defence in the Six Counties had been discussed and discarded in British decision-taking circles.[41] It had been only a peripheral matter. However the Six County Prime Minister scented the wind and, wishing to advance the claims of 'loyal Ulster', had written to Herbert Morrison, the British Home Secretary, on 4 April 1941, suggesting that conscription be extended to the Six Counties.[42] There the matter rested for a few weeks while the bombings intervened.

The appalling aftermath of the Belfast raids did not produce any sort of humanitarian reaction from the rulers of the Six County statelet. In fact, it is a matter of record[43] that one of the principal preoccupations of the Cabinet after the bombing was not to preserve the poor of Belfast from further horror, but how to ensure that the statue of Carson outside the Parliament building could be saved; they set up a committee to look into this matter. Meanwhile a pathetic phenomenon known as the 'Ditchers' began to be observed in Belfast. Night after night the poor of the city, men, women and children, climbed into the surrounding hills to sleep in the ditches where they might escape the expected return of the bombers. However, the Unionist philosophy is imbued with a 'cannon fodder' mentality where 'other ranks' are concerned. The plight of the 'Ditchers' prompted MacDermott, who had appealed to neutral de Valera as Belfast burned, to advise the Cabinet that the fact that the province was not fully in the war had created[44] 'a general feeling that we are neither one thing nor the other, and I think this has contributed to the unsettling effects of the raids. . . . There is no feeling of equality of sacrifice throughout the country. The willing horse is bearing the brunt and we are in danger of working him to death.'

At this stage death *was* working in Belfast. Corpses were still turning putrescent in its rubble. However, the Unionist establishment was discovering that the 'other ranks' were not volunteering to dig them out, or to perform other necessary civil defence tasks; instead they were taking to the hills in terror. MacDermott's panacea for sustaining the 'willing horse', therefore, was that 'the discipline of the province would stand stronger if we had conscription'. The Cabinet's principal concern was that the 'unsettling effect' of the bombings would not be turned against the administration. Conscription would provide a mechanism of control.

And here occurred a potent concatenation of desiderata: on the one hand Belfast's desire to preserve hegemony over its holding; on the other, London's eagerness to avail itself of the offer of manpower in the Six County Government's missive of 4 April. The result was that on 20 May Morrison cabled Stormont, saying that the British Government was: 'disposed to think that this [conscription] might produce substantial accession of strength to armed forces'. What did the Stormont Government think? asked Morrison. Stormont replied that it was:[45]

> . . . emphatically of opinion that conscription *should* [author's italics] be applied to Northern Ireland. It considers that in this matter a common basis for the whole of the United Kingdom is just. It further considers, particularly in the light of recent heavy enemy attacks, that the principle of equality of sacrifice and service underlying conscription is essential to promote the degree of *corporate discipline* [author's italics] which is necessary if our people are to withstand the tide of total war and play their full part in the national effort.

The only drawback to conscription which the Unionists had perceived was the possibility of workers from the South filling the jobs of conscripts. A far greater objection was completely overlooked: the Unionist politicians had neglected to seek either police or Army evaluations of the issue. Hence the cable contained a gross miscalculation of the Catholic minority's response: '. . . there may be Nationalist opposition to conscription. It is impossible to forecast the extent of such opposition accurately. It [Stormont] feels, however, that the difficulties of such opposition would be more than offset by the advantages gained.'

The head of the RUC, Colonel Wickham, flatly contradicted this assessment when his views were sought by the British Cabinet. He said that it was:[46]

> . . . extremely doubtful if conscription has the whole-hearted support of either section of the population . . . . It will fall more heavily upon the Roman Catholic section than the Protestant because a greater proportion of the latter are in reserved occupations . . . active organisation to resist it will commence at once in every parish . . . . Many will cross the Border but from those who remain wide resistance to the enforcement of the Act may be expected . . . conscription will give new life to the IRA . . . . It will . . . increase the risk of Protestants adopting the attitude that they go only if the Roman Catholics are taken . . . .

In fact when Churchill announced that the Cabinet were considering conscription, on the same day that Morrison sent his enquiry (20 May 1941), the Nationalists exploded in outrage. Cardinal MacRory and the Northern bishops issued a denunciation of the proposal. Nationalist leaders drew up a version of the anti-conscription pledge which had been read at churches in 1918. Although he had made no protest to Germany over the carnage in Belfast that one can discover, De Valera was galvanized into protesting to Britain against the conscription proposal. The bombings affected the North, but conscription might have affected the South. His official biography states:[47]

> It was a crisis of the first magnitude, carrying a threat to the whole internal peace of Ireland. The IRA which had been rendered ineffective . . . would be assured of an accretion of sympathy and strength if conscription were enforced . . . . Herman Goertz [a German agent] . . . continued to evade capture . . . . The crisis of conscription . . . might have made him really dangerous . . . .

There was some question of de Valera's going to London to see Churchill personally, but he showed no more eagerness to negotiate with the Englishman in 1941 than he had during the Treaty negotiations of 1921. He is reported to have said that:[48] 'his personal arrangements with Churchill were very different from those with Chamberlain'. That remark certainly qualifies as one of the all-time great pieces of understatement. Had he met Churchill at this time the exchanges would certainly have exceeded the acrimony of his worst moments with Gray by a factor of ten. As it was, Dulanty, an old friend of Churchill's, had two interviews with the British Prime Minister, the first of which might be classed as stormy, the second as a gale force affair.

587

At the first, on 22 May, Dulanty made the case that conscription would bring untold chaos to Ireland and that it would be outrageous to force the Six County Nationalists to fight for a freedom they had never known. Churchill replied to the effect that he could not be expected to be greatly concerned at the prospect of disturbances in Northern Ireland in view of the disturbances in other parts of Europe. If the democratic Government of Northern Ireland asked the British Government to impose conscription, he did not see how this could be refused. He nettled Dulanty by saying that, if members of the minority wished to 'run away' to Eire, they could do so. Dulanty retorted that the Irish had never shown any inclination to run away – least of all when they were fighting the might of England. Churchill instantly agreed with this. The Irish were 'one of the world's finest fighting races'. It was lamentable that they were not now in the world fight for freedom 'through the ignoble fear of being bombed'. He had always been in favour of a united Ireland, but there was little hope of this now with the Northerners fighting alongside the British while the Southerners stood aside, perpetuating partition. He said: 'You should tell your Government that we are fighting for our lives, and owing to the imprudence of Mr. Chamberlain we are denied the use of the ports which were given you.'

Dulanty made the point that the ports were Irish in the first place and could hardly be referred to as being 'given' to them. Churchill did not deign to reply. In sub-conference with Michael Collins, he had personally conducted the portion of the Treaty negotiation concerning the ports. What he did say was that he had no doubt that de Valera intended to 'do us as much harm as he can' in the United States, and that the South was only keeping out of the war because it was thought that Britain would lose. While this discussion took place the normal daily Cabinet meeting was delayed for some twenty minutes; but it yielded nothing except a declaration by Churchill that he would inform his colleagues of the Irish Government's viewpoint.

Dulanty brought a direct appeal from de Valera to Churchill for the second meeting, on the 26th. Very little of it appears to have been based on the reality of the Anglo-Irish relationship of the period:

> A feeling of better understanding and of mutual sympathy which held in it the promise of ultimate close friendship has grown up between our peoples in recent years. The existence of Partition was the only stumbling block, and there was the hope that in the improved conditions it too would disappear. The imposition of Conscription will inevitably undo all the good that has been done and throw the two peoples back into the old unhappy relations. The conscription of the people of one nation by another revolts the human conscience . . . an act of oppression upon a weaker people . . . .
>
> The Six Counties have towards the rest of Ireland a status and relationship which no Act of Parliament can change. They are part of Ireland. They have always been part of Ireland, and their people, Catholic and Protestant, are our people . . . .

588

Churchill took fire: 'Does Mr. de Valera want an answer to this message, because if he does I will give him one – an answer that will resound throughout the world.' Without waiting for an answer, he began pacing up and down the room. Amongst the statements he made were:

> When I think of the fine men with whom I worked in past years, men who gave their lives for Ireland – the two Redmonds, Dillon and Kettle – one of your finest modern minds – and all those other Irish who showed such courage and valour in the last war, my blood boils to think of your present position.

Dulanty described the two conversations as taking place in an 'unfriendly' atmosphere. He said that it was 'difficult, such was the Niagara-like rush of his talk, to make any reply' to Churchill. The Prime Minister became at times 'emotional. . . . I did not think,' wrote Dulanty, 'there was any play-acting because this tendency of his to emotion is the cause of some apprehension amongst his own supporters.' Dulanty noted that some, 'not in any fault-finding way', described Churchill as having an 'eighteenth-century mind'. He recalled hearing Churchill make a speech thirty years earlier during which he urged his listeners to look upon Ireland with a modern, unprejudiced mind. However, Dulanty summed up the two encounters by saying: 'He himself looks today on Ireland with a mind which is neither. What he said against our Government lost nothing from the acerbity with which he said it. His feeling of hostility was known; these conversations made crystal clear the depth and bitterness of that hostility.'

Yet, despite their binary opposition, Churchill ultimately came down on de Valera's side of the argument. Amongst those who added their voices to the skilfully orchestrated chorus of opposition emanating from Dublin were Cardinal MacRory; the Head of the Royal Ulster Constabulary; the Canadian Prime Minister, Mackenzie King; Gray and Maffey. The last two agreed that the conscription hare had been started by what Gray described to Washington on 24 May as 'the weak and faltering Ulster Government' for its own purposes, and that these were damaging to British, American and Irish interests. They informed their governments accordingly, and ultimately their views prevailed. Gray was particularly supportive of de Valera's position, although the pair had their inevitable row[49] while, for once, fighting alongside each other.

The row had its genesis in a long telegram sent by Gray to the State Department on 24 May 1941. Two days earlier, on learning that Churchill was about to introduce conscription, he had warned the State Department against the move, saying that its introduction would: 'seriously hamper the Opposition on which we must rely'. His personal view was that he would[50] 'like to see them all drafted and put in the front line'. But he felt that, given the current state of Irish American opinion, this would be 'madness'.[51] Accordingly, he told the State Department:

> Opposition leaders yesterday informed me that conscription without a

conscientious objector's clause for minority Catholic nationalists will constitute a major irretrievable and probably fatal political blunder at this time and play directly into de Valera's hands with grave possibilities for American interests. They predict draft riots, the escape of draft dodgers to Southern Ireland who will be acclaimed as hero martyrs by three-quarters of the population and the fomenting of trouble by Republicans and Fifth Columnists. The clearest headed leader predicts that de Valera will seize the opportunity to escape from economic and political realities by proclaiming himself the leader of the oppressed minority and with the blessings of the Cardinal will rouse anti-British feeling and call a Holy War. I think it a very likely prediction. All classes of opinion here unite in condemning the move as calamitous . . . a repetition of the same fatal blunder made during the last war . . . .

Eighty thousand Irish volunteers in British Army will be disaffected, there will be no material number of Nationalist conscripts, a popular majority and an army inclined to be friendly to Great Britain rather than the Axis will become definitely hostile, possibly giving active aid to Germany, and most important of all the pro-British opposition will be helpless and the opportunity for dividing the country on the question of the ports will be lost for the duration . . . effect on Irish-American opinion at this juncture is not for me to estimate. This is a grave situation.

Gray sent a sanitized version of this telegram to de Valera on the day of despatch, saying he would be glad to receive constructive suggestions. De Valera was delighted. He phoned Gray that afternoon to thank him but said that he had no constructive suggestion, as Gray had stated the matter exactly as he would have done. However, later in the day he made another call to Gray asking him to contact him that night. Gray did so at 11.30 and records the following conversation in 'Behind the Green Curtain'.

De Valera began by saying that Gray had asked for constructive suggestions. He had one: the escape clause for Catholic objectors – that his Government could not concede the right of another Government to conscript Irishmen, whether in Ulster or elsewhere – would not be satisfactory. Gray writes that he replied: 'with some astonishment': ' . . . you took no exception to this clause this afternoon. This is not a discussion of the issue of Partition.'

De Valera: 'I didn't really note the clause, or grasp its significance.'
Gray: 'Do you mean to take the position that Orangemen cannot conscript themselves?'
De Valera: 'Why should they? They can volunteer.'
Gray: 'Some volunteer, and others need to be conscripted.'
De Valera: 'Don't say that; it's not true.'
Gray: 'It is true. You rule this country. You are far and away its most powerful man and you have to take responsibility for what it thinks.'
De Valera: 'That is not so.'
Gray: 'Are you trying to tell me that you insist on bring up partition in principle in this emergency and refuse to compromise in the interest of humanity and to save bloodshed?'
De Valera: 'No, but I cannot ignore the conviction of the Irish people.'

The conversation terminated with Gray saying that, while he would continue trying to block conscription, he would have to inform his Government of de Valera's change of position since the afternoon. De Valera insisted that he had not changed his position, but had merely overlooked the significance of the conscientious objector's clause. Gray, who would appear to have recorded the conversation, typed up the exchange before going to bed. The expenditure of much other midnight oil in the capitals involved, including Gray's own continuing and strenuous efforts, finally soothed the conscription crisis. Churchill announced in the House of Commons, to the sound of loud cheers, as the *Irish Press* pointedly noted, that:[52] 'it would be more trouble than it was worth to enforce such a policy in Northern Ireland'. Three days later the, literally, off-beam German planes bombed Dublin.

De Valera and Gray jousted again later in the summer of 1941 over the question of recognizing de Valera's right to intervene in Six County affairs. The question arose following America's assumption of the defence of Iceland. In July, reports circulated in Dublin that American 'technicians' were building a base in Derry to aid in Iceland's defence. De Valera inquired from Gray whether the reports were true. He felt he had a standing in the matter because 'while he recognised the de facto occupation of that part of Ireland, he could not waive Irish rights of sovereignty over it'.[53] Gray refused to entertain discussions about partition, and suggested the matter be taken up in Washington through Robert Brennan. Thus rebuffed, de Valera allowed the matter to rest for the time being. Roosevelt's reaction on hearing from Gray about the approach was:[54]

> It is a rather dreadful thing to say but I must admit that if factories close in Ireland and there is a great deal more suffering there, there will be less general sympathy in the United States than if it had happened six months ago. People are, frankly, getting pretty fed up with my old friend Dev.

De Valera's own state of mind was described in a letter from Gray to Roosevelt:[55] 'Dev. is still grim and obstinate and blind, I keep pounding away on the idea that we do not like to be pressure-grouped by ANY hyphenated [i.e. Irish-American] minority. It is a good deal of a blow to them. . . .'

De Valera took up the Derry issue again in October after the *Daily Mail* had printed a report on the 13th to the effect that operations there had grown to such an extent that US marines were required to protect them. His initial approach through Brennan, made on the 15th,[56] was ignored. He made a 'more formal' request on 6 November. This time the note,[57] also delivered in Washington, said that 'the restoration of the integrity of the national territory of Ireland' was the 'primary political aim' of the majority of the people of Ireland. Roosevelt's reply, delivered on 16 November, did indeed indicate that people were getting 'fed up with Dev.'. It said: 'In as much as the inquiry contained in your communication under acknowledgement relates to territory recognised by the Government of the

United States as part of the United Kingdom . . . the inquiry in question should be addressed by the Irish Government to the Government of the United Kingdom.'

But after this bleak brush-off the year ended with the hand of friendship suddenly being extended to de Valera from an unexpected quarter – Winston Spencer Churchill. De Valera initially mistook it for the mailed fist – not un-understandably in the circumstances. At 1.30 in the morning of 8 December 1941 his phone rang. Joseph Walshe was on the line to say that Sir John Maffey had a message for him from Churchill which would not wait until daybreak; he had been instructed to deliver it at once. Pearl Harbor had been attacked the previous day. De Valera wondered if the message portended a drive on the Irish ports as a result. Maffey arrived half an hour after Walshe's call. Meanwhile de Valera had alerted the Army Chief of Staff, Major Dan McKenna, and Maurice Moynihan, Secretary to the Government, to stand by. But the mountainous message turned out to be a Churchillian mouse, and one which had apparently been at the brandy into the bargain. It read: 'Following from Mr. Churchill for Mr. de Valera. Personal, Private and Secret. Begins. Now is your chance. Now or never. "A Nation once again". Am very ready to meet you at any time.'

'A Nation Once Again' was the song of the old Irish Parliamentary Party of Tom Kettle and the Redmonds, whose virtues Churchill had extolled to Dulanty earlier in the year as opposed to the demerits of de Valera's policies. Reading the message, de Valera did not feel like singing. In his own plangent prose he recorded his reaction:[58]

> On being handed the written text I concluded that it was Mr. Churchill's way of intimating 'now is the chance for taking action which would have ultimately led to the unification of the country' . . . . I did not see the thing in that light. I saw no opportunity at the moment of securing unity, that our people were determined on their attitude of neutrality, etc.

Again he shied away from meeting Churchill. His note says:[59] 'I was not in favour of it because I considered it unwise; that I didn't see any basis of agreement and that disagreement might leave conditions worse than before and that my visit, in any case, would have the results that I had already indicated.'

An American OSS officer[60] who operated in Ireland during the war, unbeknown to the Irish, later recorded his view of the real situation concerning neutrality and the de Valera–Churchill relationship:

> Much of the problem . . . was grounded in the character of de Valera and of Churchill, each of whom hated the other from youth. Each was a kind of genius with one or more human flaws. For their personal political reasons, each said much to conceal the fact that the Eire [sic] was a significant help to the Allies and was neutral in name only – a fact clearly known to the Germans and the Japanese.

There is much truth in that assessment. At all events de Valera met Churchill's historic telegram by letting Moynihan and McKenna go back to bed. He concluded that where the message was concerned:[61] 'Perhaps a couple of days' delay would indicate that he saw no point in being awakened out of his sleep to receive it.' The reply he gave Maffey two days later, on 10 December, was to thank Churchill for his message and suggest that he send Cranborne to Dublin to gain, perhaps, a 'fuller understanding of our position here'.[62] Cranborne came, saw de Valera on the 16th, but did not conquer. Neither for that matter did de Valera. There was further discussion of partition and neutrality, and a suggestion by de Valera that, while the Irish had no wish to profiteer, they could supply more food to England – if the price was right.[63] But there was no agreement on any of these points or on giving de Valera the arms he sought. At the end of the discussion the Authorized Version records:[64] 'The Irish point of view had been demonstrated and the situation remained unchanged in respect of Irish neutrality.'

What that 'situation' meant in real terms was unlimited expressions of sympathy and minimal involvement. De Valera had spelled out in lachrymose terms his policy response to the situation created by the entry of America into the war after Pearl Harbor. But these included a subtle underlining of his own increased clout through Irish families' involvement. His rhetoric carefully avoided any suggestion that there might be questions of morality or freedom involved. The war was an insensible thing, like a plague:[65]

> Since this terrible war began, our sympathies have gone out to all the suffering peoples who have been dragged into it. Further hundreds of millions have become involved since I spoke at Limerick a fortnight ago. Its extension to the United States brings a source of anxiety and sorrow to every part of this land. There is scarcely a family here which has not a member or a near relative in that country. In addition to the ties of blood, there has been between our two nations a long association of friendship and regard . . . . It would be unnatural . . . if we did not sympathise in a special manner with the people of the United States . . . .

Nevertheless Ireland was not going to get involved: 'The policy of this State remains unchanged. We can only be a friendly neutral. From the moment this war began, there was, for this state, only one policy possible, neutrality.'

The American troops for whom the 'technicians' had been preparing began arriving in the Six Counties in January 1942. De Valera was advised by Maffey on the 26th that the arrivals were 'imminent'. Maffey said afterwards[66] that he had never seen de Valera so depressed. He was resentful over the troops' arrival, even though he had expected them; they were confirmation of growing fears he had entertained throughout 1941 of America's entry into the war – although, apparently, Aiken's immersion in isolationist circles in America had led him to inform de Valera on his return that there was no likelihood of America's entering the war. Now the loneliness of the neutral really came home to de Valera. What to do? According to Gray, Maffey suggested that he 'apply for membership in the club to which he logically belonged'.

De Valera, however, is quoted as saying that if only Ireland were attacked by Germany it would simplify matters. The day after the Maffey interview he issued a protest that was not a protest. After going back over the history of partition he said:[67]

> The people of Ireland have no feelings of hostility towards, and no desire to be brought in any way into conflict with, the United States. For reasons which I referred to a few weeks ago, the contrary is the truth, but it is our duty to make it clearly understood that no matter what troops occupy the Six Counties, the Irish people's claim for the union of the whole of the national territory and for supreme jurisdiction over it will remain unabated.

He then directed Brennan to hand this to Sumner Welles on 6 February 1942. The reply, which Roosevelt authorized, both dealt with the issue of the troop landings and contained a pointed warning about the position de Valera might find himself in after the war:[68]

> The decision to dispatch troops to the British Isles was reached in close consultation with the British Government as part of our strategic plan to defeat the Axis aggressors. There was not, and is not now, the slightest thought or intention of invading Irish territory or of threatening Irish security. Far from constituting a threat to Ireland, the presence of these troops in neighbouring territory can only contribute to the security of Ireland and of the whole British Isles, as well as furthering our total war effort.

The sting was in the last paragraph:

> At some future date when Axis aggression has been crushed by the military might of free peoples, the nations of the earth must gather about a peace table to plan the future world on foundations of liberty and justice everywhere. I think it only right that I make plain at this time that when that time comes the Irish Government in its own best interest should not stand alone but should be associated with its traditional friends, and among them, the United States of America.

That 'stand alone' reference foreshadowed the isolation and stagnation which befell Ireland after the war. Throughout 1942 Roosevelt developed his 'absent treatment' policy towards de Valera. Gray had made a number of more drastic recommendations, which included shutting off supplies of petrol in retaliation for Ireland not exporting foodstuffs to Britain, and refusing to allow unarmed neutral ships to travel in American convoys.[69] He also drew up contingency plans for an American invasion of Ireland and the setting up of a puppet Government in the event that de Valera 'went to the hills, as Aiken would probably advise him to do'.[70] He

made this proposal following the resignation of James Dillon from the Fine
Gael deputy leadership in the spring of 1942 on the neutrality issue. Prior
to this he had advised Roosevelt that, if it became necessary to seize the
ports:[71] 'the demand be publicised and forced into the Irish legislature for
debate'. He had been assured by Dillon that if such a debate occurred he
could 'split the country'. After Dillon's resignation he preferred 'the fait
accompli' approach. 'Probably a great flight of planes dropping leaflets
would be the best way of doing this about the time the demands were
presented to de Valera.' If de Valera ordered his troops to fire on
American troops: 'a few well placed bombs on the Irish barracks at the
Curragh and in the Dublin area would be the most merciful way of shutting
off opposition'.[72]

Roosevelt 'read with interest' Gray's views on the possibility of it
becoming 'necessary for us to follow a more positive course in Ireland'.[73]
However, he decided to take a less sanguinary route than that advocated
by Gray. Although, as he made quite clear, everything Gray did was done
with his approval – and his post-war plans for Ireland in partnership with
Churchill have already been noted on p. 546 – Roosevelt's choice of policy
has to be regarded as being actuated more by concern for South Boston's
reaction than for that of Southern Ireland. He wrote Gray a letter on
16 September 1942 which both outlined the 'absent treatment policy' and
illustrates the background for what blew up into the greatest Dublin–
Washington crisis of the entire war, the 'American note' affair of February
1944.

The President began by complimenting Gray on his work:[74] 'Several
people who have come back from, or passed through Ireland, have told me
what a perfectly magnificent job you are doing. I did not have to be told
that because I knew it, for the very simple fact that you have not given me
the remote shadow of a headache all these years.' Not so Eamon de
Valera. The letter continued:

> I am inclined to think that my policy of giving Dev the absent treatment is about
> as effective as anything else. The other day one of his friends over here – a typical
> professional Irish American – came in to tell me about the terrible starvation
> among the people of Ireland. I looked at him in a much interested way and
> remarked quietly 'Where is Ireland?'

The last paragraph contains the kind of thinking that led to the 'American
note':

> I do wish the people as a whole over there could realise that Dev is unnecessarily
> storing up trouble because most people over here feel that Dublin, by maintaining
> German spies and by making all the little things difficult for the United Nations, is
> stirring up a thoroughly unsympathetic attitude toward Ireland as a whole when
> we win the war. That is a truly sad state of affairs.

By coincidence, in his acknowledgement Gray describes[75] an incident involving de Valera which may provide at least part of the reason he was so resolute in 'storing up trouble'. Gray told Roosevelt:

> A very nice fellow, Matthews, editor of a Tucson newspaper, was here a week ago. In his talk with the Prime Minister, the latter let the cat out of the bag. Matthews said, 'Aren't you afraid that your policy which operates almost wholly in the interest of Germany will cause trouble for you after the war?' Dev answered, 'No, because when the war ends, Britain and America will quarrel and then America will see that we were right.'

Gray commented: 'At that, Dev may get away with it.' But in the same letter he warned Roosevelt prophetically: 'Dev will try to get me.' As his diary entry in 'Behind the Green Curtain' shows, he had recently been told by Mulcahy that de Valera had said at a meeting of the Defence Council that he would have asked for Gray's recall were it not for his relationship with Roosevelt.

A notable example of the 'absent treatment' occurred later that month when Eleanor Roosevelt visited the American installations in the Six Counties. On 26 October, Gray informed Joseph Walshe[76] that it would not be possible for her to accept the Irish Government's offer to 'recognise her presence here in some appropriate and gracious manner'. His explanation was that, though she was the President's wife, she had no official status and that once her designated task of visiting the Six Counties was over she would revert to private citizenship and as such could not be 'received officially'. However, as he told Roosevelt, he was less diplomatic at a lunch with Sean T. O'Ceallaigh, who had tested him by remarking innocently how 'shocked' he was that Eleanor Roosevelt had passed through Ireland and his Government had accorded her no honour:[77] 'I started to say that as her husband was Commander in Chief of the United States forces whose presence in Northern Ireland the Irish Government had protested – At that point your aunt shushed me violently but I think the point got over.' In his reply Roosevelt saw nothing in the incident to criticize, but thanked the Grays for their gift of Irish linen handkerchiefs, saying, in terms that indicated little regard for de Valera:[78] 'I am proud to know that the Irish still can turn out linen like that. A practical virtue under an impracticable or perhaps unpractical leadership.' Nor did he contradict a statement of Gray's in another letter to him that month:[79] 'Of course you know better than I that British policy towards Eire follows our lead and intends to for the Duration [of the war].'

In this climate of opinion, with American troops very visible in Northern Ireland and Roosevelt making himself equally conspicuously 'absent' in Washington, Gray received an invitation to dinner at Claridge's Hotel in London from the American Ambassador to Britain, John Winant. The purpose of the dinner, which took place on 17 November 1942, was 'to discuss the Irish question with special reference to American interests'.[80] Present were Clement Attlee, Minister of State for the Dominions;

Herbert Morrison, Home Secretary; Lord Cranborne, then Minister for the Colonies and shortly to become Lord Privy Seal; and Sir John Maffey. The group discussed the larger issue of how, after the war, the Anglo-Irish problem could be removed from American politics and with it all the embarrassments it caused. The British, who with the exception of Maffey all seemed to be suffering from overwork and general disgust with Ireland, had no long-term strategy in mind. There was a very broad discussion of every aspect of Irish–English relationships both constitutional and economic. It was agreed from the British side that, while the North could not be coerced, the ending of partition was highly desirable. Gray told the gathering of de Valera's expectation of post-war differences between America and Britain. Ironically his central point was that, in a post-war world, whatever Ireland's status, the important point to ensure was that she could never be used as a base from which to attack Britain. The safeguarding of Britain from attack was, of course, Michael Collins' old argument, and de Valera's central plank in his neutrality policy.

But it was Maffey who suggested that, in the short term, one positive step to be taken would be to call for the removal of the Axis diplomatic representatives from Dublin. It was this idea which was destined to create the greatest storm in a teacup between de Valera and the Allies of the entire war period. It also served to provide history with one of the best examples on record of a de Valera fact.

28

GETTING DE VALERA
ON THE RECORD

THE IDEA GESTATED over the next few days throughout similar long-
and short-term discussions between Gray, Maffey and James Dillon, and
then, on 29 November 1942, at a high-level lunch in Downing Street hosted
by Churchill, at which de Gaulle was also a guest. At this Churchill
informed Gray that, though the ports would have been valuable earlier on,
the war had now reached a stage at which it could be won without them.
Thus, freed from considerations of issues like forcible seizure and puppet
Governments, Gray again developed his thesis on the need to remove the
Irish American element from US politics. It was during this conversation
that he made the suggestion to which Roosevelt was attracted about
offering Ireland a punitive self-sufficiency on the basis of both supplying
and protecting herself.

Such generalized conversations continued in British, American and
Canadian decision-taking circles. In February Maffey and John Kearney,
the Canadian High Commissioner in Dublin, told Gray they were
exchanging views on their countries' relationship with Eire. The bottom
line was that neither was happy at the prospect of de Valera being able to
take advantage of post-war benefits such as Commonwealth preference or
United Nations membership without having borne the responsibilities
involved. Gray packed the Canadian and British approach into the saddle-
bags of his Irish American hobby-horse and on 14 May 1943 produced a
lengthy memo[1] for the State Department. He recommended that the Allies
make a demand to de Valera for the ports. He did not expect it to be
granted, but he wanted the refusal on the record when, as expected, the
Irish societies, masterminded by de Valera, came to life again in the USA
after the war: 'The important thing from the view-point of Anglo-
American co-operation is to bring to the notice of the American people the
unfair and destructive policy of the de Valera politicians at the time when
British and American interests are essentially the same and to obtain a
verdict of American disapproval which will remove the pressure of the
Irish question from Anglo-American relations.' Roosevelt liked the memo.
He sent it to the Secretary of State, saying:[2] 'I think Mr. Gray is right in his
desire to put de Valera on record. We shall undoubtedly be turned down. I
think the strongest fact is that we are losing many American and British
lives and many ships in carrying various supplies to Ireland without
receiving anything in return, and without so much as a "Thank you".'

However, the matter lay fallow for several months. The military view of the ports' importance both in Britain and the USA was that expressed by Churchill – their hour of importance had passed. Politically the British Cabinet had little will for a confrontation. There were three factors weighing against making a demand for the ports. First, there was a suspicion amongst United Kingdom traders that the Americans had their eyes on Irish markets. Second, even at that late stage of de Valera's demonstration of the Twenty-six Counties' sovereignty there was:[3] 'the bureaucratic view which is reluctant to recognise Eire as not a dominion and under British tutelage'. Third, Gray wrote:[4] ' . . . possibly no one in the British Cabinet except Churchill and Morrison appreciates clearly the desirability of placing de Valera on the record from the viewpoint of the American situation. There is little accurate knowledge of de Valera or of his political strategy in British Government circles, and so long as he is making no immediate trouble, the "better not" school of thought in the Cabinet gains ground.'

What Gray did not know at this stage was that the 'better not' school included the OSS. R. Nicholas Carter, the Irish Desk officer at OSS's Washington office, was using reports from their field officers in Ireland to 'block a strident note on the issue of Irish neutrality which was being sought by Minister Gray'.[5] The military in Britain and the USA were pleased with the way Irish neutrality worked in practice, as a little-known story of the period illustrates.

Martin Quigley, an American OSS officer who used the film industry as a cover for his Irish sojourn, struck up a friendship with Emmet Dalton, who was also in the film business. Dalton, a Dubliner who had served in the British Army, was a heroic figure of the Anglo-Irish war. A friend of Collins, he had accompanied him on his fatal last journey to Beal na mBlath and was ever afterwards accused by some of having shot Collins at the behest of British intelligence. Of my own knowledge Dalton was approached by Lord Mountbatten to command an Irish 'special operations' unit under him during World War II – the idea was that there would be Irish, Scottish, Welsh and English divisions; but Dalton declined this role. His family's understanding of his wartime activity is that he was a professional gambler, travelling from one race meeting to another. Whatever he was doing, he obviously had high-level access to British decision-takers. For Quigley, whose father also had high-level American access – to Roosevelt – devised a scheme:[6] ' . . . the British Government – with consent of the Eire Government [meaning at that time consent of de Valera] turning over the bases to the U.S.A. This would be in exchange for the guarantee of the American Government using its good offices at the end of the war to bring about the end of Partition.' Quigley believed, rightly, that: 'Neither the British Government nor the Government in Belfast could have resisted determined American pressure.'[7] However, the level of real co-operation between the Irish and the British, as opposed to the top-level sparring between Churchill and de Valera, was such that:[8] 'The plan died after Dalton had it referred directly to the top officials of the Imperial General Staff in England. The word sent back to Dalton . . . was that the British Military wanted no alteration to the existing situation.' As Quigley says, the 'aggressive Nazi bombings' would have 'devastated' the bases if the USA had taken them over; and the devastation, which of course would not have been confined to the bases, would have 'required relief and scarce materials and supplies if Eire became an official belligerent. Nazi bombings would require the diversion of military equipment.'

On top of this another OSS agent, Ervin Marlin, based in the American Embassy, had already informed his superiors that, contrary to Gray's beliefs, Irish intelligence efficiency was such that the threat from German spies was non-existent. Gray was displeased and asked for Marlin's recall.[9] However, as the Normandy landings approached it was finally decided that a note should be presented by the Americans with which the British would concur. This American-British approach was to contain a different demand from that which Gray had originally prepared, though it had the same object: getting de Valera's refusal of co-operation on the record. The Allies both wanted to continue the *de facto* wartime co-operation with the Irish and brand them (or at least de Valera) *de jure* as Nazi collaborators. The demand was, in fact, Maffey's original suggestion about removing the Axis diplomats. It was:[10] ' . . . Prepared in the first instance by Mr. David Gray . . . submitted to the British Government . . . . Mr. Eden . . . replied that the British Government concurs in this proposed draft and . . . will send a separate note supporting our request . . . . '

Gray presented it on 21 February 1944. Maffey fired the second barrel the following day. However, here it should be noted that, between the initial conversations about long-term political considerations held in Claridge's Hotel and No. 10 Downing Street an important security factor had been added to the equation. Shortly beforehand, on 16 and 19 December 1943, two Irishmen[11] captured by the Germans had been parachuted into Clare for espionage purposes. Both were captured and interned within hours of landing. However, they had both been provided with radio sets and this fact served to train the spotlight on a transmitter which had been troubling the Allies for years – that in the German Legation.

It had also been troubling de Valera, both because of Allied pressure and because the Irish security forces guessed that it had been used to supply intelligence about Irish defence matters to Berlin. The British had cracked Hempel's codes and supplied copies of the transcripts to Dublin. A broadcast of Hempel's in September 1939 is thought[12] to have been responsible for the sinking of the American ship *Iroquois* shortly after it sailed from Cobh. A British protest to Dublin about the use of the transmitter in 1941 caused de Valera to ask that the transmitter 'at least be limited to very urgent cases'.[13] The German air attacks on Northern Ireland hardened de Valera's attitude, and further pressure was exerted on Hempel by Walshe on 12 May 1941. Although still denying its existence, Hempel cabled Berlin in an apparently unsuccessful attempt to get permission to discontinue sending weather reports.[14] The transmitter is believed[15] to have been used to send a stream of weather reports in February 1942 which are said to have facilitated the escape of three important German warships through the English Channel from Brest: the *Scharnhorst*, the *Prinz Eugen* and the *Gneisenau*. Certainly in that month de Valera delivered an ultimatum to Hempel via Walshe:[16] ' . . . he must cease absolutely using the transmitter'. Otherwise de Valera would require its transfer 'to the custody of the Department'.[17]

However, even after this, Irish intelligence[18] found that the Germans were transmitting from Bettystown, Co. Meath, a coastal area in the north of the county within striking distance of the border. The episode of the Clare parachutists sealed the fate of the transmitter. It was handed over to an Irish intelligence officer and placed in a safe in the Munster and Leinster Bank in Dublin on 21 December 1943. Hempel and the Department of Foreign Affairs each held a set of keys; neither could open the safe except in the presence of the other.

It was against this background that Gray entered de Valera's study bearing his long-gestating note.[19] It referred to the common reports of impending Allied military activity on which the expulsion of the diplomats was based. It also made reference to the transmitters found on the captured parachutists and to the one in the German Legation which, though Gray did not realize it, was also under lock and key. The note continued as follows:

> We request, therefore, that the Irish Government take appropriate steps for the recall of German and Japanese representatives in Ireland. We should be lacking in candour if we did not state our hope that this action will take the form of severance of all diplomatic relations between Ireland and these two countries. You will readily understand the compelling reasons why we ask, as an absolute minimum, the removal of these Axis representatives, whose presence in Ireland must inevitably be regarded as constituting a danger to the lives of American soldiers and to the success of Allied military operations.

Gray reported that de Valera 'betrayed no anger as he had often done when confronted with an unacceptable proposal but looked very sour and grim'. He asked: 'Is this an ultimatum?' Gray replied to the effect that it was not, pointing out that the note contained no 'or else' clause. Gray summarized de Valera's reaction as follows: 'We have done all we could to prevent espionage directed against your interests and we can do and will do no more. As long as I am here my answer to this request must be – no.'

Substantively he gave the same answer to Maffey next day, but his style of receiving the British note was different. Maffey said: 'After perusing it he turned to me, white with indignation, and exclaimed, "This is an ultimatum. This is an outrage."' Maffey riposted that he would do the same were he in General Eisenhower's shoes with the same anxieties. De Valera argued that he had done everything possible to spare the British from such anxieties. When Maffey interjected: 'Everything except removing the root of them', he switched his attack. He objected to the presentation of a note on the grounds that Maffey and he had established a good working relationship which should have precluded such a step. But Maffey could recognize an effort to divide allies when he saw one, and refused to be cast as the Good Guy to Gray's Baddie. He said that the note was fully justified in view of the flagrancy of the Nazis' action in sending planes to Eire on espionage missions.

This shook de Valera and he abated the emotional tone of his response; but he made no concession to the subject matter of the note. His position was that it was an attempt to deprive Eire of both her neutrality and her independence. His official biography, however, makes it clear that he understood exactly the motive behind the démarche, and that he knew from Warnock's despatches and other sources that a German defeat was inevitable:[20] 'He knew, too, that the Note was drafted with a purpose in mind, beyond that of getting rid of the legation in Dublin. In a draft for a reply . . . he said: "The request was one to which it must have been known by the American Minister here, the Irish Government could not possibly accede . . . . It seemed designed therefore to put the Irish people in the wrong before the American public."'

He decided to defeat Gray's purpose by magnifying the calamity – by treating the note as if it were an ultimatum and attempting to divide the Allies. To this end he unleashed a mighty force-field of tension and speculation. As James Reston wrote in the *New York Times*:[21] All leaves in the Irish Army were cancelled immediately . . . . Special guards were placed over airfields, ports and other strategic positions. Bridges leading from Ulster into Southern Ireland were mined and the Irish Local Defence Volunteers were mobilised and armed.' The Cabinet held marathon sittings. The Defence Council were informed of the démarche. Word of a threatened invasion was leaked. Moving swiftly, de Valera called in the Canadian High Commissioner, John Kearney, before either Gray or Maffey had a chance to brief him, and lectured the surprised Kearney for an hour and a half on the iniquity of what had befallen. He asked his help in getting the notes withdrawn. Kearney, who thought the request reasonable and felt that the diplomats should be expelled, reported to Ottawa that the centrepiece of de Valera's indignation lay in the fact of formal notes being presented. These required formal answers, for the record. Kearney afterwards described his interview with de Valera to Maffey:[22]

> Mr. de Valera, very emotional and stubborn, complained that the notes were merely a political move, that they implied a direct threat to which Eire would

react, that interference with sovereignty of Eire would be resisted, and that the army and the country would fight . . . . He intended to summon the Dail and receive their endorsement of this renewal of the old struggle, this time against England, against America, against anybody.

This is exactly what he did. On the international front he attempted to parlay the American note into another Chanak incident involving the Dominions.[23] Making use of the phrase in Gray's document, 'as an absolute minimum', he succeeded in getting a degree of understanding. The use of the note methodology was queried, though there was fundamental agreement with its stated objectives. However, speaking at Cavan on 27 February de Valera sounded the tocsin: 'At any moment the war may come upon us and we may be called upon to defend our rights and our freedom with our lives. Should the day come we will all face our duty with the traditional courage of our race.'

All this was done and said with the world's media in one hand and the ballot box in the other. The day before his Cavan histrionics he had been officially informed that there was no question of an invasion involved. In Washington, Brennan had been formally told that American policy was still governed by the statement made by Roosevelt in 1942, after US troops arrived in the Six Counties; this guaranteed there would be no aggression against Ireland. There was no ultimatum. All de Valera would have to fear in this connection, a State Department spokesman said, was 'the wrath of American mothers' if the Axis mission resulted in the loss of their sons' lives. On top of this, Kearney had been cleared by both Ottawa and London to tell him that there was no question of an invasion.

Most telling of all was an embarrassing incident which occurred the night Gray delivered his note. This being an Irish crisis, an element of farce was a near-essential. While the Defence Council were in all-night session preparing to unleash the Legions of the Gael in a last stand against the forces of the Murdering British Oppressor, the phone rang. It was the British military attaché. He knew nothing about any note. All he wanted to find out was:[24] 'where the Irish Army would take delivery of the 500 motorcycles which he had procured for them'.

Both Maffey and Gray had forecast this reaction on de Valera's part. As we shall shortly examine, normal political life had to some extent continued in the Twenty-six Counties. At this stage a general election had left de Valera in a minority government situation. Maffey was afraid that de Valera would make use of the censorship to generate fresh martyrs, and certainly to create the atmosphere of 'a new blood sacrifice'. He warned London that de Valera was[25] 'a strange mixture of sincerity, hysteria and astuteness; from having led the country into a wilderness he now, as an Irish politician, sees new dynamic forces in the pent-up frustration of war years, in partition, fanned in the Catholic feelings of the moment'.

The 'Catholic feelings' were those excited by a statement in Cardinal MacRory's Lenten Pastoral which had given de Valera a boost and Fleet

Street a bone to gnaw on. The Cardinal had said that, in view of England's record in Ireland: 'Eire deserves credit for not having allied herself with the Axis nations and offered them hospitality and assistance.' Gray read the signs correctly and urged the State Department against leaving the Crown of Martyrdom anywhere within de Valera's reach. He advocated the 'token release of strategic materials' to sweeten Irish public opinion. And knowing the state of the British Prime Minister's emotions where de Valera was concerned, he warned of the dangers of a Churchillian denunciation: 'We might lose more than we have gained by such action.' Gray was an accurate prophet.

De Valera and he had another session when Gray called on him on 29 February to pass on formally what had already been told to Brennan in Washington – namely that there was no question of an American invasion. But now de Valera was moving the goalposts. He focused his criticism, not on the notes but on what he termed the State Department official's 'sinister' warning about the wrath of American mothers. He could see the implications of having such a remark stitched into the record. Gray too was alive to what de Valera was doing behind the smokescreen of invasion scares. He pointedly warned de Valera that if the story of the notes got into the papers it would not have come from either American or British sources. Dublin was awash with rumours, some of them remarkably well informed. A Legation official had been able to give Gray an accurate account of the contents of the American, British and Canadian communications to de Valera. The official had been given them from someone whom the normally closed-mouthed de Valera had apparently briefed.

He also briefed members of the Opposition on the contents of the American note, but made it clear that he was informing them and not consulting them about the terms his reply would take. However, he magnanimously agreed to allow them to see it, 'shortly *after* [author's italics] it was sent'.[26] Then, three days after he had spoken at Cavan, and a day after he had seen Gray again, with the rumour factory at full production, as the *Daily Express* records,[27] he brazenly 'hit out in the Dail at rumour mongers and appealed to deputies not to ask questions that could not be answered without embarrassing neutrality'. By this stage, as the *Express* said in its report, the stories had become: ' . . . still more fantastic, "The Allies have presented an ultimatum", "Mulcahy has been arrested and Deputy Dillon shot".' The report speculated that de Valera had been asked to make a démarche to Hempel and that he had been informed of his responsibility not to allow security leaks about the Second Front. The *Express* scoop caused some soreness between London and Washington: Eden had promised the Americans there would be no publicity without prior consultation between the Allies. The Ministry of Information became alarmed at the opportunities for German propaganda, and the censor was hurriedly sent around Fleet Street to ensure that the *Express* story was not followed up.

Then, with the heat turned up nicely to his liking, de Valera despatched his note of reply.[28] It was lengthy, and in tones of pained indignation confirmed his verbal rejection to Gray and Maffey. The Irish Government was surprised at a note of such grave character being addressed to it, in view of the tradition of friendship between the Americans and the Irish. There was a strong hint that the Americans had been misinformed. The Irish Government doubted whether such a note could have been presented if the American Government knew of 'the uniform friendly character of Irish neutrality in relation to the United States'.

> They [the Government] felt, moreover, that the American Government should have realised that the removal of representatives of a foreign state on the demand of the Government to which they are accredited is universally recognized as the first step towards war, and that the Irish Government could not entertain the American proposal without a complete betrayal of their democratic trust. Irish neutrality represented the united will of the people and parliament. It is the logical consequence of Irish history and of the forced partition of national territory.

This and the text of the American and British notes were published simultaneously on 11 March. The notes made a considerable impact in the press everywhere. Ireland's willingness to resist invasion made world headlines. And then, from Gray's point of view, Murphy's Law set in. The thing he had most dreaded occurred – Churchillian intervention. As part of the Normandy preparations the Allies had been contemplating curtailing communications with Ireland; but they overlooked the possibilities of these becoming mixed up with the notes controversy. Now, in the aftermath of the notes' publication, speculation began to appear in the papers concerning travel restrictions between Ireland and England and the possibilities of economic restrictions also.

The day after the travel restrictions forecast appeared, Churchill spoke in the House of Commons on 14 March in terms which transported the restrictions from the realms of juxtaposition to becoming the central issue. He said frankly that the note had been initiated by the Americans with British support. Measures had been taken to restrict the security risks posed by the Axis missions in Dublin, but now:

> ... these measures must be strengthened, and the restrictions on travel announced in the press yesterday are the first step in the policy designed to isolate Great Britain from Southern Ireland, and also to isolate Southern Ireland from the outer world during the critical period which is now approaching. I need scarcely say how painful it is to us to take such measures in view of the large numbers of Irishmen who are fighting so bravely in our armed forces and the many deeds of personal heroism by which they have kept alive the martial honour of the Irish race. No one, I think, can reproach us for precipitancy. No nation in the world would have been so patient.

De Valera could not have hoped for better had he timed and written the speech himself. Domestically it was worth an incalculable number of votes per syllable. Internationally it set the fires of the Chanak controversy blazing once more. The Canadian Government telegrammed the Dominions office:[29] 'In general it seems to us that the recent developments concerning Ireland are matters of high concern to all the members of the Commonwealth. We were not consulted in advance of the attempts to secure the removal of the Axis representatives nor were we informed of your intentions respecting travel restrictions . . . . If Ireland is moved to leave the Commonwealth this is a matter of serious moment to us.' In South Africa, Parliament was convulsed by an angry debate on the issue. The Opposition leader, Dr Malan, had sent de Valera a telegram of support. He foreshadowed his own breakaway from the Commonwealth in 1961 by arguing against Smuts, the Prime Minister, that Eire had the right to control its own external affairs and to remain neutral even if Britain went to war. This was not what Roosevelt had had in mind; the whole thing was travelling far from the original objective of simply putting de Valera on the record. He let Churchill know via Halifax that he did not wish to see sanctions imposed against Eire. Gray did not either, and he provoked a further outburst of Churchillian wrath when it was learned through Maffey that he was planning to write a letter to the Irish papers stating that no economic sanctions were envisaged. He also opposed the sending of a second note, as Cordell Hull advised, denying de Valera's contention 'that the American Government had been misinformed' and that the issue was one of 'Ireland's right to remain neutral'.[30] The British felt he was getting a 'bad attack of cold feet'.

Churchill told Cranborne that it would be 'very wrong for them [the Americans] to explain it all away and leave us out in the open'. To Roosevelt he wrote:[31]

> Gray's lead in Ireland has been followed by us and it is too soon to begin reassuring de Valera. A doctor telling his patient that medicine prescribed for his nerve trouble is only coloured water is senseless. To keep them guessing for a while would be much better in my opinion. I think that we should let fear work its healthy process, rather than allay alarm in de Valera's circles. In that way we shall get a continued stiffening up of the Irish measures behind the scenes. At the moment these are not so bad as to prevent a leakage.

All Churchill envisaged, he said, was the cutting of outgoing communications – phone calls, shipping from Ireland – and not essential supplies inward. A new generation of British officialdom was becoming uneasily aware of the truth of what a former colleague of Churchill's, Lloyd George, had once said of de Valera: 'Negotiating with him is like trying to pick up a blob of mercury with a fork.' A civil servant minuted Churchill's communication to Roosevelt: 'This will require very careful watching. President Roosevelt having got what he wanted, i.e. Mr. de Valera on the record as careless of the lives of American soldiers, is now endeavouring to place his own baby firmly in our arms, and what is more, to make us pay the paternity order.' Maffey too was aghast: the failure to make it clear that the planned restrictions were military, not punitive, meant that:[32] 'British and American Governments are now on different courses. American Note has fallen into the background. American Minister has given the Eire Government every assurance that there is no intention of following it up in any way. Indeed I see signs of desire to assist Eire e.g. in permitting importation of steel for Irish Sugar Co. Action in the field of restriction is to be British action.'

Finally, on 27 March 1944, despite Churchill's pronouncements on the virtues of fear's 'healthy process', Maffey was given clearance by London to tell de Valera all was well. The planned restrictions and any consequential shortages would be temporary and of a military character. There was a passage of arms during which de Valera spoke 'bitterly' of the wording of the American note, but the meeting ended amicably. De Valera informed Maffey that, though it had suffered, their old relationship would be re-established. Maffey reported to London:[33] 'Having latterly grown somewhat doubtful as to whether the episode of the notes would after all work out to our advantage, I now feel satisfied that the instructions given me have turned the scales to our great advantage, now, and I trust, in the future.'

Gray was inclined to a similar interpretation, albeit expressed in his own inimitable way. De Valera had tried to subject him to pressure during the crisis. The *Irish Press* attacked him editorially and splashed Brennan's charge that the American action had been taken on 'inaccurate information' supplied by him.[34] He was told that it would be desirable in view of the state of public feeling for him to have an armed guard in the grounds of Phoenix Park and an escort car. However he declined both,[35] pointing out that after delivering the note to de Valera he had gone fishing in Adare, Co. Limerick and driven through Ireland with the American flag flying without encountering any hostility. (Had de Valera realized where he was going there might have been some hostility. Gray went to the Maigue, which flows through Bruree!) Nor did he ever encounter anything untoward in his normal peregrinations around Dublin. He thought that whatever tension there was would 'steadily decline if not kept alive by designed agitation'. Had there been no leaks, he pointed out, 'our request would have been made and refused and no one would have been the wiser until the post-war white papers were issued'. And, with a pointed thrust worthy of de Valera himself, he turned down the offer of protection because of 'the probable effect on American public opinion if the story got to America that an American Minister was not safe in Eire'. He told Roosevelt that:[36]

As far as I can see the Irish note has been a success and in a long range view of things I do not think that De Valera will have much chance of making us trouble over partition . . . . The way to handle this ugly group of bad hats is to tell them to

607

go sit on a tack . . . . I have given up appeasing which gets one nowhere . . . . At the same time in looking ahead we must not allow any food shortages though we must make them sit up and ask . . . . They are entirely without gratitude and what we give must be used primarily for the play of our own hand.

So who really won the match? Gaelic football terminology would seem appropriate in determining the result. Gray and Roosevelt did score a point. They had de Valera on the record. Gray felt that:[37] ' . . . the time may come when it would be advisable for you [Roosevelt] to characterise it as an insult to the American people that any foreigner should attempt to inject himself into American politics with racial pressure group methods. This war should have put an end to hyphens.' However in Gaelic football a goal counts as three points. De Valera scored the decisive goal. The 'cute hoor' had put on the jersey of Statesman throughout the note crisis. He had united the country behind his stand. On top of this, the Irish Labour Party was going through a bad patch at the time of the controversy. In January it had split into two factions: one led by James Connolly's old colleague, Jim Larkin, the other by William O'Brien who led the powerful Irish Transport and General Workers' Union. Moreover, W. T. Cosgrave resigned from politics; his health had never recovered from the strain of the civil war following on 'the troubles'. Less than a month after Gray had sent his letter about the 'hyphens' to Roosevelt de Valera saw his chance of putting a full stop to minority government.

Gallagher described what happened in a note, made for biographical purposes, which shows how completely his mind had become infused with de Valera thought:[38] 'Irish backs were straighter because of de Valera's reply, and the necessity for a general election having arisen soon afterwards the memory of it gave de Valera the second-greatest victory he had ever had at the polls.' What happened was that on 9 May he was defeated in the Dail on an unimportant vote on a transport bill. He immediately resigned, although his biography says he could have carried a vote of confidence the following day. A general election was held on 30 May and de Valera emerged with a far more glittering prize than a mere vote of confidence: Fianna Fail won 76 seats, 14 more than all other parties combined.

A week later D-Day occurred; the Allies landed in Normandy and eventually swept on to Berlin and victory. And so the man of impractical leadership whose comparison with the good people of Dutchess County would have been 'unfair' to the latter, in Roosevelt's eyes, survived not only Roosevelt's pressures but also those of Churchill, Hitler and David Gray. True, as the war blew over there were a few retreating squalls between the Allies and de Valera, one of them a tempest, but Bernard Shaw's well-known comment summed up his achievement correctly. Writing in the wake of the notes controversy, he said: 'Neutrality seemed a crack-brained line to take, yet Mr. de Valera got away with it . . . that powerless little cabbage garden called Ireland wins in the teeth of all the mighty Powers. *Erin go Bragh* [Ireland for ever].'

By one of the ironies of history Roosevelt did not live to see the victory of which he was the principal architect, and died of a brain haemorrhage on 12 April 1945. De Valera immediately sent a message of sympathy to President Truman, saying: 'America has lost a great man and a noble leader.' Despite all that had passed between Roosevelt and himself during the war de Valera had his biographers say for the record[39] that 'he had held Roosevelt in great esteem'. And in the Dail he paid tribute to the fallen titan in a speech whose priorities showed what he believed a politician's greatest attribute to be – winning: 'President Roosevelt will go down to history as one of the greatest of a long line of American Presidents with the unparalleled distinction of having been elected four times as head of the United States. That was the greatest tribute that could be paid to any man. It is also a measure of his loss. Personally, I regard his death as a loss to the world . . . . ' He went on to say that Roosevelt could have been relied upon to throw his great powers into the creation of a new world order which would possibly save mankind from 'recurring calamities' like the present war. Gray was moved by his oratory and wrote to Eleanor Roosevelt next day:[40] 'This is indeed a strange country. All this afternoon members of the Government, their wives and leaders of the opposition have been coming in a stream to pay their respects. Mr. de Valera made a very moving tribute to the President in the Dail this morning and moved an adjournment till tomorrow. I thought I knew this country and its people but this was something new. There was a great deal of genuine feeling.'

However a couple of weeks later, on 30 April 1945, the de Valera–Gray duelling resumed. Renewing his campaign against the Axis diplomats, the previous September Gray had tried and failed to get de Valera to give assurances that 'Axis war criminals' would not be given asylum in Ireland after the war ended. Now, before Hempel had a chance to destroy archive material, he wanted the keys of the German Legation to be handed over. He claimed that the material in the Legation would yield information on submarine warfare. The interview evidently did not go well. Gray said afterwards that as he read the memorandum:[41] 'Mr. de Valera grew red and looked very sour. He was evidently annoyed, but his manners were correct. When I finished, he slapped the copy of the memorandum which I had presented on his desk and said "This is a matter for my legal advisors. It is not a matter that I can discuss with you now . . . ."'

Once again, apparently, Gray had scored a point. He reported to the State Department that the Irish Government was on the record once more for refusing 'the opportunity of co-operating with us in a friendly and non-legislative way'.[42] This time, however, he may have been instrumental in doing more: this visit and his overall bad relationship with de Valera may have had some bearing on the fact that shortly afterwards de Valera scored an uncharacteristic own goal. Unknown to either Gray or de Valera, Hitler was in his bunker preparing to commit suicide as they were talking. Two days later, on 2 May 1945, the Irish papers carried the news of the Führer's death. On the same day, despite strong representations from Boland and Walshe, de Valera called on Hempel 'to express condolence'. But by now the advancing Allied armies had uncovered the horrors of the Nazi death camps and the visit aroused worldwide criticism. De Valera defended his action in a letter to Brennan in which he bracketed his action with Gray's attitude:[43]

> I have noted that my call on the German Minister on the announcement of Hitler's death was played up to the utmost. I expected this. I could have had a diplomatic illness but, as you know, I would scorn that sort of thing . . . . So long as we retained our diplomatic relations with Germany, to have failed to call upon the German representative would have been an act of unpardonable discourtesy to the German nation and to Dr. Hempel himself. During the whole of the war, Dr. Hempel's conduct was irreproachable. He was always friendly and inevitably correct – *in marked contrast to Gray* [author's italics]. I certainly was not going to add to his humiliation in the hour of defeat.

He went on to say that his action should not have 'special significance' attached to it: ' . . . such as connoting approval or disapproval of the State in question, or of its head'. Maffey's interpretation of the visit was that de Valera:[44]

> . . . had taken a very unwise step. Obstinately and mathematically consistent – stung perhaps by the most recent assault on his principles, ie, by the request for . . . the German archives before VE day – he decided to get a mention for a conspicuous act of neutrality in the field. He would at least show that he was no 'bandwaggoner'. He therefore called on the German Legation in Dublin to express his personal condolences on the death of Hitler . . . but . . . with the sudden end of the censorship there came also atrocity stories, pictures of Buchenwald etc. . . . . a sense of disgust slowly manifested itself . . . .

It is not likely that this disgust would have ever manifested itself in damaging electoral form, given the size of de Valera's parliamentary majority, but in any case the question of retribution for his blunder was suddenly rendered otiose. Churchill snatched him from the fires of contumely more dramatically, and with even greater reward, than he had done during the notes issue. In the course of his victory speech on 13 May 1945 Churchill referred to the Battle of Britain, the blitz and the Battle of the Atlantic, when it seemed that the U-boat wolf packs were about to cut Britain's lifelines to the USA. He said:

> This sense of envelopment which might at any moment turn to strangulation, lay heavy upon us . . . . Owing to the action of Mr. de Valera, so much at variance with the temper and instinct of thousands of Southern Irishmen who hastened to the battle-front to prove their ancient valour, the approaches which the southern Irish ports and airfields could so easily have guarded were closed by the hostile aircraft and U-boats. This was indeed a deadly moment in our life, and if it had not been for the loyalty and friendship of Northern Ireland we should have been

forced to come to close quarters with Mr. de Valera or perish for ever from the earth. However with a restraint and poise to which, I say, history will find few parallels, His Majesty's Government never laid a violent hand upon them, though at times it would have been quite easy and quite natural, and we left the de Valera Government to frolic with the Germans and later with the Japanese to their heart's content.

As the *Irish Press* reported on 17 May, de Valera's reply was the 'most eagerly awaited public pronouncement for many years'. Excitement mounted in the country as he deliberately delayed his reply. In Dublin the streets became deserted as the time for the broadcast approached. Pubs, and dancehalls fitted with loudspeakers, filled to capacity. Neighbours congregated in each other's homes to crowd around radios. It was remarked that, when he came to the portion of his speech replying to Churchill, there was absolute silence in bars and homes. After a lengthy review of the course of the war, prefaced by a tribute in Irish to the Gaelic speakers who had helped to throw a shield around the country, he said:[45]

Certain newspapers have been very persistent in looking for my answer to Mr. Churchill's recent broadcast. I know the kind of answer I am expected to make. I know the answer that first springs to the lips of every man of Irish blood who heard or read that speech, no matter in what circumstances or in what part of the world he found himself. I know the reply I would have given a quarter of a century ago. But I have deliberately decided that it is not the reply I shall make tonight.

Allowances can be made for Mr. Churchill's statement, however unworthy, in the first flush of his victory. No such excuse could be found for me in this quieter atmosphere . . . . Mr. Churchill makes it clear that in certain circumstances he would have violated our neutrality and that he would justify his action by Britain's necessity. It seems strange to me that Mr. Churchill does not see that this, if accepted, would mean that Britain's necessity would become a moral code and that when this necessity became sufficiently great, other people's rights were not to count . . . this same code is precisely why we have the disastrous succession of wars . . . shall it be world war?

It is indeed fortunate that Britain's necessity did not reach the point where Mr. Churchill would have acted. All credit to him that he successfully resisted the temptation . . . . By resisting his temptation in this instance, Mr. Churchill, instead of adding another horrid chapter to the already bloodstained record of the relations between England and this country, has advanced the cause of international morality an important step – one of the most important, indeed, that can be taken on the road to the establishment of any sure basis for peace.

Mr. Churchill is proud of Britain's stand alone, after France had fallen and before America entered the war. Could he not find in his heart the generosity to acknowledge that there is a small nation that stood alone, not for one year or two, but for several hundred years against aggression, that endured spoliations, famines, massacres in endless succession, that was clubbed many times into insensibility, but that each time on returning consciousness took up the fight anew, a small nation that could never be got to accept defeat and has never surrendered her soul?

Cheering broke out all over the city as he finished. When he appeared outside the radio station in Henry Street a large crowd jostled his protecting Gardai aside to shake his hand and congratulate him. The telephone in his office rang all night with messages of congratulation. He got a standing ovation when he entered the Dail the next day. The *Irish Times*, which, being accused of outspokenness, had suffered most under the censorship, said on 18 May: 'The Taoiseach's broadcast reply to Mr. Churchill was as temperate as it was dignified. Mr. de Valera has his faults as a statesman and as a politician; but he has one outstanding quality. He is a gentleman.'

The lion's tail had been used to unprecedented effect, and one man who realized this was Winston S. Churchill. Discussing the speech shortly after it had been made, his son Randolph told Frank Gallagher that his father 'didn't like it and . . . was very quiet for a long time after it was delivered'. Another was Sir John Maffey. He wrote to Sir Eric Machtig, the Dominions Office Permanent Under Secretary: 'How are you to control Ministerial incursions into your china shop? Phrases make history here.' Maffey's considered opinion was:[46]

'Absent treatment' would not have presented Mr. de Valera with this opportunity of escape from the eclipse which had closed down on him and the Irish Question . . . . Mr de Valera assumed the role of elder statesman and skilfully worked on all the old passions in order to dramatise the stand taken by Eire in this war. So long as he can work his mystique over Irishmen in all parts of the world Mr. de Valera does not worry about the rest of humanity.

Kearney was similarly affected. He had been horrified by the Legation visit after Hitler's death, regarding it as a 'slap in the face', but as a Commonwealth diplomat he could recognize that there were advantages to be gained from it. Now, however, his reaction to Churchill's speech and de Valera's reply was: 'We had him on a plate. We had him where we wanted him. But look at the papers this morning!'

There had been another moment during the war when de Valera had displayed nobility, and it had apparently found a measure of accord on the part of all the belligerents: the saving of Rome.[47] In March 1944 he had circulated the belligerent powers with an appeal to save the Eternal City, on behalf of both Irish Catholics and 'the three hundred million Catholics throughout the world'. What part his initiative played in the Powers' decision to spare Rome cannot be stated with accuracy, but he did receive from the city's artistic community a note of thanks saying: 'The memory of this noble gesture on the part of Ireland's Prime Minister will pass on also to future generations.'

And so World War II ended for Eamon de Valera. Its conclusion had been marked by some Protestant students burning the Irish tricolour from the roof of Trinity College. For those with a taste for symbolism, there is significance in the fact that two Catholic students riposted by burning a

Union Jack in College Green. The young tigers were reaching for the lion's tail. One of the two was Charles Haughey, who was destined one day to become Taoiseach. But at that time, questions of who would succeed him in the future were not troubling Eamon de Valera. He was concerned with those who dared oppose him in the present.

In 1946 he told the Dail:[48] 'Ultimately in my opinion, the question whether our neutrality was going to be accepted depended upon the concurrence of wills of two individuals.' He made it clear that this was 'a very serious and a very anxious situation in which to have this country'. Then he explained to the Parliament that the two were Franklin Delano Roosevelt and Winston Spencer Churchill. He did not mention Adolf Hitler in this regard. Nor did he mention David Gray. But from the end of the war he turned his full force against Gray, with whom he most emphatically had not had a concurrence of will.

His campaign began less than a month after his triumphant rejoinder to Churchill. On 11 June 1945 Walshe cabled Brennan in Washington, inquiring if he could[49] 'talk strongly to some influential politician who would put an end to Gray's career'. Amongst the many reasons advanced why this should be done were:

> ... the continued unfitness of David Gray for promoting good relations between this country and the United States. It would be quite inconceivable for any other country in the world to send and maintain a Minister who has been doing such harm to his country as this gentleman. He has never missed an opportunity of showing his anti-Irish spleen and of encouraging anti-Irish elements in this country to take an attitude hostile to the State .... The general attitude of the Irish people towards David Gray is one of complete astonishment that the representative of the democratic United States of America should pass at least four days out of every seven with a group of effete nobles who are more violently anti-Irish than the worst John Bull in Britain. He is a toady of the worst type ....

Brennan replied on 18 June: 'I will see what I can do about G, in the next few weeks', and drew Walshe's attention to some of Gray's misdemeanours. These included accusing de Valera of keeping the Irish people in ignorance of the moral issues involved in the war for five years and not acknowledging how his country had been 'dependent on the Allies for supplies'. Heinous crimes indeed. But not sufficient to cause the Truman administration to shift Gray. Walshe was told to try again.

On 24 April 1946 he cabled Brennan that, amongst a litany of crimes, Gray had 'even handed out to visiting journalists propaganda hostile to the Taoiseach and the Irish Government ... '. What Gray had done was given out copies of Donal O'Sullivan's book *The Irish Free State and Its Senate*. It was in this cable that Walshe referred to Gray as being persona non grata with the Irish Government. But the Truman administration had dropped the bomb on Japan and were inured to the horrors of the world. Not only did Gray stay, he was empowered to call on de Valera to ask for 'such measure of co-operation in regard to German property and personnel as would indicate the acceptance of the principle that Germany and Italy criminally conspired against the peace of the world and world civilisation'. What Gray sought was the sequestration of the former and the return of the latter to their country of origin. Worse, he said that 'the American Government and the American people hoped earnestly that the frictions which had developed between the United States and Ireland during the war might cease and that the long-standing friendship between the two nations might be resumed'.

De Valera had certain ideas as to the basis on which the 'long-standing friendship' might be restored. They included neither Gray, nor the principle that he advocated. Even though the American threw out a pretty broad hint about the 'excepting on compassionate grounds of specific individuals' – which, decoded, meant Hempel – de Valera replied:

> ... the Irish people set great store by the right of asylum and would be unable to understand his actions in the case that he gave up German officials and agents ... the German Minister, to the best of his knowledge and belief, had behaved with correctness during the period of the war ... the Minister was a very decent man and ... he could not bring himself to return him to a Germany without a government of its own and in extreme economic disorder.

Eventually de Valera's pressure began to tell, even against a member of the Roosevelt clan. As America went into a presidential election period, during which the Irish American societies were again beginning to put their heads over the parapet following the war, the administration sent a signal to Dublin. On 31 December Brennan cabled Walshe a report on an overture made by the State Department. Two junior officers from the Irish section of the Department had taken M. L. Skentelbery from the Irish Legation to lunch to inform him that: 'They were both very perturbed at the present state of Irish–American relations, and they feel that Gray is to blame ... neutrality had not been properly understood by the American people and had been wrongly interpreted, which was a great pity .... Gray has a sincere love for the country ... [but] does not appreciate Irish Nationalism, and is blind to present day Irish politics and realities ... '. Skentelbery's report concluded: 'Naturally I was very surprised at two officers of the State Department going out of their way to say all these things to me, and I wondered whether it was pure altruism on their part or whether the whole thing was done at the instance of persons on a higher level ... '. Indeed!

The issue was pressed home by de Valera a few weeks later when a new Secretary of State was installed in Washington. Brennan was instructed on 25 January 1947 to use the occasion 'to mention G. You might say we regret relations with U.S.A. are not more warm and cordial. We attribute this entirely to influence of Gray and see no prospect of improvement so long as he remains. He has done more than any American in history to create misunderstanding and bad feeling between the two countries.' On

19 February Brennan reported that contacts had informed him that efforts by leading Democrats to get Gray removed had proved unsuccessful in the face of 'Mrs. Roosevelt's influence'. Even the powerful John McCormack, Chief Whip of the Democratic Party in the House, said he could not touch the question of Gray 'because of the Roosevelt connection'.[50] However, Brennan was informed by a close confidant of Truman's that: 'I don't think it can go on much longer.'

It did not: David Gray left Ireland on 28 June 1947. Sinead de Valera sent Maude Gray a charming note in which she said: 'My prayers and good wishes go with you and the Minister for every happiness and good fortune.'[51] But according to Joseph Walshe, 'no tears were shed' at the departure of this 'turbulent representative'.[52] However, at an official dinner to mark his departure de Valera delivered a speech:[53] 'which everyone present – including David Gray himself – acclaimed as a masterpiece . . . . There was not an insincere word in it, but it was without the slightest trace of bitterness or ill-feeling . . . . David was moved by the speech and replied not ungenerously . . . describing the Taoiseach as one of the greatest living statesmen.'

The veneer of official courtesy was heightened by a last felicitous touch from de Valera, who ordered an Irish Navy corvette to take Gray to the SS *America* off Cobh instead of 'leaving him to the discomforts of the public tender'.[54] However, a truer indication of the state of the two men's leave-taking emerges from the record which Gray, wary to the end, kept of their last conversation.[55] De Valera said that he had attached peculiar significance to Gray's arrival in 1940 since he knew Gray was a close friend of President Roosevelt. The suggestion that he had been selected for Ireland on that account he believed to be baseless. He hoped that past differences could now be adjusted. De Valera knew, of course, that Gray was aware of his having spoken publicly of Gray's recall being demanded were it not for the Roosevelt connection. The adjustment of differences reference clearly implied that the improvement was contingent on Gray's departure.

However, Gray gave as good as he got. He pointed out to de Valera that, so long as he maintained a propaganda agitation in the United States which put pressure on the American administration, grievance and irritation would result. No Government enjoyed having its foreign policy influenced by minority pressure groups. He went on to point out that in future Ireland and Britain would constitute a strategic bridgehead in Europe which could be crucial in case of war with Russia. Ireland's security, like the economy, being bound up with Britain dictated a recognition of some principle of co-operation. At this Gray noted: 'Mr de Valera broke in here, with some vehemence, and said: "We are free but only in part. We can take no part in the kind of thing you suggest while this wrong to our six north eastern counties continues."'

Gray did not abate the 'vehemence' by asking him if he wanted the USA to conquer the Six Counties and hand them over to him. After de Valera had replied: 'Of course not', Gray then suggested that: 'The only other course is in your own hands; that is to make conditions so desirable in Eire that the North will wish to join you.' To which de Valera replied: 'But if we cannot ask you to coerce the six counties why should the Protestant majority coerce the Nationalist minorities in two of them?' Gray said of their exchange: 'As so often before he stood adamant on what he calls his "rights" and we go nowhere.' As they were being photographed shaking hands, he said to de Valera: '"I am going to be repeating "God bless you" so as to give me a benign expression", and, I added, "I do really mean it."'

Gray noted: 'At that we parted.' He ended his memorandum by making the following assessment of de Valera's thinking:

1) He believes that his mission is to save Ireland.
2) Believing this, it is essential that he should remain in power.
3) To continue in power the Nationalistic issue of partition is essential.
4) To achieve the ending of partition would be equivalent to relinquishing power since the Northern Counties would be represented in the Dail by 36 Protestant members.

Another diplomat also excited de Valera's wrath during the war years; this time it was an Irishman, L. H. Kearney, who was Minister to Madrid. That some serious cloud hung over Kearney's name in de Valera's Department is evidenced by a reference in a letter from Walshe:[56] 'The Madrid betrayal, so far, has been glossed over. It would be a pity to have the whole ugly business brought on the tapis just now. Have you spoken to Dan Bryan? He will remember the recurrence of the name in question in the British black list, and the fact that the chief British agents insisted on showing it both to him and to me.' Walshe was referring to an important series of articles in the *Irish Press* by the distinguished Irish historian Professor Desmond Williams. These articles, an extended version of a series that Williams had previously written for the opinion journal, the *Leader* throughout January and April, appeared in the *Irish Press* in June and July 1953. They aroused enormous interest and their worth was assessed by Walshe as follows:[57] 'For the first time a qualified historian, trained in England and, therefore, more likely to be accepted as impartial in this matter, writes what is, on the whole, a serene, impartial, concrete and really splendid account of the policy of neutrality as conceived and executed by the Taoiseach during the war.'

Kearney did not share this view and asked that a lengthy report made by him in August 1942 should be published 'so as to obviate the necessity of his taking legal action'.[58] His request was turned down by the Department of External Affairs. The reason Kearney contemplated legal action was contained in allegations about his activities which, though worded differently, appeared in both the *Leader* and the *Irish Press*:[59]

It was at this precise moment that the indiscreet contacts by an Irish diplomat in a neutral European country with Herr Veesenmayer, one of Ribbentrop's most experienced agents for special missions [Veesenmayer was a coup d'état specialist] awakened the interest of German military circles in Ireland. On the basis of optimistic reports given on Mr. de Valera's secret sympathies with the Germans, preparations for a study of a special landing to assist revolutionary anti-British forces in Southern Ireland were ordered . . . if it were not for the great failure on the Eastern front, Hitler might have been encouraged to reject the advices of his resident Minister in Dublin and to rely on Mr. de Valera's 'promised' support provided his hand was at first forced. The danger of irresponsible theorising about the Taoiseach's ultimate political aims could hardly have been greater.

Kearney's own report to the Department contradicts this account completely. It says he told Veesenmayer that:[60] 'public declarations of the Taoiseach proved clearly that Ireland would resist the violation of her neutrality by Americans, English or Germans, and that he lost no opportunity of warning the people that they must be ready at all times to find themselves at war . . . there could be no question for us of abandoning neutrality in exchange for concessions of any kind.'

At this stage of the availability of evidence the Scottish verdict of 'not proven' is all that one can advance regarding Walshe's statement about 'treachery' in Madrid. Was it based on disinformation or on wrongful extrapolation? Kearney was known to be in touch with Frank Ryan, the former IRA leader. Ryan was at that time living in Germany, where he had been taken partly because of de Valera, who had authorized Kearney to pay for his defence before a Spanish court after the Spanish Civil War ended. De Valera had sanctioned Kearney's co-operation with the Red Cross and other bodies in securing Ryan's 'escape' from prison and subsequent release to Germany.[61] Kearney also had contacts with Helmut Clissman, a friend of Ryan's who had married an Irishwoman. During a spell of home leave in 1941 Kearney, apparently at de Valera's suggestion, visited Ryan's parents, and finding them both in bad health, had this information conveyed to Ryan via Mrs Clissman. According to a document in the Department of External Affairs records, Kearney gave military intelligence a 'full account' of how Ryan's escape was engineered.[62]

However, there was unease in the Department about Kearney's contacts with Ryan 'and others considered dangerous to the State . . . there was a feeling that the information he furnished to the Department about these contacts lacked amplitude and candour'.[63] Also, the British would appear to have found out about the Veesenmayer visit. In February 1943 Kearney was brought back to Dublin for consultation. The ostensible reasons for his return were a dispute over pay and a proposal which he had forwarded to Dublin from the Spanish Government that Ireland should join with Spain in forming a 'neutral bloc'. The other participants were said to be Argentina and the Holy See. De Valera had been informed by the British that this idea emanated from the Germans; in fact it was a Spanish–Vatican creation. But de Valera took no action on it. The main reason for bringing Kearney back:[64] 'was to use his presence in Dublin to talk to him seriously about the need for extreme care and prudence in security matters, particularly in view of the prospect of a second front being opened'. De Valera spoke to him 'very seriously indeed'. But not so seriously, apparently, as to prevent Kearney returning to his post in Madrid. Moreover Boland, who saw a lot of Kearney during this visit, said he heard nothing from him of any talks with German emissaries.

Having failed to get his report into the public domain Kearney brought a libel action against Williams, the *Leader* and the *Irish Press*; as the records show, this led to a great deal of activity in the Department of External Affairs and between the Department and the Office of the Taoiseach. As a result of it Boland, who in 1954 was in Britain as Ambassador to the Court of St James, was shown the captured German documents on which it was thought Williams had based his statements. They were produced for him at the Commonwealth Relations Office on 15 March that year. Having perused them, he agreed with the view of the Foreign Office's legal adviser that they did not support the Williams allegations:[65] 'The legal adviser commented that Mr. Kearney's attitude, in the conversations he had with the emissaries from Germany, seemed to him to have been cautious and perfectly proper in every way.'

Boland advised Sean Nunan, who was now Secretary of the Department (De Valera having acceded to a request by Walshe, a former Jesuit student, that he be appointed Ambassador to the Holy See), that if Williams was relying on the documents to substantiate his case it was doubtful whether he would 'find them of very much use to him'.[66] Later that year Dr Conor Cruise O'Brien, then a member of the Department of External Affairs, encountered Kurt Haller while on a visit to Germany. At the time of the Veesenmayer–Kearney meeting Haller had been section leader in Abwehr (11) Office 1 West in Berlin. He had overseen the Ryan escape and was fully conversant with all aspects of the Veesenmayer mission. He said that Veesenmayer's report on the Kearney meeting had been 'disappointing' from the German point of view:[67] 'Mr Kearney had simply adopted the formally correct attitude of a neutral head of mission and declined to hold out any hope that Ireland would be likely to come in on the German side, or at all. This account runs, of course, contrary to the version published by Professor Desmond Williams in his articles in the *Leader* and in the *Irish Press*.'

The month after O'Brien made his report Kearney's solicitors[68] wrote to the Secretary of the Department of External Affairs asking two questions. One, would the Department claim privilege if a subpoena was served on them to produce Kearney's account of his meeting with Veesenmayer? Two, was Kearney at liberty to disclose the contents of the interviews he had had with representatives of the German Government, or would he too be made subject to privilege? This inquiry resulted in a high-powered meeting in de Valera's office.[69] Apart from de Valera himself, those present were the Attorney General and a member of his staff, Boland from London and W. P. Fay on behalf of the Department of External Affairs. After this colloquy Kearney's solicitors were informed that:[70] 'The Minister for External Affairs . . . will be obliged to claim privilege . . . in the public interest' in respect of the Kearney report. As to Kearney's own evidence: '. . . the Minister assumes that your client will be guided by the advice of his counsel, his own discretion as the former Head of an Irish diplomatic mission, and the directions of the trial judge'. The minute taken by Moynihan of his conversation with de Valera says:[71] 'In coming to the conclusion that privilege should be pleaded for the report of the 24th of August, 1942, the Taoiseach was influenced by considerations of the public interest and the view, which he takes, that Mr. Kearney will not, in consequence, be materially hampered in seeking to vindicate his reputation.'

Obviously without his centrepiece document Kearney *was* severely hampered in proving that he had acted correctly as 'Head of an Irish diplomatic mission'. On 5 November 1954 he settled, before the case went to hearing, for an apology, £500 and costs[72] – a modest sum for an action that involved the Taoiseach, two Departments of State in Ireland, the Attorney General's Office, and some of the most senior members of both the Irish public service and the British foreign service. At this stage a reader might be forgiven for wondering what all this had to do with de Valera and with the basic question of whether Williams misread the official documents. The answer probably says as much or more for de Valera's character as does the account of his more important duel with Gray. Williams was one of the most brilliant academics of his time: he did not misread documents. I know that he averred privately that his informant about the Veesenmayer–Kearney episode, as about much more in the *Irish Press* series, was none other than the editor-in-chief of the *Irish Press* – Eamon de Valera. However as Frank Aiken noted at the outset of the war:[73] '. . . one of the most important weapons of war is propaganda . . . . Neutrality . . . is regarded . . . with hatred and contempt. "he who is not with me is against me". In the modern total warfare it [neutrality] is not a condition of peace with both belligerents, but rather a condition of limited warfare with both . . . . ' With the conclusion of the Kearney incident, de Valera may be said to have rung down the curtain on a sustained, successful interpretation of those sentiments.

29

HARSH JUSTICE

ANOTHER ASPECT OF de Valera's wartime rule which has received little attention from biographers is his policy towards the IRA. It was important not only in itself but also because it rebounded on him to such an extent that after the war it played a part in his electoral defeat. Faced with a double-edged threat from the militant Republicans – internal subversion, and the potential for a link-up with the Nazis – he was relentless in dealing with both. On the internal front the clash between IRA and police was brutal. Six policemen were shot in the course of the war. Six members of the IRA were executed, three allowed to die on hunger strike and three shot dead by detectives. At least one member of the IRA was shot dead by the organization on suspicion of being a spy. A number of civilians who gave evidence against the IRA were shot and wounded. During the course of the war some eleven hundred persons were interned or imprisoned at different times, the largest number in custody at any one time being around six hundred. All this attrition had the desired effect: it rendered the IRA impotent for the whole of the war.

Externally, it took the Nazis some time to realize this. Apart from Ryan, another IRA leader was smuggled into Germany on 3 May 1940: Sean Russell, who had been touring America under Joe McGarrity's tutelage. Hempel objected to his superiors becoming involved with Russell, because of his knowledge of the IRA's position in Ireland. But at this early stage of the war he was over-ruled by the viewpoint that 'by reason of their militant attitude towards England, the IRA is Germany's natural ally.'[1] The result was an abortive U-boat voyage to Ireland during which Russell died, seemingly of a perforated ulcer. Ryan returned to Germany and subsequently died there, also of natural causes, without making any further contribution to an IRA campaign. The handful of agents whom the Nazis later despatched included an ex-circus strongman and a trio of sailors, among them an Indian. This latter addition to the wartime Irish countryside came to the attention of the vigilant Irish security forces with even more than ordinary efficiency and removed all uncertainty concerning board and lodging for the three for the duration.

The one first-class agent whom the German did succeed in landing was Herman Goertz, who before the war had been engaged in intelligence-gathering in England. Goertz was parachuted into Co. Meath on 5 May 1940, and succeeded in remaining at liberty for nineteen months. But he did not succeed in promoting any action against either the British or Irish

Governments, or in getting any reports of significance back to Berlin. Elements in the Irish Army, whom he succeeded in contacting, refused to collaborate with him because of their contempt for the IRA. Goertz came to share this view and wrote:[2] 'The IRA had become an underground movement in its own national sphere, heavily suppressed by men who knew all their methods. . . . In spite of the fine qualities of individual IRA men, as a body I considered them worthless.'

This was a correct assessment. The Irish Army intelligence team was largely officered by men who had learned their trade under Michael Collins. I interviewed them at different times and have no reason to doubt that they completely eliminated the IRA-Nazi threat from the Irish neutrality equation. To their skills were added all the resources of the state, police and public co-operation, combined with wartime measures such as widespread phone tapping, opening of letters, censorship and so on. A combination of the aborted Russell mission, and the reaction to the landing of Goertz, helped Hempel to convince Berlin of these facts also. From the summer of 1940 onwards his assessment of the Irish situation was the one that prevailed in Berlin: de Valera was serious about neutrality; he had all-party support in maintaining it, and the IRA could do nothing but harm to Germany's interests by provoking a British reaction.

De Valera was even more aware of the foregoing facts. He knew that, apart from the occasional isolated fatal incident, the IRA was virtually destroyed as a significant force from early 1940. Once Goertz was captured, de Valera's worries concerning the organization were few. Knowing this, two aspects of his handling of the IRA situation are difficult to justify – in particular the question of prison conditions, and his very public defence of IRA men outside his jurisdiction. This contrasts very sharply with his own use of capital punishment.

Prior to the hanging of Barnes and McCormick on 7 February 1940 for their role in the Coventry bombings he allowed Fianna Fail TDs (deputies) to appear on protest platforms, and permitted massive coverage of the affair in the *Irish Press* which said on 7 February: 'Up to the last minute everything that the Irish Government could do had been done.' He made personal appeals for their reprieve to both Eden and Chamberlain. To Eden he said:[3] 'It will matter little that Barnes and McCormick have been found guilty of murder. With the background of our history and the existence of partition many will refuse to regard their action in that light.' When the appeal was rejected he wrote to Chamberlain:[4]

> I have received your decision with sorrow and dismay. The reprieve of these men would be regarded as an act of generosity, a thousand times more valuable to Britain than anything that can possibly be gained by their death. The latter will be looked upon as fitting only too sadly into the historic background of our relations. Almost superhuman patience is required on both sides to exorcise the feelings which the knowledge of centuries of wrong-doing have engendered.

Later in the year, on 12 August, he very publicly attended a memorial

Mass for Joe McGarrity in the Franciscan church on Merchant's Quay in Dublin; it was McGarrity who had sponsored the bombing campaign which ultimately led to the executions of Barnes and McCormick. De Valera used arguments similar to those he had advanced with Chamberlain and Eden two years later, when a young IRA man was awaiting hanging in Belfast. Thomas Williams was the only one of six men convicted of shooting a policeman the previous Easter not to be reprieved. On 1 September 1942 de Valera instructed Walshe to send this message to Churchill:[5] 'The saving at this last moment, through your personal intervention, of the life of young Williams, who is due to be executed on Wednesday morning in Belfast, would profoundly affect public feeling here. I know the difficulties, but results would justify, and I urge strongly that you do it.' Meanwhile he put such an intercessionary effort into force in America that it took Bob Brennan three closely typed foolscap pages to report[6] on all the efforts that were made. The President, congressmen, senators, trade union leaders, the Mayors of Boston and New York, the Treasurer of Harvard, the British Embassy, the Secretary of State, and the leading Irish societies were but a few of those contacted – in the middle of a presidential election campaign.

The contrast between these publicity drives and those permitted in the case of men whose executions de Valera had himself sanctioned was stark. A bleak message from the Secretary of the Department of Justice, T. J. Coyne, tells the story:[7] ' . . . he has looked up the papers to see what line they took as regards the censoring of publicity in connection with agitations for the reprieve of the men we had ourselves executed in recent years. Mr. Coyne finds that they had suppressed *all* such publicity, merely permitting the announcement of the sentences and of their execution.' Yet the arguments which de Valera used to Chamberlain, Churchill and Eden could equally well have been applied to the cases of the men he had executed, and would execute. True, at the time of the Barnes and McCormick hangings the war was at an early stage and there was widespread sympathy for them. But the difference lay not in argument, or in morality, but in circumstance. The men whom de Valera had shot represented a challenge to his authority and fiefdom. Barnes, McCormick and Williams threatened other states and afforded opportunities for making use of the lion's tail. Politically speaking, they stood in the same relation to de Valera as did their precursors whom he had incited against the provisional Government in his 'wading through blood' phase.

Similarly, the conditions in which some IRA prisoners were held raise questions of double standards. De Valera's official biography[8] recalls how he arranged with Malcolm MacDonald to send some of his ideas on prison reform to Sir Samuel Hoare, the British Home Secretary, who, prior to the war, was drafting a Penal Reform Bill. De Valera 'knew quite a lot about the prisons of England'. Sir Samuel was 'delighted' and 'some of de Valera's ideas were incorporated in Sir Samuel Hoare's Bill'.

Had they known of this interest in prison reform on de Valera's part, at least one group of IRA prisoners in Portlaoise Jail during the war would have found it distinctly odd. They had been sentenced by either the military tribunal or the Special Criminal Court under the Offences Against the State Act and did not wish to be regarded as ordinary criminals. They wanted to wear their own clothes, not convict uniform. This was allowed in the Curragh internment camp, Arbour Hill Jail and Mountjoy Jail, but not in Portlaoise. The affected men refused prison clothing and went 'on the blanket'. This type of protest, traditional to Irish Republicans, has become familiar through the world's media since the Bobby Sands-led hunger strikes at Long Kesh prison in the Six Counties in the 1980s led to ten deaths. But no media coverage was allowed in de Valera's Twenty-six Counties for the ten top IRA prisoners in Portlaoise Jail during the war years. From July 1940[9] to April 1943 the 'blanket' prisoners, being in breach of prison regulations, were denied all privileges. They were kept in solitary confinement, which was made particularly rigorous by having an empty cell on either side of them. They were not allowed out to the lavatory or to exercise. Nor did they get any letters, visits or newspapers.

In 1943 their conditions were relaxed somewhat to enable them to receive a newspaper once a week, to write a letter once a month and to receive a reply. They were also permitted to associate with each other for two periods of one and a half hours[10] a day, but not in the open air. They were allowed to exercise in a disused workshop. Some of them missed Mass during their incarceration because they would have had to wear convict clothing in order to attend.

These conditions produced one of the two most disturbing IRA incidents of the war years and their immediate aftermath in Ireland. The first was the hunger *and thirst* strike to the death, after twenty-five days, of Sean McCaughey in 1946. In 1944 a doctor had reported[11] that McCaughey complained 'that he had not been sleeping for some days past'. However he declined a sleeping mixture, saying that his trouble 'could not be cured by a doctor'. The doctor discovered from other prisoners that McCaughey suspected them 'of disloyalty to the IRA'. It was this suspicion which had led to McCaughey's being imprisoned in the first place. It was also this suspicion which led to the other disturbing IRA case of the war years, that of the execution by de Valera of George Plant. Both McCaughey's death and Plant's execution were inextricably mixed up in the infamous Stephen Hayes affair.

On the morning of 30 June 1941, Stephen Hayes was Chief of Staff of the IRA. By nightfall that same day he had been kidnapped on the orders of Sean McCaughey and charged with being a stool pigeon for the de Valera Government. He was found guilty and sentenced to death. However McCaughey, who had been in charge of the Northern Command of the IRA which had its headquarters in Joe McGarrity's home district of Carrickmore, decided that a confession was necessary. This was beaten out of Hayes over the next two months. Its character may be gauged from a refutation of it which he gave me:[12] 'I am prepared to swear an oath that I never entered into any conspiracy with the Free State Government, through Dr. James Ryan, TD, Minister for Agriculture, Thomas Deirg, TD, Minister for Education, Senator Chris Byrne or Laurence de Lacy, to wreck the Irish Republican Army. . . .'

In assessing the Hayes affair we are again in a Scottish 'not proven' situation. The actual Hayes confession[13] contains so many falsehoods that it is easy to accept Hayes' assertion of innocence. He gave me a point-by-point refutation of the charges which is readily acceptable.[14] He told me he had answered 'Yes' to everything that McCaughey and the other inquisitors put to him, in order to save his life and give him an opportunity of buying time as he wrote and rewrote agonizingly. These charges included Fianna Fail complicity in both the Coventry bombings and the Magazine Fort raid, in which the IRA made off with a large proportion of the Irish Army's ammunition. (Fianna Fail were said to have acted thus in order to discredit the IRA.) But the confession does not prove or disprove that he was a traitor.

Eventually Hayes broke free of his captors and made his way to a police station. Arrested and tried before a military tribunal on 18 September that year, McCaughey was sentenced to death by shooting on Hayes' evidence. This sentence was later commuted and McCaughey fetched up in jail. So did Hayes, who spent five years in Mountjoy with no remission for good behaviour. He was segregated from the other IRA prisoners and this circumstance added to the belief in Republican circles that he was a traitor in custody for his own protection. The very best legal brains available in Ireland at that time[15] had offered themselves to him, but Hayes refused to plead. Therefore there was no defence and no cross-examination. The confession was not probed.

So where did the truth lie? I do not profess to know – though I must confess to wondering why, or how, by underground routes, a message was apparently sent to the IRA during the time of Hayes' captivity, to the effect that if he were released, the much sought after IRA man Richard Goss would not be shot. In the event Goss was executed.[16] The fact that Fine Gael could always be relied upon to support the Government of the day against the IRA, coupled with de Valera's censorship, has tended to militate against any rigorous analysis of the evidence, and always will. Watching the drama unfold, David Gray noted the unsatisfactory character of the Hayes trial, which he likened to the sort of tribunal which Arthur Balfour created in the days of British 'coercion', and remarked of what he saw as its sequel:[17] 'What was one to believe? In the course of the trial of an inconspicuous IRA member on the charge of circulating an illegal document, the confession, the two cabinet ministers and Senator Byrne took the stand and made ex parte statements, denying the Hayes allegations. They were not cross examined.'

There was, however, a more grievous sequel. The Hayes confession described how an IRA officer, Michael Devereux of Wexford, where Hayes came from, had been allegedly set up by the Government as a spy and shot. Detectives, put on the trail by the confession, were guided to his burial place by an IRA man who could not read or write. The upshot was that George Plant was arrested and 'Balfoured' with his murder. Two members of the IRA who had made statements implicating him rescinded their evidence. However, de Valera met this challenge by issuing an Emergency Powers Order on 30 December 1941. This provided that: 'if a statement was made voluntarily, lawfully . . . then at any stage of the trial the prosecution may read such a statement as evidence'.[18] Furthermore the Order empowered the court to 'act on the statement against the accused'. And to make assurance doubly sure:[19] ' . . . if a military court considered it proper on any occasion during a trial that it should not be bound by the laws of evidence, whether of military or common law, then the court should not be bound by such a rule.'

The goalposts moved thus, Plant was put on trial again with the two men who had withdrawn their statements. All were sentenced to death. The two witnesses were reprieved, but on 5 March 1942 Plant was executed in what Republican folklore has subsequently referred to as 'judicial murder'. Despite the charge against him, Plant seems to have been a particularly pleasant person. Apart from Sean MacBride, his counsel, the officer in charge of him in the jail on the night before his execution spoke highly of him to me. The feeling occasioned by his execution may have been a factor in de Valera's decision not to use the Irish Army in the last IRA execution (for shooting a policeman) of the war. In December 1944 Charles Kerins, described as 'The Boy from Tralee' in the ballad named after him, was despatched in Mountjoy Jail, in a grisly display of Anglo-Irish co-operation, by Albert Pierrepoint, the English hangman.

Why in the latter stages of the war de Valera behaved as he did towards the IRA leadership, which he had safely under lock and key, must naturally remain a matter of conjecture. At McCaughey's inquest Sean MacBride, acting for the next of kin, was not allowed to cross-examine the Governor of the prison, but he participated in one of the best-known exchanges in Irish legal history with the prison doctor:[20]

> MacBride: 'If you had a dog would you treat it in that fashion?'
> Doctor: (After a pause) 'No.'

McCaughey's fatal hunger strike, intended to result in his release, was embarked on well after the war had ended; it began on 19 April 1946. There was no question of any danger to Irish neutrality being involved. In fact I was told by some of those in jail with him that, had he been transferred to the Curragh, he would have abandoned the strike. Perhaps he was a man who had been medically reported as suffering from nervous strain. But, perhaps also, too much power had made a stone of the heart that de Valera looked into to know the wishes of the Irish people. Certainly Sean McCaughey, inconspicuous on the stage of history compared to Churchill and Roosevelt, did what they could not do – he helped to put de Valera out of power. However, before moving on to see how this came about, let us take a brief backward look at the conditions which sustained him in office before ultimately combining to dethrone him.

'Backward' is not an inappropriate term to describe the electoral climate of the people. Educationally, as de Valera himself pointed out in a speech to a teachers' conference in 1940:[21] 'For at least nine-tenths of the people the primary school is the sole source of education. . . . What the National Schools are, the Nation must be.' How strongly de Valera rated the priorities of the nation may perhaps be gauged from the fact that at this stage (from September 1939 to June 1940) he had decided that the burden of being Minister of Education could safely be added to his other cares. The curriculum was an intellectual division of the spoils between the claims of Fianna Fail's brand of nationalism and the Roman Catholic Church. Or, as de Valera put it:[22] 'Of the influence of religion in the education of the child, it is not necessary for me to speak. It is the heart of all real education, the centre from which the life-force of education must come, if it is to have any permanent value, and the family is, or should be, its most natural ally in the shaping of the child.'

What this meant in effect was that the average twelve-year-old, leaving formal education behind for ever, would have devoted a high proportion of classroom time to a study of the Irish language and the catechism, and whatever was left over to the 'three Rs'. The dangers posed to de Valera's regime by whatever native Irish genius and questioning spirit the system left intact were countered in a number of ways. First there was emigration, largely into Britain's wartime production machine and into her armed services. Next there was the absorption of potentially troublesome manpower into the Twenty-six Counties' own defence forces

The fall of France caused a reversal of the decision to cut the defence forces (and made de Valera hand over the Education portfolio to Thomas Derrig), and the establishment was raised to 42,000. There was also a part-time militia, a local defence force which was said to have reached a membership of 142,000. In addition potentially dangerous energies were subsumed to a degree by wartime activities such as increased turf production (much of which was stored in Phoenix Park under local resident David Gray's indignant gaze) and a legal requirement to cultivate all available land. Incomes were frozen under the emergency decrees – not that there was a great deal to spend them on. Consumer goods vanished from the shops as rationing was introduced for food, clothing and petrol; private motoring ceased. Rail travel, too, dwindled as coal stocks became depleted: the eight-mile journey from my local railway station to Dublin sometimes took seven hours to complete. It was not uncommon for trains to set off for the country and take three or four days to get there. The rigorous censorship heightened feelings of acceptance, encapsulation, obedience to authority. Dissent, like morality, is often a matter of opportunity. Lack of mobility and the crushing weight of the censorship militated against the growth of either new ideas or organized opposition to Fianna Fail rule.

Moreover, there was de Valera's omnipresence at the levers of power. On taking office in 1932 he had been careful to stir up as little opposition as possible by largely rejecting his wilder followers' advice to go in for widespread sackings of Cosgrave's supporters. Instead he introduced a more subtle, and more effective, appointment and patronage policy.

The Constitution created a sixty-member Seanad. Eleven of its members were nominated by the Taoiseach, six by the universities. In a typically de Valera move the remaining forty-three were to be returned in two different ways. If the Oireachtas (Parliament) so decided, they could be elected under the terms of Article 19 'by any functional or vocational group or association'. As the Oireachtas never did get round to so deciding they were, and are, under the terms of Article 18, drawn from a number of panels controlled by County Councillors and TDs – in other words on a party basis in which the ruling party, normally Fianna Fail, gets the lion's share of the spoils. Although the skulduggery thus engendered only resulted in one successful prosecution for bribery,[23] it nevertheless helped to give lasting political life to many who had either failed to get re-elected to the Dail or devoted themselves to the trade of carpet-bagger – intent, that is, on obtaining government contracts, planning permissions and preferments at public expense.

Obviously one of the great dangers for someone like de Valera, hoping to continue in control of a society such as this, would be a sudden collective realization of the fact that the Emperor had no clothes – particularly if such an awareness dawned at a moment of national crisis such as an election or a war. Uncharacteristically he revealed his hand on the subject of character formation, de Valera-style, at the outbreak of the war. He warned teachers against the improper exposure of children to the use of reason:[24]

> Just as there are stages in the life of a nation in which different sides of capacity have to be trained, so there are stages in the life of the pupil in which one faculty should be trained rather than another. In the earlier stages the memory is the strongest faculty, the reasoning power the weakest. Common sense dictates that at this stage we should not try to appeal to reasoning power . . . the stress should be on memorising . . . habit is the foundation of character, the training of character is your greatest task, more fundamental than any training in any particular branch of knowledge. . . .

The sort of character desired was one which paid its rulers the homage of its understanding.

The particular 'capacity' which de Valera depended on for his continuance in power was the suspension of disbelief. Even though, in substance, he acted in the most flint-edged, self-interested way, his style was other-worldly – that of someone 'impractical', 'a dreamer'. No single utterance of de Valera's contributed so much to his other-worldly persona as did his St Patrick's Day address of 1943. This was the year of the fiftieth anniversary of the foundation of the Gaelic League by Douglas Hyde. Hyde was still President of the Twenty-six Counties but had suffered a stroke, and de Valera was active throughout the country in attending Gaelic League commemorations of various sorts. In between these activities, bending laws, signing death warrants and internment orders, and fending off Churchill, Hitler and Roosevelt, de Valera went on air over Radio Eireann to describe That Ireland Which We Dreamed Of in these terms:[25]

> ... let us turn aside for a moment to that ideal Ireland that we would have. That Ireland which we dreamed of would be the home of a people who valued material wealth only as the basis for right living, of a people who were satisfied with frugal comfort and devoted their leisure to the things of the spirit – a land whose countryside would be bright with cosy homesteads, whose fields and villages would be joyous with sounds of industry, with the romping of sturdy children, the contests of athletic youths and the laughter of comely maidens, whose firesides would be forums for the wisdom of serene old age. It would, in a word, be the home of a people living the life that God desires that man should live.

Nothing in de Valera's entire public career ever drew anything like the comment and ridicule that that speech, made in those circumstances, elicited over the years. David Gray nearly blew a gasket, and wrote to Roosevelt:[26]

> Your friend Mr. de Valera is continuing to ignore those little events of history which in spite of him keep occurring. He is in fact too busy attending meetings celebrating the revival of the Gaelic language to give his attention to such matters. It is fifty years since Douglas Hyde, the Protestant Anglo-Irish squire from the West, founded the Gaelic league. He has his reward in being the paralysed, dummy President of an Eire which would have seen Britain overrun by Hitler with a degree of satisfaction and without lifting a finger to prevent it.
>
> Meanwhile the Censor is loose again. The American flag was recently cut out of a film called 'Good luck Mr. Yates'. ... Meanwhile I am surrounded by mountains of turf, some two hundred and fifty thousand tons, all brought from the interior with American gasoline. If I go nuts can you blame me?

In the circumstances Mr Gray may be forgiven a little pardonable nuttiness. But what Gray and the mockers overlook are two facts. The first was the forces of conservatism in the Irish society of the time. All those celibate Christian brothers and nuns, and priests and Gaelic revivalists, and almost equally asexual turned-off mothers of ten (or twelve), nodding approvingly. Not an impure thought or an orgasm in sight. In Gaelic and Catholic Ireland conception would take place through the medium. Think of all those small-time capitalists created by Fianna Fail's protected industries. They could mock, but, with the backing of a wage freeze, they could also tell their workers that they should be satisfied with 'frugal comfort' and aspire to 'right living'.

The second fact overlooked by the mockers, even allowing de Valera a percentage of Bruree nostalgia and Arcadian escapism as the jaws of reality closed on him, was that an election was inescapable that year. Normally de Valera nipped these disagreeable occurrences in the bud at a moment favourable to himself; but in 1943 no such moment occurred. It had been five years since the last general election. He hung on desperately waiting, fruitlessly, for something to turn up until June, the last month beyond which the inevitable was no longer constitutionally postponable. On the left, since he had swept the boards in 1938, Labour had grown stronger on the wings of dissatisfaction with wartime conditions. On the right a new party, Clann na Talmhan (the Party of the Land), had emerged to represent the interests of the bigger farmers. It advocated reafforestation and land drainage, and would probably not have come into being had the British not been unsporting enough to take steps, at the outset of the war, to prevent Irish farmers profiteering as they had done during World War I.

In the event de Valera emerged from the 1943 general election in a minority Government situation, having lost support to both Labour and the Clann. He had 67 seats compared to Fine Gael's 32, Labour's 17, Clann na Talmhan's 14 and the Independents' 8. But, as we have seen, poor old blind de Valera groped his way past the mockers and David Gray, through the Celtic mists, and, guided by the bitter sheen of the American note, found his way back into majority Government less than a year later. Sure, where would a decent man be without a few comely maidens and the occasional athletic youth? Nowhere, as we shall see in Chapter 30, if he lost his bedrock Republican and teacher support.

30

DE VALERA CLINGS ON, AND ON

WHEN THE WAR ended in 1945 de Valera was sixty-three. From then until 1959 he continued to dominate the Irish political landscape; but the exhausting experiences of the 'emergency', combined with the strain of his eye condition, had drained whatever innovative spirit was left to him. During the last fourteen years of his life in party politics he rarely showed either the ability or the inclination to confront the great challenges of Irish life: unemployment – and its concomitant evil, enforced emigration – partition, and Church–State relationships. Towards the end of this period he had to confront, privately, the possibility of a rebellion against his continued leadership of Fianna Fail, and publicly, and far more tangibly, objections to his control of the *Irish Press*.

Starting with unemployment, one can point to a period of roughly a month's duration which may be taken as symbolizing the death of innovation and the enthronement of reaction. The time in question was April–May 1945, when he made his highly publicized reply to Churchill. But of far more lasting significance was his unpublished reaction to a plea for initiative made by Sean Lemass. De Valera's rejection took the form, not of a statement, but of a manoeuvre[1] that successfully subverted the process of post-war economic improvement which, as we shall see shortly, Lemass had been strongly advocating since 1942.

The end of the war found the Twenty-six Counties a small, open economy, highly vulnerable to outside influences, with a limited home market and no industrial base to speak of. A government memo[2] of this period described Ireland's industries as consisting of brewing, distilling, wool and linen weaving and agricultural produce. History and the transportational costs for both imports and exports caused by Ireland's geographical position – an island, lying off an island, on the edge of Europe – had resulted in an undue trade dependence on Britain. This was, and still is, accurately described in the commonly heard expression: 'When England sneezes Ireland catches pneumonia.'

Lemass favoured the setting up of an economic planning committee consisting of the Secretaries of the major governmental economic Departments: Finance, Agriculture, and Industry and Commerce. The Secretary of Lemass's Department, John Leydon, had hurled the Lemass-made snowball, outlining the idea, to de Valera in September 1942. A negative decision was duly thrown back at him, with unusual speed, only six days later, on the 28th. De Valera, Man of Power, believed that power slipped through the fingers of those who did not exercise it. He was not going to allow the fingers of others on the levers of economic decision-taking. Instead he established a committee consisting of himself, Lemass and Sean T. O'Ceallaigh, who was then Minister for Finance. O'Ceallaigh was a small man of whom it was once observed unkindly that it would have been the height of absurdity to imagine him standing up to the Tall Man. Thus, with O'Ceallaigh's lack of opposition automatically built into the committee, de Valera proceeded to blunt Lemass's thrust by adopting a policy of sending the fool further. Over the next two years the committee's attention was taken up with discussions of such items as 'the Dun Laoghaire refuse dump'.[3]

Similar futility had attended Lemass's efforts to galvanize de Valera and his aging Cabinet colleagues into a sense of urgency concerning the problems which the ending of the war would pose on the labour front. There were fears of social revolution attendant on the ending of the war and the return of Irish emigrants from Britain. F. H. Boland prepared a memo for the Government saying:[4] ' . . . immediately the "cease fire" order is given, the whole aim and purpose of the British authorities will be to rush all these workers back to this country as quickly as they can. . . . ' Arising out of the ensuing discussions was a proposal by Lemass[5] to set up a wide-ranging Ministry of Labour that would have cut across existing Departments and revolutionized Irish labour policy. De Valera shot this down in a memo which advocated making haste slowly:[6] ' . . . we should plan at once such use and development of our resources and potentialities as seemed reasonably practical *without* [author's italics] a revolutionary change in the foundations.' There was no revolutionary change in the foundations or anywhere else. British post-war reconstruction kept the potentially troublesome Irish emigrants in Britain, where de Valera's governmental policy ensured that they were joined by many more like them.

However, Lemass gamely continued his efforts to alter this scheme of things. He was greatly stimulated by the 1944 British White Paper on Full Employment, and detached himself from the problems of the Dun Laoghaire refuse dump and similar intricacies to produce an Irish version[7] of the British document. His recommendations included overhauling the tax system so as to provide the 'maximum inducement to industrialists to accumulate funds for the replacement of obsolete plant'; as well as setting up a state export board to help in the establishment of markets abroad and, at home, founding industries to serve them. He warned that budget deficits would have to be allowed for: 'The essential part of the Full Employment Policy outlined in this Memorandum is the preparation of a new kind of Budget.' He proposed that banking and government policy would have to work in tandem. And to support his contention that: 'It is to be assumed that in the case of this creditor country, the problem of Government borrowing need offer no insuperable difficulty' he quoted from a range of authorities including a report by Unilever, J. M. Keynes, P. Lamartine Yates, Sir William Beveridge and Nicholas Kaldor. All were designed to 'show that a Full Employment Policy is practicable, that it is in line with modern economic thought, that it involves no departure from democratic principles'. A full employment policy would ensure that 'the output capacity of the country should be so expanded that on the basis of the most efficient production it will require, when fully utilised, the employment of the whole available manpower'.

The first section of the 'available manpower' which Lemass discovered to be 'fully utilised' consisted of the Department of Finance and his own Cabinet. De Valera did not confront him head on; his technique was partly to allow others to do this for him and partly to smother Lemass in the general web of a deeply conservative Cabinet's disapproval. He had always worked like this. Noel Browne has recorded a telling description by a then member of Fianna Fail, Noel Hartnett, of how de Valera used similar tactics in an incident involving Lemass even in the early days of Fianna Fail's reign:[8]

> Sean Lemass had made a speech . . . pounding our the simple grating truth – the romantic struggle to liberate Ireland is over; we must forget our old grievances, bind up our wounds, and get on with the work of building a new and prosperous Ireland. These sentiments dismayed many of the old soldiers, inflamed by memories of their real and imagined heroics in the national struggle.
>
> A call was made to discipline Lemass. Hartnett, who sided with Lemass, noted that de Valera sat through the long and heated executive debate and made no attempt to rescue Lemass from the old soldiers snapping at his heels. Late in the night, de Valera proposed to adjourn the debate. Lemass, who had sat silent, spoke for the first time and said. 'No, finish the debate. Make your minds up.' In the end, after a close vote, he survived. What was clear to Hartnett was that while de Valera had feared no rival since Collins, he did not disapprove of Lemass's power in the party being visibly curbed.

De Valera's relationship with Lemass was not that clear to Maurice Moynihan, who worked closely with both men. He told me that he:[9] ' . . . often wondered about the relationship between de Valera and Lemass. Lemass was very un-Irish. He had the Huguenot strain in him. He was very determined, confident in himself, hard working. Lemass barked a lot. He fought continuously with MacEntee in Cabinet. Dev. was reluctant to interfere at all.'

By not interfering in this case de Valera ensured that the Warriors of Destiny carried the opposition for him. Points 8 and 9 of Lemass's programme took on central Fianna Fail dogma full frontally. Point 8 openly recognized the Fianna Fail tenet that: 'Land policy has for its aim the placing of as many families as possible on the land.' But it then went on to introduce an alarming heresy: the concept that there was an expectation of the farmer 'working the farm diligently and efficiently'. Point 9 stipulated that, in cases where this did not occur over a 'number of consecutive years', powers to effect 'compulsory transfer' should be acquired by the state. That paragraph concluded with a statement that must have bounced around de Valera's desk like a hand grenade with the pin out: 'The rights of owners should not allow the right to allow land to go derelict or to be utilised below its reasonable productive capacity. Only a limited number of families can be settled on the land, on economic holdings, and policy must be directed to ensuring that ownership will be confined to persons willing and capable of working them adequately.'

The memo was circulated to all Cabinet members for their comments – after de Valera himself had made a significant comment to Lemass, who had been advocating larger, more economic, holdings. He said:[10] 'On the question of the size of farms . . . there was more real work and thrift on *small* [author's italics] farms.' James Ryan, the Minister for Agriculture, agreed with these sentiments:[11] 'In paragraph 9 Mr. Lemass deals with the matter of displacement of bad farmers. This would be a most delicate and difficult matter. . . . If displacement were done on a small scale only it would have little or no effect on output and if it were done to such an extent as to have a substantial effect on output there would be danger of serious agitation and public disturbances.'

Decoded, this of course meant: if Lemass succeeds in thinning out the inefficient farmers the effect will be felt most amongst small farmers, particularly in the west, which will erode Fianna Fail's dole-and-subsidy-erected electoral bulwark. Accordingly Ryan argued for the preservation of uneconomic holdings in terms which would raise eyebrows today, but which found an approving echo around the Cabinet table in 1944. He conceded that in some cases involving 'senility or mental trouble, there would be a good case for the State taking over', but:

> There are a number of holdings, however, in every parish, falling below a reasonable productive capacity due to some failing on the part of the present owner but who probably has a young family growing up, one member of which would in time pull the place together and become in due course a first-class farmer. In the meantime the family somehow or other are reared and set out in life as useful citizens. Indeed, the lessons *which the poverty of the home teaches them very often make them good workers wherever they go* [author's italics]. It would be unthinkable to disturb the family in such cases no matter how much below the desired standard the farm might presently be.

In the absence of any lead from de Valera, the electoral implications of this 'comely maidens' and 'frugal comfort' doctrine killed any hope that Lemass's colleagues might support his approach.

The change-resistant Department of Finance naturally attacked Lemass's proposals. He prepared a point-by-point refutation of their arguments, but de Valera moved the goalposts so that his shots went harmlessly wide. In the month before the celebrated rejoinder to Churchill, April 1945, he altered the structure of the Planning Committee so that instead of being composed just of him, O'Ceallaigh and Lemass it became a committee of the Cabinet. In this enlarged forum the necessity for preserving as many small farmers as possible on the land (that is, in the polling booths) overlay any discussion of Lemass's vision concerning banks, trade unions, budgets, whatever. 'When a verdict was pronounced in June it registered a clear defeat for Lemass.'[12] To use an agricultural metaphor, a full employment policy was a dead duck.

As a result the Irish economy nearly died with it. Let us briefly move forward to look at the country's position as it was described towards the end of the following decade:[13] ' . . . the years 1955–56 had plumbed the depths of hopelessness. One of the recurring series of balance of payments crises was overcome but only at the cost of stagnation, high unemployment and emigration.' And in 1957:

> A sense of anxiety is indeed justified. But it can too easily degenerate into feelings of frustration and despair. After 35 years of native government people are asking whether we can achieve an acceptable degree of economic progress. The common talk amongst parents in the towns, as in rural Ireland, is of their children having to emigrate as soon as their education is completed in order to be sure of a reasonable livelihood .... All this seems to be setting up a vicious circle – of increasing emigration, resulting in a smaller domestic market depleted of initiative and skill. ...

This dismal state of affairs was caused by: ' . . . the absence of a comprehensive and integrated programme . . . tending to deepen the all-prevalent mood of despondency about the country's future'.

The author of the foregoing comments was not a political opponent of de Valera's but the country's most important civil servant, T. K. Whitaker, then Secretary of the Department of Finance. On the eve of his departure from parliamentary politics de Valera accepted both Whitaker's diagnosis and his prescription – without, of course, acknowledging the condition of the patient. Effectively speaking, between the time de Valera turned down Lemass's recommendations for a 'comprehensive and integrated programme', and the provision of one by Whitaker, the Twenty-six Counties' economy and society were like rotting meat in a sandwich. The people were caught between de Valera's increasing incapacity for original thought and the opposition parties' matching inability to provide any alternative.

Mary Bromage has described de Valera's circumstances and mind set as the post-war era dawned. Swaddled in frugal comfort he gazed sightlessly, resentfully, on the breaking of old moulds:[14]

> 'I believe that I live as simply as most people,' Dev commented. 'A number of expenses that the average person has, I have not got. I do not smoke or drink; I do not entertain to any extent.' ... It was privacy that de Valera cherished. 'The newspapers, the opening up of areas by buses, the radio, and the cinema, all these things,' he complained, 'are breaking in.' The frugality of his Limerick boyhood was the preference if not the necessity of his old age. Anyone brought up in the

country might, he supposed, say, 'You are in the country all your life because you understand fully what country life means.'

The stifling effect of de Valera's dead hand in the post-war years contrasts starkly with his own words to Joe McGarrity in 1926 when he split Sinn Fein in order to achieve power: 'Ten years are worth saving to the nation.' Twenty years later he did not feel that fifteen wasted years were too high a price to pay for his determination to hold on to that power. Nothing that his economic incompetence could do to the state was going to intimidate him! However, though change did not come with the sudden rush that unseated Churchill, powerful forces were working against de Valera in the years after the war.

On the one hand there was the reaction to two widely publicized scandals, on the other the backlash against his treatment of the IRA and his intransigence towards trade unions, that of teachers in particular. The first scandal concerned a prominent Fianna Fail politician in the bacon-curing business, Dr F. C. Ward, who was forced to resign his junior ministerial position as Parliamentary Secretary. Another doctor had sent a list of allegations to de Valera, who immediately directed that a Tribunal of Inquiry should be set up, on 7 June 1946. Most of the allegations, including charges of local government corruption in Ward's native Co. Monaghan, were disproved. However, it was found that Ward and his fellow directors (it was a family concern) made payments to themselves which 'were not brought to account for income tax purposes'. The Wards were forced[15] to make restitution to the Revenue Commissioners. The tribunal conducted its business with such despatch that de Valera was tempted to try a 'cute hoor' manoeuvre to damp down discussion of the affair. He attempted to announce its findings minutes before the Dail's summer recess for 1946. The Opposition, however, were keeping watch and Ward on de Valera. Dr T. F. O'Higgins of Fine Gael summed up a widespread feeling when he said:[16]

There was a very general effort to make him [Ward] the scapegoat for administrative inefficiency in many Government Departments, to brand him as the one black sheep in a flock of Ministerial white sheep. Part of the plot was the rather unworthy attempt by Mr. de Valera to suppress all debate and reference to the matter by his plan, which was frustrated, to announce the findings at one quarter of an hour before the adjournment of the Dail, and his statement that no person other than himself had a right to speak.

. . . The country has for too long been the paradise of profiteers exploiting the consumers, but the reaction is setting in, public opinion is awake.

The public got a further dose of wakefulness the following year because of allegations concerning the sale of Locke's whiskey distillery. These too necessitated the setting up of a tribunal, which too largely exonerated the main targets of the accusations. But some of the mud stuck. It had been alleged under the cloak of Dail privilege by Oliver Flanagan, originally an

Independent TD for Laois-Offaly but who later joined Fine Gael, that de Valera, his son Eamon, Lemass and Gerry Boland were all involved in bribery and corruption in the attempted sale of the distillery to foreigners. The tribunal report,[17] published on 18 December 1947, dismissed Flanagan's allegations most comprehensively. He was accused of 'complete irresponsibility' and 'extravagant recklessness', of being 'uncandid' and giving 'untrue' evidence. But the luridity of the three foreigners who made the abortive purchase attempt ensured that the case became a *cause célèbre*, even without the allegations of high-level political involvement. It was revealed that they were using false names. One left the country and disappeared. Another was deported. The third, calling himself Smith, was in fact one Alexander Maximoe who was wanted in England. He threw himself off the Irish mail boat while being taken back to the UK under police escort, and drowned. Despite the strictures of the tribunal, Flanagan topped the poll in Laois-Offaly in a general election held two months after it reported. As Patrick McGilligan, Minister for Finance in the incoming Cabinet, said: 'the people of the country disagreed with the Tribunal'.[18]

There was also disagreement with the Government in the ranks of the trade unions. In one notable case, which occurred in June 1947, de Valera displayed flexibility in dealing with a threatened strike at the country's flour mills: he met union leaders and helped to bring about a settlement. But this was in contrast to his attitude the previous year to the national teachers, whom he had once addressed so eloquently. Government refusal to concede their pay demands resulted in a bitter strike lasting from March to October.

The strike was like an electoral runway rolled out in front of a new party waiting to take off. In July, Sean MacBride founded Clann na Poblachta (clan, or family, of Republicans). It was like a new version of the old Fianna Fail. Most of its principal figures had been prominent in the IRA. Its organization was built on the network, set up from the time of the Barnes and McCormick trials, to agitate on behalf of Republican prisoners. Sean McCaughey's death a few months earlier, and the plight of his colleagues still in jail, were potent emotional wellsprings for the new party to draw strength from. Like Fianna Fail, the Clann advocated social reform. It also had an eye-catching plan to eradicate tuberculosis, which in those years claimed many lives in Ireland and carried a far greater social stigma than does Aids today. And it had the teachers.

Either then or now, it would be difficult to imagine two other groups in Ireland which could match the commitment and energy of a combination of the Republicans and the teachers. Disillusioned with Fianna Fail, a significant proportion of the membership of the teachers' trade union, the Irish National Teachers' Organization (INTO), swung over to the new party. The Teachers' Club in Dublin's Parnell Square virtually became Clann na Poblachta's headquarters, from which a nationwide campaign was directed. Apart from the Government's failure to live up to its

Republican ideals Clann na Poblachta was able to capitalize on the whiff of corruption emanating from Fianna Fail and to contrast this with its own clean, Republican image symbolized by its leader, Sean MacBride. A son of John MacBride, the executed 1916 leader, he carried a romantic aura akin to that of de Valera in his heyday. A former Chief of Staff of the IRA, he had an attractive French accent acquired during his boyhood in Paris. On top of this there was his more recently acquired reputation as the fearless lawyer who fought to save men's lives from firing squad and hangman, and their reputations at inquests like that on McCaughey.

Fianna Fail's response to the challenge might be thought of as a negative formula consisting of two parts stymied Lemass and one part 'cute hoor'. Neither of Lemass's initiatives, both of which were introduced in 1947, affected the issue of the day: how to stay in power. Some of Lemass's ideas, contained in the two plans he submitted to Cabinet, did surface in succeeding decades. His plans were intended, firstly, to stimulate exports. This would have involved setting up a Trade Advisory Council which would have provided grants and advice to exporters. The second project was an Industrial Efficiency Bill. After passing through some departmental and Cabinet trench warfare this boiled down to a number of concrete proposals to encourage industry, which included stimuli for market research, training, co-operation within industry on buying and selling policies, and improvements in design and in production methods. Both Lemass's projects were curtailed by the calling of the 1948 election. Neither party nor public was ready for him.

But the party was ready for a dose of 'cute hoorism'. The method chosen to stem the rise of Clann na Poblachta was the Electoral Amendment Bill of 1947. Since electoral revisions carried out in 1935, the number of deputies had been 138. Now, despite the fact that the population had fallen, de Valera unblushingly presided over an increase in the number to 147. Moreover, the number of three-member constituencies was increased from fifteen to twenty-two, which favoured Fianna Fail over smaller parties. It was a blatant attempt at gerrymander which no Six County Unionist could have bettered. In October de Valera lost two by-elections to Clann na Poblachta, one of which returned Sean MacBride to the Dail. Banking on the new Electoral Act, de Valera went to the polls earlier than he was constitutionally obliged to, hoping to embroil Clann na Poblachta in an election before it was ready for one. And, in the general election of 4 February 1948, 'cute hoorism' achieved a qualified success. As one commentator wrote:[19] ' . . . constituency revision achieved its purpose. The Clann would have won 19 seats instead of 10 had it secured representation proportional to its vote.'

However, ten were enough. De Valera had correctly targeted the enemy who would unhorse him. Fianna Fail's total of seats fell to 68. He still hoped for a rerun of 1932, the achievement of office with Labour support.[20] His hopes were based on sand: after sixteen years in power he could not bring himself to face the fact that he was widely disliked. Even the Authorized Version admits:[21]

> In the days following the General Election, alliances and bargains were explored with eagerness – based less on compatibility of policy than on intense opposition to de Valera, much of it highly personal . . . . Even on the day when the Dail assembled a coalition seemed far from certain. De Valera understood up to a short time before the meeting that National Labour had refused to participate. Then he was told that agreement had been reached. There was a hustle to prepare his office for his departure. His papers had to be gathered up hurriedly.

Having helped to gather up the papers, Kathleen O'Connell gave up her secure civil service job to follow him into the wilderness as his secretary.

Richard Mulcahy was the official leader of Fine Gael, the largest party in the inter-party Government which was now formed. However John A. Costello, a leading barrister, became Taoiseach in de Valera's stead. Clann na Poblachta had put de Valera out after his wartime executions, and they would not install Mulcahy after those of the civil war. Sean MacBride became Minister for External Affairs. But nobody became more external than one Eamon de Valera. Alas for David Gray's hopes. No sooner had the dust of Cabinet formation settled than de Valera and his first mate, Frank Aiken, set sail in the good ship *Partition* on a world tour, 'as a guest of the Irish Societies',[22] in which his first port of call was America. One commentator, Professor Lee, in a judgement that made up in cynicism what it lacked in charity, said:[23] 'It was necessary to pre-empt the danger of MacBride purloining the partition issue for himself and despoiling Fianna Fail of such winnings as it had made on the partition stakes.'

His month in the USA, after which he moved on to Australia, New Zealand and India, was:[24] 'treated with supreme importance by Irish Americans'. Everywhere there were 'wildly welcoming greetings from friends gone mad with excitement'. His arrival at La Guardia Airport in New York on 8 March 1948 was greeted by thousands of Irish and Irish Americans who had waited for him since 'early dawn'. It was 1919–20 all over again. The hopes of Gray and Roosevelt were like dust beneath the de Valera chariot wheels. Cardinals, Governors, Mayors, all vied to do him honour. 'New York staged the biggest parade since the one celebrating the end of the war.' He and Aiken led the procession in an open car, accompanied by Governor Grover Whelan, to City Hall where he was once again made an Honorary Citizen. He was described as 'Eamon de Valera the boy from Manhattan who made good in Ireland'.

In Washington in presidential election year, he was cordially received by Truman and Marshall. It didn't matter that de Valera's wartime policies meant that the Twenty-six Counties were virtually excluded from Marshall Aid. This was For the Optics time. In Philadelphia, Joe McGarrity's old city, he asked for American aid – not for combatting TB, stemming emigration, rehabilitating ex-IRA prisoners or improving the educational system, but because: 'The struggle is not over ... the British are still occupying Six of our Counties ... we are asking the people of America, those of goodwill, to help us in that fight.' All his visits to American cities were successful. Some were simply more successful than others:

> Boston's million Irish smashed parade records of all the U.S. cities in honouring Mr. de Valera – 200 bands, old IRA men ... steady fall of ticker tape and confetti in bright colours, half a million marched, half a million cheered. ...
>
> San Francisco saw: ... 1,000 horses take part in biggest ever St. Patrick's Day Parade. One hundred thousand marched. They cheered 'up Dev' in 20 different languages. They cheered for 'The leader of Irish Republicanism.'

The defence of the 'leader of Irish republicanism' to any charges by those who thought like Gray and Roosevelt concerning what some uniformed persons referred to as World War II, rather than by its proper title, 'the emergency', was summed up on 23 March in Detroit:

> We refused to fight in World War I for what they called the freedom of small nations because our territory was occupied by Britain and we resented the injustice. We could not have been expected to fight in World War II unless we were attacked. Our territory was still occupied by Britain, and the injustice continued ... you cannot ask a small nation to fight with you for justice when you are inflicting an injustice on the small nation.

And then, after attending the enthronement of Cardinal MacIntyre in Los Angeles, and broadcasting to the nation from Chicago for a full hour on 'Irish Partition', de Valera was off to be photographed with Nehru in New Delhi and lionized in the Antipodes. His last night in India was spent as a guest of the Mountbattens. It was also the last night of British rule in India. Given the part played by 1916, and the subsequent Anglo-Irish war, in the break-up of the British Empire, there was an extraordinary congruency in de Valera's being the Viceroy's last guest.[25]

The grip on the lion's tail was never relinquished. De Valera told the Catholic Luncheon Club of Adelaide that: 'only a bandit would cut one part of Ireland from another'. He told an *Advocate* reporter who questioned him on neutrality: 'The question had to be restated. It was wrong to speak of the necessity of justifying neutrality. What had to be justified was a nation's entry into war.' He renewed his acquaintance with a kindred spirit, his old friend Daniel Mannix, Archbishop of Melbourne, who, according to what Tom Kiernan, the Irish Ambassador to Australia, told Frank Gallagher, had not spoken for two days after learning of what had befallen in the general election of February 1948.[26] Other manifestations of respect in Australia included the fact that Aiken and de Valera were invited to sit in the National Parliament at Canberra while it was in session. Only General MacArthur had received that honour before them.

However, though his tour helped to safeguard the Fianna Fail investment in partition, it was the inter-party Government which made the most capital out of the issue that year. The exact status of the Twenty-six Counties, their relationship to King and Commonwealth and whether they constituted a republic or not had all come into question again after the war's end. On 11 July 1945 James Dillon inquired in the Dail: 'Are we a Republic or not, for nobody seems to know?' De Valera gave him a short answer: 'We are, if that is all the deputy wants to know.' Subsequently de Valera apparently became exercised in equal measure by both the complexities of the external association relationship with the Crown, and the fact of having given a straight answer to anyone. There *had* to be more that Dillon wanted to know. It was rumoured that Gray had put Dillon up to asking the question. Accordingly on 17 July, while speaking on the external affairs estimate, he set about defining the status of the Twenty-six Counties.

To save the Dail 'the trouble of looking up references',[27] he said he had himself consulted a number of dictionaries and encyclopaedias. He then proceeded to read out the definitions of the term 'republic' according to the Encyclopedia Britannica, Webster's and so on. The net result of all this was that the wags christened the state a 'Dictionary Republic'. However, in the course of his exposition de Valera did make the point that: 'This External Relations Act is a simple statute repealable by the legislature and not a fundamental law.' The only fundamental law was his Constitution. According to his official biography, he had been moving towards repealing the Act when he was ousted by the general election. He had told Maffey that the Act was not serving the purpose for which he had designed it: to provide a bridge between North and South. Worse, it was causing confusions and divisions in Southern politics. Accordingly he was being driven back to the drawing-board, via the dictionary. The official version is that he stayed his hand to allow Maffey time to try to get the British Government to revive the concept of a Council of Ireland which had been contained in the Government of Ireland Act.

Now, on his return from his world tour, he found that the new Government was laying impious hands on the lion's tail. They were thinking of repealing the External Association Act. During the adjournment debate, on 6 August, William Norton, the Tanaiste, Deputy Leader of the inter-party Government, said he thought it would be good for 'national self-respect . . . at home and abroad if we were to proceed without delay to abolish the External Relations Act.' Given his record on the issue, De Valera's reply could only be: 'You will get no opposition from us.'

'Without delay' turned out to mean what it said. Although Fine Gael had fought the election on a reaffirmation of its old fidelity to the Commonwealth, at a meeting of the Canadian Bar Association in Ottawa on 1 September the Fine Gael Taoiseach, John A. Costello, denounced the External Relations Act as being: 'full of inaccuracies and infirmities'. And a week later, at a press conference, he confirmed a report in the Dublin *Sunday Independent* that the Government intended to repeal the Act. There was a good deal of confusion and political point-scoring subsequently; in the end de Valera had no option but to vote for the demise of the Act. The Dail was thus unanimous, and the Republic of Ireland Act was signed into law by the President on 21 December 1948. The date of its enactment was, however, held over until the following year. All of the foregoing was to have a significant impact on today's Ireland and on Anglo-Irish relationships.

This came about as follows. First, the Unionists took a hand. Sir Basil Brooke declared a general election for 10 February 1949. Five days after he announced this Costello called an all-party meeting at the Mansion House, at which those present decided to launch a root-and-branch onslaught on partition. Anti-partition candidates were sponsored in the forthcoming Six County elections. A major propaganda campaign was instituted in Ireland, England and America. Large sums of money were collected and masses of information collected and disseminated about discrimination and gerrymandering. De Valera himself spoke at several British venues.

The Mansion House initiative had a number of important results: presumably none but the first was in any way intentional. In the Twenty-six Counties it created so much publicity that all light-minded considerations such as unemployment and emigration were overshadowed. In the Six Counties the combination of a Republican renewal in the South, and intervention by Dublin in a Belfast-run election, wiped out every consideration save the Union in loyalist eyes. The Labour Party was decimated and the Unionists were returned to power with the same majority as in 1921: 42 seats to 12. The disorganized IRA received a sudden accession of strength in both propaganda terms and recruitment. And, last but not least, the British Government hung an albatross around its neck which it still wears, the celebrated 'guarantee' to the Unionists. This last requires some explanation.

One of the Mansion House Committee's efforts to win friends and influence people in the Six Counties was to announce on 10 February 1949, polling day in the North, that the Republic of Ireland Act would come into force on Easter Monday, 18 April, the anniversary of the Easter Rising. Although de Valera was party to the Committee, and had not opposed the passing of the Bill in the Dail, he boycotted the Easter ceremonies which transformed the Twenty-six Counties into a republic. Fianna Fail was not permitted to participate in the official ceremonies at the GPO. Instead, he led his colleagues in a wreath-laying ceremony at Arbour Hill to commemorate the executed 1916 leaders.

In London, British reactions were equally negative, but with longer-lasting effect. Under pressure from the Unionists the Labour Government moved to respond to the disappearance of the link with the Crown. The Ireland Act which, on 3 May 1949, Prime Minister Clement Attlee introduced in the House of Commons, contained the following provision: 'It is hereby declared that Northern Ireland remains part of Her Majesty's Dominions of the United Kingdom and it is hereby affirmed that in no event will Northern Ireland or any part thereof cease to be a part of Her Majesty's Dominions and the United Kingdom without the consent of the Parliament of Northern Ireland.'

So, in their joint anxiety to score off each other on the partition issue, both de Valera and the inter-party Government succeeded in contributing to a copper-fastening of the division. Practically everyone in Twenty-six County political life erupted in indignation over the Attlee initiative, but to no avail. No matter what speech-making and propagandizing was done, Dublin policy-makers had unwittingly conspired to ensure that henceforth the Unionists would end up with a veto on change.

At this stage some kind of assessment of de Valera's lifelong policy towards partition becomes incumbent on a biographer, if for no other reason than that the ending of partition was defined by him as his 'primary and fundamental national aim.'[28] Though it was the inter-party Government that took the final step, de Valera was at pains to let the world know, via his biography, that it was he who had first thought of repealing the External Relations Act. How did a man who in a very real sense had made a political career out of partition, denouncing its evil to the four corners of the world, fetch up in such a cul-de-sac? Leaving his public lion Act to one side, what did he really see when he looked into his own heart to know the wishes of the people of Northern Ireland? The truth is the short answer. The tragedy is that he never acted on it.

He told Frank Gallagher what made partition 'such a grievous wrong'.[29] The 'deepest wound' was the division not of territory, but of people, the division of the personnel of the nation. In an earlier talk he had told Gallagher that the position of the majority was one of a group, now in power, fearing to become a minority inside a temperamentally different state. This was the essence of partition's persistence and it should be approached from that point of view. However, having thus accurately diagnosed the problem, what did de Valera do about making the state he ruled for so long less 'temperamentally different' from that of the Protestants of Northern Ireland?

The truthful answer is that by the introduction of his theocratic and sectarian Constitution he helped to make a bad situation worse. And the situation as Southern Protestants saw it *was* bad. De Valera was once warned by the head of the Irish Statistics Office, Roy C. Geary, that it could be argued that the worst discrimination in the whole island was directed not against Six County Catholics, but against Twenty-six County Protestants.[30] The shock of a British departure coupled with the progressive introduction of Roman Catholic legislation drove many Protestants from the state immediately after independence. In 1911 census returns[31] showed that there were 327,171 Protestants in Southern Ireland.

By 1926 this figure had fallen sharply, to 220,723. And at the time of Geary's warning, 1951, the number had dropped to roughly half the 1911 total. The difficulties confronting de Valera, or any Southern legislator, in attempting to check the imposition of a Catholic ethos on their Protestant fellow citizens will be more easily grasped by readers who follow the intricacies of Church–State relations detailed in Chapter 31. Nevertheless – quite apart from the fact that de Valera's Constitution and general conduct in office furthered rather than checked the legislative drift – there was something curmudgeonly and ungenerous about de Valera's whole approach to Northerners.

Although an offer of co-operation had come from Belfast his response, in the words of the director of Radio Eireann, made it clear that: 'There is no intention of making noticeable or ostentatious progress in developing a close understanding between the Dublin and Belfast broadcasting organisations.'[32] Lack of co-operation and denial of official recognition remained settled Fianna Fail policy towards the Six County authorities. Cabinet Minutes recorded twelve years[33] after the Radio Eireann decision noted that the Government 'did not approve' of Bord Failte, the Tourist Board, seeking the co-operation of 'public representatives and other prominent persons in the Six Counties' in connection with An Tostal, a major festival being planned for the Twenty-six Counties. However the Government felt that the festival would provide an 'excellent opportunity' to distribute anti-partition propaganda to foreign visitors.

When Sir James Craig died, de Valera was represented at the funeral on 28 November 1940 by a Protestant member of the Seanad, Senator Robinson. Robinson was so well received by the Unionists, in particular by J. M. Andrews, Craig's successor, that he asked for a note to be sent to the Secretary of the Northern Ireland Government expressing official appreciation for the consideration shown him. Maurice Moynihan prepared a draft for his opposite number along the lines suggested. However, de Valera refused to allow it to be sent on the grounds that 'a letter from the Secretary of this Department [of the Taoiseach] to the Secretary of the Northern Government would be too formal'. He directed Robinson to write himself.[34]

De Valera once told David Gray[35] that the people of the Twenty-six Counties got on better with the English as individuals, and understood them better, than their Nationalist brethren in the Six Counties. There was 'something about' the Six County Nationalists. It might have been more accurate to state that he had 'something' concerning the Northern Nationalists. We have seen how he rebuffed their representations during the ports negotiations. This was perhaps understandable in the circumstances, but it is hard to justify his rejection of other suggestions made by Nationalist leaders years later when no great issue hung in the balance.

Twice in successive years he refused to allow Six County representatives to sit in the Seanad. Given that he had drafted a Constitution claiming the Thirty-two Counties, one would have thought it axiomatic that he should have acknowledged the right of representation from all those Thirty-two counties – even welcomed it – to prove his point. But when he was visited by a deputation of Nationalists in January 1952 he flatly rejected a suggestion that two Nationalists, recently elected to the Westminster Parliament, should sit instead in the Senate. He thought they should abstain from Westminster, but rejected suggestions that Dublin should defray their salaries so that they could devote themselves to constituency work in the Six Counties. Beyond this negative advice he had nothing to offer the delegation save a lecture on how much he 'resented statements' that he had done nothing to end partition.[36] He stated that a 'steady policy in the direction of re-unification had been, and would continue to be, pursued. . . '.

The following year he told another delegation that the policy of abstention from Westminster was not necessarily a negative one, and again turned down suggestions of any form of representation in the Dublin Parliament. Eddie McAteer MP, the delegation's leader, had proposed that, if it were decided that Nationalists should not take their seats in Westminster, they should get a 'symbolic' attendance in Dublin – a 'right of audience of some kind'. De Valera had a litany of objections to the idea, including no 'representation for Six County members without taxation or responsibility'. He feared that 'symbolic representation' would be followed by a demand for 'fuller representation'. Also he was apprehensive about upsetting 'the idea of representation in the Twenty-six Counties'.

Decoded, what this meant was that de Valera did not want the Northern Nationalists making of partition a substantive issue which he might have to act on, as opposed to securing electoral kudos for mere verbal republicanism. Not that he had any particular time for Northern Unionists. On another occasion[37] he told Gray that he was optimistic about a united Ireland because 'even exchanges of population were not impossible these days'. As Gray made 'no comment on this suggestion', no further conversation ensued. Therefore we do not know whether de Valera really visualized the British swapping Irish Catholics for Irish Protestants: Kilburn for East Belfast – a beguiling thought.

What we do know is that in his last days in power de Valera decided in effect to do nothing about partition. The inter-party Government had put in train a study of the 'practical problems arising on re-integration of the national territory'.[38] De Valera directed that the work should continue[39] and on 1 August 1957 received a progress report. The Ministers for Justice, Lands, Health, Education and the Gaeltacht said that in the existing circumstances there was 'no value' in pursuing the study.[40] Industry and Commerce felt it should be deferred in view of the impending European Free Trade Association (EFTA) proposals. Finance was in favour of such a study, but not as a matter of 'urgency'. Agriculture thought it a good idea

644

to have up-to-date comparative studies on the subsidies available in the Six Counties, and on allied matters. Local Government, Social Welfare, and Posts and Telegraphs made no reply, but all was compensated for by the Department of Defence! Here: 'a study of the military problems arising on the re-integration of the national territory has already been well advanced'.

On 29 January 1958 de Valera made a major speech[41] in the Seanad opposing the following motion by Senator Stanford: 'That Seanad Eireann requests the Government to set up a Commission or to take other decisive and energetic steps to consider and report on the best means of promoting social, economic and cultural co-operation between the Twenty-six Counties and Six Counties.' Stanford, a Trinity College senator, had been trying to get the motion debated since the previous July.[42] De Valera manipulated him into withdrawing the motion by proposing instead a Joint Commission from both the Six and Twenty-six Counties. The *Irish Times* applauded his wisdom in this: ' . . . we cannot see why such a body should not be constituted'.[43] In the course of his speech de Valera had said:[44] 'The Government is in duty bound – certainly in my opinion and in the opinion of the present Government – to do everything in its power to foster economic, social and cultural relations. . . . It was the duty of Departments of State. . . .'

However, after the debate there was no tangible sign of activity on the Great Issue from de Valera. The faithful Moynihan kept reminding him of the departmental studies and the question of 'whether and in what direction co-operation [social, economic and cultural] with the Six Counties is possible'. Finally he got his answer.[45] De Valera decided that: ' . . . it is *not* [author's italics] necessary to raise the matter at a Government meeting. It may be presumed that Departments will keep the matter in mind without any explicit directions.' Moynihan noted that in support of this judgement de Valera quoted a statement of his own during the Stanford debate: 'It is the duty of the Departments of State. . . '. A few days later, on 14 March, the Irish Ambassador in London, Hugh McCann, received his instructions concerning a suggestion by Lord Longford that an Anglo-Irish Society be set up: ' . . . it is a case where we should advance very cautiously and, for the time being, not at all'.[46] The objection to Longford's suggestion[47] was that the society would be composed of 'Anglo-Irish' and thus the Government 'might easily become prisoners of a particular way of thinking on Ireland'.[48]

Almost at the same time that this letter was being delivered, de Valera seems to have upscuttled his own entire 'way of thinking on Ireland'. During a three-day visit to London for the St Patrick's Day celebrations, in the course of which he visited Prime Minister Harold Macmillan, he is said to have paid an unheralded call on Lord Home, the British Foreign Secretary. Only his Macmillan visit was reported in the press of the time. But a lead story in the *Irish Times*[49] many years afterwards, ascribed to official British sources, describes another 'visit' to Home, which, if it

645

occurred, was the more newsworthy happening. It may be that, instead[50] of paying a visit to Home, he simply made use of the opportunity presented by Home's presence at an Irish Embassy dinner on the 18th to throw out his weighty sprat.[51] According to the *Irish Times* he proposed that, in return for unity, Ireland would rejoin the Commonwealth. The previous year his old schoolmate, Cardinal d'Alton, had made similar suggestions which the more knowledgeable remarked could not have been made without approval from 'persons of influence'.[52] Now de Valera 'made it a condition of the Commonwealth proposal that the United Kingdom should take the initiative towards such a solution'.[53] 'Cute hoor' to the end.

The proposal was, of course, facilitated to a degree by the fact of India's both becoming a republic and remaining a member of the Commonwealth. In a sense external association was coming into vogue. But above all there was de Valera's sense of impending dissolution. In July[54] Aiken saw Home again and pointedly remarked that, while any solution which de Valera endorsed would probably succeed, 'he would not live for ever'. Ironically, in turning down the suggestion, though he did admit that a united Ireland would be in everyone's interest, Home bolstered his arguments by using de Valera's own newspaper, the *Sunday Press*:[55] ' . . . judging from the inflammatory material appearing . . . there could be no assurance that a United Ireland would stay in the Commonwealth. Lord Home produced as an example the *Sunday Press*. . . . ' He also objected to the history that was taught in Irish schools, to which Aiken replied that the Scots had not burned their history books. It was a good answer – but not, unfortunately, a solution to partition.

Nor did de Valera have one. The Commonwealth suggestion was his parting shot. He relinquished his grip on the lion's tail the following year and retired as Taoiseach to become President. He had profited from the issue. His country of adoption had not. In the course of his long life in politics Eamon de Valera had, in reality, not advanced the partition issue one centimetre beyond the point where it lay on the morning of 6 December 1921 when Michael Collins put his signature to the Treaty.

Partition, and a few trips abroad, were de Valera's main occupations during his three years in opposition under the first inter-party Government's reign. One of these trips, which occurred in 1949, brought him face to face with Churchill when both men were attending a Council of Europe meeting at Strasbourg. However, he refused either to be photographed or to fraternize with him.[56] During 1950, a Holy Year, he attended celebrations at Luxeuil in France commemorating the Irish saint Columbanus. After these he visited the Holy Land as a guest of the Israeli Government. He stayed in the King David Hotel in Jerusalem, which, during the Israeli war of independence against the British, was blown up by guerillas who had studied Michael Collins' methods. 'When he left Israel he made sure to cross into Jordan. He was persona grata with both sides and felt sympathy for both.'[57]

31

WHEN BISHOPS WERE BISHOPS

DE VALERA'S PRAYERS during the Holy Year would appear to have been answered. Certainly religion was to play a part in his return to power in 1951, after what was known as the Mother and Child controversy brought down the inter-party Government. The 1950s were a period during which an observer might have been forgiven for thinking that the Church had decided to settle the constitutional confusions surrounding the status of the Twenty-six Counties by converting them into a Green Vatican state. The Mother and Child row was but one, albeit the most significant, of a decade of continuous interventions by the Church into the State arena.

The controversy arose through the detonation of a legislative time bomb that de Valera had left ticking away in the Department of Health on leaving office. It was a draft Health Bill, the brainchild in the first place of the chief medical adviser to the Government, Dr James Deeny, and Ward, the politician who fell in the wake of the tribunal investigating his affairs. Dr James Ryan had brought the project forward to the point where a memorandum was prepared for de Valera.[1] Blind or not, he saw its implications clearly and wrote across the memo: 'Confidential. I would not transmit this as it stands. It requires considerable revision.'[2] The memorandum was duly amended, so that it became an unusual Christmas present. Another note reads: 'A later corrected draft given to A.B. [Archbishop McQuaid] 24.12.47'. But the corrections were not sufficient to prevent the Bill being objected to in clerical and medical circles. Amongst its laudable objectives the Bill included a free medical service for mothers and for children up to sixteen. There were to be improved medical services for schools, and better protection against infectious diseases. There was also to be a means test. The doctors were worried about the potential loss of fees, the hierarchy about what they saw as a broad range of intrusions on their turf. In 1947 they had summarized these in a letter to de Valera:[3] '. . . for the State, under the Act, to empower the public authority to provide for the health of all children, and to treat their ailments, and to educate women in regard to health, and to provide them with gynae-cological services, was directly and entirely contrary to Catholic social teaching, the rights of the family, the rights of the Church in education, and the rights of the medical profession, and of voluntary institutions.'

Loss of office meant that de Valera could afford to let this chalice pass. However the inter-party Government Minister for Health, Dr Noel Browne, a young Trinity graduate, gripped it with both hands. Browne had successfully introduced a most ambitious scheme to curb TB by using the assets of the Irish Hospitals Sweepstakes and of the Department of Health itself to raise some £30 million for increased expenditure on sanatoria, BCG vaccinations and the use of streptomycin. The effects were seen in the statistics long after he had ceased to be a political force: TB claimed 3,103 lives in 1948, but by 1961 the figure had fallen to 432. Having launched the TB scheme into orbit, Browne, known in Dublin's slums as 'the man who gave us the free TB', turned his formidable energies to implementing his predecessors' Act.

The effect was similar to that of a man standing on the end of a plank. The objections which bishops and doctors had made privately to de Valera now hit Browne, and the Government, in the face very publicly. The Irish Medical Association condemned 'socialized medicine'. The hierarchy developed the arguments earlier put to de Valera in a letter to the Government dated 10 October 1950:[4]

> ... the powers ... in the proposed Mother and Child Health Service are ... liable to very great abuse ... no assurance that they would be used in moderation could justify their enactment. If adopted in law they would constitute a ready-made instrument for future totalitarian aggression. The right to provide for health of children belongs to parents, not to the State.
>
> The State has the right to intervene only in a subsidiary capacity, to supplement, not to supplant. It may help indigent or neglectful parents, it may not deprive 90 per cent of parents of their rights because of 10 per cent necessitous or negligent parents.
>
> It is not sound social policy to impose a state medical service on the whole community on the pretext of relieving the necessitous 10 per cent from the so-called indignity of the means test.

Those were the days when bishops were bishops in Ireland – when their lordships could pronounce it a mortal sin for Catholics to attend Trinity College, Dublin. This ban was of long standing, and had in fact been given a form of legal backing as far back as 1928 by the then Chief Justice, Hugh Kennedy.[5] He asked the Roman Catholic Archbishop of Dublin, Dr Byrne, to guide him in deciding whether Catholic minors who were wards of court might be allowed to go to Trinity. Predictably the Archbishop confirmed Kennedy's feeling that they should not, and the Chief Justice subsequently ruled accordingly. However, through custom and usage, by 1944 the ban had become considerably relaxed, to the point where most enlightened Irish Catholics regarded it as no more than what it was – an outdated outcropping of the great controversies surrounding university education which had raged in the late nineteenth and early twentieth centuries. However, the Lenten Pastorals that year ended the relaxation process. Dr McQuaid's pastoral spoke of Trinity as being a 'Protestant' university[6] and Catholics were forbidden to enter the College without his express permission and subject to a number of safeguards.[7]

Not surprisingly, therefore, a section in the proposed legislation that dealt with sex instruction created intense disquiet: 'We regard with the greatest apprehension the proposal to give to local medical officers the right to give instruction to Catholic girls and women in regard to this sphere of conduct. . . . Gynaecological care may be and in some countries is interpreted to include provision for birth limitation and abortion. We have no guarantee that State officials will respect Catholic principles in regard to these matters.'

The belts from the croziers, combined with the attrition from the doctors, drove MacBride into demanding and getting Browne's resignation, on 10 April 1951. Two days later there was a turbulent debate on the resignation in the Dail. Inter-party speakers dismembered each other in equal measures of passion and pusillanimity. Then came the Supreme Moment:[8] 'There was a sense of occasion as Mr. de Valera slowly rose to his feet.' It was not to be fulfilled. Browne has recorded:[9] '. . . de Valera muttered inaudibly one sentence only, "We have heard enough."' Pilate had not so much washed his hands as extended them to catch the falling fruits of power. The Dail was dissolved on 7 May 1951. Clann na Poblachta lost eight seats. MacBride was tarnished by the affair and barely managed to retain his seat. Fianna Fail only gained a single seat, but with the aid of Browne, who voted with the Independents, de Valera was able to form a minority Government.

His greatest challenges on taking up office were not political but physical and psychological. His eyesight worsened dramatically. As far back as 1936 he had had an operation in Zurich to remove the lens from the better of his eyes, after which his sight 'became extremely good'.[10] Prior to this his eye, apparently, had three symmetrical foci. The result of this was that on one occasion as he was driving in Dublin he saw two identical twin girls walking on the footpath. Just as he was commenting to himself on their extraordinary similarity he saw to his horror that a third identical girl had appeared walking above the shoulder of the two girls on the path, so as to form a triangle.[11] His interlude of good sight lasted until the outbreak of war when his eyes began to film over, causing lack of vision. This condition was successfully operated on at the Mater Hospital in Dublin in 1940. The third and most serious bout of eye trouble necessitated a series of six painful operations in Utrecht to reattach a detached retina. The manner in which he faced this trauma may be gauged from a description by the Irish Ambassador to The Hague, Josephine McNeill, who visited him after the second operation:[12]

The Taoiseach has come through his ordeal – for the two operations were a severe ordeal – very well. Despite the great skill of Dr. Weve which reduced the actual pain suffered during the operations (performed with local anaesthetic) to a minimum, nevertheless, the operations which were delicate and necessarily protracted constituted a severe psychological strain. The Taoiseach's most admirable courage brought him through splendidly and his great patience and fortitude in these trying days of convalescence is helping him to recover from his ordeal.

The operations left him with only peripheral vision, and he could not read. This disability was overcome by the 'oral reporting', as he termed it, of devoted public servants like Maurice Moynihan. Where mobility was concerned, de Valera got around places he was familiar with astonishingly well. Those which he did not know he managed to negotiate with the help of aides. Sometimes he would astound people by striding through a strange building unassisted. He accomplished this seeming miracle by sending his aide de camp, Colonel Sean Brennan, to inspect the location beforehand, pacing the distances and counting the steps involved.

Politically, too, de Valera remained as sure-footed as ever; he gave a notable demonstration of this in coping with a renewed onslaught from the Church the year after his operations. De Valera had allowed Ryan to press ahead with the fundamentals of the Bill which had destroyed the previous Government. The Minister, it seemed, had met with success in dealing with the obstacles placed in its way. Unlike the impetuous Browne, Ryan had first secured the assent of his colleagues to what he was doing. He also sought to compromise rather than to confront publicly on the episcopal and medical fronts. When the Lenten Pastoral of Bishop Browne of Galway emerged containing criticisms of his Department's disposal of Hospital Sweepstakes' monies he replied toughly but privately:[13] 'A Lenten Pastoral is the last place in which I would expect false or uncharitable statements, and I still find it hard to credit the evidence that I see before me.' Browne wrote back equally firmly and privately, assuring Ryan that he bore him no personal ill will but still sticking to his guns.[14]

However, as a result of these and other behind-the-scenes manoeuvrings certain compromises were made. Sex education, for example, no longer reared its priapic head. To placate the doctors, the means test was dropped. But, unknown to Ryan or de Valera, the croziers were again being prepared for battle in the incense-filled back rooms. The mighty engine, having struck once successfully in 1951, was moved into striking mode again in April 1953. An embargoed letter detailing their lordships' objections to Fianna Fail's handiwork was sent to the newspapers. Vivion de Valera, who was managing director of the *Irish Press*, was shown a copy and immediately alerted his father.[15] De Valera promptly phoned his old Blackrock College classmate, John Cardinal d'Alton. Was it to be a case of public war or private discussion? he asked. D'Alton settled for private discussion. The Cardinal drove from Armagh, de Valera literally meeting him halfway, in Drogheda. This venue was selected because Drogheda was in the diocese of Armagh, which meant that the Cardinal did not have to leave his Metropolitan area to see de Valera; nor did de Valera have to leave his territory to cross the border. Mahomet did not go to the Mountain, nor the Mountain to Mahomet. They just met, privately. In a way it was a meeting of two cardinals, one lay, one clerical. The official biography described the outcome:[16] 'An amicable solution followed.'

It was, however, not quite that easy. The 'amicable solution' was only reached after a number of other bargaining sessions not referred to in the biography. In fact[17] de Valera had alerted Joseph Walshe, now Ambassador to the Holy See, to stand by in case the lay cardinal found it necessary to appeal over the head of the clerical one to his superiors in Rome. And Cardinal d'Alton only agreed to withhold publication of the letter from the bishops after de Valera had promised to arrange a meeting between the hierarchy and himself the following day at no less a venue than Arus an Uachtarain, the President's official residence. De Valera complained of the bishops' letter that: ' . . . the terms of the statement have caused me no little concern, and surprise, since I was aware that the proposals for health legislation had, on a number of occasions, been discussed by representatives of the Hierarchy, with the Tanaiste, and with the Minister for Health, and since I understood that at no stage in these discussions did it appear that any fundamental or irreconcilable difference of opinion existed.'

Browne had had exactly the same experience at the hands of the bishops. He claimed that he understood he had satisfied their objections before the croziers were unsheathed. But while this misapprehension could be ascribed to political immaturity in the case of the youthful Browne, no such explanation could be advanced in the case of negotiations involving a Fianna Fail father figure with the experience of the wise and wily James Ryan. De Valera realized that their lordships felt they were dealing from such a position of strength that he must either confront them as Browne had done – and risk his fate – or capitulate. He chose the latter course.

He opened the proceedings at Arus an Uachtarain by declaring himself in agreement with the obligation to accept the teaching authority of the bishops as laid down[18] by the hierarchy after the Mother and Child controversy. This statement had boldly asserted the correctness of the ban on Catholics attending Trinity College: 'The prohibition is not a mere arbitrary one; it is based on the natural divine law itself.' And it had then gone on to say: ' . . . Subjects should not oppose their bishops' teaching by word, by act or in any other way, and positively they should carry out what is demanded by it. . . . It is the province, then, of the Church Hierarchy to decide authoritatively whether political, social and economic theories are in harmony with God's law.'

Accordingly, the 'amicable solution' finally agreed upon the following October made certain that the new Health Bill was 'in harmony with God's law'. In other words, it left a very large slice of the Irish hospital system in the hands of nuns, priests and the Roman Catholic ethos. Significantly, Noel Browne recorded in his autobiography that the only comment de Valera ever made to him on the Mother and Child controversy was:[19] 'You should not have published the correspondence with the Hierarchy.' The route which de Valera favoured in matters of Church–State controversy was the one which led to the Drogheda meeting with Cardinal d'Alton. He had to travel it again before 1953 was out.

On 16 November that year he received a letter[20] from the Archbishop of Dublin, Dr John Charles McQuaid, seeking a meeting with him on behalf of the hierarchy on 'a matter of grave social import'. De Valera wasted no time in phoning Dr McQuaid to find out what this new enormity might be; it was the 'importation and circulation of newspapers and periodicals objectionable on moral grounds'.[21] When the Archbishop was ushered into de Valera's office three days later he brought with him two 'paper-back novels of a highly indecent nature'.[22]

Like de Valera, McQuaid was an extremely complex character. He was highly intelligent, not devoid of humour, and very often remarkably far-seeing. His standing in the history of Blackrock College could be described as an Irish variation of that of Dr Arnold of Rugby. Privately he was charitable to the point of being princely in his disbursements. As a bishop, however, he was authoritarian, convinced of his right and responsibility to play a strongly interventionist role in Irish society. He was particularly zealous in his efforts to protect that society from the contagion of sex. But he had a strange attitude towards sexuality in print. He had been particularly kind to Vivion de Valera while the latter was a student at Blackrock (this was the source of a friendship with de Valera himself, which cooled[23] somewhat after the Archbishop repaid de Valera's role in helping to secure the archbishopric for him by championing the teachers – against de Valera – in the great post-war strike). One day he had brought Vivion, who, while still a student, had been appointed a director of the *Irish Press*, to his room to show him a pile of cuttings from that newspaper which he wished Vivion to study – and proceed against. They were mainly full-page advertisements for the big Dublin drapery store, Clery's. A number included small line drawings of women modelling underwear of a design which reflected the modest standards of the Ireland of that era. McQuaid, however, pointed out the insidious immorality of the drawings. Some of them, if one used a magnifying glass, indicated the outline of a mons veneris.

Therefore when McQuaid produced the trashy novels de Valera realized that Something Must be Done. McQuaid said the books were 'known to be on sale in twenty-one shops in Dublin.' Peripheral vision meant that there was no question of de Valera himself reading the offending works. But his political vision was unimpaired. In a letter to McQuaid on 21 December de Valera described the steps taken:[24]

> . . . towards preventing the importation of indecent paper-backed novels. Instructions have been given to Customs Officers to detain suspected consignments pending a decision of the Censorship of Publications Board, to whom a copy of each suspected book is to be forwarded. Periodicals are likewise to receive special attention. These instructions are, of course, in addition to the existing instructions concerning consignments of books in general.

The way the system worked in practice was described to me by a former

Customs official. I asked him to explain how an author like Brendan Behan could be banned. 'Well, you're given a list,' he explained, 'an' you look up under B, for Behan. Then if his book is on the list you go through the book and see is there any dirty words or obscenity. Then you mark them, an' it goes up to the Censorship an' they ban it.' Readers may find a certain irony in the fact that I was interviewing the gentleman in question as part of some research I was doing on crime in Ireland. His competence in this area has since been attested to by the bestowal of a lengthy jail sentence. But the censorship mechanism was the same for him as for a member of the Legion of Mary. Even without a list or Customs officials, voluntary Catholic thought police were diligent in sending potentially 'objectionable material' to the Censorship Board, so it is not surprising that 'pornographers' banned included:[25] Faulkner, Hemingway, Sartre, Ehrenburg, Tennessee Williams, Scott Fitzgerald, Beckett, Joyce, Graham Greene, Dylan Thomas, Orwell, C. P. Snow, Muriel Spark, Joseph Heller, Danilo Dolci, Frank O'Connor, John McGahern, Sean O'Faolain, Edna O'Brien, Kate O'Brien, Liam O'Flaherty and, of course, Brendan Behan.

In those years, outside of a very small circle, books were seldom discussed on their literary merits. The more general discussion point was: 'Should it have been banned or not?' But even the type of censorship indicated by the foregoing selection did not satisfy bishops intent on creating an ultramontane Catholic state, and invoking de Valera to justify their actions. Some six months before de Valera returned to power in 1957 the country had been swept by controversy arising from the Clonlara case. The case and its aftermath perfectly illustrate the temper of rural Irish Catholicism of the time. It arose out of an assault on two Jehovah's Witnesses at Clonlara in Co. Clare in May 1956 by a group which included the local parish priest. The Witnesses' Bibles and other literature were publicly burned. When the case came to trial on 27 July 1956 the courtroom was packed. The Bishop of Killaloe, Dr Rogers, attended the hearing, and it was reported that: 'The crowded Courtroom rose to their feet as His Lordship entered.'[26]

The assaults and burnings were admitted, but the charges were dismissed under the Probation of Offenders Act. The District Justice, however, found the two Jehovah's Witness plaintiffs guilty of blasphemy and bound them to the peace on bonds of £200 each! What troubled Dr Rogers was the fact that his priest had been brought to court. He wrote to Costello, the then Taoiseach, invoking de Valera's Constitution to protest against the action of the Attorney General in proceeding:[27]

> . . . against one of my priests for upholding and defending the fundamental truths of our treasured Catholic Faith. . . . I also find it passing strange that, despite the fact that the preamble to our Constitution invokes and honours the Blessed Trinity, your Attorney-General should arraign in Court an excellent priest of my diocese and the other loyal Catholics of Clonlara Parish, for their defence of the doctrine of the Blessed Trinity, a doctrine so nobly enshrined in our Constitution.

Are we to have legal protection in future against such vile and pernicious attacks on our faith? We censor obscene literature: your Attorney-General prosecutes one of my priests for doing what I, and all good Catholics here, regard as his *bounden duty and right* [author's italics]. The matter cannot rest.

Costello replied[28] to Rogers, stating that while he appreciated the 'just indignation' of 'the clergy and people', nevertheless 'the law provides a means of dealing with persons whose conduct is calculated to lead to a breach of the peace or who utter blasphemy'. Once complaints had been laid arising from the Clonlara incident, the state had no option but to investigate and take appropriate action. It is unlikely that this of itself would have caused Rogers to 'rest'. Appeasement seems to have been achieved through the intercession of John Charles McQuaid,[29] whom Costello approached. De Valera was fully aware of the details of the Clonlara case: it had occurred in his constituency and he had access to all the files. The implications of the invocation of his Constitution in connection with matters of faith were more telling when directed towards himself than towards Costello. He realized, therefore, that he had to tread warily when McQuaid, with the backing of the hierarchy, once again entered the lists on the censorship issue during 1957. Earlier that year a far more serious religion-based controversy – which we will turn to in a moment – had underlined the sort of influence that McQuaid wielded at the time.

On 4 December 1957 the Archbishop launched an 'organised campaign' against 'foul books'.[30] This had its origins in a split on the Censorship Board between a conservative chairman, Professor J. J. Pigott, and two like-minded colleagues, and a minority of two liberals,[31] one of whom was a Protestant, R. R. Figgis. Figgis had been appointed by the coalition administration, which had also erred by failing to replace a departing Catholic clergyman with another priest. In consequence, Pigott's campaign took the form of objecting to the provision in the Censorship Act that a book could only be banned when there were three votes in favour and not more than one against. In a nutshell, the two liberals could veto the three conservatives' bans. Matters came to a head in September 1957 when Pigott refused to convene meetings of the Board unless the Government removed the offending liberals. His resignation was asked for, and its acceptance was followed by the immediate resignation of the remaining two conservatives. Three replacements were appointed in October, all exemplary Catholics; none, however, were priests or nuns. Worse, under the new chairman, Judge Conroy, the Board developed a reprehensible trend towards liberalism (liberalism in the Irish context, that is; it was this Board which banned Spark, Dolci, McGahern and Heller). These liberal attitudes were what elicited the belt of the crozier on 4 December.

There followed a flood of protests against the 'tide of filth' admitted by the Censorship Board. Such fonts of critical theory as Secondary Schools Past Pupils' Unions, Football Clubs, the Catholic Boys' Brigade, the

Belvedere Newsboys' Club, St Vincent de Paul and Legion of Mary groups all erupted in spontaneous indignation, calling for a tightening of the censorship laws and reform of the Censorship Board. These culminated in a letter from the hierarchy to the Government on 30 January 1958, echoing the protests and demands for 'reform'. However, the impression of spontaneity was lessened when the Government discovered that a 'number of these were date-lined the 4th December, 1957'.[32] Furthermore, no samples of the evil tide were furnished to the Censorship Board. It was clear that the campaign was 'the direct consequence of the Minister for Justice in calling for Professor Pigott's resignation'.[33] Accordingly, de Valera parried the hierarchy's thrust in a finely crafted reply[34] that could be read either as an explanation or as a rebuke. It adroitly made the connection between the campaign and the reconstitution of the Censorship Board: 'As regards the extent to which the number of these publications has been increased, although the evidence is not conclusive, I do not doubt that some increase has taken place as a result of difficulties that existed for a time concerning the membership and functioning of the Censorship of Publications Board. *Of these difficulties I think Their Lordships are aware* [author's italics].' But de Valera refused to allow an episcopal presence on the Censorship Board: 'I am afraid that a considerably larger number of members, working in groups, as suggested by the Bishops, would find it very difficult to maintain uniform standards of judgement and that, in consequence of this, there might be a serious growth in adverse criticism of the censorship arrangements.' He ended with a pointed reminder that it would be easier to deal with the problem of censorship if 'complaints by individuals and societies were made in a specific rather than a general form'.

De Valera's reply to the hierarchy deserves to be remembered; it could be taken as marking the point where the Irish censorship began to mend its lamentable ways. Those months of 1957–8 also marked a nadir in Catholic–Protestant relationships in Southern Ireland. The general public knew nothing of the exchanges between Government and hierarchy over censorship, but they were all too well aware of a husband and wife row in the quiet Co. Wexford village of Fethard-on-Sea that grew into a national tempest. The conflict arose out of the Roman Catholic Ne Temere decree (the Latin phrase is from the first words of the decree promulgated in 1907–8, which translate as 'not rashly'; the theologically correct term in these more emollient days is 'motu proprio', meaning of one's own volition) whereby consent to a Catholic's marrying a non-Catholic was granted by the Church only on condition that children of the marriage would be reared as Catholics. The principal Catholic newspaper, the *Catholic Standard*, stated, incorrectly, that this promise:[35] 'was legally binding in this country'. Simple people buying the *Standard* at Mass on Sundays were therefore led to believe that if the decree were not observed the laws of both God and man were being breached.

Sean Cloney, of Fethard-on-Sea, had married his wife Shiela, a Protestant, in London in 1949. They had two children, both girls. By 27 April 1957 Mrs Cloney's objections to rearing the children as Catholics had reached the point where she left home with them. Three days later Desmond Boal, a Belfast barrister who later became nationally known as a close associate of Ian Paisley, called upon Sean Cloney with a list of what were described as 'settlement proposals'. These predictably required Cloney to agree to the children being brought up as Protestants. However, the Boal formula[36] also suggested that Cloney consider changing his own religion, selling his farm and emigrating to either Australia or Canada with his wife and children.

Boal's initiative found favour neither with Cloney nor with the local Catholic community. An unofficial boycott of Protestants began in the area on 13 May. The boycott rolled on through the summer, generating more heat than light as attitudes hardened throughout the country. A Protestant teacher found a notice on his school door telling him that he would 'get a bullet'. The *Catholic Standard* said that the taking away of the Cloney children had 'cut a deep wound in the Catholic heart of the village'.[37] By the end of June the issue was reaching serious proportions. Memories of Catholic and Protestant atrocity during the 1798 rebellion – only yesterday in folkloric time – were stirring to life. The local Catholic clergy were encouraging their parishioners to continue the boycott. The Protestant bishop of the area, Dr Phair, sought a meeting with President O'Ceallaigh.[38] But before his request could be acted on an influential Catholic bishop, Dr Michael Browne of Galway (known as Cross Michael in his diocese), made a significant and temperature-raising intervention.

Preaching during High Mass at the closing of the Catholic Truth Society's Annual Conference in Wexford, Dr Browne asked:[39] 'Do non-Catholics never use this weapon of boycott in the North? Here in the South do we never hear of them supporting only their own co-religionists in business and in professions? Those who seek the mote in their neighbour's eye, but not the beam in their own, are hypocrites and Pharisees.' Dr Browne said he believed that there was a 'concerted campaign to kidnap Catholic children, and deprive them of their faith, against which non-Catholics had not protested'. However, they had sought to make political capital out of a 'peaceful and moderate protest'. The Bishop made these remarks in the presence of several, seemingly assenting, members of the hierarchy including Cardinal d'Alton and Archbishop McQuaid. What Dr Browne did not know was that some days earlier de Valera had gone secretly to Archbishop's House in Drumcondra to discuss the matter with McQuaid. So far he had managed to avoid saying anything in public about the affair, but the pressures on him to do so were mounting. In view of the delicacy of the situation the Archbishop requested that the discussion be 'strictly confidential'. De Valera agreed, and afterwards gave instructions that the record of the visit should be kept apart from the official file.[40]

However from what little was noted[41] it appears that McQuaid shared de Valera's view on the situation. The boycott was unjustified; moreover, both nationally and internationally it was damaging to Ireland's reputation for religious toleration. De Valera was forced into commenting publicly a few days later when Noel Browne put down a question on the matter in the Dail. Before doing so he made sure to keep McQuaid on side by sending him – marked 'personal' – both a copy of the question and his statement in reply.[42] As these were dated 4 July 1957, the same day on which he replied to Browne, one wonders whether he was avoiding charges of lack of consultation while denying opportunities of intervention!

Browne asked whether representations about the boycott had been made to him and whether he proposed to make a statement. In reply de Valera said:

> Certain representations have been made to me.
>
> I have made no public statement because I have clung to the hope that good sense and decent neighbourly feeling would, of themselves, bring this business to an end. I cannot say that I know every fact, but, if, as Head of the Government, I must speak, I can only say, from what has appeared in public, that I regard this boycott as ill-conceived, ill-considered and futile for the achievement of the purpose for which it seems to have been intended; that I regard it as unjust and cruel to confound the innocent with the guilty; that I repudiate any suggestion that this boycott is typical of the attitude or conduct of our people; that I am convinced that 90 per cent of them look on this matter as I do; and that I beg of all who have regard for the fair name and good repute of our nation to use their influence to bring this deplorable affair to a speedy end.
>
> I would like to appeal also to any who might have influence with the absent wife to urge on her to respect her troth and her promise and to return with her children to her husband and her home.

This cleverly worded statement was also courageous. As the man in the eye of the storm, Sean Cloney, wrote when congratulating de Valera:[43]

> At Mass this morning we heard from the altar the outworn Unionist cry 'Not an inch', the clergy apparently authorise no relaxation of the boycott, and I doubt if it shall ever cease unless and until they so direct. . . . Naturally the Protestants are pleased and appreciative, in Fianna Fail many agree with you completely, others are in a dilemma between 'what the priest says' and 'what Dev. says', still others say in effect that your statement was ill-advised.

However, after de Valera had spoken the bishops fell silent, and, we may assume, John Charles McQuaid did what he could to ensure they stayed that way. Fianna Fail Cummain in Wexford discreetly urged an end to the boycott, and by the end of the year all was quiet again in Fethard-on-Sea. On New Year's Eve Mrs Cloney returned[44] to her home and 'her promise', to obey the dictates of the Ne Temere decree.

Eamon de Valera was, as he had pointedly described himself, 'Head of Government', but, as has been demonstrated, he was primarily a Catholic

Head of Government. Of all the forces which were shortly to transform Ireland, so that the religious sobriquet would no longer be quite so essential, television was one of the most powerful. It was perhaps fitting, therefore, that one of de Valera's last gestures of respect towards Rome whilst in power should have concerned television. In the summer of 1958 a Commission of representative Irish persons was nearing the end of its investigations into the question of setting up an Irish television service. When word of this Commission reached the Pope[45] two Vatican emissaries were despatched to Dublin. They were Monsignor Georges Roche, Prelate of the Papal Household and Superior General of Opus Cenaculi, and Monsignor Andrea Maria Deskur, Executive Vice Secretary of the Pontifical Commission on the Cinema, Radio and Television. After making a formal submission to the Television Commission itself they made more significant representations, informally, to the Government through Sean MacEntee, whose brother-in-law, Dr Michael Browne, was Master-General of the Dominicans.

In a nutshell, the Pope wanted to preserve the ethos which was serving the papacy so well in the provision of money, clergy, nuns and an ever-swelling tide of energetic, white, English-speaking Irish emigrants who took the faith with them to some of the more important parts of the world, chiefly the USA, Canada, Britain, Australia and New Zealand. The Vatican envoys impressed on MacEntee the 'great personal interest' which His Holiness had in the proposed service as a vehicle for 'combatting irreligion and materialism', because, apart from Vatican Radio and a station in Portugal, broadcasting systems were not greatly concerned with 'moral issues': 'the Holy Father had been particularly struck by the potentialities of an Irish television service'. Monsignor Deskur made the highly significant observation that:[46]

> ... the influence of radio and television as media of mass communication had been particularly bad in traditionally Catholic countries in South America and Europe, because of programmes which in their treatment of moral and religious issues had been highly objectionable. .... His Holiness felt that, by reason of its geographical situation, the Irish television could be of great service to the Christian religion provided that a transmitter be installed which would be sufficiently powerful to transmit its programmes to trans-oceanic territories. He trusted, therefore, that when the type, power and site of the television transmitter was being determined this consideration would be given great weight by those responsible.

On the one hand the Vatican was obviously under the impression that the type of censorship-controlled Roman Catholic ethos which then prevailed in Ireland was going to continue; and on the other hand a pretty broad hint was being given that the Pope expected the Irish Government to make sure that the new television service would assist, rather than disrupt, this continuation. The priests asked that the Pontifical Commission on Radio and Television be given the opportunity of studying the Report '*before* [author's italics] the Government made a decision in regard to it'. Not only did de Valera readily agree with this suggestion (he had, after all, arranged for the Irish Constitution to be shown to the Pope of the day before it was shown to the Irish people); he also directed that it be sent 'if possible *in advance of* [author's italics] the final signatures of the Commission'.

However, he was not in power long enough to affect the implementation or otherwise of papal desiderata. By the time the lengthy public debate on the proposed service had ended, de Valera was 'up in the Park'.[47] As President it fell to him to inaugurate the opening of the new TV station. It at least afforded him the opportunity of making a statement the Vatican would have approved of:[48]

> Never before was there in the hands of man an instrument so powerful to influence the thoughts and actions of the multitude. A persistent policy pursued over radio and television, in addition to imparting knowledge, can build up the character of a whole people, including sturdiness and vigour and confidence. On the other hand, it can lead, through demoralisation, to decadence and dissolution.

Unfortunately it was not a path which led to a solution of economic difficulties.

A few months after assuaging the Cardinal's fears, de Valera explained to the electorate where the problem lay. Speaking during a by-election campaign in East Cork, he said:[49]

> When the war ended . . . we recognised that we were presented with a splendid opportunity for a new economic advance. Our homes, our factories and our transport were intact, not as in other countries destroyed. Most of the plans for further developments had already been made and many of them issued as White Papers. All was ready for a flying start. The manoeuvring that brought about the Coalition, however, took out of our hands the direction of affairs, and the plans which we had made were largely set aside or mishandled by the Coalition. Some of the damage thus done may prove irreparable.

The speech was a classic example of de Valera fact: the skilful indication of where credit lay for homes and factories being intact – his neutrality policy; the blaming of other parties for the present state of affairs; and, needless to say, not the slightest hint that his setting aside of Lemass's plans might have had a bearing on the 'damage thus done' which might 'prove irreparable'. His other whipping boy for the unsatisfactory state of affairs was proportional representation:[50] 'The multiplicity of small parties which had grown up, particularly since 1943, appeared to him to militate against effective government.' Decoded, this meant PR was making it difficult in the existing conditions for Fianna Fail to secure an overall majority. He decided, as we shall see, to get rid of PR when opportunity offered.

The country was sinking into an economic and psychological slough of despond. Outside stimuli were virtually denied to it following the war years. The 1948–51 coalition did make two important initiatives in the field of international trade. One was the creation of the Industrial Development Authority, set up in 1949–50 to encourage new industries to come to Ireland. Second, in an effort to stimulate Irish exports to América the coalition set up in 1950 the Dollar Exports Advisory Committee. This led to the establishment the following year of an organization which rivalled the IDA in significance – Coras Trachtala, the Export Board. Some residue of the seeds which Lemass and Leyden had scattered had not fallen on stony ground.

But a good deal of the seed which it was hoped that Marshall Aid would deposit on Irish soil never came. Not that those charged with sowing it had much idea of how this should be done. As T. K. Whitaker, a man who, under MacBride, helped to work out the Irish Marshall Aid White Paper, later admitted:[51]

> It was never conceived of as a programme for policy. It was conceived as something to satisfy the Americans so that we could get Marshall Aid. It did not have, as far as I know, any commitment of the government to do any of the things. There was simply a group of civil servants, of whom I was one, working under the auspices of the Department of External Affairs. We were with MacBride, putting together the most plausible memo we could about gradual progress towards a more viable economy. We were told that, in order to get aid, you have to show that you will be viable in four years' time. So you worked to that schedule. But what you were saying had a very limited influence on government policy.

It also had a limited effect on the dispensers of Marshall Aid largesse. MacBride hoped to gain a grant of £120 million from his application. What actually arrived was some £36 million, of which only something of the order of £5 million was a grant and the rest a loan. This was the real price tag which official Washington placed on neutral Ireland's worth, behind the facade of the genuine welcome the Irish Americans had innocently put on for de Valera. However, money is money, and it is estimated that Marshall Aid paid for half of what was invested by the state in the first inter-party Government period. Much of the money went on land reclamation, clearance, drainage, fertilizers and lime, farm machinery and spreading rural electrification. But it only delayed rather than stemmed the flight from the land, and the long-term effect of Marshall Aid was negligible. National income went up by only 1 per cent during 1949–53. The change-resistant agricultural sector increased production by a mere 8 per cent between 1948 and 1960. Industrial production remained largely a matter of small, family-owned, light manufacturing operations which depended on protection to survive, and exported comparatively little.

Meanwhile emigration and unemployment were rising, as was inflation. Numerous causes were advanced for the poor economic performance in the Ireland of the early fifties: they included rising inflation, British devaluation, the effects of the Korean War and the absence of an entrepreneurial spirit. The presence of a dead hand on the levers of power contributed to and magnified all these ills. In the Cabinet which de Valera formed in June 1951, Sean MacEntee was appointed Minister for Finance. Charming, literate and witty socially, MacEntee was a conservative of the deepest dye politically. He had fought a ferocious bureaucratic battle with Lemass against the introduction of children's allowances (2s 6d per week per child in pre-decimalization coinage – about 15p – starting with the third child) during the war. A memo of his to de Valera on the subject of family allowances illuminates his view of both authority and society. Such allowances, he told de Valera on the outbreak of World War II, were undermining parental authority:[52] ' . . . without the firm exercise of such authority a peasant economy such as ours, based upon the patriarchal principle, cannot exist'. Translated into political terms this meant ' . . . a peasant *following* such as ours, based upon the patriarchal principle, cannot exist'.

Lemass ultimately won the argument over children's allowances because de Valera supported him. Now, more than a decade later, de Valera supported MacEntee in his calcified economic thinking. The Government accepted his recommendation that a flat economy should be taxed. Taxed it duly was in his first Budget of 1952. Income tax went up and basic essentials such as food, petrol and alcohol were all increased in price. The aim was to cut imports, inflation and the trade deficit. In agriculture the objective became a return to protection and subsidization. Wheat and sugar beet production were encouraged, producing surpluses which had to be sold internationally at a loss. Exports and income growth suffered as a result of these policies. Stagnation was the order of the day. De Valera's 1951–4 administration was the shakings of the bag of Fianna Fail policies since its formation. There was nothing of substance left, except the power structure of the political party itself.

Nothing better illustrates the combination of empty sloganizing and callous politicking which formed the real basis for de Valera's approach to the challenges of the fifties than does his treatment of the emigration problem.[53] A parliamentary reply[54] delivered on de Valera's behalf during 1951 stated his policy on emigration as follows: 'The whole objective of the economic and social policy of the Government and of the implementation of that policy through the various Departments of State concerned is to create such economic and social conditions in this country as will lead to the stopping of emigration.'

The appalling record of the decade says all that is required about Irish governmental lack of success in achieving 'such economic and social conditions'. But to be fair to de Valera, few in the state showed much awareness of how the problem might be tackled. A governmental Commission on Emigration and Other Population Problems was set up in

April 1948 and did not report until May 1954. The Report found that the Twenty-six Counties suffered from having the highest dependent group (that is, below the age of fourteen and over sixty-five) of twenty-five countries listed. The Commission noted the conservative effect of so many elderly people in a society and the retarding effect of the dependency ratio – two non-earners to every three producers. Its recommendations for remedying this state of affairs varied from the fields of practicality to those of morality. The practical recommendations included the setting up of a Land Utilization Body, an Export Corporation, an Investment Council to decide on public investment priorities and the giving of old age pensions to small farmers who transferred their holdings to their children on reaching the age of sixty-five. The Report's moral stance may be gleaned from the following:[55] 'In general it may be said that those who remain single through selfishness, or through over-anxiety about the future, or for any other such reason – for instance, the woman who does not want to give up her independence or her job, or the man who does not want the burden of supporting a home – are failing in their duty to God, themselves and the race.' For all the effect the Report had on emigration, the moralistic aspects of the Commission's thinking may be adjudged no more effective than its practical suggestions. Its main effect was to enable various Government spokesmen to avoid Dail questions on emigration by saying they were awaiting the Report before formulating policy. De Valera was an arch-practitioner of this general philosophy of never putting off until tomorrow anything which could safely be deferred for much longer. As we shall see, he showed himself fully aware of the scale of the emigration challenge in a famous speech delivered in Galway, but he chose to address it with an empty formula based on equal measures of audacity, cant and procrastination.

The speech had its genesis in the initiative of F. H. Boland, then Irish Ambassador to the Court of St James, and Maurice Foley, a young Irish social worker who had prepared a scarifying report on the conditions of Irish workers in Birmingham. On 23 July 1951 Boland notified the Government of the report and its contents, which he authenticated. The findings showed that, as a result of the rearmament boom, Irish emigrants had been flocking to Birmingham, Coventry and Wolverhampton. Some fifty thousand had concentrated on Birmingham, where post-war housing conditions were already bad. As a result Foley found the accommodation for Irish workers to be 'grossly over-crowded, ill-kept, dirty'. Its cost was 'exorbitant'. In one house in which fifty young Irishmen lived, fifteen slept to a room, supplying and cooking their own food and paying a rent of £2 per week each. In other houses boys on shift work slept by day in beds which at night were occupied by girls. Sanitary conditions were often 'appalling'. If the young labourers provided their own food, they often subsisted on a diet of tea and buns. If it was supplied by landladies, kippers, meat paste and Marmite were the order of the day. As a consequence there was a high incidence of alcoholism, TB and gastro-enteritis amongst the Irish community. The pub, or overtime, was the only means of escape from these conditions.

Boland had suggested that the report might be highlighted in a series of articles in the *Sunday Press*. However Frank Gallagher, then Head of the Government Information Bureau, advised against this, obviously foreseeing the problems arising from publicizing in a Government newspaper the failure of said Government to provide for its citizens. But when the report was read to de Valera, on 20 August, he decided to pre-empt bad publicity by making a statement on the Irish workers' conditions. The civil servant who briefed him on the Foley Report diplomatically pointed out that he could be[56] 'put in a false position if he spoke in public about the contents of these reports unless some definite action had been taken by the Government beforehand'. De Valera took his advice. First, on 24 August he wrote to Bishop Staunton, the Secretary of the hierarchy, sending him a copy of the Foley Report because: 'it refers, in part, to moral and religious aspects of the conditions in which some of these workers find themselves'. He informed the hierarchy that he was instructing the Irish Ambassador to make 'suitable representations to the British Government'. A note detailing the conditions highlighted by Foley was duly handed to the Secretary of State for Commonwealth Relations on the 28th. Then, being now able to claim that he had taken 'definite action', de Valera delivered his speech at a Fianna Fail dinner in Galway the following day.

He began by hailing the achievements of the Irish in bestowing their spiritual and artistic gifts on western European civilization in the 'golden age'. Presumably he meant the period during the Dark Ages when Irish monasticism flourished and Irish monks brought Christianity and scholarship to parts of Europe. He went on to say that Ireland's contemporary aim should be to work in the same spiritual field and to win distinction in that field, rather than in the material one. To do this effectively, the fount would have to be kept pure by the preservation and restoration and development of their own language. Having established the priorities, he turned to the 'alarming dimensions' of emigration – now 50 per cent above what it had been between 1936 and 1946, and averaging forty thousand a year. He then informed his Galway listeners that:

> The saddest part of all this is that work is available at home, and in conditions infinitely better from the point of both health and morals. In many occupations, the rates of wages are higher at home than they are in Britain . . . an Irish worker's . . . conditions . . . are so unattractive that he prefers unduly long hours of overtime to a leisure which he cannot enjoy. There is no doubt that many of those who emigrate could find employment at home at as good, or better, wages – and with living conditions far better – than they find in Britain.

After this he cited the conditions described in the Foley Report. In describing how the accommodation shortage was exploited by 'avaricious landlords', he said that the 'prestige of our people generally suffers by the suggestion that "anything is good enough for the Irish" '.

The speech made headlines in both Ireland and England, particularly in the British Midlands where Coventry and Wolverhampton representatives took exception to being branded with the stigma of the Birmingham conditions. Irish Opposition spokesmen also attacked the speech on lines summarized by Oliver Flanagan:[57] 'It is indeed a great pity that you did not display the same active interest in the emigrants during the former 16 years of your administration and you would have prevented the breaking of many an Irish mother's heart at the sight of the emigrant ship taking her loved ones to a foreign land for a livelihood.' But de Valera was unrepentant. On 30 August he issued via the Government Information Service a widely quoted press release saying that he had made a public statement as the[58] 'quickest and most effective way . . . of ensuring that a remedy will be provided . . . also for giving the necessary warning to Irish youths and girls who may be tempted to go to Britain without having assured themselves that proper accommodation is available there. . . . That my statement has caused anger to certain people does not surprise me, but their anger is certainly not greater than mine when I read the report.'

Alas for the provision of a remedy. Over a year later, on 11 November 1952, the files show Boland reporting that[59] 'no appreciable improvement has taken place'. The British had not replied to the Irish note. Nor was it likely that the authorities could be expected to discriminate in favour of Irish workers while the housing shortage was so bad that British citizens were themselves living in 'sub-human conditions'. Boland warned that it would be a mistake for Dublin to argue that the British were failing in their duty to provide housing for Irish workers: 'They would have no difficulty in arguing that our position was an unreal and an unreasonable one.' He went on to draw attention to a factor which would be central to de Valera's approach to dealing with the emigrant problem: the influence of the Catholic clergy, who were very active on the housing issue. Boland made the important point that the clergy's interest lay in keeping the Irish together in individual houses, as opposed to taking digs in English households where, though 'materially better off, the atmosphere would often be destructive of spiritual values'. He cited a case in Southwark, south London, where the local canon approved of having 150 Irishmen living in 'three smallish houses' because 'the men were kept together in accommodation run by a man of good character'.

The Irish in Britain continued to lobby the Government in Dublin to do something about the emigrants' plight. The *Irish Press* of 3 December 1953 recorded that twenty thousand people had signed a petition urging the Government to assist in the setting up of an emigrant information centre in Birmingham. After the sponsors of this petition had presented it to the Government – along with a request for a grant, which was refused – the Department of External Affairs prepared an important document for de

Valera's perusal. It was read to him on 5 January 1954. While disclaiming all financial responsibility for providing hostel or welfare centres 'for young Irish boys and girls in the various large British centres', the document contained one constructive proposal: the setting up of an Irish Community Trust Fund. This fund was to be financed, not by the Government, but by voluntary subscription in Ireland, and (particularly) in Britain amongst the emigrants themselves with the support of the Catholic clergy.

Although de Valera was now blind and in his seventies, the changes he caused to be made in the draft as it was read to him show that he had lost none of his skills in word-play. One paragraph of the original read:[60] ' . . . no Irish Government wished the Irish people to go to England or could take responsibility for keeping them there; the Irish Government would, of course, be only too happy to look after them if they came home'. In de Valera's reply, dated 7 January, the reference to the Irish Government's happiness at the prospect of looking after its returned emigrants was omitted. The lion's tail syndrome showed itself in another deletion. The original read: 'The work of catering for the welfare of Irish workers in Britain would however, to be effective and permanent, have to be done by the Irish in Britain with the help and cooperation of their English friends.' In de Valera's version the 'however' quite properly disappeared; but so did 'their English'. In the first draft, which referred to turning down the Birmingham social workers' request, another sentence read: 'The Minister pointed out to them that their request could not be granted but he promised to endeavour to have a fund raised by voluntary subscription in Ireland, which would be handed over to trustees, drawn from England, Scotland and Wales, who would administer it for the purpose of encouraging and assisting organisation among Irish people in Great Britain for social and welfare purposes.' De Valera had this amended to contain what in effect amounted to a policy statement on what he was prepared to do for the emigrants:

> The Minister informed them that the Government could not undertake *any* [author's italics] responsibility for the financing of such a project. If, however, suitable trustees were appointed in Britain with a view to the raising of a fund by public subscriptions in that country and here, he would consider what might be done towards assisting in the collection of money in this country. The object of the fund would be to encourage and assist organisation among Irish people in Britain for social and welfare purposes.

And so Caesar washed his hands of responsibility and turned the matter of Irish emigrant welfare over to Christ. Another year went by, and on 20 January 1955 Cardinal Griffin launched a fund to build an Irish Centre in Camden Town, north London, with a £1,000 cheque (Cardinal d'Alton sent a contribution of £200, Archbishop McQuaid £500). The *Irish Press* of the following day reported the Cardinal as saying of the Irish: ' . . . we should always be grateful for what they have done to help us . . . Ireland's tragedy had under God's providence led to an immense strengthening of the Church in this country . . . the contribution which the Irish immigrants have made to the development of the Church in this country is incalculable.' By the end of the 1950s some four hundred thousand more emigrants would have increased that contribution over the decade.

I was reared in the Dun Laoghaire area of Co. Dublin whence the mailboat, in those days the principal method of emigrant transportation, sailed for Holyhead. The image of the tide of human misery that daily poured on to that ship is symbolized for me by the Bursting Suitcase man. Pale-faced, shabby, low-sized, in his forties and late for the boat, he puffed along in front of his wife and the clutch of small children who had come to see him off. Evidently (oh treacherous crutch of the Irish) he had tarried in a pub for some parting courage. Suddenly, as he came to the busy crossroads just above the ship's berth, his large suitcase burst open. There was surprisingly little in it – a few shirts, a sweater, underwear. Flustered, the family helped him gather up his things amidst the traffic; then, holding his suitcase in both arms, he gasped on to the boat as the gangplank was hauled in. The family wept as they waved him goodbye at the end of what was probably his annual holiday. Very likely there would be another baby to greet him when he returned the following year, a little paler, a little shabbier. That was the reality of thousands of Irish emigrants behind the rhetoric about 'comely maidens' and the 'cute hoorism' of de Valera's true approach to their situation.

With the help of the British hierarchy, an Irish Centre was finally opened in Camden Town on 27 September 1955. De Valera was no longer Taoiseach when it did so. In a general election held on 13 May 1954, Fianna Fail's representation had fallen to 65. Another inter-party Government rose from the ashes of Fianna Fail's defeat. Its performance would call to mind, not a phoenix, but a raven flying over a stricken field. Costello was again Taoiseach, but he found that neither of his first choices for Finance, Patrick McGilligan and John O'Donovan, would take the job. It eventually went to Gerard Sweetman, a lawyer, who had ability and drive but no political sensitivity. It was the era of Suez, credit restriction and a balance of payments crisis. Sweetman set out to tackle these last as though the electorate were not a factor in his calculations. He curbed exports by introducing swingeing levies on a wide variety of goods and produce. The balance of payments deficit duly went down from £35 million in 1955 to £14 million in 1956. But unemployment went up and so did emigration. There were protest marches and police baton charges against unemployed demonstrators in Dublin as the building industry virtually collapsed.

A climate of depression, verging on despair, became almost a tangible thing throughout the country. Two factors militated against revolution. One was the safety valve of emigration: at this time the annual emigration total rose to around eighty thousand. In this climate revolution did stir into life. But it was revolution Irish-style, directed against the border and not against social and economic conditions. A new generation of IRA men were coming on stream, and from 1954 attacks against Northern installations recommenced. These intensified in 1956 and, as will shortly be indicated, were a factor in bringing down the inter-party Government.

We are now reaching the point where the Fianna Fail matchmakers were finally forced to abandon their efforts to pair Comely Maiden with Peasant Patriarch. That stern ethnarch, Economic Reality, not only refused to marry them but rendered it impossible for them even to cohabit. The first figure in the party to attempt to produce a plan to deal with this situation was, predictably, Sean Lemass. He made what became known as the 'hundred thousand jobs speech' at Clery's restaurant in Dublin on 16 October 1955. After seeing an item in a newspaper about the Italian Vanoni plan he got a translation of the document, which proposed a ten-year development scheme, from the Embassy and produced his own variant of the Italian blueprint. He proposed an investment programme which would set up a fund of some £67 million of Government money and private savings to create a hundred thousand new jobs in the private sector within five years. This was to be financed in two ways: through 'external assets' (the transfer of monies tied up in British holdings to Irish Government liabilities), and by persuading Irish savers to invest their money in the creation of industry and jobs in Ireland rather than England.

The immediate effect of the Lemass speech was to prompt a wide-ranging economic debate in all political circles which eventually spurred Costello into producing a Fine Gael response. Almost a year later, on 5 October 1956, Costello suggested that the way forward should be based on agricultural research and increased production. But he also had suggestions for industry. He proposed tax incentives for exports and Government grants towards plant and factories. As he said later:[61] 'I had been fully aware that unless we produced a plan soon we were heading for trouble.' The Costello initiative was well received in farming and trade union circles, though not by Eamon de Valera. His reaction was:[62] 'The Taoiseach has treated us to another of his coalition blueprints for prosperity tomorrow. . . . If professions, programmes and promises with commissions, councils and consultations were a cure for our ills, or a substitute for decision and effective action, this country should never be in bad health.' The problem was that in the economic sphere de Valera no longer had any realistic concept of what that 'effective action' should be.

During the fifties there was, however, one area in which de Valera continued to exert a lively, constructive and indeed courageous influence – that of foreign affairs. Ireland's period of isolation from world affairs may be said to have come to an end with the start of the 1956 session of the UN General Assembly, in which Irish representatives took their seats for the first time. A deal had been struck between the Eastern and Western blocs, in which the republic was one of the pro-Western countries traded off against a group of admissions favoured by the USSR.

After a year in which the contributions of Liam Cosgrave, a son of W. T. Cosgrave, proved that Irish foreign policy had lost none of its independence,[63] Fianna Fail's return to power saw Aiken become Minister for External Affairs in de Valera's new Cabinet. The Aiken–de Valera partnership put in train an era of high-profile Irish position-taking which lasted for several years until about 1968, when the economic considerations involved in Ireland's decision to join the EEC resulted in a less independent stance.

Ironically, 1968 was also the year in which, on 1 July, in Moscow, the Treaty for the Non-Proliferation of Nuclear Weapons was signed by the members of the UN. The Treaty was the culmination of ten years' effort by Aiken, beginning in 1958 at the UN, to restrict the spread of nuclear weapons. To this day, though more honoured in the breach than in the observance, it remains the only statutory instrument devised by man to prevent a nuclear holocaust.

In 1958 also (on 14 August), Ireland proposed the 'neutralization' of the Middle East by withdrawing foreign troops and voting UN funds to help the Palestinian refugees. Ireland also supported the Algerians against the French, in their struggle for independence, which annoyed those in Ireland who were beginning to look towards the EEC and knew the importance of French support in this area. How much de Valera cared for the European Economic Community is a moot point. Though he was careful to guard his thoughts to the world at large, people close to him sensed a lack of enthusiasm for the move into Europe, with its risks of submersion of national identity and loss of freedom of manoeuvre. Maurice Moynihan recalled at least one specific conversation wherein: 'While not saying anything which might be considered improper, or intruding into policy considerations outside his sphere, the President did indicate to me, at the time we were approaching the joining stage, that he would have preferred to maintain the independent national position.' In other words, de Valera was something of an Irish de Gaulle where Europe was concerned. A member of the family who visited him towards the end of his life told me a story which tends to corroborate this view: 'He was lying on the bed, sort of coming and going into consciousness. I thought he had gone asleep, but he suddenly opened his eyes and said in quite a strong voice, as though he were making a statement to someone, "You know I'm probably the last President of an independent Irish Republic."'

De Valera's last setting of the cat amongst the international pigeons came on 23 September 1957. Ireland supported an Indian amendment urging discussion of the admission of China to the UN. This created considerable right-wing anger in the USA, which duly filtered back to Ireland.[64] For some six months Aiken had to weather a storm of confused wrath at Ireland's inexplicable support for the godless Chinese who had persecuted Irish missionaries. The bewilderment was perfectly summed up by the *National Hibernian Digest*,[66] which prefaced its comments by saying that: 'It must be understood that Mr. Aiken did what he did with the express permission and consent of his superior officer, Prime Minister Eamon de Valera, undoubtedly the world's foremost Catholic leader.' Then the *Digest* went on to speculate that de Valera's real motive in raising the discussion issue was to 'expose before the entire world the brutal and criminal leadership in Peking'. This discussion would lead to 'the second and most important step . . . a discussion of British rule in Ireland'!

In fact, voting in favour of discussing China's admission to the UN was on all fours with the attitude towards admitting the Soviet Union to the League of Nations which de Valera had adopted in the thirties. In the interval, while maintaining his firm grip on the lion's tail for domestic purposes, the Long Fellow had also held on to a vision of an international order wherein rational discourse held sway over prejudice. Several years after de Valera had 'gone to the Park' Aiken told me:[66] 'We are only carrying on his work.'

Meanwhile, on the domestic front, the IRA campaign had produced two examples of the customary daring exploits and tragic aftermaths. One was a raid on Roslea RUC Barracks in which one of the attackers, Connie Green, was killed; he was subsequently buried in the Twenty-six Counties after a secret inquest. The circumstances of the inquest caused great controversy in the South, though not nearly as much as would have been occasioned by disclosure of the fact that the raid had been led by one of the Northern senators whom Sean MacBride had appointed to the Seanad, Liam Kelly. The second exploit was a raid on Brookeborough Barracks in Co. Fermanagh, as a result of which two young IRA men, Sean South and Fergal O'Hanlon, were killed on the New Year's Eve after Costello's speech. Their funerals were two of the most emotional in Irish history.

When Costello then began a crackdown on the IRA MacBride and Clann na Poblachta could no longer support the coalition. On 28 January 1957, MacBride tabled a motion of no confidence in the Government both on economic policy and because of its failure to 'formulate and to pursue any positive policy to bring about the unification of Ireland'. At the ensuing general election, on 5 March, Fianna Fail's campaign was based almost exclusively on the need for 'single party Government'. The attempt to identify the country's problems solely with coalition Government succeeded in bringing out the protest vote. Fianna Fail came back with 78 seats, a majority of 9. This effectively became 13 because four victorious Sinn Fein candidates did not take their seats.

Although now seventy-five and blind de Valera had no difficulty in exercising control over both Government and country. He demonstrated this effectively by the almost routine manner in which he dealt with the IRA. The Curragh internment camp was reopened. Part II of the Offences Against the State Act was reactivated, allowing for arrest and detention without trial. Because of this, and the more significant fact that in the fifties, unlike the period since 1969, the Nationalists of the Six Counties did not support the IRA, the campaign was broken before the year was out. Exercising control was one thing, however; giving direction was another.

All this for what? If someone in 1957 could have taken Eamon de Valera aboard a political spacecraft on a flight over the Irish political and economic landscape, and left him afterwards to look into his own heart for the answer to that question, the answer would probably have been given in two versions, to say nothing of two languages. The public one is likely to have contained references to the destiny of the Gael, Irish unity, the Irish language, frugal comfort, spiritual values and the rest of it. The private answer could have been expressed in one word: power. In effect all the public protestations were but outworks, protecting a tabernacle wherein rested the Holy Grail of Power.

However, there were those within the Cabinet who realized that 'all that delirium of the brave' was in danger of passing into nightmare. Economic collapse and a loss of sovereignty were round the corner. Shortly after the election, on 1 April 1957, the Minister for Finance, James Ryan, circulated a 'Memorandum for the Information of the Government'. The memo was in fact the script of a highly critical address by the economist Professor C. F. Carter to the Irish Association in Dublin on 19 March. Amongst other things Carter said:[67]

> Income per head in the Republic is about 55% of that in the United Kingdom, but since the ratio is about 65% for the Province of Leinster, it must be less than half for the rest of the country . . . the Republic is falling further behind . . . . Unique in the world, the Republic combines a large excess of births over deaths with a small and declining population. . . . This is a situation dangerous both to the Republic and to her neighbours. Faced by it, the universal resort of politicians is to seek refuge in fantasy, and usually in the dreary fantasy that prosperity must await the re-union of Ireland.

Carter then went on to make a well-reasoned case for economic development: for better management in industry, increased and improved technical training, the attraction of foreign business and a more efficient deployment of resources in agriculture. The mere fact that such a hard-hitting analysis should be circulated to the Cabinet by a pillar of Fianna Fail orthodoxy such as Ryan, a man completely loyal to de Valera, says all that needs to be said about the depth of the crisis. It also explains why the new Secretary of the Department of Finance, T. K. Whitaker, whom Sweetman had appointed in 1956, took it upon himself, with the aid of his colleagues, to draw up some sort of economic programme for the Government. He had read Lemass's Clery's restaurant speech with enthusiasm. Even though he regarded the approach as both opportunistic and simplistic he correctly reasoned that if, as seemed likely at the time, Fianna Fail were returned to power, Lemass would be a potential ally.

Whitaker was not certain how his ideas would be received. He planned to acquaint Ryan of them on 12 December 1957. Also that day he sent a

670

colleague a note with the memorandum outlining his thinking. The note asked for suggestions because, he said, the memo:[68] 'may be circulated to the Government'. The 'may' was underlined, and the underlining was understandable. Whitaker's document was entitled: 'Has Ireland a Future?' It contained a twenty-one-point proposal headed 'Scheme of Work', containing suggestions on how every aspect of the Irish economy might be revivified. Its Introduction began:[69]

> On my way to Washington for the first annual meeting of the International Monetary Fund and World Bank at which Ireland was represented I had with me a copy of the September, 1957, issue of 'Dublin Opinion'. The cover cartoon showed Ireland as a mature, but still attractive lady, consulting a fortune-teller and admonishing her: 'Get to work! They're saying I've no future.' As so often with humorous journals, 'Dublin Opinion' had caught, and vividly expressed, the mood of the moment.

Nor did the straight talking stop there. Whitaker's other pointed observations included the fact that: 'The Irish people . . . are falling into a mood of despondency. After 35 years of native government can it be, they are asking, that economic independence achieved with such sacrifice must wither away?' Rarely can a senior Treasury official have felt the underlining of doubt as to governmental receptivity to his proposals more justified. But in the event Whitaker had nothing to fear. Ryan, who had been impressed with the extern Carter in April, was delighted to discover that he had an even more potent intern in December. He put the proposals before the Cabinet only five days later. The Cabinet was a democracy in which one vote counted – Eamon de Valera's. As one commentator who interviewed him concerning the decisions of that December described the position:[70]

> The Taoiseach, Eamon de Valera, carried the most weight in the decision-making process. As head of the government and of Fianna Fail, he had to approve all major political announcements. His objection alone would be enough to doom the entire proposal. At seventy-six and almost blind, de Valera still maintained absolute party discipline. No minister or group of ministers could force him to accept a policy which he found fatally flawed.

In the event de Valera did not find Whitaker's proposals 'fatally flawed'. Not only did he endorse them, he subsequently pronounced them a continuation of long-established policy, claiming:[71] 'We set out those policies in 1926 at the formation of Fianna Fail.' It was a last and most significant example of de Valera fact. Protection, self-sufficiency, keeping people on the land, retaining industry in Irish hands only; these sacred Fianna Fail tenets all went out the window. Whitaker's Programme for Economic Development ultimately escaped through the thickets of bureaucratic and Cabinet delay and, adopted as Government policy, was published on 21 November 1958. Interestingly de Valera – against some opposition, notably that of Sean MacEntee – decreed that Whitaker be allowed to sign the document, which was a break with precedent. Various reasons were advanced for this: a desire to gain all-party support, and the fact that Whitaker deserved the credit. Was there another reason? During the course of discussions on the Whitaker proposals Lemass is remembered as having made a rueful point to his Cabinet colleagues:[72] 'I told you all these things. I put these ideas before you.' Did de Valera feel a new name, denoting new ideas, would help to head off 'I told you so's' and accusations of wasted opportunity?

The Whitaker plan would not have appeared remarkable in any other western European country. In Ireland, however, it was of profound importance, creating a revolution in confidence. As it began to take effect people began to feel that things could improve rather than get worse. Helped by the sixties' boom, Ireland entered a new era – not as enduringly prosperous as was once hoped, but highly significant none the less. Its introduction may also be taken as marking the end of the de Valera era in party political terms. The type of political leadership and management it called for, the circumstances which elicited it, all conspired to write 'finis' to that lengthy career. Significantly, out of the ten pages in his official biography devoted to this period of his life, only one paragraph refers to Whitaker and the Programme for Economic Development.

Meeting Whitaker at a reception at a stage when the plan had visibly begun to work, de Valera complimented him on Economic Development. But he then went on, speaking in Irish:[73] '*Ach ta rudai eile nios tabhachtai*' (But there are more important things). The nature of the 'important things' may be guessed from a matter that does take up a great deal of space in the authorized biography, proportional representation. Despite his unrivalled success in getting and holding power, de Valera knew that he had only won an overall majority in four out of twelve elections. Without his presence it was going to be considerably more difficult to impress Fianna Fail's Divine Right to Rule on the Irish electorate. But adoption of the British system of first past the post would mean that, as the largest party, Fianna Fail would be virtually assured of majorities long into the future. Accordingly, on 2 November 1958 he introduced a bill in the Dail with a view to securing the required amendment to the Constitution.

He was aware that he could not stay on much longer. But in his usual quirky fashion he chose to make the prospect of departure appear unthinkable. Speaking at the Fianna Fail Ard Fheis two weeks after the introduction of the Bill, on 19 November, he pooh-poohed the increasing rumours of his resignation:[74] 'I do not feel ill. I know I am hampered by the fact that I cannot read. This imposes many tasks upon me – it makes more difficult many tasks that could otherwise be easy. But so long as this organisation wants me (if they do not want me, they can get rid of me very easily) and as long as Dail Eireann thinks I am doing my work and can do my work, then I stay.'

Charles Haughey, at the time one of the rising stars of Fianna Fail, once described to me the attitude within the party to the Chief in those closing days. He had attended a National Executive meeting in the company of Oscar Traynor. 'Dev. had been going on about the usual stuff, the national aims, the need to restore the language. Oscar was very down afterwards. "It won't do," he said. "It won't do. The young people need jobs." Imagine, *Oscar!*' Traynor was not much in the public eye, his Cabinet posts tended to be of the level of Defence, but he was a revered figure within Fianna Fail.[75] He was still looked up to by the old guard as the former OC of the Dublin Brigade of the IRA. His loyalty to de Valera was legendary. It would be Traynor who would be chosen to bell the cat. Ironically, the final factor in the decision that the cat should be belled was the very instrument which first put de Valera into power – the *Irish Press*. Now it would help to put him out.

32

BORNE DOWN BY
WHAT BORE HIM UP

DE VALERA'S HUMILIATION over the Irish Press came about because Dr Noel Browne was given a present[1] of one Irish Press share. He remarked afterwards[2] that the gift, the only share he had ever owned, gave him an insight into the true meaning of the word 'serendipity'. He used the share to exercise his right to consult the Irish Press records to discover who had bought and sold shares over the years. After a lengthy struggle to make known the results of his research by means of a Dail debate, on 12 December 1958 he finally succeeded in moving a private member's motion which said that de Valera: ' . . . in continuing to hold the post of controlling director of the Irish Press Ltd while acting as Taoiseach . . . has rendered a serious disservice to the principle of integrity in parliamentary government and derogated from the dignity and respect due to his rank and office as Taoiseach'. In the course of the subsequent debate Browne pointed out that, in reply to an earlier question put to de Valera about his financial interest in the Irish Press, de Valera had replied:[3] 'I have no financial interest.' Furthermore, Browne reminded the House, de Valera had given the impression that his holding in the company was only 500 shares. And he quoted de Valera's own statement that he had only a 'fiduciary interest' in the newspaper empire. However, Browne's researches had revealed that since 1929 first de Valera himself, and then his son Vivion, had been buying up shares in the company so that their grand total of holdings was approaching 150,000. Moreover, by not allowing the shares to be quoted on the Stock Exchange the de Valeras had prevented their true commercial value being established and thus secured them from the unfortunate shareholders at a 'grossly deflated undervaluation'.[4]

In the circumstances there was not a great deal that de Valera could say in reply to the disclosure of these facts, so damningly at variance with the high-minded motives of those who had subscribed to either bonds or newspaper in the first instance. He claimed that he regarded himself as exercising a 'moral trusteeship',[5] and argued that he did not derive remuneration either as a director or from his shareholdings. He said:[6] 'I am quite satisfied in my conscience, and I believe that any fair-minded person will be similarly satisfied, that in the circumstances, knowing the position in which I was placed with regard to the *Irish Press* before I came here there was nothing to suggest that I had been acting all these years in a manner which was inconsistent with the dignity of the office which I hold.'

The remuneration argument was of course akin to a man with gold bars in a safe disregarding their appreciation in value and claiming that he was getting no return from them. Nor was he 'placed' in a position with regard to the Irish Press. He himself had created and fought to maintain his position even to the extent of getting public money voted to maintain it (see Chapter 20). Browne pointed out that, apart from the vast political value of the papers to de Valera down through the years, the company was worth around a million pounds:[7] 'a very solid nest egg for the days of his retirement'. He drew attention to the fact that by bringing Vivion's brother-in-law on to the board the de Valeras had effectively turned the company into a family concern. He also made telling use of the point that on its inside pages the *Sunday Press* pursued a policy of glorifying IRA activities of earlier days, while the news pages recorded the fact that his Government was locking up young men who sought to emulate this militarism. It is a historical fact[8] that in the mid-1950s some of the new generation IRA, in their inexperience, deduced from de Valera's position with Irish Press Ltd, and the fact that the *Sunday Press* Editor, Colonel Matthew Feehan, was a member of the Fianna Fail National Executive, that a blind eye would be turned to their activities.

After giving a denatured and unconvincing parliamentary performance in his own defence de Valera turned the debate over to Sean MacEntee, who fought a doughty rearguard action against this 'slimy private member's motion'.[9] Fianna Fail's numbers told in the division, and the motion was defeated by 71 votes to 49. But a vote in Dail Eireann did not mean that discussion on 'slimy motions' could be clotured in the wider world outside the chamber. Something bigger was needed to distract minds from the Browne revelations.

Age and circumstances were combining to ensure that there could be no question of de Valera leading the party into the next general election. Sean T. O'Ceallaigh second and final term as President was drawing to a close. It was Traynor who conveyed to the Chief the 'suggestion'[10] that Arus an Uachtarain would be a suitable retirement home. Discussion on the issue was kept to a minimum. No one outside a very small circle knew what was intended. Moynihan, whose antennae had been refined and sensitized by a lifetime working with de Valera in the corridors of power, was a witness to the vital conversation. He told me[11] that he 'just happened' to be getting a breath of air when he saw de Valera and Traynor walking up and down on Leinster Lawn, outside the Dail. They were deep in conversation, and by 'guesswork' he intuited that de Valera was being confronted with the ineluctable dialectic of history. It was literally a moving moment. Ironically, the offer that de Valera could not refuse was made in an enclosure dominated by a cenotaph erected to the memory of Collins and Griffith. De Valera had once put a dramatic halt to O'Duffy's attempt to march to the cenotaph, but he could not halt the march of time.

This is how de Valera wanted history to record the circumstances of his departure. His official biography does not contain one word of Browne's motion, or the revelations about the Irish Press. What it does say is:[12]

> ... he went to a meeting of the Fianna Fail Parliamentary Party in mid-January, 1959, and told them of his determination to retire from office. . . . He had for a considerable time made up his mind that it would not be in the interests either of the country or the Party that he should lead Fianna Fail in the next general election. For that reason he thought that it would be necessary for him, in any case, at least a year before the general election was due, to resign so as to enable the new leader of the Party and the Party to decide on policy and prepare their plans and organisation for the election. There was something more to come. Recently since the Presidential election became a matter of general public interest he had been approached by some members of the Party urging him to consent to go forward if the Party so desired. He was in this matter completely in the hands of the Party.

After stating that there was 'no move to unseat him from his undisputed leadership'[13] the biography goes on to say that, though de Valera was an 'obvious Fianna Fail nominee',[14] his retirement announcement was a 'bombshell'[15] which resulted in:

> ... the most moving scenes. After following him throughout their political lives the party members were, in general, dumbfounded that he should ever think of retiring. Cabinet ministers and others emerged from the meeting with tears in their eyes; for the first time the years seemed to have suddenly caught up with their well-nigh indestructible leader. The man who had always been 'the Chief' to them was determined on his course, but they could visualise no other Chief than he.

The official records omit the fact that the moving scenes took place on the morning of the Dail vote on Browne's motion. The result was that the following day, 15 January 1959, the news of de Valera's resignation as Taoiseach and impending candidacy as President occupied a prominent position on page one of the newspapers, while the proceedings in the Dail were given inside, down page. Normally the debate would have received far greater prominence, particularly since Oliver Flanagan was expelled from the House for making a series of interruptions which included proposing a judicial inquiry into the matter, and suggesting that the Minister for Justice should take action on Browne's charges.

De Valera absented himself from the final vote but then sent round a letter to the Dublin papers:[16] 'At a late hour when there was no opportunity of replying in the Dail Dr. Browne made a number of personal charges against me which time now permits me to deal with only in brief . . . .' He went on to aver that 'I have not and never had any beneficial interest' in Irish Press shares. The block of 90,000 to which Browne referred was held by himself and Vivion 'on behalf of the persons who subscribed the money and to whom any dividends or profits on these shares must be paid'. There was no question of deriving profit from these shares.

They were held 'so that the purposes for which the money was subscribed will not be departed from'. Browne's allegations that he and Vivion had been buying up shares was 'completely untrue'. The letter was an unimpressive footnote to a debate which had been going on since the previous November. Moreover Vivion, who was in the House to vote against Browne's motion, had an 'opportunity of replying in the Dail' to the 'personal charges', but did not avail himself of it.

What de Valera availed himself of was the opportunity to deal with what his biography termed his 'immediate concern', namely to pilot through the legislature his Bill to amend the Constitution to get rid of PR. He gave a good account of himself in piloting his proposals through the Dail – far better than his limping performance over the Irish Press disclosures. He got round the disability of his blindness by memorizing anti-PR speeches made by the Opposition thirty years earlier, so as to discredit their attacks. But it took all his force, and Fianna Fail's majority, to get it through unexpectedly determined opposition. The uproar startled the normally supine Seanad into unexpectedly successful resistance, and the Bill was rejected by a single vote on 19 March 1959. De Valera attempted to abort this decision by proposing that the Dail pass a resolution deeming the Bill passed by both Houses. Further debate and dissension ensued, but the Seanad's powers of delay expired after ninety days and the Bill passed into law.

Then came the final throw of 'cute hoorism'. The presidential election date was set for 17 June. Fine Gael chose Sean MacEoin to be his opponent. It was an ironic choice. MacEoin was the man who, reading from an Irish text prepared for him by Michael Collins, had proposed de Valera as President of the Irish Republic in 1921. He was a good candidate, well known both through the Anglo-Irish war and his subsequent political career, which included spells in Cabinet during the inter-party Governments. But he was overshadowed by de Valera, who sought to profit from his lead in the popularity stakes by embroiling the PR issue with the presidency. The PR vote was fixed for the same day as the election. 'Vote Yes and de Valera' was the Fianna Fail slogan.

The people, however, decided to vote 'no' and de Valera. He won by 538,000 votes to 417,636, but the proposal to drop PR was defeated. It was an appropriate end to his parliamentary career. The people rewarded de Valera Nice Guy and gave de Valera Man of Power a slap on the wrist. Power and the perpetuation of power had concerned him to the end. One of the great insiders[17] of Irish politics, his then secretary, Padraig O'hAnrachain, told me a revealing anecdote about his last moments as Taoiseach. Earlier in the day he had made his will and settled his affairs, including turning over the by now immensely valuable shares he held in the Irish Press to Vivion, who was also awarded the post of controlling director. Oliver Flanagan's intervention in the Browne debate probably had a bearing on the handover: Flanagan had tried to raise a question concerning the propriety of de Valera's holding his Irish Press position if he became President.

A photocall had been arranged to record his departure from Government Buildings. He had asked Padraig to leave him alone at his desk for a moment before facing the photographers. The moment became a long one and O'hAnrachain decided that he would have to re-enter the office, one of the features of which was an antiquated but highly efficient communications system. Standing beside the Taoiseach's desk was a switchboard with a set of brass levers that enabled de Valera to communicate with ministers, heads of Departments, the Army and Gardai at the flick of a switch. O'hAnrachain made a determinedly light-hearted entrance, calling out: 'Come on now, Chief. Don't be shy. You're *boooutiful* – they're all dying to make a film star out of you.' He discovered de Valera with his arms around the switchboard. There were tears in his eyes. 'Oh, Padraig,' he exclaimed. 'It's awfully hard to leave the levers of power.'

The British historian Sir John Wheeler-Bennett[18] visited him a few months after he 'went to the Park' and has left a revealing picture of how the change to the presidency had affected de Valera. Sir John found him 'impressive' but 'irked by the trivial duties of his new office which fill his day without giving any of the satisfaction of accomplishment'. De Valera, then seventy-seven, was increasingly preoccupied with the past, with memories of Michael Collins and the days of thunder and lightning. He was still attempting to rewrite history according to de Valera fact. Sir John has recorded that, when he mentioned that he knew Collins and Griffith had met the leading British civil servants Anderson and Cope before the truce, 'the President became very animated':

> He turned suddenly in his chair and fixed his bright, unseeing eyes on me. 'Are you sure of that?' he said in a very low voice. 'Perfectly,' I replied. 'When was it?' he asked, still in that low, tense voice. I answered that I couldn't give him the exact dates but that it must have been in early spring of 1921. 'After I had returned from America,' he said, almost to himself. 'I wonder were they double-crossing me even then, those two.' I said that I would look up the exact date and let him know. He sat for a few moments in a reverie and then broke out into almost a lament for the soul of the Sinn Fein Party as it had been 'before the British savaged it'.

In the knowledge that he was talking to a historian, de Valera went on: '"You could not beat us in war but you defeated us in negotiation. . . . Those three men, Lloyd George and Churchill and Smith, made dupes of Griffith and Collins. I can never forgive the ruthless, pitiless way in which they pushed them over the edge, without a thought as to what would happen to them or to Ireland afterwards."' Wheeler-Bennett was duly awed: 'The room was growing dark and the atmosphere within it was tense and almost eerie. The President was not talking to me, he was apostrophising the past. He had forgotten that I was there. His blind eyes seemed to be focused on some point in infinity behind my head. I felt quite incapable of breaking through this trance-like concentration.' However, the trance passed 'as quickly as it had come'.

Although he did not know it, Wheeler-Bennett also elicited a prime, in fact possibly *the* prime, example of de Valera fact. The historian records that he urged de Valera to write his memoirs. De Valera told him that he had hesitated because he did not wish to criticize the dead. 'After all,' he said, 'they *are* dead and I, by the blessing of God, am alive.' Much moved, Wheeler-Bennett replied that de Valera 'owed it to himself, his cause, his nation and to history to put down his own story, not for immediate publication, but to be published after his death'.

De Valera solemnly assured him that he would give the matter 'serious consideration'. What he did not tell the Englishman was that Frank Gallagher had been working on preparing his biography for several years. But Gallagher's health was failing, and in 1954 a sinecure position was found for him on the staff of the National Library. He died, without being able to complete the biographical project, in 1962.

However, his work in the Library had brought him into contact with the historian Thomas P. O'Neill, another staff member and a keen 'Dev' man who had impressed Gallagher as a writer and researcher for the all-party Mansion House Anti-Partition Committee. De Valera knew of O'Neill's reputation and of his standing in Gallagher's eyes; he had also had dealings with him through the Library. Accordingly O'Neill was chosen to produce de Valera's official biography.

A contract[19] was signed between O'Neill and the publishers Hutchinson the year after Gallagher died, on 31 May 1963. O'Neill, a gentle and scholarly man, gave up his job in the National Library and moved to Arus an Uachtarain to work on the book. I cannot presume to state the effect of this arrangement on Dr O'Neill, but I know I would find both the surroundings and the constant proximity of the subject of the work inhibiting in the extreme – particularly so in the case of a subject with de Valera's formidable personality. Working so closely, with both the papers and the subject of a biography, might appear to some to be an advantage, but to me – and I have considerable experience of both forms of writing – it resembles less the role of biographer to subject than that of a leader writer to his Editor. The directive appearance of the de Valera–biographer relationship is heightened by paragraph 21 of the contract, which stipulated that the contract was 'contingent'[20] on compliance with conditions laid down by de Valera in a letter dated 30 April 1963. De Valera said that he would:[21] 'recognise this work, *if satisfactory* [author's italics], as my official biography and will make available to Mr O'Neill all the papers and give him all the *general directions* [author's italics] necessary for his work'. Dr O'Neill was required to sign a copy of this letter.

In the event Hutchinson became dissatisfied with the outcome of the arrangement; after further negotiation with de Valera, carried out on behalf of the publishers by Harold Harris,[22] a new contract was agreed upon on 26 April 1965.[23] This time the Earl of Longford was brought in as co-author, the royalties to be divided sixty:forty respectively between O'Neill and Longford.

Longford had won favour with de Valera for his writing as far back as 1935. On 24 July 1934 he had written to the Executive Council inquiring whether there would be governmental objection to his including hitherto unpublished material in his forthcoming work on the Treaty, *Peace by Ordeal*, for which he had consulted many of the British negotiators. In the event de Valera agreed with Longford that he would offer no objection, provided that he approved of Longford's selection of official extracts, and that Longford took responsibility for their selection!

Peace by Ordeal, published in 1935, was ultimately deemed so favourable to de Valera that he felt no further publication of Treaty documents was necessary.[24] But, where the second contract for the authorized biography was concerned, once again there was a clause stipulating that the conditions laid down by de Valera in his letter of 30 April 1963 remained in force.

We can only speculate as to what effect this *ukase* may or may not have had on creativity. But the rate of progress can be assessed by an extract[25] from a letter of Longford's to Harold Harris on 1 November 1965: 'I now enclose ten chapters beginning with "The Rising" and ending with the signature of the Treaty. This leaves me in possession of ten chapters sent me by Tom O'Neill.' Longford went on to say that that represented almost half the book. However, the book did not appear in print until 1970, five years later, and then only after a strenuous bout of editing by Harris.

So much for the biography. De Valera's discussions with Wheeler-Bennett then moved on to the Easter Rising. He told the historian that 1916 had been 'the action of a small group of dedicated men, inspired by the highest motives *but without legal basis or mandate* [author's italics]'. The mandate had been conferred by the general election of 1918, after which, de Valera alleged, he had been elected 'President of the Republic' along with other titles. He then went on to make the following amazing claim, a retrospective justification for the position he took prior to and during the civil war. ' "There are men," said Dev., "who will attempt to contradict today what I am saying, but that is the truth. I was President of the Republic of Ireland from 1918 till the establishment of the Free State under the Treaty. This is, as you might say, my second term of office." '

De Valera fact at its best! There is no need to dwell on the fact that de Valera proclaimed himself 'President of the Republic' when he got to America, long after the 1918 general election; nor on the point that he only succeeded in getting the title conferred on him by the Dail in August 1921, after he had met Lloyd George and had clearly determined that he did not want to meet him again in a hopeless defence of his Republic of the Mind. What is significant is that at that stage of his career de Valera's eyes, blind as they were, were filled nevertheless with a vision of himself as he would appear standing before the bar of history. He knew that the levers of power were now largely beyond his grasp. The levers of the past preoccupied him.

And his religious practices gave him a certain symbolic sense of power. De Valera's official biography tells us:[26] 'He had long been known as a daily communicant. Once installed in the President's Residence he usually visited the Oratory five times a day. One of his first steps was to obtain permission for the Blessed Sacrament to be reserved. He was characteristically scrupulous about its custody. He felt strong personal satisfaction when it was decided that his desk was the safest place for the key of the Tabernacle.'

However, even in the semi-retirement of Phoenix Park de Valera still managed the occasional touch on the political levers of the present. Although he had vacated the producer's box he had moved to one overlooking the stage. Here, apart from a monthly briefing on matters political from the Taoiseach of the day, he received a stream of visitors. Some were national, others international, figures – John F. Kennedy, King Baudouin of Belgium and Queen Fabiola, Princess Grace of Monaco, General de Gaulle, the Presidents of India and Pakistan, the Secretary General of the UN (U Thant) and many other dignitaries. He got on particularly well with Kennedy and de Gaulle; the latter paid de Valera the rare compliment of conversing with him in English – other foreign statesmen were invariably addressed in French. Kennedy's visit sent a glow through Irish society. For Ireland and the Irish it was as though not one family, but the whole country, had made good.

Kennedy's schedule included the planting of a tree in Arus an Uachtarain, alongside one that Queen Victoria had planted during the famine. The strong, stylish young man in the grey pinstriped suit, who smiled at the travelling White House press corps shouting 'Jack' to attract his attention, made a particular impact on Irish journalists. The world of Irish journalism then was one in which if a reporter asked an embarrassing question his Editor could be reprimanded. The idea that either question or answer might ever appear in print was questionable. Imagine shouting 'Eamon'! Compared to Kennedy de Valera seemed a fading, olive-complexioned old man. But Kennedy was impressed with Ireland and the de Valeras – he turned back from the steps of Airforce One to hug Sinead impulsively. More importantly, he told some of his closest advisers that in his second term he was going to 'do big things for Ireland'.[27] But the tree died – Irish Press newspapers were forbidden to print the fact – and the following year de Valera was in Washington, representing the Republic at Kennedy's funeral. He scorned to take a car to follow the cavalcade to Arlington Cemetery and presented an unforgettable picture on Irish television as he strode along sightlessly, arms swinging, lurching slightly, like a huge heron in a high wind, going at a pace that would have left a man twenty years younger gasping.

Less than a year later, at the invitation of President Johnson, he was back in Washington on a State Visit from 26 May to 3 June 1964. Johnson introduced him to a joint session of both Houses of Congress, saying: 'We consider this to be your second country and you are always welcome on this soil.' De Valera subsequently spoke without notes for twenty-five minutes. He quoted James Clarence Mangan:[28]

> Oh, Ireland be it thy high duty
> To teach the world the might of
> moral beauty,
> And stamp God's image truly on the
> struggling soul

He made a *tour d'horizon* speech on US–Irish relationships throughout the twentieth century. The only period omitted was that in which occurred the little unpleasantness referred to in Ireland as 'the emergency' and elsewhere as World War II. Amongst other things he said:

> I would like to confess, and confess freely, that this is an outstanding day in my own life, to see recognised, as I have here in full, the rights of the Irish people and the independence of the Irish people in a way that was not at all possible forty-five years ago. I have longed to come back and say this to you and, through you, to the people as a whole. I would, indeed, be fully happy today were there not one serious set-back that had occurred in these forty-five years. When I was addressing you here in 1919 and 1920, our ancient nation, our ancient Ireland, was undivided. Since then it has been divided by a cruel partition.

History does not record the reaction of David Gray. But 1964 was a presidential election year. World War II was a long way away and, as Lyndon B. Johnson strove to make the transition from inheriting to winning John Fitzgerald Kennedy's mantle, a rub of the Green was especially welcome.

Possibly because by that stage the sound of the oft-beaten anti-partition drum was beginning to sound accusingly, or at best increasingly hollow, to his ears, de Valera in his last years seems to have developed something of a conscience about Northern Ireland. Apart from revivifying the Irish economy, T. K. Whitaker was the inspiration behind the historic Lemass–O'Neill meetings of 1965 in which, for the first time since the 1920s, the Prime Ministers of Northern and Southern Ireland held talks. In the course of their cordial discussion de Valera openly confessed[29] to O'Neill that he had never understood the North. He told Whitaker and O'Neill that he had principally relied on Erskine Childers for advice about the Unionists. This revelation was made all the more sigificant by an incident which took place as he was nearing the end of his presidency. He invited Robert Barton and a Childers family[30],[31] party to Aras an Uachtarain for a private dinner. When the meal was ended he ordered the servants to leave the room. Then, alone with the family and speaking with obvious emotion, he told his hearers for the first time that Erskine Childers had written a letter[32] to him on the night before his execution. In it he had warned de Valera that his greatest challenge would be Northern Ireland. Childers had advised him that the Northern Protestants could not be coerced, saying that they were a special people with special fears and ideals which needed to be understood and allowed for. De Valera told his hearers, one of whom was Erskine Childers' son, also Erskine, who succeeded him as President, that he deeply regretted not having followed Childers' advice.

On a sleety March day in 1965 de Valera got out of a sickbed against the advice of his doctor to attend the ceremonies for the reinterment of Roger Casement in Glasnevin Cemetery. He had finally buried the hatchet with Churchill in 1953 when, after considerable arm-twisting by F. H. Boland, he accepted an invitation to lunch at which his old sparring partner was determinedly friendly and courteous. At this meeting, after urging an end to partition, de Valera asked that Casement's remains be returned to Ireland. Churchill's advisers ruled against granting this request, which had been Casement's last wish – he did not want to be left to rest in Pentonville. One of de Valera's last acts before leaving Pentonville himself had been to pray over Casement's grave.[33] It was Harold Wilson who finally cut through the red tape and sent the bones home. At Glasnevin de Valera said:[34]

> This grave, like the grave of the other patriots who lie in this cemetery, like the graves in Arbour Hill, like the graves in Bodenstown, the grave at Downpatrick, the grave at Templepatrick, and the grave at Greyabbey[35] – this grave, like these others, will become a place of pilgrimage to which our young people will come and get renewed inspiration and renewed determination that they also will do everything that in them lies so that this nation which has been one in the past will be one again in the future. . . .

Funerals brought out some essential element in de Valera's charisma. One could only understand it if one had seen the attendance gather round to worship him through tear-filled eyes – not for the departed, but for the immensity of the fact that 'Dev Came to the Funeral'. Rain, God, graves, the Irish language, and de Valera: these were the five fingers of a fist that maintained and symbolized a man, an era, a culture. To me these elements meshed in a perfect tableau in Limerick in 1968 as Donough O'Malley, the Minister of Education, was buried. The space around the open grave was roped off. Making daring use of his limited peripheral vision de Valera strode imperiously through the gap in the rope, walked to the end of the rectangle, jabbed his umbrella into the ground and used its leverage to swing around proudly, face towards the grave, finally coming to rest with a parade ground thump of heels that could be heard yards away. It *was* his turf. Robed in purple, members of the Irish hierarchy had poured through the gap after him; men before whom every knee should bend. But they did not dare approach de Valera's end of the rectangle. Instead they all scuttled to the opposite end of the enclosure, like a flock of plump, pink scratching birds keeping out of range of a heron.

> Matter for old age meet;
> Might of the Church and the State.
> Their mobs put under their feet.[36]

The man who lay in the yawning grave between Church and State had died suddenly while engaged in helping to create an Ireland that would radically change the character of both. Three years earlier, in 1965, a committee under the chairmanship of Patrick Lynch had recommended radical reforms in the Irish educational system. Even at that stage, half of Ireland's children still left school at the age of twelve. Lemass had empowered O'Malley to implement the report. Though both he and O'Malley predeceased de Valera, their work would live after him.

De Valera used his presidency to make at least one notable conciliatory gesture. W. T. Cosgrave accepted an invitation to meet a new Papal Nuncio, and the two old adversaries shook hands and afterwards had a private chat.[37] De Valera was a generous host, surprising many with his conviviality. He liked a glass of brandy for himself, and surprised and disarmed many a visitor with a gladiatorial measure of Paddy whiskey. One cannot state with accuracy whether he liked the whiskey for itself or for the fact that the map of Ireland on the bottle has Ulster coloured not in orange, but in green!

People who were present at either official functions, or more relaxed occasions such as a dinner for old school friends, agreed that de Valera was a 'princely'[38] host. Father Farragher, who saw him in operation both at Blackrock and at Arus an Uachtarain, described him as being 'charming and hospitable, making everyone feel at home. But not in any "come-all-ye" way.'

Mathematics apart, de Valera did not devote much time to pursuits other than politics. In middle life, one might have expected to see him at an occasional GAA or rugby match, but not on a golf course. He would sometimes walk from his home in Blackrock to Government Buildings, a distance of approximately five miles. And at weekends he could have been encountered, at the head of a perspiring posse of bodyguards, striding across the Dublin mountains. His acquaintances were myriad, his near friends few. Patrick Ruttledge, whom he had appointed to succeed him after his arrest in Clare, remained close to him as a friend and Cabinet colleague until he died on 8 May 1952. De Valera's feelings for Ruttledge may be gauged by an extract from his graveside oration:[39] 'We honoured him for the part he played in the effort to win freedom for our country and to secure for her a fitting place among the nations. We admired him as a brave soldier and a wise counsellor. We loved him as a comrade whose intimate companionship in days of stress and danger made him more than a friend.'

After Ruttledge's death Aiken took his place as de Valera's closest political friend and associate. For such a seemingly aloof and self-contained man, confident of the worth of his own judgement, de Valera had a surprising need for companionship. Vivion once advised me to: 'Follow my father's example. Get yourself someone whose advice you can rely on from outside your own sphere, an older man if possible.' De Valera's principal friend and confidant outside politics was Dr Farnan. Vivion also told me that his father counselled him to select a younger man to work close to him. The principle in selecting this man was that he should be old enough and intelligent enough to be relied on, but young enough 'to control'. How to control either men or movements was always a primary concern with de Valera.

Apart from the early rumours about Kathleen O'Connell there was never even a hint of any extra-marital liaison. In some respects Sinead's influence over de Valera appears to have grown rather than diminished with the years. 'The way to Dev. was via Mrs. Dev.' was how Father Michael O'Carroll put it to me.[40] On one memorable occasion he took the route on behalf of Dave Neligan. Neligan was nearing retirement, and Father O'Carroll wrote to Sinead seeking her intercession in having the promotional bar which de Valera had imposed removed so that Neligan's pension position might be improved. By way of reply Father O'Carroll received a telephone call from de Valera himself, saying that he would do whatever he could to assist in the situation. Neligan subsequently found himself promoted within the Land Commission to become something known as an Assistant Registrar. He never found out what the job was supposed to entail, but it meant more money and an enhanced pension entitlement.

While one can ascribe a special relationship to Ruttledge and Aiken, de Valera's control of his Cabinet was extended through parallel reins of awe and comradeship. His ministers were rooted in a revolutionary background from which he had led them to positions of power and respect. Moynihan would say that 'he ruled by respect, like a father figure'.[41] But there was adroit man management in de Valera's rule. Apart from ploys such as retaining External Affairs, which he understood, in his own grasp, and ensuring that the able Lemass never got control of Finance, which he did not, he used his personality and mastery of psychology to such effect that, buttressed by his command of patronage, none of his ministers would dream of going against him. Strong opinions might be expressed in Cabinet, but the opinions did not translate into policy unless de Valera shared them. Figures such as Gerry Boland, Sean MacEntee, James Ryan, Sean T. O'Ceallaigh, Oscar Traynor or Sean Lemass were far from being yes-men, but with de Valera there was a displeasure line, as much as one of authority, which was undrawn, but well understood and therefore untransgressed. The extraordinary deference extended to him by subordinates which was noted by Geoffrey Shakespeare, while de Valera was visiting Lloyd George in 1921, continued to be extended right to the end of his days.[41a]

In one area of his life only was de Valera unfailingly relaxed and at ease – in his relationships with Blackrock College. It was commonly said in the College that: 'If there was a dogfight on Dev. would come to it.' To the end of his life Blackrock remained a second home to him, the place he would choose to spend Christmas in. No function was too trivial for him to attend. The annual school sports were a 'must'. If de Valera was in the country, the Fathers knew, when arranging a lunch or dinner for a visiting dignitary, that a phone call to Government Buildings, or to Arus an Uachtarain, would ensure the presence of their most famous alumnus. He himself had no hesitation in ringing up the College 'at all hours'[42] to check some point of detail, like the wording of the inscription on the cups presented for Middle Grade English.

His conversation on visits to the College could fairly be described as escapist – anecdotal, humorous, nostalgic. He would talk about old friends, deriving particular enjoyment from dwelling on their foibles and eccentricities; reminisce about Limerick and Tipperary in a folksy, Bruree fashion; and recall odd childhood anecdotes that portrayed him as a rustic innocent. For example, Father Farragher remembers him[43] regaling a group of priests with his scruples over how he allowed his mind to wander on one occasion while serving Mass. According to himself, de Valera felt guilty at allowing his mind to wander to memories of 'the geese in Halpin's garden.'

In old age de Valera liked travelling around the country by train in the presidential coach; it was a mode of travel which suited his dignified persona. The rail company's Head of Information, Sean J. White, was generally chosen to accompany him on these trips because of his excellent command of Irish. Eventually de Valera became so friendly with him that on a memorable day he told White it was no longer necessary to address him as 'A Holise' (Your Excellency). White struggled for words to express his gratitude at the prospect of being allowed to address the Olympian One as 'Dev.' – even, dizzyingly, as 'Eamon'. De Valera continued: 'You need just call me Chief!'

Despite his aloof, dignified mien, the minutiae of politics continued to fascinate him. He and Padraig O'hAnrachain, a Clare man, on one occasion spent most of a morning deep in discussion concerning some skulduggery current at the time in Dev's old constituency. 'Look here, Chief,' O'hAnrachain said finally, 'you're supposed to be above politics, not sitting here discussing dirty politics with me.'[44] They both laughed and turned to matters ceremonial. However on at least three other occasions his interest in politics, combined with his position as the Elder Ayatollah of Fianna Fail, went beyond mere gossiping and had important political consequences.

The first of these occurred in 1964 when the Fianna Fail Minister for

Agriculture, Patrick Smith, suddenly announced his resignation in displeasure at Lemass's economic policies. This was an unheard-of happening in Irish politics generally and in Fianna Fail in particular. Rumours of a right–left split in Fianna Fail swept the country. People held their breaths waiting for the next announcement. But Smith's first step had been to call on his old mentor, President de Valera. The two men talked, and there was no further public announcement. Lemass moved quickly to replace Smith with Neil Blaney, one of the younger, rising men, and the party closed ranks. No split occurred.

De Valera also spoke to Kevin Boland, Gerry's son, when a crisis threatened over his intention to resign in 1969 when the Northern Ireland troubles erupted. Boland advocated a more 'forward' policy than that taken by Jack Lynch, who had succeeded Lemass in 1966. He stayed on-side for several months after talking to de Valera, but ultimately resigned over a fresh crisis that broke out in 1970 over what became known as the Arms Trial affair. De Valera also played a part in this saga. Information was conveyed to Lynch that Blaney and Charles Haughey had allegedly tried to import guns into the Six Counties. He asked for their resignations, and when they refused called on de Valera to remove them formally. De Valera did so. Arising out of the allegations, the pair were subsequently unsuccessfully charged with illegal arms importation.

Aiken mistrusted Haughey[45] and threatened to resign when he was allowed to stand for Fianna Fail in the 1973 general election. He had intended to accompany his resignation with a statement to the papers explaining the reason for his action. But after Jack Lynch had sought de Valera's intervention de Valera persuaded him to announce that he was leaving politics 'on doctor's orders'. No one except de Valera would have succeeded in getting Frank Aiken – a man who was prepared to stand up to Roosevelt in his own office – to die in silence.[46] Haughey had master-minded de Valera's second presidential campaign, in 1966. The strategy chosen was a monumental example of 'cute hoorism'.

De Valera had had reason to hope that a contest would not have proved necessary. Sean T. O'Ceallaigh had been allowed a second term unopposed, but O'Ceallaigh had aroused less animosity in Fine Gael. The party chose T. F. O'Higgins, a lawyer and nephew of the murdered Kevin O'Higgins, as de Valera's opponent. He was a good candidate, an articulate, forceful speaker, and, of course, far younger and better able to get around the country than de Valera. Fianna Fail nullified these campaigning advantages by having the President Who Was Above Politics simply not campaign. His age and blindness were thus turned to advantages. In the interests of 'fair play', Fianna Fail-style, RTE (Radio Telefis Eireann, the Irish broadcasting service), which was heavily influenced by the Government, gave very little coverage to the candidate who *was* campaigning.

However, 1966 was also the fiftieth anniversary of the Easter Rising.

President de Valera, the last surviving Commandant of 1916, was naturally expected to take part, in fact to be the centrepiece, of the plethora of commemorations which broke out all over the country. These were covered extensively and reverentially by RTE and the newspapers. Such occasions were, of course, separate from his normal official duties, which also brought media attention; as did a myriad of attractive photocall opportunities such as visits to the Arus to see their famous grandfather by little de Valeras on First Holy Communion Day. Yet despite all this, and the enthusiastic contribution of Cabinet members and Party to the generation of pro-de Valera meetings and rallies, he barely squeaked through on election day. O'Higgins, out of a poll of roughly a million, came to within twenty thousand votes of defeating him. With its subject eighty-four and blind, the slogan 'Up Dev' was losing some of its resonance for a newer generation of Irish voters.

Ironically, the less history-laden generation decided against O'Higgins too in his turn. An increasingly ecumenically minded electorate ensured that it was a son of Erskine Childers who succeeded de Valera at the conclusion of his second term in 1973. Erskine Childers Jnr was a Protestant and this factor, more than his creditable ministerial record, ensured that Eamon de Valera handed over to the son of the man he once admired most. He and Sinead then retired, not to the old home in Blackrock, but to a nursing home, Talbot Lodge, run by the Sisters of Charity close by. A biographer has written of his final days:[47]

> He had already sold his old home in Blackrock and he had essentially given away most of his possessions. He had handed over the Irish Press to his son Vivion, and had donated his personal papers and various memorabilia to the Franciscan Fathers. Those would have been worth a fortune on the open market, which prompted some cynics to describe his gesture as his insurance policy for the next life. At the end he left only £2,800 in his will, which could be compared with over £380,000 left by Vivion, when he died little over five years later.

It was not *quite* like that. Noel Browne had made it unwise for him to consider retaining the Irish Press shares while holding the post of President. His personal papers were left to the Franciscans, but without any money towards the significant costs of storing and cataloguing them. The old home was signed over to Vivion. Granted Eamon de Valera only left £2,800, but what is not left behind is not subject to death duties.

The nuns remarked on the affection displayed by Sinead and Eamon in the last days of their life together. They may truly be said to have finished their days in frugal comfort. The nuns had fixed up modest quarters for the old pair: two adjoining bedrooms and a bathroom and lavatory. No reception rooms. It had been generally accepted that their marriage was not a serene affair. Apart from the general turmoil of de Valera's early revolutionary days, the split with Michael Collins etched a deep furrow in their relationship. Shortly before she left Arus an Uachtarain Sinead sent for a senior member of the Collins family and, under promise of secrecy, had a long talk with him about 'Mick', as she still called him. What Sinead had to say on that occasion would provide a fascinating and significant insight into a vital period of Irish history. But, as they made their souls in their ebbing days, a Darby-and-Joan-type relationship was certainly discernible. Sometimes the old couple could be observed walking hand in hand together in the grounds. And they said the rosary together with obvious piety and fervour. But this phase did not last long. Sinead was removed to the Mater Hospital some six months after the move to Blackrock, and never returned.

Left to himself, de Valera made his soul. 'You'd see him down on his two knees, saying the rosary,' a nun remarked. His spiritual adviser was Father Willie O'Meara from nearby Blackrock College. Both Father O'Meara and other priests from the College were impressed with his spirituality and faith. He seemed a man at peace with himself. He had no fear of the next world and made few demands on those who accompanied him out of this one. 'Anything would please him,' said one of the sisters who attended to him. 'He was a good man, easy to get on with and in no way troublesome.' Marie O'Ceallaigh came to the nursing home each morning and stayed with him late into the evening. She read to him – the Bible, his letters, newspapers and the occasional detective story. He had never learned to read braille, apart from a braille watch, and had no televison. His visitors were not numerous. Aiken visited him regularly, as did Moynihan and Padraig O'hAnrachain. Of his family, his daughter Emer impressed the nuns as being his most frequent visitor. He was able to find his way around the area in the vicinity of his bedroom, but when he went out he had to be helped down the steps, usually by the detectives who were provided for him to the end.

Sinead predeceased Eamon, on the eve of their sixty-fifth wedding anniversary. She had lost consciousness for some days and her death had been expected. De Valera had given instructions that if the end approached while he was asleep he was to be woken up. His instructions were obeyed in the early hours of 7 January 1975. It was the anniversary of the Dail's vote in favour of the Treaty. De Valera was not long in following her. As the summer drew to a close, so did his life. Word was sent to Maynooth, where Cardinal William Conway was visiting. He came immediately to de Valera's room and said Mass. De Valera remained conscious almost to the end. At midday on 29 August 1975, without a struggle, he was reunited with Sinead.

ET VALE

Brendan Kennelly only met de Valera six weeks before he died. As he says himself, his childhood had been 'fiercely bigoted against him'. His father had been wounded in the civil war and refused to have a bullet fragment extracted from his hand because it reminded him 'of his hate'. But, he says, 'in that late afternoon I grew to like and admire him'. The poem is in the form of answers by de Valera to a series of questions which Kennelly put to him, based on the attitudes of his childhood. Kennelly says 'the effect of the poem should be of a monologue in which my questions to him are all burned up in his thoughtful, wandering response'.[49]

De Valera at Ninety-Two

To sit here, past my ninetieth year,
Is a joy you might find hard to understand.
My wife is dead. For sixty years
She stood by me, although I know
She always kept a secret place in her heart
For herself. This I understood. There must always be
A secret place where one can go
And brood on what cannot be thought about
Where there is noise and men and women

Some say I started a civil war.
There are those who say I split the people.
I did not.
The people split themselves,
They could not split me.
I think now I was happiest when I taught
Mathematics to teachers in their training.
From nineteen hundred and six to nineteen sixteen
I taught the teachers.
Then the trouble started.
In jail, I often sat for hours
Especially at evening
Thinking of those mathematical problems
I loved to solve.
Here was a search for harmony,
The thrill of difficulty,
The possibility of solution.
Released from jail, I set about
Making a nation,
A vicious business,
More fools among my friends than in my enemies,
Devoted to what they hardly understood.

Did I understand? You must understand
I am not a talker, but a listener.
Men like to talk, I like to listen.
I store things up inside.
I remember what many seem to forget.
I remember my grandfather
Telling of his brother's burial in Clare.
The dead man was too tall
To fit in an ordinary grave
So they had to cut into a neighbour's plot,
Break the railings round a neighbour's grave
To bury a tall man.
This led to war between the families,
Trouble among the living,
Over a patch o' land for the dead.
The trouble's still there. Such things, as you know,
Being a countryman yourself,
Are impossible to settle.
When my grandfather scattered things on the kitchen floor
He used strange words from the Gaelic.
I wonder still about the roots of words.
They don't teach Latin in the schools now.
That's bad, that's very bad.
It is as important to know
Where the words in your mouth come from
As where you come from yourself.
Not to know such origins
Is not to know who you are[50]
Or what you think you're saying.
I had a small red book at school,
'Twas full of roots,
I still remember it.

Roots . . . and crops. Origins . . . and ends.

The woman who looks after me now
Tells me to sip my brandy.
Sometimes I forget I have a glass in my hand
And so I do what I'm told.
I have been blind for years.
I live in a world of voices
And of silence.
I think of my own people, the tall men,
Their strange words, the land
Unmoved by all our passions about it,

This land I know from shore to shore,
The Claremen roaring their support
And all the odds and ends
(What was that word he had for them?)
Scattered on my grandfather's kitchen floor.

33

THE SUMMING-UP

AND SO WE come to the final question: how does the figure of Eamon de Valera stand in history as we approach the year 2000? This biographer's answer is: bulking large, etched in light and shade, with the light dimmer and the shade darker than official portraits have hitherto depicted. Inevitably other writers will arrive at different conclusions, and give different opinions from those which I have recorded. Some are known to have been at work on biographies of their own for several years. Apart from questions of what fresh evidence may be turned up, it will be interesting to see what new verdicts may be arrived at.

But the evidence I have unearthed drives me to say that, on the great challenges which confronted him during his years in office, de Valera did little that was useful and much that was harmful. Emigration, partition, the economy: even if we start by conceding that his freedom of manoeuvre in these areas was limited, his policies appear to have been framed not for substantive action, but for the eye of the beholder. Rhetoric rather than reality were the hallmarks of de Valera's style, symbolized where emigration was concerned by palming off the responsibilities of Caesar on to Christ – getting the Roman Catholic Churches of England and Ireland to build an emigrant centre.

Granted that the Irish economy had been ravaged by war and civil war and afflicted by partition, and was in any case small, open, agriculture-based and on the periphery of Europe, there was another complicating reality – de Valera's lust for power. Even as an old man, he tenaciously denied the reins to Lemass until, with society nearing collapse, he was forced to relinquish them.

He lacked the capacity to act on the economic challenge but he cloaked this with the lofty pretence that his vision was set on higher things than the mundane matter of the economy. His remark to Whitaker after the latter had succeeded in getting his development plan into action, and as a result an unflattering contrast with the de Valera years was beginning to appear, epitomized this: 'There are more important things.' Where economic pressures touched de Valera himself, however, few things showed themselves 'more important', as he amply demonstrated both in the manner in which he got money from the bonds to found the *Irish Press* and in the parsimonious way in which he subsequently ran the company.

Something of the evolution towards conservatism in Fianna Fail policy may be gauged from the career of Joseph Connolly. Though a senator and

693

a member of the Cabinet he was not a member of the Dail; with the abolition of the Senate in 1936 he ceased to be a minister and became instead Chairman of the Commissioners of Public Works. In his memoir he describes refusing the offer of a constituency from a deputy who offered to retire in his favour. A self-made man who had left school at the age of fourteen, Connolly had all the bluntness of his native Belfast. His departure from politics is popularly believed to have been caused by the manner in which big business contributions to Fianna Fail were multiplying. It is said that when he voiced his displeasure to de Valera the Chief replied: 'But we have to be practical. . . . '

Connolly does not refer to this incident in his memoirs, but he does cite another disagreement to indicate a policy change on de Valera's part. De Valera had continued to seek Connolly's advice after he took on the Public Works job. But Connolly notes:[1] 'I cannot flatter myself that either my talk or advice had any appreciable influence . . . we seemed to agree that radical change was essential but no change or action followed. . . . What I did realise was that most of our economic and land policy of 1932 was rapidly disappearing and that the drift from internal self-reliance and development had become a steady stream in the opposite direction.'

At what proved to be their final *tête-à-tête* de Valera raised with Connolly his concern over the slow pace of land division by the Land Commission. Connolly asked him if he was serious. De Valera 'seemed irritated' and replied that 'of course he was serious'. Connolly then pointed out to him that they had discussed this problem 'frequently'. They had received advice from the Land Commissioners, but nothing had been done. Connolly said he concluded that de Valera had changed his policy. This 'sparked off a minor fireworks display'. It was Connolly's 'last private talk or conference with de Valera'. He commented that it was the 'most bewildering problem' of his political career to understand de Valera's change on the land issue and other matters which had been articles of faith to which de Valera had pledged himself. Connolly writes that:[2] 'In my later talks with de Valera, I formed the opinion that he no longer welcomed discussion, much less criticism, and that what he wanted beside him was a group of "yesmen" who agreed with everything and anything that the party (with himself as leader) approved. I think he achieved this!' Connolly said that he found writing this judgement 'the most unpleasant section' of his memoir. He would have been glad, he said, to have omitted this aspect of his relationship with de Valera, but for the fact that it was[3] 'a vital part of my experiences and seems to me to shed some light on the trend of things since war broke out in 1939 and a trend that has been alarmingly accelerated in recent years'.

The extent of the sclerosis in Fianna Fail policy towards employment may be gleaned from a prepared speech delivered by Sean MacEntee to a student society in University College, Dublin on 8 May 1945. Replying to a paper entitled 'Should Eire Plan for Full Employment', MacEntee said that he:[4] 'hesitated to give an affirmative answer to the Auditor's question. Supposing they succeeded temporarily, one of two things would happen. The first would be that the too few men available would immediately demand higher wages in return for their labour.' MacEntee's second ground for hesitation was based on the belief that workers would push their demands so high that employers would be forced to use machines to do men's work. The result of this would be that in the absence of workers there would be no growth or economic progress.

Commenting on this type of thinking, Sean O'Faolain wrote:[5] 'Two minutes' walk from Mr. de Valera's office would bring him to the door of 30, Merrion Sq., the United Kingdom Permit Office, and if he were to push open that door and see the tired, dumb faces in the crowded waiting rooms and up the stairs lifted to see him enter. . . .'

Sean O'Faolain summed up the Ireland which de Valera had created in a memorable polemic which appeared in the *Bell* in June 1945. Having described de Valera's policy as one of 'masterly inactivity', he wrote:

> His Ministers do the best they can. He who should creatively and imaginatively initiate as leader an all-over, all embracing social plan has lost the power to initiate anything . . . we see the Irish nature so adventurous, so eager, so gay, being chilled and frustrated by constant appeals to peasant fears, to peasant pietism, to the peasant sense of self-preservation and all ending in a half-baked sort of civilisation which taken all over is of a tawdriness a hundred miles from our day of vision – when we see all that we have no option but to take all these things in one angry armful and fling them at the one man who must accept them as his creation, his reflex, his responsibilty.

On partition, again an area in which his freedom of manoeuvre was severely limited, he showed a consistently ungenerous spirit towards the Protestants of Northern Ireland. Granted that their record of bigotry and discrimination rivals that of the South African Boers, de Valera was the one allegedly seeking unity. Excluding the sending of the Dublin fire brigade to Belfast, what co-operative gestures did he ever make to conciliate the Unionists? Some will argue, of course, that it was the gestures of conciliation made by Lemass in going to speak with Captain Terence O'Neill, the then Six County Prime Minister, at Stormont in 1965 that led to the present troubles. But this is an untenable argument. It was not the visit but the cynical manipulation of it by that disturbing personality, Ian Paisley, which provoked the turmoil. Craig spoke of a vision of a Protestant Parliament for a Protestant people. De Valera's Constitution indicates a vision of a Catholic Constitution for a Catholic people. On the partition issue, as on much else, his was a policy of activity without movement. He realized that the line drawn on the map of Ireland by the Government of Ireland Act and enshrined in the Treaty a year later was there to stay. It could only be removed by either overwhelming force on an imaginative policy of reconciliation. He had not the troops for the former nor the creativity and flexibility for the latter. Self-righteous propaganda that stirred the pot of anti-British sentiment without adding anything fresh to the ingredients became his stock-in-trade.

And here we come to the crucial turning point of his entire career – his attitude towards the British peace package that Lloyd George first showed him in July 1921 and which subsequently formed the basis of the Treaty. This was the hub around which all else revolved: the civil war; the type of state which emerged; the parameters of political and economic advance, North and South; and his refusal to face up to the responsibility for accepting the British proposals. His disowning of those who did, and the attitude he subsequently displayed towards democracy, helped to determine the course of Irish history to this very day. It is impossible to avoid the conclusion that part of that determination was born out of a reckless pride. De Valera was a Disturber. The ego he had already shown in shouldering Arthur Griffith aside in his hour of triumph from the presidency of the Sinn Fein Party, which Griffith had founded, was heightened by his reception in America and by the battles which he fought there.

Having played a leading role in one type of civil war in America, he returned to Ireland to play an even more fateful part in a far bloodier kind. He could not stoop to accept the blame for the inevitable compromise in London; instead he sent his rival, Collins – whom, be it remembered, he did not take to see Lloyd George in the first place – and turned once more to Griffith. His behaviour after the Treaty was signed was irresponsible and caused lasting damage to his colleagues and to Ireland. The wading-through-blood speeches, though they chillingly articulated his pique and pride, were not an aberration. They were fiery, but cold-blooded, on all fours with his deliberate decision to utilize 'extremist support' – the IRA – for his purpose. Criticism made him desist from the use of such wild and swirling words, but not from his policy of making use of the IRA until he got into power and a break became inevitable.

But by then Ireland's course was set in bitterness and small horizons. His tinkering with constitutional forms, abolishing the Oath and so forth, was nothing more than a 'stepping stone' policy that could, and should, have been followed without either a civil war or the creation of the ideological baggage with which the Twenty-six Counties is still burdened. During the civil war, when he was writing in confidence to his friend, Father Byrne, at the time of the Luzio visit, he spelled out that what he was fighting for was about power: 'a usurpation that got into power by a "coup d'etat" – by fraud and force.'

Whence came that almost insatiable drive for power? We cannot say for certain why any man pursues that grail, but in de Valera's case it would appear that uncertainties about his origins, coupled with the hero worship and respect shown for his leadership qualities and political skills after 1916, combined to create an unshakable determination that so long as he lived there would be no doubt as to who was the Chief. De Valera did not do or say anything that can be pointed to as enriching Irish culture or bringing Ireland into the mainstream of Western thought, never mind contributing to that intellectual development. The view of culture he promoted was isolationist, parochial almost. Sean O'Faolain's polemic contains much uncomfortable truth. Ill fares the land where culture languishes and censors multiply.

De Valera sought deliberately to create an identity based on being the Boss – on Bruree Man, Blackrock College, the Irish language and Irish Catholicism. This last took a more authoritarian, rigorous and unquestioning form than that found elsewhere in western Europe. Even though one concedes that de Valera himself was a sincere and devout Catholic, the form of the Irish Church, in a pre-television age, was essential to de Valera, Man of Power. It provided him with an electorate indoctrinated by a catechism which spoke of the necessity for having 'respect for kings and those who rule over us',[6] and trained people to look for their rewards in the next life.

A fusion of these elements and his own unshakable belief in himself carried him successfully through shooting wars, political wars and his most praised achievement, neutrality. This last, as Frank Aiken pointed out, was a sort of warfare carried on against both sets of belligerents. Without even attempting to evaluate the important moral issue of where right lay in the question of opposing the Nazis (an issue which was also evaded by ethical nations such as Sweden), what was the long-term effect of neutrality on Ireland? Had Ireland been on the side of the Allies, what would have been the outcome? Initially at least, until the British introduced to the South the sort of defence systems which spared Belfast from further horrors, there would certainly have been incalculable loss of life from aerial bombardment. Whether this would have had the saving grace of ending partition and thus avoiding what has befallen Northern Ireland over the last twenty years is simply an unanswerable question.

Patrick Lynch reckoned that central to de Valera's maintenance of power was the fact that 'he never told his colleagues anything'. Shortly after speaking to Lynch[7] I received an excellent indication of the worth of the former civil servant's judgement. While going through Sean MacEntee's papers, I discovered that while Minister for Finance he had twice tendered his resignation during the 1930s. On one occasion he complained that his colleagues were putting forward proposals which would make of him a 'cypher'.[8] On another he wrote that the Cabinet was 'spending excessively' and that his continuation in office would be 'incompatible with the views' held by de Valera.[9]

Even a suspicion of resignation concerning a figure of McEntee's standing within Fianna Fail would have sent seismic waves through Irish political life. But de Valera so successfully defused the McEntee bombshell that – along, of course, with talking him into withdrawing his threat – I found that[10] even Maurice Moynihan had been unaware that it had ever existed. And on the surface Moynihan was as close as de Valera, both personally and professionally, as any man could be. He was secretary of the Government at the time of the McEntee affair, and remained so for twenty-three years – from 1937 to 1960. Apart from Moynihan's own service, his brother Sean also served de Valera as private secretary for several years. Furthermore, after Maurice Moynihan's retirement, during which he kept in constant touch with the President, he devoted eight years of his life to what was literally a labour of love, producing the monumental and indispensable *Speeches and Statements of Eamon de Valera*.

Moynihan's Delphic comment on how *omertà* was maintained over the McEntee incident, and much else, was worthy of de Valera himself:[11] 'Kathleen kept her own files.' But he did not attribute de Valera's success solely to his ability to keep his own counsel:[12]

> He was a very close man, he learned that as a revolutionary, but he was also a great strategist. He always had a plan. There was strategy behind every tactic. He was chess-like, some minor move here, then a big step forward. His thought was political. I doubt if he ever read a serious novel in his life. Of course Marie O'Kelly read detective stories and other things to him towards the end. It was amazing how much he got from the papers about international affairs. He was a very good listener, and he got a lot from people like Frank Gallagher, or in long talks with the Secretary of External Affairs. I would sum up his thought as being primarily political and Catholic. If he was not a daily communicant he certainly went very frequently, and he attended Mass practically every day.

Archbishop Lefevre, who had met de Valera at various functions run by the Holy Ghost Fathers and for whom de Valera served Mass, concurred in Moynihan's assessment of de Valera's cast of mind as being essentially Catholic. He described de Valera as 'the ideal Christian statesman'.[13] It was therefore appropriate that, late in life, de Valera should choose to make a significant assessment of how he saw his own role, and its challenges, to a Roman Catholic bishop, the Bishop of Montpellier, who visited him at Arus an Uachtaran. The bishop posed two questions to him:[14] (1) What was the most difficult decision you had to face? (2) What is the most important quality needed for leadership? De Valera's reply to (1) was: 'Going against friends one was close to.' And to (2): 'The most important quality needed in a leader is judgement. I was a judging machine. They were always referring things to me.'

One wonders what visions of Collins, Griffith, Joseph McGarrity even, swam before de Valera's vision as he replied to (1). But there can be no doubt that his answer to (2) is a precise description of how he operated in Cabinet and elsewhere. Everyone got their say, and when he was satisfied that he was in possession of all the facts he gave his verdict – and it was as final as that of any judge.

Lynch and Moynihan may be regarded as two knowledgeable translators of the same text who differ somewhat in their emphasis. Moynihan would concede that de Valera was 'a very complex man'. Yet he pointed to only one period in which he thought de Valera's judgement failed him: the 'wading through blood' speeches he delivered in 1922. Moynihan would argue, however, that de Valera's main contribution to Irish political life was 'honesty', and that he was capable of changing his mind although: 'He placed a tremendous reliance on the soundness of his own judgement.'

Lynch's analysis was that when de Valera said: ' "That is my decision" – that was that.' His abiding memories of the pluses and minuses on the de Valera balance sheet included:[15] 'His great courtesy and charm; his incredible performance during World War II and, many people don't know this, he was a great Chancellor of the National University, never missed a meeting, though he was no use insofar as primary or secondary level education was concerned. It just did not seem to interest him.'

Lynch, who is himself a distinguished economist – after the war he left Government service for a chair in the subject at University College, Dublin – adjudged de Valera's greatest demerit to be the fact that he had no grasp of economics. In the absence of a lead from the head of Government, policy formulation in this field for much of de Valera's reign, as with that of his predecessors, devolved, as we have seen, on the shoulders of the conservative British Treasury-minded civil servants who headed the Department of Finance, notably Joseph Brennan and Joseph McElligott. But it may be remarked here that, though he had no grasp of economics as a science, de Valera had a very shrewd view of the subject in terms of the pound in his pocket. We find him replying to a lawyer who had written to him in connection with the will of an admirer:[16] 'I will be very pleased if you take steps as you think necessary for the protection of my interest, provided of course that *I incur no personal responsibility for any expenses that may accrue* [author's italics].'

Perhaps it was his lack of insight into economics, coupled with his twin preoccupations with mathematics and power, which led him to set Lynch a task redolent of the odd-ball side of his character. Lynch was instructed to prepare a paper showing how the theory of relativity could be applied to politics. Lynch was briefed by Moynihan that he would: '. . . find plenty of books on the subject in the National Library. Lynch did as he was directed, consulted the shelves of the National Library, and duly produced a solemn piece of nonsense on his assignment. History does not record any subsequent instance of the successful application of Einstein to Fianna Fail; nevertheless, Lynch recalled, 'de Valera was delighted with the paper.'

The Einstein episode probably owed less to de Valera's *le calcul* days than to a desire to have something with which to impress Dr Erwin Schrödinger, the distinguished Austrian physicist, whom he had brought to Dublin. De Valera had been warned by Father Paddy Browne of Maynooth that Schrödinger was in danger from the Nazis; he made contact with him in Geneva and offered him sanctuary in Ireland. He then got Schrödinger to furnish him with arguments as to why the somewhat bewildered Dail should mark the outbreak of world war by sanctioning the creation of an Institute for Advanced Studies. Armed with these, he personally piloted the Institute for Advanced Studies Bill through both the Dail and the Seanad. Despite some strong criticism to the effect that the new Institute would harm the universities and the Royal Irish Academy, and was unnecessary anyhow, the Bill was enacted in June 1940. The Institute consisted of two Schools, one of Celtic Studies, the other of Theoretical Physics. Schrödinger was appointed Director of the School of Theoretical Physics on 21 November 1940.[17] He was popularly supposed to be a Jew, though in fact he was of Roman Catholic origin. In his early days in Dublin, while he was still well disposed towards de Valera, David Gray wrote to Roosevelt[18] expressing his admiration at how de Valera was more concerned with saving one Jew from the Nazis than with the problems of neutrality. De Valera did take a personal interest in Schrödinger's welfare and detailed Lynch to look after his needs. On his first visit to the physicist's office Lynch found him in a fury because 'the fools' had supplied him with a desk and chairs. Schrödinger disliked these because, he said, they only attracted people who wanted to waste his time. He preferred to work lying down on a couch. Lynch found it easier to impress Schrödinger with the success of his application for new furnishings from the Board of Works than with his efforts to help de Valera apply Einstein to Irish politics.

But if de Valera failed with Albert Einstein, he succeeded with George Berkeley – to his own satisfaction. Speaking at the bicentenary[19] of the philosopher bishop he recalled a series of Berkeley's Questions such as:[20] 'Whether there be any other nation possessed of so much good land, and so many able hands to work it, which yet is beholden for bread to foreign countries?' De Valera replied to this, and to some of the other questions which he cited, by saying that Fianna Fail accomplishments, including neutrality, had given the answers: '. . . in concrete form . . . we were able to supply our own needs in bread and sugar and other essentials of food. We were able to supply our own footwear and our own clothing and live in reasonable comfort.' Truman's dictum that there was no such thing as an awkward question, only an awkward answer, had been stood on its ear!

Among de Valera's other intangible, and tangible, legacies were his Constitution, the *Irish Press* and his political party, Fianna Fail. The Constitution is clearly outmoded and in some respects antipathetic to contemporary thought. But no one has yet shown a de Valera-like will, or ability, to replace it. As this Epilogue was being written a series of talks involving Dublin, Belfast and London broke down on the ostensible issue of de Valera's Constitution. However, much of the controversy thus generated was of a sort that de Valera himself would have fully understood: for the optics. Ian Paisley used the Articles as a figleaf to cloak his refusal to enter talks, for the benefit of British public opinion. Even if the much discussed Articles 2 and 3 were removed, the Unionists would still not move towards a united Ireland. So long as they retain the veto on change conceded to them by the Attlee Government, they have no inducement to do so. Of more real significance are the provisions prohibiting divorce and relating to the status of women. Here it is almost certain that the next few years will see the Ireland of the Nineties moving decisively to lessen the shade of the Long Fellow's Long Shadow. Lessen, but not remove totally: De Valera's Constitution will continue to exert an influence on Ireland, North and South, for a long time to come.

The most visible sign of de Valera's legacy, the Irish Press Group newspapers, have had a depressing history. Control of the Group passed from Vivion to his son Eamonn. He purchased a block of Irish Press shares from his uncle Terry (Vivion's youngest brother) in 1985, when his control of the family newspaper empire was threatened by a boardroom power struggle. The share acquisition enabled Eamonn to resist a demand from his directors that a new chief executive be appointed in his place. However, this particular de Valera triumph was short-lived. As a result of the deal Terry de Valera's son-in-law, Elio Molocco, a solicitor, was made a director. He was also entrusted with the firm's lucrative legal business which had hitherto been handled by the old-established firm of John S. O'Connor, who had acted for both Eamon de Valera and Vivion in legal and political matters for several years. However, at the time of writing he is before the courts on a number of charges involving both the Irish Press and others concerning large sums of money. In addition, as this book goes to press de Valera III is engaged in costly litigation with his co-owner, Ralph Ingersoll.

Eamonn de Valera III also changed the *Irish Press* into a tabloid, having first consulted a Mr Giles, a newspaper doctor, who likes to boast about having introduced Page Three to the *Sun*. Thus was furthered the 'purpose for which the papers were founded', about which de Valera spoke so convincingly. The net result of these manoeuvres on the expertise front has been such huge circulation losses that the Group's three papers are now selling less than 50 per cent of what they were when young de Valera inherited them from his father, Vivion. There has been a massive outflow of talent from the company, unprecedented in the history of Irish journalism. All that remains of its past is a recrudescence of the atmosphere which M. J. MacManus described in 1935, on succeeding Frank Gallagher:[21] 'desolation, doom, suspicion and intrigue'. The pay of *Irish Press* journalists is markedly below that offered by other Dublin newspapers.

The courts are being asked in effect to decide who controls the company, Ingersoll or de Valera. Who is entitled to the bonds . . . ? In addition – again shades of the past – just as in a notably swift-footed operation the founding de Valera secured money to float the company, so has his grandson secured funds against its sinking. Although the newspaper company has lost more than £11 million since 1989, some £9 million of it

Ingersoll's money, de Valera III has constructed a very substantial life-raft: Irish Press PLC. This is an investment company, separate from the Irish Press Newspapers, which has assets of some £4 million. It has no financial responsibility for Irish Press Newspapers, although it owns a 50 per cent stake in the papers, having written off its investments in the company. Irish Press PLC has been described as a 'very liquid and very solvent little investment company'.[22] One would not have to be unduly fanciful to imagine the shadow of the Long Fellow falling somewhat darkly across the boardroom of today's Irish Press newspapers.

Where it falls rather more lightly is over Fianna Fail. De Valera, Man of Power, wrought for the future in setting up that which he understood best: a power structure. The party has suffered splits and currently governs, as it has done for some time, only by being in coalition. But it governs. Despite internal upheavals, and a more or less permanent aroma of corruption, Fianna Fail is still the largest political party in Ireland, north or south of the border. It has shown a pragmatic willingness to stay in power with either left- or right-wing partners. Its current bed-fellows are the Labour Party, who ousted the previous occupants, the right-wing Progressive Democrats Party. This in turn was an Adam's Rib party born out of Fianna Fail itself. The current leader of FF, and Prime Minister of the country, is a dogfood manufacturer, the amiable Mr Albert Reynolds. On account of rumours of scandal emanating from the meat industry, which were alleged to have touched some of the most important people in Irish business and political life, the state has set up a tribunal, under the aegis of a High Court judge, to try to get at the truth. All that can be said with complete certainty so far is that the presence of most of the country's top lawyers has ensured that the proceedings have been both protracted and costly.

'There are other things .... ' Violence in Northern Ireland, unemployment nearing 30 per cent, and an uncertain future for Ireland, North and South, caught in world recession and the aftermath of the collapse of the Russian empire. Nevertheless the Fianna Fail Party persists. Its Green-tinted combination of organization, patronage, menace ('We'll get ye if ye don't') and a Tammany-style social conscience, admixed with corruption, still moves successfully to the tune of 'De Valera leads you'. Fianna Fail may be his most enduring epitaph. The party, like its founder, is about power.

And what else did the man leave? Some not inconsequential legacies. A tradition that courtesy pays in public life. An acknowledgement of the worth of a consciousness of being Irish and of the Irish language, albeit to the exclusion of other manifestations of Irishness. A memory of a notable furtherance of the Irish tradition of independence in world affairs. Sadly, this has been progressively lost sight of as Ireland increasingly looks toward the EC gravy train as the object of its foreign policy. Yet there are 'other things'. Along with Paudeen fumbling in his greasy till, preoccupied with tales of tax-dodging and malpractice emanating from the beef tribunal, there are Ireland's poets, playwrights, writers, film-makers and rock musicians. These were the sort of people who in their youth, in their generation, made the 1916 revolution. It was de Valera's karma to risk his life by taking part in that poets' revolt and yet later, in power, to seek, and too often to succeed, in frustrating that poetic vision. Not all defenders of artistic freedom in de Valera's Ireland were of the calibre of W. B. Yeats. Where Christ and Caesar reign, the voice of the Censor is loud in the land. Yet even though he held it for too long de Valera played a decisive, and not dishonourable, part in holding the bridge for democracy, so that other generations could pass over to their destiny, their fulfilment.

What then was de Valera? A hero or a fraud? A patriot and a statesman or a ward-heeling politician? A scholar or an obscurantist? A charlatan or a seer? He had elements of all these things in him.

Whitaker, as befits the man who did so much to reshape the Twenty-six Counties from de Valera's image, is cooler and more objective than most in describing him:

> He was the quintessential Christian Brothers boy. He had enormous courtesy, but no social graces. His early upbringing told all through his life. He'd been brought up the hard way. He was an ideologue, not like Lemass who was a pragmatic patriot, but quite a simple man really. I remember once, after we joined the International Monetary Fund, bringing a top IMF man, Charles Merwin, to see him. Dev. delivered a scaled down version of the Comely Maidens speech. I attempted to intersperse a few economic truths about exports and so on.
>
> After we left Merwin was silent for a bit. Then he turned to me and said: 'Strange man your Prime Minister.'
>
> Dev. was genuinely fond of Irish. He would normally speak to me in Irish when he'd come on the phone.
>
> I remember a typical conversation when he was president. First Marie O'Ceallaig came on, talking Irish of course. Then the old gravelly voice of Dev. himself. He asked me if I was still minding the purse, that was his usual job description of the Secretary of the Department of Finance. Then he invited me to a dinner and went through the names of everyone who'd be there. I asked after Sinead, and he said, a bit shortly: '*Ah, is i sin Sean*' ['She is old.' De Valera himself was, of course, well over eighty at the time.] He and Sinead used to put themselves out quite a bit going to Irish events.
>
> But he had leadership qualities. He wasn't Irish in his manner. He had the strange name, 1916, the mathematics. It all inspired awe.

Whitaker told a story which illustrated perfectly how, with a man of lesser calibre than Whitaker, de Valera's use of his mathematical expertise would indeed have been awe-inspiring to the point of being disconcerting.

> He had a very strange sense of humour. I remember once I was over in the Dail, in the 'bullpen' [the enclosure for top officials whose presence is required in the Chamber for important debates], advising the Minister for Finance during a Budget debate. Suddenly Paddy Lynch appeared at my shoulder. He said that the Taoiseach had sent him over to ask me did I know what an Epicycloid Circle was. Paddy said he did not know for the life of him what he meant.

703

So I said I was no expert but I thought it was a circle enclosing a smaller circle which it touched tangentially. Paddy came back later in the debate to say that Dev. was delighted. He was to tell me two things. Firstly that the Taoiseach said that it was reassuring to know there was someone in Finance who understood mathematics.[25] Secondly that the tangential nature of the two circles touching contained about the same contact with truth as did the Opposition's attack on the Budget!

The American intelligence agent whom I have already quoted came very close to the truth when he described both de Valera and this great adversary, Churchill, as possessing political genius. A respected Irish commentator, Professor Lee, summed him up as being:[26] 'in a sense, greater than the sum of his parts. Behind the ceaseless political calculation and the labyrinthine deviousness, there reposed a character of rare nobility. His qualities would have made him a leader beyond compare in the pre-industrial world. It was in one sense his misfortune that his career should coincide with an age of accelerated economic change whose causes and consequences largely baffled him.'

It was also, one might add, a misfortune for that little man heading for the emigrant ship with his bursting suitcase. But I will leave the last word to someone who loved him, Sinead. She once 'half-humorously, half-despairingly', told friends that she could write a play about him. But, she said, she did not know whether it would be 'a comedy or a tragedy'. *Sinn é, Sinead.*[27]

NOTES

Abbreviations

Author	Original in author's possession
Author's copy	Copy in author's possession
BCL	Blackrock College Library
FO	Foreign Office, London
FAK	Franciscan Archives, Killiney
NAI	National Archives of Ireland
NLI	National Library of Ireland
PRO	Public Record Office, London
TCD	Trinity College, Dublin
UCD	University College, Dublin

Sources, particularly books, are generally referred to by author only. For titles, readers should consult the Bibliography. Where there are a number of works by the same author, these are numbered both in the Notes and in the Bibliography, e.g. Bromage (1).

Chapter 1 (pp.3–39)

1. Archbishop McHale at the Vatican Council of 18 July 1870.
2. Marianne O'Brien. She was nearly forty years younger than her husband, Michael. Like him she knew Latin and spoke some French. After his death she ran their farm and looked after a large family. A fuller account of her life and that of her husband may be found in T.P. Coogan's *Michael Collins*.
3. Details of de Valera's early life can be found in a number of books referred to in the Bibliography, but readers are especially referred to his authorized biography by Lord Longford and T.P. O'Neill, *Eamon de Valera*, and to *Dev and His Alma Mater* by Sean P. Farragher Cssp.
4. Longford and O'Neill (1), p.1.
5. Ibid.
6. C. O'Brien, Introduction, p.1.
7. Mulcahy papers, P7C/57 C2, UCD.
8. These sorts of rumours can, of course, be met with in any pub in Ireland. However, I confirmed with an impeccable source that they were also common amongst both friends and enemies during the boyhood of Mark Hederman, a Benedictine monk who grew up in the shadow of Glenwilliam Castle, Ballingarry, Co. Limerick, owned by Thomas Atkinson. Atkinson, who had the reputation of being a noted cocksman, reputedly won the castle in a card game. Hederman, who became Headmaster of Glenstal Abbey, was not, of course, the author of such rumours. I merely asked him if he had heard them as a boy.
9. Letter to author from Mark Hederman, 1 December 1991: 'Gossip around Ballingeary when I was a boy.' The letter was in reply to a questionnaire about de Valera anecdotes.
10. Author's copy, dated 'Sat. Evg.'
11. Author's copy.
12. Longford and O'Neill (1), pp.1–2.
13. Ibid, p.2.
14. 'Notes on Dev.', 6 April 1946, Gallagher papers, Ms 18, 375, NLI. (See also n.28.)
15. Frank Gallagher. He recorded the incident in an unpublished diary of his American tour with de Valera in 1927. Gallagher papers, Ms 1005/115, TCD.
16. De Valera was awarded the Bible as a prize while attending Blackrock College, Dublin, where it is now preserved.
17. Longford and O'Neill (1), p.2.
18. 'Notes on Dev.', Gallagher papers, Ms 18, 375, NLI.
19. Ibid.
20. Ibid.
21. Available in US National Archives, Washington DC, and at National Archives Building, 201 Varrick St, New York.
22. According to Patrick Shalhoub, Archivist in the Jersey City public library.
23. I am indebted to both the pastor of St Frederick's, Father Jean Solomon, and Father McHale of St Paul's for permission to study their records on 27 May 1993.
24. On State of New Jersey Marriage Returns. Author's copy. The Turst–de Valera wedding

took place on 10 February 1891 at St Peter's church, Newark.

25. Author's copies.
26. From Ms Marion Touba, Reference Librarian, on 17 June 1993.
27. Dwyer (6). Author's copy of inscription.
28. The bulk of his papers are in the National Library of Ireland and in the Library of Trinity College, Dublin. Roughly speaking, the Trinity collection contains the diaries which Gallagher kept during two tours of America with de Valera in 1927–8 (Ms 1005/115), while the NLI has his 'Notes on Dev.', which consist of records of observations, interviews and anecdotes about de Valera over a period of nearly thirty years, from which it was intended to fashion a biography. These are largely, though not exclusively, in the extensive files beginning Ms 18, 375. But in both collections readers will find interesting notes, written on scraps of paper, in the writing cultivated by men who have been in prison. The difficulty of the two collections being separated is mitigated by the fact that they are only a few hundred yards from each other.
29. 'Notes on Dev.', Gallagher papers, NLI.
30. Ibid.
31. Longford and O'Neill (1), p.3.
32. Mannix Joyce compiled a lengthy and authoritative article about de Valera's Bruree associations, 'Eamon de Valera, Bruree Man', in The Capuchin Annual.
33. Ibid.
34. General Gordon, one of Britain's best-known soldiers, was known as 'Chinese Gordon' because of his suppression of the Taiping rebellion of 1860. Service to the British Empire took him to many parts of the world, including Ireland. He was killed at Khartoum in 1885 during the Mahdi's rebellion. This quotation is taken from J. L. Hammond, Gladstone and the Irish Nation and quoted in F. Lyons (1), p.162.
35. Patrick Kavanagh, Lough Derg.
36. Longford and O'Neill (1), p.3.
37. Bromage (1), pp.23 et seq.
38. Gallagher papers, Ms 1065/128, TCD.
39. Ibid.
40. Ibid.
41. Bromage (1), p.91.
42. Rochester Patriot Weekly, 11 October 1942.
43. Ibid.
44. Joyce, in The Capuchin Annual.
45. Longford and O'Neill (1), p.3.
46. 'Notes on Dev.', Gallagher papers, NLI.
47. Longford and O'Neill (1), p.4.
48. Ibid.
49. Dwane, pp.25-6 et seq., gives considerable detail concerning the youthful de Valera's leisure pursuits.
50. Joyce, in The Capuchin Annual.
51. Ibid.
52. Sean Moylan, Bureau of Military History memoir. These memoirs were recorded on the basis that they would not be made public until the last survivor of the Anglo-Irish war period had passed away, but they can be obtained in individual cases with the permission of families. Moylan's is available in Sean T. O'Ceallaigh's papers, Ms 27, 731, NLI.

53. Gallagher papers, Ms 1065/115, TCD.
54. Longford and O'Neill (1), p.5.
55. Ibid.
56. Treaty Debates, Public Session, 6 January 1922, pp.271-15, Stationery Office, Dublin.
57. Gallagher papers, NLI.
58. Ibid.
59. Ibid.
60. Longford and O'Neill (1), p.6.
61. Ibid, p.5.
62. Gallagher papers, Ms 1065/115, TCD.
63. Ibid.
64. Longford and O'Neill (1), p.6.
65. These, and other examples of British educational policy in Ireland, are discussed in O'Hegarty (2), p.395.
66. Gallagher papers, NLI.
67. The conversation with Gallagher is recorded in 'Notes on Dev.', 19 July 1952, Gallagher papers, NLI.
68. Militant Orange societies had been a feature of northern Protestant life in particular since the 1798 rebellion. Formed to defend the Protestant Ascendancy and to maintain the link with England, they were frequently involved in violent clashes with their Catholic mirror groupings.
69. Churchill (1), Vol.II, p.65.
70. Gallagher papers, NLI.
71. Healy to Liston, 31 August 1898, quoted in Farragher, p.13.
72. Gallagher papers, NLI.
73. The penal laws had been officially repealed in 1829.
74. Gallagher papers, NLI.
75. Farragher, p.28.
76. Preserved in BCL.
77. Both letters date from the early days of their marriages, 1911 et seq., and are reprinted in Farragher, pp.102-3.
78. Farragher, p.208.
79. The drawing, dated May 1908, is in BCL.
80. Gallagher papers, NLI.
81. Farragher, p.35.
82. BCL.
83. Farragher, p.45.
84. To be strictly accurate, he wrote: 'Florrie Green and Donnegan', omitting Donnegan's first name, Patrick.
85. Farragher, p.54.
86. Father Sean Farragher, Cssp. Author's interview with Father Farragher, 9 April 1993.
87. BCL.
88. He subsequently presented the paper to the College.
89. Farragher, p.35.
90. Ibid, p.73.
91. Here there was another curious parallel with Michael Collins, who also became engaged to a hotelier's daughter – Kitty Kiernan, of Granard, Co. Longford.
92. Farragher, p.77.
93. Author's interview with Farragher, 8 April 1993.
94. Gallagher papers, NLI.
95. Ibid.
96. Farragher, p.85.
97. Longford and O'Neill (1), p.13.

98. 'Problems set by Eamon de Valera to Carys-fort students in October, 1906', quoted in Dwane, p.35.
99. Ibid, p.35.
100. From a description of him by a student of the time, 1908–9, BCL.
101. Dwane, p.40.
102. Under Professors Conway and MacSweeney at UCD, and at TCD under the Irish Astronomer Royal, E.T. Whittaker.
103. Gallagher papers, Ms 1065/115, TCD.
104. Terry de Valera, *Sunday Independent*, 3 October 1982.
105. Dwane, p.41.
106. Shanahan, who through his work in Nigeria became one of the legendary figures of the Irish missionary effort, was later made a bishop.
107. Farragher, p.34.
108. Ibid, p.83.
109. Literally 'soul friend'; in this case he bared his soul to his confessor. The term is Farragher's, who describes this phase of de Valera's concern with the priesthood on pp.83–4.
110. Original in the Dublin Archdiocesan Archives, Clonliffe College. Author's copy.
111. Gallagher papers, NLI.
112. Ulick O'Connor called his book describing this literary renaissance *The Celtic Dawn*, as a counterpoint to Yeats' well-known collection of folk-tales, *The Celtic Twilight*.
113. Farragher, p.100.

Chapter 2 (pp.40–56)

1. Boylan, p.88.
2. Farragher, p.101.
3. Bromage (1), p.31.
4. Some of the illegal distillers, through a combination of laziness and police surveillance, do not now take the time needed to get the brew as clear as, say, gin or vodka. Instead of repeatedly passing it through the still, some of them have been known simply to add household bleach.
5. Longford and O'Neill (1), p.16.
6. Gallagher papers, NLI.
7. Gwynn, p.25.
8. Casement visited the school the following year, 1911.
9. Longford and O'Neill (1), p.18.
10. Eamon de Valera to Sinead de Valera, 'August 1912', author's copy. Translated from the Irish by Micheal O'Siadhail. The poem, '*An Chaoin-Rois*', actually contains five stanzas. De Valera quoted the second in full and gave the second couplet of the third stanza.
11. The importance of Clarke and of the IRB is discussed in some detail on Coogan (4), Ch.2.
12. IRB Constitution, O'Donoghue papers, Ms 31, 305 (1), NLI.
13. Quoted in Stewart (1), p.55. The siege of Derry began when the Protestant apprentice boys defied Mayor Lundy and slammed the gates of the city in the face of the Catholic King James. It ended with the breaking of the boom by ships loyal to King William (of Orange).
14. Buckland (3), p.51.
15. Bonar Law, speaking at Blenheim Palace, 24 July 1912. Quoted in Buckland (3), p.85.
16. Marjoribanks, pp.96–7.
17. Quoted in Marjoribanks, p.99. In 'Recessional', Kipling had used the phrase 'Lesser breeds without the law' to describe 'wild tongues that have not Thee in awe'. Cf. the Gentiles (Romans 11, 14) 'who have not the law'.
18. Carson to his niece, quoted in Stewart (1), p.27.
19. Irvine, p.57.
20. Quoted in Stewart (1), p.62.
21. For example, the first commander, Sir George Lloyd Reilly Richardson, was recommended for the post by Lord Roberts of Kandahar, then the most distinguished living British soldier.
22. Stewart (2).
23. Calwell, Vol.I, p.38.
24. Ibid, p.145.
25. Stewart (1), p.171.
26. 14 September 1914.
27. Gallagher papers, NLI.
28. De Valera, speaking at the opening of the Bureau of Military History, 20 December 1946, D/T. S1433, NAI.
29. Gwynn, p.26.
30. Macardle, p.907.
31. Longford and O'Neill (1), p.20.
32. Readers wishing to know more about the conditions of the time and the founding of the Irish Citizen Army are recommended to consult Greaves (1) and White.
33. John Swift, p.208.
34. Longford and O'Neill (1), p.71.
35. Stewart (1), p.59.
36. Father Curran memoir, O'Ceallaigh papers, section headed 'For Insertion on Page 172', p.5, NLI.
37. Longford and O'Neill (1), p.21.
38. Gwynn, p.25.
39. John Swift, quoted in John P. Swift, p.21.
40. Macardle, p.114.
41. Churchill (3), Vol.I, p.193.
42. *Sunday Independent*, 2 August 1940.
43. Longford and O'Neill (1), p.23.
44. Ibid.

Chapter 3 (pp.57–74)

1. Longford and O'Neill (1), p.23
2. De Valera papers, Folder 30B, FAK.
3. Gallagher papers, NLI.
4. Ibid. The emphasis is Gallagher's.
5. Ibid.
6. Ibid.
7. 'Recollections of J. O'Connor', *Irish Press*, 13 April 1950.
8. Vivion de Valera to author.
9. Macardle, p.149.
10. The 1937 edition was revised and reprinted in 1951, with a foreword by de Valera. Writing to a friend in America on 4 May 1965, he advised that this 'excellent history' should be circulated in the USA. De Valera papers, Folder 11/4, FAK.
11. Longford and O'Neill (1), p.25.
12. Ibid.
13. For full text of speech see Macardle, p.134.

14. 'Notes on Dev.', 14 August 1944, Gallagher papers, NLI. He used the term 'mad' in describing the incident, which he did in far greater detail than that given in this text. Obviously a challenge to his authority gained a certain prominence in his memory.
15. For examples see the Royal Commission of Inquiry into the 1916 Rebellion, Appendix 115, and Stewart (1), pp.213–14.
16. See Stewart (1), p.224 et seq.
17. Stewart (1), pp.227–8.
18. *Hansard*, House of Commons, 5th series, XCL, col. 1841.
19. Ibid.
20. O'Ceallaigh papers, Ms 27, 688 (16), NLI.
21. Coogan (4), p.36.
22. *Irish Press*, 8 January 1937. Account by Geraldine Plnkett, whose brothers George and Joseph helped to prepare the forgery.
23. Account by de Valera, de Valera papers, Folder 3/5, FAK.
24. Longford and O'Neill (1), p.33.
25. Eamon de Valera to Sinead de Valera, Lewes Jail, Easter Saturday 1917. Author's copy.
26. Longford and O'Neill (1), p.44.
27. The account of the Benedict–Plunkett exchange is given by Father Curran in his Bureau of Military History memoir, O'Ceallaigh papers, MS 27, 728 (1), NLI.
28. Macardle, pp.166–7.
29. Longford and O'Neill (1), p.38.
30. Ibid, pp.39–40.
31. This is the estimate of the authoritative Padraig O'Caoimh, Secretary of Sinn Fein. It is far lower than the 1,200 or so normally claimed. De Valera urged O'Caoimh to make this correction as part of a series being prepared for a new edition of Macardle. See D/T S.13162, NAI.
32. 'Mount St Bridge', memoir by Simon Donnelly, de Valera papers, Folder 29C, FAK.
33. Gallagher papers, NLI.
34. Longford and O'Neill (1), p.43.
35. *The Easter Rebellion*.
36. Quoted in Coogan (4), pp.41–2.
37. Simon Donnelly, letter to *Sunday Press*, 5 April 1964.
38. De Valera to Donnelly, Donnelly memoir.
39. Coogan (4), p.42.
40. See n.32.
41. Donnelly memoir, p.11.
42. White was then public relations officer for the national transport company, CIE. Being fluent in Irish, he got on well with de Valera and was thus often assigned to travel in his coach.
43. Dwane, p.47.
44. Longford and O'Neill (1), p.45.
45. Ibid.
46. Gwynne, p.259.
47. Longford and O'Neill (1), pp.45–6.

Chapter 4 (pp.75–106)

1. The term was used to me by a survivor of the meeting. Cuchullainn was a legendary Irish hero who tied himself to a tree so that he could stil face his enemies on his feet, although dying. His foes only dared to approach him when a raven perched on his shoulder, showing him to be dead. His statue, commemorating the Easter Rising, stands in the GPO.
2. Andrews (1), p.89.
3. The Young Irelanders awaiting their trials for high treason after the 1848 rebellion – for which the penalty was death – staged similar mock trials.
4. Longford and O'Neill (1), p.48.
5. Ibid, p.45.
6. Ibid, p.48.
7. Ibid, p.49.
8. Original in BCL.
9. Quoted in Farragher, p.113.
10. Given to Michael Lennon, 16 December 1945. De Valera papers, Folder 306, FAK.
11. Wylie gave his account to David Gray, the wartime US Ambassador to Ireland, at a lunch in the Embassy on 21 May 1941. Gray recorded the story in his diary, which he later reproduced in an unpublished book, 'Behind the Green Curtain', described in detail in Ch.8.
12. The letter is headed '33, Morehampton Tce., Tues.'. Original in BCL.
12a. Longford and O'Neill (1), p.33.
13. Ibid, p.51.
14. Ibid, p.52.
15. Ibid, pp.52–3.
16. Gallagher diary, 18 January 1928, Ms 10065/167, TCD.
17. Kathleen O'Connell to Mrs Doheny, 23 May 1967. De Valera papers, Folder 30/C, FAK.
18. Gallagher papers, NLI.
19. Longford and O'Neill (1), p.53.
20. Gallagher papers, NLI.
21. Gallagher diary, 18 January 1928, Ms 10065/167, TCD.
22. Dept of State to Father Wheelright, 11 November 1916. De Valera papers, FAK.
23. De Valera to fellow prisoners, Lewes Jail, Whit Monday, 28 May 1917. De Valera papers, Folder 36, FAK.
24. Gallagher papers, Ms 18, 375 (6), NLI.
25. De Valera to Simon Donnelly, Easter Sunday–Monday morning 1917. De Valera papers, Folder 36, FAK.
26. De Valera to Simon Donnelly, 23 April 1917, 4.30a.m. De Valera papers, Folder 36, FAK.
27. De Valera's instructions to prisoners, Easter Sunday 1917, Lewes Jail. De Valera papers, FAK.
28. Eamon de Valera to Mrs Malone, Lady's Day 1917, Lewes Jail. De Valera papers, FAK.
29. De Valera's instructions to prisoners, Easter Sunday 1917, Lewes Jail. De Valera papers, FAK.
30. Gallagher diary, TCD.
31. Ibid.
32. Ibid, 18 January 1928, Ms 10065/165, TCD.
33. Ibid.
34. Frank Thornton memoir, Bureau of Military History. Author's copy.
35. Ibid.
36. Gwynne, p.227.
37. Pieras Beaslai, a gifted journalist, member of the IRB and of the IRA GHQ staff, has left a first-hand account of the 'turning of the tide' in *Michael Collins and the Making of a New Ireland*. Dorothy Macardle's *The Irish Republic*

and T.P. Coogan's *Michael Collins* are also recommended.
38. Beaslai, Vol.1, p.126.
39. Ibid.
40. Published in every newspaper in Ireland.
41. Stewart (1), p.103.
42. John Grigg to author, 1 February 1992.
43. Quoted in Coogan (4), p.61.
44. Quoted in Macardle, p.195.
45. De Valera papers, Folder 30G, FAK.
46. Bromage (1), p.64.
47. Ibid.
48. Thornton memoir.
49. Bromage (1), p.65.
50. Longford and O'Neill (1), p.60.
51. Sinead to Valera to Frank Hughes, 26 January 1917. Quoted in Farragher, p.118.
52. Longford and O'Neill (1), p.64.
53. Beaslai, Vol.1, p.150.
54. De Valera papers, 'Sheet 25', Folder 36, FAK.
55. Unpublished memoir of Dr Thomas Dillon, de Valera papers, Folder 52, FAK. Dillon was an explosives expert who had trained the Volunteers in bomb-making prior to the 1916 rebellion.
56. Ibid.
57. Beaslai, Vol.1, p.173.
58. Dillon memoir.
59. Beaslai, Vol.1, p.175.
60. Ibid, p.174.
61. Longford and O'Neill (1), p.68.
62. Ibid, p.69.
63. Beaslai, Vol.1, p.175.
64. Brugha to Sean Matthews. De Valera papers, FAK.
65. Brugha to Michael Lynch. De Valera papers, FAK.
66. Longford and O'Neill (1), p.66.
67. Ibid.
68. Beaslai, Vol.1, p.177.
69. Longford and O'Neill (1), p.66.
70. Bromage (1), p.71.
71. Ibid, p.69.
72. Ibid, p.70.
73. Coogan (4), p.74.
74. Ibid, p.75. Roisin Dhu (Black Rose) is a poetic name for Ireland.
75. Macardle notes (p.210) that at the March Assizes the magistrates congratulated the people on the 'ordinary peaceful and satisfactory condition' of the country.
76. Lee (1), p.40.
77. Father Curran memoir, O'Ceallaigh papers.
78. Macardle, p.241.
79. Thomas Russell, 28 March 1918.
80. John Brown and Robert Laide were shot on 16 April 1918.
81. Longford and O'Neill (1), p.70.
82. Ibid.
83. Ibid, p.71.
84. Macardle, p.235.
85. Aspects of the convention report are discussed in Macardle, Ch.24, and Lee (1), p.39.
86. Coogan (4), p.85.
87. MacManus, p.74.

Chapter 5 (pp.107–123)

1. Father Curran memoir.

2. Bromage (1), p.70.
3. O'Faolain, p.3.
4. Bromage (1), p.72.
5. William O'Brien, quoted in Longford and O'Neill (1), p.72.
6. Bromage (1), p.75, quoting Tim Healy.
7. MacManus, p.75.
8. Father Curran memoir.
9. Bromage (1), p.75.
10. Longford and O'Neill (1), p.73.
11. Father Curran memoir.
12. Macardle, pp.252–3, cites various authorities for this interpretation of British policy.
13. Calwell, Vol.2, p.141.
14. Longford and O'Neill (1), p.74.
15. Ibid.
16. Beaslai, Vol.1, p.189.
17. Longford and O'Neill (1), p.75.
18. De Valera to Charles Murphy. De Valera papers, FAK.
19. Longford and O'Neill (1), p.78.
20. Eamon de Valera to Sinead de Valera, Lincoln Jail, undated. Author's copy.
21. Eamon de Valera to Sinead de Valera, Lincoln Jail, 4 June 1918. Author's copy.
22. McGuinness died in 1922.
23. Eamon de Valera to Sinead de Valera, Lincoln Jail, 2 July 1918. Author's copy.
24. This letter (18 July 1918) and those from de Valera to Sinead of 23 July and 2 August 1918: all author's copies.
25. Eamon de Valera to Sinead de Valera, 22 June 1918. Author's copy.
26. Author's copy.
27. On 22 July 1918. Author's copy.
28. Eamon de Valera to Sinead de Valera, 22 June 1918. Author's copy.
29. Eamon de Valera to Sinead de Valera, 24 August 1918. Author's copy.
30. Eamon de Valera to Sinead de Valera, 17 October 1918. Author's copy.
31. Bromage (1), p.80.
32. O'Faolain, p.13.
33. Longford and O'Neill (1), p.81.
34. Sean O'Mahony papers, Ms 24, 458, NLI.
35. From Sean O'Mahony's entry.
36. P.S. O'Hegarty, 'The Victory of Sinn Fein', quoted in O'Faolain, p.51.
37. De Valera to Donnelly, 23 April 1917. De Valera papers, FAK.
38. Bromage (1), p.86.
39. Ibid, p.91.
40. O'Mara papers, MS 21, 549 (2), NLI.
41. Ibid. Lavelle read her Mss to de Valera between 15 and 30 November 1954.
42. Longford and O'Neill (1), p.88.
43. Bondanella and Musa, p.135.
44. It was drawn up by an anonymous reporter for the Archbishop of Dublin in 1922. As condtions did not change greatly until the mid-1960s it may be taken as applying to the period under review. Archbishop Byrne papers, Diocesan Archives, Archbishop's House, Drumcondra.
45. Vivion de Valera to author.
46. Beaslai, Vol.1, p.205.

Chapter 6 (pp.124–134)

1. Longford and O'Neill (1), p.84.

2. De Valera's escape, one of the most famous prison breaks in Irish history, is well documented in several works: Beaslai, Coogan (4), Longford and O'Neill (1), Bromage (1) and O'Donoghue (3).
3. Bromage (1), p.84.
4. Fintan Murphy escape account, *Sunday Independent*, 20 January 1957.
5. Eamon de Valera to Sinead de Valera, 17 November 1918. Author's copy.
6. Sinead de Valera to Eamon de Valera, undated. Author's copy.
7. Beaslai, Vol.1, p.269.
8. Longford and O'Neill (1), p.87.
9. Bromage (1), p.75.
10. Quoted in Coogan (4), p.105.
11. Ibid.
12. Longford and O'Neill (1), p.87.
13. Beaslai, Vol.1, pp.282–4.
14. Collins papers, Ms 17090, NLI.
15. Longford and O'Neill (1), p.93.
16. Bromage (1), p.86.
17. These appointments took effect from 1 April 1919. Further details may be obtained by consulting the Minutes of Proceedings, Dail Eireann, for the period, published by the Stationery Office, Dublin.
18. Longford and O'Neill (1), p.92.
19. Minutes of Proceedings, Dail Eireann, 10 April 1919.
20. Longford and O'Neill (1), p.83.
21. F. O'Connor, p.70.
22. Quoted in Coogan (4), p.102.
23. Longford and O'Neill (1), p.97.
24. F. O'Connor, p.70.

Chapter 7 (pp.135–155)

1. F. O'Connor, p.70.
2. Ibid.
3. Eamon de Valera to Sinead de Valera, 2 June 1919. Author's copy.
4. Dail Debates, 9 April 1919.
5. He was hit but kept running, and did not die for some days. Collins changed the Squad's revolvers to .45 calibre weapons for all subsequent assassinations.
6. Longford and O'Neill (1), p.96.
7. 'Derwent's Story'. This lengthy, detailed account of how de Valera got to America is in the de Valera papers, FAK.
8. Bromage (1), p.91.
9. Ibid.
10. Ibid.
11. Cronin (1).
12. Recounted to author by Dan Stephenson, chairman of the meeting.
13. Michael Collins to Sean Nunan, 6 October 1919. Quoted in Coogan (4), p.189.
14. Gallagher diary, Ms 10065/28, P.2, TCD.
15. Bromage (1), p.91.
16. Ibid, p.92.
17. Ambassador Spring Rice to Lord Robert Cecil, 13 April 1917. Spring Rice, Vol.II, p.392–3.
18. Macardle, p.280.
19. Tansill, p.213.
20. Lavelle, p.136.
21. Carroll, p.133.

22. Ibid, pp.135–6.
23. CAB 27/69, PRO.
24. Longford and O'Neill (1), p.99.
25. De Valera printed statement to press: widely quoted in US newspapers, most fully in *Gaelic American* and particularly *Irish Press*, Philadelphia, 28 June 1919. Extracts in Bromage (1), Longford and O'Neill (1) and Dwyer (4), p.18.
26. McCartan, p.145.
27. Bromage (1), p.92.
28. Ibid.
29. FO, 371/4249, PRO.
30. Memorandum prepared by Michael Rynne, Dept of External Affairs, Dublin, 25 April 1946, in reply to query addressed to Irish Legation in Washington by *Collier's Magazine*: 'Whether Mr de Valera is still a citizen of the United States, and, if not, whether he renounced it or lost it.' Gallagher papers, Ms 18, 375 (19), NLI.
31. Dail Debates, 1919–21, pp.72–4.
32. Dwyer (4), p.21.
33. Ibid.
34. Longford and O'Neill (1), p.98.
35. Notably at his first press conference in New York on 23 June 1919 and at Boston on 29 June 1919; there were also several other lesser occasions on which interviews were given and statements made.
36. Longford and O'Neill (1), p.98.
37. Dwyer (6), p.32.
38. *Boston Herald*, 30 June 1919.
39. McCartan, pp.140 and 147.
40. Longford and O'Neill (1), p.95.
41. Ibid.
42. Quoted in Longford and O'Neill (1), p.95.
43. Ibid, p.98.
44. McCartan, p.38.
45. Ibid.
46. McCartan, quoted in Bromage (1), p.92.
47. *San Francisco Chronicle*, 19 July 1919.
48. Dwyer (4), p.21.
49. Copies of itineraries in Gallagher papers, NLI.
50. Report of British Consulate General, 14 July 1919. Author's copy.
51. O'Doherty, pp.101–20, gives detailed accounts of places visited.
52. McCartan papers, Mss 17, 680, NLI.
53. Quoted in O'Doherty, p.173.
54. De Valera to Arthur Griffith, 13 August 1919.
55. Quoted in O'Doherty, p.115.
56. Longford and O'Neill (1), p.102.
57. Eamon de Valera to Sinead de Valera, 14 July 1919. Author's copy.
58. Eamon de Valera to Sinead de Valera, 19 July 1919.
59. Eamon de Valera to Sinead de Valera, 31 July 1919.
60. Eamon de Valera to Sinead de Valera, 13 August 1919.

Chapter 8 (pp.156–178)

1. De Valera to Arthur Griffith, 17 February 1920. This correspondence between de Valera and the Irish leaders at home during his American stay has been widely reproduced in varying detail in, e.g., Longford and O'Neill

(1), Dwyer (4 and 7), Beaslai, and Coogan (4). Copies of the actual correspondence exist in a number of archives, chiefly the National Archives, Bishop's Street, Dublin, to which the Dail Eireann Series 2/245 was transferred from the Old State Paper Office in Dublin Castle; the National Library; and the de Valera papers in the Franciscan Archives, Killiney.

2. De Valera to Judge Cohalan, 20 February 1920.
3. Judge Cohalan to de Valera, 20 February 1920.
4. Harry Boland to de Valera, 4 June 1919. Quoted in Longford and O'Neill (1), p.97.
5. Ibid.
6. McCartan, pp.141–2.
7. Ibid, p.142.
8. For these and other objections, including those of the Treasury, see F.M. Carroll, pp.152–3.
9. Quoted in Lavelle, p.148.
10. *Wall Street Journal*, 4 February 1919.
11. McCartan, p.145.
12. Ibid, p.143.
13. Minutes of FOIF, 29 September 1919, quoted in McCartan, p.144.
14. Lavelle, p.150.
15. Ibid.
16. See Senator Thomas Connolly (Texas), *New York Times*, 24 January 1920.
17. Beaslai, Bromage (1), Longford and O'Neill (1), Dwyer and others all give accounts of this controversy, but two writers in particular are recommended: McCartan, who was both an eye-witness and a participant, and Tansill, who makes good and extensive use of Judge Cohalan's papers.
18. McCartan, p.150.
19. Ibid, p.151.
20. Quoted in Dwyer (6), p.33.
21. De Valera to Arthur Griffith, 6 March 1920.
22. This correspondence is covered in Beaslai, Vol.2, pp.7–14.
23. Quoted in Beaslai, Vol.2, p.14.
24. De Valera to Arthur Griffith, 10 March 1920.
25. De Valera to Arthur Griffith, 25 March 1920.
26. McCartan, p.151.
27. Ibid, p.153.
28. Ibid, p.155.
29. De Valera to Arthur Griffith, 17 February 1920.
30. Both examples quoted in McCartan, p.143.
31. Michael Collins to de Valera, 6 and 13 October 1919. Quoted in Beaslai, Vol.1, pp.355–6.
32. Vivion de Valera to author. Collins used to let Vivion play with his revolver, thereby heightening the boy's hero-worship.
33. The de Valera–Collins Fenian correspondence is quoted more fully in Beaslai, Vol.1, pp.327–8.
34. Longford and O'Neill (1), p.101.
35. Correspondence quoted in full in Beaslai, Vol.1, pp.353–7.
36. Beaslai, Vol.2, p.7.
37. McCartan, pp.152 and 155.
38. James O'Mara to de Valera, 1 March 1920. Quoted in Lavelle, p.153.
39. Ibid. Quoted in Lavelle, p.155.
40. McCartan, p.144.
41. De Valera to James O'Mara, 4 March 1920. Quoted in Lavelle, p.156.

42. Quoted in Beaslai, Vol.2, p.15.
43. De Valera to James O'Mara, Easter Sunday 1920. Quoted in Lavelle, p.158.
44. Dwyer (4), p.28.
45. F.M. Carroll, p.147.
46. De Valera to Arthur Griffith. Quoted in McCartan, pp.166–7.
47. De Valera to Arthur Griffith, 25 March 1920.
48. Dwyer (4), p.28.
49. Macardle, pp.366–7.
50. Quoted in McCartan, pp.165–6. Original in McGarrity papers, NLI.
51. Considering its significance, de Valera's various biographers have described the Park Hotel meeting in less detail than one would have expected. Readers will find accounts in Dwyer (6) and in the authorized Longford and O'Neill biography. For more vivid descriptions, however, McCartan can be recommended, as can Tansill, and Sean Cronin's *The McGarrity Papers* (Cronin (1)), which gives the longest and most colourful account. For those who can get access to it, the best source of all is the NLI collection of McGarrity papers.
52. Cronin (1), p.78.
53. Ibid.
54. Dwyer (6), p.39.
55. John H. Splain memorandum, quoted in Tansill, p.367.
56. Quoted in Cronin (1), p.79.
57. Andrew J. Ryan. Grace's letter to Ryan, dated 29 June 1920, is quoted extensively in Tansill, pp.367–8.
58. Quoted in Cronin (1), p.80.
59. McCartan, p.169.
60. Tansill drew on Cohalan's papers.
61. Dwyer (6), p.39.
62. Ibid.
63. De Valera to Arthur Griffith, 25 March 1920.
64. McCartan, p.182.
65. Ibid.
66. Ibid, p.186.
67. Lavelle, p.165.
68. McCartan, p.188.
69. Bondanella and Musa, p.13

Chapter 9 (pp.179–196)

1. The description of de Valera's activities is largely based on McCartan's eye-witness account (McCartan, p.191 et seq.), the source for most other biographical work of consequence. But there is some valuable information in Beaslai, Vol.2, pp.16–17, which gives the full text of Cohalan and de Valera's resolutions; Dwyer (6) contains some interesting insights into de Valera's psychological state; and Longford and O'Neill (1) give his own interpretation of his actions.
2. De Valera to Frank Gallagher, quoted in Dwyer (4), p.45.
3. Quoted in O'Doherty, p.154.
4. Geddes to Earl Curzon of Kedleston, 16 June 1920. Author's copy.
5. *Chicago Tribune*, 12 June 1920.
6. Report of conversation between Harding and Geddes is in F.M. Carroll's pamphlet, 'The American Committee for Relief in Ireland, 1920–21'.

7. McCartan, p.199.
8. Ibid, p.219.
9. F.M. Carroll, p.149.
10. McCartan, p.197.
11. Quoted in Coogan (4), p.156.
12. McCartan, p.211.
13. Ibid.
14. Quoted in Lavelle, p.172.
15. Longford and O'Neill (1), p.113.
16. Dwyer (4), pp.51–2.
17. I heard this anecdote told on different occasions by several people who claimed to have been present in the House at the time; they included the late political correspondent of the *Irish Times*, Michael McInerney, and the current Irish Ombudsman, Michael Mills, then political correspondent of the *Irish Press*.
18. Longford and O'Neill (1), p.113.
19. Lavelle, p.173.
20. Ibid.
21. Sinead de Valera to James O'Mara, 29 October 1920. Quoted in Lavelle, p.181.
22. Patrick McCartan to Joseph McGarrity, 12 July 1920.
23. *New York Times*, 11 August 1920.
24. Longford and O'Neill (1), p.114.
25. Rossa Downing described the happenings in his pamphlet 'A Report by Rossa F. Downing', pp.19–20.
26. McCartan, p.212.
27. Longford and O'Neill (1), p.114.
28. James O'Mara to de Valera, 25 April 1921. Quoted in Lavelle, p.247.
29. R.C. Lindsay, Chargé d'Affaires at the British Embassy in Washington, to Curzon, 5 March 1920. Author's copy.
30. Michael Collins to John Devoy, 30 September 1920.
31. Extract from letter written by Mellows from Mountjoy Jail, Dublin, 26 August 1922. He was executed in the jail reprisal for an IRA killing on 8 December 1922.
32. Quoted in Longford and O'Neill (1), p.xxi.
33. Quoted in Coogan (4), p.193.
34. Moylan, Bureau of Military History memoir.
35. Thwaites, pp.191–2.
36. DE 2/450, NAI.
37. De Valera papers, Ms 17, 439, NLI.
38. David Gray, in 'Behind the Green Curtain'.
39. De Valera to James O'Mara, 3 February 1921, O'Mara papers, NLI. Quoted in Lavelle, p.236.
40. FO 371/4249, PRO.
41. De Valera to Frank Gallagher, Gallagher papers, NLI. Conversation of 9–10 August 1944. Another version appears in O'Doherty, p.197, which has him nearing Liverpool when word came that the ship was to be searched. He was heading for the tank, but stopped to pick up some books, thus giving a sailor time to warn him that the tank was being filled 'for the first time in eighteen trips'.
42. 'Derwent's Story', de Valera papers, FAK.
43. Ibid.
44. Ibid.
45. Ibid.

Chapter 10 (pp.197–229)

1. De Valera to Frank Gallagher, 2 April 1955, Gallagher papers, NLI.

2. The incident is described in more detail in Coogan (4), p.166.
3. In a celebrated scene in *Ulysses*, Leopold Bloom lusts after Gertie MacDowell.
4. Longford and O'Neill (1), p.17.
5. Ibid.
6. Ibid, p.122.
7. De Valera to James O'Mara, 3 February 1921. Quoted in Lavelle, p.236.
8. Quoted by Richard Mulcahy in 'Interpolations to Pearse Beasley Mss', Mulcahy papers, UCD. Reprinted in Dwyer (3), p.120.
9. Memoir of John McCoy, second-in-command, 4th Northern Division. Author's copy.
10. This was the assessment of Michael Brennan of Clare, one of the leading IRA commanders, in his memoir for the Bureau of Military History.
11. Quoted in Dwyer (3), p.131.
12. De Valera to Frank Gallagher, 2 April 1955, Gallagher papers, NLI.
13. It was in fact Collins who was head of the IRB. McGarry was more likely the Brotherhood's Secretary and certainly a member of the Supreme Council.
14. F. O'Connor, p.134.
15. Beaslai, Vol.2, pp.19–20.
16. Described in Coogan (4), p.143.
17. Longford and O'Neill (1), p.118.
18. F. O'Connor, p.114. NB O'Connor's insights into the events and relationships of the time are not merely those of a contemporary novelist, albeit a distinguished one. Some of Collins' closest associates, including Richard Mulcahy, David Neligan and, above all, his personal assistant, Joe O'Reilly, provided him with meterial. He was also given unprecedented access to what were then classified Government files.
19. Coogan (4), p.175. A description of Dowling's career and a fuller version of this quotation can be found in MacEoin (1), p.405.
20. F. O'Connor, p.133.
21. Ibid.
22. Ibid.
23. Longford and O'Neill (1), p.118.
24. De Valera to Michael Collins. Quoted in Longford and O'Neill (1), p.118.
25. De Valera to Michael Collins. The letter is reprinted in full in Beaslai, Vol.2, p.141.
26. Longford and O'Neill (1), p.119.
27. Point F of de Valera letter to Collins, 18 January 1921. Quoted in Coogan (4), p.205.
28. Coogan (4), p.205.
29. F. O'Connor, p.134.
30. Longford and O'Neill (1), p.127.
31. F. O'Connor, p.132.
32. Forester, p.181, records the reactions of a participant at the meeting. Richard Mulcahy's papers (UCD) also contain references to de Valera's performance.
33. *Irish Independent*. 30 November 1920, p.6, col.2.
34. *Freeman's Journal*, 4 June 1929, p.5, cols 6–7.
35. Coogan (4), p.206.
36. Longford and O'Neill (1), p.118.
37. Quoted in Longford and O'Neill (1), p.119.
38. O'Malley (2), pp.293–4.

39. The accounts controversy involving Mellows with Collins and Brugha may be followed in more detail in either Coogan (4), pp.174–6, or F. O'Connor, pp.139–41.
40. Coogan (4), p.174.
41. F. O'Connor, p.141.
42. Dwyer (2), p.31.
43. In after life Mulcahy devoted a prodigious amount of energy to annotating Pieras Beaslai's mammoth work on Collins with his own interpretations of events, and sometimes, as in this case, with his own experiences. These annotations are to be found in Mulcahy's papers in UCD. The quotation was reprinted in Dwyer (3), p.130.
44. Mulcahy papers, quoted in F. O'Connor, p.141.
45. Longford and O'Neill (1), p.149.
46. Ibid.
47. Macardle, p.436.
48. Ibid, p.437.
49. Coogan (4), p.250.
50. Dwyer (3), p.125.
51. De Valera to James O'Mara, 3 February 1921. Quoted in Lavelle, p.237.
52. James O'Mara to de Valera, 22 March 1921, 'not sent'. The originals of the de Valera correspondence and related letters, to Harry Boland and others, are in the O'Mara papers in the NLI. Lavelle, p.234 et seq., reprints an extensive series of extracts from the correspondence.
53. De Valera to Harry Boland, 29 April 1921, O'Mara papers, NLI. Quoted in Lavelle, p.254.
54. Lavelle, p.238.
55. Ibid.
56. James O'Mara to Michael Collins, 2 April 1921. Quoted in Lavelle, p.244.
57. Lavelle, p.239.
58. De Valera to Harry Boland, 8 April 1921.
59. Diary of Agnes O'Mara, 29 April 1921. Quoted in Lavelle, p.243.
60. James O'Mara to de Valera, 25 April 1921.
61. Harry Boland to James O'Mara, 27 April 1921.
62. James O'Mara to Harry Boland, 29 April 1921.
63. O'Mara papers, Ms 21, 550, NLI.
64. Contained in O'Mara papers, Ms 21, 550, NLI.
65. Quoted in Lavelle, p.255.
66. Both telegrams quoted in Lavelle, p.256.
67. O'Mara papers, Ms 21, 550, NLI.
68. Quoted in Lavelle, p.245. Original in O'Mara papers, NLI.
69. Beaslai, Vol.2, p.168.
70. This is the sequence as given by Longford and O'Neill (1), p.122, but in talking to Gallagher (2 April 1952) de Valera said that Derby was to see the Cardinal after meeting him.
71. De Valera to Frank Gallagher, 2 April 1952. 'Conversations with Dev.', Gallagher papers, NLI.
72. De Valera to Harry Boland, 29 April 1921. Quoted in full in Lavelle, pp.251–4.
73. Derby–de Valera–Lloyd George exchange, quoted in Macardle, pp.449–51.

74. Emmet Dalton interview, RTE, 6 January 1978.
74a. Sir James Craig became Lord Craigavon.
75. Several accounts of the meeting occur in biographies of Craig and de Valera, notably in Longford and O'Neill (1). Readers are also recommended to read Bowman, pp.246–8.
76. Coogan (4), pp.204–6.
77. Longford and O'Neill (1), p.124.
78. 'I.O.', p.83.
79. Coogan (4), pp.177–8.
80. Longford and O'Neill (1), p.124 et seq.
81. De Valera to Frank Gallagher, 7 May 1952, Gallagher papers, NLI.
82. In the version given in Longford and O'Neill (1), p.125, the dignitary is referred to as an officer, possibly a general. But, twenty years earlier, Gallagher wrote 'Sir Brian MacMahon' in his notes. General Sir Bryan Mahon had been replaced as Commander-in-Chief in Ireland in 1918, so either he was paying an unlikely return visit or Gallagher was confusing him with the Under Secretary and ex-Blackrock man Sir James MacMahon.
83. Gallagher papers, NLI.
84. Churchill (2) quoted in Longford and O'Neill (1), p.129.
85. CO 704/188, PRO.
86. CO 704/100, PRO.
87. CAB 22/23, PRO.
88. The various peace initiatives are described in Coogan (4), pp.185–236.
89. Quoted in Coogan (4), p.203.
90. Longford and O'Neill (1), p.121.
91. Ibid.
92. This election campaign and its outcome are described by several writers, amongst them Macardle, Coogan (4) and Buckland (1).
93. The proceedings are described in Coogan (4), pp.212–13.
94. Quoted in Longford and O'Neill (1), p.113.
95. Philadelphia Public Ledger, 22 April 1921.
96. Dwyer (2), p.31.
97. De Valera to Harry Boland, 29 February 1921, O'Mara papers, Ms 21, 549, NLI.
98. New York Evening World, 28 January 1921.
99. New York Herald, 17 May 1921.
100. Quoted in Dwyer (4), p.55.
101. Sean T. O'Ceallaigh to de Valera, 17 April 1921, D/E Series, NAI.
102. De Valera to Sean T. O'Ceallaigh, 28 April 1921, D/E Series, NAI.
103. Longford and O'Neill (1), p.148.
104. Jones (1), p.60.
105. Lord Riddle, p.238.
106. Quoted in Coogan (4), p.213.
107. De Valera papers, FAK.
108. Longford and O'Neill (1), p.130.
109. Millin, pp.319–33.
110. Diary of Sir Mark Sturgis, 26 June 1921, NLI.
111. Diary of Sir Roger Casement, 23 June 1921.
112. Quoted in Macardle, p.472.
113. Longford and O'Neill (1), p.129.
114. The de Valera–Lloyd George–Unionist correspondence is quoted in Macardle, pp.471–3.
115. Diary of Lady Craig (later Lady Craigavon), 20 June 1921. Sturgis diary, 20 June 1921, Sturgis papers, PRO 30/59/4.

116. Sir Mark Sturgis, quoted in Coogan, p.216.
117. The inaccuracy is pointed out in Longford and O'Neill (1), p.131.
118. Quoted in Dwyer (4), p.62.
119. Ibid, pp.62–4.
120. Diary of H.A.L. Fisher, 6 July 1921, Bodleian Library, Oxford.
121. Smuts to Lloyd George, 6 July 1921. Quoted in Jones (1), p.83.
122. Longford and O'Neill (1), p.131.
123. Quoted in Coogan (4), p.217.

Chapter 11 (pp.230–243)

1. Longford and O'Neill (1), p.132.
2. Collins wrote, but did not send, the note to Moya Llewelyn Davies in London.
3. Longford and O'Neill (1), p.132.
4. Stevenson, 12 July 1921.
5. *The Treaty*, shown first on RTE on 5 December 1971, and subsequently on ITV a month later. The author, on whose book on Michael Collins the film was largely based, headed a list of historical consultants who included de Valera's biographers, Lord Longford and T.P. O'Neill, and John Grigg, Lloyd George's biographer.
6. Longford and O'Neill (1), p.133.
7. Shakespeare, p.75.
8. Extracts from this and other letters connected with the July negotiation have appeared in several works, including those most frequently quoted hitherto (Coogan (4), Longford and O'Neill (1), Macardle etc.), but the full correspondence may be examined in Dail Eireann, Correspondence Relating to Peace Negotiations, June–September 1921, Dublin, 1921.
9. Quoted in Macardle, p.180.
10. De Valera to Michael Collins, 19 June 1921.
11. Longford and O'Neill (1), pp.135–6.
12. Ibid, p.134.
13. Ibid, p.137.
14. Ibid, p.135.
15. Ibid, p.133.
16. Longford (2), p.74.
17. CAB 23/27, PRO.
18. Shakespeare describes the events of 14–20 July in *Let Candles Be Brought In*, and Jones records them in *Whitehall Diaries*.
19. H.A.L. Fisher diary, 20 July 1921, Fisher 17 and 18M, Bodleian Library, Oxford.
20. Longford (2), p.74.
21. Longford and O'Neill (1), p.137.
22. Ibid.
23. Longford and O'Neill (1), p.137.
24. Dangerfield, p.341.
25. Macready to Jeudwine, 10 December 1920. Quoted in Coogan (4), p.353.
26. Dwyer (6), p.58.
27. J.J. O'Kelly, Minister of Education and a well-known writer under the pseudonym 'Sceilig'.
28. Brugha's reaction is in fact not contained in any official record, but in a pamphlet, 'Stepping Stones' (pp.15–16), issued by Sceilig himself through the Irish Book Bureau (Dublin, n.d.). As Sceilig was himself a participant in what is generally agreed to have been a noisy and confused meeting, this biographer, who has had some experience of the difficulties of verbatim note-taking at heated political gatherings, is inclined to question whether the dialogue as quoted is exactly that spoken. However, something of the sort certainly happened, as the episode is entirely in keeping with Brugha's character and subsequent behaviour.
29. Longford and O'Neill (1), p.139.
30. Lloyd George to King George V, 21 July 1921. Quoted in Nicolson, p.357.
31. De Valera to Smuts, 21 July 1921, Series D/E2/262, NAI.
32. Smuts to de Valera, 22 July 1921, Series D/E2/262, NAI.
33. Longford and O'Neill (1), p.131.
34. Dail Eireann, Private Sessions, 22 August 1921.
35. Ibid.
36. Smuts to de Valera, 4 August 1921.
37. Longford and O'Neill (1), p.139.
38. Ibid.
39. Ibid, p.140.
40. CAB 23/26/66. C.P. 3149, 13 August 1921, PRO.
41. Macardle, p.477.
42. The state of being kept going by whatever hospitality could be found whilst on the run.

Chapter 12 (pp.244–254)

1. Longford (2), p.79.
2. Dail Eireann, Private Sessions, 14 September 1921.
3. Longford and O'Neill (1), p.138.
4. Ibid, p.140.
5. Quoted in Coogan (4), p.223.
6. De Valera to Lloyd George, 10 August 1921. Quoted in Coogan (4), p.234.
7. Dail Eireann, Private Sessions, 22 August 1921.
8. Speaking in the Dail on 23 August 1921.
9. Ibid.
10. De Valera speaking in the Dail, Private Sessions, 14 September 1921.
11. De Valera to Joseph McGarrity, 11 December 1921, de Valera papers, Ms 17, 440, NLI. Quoted in Coogan foreword to new edition of Longford (2), p.xii.
12. De Valera to Long Longford, 14 September 1963, Childers papers, 7848/302, TCD. Quoted in Coogan foreword to new edition of Longford (2), p.xii.
13. Dail Eireann, Private Sessions, 14 September 1921.
14. Lee (1), p.49.
15. Longford and O'Neill (1), p.147.
16. De Valera apologists would, of course, need no urging to accept this assessment, but it is also advanced by more objective sources, e.g. Dwyer (7), pp.11–13.
17. Michael Collins to Hayden Talbot, quoted in Coogan (4), p.227.
18. Coogan (4), p.227.
19. An account of the conversation, given to the author by O'Connor's daughter, Sister Margaret Mary, a Carmelite nun, can be found in Coogan (4), p.228.
20. Revealed to the Dail on 17 December 1921 by Mrs Tom Clarke. See Dail Eireann, Private Sessions, p.262. De Valera at first attempted a denial, but finally admitted the remark, saying:

'I forget what particular idea was in my mind at the time.'

21. Michael Collins to Joe O'Reilly, 11 November 1921. Quoted in Coogan (4), p.229.
22. Coogan (4), pp.242–3.
23. Described in Coogan (4), especially Ch.11.
24. O'Hegarty (3), pp.86–7.
25. Macardle, p.530.
26. De Valera to Joseph McGarrity, 27 December 1921.
27. Beaslai, Vol.2, p.291.
28. Ibid, p.290.
29. Cathal Brugha to Richard Mulcahy, 13 September 1921. Mulcahy papers, UCD.
30. Described in Coogan (4), p.232.
31. Dail Eireann, Private Sessions, 18 August 1921, p.12, col.2.
32. Copies of the lengthy exchange may be found in the PRO and NAI. It is also extensively reprinted in Macardle, Chs 51–2.
33. Louis MacNeice's poem 'Bagpipe Music' begins: 'It's no go the merry-go-round, it's no go the rickshaw . . . '.
34. Longford (2), p.79.

Chapter 13 (pp.255–280)

1. I came across the letter in O'Briain's papers in the NLI while I was researching *Michael Collins*. At the time Collins' correspondence with O'Briain was of greater interest to me than de Valera's and I merely took a few brief notes, intending to have the letter photocopied in its entirety when an industrial dispute affecting the library's copying services was over. However, other matters intervened and I did not return to the collection until a year later. When I did so the letter had disappeared.
2. Quoted in Coogan (4), p.235.
3. Ibid, p.230.
4. De Valera to Arthur Griffith, 14 October 1921, D/E Series, 2/304, NAI.
5. R. Taylor (1), p.132.
6. Conversation with author, 11 May 1992.
7. These manoeuvrings are described in Coogan (4), pp.135–76; much of the background to the Treaty negotiations is illuminated also in Longford (2) and Macardle. The various telegrams are quoted in Macardle, pp.535–6. De Valera's version of events is contained in Longford and O'Neill (1).
8. This description of the Sixth Plenary Session is taken from Austen Chamberlain's notes of 21 October 1921. Author's copy.
9. De Valera to Arthur Griffith, 22 October 1921. The letter is part of a compilation of the Treaty negotiation documents made by Robert Barton, of which a copy is in the author's possession.
10. Father Curran's recollections are contained in the Sean T. O'Ceallaigh papers in the NLI. He says that Hagan was sent for by Monsignor Pizzardo, who, acting on behalf of the Pope, asked what he thought of the telegram. Hagan is quoted as saying that he thought it would do harm because of the implication of 'allegiance owed by the Irish to the King'. By coincidence, Hagan's audience with the Pope occurred on the same day that de Valera sent his telegram.

11. Griffith–de Valera correspondence, 10–12 October 1921, Barton compilation.
12. De Valera to Arthur Griffith, 14 October 1921, Barton compilation.
13. De Valera to Arthur Griffith, 16 October 1921, Barton compilation.
14. De Valera to Arthur Griffith, 19 October 1921, Barton compilation.
15. Barton compilation.
16. Ibid.
17. The description of the exchange of documents and the scene they created are described in the Barton papers.
18. Barton compilation.
19. Ibid.
20. Quoted in Coogan (4), p.256.
21. Arthur Griffith to de Valera, 31 October 1921, Barton compilation.
22. Quoted in Coogan (4), p.258.
23. Arthur Griffith to de Valera, 9 November 1921, Barton compilation.
24. Arthur Griffith to de Valera, 12 November 1921, Barton compilation.
25. Ibid.
26. Ibid.
27. Longford and O'Neill (1), p.164.
28. De Valera to Arthur Griffith, 23 November 1921, Barton compilation.
29. Arthur Griffith to de Valera, Barton compliation, p.68.
30. De Valera to Arthur Griffith, 9 November 1921, Barton compilation.
31. Cable from Sir John Anderson to the Chief Secretary, CO 904/188, PRO.
32. M. Farrell, p.76.
33. The full collection subsequently passed out of the Collins family into the hands of a researcher who lost them. The extracts given here form part of a longer selection in Coogan (4), pp.256–7.
34. Dail Eireann, Private Sessions, 15 December 1921, p.155.
35. Father Curran diary, O'Ceallaigh papers, NLI.
36. Michael Collins to Richard Mulcahy, 23 November 1921. Quoted in Coogan (4), p.250. Original in Mulcahy papers, UCD.
37. Accounts of the New Army meeting appear in Coogan (4), pp.150–1 and O'Broin (8), pp.100–3. There is extensive material relating to the issue in the Mulcahy papers, UCD.
38. Barton compilation.
39. In his pamphlet 'The American Committee for Relief in Ireland, 1920–21', p.47.
40. In a letter to Lavelle, O'Mara papers, Mss 21, 550, NLI.
41. Original in Bodleian Library, Oxford (Fisher 17 and 18 M). Author's copy.
42. Arthur Griffith to de Valera, 3 April 1921, Barton compilation.
43. Arthur Griffith to de Valera, 29 November 1921, Barton compilation.
44. Ibid.
45. Lloyd George to Arthur Griffith, Proposed Articles of Agreement, 1 December 1921. Author's copy.
46. British memorandum, 27 October 1921, quoted in Coogan (4), p.251. Author's copy.
47. Longford and O'Neill (1), p.160.

48. Ibid.
49. Ibid.
50. Ibid.
51. Ibid.
52. Gallagher (2), quoted in Longford and O'Neill (1), p.162.
53. Barton compilation.
54. Childers diary, TCD.
55. Barton compilation.
56. Dail Eireann, Private Sessions, p.176.
57. Dail Eireann, Private Sessions, p.187.
58. Barton compilation.
59. Ibid.
60. Longford and O'Neill (1), p.162.
61. Longford (2), p.210.
62. Longford and O'Neill (1), p.162.
63. Barton compilation.
64. Quoted in Longford and O'Neill (1), p.162.
65. The first quotation is from F. O'Connor, p.168. Both it and the remark about confusion are quoted in R. Taylor (1), p.147.
66. Coogan (4), p.268.
67. Dail Eireann, Private Sessions, p.177.
68. Longford and O'Neill (1), p.164.
69. Ibid.
70. CAB 27/23, PRO.
71. Shakespeare, p.89.
72. Coogan (4), p.276.
73. R. Taylor (1), p.152.
74. Michael Collins to 'O'Kane', quoted in Longford and O'Neill (1), p.166.

Chapter 14 (pp.280–299)

1. The term 'Rock of the Republic' was originally coined by Frank Owen in his life of Lloyd George and subsequently quoted with approval in Longford and O'Neill (1), pp.128–9.
2. *Freeman's Journal*, 5 December 1921, quoted in Longford and O'Neill (1), p.163.
3. *Irish Independent*, 6 December 1921.
4. Ibid.
5. Lavelle, p.272.
6. Ibid.
7. Lee (3), pp.115–16.
8. Mulcahy later frequently described this incident in detail to his son, Professor Risteard Mulcahy, who both informed me verbally of what his father had said and subsequently wrote down for me an extensive account of his father's memories of the circumstances of the telephone call to the O'Mara home. The aide de camp, Michael Rynne, also confided his memories to his son Xavier, who like Risteard Mulcahy is an academic, Professor of Archaeology at University College, Galway. Rynne's account corroborates that of Mulcahy.
9. De Valera to Joseph McGarrity, 21 December 1921, McGarrity papers, NLI. Quoted in Cronin (1), pp.106–7.
10. Longford and O'Neill (1), p.166.
11. Michael Rynne (the ADC's son) to author.
12. Lavelle, p.272.
13. Ibid.
14. Longford and O'Neill (1), pp.166–7.
15. Ibid, p.167.
16. Beaslai, Vol.2, p.308.
17. De Valera to Joseph McGarrity, 27 December 1921, McGarrity papers, NLI.

18. De Valera to Frank Gallagher, 16 May 1952, Gallagher papers, NLI.
19. Jack Lynch in conversation with author, May 1992.
20. Longford and O'Neill (1), p.168.
21. Macardle, p.594.
22. Stack memoir, quoted in Dwyer (6), p.85.
23. Childers diary, 8 December 1921, TCD.
23. Frank Gallagher in 'The Anglo-Irish Treaty', quoted in Longford and O'Neill (1), p.169.
24. Frank Gallagher in 'The Anglo-Irish Treaty', quoted in Longford and O'Neill (1), p.169.
25. Dail Eireann, Private Sessions, 15 December 1921, p.173.
26. Dail Eireann, Private Sessions, p.212.
27. The term is used to describe the document in Longford and O'Neill (1), p.169.
28. Beaslai, Vol.2, p.312.
29. Dail Eireann, Private Sessions, p.212 et seq.
30. Ibid, p.241. Statement by Collins to Dail.
31. Dail Eireann, Private Sessions, pp.128–9.
32. Dail Eireann, Private Sessions, 14 December 1921, p.137.
33. There are two separate volumes giving the proceedings of the public and private sessions, the fruits of a remarkable feat of note-taking by long-dead parliamentary reporters and of the scholarship of Dr T.P. O'Neill, de Valera's co-biographer. In the heat of the moment the note-takers sometimes attributed statements to deputies who did not exist. Apart from dealing with these and other problems Dr O'Neill had to contend with the fact that sometimes private and public sessions took place on the same day, as on 14 December 1921, the date of the opening session. De Valera's remarks about the use of Irish and his manoeuvre with the 'Cecil' document both occurred in the first, public, portion of the 14 December session.
34. De Valera to Joseph McGarrity, 21 December 1921: 'The only hope was to try in private session to get the Dail to turn down by a large majority the treaty as signed and to offer our counter proposals to the British.' Quoted in Cronin (1), p.108.
35. Dail Eireann, Private Sessions, p.101.
36. Ibid, p.132.
37. Ibid, pp.131–3.
38. De Valera to Joseph McGarrity, 21 December 1921.
39. Dail Eireann, Private Sessions, pp.110–11.
40. Coogan (4), p.299.
41. Dail Eireann, Private Sessions, p.153.
42. Ibid, p.123.
43. Ibid, p.137, col.1 contains the two statements.
44. Ibid, p.155.
45. Ibid, p.197.
46. Ibid, p.221.
47. Ibid, p.197.
48. Coogan (4) p.300.
49. Dail Eireann, Public Sessions, pp.24–6.
50. Parnell's statue stands at the foot of Parnell Street in Dublin. Inscribed on the plinth are the famous words ' . . . no man can set a boundary to the onward march of a nation . . . ', while Parnell's outstretched arm is pointing to the nearby Rotunda Hospital.
51. Dail Eireann, Public Sessions, p.32.

52. Childers diary, 28 December 1921, TCD.
53. *Irish Times*, 4 January 1922.
54. Dwyer (6), p.92.
55. Dail Eireann, Public Sessions, 4 January 1922, p.217.
56. *Freeman's Journal*, 5 January 1922.
57. Beaslai, Vol.2, p.335.
58. See Ibid, p.333, and Dail Eireann, Private Sessions, pp.273–83.
59. Coogan (4), p.303.
60. *Freeman's Journal*, 5 June 1922.
61. Dail Eireann, Public Sessions, pp.271–5.
62. Dail Eireann, Private Sessions, p.282. The speaker was Joseph McGuinness.
63. Dwyer (2), p.106.
64. Longford and O'Neill (1), pp.177–8.
65. Dail Eireann, Public Sessions, p.203.
66. Beaslai, Vol.2, p.335.
67. Dail Eireann, Private Sessions, 16 February 1921, p.216.
68. Longford and O'Neill (1), p.177.
69. Dail Eireann, Public Sessions, p.344.
70. Ibid, p.346.
71. Ibid.
72. Beaslai, Vol.2, p.342. See also Dail Eireann, Public Sessions, p.347.
73. Dail Eireann, Public Sessions, p.347.

Chapter 15 (pp.300–321)

1. Moynihan, p.92.
2. The original proofs of the article are contained in the Gallagher papers, Ms 22, 93X, NLI. The Editor of the *Sunday Press* at the time was Colonel Matt Feehan, a member of Fianna Fail's influential Committee of Fifteen, and copy boys plied between Government Buildings and the *Sunday Press* offices both frequently and unremarkedly.
3. Quoted in Coogan (4), p.319.
4. Dail Eireann, Public Sessions, 9 January 1922.
5. Dail Eireann, Public Sessions, p.375 et seq.
6. Dail Eireann, Public Sessions, 10 January 1922.
7. *Freeman's Journal*, 12 January 1922.
8. Labour Party submission to Collins and Griffith, 10 January 1922. Stationery Office, Dublin.
9. For the full story of the Monaghan footballers and the Derry prisoners saga see Coogan (4), p.343.
10. *Poblacht na hEireann*, 17 January 1922.
11. Macardle, p.665.
12. Longford and O'Neill (1), p.183.
13. Ibid.
14. Ibid.
15. Macardle, p.665.
16. Ibid, p.666.
17. The development of the crisis in the Army is documented by Valiulis in her biography, *General Richard Mulcahy*.
18. Dail Eireann, Public Sessions, 10 January 1922.
19. Abstract of memorandum from de Valera to Mulcahy. Quoted in Valiulis (1), p.123.
20. Mulcahy papers, P7/B/191, UCD.
21. Hopkinson, p.16.
22. Valiulis (1), p.243.
23. Beaslai, Vol.2, p.372.
24. Bromage (1), p.165.

25. Ibid, p.166.
26. Ibid, p.165.
27. Ibid, p.166.
28. Patrick McCartan to Joseph McGarrity, 29 March 1922. Quoted in Tarpey, p.158.
29. Quoted in Dwyer (2), p.104.
30. Maurice Moynihan.
31. Longford and O'Neill (1), p.186.
32. *Irish Independent*, 17 March 1922.
33. Ibid, 18 March 1922.
34. Ibid.
35. Dail Eireann, 19 May 1922.
36. Macardle, p.669.
37. Patrick McCartan to John Devoy. Quoted in Tarpey, p.154. Original in Devoy papers, NLI.
38. Ibid.
39. Unpublished memoirs of Joseph Connolly, then the Irish Consul in Philadelphia, who persuaded McGarrity to undertake the peace mission. Quoted in Tarpey, p.155.
40. *Irish Independent*, 7 April 1922.
41. The *Manchester Guardian* interview of 11 April 1922 was subsequently reproduced in *Poblacht na hEireann* on 20 April by Erskine Childers, so it clearly contained an accurate representation of de Valera's views.
42. Macardle, p.695.
43. O'Malley (1), p.155.
44. Ibid.
45. Quoted in D. O'Sullivan, p.59.
46. Macardle, p.695.
47. Eamon de Valera Proclamation, dated Easter 1922. Author's copy.
48. Longford and O'Neill (1), p.188.
49. Quoted in Tarpey, p.161.
50. Dr Byrne's notes of the conference are in the Archdiocesan Archives, Archbishop's House, Drumcondra.
51. From 'Parnell's Funeral'.
52. *Poblacht na hEireann*, 18 May 1922.
53. Described by a number of contemporaries, among them Frank O'Connor and his Cabinet colleague Ernest Blythe, in a variety of articles and conversations, including interviews with this author. See also O'Luing, p.396.
54. Hugh Kennedy to Michael Collins, 20 May 1922, Kennedy papers, UCD.
55. Churchill to Michael Collins. Author's copy.
56. Lee (1), p.60.
57. Quoted in Coogan (4), p.317.
58. O'Muirthuile memoir, Mulcahy papers, UCD.
59. Lionel Curtis, who made the assessment, was at the time (6 June 1922) Secretary of the British Government's Provisional Government of Ireland Committee. See CAB 27/154, PRO.
60. CAB 21/49, PRO.
61. Longford and O'Neill (1), p.189.
62. Macardle, p.719.
63. Downing Street, 27 May 1923, CAB 21/49, PRO.
64. Dail Debates, i, 358.
65. Ibid, col.536.
66. Coogan (4), p.329.

Chapter 16 (pp.322–355)

1. The letter, dated 21 March 1922, is in a series of Michael Collins documents released during

April 1993 by the Irish Dept of Foreign Affairs. They were not catalogued at the time of writing, but the boxes in which they were kept were kindly made available to me by Ms Deirdre Crowe, a member of the staff of the National Archives at Bishop's Street, Dublin.

2. Quoted in Macardle, pp.736–7.
3. Longford and O'Neill (1), p.195.
4. Quoted in Ibid.
5. His memoirs are in Archbishop Byrne's papers, Archdiocesan Archives, Archbishop's House, Dublin.
6. Longford and O'Neill (1), p.199.
7. Tarpey, p.179.
8. Longford and O'Neill (1), p.197.
9. Quoted in Ibid.
10. Bromage (1), p.188.
11. Quoted in Longford and O'Neill (1), p.197.
12. Ibid, p.198.
13. Longford and O'Neill (1), p.196.
14. Bromage (1), p.179.
15. Ibid.
16. Ibid.
17. Ibid, p.182.
18. Ibid, p.191.
19. Ibid, p.182.
20. Ibid.
21. Ibid, p.183.
22. Ibid, p.176.
23. Quoted in Longford and O'Neill (1), p.198. De Valera was an inveterate hoarder of documents, sometimes retaining subway tickets as mementoes of journeys undertaken fifty years earlier, but he did not normally keep a diary. The fact that he recorded his thoughts at this time is an indication of the impact on him of the outbreak of the civil war.
24. Peter Golden, 'Impressions of Ireland', quoted in Longford and O'Neill (1), p.198.
25. Coogan (4), p.147.
26. De Valera's reactions, the reasons for Collins' presence in the area and the controversial circumstances surrounding his death are described in detail in Coogan (4), pp.386–415.
27. Coogan (4), p.407.
28. Valiulis (1), p.174.
29. Quoted in Coogan (4), p.427.
30. Coogan (4), pp.426–7.
31. Longford and O'Neill (1), p.199.
32. Valiulis (1), p.174.
33. Mulcahy's papers (UCD) give accounts of the meeting and of its outcome. A good short account appears in Valiulis (1), pp.175–6.
34. Bromage (1), p.187.
35. De Valera to Joseph McGarrity, 10 September 1922. Quoted in Cronin (1), p.125.
36. Provisional Government Minutes, 15 September 1922, NAI.
37. Quoted in Macardle, p.804.
38. Quoted in Bromage (1), p.186.
39. De Valera to Colm O'Murchadha. Quoted in Bromage (1), p.187.
40. Quoted in Bromage (1), p.186.
41. The original of this letter is in the McGarrity papers in the NLI. Extracts have appeared in several works, probably most fully in Cronin (1).
42. Coogan (4), pp.399–400.

43. Quoted in Bromage (1), p.188.
44. The de Valera–O'Murchadha correspondence was captured, along with a number of other documents, and published by the Provisional Government under the title 'Correspondence of Mr Eamon de Valera and others'.
45. Bromage (1), p.189.
46. Macardle, p.806.
47. Longford and O'Neill (1), p.200.
48. Macardle, p.807.
49. Longford and O'Neill (1), p.200.
50. Dail Eireann, 27 September 1922, col. 807 et seq.
51. *Irish Independent*, 18 November 1922.
52. O'Malley's *The Singing Flame* gives his own account of the raid.
53. Three of his books, *On Another Man's Wound*, *The Singing Flame* and *Raids and Rallies*, are probably the best autobiographical works to emerge from the period. His unpublished notebooks in the UCD Archives, filled with first-hand recollections of survivors from the Anglo-Irish war and from both sides in the civil war, are a historical treasure trove.
54. Bromage (1), p.191.
54a. An incident which occurred in November 1922 gave an extraordinary insight into the perfervid pitch which de Valera's mind sometimes reached. Mary MacSwiney had been caught up in the waves of arrests which were going on as a result of the civil war. She decided to do as her brother had done and go on hunger strike in protest. De Valera urged her to continue, in the following terms (letter quoted in Dwyer (4), p.129): 'When Terry was dying, knowing how conscientious he was and how good, I feared that he might have some scruples about what he was doing, and intended giving him an official *order* [author's italics] to continue, as I might to a soldier running great risk on the battlefield. For him to surrender having begun would have been not personal defeat, but defeat for his cause. Your case is the same and may the God of Calvary give your spirit the necessary strength to endure to the last if need be and take you to Himself when your ordeal is ended.'

In the event, the Free State authorities released MacSwiney after three weeks (her sister Annie had meanwhile joined the protest, going on hunger strike outside the jail for ten days – no mean feat of endurance in an Irish winter). Apart from the fact of ordering a woman to continue hunger striking to the death, lest she suffer not *personal* defeat, but defeat for the cause – that is, *his* cause – de Valera's reference to Terence MacSwiney is a remarkable disclosure of cold-bloodedness. That a man who was at the time living in luxury hotels, a continent away from the jailed and withering MacSwiney, should write that he contemplated ordering him to continue fasting unto death is one of the most significant insights we have into de Valera's character. This is certainly de Valera Man of Power speaking.
55. Quoted in Cronin (1), p.129.

56. The four men's executions formed the subject of Ulick O'Connor's play *Executions*, first staged by the Abbey Theatre Company at the Peacock Theatre, Dublin in 1984. The play was based on contemporary material and interviews with survivors.

57. Author's copy.

58. The letter, which Connolly reproduces in his memoir, is dated 26 December 1922 and uses the Irish form, 'Uachtarain', for the title of President.

59. Bromage (1), p.191.

60. De Valera to P.J. Ruttledge, 12 December 1922. Quoted in Longford and O'Neill (1), p.208.

61. Longford and O'Neill (1), p.209.

62. Liam Lynch, Operational Order, 3 February 1923.

63. De Valera to M. Twomey, 14 March 1923.

64. De Valera to Liam Lynch and P.J. Ruttledge, 15 December 1922. Quoted in Longford and O'Neill (1), p.210.

65. De Valera to Joseph McGarrity, 28 November 1922. Quoted in Longford and O'Neill (1), p.207.

66. Reprinted in *Irish Independent*, 3 February 1923.

67. Quoted in Longford and O'Neill (1), p.215.

68. Quoted in Macardle, p.830.

69. Liam Lynch to de Valera, 28 February 1922. Quoted in Longford and O'Neill (1), p.215.

70. *Irish Independent*, 12 February 1923.

71. De Valera to Liam Lynch, 7 March 1923. Quoted in Longford and O'Neill (1), p.216.

72. De Valera to P.J. Ruttledge, 7 March 1922. Quoted in Longford and O'Neill (1), p.216.

73. De Valera to Father McKenna, 18 January 1923. Quoted in Longford and O'Neill (1), p.210.

74. De Valera to Edith Ellis, 26 February 1923. Published in the *Irish Independent*, 10 March 1923.

75. Longford and O'Neill (1), p.211.

76. De Valera to Liam Lynch. Quoted in Longford and O'Neill (1), p.210. Original in possession of Mr Eamon de Barra. See also Coogan (4), p.427.

77. All four letters to Lynch quoted in Longford and O'Neill (1), p.213.

78. De Valera to Liam Lynch. Quoted in Longford and O'Neill (1), p.216.

79. O'Donoghue (2), p.294. Florence O'Donoghue, one of the leaders of the famous Cork No.1 Brigade during the Anglo-Irish war, later became a historian of the period, a noted collector of military documents and a founder of the Irish Military History Bureau.

80. Ibid.

81. Ibid, p.297.

82. Longford and O'Neill (1), p.217.

83. Ibid, p.218.

84. O'Donoghue (2), p.301.

85. Quoted in Bromage (1), p.197.

86. 'Conversations with Dev', 2 April 1955, Gallagher papers, NLI. Possibly because the conversation took place on 2 April, Gallagher also ascribes the 1923 meeting, wrongly, to April.

87. As is the authoritative O'Donoghue, who from my own knowledge spoke with survivors of the meeting, including Tom Barry. O'Donoghue's account corroborates that in the official biography (Longford and O'Neill (1)).

88. Bromage (1), p.199.

89. De Valera diary, quoted in Longford and O'Neill (1), p.218.

90. Quoted in Macardle, p.976.

91. Longford and O'Neill (1), p.218.

92. De Valera to Monsignor Luzio, 30 April 1923. Quoted in Longford and O'Neill (1), p.220.

93. De Valera to Monsignor Luzio, 23 May 1923. Quoted in Longford and O'Neill (1), p.221.

94. D. O'Sullivan, p.112.

95. Macardle, p.849.

96. D. O'Sullivan, p.112.

97. Bromage (1), p.200.

98. D. O'Sullivan, p.114.

99. *Irish Times*, 29 May 1923.

100. Quoted in Macardle, p.858.

Chapter 17 (pp.356–383)

1. Longford and O'Neill (1), p.225.

2. *Freeman's Journal*, 21 November 1923, quoting statistics.

3. *Irish Independent*, 24 July 1923.

4. De Valera to Molly Childers, 31 July 1973. Quoted in Longford and O'Neill (1), p.226.

5. Statement made 23 July 1923. Quoted in Longford and O'Neill (1), p.226.

6. Memorandum for Cosgrave's attention from Sean Lester, Free State Director of Publicity, 9 August 1923, incorporating comments of Lindsay Crawford. D/T S.1369/15, NAI.

7. Ibid.

8. Longford and O'Neill (1), p.226.

9. Connolly memoir.

10. De Valera papers, Ms 13, 332, NLI.

11. 16 August 1923.

12. Ibid.

13. Longford and O'Neill (1), p.228.

14. Ibid.

15. Bromage (1), p.203.

16. Longford and O'Neill (1), p.228.

17. Neligan eventually ended up drawing five pensions: from the British Secret Service, the RIC, the IRA, the Civic Guards and, after de Valera transferred him to the Land Commission, a civil service pension. He described his undercover work for Collins in *The Spy in the Castle*.

18. David Neligan to Minister of Defence, 23 June 1923. D/T S.1369, NAI.

19. Longford and O'Neill (1), p.228.

20. Sinead de Valera to Kathleen O'Connell, 24 August 1923. Quoted in Longford and O'Neill (1), p.228.

21. Bromage (1), pp.205–6.

22. De Valera to Kathleen O'Connell, 19 January 1924. Quoted in Longford and O'Neill (1), pp.229–30.

23. De Valera to Kathleen O'Connell, 2 February 1924. Quoted in Longford and O'Neill (1), pp.229.

24. Longford and O'Neill (1), p.229.

25. Mulcahy papers, P7/B/286, UCD.

26. Maude Gonne, widow of the executed 1916

leader, John MacBride, and mother of Sean MacBride, the IRA leader who later won the Nobel Peace Prize for his work in founding Amnesty International, was the great unrequited love of W. B. Yeats' life. She was also a formidable agitator and publicist.

27. T.A. Smiddy to Ministry of External Affairs, 14 April 1924. D/T S.1369/15, NAI.

28. Tammany Hall, the New York County HQ of the Democratic Party, was originally founded as a benevolent society but became notorious for corruption.

29. Longford and O'Neill (1), p.230.

30. Bromage (1), p.209.

31. Ibid.

32. Diary of Austin Stack, 25 April 1924, NLI.

33. Sinead de Valera to Kathleen O'Connell, 7 May 1924. Quoted in Longford and O'Neill (1), p.231.

34. Bromage (1), p.208.

35. Ibid.

36. Longford and O'Neill (1), p.420.

37. Bromage (1), p.210.

38. Longford and O'Neill (1), p.424.

39. Ibid.

40. Ibid, p.420.

41. Jack O'Sheehan, in Hare Park Prison Camp, Kildare.

42. Bromage (1), p.210.

43. It can be studied in detail in Valiulis (1) and (2). Lee (1) also deals with the crisis.

44. Provisional Government Minute No.94, 19 August 1922, NAI. Quoted more fully in Coogan (4), p.384.

45. At Glandore House in Glandore, Co. Cork. See W.T. Cosgrave to Judge Cohalan, 11 September 1924, D/T S.11724, NAI.

46. Dept of Justice file J H99/176, NAI.

47. Deputy Commissioner Eamonn Coogan to E. O'Frighil, 3 May 1923. Dept of Justice file J H99/176, NAI.

48. See O'Neill–O'Frighil exchange, 4 and 5 May 1923. Dept of Justice file J H99/176, NAI.

49. E O'Frighil to Eamonn Coogan, 16 May 1923. Dept of Justice file J H99/176, NAI.

50. Eamonn Coogan to E O'Frighil, 31 January 1924. Dept of Justice file J H99/176, NAI.

51. Ibid.

52. E O'Frighil to Commissioner, Garda Siochana, 8 February 1924. Dept of Justice file J H99/176, NAI.

53. Quoted in Macardle, p.873.

54. Ibid.

55. W.T. Cosgrave to Judge Cohalan, 11 September 1924.

56. Longford and O'Neill (1), p.235.

57. Minutes of Comhairle na d'Teachtai, 7 August 1924. Quoted in Longford and O'Neill (1), p.236.

58. Gaughan (1), pp.319–35, quoted in Dwyer (6) pp.133–4.

59. Notes of executive meeting, 10–12 August 1924. Quoted in Longford and O'Neill (1), p.236.

60. Gwynn, p.202.

61. Sinead de Valera to Kathleen O'Connell, 11 August 1924. Quoted in Longford and O'Neill (1), p.237.

62. Quoted in Longford and O'Neill (1), p.237, from script supplied by de Valera.

63. Mary MacSwiney papers, P48/C/8, UCD

64. Dwyer (6), p.136.

65. Ibid.

66. Longford and O'Neill (1), p.238.

67. Michael Murney, who was defeated.

68. Longford and O'Neill (1), p.238.

69. South Dublin, Cork City, East Cork, Donegal and North Mayo.

70. His 1916 comrade Eamonn Donnelly, who won in South Armagh, was the only other Sinn Fein candidate to win a seat.

71. Vivion de Valera to author.

72. Bromage (1), p.114.

73. Script of de Valera speech at Gorey, Co. Wexford, 14 December 1924. Quoted in Longford and O'Neill (1), p.239.

74. Open letter to de Valera from Thomas Johnson, 15 January 1925, Johnson papers, Ms 17, 230, NLI.

75. Quoted in Coogan (4), p.76.

76. Ibid.

77. Ibid.

78. Foley, p.58.

79. Ibid.

80. *Belfast Newsletter*, 16 November 1925.

81. Ernest Blythe, Free State Minister for Finance, in a written reply to Thomas Johnson, 8 December 1925.

82. Script of de Valera statement, 5 December 1925. Quoted in Moynihan, pp.122–5.

83. Addendum North-East Ulster, Document No.2, reproduced in full in Appendices to this book.

84. Austin Stack to de Valera, 4 December 1925. Quoted in Dwyer (6), p.138.

85. *Irish Times*, 10 October 1968. Quoted in Dwyer (6), p.138.

86. Moynihan, p.126.

87. Quoted in MacEoin (1), pp.100–1.

88. Quoted in Foley, p.55.

89. O'Donnell's manoeuvre and the development of the IRA both militarily and philosophically, from the ending of the civil war to de Valera's taking power in 1932, are described in Coogan (3). pp.59–90.

90. On 20 June 1925, under the editorship of Maurice Twomey.

91. See Coogan (3), pp.124–50.

92. Bromage (1), p.215.

93. Coogan (3), p.78.

94. Bromage (1), p.218.

95. Ibid.

96. Foley, p.61.

97. Script of de Valera speech to Sinn Fein Ard Fheis, 10 March 1926. Quoted in Moynihan, p.126.

Chapter 18 (pp.384–407)

1. Tarpey, p.228.

2. Quoted in Cronin (1), pp.141–2. Original in NLI.

3. De Valera Ard Fheis speech, 10 March 1925. Quoted in Moynihan, p.130.

4. Aiken–McGarrity correspondence quoted in Cronin (1), p.144. Originals in NLI.

5. Cronin (1), p.144.
6. Joseph McGarrity to Frank Aiken, 1 September 1926. Quoted in Cronin (1), p.144. Original in NLI.
7. The extracts given here are from the 'expanded version' of the statement in Moynihan, pp.131–2.
8. Later the Capitol Cinema, and now demolished.
9. Moynihan, p.130.
10. Ibid, p.133.
11. Ibid, pp.144–5.
12. Foley, p.65.
13. Gallagher papers, diary entry for 25 February 1927, Ms 1006/113, TCD.
14. De Valera to John Hearn, 13 May 1922. Author's copy.
15. Macardle, p.986.
16. Longford and O'Neill (1), p.249.
17. Sean T. O'Ceallaigh to John Hearn, 5 August 1925. Author's copy.
18. Longford and O'Neill (1), p.249.
19. Shannon, p.193.
20. The Irish form of 'Dear Sir'.
21. Gallagher, Ms 10065/178, TCD.
22. Frank Gallagher to Celia Gallagher, 31 March 1927, Gallagher papers, Ms 21, 209, NLI.
23. Foley, p.65.
24. In Coogan (1), p.65, I quote the experience of political correspondent Edward Lawlor on the use and distribution of these weapons.
25. Irish Independent, 8 June 1925.
26. D. O'Sullivan, p.193.
27. Longford and O'Neill (1), p.252.
28. George Gavan Duffy, Ernest Woods KC and Arthur C. Meredith KC.
29. Coogan (1), p.64.
30. The Countess did not survive long within the ranks of Fianna Fail. She died, in the public ward of a hospital for the poor, on 5 July 1927. Her funeral was one of the largest ever seen in Dublin: over 100,000 people are said to have attended.
31. De Valera to Joseph McGarrity, quoted in Cronin (1), p.145. Original in NLI.
32. Coogan (4), p.290.
33. Johnson papers, Ms 17, 162, NLI.
34. Quoted in D. O'Sullivan, p.192.
35. Lee (1), p.157.
36. Coogan (1), pp.64–5.
37. Johnson statement, 3 June 1927, Johnson papers, Ms 17, 164, NLI.
38. Johnson address to National Executive, Labour Party, 5 July 1925, Johnson papers, Ms 17, 230, NLI.
39. The negotiations are described in the Johnson papers, Ms 17, 168, NLI.
40. Ibid.
41. Longford and O'Neill (1), p.254.
42. Ibid, p.255.
43. Ibid.
44. Statement by de Valera, 11 August 1927. Quoted in Longford and O'Neill (1), p.256.
45. The foregoing quotations appear in Dwyer (6), p.147.
46. Longford and O'Neill (1), p.256.
47. D. O'Sullivan, p.219.
48. Austin Stack to de Valera, 15 August 1927, Stack papers, Ms 21, 568, NLI.
49. Moynihan, p.150.
50. Quoted in Longford and O'Neill (1), p.260.
51. De Valera statement, 25 August 1927.

Chapter 19 (pp.408–438)

1. In the Fianna Fail weekly, the Nation, 26 April 1930.
2. See Coogan (3), pp.68–75.
3. Foley, p.78.
4. Daily Express, 31 August 1931.
5. Patrick Carroll (30 January 1931), Superintendent Curtin (3 March 1931) and John Ryan (20 July 1931).
6. Coogan (3), p.86.
7. Longford and O'Neill (1), p.278.
8. Moynihan, p.152.
9. Quoted in Coogan (3), p.89.
10. Quoted in Foley, p.73.
11. Ibid, p.94.
12. Quoted in MacEoin (1), p.32.
13. Quoted in Moynihan, p.140.
14. During the sixties for The IRA (Coogan (3)), published 1970. The IRA viewpoint on 'legitimacy' is described on p.82.
15. Quoted in MacEoin, p.33.
16. Quoted in Foley, p.92.
17. Coogan (3), p.82.
18. Ibid, p.86.
19. Quoted in Foley, p.62.
20. Longford and O'Neill (1), p.269.
21. Gallagher diary, 20 November 1927, Ms 10065/151, TCD.
22. Ibid, Ms 10065/155, p.20.
23. On 19 December 1927. Gallagher diary, Ms 10065/155, TCD.
24. Author's copy.
25. Gallagher diary, Ms 165/200, TCD.
26. Michael S. Robinson. Author's copy.
27. Joseph McGarrity to de Valera, 23 December 1927, McGarrity papers, Ms 17, 441, NLI.
28. De Valera statement on bonds case, 12 May 1927. Author's copy.
29. Frank P. Walsh to potential subscribers to Irish Press, 30 January 1930, addressed from 'Irish Press Limited, American Office (Room 3907), 225 Broadway, New York City'.
30. Author's copy.
31. Diarmuid O'Hegarty, Secretary to Executive Council, to W.T. Cosgrave, President of Executive Council, 14 April 1930.
32. No.84, Serpentine Avenue, Sandymount, Co. Dublin.
33. Brutus, in Shakespeare's Julius Caesar, Act II, Scene I, lines 14–15: 'It is the bright day that brings forth the adder, and that craves wary walking.'
34. Joseph McGarrity to de Valera, McGarrity papers, Ms 17, 441, NLI.
35. De Valera to Joseph McGarrity, 8 September 1928, McGarrity papers, Ms 17, 441, NLI.
36. Gallagher papers, Ms 18, 345/D, 16 December 1929, NLI.
37. 'Need for a National Daily Newspaper in Ireland', circulated by de Valera throughout USA from 1930. Author's copy.
38. This antipathy towards the boy scouts was deep-rooted and widespread at the time. When

founding Fiann na hEireann, the Volunteers'
youth section, Liam Mellows and Countess
Markiewicz used to advise their youthful recruits to obtain uniforms by stripping boy scouts
of theirs.

39. Jim McCoy, a reporter with the *Cleveland Press*
in Cleveland, Ohio, at the time when de Valera
visited the paper's offices in 1930, told me: 'All
the guy seemed to want to know was: "How do
you control the goddam thing?"' '

40. *Irish Press* leading article, 5 September 1931.

41. James Dowdall, Henry Gallagher, John
Hughes, Stephen O'Mara, Philip Busteed
Pierce, James Lyle Stirling and Edmund
Williams.

42. Such papers as would accept them. The largest
Irish daily, the *Irish Independent*, did not.

43. Dail Eireann, 11 December 1958, col. 2179.

44. Gallagher diary, 21 January 1928, TCD.

45. Kathleen O'Connell, quoted in Longford and
O'Neill (1), p.269.

46. *Irish Times*, 13 February 1929.

47. The *Nation*, 23 February 1929.

48. I persuaded Lemass to agree to be interviewed
for a major series on his life, which was
published in the *Irish Press* in January 1969. In
the course of the series he told the writer,
Michael Mills, later the first Irish Ombudsman,
that Fianna Fail was not ready for Government
in those years. Boland, who was helping me
with my researches into the IRA, later said
much the same thing in the *Irish Times* on 10
October 1968.

49. Memorandum by J.P. Walshe, 1 December
1924. Quoted in Harkness, p.58.

50. Ibid.

51. Ibid, pp.67–8.

52. Desmond Fitzgerald to his wife, 20 October
1930. Quoted in Harkness, p.187.

53. Ibid, pp.177–8.

54. Quoted in Ibid, p.238.

55. Harkness, p.229.

56. Taken from the Act as published, December
1931.

57. The amendment read: 'Nothing in this Act shall
be deemed to authorise the legislature of the
Irish Free State to repeal, amend or alter the
Irish Free State Agreement Act, 1923, or the
Irish Free State Constitution Act, 1922, or so
much of the Government of Ireland Act, 1920,
as continues to be in force in Northern Ireland.'
Hansard, House of Commons, col.303.

58. Ibid, col.311.

59. By the Bishop of Killaloe, while unveiling a
portrait of Kevin O'Higgins at Leinster House,
21 January 1944.

60. In 1930 and 1931. See Dail Eireann, 36, cols
1229–30 and 1620–1, and 39, col.2360.

61. Sean Murphy, Assistant Secretary, Dept of External Affairs.

62. Harkness, p.253. Before making this assessment Harkness consulted some of the most
prominent foreign affairs personnel of the
period.

63. Senate Debates, Vol.15, col.938.

64. Dail Eireann, Vol.9, col.562 (10 October 1924).

65. Lee (1), p.105.

66. Chubb (1), p.78.

67. Whitaker, in F. Lyons (2), p.77.

68. Lee (1), pp.109–10.

69. During a debate on economic policy in the Dail
on 12–13 July 1928. Quoted in Moynihan,
p.154.

70. Ibid.

71. Longford and O'Neill (1), p.271.

72. In the Franciscan Archives at Killiney, but not
in the papers open to the public at the time of
writing.

73. Sherwood anecdote.

74. Foley, pp.79–80.

75. *Irish Press*, 15 February 1922.

76. Foley, p.102.

77. Longford and O'Neill (1), p.274.

78. Bromage (1), p.234.

79. Quoted in full in Moynihan, p.189.

80. A joint Pastoral, which equally condemned the
IRA and the left-wing Saor dEire organisation
which emanated from the ranks of the IRA,
was read in all Roman Catholic churches on 18
October 1931.

81. Lee (1), p.169.

82. Longford and O'Neill (1), p.274.

83. Reprinted in the *Irish Press*, 23 February 1932.

84. 4 March 1932, reprinted in Moynihan,
pp.191–3.

85. Longford and O'Neill (1), p.274.

86. Quoted in Beresford Ellis, pp.274–5.

87. Foley, p.105.

88. Longford and O'Neill (1), p.274.

89. Foley, p.107.

90. Ibid.

91. O'Ceallaigh papers, Ms 27, 702.

92. MacSwiney to Hearn, Hearn papers, Ms 15,
987, NLI.

93. 'Conversations with Dev.', 24 March 1950, Gallagher papers, NLI.

94. De Valera, speaking in the Dail, 29 April 1932.
Quoted in Moynihan, p.203.

95. Ibid, p.209.

96. Ibid, p.204.

97. Ibid.

98. On 29 April 1932.

99. Longford and O'Neill (1), p.288.

Chapter 20 (pp.439–460)

1. Belgium, France, Hungary and Poland.

2. 16 December 1932.

3. Dwyer (6), p.178.

4. Press release from Michael MacWhite, Minister
of the Irish Free State, issued New York, 3
April 1935. Author's copy.

4a. There was a double benefit for de Valera in
the bonds repayment: apart from the financial
advantage to the *Irish Press* he also drew a
political dividend from America. Following his
triumph in the 1933 general election he sent
Joseph Connolly to the USA on a cleverly conceived PR mission. The brief which he gave
Connolly to argue was that, far from reneging
on its lawful commitments as Britain alleged,
Ireland, unlike Britain, which was defaulting
on its wartime loans from America, was so
punctilious about her debts that she was repaying a loan which she was under no legal
obligation to discharge. Roosevelt was

amongst those who were impressed at Ireland's sense of morality. He made a point of telling Connolly so, and drew his attention to the fact that he had publicly commended Ireland and Finland, 'two of the smallest countries in Europe' (Roosevelt to Connolly, quoted in Connolly memoir), for paying their debts.

5. Boake Carter, Philco Radio, 4 April 1935. Author's copy.

5a. Not everyone approved of his using the Dail funds for his own purposes. Mary MacSwiney thought it 'flagrantly wrong to ask for the Dail money for his new paper' (MacSwiney to Hearn, 15 December 1927, Hearn papers, MS 15/987, NLI). And even a lifelong admirer like Dr C. S. 'Tod' Andrews noted in his autobiography (Andrews (2), p.232) that he felt the only point at which de Valera 'failed' him was in not putting the paper into some sort of trust arrangement for the Fianna Fail Party. Andrews pointed out that, although de Valera's American collections had been substantial, the paper could not have got off the ground without the dedicated efforts of ordinary Fianna Fail workers. Nevertheless it was not until the closing stages of his parliamentary career that anyone seriously challenged his right to control the Irish Press Group; and that challenge came from outside the Fianna Fail Party.

6. Dail Eireann, Loans and Funds Bill, 1933, Vol.48, cols 1735–1986, 5–6 July 1933.

7. The Marconi scandal was a British *cause célèbre* of 1912. Four prominent Liberal politicians were accused of having bought shares in the Marconi company prior to one of them, Herbert Samuel, the Postmaster General, awarding the company a government contract.

8. Following the case it was explained to the Free State lawyers by the American lawyer Russell S. Coutant that the Peters verdict prevented the 'hostile use of the funds' by de Valera. Moreover, it prevented the Free State from inheriting the obligations of the original borrower as well as the benefits. Russell Coutant to William Norman, 13 May 1927, D/T S.9592, NAI.

9. The crib was later transferred to the Bank of Ireland.

10. Unsigned, dated '10.30 p.m. Sunday', McGarrity papers, Ms 17, 441.

11. During the 1970s, a good period for newspapers, Vivion de Valera felt compelled to pay dividends for a few years. The custom has not been continued.

12. Gallagher papers, Ms 18, 361 (3), NLI.

13. Ibid, Ms 18, 340, NLI.

14. Frank Gallagher to de Valera, 17 July 1933, Gallagher papers, Ms 18, 361 (6), NLI.

15. Gallagher papers, Ms 18, 361 (5), NLI.

16. Memoir of Maire Comeford, who acted as women's editor, quoted in MacEoin (1), p.54.

17. Ibid.

18. Brendan Malin to author, 19 October 1991. Author's.

19. Frank Gallagher to the board of Irish Press Ltd, 8 July 1934, Gallagher papers, Ms 18, 361 (5), NLI.

20. Quoted in Bromage (1), p.250.

21. Ibid, pp.250–1.

22. Connolly memoir.

23. DO 35/397/36, PRO.

24. Oldham letter in Ministry of Pensions file DO 35/397/261, PRO.

25. CAB 24/228, PRO.

26. As the matter was deemed 'domestic' to Dublin Dulanty was instructed not to hand over a document. The quotations are from a 'verbal note' of Dulanty's which de Valera presented to the Oireachtas in April 1932. Author's copy.

27. Michael Collins, speaking in the public session of the Treaty debate, p.32 of the official record.

28. Whereon, according to the legend in the Bible, St Paul underwent a conversion to Christianity.

29. De Valera put forward this argument both in an interview with the *Irish Times* on 6 March 1932 and in parliamentary debate.

30. Quoted in Bromage (1), p.257.

31. Bromage (1), p.237: 'The Senators would, the President fumed, wait to act till Tibb's Eve; the Seanad itself would have to go if it was bent upon perpetuating the imperial ties. "*Fan go foil*" – we shall see – he said.'

32. De Valera–Thomas exchange, Cmnd 4056 (1932), Vol.XIV, 5 and 9 April 1932.

33. Longford and O'Neill (1), p.266.

34. Quoted in Dwyer (6), p.166.

35. *Irish Press*, 14 June 1935.

36. The Boundary Commission Agreement exempted Dublin from 'liability for the service of the Public Debt of the United Kingdom, and [stated] that the Irish annuities form part of the Public Debt'.

37. Chamberlain memorandum, 8 March 1932. Quoted in Fanning (1), p.227.

38. Dwyer (6), p.165.

39. Gwynn, p.255.

40. Ibid.

41. Thomas/Hailsham memorandum, 8 March 1932, CAB 27/525, PRO.

42. Connolly memoir.

43. Longford and O'Neill (1), p.279.

44. Thomas, p.188.

45. In July 1932.

46. De Valera to William Norton, 14 July 1932. Author's copy.

47. 'Introductory Note' and Note of Discussion on de Valera meeting, DT/S.6298, NAI.

48. Ibid.

49. Quoted in Dwyer (6), p.169.

50. Ibid, p.191.

51. Moynihan, pp.217–18, gives the English text of de Valera's remarks in Latin.

52. Gwynn, p.258.

53. *Irish Press*, 9 November 1932.

54. Lemass memorandum on Economic War, 7 November 1932, D/T S.6274, NAI.

55. Dwyer (6), pp.182–3.

56. *Irish Times*, 16 September 1932.

57. Gallagher papers, Ms 18, 375 (2), NLI.

58. Longford and O'Neill (1), p.287.

59. *Irish Press*, 11 January 1933.

60. Ibid, 18 January 1933.

61. D. O'Sullivan, p.321.

62. Maurice Twomey, Chief of Staff at the time, to author.

63. Literally Sean of the Brushes – a figure of contempt.
64. The full correspondence between de Valera and O'Neill appeared in the Dublin papers on 12 July 1932.
65. This phase of the Governor General saga is documented in a Dept of External Affairs memorandum, 'The Governor-Generalship, 1932–1936', Summary of Departmental Files, DFA, S.22, NAI.
66. Ramsay MacDonald papers, 30/69/678/782, PRO.
67. Hugh Kennedy to de Valera, 1 November 1932, D/T S.8532, NAI.
68. Paragraph 7, DFA memorandum, 'The Governor-Generalship, 1932–1936', S.22, NAI.
69. Ibid.
70. Ibid.
71. A senior External Affairs official, John Hearne, and the Attorney General, Conor Maguire, saw Kennedy on 20 November 1932 to discuss the matter. However, he again stated that it would be obligatory on him to take oaths which he did not wish to take, and Hearne and Maguire reported accordingly to de Valera. D/T S.8532.
72. Hugh Kennedy to de Valera, D/T S.10550, NAI.
73. De Valera to Hugh Kennedy, 12 October 1932, D/T S.10550, NAI.
74. DFA memorandum, 'The Governor-Generalship, 1932–1936', S.22, NAI.

Chapter 21 (pp.461–485)

1. Longford and O'Neill (1), p.336.
2. *Irish Times*, 27 September 1932.
3. A.J. Cummings in the *News Chronicle*, quoted in Longford and O'Neill (1), p.337.
4. Moynihan, pp.219–33.
5. *New York Herald Tribune*, 28 September 1932.
6. *Daily Herald*, 27 August 1932.
7. *New York Times*, 27 September 1932.
8. De Valera broadcast on League of Nations Radio, Geneva, 2 October 1932.
9. *Irish Times*, 14 March 1932.
10. Described in Cronin (1), pp.154–5.
11. Tarpey, p.278.
12. Foley, p.107.
13. *Irish Press*, 15 July 1932.
14. *An Phoblacht*, 23 July 1932.
15. Both quotations in Coogan (3), p.91.
16. Dail Eireann, Vol.44, col.1573.
17. D. O'Sullivan, p.322.
18. Published in 1933.
19. Foley, p.121.
20. Dail Eireann, Vol.46, cols 796–7.2.
21. Much of my knowledge of the O'Duffy–IRA interaction comes from interviews with police and IRA survivors of the period for my book on the IRA. Cronin (1), p.155, refers to the de Valera–IRA contacts of the period, in connection with both O'Duffy and other matters.
22. D. O'Sullivan, p.330.
23. Quoted in full in Coogan (3), pp.93–7.
24. Quoted in Coogan (1), p.81.
25. Quoted in Foley, p.121.
26. Ibid, p.61.
27. MacManus, p.302.

28. Quoted in Coogan (3), p.98.
29. Ibid.
30. *Irish Press*, 3 September 1933.
31. 'Dev and His Alma Mater'.
32. It occupies over twelve pages in Moynihan, pp.345–58.
33. Ibid, p.246.
34. Dail Eireann, Vol.50, col.2237.
35. D. O'Sullivan, p.344.
36. Dail Eireann, cols 2523–5.
37. D. O'Sullivan, p.361.
38. Dwyer (6), p.187.
39. Delivered on 5 April 1937.
40. The reaction of P.J. Ruttledge, the Minister for Justice, on reading the newspaper reports of the case was to write immediately to the Attorney General, Patrick Lynch, asking if anything could be done to 'remedy the situation' created by the 'mischievous impression that there is within the police force an undesirable class recruited in recent years with whom the ordinary police do not wish to associate . . .'. A copy of the letter was sent to de Valera also. Ruttledge to Attorney General, 10 March 1937, D/T S.9878.
41. *Cork Examiner*, 1 September 1934.
42. O'Duffy's policy, described in the *Irish Independent* of 10 June 1935, included a 'Republic de jure for thirty-two counties and de facto for twenty-six'.
43. The course of the debate is traced in Coogan (3), pp.90–107.
44. Coogan (3), p.104.
45. Dail Eireann, Vol.55, col.1.
46. Ibid, cols 389, 381, 3 May 1935.
47. *Irish Independent*, 18 March 1936.
48. Barry told me that, at precisely the moment of the shooting, he and a companion went up to a Garda on duty outside the Metropole Hotel in faraway Cork city to ask him the time, thereby establishing an alibi.
49. Conway subsequently became a Cistercian Brother. I received special permission from the Order to interview him.
50. Quoted in Coogan (3), p.123.
51. Dail Eireann, Vol.63, col.112.
52. Quoted in Cronin (1), pp.152–3.
53. Ibid, p.153.
54. Ibid, p.157.
55. Ibid. Many of these letters are available in their original form in various collections in the National Library of Ireland, chiefly in the McGarrity and O'Ceallaigh papers. For ease of access for the general reader, however, I have quoted only from the extracts which appear in Cronin's published work (Cronin (1)).
56. Cronin (1), p.156.
57. Joseph McGarrity to de Valera, 2 October 1932, McGarrity papers, NLI.
58. De Valera to Joseph McGarrity, 31 January 1934. Original in NLI.
59. McGarrity was subsequently restored to both his fortune and good name by another Irish American lawyer, Thomas O'Neill, who secured a settlement in his favour on 20 February 1934.
60. Tarpey, p.299.
61. Coogan (3), p.153.

62. Twomey to McGarrity, 7 October 1935. Quoted in Tarpey, p.298.
63. Quoted in Tarpey, p.299.
64. Tarpey, p.300.
65. Quoted in Coogan (3), p.152.
66. In the *Evening Public Ledger*, 16 September 1936.
67. Joseph McGarrity to Mick McDonnell, 13 February 1940. Quoted in Tarpey, p.339.
68. Longford and O'Neill (1), p.288.

Chapter 22 (pp.486–506)

1. The full text of the speech is given in Moynihan, pp.236–7.
2. Ryan (2).
3. *Irish Press*, 1 July 1935.
4. 8 June 1936. Quoted in Longford and O'Neill (1), p.290.
5. The wording is actually in the Preamble to the Statute.
6. Walshe memorandum quoted in Longford and O'Neill (1), p.292.
7. Longford and O'Neill (1), p.293.
8. Dail Eireann, Vol.64, col.1263.
9. Dwyer (6), p.199. Readers may follow the genesis of the Constitution and its reception by the public in D. O'Sullivan, Lee (1) or Longford and O'Neill (1). One of the best and most objective analyses can be found in Chubb (1).
10. Longford and O'Neill (1), p.296.
11. De Valera broadcast on Constitution, 15 June 1937, D/T S.9868, NAI.
12. *Irish Press*, 13 October 1937.
13. Moynihan, pp.330–44.
14. Ibid, p.331.
15. On 20 December 1939. Gallagher papers, Ms 18, 375 (11), NLI.
16. Dail Eireann, Vol.67, cols 951–2, 25 May 1937.
17. Quoted by Whitaker in F. Lyons (2), p.83.
18. Maurice Moynihan to author, 1 May 1991.
19. The MacElligott submissions were made in March and April 1937. They are quoted in various works dealing with the period, including Bowman, p.148.
20. Ibid.
21. Ibid.
22. Whitaker, in F. Lyons (2), p.83 (Whitaker's italics).
23. If only because of the opinion of a senior Provisional IRA man I once interviewed: 'As a practising terrorist I'd like to see those Orange bastards all cooped up in the one small area – it'd be easier to have a crack at them!'
24. MacMahon, p.215.
25. Bowman, p.150.
26. Ibid.
27. Dail Eireann, Vol.68, col.430, 14 June 1937.
28. Moynihan, pp.332–3.
29. Frank Gallagher replying to Mary S. Kettle, *Irish Press*, 17 May 1937.
30. 'A Woman's View of the Constitution', *Irish Independent*, 7 May 1937.
31. In a widely reported speech at Ennis on 11 May 1937.
32. *Irish Press*, 11 May 1937.
33. Six Point Group to de Valera, 14 June 1937. Author's copy.
34. Published in the *Irish Press*, 12 May 1937.
35. *Irish Press*, 17 May 1937.
36. Lee (1), p.270.
37. Dorothy Macardle to de Valera, 21 May 1937.
38. Copies of the correspondence are preserved both in BCL and in the de Valera papers in FAK.
39. These included the ultra-conservative Catholic newspaper the *Catholic Standard* and a Father Timothy Traynor of Sandymount, who took the trouble to telephone de Valera's office; author's copy of transcript of message. The most significant Catholic intellectual to contribute to the debate was Professor Alfred O'Rahilly of Cork University, who had been involved in the drafting of the Collins Constitution.
40. The register did not come into operation at precisely the same time as the constitutional plebiscite: 15 December as opposed to 1 July. *Ulster Year Book, 1938*, p.308.
41. The *Nation*, 13 December 1930.
42. The Dunbar-Harrison case is dealt with in files D/T S.2547A and B, NAI, and in the newspapers of the period.
43. Lee (1), p.211.
44. *Irish Press*, 5 May 1938.
45. The original letter, dated 29 March 1939, is in the Archdiocesan Records, Archbishop's House, Drumcondra. Author's copy.
46. Interview with author, 11 June 1991.
47. Interview with author, 21 April 1993.
48. Smiddy to External Affairs, 5 May 1924, DFA, GR 204, NAI.
49. Gallagher diary, 23 December 1927, Gallagher papers, TCD.
50. De Valera, speaking on 12 December 1944, Gallagher papers, Ms 18, 375 (11), NLI.
51. Fianna Fail resolution, passed at 334 Lennox Street, New York, 21 December 1932. The resolution and much other material relating to the Abbey tour and subsequent controversy involving de Valera are contained in D/T S.8208, NAI.
52. Yeats and Lady Gregory were co-directors of the Abbey, with J.M. Synge. The theatre's first production, on 27 December 1904, was a double bill consisting of Yeats' *On Bailie's Strand* and Lady Gregory's *Spreading the News*. Over the years the Abbey became known as the 'Cradle of Genius'. The company drew international acclaim, mingled with controversy, for productions such as Synge's *The Playboy of the Western World* and Sean O'Casey's *The Plough and the Stars*.
53. In a letter to de Valera dated 13 March 1934 MacEntee noted that 'you are not disposed to meet them unless there are very special grounds'.
54. *Sunday Times*, 8 April 1934.
55. On 17 April 1934.
56. Robinson to de Valera, 28 April 1934.
57. *Irish Press*, 28 August 1935.
58. Ibid, 2 October 1934.
59. De Valera to John Devine, 20 October 1934. Author's copy.
60. Frank O'Connor, in foreword to Eric Cross's *The Tailor and Ansty*, Chapman & Hall, London, 1964.

61. Fanning, in F. Lyons (2), p.84.
62. Ibid.
63. First Interim Report on Banking and Currency, Banking Commission, 1926.
64. 'Legal aspects of the Anglo-Irish dispute and the possibility of its adjustment', D/T S.14145, NAI.

Chapter 23 (pp.507–520)

1. Readers looking for a detailed study of Anglo-Irish negotiations on these and other issues of the 1930s are especially recommended to McMahon's *Republicans and Imperialists*. Bowman's *De Valera and the Ulster Question* also contains much useful information. De Valera's own view of the negotiations is given in Longford and O'Neill (1).
2. MacDonald to Cabinet, May 1936, CAB 24/262, PRO.
3. Committee of Imperial Defence, 4 February 1936, CAB 24/262, PRO.
4. Quoted in Fisk, p.25. This fine book gives a comprehensive insight into both the negotiations which led to the settlement of the annuities issue and the subsequent period of neutrality during World War II. Readers are also recommended to J. Carroll, Duggan (2), Coogan (3) and Longford and O'Neill (1).
5. *Times*, 29 October 1935.
6. 7 February 1934.
7. *Irish Times*, 7 October 1935.
8. Cabinet minutes, 20 August 1935 and 22 October 1935, NAI.
9. Survey of International Affairs, 1935–6, quoted in J. Carroll, p.29.
10. Dail Eireann, 18 June 1936. Quoted in Moynihan, pp.276–7.
11. Fisk, p.26.
12. Ibid, p.36.
13. Irish Situation Committee, 25 June 1936, CAB 24/523, PRO.
14. McMahon, p.30.
15. Fisk, p.26.
16. Ibid.
17. Longford and O'Neill (1), p.304.
18. Fisk, p.28.
19. Committee of Imperial Defence, 4 February 1936, CAB 24/262, PRO.
20. Quoted in Moynihan, p.277.
21. Lord Longford summarising Collins in Longford (2), p.141.
22. Committee of Imperial Defence, 4 February 1936, CAB 24/262, PRO.
23. MacDonald memorandum, May 1936, CAB 24/262, PRO.
24. Fisk, p.28.
25. Ibid.
26. Ibid.
27. Longford and O'Neill (1), p.307.
28. The American Minister, Alvin Owsley, quoted in McMahon, p.203.
29. Quoted in McMahon, p.247.
30. Keatinge (1), p.70.
31. Quoted in Longford and O'Neill (1), p.311.
32. Longford and O'Neill (1), p.311.
33. 3 March 1938, CAB 27/642, PRO.
34. Longford and O'Neill (1), p.311.

35. O'Neill and O'Fiannachta, Vol.2.
36. Fianna Fail Ard Fheis agenda, resolution 4.
37. McMahon, p.239.
38. MacDonald memorandum, 19 January 1938, CAB 27/642, PRO.
39. Peters to Batterbee, DO 35/397/36, PRO.
40. MacDonald note of de Valera conversation, 6 October 1937, CAB 24/271, CP 228 (37), PRO.
41. Longford and O'Neill (1), pp.309–10.
42. The quotations are from McMahon, p.246.
43. Cudahy to Roosevelt, 22 January 1938, Roosevelt papers, Roosevelt Library, Hyde Park, New York.
44. De Valera to Roosevelt, 25 January 1938, Roosevelt papers, Roosevelt Library, Hyde Park, New York.
45. Roosevelt to Cudahy, 9 February 1938, Roosevelt papers, Roosevelt Library, Hyde Park, New York. Author's copy.
46. Roosevelt to de Valera, 22 February 1938, Roosevelt papers, Roosevelt Library, Hyde Park, New York. Author's copy.
47. De Valera to Roosevelt, 22 April 1938, Roosevelt papers, Roosevelt Library, Hyde Park, New York. Author's copy.
48. Longford and O'Neill (1), p.321.
49. Patrick Quinn to Editor, *Irish Independent*, 23 February 1938. Quoted in Bowman, p.175. Original in possession of Brian Quinn, Dublin.
50. Quoted by Brian Quinn in 'Dev's last ditch stand on Partition', *Sunday Independent*, 4 March 1979.
51. Cudahy to Secretary of State, 24 January 1938, National Archives, Washington, State Department Records.
52. Minutes of Irish Negotiating Committee, 17 January 1938. CAB 27/642, PRO.
53. Longford and O'Neill (1), p.321.
54. Ibid, p.320.
55. Quoted in Bowman, p.181.
56. Cudahy to Secretary of State, 24 January 1938.
57. Ibid.
58. Longford and O'Neill (1), p.320.
59. Minutes of Irish Negotiating Committee, 17 January 1938. Quoted in McMahon, p.243.
60. Hoare, p.257.
61. 14 December 1937, CAB 27/524 ISC, PRO.
62. Committee of Imperial Defence, 12 January 1938, CAB 53/35, PRO.
63. Cudahy to Roosevelt, 29 April 1938, Roosevelt papers, Roosevelt Library, Hyde Park, New York. Author's copy.
64. *Hansard* (House of Commons), col.335, cols 1094–1105.
65. Fisk, pp.35–6.
66. J. Carroll, p.37.
67. Longford and O'Neill (1), p.468.
68. Cudahy to Secretary of State, 24 January 1938.
69. McMahon, p.264.
70. Quoted in Fisk, p.341, from *The Diaries of Sir Alexander Cadogan* (Permanent Under Secretary at the Foreign Office), ed. David Dilkes, Cassell, London.

Chapter 24 (pp.521–541)

1. The title was deliberately pejorative: 'West Brits' were those who supported the British

connection, attitude and *mores*. Inglis, born in a predominantly Protestant 'West British' enclave, Malahide, Co. Dublin, used that term to describe not only his geographical but his mental origin, and how he evolved from it.

2. F.H. Boland to Secretary, Dept of External Affairs, 10 July 1953, DFA files, NAI.
3. Gallagher papers, Ms 18, 375 (5), NLI.
4. Ibid, Ms 18, 375 (6).
5. Coogan (3), pp.155–6.
6. On 8 December 1938. Described in Coogan (3), p.159.
7. Ibid, p.166.
8. The corresponding British legislation, the Prevention of Violence (Temporary Provisions) Bill, was not introduced to the House of Commons until 24 July 1939.
9. The identity of the man responsible only became known more than thirty year later, by which time he had undergone treatment in a mental institution and was never charged.
10. Quoted in the London *Evening Standard*, 17 October 1938.
11. Quoted in Moynihan, p.417.
12. Coogan (3), p.174.
13. Hempel interview, *Sunday Press*, 17 November 1963.
14. The telegrams were seized by the Allies after the war and were published in *Documents on German Foreign Policy, 1918–45*, Series D, Vol.VII, HMSO, London, 1952. The German telegrams quoted in this chapter are taken from this publication.
15. Roosevelt to David Gray, 8 May 1940, Roosevelt papers, Roosevelt Library, Hyde Park, New York.
16. The original manuscript is in the David Gray papers, American Heritage Center, University of Wyoming, Laramie, Wyoming. The quotations are from the author's copy of 'Behind the Green Curtain', Ch.1, p.17 and pp.66–7.
17. Moynihan, p.356.
18. Ibid, p.357.
19. De Valera's closing address to League of Nations General Assembly, 30 September 1938.
20. Gerrymandering involved penning Catholics into electoral districts where their numbers were diluted so that they could not return a candidate of their choice. Protestants, on the other hand, were so placed that in predominantly Catholic areas, such as Derry, they were able to return a Unionist candidate.
21. Devonshire minute of de Valera conversation, 4 October 1938, DO 35/893/XII/247, PRO.
22. Ibid.
23. Dwyer (6), p.221.
24. Committee of Imperial Defence, Report and Index, CAB 53/36, PRO.
25. MacDonald minute, 12 October 1938, CAB 53/41, PRO.
26. Inskip minute, 20 October 1938, CAB 53/42, PRO.
27. MacDonald minute, 12 October 1938, CAB 53/41, PRO.
28. Chamberlain minute, 27 March 1938, FO 800/310, PRO.
29. MacDonald minute, 23 December 1938, FO 800/310, PRO.

30. Ibid.
31. Cudahy to Roosevelt, 17 August 1939, Roosevelt papers, Roosevelt Library, Hyde Park, New York.
32. Cudahy to Roosevelt, 6 April 1938, Roosevelt papers, Roosevelt Library, Hyde Park, New York.
33. Cudahy to Roosevelt, 1 March 1938, Roosevelt papers, Roosevelt Library, Hyde Park, New York.
34. Cudahy to Roosevelt, 6 April 1939, Roosevelt papers, Roosevelt Library, Hyde Park, New York.
35. Memorandum for Summerlin and others, 19 April 1939, Roosevelt papers, Roosevelt Library, Hyde Park, New York.
36. *Irish Press*, 3 May 1939.
37. Quoted in Shirer, p.577.
38. *Manchester Guardian*, 29 April 1939.
39. *Daily Mirror*, 1 May 1939.
40. Quoted in Ervine, p.547.
41. Ibid.
42. Dept of Industry and Commerce memorandum, 18 April 1939, S11394, NAI.
43. Churchill (4), p.335.
44. Churchill to Halifax, 23 October 1939, FO 800/310, PRO.
45. Malkin memorandum, 19 October 1939, FO 800/310, PRO.
46. Eden to Malkin, 20 October 1939, Ibid.
47. Longford and O'Neill (1), p.351.
48. Government minutes, 22 September 1939, G 3/3 2nd Govt. G 2/56–113, NAI.
49. Maffey minute, 14 September 1939, CAB 6/1, PRO.
50. Ibid.
51. Ibid.
52. Eden memorandum, 16 September 1939, CAB 55/1, PRO.
53. Avon, p.69.
54. Maffey minute, 20 September 1939, CAB 66/1, PRO.
55. Churchill's own account of this period can be read in Churchill (4), pp.582–3.
56. Maffey minute, 20 October 1939, CAB 66/2, PRO.
57. Maffey minute, 21 October 1939, CAB 62/2, PRO.
58. Quoted in J. Carroll, p.30.

Chapter 25 (pp.542–554)

1. Gray, 'Behind the Green Curtain', Ch.3.
2. David Gray to Roosevelt, 12 March 1992, Roosevelt papers, Roosevelt Library, Hyde Park, New York.
3. Cummins came of a prominent Cork medical family. She played hockey for Ireland and was the author of a series of books describing the life and times of St Paul. The information in these was said by Gray (in a letter to Roosevelt, 15 February 1942) to have come to her supernormally, a million words in all, at the rate of fifteen hundred words an hour.
4. Roosevelt to David Gray, 9 April 1942, Roosevelt papers, Roosevelt Library, Hyde Park, New York.
5. David Gray to Roosevelt, 2 October 1940.

Gray thought the poem might have been written by A.P. Herbert, Roosevelt papers, Roosevelt Library, Hyde Park, New York.
6. Joseph Walshe to Robert Brennan, 11 June 1945, DFA, P 48-A, NAI.
7. Dept of External Affairs minute, 24 April 1946, DFA, P 48-A, NAI.
8. David Gray to Eleanor Roosevelt, 10 February 1940, Roosevelt papers, Roosevelt Library, Hyde Park, New York.
9. 15 August 1940.
10. Ibid.
11. Boland, who later became the Irish Ambassador to the UK, presided over the famous UN General Assembly meeting at which Khrushchev pounded the desk with his shoe. Boland broke his gavel in an unsuccessful attempt to pound the Secretary General of the Russian Communist Party into silence. His daughter, Evan Boland, is a leading Irish poet.
12. David Gray to Eleanor Roosevelt, 15 August 1940, Roosevelt papers, Roosevelt Library, Hyde Park, New York.
13. 'Behind the Green Curtain', Ch.2, p.5.
14. Oscar Cox to Harry Hopkins (copied to Henry Morgenthau Jnr), Morgenthau papers, Book 433, p.92, Roosevelt papers, Roosevelt Library, Hyde Park, New York.
15. Roosevelt to David Gray, 6 March 1941, Roosevelt papers, Roosevelt Library, Hyde Park, New York.
16. David Gray to Roosevelt, 29 November 1942, Roosevelt papers, Roosevelt Library, Hyde Park, New York.
17. Roosevelt to David Gray, 18 December 1942, Roosevelt papers, Roosevelt Library, Hyde Park, New York.
18. Maffey minute, 11 May 1940, CAB 67/6, PRO.
19. Ibid.
20. Moynihan, p.435.
21. 'Behind the Green Curtain', Ch.3, p.8.
22. Ibid.
23. Memorandum from Woermann, Director Political Dept, German Foreign Ministry, Berlin, 21 May 1940. Copies of this correspondence are also available in the Foreign Affairs records in the National Archives of Ireland.
24. Longford and O'Neill (1), p.361.
25. Ibid, pp.361-4.
26. J. Carroll, p.70.
27. In a letter to Sean Nunan, 10 July 1953, DFA, NAI.
28. CAB 66/8, PRO.
29. The minutes of these meetings are available in DFA A/3, NAI.
30. Minute for meeting of 24 May 1940, DFA A/3, NAI.
31. Desmond Morton, Churchill's intelligence adviser, sent him a distillation of Tegart's report on 10 June 1940, PREM 3/131/2, PRO.
32. MacDonald minute, 16 June, PREM 3/131/1, PRO.
33. Mulcahy minute, 1 February 1941, P7/C/111, Mulcahy papers, UCD.
34. Cabinet record, 20 June 1940, CAB 66/9, PRO.
35. MacDonald minute, 21 June 1940, PREM 3/131/1, PRO.
36. Chamberlain memorandum, 25 June 1940, CAB 66/9, PRO.
37. MacDonald to Cabinet, 26 June 1940, PREM 3/131/1, PRO. MacDonald's conversation with Aiken, Lemass etc., CAB 2/3, Cabinet minutes, 27 June 1940, NAI.
38. Fisk, pp.177-81, quotes the official records of Belfast, Dublin and London.
39. Ibid.
40. Maffey minute, 17 July 1940, CAB 60/10, PRO.
41. Longford and O'Neill (1), p.366.
42. Ibid, p.368.

Chapter 26 (pp.555-570)

1. Telegram no.473, Woermann to 'Legation in Eire', 15 June 1940, D/T S.15469A, NAI.
2. Hempel to Foreign Ministry, 17 June 1940, D/T S.15469A, NAI.
3. Hempel to Foreign Ministry, 21 June 1940, D/T S.15469A, NAI.
4. Ibid.
5. Ibid.
6. Weizsäcker to Hempel, 24 June 1940, D/T S.15469A, NAI.
7. J. Carroll, pp.67-8.
8. Morgenthau diary, Book 276, 26-27 June 1940, p.158, Roosevelt papers, Roosevelt Library, Hyde Park, New York.
9. Morgenthau diary, 15 August 1941.
10. Eden minute, 'Equipment for Eire', 25 July 1940, CAB 66/10, PRO.
11. Caldecote to War Cabinet, 20 July 1940, CAB 66/10, PRO.
12. Longford and O'Neill (1), p.374.
13. Moynihan, pp.451-2.
14. Longford and O'Neill (1), p.174.
15. Bowen letter, 9 November 1940, FO 800/310, PRO.
16. The Nation, January 1942.
17. Despite the rigorous censorship the Shavian dart was reproduced in the Irish Press of 14 December 1940. Contemporary readers will find it more accessible in J. Carroll, p.71.
18. J. Carroll, p.71.
19. Readers seeking more information on the overtures which Hitler put in train – or, indeed, on the course of German-Irish relationships during World War II – are recommended to both Fisk and J. Carroll. Ch.4 of the former and Ch.8 of the latter give admirable insights into this phase of the war.
20. J. Carroll, p.75.
21. Documents on German Foreign Policy, 1918-45, Series D, Vol.XI, pp.572-3.
22. David Gray to Joseph Walshe, 3 September 1941, listing answers to questions which he gave to American journalists, DFA, NAI.
23. Hempel to Ribbentrop, 21 December 1940.
24. J. Carroll, p.76.
25. Ibid, p.77.
26. Ibid, p.78.
27. Churchill (5), Vol.2, Their Finest Hour, p.614.
28. Spender diaries, D 715/15, PRO Northern Ireland.
29. Ibid.
30. Ibid.
31. Fisk, p.253.
32. Kingsley Wood to Churchill, 16 December 1940, CAB 66/14, PRO.

33. Ibid.
34. PREM 3/131/3, PRO.
35. Cranborne–Churchill exchange, PREM 3/131/3, PRO; also Churchill (5), Vol.3, p.645.
36. Donal MacLachlan in *Room 39*, quoted in J. Carroll, p.79.
37. J. Carroll, p.127.
38. F.H. Boland to Sean Nunan, 10 July 1953, DFA, NAI.
39. Fisk, p.269.
40. J. Carroll, p.90.
41. On 6 September 1939.
42. Churchill (5), Vol.2, p.536.
43. Dept of Supplies memorandum, 16 August 1943, S.11394, NAI.
44. Records of CEPTE, 14 August 1942 and 11 September 1942, CAB 72/25. PRO.

Chapter 27 (pp.571–597)

1. *Foreign Relations of the United States, Diplomatic Papers, 1940*, iii, pp.169–70.
2. The Brennan–Welles interlude and its sequel are described in Longford and O'Neill (1), pp.375–6.
3. It is true that Cosgrave and de Valera were not on speaking terms for most of their lives, but the reasons for this were rooted in the civil war and predated the annuities controversy. De Valera's use of the 'Secret Agreement' document could be taken as heightening existing antagonisms, rather than as initiating them.
4. FO371, 29108, PRO.
5. David Gray to Roosevelt, 31 December 1940, Roosevelt papers, Roosevelt Library, Hyde Park, New York.
6. In *Foreign Affairs*, Washington, 1946.
7. F.H. Boland to Sean Nunan, 10 July 1953, DFA, NAI.
8. David Gray to Roosevelt, 31 December 1940.
9. David Gray to Frank Aiken, 24 February 1941. Letter quoted in 'Behind the Green Curtain', Ch.22, p.20.
10. De Valera to Roosevelt, 4 March 1941, DFA, NAI. Author's copy.
11. Hempel to Foreign Ministry, 31 July 1940, *Documents on German Foreign Policy, 1918–45*.
12. Quoted in J. Carroll and Fisk; he subsequently described his reception at length in an interview with Carroll.
13. Fisk, p.265.
14. FO371, 29108, quoted in J. Carroll, p.103.
15. Longford and O'Neill (1), p.379.
16. The row with Roosevelt was described by an eye witness, Robert Brennan, who accompanied Aiken to the meeting and later wrote about the incident in a series of articles in the *Irish Press* in April and May 1958.
17. Roosevelt to de Valera, 15 April 1941, Roosevelt papers, Roosevelt Library, Hyde Park, New York. Author's copy.
18. The broadcast also gave the impression that the Government had taken every precaution to build up stocks and make all necessary arrangements 'for a year before the outbreak'. See Moynihan, p.452 et seq.
19. Moynihan, p.452.

20. Apart from his description of his instructions from Hull and the subsequent interview with de Valera in his unpublished memoir 'Behind the Green Curtain', Gray preserved in his papers a typewritten account, 'Notes for conversation with the Irish Prime Minister', which he marked 'Delivered, April 26th, 1941'. Author's copy. Gray reprinted his despatches to Washington, in which he described the meeting, in 'Behind the Green Curtain'. They are publicly available in *Foreign Relations of the United States, Diplomatic Papers, 1941*, iii, p.23.
21. Roosevelt sent the card to the State Department on 27 December 1943 to inquire whether it was felt he should reply. The answer was: 'It is believed that this greeting does not call for any acknowledgement.' FDR accepted the advice. Original card and correspondence in Roosevelt papers, Roosevelt Library, Hyde Park, New York.
22. De Valera's attitude to Gray is described in J. Carroll, p.107.
23. Brennan to Secretary of State, 22 September 1941, DFA, NAI. Author's copies.
24. As Fisk has noted (p.272), Ireland started the war at a disadvantage where shipping was concerned 'because of de Valera's lack of foresight'. The Irish Government attempted to rectify the shortage by setting up Irish Shipping Ltd in March 1941, the month before Gray conveyed Roosevelt's barbed offer of ships to him. But though Irish Shipping did manage to maintain a small fleet of obsolete vessels all through the war, it failed to get any new ones from Washington.
25. State Department to US Legation, Dublin, 23 December 1943. Author's copy.
26. Longford and O'Neill (1), p.381.
27. Darryl F. Zanuck to Stephen Early, Secretary to President, 14 May 1942, Roosevelt papers, Roosevelt Library, Hyde Park, New York.
28. Document 218-a, Roosevelt papaers, Roosevelt Library, Hyde Park, New York.
29. J. Carroll, p.266.
29a. Mulcahy papers, P7/C/113, UCD. Quoted in Fisk, p.266.
30. There is a copy of Aiken's set-piece speech, delivered in Boston, in the Mulcahy papers, UCD.
31. Secretary, Dept of External Affairs, to Washington (codename 'Estero'), 17 June 1941, DFA, NAI.
32. The text of Cohalan's speech was cabled to de Valera, in clear, on 26 June 1941 and received in Dublin the following day. DFA, NAI. Author's copy.
33. *New York Times*, 28 June 1941.
34. David Gray to Roosevelt, 18 July 1941, Roosevelt papers, Roosevelt Library, Hyde Park, New York.
35. Longford and O'Neill (1), p.383.
36. Fisk, p.422, quoting RAF records in the Blake papers, PRO Northern Ireland.
37. David Gray to Roosevelt, 24 March 1942, Roosevelt papers, Roosevelt Library, Hyde Park, New York.
38. Moynihan, p.458.
39. Hempel memoirs, *Sunday Press*, 8 December 1963.

40. J. Carroll, p.109.
41. Ibid, p.107.
42. Fisk, p.441, quoting Blake papers, PRO Northern Ireland.
43. Draft conclusion of the Northern Ireland Cabinet, 23 September 1941, CAB 41/482/5, PRO Northern Ireland.
44. MacDermott's words are taken from his memorandum to Cabinet, 12 May 1941, CAB 4/473/10, PRO Northern Ireland.
45. North of Ireland Government to Morrison, 21 May 1941, CAB 4/475/15, PRO Northern Ireland.
46. Wickham 'secret' memorandum, 24 May 1941, CAB 66/16, PRO.
47. Longford and O'Neill (1), p.384.
48. The de Valera–Churchill exchange and that between Dulanty and Churchill are described in Dulanty to External Affairs, 22 and 26 May 1941, DFA, pp.12–14, NAI. The originals of Dulanty's excellent memoranda detailing both are in the DFA file, NAI. Author's copies.
49. In 'Behind the Green Curtain' Gray draws on memoranda and diary entries for 24 May et seq., in which he describes his exchanges with de Valera and how he sent him copies of his State Department telegrams, 'obviously reserving certain details'.
50. David Gray to Roosevelt, 28 May 1941. Quoted in 'Behind the Green Curtain'. Author's copy.
51. Ibid.
52. *Irish Press*, 28 May 1941.
53. Longford and O'Neill (1), p.390.
54. Roosevelt to David Gray, 21 August 1941, Roosevelt papers, Roosevelt Library, Hyde Park, New York. Author's copy.
55. Author's copy.
56. Author's copy.
57. Author's copy.
58. Longford and O'Neill (1), p.393.
59. Ibid.
60. Quigley, p.21.
61. Longford and O'Neill (1), p.394.
62. Ibid.
63. Ibid, p.329.
64. Ibid, p.395.
65. Moynihan, p.461.
66. He apparently discussed his meeting in some detail with David Gray the next day, 27 January 1942. Gray immediately wrote personally to Roosevelt giving him the facts on which this account of de Valera's reaction to the troop arrivals is based. Original in Roosevelt papers, Roosevelt Library, Hyde Park, New York. Author's copy.
67. Moynihan, p.465.
68. Welles draft to Roosevelt, 24 February 1942, Roosevelt papers, Roosevelt Library, Hyde Park, New York. Author's copy.
69. David Gray to Roosevelt, 27 January 1941.
70. David Gray to Roosevelt, 20 May 1942. Author's copy.
71. Ibid.
72. Ibid.
73. Roosevelt to David Gray, 6 June 1942. Author's copy.
74. Roosevelt to David Gray, 16 September 1942. Author's copy.
75. David Gray to Roosevelt, Roosevelt papers, Roosevelt Library, Hyde Park, New York. Author's copy.
76. Roosevelt papers, Roosevelt Library, Hyde Park, New York. Author's copy.
77. Ibid.
78. Roosevelt to David Gray, 19 November 1942, Roosevelt papers, Roosevelt Library, Hyde Park, New York.
79. David Gray to Roosevelt, 19 October 1942, Roosevelt papers, Roosevelt Library, Hyde Park, New York. Author's copy.
80. Memorandum by David Gray on 'Discussion of Anglo-Irish Problems at Ambassador Winant's Dinner', Roosevelt papers, Roosevelt Library, Hyde Park, New York. Author's copy.

Chapter 28 (pp.598–620)

1. Roosevelt papers, Roosevelt Library, Hyde Park, New York. Author's copy.
2. Roosevelt to Cordell Hull, 15 June 1943, Roosevelt papers, Roosevelt Library, Hyde Park, New York. Author's copy.
3. David Gray (Personal) to Acting Secretary of State, 1 November 1943, Roosevelt papers, Roosevelt Library, Hyde Park, New York. Author's copy.
4. Ibid.
5. Quigley, p.19.
6. Quigley to author, 9 March 1993.
7. Ibid.
8. Ibid.
9. Fisk, pp.458–9.
10. Under Secretary of State, Edward Street, to Roosevelt, 15 February 1944. Author's copy.
11. The two were John O'Reilly and John Kenny. O'Reilly's father was one of the policemen involved in the arrest of Roger Casement. Now in the Garda Siochana, he immediately advised his son to give himself up. O'Reilly, who had been one of a group of Irishmen over-run by the Germans while fruit-picking in the Channel islands, had been broadcasting to Ireland on German Radio.
12. Fisk, p.135.
13. Hempel to Berlin, 9 May 1941, announcing that 'Legation discovered to be the location' of transmitter.
14. Hempel to Berlin, 12 May 1941.
15. J. Carroll, p.141.
16. Longford and O'Neill (1), p.397.
17. Ibid.
18. Fisk, p.318.
19. The episode of the notes is described in 'Behind the Green Curtain' and in *Foreign Relations of the United States, Diplomatic Papers, 1943*, iii, pp.132–44, 211–22 and 226–40. See also Longford and O'Neill (1), p.404.
20. Longford and O'Neill (1), p.405.
21. *New York Times*, 10 March 1944.
22. Maffey memorandum to Foreign Office, FO371, 42679, PRO. This memorandum is quoted extensively in J. Carroll, p.143.
23. In August 1922 Mustapha Kemal's Turkish forces threatened the British troops stationed at Chanak in the Dardanelles. Churchill's belligerent speeches during the confrontation, which

eventually ended peacefully through the good sense of the British officer in command, General Sir Charles Harington, appeared to commit the Dominions to support Britain against the Turks in the event of war – without consultation. The feeling that Churchill, Lloyd George and Birkenhead were warmongering provoked not just the Dominions but the final crisis in the Tory ranks, which brought down the coalition in October 1922.

24. David Gray to Roosevelt, 14 April 1944. Author's copy.
25. Maffey memorandum to Foreign Office, FO371, 42679, PRO.
26. Longford and O'Neill (1), p.406.
27. *Daily Express*, 4 March 1944.
28. On 7 March 1944, via Brennan in Washington.
29. Quoted in J. Carroll, p.153.
30. Cordell Hull to Roosevelt, 24 March 1944. Author's copy.
31. Quoted in J. Carroll, p.155.
32. Ibid, p.156.
33. Ibid, p.157.
34. David Gray to Roosevelt, 24 March 1944. Author's copy.
35. David Gray to Boland, 14 March 1944, DFA P-40F, NAI. Author's copy.
36. David Gray to Roosevelt, 24 March 1944. Author's copy.
37. David Gray to Roosevelt, 14 April 1944. Author's copy.
38. Gallagher papers, Ms 18, 375 (8), NLI.
39. Longford and O'Neill (1), p.411.
40. Gray to Eleanor Roosevelt, 13 April 1945, Gray papers, University of Wyoming, Laramie.
41. Gray to State Department, 3 May 1945, quoted in Fisk, p.460.
42. Maffey to Dominions Office, quoting Gray, 3 May 1945, DO 35/1229/WX 130/3/40, PRO.
43. Longford and O'Neill (1), p.415.
44. Maffey to Dominions Office, 21 May 1945, DO 35/1229/WX 910/3, PRO.
45. Moynihan, pp.474–5.
46. DFA, P48A, NAI. Subsequent correspondence between Dublin and its Washington representatives is also taken from this file.
47. Longford and O'Neill (1), pp.408–9.
48. Ibid.
49. Robert Brennan to Joseph Walshe, 15 March 1947. Author's copy.
50. Ibid.
51. Sinead de Valera to Maude Gray, 27 June 1947, Roosevelt papers, Roosevelt Library, Hyde Park, New York. Author's copy.
52. Joseph Walshe to Sean Nunan ('Personal and Confidential'), 2 July 1947, DFA, P48A, NAI.
53. Ibid.
54. Ibid.
55. On 25 June 1947 at Leinster House. Original of Gray memorandum in Roosevelt papers, Roosevelt Library, Hyde Park, New York. Author's copy.
56. Joseph Walshe to Sean Nunan ('Very Secret'), 6 July 1953, DFA, NAI.
57. Joseph Walshe to Sean Nunan ('Secret and Personal'), 1 July 1953, DFA, NAI.
58. Sean Nunan to Joseph Walshe ('Secret'), 10 March 1954, DFA, NAI.

59. *Leader* version of 31 January 1953. The issues of the *Irish Press* for 10, 11 and 17 July carry amplified versions of the same allegations.
60. L.H. Kearney to Joseph Walshe, 24 August 1942, DFA, NAI. Author's copy.
61. Coogan (3), p.269 et seq.
62. Extract from Colonel Bryan memorandum, 20 October 1941, DFA, NAI.
63. Government Report of 20 October 1941, A20, referred to in Kearney file, DFA, NAI.
64. Boland to Nunan, 3 March 1954, DFA, NAI.
65. Boland to Nunan, 23 March 1954, DFA, NAI.
66. Ibid.
67. Conor Cruise O'Brien, report of visit to Germany, September 1954, DFA, P168, NAI.
68. OhUadhaigh & Co. to Secretary, Dept of External Affairs, 20 October 1954, DFA, NAI.
69. On 1 October 1954, minute of meeting by Maurice Moynihan, 2 November 1954. Copy, Dept of External Affairs.
70. Secretary, Dept of External Affairs to OhUadhaigh & Co., 2 November 1954.
71. Moynihan minute, 2 November 1954, D/T 315469, NAI.
72. The jury had been sworn in but the case was adjourned for forty-five minutes to allow negotiations to continue. Reports in the Irish newspapers: *Irish Independent, Irish Press* and *Irish Times*.
73. Aiken memorandum on censorship, 23 January 1940, D/T S.11586A, NAI.

Chapter 29 (pp.620–629)

1. See Coogan (3), pp.269–79.
2. Quoted in Coogan (3), pp.275–6. The quotation is from a series of articles allegedly written by Goertz in the *Irish Times* during August 1947. They were in fact written by a Dublin accountant who had befriended him.
3. Longford and O'Neill (1), p.359.
4. Ibid.
5. Ibid, p.399.
6. Robert Brennan to Secretary, Dept of External Affairs, 4 September 1942, DFA, p.60, NAI.
7. Ibid, p.60A.
8. Longford and O'Neill (1), pp.325–6.
9. The first prisoner to go 'on the blanket' was Thomas McCurtain, beginning on 29 July 1940.
10. This, according to a Dept of Justice memorandum prepared on 28 February 1945 (author's copy; available also in D/T S.11443, NAI) was one and a half hours per period. My informants, however, some of whom had experienced the regime, said one hour.
11. According to the Dept of Justice memorandum already quoted, this took place on 25 January 1944.
12. Coogan (3), p.201.
13. Author's copy.
14. See Coogan (3), 'The Years of Disaster'.
15. These included Cecil Lavery KC, Sean MacBride and my own solicitor, Con Lehane.
16. On 9 August 1942, by firing squad.
17. 'Behind the Green Curtain', p.29.
18. Coogan (3), p.205.
19. Ibid, p.206.
20. George Kerr, later news editor of the *Irish*

Press, recalled an inquest one night when I brought MacBride to visit the paper's offices shortly before his death. The reporters read the transcript over to MacBride after the very tense proceedings, with Special Branch police very much in evidence. MacBride had no corrections to make – only one suggestion: 'Before Dr Duane's reply, put "after a pause".'

21. The annual conference of the Irish National Teachers' Organization, Killarney, 26 March 1940. Moynihan, pp.425–33.
22. Moynihan, p.30.
23. John Corr, a Dublin shopkeeper, was sentenced to three months' imprisonment in 1944.
24. Moynihan, p.431.
25. Ibid, p.468.
26. David Gray to Roosevelt, 4 November 1943, Roosevelt papers, Roosevelt Library, Hyde Park, New York. Author's copy.

Chapter 30 (pp.630–646)

1. Cabinet Committee on Economic Planning memorandum, D/T S.13026B, NAI.
2. Dept of Foreign Affairs memorandum, 6 May 1948, FAS.14319, NAI.
3. Lee (1), p.229. See also Cabinet Committee on Economic Planning, 3 March 1943, D/T S.13026A, NAI.
4. Transmitted to de Valera 18 May 1942, D/T S.1258A, NAI.
5. Lemass memorandum, 18 June 1942, D/T S.12882A, NAI.
6. De Valera drafts and memoranda elicited by Lemass memorandum above, 6–9 July 1942, Ibid.
7. Lemass memorandum, D/T S.13101A, NAI.
8. Browne, p.91.
9. Interviews 1 May 1991 and 11 June 1991.
10. Quoted in Lee (1), p.231.
11. Comments of the Minister for Agriculture on the memorandum on Full Employment prepared by the Minister for Industry and Commerce.
12. Lee (1), p.232.
13. Whitaker (1). The genesis of economic development and its evolution may be studied in D/T S.16541A-B (Progress Reports); D/T S.1656A-B (Discussions with Taoiseach); and D/T S.16066B (Economic Development Schemes). All NAI.
14. Bromage (1), p.288.
15. Memorandum to Taoiseach, 19 January 1948, D/T S.13866B, NAI.
16. *Irish Press*, 22 July 1946.
17. Apart from the newspaper reports, a succinct report of both allegations and findings exists in D/T S.14153C, NAI.
18. Ibid.
19. Lee (1), p.297.
20. Longford and O'Neill (1), p.431.
21. Ibid.
22. Longford and O'Neill (1), p.435.
23. Lee (1), p.301.
24. The quotations are taken from the *Irish Press*, which sent a reporter, Liam McGabhann, to cover the tour. Apart from daily reports the *Irish Press* published a special supplement to

mark the tour's conclusion in June. Copies of these supplements were sought from all quarters of the globe and are now collectors' items. There is a copy in the Gallagher papers in the NLI.
25. The symbolism of the importance of the Irish issue in imperial affairs was carried to a grim conclusion when an IRA bomb killed Lord Mountbatten at Mullaghmore, Co. Sligo, on 27 August 1979.
26. Kiernan to Gallagher, 20 April 1948, Gallagher papers, Ms 18, 337, NLI.
27. Moynihan, p.478.
28. De Valera reply to Sean Collins TD, Dail Eireann, 31 October 1951.
29. De Valera conversation with Gallagher, 20 December 1938, Gallagher papers, Ms 18, 375 (11), NLI.
30. Geary to O'Muimhneachain (Moynihan), 7 December 1951, D/T, NAI. Geary was advising the Taoiseach's office about the dangers involved in a Dail question from Sean MacBride which suggested that Unionist discrimination was causing a Catholic exodus from the Six Counties.
31. These figures and their implications are discussed more extensively in Coogan (1), pp.247–54.
32. T. Kiernan, Director, Radio Eireann to Moynihan, 27 May 1938, D/T S.1077A, NAI.
33. Cabinet minutes, 17 October 1952, D/T S.15297, NAI.
34. Moynihan minutes on Craig funeral, D/T S.12193, NAI.
35. David Gray memorandum of conversation with de Valera, 19 August 1941, Gray papers, University of Wyoming, Laramie, Wyoming. Author's copy.
36. Fermanagh-Tyrone deputation to Taoiseach, 9 January 1952, D/T S.61B, NAI.
37. 3 June 1943, D/T S.61B, NAI.
38. Memorandum for Government, 16 April 1957, D/T S.16220, NAI.
39. Ibid.
40. D/T S.16272A, NAI.
41. Seanad Eireann, 29 January 1958, cols 1411–21.
42. See O'Muimhneachain to Foreign Affairs, D/T S.16272, NAI.
43. *Irish Times* leading article, 31 January 1958.
44. Seanad Eireann, 29 January 1958, col. 1412.
45. Moynihan minute, 7 March 1958, D/T S.16272, NAI.
46. Cremin to McCann, DFA, P.288, NAI.
47. It was appreciated that Longford himself was 'inspired in this as in other matters by the best of intentions'. Ibid.
48. Ibid.
49. *Irish Times*, 1 and 2 January 1992.
50. The Irish Embassy in London prepared a very detailed memorandum marked 'Confidential', detailing the de Valera/Aiken visit to London. It states that: 'In the afternoon the Taoiseach called upon the Prime Minister at Downing St and the Minister upon the Secretary of State for Commonwealth Relations in the House of Lords.' There is no mention of de Valera's having called on Home after seeing Macmillan. However, Home is mentioned amongst the

guests at the Irish Embassy dinner party later that day. See DFA, P.302, NAI.

51. That something of major importance was proposed is evidenced by a private letter from Joseph Walshe, then Irish Ambassador to the Vatican, to Con Cremin, dated 28 March 1958, in which he refers to 'terrific top news. I always guessed that he was coming. ... ' DFA, p.203/2, NAI.

52. March 1957.

53. Ibid.

54. 4 July 1958, DFA P.203, NAI.

55. Ibid.

55. Longford and O'Neill (1), p.432.

56. Longford and O'Neill (1), p.435.

Chapter 31 (pp.647–673)

1. Documents dealing with the background to the dispute and correspondence between the hierarchy and the Government are contained in D/T S.14227, NAI.

2. Ibid.

3. Ibid.

4. Quoted in Coogan (1), p.98.

5. See Kennedy to Byrne, 22 April 1928 and 19 May 1928, Archdiocesan Archives, Archbishop's House, Dublin.

6. See Dulanty to Secretary, Dept of External Affairs, 14 April 1944, DFA P.84, NAI.

7. The ban disappeared in the wake of the Second Vatican Council. The current Provost, Dr Thomas Mitchell, is a Catholic, the first to hold the post.

8. Browne, p.188.

9. Ibid.

10. Longford and O'Neill (1), p.442.

11. Ibid.

12. MacNeill to Secretary, Dept of External Affairs, 22 September 1952. DFA P.240, NAI.

13. Ryan to Browne, 5 March 1952, D/T S.14227, NAI.

14. Browne to Ryan, 11 November 1952, Ibid.

15. Vivion de Valera to author.

16. Longford and O'Neill (1), p.442.

17. The relevant Government papers ultimately surfaced under the thirty-year rule and were used with devastating effect by Dr Browne in *Against the Tide*, p.216 et seq.

18. Spokesman for the hierarchy, *Irish Independent*, 2 June 1951.

19. Browne, p.168.

20. McQuaid to de Valera, 14 November 1953, D/T S.2321A, NAI. Author's copy.

21. Ibid.

22. Ibid.

23. Conversations between author and Dr McQuaid. I would not presume to claim intimacy with the Archbishop, but I was probably on friendlier terms with him than any other journalist at that time.

24. Ibid.

25. Coogan (1), p.169 et seq., gives an extended list of banned works, a description of the censorship and an interview with a censor of the period.

26. *Clare Champion*, 4 August 1956.

27. Rogers to Costello, 27 July 1956, D/T S.16073A, NAI.

28. Costello to Rogers, 14 August 1956, Ibid.

29. McQuaid to Costello, 16 August 1956, Ibid.

30. Dept of Justice memorandum, 20 February 1958, D/T S.2321B, NAI.

31. The other two conservatives were C.J. O'Reilly and D.J. Flynn. The second liberal was A.F. Comyn.

32. Dept of Justice memorandum, 20 February 1957, D/T S.2321B, NAI.

33. Ibid.

34. De Valera to Bishop MacNeely, 8 March 1958, D/T S.2321B, NAI.

35. *Catholic Standard*, 21 June 1957.

36. Ibid.

37. Ibid.

38. *Irish Press*, 3 July 1957.

39. Ibid, 1 July 1957.

40. D/T S.16247, NAI.

41. Ibid.

42. De Valera to McQuaid, 4 July 1957, D/T S.16247, NAI.

43. Cloney to de Valera, 7 July 1957, D/T S.16247, NAI.

44. *Irish Press*, 10 January 1958.

45. Aide-memoire, MacEntee to de Valera, 21 July 1958, D/T S.16247, NAI.

46. Monsignor Deskur's approach and de Valera's response are contained in D/T S.14996B, NAi.

47. Because Arus an Uachtarain, like the US Embassy and the Papal Nunciature, is located in Phoenix Park, the incumbent in any one of the three is generally referred to as being 'up in the Park'.

48. Quoted in Dwyer (6), p.314.

49. *Sunday Press*, 7 June 1953.

50. Longford and O'Neill (1), p.439.

51. T.K. Whitaker, quoted in McCarthy, p.20.

52. MacEntee to de Valera, 14 August 1939, D/T S.11265A, NAI.

53. Readers wishing to learn more about de Valera's, and indeed Ireland's, attitude towards emigration are advised to consult the files of the Dept of the Taoiseach in the NAI, in particular the files in the series S.11S82A, B, C, D, E, F and G. Amongst the many other files dealing with emigration the series S.1429 A/1 and A/2, concerning the Commission on Emigration, and the subsequent B, C and D files, containing either newspaper comment or consequential inter-governmental correspondence, are of considerable interest. The references to the Birmingham report, the Galway speech and the Irish Centre are all taken from these files.

54. Dail Eireann, 31 October 1951, Vol.127, No.1, cols 3 and 4.

55. Commission on Emigration Report, D/T S.14249 A/2, NAI.

56. Government minute, 22 August 1951. This note and much other material on emigration is contained in the series D/T S.11582A-F, NAI.

57. Oliver Flanagan to de Valera, 13 September 1951. Author's copy.

58. Quoted in Irish newspapers 31 August 1951, D/T S.1182, NAI.

59. Boland to Secretary, Dept of Foreign Affairs, 11 November 1952.

60. D/T S.11582, NAI.

61. Quoted in McCarthy, p.29.

62. Ibid.
63. Ireland voted to condemn both the Russian invasion of Hungary and the Anglo-French invasion of Egypt.
64. Irish and American reactions are catalogued in the series D/T S.1607A–F, NAI.
65. *National Hibernian Digest*, January/February 1958.
66. In 1965, during the course of a long interview, later fleshed out by material supplied from the Irish Dept of Foreign Affairs, for Coogan (1), pp.114–35.
67. Carter script, D/T S.16211, NAI. This is the complete text – abbreviated versions appeared in the newspapers.
68. Whitaker memorandum, D/T S.16066A, NAI.
69. Ibid.
70. McCarthy, p.50.
71. Ibid.
72. Moynihan in interview with author, 11 June 1991.
73. Quoted in McCarthy, p.51.
74. Moynihan, p.581.
75. 'They all respected him': Moynihan to author, 1 May 1991.

Chapter 32 (pp.674–692)

1. In his biography *Against the Tide* Dr Browne says (p.234) that he got the share in 1958 and finally succeeded in forcing a Dail debate on his consequential discoveries a year later. The debate in fact commenced on 12 December 1958 and was adjourned until the following January; it resumed on the 7th of that month and was again adjourned until the 14th.
2. In the course of an interview with the author for *Ireland Since the Rising*.
3. Dail Eireann, 12 December 1958, col.2182.
4. Dail Eireann, 14 January 1959, col.589.
5. Dail Eireann, 7 January 1959, col.129.
6. Dail Eireann, 7 January 1959, col.133.
7. Dail Eireann, 14 January 1959, col.590.
8. I interviewed many of these men and there is no doubt that in those pre-television times the *Sunday Press*, which in those days sold nearly half a million copies a week, did have a bearing on the decision to launch a new Border campaign.
9. Dail Eireann, 7 January 1959, col.141.
10. Longford and O'Neill (1), p.447.
11. Interview with author, 12 April 1993.
12. Longford and O'Neill (1), p.446.
13. Ibid, p.447.
14. Ibid.
15. Ibid.
16. *Irish Times*, 15 January 1959.
17. O'hAnrachain served under four Taoisigh: de Valera, Lemass, Lynch and Haughey. I was helping him to write his memoirs when he died suddenly in 1988.
18. Sir John Wheeler-Bennett's account of the de Valera interview, 9 October 1959, was given to the National Library in early 1993 and had not been awarded a Ms number at the time of writing. However, access to the manuscript may be had on request.
19. Author's copy.
20. Author's copy.
21. De Valera to Robert Lusty, Chairman of Hutchinson, 30 April 1963. Author's copy.
22. Conversations between Harris and author, 30 October 1992 and subsequent dates.
23. Author's copy.
24. D/T S.6295A, NAI.
25. Contained in letter from Harris to author, 27 October 1992.
26. Longford and O'Neill (1), p.xxii.
27. My late friend William V. Shannon, a friend of the Kennedy family, who became the US Ambassador to Ireland under President Carter and wrote the speeches that Kennedy delivered in Ireland, verified for me that this sentiment was JFK's wish and intention.
28. Moynihan, pp.597–602. The lines are from 'Irish National Hymn' by James Clarence Mangan (1803–49).
29. Whitaker to author, 14 May 1993.
30. By coincidence Rita Childers, Erskine Childers' widow, told me the story on the same day that Whitaker had described for me O'Neill's visit to de Valera, 14 May 1993.
31. One of his children, also Erskine, would succeed him as President. The anecdote was told to me by Childers' widow, who was present at the dinner.
32. The letter is not with de Valera's papers in the FAK, and may have been destroyed.
33. After the ceremonies had concluded an considerable furore was aroused in Ireland by the revelation of an ex-convict from Pentonville that he had been one of a work party detailed to dig up the remains. The prison graveyard was so full of bones that there was no way of identifying individual remains, he said, so prisoners simply gathered up the makings up the skeleton, which was then solemnly returned to Dublin.
34. Moynihan, p.604.
35. The graves mentioned are: Arbour Hill, the 1916 leaders; Bodenstown, Wolfe Tone; Downpatrick, Thomas Russell; Templepatrick, William Orr; Greyabbey, the Rev. James Porter. The last three were, like Casement, all Protestants and were executed by the British.
36. From 'Church and State' by W.B. Yeats.
37. Longford and O'Neill (1), p.456.
38. The term is Father Farragher's, in interview with author, but several other witnesses, among them Maurice Moynihan and Padraig O'hAnrachain, concur that de Valera was a generous and impressive host.
39. At Glasnevin Cemetery, Dublin, 10 May 1952.
40. Author's interview with Father O'J. Carroll, 16 April 1993.
41. Moynihan interview with author already cited.
41a. As we have seen, in his earlier life de Valera could sometimes react badly under pressure, be it pressure from peril or from pride. His behaviour during the 1916 Rising, or when thwarted over the New Army manoeuvre, could be studied under both headings; as indeed could his entire performance during the civil war. But as he got older, particularly from the time he achieved governmental responsibility, he showed an ability to withstand pressure more and more successfully, as his behaviour

during World War II indicates. He still lost his cool, occasionally even in front of witnesses, but more and more he developed an ability to turn this failing to advantage.

Two examples may be cited to illustrate how he profited from his temperament. One relates to his first meeting with a man whom he relied on absolutely during World War II, the other to a man whom he fought continuously during the same period. The two were Dan McKenna, Chief of Staff of the Irish Army, and David Gray, the American Minister – in effect the Ambassador to Ireland – throughout the same period. De Valera's meeting with McKenna occurred shortly after he came to power, 'early in 1933'. (Longford and O'Neill (1), p.334. The McKenna saga is detailed on pp.334–5. Subsequent quotes in this note not attributed to Gallagher are from the same source.) A Professor John Nolan, who had been studying ions in the Dublin mountains, had been cut off by a heavy snowfall. De Valera, who had been approached for assistance, contacted the Department of Defence on a Friday. Receiving no progress reports, de Valera became impatient and set off to the mountains the next afternoon, a Saturday, normally a half-day in government circles. He took Vivion and Eamonn with him in the state car.

At Enniskerry village he noticed an Army lorry and a group of soldiers outside a pub 'showing more interest in the premises than in the hills behind'. He inquired whether they were involved with the Nolan rescue attempt, and was informed that their lorry had got stuck in the snow and they had had to turn back. 'De Valera was angry.' He ordered his driver on up the mountain. He too got stuck, but de Valera pressed on, borrowing two horses from a nearby farm for himself and Vivion and leaving Eamonn at the farmhouse. He pressed on up the icy mountain, expecting to find Nolan 'suffering from exposure in an open shed'. Instead he found him in 'a comfortable country kitchen, with a bright fire glowing on a hearth behind him and bottle of whiskey in his hand as he poured a drink for two army officers in uniform who had made their way to the house on foot'. Because of the snow the senior officer, Dan McKenna, then Major McKenna, had sent back the lorry and gone on, on foot, with his companion. 'De Valera realised that he had foolishly jumped to conclusions. ... He admired the spirit and initiative shown by the officer in charge whom he first met on that occasion.' That character assessment formed part of the reason why McKenna was placed in charge of the Irish defence forces during World War II.

David Gray, however, de Valera did not admire, and he took the opportunity of letting him know as much when Gray presented him with a chance of so doing – in private. The ubiquitous Gallagher recorded the occasion (Gallagher papers, Ms 18, 375, NLI), which arose because Gray had been informed, as he told Gallagher, that: 'The right way to treat de Valera was to thump the table at him.' (As previous source.) Gallagher was present when Gray emerged from de Valera's room 'with a startled face'. (As previous source.) 'The bloody fool!' Gray exclaimed, citing the name of whoever it was had told him to handle de Valera by thumping the table. 'And did you?' asked the kindly Gallagher hopefully. Gray 'drew his hands across his face' and replied brokenly, 'I did!' (As previous source.) Gallagher's note on the incident concludes: 'What de Valera's response was I never heard. Judging by Gray's swift departure it must have been terrible.' In that case de Valera's flash of temper made the point, in the privacy of his office, that no one, not even the Americans, told Eamon de Valera, the head of a sovereign state, what he should or should not do.

But, even when he had assumed the role of elder statesman and had retired from active politics in preparation for going to 'the Park', the temperament could still peep through. Colman Doyle, the top photographer of the Irish Press Group, was assigned by the Editor of the *Sunday Press* to do a portrait of Eamon and Sinead. Vivion was furious. He was feuding with Feehan at the time, and in any case wished all contact with his father by Irish Press employees to be channeled through himself. The strong-minded Feehan, who had his own contacts with the President-to-be from their work together in Fianna Fail, had not approached Vivion for permission to arrange the photograph.

As Doyle prepared to take the photograph, in the grounds of the family home at Cross Avenue, Vivion appeared and began to inquire what Colman was doing. De Valera, who had some knowledge of the state of relationships between Vivion and Feehan, cut him off. Waving his stick he thundered at his eldest son, then controlling director of Irish Press Ltd: 'Get in the house! Get in the house!' Vivion attempted a demur, but The Voice rose and the stick was brandished more ferociously: 'GET INTO THE HOUSE!' Vivion slunk off like a small boy told to await his father's wrath in the study. The photo session continued. But it was one of the incidents which led to Feehan's departing the *Sunday Press* editorship a few years later.

42. Father Farragher's phrase.
43. Interview with author, 7 April 1993.
44. Amongst of the most respected Government advisers of his day, O'hAnrachain concealed one of the best political minds in Ireland behind a facade of jocularity and occasional obscenity. At a time when he was principal political adviser to the then Taoiseach, Charles Haughey, he was once overheard in the corridors of Government Buildings discussing the arrangements for his attendance at a funeral representing Haughey. Haughey's list of requirements eventually irritated O'hAnrachain to the point where he turned on the Taoiseach wrathfully to inquire: 'Jasus, do you want me to lay out the bollocks?'
45. Dwyer (6), p.321.
46. In the event Aiken's action did not save Fianna

Fail – Fine Gael and Labour won enough votes to form a coalition Government.

47. Dwyer (6), p.322.

48. As he would one day acknowledge (Coogan (4), p.432), Valera was well aware that Collins' memory could only shine at the expense of his being dimmed. The entire basis of his power stemmed from his attempts to prove Collins wrong and himself right over the Treaty and the subsequent civil war. While he was in power, therefore, he did everything possible to ensure that Collins' memory was not exalted.

Apart from a public policy, which took the form of actions such as preventing the Army (of which Collins had been the first Commander-in-Chief) from attending the annual Collins commemoration ceremonies at Beal na mBlath, in private de Valera personally handled a matter concerning his dead rival in a manner that does no credit to his own memory. Johnny Collins tried without success from 1935 to 1938 to get official permission to erect a marble cross over his famous brother's grave in Glasnevin Cemetery. Official permission was necessary because Collins was buried in a military plot. The marble would have been supplied and shipped from Carrara by a millionaire admirer of Collins, Joseph McGrath. But de Valera refused to allow a marble cross. All he would agree to was a limestone cross and surrounds, not to exceed £300 in cost. No public subscription was allowed, nor any publicity. He sent for Johnny Collins to inform him that the wording on the front of the cross would have to be in Irish and that it would have to be submitted to him before being unveiled. The inscription at the back of the cross had to include the words 'M. Collins erected by his brothers and sisters'.

No member of the Collins family, except Johnny himself, was to attend the blessing of the cross. De Valera also stipulated that only one altar boy should accompany the cemetery chaplain, to carry the holy water. Even though the outbreak of World War II was only a few weeks away, de Valera monitored the Collins project to the extent of personally signing, on 31 July 1939, the certificate of authorization for the cross. It was duly blessed in the presence of Johnny Collins and two gravediggers. As no press were allowed, the only record of the melancholy little scene is a snapshot taken by an American tourist whom one of the gravediggers called over. (The story is described in detail in Coogan (4), which also reproduces the tourist's photograph.) Judging by attendances at other Collins commemorations it is probable that, had the normal courtesies and publicity been allowed, the event would have been a national occasion and the crowd would have run into tens of thousands.

Even late in life his sensitivity about Collins continued to manifest itself. There was a nasty little controversy in 1965 when it was discovered that a booklet called 'Facts about Ireland', put out by Frank Aiken's Department of Foreign Affairs, had omitted all reference to Collins' role in the setting up of the state. The book was withdrawn and republished with the

omission made good. Later still, nearing the end of his presidency, de Valera revealed something of the reasoning behind his attitude. He was asked by Joseph McGrath, who had just been diagnosed as having cancer, to become a patron of a project suggested by Michael's brother Johnny – a Collins commemorative scholarship. But de Valera declined, saying that 'in the fullness of time' Collins' greatness would be acknowledged, but that it would be 'at my expense'. History had cast some long shadows on the Long Fellow.

49. Letter from Brendan Kennelly to author, 20 April 1993.

50. Author's italics.

Chapter 33 (pp.693–704)

1. Connolly memoir.

2. Ibid.

3. Connolly completed his memoir in 1958. The row with de Valera over land division seems to have occurred about 1945.

4. *Irish Times*, 9 May 1945.

5. The *Bell*, June 1945.

5a. BCL.

6. The quotation is from the 'threepenny' catechism which I learned as a schoolboy. It carried the 'Permissu Ordinem' of the Archbishop of Dublin, Dr John Charles Mcquaid.

7. On 14 April 1993.

8. MacEntee papers, Ms P67/121 (1), UCD.

9. Ibid, Ms P67/125 (1).

10. In conversation with Maurice Moynihan, 21 April 1993.

11. Moynihan interview, 24 April 1993.

12. Ibid.

13. Father Michael O'J. Carroll Cssp, Blackrock, to author.

14. The incident is vouched for by Father Michael O'J. Carroll, who acted as cicerone during the Bishop's Irish visit. Conversation with author, 16 April 1993.

15. Lynch to author, 14 April 1993.

16. De Valera to Taheny and Taheny, 25 April 1951, D/T S.15218, NAI.

17. He held the post until the end of the war, resigning as Director on 14 December 1945 and becoming Senior Professor in order to devote himself exclusively to pure research.

18. Quoted by Gray in 'Behind the Green Curtain'.

19. On 7 June 1953, at Cloyne, Co. Cork.

20. In all, Berkeley composed some five hundred questions on Ireland's social and economic condition; they appeared in a three-volume work, *The Querist*, which began publication in 1735.

21. MacManus to Gallagher, Ms 18361 (7), 28 August 1935, NLI.

22. *Phoenix* magazine, 18 September 1992.

25. The dictionary definition of an epicycloid circle is: the curve described by a point on the circumference of a circle as this circle rolls around the outside of another fixed circle, the two circles being coplanar.

26. Lee (1), p.340.

27. Irish for (literally): 'That's it, Sinead.'

APPENDICES

ARTICLES OF AGREEMENT AS SIGNED
on December 6th 1921

1. Ireland shall have the same constitutional status in the Community of Nations known as the British Empire as the Dominion of Canada, the Commonwealth of Australia, the Dominion of New Zealand, and the Union of South Africa, with a Parliament having powers to make laws for the peace, order and good government of Ireland and an Executive responsible to that Parliament, and shall be styled and known as the Irish Free State.

2. Subject to the provisions hereinafter set out the position of the Irish Free State in relation to the Imperial Parliament and Government and otherwise shall be that of the Dominion of Canada, and the law, practice and constitutional usage governing the relationship of the Crown or the representative of the Crown and of the Imperial Parliament to the Dominion of Canada shall govern their relationship to the Irish Free State.

3. The representative of the Crown in Ireland shall be appointed in like manner as the Governor-General of Canada and in accordance with the practice observed in the making of such appointments.

4. The oath to be taken by Members of the Parliament of the Irish Free State shall be in the following form:

I .... do solemnly swear true faith and allegiance to the constitution of the Irish Free State as by law established and that I will be faithful to H. M. King George V, his heirs and successors by law, in virtue of the common citizenship of Ireland with Great Britain and her adherence to and membership of the group of nations forming the British Commonwealth of Nations.

5. The Irish Free State shall assume liability for the service of the Public Debt of the United Kingdom as existing at the date hereof and towards the payment of war pensions as existing at that date in such proportion as may be fair and equitable, having regard to any just claims on the part of Ireland by way of set-off or counter-claim, the amount of such sums being determined in default of agreement by the arbitration of one or more independent persons being citizens of the British Empire.

6. Until an arrangement has been made between the British and Irish

737

Governments whereby the Irish Free State undertakes her own coastal defence, the defence by sea of Great Britain and Ireland shall be undertaken by His Majesty's Imperial Forces. But this shall not prevent the construction or maintenance by the Government of the Irish Free State of such vessels as are necessary for the protection of the Revenue of the Fisheries.

The foregoing provisions of this Article shall be reviewed at a Conference of Representatives of the British and Irish Governments to be held at the expiration of five years from the date hereof with a view to the undertaking by Ireland of a share in her own coastal defence.

7. The Government of the Irish Free State shall afford to His Majesty's Imperial Forces:

(a) In time of peace such harbour and other facilities are are indicated in the Annex hereto, or such other facilities as may from time to time be agreed between the British Government and the Government of the Irish Free State; and

(b) In time of war or of strained relations with a Foreign Power such harbour and other facilities as the British Government may require for the purposes of such defence as aforesaid.

8. With a view to securing the observance of the principle of international limitation of armaments, if the Government of the Irish Free State establishes and maintains a military defence force, the establishments thereof shall not exceed in size such proportion of the military establishments maintained in Great Britain as that which the population of Ireland bears to the population of Great Britain.

9. The ports of Great Britain and the Irish Free State shall be freely open to the ships of the other country on payment of the customary port and other dues.

10. The Government of the Irish Free State agrees to pay fair compensation on terms not less favourable than those accorded by the Act of 1920 to judges, officials, members of Police Forces and other Public Servants who are discharged by it or who retire in consequence of the change of Government effected in pursuance hereof.

Provided that this agreement shall not apply to members of the Auxiliary Police Force or to persons recruited in Great Britain for the Royal Irish Constabulary during the two years next preceding the date hereof. The British Government will assume responsibility for such compensation or pensions as may be payable to any of these excepted persons.

11. Until the expiration of one month from the passing of the Act of Parliament for the ratification of this instrument, the powers of the Parliament and the Government of the Irish Free State shall not be exercisable as respects Northern Ireland and the provisions of the Government of Ireland Act, 1920, shall so far as they relate to Northern

Ireland remain of full force and effect, and no election shall be held for the return of members to serve in the Parliament of the Irish Free State for constituencies in Northern Ireland, unless a resolution is passed by both Houses of the Parliament of Northern Ireland in favour of the holding of such election before the end of the said month.

12. If before the expiration of the said month, an address is presented to His Majesty by both Houses of the Parliament of Northern Ireland to that effect, the powers of the Parliament and Government of the Irish Free State shall no longer extend to Northern Ireland, and the provisions of the Government of Ireland Act, 1920 (including those relating to the Council of Ireland) shall, so far as they relate to Northern Ireland, continue to be of full force and effect, and this instrument shall have effect subject to the necessary modifications.

Provided that if such an address is so presented a Commission consisting of three persons, one to be appointed by the Government of the Irish Free State, one to be appointed by the Government of Northern Ireland and one who shall be Chairman to be appointed by the British Government shall determine in accordance with the wishes of the inhabitants, so far as may be compatible with economic and geographic conditions, the boundaries between Northern Ireland and the rest of Ireland, and for the purposes of the Government of Ireland Act, 1920, and of this instrument, the boundary of Northern Ireland shall be such as may be determined by such Commission.

13. For the purpose of the last foregoing article, the powers of the Parliament of Southern Ireland under the Government of Ireland Act, 1920, to elect members of the Council of Ireland shall after the Parliament of the Irish Free State is constituted be exercised by that Parliament.

14. After the expiration of the said month, if no such address as is mentioned in Article 12 hereof is presented, the Parliament and Government of Northern Ireland shall continue to exercise as respects Northern Ireland the powers conferred on them by the Government of Ireland Act, 1920, but the Parliament and Government of the Irish Free State shall in Northern Ireland have in relation to matters in respect of which the Parliament of Northern Ireland has not power to make laws under that Act (including matters which under the said Act are within the jurisdiction of the Council of Ireland) the same powers as in the rest of Ireland, subject to such other provisions as may be agreed in manner hereinafter appearing.

15. At any time after the date hereof the Government of Northern Ireland and the provisional Government of Southern Ireland hereinafter constituted may meet for the purpose of discussing the provisions subject to which the last foregoing article is to operate in the event of no such address as is therein mentioned being presented and those provisions may include:

739

(a)   Safeguards with regard to patronage in Northern Ireland:

(b)   Safeguards with regard to the collection of revenue in Northern Ireland:

(c)   Safeguards with regard to import and export duties affecting the trade or industry of Northern Ireland:

(d)   Safeguards for minorities in Northern Ireland:

(e)   The settlement of the financial relations between Northern Ireland and the Irish Free State:

(f)   The establishment and powers of a local militia in Northern Ireland and the relation of the Defence Forces of the Irish Free State and of Northern Ireland respectively:

and if at any such meeting provisions are agreed to, the same shall have effect as if they were included amongst the provisions subject to which the Powers of the Parliament and Government of the Irish Free State are to be exercisable in Northern Ireland under Article 14 hereof.

16. Neither the Parliament of the Irish Free State nor the Parliament of Northern Ireland shall make any law so as either directly or indirectly to endow any religion or prohibit or restrict the free exercise thereof or give any preference or impose any disability on account of religious belief or religious status or affect prejudicially the right of any child to attend a school receiving public money without attending the religious instruction at the school or make any discrimination as respects state aid between schools under the management of different religious denominations or divert from any religious denomination or any educational institution any of its property except for public purposes and on payment of compensation.

17. By way of provisional arrangement for the administration of Southern Ireland during the interval which must elapse between the date hereof and the constitution of a Parliament and Government of the Irish Free State in accordance therewith, steps shall be taken forthwith for summoning a meeting of members of Parliament elected for constituencies in Southern Ireland since the passing of the Government of Ireland Act, 1920, and for constituting a provisional Government, and the British Government shall take the steps necessary to transfer to such provisional Government the powers and machinery requisite for the discharge of its duties, provided that every member of such provisional Government shall have signified in writing his or her acceptance of this instrument. But this arrangement shall not continue in force beyond the expiration of twelve months from the date hereof.

18. This instrument shall be submitted forthwith by His Majesty's Government for the approval of Parliament and by the Irish signatories to a meeting summoned for the purpose of the members elected to sit in the House of Commons of Southern Ireland, and if approved shall be ratified by the necessary legislation.

On behalf of the British Delegation. *Signed*	On behalf of the Irish Delegation. *Signed*
D. LLOYD GEORGE.	ART Ó GRÍOBHTHA (ARTHUR GRIFFITH).
AUSTEN CHAMBERLAIN.	MICHEÁL Ó COILEÁIN.
BIRKENHEAD.	RIOBÁRD BARTÚN.
WINSTON S. CHURCHILL.	EUDHMONN S. Ó DÚGÁIN.
L. WORTHINGTON-EVANS.	SEÓRSA GHABHÁIN UÍ DHUBHTHAIGH.
HAMAR GREENWOOD.	
GORDON HEWART	*December 6th*, 1921

ANNEX

1. The following are the specific facilities required:

Dockyard Port at Berehaven

(a) Admiralty property and rights to be retained as at the rate hereof. Harbour defences to remain in charge of British care and maintenance parties.

Queenstown

(b) Harbour defences to remain in charge of British care and maintenance parties. Certain mooring buoys to be retained for use of His Majesty's ships.

Belfast Lough

(c) Harbour defences to remain in charge of British care and maintenance parties.

Lough Swilly

(d) Harbour defences to remain in charge of British care and maintenance parties.

Aviation

(e) Facilities in the neighbourhood of the above Ports for coastal defence by air.

Oil Fuel Storage

(f) Haulbowline and Rathmullen. To be offered for sale to commercial companies under guarantee that purchasers shall maintain a certain minimum stock for Admiralty purposes.

2. A Convention shall be made between the British Government and the Government of the Irish Free State to give effect to the following conditions:

(a) That submarine cables shall not be landed or wireless stations for communications with places outside Ireland be established except by agreement with the British Government; that the existing cable

741

landing rights and wireless concessions shall not be withdrawn except by agreement with the British Government; and that the British Government shall be entitled to land additional submarine cables or establish additional wireless stations for communication with places outside Ireland.

(b) That lighthouses, buoys, beacons, and any navigational marks or navigational aids shall be maintained by the Government of the Irish Free State as at the date hereof and shall not be removed or added to except by agreement with the British Government.

(c) That war signal stations shall be closed down and left in charge of care and maintenance parties, the Government of the Irish Free State being offered the option of taking them over and working them for commercial purposes subject to Admiralty inspection, and guaranteeing the upkeep of existing telegraphic communication therewith.

3. A Convention shall be made between the same Governments for the regulation of Civil Communication by Air.

			A. G.
D. LL. GB.	B.	W. S. C.	M. O. C.
A. C.		E. S. O. D.	R. B.
			S. G. D.

DOCUMENT NUMBER TWO
The Counter-proposal drafted by de Valera

'That inasmuch as the "Articles of Agreement for a treaty between Great Britain and Ireland", signed in London on December 6th, 1921, do not reconcile Irish National aspirations and the Association of Ireland with the Community of Nations known as the British Commonwealth, and cannot be the basis of an enduring peace between the Irish and the British peoples, DAIL EIREANN, in the name of the Sovereign Irish Nation, makes to the Government of Great Britain, to the Government of the other States of the British Commonwealth, and to the peoples of Great Britain and of these several States, the following Proposal for a Treaty of Amity and Association which, DAIL EIREANN is convinced, could be entered into by the Irish people with the sincerity of goodwill':

Proposed Treaty of Association Between Ireland and the British Commonwealth

In order to bring to an end the long and ruinous conflict between Great Britain and Ireland by a sure and lasting peace honourable to both nations, it is agreed

Status of Ireland.

1. That the legislative, executive, and judicial authority of Ireland shall be derived solely from the people of Ireland.

Terms of Association

2. That, for purposes of common concern, Ireland shall be associated with the States of the British Commonwealth, viz: – The Kingdom of Great Britain, the Dominion of Canada, the Commonwealth of Australia, and Dominion of New Zealand, and the Union of South Africa.

3. That when acting as an associate the rights, status, and privileges of Ireland shall be in no respect less than those enjoyed by any of the component States of the British Commonwealth.

4. That the matters of 'common concern' shall include Defence, Peace and War, Political Treaties, and all matters now treated as of common concern, amongst the States of the British Commonwealth, and that in these matters there shall be between Ireland and the States of the British Commonwealth 'such concerted action founded on consultation as the several Governments may determine.'

5. That in virtue of this association of Ireland with the States of the British Commonwealth, citizens of Ireland in any of these States shall not be subject to any disabilities which a citizen of one of the component States of the British Commonwealth would not be subject to, and reciprocally for citizens of these States in Ireland.

743

6. That, for purposes of the Association, Ireland shall recognise His Britannic Majesty as head of the Association.

Defence

7. That, so far as her resources permit, Ireland shall provide for her own defence by sea, land and air, and shall repel by force any attempt by a foreign Power to violate the integrity of her soil and territorial waters, or to use them for any purpose hostile to Great Britain and the other associated States.

8. That for five years, pending the establishment of Irish coastal defence forces, or for such other period as the Governments of the two countries may later agree upon, facilities for the coastal defence of Ireland shall be given to the British Government as follows:-

(a) In time of peace such harbour and other facilities as are indicated in the Annex hereto, or such other facilities as may from time to time be agreed upon between the British Government and the Government of Ireland;

(b) In time of war such harbour and other naval facilities as the British Government may reasonably require for the purposes of such defence as aforesaid.

9. That within five years from the date of exchange of ratifications of this Treaty a Conference between the British and Irish Governments shall be held in order to hand over the coastal defence of Ireland to the Irish Government, unless some other arrangements for naval defence be agreed by both Governments to be desirable in the common interest of Ireland, Great Britain, and the other Associated States.

10. That, in order to co-operate in furthering the principle of international limitation of armaments, the government of Ireland shall not

(a) Build submarines unless by agreement with Great Britain and the other States of the Commonwealth;

(b) Maintain a military defence force, the establishments whereof exceed in size such proportion of the military establishments maintained in Great Britain as that which the population of Ireland bears to the population of Great Britain.

Miscellaneous

11. That the Governments of Great Britain and of Ireland shall make a convention for the regulation of civil communication by air.

12. That the ports of Great Britain and of Ireland shall be freely open to the ships of each country on payment of the customary port and other dues.

13. That Ireland shall assume liability for such share of the present public debt of Great Britain and Ireland, and of payment of war pensions as

existing at this date as may be fair and equitable, having regard to any just claims on the part of Ireland by way of set-off or counter-claim, the amount of such sums being determined in default of agreement, by the arbitration of one or more independent persons, being citizens of Ireland or of the British Commonwealth.

14. That the Government of Ireland agrees to pay compensation on terms not less favourable than those proposed by the British Government of Ireland Act of 1920 to that Government's judges, officials, members of Police Forces and other Public Servants who are discharged by the Government of Ireland, or who retire in consequence of the change of government elected in pursuance hereof:

Provided that this agreement shall not apply to members of the Auxiliary Police Force, or to persons recruited in Great Britain for the Royal Irish Constabulary during the two years next preceding the date hereof. The British Government will assume responsibility for such compensation or pensions as may be payable to any of these excepted persons.

15. That neither the Parliament of Ireland nor any subordinate Legislature in Ireland shall make any law so as either directly or indirectly to endow any religion or prohibit or restrict the free exercise thereof, or give any preference or impose any disability on account of religious belief or religious status, or affect prejudicially the right of any child to attend a school receiving public money without attending a religious instruction at the school, or make any discrimination as respects State aid between schools under the management of different religious denominations, or divert from any religious denomination or any educational institution any of its property except for public utility purposes and on payment of compensation.

Transitional

16. That by way of transitional arrangement for the Administration of Ircland during the interval which must elapse between the date hereof and the setting up of a Parliament and Government of Ireland in accordance herewith, the members elected for constituencies in Ireland since the passing of the British Government of Ireland Act in 1920 shall, at a meeting summoned for the purpose, elect a transitional Government to which the British Government and Dail Eireann shall transfer the authority, powers, and machinery requisite for the discharge of its duties, provided that every member of such transition Government shall have signified in writing his or her acceptance of this instrument. But this arrangement shall not continue in force beyond the expiration of twelve months from the date hereof.

Ratification

17. That this instrument shall be submitted for ratification forthwith by His Britannic Majesty's Government to the Parliament at Westminster, and by the Cabinet of Dail Eireann to a meeting of the members elected

for the constituencies in Ireland set forth in the British Government of Ireland Act, 1920, and when ratifications have been exchanged shall take immediate effect.

ANNEX

1. The following are the specific facilities referred to in Article 8 (a):

Dockyard Port at Berehaven

(a) British Admiralty property and rights to be retained as at the date hereof. Harbour defences to remain in charge of British care and maintenance parties.

Queenstown

(b) Harbour defences to remain in charge of British care and maintenance parties. Certain mooring buoys to be retained for use of His Britannic Majesty's ships.

Belfast Lough

(c) Harbour defences to remain in charge of British care and maintenance parties.

Lough Swilly

(d) Harbour defences to remain in charge of British care and maintenance parties.

Aviation

(e) Facilities in the neighbourhood of the above Ports for coastal defence by air.

Oil Fuel Storage

(f) Haulbowline and Rathmullen. To be offered for sale to commercial companies under guarantee that purchasers shall maintain a certain minimum stock for British Admiralty purposes.

2. A Convention covering a period of five years shall be made between the British and Irish Governments to give effect to the following conditions:

(a) That submarine cables shall not be landed or wireless stations for communications with places outside Ireland be established except by agreement with the British Government; that the existing cable landing rights and wireless concessions shall not be withdrawn except by agreement with the British Government; and that the British Government shall be entitled to land additional submarine cables or establish additional wireless stations for communication with places outside Ireland.

(b) That lighthouses, buoys, beacons, and any navigational marks or navigational aids shall be maintained by the Government of Ireland as at the date hereof and shall not be removed or added to except by agreement with the British Government.

(c) That war signal stations shall be closed down and left in charge of care and maintenance parties, the Government of Ireland being offered the option of taking them over and working them for commercial purposes subject to British Admiralty inspection and guaranteeing the upkeep of existing telegraphic communication therewith.

(The following addendum concerning N.E. Ulster was to be proposed as a separate resolution by the President.)

ADDENDUM
NORTH-EAST ULSTER

Resolved:

That, whilst refusing to admit the right of any part of Ireland to be excluded from the supreme authority of the Parliament of Ireland, or that the relations between the Parliament of Ireland and any subordinate Legislature in Ireland can be a matter for treaty with a government outside Ireland, nevertheless, in sincere regard for internal peace, and in order to make manifest our desire not to bring force or coercion to bear upon any substantial part of the Province of Ulster, whose inhabitants may now be unwilling to accept the national authority, we are prepared to grant to that portion of Ulster which is defined as Northern Ireland in the British Government of Ireland Act of 1920, privileges and safeguards not less substantial than those provided for in the Articles of Agreement for a Treaty between Great Britain and Ireland signed in London on December 6th, 1921.

LETTER TO PATRICK KENNEDY IN DEPT OF THE TAOISEACH
with enclosures detailing the extent of
wartime co-operation with the British Government

MOST SECRET

24 May, 1941.

Dear Paddy,

I enclose the note we got from Sean Leydon on co-operation with the British Government, and the second note you asked for. This second list has never been compiled before, and I think it might be well to ask the Taoiseach whether we should leave it in existence at all once he has seen it.

Yours sincerely,

P. Kennedy Esq.,
Department of the Taoiseach.

MOST SECRET

Help Given by Irish Government to the British
in Relation to the Actual Waging of the War

1. A large volume of detailed information about roads, railways and military facilities of every kind in the Twenty-Six County area.

2. Broadcasting of information relating to German planes and submarines in or near our area.

3. Permission to use the air for their planes over a certain specified area.

4. Abstention from protest in regard to very frequent over-flying of other parts of our territory.

5. A constant stream of intelligence information in reply to an almost daily series of questions.

6. Placing at their disposal the information gathered by an elaborate coast-watching service.

7. Routeing of German and Italian official communications through Britain.

8. Suppression of wireless transmitters and capture and internment of real or potential spies.

9. Use of Shannon airports for West African Service, and presumably trans-Atlantic services, though both these services cannot fail to be used for largely military purposes.

10. Allowing the British Legation to have two secret wireless sets and a private line to London and Belfast.

11. Complying with requests of the British Naval and Military Attachés for information and visits to special districts to satisfy themselves that British interests were being safeguarded.

12. Obscuring our lighting system at the request of the British military authorities.

13. Allowing the setting up of apparatus which has resulted in the destruction and decreased efficiency of our broadcasting system in order to prevent it being used by the Germans as a guide to British objectives.

24 May, 1941

[At the end of this list Maurice Moynihan wrote the following in longhand:]
150,000 men to British bases   (given to Grattan O'Leary
                                                                by British Ministry of Infn)

About 60,000 workers (men) have collaborated
We have 250,000 men in all our military forces
i.e. 400,000 men in military defence of island
& we could not do more if we were in the war
All our surplus production going to them.

SECRET
CO-OPERATION WITH BRITISH GOVERNMENT
1. Since the outbreak of war, the Irish Meteorological Service has continued to supply to the British Meteorological Service weather reports and meteorological data generally. These are not being supplied to any other country. They are of course extremely important as a basis for weather forecasts.

NOTE:- It should be borne in mind that the British Meteorological Service supplies us with weather forecasts, etc. which are important for the Army Air Corps and for the Commercial Air Service between Dublin and Manchester. There is therefore an element of reciprocity about the arrangement.

2. The necessary authorisation was given to the Air Ministry last Summer to establish the trans-Atlantic Air Service and no embarrassing restrictions were imposed.
3. There is also co-operation in the operation of the Broadcasting Service.
4. A system of petrol rationing was introduced in this country at the outbreak of war and has been maintained ever since. It is understood that New Zealand has a petrol rationing system in operation but that Australia, South Africa, and Canada have not. The United Kingdom has a petrol rationing scheme but the reduction in consumption for ordinary civilian purposes has been much more than offset by the increase in the consumption of the Defence Services so that the total United Kingdom consumption is very much greater than it was before the war. The total consumption in this country is very much less than it was before the war, and the saving is in effect a contribution to the requirements of the British Defence Services.
5. At the request of the United Kingdom Government we agreed to the transfer to the British Shipping Register of seven tankers which were registered in Dublin at the outbreak of war. Four of these would probably have been quite sufficient to import to this country all our requirements of petroleum products.
6. At the suggestion of the United Kingdom Government we agreed to a scheme of combined purchasing for sugar, wheat, maize, and animal feeding stuffs (other than cereals). These arrangements were designed to eliminate competition and to keep down prices. They are advantageous to both countries; but they are much more advantageous to Great Britain than they are to this country because of the magnitude of the saving effected by any reduction in price as a result of the elimination of competition; the British requirements of all these products are of course very much greater than ours; and they are *relatively* much greater in the case of sugar, wheat, etc. where we produce a much higher percentage of our own requirements than the United Kingdom does.

7. A similar arrangement was made, again at the suggestion of the United Kingdom Government, regarding the chartering of ships. This arrangement again was designed to eliminate competition and keep down freights but in practice it has brought us a rather painful experience.

8. The Irish Government have also imposed restrictions on the purchase of Foreign Exchange and have followed the same general principles as the British Government with a view to economising the available resources of Foreign Exchange. Newspapers for example have, at the instance of the Department of Supplies, reduced their consumption of newsprint to about one-half of the pre-war consumption.

9. It is understood that generally the British Government made provision for normal supplies to continental neutrals provided those countries did not allow re-export to belligerents. We have had since the beginning of the war rigid control of exports but we are in effect now finding ourselves blockaded more rigidly than any of the continental neutrals were since the war began.

BIBLIOGRAPHY

PRIMARY SOURCES

CHAMBERLAIN, Austen, copies of Treaty papers in author's possession.
Compilation of Treaty documents; original drafts of MSS for de Valera biography; some correspondence with Harry Boland and Michael Collins; memoir by Gerry Boland. Supplied by Dr T.P. O'Neill.
CONNOLLY, Joseph, unpublished memoirs (Connolly papers).

ARCHIVES

ARCHDIOCESAN RECORDS, Dublin
Archbishop Byrne papers, Archbishop Walsh papers.
BLACKROCK COLLEGE ARCHIVES
De Valera papers, Archbishop McQuaid papers.
CHURCH RECORDS
St Agnes, Lexington Avenue, New York; St John Baptist, Kennedy Boulevard, Jersey City; St Paul's, Bergen Road and Greenville Avenue, Greenville, New Jersey; St Patrick's, Bramhall Road, Jersey City.
NEW JERSEY ARCHIVES, Trenton
PUBLIC RECORD OFFICE, London
British Cabinet, Dominion Office and Foreign Office papers. The PRO also contains relevant letters from Birkenhead, Austen Chamberlain, Balfour, Churchill, Andew Cope, Lionel Curtis, H. A. L. Fisher, Tom Jones, General Macready, Lord Midleton and Mark Sturgis.
BUREAU OF MILITARY HISTORY, Dublin
Memoirs of Michael Brennan, Paddy Daly, Joe Dolan, Joe McGuinness, Jim Slattery, Frank Thornton and Liam Thornton; Chronologies, Vols 1–3, 1898–1921.
DEPARTMENT OF DEFENCE, Dublin
Correspondence relating to erection of Collins memorial.
DEPARTMENT OF FINANCE, Dublin.
Correspondence relating to erection of Collins memorial.
DUBLIN UNIVERSITY
Papers and diaries of Erskine Childers and Frank Gallagher.
FRANKLIN DELANO ROOSEVELT LIBRARY, Hyde Park, New York
Some of David Gray's papers.
FRANCISCAN ARCHIVES, Killiney
Photocopies of de Valera letters from anonymous source.
HM STATIONERY OFFICE, London
Hansard, from period of Home Rule crisis, c. 1900–75, for both House of Commons and House of Lords.
NATIONAL ARCHIVES OF IRELAND
Dail Eireann papers, Departments of President of Executive Council, Taoiseach and Foreign Affairs, and Cabinet Minutes. Proceedings of North Eastern Advisory Committee, background to undercover police activity in Northern Ireland, the Craig/Collins pacts, treatment of Nationalists in the Six Counties. The Boundary Commission, the Sinn Fein funds case. Dail Debates, First Dail 1919–21; Second Dail 1921–22. Treaty debates (public and private sessions) and subsequent proceedings of Dail, until 1975.

NATIONAL ARCHIVES, Washington, DC
Immigration records, State Department papers.
NATIONAL LIBRARY OF IRELAND
Papers of de Valera, F.S. Bourke, Joseph Brennan, Daniel F. Cohalan, Michael Collins, Father Curran, John Devoy, Frank Gallagher, John J. Hearne, Sir John and Lady Lavery, Patrick McCartan, Joseph McGarrity, Kathleen Napoli Mackenna, Mary MacSwiney, Sean Moylan. Art O'Brien, William O'Brien, Leon O'Broin, Sean T. O'Ceallaigh, Florence O'Donoghue, John O'Mahony, James O'Mara, Austin Stack, W.B. Yeats.
PUBLIC RECORD OFFICE, Belfast
Londonderry papers and Spender papers relating to Collins' Northern activities and to those of the B-Specials.
UNIVERSITY OF WYOMING, Laramie
Some of David Gray's papers, including his unpublished memoirs, 'Behind the Green Curtain'.
UNIVERSITY COLLEGE, Dublin
Papers of Ernest Blythe, Dan Bryan, Desmond Fitzgerald, Hugh Kennedy, Sean MacEntee, Eoin MacNeill, Richard Mulcahy, Ginger O'Connell, Patrick McGilligan.

NEWSPAPERS AND PERIODICALS

Belfast Newsletter, Bell, Capuchin Annual, Catholic Herald, Catholic Standard, Chicago Tribune, Christus Rex, Daily Herald, Derry Journal, Doctrine and Life, Evening Herald, Freeman's Journal, Furrow, Gaelic American, Hibernia, Irish Bulletin, Irish Catholic Directory, Irish Ecclesiastical Record, Irish Independent, Irish News, Irish Press, Irish Times, Irish World, Limerick Weekly Echo, Magill Magazine, Manchester Guardian, Mayo News, Morning Post, New York Times, Northern Whig, Phoenix, Poblacht na hEireann, Studies, Sunday Independent, Sunday Press, Times, Tuam Herald.

PAMPHLETS AND ARTICLES

AKENSON, D.H., and Fallin, F.P., (1) 'The Irish Civil War and the Drafting of the Irish Constitution', *Eire Ireland*, Irish American Cultural Institute, Minnesota, Vols 1, 11, 1V, 1970; (2) 'Was de Valera a Republican?)', *Review of Politics*, 33, 2, 1972.
BAKER, S. 'Nationalist Ideology and the Industrial Policy of Fianna Fail', *Irish Political Studies*, 1, 1986.
BARTON, Robert, 'The Truth about the Treaty', Republican Press, n.d.
BOYCE, D.G. 'British Conservative Opinion, the Ulster Question, and the Partition of Ireland', *Irish Historical Studies*, Vol. XVII, No.65, 1970–1.
CARROLL, F.M., 'The American Committee for Relief in Ireland, 1920–21', *Irish Historical Studies*, Vol. XXIII, No.89, May 1982.
CHARLETON, Joseph, articles on IRA and Goertz mission to Ireland, *Irish Times*, August 1947.
DE VALERA, Eamon, 'The Alternative to the Treaty, Document No.2', Irish Nation Committee, Dublin, 1923.
DOWNING, Rossa, 'A Pamphlet by Rossa F. Downing', American Association for the Recognition of the Irish Republic.
GALLAGHER, Frank, 'The Partition of Ireland', Gill & Macmillan, Dublin, 1947.
HAYES, Michael, 'Dail Eireann and the Irish Civil War', *Studies*, Dublin, Spring 1969.
HOGAN, James, 'Could Ireland Go Communist?', Fine Gael, Dublin, 1933.
HOPKINSON, Michael, 'The Craig, Collins Pacts', *Irish Historical Studies*, Vol. XXVII, No.106, November 1990.
JOYCE, Mannix, 'Eamon de Valera, Bruree Man', *The Capuchin Annual*, Dublin, 1964.
LYNCH, Patrick, 'The Economist and Public Policy', *Studies*, Autumn 1953.
O'BEIRNE, John Ranelagh, 'The IRB: Treaty to 1924', *Irish Historical Studies*, Vol.XX, 1976.
O'RAHILLY, Alfred, 'The Case for the Treaty', n.d.

STATIONERY OFFICE, Dublin, White Paper on the Irish Language, 1965.
STUART, Francis, 'Frank Ryan in Germany', *Bell*, Dublin, November/December 1950.
VINEY, Michael, 'The Five Per Cent', series of articles in *Irish Times*, reprinted as pamphlet 1965.

IRA PUBLICATIONS

Stephen Hayes Confession, *An Phoblacht* (1930s), *Easter Week, Republican Congress, United Irishman, Wolfe Tone Weekly, Republican News, An Phoblacht* (1980s), *Resistance*.

TELEVISION DOCUMENTARIES

The Age of de Valera, de Valera centenary series, RTE, 1982; *The Treaty*, Thames, 1991; *The Shadow of Beal na mBlath*, RTE, 1989.

SELECT BIBLIOGRAPHY

ADAMS, Michael, *Censorship, The Irish Experience*, Sceptre, Dublin, 1968.
AKENSON, D.H., (1) *Education and Enmity, The Control of Schooling in Northern Ireland 1920–50*, David & Charles, Newton Abbot, 1973; (2) *A Mirror to Kathleen's Face*, David & Charles, Newton Abbot, 1975; (3) *The US and Ireland*, Harvard University Press, 1973.
ANDREWS, C.S. 'Tod', (1) *Dublin Made Me*, Mercier, Dublin and Cork, 1979; (2) *Man of No Property*, Mercier, Dublin and Cork, 1982.
ARENSBERG, C., and Kimball, S., *Family and Community in Ireland*, Harvard University Press, 1940.
ARTHUR, Sir G., *General Sir George Maxwell*, John Murray, London, 1932.
ASH, B., *The Lost Dictator*, Cassell, London, 1968.
AVON, Lord, *The Eden Memoirs*, Cassell, London, 1965.
BARRY, Tom, (1) *Guerilla Days in Ireland*, Anvil, Tralee, 1962; (2) *The Reality of the Anglo Irish War*, Anvil, Tralee, 1974.
BEASLAI, Pieras, *Michael Collins and the Making of a New Ireland*, 2 vols, Phoenix, Dublin, 1926.
BELL, J. Bowyer, (1) *The Secret Army, The IRA 1916–1979*, Academy Press, Dublin, 1983; (2) *The Irish Troubles*, St Martin's Press, New York, and Gill & Macmillan, Dublin, 1993.
BEAVERBROOK, Lord (Max Aitken), *Decline and Fall of Lloyd George*, Collins, London, 1963.
BENNETT, Richard, *The Black and Tans*, New English Library, London, 1970.
BERESFORD ELLIS, P., *History of the Irish Working Class*, Pluto, London, 1985.
BIRKENHEAD, Earl of (F.E.), *The Life of F.E. Smith: First Earl of Birkenhead*, Eyre & Spottiswoode, London, 1950.
BLANSHARD, Jean, *The Church in Contemporary Ireland*, Clonmore & Reynolds, Dublin, 1963.
BLANSHARD, Paul, *The Irish and Catholic Power*, Beacon Press, Boston, 1953, and Verschoyle, London, 1954.
BOURKE, Marcus, *John O'Leary*, Anvil, Tralee, 1967.
BONDANELLA, Peter, and Musa, Mark (eds), *The Portable Machiavelli*, Penguin, London, 1979.
BOWMAN, John, *De Valera and the Ulster Question 1917–73*, Clarendon Press, Oxford, 1982.
BOYCE, D.G., (1) *Englishmen and Irish Troubles*, Cape, 1972; (2) *Nationalism in Ireland*, Gill & Macmillan, Dublin, 1982; (3) *Separatism and Irish Nationalist Tradition* (ed. C.H. Williams), University of Wales Press, 1982.
BOYLAN, H. *Dictionary of Irish Biography*, Gill & Macmillan, Dublin, 1978.
BOYLE, Andrew, *The Riddle of Erskine Childers*, Hutchinson, London, 1977.
BRADY, Conor, (1) *Guardians of the Peace*, Gill & Macmillan, Dublin, 1974; (2) *Worsted in the Game*, Lilliput, Dublin, 1989.
BREEN, Dan, *My Fight for Irish Freedom*, Talbot Press, Dublin, 1926.

BRENNAN, Nial, *Dr Mannix*, Angus & Robertson, Sydney, and Tri-Ocean, San Francisco, 1965.

BRENNAN, Robert, *Allegiance*, Irish Press, Dublin, 1950.

BROMAGE, Mary C., (1) *De Valera and the March of a Nation*, Hutchinson, London, 1956; (2) *Churchill and Ireland*, University of Notre Dame Press, Indiana, 1964.

BROWNE, Noel, *Against the Tide*, Gill & Macmillan, Dublin, 1986.

BUCKLAND, Patrick, (1) *James Craig*, Gill & Macmillan, Dublin, 1980; (2) *Irish Unionism 1, The Anglo-Irish and the New Ireland, 1885–1922*, 1972; (3) *Irish Unionism 2, The Origins of Northern Ireland 1886–1922*, 1973, both Gill & Macmillan, Dublin, and Barnes & Noble, New York; (4) *The Factory of Grievances*, Gill & Macmillan, Dublin, and Barnes & Noble, New York, 1979; (5) *A History of Northern Ireland*, Gill & Macmillan, Dublin, 1981.

CALWELL, C.E., *Field Marshal Sir Henry Wilson, His Life and Diaries*, 2 vols, Cassell, London, 1927.

CAMPBELL, John, *F.E. Smith*, Cape, London, 1983.

CARROLL, Francis M., *American Opinion and the Irish Question, 1910–23*, Gill & Macmillan, Dublin, and St Martin's Press, New York, 1978.

CARROLL, Joseph T., *Ireland in the War Years, 1939–45*, David & Charles, Newton Abbot, and Crane, Russak, New York, 1975.

CAULFIELD, Max, *The Easter Rebellion*, Frederick Muller, London, 1964.

CHUBB, Basil, (1) *A Source Book of Irish Government*, Institute of Public Administration, Dublin, 1964; (2) *The Government and Politics of Ireland*, Oxford University Press, 1974; (3) *Cabinet Government in Ireland*, Institute of Public Administration, Dublin, 1974.

CHURCHILL, Winston, (1) *Lord Randolph Churchill*, 2 vols, Odhams, London, 1906, and 1 vol., Heinemann, London, 1966; (2) *The Aftermath*, Butterworth, London, 1929; (3) *The World Crisis*, several vols, Thornton Butterworth, London, 1923–9; (4) *The Gathering Storm*, Cassell, London, 1949; (5) *The Second World War*, several vols.

CLARK, Wallace, *Guns in Ulster*, Belfast Constabulary Gazette, 1967.

CLARKSON, J.D., *Labour and Nationalism*, Columbia University Press, New York, 1925.

COLLINS, Michael, *The Path to Freedom*, Talbot Press, Dublin, and T. Fisher Unwin, London, 1922.

COLUM, Padraic, *Arthur Griffith*, Browne & Nolan, Dublin, 1959.

CONNOLLY, James, *Labour in Irish History*, New Books, Dublin, 1983.

COOGAN, Tim Pat, (1) *Ireland Since the Rising*, Pall Mall, London, 1966; (2) *Ireland and the Arts* (ed.), Namara Press, London, n.d.; (3) *The IRA*, Fontana, London, 1986; (4) *Michael Collins*, Arrow, London, 1991; (5) *The Irish, a Personal View*, Phaidon, London, 1975; (6) *On the Blanket, The H-Block Story*, Ward River Press, Dublin, 1980; (7) *Disillusioned Decades*, Gill & Macmillan, Dublin, 1987.

CORFE, Tom, *The Phoenix Park Murders*, Hodder & Stoughton, London, 1968.

COXHEAD, Elizabeth, *Lady Gregory*, Macmillan, London, 1961.

CRAWFORD, Robert, *Loyal to King Billy*, Gill & Macmillan, Dublin, 1987.

CRONIN, Sean, *Ideology of the IRA*, Ann Arbor University Press, Michigan, 1972.

CRONIN, Sean, (1) *The McGarrity Papers*, Anvil, Tralee, 1972; (2) *Washington's Irish Policy, 1916–1986*, Gill & Macmillan, Dublin, 1987; (3) *Frank Ryan*, Repsol Press, Dublin, 1980; (4) *Irish Nationalism*, Academy, Dublin, 1980.

CROZIER, Brigadier F.P., (1) *Impressions and Recollections*, Laurie, London, 1930; (2) *Ireland for Ever*, Cape, London, 1932.

CURRAN, Joseph, *The Birth of the Irish Free State, 1921–23*, Alabama University Press, 1988.

DALTON, Charles, *With the Dublin Brigades 1917–21*, Peter Davies, London, 1929.

DANGERFIELD, George, *The Damnable Question*, Constable, London, 1977.

DE BURCA, Padraic, and Boyle, John F., *Free State or Republic?*, Talbot Press, Dublin, and T. Fisher Unwin, London, 1922.

DE VERE WHITE, Terence, *Kevin O'Higgins*, Methuen, London, 1948.

DILLON, Martin, *Stone Cold*, Arrow, London, 1992.

DOHERTY and HICKEY, *Chronology of Irish History since 1500*, Gill & Macmillan, Dublin, 1989.

DONNELLY, J., (1) *Landlord and Tenant in 19th Century Ireland*, Gill & Macmillan, Dublin, 1973; (2) *19th Century Land and People of Cork*, Routledge & Kegan Paul, London, 1975; (3) with S. Clarke, *Irish Peasants*, Manchester University Press, 1985.

DRIBERG, Tom, *Study in Power and Frustration*, Weidenfeld & Nicolson, London, 1956.

DRUDY, P.J. (ed.), *The Irish in America*, Cambridge University Press, 1985.

DUGGAN, J.P, (1) *Neutral Ireland and the Third Reich*, Lilliput, Dublin, 1989; (2) *A History of the Irish Army*, Gill & Macmillan, Dublin, 1991.

DWANE, David T., *Early Life of Eamon de Valera*, Talbot Press, Dublin, and T. Fisher Unwin, London, 1922.

DWYER, T. Ryle, (1) *Irish Neutrality and the USA 1939–1947*, Gill & Macmillan, 1977; (2) *Michael Collins and the Treaty, His Differences with de Valera*, Mercier, Cork and Dublin, 1981; (3) *Michael Collins, The Man Who Won the War*, Mercier, Dublin, 1990; (4) *De Valera's Darkest Hour*, Mercier, Cork and Dublin, 1982; (5) *De Valera's Finest Hour, In Search of National Independence, 1932–59*; (6) *De Valera, The Man and the Myths*, Poolbeg, Dublin, 1991; (7) *Eamon de Valera*, Gill's Irish Lives Series, Gill & Macmillan, Dublin, 1980.

EDWARDS, Ruth Dudley, (1) *Patrick Pearse, The Triumph of Failure*, Gill & Macmillan, Dublin, 1981; (2) *James Connolly*, Gill's Irish Lives series, Gill & Macmillan, Dublin, 1981.

ELLIOT, Marianne, *Wolfe Tone, Prophet of Irish Independence*, Yale University Press, London, 1989.

ERVINE, St John, *Craigavon, Ulsterman*, Allen & Unwin, London, 1949.

FAIRFIELD, Leticia, *The Trial of Peter Barnes*, Hodges, London, 1953.

FANNING, Ronan, (1) *Irish Department of Finance*, Institute of Public Administration, Dublin, 1978; (2) *Independent Ireland*, Helicon, Dublin, 1983.

FARRAGHER, Sean P. Cssp., *Dev and his Alma Mater*, Paraclete Press, Dublin and London, 1984.

FARRELL, Brian, (1) *Chairman or Chief*, Gill & Macmillan, Dublin, 1971; (2) *Sean Lemass*, Gill & Macmillan, Dublin, 1983; (3) *De Valera's Constitution and Ours* (ed.), Gill & Macmillan, Dublin, 1988.

FISK, Robert, *In Time of War*, Deutsch, London, 1983.

FITZPATRICK, David, *Politics and Irish Life 1913–21*, Gill & Macmillan, Dublin, 1977.

FLACKES, W.D., *Northern Ireland: A Political Directory*, Ariel Books, London, 1980.

FOLEY, Conor, *Legion of the Rearguard*, Pluto, London, 1992.

FORESTER, Margery, *Michael Collins, the Lost Leader*, Sidgwick & Jackson, London, 1971.

FOSTER, Roy, *Modern Ireland, 1600–1972*, Allen Lane, London, 1988.

GALLAGHER, Frank, (1) *The Indivisible Island*, Gollancz, London, 1957; (2) *The Anglo-Irish Treaty*, Hutchinson, London, 1965.

GAUGHAN, Anthony, (1) *Austin Stack*, Kingdom Books, Dublin and Tralee, 1977; (2) *Thomas Johnson*, Anvil, Dublin, 1980.

GEARY, Laurence, *Plan of Campaign*, Cork University Press, 1986.

GILBERT, Martin, (1) *Winston Churchill, Vol.III, The Challenge of War 1914–1916*, Heinemann, London, 1971; (2) *Companion*, Heinemann, London, 1977; (3) *World in Torment, W.S. Churchill, 1917–22*, Minerva, London, 1990.

GLEESON, James, *Bloody Sunday*, Peter Davies, London, 1962.

GOLDRING, Maurice, *Faith of Our Fathers*, Repsol, Dublin, 1982.

GREAVES, Desmond C., (1) *The Life and Times of James Connolly*, Lawrence & Wishart, London, 1961; (2) *Liam Mellows and the Irish Revolution*, Lawrence & Wishart, London, 1971.

GREELEY, Andrew, *That Most Distressful Nation*, Quadrangle, Chicago, 1972.

GRIFFITH, Kenneth, and O'Grady, Timothy, *Curious Journey*, Hutchinson, London, 1982.

GWYNN, Denis, *De Valera*, Jarrolds, London, 1933.

GWYNNE, Stephen, *John Redmond's Last Years*, Edward Arnold, London, 1919.

HAMBRO, C.J., *Newspaper Lords in British Politics*, Macdonald, London, 1958.

HARKNESS, D.W., *Restless Dominion*, New York University Press, 1970.

HEZLET, Sir Arthur, *The B-Specials*, Stacey, London, 1972.

HOLT, E., *Protest in Arms, 1916–21*, Putnam, New York, 1960.

HOPKINSON, Michael, *Green Against Green*, Gill & Macmillan, Dublin, 1988.

HYDE, Montgomery, *The Londonderrys*, Hamish Hamilton, London, 1979.

'I.O.' (C.J.C. Street OBE, MC), *Ireland in 1921*, Philip Allan, London, 1922.

IRVINE, Maurice, *Northern Ireland, Faith and Faction*, Routledge, London and New York, 1991.

JENKINS, Roy, *Asquith*, Collins, London, 1965.

JONES, Tom, (1) *Whitehall Diaries, Vol. III: Ireland* (ed. K. Middlemass), Oxford University Press, 1971; (2) *Lloyd George*, Harvard University Press, 1951.

KEATINGE, Patrick, (1) *A Place Among the Nations*, Institute of Public Administration, Dublin, 1978; (2) *A Singular Stance*, Institute of Public Administration, Dublin, 1984.

KEE, Robert, *The Green Flag*, Weidenfeld & Nicolson, London, 1972.

KILFEATHER, T.P., *The Connacht Rangers*, Anvil, Tralee, 1919.

KITSON, F.E., *Low Intensity Operations*, Faber, London, 1971.

LAFFAN, Michael, *The Partition of Ireland*, Dundalgan Press, Dundalk, 1983.

LARKIN, Emmet, *James Larkin*, Routledge & Kegan Paul, and MIT Press, Cambridge, Mass., 1965.

LAVELLE, Patricia, *James O'Mara: A Staunch Sinn Feiner*, Clonmore & Reynolds, Dublin, 1961.

LEE, J., (1) *Ireland 1912–1985, Politics and Society*, Cambridge University Press, 1989; (2) *Ireland 1945–70* (ed.), Gill & Macmillan, Dublin, and Barnes & Noble, New York, 1979; (3) *The Modernisation of Irish Society, 1848–1918*, Gill & Macmillan, Dublin, 1973; (4) with Gearoid O'Tuathaigh, *The Age of de Valera*, Ward River, Dublin, 1982; (5) *Towards a Sense of Place*, Cork University Press, 1985.

LE ROUX, Louis N., (1) *Tom Clarke and the Irish Freedom Movement*, Talbot Press, Dublin, 1926; (2) *Patrick H. Pearse*, trans. Desmond Ryan, Phoenix, Dublin, 1932.

LLOYD GEORGE, David, *War Memoirs*, 2 vols, Odhams, London, 1934.

LONGFORD, Earl of, and O'Neill, T.P., (1) *Eamon de Valera*, Hutchinson, London, 1970; (2) Longford, *Peace by Ordeal*, Pimlico, London, 1992.

LUCEY, Charles, *Ireland and the Irish*, Doubleday, New York, 1970.

LYNCH, Diarmuid (ed.), (1) *Florence O'Donoghue*, Mercier Press, Cork, 1957; (2) *The IRB and the 1916 Rising*, Doubleday, New York, n.d.

LYONS, F.S.L., (1) *Ireland Since the Famine*, Charles Scribner's Sons, New York, 1971; (2) (ed.), *Bicentenary Essays, Bank of Ireland, 1783–1983*, Gill & Macmillan, Dublin, 1983.

LYONS, J.B., (1) *Oliver St John Gogarty*, Blackwater Press, Dublin, 1980; (2) *Tom Kettle*, Glendale, Dublin, 1983.

MACARDLE, Dorothy, *The Irish Republic*, Irish Press, Dublin, 1951.

McCAFFREY, Lawrence J., *The Irish Diaspora in America*, Indiana University Press, Bloomington and London, 1976.

McCANN, John, *War by the Irish*, Kerryman, Tralee, 1946.

McCARTAN, Patrick, *With de Valera in America*, Brentano, New York, 1932.

McCARTHY, John F., *Planning Ireland's Future*, Glendale, Dublin, 1990.

McCARTNEY, Donal, *The Dawning of Democracy, Ireland 1800–1870*, Helicon, Dublin, 1987.

McCOLGAN, John, *British Policy and the Irish Administration, 1920–22*, Allen & Unwin, London, 1983.

McCONVILLE, Michael, *Ascendancy to Oblivion*, Quartet, London, 1986.

McCRACKEN, J.P., *Representative Government in Ireland*, Oxford University Press, 1958.

MACDONAGH, Oliver, *Ireland, the Union and its Aftermath*, Allen & Unwin, London, 1977.

McDONNELL, Kathleen Keyes, *There is a Bridge at Bandon*, Mercier, Cork, 1971.

MACEOIN, Uinseann (ed.), (1) *Survivors*, Argenta, Dublin, 1987 (revised edition); (2) *Harry*, Argenta, Dublin, 1985.

MACLOCHLAINN, Piaras F., *Last Words*, Kilmainham Jail Restoration Society, Dublin, 1971.

McMAHON, Deirdre, *Republicans and Imperialists*, Yale University Press, New Haven and London, 1984.

MACMAHON, Sean, *Rich and Rare*, Ward River, Dublin, 1984.

MACMANUS, M.J., *Eamon de Valera*, Talbot Press, Dublin and Cork, 1944.

MACREADY, General Sir Nevil, *Annals of an Active Life*, 2 vols, Hutchinson, London, 1924.

MANSERGH, Nicholas, *The Irish Question 1840–1921*, Allen & Unwin, London, 1965.

MANSFIELD, Michael, *Presumed Guilty*, Heinemann, London, 1993.

MARJORIBANKS, Edward, *The Life of Lord Carson*, Gollancz, London, 1932.

MARTIN, F.X., (1) *The Irish Volunteers 1913–15* (ed.), Dublin, 1963; (2) *Howth Gun-running*, Browne & Nolan, Dublin, 1964; (3) *Leaders and Men of the Easter Rising*, Dublin and Methuen, London, 1965.

MIDDLEMASS, Keith, and Barnes, John, *Baldwin*, Weidenfeld & Nicolson, London, 1969.

MILLER, David, *Queen's Rebels*, Gill & Macmillan, Dublin, 1971.

MILLIN, Sarah, *General Smuts*, London, 1936.

MITCHELL and O'SNODAIGH, *Irish Political Documents, 1916–49*, Irish Academic Press, Dublin, 1985.

MOODY, T.W., *The Ulster Question, 1603–1973*, Mercier, Cork, 1974.

MOYNIHAN, Maurice (ed.), *Speeches and Statements by Eamon de Valera, 1917–73*, Gill & Macmillan, Dublin, and St Martin's Press, New York, 1990.

MUIR, D. Erskine, *Machiavelli and His Times*, Heinemann, London, 1936.

MURPHY, Brian P., *Patrick Pearse and the Lost Republican Ideal*, James Duffy, Dublin, 1991.

NEESON, Eoin, (1) *The Civil War in Ireland 1922–1923*, Mercier, Cork, 1967; (2) *The Life and Death of Michael Collins*, Mercier, Cork, 1968.

NELIGAN, David, *The Spy in the Castle*, McGibbon & Kee, London, 1968.

NICOLSON, Harold, *King George V*, London, 1952.

O'BRIEN, Conor Cruise, (1) *Parnell and His Party*, Oxford University Press, London, 1957; (2) *States of Ireland*, Granada, London, 1974.

O'BRIEN, John (ed.), *The Vanishing Irish*, McGraw-Hill, New York, 1953.

O'BROIN, Leon, (1) *The Chief Secretary*, Chatto & Windus, London, 1969; (2) *Revolutionary Underground*, Gill & Macmillan, Dublin, 1976; (3) *Fenian Fever*, Chatto & Windus, London, 1979; (4) *Dublin Castle and the 1916 Rising*, Helicon, Dublin, 1986; (5) *No Man's Man*, Institute of Public Administration, Dublin, 1982; (6) *In Great Haste, The Letters of Michael Collins and Kitty Kiernan* (ed.), Gill & Macmillan, Dublin, 1983; (7) *Protestant Nationalism in Ireland*, Gill & Macmillan, Dublin, 1985; (8) *Michael Collins*, Gill & Macmillan, Dublin, 1980.

O'CONNOR, Batt, *With Michael Collins in the Fight for Irish Independence*, Peter Davies, London, 1929.

O'CONNOR, Frank, *The Big Fellow*, Corgi, London, 1969.

O'CONNOR, Sir James, *History of Ireland, 1798–1924*, 2 vols, Arnold, London, 1925.

O'CONNOR, Ulick, *Oliver St John Gogarty*, Cape, London, 1964.

O'DOHERTY, Kathleen, *Assignment America*, De Tanko, New York, 1957.

O'DONNELL, James, *How Ireland Is Governed*, Institute of Public Administration, Dublin, 1974.

O'DONOGHUE, Florence, (1) *Rebel Cork's Fighting Story*, Kerryman, Tralee, 1947; (2) *No Other Law*, Irish Press, Dublin, 1954; (3) *Famous IRA Jailbreaks, 1918–21* (ed.), Anvil, Tralee, 1971.

O'DONOVAN, Donal, *Kevin Barry*, Glendale, Dublin, 1984.

O'FAOLAIN, Sean, *De Valera*, Penguin, London, 1939.

O'FARRELL, Patrick, (1) *Ireland's English Question*, Schocken, New York, 1971; (2) *England and Ireland Since 1800*, Oxford University Press, London and New York, 1975.

O'HALLORAN, Clare, *Partition and the Limit of Ideology*, Gill & Macmillan, Dublin, 1989.

O'HANLON, Thomas. J, *The Irish*, Deutsch, London, 1976.

O'HEGARTY, P.S., (1) *The Indestructible Nation*, Maunsel, Dublin, 1918; (2) *A History of Ireland Under the Union, 1801–1922*, Methuen, London, 1922; (3) *The Victory of Sinn Fein*, Talbot Press, Dublin, 1924.

OLIVER, John, *Working at Stormont*, Institute of Public Administration, Dublin, 1978.

O'LUING, Sean, *Art O'Griofa*, Sairseal agus Dill, 1953.

O'MAHONY, Sean, *Frongoch*, FDR Teoranta, Dublin, 1987.

O'MAHONY, Tom, *Jack Lynch, a Biography*, Blackwater, Dublin, 1991.

O'MALLEY, Ernie, (1) *The Singing Flame*, Anvil, Dublin, 1978; (2) *On Another Man's Wound*, Anvil, Dublin, 1979; (3) *Raids and Rallies*, Anvil, Dublin, 1982.

O'NEILL, Marie, *From Parnell to de Valera*, Blackwater, Dublin, 1991.

O'NEILL, T.P., and O'Fiannachta, P., *De Valera*, 2 vols, Dublin, 1970. (Irish translation of Longford and O'Neill (1).)

O'SULLIVAN, Donal, *The Irish Free State and Its Senate*, Faber, London, 1940.

O'SULLIVAN, Harold, with Gavin, Joseph, *Dundalk, a Military History*, Dundalgan Press, Dundalk, 1987.

O'SUILLEABHAIN, Michael, *Where Mountainy Men Have Sown*, Anvil, Dublin, 1965.

QUIGLEY, Martin, *Peace Without Hiroshima*, Madison Books, New York, 1991.

RIDDELL, Lord George, *Intimate Diary of the Peace Conference*, Gollancz, London, 1933.

RIDDLE, Patrick, *Fire over Ulster*, Hamish Hamilton, London, 1970.

ROSKILL, S.W., *Hankey, Man of Secrets*, Vol. II, Collins, London, 1972.

RYAN, Desmond, (1) *Remembering Sion*, Barker, London, 1934; (2) *Unique Dictator*, Barker, London, 1936; (3) *Michael Collins and the Invisible Army*, 1932, reprinted Anvil, Dublin, n.d.

RYAN, Meda, *The Day Michael Collins Was Shot*, Poolbeg, Dublin, 1989.

SALVIDGE, Stanley, *Salvidge of Liverpool 1890–1928*, Hodder & Stoughton, London, 1934.

SCOTT, C.P. (ed.), *T. Wilson, Political Diaries, 1911–28*, Collins, 1970.

SENIOR, Hereward, *Orangeism in Ireland and Britain*, Routledge & Kegan Paul, London, 1966.

SHAKESPEARE, Sir Geoffrey, *Let Candles Be Brought In*, Macdonald, London, 1949.

SHANNON, William V., *The American Irish*, Collier Macmillan, New York, 1970.

SHAW, G.B., (1) *How to Settle the Irish Question*, Talbot Press, Dublin, 1917; (2) *Autobiography 1898–1950*, Reinhardt Books, London, 1970; (3) *Collected Letters*, Vol. III, Reinhardt Books, London, 1985.

SHERMAN, Hugh, *Not an Inch*, Faber, London, 1942.

SHIRER, William L., *The Rise and Fall of the Third Reich*, Pan, London, 1960.

SPRING RICE, Sir Cecil (ed. Stephen Gwynne), *Letters and Friendships of Sir Cecil Spring Rice*, 2 vols, London, 1929.

STREET, Major C.J., (1) *The Administration of Ireland, 1920*, Philip Allen, London, 1921; (2) *Ireland in 1922*, Philip Allen, London, 1922.

STEVENSON, Frances (ed.), *Lloyd George, A Diary*, Hutchinson, London, 1971.

STEWART, A.T.Q., (1) *The Ulster Crisis*, Faber, London, 1967; (2) *Edward Carson*, Gill's Irish Lives series, Gill & Macmillan, Dublin, 1981.

SWIFT, John, *Age of de Valera*, Lee & Tuathaig/RTE, Dublin, 1982.

SWIFT, John P., *John Swift, An Irish Dissident*, Gill & Macmillan, Dublin, 1991.

SWIFT, Roger, and Gilley, Sheridan (eds), *The Irish in Britain, 1815–1939*, Pinter, London, 1989.

TALBOT, Hayden, *Michael Collins's Own Story*, Hutchinson, Dublin, 1932.

TANSILL, Charles Callan, *America and the Fight for Irish Freedom, 1866–1922*, Devin-Adair, New York, 1957.

TARPEY, Marie Veronica, *The Role of Joseph McGarrity in the Struggle for Irish Independence* (doctoral thesis), Arno, New York, 1976.

TAYLOR, A.J.P., (1) *English History, 1914–45*, Oxford University Press, 1965; (2) *War by Timetable*, Macdonald, London, 1969; (3) *Churchill, Four Faces and the Man*, Allen Lane, London, 1969; (4) *Beaverbrook*, Hamish Hamilton, London, 1972.

TAYLOR, Rex, (1) *Michael Collins*, Four Square, London, 1961; (2) *Assassination, the Death of Sir Henry Wilson*, Hutchinson, London, 1961.

THOMAS, J.H., *My Story*, London, 1937.

THWAITES, Lt-Col Norman, *Velvet and Vinegar*, London, 1932.

TOWNSHEND, Charles, (1) *The British Campaign in Ireland, 1919–21*, Oxford University Press, 1975; (2) *Political Violence in Ireland*, Oxford University Press, 1983.

URBAN, Mark, *Big Boys' Rules*, Faber, London, 1992.

USHER, Arland, *The Face and Mind of Ireland*, Gollancz, London, 1949, and Devin-Adair, New York, 1950.

VALIULIS, Maryann, (1) *General Richard Mulcahy, Portrait of a Revolutionary*, Irish Academic Press, Dublin, 1992; (2) *Almost a Rebellion*, Tower Books, Cork, 1985.

WALDRON, Jarlath, *Maamtrasna, the Murders and the Mystery*, Edmund Burke, Dublin, 1992.

WALSH, Rev. P.J., *William J. Walsh, Archbishop of Dublin*, Talbot Press, Dublin, 1928.

WATT, David (ed.), *The Constitution of Northern Ireland*, Heinemann, London, 1981.

WEITZER, Ronald, *Transforming Settler States*, University of California Press, 1980.

WHITAKER, T.K., (1) *Economic Development*, Government Publications, Dublin, 1958; (2) *Interests*, Institute of Public Administration, Dublin, 1983.

WHITE, Captain J.B., *Misfit*, Cape, London, 1930.

WHYTE, J.H., *Church and State in Modern Ireland*, Gill & Macmillan, Dublin, 1971.

WILLIAMS, T. Desmond (ed.), *Historical Studies*, Gill & Macmillan, Dublin, 1970.

WINTER, Sir Ormonde, *Winter's Tale*, Richards Press, London, 1955.

YOUNGER, Calton, (1) *Ireland's Civil War*, Muller, London, 1968; (2) *A State of Disunion*, Muller, London, 1972; (3) *Arthur Griffith*, Gill & Macmillan, Dublin, 1981.

INDEX